INSTRUMENTAL MUSIC

PRINTED BEFORE 1600

INSTRUMENTAL MUSIC PRINTED BEFORE 1600

A Bibliography

HOWARD MAYER BROWN

HARVARD UNIVERSITY PRESS
CAMBRIDGE, MASSACHUSETTS
1967

Second Printing

Distributed in Great Britain by Oxford University Press, London

Library of Congress Catalog Card Number 65-12783

Printed in the United States of America

For John Ward

ACKNOWLEDGMENTS

My first debt of gratitude is to Professor John Ward of Harvard University. He began this bibliography, and many of the crucial, initial decisions about style and content were his. Since I assumed responsibility for the work, he has been extremely generous with his time, materials, and ideas. The bibliography is, then, in a very real sense his as well as mine, and I am deeply grateful to him for his help.

Three dissertations written at Harvard University, those by Lawrence Moe, Daniel Heartz, and H. Colin Slim, were especially helpful to me and I acknowledge with thanks the contributions their authors made to this work. Moreover Professor Slim has been extraordinarily generous with suggestions and advice; he undertook the thankless task of proofreading the entire typescript, an immense labor for which I am duly grateful.

I cannot list here all of the librarians who so kindly verified the existence of volumes in their libraries, but my thanks to all of them is nonetheless sincere.

Among the other friends and colleagues who have helped me, I should like to thank especially Madame la Comtesse de Chambure, Edna Christopher of the University of Chicago Library, Alan Curtis of the University of California, Vincent Duckles of the University of California Library, David Fuller of the University of Buffalo, Elizabeth Henderson, Reference Librarian at the University of Rochester, François Lesure of the Bibliothèque Nationale in Paris, Professor Edward Lowinsky of the University of Chicago, who allowed me to check various concordances against his index of sixteenth-century motets, and Larry Mowers of the Isham Memorial Library of Harvard University.

Publication of this volume was assisted by a grant from the American Council of Learned Societies as a result of a contribution from the United States Steel Foundation. I am pleased to acknowledge also the financial assistance of the Research Committee of the Division of the Humanities of the University of Chicago, and Wellesley College. Their grants of money enabled this book to be prepared.

Without the help of Katherine Bowers, Lenore Coral, Raymond Rosenstock, and William Spady, the index of musical incipits from which the concordances were made would probably never have been completed. And, finally, it is a pleasure to thank two people whose assistance has been literally invaluable: Bonnie Blackburn, who not only typed the manuscript superbly well but also saw to innumerable details, and Blair McElroy, whose expert editorial help made the final stages much less painful than they otherwise would have been.

September 1964 HOWARD MAYER BROWN

CONTENTS

ILLUSTRATIONS

Additions to the Second Printing

Many of the additions below were called to my attention by Claudio Sartori. I gratefully acknowledge his assistance in preparing this list. Mr. Sartori points out that the Cortot Library (CH: Lcortot) has been dispersed; the following volumes are now in the Newberry Library in Chicago: 1542_1, 1546_{10}, 1546_{15}, 1555_1, and 1584_5. Various other volumes from the Cortot Library are said to be in F: Pthibault.

The pages on which the additions occur are marked with a dagger (†).

Page

28 All of the solo lute music from 1529_3 has been printed in a modern edition in Daniel Heartz, ed., *Preludes, Chansons and Dances for Lute* (Neuilly-sur-Seine, 1964), which includes facsimiles of the title page and several other pages.

31 A facsimile of the entire treatise by Finé (1530_2) appears in Heartz, *Preludes*, pp. 129–130.

All of the music in 1530_3 has been printed in a modern edition in Heartz, *Preludes*, which includes facsimiles of the title page and several other pages.

37 All of the music in 1531_4 has been printed in a modern edition in CEK VIII (Daniel Heartz, ed., *Keyboard Dances from the Earlier Sixteenth Century*, 1965).

56 A modern edition of 1536_9, no. 19, appears in Heartz, *Preludes*, p. 120.

119 A modern edition of 1549_8, no. 40, appears in Heartz, *Preludes*, p. 126.

130 All of the music in 1551_5 has been printed in a modern edition in CEK VIII (Heartz, *Keyboard Dances*) and in an edition by Thurston Dart and William Oxenbury (London, 1966).

137 Two folios (33 and 34, wrongly numbered 31 and 32) from 1552_4 are in US: R. I am grateful to Jeremy Noble for pointing out to me the existence of this fragment.

151 Another copy of 1553_6 is in I: Bc.

173 Another copy of 1556_9 is in the Episcopal Library at Szombathely.

225 Other copies of 1568_2 are in the Biblioteca Civica at Bergamo and in US: NYp.

265 Another copy of 1572_2 is in I: PCd.

300 Another copy of 1580_3 is in I: Nc.

331 Other copies of 1584_5 are in F: Pa, I: Rvat, and the Collezione Greggiati in Ostiglia.

Page

345 A copy of $[1586]_6$ is in I:PCd.

346 Another copy of 1586_8 is in I:Pu.

354 Another copy of 1589_3 is in I:VEcap.

363 Other copies of 1590_8 are in I:MOe, I:PCd, and the Collezione Cini in Venice.

385 The Polish dances in 1592_{12} (nos. 5–16) are printed in a modern edition in Zofia Steszewska, ed., *Tance Polskie z tabulatur lutniowych* (Warsaw, 1962).

388 Another copy of 1593_3 is in F:Pthibault.

398 The running heads said to appear on various folios of 1594_5 (see, for example, footnotes 3, 4, and 6) actually appear only in the table of contents on fol. *3^{v}.

407 All of the music in 1596_4 has been printed in a modern edition in Wilburn W. Newcomb, ed., *Lute Music of Shakespeare's Time* (University Park, Penn., 1966).

408 All of the music in 1596_5 has been printed in a modern edition in Newcomb, *Lute Music*.

409 All of the music in 1596_6 has been printed in a modern edition in Newcomb, *Lute Music*.

411 *Di Antonio Il Verso siciliano il Primo Libro della Musica a due voci* (Palermo, 1596) should be included as 1596_{12}. A copy, which I have not seen, is in the Biblioteca Comunale of Palermo.

412 Another copy of 1597_2 is in the Biblioteca Comunale of Lodi.

412 Another copy of 1597_3 is in US:Wc.

414 Another copy of 1597_5 is in the Archivio del Duomo at Ferrara.

425 Another copy of 1598_9 is in US:Wc. A modern edition of no. 5 (*Secondo tuono. Toccata Quinta*) is printed in ParrishT, p. 152.

INSTRUMENTAL MUSIC
PRINTED BEFORE 1600

INTRODUCTION

A definitive history of sixteenth-century instrumental music has not yet been written. Joseph W. Wasielewski's pioneering study, *Geschichte der Instrumentalmusik im XVI. Jahrhundert* (1878), remains the only book-length survey of the subject, and it is now almost hopelessly out of date, for only a limited amount of the music was accessible to the author. An over-all view of the field is attempted in some general histories. Hugo Riemann in his *Handbuch der Musikgeschichte* (2nd ed., 1920–1923), Wilhelm Fischer in Guido Adler's *Handbuch* (2nd ed., 1929), Gustave Reese in *Music in the Renaissance* (1954), Geneviève Thibault in the *Encyclopédie de la Pléiade: Histoire de la musique*, vol. I (1960), and Yvonne Rokseth in volume III of *The New Oxford History of Music* (1960)—all present a summary of Renaissance instrumental music. But these are more accurately reports on the current state of research rather than genuinely comprehensive surveys; lack of space has prevented the authors from writing very detailed studies.

The fact that there are almost no syntheses of all of the available material does not mean that the subject of sixteenth-century instrumental music has been entirely neglected by scholars. A number of articles and monographs treat a single aspect of the larger field, and some of these are exhaustive within their self-imposed limitations.[1] Moreover, interest in the subject has recently grown very rapidly. New editions of the music are appearing in greater quantities than at any time since the sixteenth century itself. For example, the Centre National de la Recherche Scientifique in Paris has stimulated research on lute music. Thanks to one of its directors of research, Jean Jacquot, a study group has been formed, and a series of modern editions of music with lute ("Le Choeur des Muses") is now under way. And the American Institute of Musicology has recently begun to publish a corpus of early keyboard music, with Willi Apel as general editor.

Before a comprehensive survey of the field can be made, however, the music must be assembled, sorted, and studied. The present volume, cataloguing and describing all of the instrumental music published before 1600, is a first step in that direction. Using the bibliographical techniques developed mainly by Robert Eitner, Emil Vogel, Alfred Einstein, Claudio Sartori, and, most recently, by the compilers of the first volume of the *Répertoire international des sources musicales* (RISM), my aim has been to gather in one place information relevant to a study of this repertoire, describing each volume, making an inventory of the contents, and listing modern editions and studies of the music.[2] This is, in other words, a workbook, designed to make easily accessible to the student of this music all of the pertinent data.

The bibliography lists volumes of instrumental music known to have existed but now lost, as well as those still extant. Perhaps hitherto unknown copies will turn up as a result and in any case including these lost volumes helps to complete our picture of the period. In an effort to collect as many such "ghosts" as possible, I have combed various reference works, notably Robert

[1] Most of these articles and monographs are mentioned in the List of Works Cited, with their sigla. Only the sigla will be used to refer to these works throughout this bibliography.

[2] The editors of RISM intend to publish bibliographies of lute music and of keyboard music, manuscripts as well as prints, of the sixteenth and seventeenth centuries. The RISM bibliographies will apparently not list the individual compositions in each collection, nor will they contain an index of composers. Therefore there is a point in making this present bibliography more detailed within narrower chronological limits and not restricted to volumes of music for one particular kind of instrument. And bibliographical control of the printed sources is a necessary preliminary to detailed studies of the manuscript instrumental music of the period.

Eitner's *Biographisch-bibliographisches Quellenlexikon* (1899–1904) and François J. Fétis' *Biographie universelle des musiciens* (1860–1865), and have searched through sixteenth- and seventeenth-century book lists and catalogues, such as the inventories prepared by Georg Draudius for the Frankfurt book fairs (*Bibliotheca classica*, 1625 ed.; *Bibliotheca exotica*, 1625 ed.; *Bibliotheca librorum germanicorum*, 1625 ed.), and inventories of private libraries like those of the Fugger family (see Richard Schaal, "Die Musikbibliothek von Raimund Fugger d. J.," *Acta musicologica*, XXIX [1957], 126) and of King John IV of Portugal (see Josquim de Vasconcellos, *El Rey D. João o* 4to, 1900, and Vasconcellos, *Primeira parte do index da libraria de musica do Rey Dom João IV*, 1873). I have included notices of licenses granted to issue volumes of instrumental music (for example, $[1505]_1$, $[1536]_1$, $[1565]_6$, and $[1574]_4$), even when no evidence is available to prove that the volumes ever were actually printed. And for cases of particularly dubious "ghosts" and of obvious mistakes, I have invented a category of "Doubtful Works," lumping several volumes under the one heading at the end of the year involved (see, for example, the end of 1535 and 1536).[3]

The bibliography cites volumes of music for instruments and voices—lute songs, for example—and anthologies that contain some vocal music and some instrumental music. These mixed anthologies are described fully, but only the instrumental pieces are inventoried.[4]

Theoretical treatises that deal wholly with instruments or with the music written for them are included in the bibliography. These volumes either survey the instruments in use during the sixteenth century, such as Sebastian Virdung's *Musica getutscht* (1511_3), or deal with specific kinds of instruments, their construction, and use, such as Arnolt Schlick's *Spiegel der Orgelmacher* (1511_2); or else they are instruction books explaining how to play various instruments, such as Silvestro di Ganassi's *Regola Rubertina* (1542_2). Dance treatises are cited here only if they contain music. Thus Antonio Arena's *Ad suos compagniones studiantes* (1529 and later) and the Jacques Moderne *basse dance* book (reprinted in François Lesure, "Danses et chansons à dancer au début du XVIe siècle," in *Recueil de travaux offerts à M. Clovis Brunel*, 1955) are omitted, while the choreographic instructions of Michel Toulouze ($148?_1$) and of Thoinot Arbeau (1589_1) are included.

Treatises that discuss instrumental music as part of a more general study have not been described in the bibliography. Even though chapter 33 of Claudio Sebastiani's *Bellum musicale* (1563), for example, contains valuable information about instrumental practices,[5] the central issues of the book do not concern instruments, and so it has not been listed; nor has Pater Johann Lengenbrunner's *Musices haud vulgare compendium* (1559), in spite of its appendix on the transverse flute.[6] Some treatises include musical examples without text, but I have not felt that fact sufficient to justify adding those volumes to the bibliography, and so Nicolaus Listenius, *Musica...ab authore denuo recognita* (1537 and later), Giovanni Paduani, *Institutiones ad diversas ex plurium vocum harmonia cantilenas* (1578), Orazio Tigrini, *Il Compendio della musica* (1588), and Thomas Morley, *A plaine and easie introduction to practicall musicke* (1597), for example, are all omitted.[7] Even when textless examples are as clearly instrumental in character as the twelve "ricercares" *a2*

[3] Three "ghosts" are dubious enough not even to have merited inclusion in one of the "Doubtful Works" lists: (1) a volume listed under "Paduana" in DraudiusBC, p. 1647, as "Cantiones Italicae quas Paduana Itali vocant, 4. vocum. Venet. 1565. 4°.," which might contain instrumental music, but might as well be vocal; (2) a collection of "Teutsche Lieder auf die fletten. Und ande Instrument" listed in SchaalM, p. 129, no. 67, as having been in the Fugger library; and (3) an otherwise unknown collection by Costanzo Antegnati, *Inni d'intavolatura d'organo* (Venice, n.d.), listed in FétB I, 116, which may have been printed after 1600, if it ever in fact existed.

[4] In cases where inventories were not available in any standard reference work I have sometimes included the vocal music as well as the instrumental music for these mixed anthologies.

[5] A German translation of Sebastiani by Hermersdorff appeared in *Cäcilia* XV–XVIII (1875–1878), and also separately. An English translation of chapter 33 may be found in YoungBS, p. 66.

[6] The full title of Lengenbrunner's lost treatise is given in DavB, p. 48; EitQ VI, 132; and FétB V, 271.

[7] The Listenius treatise was reprinted in a facsimile edition by Georg Schünemann in 1927. Both the Tigrini and the Morley treatises are listed in WolfH II, 308, as containing instrumental scores. The Paduani treatise is described in SartMS, p. 33.

illustrating the modes in Book IV of Gioseffo Zarlino's *Le Istitutioni harmoniche* (1588 and later), the treatise has not been included in this bibliography, since under no circumstances could it be considered to be principally about instrumental music. The only exceptions to the practice of excluding treatises unless they deal wholly with instruments or instrumental music are the first two editions of Juan Bermudo's *Declaración de instrumentos musicales* (1549_3 and 1550_1), and Adam Gumpelzhaimer, *Compendium Musicae* (1591_6 and 1594_4).

This bibliography lists volumes of music written specifically for one kind of instrument, or for one family of instruments, as well as music written with no particular kinds of instruments in mind. Thus there are entries for collections of keyboard music, of lute music and music for other plucked stringed instruments, of viol and recorder music, and of music for miscellaneous instrumental ensembles. Some idea of the number of volumes published for each kind of instrumental combination may be obtained by referring to Index III, Volumes Described, Arranged by Performing Medium.

The development of music written specifically for instruments is one of the distinguishing characteristics of the sixteenth century, and yet no hard and fast distinctions between instrumental and vocal music exist. Some arbitrary decisions have had to be made concerning which volumes to include and which ones to omit. Throughout the century publishers added on the title pages of vocal anthologies notes stating that the music was fit to be played on instruments as well as to be sung. To have listed all of the volumes would have meant citing a far greater number of printed music books of the century, and would have obscured the central purpose of this bibliography. On the other hand, to omit these volumes of music suitable for voices or instruments is to risk distorting the reader's view of sixteenth-century instrumental practices, for without these anthologies the innocent reader might suspect that comparatively little music originally conceived for voices was capable of being performed by instrumental ensembles, when exactly the reverse is true. There is scarcely any vocal music at all that cannot be played on instruments and that was not so performed. In other words, the ensemble counterpart of the lute and keyboard intabulation is missing completely from the present volume; to understand what actually happened during the century the reader should remember that the instrumentalist also performed "vocal" music.[8]

Even with the distinction between instrumentally performed songs and originally instrumental pieces clearly in mind, it has not always been possible to make clear-cut decisions. What should be done, for example, with the *Odhecaton*, *Canti B*, and *Canti C* (1501_1, 1503_1, 1504_1, and 1504_2)? The pieces in these anthologies are not texted and scholars have disagreed about whether or not they were intended for instrumental performance. On the one hand text can easily be added to many of the pieces, and many are effective as vocal compositions. On the other hand texts are not actually present, some of the pieces might have been written as instrumental arrangements of vocal melodies, and some may well have been originally conceived for instruments. My solution has been to describe these volumes, and to inventory only those pieces which *probably* did not have words originally (in this case those pieces which have been called, for want of a better term, *carmina*, like "La Morra," "La Stanghetta," and "La Alfonsina"). But this general principle is admittedly difficult to apply, and there is much room for disagreement about some of the volumes I have omitted, and some of the individual compositions I have listed.

I have listed as 1533_2 and 1533_3, for example, the two volumes of chansons published by Pierre Attaingnant which are described on the title page as being particularly suitable for recorders and transverse flutes, since certain of the individual chansons are marked as being better for the one instrument or for the other. And I have listed the volume of music performed at the marriage of Cosimo de' Medici and Leonora of Toledo in 1539, since the instruments that performed specific pieces are described in detail in the table of contents (see 1539_1).

[8] See SchneidA for a discussion of this point, and for an exploration of other borderline areas between instrumental and vocal music.

I have omitted, on the other hand, several volumes of music that might, using similar criteria, have been included. Several volumes of Nicolas Gombert's motets were published with the title *Musica Quatuor Vocum* (*vulgo Motecta nuncupatur*), *Lyris maioribus, ac Tibiis imparibus accommodata.* This statement that they are arranged for viols or recorders (?) is much more specific than the usual vague note that the music is apt for voices and instruments; and yet the volume contains vocal music, and so it was not included in the bibliography; nor was Giovanthomaso Cimello's *Libro primo de canti a quatro voci sopra Madriali*, even though the title promises information about instrumental practices, and about the combination of voices with instruments ("le piu necessarie osservanze instromentali, e piu convenevoli avvertenze De toni accio si possano anchora Sonare, & Cantare insieme"), a promise it does not fulfill. Girolamo dalla Casa, head of the wind band in Venice, published a volume of madrigals *a 5* decorated with *passaggi*, but like the Cimello and the Gombert volumes, Dalla Casa's madrigals are essentially vocal music, even with ornaments, and so the volume has been omitted.[9]

In the last quarter of the sixteenth century vocal music began to be published taking into account the practice of accompanying a chorus by a keyboard instrument. An accompaniment could be entirely written out, as in at least one volume of Victoria motets. Or the composer, or publisher, could merely write in suggestions, as in Francisco Sale's *Patrocinium Musices* (1598), where the alternation between voices and instrument is marked in the music: "Chorus," "Organ," or "Organista cum suis Cantoribus." More commonly, the set of part books would include a separate "Basso per l'organo," usually a simplified score of two staves, showing the highest and lowest sounding voices at any given moment, from which the organist could improvise his accompaniment. But even though the advent of the figured bass is of great significance to the history of instrumental music, organ basses and organ scores are not catalogued in this bibliography unless they contain music not originally conceived with words (such as canzonas).[10]

Volumes containing hunting calls of the sixteenth century do not figure in the bibliography, although hunting calls deserve to be classified as instrumental music. But in fact only two books fall into this category: George Turberville, *The noble art of Venerie*, and Jacques du Fouilloux, *La Vénerie*, both of which went through several editions in the sixteenth century.[11]

And I have omitted Antonio Gardane's 1539 volume of two-voiced chansons (RISM 1539_{21}), which Claudio Sartori includes in his *Bibliografia della musica strumentale italiana* (1952, p. 5), although the volume may well have been intended for instrumental performances. Indeed, the collections of duos printed from time to time throughout the century are all rather difficult to justify as "instrumental" music; many of them might more properly be called exercise books for counterpoint students. But, following the principle that pieces which did not originally have words should be included I have listed many of these collections of duos (see, for example, 1559_6, 1577_2, 1590_{11}, and 1590_{12}). They may well have had two functions: to provide both beginning instrumentalists and counterpoint students with material for study and performance.

The main body of this bibliography is arranged chronologically. As with other similar bibliographies each entry is labeled with the year of publication and a subscript number. Within any given year the volumes are listed alphabetically by composer or editor, with the anonymous anthologies

[9] For the Gombert volumes, see SchmidtgG, pp. 348–349; for descriptions and inventories of the volumes by Cimello and Dalla Casa, see Vogel.

[10] The Victoria motets are discussed in ReMR, pp. 604, 607, and 629, and in the introduction to VicO I. Sale's *Patrocinium Musices* is described in BohnMD, p. 350. KinO, pp. 94ff, lists and discusses late sixteenth-century editions with organ bass parts. Those editions with *basso continuo* parts that do not otherwise appear in this bibliography are listed in the Appendix.

[11] Undated copies of the Turberville volume are in the Yale University Library and in the Henry E. Huntington Library, San Marino, California. A diplomatic reprint of the 1576 ed. was published in the Tudor & Stuart Library (Oxford, 1908); for a discussion of the work, see HalfT. A copy of a 1561 ed. of the Du Fouilloux work, printed in Poitiers, is now in the Library of Congress. For a bibliography of editions of the Du Fouilloux volume, see the new edition of 1844; for a discussion of the work, see TautA.

grouped at the end. Thus 1546 begins with the volume of lute dances by Julio Abondante, continues with volumes by Melchiore de Barberiis, Dominico Bianchini, Francesco da Milano, and so forth to Francesco Vindella, and ends with the lute anthologies published by the firm of Pierre Phalèse. If the title page or the colophon carries no year, then the date of the dedication is used instead. Undated volumes are grouped at the end of the decade in which they were probably published. That is, all of the undated collections published during the 1540's are arranged after 1549 under the rubric 154?. The one exception to this approximate dating is $154?_4$, a volume of lute music by Francesco da Milano. The probable date of that collection is impossible to determine. I have included it under 154? only because the majority of Francesco's works were published during that decade. Late discoveries and changes of policy in the course of preparing this bibliography have pushed some volumes out of alphabetical order. I have left them that way in order to avoid changing all of the cross-references for a whole year.

If a collection was reprinted, the later editions are mentioned at the end of the description of the first edition. Such cross-references are given even when the collection was later revised or augmented, and the changes are listed in the description of the revisions. Whenever editions after 1600 are cited a reference to them in some standard bibliographical work is given (Eitner's *Quellenlexikon*, RISM, Sartori's *Bibliografia della musica strumentale italiana*, or Emil Vogel, *Bibliothek der gedruckten weltlichen Vocalmusik Italiens, 1500–1700*, 1892). Sixteenth- and seventeenth-century catalogues and book lists are cited only when they mention volumes that are now lost, or when they disagree with known facts. For example, that Draudius dated the volume of Mainerio dances incorrectly is noted in the description of that volume (1578_8).

Each entry begins with the title page. Line divisions and punctuation of the original title pages are indicated, as well as the distinction between upper- and lower-case type. The only exception to this practice has been to substitute commas for diagonal slashes in the original German title pages, in order not to confuse punctuation marks with line divisions. Cuts are described and printers' marks are indicated. But, since this is a workbook designed for the student of music rather than for the professional bibliographer, some features of the title pages are ignored in the catalogue entries. Distinctions between Roman and italic types are not made. Ornamental borders, fleurets, and other decorative features are not always indicated. Abbreviations are resolved without comment. If the collection is printed in part books, the abbreviations SATB, 5, 6, 7, and so on are used for the various part books. In the inventories, however, the designation of the part used as the model is not included. Normally the cantus part book was used in such cases, and variants with the other part book title pages are indicated in footnotes. Following the title page each entry describes a perfect copy of the volume, indicating the number of folios and the kind of musical notation, and briefly describing the prefatory material (dedication, illustrative plates, table of contents, rules for performance, observations on notation, laudatory poems, and the like), and the closing material (colophon, index, and so on). Throughout the bibliography I have used the term "mensural notation" to describe the normal staff notation in common use for polyphonic music during the fifteenth and sixteenth centuries, as opposed to the various tablatures devised for specific instruments. The term "mensural notation," therefore, is not meant to suggest that tablatures are not measured.

Modern editions and facsimile editions of complete volumes are listed if they exist, as well as monographs and articles dealing with the contents of the volumes. If single pieces from a volume are reprinted in modern editions they are indicated in footnotes. If several pieces from the same source are reprinted in a single place they are identified by a superior letter preceding the footnote numbers. Curiously enough some of the modern editions of sixteenth-century instrumental music are more difficult to find than the original sixteenth-century editions. The reason for this state of affairs is that much sixteenth-century instrumental music has been reprinted only in popular editions, which libraries do not usually collect, and which soon go out of print. I have tried to include as many of these popular editions as I could, in spite of their rarity, but I have probably not been able to control them all. I have omitted modern editions when the editor has drastically arranged the sixteenth-century original, such as the Susato and Phalèse dances arranged for piano, four hands, in volumes XXV and XXVII of *Vereeniging vor Nederlandsche Muziekgeschiedenis* (1896—), and the lute music reprinted in modern schools of guitar playing like José de Azpiazu, *Gitarrenschule* (1954–1958), and Bruno Henze, *Das Gitarrespiel* (1950), but I have not been neurotically consistent about this policy.

At the end of each description there is a list of the libraries where copies of the volume are now located. I have included libraries that once owned copies which are now lost, indicating that fact (for example, see 1546_1 for the collection that was in Sorau), as well as the previous locations of volumes when that information has been available (see, for example, 1542_2). Thus all of the copies known to have existed should be listed among the exemplars. If a library owns a defective copy that fact is noted, although the imperfections are not always specified. It has not always been possible to discover whether or not a copy is defective, since I have made the entries mostly from microfilms of one or at most two or three exemplars of each volume. If a library owns an incomplete set of part books, its holdings are indicated in parentheses by the abbreviations SATB 5, 6, 7, and so on. Whenever possible manuscript appendixes to the printed volume are inventoried if they contain instrumental music, but no attempt has been made to identify further the individual compositions in these manuscript appendixes.

Finally, the contents of each volume are inventoried. Titles of the pieces have been taken from the body of each volume and not from the tables of contents. Where the information in the two places differs significantly, that fact has been noted. The original spelling and punctuation of titles have always been preserved. Especially in the case of the intabulations that fact may occasionally create ambiguity. If the original is so garbled that the actual title of a piece remains obscure, then the actual title is also given. If the title includes directions for accordatura tunings or other instructions for the players, it has been shortened to omit this information. And occasionally the entries have been made consistent where they were not in the original.

The pieces in each volume have been numbered, and either pagination or foliation, whichever appears in the original, is also included. Errors in the original numbering have been corrected here without comment.

Regardless of medium, sixteenth-century instrumental music falls into a few clearly defined categories. Each of these categories has been treated in a slightly different way in the inventories of the volumes. There are pieces originally conceived for voices but arranged for instruments (for example, intabulations and lute songs), music originally conceived for instruments (for example, "abstract" instrumental pieces: ricercares, fantasies, and preludes), and dance music. Each sort of music is represented by examples for each kind of performing medium, with the exception explained above that the reader will look in vain for vocal compositions directly transferable to instruments.

Wherever possible the vocal model of the intabulations and other compositions originally conceived for voices is identified in the inventories. Instrumental pieces are identified in the bibliography in one of four different ways:

1. Vocal models of intabulations are identified thus: "*Susanne ung jour* (LevyS, p. 403: Didier Lupi Second)."

2. When the vocal model could not be found, but a closely related piece is known, the identification is preceded by "compare": "*Je ne veux plus* (compare LesLRB, art. 3, no. 13: Certon)." The word "compare" also precedes identifications of monophonic melodies on which instrumental compositions are based, and references to sources related in some other significant way to the composition in question.

3. Pieces that are exactly reprinted are identified by equals signs; for example, the first fantasia in 1570_3 was reprinted from 1568_6, so the entry in 1570_3 reads: "*Fantasia* = 1568_6, no. 2."

4. When a dance or an abstract piece is arranged for a different performing medium,

the original is cited as though it were a vocal model. For example, in 1599 Giovanni Terzi arranged for solo lute two of Guami's instrumental ensemble fantasias; thus the entry for the first of them in 1599_{11} reads: "*Fantasia in modo di Canzon Francesa* [Francesco] Guami (1588_{8}, no. 4)."

The identifications refer the reader to modern editions of the vocal models whereever these exist, and otherwise to sixteenth-century editions cited by their RISM numbers, Vogel numbers, or, in rare cases, by their Eitner numbers. The identifications include volume, page number, and composer if he is not cited in the instrumental volume, and the correct title of the model if the intabulator has changed it enough to cause serious ambiguity. Identical intabulations are cross-referenced. Different intabulations of the same vocal models can be collated by consulting the index of text incipits (see, for example, the many different versions of "Susanne ung jour"). *Secundae partes* are not given separate numbers in the inventories. A motet, chanson, or madrigal in more than one part is numbered as one composition, and references elsewhere to an individual part are made by number followed by a letter. Thus "1573_{3}, no. 23b," refers to "Et valde mane," the *secunda pars* of Christian Hollander's motet "Dum transisset Sabbathum." The job of making the identifications and cross-references has been done mostly through incipits. Some mistakes will inevitably have crept in because of this procedure, for occasionally a piece will begin in the same way as another and continue differently. This possibility of confusion is particularly acute, for example, in the Hans Newsidler volumes (1536_{6}, 1536_{7}, and so on), in which several slightly different versions of the same pieces occur.

Vocal models have not been found for all of the intabulations. For some of these unidentified intabulations different arrangements of the same thematic material, or perhaps a monophonic melody related to the intabulation, do exist. In such cases the reader is advised to "compare" the other version. Wherever the word "compare" precedes an identification, then, the vocal source is not the exact model on which the intabulator has based his instrumental arrangement, but the two versions are related in some significant way. The reader should also take into account the fact that not all of the compositions listed in this bibliography were originally conceived for voices; some, and perhaps many, of the otherwise unidentified "intabulations" may have been originally conceived for instruments, or for instruments with voices.[12] In those cases where a number of vocal compositions have been compared with an intabulation and the model has still not been identified, all of the false leads are listed in a footnote. That the "Bergerette savoysienne" in 1507_{2}, for example, is not related to the monophonic tune, nor to the three polyphonic arrangements known, is almost as informative as having found the model; in any case, stating the fact may save scholars some time and effort.

Abstract pieces, fantasias, and ricercares that are reprinted in later volumes are cross-referenced in the same manner as the intabulations. Often the pieces in question have been republished without acknowledgment of the editor or printer, so that the cross-references sometimes bring out surprising relationships. No further identifications of the abstract pieces seemed necessary or possible. On the few occasions where a fantasia has been based on a vocal model, and the vocal model is cited, that fact appears, of course, in the title. The task of cross-referencing all of the abstract pieces has been greatly facilitated by consulting H. Colin Slim, "The Keyboard Ricercar and Fantasia in Italy, ca. 1500–1550" (unpub. diss., Harvard University, 1961), which includes a thematic index of all of the fantasias from the first half of the century, and some examples from the second half. I here acknowledge my debt to Professor Slim.

Dance pieces have been cross-referenced only if they are identical settings of the same melodies. Many of these compositions are rearrangements of some one given element. That is, the melodies of many dances are similar to each other, but the harmonizations differ, or else the bass patterns

[12] See, for example, the introduction to Le RoyP, and my review of that volume in *Music Library Association Notes*, XX (1963), 558. In this case stylistic evidence strongly suggests that the compositions were originally conceived for lute, or for lute and voice.

resemble each other, or the harmonies are the same. It has not been possible to include all of these resemblances in the inventories of the present bibliography. The reader is referred to Lawrence Moe, "Dance Music in Printed Italian Lute Tablatures from 1507 to 1611" (unpub. diss., Harvard University, 1956), for concordances for all of the Italian lute dances, and to Daniel Heartz, "Sources and Forms of the French Instrumental Dance in the Sixteenth Century" (unpub. diss., Harvard University, 1957), for concordances for all of the French dances. I am grateful to Professors Moe and Heartz for their important contributions to this bibliography. Vocal melodies used as a basis for dances are cited comparatively infrequently (and usually with the admonition to compare the melody with the dance—see, for example, 148?$_1$). Such relationships are listed here only when they can be proven beyond the shadow of a doubt. One number in the inventories has been given to each group of dances. Pavane-gaillarde pairs and Pavana-saltarello pairs are numbered as one composition, and so are suites of three and four dances, while series of branles, allemandes, and courantes have been numbered separately. The reader may complain that this system is sometimes arbitrary and involves interpreting the contents. It is not always clear from the original volumes which dances are to be grouped into units, but, in spite of this drawback, such a numbering system reveals the conventional groupings more easily, and allows the reader to see at a glance how a volume is organized. Smaller sections within a single dance movement—those sections marked "reprise" or "alio modo" for example—have been omitted from the inventories.

CHRONOLOGICAL BIBLIOGRAPHY

148?1

TOULOUZE, MICHEL DE, PUBLISHER

Sensuit lart et instruction de bien dancer.

12 fols. Mensural notation. On fol. B6v: cut of a couple dancing and the colophon, "Cy finissent les regles de dancer toutes dances avecques celles regles sont notees pour Jouer a tous Instrumens nouvellement imprimees a paris aumont sainct hylaire par Michiel tholouze a lenseigne de la corne du cerf." Beginning on fol. A1: instructions for dancing, including choreographies with monophonic melodies (dance tenors). TouA is a facsimile reprint of this dance manual. All but four of the tenors (nos. 10, 11, 45, and 46) are also in the "Brussels Basse Dance Manuscript" (B:Br, MS 9085; printed in facsimile in ClosBD). For further information see MeM, SmithFC (which includes a facsimile of fol. B6v and of no. 20), and the bibliography in BukMR, pp. 212–216. For a detailed comparison of the Toulouze choreographies with those in the Brussels Manuscript, see HeartzBD, pp. 331–332. A modern edition of the Toulouze and Brussels choreographies appears in JackBD.

Copy in: GB:Lrc.

	fol.	
1	A3v	*Le petit Rouen*
2	A3v	*Filles a marier* (compare GomVC, p. xxxvii, and PlamSC, pp. 119–121)
3	A3v	*Ma maistresse*
4	A4	*Le hault & bas*
5	A4	*Le moys de may*
6	A4v	*Triste playsir* (compare BinchoisC, no. 45, and GurB, pp. 160–161)
7	A4v	*La poytevine*
8	A5	*Langueur en nul soit destresse*[1] (compare the Rostocker Liederbuch, "Mir ist mein Pferd" [RanR, no. 38], and the Lochamer Liederbuch, no. 48: "Virginalis flos" [SalmL, p. 90])
9	A5	*Le joyeulx espoyr* (compare no. 34 below)
10	A5	*Casulle la novele* (= "La Spagna"; see GomVC, pp. lxii–lxiii, and BukMR, pp. 190–216)
11	A5v	*Torin*
12	A5v	*Le grand roysin*
13	A5v	*Avignon*
14	A6	*Je languis*
15	A6	*Le petit roysin*
16	A6v	*Ma myeulx aymeye*
17	A6v	*Le grant thorin*
18	A6v	*Ma doulce amour* (compare GB:Ob, MS Canonici misc. 213, no. 290 [see ReaneyMS], and GurB, pp. 160–161)
19	B1	*La beaulte de castille*
20	B1	*Roti bolli joieulx*[2] (compare KinDT, p. 22)
21	B1v	*Lesperance de bourbon en pas de barbain* [sic]
22	B1v	*Sensuit la basse dance Lesperance de bourbon*
23	B1v	*Aliot novelle*
24	B2	*La basse dance du roy*
25	B2	*Lespoyr* (compare BinchoisC, no. 30: "Mon doulx espoir," and GurB, pp. 160–161)
26	B2v	*Beaulte*
27	B2v	*Mamie*
28	B2v	*La verdelete*
29	B3	*Le joyeulx de brucelles*
30	B3	*Engolesme*
31	B3	*La belle*
32	B3v	*Bayonne*
33	B3v	*La navaroyse*
34	B3v	*Barcelone* (compare no. 9 above)
35	B4	*Florentine*
36	B4	*La tantayne*
37	B4	*Barbesieux*
38	B4v	*La rochele*
39	B4v	*Orlyans*
40	B5	*Mamour*

41 B5 *Alenchon*
42 B5 *La portingaloyse*[3]
43 B5 *Vatem mon amoureux desir*[4]
44 B5v *Joyeusement*
45 B5v *Passe rose*
46 B5v *La basine*
47 B5v *Ma souverayne* (compare PlamF, p. 6, no. 102)
48 B6 *La marguerite*
49 B6 *Vyses*

[1] Facs. of fol. A5 in BukMR, opp. p. 128.
[2] Mod. ed. in KinDT, p. 102. Facs. of fol. B1 in PN, p. 63.
[3] Apparently not related to Dufay's "Portugaler" (mod. ed. in BorD, pp. 297–302).
[4] Apparently not related to "Va tost mon amoureux desir," in I:Fr, MS 2356; see PlamSC, no. 30.

1501₁

PETRUCCI, OTTAVIANO, PUBLISHER

Harmonice Musices / Odhecaton / A[1]

104 fols. Mensural notation. Dedication to Girolamo Donato on fol. 1v headed "Octavianus petrutius forosemproniensis Hieronymo Donato patricio Veneto Felicitatem," and dated "Venetiis decimo octavo cal. iuias. Salutis anno. MDI." (May 15, 1501). On fol. 2: a letter from Bartolomeo Budrio to Girolamo Donato, headed "Bartholomaeus Budrius Justinopolita Hieronymo donato patricio Veneto. S." On fol. 2v: table of contents. All of the prefatory material is reprinted in SartP, pp. 34–37. PetrO is a facsimile reprint (made from 1504₂) of the entire collection, Petrucci's first publication, and the first volume of polyphonic music ever printed. HewO is a modern edition of the entire collection, with an extensive introduction, several facsimile pages, and complete concordances. For further information, see also ReO and SartP, pp. 34–42. The volume contains 96 compositions, most of them with text incipits only. At least four of these were almost certainly originally conceived for instruments (see the statement of policy in the Introduction, above, and also CauO, CauT, and HewO, pp. 74–78, where seven such pieces from this volume are listed and discussed). Contents = 1503₁ and 1504₂.

Copy in: I:Bc (imperfect).

fol.
1 20v *Dit le burguygnon* *a4*
2 49v *La morra*[2] Yzac *a3*
3 54v *La stangetta*[3] Werbach [or Obrecht?] *a3*
4 87v *La alfonsina*[4] Jo. ghiselin *a3*

[1] Facs. of title page in GrandT, p. 7. Facs. of title page and one other page in MagniSM I, 239. Facs. of several pages in AbbS I, 331; PN, p. 66; ReO; and VernO, fig. 3.
[2] Mod. ed. also in DTO XIV/28, p. 90, and RieM, no. 18.
[3] Mod. ed. also in ObrWW, p. 45.
[4] Mod. ed. also in AmbG V, 190, and GiesS, p. 92.

1502₁

PETRUCCI, OTTAVIANO, PUBLISHER

Motetti A numero / trentatre. / A

56 fols. Mensural notation. On fol. 1v: table of contents. Colophon on fol. 56: "Impressum Venetiis per Octavianum Petrutium Forosemproniensem die 9 Madii Salutis anno 1502. Cum privilegio invictissimi Dominii Venetiarum quod nullus possit cantum Figuratum Imprimere sub pena in ipso privilegio contenta," followed by the register of signatures. For further information see SartP, pp. 44–46. The volume contains 32 compositions with Latin text, two vocal compositions ("O flores rosa" and "De tous biens") with text incipit only, and one composition for instruments. SartP gives a complete list of the contents.

Copy in: I:Bc.[1]

fol.
1 32 *La spagna*[2] Ghiselin *a4*

[1] A copy was in E:S; see SartN, no. 11.
[2] The beginning is pr. in GomVC, p. 1.

1503₁

PETRUCCI, OTTAVIANO, PUBLISHER

Harmonice Musices / Odhecaton / A

104 fols. Mensural notation. The prefatory material is identical with that in the first edition (1501₁). Colophon on fol. 104: "Impressum Venetiis per Octavianum Petrutium Forosemproniensem 1502 die 14 Januarii. Cum privilegio invictissimi Dominii

Venetiarum quod nullus possit cantum Figuratum imprimere sub pena in ipso privilegio contenta," followed by the register of signatures. For further information see SartP, pp. 52–55. Contents = 1501_1.

Copy in: E:S (imperfect).

1504_1

PETRUCCI, OTTAVIANO, PUBLISHER

Canti. C. N° cento / Cinquanta. / C [1]

168 fols. Mensural notation. On fol. 2: table of contents. Colophon on fol. 168: "Impressum Venetiis per Octavianum Petrutium Forosemproniensem 1503 die 10 Februarii. Cum privilegio invictissimi Dominii Venetiarum quod nullus possit cantum Figuratum imprimere sub pena in ipso privilegio contenta," followed by the register of signatures. For further information see SartP, pp. 69–74. The volume contains 139 compositions, including at least four which were almost certainly originally conceived for instruments. SartP gives a complete list of the contents.

Copies in: A:Wn, F:Pc, I:TVcap (imperfect).[2]

	fol.	
1	131ᵛ	*Vive le roy* [3] Josquin *a4*
2	147ᵛ	*La spagna* [4] *a3*
3	151ᵛ	*Le hault dalemaigne* Mathurin *a3*
4	157ᵛ	*La bernardina* [5] Josquin *a3*

[1] Facs. of title page in SchmidOP, fig. 1. Facs. of several pages in CesF, p. viii, and IMAMI I, viii.

[2] A copy was in E:S; see SartN, no. 12.

[3] Mod. ed. in ChilS, no. 13, and ScherG, no. 62a.

[4] The beginning is transcribed in BukMR, p. 205; this piece is intabulated in 1507_2, no. 24; see also GomVC, p. lxii.

[5] Mod. ed. in KiesS, app., no. 20; KiesT, app., p. 64; and ScherG, no. 62b.

1504_2

PETRUCCI, OTTAVIANO, PUBLISHER

Harmonice Musices / Odhecaton / A [1]

104 fols. Mensural notation. The prefatory material is identical with that in the first edition (1501_1). Colophon on fol. 104: "Impressum Venetiis per Octavianum Petrutium Forosemproniensem 1504 die 25 Maii. Cum privilegio invictissimi Dominii Venetiarum quod nullus possit cantum Figuratum imprimere sub pena in ipso privilegio contenta," followed by the register of signatures. For further information see SartP, pp. 77–82. PetrO is a facsimile of the entire collection, made from the Treviso copy. Contents = 1501_1.

Copies in: E:Mmc, F:Pc, I:TVcap (imperfect), NL:DHg, US:Wc.[2]

[1] Facs. of title page in ZurM, p. 12.

[2] The Hague copy was in the Wolffheim library (see WolffC II, no. 1909).

$[1505]_1$

MARCO D'AQUILA

[Intabulatura de lauto]

In 1505 Marco d'Aquila received a ten-year privilege from the Signoria of Venice to print lute books. No volumes are known to have been printed by him. The privilege (reprinted in SchmidOP, pp. 12–13, after Venice, Archivio dell'Ex-Veneta Cancelleria Ducale, Registro Notatorio XXIII, 1499–1506, fol. 141) reads:

Serenissimi Principi ejusque Sapientissimo Consiglio.

Humiliter supplica et servitor de la Sublimità Vostra Marco da l'Aquila cum sit che cum grandissima sua fatica et spesa non mediocre se habii inzegnato a comune utilitate de quelli che se delectarono sonar de Lauto nobilissimo Instrumento pertinente a Vary Zentilhomini far stampar la tabullatura, et rasone de metter ogni Canto in lauto cum summa industria, et arte; et cum molto dispendio de tempo, et facultade sua: la qual opera non mai e sta stampata: Se degni la Illustrissima Signoria Vostra concieder de special gratia al prefato supplicante vostro fidelissimo: che alcun chi esser se vogli si in questa Cità de Venetia, come in tutte altre terre, et lochi nel Dominio de la Sublimità Vostra non ardisca, over prosama far stampar alcuna tabullatura de lauto de alcuna sorte, nec etiam se alcuno la stampasse extra ditionem Illustrissimi Dominii Vestri, possi quella vender, over far vender in questa Cità ne altrove nel predicto Dominio, sotto pena, si a quelli, che la stampasseno in le terre de la Sublimità Vostra, come a quelli la conducesseno a vender in ipse terre de perder irrimissibiliter le loro opere et libri tabullati, et per cadauno de quelli stampati, over venduti pagar Ducati X. Il terzo de la qual pena sia del accusator, un terzo de quel rector, over Magistrato a chi sara facta la accusa, et l'altro terzo de epso supplicante aciò el possi cum tal gratia de Vostra Celsitudine continuar a vender le ditte opere et libri tabullati, et che alcun non li togli la industria et utilità che cum tanti sudori, et vigilie el prefato fidelissimo supplicante se ha acquistato, et questa prohibitione se intendi valer per anni X. come in similibus ad altri e sta concesso: ai piedi de la qual Sublimità Vostra humiliter se ricomanda.

Die 11. Martii 1505.

Infrascripti Domini Consiliarii intelecta suprascripta suplicatione terminaverunt quod suprascripto suplicanti, fiat quod petit.

Consiliarii.
Ser Franciscus Barbadico.
Ser Nicolaus Foscareno.
Ser Marcus de Molino.
Ser Andreas Gritti.

1507$_1$

SPINACINO, FRANCESCO

Intabulatura de Lauto / Libro primo.

56 fols. Italian lute tablature. Colophon on fol. 56: "Impressum Venetiis: Per Octavianum Petrutium Forosemproniensem: 1507. Cum privilegio invictissimi Dominii Venetiarum quod nullus possit imprimere intabulaturam lauti. ut in suo privilegio continet." On fol. 2: "Regula pro illis qui canere nesciunt" (in Latin and Italian); the same instructions "for those who cannot sing" appear in 1507_2, 1508_2, 1509_1, 1511_1, and $152?_1$.[1] On fol. 2^v: a preface by the printer, dated "Venetiis. iii. Calendas Martias. Anno Salutis. M. D. VII," a poem headed "Christophorus Pierius Gigas Forosemproniensis in Laudem Francisci Spinacini," and the table of contents. The initials F. S. (Francesco Spinacino) appear in the volume over the pieces followed here by an asterisk. The compositions identified by the superior letter *a* ([a]) are reprinted in DiseF, pp. 176–247. SlimK II, 434, contains a thematic index of the ricercares. All of the compositions are for solo lute except nos. 8–12, which are for two lutes.[2]

	fol.	
1	3	*Ave Maria de Josquin** [3] [a] (JosqMT, no. 2)
2	4	*Benedictus de Isach** [a] (HewO, no. 76)
3	5	*Le desproveu infortune** (RISM 1504_3, no. 94: Caron?)
4	6^v	*Come feme** (RISM 1504_3, no. 120: Alexander Agricola)
5	8	*Fortuna dun gran tempo** [4] [a] (HewO, no. 74: Josquin?)
6	9	*Una maistres** (RISM 1504_3, no. 129: Brumel)
7	10	*Vostre a Jamays** [5] (RISM 1504_3, no. 130: "Vostre a jamais / J'en ay dueul," Ghiselin)
8	11	*Juli amours** [a] [two lutes] (RISM 1504_3, no. 115: Ghiselin; compare no. 23 below)
	13	2a pars
9	16	*De tous biens** [a] [two lutes] (HewO, no. 20: Hayne; compare no. 22 below)
10	19	*La Bernardina de Josquin** [two lutes] (ScherG, no. 62b; see no. 15 below)
11	21	*Je ne fay** [two lutes] (HewO, no. 8)
	22^v	2a pars [*De lyvres plains*]
12	23^v	*Jay pris amours** [a] [two lutes] (DrozT, no. 2)
	24^v	2a pars [*Heureux seray*]
13	26	*La Mora** (HewO, no. 44: Isaac)
14	27	*O Venus banth** (HewO, no. 78: Josquin [or Gaspar?])
15	27^v	*La Bernardina de Josquin** [6] (ScherG, no. 62b; see no. 10 above)
16	28^v	*Bassadans* [7] (1504_1, no. 2: "La Spagna")
17	31	*Ma buche rit* (HewO, no. 54: Ockeghem)

18 32^v *Adiu mes amours**[8] (HewO, no. 14: Josquin)
19 33^v *Nunquam fuit pena maior* (HewO, no. 4: Juan Urrede)
20 35^v *Non sovenir* (HewO, no. 83: "Mon souvenir," Hayne)
36 *Replica* (= coda)
21 36^v *Fortuna per te crudele*[a] (HewO, no. 60)
22 37^v *Recercare de tous biens**[9] (compare no. 9 above)
23 38 *Recercare a Juli amours**[10] (compare no. 8 above)
24 39 *Recercare**[11]
25 39^v *Recercare*
26 40^v *Recercare de tutti li Toni*[12]
27 42^v *Recercare*
28 43 *Recercare*
29 44 *Recercare*
30 44^v *Recercare*[13]
31 46^v *Recercare*[14]
32 47 *Recercare*
33 47^v *Recercare*
34 49 *Recercare*
35 50 *Recercare*
36 51 *Recercare*
37 52 *Recercare*
38 53^v *Recercare*

[1] The "Regula" are repr. in SartP, pp. 140 (from 1508$_2$) and 148 (from 1509$_1$); facs. and German transl. (from 1507$_2$) in WolfH II, 53; Eng. transl. (after 1511$_1$) in SartFB.

[2] Copies were in D:Bds and E:S (see SartN, p. 193, and PlamEC, p. 679). A photostat of the Berlin copy is now in F:Pn. For further information see SartP, no. 30. Sartori is mistaken in stating that a copy is in A:Wn.

[3] Partial transcription in PirH, p. 135.

[4] Partial transcription in LowG, p. 62. See there for an extended discussion of the vocal model.

[5] No. 7 is listed as "Vostre a maistres" in the table of contents.

[6] Mod. ed. in ScherG, no. 63a.

[7] Partial transcription in GomVC, pp. li–lii, and ApelR, p. 143. Incipit in MoeDM, p. 348.

[8] Although Spinacino's name does not appear in the body of the print, this title in the table of contents is initialed "F. S." Facs. of fol. 32^v in WolfMS, no. 28.

[9] Mod. ed. in SlimK II, 601.

[10] Mod. ed. in SlimK II, 602.

[11] Mod. ed. in BarthaZ, no. 41; NeemAM I, no. 1; and ScherG, no. 63b. Facs. of fol. 39 in ApelN, facs. 19.

[12] Mod. ed. in KörL, p. 129.

[13] Mod. ed. in SlimK II, 598.

[14] Facs. of fol. 46^v in WolfH II, 55. Mod. ed. in HAM, no. 99b, where the source is incorrectly given as 1507$_2$, and in ZanG I, 14.

1507$_2$

SPINACINO, FRANCESCO

Intabulatura de Lauto / Libro secondo.

56 fols. Italian lute tablature. Colophon on fol. 56: "Impressum Venetiis: Per Octavianum Petrutium Forosemproniensem: Cum privilegio invictissimi dominii Venetiarum: quod nullus possit intabulaturam Lauti imprimere: sub peni: in ipso privilegio contentis. Die ultimo Martii 1507," followed by the register of signatures. On fol. 1^v: "Regula pro illis qui canere nesciunt" (in Latin and Italian; for concordances see 1507$_1$), followed by the table of contents (facsimile of fol. 1^v in WolfH II, 53, along with German translation of the "Regula"). The entire volume is by Francesco Spinacino. The compositions identified by the superior letter *a* ([a]) are reprinted in DiseF, pp. 184–242. SlimK II, 437–438, contains a thematic index of the ricercares. All of the compositions are for solo lute except no 29, which is for two lutes.[1]

fol.
1 2 *Bergirette savoyene*[2]
2 3 *Je ne cuide* (HewO, no. 2: "Je cuide se ce tamps me dure")
3 4^v *Christe de si dedero*[3a] (ObrMS III, Mass 9: Obrecht)
4 5^v *Agnus de ut re mi fa sol la* (SartP, no. 8: Mass 3, Agnus III: Brumel)
5 7 *Tandernaken*[a] (GomO, no. 25: Alexander Agricola)
6 9 *Je ne demande* (HewO, no. 42: Busnois)
7 10^v *Leure et venue* (HewO, no. 81: A. Agricola)
8 13 *Jay pris amours* (DrozT, no. 2)
9 14^v *Le sovenir* (JepK, no. 20: Morton?)
10 15^v *Haray tre amours* (HewO, no. 86: "Ha traitre amours," Stockhem)
11 16 *Palle de ysach*[4a] (DTO XIV/28, p. 98)
12 17^v *Cent mil escus* (RISM 1504$_3$, no. 96: Busnois?)
13 18^v *Malor me bat* (HewO, no. 63: Ockeghem?)

14 19[v] *Coment peult avoir Joye*[a] (RISM 1502_2, no. 19: Josquin)
15 20[v] *Dung autramer* (DrozT, no. 36: Ockeghem)
16 21[v] *A le regretz* (HewO, no. 48: A. Agricola)
17 22[v] *Amours amours* (HewO, no. 9: Hayne)
18 23[v] *Mo mari ma defame* (GB:Lbm, Add. MS 35087, fol. 21[v])
19 24[v] *Helogeron nous* (HewO, no. 40: Isaac)
20 25 *Kyrie de lez armes* (SartP, no. 9: Mass 2: Ghiselin)
21 26 *Marguerit* (HewO, no. 85)
22 27[v] *Motetto o dulcis Jesu de sopra el pater nostro* (RISM 1504_1, fol. 15)
23 29[v] *Si dedero* (HewO, no. 56: Alexander [Agricola])
24 31 *Bassadanza*[5] (RISM 1504_3, no. 121: "La Spagna")
25 33[v] *Mater patris & filia*[a] (HewO, no. 62: Brumel)
26 35 *Lome bani* (HewO, no. 47: A. Agricola)
27 36[v] *Pensi che mai* (HewO, no. 43: "Pensif mari," Tadinghen)
28 37[v] *La stanghetta* (HewO, no. 49: Weerbecke or Obrecht?)
29 38[v] *Fortuna desperata* [two lutes] (JosqMS I, 106: anon.)
30 41[v] *Si fays viey* (I:Fn, MS Magl. XIX, 59, fol. 82[v]: "Se je fais bien," A. Agricola)
31 42[v] *Je ne fay cont damer*
32 43[v] *La Mignonne [de fortune]* (I:Fn, MS Magl. XIX, 59, fol. 130[v]: A. Agricola)
33 45[v] *In pace in idipsum* (I:Fn, MS Magl. XIX, 59, fol. 43[v]: Josquin)
34 47 *Recercare*
35 48 *Recercare*
36 48 *Recercare*
37 49[v] *Recercare*
38 50[v] *Recercare*
39 51[v] *Recercare*[6] = 1568_1, no. 44
40 52[v] *Recercare*
41 53[v] *Recercare* = 1568_1, no. 42
42 54[v] *Recercare* = 1568_1, no. 41
43 55[v] *Recercare*[7]

[1] Copies were in D:Bds and E:S (see SartN, p. 193, and PlamEC, p. 679). A photostat of the Berlin copy is now in F:Pn. For further information on 1507_2, see SartP, no. 131. Sartori is mistaken in stating that a copy is in A:Wn.

[2] No. 1 has no apparent musical relation to the chanson "Bergerette savoisienne," a monophonic version of which is pr. in ParisC, no. 12. This melody is incorporated in the anon. setting in RISM 1504_3, no. 42, and in the settings by Josquin (HewO, no. 10) and by Compère (Segovia Chansonnier [E:SE, MS s.n.], fol. 154).

[3] Facs. of fol. 4[v] in WolfH II, 52.

[4] Mod. ed. in DTO XIV/28, p. 90.

[5] Incipit in MoeDM, p. 348.

[6] Mod. ed. in BruAL I, 17; EnI, p. 7; and NeemAM I, no. 2.

[7] Mod. ed. in GomVC, p. xxxi.

$[1508]_1$

GIOVAN MARIA[1]

Intabulatura di Lauto, Libro Tertio.

The third of Petrucci's lute tablatures is now lost. Knowledge of the work is limited to the information contained in an entry made by Fernando Colón in the *Regestrum B* of the Biblioteca Colombina, Seville (see HuntingC, no. 2582, and PlamEC, p. 679): "Intabulatura de lauto libro tertio. et opera quae continet sunt Joannis marie alemani cuius epistola I. Come la musica. Cantilene sunt 25 quorum tabula est in principio. Item Regula pro illis qui canere nesciunt Italice et Latine. Italice I. prima deve. Latine I. intelligendum est. prima cantilena I. come feme. ultima I. Recercare giovan maria. Imp. venetiis anno 1508 Junii 20. est in 4° ad longum. Costo en Roma 110 quatrines por Setiembre de 1512."

[1] On the identity of this composer see SlimK I, 383.

1508_2

DALZA, JOAN AMBROSIO

Intabulatura de Lauto / Libro Quarto. / Padoane diverse. / Calate a la spagnola. / Calate a la taliana. / Tastar de corde con li / soi recercar drietro [*sic*]. / Frottole. / Joanambrosio.

56 fols. Italian lute tablature. On fol. 1[v]: "Regula per quelli che non sanno cantare" (in Italian only; for concordances see 1507_1), followed by a note stating that "tutte le pavane hanno el suo saltarello e piva,"

followed by the table of contents headed "Tavola de la presente opera composta per lo excelente musico e sonator de lauto. Joanambrosio dalza milanese." The "Regula" and table of contents are reprinted in SartP, pp. 140–142. Colophon on fol. 56: "Impressum Venetiis: Per Octavianum Petrutium Forosemproniensem: Cum privilegio invictissimi dominii Venetiarum: quod nullus possit intabulaturam Lauti imprimere: sub penis in ipso privilegio contentis. Die ultimo Decembris. 1508." SlimK II, 438, contains a thematic index of the ricercares. MoeDM contains a thematic index (p. 349) and a table of concordances of the dances (p. 220). All of the compositions are for solo lute except nos. 24–26, which are for two lutes.

Copies in: A:Wn, B:Br, US:Cn (imperfect).[1]

	fol.	
1	2	*Caldibi castigliano*[2]
2	3	*Recercar*[3]
3	3^v	*Tastar de corde*[4]
4	3^v	*Tastar de corde*[5]
5	3^v	*Recercar dietro*
6	4	*Tastar de corde*
7	4^v	*Recercar dietro* = 1545_3, no. 11
8	5	*Tastar de corde*[6]
9	5^v	*Recercar dietro*[7]
10	6	*Tastar de corde*[8]
11	6^v	*Recercar [dietro]*[8]
12	7	*Recercar*[9]
13	8	*Recercar*
14	8	*Recercar*
15	9	*Pavana alla venetiana*[10]
	9^v	*Saltarello*
	10^v	*Piva*
16	11^v	*Pavana alla venetiana*
	12^v	*Saltarello*
	13^v	*Piva*
17	14	*Pavana alla venetiana*[11]
	14^v	*Saltarello*
	15^v	*Piva*
18	16^v	*Pavana alla venetiana*[12] (compare 1523_2, no. 5)
	17	*Saltarello*
	17	*Piva*
19	18	*Pavana alla venetiana*
	19	*Saltarello*
	20	*Piva*
20	21	*Pavana alla ferrarese*[13]
	22	*Saltarello*
	23^v	*Piva*
21	24^v	*Pavana alla ferrarese*
	25^v	*Saltarello*
	26^v	*Piva*
22	27^v	*Pavana alla ferrarese*
	29^v	*Saltarello*
	31^v	*Spingardo*
23	33	*Pavana alla ferrarese*
	34^v	*Saltarello*
	36	*Spingardo* (D:Mbs, Mus. MS 1511b, fol. 13^v: "Saltarello ala ferrarese")
24	37	*Saltarello* [two lutes]
25	39	*Piva* [two lutes]
26	41	*Calata* [two lutes]
27	43	*Calata dito zigonze*
28	44^v	*Calata de strambotti*[14]
	44^v	2a pars
29	45	*Calata*[15]
30	46	*Calata*
31	46^v	*Calata*
32	47	*Calata*
33	47^v	*Calata ala spagnola* = 1523_2, no. 33
34	48^v	*Calata spagnola* (at end: *Recercar detto coda*)
35	49	*Calata ala spagnola*
36	49^v	*Calata ala spagnola*
37	50	*Calata spagnola*
38	50^v	*Calata ala spagnola ditto terzetti di zuan ambroso dalza*
39	52	*Poi chel ciel contrario adverso*[16] (CesF, p. 18: B[artolomeo] T[romboncino])
40	53^v	*Poi che volse la mia stella*[17] (CesF, p. 107: B[artolomeo] T[romboncino])
41	54	*Patientia ognun me dice* (F:Pn, Rés. Vm^7 676, fol. 18^v)
42	55^v	*Laudato dio*[18]

[1] A copy was in E:S (see SartN, p. 206, and PlamEC, p. 679).

[2] A corruption of "Calvi vi valvi, calvi arravi," the "Arabic" tune quoted in SaliM, p. 339, in connection with the Spanish text "Rey don Alfonso Rey me senor."

[3] Mod. ed. in WasG, no. 12.

[4] Mod. ed. in ApelM I, 20, and WolfH II, 54, with a quasi-facs.

[5] Mod. ed. in EP, p. 1209; HAM, no. 99a; and KörL, p. 132.

[6] Mod. ed. and facs. in AdlerH I, 398.

[7] Mod. ed. in ZanG II, 16.

[8] Mod. ed. in BruS II, no. 73, and TapS, pp. 4–5.

[9] Mod. ed. in SlimK II, 603.

[10] Melody only of nos. 18a and b in KörL, pp. 148–149. Melody only of first phrase of nos. 15a, 16a, 17a, 18a, and 19a in GomVC, p. lxv; melody only of first phrases of nos. 20a, 21a, 22a, and 23a

in GomVC, p. lxiv. Mod. ed. of nos. 15a–c in MoeDM, p. 319.

[11] Facs. of fol. 14 in PN, p. 67.

[12] Mod. ed. (somewhat arranged) in ApelM I, 20.

[13] Mod. ed. in LowT, p. 63, and ZanG II, 4.

[14] Mod ed. in BruS I, no. 28; EC, pt. I, vol. III, p. 1220; and WasG, no. 2.

[15] Mod. ed. in MoeDM, p. 322.

[16] Mod. ed. in PirF, pp. 6–9, and DiseF, p. 225.

[17] Mod. ed. in PirF, p. 10, and DiseF, p. 223.

[18] Mod. ed. in DiseF, p. 228.

1509_1

BOSSINENSIS, FRANCISCUS

Tenori e contrabassi intabu/lati col sopran in canto fi/gurato per cantar e so/nar col lauto Li/bro primo. / Francisci Bossinensis / Opus.

56 fols. Italian lute tablature and mensural notation. On fol. 1ᵛ: table of contents including a list of the "Recercar li quali serveno a le frottole secondo lordino de le littere sottoscripte." On fol. 2: "Regola per quelli che non sanno cantare" (in Italian only; for concordances see 1507_1). On fol. 2ᵛ: dedication to "Reverendo in Cristo Patri Domino .D. Hieronymo Barbadico Prothonotario appostolico ac primicerio .S. Marci Venetiarum dignissimo patrono singulari Franciscus bossinensis. S. P. D.," followed by a poem in Italian signed B. M. F. On fols. 55ᵛ–56: extra verses of text for some of the intabulations. Colophon on fol. 56: "Impressum Venetiis: Per Octavianum Petrutium Forosemproniensem: Cum privilegio invictissimi dominii Venetiarum: quod nullus possit intabulaturam Lauti imprimere: sub penis in ipso privilegio contentis. Die 27 Martii. 1509," followed by the printer's mark. The entire collection is reprinted in DiseF, which includes facsimiles of the title page, fols. 49ᵛ and 50, the table of contents, and the colophon. For further information see SartP, pp. 146–151, which reprints the table of contents, the "Regola," the dedication, and the poem. SlimK II, 441, contains a thematic index of the ricercares. Nos. 1–70 are for solo voice (written in mensural notation) and lute; nos. 71–96 are for solo lute. In the following inventory the composers' initials are resolved the first time they appear only.

Copies in: A:Wn, E:S, F:Pc, US:Cn (imperfect).

SONGS FOR SOLO VOICE AND LUTE

	fol.	
1	3	*Afflitti spirti miei* [1] B[artolomeo] T[romboncino] (RISM 1507_3, fol. 2)
2	3ᵛ	*Sel morir mai de gloria* B. T. (RISM 1507_3, fol. 3ᵛ)
3	4	*Accio chel tempo e i cieli* B. T. (RISM 1507_3, fol. 4)
4	4ᵛ	*O dolce e lieto albergo* (RISM 1505_5, fol. 45ᵛ)
5	5	*Si e debile il filo a cui* B. T. (RISM 1507_3, fol. 4ᵛ)
6	6	*Con pianto e con dolore* (RISM 1505_5, fol. 42)
7	6ᵛ	*Sil disi mai chio venga in odio* B.T. (RISM 1507_3, fol. 31ᵛ)
8	7ᵛ	*Che debo far che mi consigli* B.T. (RISM 1507_3, fol. 13ᵛ)
9	8ᵛ	*Haime per che mhai privo* (RISM 1507_3, fol. 47)
10	9	*Voi che passate qui* F[rancesco d'Ana] V[enetus organista] (RISM 1507_3, fol. 18: B. T.)
11	9ᵛ	*Non peccando altri chel core* B.T. (RISM 1507_3, fol. 26ᵛ: M[arco] C[ara])
12	10ᵛ	*Cade ogni mio pensier* B. T. (RISM 1507_3, fol. 46ᵛ)
13	11	*Ala fama si va per varie scale* (RISM 1509_2, fol. 9: B. T.)
14	11ᵛ	*Chi in pregion crede tornarmi* B. T. (RISM 1507_4, fol. 3ᵛ)
15	12ᵛ	*Spargean per lariale annodate* B. T. (RISM 1507_4, fol. 5ᵛ)
16	13	*Zephyro spira e il bel tempo rimena* B. T. (RISM 1507_4, fol. 6ᵛ)
17	14	*Ho scoperto il tanto aperto* B. T. (RISM 1507_4, fol. 16ᵛ)
18	14ᵛ	*Deh non piu deh non piu mo* M. C. (RISM 1507_3, fol. 44ᵛ)
19	15ᵛ	*O despietato tempo* P. Zanin [Bisan] (RISM 1507_3, fol. 50ᵛ)
20	16ᵛ	*Io cercho pur la insupportabil* B. T. (RISM 1507_3, fol. 52ᵛ)
21	17	*Chi lharebbe mai creduto* (RISM 1509_2, fol. 17: M. C.)
22	17ᵛ	*Arma del mio valor* [2] M. C. (RISM 1509_2, fol. 16ᵛ)
23	18	*Lacrime e voi sospir* (RISM 1505_5, fol. 42ᵛ)

24 18^v *Nasce laspro mio tormento* F. V. (CesF, p. 52)

25 19 *O mia cieca e dura sorte* (CesF, p. 5: M. C.)

26 20 *Se per chieder merce gratia simpetra* M. C. (RISM 1507_4, fol. 10^v)

27 20^v *Ostinato vo seguire* (RISM 1509_2, fol. 12^v: B. T.)

28 22 *Tu dormi io veglio a la tempesta* B. T. (RISM 1506_3, fol. 9)

29 22^v *Deus in adiutorium meum intende* B. T. (RISM 1505_5, fol. 9^v)

30 23 *Mia benigna fortuna el viver lieto* (RISM 1509_2, fol. 37^v)

31 23^v *Come chel bianco cigno* M. C. (CesF, p. 11)

32 24 *Aqua aqua aiutal foco* B. T. (RISM 1509_2, fol. 40^v)

33 24^v *Sera forsi ripreso il pensier mio* B. T. (RISM 1509_2, fol. 30^v)

34 25 *Chi vi dara piu luce* F. V.

35 25^v *Son piu tua che non son mia*[3] M. C. (RISM 1507_4, fol. 33^v)

36 26^v *Chi vi dara piu luce* B. T. (RISM 1507_4, fol. 54)

37 27 *Poi che volse la mia stella*[4] B. T. (CesF, p. 107)

38 28 *Deh si deh no deh si* B. T. (CesF, p. 12: M. C.)

39 28^v *Sio gel dico che dira* B. T. (RISM 1507_4, fol. 2^v)

40 29^v *Crudel come mai potesti*[5] (CesF, p. 18: B. T.)

41 30^v *Scopri lingua el cieco ardore* B. T. (CesF, p. 14)

42 31 *Se de fede vengo ameno* M. C. (CesF, p. 7)

43 32 *Oime il cor oime la testa*[6] M. C. (CesF, p. 3)

44 32^v *Non e tempo daspetare*[7] M. C. (CesF, p. 3)

45 33 *Hor venduto ho la speranza* M. C. (CesF, p. 6)

46 34 *Io non compro piu speranza*[8] M. C. (CesF, p. 8)

47 34^v *La fortuna vol cosi* (CesF, p. 13: M. C.)

48 35 *In hospitas per alpes* D. M[ichele Pesenti] (CesF, p. 34)

49 35^v *Se me grato il tuo tornare* Phi[lippo] de Lu[prano] (CesF, p. 41)

50 36 *Integer vite scelerisque purus*[9] D. M. (CesF, p. 35)

51 36^v *Ben chamor me facci torto*[10] B. T. (CesF, p. 22)

52 37 *Ognun fugga fugga amore* Ant[onio] Cap[rioli Brixiensis] (RISM 1505_5, fol. 36^v)

53 38 *Poi chel ciel contrario adverso*[11] B. T. (CesF, p. 18)

54 38^v *In te domine speravi* Josquin [des Prez] Dascanio (CesF, p. 38)

55 39^v *Ala guerra ala guerra* B. T. (CesF, p. 26)

56 40 *El convera chio mora* B. T. (CesF, p. 21)

57 40^v *Udite voi finestre*[12] M. C. (CesF, p. 10)

58 41 *Poi che per fede manca* Ant. Cap. Brixiensis (CesF, p. 13)

59 41^v *Aime chio moro* D. M. C. (CesF, p. 33: Micha[el Pesenti])

60 42^v *Ben chel ciel me thabbi tolto*[13] B. T. (RISM 1509_2, fol. 7^v)

61 44 *O cara libertade* (RISM 1506_3, fol. 49)

62 44^v *Piu non tamo aibo aibo* M. C. (RISM 1509_2, fol. 18^v)

63 45^v *Sel affannato cor in foco giace* F. V. (RISM 1505_5, fol. 22^v)

64 46 *Ti par gran maraveglia* N[icolaus] P[ifaro] (RISM 1505_5, fol. 17^v)

65 46^v *Chi me dara piu pace* M. C. (CesF, p. 11)

66 47 *Pieta cara signora* M. C. (CesF, p. 12)

67 47^v *Non som qual chio solea* Phi. D. L. (RISM 1506_3, fol. 2)

68 48 *Se ben il fin de la mia vita asento* M. C. (RISM 1506_3, fol. 42^v)

69 48^v *Non si po qual che si vole* Phi. D. L. (RISM 1506_3, fol. 47^v)

70 49 *De che parlera piu la lingua mia* M. C.

SOLO LUTE PIECES

71 49^v *Recercar primo*

72 49^v *2.*[14]

73 50 *3.*[15]

74 50 *4.*

75 50 *5.*[16]

76 50^v *6.*

77 51 *7.*[17]

78 51 *8.*

79 51 *9.*

80	51	*10.*
81	51^{v}	*11.*
82	52	*12.*
83	52	*13.*
84	52	*14.*[18]
85	52	*15.*[19]
86	52^{v}	*16.*[20]
87	52^{v}	*17.*
88	53	*18.*
89	53	*19.*
90	53^{v}	*20.*
91	53^{v}	*21.*
92	54	*22.*
93	54	*23.*
94	54^{v}	*24.*[21]
95	55	*25.*
96	55	*26.*

[1] Facs. of fol. 3 in SchmidOP, fig 3.
[2] Facs. of fol. 17^{v} in PirH, pl. XVI.
[3] The title is given here as it appears in the table of contents. The text under the voice line reads "Som pi tua che non sia mia."
[4] Mod. ed. in PirF, pp. 6–9.
[5] Mod. ed. in FerandIM, pp. 383–384.
[6] Mod. ed. in ReMR, pp. 163–164.
[7] Mod. ed. in ScherG, no. 72.
[8] Mod. ed. in BruAL I, 13, and in MagniSM I, 249–250. Quasi-facs. in WolfH II, 60.
[9] Mod. ed. in BruS III, no. 116; ScherG, no. 74; and TapS, pp. 6–7 (with a quasi-facs. of fol. 36).
[10] Mod. ed. and facs. of fols. 36^{v} and 37 in NoskeS, pp. 11, 17.
[11] Mod. ed. in PirF, p. 10.
[12] The table of contents reads "Odite voi finestre."
[13] The initials "D. M." appear on fol. 43^{v} over the last page of no. 60.
[14] Mod. ed. in ApelM I, 21.
[15] Mod. ed. in BruS I, no. 33, and WasG, no. 13.
[16] Mod. ed. in SlimK II, 605.
[17] Mod ed. in TapS, p. 7.
[18] Mod. ed. in FerandIM, p. 382.
[19] Mod. ed. in EC, pt. I, vol. III, p. 1220.
[20] Mod. ed. in ReMR, p. 163.
[21] Mod. ed. in FerandIM, p. 382.

1511_1

BOSSINENSIS, FRANCISCUS

Tenori e contrabassi intabu/lati col sopran in canto fi/gurato per cantar e so/nar col lauto Li/bro Secundo. / Francisci Bossinensis / Opus.

64 fols. Italian lute tablature and mensural notation. On fol. 1^{v}: table of contents including a list of the "Recercar li quali serveno a le frottole secondo lordine de le littere sottoscripte." On fol. 2: "Regola per quelli che non sanno cantare" (in Italian only; for concordances see 1507_1). On fol. 2^{v}: the same dedicatory letter addressed to Girolamo Barbadico and poem in Italian as appear in 1509_1. Colophon on fol. 64: "Impressum in Forosempronii per Octavianum Petrutium Forosemproniensem Anno domini M D XI Die 10 Madii," followed by the printer's mark. For further information see SartP, pp. 152–159, which reprints the prefatory material. Facsimiles of fols. 1^{v} and 3 appear in SartFB, opposite p. 240; the same article contains an English translation of the prefatory material. The entire collection is reprinted in DiseF, which includes facsimiles of the title page, the "Regola," the dedication, fol. 48^{v}, and the colophon. BossR is a modern edition of the 20 ricercari in this volume. SlimK II, 445–449, contains a thematic index of the ricercares. Nos. 1–56 are for solo voice (written in mensural notation) and lute; nos. 57–76 are for solo lute. In the following inventory composers' initials are resolved the first time they appear only.

Copy in: I:Mb.[1]

SONGS FOR SOLO VOICE AND LUTE

	fol.	
1	3	*Felice fu quel di felice il ponto*
2	3^{v}	*Per dolor me bagno il viso* B[artolomeo] T[romboncino] (RISM 1514_2, fol. 24^{v}: M[arco] C[ara])
3	4^{v}	*Il bon nochier sempre parla de venti*
4	5	*Io tho donato il core* Jo[an] Ba[ttista] Ze[sso] (RISM 1507_3, fol. 2)
5	5^{v}	*Se mai per maraveglia*[2]
6	6^{v}	*Si oportuerit me teco mori* M. C.
7	7^{v}	*Ochi mei lassi mentre chio* B. T. (RISM 1510, fol. 40^{v})
8	9	*Per fuggir damor le punte* M. C. (RISM [c. 1516]$_2$, fol. 8^{v})
9	10	*Se per colpa di vostro fero*[3]
10	11^{v}	*Amando e desiando*[4] Cariteo (RISM 1509_2, fol. 55^{v})
11	12^{v}	*Dopoi longe fatiche & longi* (I:Vnm, MSS It. Cl. IV, 1795–98, no. 11: Galeotto del Carretto)
12	13^{v}	*Deh chi me sa dir novella* D. Mi[chele Pesenti][5] (RISM 1507_4, fol. 45^{v})

13 15 *He le nata aime colei* Pie[tro] da Lodi

14 16 *Poi chel ciel e la fortuna* Michel [Pesenti] V[eronensis] (CesF, p. 29)

15 17 *Pregovi frondi fiori aque*[6] B. T. (RISM 1507_3, fol. 11)

16 17^v *Come val mondo fior tu che beato* T. B. [*sic*] (RISM 1507_3, fol. 11^v: B. T.)

17 18 *Passato el tempo jocondo* B. T.

18 18^v *Vidi hor cogliendo rose* Alexan[dro] Demophon (RISM 1507_3, fol. 49^v)

19 19^v *Venimus e romeria* (RISM 1506_3, fol. 45^v)

20 20 *Con pianto e con dolore* (RISM 1505_5, fol. 42)

21 20^v *Io non manchi di fede* Jo. Ba. Ze.

22 21^v *Poi che mia sincera fede* Ant[onio] Cap[rioli] (RISM 1505_5, fol. 4^v)

23 23 *O bon egli e bon o bon* M. C. (RISM 1505_6, fol. 4^v)

24 24 *Non val aqua al mio gran foco* B. T. (CesF, p. 15)

25 25 *Ite in pace suspir fieri* B. T. (RISM 1505_6, fol. 13^v)

26 26^v *Sel partir mincrebe e dolse* (RISM 1505_6, fol. 25^v)

27 27 *Fate ben gente cortese* B. T. (RISM 1507_4, fol. 39^v)

28 28 *Non si vedra mai stanca ne satia* A. C. (RISM 1507_3, fol. 8^v)

29 29 *Spenta mhai del petto amore* D. M. (RISM 1507_3, fol. 20^v)

30 30^v *Liber fui un tempo in foco* M. C. (CesF, p. 122)

31 31^v *Sio son stato a ritornare* D. Mi. (CesF, p. 30)

32 32^v *Ai ceco e crudo amore* Helias Dupre

33 33 *Chi non sa chi non intende* B. T. (RISM 1506_3, fol. 19^v)

34 35 *Soto un verde e alto cupresso* Anto. Capri. (RISM 1507_4, fol. 13^v)

35 36 *Chi promete e debitore* (RISM 1507_4, fol. 12^v)

36 37 *Quei che sempre han da penare* M. C. (CesF, p. 120)

37 38^v *Fuggitiva mia speranza* M. C. (CesF, p. 121)

38 39^v *Cosi confuso e il stato* B. T.

39 40^v *Dolce amoroso foco* (RISM 1505_6, fol. 32^v)

40 41 *Quando andaratu al monte* Jo. Pie. Man. (AmbG V, 534: "E quando andare tu al monte," Giovanni Battista Zesso)

41 42^v *Dolermi sempre voglio* B. T. (RISM 1509_2, fol. 3)

42 43^v *Quella bella e bianco mano* A. C. (RISM 1507_4, fol. 14^v)

43 44 *Starala ben cussi* Jo. Ba. Ze.

44 44^v *Ite caldi o miei suspiri* B. T. (RISM 1509_2, fol. 11^v)

45 46 *Suspir io themo ma piu theme il core* B. T. (RISM 1505_6, fol. 54^v)

46 47 *Se mai nei mei pochi anni* B. T. (RISM 1507_4, fol. 27)

47 47^v *Ala fe per la mia fe* Pele[grino] Cesena (RISM 1505_6, fol. 5^v: anon.)

48 48^v *Sio sedo a lombra amor*[7] M. C. (RISM 1505_6, fol. 53)

49 49 *Ameni colli* Ludo[vico] Mila[nese] (RISM 1507_4, fol. 29^v)

50 49^v *Non e pensier chel mio secreto* D. Mi. (RISM 1507_4, fol. 54^v)

51 51 *Ahime lasso ahime dolente* Mi. C. (RISM 1505_6, fol. 2^v: Michele Pesenti)

52 52^v *Vale diva vale in pace* B. T. (CesF, p. 17)

53 53 *Deh per dio non mi far torto* B. T. (CesF, p. 19)

54 54 *Son pur congionto a tanto* (RISM 1505_6, fol. 52^v)

55 54^v *O selve o sparse gregge* [Onofrio] An[tinori] Pattavinus (RISM 1505_6, fol. 49: anon.)

56 55 *O tempo o ciel volubil* Pauli Scotti (RISM 1509_2, fol. 8^v: anon.)

SOLO LUTE PIECES

57 55^v *Recercar primo*

58 55^v *R2*

59 56 *3*

60 57 *R4*

61 57^v *R5*

62 58 *6*

63 58 *7*

64 58^v *R8*

65 58^v *9*

66 59^v *10*

67 60 *R11*
68 60ᵛ *R12*
69 60ᵛ *13*
70 60ᵛ *14*
71 61 *15*
72 61ᵛ *16*
73 62 *17*
74 62ᵛ *18*
75 63 *R19*
76 63ᵛ *R20*[8]

[1] A copy was in E:S (see PlamEC, p. 683).
[2] Mod. ed. in BossR, p. 17.
[3] No musical relation to the setting of the same text by Marco Cara in RISM 1514_2.
[4] Mod. ed. (with vocal model) and analysis in DiseCT.
[5] A note indicates that Pesenti wrote the text as well as the music of no. 12.
[6] Mod. ed. in GallLP, p. 137.
[7] Mod. ed. in BossR, p. 18.
[8] Mod. ed. in GallLP, p. 137.

1511_2

SCHLICK, ARNOLT

Spiegel der Orgelmacher und Organisten allen Stifften und kirchen / so Orgel halten oder machen lassen hochnützlich, durch den hochbreüm/pten und künstreichen Meyster Arnolt Schlicken Pfaltzgravischen / Organisten artlich verfasst. und uss Römischer Kaisserlicher maiestat / sonder löblicher befreyhung und begnadung auffgericht und aussgangen. / [Cut of performing musicians][1]

30 fols. Colophon lacking. The "Privilegium" is signed: "Gegeben in unserer und des Reichs Stadt Strassburg, am 3. April Anno 1511, unserer Herrschaft im Römischen Reiche des 26. und im Ungarischen des 21. Jahres. Für den König: Im Auftrag Seiner Kaiserlichen Maiestät eigenhändig: Serentiner sszt." After SchlickS (Eitner) it has been assumed that the work was printed in Mainz by Peter Schöffer in 1511; SchlickS (Smets) states that Peter Drach in Speyer was the printer. This short treatise deals with organ construction; it includes information on building materials, tuning, registration, and use of the instrument, and descriptions of contemporary organs. SchlickS (Eitner), SchlickS (Flade), and SchlickS (Smets) are modern editions of the complete treatise. SchlickS (Miller) is an English translation. For further information see BraunS; FrotO, p. 86; KenN; MendP; ReFS, no. 34; and SchlechtB.

Copies in: D:HAmk, GB:Lbmh.

[1] Facs. of cut in CollaerAH, p. viii, and MGG VII, col. 639. Facs. of title page in KleinO, p. 48; KommaM, p. 82; and SumnO, pl. 9.

1511_3

VIRDUNG, SEBASTIAN

Musica getutscht und / aussgezogen durch Sebastianum virdung Priesters / von Amberg und alles gesang auss den noten in die tabulaturen diser benanten dryer Instrumenten der Or/geln: der Lauten: und den Flöten transferieren zu lernen / Kurtzlich gemacht zu eren dem hochwirdigen hoch / gebornen fürsten unnd herren: herr wilhalmen / Bischove zum Strassburg seynem gnedigen herren.[1]

56 fols. On fol. A1ᵛ: heraldic shield. On fol. A2: dedication to "Dem hochwirdigen hochgebornen fürsten und herrenherr Wilhelmen Bischove zu Strassburg," and signed on fol. A2ᵛ, "Geben zü Basel uff zinstag Margarethe. Tusent fünff hundert und xi Jar." No printer is named.[2] This treatise in dialogue describes various types of instruments and teaches the student to transcribe vocal music for organ, lute, and flute. The text is profusely illustrated with woodcuts of the instruments. On the illustrations see EisenV.[3] On the "instruments of Saint Jerome" see HammerI. The volume contains one complete composition, a German religious song "O haylige, onbeflecte, zart junckfrawschafft marie," printed in mensural notation on fols. H4ᵛ–J1; in organ tablature on fols. J1ᵛ–J2; and in German lute tablature on fols. M2ᵛ–M3.[4] The second part of this treatise was translated into French (see 1529_2), Latin (see 1536_4), and Flemish (see 1554_9 and 1568_8). Agricola's *Musica instrumentalis deudsch* (for various editions see 1529_1) is based on Virdung. PubAPTM XI and VirdungM are facsimile editions of the complete treatise. For further information see LenneCC (which includes a modern

edition of the lute intabulation); NefV; ReFS, no. 33; and WalS.

Copies in: A:Iu, A:Wgm (imperfect), A:Wn, CH:Bu (imperfect), D:Bds-Tü, D:KA, D:Mbs, D:Ngm, D:W, F:Pc, GB:Eu, GB:Lbm, GB:Lbmh (imperfect), NL:DHgm.[5]

[1] Facs. of title page and three other pages in KinsP, pp. 118, 132.

[2] DavB names Michael Furter as the printer.

[3] Some of the illustrations are repr. in AbbS I, 426; DegenB, pl. 2; EC, pt. II, vol. III, p. 1488; LittC, p. 8; MGG VIII, col. 357; PinchIH, p. 40; and WinterR, p. 469.

[4] Facs. of fol. M2ᵛ in MGG VIII, col. 358 (incorrectly labeled "Maria zart"); mod. ed. in ChilHN, p. 52.

[5] Copies were in the libraries of W. H. Cummings (see CummC, no. 1153), Alfred Littleton (see LittC, p. 8, and MLE, 1904, p. 12), J. E. Matthew (see MLE, 1904, p. 32), and in E:S (see HuntingC, no. 922, and PlamEC, p. 670, where the title is given as "Musica theutonica sebastiani virdvarg"). Just possibly this is the volume referred to as "Teutsche Lieder auf die fletten. Und ande Instrument" in the Raimund Fugger library (see SchaalM, p. 129).

1512_1

SCHLICK, ARNOLT

[Cut of a swan and a lady playing a recorder; at her feet are an organ, a harp, a lute, and several other instruments.] Tabulaturen Etlicher lob/gesang und lidlein uff die orgeln und lau/ten, ein theil mit zweien stimen zü zwicken / und die drit dartzu sungen, etlich on gesangk / mit dreien, von Arnolt Schlicken Pfaltz/gravischem Chürfürstlichem Organisten / Tabulirt, und in den truck in der ursprungk/lichen stat der truckerei zü Meintz wie hie/nach volgt verordent.

4 + 42 fols. Mensural notation, German keyboard tablature (mensural notation and letters), and German lute tablature. On fol. 1ᵛ: poem in German beginning "Diss artlich büch und künstlich wergk." On fol. 2: a letter addressed to "meinem lieber vatter," and signed "Arnolt Schlick der Jung, dein undertheniger sone," followed (on fols. 2ᵛ–4) by the "Antwort Arnolt Schlicken uff die bitt seines sons," dated "Datum Andree apo. anno 1.5.11." On fol. 4ᵛ: table of contents and a satirical poem in German against Sebastian Virdung beginning "Ir Musici senger orgler" (see LenneCC for information about their quarrel). Fol. 5 = p. 1. Colophon on p. 83: "Getruckt zü Mentz durch Peter Schöffern. Uff sant Matheis abent. Anno. M. d. xii." SchlickT (Eitner) is a modern edition of most of the collection. SchlickT (Harms) is a modern edition of the entire collection, and includes facsimile pages of the prefatory matter and some of the music. Nos. 1–14 are cantus firmus settings for solo keyboard (written in keyboard tablature); nos 15–26 are for solo voice (written in mensural notation) and lute; and nos. 27–29 are for solo lute.

Copies in: D:Bds-Tü (imperfect), D:LEm, F:Pn (imperfect).

SOLO KEYBOARD PIECES

	p.	
1	1	*Salve regina*[1]
2	4	*Ad te clamamus*
3	6	*Eya ergo advocata*
4	10	*O pia*
5	13	*O dulcis Maria*
6	18	*Pete quid vis*
7	24	*Hoe losteleck*[2]
8	29	*Benedictus*[3]
9	34	*Primi toni*
10	37	*Maria zart*[4] (compare BäumK II, 89; ZahnM, no. 8552; and no. 26 below)
11	42	*Criste*
12	45	*Da pacem*[5]
13	49	*Da pacem*[5]
14	53	*Da pacem*[5]

SONGS FOR SOLO VOICE AND LUTE

15	57	*Mein M. ich hab*[6] (MosL, no. 41)
16	59	*Cupido hat* (MosL, no. 24)
17	61	*Hertzliebstes pild*[7] (MosPH, no. 9: Hofhaimer)
18	62	*Nach lust hab ich*[8] (MosL, no. 25: Georg Forster)
19	64	*Vil hinderlist*[9] (MosL, no. 4)
20	65	*Möcht es gesein*[10]
21	66	*Mein lieb ist weg*
22	67	*Ich schrei und rieff* (MosL, no. 45)
23	68	*Metzkin isack*[11] (HewO, no. 27: "Tmeiskin was jonck," Isaac, Japart, or Obrecht?)

24 71 *Philips zwolffpot auss not hilff mir*[12]

25 73 *Nun hab ich all mein tag gehört*[13] (SchlickT [Harms], p. 61)

26 75 *Maria zart*[14] (compare no. 10 above)

SOLO LUTE PIECES

27 79 *All ding mit radt*[15]

28 81 *Wer gnad durch klaff*[16] (MosL, no. 62)

29 81 *Weg wart dein art*[17] (CH:SGs, Cod. 463, no. 61)

[1] Mod. ed. in ApelMK, p. 38; HAM, no. 100; MOM LI; and OL VIII, 5. Facs. of p. 1 in ApelN, p. 27, and PinchIH, p. 41. Facs. of parts of several pages in ChrysS, p. 472.

[2] Mod. ed. and partial quasi-facs. in WolfH II, 20.

[3] Facs. of p. 29 in GottronMM, pl. III.

[4] Mod. ed. in ApelMK, p. 39; HAM, no. 101; KleinO, p. 50; MU II, Supplement, "Musik im Anfang," p. 30; OL XIV, 7; RitZ II, 96; RoyM, p. 38; and StraubeM II, no. 25.

[5] Mod. ed. of nos. 12–14 in LitaDP, p. 3; mod. ed. of one "Da pacem" in OL II, 4. Facs. of p. 52 in KinsP, p. 77.

[6] Mod. ed. and quasi-facs. of p. 57 in TapS, p. 8. Heading on p. 56: "Hienach fahet an Tabulatur uff die Lauten. Ein Stim zu singen die andern zwicken."

[7] Mod. ed. in BruAL, p. 2; DTO XXXVII/72, p. 82; and MU II, app., p. 25.

[8] Mod. ed. in BruAL, p. 4.

[9] Mod. ed. in BruS I, no. 15, and KörL, p. 155.

[10] Mod. ed. in KörL, p. 154.

[11] Mod. ed. in DTO XIV/28, p. 159.

[12] Partial quasi-facs. in WolfH II, 42.

[13] Mod. ed. in BruS II, no. 85, and GünthB, 1936.

[14] Mod. ed. in BruS II, no. 46.

[15] Heading on p. 79: "Zwicken mit dreien."

[16] Mod. ed. in TapS, p. 10.

[17] Only the discant and altus of the vocal model are extant. The altus does not appear in the Schlick arrangement.

1517_1

ANTICO, ANDREA, PUBLISHER

FROTTOLE INTABULATE DA SONARE ORGANI / LIBRO PRIMO. / [Cut of a man playing a harpsichord decorated with the arms of Leo X. A lady in the background holding music points to a monkey with a lute crouching on top of the harpsichord.][1]

40 fols. Keyboard score. On fol. 2: table of contents. On fol. 38v: printing privilege granted by Leo X, dated and signed (on fol. 39): "Romae apud sanctum Petrum sub annulo Piscatoris. Die .XXVII. Decembris. M. D. XVII. Pontificatus. nostri Anno Quarto. Jacobus Sadoletus," followed by the printer's mark (two intertwined *A*'s within an ornamental border) and the colophon: "Impresso in Roma per Andrea Anticho de Montona. Nel anno. M. D. XVII. A di .XIII. di Genaro." The printing privilege and a facsimile of the title page and the colophon appear in SartMS, opposite p. 1, and pp. 1–2. For further information on this volume see GravA, pp. 141ff, and TomasA. The compositions identified by the superior letter *a* ([a]) are reprinted in JepO, which includes facsimiles of the title page and fols. 19v and 33v, an introduction to the volume (I, 47–75), and thematic incipits and concordances for the entire collection (I, 50–53). The compositions identified by ([b]) are reprinted in DiseF, pp. 271–303, which includes (between pp. 32 and 33) facsimiles of fols. 7v, 14, and 39. All of the compositions are for solo keyboard. In the following inventory the composers' initials are resolved the first time they appear only.

Copies in: CS:Pdobr, I:Rpol (fol. 37 wanting).[2]

fol.

1 2v *Amor quando fioriva mia speme*[3] B[artolomeo] T[romboncino] (RISM [c. 1516]$_2$, fol. 2v)

2 4v *Per mio ben te vederei*[a] T. B. [*sic*] (RISM 1510, fol. 40v)

3 5v *Chi non crede* B. T.

4 6v *Frena donna i toi bei lumi*[b] (RISM [c. 1516]$_2$, fol. 30v)

5 7v *Virgine bella che del sol vestita*[b] B. T. (RISM 1510, fol. 38v)

6 10 *Gentil donna* B. T. (RISM [c. 1516]$_2$, fol. 6v)

7 12 *Che debbio fare*[b] B. T. (RISM 1507_3, fol. 13v)

8 14 *Si e debile el filo*[b] B. T. (RISM 1507_3, fol. 4v)

9 16 *Ochi miei lassi*[b] B. T. (RISM 1510, fol. 40v)

10 18v *Odi cielo el mio lamento* B. T. (RISM [c. 1516]$_2$, fol. 29v)

11 20 *Animoso mio desire* B. T. (RISM [c. 1516]$_2$, fol. 13^v)
12 21 *Stavasi amor* B. T. (RISM [c. 1516]$_2$, fol. 14^v)
13 22 *Fiamma amorosa* B. T. (RISM [c. 1517]$_1$, fol. 8^v: anon.)[4]
14 24 *Non resta in questa*[a 5] (RISM 1510, fol. 36)
15 25 *O che aiuto o che conforto*[b] M[archetto] C[ara] (RISM [c. 1517]$_1$, fol. 5^v)
16 27 *Per dolor mi bagno el viso*[ab] M. C. (RISM 1514$_2$, fol. 24^v)
17 29 *Non piu morte al mio morire*[a] B. T. (RISM [c. 1516]$_2$, fol. 15^v)
18 30 *Dolce ire dolce sdegni* B. T. (RISM 1510, fol. 37^v)
19 31 *La non vol esser* B. T. (RISM 1514$_2$, fol. 8)
20 32^v *Son io quel che era quel di* B. T. (RISM [c. 1516]$_2$, fol. 28)
21 33 *Che farala che dirala*[a] B. T. (RISM 1514$_2$, fol. 28: D. M[ichele Vicentino])
22 33^v *O che dirala mo* B. T. (RISM [c. 1517]$_1$, fol. 7^v)
23 35 *Crudel fugge se sai* M. C. (RISM 1519$_4$, fol. 42^v)
24 35^v *Me lassera tu mo*[a] Ranier (RISM 1519$_4$, fol. 39^v)
25 36 *Hor chel ciel e la terra* B. T. (RISM [c. 1516]$_2$, fol. 10^v)
26 37 *Cantai mentre nel core* (RISM [c. 1517]$_1$, fol. 45^v: Marco Cara)

[1] Facs. of cut in EF I, 280, and MagniSM I, 303. Facs. of title page in PirC, p. 33.

[2] A copy was in E:S (see JepL, p. 74). In the Rome copy there is a manuscript addition to the title page: "Impresso in Roma da Andrea Anticho da Montona .Chierico. Con privileg. di PP Leone X. MDXVIII...." On fol. 3 there is the manuscript addition: "Questo libro si e de canto d'organo." Three folios have been bound in at the end of the volume: fol. 41: Four seven-line staves without music; 41^v: Four seven-line staves: on the bottom stave in chant notation: "Celerius urbs sevecale (?)"; 42: Blank; 42^v: In manuscript: "recetta d'accorssar el umo et ha la muffa et sappia & moscanello"; 43: An index of pieces with Italian titles, along with an "Agnus voi clamo ne cesses" (superius from the "Agnus" of the *Missa L'Homme armé super voces musicales* by Josquin des Prez; written in mensural notation with Arabic numerals added); 43^v: Two measures of "Multi sunt vocati pauci vero electi," in Italian organ tablature.

[3] Facs. and mod. ed. in TomasA.

[4] Attributed to Marco Cara in RISM 1518$_1$.

[5] Mod. ed. in FuserC, no. 1.

151?$_1$

JUDENKÜNIG, HANS

Utilis & compen/diaria introductio, qua ut fun/damento iacto quam facillime mu/sicum exercitium, instrumentorum / & Lutine, & quod vulgo Gey/gen nominant, addiscitur labore / studio & impensis Joannis Ju/denkunig de Schbebischen / Gmundt in communem omnium / usum & utilitatem typis ex/cudendum primum exhi/bitum. Viennae. / Austriae.

12 fols. German lute tablature. On fols. A1^v–A4: instructions for playing the lute. On fol. A4^v: cut of two men, one playing a lute and the other a viol, with the inscription: "HANS. JUDENKUNIG. BIRTIG. VON. S. G. LUTENIST. I. Z. W." The same cut appears in 1523$_2$, fol. a2. Note on fol. B1: "Harmonie super odis Horatianis secundum omnia Horatii genera, etiam doctis auribus haud quaquam aspernandae. Nota tamen, bone Tyro, quaecunque eiusdem generis sunt carmina, sub una eademque harmonia fidibus esse pulsanda." On fol. B4^v: rules for tuning the lute, headed "Regula qua cordas congrue aptare." Hans Singriener of Vienna was probably the printer, although he is not named (see 1523$_2$). All of the odes of Horace (nos. 1–19) are intabulations of the settings by Peter Tritonius published in *Melopoiae* (Augsburg, Erhard Öglin, 1507); these vocal models have been reprinted in LiliH. The compositions identified by superior letters are reprinted as follows: ([a]) in BruS; ([b]) in DTO XVIII/37, p. 1; and ([c]) in ZanG I, 7. For further information on Judenkünig see 1523$_2$ and KoczJ. All of the compositions are for solo lute.

Copies in: A:Wn, D:Mbs.

	fol.	
1	B1^v	*Ode prima Mecoenas atavis*[bc 1]
2	B1^v	*Ode 2. Iam satis terris*[a] = 1523$_2$, no. 10: "Saphica"
3	B1^v	*Ode 3. Sic te diva potena Cypri*
4	B1^v	*Ode 4. Solvitur acris hyems*[a]
5	B2	*Ode 5. Quis multa gracilis*
6	B2	*Ode 6. Scriberis vario*
7	B2^v	*Ode 7. Laudabunt alii*[a]
8	B2^v	*Ode 8. Lydiadic per omnes*
9	B2^v	*Ode 9. Vides ut alta stet*[a]
10	B2^v	*Ode 11. Tu ne quesieris*[a]

11 B3 *Ode 18. libri secundi. Non ebur neque aureu*
12 B3 *Ode 12. li. tertii. Miserarum est*
13 B3 *Ode 7. libri quarti. Diffugere nives*[bc]
14 B3 *Ode prima ex libro Epodon. Ibis liburnis inter alta navium*
15 B3ᵛ *Ode 11. Pecti nihil me sicut*
16 B3ᵛ *Ode 13. Horrida tempestas*
17 B3ᵛ *Ode 17. Mollis inertia*
18 B4 *Ode 16. Altera iam bellis*
19 B4 *Ode 17. Iam iam efficaci dominus*
20 B4 *Phaleutium Hendecasyllabum. Vivamus mea lesbia atque amemus*[b2]
21 C1 *Madonna katerina. Oder hast du mich genummen* (compare no. 31 below, and also 1540_1, no. 3)[3]
22 C1 *Christ ist erstanden*[abc 4] (compare BäumK I, 502, and ZahnM, no. 8584)
23 C1 *Und wer er nit erstanden*[abc 4] (second strophe of no. 22)
24 C1ᵛ *Der hoff dantz* [5]
C2 *Der hoff dantz* (= Nach Tantz)
25 C2 *Ich traw der lieben woll*
26 C2ᵛ *Zart schönste fraw* (CW XXIX, 28; compare 1536_6, no. 7)
27 C2ᵛ *Nach lust* (MosL, no. 25: Georg Forster)
28 C3ᵛ *Nach willen dein* (MosPH, p. 74: Hofhaimer; compare 1536_6, no. 12)
29 C3ᵛ *Zucht er und lob* (MosPH, p. 99: Hofhaimer)
30 C4 *Von edler art*[a] (MosPH, p. 180: J. Schönfelder or Hofhaimer; compare 1536_6, no. 13)
31 C4ᵛ *Hast du mich genumen* (compare no. 21 above, and also 1540_1, no. 36)
32 C4ᵛ *Wo sol ich mich hin keren*[a] (PubAPTM XXIX, 90: Georg Vogelhuber)

[1] Mod. ed. also in ApelM I, 6.
[2] This is a setting of an ode by Catullus (text in CatalP, p. 6).
[3] The compositions in $151?_1$ identified as having concordances with 1536_6 and 1540_1 (lute books of Hans Newsidler) are very similar to but not identical with these later versions. In most cases Newsidler has added more ornaments to the music borrowed from Judenkünig.
[4] Mod. ed. of nos. 22 and 23 also in BehD, p. 5 (arr. for guitar), and MU III, app., p. 32.
[5] Mod. ed. and identification of the tune (= "Schwartz knab") in GomH, p. 60.

1521_1

EUSTACHIO ROMANO

Musica di Eustachio / Romano. / Liber primus.

47 fols. Mensural notation. On fol. 1ᵛ: table of contents. On fol. 2: dedication to "Reverendissimo domino Jovani Marie de Monte Pontici: Sipontino ac Papiensis." Colophon on fol. 47ᵛ: "Musica Duorum Eustachii Romani de Macionibus excusit... Ingenti cura & industria magistri Johanis Jacobi de pasotis de Monticulo Regiensis Impressum fuit hoc opus Musicae. A Romae Anno domini M. D. xxi de mense VIIbris die xvi regnante Leone decimo pontifice Maximo." SartMS, pp. 2–3, reprints the dedication and the colophon. All of the pieces are *a 2* and without text (but see nos. 2, 11, 13, 22, and 26). Information added in brackets is from the table of contents. For a brief discussion of the volume see JepO, p. 18.

Copy in: A:Wn.[1]

fol.
1 2ᵛ [*a. Tenor cum basso*]
2 3ᵛ [*b. Tenor cum basso*] (RISM 1549_{16}, no. 29: "Non opus habent," Eustachius Romanus)
3 4ᵛ *c.* [*Tenor cum tenor*]
4 5ᵛ *d.* [*Tenor cum basso*]
5 6ᵛ *e.* [*Tenor cum tenor*]
6 7ᵛ *f.* [*Tenor cum tenor*]
7 8ᵛ *g.* [*Tenor cum tenor*]
8 9ᵛ *h.* [*Tenor cum tenor*]
9 10ᵛ *i.* [*Tenor cum basso*]
10 11ᵛ *k.* [*Bassus cum basso*]
11 12ᵛ *l.* [*Cantus cum tenor*] (RISM 1549_{16}, no. 28: "Haec est vita aeterna," Meistre Gosse)
12 13ᵛ *m.* [*Bassus cum basso*]
13 14ᵛ *n.* [*Tenor cum basso*] (RISM 1549_{16}, no. 30: "Ecce mysterium," Eustachius Romanus)
14 15ᵛ *o.* [*Tenor cum basso*]
15 16ᵛ *p.* [*Tenor cum tenor*]
16 17ᵛ *q.* [*Tenor cum basso*]
17 18ᵛ *r.* [*Bassus cum basso*]
18 19ᵛ *s.* [*Tenor cum basso*]
19 20ᵛ *t.* [*Bassus cum basso*]
20 21ᵛ *u.* [*Tenor cum tenor*]
21 22ᵛ *x.* [*Cantus cum tenor*]

22	23v	*y*. [*Tenor cum tenor*] (RISM 1549₁₆, no. 12: "Prande bis tecum," Meister Jan)
23	24v	*z*. [*Cantus cum tenor*]
24	25v	*A*. [*Cantus cum tenor*]
25	26v	*B*. [*Tenor cum basso*]
26	27v	*C*. [*Cantus cum tenor*] (RISM 1549₁₆, no. 24: "Mulier cupido," Eustachius Romanus)
27	28v	*D*. [*Bassus cum basso*]
28	29v	*E*. [*Cantus cum tenor*]
29	30v	*F*. [*Tenor cum basso*]
30	31v	*G*. [*Tenor cum basso*]
31	32v	*H*. [*Cantus cum tenor*]
32	33v	*J*. [*Tenor cum tenor*]
33	34v	*K*. [*Tenor cum basso*]
34	35v	*L*. [*Tenor cum tenor*]
35	36v	*L*. [sic] [*Cantus cum canto*]
36	37v	*M*. [*Tenor cum basso*]
37	38v	*N*. [*Bassus cum basso*]
38	39v	*O*. [*Tenor cum basso*]
39	40v	*P*. [*Tenor cum basso*]
40	41v	*Q*. [*Tenor cum tenor*]
41	42v	*R*. [*Tenor cum tenor*]
42	43v	*S*. [*Bassus cum basso*]
43	44v	*T*. [*Bassus cum basso*]
44	45v	*U*. [*Cantus cum tenor*]
45	46v	*X*. [*Cantus cum tenor*]

[1] The unique copy has manuscript corrections in various places, and on fol. 2v a hymn *a2*: "Herodes hostis impie," with both voices texted.

1523₁

CAVAZZONI, MARCO ANTONIO

RECERCHARI / MOTETTI / CANZONI / Composti per Marcoantonio / di Bologna. / LIBRO PRIMO[1]

38 fols. Keyboard score. On fol. A1v: Dedication "AL MOLTO MAGNIFICO CAVALIERO, MESSER FRANCESCO CORNARO PROCURATORE DI SAN MARCO." On fol. K1: the printing privilege of Pope Adrian VI, followed by the colophon: "Venetiis apud Bernardinum Vercelensem mense Aprili. M. D. XXIII." SartMS, pp. 3–4, reprints the dedication and the printing privilege. None of the vocal models has yet been identified. The entire collection has been reprinted twice: in CMI I, and in JepO, which includes facsimiles of the title page, the decication, and fols. A2 and D3. SlimK II, 450, contains a thematic index of the ricercares. All of the compositions are for solo keyboard.

Copies in: GB:Lbm, US:Cn (imperfect).

	fol.	
1	A2	*Recercare primo*[2]
2	B2	*Salve Virgo*[3]
3	C1	*Recercare Secondo*
4	D3	*O Stella maris*
5	E4v	*Perdone. Moi sie. folie.*
6	G1v	*Madame vous. aves. mon. cuor.*[4]
7	H1	*Plus. de regres.*
8	H4	*Lautre. yor. per un matin.*[5]

[1] Facs. of title page in MGG VII, col. 654, and KinsP, p. 132. A facs. of fol. C2 appears in ApelN, p. 5, and of fol. D3 in MGG II, col. 935. A part of one page in facs. is repr. in PN, p. 68.
[2] Mod. ed. in BedbI II, no. 3.
[3] Mod. ed. in FroideA I, 14–17.
[4] Mod. ed. in BedbI II, no. 1.
[5] Mod. ed. in BedbI II, no. 2.

1523₂

JUDENKÜNIG, HANS

1.5.2.3. / Ain schone / kunstliche under/weisung in disem / büechlein, leychtlich zu be/greyffen den rechten grund / zu lernen auff der Lautten / und Geygen, mit vleiss ge/macht dürch Hans Juden/künig, pirtig von Schwe/bischen Gmünd Lutenist, / yetz zu Wien in Osterreich

46 fols. German lute tablature. On fol. a2: the same cut that appears in 151?₁, fol. A4v.[1] Instructions for playing the lute are interspersed throughout the volume (on fols. a3v–b2, c1–c1v, d1–d1v, e3v, f4v, h2v, and i3–i3v).[2] The compositions introduced by these instructions are arranged in progressive order of difficulty; the first six numbers are *a2*, the rest *a3*. On fol. i4: table of contents. The second part of the volume (fols. k1v–l4) is introduced by a separate title page (on fol. k1):

> Item das ander puechlein zuver/nemen, darinnen du underrichtt / wierdest, den gesang züversteen was ayn yedliche / noten oder pawss bedeüt, under aynem yedlichen / zaichen welcher nit singen kan,

auch wie ain yedli/cher gesang anfecht, auff der Lautten oder Geygen / und wievil, ain yedliche noten, in den Ligereturen / an ainander gepunden, gilt, darnach wie du zwo / oder drey stym züsamen setzen soldest auss dem ge/sang, in die Tabalatur under ain mensur einge/taylt, und gerechnet muess werden. Und wie / die noten, unvolkumen gemacht werden, / in den volkhumen zaichen, und welche / gealterieret wierdt, das ist aine yedli/chen nutz züwissen, Wiewol es jetzt / wenig der gebrauch ist in dem ge/sang, noch ist gemainiklich der / aller pesst gesang, in mani/cherlay zaichen versatzt, / darumb ist es dier / von noten zu / wissen.

Colophon on fol. l4: "Vollendet und getrückht zu Wien yn Osterreich dürch Hanns Singryener. im 1.5.2.3. Jar." The compositions identified by the superior letter *a* ([a]) are reprinted in DTO XVIII/37, pp. 2–14. SlimK II, 449–450, contains a thematic index of the ricercares. For further information on Judenkünig, see $151?_1$. All of the compositions are for solo lute.

Copies in: A:Wgm (imperfect), A:Wn, B:Br, CS:B, D:Mbs, US:Wc.[3]

	fol.	
1	b2v	*Wo soll ich mich hin keren ich armes* (PubAPTM XXIX, 90: Georg Vogelhuber)
2	b2v	*Mag ich unglück nit widerston*[4] (SenflW V, no. 13: Senfl; see no. 11 below)
3	b2v	*Ich bin ir lange zeyt hold gewesen* (CH:SGs, MS 463, no. 173)[5]
4	b3	*Woll kumbt der may*[6] (EDMR XX, no. 66: Wolff Grefinger) = 1536_6, no. 19
5	b3v	*Pavana alla Veneciana* (compare 1508_2, no. 18a)
6	b4	*Ain hoff dantz mit zway stimen*[7]
	b4v	[*Nach Tantz*]
7	c2	*Das erst Priamell*[a 8] = 1532_2, no. 25
8	c2v	*Rossina ain welscher dantz*[a 9]
	c3	*Rossina* [*Nach Tantz*][a]
9	c3	*Ain niderlendisch runden dantz*[a 10]
10	c3v	*Saphica*[a] = $151?_1$, no. 2: "Iam satis terris," Tritonius[11]
11	c3v	*Mag ich unglück nit widersten*[12] (see no. 2 above)
12	c4v	*Elslein liebes Elslein*[13] (SenflW IV, no. 17: Senfl)
13	d2	*Das ander Priamell*[a 14] = 1532_2, no. 32
14	d2v	*Zucht er und lob*[a 15] (MosPH, p. 99: Hofhaimer)
15	d3v	*Mein hertzigs* (MosL, no. 6: Heinrich Finck)
16	d4	*Nach willen dein*[a 16] (MosPH, p. 74: Hofhaimer)
17	e1	*Der hoff dantz*[a]
	e1v	[*Nach Tantz*]
18	e2	*Der ander hoff dantz*[a]
	e3	[*Nach Tantz*]
19	e4	*Das drit Priamel*[a 17]
20	e4v	*Freüntlicher gruess* (PubAPTM IX, 25)
21	f1	*Erwelt hab ich mir* (PubAPTM IX, 7)
22	f1v	*Ellend bringt peyn* (EDMR XX, 126: Benedictus Ducis)
23	f2v	*Nerrisch don ist mein munier* (PubAPTM XXIX, 106: "Nur nerrisch sein ist mein monier," Sixt Dietrich)
24	f3v	*Weyplich art*[a] (MosL, p. 50)
25	g1	*Das fierd Priamel*[a 18]
26	g1v	*Ain trium*[a]
27	g2v	*Tota pulchra*
28	g4	*Tota pulchra*
29	h2	*Ain Spaniyelischer hoff dantz*[a]
30	h3	*Das fünfft Priamel*[a]
31	h3	*Tropolus secret*[a] (CH:Bu, MSS F. X. 1–4, no. 108: "Trop plus secret," Pierre de la Rue)
32	h4v	*Mein hertz all dit* (ObrWW, no. 21: "Mijn hert heest altijts verlanghen," Obrecht [Pierre de la Rue?])
33	i2	*Kalata ala spagnola* = 1508_2, no. 33

[1] The cut is repr. in EF II, 639; KommaM, p. 82; PanS, p. 338; and SubHM I, 442.

[2] Some of the diagrams illustrating the instructions are repr. in facs. in DTO XVIII/37, pl. A. Facs. of fols. a2 and e1 appear in *Library of Congress. Annual Report*, 1928, opp. p. 124.

[3] The Washington copy was in the Wolffheim library (see WolffC I, no. 1194); a copy was in the library of Alfred Wotquenne-Plattel (see ThibaultC).

[4] Mod. ed. in SenflW VII, no. 41a, and BruS II, no. 43.

[5] Judenkünig gives only bass and tenor for no. 3; only the discant and altus part books of the St. Gall manuscript are preserved. But the two sources fit together perfectly.

[6] Mod. ed. in BruD, no. 15; DTO XXXVII/72, p. 79; and SenflW VII, no. 35a.

[7] Mod. ed. in NeemAM I, no. 3, and ZanG I, 12.

[8] Mod. ed. and identification of the tune (= "Bentzenawer") in GomH, p. 61 (main dance only).

[9] Mod. ed. in BruS I, no. 25, and MFH II, 9.

[10] Mod. ed. in BruS IV, no. 130, and ZanG I, 19.

[11] The title is derived from the poetic meter on which this ode is based.

[12] Mod. ed. in SenflW VII, no. 41c.

[13] Mod. ed. in BruAL I, p. 6; SenflW VII, no. 29a; and TapS, p. 11.

[14] Mod. ed. in EC, pt. I, vol. III, p. 1221; MU II, app., p. 8 (incorrectly labeled); MülleG, no. 13; NeemAM I, no. 4; and WasG, no. 3.

[15] Mod. ed. in DTO XXXVII/72, p. 90.

[16] Mod. ed. in DTO XXXVII/72, p. 84; the beginning is repr. in MosPH, p. 76. For a comparison of this intabulation with various others, see NowakII.

[17] Facs. of fol. e4 in ApelN, p. 79.

[18] Facs. of fol. g1 in DTO XVIII/37, pl. B, and NeemAM I, no. 5.

1528_1

AGRICOLA, MARTIN

Musica / Instru/menta/lis. / Deudsch. / Martinus Agricola.

60 fols. plus four inserted tables (?). Contents = 1529_1, except for the different title page. The dedication is dated 1528, the only date given in this edition.

Copy in: D:Dl (imperfect).

1529_1

AGRICOLA, MARTIN

Musica instru/mentalis deudsch / ynn welcher begrif/fen ist, wie man / nach dem gesange auff mancherley / Pfeiffen lernen sol, Auch wie auff / die Orgel, Harffen, Lauten, Gei/gen, und allerley Instrument und / Seytenspiel, nach der recht/gegründten Tabelthur / sey abzusetsen. / Mart. Agricola.[1]

60 fols. plus four inserted tables. On fol. 1v: the preface ("Vorrhede"). On fol. 3: dedication to "Georgio Rhaw buchdrücker zu Wittemberg," signed "Geben zu Magdeburg, am tage Bartholomei. 1528. Mart. Agric." Colophon on fol. 60: "Gedrückt zu Wittemberg durch Georgen Rhaw. M. D. xxix." This treatise on musical instruments in rhymed verse is based on Virdung's *Musica getutscht* (1511_3). The only complete composition that Agricola includes is "Ach gott von hymel sich dar eyn" in German lute tablature on fols. 38v–40. For other editions of this treatise see 1528_1, 1530_1, 1532_1, 1542_1, and 1545_1 (the last a completely revised version). The 1529 edition and the 1545 edition have been reprinted in a quasi-facsimile as PubAPTM XX. For further information on Agricola see FunA.

Copies in: A:Wgm, A:Wn, B:Br, CH:E, D:As, D:Bds-Tü, D:DS, D:G, D:LEm,[2] D:Mbs (imperfect), D:W, GB:Lbm (imperfect), NL:DHgm, S:Uu, US:CA (imperfect).[3]

[1] Facs. of title page and two other pages in KinsP, p. 118. Illustrations of instruments from this volume appear in AbbS I, 430; EC, pt. II, vol. III, p. 1488; EF I, 250, and II, 83; MGG I, col. 165; ReissmA, p. 198; and ScheurC, opp. p. 216. One of the tables, showing how to transcribe a line from mensural notation into German keyboard tablature, is repr. after the 1532 ed. in PN, p. 57.

[2] At the end of the Leipzig copy (call number: I. 191), which is bound with Martin Agricola's *Ein Kurtz Deudsche Musica* (1528), there are 43 fols. of manuscript music in German keyboard tablature: fol. 1v: [Diagrams explaining the tablature]; 4: *Der stad pfeyffer tancz;* 7v: *Der Trippel;* 9v: *Si ist meyn bull;* 11v: *Ich het mir eyn anelein fürgnommen;* 13v: *Elssleyn libes elssley;* 15v: *Eyn Tancz;* 17v: *Der trippel;* 19v: *Unser magdt kann ausdermassen* [*kochen*]; 21v: *Nach wyllen deyn;* 24v: *Ach Lieb mit laidt;* 27v: *Von edler arth;* 30v: *Zarth schone fraw;* 33v: *Meyn eyniges a;* 36v: *Deyn murren macht;* 38v: *Wo ich mith leyb;* 40v: *Preludium;* 41: *Eyn Final;* 41v: *Preambel;* 42v: *Sive Preludia.*

[3] A copy was in the library of Alfred Littleton (see LittC, p. 9, and MLE, 1904, p. 34), and in D:HAL (see EitQ I, 61).

1529_2

VORSTERMAN, GUILLAUME, PUBLISHER

Livre plaisant et tres/utile pour apprendre a faire & ordonner toutes tabu/latures hors le discant, dont & par lesquelles / lon peult facilement et legierement apren/dre a jouer sur les Manicordion, Luc, / et Flutes. / [Cut of a man playing the lute, with two recorders and a clavichord forming a border]

40 fols. Colophon on fol. K4: "Imprime en Anvers par moy Guillaume Vorsterman

demourant en la rue de la chambre a la Licorne dor Lan de nostre Seigneur. M. CCCCC. & xxIx Le douziesme jour Doctobre. [Cut with the double-headed eagle of the Holy Roman Empire] Cum gratia et privilegio." This volume is a free translation of the second part of Virdung's *Musica getutscht* (1511_3), using French rather than German lute tablature, and replacing Virdung's musical example with "Een vrolijc wesen" (by Barbireau, Isaac, or Obrecht; see 1538_2, no. 28), in mensural notation on fols. D1–D2^v; in organ tablature on fols. D3–E1^v; in French lute tablature on fols. G2^v–G4; and the superius only in mensural notation again on fol. K3. The treatise was later translated into Flemish (see 1554_9 and 1568_8). For further information see FoxP, FoxED (which includes a transcription of "Een vrolic wesen" for recorder and guitar), and NijM (which includes facsimiles of the title page and five other pages).

Copy in: E:S.[1]

[1] Manuscript note on fol. K4^v of the unique copy (from the library of Fernando Colón): "Este libro costo 12 negmit en bruselas a 26 de agosto de 1531 y el bucado de oro vale 320 negmit."

† 1529_3

ATTAINGNANT, PIERRE, PUBLISHER

Tres breve et familiere introdu/ction pour entendre & apprendre par soy mesmes a jouer toutes chansons reduictes en la tabu/lature du Lutz, avec la maniere daccorder le dict Lutz. Ensemble .xxxix. chansons dont la plus / part dicelles sont en deux sortes, cest assavoir a deux parties & la musique. Et a troys sans musique / Le tout acheve dimprimer le .vi. jour doctobre .1529. Par Pierre Attaingnant demourant a / Paris en la rue de la Harpe pres leglise saint Cosme. Desquelles la table sensuyt. / [Table of contents] / Avec privilege du Roy nostre sire pour troys ans, que nul ne pourra / imprimer ou faire imprimer en ce royaume la mu/sique & jeu du lutz fors le dict Attaingnant. soubz les / peines contenues es lettres du dict privilege.

60 fols. Mensural notation and French lute tablature. On fol. 1^v: "Troys breves rigles pour estre tost & facillement introduict en la tabulature du lutz," reprinted in WolfH II, 72–73. SlimK II, 450–451, contains a thematic index of the preludes. The compositions followed by an asterisk are for solo voice (written in mensural notation) and lute; they are all reprinted in LauC, which includes facsimiles of the title page and fol. 50^v. All of the other compositions in the volume are for solo lute.

Copy in: D:Bds–Tü.[1]

	fol.	
1	2^v	*Prelude*[2]
2	3^v	*Prelude*[3]
3	4^v	*Prelude*
4	5^v	*Prelude*
5	6^v	*Alsovverdonont / A toy me rendz* (MB XVIII, no. 42: "Ough warder mount")
6	7^v	*Dulcis amica* (RoksT, no. 4: Prioris)
7	8^v	*Cest boucane*[4] (AttainCK III, no. 2)
8	9	*Prelude*
9	9^v	*Fortune laisse* (AttainCK II, no. 23) = 1546_{18}, no. 12
	10^v	*Fortune laisse moy la vye**
10	11^v	*Amy souffres* (AttainCK III, no. 7: Moulu)
	12^v	*Amy souffres que je vous ayme**
11	13^v	*Jay trop ayme* (AttainCK I, no. 12) = 1546_{18}, no. 14
	14^v	*Jay trop ayme vrayment je le confesse**
12	15^v	*Si vostre cueur* (RISM [c. $1528]_5$, no. 30)
	16^v	*Si vostre cueur prent le tane**
13	17^v	*De retourner* (AttainCK III, no. 10)
	18^v	*De retourner mon amy je te prye**
14	19^v	*Languir me fais* (AttainCK II, no. 12: Claudin de Sermisy)
	20^v	*Languir me fais**
15	21^v	*Vivray je tousjours en soucy* (AttainCK III, no. 17: Sermisy) = 1549_8, no. 18
	22^v	*Vivray je tousjours en soucy**
16	23^v	*Jatens secours* (AttainCK II, no. 11: Sermisy)
	24^v	*Jatens secours**
17	25^v	*Ces fascheux sotz* (AttainCK II, no. 25)
	26^v	*Ces fascheux sotz**

18 27^v *Dolent depart* (AttainCK I, no. 15) = 1545$_3$, no. 19

28^v *Dolent depart**

19 29^v *Je me repens*[5]

30^v *Je me repens de vous avoir ayme**

20 31^v *Je demeure seule esgaree* (AttainCK III, no. 4)

32^v *Je demeure seule esgaree**

21 33^v *Amour vault trop* (AttainCK III, no. 5) = 1545$_3$, no. 18

34^v *Amour vault trop**

22 35^v *Secoures moy* (AttainCK II, no. 22: Sermisy)

36^v *Secoures moy**

23 37^v *Dou vient cela* (AttainCK III, no. 22: Sermisy)

38^v *Dou vient cela**

24 39^v *Il me suffit*[6] (AttainCK I, no. 9: Sermisy) = 1545$_3$, no. 21, and 1563$_{12}$, no. 109

40^v *Il me suffit**

25 41 *Las las pourquoy* (RISM [c. 1528]$_5$, no. 18)

41^v *Las las pourquoy mestes vous si dure**

26 42^v *Fortune a bien couru sur moy*[7] (compare 1554$_4$, no. 14: "Si j'ayme ou non")

43 *Fortune a bien couru sur moy**

27 43^v *Le dur regret* (compare RISM 1530$_4$, no. 12: Cochet) = 1549$_8$, no. 21

28 44^v *Une bergerote*[8] (RISM 1530$_5$, no. 30: Sermisy)

45 *Une bergerote*

29 45^v *Las il fauldra* (RISM [c. 1528]$_7$, no. 20)

46^v *Las il fauldra**

30 47^v *Le jaulne & blanc* (AttainCK II, no. 15: "Le jaulne & bleu")

48^v *Le jaulne & blanc**[9]

31 49^v *Jouissance* (AttainCK III, no. 24: Sermisy)

50^v *Jouissance vous donneray**

32 51^v *Destre amoureux*[10] (compare RISM 1529$_3$, no. 23) = 1549$_8$, no. 19

52^v *Destre amoureux**[11]

33 53^v *Tant que vivray*[12] (AttainCK II, no. 10: Sermisy) = 1545$_3$, no. 30

54^v *Tant que vivray**[13]

34 55^v *Si jay pour vous* (AttainCK III, no. 12: Sermisy)

56^v *Si jay pour vous**

35 57^v *Damour je suys* (compare CM II, 5) = 1545$_3$, no. 17

36 58 *De toy me plains* (AttainCK II, no 24)

37 58^v *Elle sen va* (AttainCK I, no. 8: Sermisy)

38 59 *La guerre*[14]

39 60 *Tresoriere* [*de plaisir amoureux*] (RISM [c. 1528]$_5$, no. 3)

[1] The unique copy has manuscript additions in lute tablature on fols. 54, 55, 59^v, and 60^v.

[2] Mod. ed. in KörL, p. 133.

[3] Mod. ed. in KörL, p. 135.

[4] Mod. ed. in BruA, no. 16.

[5] A different text beginning "Je me repens" may be found in ParisC, no. 23 (monophonic), and DK:Kk, Ny. Kgl. S. 2°. MS 1848, p. 149 (*a3*).

[6] Quasi-facs. and mod ed. in WolfH II, 77–78.

[7] Quasi-facs. and mod. ed. in WolfH II, 76–77; facs. of fols. 42^v and 43 in ApelN, p. 65, and in WolfMS, pl. 61.

[8] The second version of this chanson (no. 28b) is the intabulation for solo lute. The first version is a somewhat modified arrangement of the lower two voices. Perhaps the voice part was omitted through an oversight.

[9] Mod. ed. in LowT, p. 30.

[10] Mod. ed. in BruA, no. 23.

[11] Mod. ed. in BruAL I, 28, and KörL, p. 157.

[12] Mod. ed. in ApelM II, 23, and BruA, no. 24.

[13] Mod. ed. in BruAL I, 29; KörL, p. 156; LowT, p. 27; and NoskeS, p. 18.

[14] Mod. ed. in KörL, p. 153.

152?$_1$

TROMBONCINO, BARTOLOMEO, AND MARCO CARA

Frottole de Misser Bortolomio Trombon/ cino & de Misser Marcheto Carra / con Tenori & Bassi tabulati & con / soprani in canto figurato per / cantar & sonar col / lauto. / Sanctissimus dominus sominus noster Papa Leo .x. / vetat nequis alius hos cantus imprimat to/to decennio sub excommunicationis pena. / [Cut with fleur-de-lis]

48 fols. Mensural notation and Italian lute tablature. On fol. 1^v: table of contents. On fol. 2: "Regula per quelli che non sano cantare" (in Italian only; for concordances see 1507$_1$). Thirteen folios, including that containing the printer's colophon, are missing from the unique copy; these are indicated in the following list of contents by an asterisk. The composers' initials are

resolved the first time they appear only. For further information see Vogel Einstein $[152\grave{o}]_2$, WolfEA, and GanB. All of the compositions are for solo voice (written in mensural notation) and lute.

Copy in: I:Fc (fols. 14–19, 30–34, 47–48 wanting).

fol.

1 2^v *Chi se po slegar damore*[1] B[artolomeo] T[romboncino]

2 3^v *Se gliel dico che dira*[2] M[arco] C[ara]

3 5 *Come haro donque ardire* B. T. (RISM 1519_4, fol. 29^v: text by Michelangelo Buonarroti)

4 7^v *Per fugir la mia morte alma* M. C. (I:Vnm, MSS It. Cl. IV, 1795–1798, no. 74: anon.)

5 8 *Almen vedesti el cor mio* B. T.

6 9 *Aqua non el humor* B. T. (RISM 1514_2, fol. 71^v)

7 10 *Se alcun tempo da voi* M. C. (RISM 1518, fol. 42)

8 10^v *Piu volte fra me stesso* B. T. (CesF, p. 75: anon.)

9 11^v *Se la lumacha che sabrusa* B. T. (RISM 1517_2, fol. 6^v)

10 12^v *Amor se dora in hor* B. T. (RISM 1517_2, fol. 26^v: M. C.)

11 13^v *Se amor non e, che adunque* M. C. (RISM 1517_2, fol. 5^v: text by Petrarch)

12 *La non vol perche** (RISM 1519_4, fol. 21^v: M. C. [?])

13 *Nel foco tremo** (RISM 1517_2, fol. 39^v: B. T. [?])

14 *Signora un che v'adora** (RISM 1519_4, fol. 32^v: M. C. [?])

15 *Dura passion che per amor** (RISM 1519_4, fol. 40^v: B. T. [?], text by Sannazar)

16 *La speranza in tutto** (RISM 1519_4, fol. 36^v: B. T. [?])

17 *Cangia sperar mia voglia**

18 20^v *Cum rides mihi* B. T. (RISM 1519_4, fol. 25^v: anon., text by Pontano)

19 22 *Madonna la pietade* B. T. (RISM 1517_2, fol. 8^v)

20 23^v *Mia ventura al venir* B. T.

21 26 *Ogni mal d'amor procede*[3] B. T.

22 27 *Quando i piango e mecho amore* B. T. (RISM 1519_4, fol. 41^v: anon.)

23 28 *Movessi il vechiarel* B. T. (I:Vnm, MSS It. Cl. IV, 1795–1798, no. 27: anon.)

24 29^v *Facto son per affanni* B. T. (I:Vnm, MSS It. Cl. IV, 1795–1798, no. 26: anon.)

25 *Donna non me tenete**

26 *Donna sol per voi**

27 *Queste lachrime mie**[4] B. T. (RISM 1514_2, fol. 63^v: text by Castiglione)

28 35^v *Voi gentil alme accesse* B. T.

29 37 *Gli e pur cocente il fier* B. T. (RISM 1519_4, fol. 44^v)

30 38 *Ecco colui chi marde* M. C. (RISM 1519_4, fol. 43^v)

31 39^v *Forsi e ver forsi che non*[5] F. T. [*sic*]

32 40^v *Munchos son damor per dicios* B. T. (RISM 1519_4, fol. 27^v)

33 41 *Ben mi credea passar mio tempo* F. T. [*sic*] (RISM 1514_2, fol. 6^v: B. T., text by Petrarch)

34 43 *De fusse almen si nota* B. T. (RISM 1514_2, fol. 4^v)

35 45 *Queste non son piu lachrime* B. T. (RISM 1517_2, fol. 3^v: text by Ariosto)

36 45^v *Longi dal mio bel sol chiaro*[6] B. T. (RISM 1517_2, fol. 52^v)

37 46^v *Piangea la donna mia*[7] M. C. (I:Vnm, MSS It. Cl. IV, 1795–1798, no. 85: anon.)

[1] Mod. ed. in KörL, p. 158.

[2] This is not related musically to the Tromboncino setting of the same text in RISM 1507_4.

[3] Mod. ed. in KörL, p. 159.

[4] The end of this piece is preserved on fol. 35.

[5] Mod. ed. in KörL, p. 160. This is not related musically to the Cara setting of the same text in CesF, p. 118.

[6] Mod. ed. in KörL, p. 161, and LowT, p. 59.

[7] Only the beginning of this piece is preserved.

1530_1

AGRICOLA, MARTIN

Musica instru/mentalis deudsch / ynn welcher begrif/fen ist, wie man / nach dem gesange auff mancherley / Pfeiffen lernen sol, Auch wie auff / die Orgel, Harffen, Lauten, Gei/gen, und allerley Instrument und / Seytenspiel, noch der recht/gegründten Tabelthur / sey abzusetzen. / Mart. Agricola.

60 fols. plus four inserted tables. Contents = 1529_1.
Copy in: US:Wc.

† 1530_2

FINÉ, ORONCE

Epithoma musice instrumentalis / ad omnimodam Hemispherii seu Luthine & theoricam et practicam / Per Orontium fineum Delphinatem studiose collectum. 1530 / Venit Pat. in officina libraria Petri Attaingnant / in vico cythare.

8 fols. Several diagrams, but no complete compositions appear as musical examples in this instruction book (in Latin) for the lute.
Copies in: A:Wn, D:Bds-Tü.

† 1530_3

ATTAINGNANT, PIERRE, PUBLISHER

1529 'Kal. Februarii / Dixhuit basses dances garnies de / Recoupes et Tordions, avec dixneuf Branles, quatre que Sauterelles que / Haulberroys, quinze Gaillardes, & neuf Pavennes, de la plus grant part / desquelles le subject est en musique. Le tout reduyt en la tabulature / du Lutz nouvellement imprime a Paris par Pierre Attaingnant demourant / en la rue de la Harpe pres leglise saint Cosme, desquelles la table sensuyt. / [Table of contents] / Avec plusieurs aultres chansons nouvelles tant en tablature du Lutz, que en musique. / Cum privilegio regis ad triennium.

40 fols. French lute tablature and mensural notation. See HeartzSF, chap. i, for a discussion of the possibility that the volume was printed in an incorrect order, and p. 315 for some dance concordances (see also HeartzS, p. 76). The compositions identified by superior letters are reprinted as follows: ([a]) in BlumeS, app. B; ([b]) in BruS; and ([c]) in BruA. All of the compositions are for solo lute; those identified by an asterisk include the melody (called "Subjectum") notated separately in mensural notation. The composer's initials are resolved the first time they appear only.
Copy in: D:Mbs.[1]

	fol.	
1	1^{v}	*La Magdalena. Basse dance*[a] [2] P[ierre] B[londeau] (1530_5, no. 6)
	1^{v}	[*Recoupe*]
	2	[*Tordion*]
2	2^{v}	*Puisquen deux cueurs. Basse dance*[c] P. B. (compare AttainCK III, no. 13)
3	3	*Basse dance* P. B.
4	3^{v}	*La brosse. Basse dance*[ac] P. B.
	4	[*Recoupe*][c]
	4	[*Tordion*][c]
5	4^{v}	*Le cueur est bon. Basse dance*[a] (compare AttainCK I, no. 11)
6	5	*Lespoir. B*[*ran*]*l*[*e*] (compare AttainCK III, no. 20: "L'espoir que jay")
7	5^{v}	*Foves basse dance*
8	6	*La roque*[c] P. B.
9	6^{v}	*Basse dance. Le corps sen va* P. B. (compare RISM [c. 1528]$_5$, no. 9: Conseil)
10	7	*Tous mes amys. Basse dance**[c] P. B. (compare RISM [c. 1528]$_5$, no. 4: Sermisy)
11	8	*Sansserre. Basse dance*[c]
12	8^{v}	*Cueur angoisseux. Basse dance* [3] P. B.
13	9	*Basse dance. s*[*ans*] *roch*[ac] [4]
	9^{v}	*Recoupe*[ac]
	10	*Tordion*[ac]
14	10^{v}	*Basse dance de lespine*[a] [5]
	11	*Recoupe*
	11^{v}	*Tordion*[b]
15	11^{v}	*Basse dance*[c]
	12^{v}	*Recoupe*[c]
	13	*Tordion*[c]
16	13^{v}	*Basse dance*[c]
	14	*Recoupe*
	14^{v}	*Tordion* [6]
17	15	*Branle gay*
18	15^{v}	*Branle gay*
19	16	*Branle*
20	16^{v}	*Branle gay. Cest mon amy* (compare RISM 1578_{15}, fol. 15: Janequin)

21	17	*Branle*
22	17^v	*Branle gay*[c]
23	18	*Branle gay*
24	18^v	*Haulberroys*
25	19	*Haulberroys*[c]
26	19	*B[ranle de] Poictou*
27	19^v	*Branle [de] Poictou*[c]
28	19^v	*B[ranle de] Poictou*
29	20	*B[ranle de] Poictou*[c]
30	20^v	*Branle*
31	21	*Branle Nicolas mon beau frere*
32	21^v	*Gaillarde*[c]
33	21^v	*B[ranle de] Poictou*
34	22	*Gaillarde*
35	22^v	*Branle gay*[c]
36	22^v	*B[ranle] Allez dire a c. damboyse*
37	23	*Branle gay*[c] (compare RISM 1535_6, no. 10: "Je ne seray jamais bergere," Passereau)
38	23^v	*Sauterelle*
39	24	*Gaillarde*[c 7]
40	24^v	*Branle Sil est a ma poste*[c] (compare MMRF V, no. 27: Hesdin)
41	25	*Pavane*[8]
42	25^v	*Basse Dance Patience*[c 9]
	25^v	*Recoupe*[b]
	26	*Tordion*
43	26^v	*Pavane*[c 10] = 1546_{20}, no. 18
44	27^v	*Basse dance. Beure frais*[a 11]
	27^v	*Recoupe*
	28	*Tordion*[12]
45	28^v	*Pavane*[c 13]
46	29	*Sauterelle*[c]
47	29^v	*Gaillarde*[bc]
48	30	*Pavane*[c 14]
49	30^v	*Gaillarde*[15]
50	30^v	*Gaillarde*
51	31	*Gaillarde*[bc]
52	31^v	*Basse dance. Verdurant*
	31^v	*Recoupe*
	32	*Tordion*[b16]
53	32^v	*Gaillarde*
54	33	*Pavane*[17]
55	33^v	*Gaillarde**[18] P. B. (1530_4, no. 4)
56	34^v	*Balle*
57	35	*Pavane*[c] P. B. = no. 63 below
58	35^v	*Gaillarde** P. B. = no. 64 below
59	36^v	*Pavane* P. B.
60	37	*Pavane*[b] Blondeau
61	37^v	*Gaillarde** P. B.
62	38	*Gaillarde**[c] (1530_4, no. 6)
63	38^v	*Pavane* P. B. = no. 57 above
64	39	*Gaillarde* = no. 58 above
65	39^v	*Gaillarde** P. B. (compare 1530_5, no. 5: "La scarpa my faict mal Basse dance")
66	40^v	*La Rote de Rode**[bc 19]

[1] Manuscript addition on fol. 13: "Le Nomi delle note sono sette: A.lasolre. B.mi. C.solfaut. D.lasolre. Elami. F.faut e G.solreut." Manuscript addition on fol. 40: examples of notes, rests, and accidentals.

[2] Mod. ed. in BruAL I, 30, and WasG, no. 4a. I am grateful to Daniel Heartz for resolving the initials.

[3] Facs. and mod. ed. in WolfH II, 75; mod. ed. in NeemAM I, no. 8.

[4] Mod. ed. in KörL, p. 150; ScherG, no. 90; and ZanG I, 7.

[5] Mod. ed. in KörL, p. 151.

[6] Mod. ed. and quasi-facs. of the beginning in TapS, p. 12.

[7] Mod. ed. in NeemAM I, no. 7.

[8] Mod. ed. in NeemAM I, no. 6.

[9] Mod. ed. (arranged) of nos. 42a–c in DolDE, p. 39.

[10] Mod. ed. in HeartzS, p. 71.

[11] Facs. in WolfMS, pl. 68; mod. ed. in ApelN, p. 68, and SachsRD, p. 111.

[12] Mod. ed. in ZanG I, 4.

[13] No. 45 is related thematically to no. 46.

[14] Mod. ed. in ZanG I, 6.

[15] Mod. ed. in GomVC, p. lxxi.

[16] Mod. ed. in BehF, p. 5 (arr. for guitar), and MU III, app., p. 36.

[17] Mod. ed. in HeartzS, p. 67.

[18] Facs. and mod. ed. in WolfH II, 79.

[19] Mod. ed. in TapS, p. 13.

1530_4

ATTAINGNANT, PIERRE, PUBLISHER

Six Gaillardes et six Pavanes / avec Treze chansons musicales a quatre parties le tout nouvellement / imprime par Pierre Attaingnant imprimeur et libraire demourant a / Paris en la rue de la Harpe devant le bout de la rue des Mathurins / pres leglise saint Cosme. desquelles la table sensuyt. / [Table of contents] / Superius

Four part books in mensural notation, each of 16 fols. On the title page of the bassus and contratenor parts: lists of errata. As the title explains, the volume contains 12 dances, presumably for instrumental ensemble, and 13 chansons. The 12 dances are reprinted in GiesA I. On dating the volume, see HeartzC.[1] For some concordances see HeartzS, p. 76, and HeartzSF, p. 323.

Copies in: D:E (A only), D:Mbs.[2]

	fol.	
1	1^v	*Gaillarde 1* = 1555_2, no. 290
2	1^v	*Gaillarde 2* = 1555_2, no. 291
3	2	*Gaillarde 3*[3] = 1555_2, no. 320
4	2^v	*Gaillarde 4* = 1530_5, no. 45 (1530_3, no. 55)
5	2^v	*Gaillarde 5* = 1530_5, no. 43
6	3	*Gaillarde 6* (1530_3, no. 62, and 1531_4, no. 17) = 1555_2, no. 191
7	3^v	*Pavane 1* = 1555_2, no. 197
8	3^v	*Pavane 2*[4]
9	4	*Pavane 3* (compare LesAC, no. 18: "J'ay le rebours," Certon) = 1555_2, no. 65
10	4	*Pavane 4* = 1555_2, no. 158
11	4^v	*Pavane 5*
12	4^v	*Pavane 6*
13	5	*A laventure lentrepris* Willart
14	5^v	*Mon cueur mon corps* Willart
15	6^v	*En lombre dung buyssonnet* M. lasson
16	7	*Hellas hellas madame* Moulu
17	7^v	*Alleluya my fault* Gombert
18	8^v	*Voulez ouyr les cris de paris* Jannequin
19	11^v	*Ian petit ian ian* Lhiretier
20	12^v	*Dessus le marche darras* Willart
21	13	*Si vous estes mamye*
22	14	*Cest tout abus*
23	15	*Du feu damours* Jacotin
24	15^v	*Vion viette sommes nous* Claudin
25[4]	16^v	*En regardant*

[1] The tenor part book bears the date 1529, but Heartz shows that it was printed before Easter, that is, in 1530 N.S.

[2] A copy of the superius part book was in D:WEs (see EitQ I, 230).

[3] Mod. ed. in MGG IV, col. 1286.

[4] Mod. ed. in RieT, no. 1, and WohlT, no. 2.

1530_5

ATTAINGNANT, PIERRE, PUBLISHER

Neuf basses dances deux branles / vingt et cinq Pavennes avec quinze Gaillardes en musique a quatre / parties le tout nouvellement imprime a Paris par Pierre Attaingnant / libraire demourant en la rue de la Harpe au bout de la rue des Matu/rins pres leglise saint Cosme. 1530 / Superius. / Cum privilegio

Four part books in mensural notation, each of 16 fols. On the title page of the tenor and contratenor part books: the printer's privilege.[1] The entire volume is reprinted in GiesA I–II. The compositions identified by superior letters are reprinted as follows: ([a]) in BlumeS, app. B; ([b]) in RieT; and ([c]) in WohlT.[2] For some concordances see HeartzS, p. 76, and HeartzSF, p. 324. For a possible later edition see $[1538]_3$. All of the dances are for instrumental ensemble *a 4*, except for no. 1 (*a 5*) and no. 29 (*a 6*).

Copies in: D:Mbs, E:S (A only).

	fol.	
1	1^v	*Basse dance 1*[abc] (*a 5*) (compare no. 3 below) = 1555_2, no. 30
2	1^v	*Basse dance 2*[abc] = 1555_2, no. 239
3	2	*Basse dance 3* (compare no. 1 above)
4	2	*La gatta en italien Basse dance 4*[abc] = 1555_2, no. 314
5	2^v	*La scarpa my faict mal Basse dance 5*[abc 3] (compare 1530_3, no. 65: "Gaillarde," P. B.)
6	2^v	*La magdalena Basse dance 6*[abc 4] (1530_3, no. 1) = 1555_2, no. 249
7	3	*Tourdion*[5] = 1555_2, no. 250
8	3^v	*Basse dance 8*[bc]
9	3^v	*La brosse Basse dance*[ab 6]
10	4^v	*Branle 1*[bc]
11	4^v	*Branle 2* (1547_6, no. 17, and $154?_6$, no. 43: "Branle simple")
12	5	*Pavenne 1* = 1555_2, no. 276
13	5	*Pavenne 2*
14	5^v	*Pavane 3*
15	5^v	*Pavane 4* = 1555_2, no. 313
16	6	*Pavane 5* = 1555_2, no. 194
17	6^v	*Pavenne 6*
18	7	*Pavenne 7* = 1555_2, no. 254
19	7^v	*Pavane 8* = 1555_2, no. 248
20	7^v	*Pavane 9* = 1555_2, no. 268
21	8	*Pavane 10*
22	8	*Pavane 11*
23	8^v	*Pavenne 12*[7] = 1555_2, nos. 218 and 319
24	8^v	*Pavenne 13* = 1555_2, no. 175
25	9	*Pavenne 14*
26	9	*Pavenne 15*
27	9^v	*Pavane 16*[abc 8]
28	9^v	*Pavane 17* = 1555_2, no. 184
29	10	*Pavane 18*[9] (*a 6*) = 1555_2, no. 6
30	10^v	*Pavenne 19*[10] (1531_4, nos. 26, 30)

31 11 *Gaillarde 1*[a] (compare AttainCK III, no. 22: "Dont vient cela," Sermisy)
32 11v *Gaillarde 2* = no. 44 below, and 1555_2, no. 277
33 11v *Gaillarde 3*
34 12 *Gaillarde 4* (1531_4, no. 29) = 1555_2, no. 270
35 12v *Gaillarde 5*
36 12v *Gaillarde 6*[11] = 1555_2, no. 321
37 13 *Gaillarde 7* (1531_4, no. 32)
38 13 *Gaillarde 8*
39 13v *Gaillarde 9*
40 13v *Gaillarde 10*
41 14 *Gaillarde 11*
42 14v *Gaillarde 12*
43 14v *Gaillarde 13* = 1530_3, no. 5
44 15 *Gaillarde 14* = no. 32 above, and 1555_2, no. 277
45 15v *Gaillarde 15* = 1530_3, no. 4, and 1555_2, no. 271
46 15v *Pavenne 20*[b]
47 16 *Pavenne 21*[bc]
48 16 *Pavenne 22*
49 16 *Pavenne 23*[b] = 1555_2, no. 258
50 16v *Pavenne 24*
51 16v *Pavenne 25 La rote de rode*[12]

[1] The privilege reads: "Le Roy a donne privilege de troys ans audit Attaingnant apres limpression de chacun livre quil imprimera. Et deffent a tous libraires, imprimeurs & aultres quilz nayent a imprimer & contrefaire lesdits livres par ledit Attaingnant imprimez ne aulcune partie diceulx sur peine de confiscation & damende arbitraire."

[2] WohlT also includes a dance labeled "La brosse," which is not no. 9 of this volume nor any other dance from the volume.

[3] Mod. ed. in MoeDM, p. 336, and ZanG I, 6 (arr. for guitar).

[4] Mod. ed. in WasG, app., no. 4b.

[5] Mod. ed. in MoeDM, p. 336, and ZanG I, 6 (arr. for guitar).

[6] Mod. ed. in GomVC, p. lxxii.

[7] Mod. ed. in OppelF, p. 215.

[8] Mod. ed. (arranged) in RieM, no. 31.

[9] Mod. ed. in DolDE, p. 85 (arranged), and OppelF, p. 214.

[10] Mod. ed. in HeartzS, p. 67.

[11] Mod. ed. in SteinitA, no. 14.

[12] Mod. ed. (arranged) in DolDE, p. 85.

1530_6

CORNYSH, PYGOT, ASHWELL, AND OTHERS

In this boke ar conteynyd .xx. songes .ix. of .iiii. partes, and .xi. of thre partes. /

iiii. partes.
Pater noster Cornysh [A1]
By by Pygot [A4]
She may be callyd Ashwell [C2]
The bella Tavernar [C3v]
My love mournyth Gwynneth [H1v]
Pleasure it is Cornysh [J1]
Concordans musycall. Cornysh [J1v]
Ut re my fa sol la. Fayrfax [K2]
Ut re my fa sol la Cowper [L3]

iii partes.
In youth. Cowper [A2]
Beware my lytyll fynger [B1v]
So great unkyndnes Cowper [D2v]
Who shall have my fayr lady. Jones [E1v]
Mynyon goo trym [E3]
Joly felow Joly [F1v]
And wyl ye serve me soo [F3v]
My harte my mynde Tavernar [G1v]
Love wyll I Tavernar [G4v]
My hartes lust Fayrfax [J3]
Fa la soll Cornyshe [L1]

Anno domini. M. ccccc .xxx. Decimo die mensis Octobris.

Four part books in mensural notation. (Bassus of 45 fols.) On fol. 1 of each part book (?): designation of part (triplex, medius, bassus, and a fourth). On fol. 1v of each part book (?): title page. Fol. 2 = fol. A1. Folio numbers in brackets have been added to the title page above from the bass part book, which contains one composition with Latin text, 16 with English text, and three textless compositions, presumably for instrumental ensemble.[1] For further information see ImelS.

Copies in: GB:Lbm (fol. 1 of triplex and complete bassus),[2] GB:Lwa (medius, fols. 1 and 45).[3]

fol.
1 K2 *Ut re my fa sol la* Fayrfax *a 4*
2 L1 *Fa la soll*[4] Cornyshe *a 3*
3 L3 *Ut re my fa sol la* Cowper *a 4*

[1] This volume was formerly thought to have been printed by Wynkyn de Worde. Facs. of bass, fol. E1v, in PN, p. 73; facs. of fols. 1v, C2, C2v, C3, and C3v in ReedC, pls. B–F; facs. of bass, fol. C2, in SteeleE, pl. 6.

[2] The bass parts of two songs, "Behold and se how byrds dothe fly," and "By a banke as I ley," have been added in manuscript to the bass part book. At the end of the first song the composer's name,

Thomas Stretton, has been written backwards ("Samoht notterts").

[3] The medius title page (repr. in facs. in NixB, pl. XVI) has the colophon: "Impryntyd in London at the signe of the black Morens," and the initials "TB" and "S"; see NixB for further details.

[4] Mod. ed. of all three voices after GB:Lbm, Add. MS 31922, in MB XVIII, no. 6.

1530

DOUBTFUL WORKS

1. FétB III, 460, lists the following volume of lute music by Hans Gerle: "Lauten-Parthien in der Tabulatur, Nuremberg, 1530, petit in-4° obl." See 1532_2, note 1.

1531_1

ATTAINGNANT, PIERRE, PUBLISHER

Dixneuf chansons musicales redui/ctes en la tabulature des Orgues Espinettes Manicordions, et telz / semblables instrumentz musicaulx Imprimees a Paris par Pierre / Attaingnant demourant en la rue de la Harpe pres leglise saint Cosme / Desquelles la table sensuyt. Idibus Januarii 1530 / [Table of contents] / Le roy a donne permission et privilege audit Attaingnant des livres quil / a par cy devant imprimez & espere imprimer cy apres tant en musique / ieux de Lutz, Orgues, et semblables instrumentz que nul ne les pourra / imprimer contrefaire ne aulcune partie diceulx vendre ne distribuer / jusques a troys ans apres limpression de chacun diceulx. Et le tout sur / peine de confiscation et damende arbitraire.

40 fols. Keyboard score. Tables of contents for all seven of the 1531 Attaingnant keyboard tablatures are given in SchlechtK. For a discussion of all seven volumes see RoksMO, chaps. 6 and 7; on the chansons see BroC. AttainC I is a facsimile of the entire volume. AttainCK I is a modern edition of the volume, and includes the vocal models, printed above the intabulations. Therefore, the inventory below lists sixteenth-century sources of the vocal models. All of the compositions are for solo keyboard.

Copy in: D:Mbs.

	fol.	
1	1v	*Ung grant plaisir* (RISM 1536_5, no. 13: Sermisy)
2	4v	*Hau hau le boys* (RISM 1529_2, no. 5: Sermisy)
3	7	*Mon cueur en souvent bien marri* (RISM 1531_2, no. 21: Sermisy)
4	8	*Amours partes* (RISM 1529_2, no. 16: Sermisy)
5	9	*A bien grant tort* (RISM [c. $1528]_7$, no. 9)
6	11	*Celle qui ma tant pourmene* (RISM 1529_3, no. 14: Sermisy)
7	13v	*Je ne scay point comment* (RISM 1529_4, no. 9)
8	15v	*Elle sen va de moy tant reg* (RISM 1529_2, no. 9: Sermisy)
9	17v	*Il me suffit*[1] (RISM 1529_3, no. 34: Sermisy)
10	18v	*Fors seulement* (I:Fn, MS Magl. XIX, 164–167, no. 61: anon. [Pipclarc])
11	21v	*Le cueur est bon* (RISM 1531_2, no. 34)
12	23v	*Jay trop ayme* (RISM 1529_4, no. 14)
13	25	*Au desiuner*[2] (RISM 1531_2, no. 2: "A desiuner la belle")
14	26	*Mauldicte soit la mondaine richesse* (RISM 1529_2, no. 15: Sermisy)
15	28	*Dolent depart* (RISM 1529_4, no. 16)
16	30	*Aupres de vous* [*secretement*] (RISM 1529_3, no. 3: Sermisy or Jacotin)
17	33	*Cest grant plaisir* (RISM 1529_4, no. 42)
18	35v	*Dung nouveau dart* (RISM [c. $1528]_4$, no. 5)
19	38	*Je le disoies* (RISM [c. $1528]_5$, no. 29)

[1] Mod. ed. in RitZ II, 75.

[2] Mod. ed. in AttainC V, pl. H.

1531_2

ATTAINGNANT, PIERRE, PUBLISHER

xli / Vingt et cinq chansons musicales / reduictes en la tabulature des Orgues Espinettes Manicordions & / telz semblables instrumentz musicaulx Imprimees a Paris par Pierre / Attaingnant demourant en la rue de la Harpe pres leglise saint Cosme / Desquelles la table sensuyt. Kal. Februarii 1530 / [Table of contents] / Avec privilege du Roy nostre / sire pour trois ans.

40 fols. Keyboard score. AttainC II is a facsimile of the entire volume. AttainCK II is a modern edition of the volume, and includes the vocal models, printed above the intabulations. Therefore, the inventory below lists sixteenth-century sources of the vocal models. For further information see 1531_1. All of the compositions are for solo keyboard.

Copy in: D:Mbs.

	fol.	
1	41^v	*Aller my fault sur la verdure* (RISM 1529_3, no. 9: Janequin)
2	44	*Jay contente ma volunte* [1] (RISM 1531_2, no. 35: Sermisy)
3	45^v	*Cest une dure departie* [2] (RISM 1529_2, no. 18: Sermisy)
4	47	*Le cueur de vous* (RISM 1529_3, no. 8: Sermisy)
5	49	*Contre raison* [3] (RISM 1529_3, no. 19: Sermisy)
6	51	*Lheur de mon bien* (RISM [c. 1528]$_7$, no. 19)
7	52	*Du bien que loeil* (RISM 1529_2, no. 19: Sermisy)
8	53^v	*Mon cueur en vous* (RISM [c. 1528]$_5$, no. 25)
9	55	*Dessus le marche darras* (1530_4, no. 20: Willaert)
10	57	*Tant que vivray* (RISM 1531_2, no. 37: Sermisy)
11	58^v	*Jatens secours* (RISM 1531_2, no. 28: Sermisy)
12	59^v	*Languir me fais* (RISM 1531_2, no. 29: Sermisy)
13	61	*Au joly bois* [4]
14	61^v	*Vignon vignon vignette* (RISM [c. 1528]$_7$, no. 3)
15	63	*Le jaulne & bleu* (RISM [c. 1528]$_7$, no. 24)
16	64	*Le cueur est myen* (RISM 1529_4, no. 7)
17	65	*Ung jour robin* (RISM 1531_2, no. 31: Sermisy)
18	67	*Cest a grant tort* (RISM 1529_3, no. 31: Sermisy)
19	68^v	*Changeons propos* (RISM 1531_2, no. 27: Sermisy)
20	71	*Maulgre moy viz* (RISM [c. 1528]$_7$, no. 23: Sermisy)
21	73	*Long temps ya que je viz* (RISM [c. 1528]$_7$, no. 18)
22	75	*Secourez moy* (RISM 1531_2, no. 1: Sermisy)
23	76^v	*Fortune [lesse moy la vie]* (RISM 1529_4, no. 13)
24	78	*De toy me plains* (RISM 1529_3, no. 26)
25	79^v	*Ces facheux sotz* (RISM 1529_4, no. 8)

[1] Facs. of fol. 44 in WolfH II, opp. p. 250.
[2] Mod. ed. in OppelF, p. 216.
[3] Mod. ed. in ScherG, no. 91c.
[4] Mod. ed. in SchlechtB II, 123, and TapS, p. 14. A different version of the same melodic material is in RISM 1529_4, no. 35, by Clemens non Papa.

1531_3

ATTAINGNANT, PIERRE, PUBLISHER

lxxxi / Vingt et six chansons musicales / reduictes en la tabulature des Orgues Espinettes Manicordions & / telz semblables instrumentz musicaulx Imprimees a Paris par Pierre / Attaingnant demourant en la rue de la Harpe pres leglise saint Cosme / Desquelles la table sensuyt. Non. Februarii 1530 / [Table of contents] / Avec privilege du Roy nostre / sire pour trois ans.

40 fols. Keyboard score. AttainC III is a facsimile of the entire volume. AttainCK III is a modern edition of the volume, and includes the vocal models, printed above the intabulations. Therefore, the inventory below lists sixteenth-century sources of the vocal models. For further information see 1531_1. All of the compositions are for solo keyboard.

Copy in: D:Mbs.

	fol.	
1	81^v	*Mon cueur gist tousiours* (RISM [c. 1528]$_7$, no. 26)
2	83	*Cest boucane* (RISM 1529_4, no. 10)
3	84	*Las voulez vous* (RISM 1531_2, no. 20: Vermont)
4	86^v	*Je demeure seule esgaree* (RISM 1529_4, no. 6)
5	87^v	*Amour vault trop* (RISM 1529_4, no. 18)

6 89 *Las je my plains* (RISM 1531_2, no. 36)

7 90 *Amy souffrez* (RISM 1529_4, no. 12: Moulu)

8 91 *Je ne fais rien que requerir* (RISM [c. $1528]_4$, no. 2: Sermisy)

9 92^v *Le content est riche*[1] (RISM 1531_2, no. 15: Sermisy)

10 94^v *De retourner* (RISM 1529_3, no. 24)

11 95^v *Ung grant plaisir* (RISM [c. $1528]_7$, no. 6)

12 97 *Si jay pour vous* (RISM 1531_2, no. 13: Sermisy)

13 98^v *Puis quen deux cueurs* (RISM [c. $1528]_7$, no. 33)

14 100 *Puis quen amours* (RISM 1529_2, no. 26: Sermisy)

15 102 *Il est jour dit lalouette* (RISM 1531_2, no. 14: Sermisy)

16 103^v *Jay mis mon cueur*[2] (RISM 1529_4, no. 11)

17 104^v *Vivray je tousiours* (RISM 1531_2, no. 11: Sermisy)

18 105^v *Jay le desir content* (RISM 1529_2, no. 20: Sermisy)

19 107^v *Veu le grief mal* (RISM 1531_2, no. 23)

20 109 *Lespoir que jay* (RISM 1529_2, no. 4)

21 110^v *Ma bouche rit* (RISM 1536_5, no. 19: Duboys)

22 112 *Dont vient cela* (RISM 1531_2, no. 10: Sermisy)

23 114 *A mes ennuys* (RISM 1529_3, no. 10: "En mes ennuyz")

24 116 *Jouyssance vous donneray* (RISM 1531_2, no. 12: Sermisy)

25 117 *Nauray je jamais reconfort* (RISM 1531_2, no. 32: Jacotin)

26 119 *Le departir* (RISM 1531_2, no. 22)

[1] Mod. ed. in KinO, p. 260.
[2] Mod. ed. in AttainC V, pls. E–G.

† 1531_4

ATTAINGNANT, PIERRE, PUBLISHER

Quatorze Gaillardes neuf Paven/nes, sept Branles et deux Basses Dances le tout reduict de musique / en la tabulature du jeu Dorgues Espinettes Manicordions & telz / semblables instrumentz musicaulx Imprimees a Paris par Pierre / Attaingnant demourant en la rue de la Harpe pres leglise saint Cosme / Avec privilege du Roy nostre / sire pour trois ans.

40 fols. Keyboard score. AttainC IV is a facsimile of the entire volume. The compositions identified by the superior letter *a* ([a]) are reprinted in EitT. For some concordances see HeartzS, p. 76, and HeartzSF, p. 321. For further information see ApelQ, and 1531_1. All of the compositions are for solo keyboard.

Copy in: D:Mbs.

fol.

1 1^v *Pavane* (compare no. 31 below)

2 4 *Gaillarde sur la Pavane*[1]

3 5^v *Gaillarde*

4 6 *Gaillarde*

5 7^v *Branle commun*[2]

6 8 *Branle gay*[3]

7 9 *Gaillarde*

8 11 *Basse dance*[a][4]

9 12 *Basse dance*

10 13 *Branle*

11 14 *Gaillarde*

12 16 *Pavenne*[a][5]

13 17^v *Gaillarde*[a]

14 19 *Branle [simple]*[a][6]

15 20 *Branle*[a][7]

16 20^v *Branle [simple]*[a][8]

17 21^v *Gaillarde*[a] (1530_3, no. 62, and 1530_4, no. 6)

18 22 *Branle*[a]

19 23 *Gaillarde*[a][9]

20 23^v *Pavane*

21 24 *Gaillarde*[a][10]

22 25 *Gaillarde*[11] (compare no. 25 below)

23 26 *Pavane*[12]

24 28 *Gaillarde*

25 29^v *Gaillarde* (compare no. 22 above)

26 30^v *Pavane* (1530_5, no. 30, and compare no. 30 below)

27 31^v *Gaillarde*

28 32^v *Gaillarde*[a][13]

29 33^v *Gaillarde* (1530_5, no. 34)

30 35 *Pavane*[14] (compare no. 26 above)

31 37 *Pavane*[15] (compare no. 1 above)

32 39 *Gaillarde*[a][16] (1530_5, no. 37)

[1] Mod. ed. in ApelM II, 22.
[2] Mod. ed. (arranged) in DolDE, pp. 58–59; facs. of no. 5 in ApelN, facs. 2.
[3] Mod. ed. in HalbK, p. 7.
[4] Mod. ed. in ApelM II, 21; BesM, p. 275; BlumeS, app. B, no. 18c; and SachsPM, p. 13.
[5] Mod. ed. in ScherG, no. 91a.
[6] Mod. ed. in BöhT II, no. 141; DolDE, p. 62 (arranged); and AttainS, no. 1.
[7] Mod. ed. in EC, pt. I, vol. III, p. 1226, and AttainS, no. 2.
[8] Mod. ed. in AttainS, no. 3.
[9] Mod. ed. in ApelM II, 21; BöhT II, no. 142; and RehA I, 21.
[10] Mod. ed. in EP, p. 1284.
[11] Mod. ed. (arranged) in DolDE, p. 122.
[12] Mod. ed. in HeartzS, p. 71.
[13] Mod. ed. in ScherG, no. 91b.
[14] Mod. ed. in HeartzS, p. 67.
[15] Mod. ed. in HAM, no. 104.
[16] Mod. ed. in HalbK, p. 8.

1531_5

ATTAINGNANT, PIERRE, PUBLISHER

Tabulature pour le jeu Dorgues / Espinetes et Manicordions sur le plain chant de Cunctipotens et / Kyrie fons. Avec leurs Et in terra. Patrem. Sanctus et Agnus dei / le tout nouvellement imprime a Paris par Pierre Attaingnant de/mourant en la rue de la Harpe pres leglise sainct Cosme. / Avec privilege du Roy nostre / sire pour trois ans.

40 fols. Keyboard score. RoksO is a modern edition of the entire volume, and includes a facsimile of the title page. For further information see 1531_1. All of the compositions are for solo keyboard.

Copy in: D:Mbs.

fol.
1 A1v *Kyrie fons* [1]
A3 *Kyrie*
A4 *Christe*
B1v *Kyrie*
B3 *Kyrie*
C1v *Et in terra pax*
C2v *Benedicimus te*
C2v *Glorificamus te*
C3v *Domine deus rex celestis*
D1 *Domine deus agnus dei*
D2 *Qui tollis*
D3v *Quoniam tu solus sanctus*
D4 *Tu solus altissimus*
E1 *In gloria dei patris*
E2v *Patrem*
E2v *Visibilium omnium*
E3 *Et ex patre*
E3v *Et incarnatus*
E4 *Et homo factus est*
E4v *Et expecto*
E4v *Amen*
F1v *Sanctus*
F2 *Sanctus*
F2v *Benedictus*
F3v *Agnus dei*
F4v *Agnus dei*
G1v *Deo gratias* [2]
2 G2 *Kyrie Cunctipotens* [3]
G3 *Kyrie* [3]
G3v *Christe* [3]
G4 *Christe*
G4v *Kyrie* [3]
H1v *Ultimus Kyrie*
H2v *Et in terra pax*
H3 *Benedicimus te*
H3v *Glorificamus te*
H4 *Domine deus rex ce*
H4v *Domine deus agnus*
J1 *Qui tollis peccata*
J1v *Quoniam tu solus*
J2 *Tu solus altissimus*
J2v *In gloria dei patris*
J3 *Sanctus* [4]
J3v *Sanctus*
J4v *Benedictus*
K2 *Agnus dei*
K3 *Agnus dei*

[1] Mod. ed. of first Kyrie only in SchlechtG, no. 57b.
[2] Mod. ed. in RauQ, p. 8, and RitZ II, 77.
[3] Mod. ed. in FroideA I, 28.
[4] Mod. ed. in ScherG, no. 92.

1531_6

ATTAINGNANT, PIERRE, PUBLISHER

xli / Magnificat sur les huit tons avec / Te deum laudamus. et deux Preludes, le tout mys en la tabulature des / Orgues Espinettes & Manicordions imprimez a Paris par Pierre / Attaingnant libraire demourant en la rue de la Harpe pres leglise / saint Cosme. Kal. Martii 1530 / [Table of contents] / Avec privilege du Roy nostre sire / pour trois ans.

40 fols. Keyboard score. RoksO is a modern edition of the entire volume, and includes facsimiles of the title page and fol. 44ᵛ. SlimK II, 451, contains a thematic index of the preludes. For further information see 1531_1. All of the compositions are for solo keyboard.

Copy in: D:Mbs.

	fol.	
1	41ᵛ	*Preludium*
2	44ᵛ	*Prelude sur chacun ton* [1]
3	49	*Magnificat primi toni*
	50	*Secundus versus*
4	51ᵛ	*Magnificat secundi toni* (compare no. 10a below)
	52ᵛ	*Secundus versus*
5	53ᵛ	*Magnificat tertii toni*
	54ᵛ	*Secundus versus*
6	55ᵛ	*Magnificat quarti toni*
	56ᵛ	*Secundus versus*
	57ᵛ	*Tertius versus*
	58ᵛ	*Quartus versus*
	59ᵛ	*Quintus versus*
7	60ᵛ	*Magnificat quinti toni*
	61ᵛ	*Secundus versus*
8	62	*Magnificat sexti toni*
	63	*Secundus versus*
9	64	*Magnificat septimi toni*
	65ᵛ	*Secundus versus*
10	66ᵛ	*Magnificat octavi toni* (compare no. 4a above)
	67ᵛ	*Secundus versus*
	69	*Tertius versus* [2]
	70	*Quartus versus*
11	71ᵛ	*Te deum laudamus* [3]
	72	*Tibi omnes angeli*
	73	*Sanctus*
	73ᵛ	*Sanctus Dominus*
	74	*Te gloriosus*
	74ᵛ	*Te martyrum*
	75	*Patrem immense*
	75ᵛ	*Sanctum quoque*
	76ᵛ	*Tu patris*
	76ᵛ	*Tu devicto*
	77ᵛ	*Judex crederis*
	78	*Eterna fac*
	79	*Et rege eos*
	79ᵛ	*Miserere nostri. Et laudamus*
	80	*In te domine speravi*

[1] Mod. ed. in SchlechtG, no. 57a.

[2] Mod. ed. in RauM II, 1.

[3] Mod. ed. of versets 1, 7, and 9–11 in BiggsT, p. 63; mod. ed. of the first verset in RitZ II, 75.

1531_7

ATTAINGNANT, PIERRE, PUBLISHER

lxxxi / Treze Motetz musicaulx avec ung / Prelude, le tout reduict en la tabulature des Orgues Espinettes et / Manicordions et telz semblables instrumentz imprimez a Paris par / Pierre Attaingnant libraire demourant en la rue de la Harpe pres / leglise saint Cosme Desquelz la table sensuyt. Kal. April. 1531 / [Table of contents] / Avec privilege du Roy nostre sire / pour trois ans.[1]

40 fols. Keyboard score. RoksT is a modern edition of the volume and includes the vocal models printed above the intabulations and a facsimile of the title page and fol. 81ᵛ. Therefore, the inventory below lists sixteenth-century sources of the vocal models. For further information see 1531_1. All of the compositions are for solo keyboard.

Copy in: D:Mbs.

	fol.	
1	81ᵛ	*Manus tue domine fecerunt me*
2	83ᵛ	*Fortuna desperata* (GB:Lbm, Add. MS 35087, fol. 11ᵛ)
3	86ᵛ	*Bone jesu dulcissime* (RISM 1535_3, fol. 16: Gascongne)
4	89	*Sicut malus* [2] (RISM 1541_2, no. 20: Moulu)
5	92	*Sancta trinitas* (RISM 1514_1, fol. 9: Févin)
6	97ᵛ	*Benedictus* Fevin (RISM 1516_1, fol. 102ᵛ: Missa Ave Maria, Févin)
7	100	*Si bona suscepimus* (RISM 1535_3, fol. 7: Sermisy)
8	105	*Sicut lilium* (RISM 1538_8, no. 2: Brumel)
9	106ᵛ	*Dulcis amica dei* [3] (US:Wc, Laborde Chansonnier, fol. 142: [Prioris])
10	108	*O vos omnes qui transitis per viam* (RISM 1542_8, no. 15: Compère)
	110	2a pars [*Audite obsecro*]
11	111ᵛ	*Aspice domine* [4] (RISM 1535_3, fol. 11: De la fage)
12	115	*Consummo* [*la vita mia*] (US:Wc, Laborde Chansonnier, fol. 139)

13 117 *Parce domine* (RISM 1503_1, fol. 33v: Obrecht)
14 119v *Prelude*[5]

[1] Facs. of title page and one other page in RoksMO, pp. 214, 216.
[2] On this composition see RoksM.
[3] Mod. ed. in FroideA I, 27, and RitZ II, 76.
[4] In RISM [c. $1526]_5$, no. 5, the motet is attributed to Sermisy.
[5] Mod. ed. in RauQ, p. 8, and RitZ II, 77; musical incipit in SlimK II, 452.

1532_1

AGRICOLA, MARTIN

Musica / Instru/menta/lis. / Deudsch. / Martinus Agricola.

60 fols. plus four inserted tables.[1] The title is placed within an ornamental border. A second title page on fol. A1v:

> Musica Instru/mentalis Deudsch, ynn / welcher begriffen ist, wie / man nach dem gesange auff man/cherley Pfeiffen lernen sol, Auch wie / auff die Orgel, Harffen, Lau/ten, Geigen, und allerley In/strument und Seyten/spiel, nach der recht/gegründten Ta/belthur sey / abzuse/tzen.

Contents = 1529_1.

Copies in: A:Wn, D:Bds-Tü, D:Mbs, F:Pc, GB:Lbm (imperfect), US:R.

[1] One of the tables showing how to transcribe a single line from mensural notation into German keyboard tablature is reprinted in PN, p. 57.

1532_2

GERLE, HANS

Musica Teusch, auf die Instru/ment der grossen unnd kleinen Geygen, auch Lautten, / welcher massen die mit grundt und art irer Compo/sicion auss dem gesang in die Tabulatur zu ord/nen und zu setzen ist, sampt verborgener / applicacion und kunst, /Darynen ein liebhaber und anfenger berürter Instrument so dar zu lust und neygung / tregt, on ein sonderlichen Meyster mensürlich durch tegliche ubung leichtlich begreiffen / und lernen mag, vormals im Truck nye und ytzo durch Hans Gerle Lutinist / zu Nurenberg aussgangen. / 1532.

63 fols. German lute tablature, viola da gamba tablature, and mensural notation. The title is placed within an ornamental border containing the initials "H. G." and date 1530.[1] On fol. A2: preface headed "Allen und yeden der Lauten und Geygen kunst liebhabern, Wünsch ich Hans Gerle Lutinist burger, zu Nürmberg frydt unnd hayl, &c." Colophon on fol. Q3: "Gedruckt zu Nurenbergk durch Jeronimum Formschneyder." On fol. Q3v: errata. This instruction book is divided into five parts:

- fol. A2v: "Der Erst tayl von dem grossen Geygen" (including, on fol. A4, a cut of two Grossgeigen[2]).
- fol. E1v: "Der ander tayl diss Buchs" (dealing with notation).
- fol. H2v: "Hie hebt an der Drittayl diss Buchs und lernt wie du solt auff den kleynen Geigleyn lernen die kein Bündt [frets] haben" (including, on fol. H4, a cut of a Kleingeige with four strings[3]).
- fol. J2: "...der Viert tayl der zaygt an wie du auff der Lautten solt lernen" (including, on fol. J4, a cut of a lute).
- fol. N4: "Der Fünfft und letzt tayl diss Buchs, darinnen anzaygt wirt wie du auss dem gesang in die Tabulatur der Lautten setzen solt."

For further information see EinZ; SommL, p. 78; and TapL. The table of contents is given in MfMG III (1871), 210. The compositions identified by the superior letter *a* ([a]) are reprinted in SenflW VII. Some of the compositions are reprinted in LB, vols. 27 and 81. Nine of the pieces for Grossgeigen are reprinted in MonkS I. Contents = 1537_1. See 1546_9 for a revised and augmented edition.

Copies in: D:Bds-Tü, GB:Lbm, GB:Lbmh.[4]

PIECES FOR FOUR GROSSGEIGEN

fol.
1 C2 *Ich clag den tag*[5] (DTO XXXVII/72, p. 71: Stoltzer; another version of nos. 18 and 34 below)
2 C2v *Eyn freylein sprach ich freuntlich zu*[6] (compare EDMR XX, no. 25: "Ein Magd, die sagt mir freundlich zu," Malchinger or Senfl)

3 C3 *Pacientia[m müss ich han]*[a 7] (SenflW IV, no. 64: Senfl; another version of nos. 19 and 23 below)

4 C3[v] *Mein fleiss und müe*[a 8] (SenflW IV, no. 19: Senfl; another version of no. 24 below)

5 C4 *Mein selbs bin ich nit meer*[a] (SenflW VI, no. 6: Senfl)

6 C4[v] *Ach herre Gott wie syndt meiner feyndt so vil. Psalm iii* (another version of no. 27 below; compare BraunS, p. 46, no. 33)

7 D1 *Das ist ein fug geen all stim auss dem Discant*[9]

8 D1[v] *Auff erdt lebt nit eyn schöner weyb* (MosL, no. 56)

9 D2 *Entlaubet ist der walde*[10] (EDMR XX, no. 61: Stoltzer)

10 D2[v] *Von edler art* (MosPH, p. 180; J. Schönfelder or Hofhaimer)

11 D3[v] *Trostlicher lieb*[11] (MosPH, p. 86: Hofhaimer; another version of no. 21 below)

12 D4[v] *Elslein liebes Elselein*[a 12] (SenflW IV, no. 17: Senfl; compare no. 31 below)

13 E1 *Die Gugel*[a 13] (SenflW IV, no. 15: "Nun grüss dich Gott," Senfl)

PIECES FOR FOUR GROSSGEIGEN PRINTED ALSO IN MENSURAL NOTATION

14 G1[v] *Herr Christ der eynig Gott* (PubAPTM VII, no. 29: Johann Walther)

15 G3[v] *Mag ich hertzlieb erwerben dich*[a 14] (SenflW IV, no. 28: Senfl)

PIECES FOR FOUR KLEINGEIGEN

16 J1 *Mag ich gunst han*

17 J1[v] *Ein Maydt die sagt mir zu*[a 15] (EDMR XX, no. 25: Malchinger or Senfl)

PIECES FOR SOLO LUTE

18 K4 *Ich klag den tag*[16] (another version of no. 1 above) = 1536_6, no. 5

19 K4 *Pacientia* (another version of no. 3 above)

20 K4[v] *Nach willen dein*[17] (PubAPTM IX, 42: Hofhaimer)

21 L1 *Trostlicher lieb*[18] (another version of no. 11 above)

22 L2 *Wu sol ich mich hin keren ich armes brüderlein*[19] (PubAPTM XXIX, 90: G. Vogelhuber)

23 L2[v] *Paciencia*[a] (another version of no. 3 above)

24 L3 *Mein fleyss und müe ich nie hab gespart*[a] (another version of no. 4 above)

25 L3[v] *Priambel* = 1523_2, no. 7

26 L4[v] *Was wirdt es doch des wunderss noch*[a] (SenflW IV, no. 26: Senfl)

27 M1[v] *Ach herre Gott wie seyndt meiner feindt so vil. Psalm iii* (another version of no. 6 above)

28 M2 *Die Brünlein die do fliessen* (DTO XIV/28, p. 69: Isaac)

29 M3 *O du armer Judas* (compare BöhA, no. 539c; PubAPTM III, no. 102: Senfl; and ZahnM, no. 8187a)

30 M3[v] *Ich het mir ein Endlein für genummen*[a] (SenflW V, no. 26: Senfl)

31 M4 *Das Elselein*[a] (compare no. 12 above)

32 N1 *Priambel* = 1523_2, no. 13

33 N1[v] *Nun grüss dich Gott du mein drusserlein* (EDMR XX, no. 82: Sixt Dietrich)

34 N2[v] *Ich klag den tag*[20] (another version of no. 1 above)

35 O4[v] *Scaramella*[21] (compare AmbG V, 134: Josquin des Prez)

36 Q1 *Dich als mich selbs*[22] (EDMR XX, no. 1)

37 Q1[v] *Cenespas*[22] (RISM 1502_2, fol. 10[v]: "Ce nest pas," Pierre de la Rue)

38 Q2[v] *Ach werde frucht*[a 22] (SenflW IV, no. 66: Senfl)

[1] Facs. of title page in HeronF II, frontispiece; HeyerV II, pl. 2; KinsP, p. 133; and MGG IV, col. 561. FétB III, 460, lists a 1530 volume by Gerle: "Lauten-Parthien in der Tabulatur, Nuremberg, 1530, petit in-4° obl." The same ornamental border is used in 1537_1, 1546_9, and 1552_1.

[2] Facs. of fol. A4 in HirK IV, pl. 31; KinsP, p. 118; LM I, 389 (from 1546 ed.); and SenflW VII, x.

[3] Facs. of fol. H4 in SenflW VII, x.

[4] A copy was in D:W; the Hirsch copy was in the Heyer library (see HeyerV II, 40).

[5] Mod. ed. in BS XXXIV, no. 1; DTO XXXVII/72, p. 96; and StolI.
[6] Mod. ed. in BS XXXIV, no. 2.
[7] Mod. ed. in BS XXXIV, no. 3.
[8] Mod. ed. in BS XXXIV, no. 4.
[9] Mod. ed. in EC, pt. I, vol. III, p. 1210; MFH VII, 13; MU IV, app., p. 19; SteinitA, no. 15; and WasG, no. 19.
[10] Mod. ed. in DehnC; DTO XXXVII/72, p. 95; and StolI.
[11] Mod. ed. in DTO XXXVII/72, p. 86, and beginning only in MosPH, p. 88.
[12] Mod. ed. in EhmL, no. 1; MU IV, app., p. 12; and TapS, p. 15.
[13] Quasi-facs. in WolfH II, 223.
[14] Facs. of fols. $G3^{v}$ and G4 in SenflW VII, x.
[15] Quasi-facs. in WolfH II, 222–223.
[16] Mod. ed. in BS XXXIV, no. 1; DTO XXXVII/72, p. 96; and StolI.
[17] Mod. ed. in DTO XXXVII/72, p. 84, and beginning only in MosPH, p. 77. For a comparison of this intabulation with others see NowakH.
[18] Mod. ed. in DTO XXXVII/72, p. 86, and beginning only in MosPH, p. 88.
[19] Mod. ed. in MU IV, app., p. 11.
[20] Mod. ed. in DTO XXXVII/72, p. 96.
[21] No. 35 is an example of intabulation method.
[22] Nos. 36–38 are headed "Nun folgen etliche stucklein hernach in der Tabulatur zu den dreyzehen saytten."

1533_1

GERLE, HANS

Tabulatur auff die Laudten etli/cher Preambel, Teutscher, Wel/scher und Francösischer stück, von Liedlein, Muteten, und schönen Psalmen, mit drey und vier stym/men, Durch Hanns Gerle Luttinisten, Burger und Lauttenma/cher zu Nürenberg, ordenlich gesetzt, und in Truck / gegeben, Im M. D. XXXIII. Jar. / Mit Röm. Kaiserlicher und Kün. Mai. Freiheyt begnadet, in vier jaren nit / nach zu trücken, Bey straff und peen zehen Marck lötigs goldes.

95 fols.[1] German lute tablature. The title is placed within an ornamental border containing the initials H. G. and the date 1530. On fols. $2–2^{v}$: preface headed "Vorrede einer underrichtung." On fol. 3: cut of a lute. Colophon on fol. 94^{v}: "Gedrückt zü Nürenberg durch Jeronymum Formschneider. M. D. XXXIII." For further information see TapL. SlimK II, 453, contains a thematic index of the preambles. All of the compositions are for solo lute.

Copies in: D:Bds-Tü, GB:Lbm (title page wanting), GB:Lbmh.[2]

	fol.	
1	3^{v}	*Ein güt Preambel auff allerley Claves*
2	9	*Nochlauff auff das Priambel*
3	9^{v}	*Preambel* = 1545_3, no. 4
4	9^{v}	*Preambel*
5	11	*Preambel*
6	11^{v}	*Preambel*
7	13^{v}	*Herr thu uns hilff*[3] (compare BraunS, p. 77, no. 505)
8	14^{v}	*Jhesus Christus unser heyland* (PubAPTM VII, no. 24: Johann Walther)
9	15^{v}	*O herre Gott*
10	16^{v}	*Ellend ich rüff* (EDMR XX, no. 100: Arnoldus de Bruck)
11	17^{v}	*Ellend du hast umbfangen mich* (EitD II, no. 21)
12	18^{v}	*Ich stund an einem morgen* (RISM $[c. 1535]_{14}$ III, no. 40 [compare BridgmE, p. 160])
13	19^{v}	*Ein frölich wesen* (DTO XIV/28, p. 5, and LenN, p. [28]: Isaac, Barbireau, or Obrecht)
14	21	*Ein büler schmaycht*
15	21^{v}	*Mein selbs bin ich nit mer* (SenflW VI, no. 6: Senfl)
16	22	*An dich hab ich ergeben mich* (compare LeMaiG, no. 74: Le Maistre)
17	23	*Mein hertz thut alezeit verlangen* (GomO, no. 31: anon.) = 1545_3, no. 33
18	24	*Nicht lass mich hart entgelten* (EitD II, no. 109)
19	24^{v}	*Capitan [Herre Gott]* (PubAPTM II no. 67: Lupus Hellinck)
20	25^{v}	*Glück eer und gut*
21	26^{v}	*Wie mag es in der karten sein*[4] (RISM 1534_{17}, no. 116: Wilhelm Breitengraser)
22	27^{v}	*Wie das glück wil* (SenflW V, no. 30: Senfl)
23	28^{v}	*Auff erd lebt nit ein schöners weyb* (MosL, no. 56)
24	29^{v}	*Welt gelt* (SenflW IV, no. 32: Senfl)
25	30^{v}	*Es mag mein freud*
26	31^{v}	*Mich zwingt dein lieb*[5]

27 31^{v} *Elssle liebes Elselein*[5] (compare SenflW IV, no. 17: Senfl)

28 32^{v} *Brüder Steffan*

29 33^{v} *Der alt Tandernack* (HewO, no. 69: Obrecht)

30 37 *Tandernack* (compare HewO, no. 69)

31 39 *Adieu mes amours*[6] (HewO, no. 14: Josquin)

32 40^{v} *Mile regres* (JosqWW, no. 24: Josquin) = 1546_{18}, no. 19.

33 41^{v} *Plus mile regres* (JosqWW, no. 29: "Plus nulz regretz," Josquin) = 1562_3, no. 9.

34 43^{v} *Ales regres* (HewO, no. 57: Hayne)

35 45 *En lombre* (RISM 1536_1, no. 14: Josquin)

36 46 *En lombre* (CM II, 46: M. Lasson)

37 47^{v} *Ein Mutetlein* (AttainCK III, no. 9: "Le content est riche," Sermisy)

38 48^{v} *Le le fairay* (D:Mbs, Mus. MS 1516, no. 24: "Je le feray")

39 49 *Alaventure* (CM II, 16: "A l'aventure l'entrepris," Adrian Willaert)

40 50^{v} *Tant rentoereist*

41 52 *Fors seulement* (ObrWW, p. 90: Josquin or Févin) = 1546_{18}, no. 17

42 53^{v} *In illo tempore accesserunt*[7] (RISM 1537_1, no. 50: Jean Mouton)

55 2a pars *Propter hoc*

43 56^{v} *Deus qui sedes* (PubAPTM VII, no. 40: Johann Walther)

44 58^{v} *Alma redemptoris*

61^{v} 2a pars

45 64 *Si dormiero* (DTO XIV/28, p. 104: Isaac [Agricola or La Rue?])

66^{v} 2a pars

69 3a pars

46 71 *Si Deus pro nobis* (RISM 1564_5, no. 40)

72^{v} 2a pars *Certum est*

47 74^{v} *Qui habitat* (JosqMT, no. 52: Josquin)

78 2a pars *Non accedat*

48 80^{v} *Nisi dominus*[8] (SenflW III, no. 10: Senfl)

82^{v} 2a pars *Cum dederit*

49 84^{v} *O Maria mater Christi* (RISM 1520_4, no. 21: Isaac)

86^{v} 2a pars *Ave domina*

87^{v} 3a pars *O jocunda*

89 4a pars *Ave sanctissima*

50 90^{v} *Inviolata*[9] (JosqMT, no. 42: Josquin)

92^{v} 2a pars *Nostra ut pura*

93^{v} 3a pars *O benigna*

[1] The gatherings are signed A^{1}–Z^{4} and a$^{1-4}$. The A gathering has only three folios, and two folios are numbered 31, an error uncorrected in the inventory. A facs. of the title page appears in KinsP, pl. 133, and in HeyerV II, pl. 3. MGG IV, col. 561, lists a *Tabulatur auff die Laudten* pr. in 1553; the date is probably a typographical error, and the notice refers to 1533_1.

[2] The Berlin copy was in the Wolffheim library (see WolffC I, no. 1192); the Hirsch copy was in the Heyer library (see HeyerV II, 40).

[3] Heading on fol. 13^{v}: "Folgen hernach Teutsche stücklen."

[4] Facs. of fol. 26^{v} in CollaerAH, p. 62; MagniSM I, after p. 274; and EF III, 113.

[5] No. 26 is on the verso of the first folio numbered 31; no. 27 is on the verso of the second folio numbered 31 (see n. 1 above).

[6] Heading on fol. 39: "Nun volgen hernach etliche Welsche stücklein, und etliche trium."

[7] Heading on fol. 53: "Nun volgen hernach Lateinische stück Psalmen und Muteten."

[8] Heading on fol. 80^{v}: "Nun volgen etliche stück mit vier stymmen."

[9] Heading on fol. 90^{v}: "Das nachvolgend stück gehet im abzug."

1533_2

ATTAINGNANT, PIERRE, PUBLISHER

Chansons musicales a quatre parties / desquelles les plus convenables a la fleuste dallemant sont / signees en la table cy dessoubz escripte par a. et a la fleuste / a neuf trous par b. et pour les deux fleustes sont signees / par ab. Imprimees a Paris en la rue de la Harpe devant / le bout de la rue des Mathurins prez leglise sainct Cosme / par Pierre Attaingnant. / Mense april. MD. XXXIII. / [Table of contents] / Superius. / Cum privilegio ad sexennium

Four part books in mensural notation, each of 16 fols. (?). As the title page states, those chansons marked with *a* are suited for transverse flute, those with *b* for recorder, and those with *ab* for both. Since only a single part book now exists concordances with extant copies of the chansons are indicated in the following inventory.

Copy in: CH:Lcortot (S).[1]

	fol.		
1	1^v	*ab*	*Per ch'el viso*
2	2	*a*	*J'aymeray qui m'aymera* Gombert
3	2^v		*O passi sparsi* (RISM 1526_6, no. 4: Sebastian Festa)
4	3^v		*Or vien ca vien*[2] Jannequin (RISM 1540_{17}, fol. 6^v)
5	4^v	*a*	*Je l'ay aymé* (RISM 1536_3, no. 6: Certon)
6	5	*b*	*De noz deux cueurs* (RISM 1536_3, no. 10: Guyon)
7	5^v	*a*	*Si par fortune* Certon (RISM 1555_{23}, fol. 8)
8	6	*a*	*Desir m'assault* Manchicourt
9	6^v	*b*	*O desloialle dame* Bourguignon
10	7	*a*	*En espoir d'avoir* Gombert (F:CA, MS 124, fol. 40)
11	7^v	*a*	*Aultre que vous de moyne* (RISM 1534_{12}, no. 3: Sermisy, or RISM 1535_6, no. 18: Gombert)
12	8	*ab*	*J'ay tant souffert* (RISM 1536_3, no. 17: Jacotin)
13	8^v	*a*	*Hors envieux retirez* Gombert (EngL, p. 51)
14	9	*a*	*Sur tous regretz* Richafort (PubAPTM II, no. 78)
15	9^v	*a*	*Vostre beaulté*[3] Lupus
16	10	*b*	*Puis que j'ay perdu* Lupi (RISM 1536_3, no. 24)
17	10^v	*a*	*Vous l'ares s'il vous plaist*[4] Adorno
18	11^v	*ab*	*Mille regretz* J. le maire (Josquin)
19	11^v	*a*	*Le printemps faict* Benedictus (NL:DHk, MS 74, H. 7, no. 13: "Le printtamps fait florir," anon., tenor only)
20	12	*a*	*Si ung oeuvre parfait* Claudin [de Sermisy]
21	12^v	*ab*	*Faict ou failly* Bridam (RISM 1529_3, no. 30: Sermisy, or more probably 1549_8, no. 31)
22	13	*b*	*Eslongné suys de mes amours*
23	13^v	*ab*	*Content desir qui cause* Claudin (RISM 1536_3, no. 8)
24	13^v	*ab*	*Vivre ne puys content* Claudin (RISM 1536_3, no. 9)
25	14	*a*	*Veu le grief mal* Heurteur (AttainCK III, no. 19: anon.)
26	14^v	*a*	*Par trop aymer* Benedictus
27	15	*a*	*La plus gorgiase du monde* (compare 1536_3, no. 21)
28	15^v	*ab*	*Changer ne puys* Lupi (RISM 1554_{24}, no. 13)
29	16	*a*	*Souvent amour me livre* Heurteur (RISM 1537_3, no. 15)
30	16^v	*a*	*Si je ne dors je ne puis vivre* Legendre

[1] A copy of the superius part book only was in D:WEs.

[2] Listed in the table of contents as "M'amye perrette." EitS, 1533a, states that the volume contains 31 chansons. Eitner probably counted "Or vien ca vien" and "M'amye perrette" as two compositions.

[3] A version of "Vostre beaulté" by Certon is pr. in LesAC, no. 21. Another "Vostre beaulté" was set by Gombert, pr. in PubAPTM II, no. 79.

[4] See the Josquin setting in JosqWW, no. 16.

1533_3

ATTAINGNANT, PIERRE, PUBLISHER

Vingt & sept chansons musicales a qua/tre parties desquelles les plus convenables a la fleuste dal/lemant sont signees en la table cy dessoubz escripte par a. / et a la fleuste a neuf trous par b. et pour les deux par a b. / Imprimees a Paris en la rue de la Harpe devant le bout / de la rue des Mathurins prez leglise sainct Cosme par / Pierre Attaingnant. Mense April: m. D. xxxiii. / [Table of contents] / Superius. / Cum privilegio ad sexennium.

Four part books in mensural notation, each of 16 fols. All of the compositions are fully texted in all voices. As title page states, those chansons marked with *a* are suited for transverse flute, those with *b* for recorder, and those with *ab* for both.

Copy in: D:Mbs.[1]

	fol.		
1	1^{v}	*ab*	*De vous servir* Claudin [de Sermisy]
2	1^{v}		*Mirelaridon don don* Heurteur
3	2^{v}	*a*	*Parle qui veult* Claudin
4	3		*Va mirelidrogue va* Passereau
5	3^{v}		*Gentil mareschal* (text beg.: A paris prez des billettes)
6	4	*ab*	*Les yeulx bendez* Vermont
7	4^{v}	*a*	*Amours amours vous me faictes grant tort* Gombert
8	5	*ab*	*Amour me poingt* Claudin
9	5^{v}	*ab*	*Allons ung peu plus avant* Heurteur
10	6^{v}	*ab*	*Je ne puis pas* Heurteur
11	7	*ab*	*Tous amoureux* Passereau
12	7^{v}	*ab*	*Par ung matin* Heurteur
13	8	*a*	*Pren de bon cueur* P. de manchicourt
14	8^{v}	*ab*	*Hellas amour* Heurteur
15	9	*ab*	*Amour me voyant* Claudin
16	9^{v}	*a*	*Jectes moy sur lherbette* Lupi
17	10	*ab*	*Jamais ung cueur*
18	10^{v}	*b*	*Troys jeunes bourgeoises* Heurteur
19	11	*b*	*Allez souspirs* Claudin
20	11^{v}	*a*	*Elle veult donc* Claudin
21	12	*ab*	*On dit quamour* Vermont
22	12^{v}	*ab*	*Voyant souffrir* Jacotin
23	13	*a*	*Hayne et amour* Vermont
24	13^{v}	*a*	*Pourquoy donc ne fringuerons* Passereau
25	14^{v}		*Je nen diray mot* Passereau
26	15	*a*	*Je navoye point* Claudin
27	15^{v}		*Ung petit coup* Passereau
28	16^{v}	*a*	*Si bon amour* Jacotin

[1] A copy of the superius part book only was in D:WEs.

1535$_{1}$

GANASSI, SILVESTRO DI

Opera Intitulata Fontegara / Laquale insegna a sonare di flauto chon tutta l'arte opportuna a esso instrumento / massime il diminuire il quale sara utile ad ogni instrumento di fiato et chorde: et anchora a / chi si dileta di canto, composta per sylvestro di ganassi dal fontego sonator della Illma. S^{a}. D. V^{a}. / [Cut of five men grouped around a table, upon which are three part books; three of the men are playing recorders, and one is singing; hanging on the wall in back of them are three violas da gamba and a lute; two cornetti are pictured in the foreground.][1]

8 + 72 fols. On fol. $*1^{v}$: dedication "Allo Illustrissimo & Serenissimo Principe di Venetia Andrea Gritti," printed in SartMS, p. 4. On fol. S3^{v}: table of contents and colophon: "Impressum Venetiis per Sylvestro di ganassi dal fontego sonator della illustrissima Signoria di Venetia hautor proprio. MDXXXV. + +iiabcdefghiklmnopqrs." Although Ganassi's instruction method for the recorder contains no complete compositions, it does contain numerous musical examples in mensural notation, most of them illustrating techniques of diminution. GanaF is a facsimile reprint of the volume; GanaOF is a German translation and includes several facsimile pages; GanaOFE is an English translation of the German edition. Some of the musical examples are reprinted in KuV, p. 89. On this and the later volumes by Ganassi see EitSW.

Copies in: D:Bds-Tü, D:J, D:W,[2] I:Bc, I:Fc, US:Wc.[3]

[1] The cut on the title page is repr. in DegenB, pl. 7; HuntR, p. 3; and MGG IV, col. 341. Facs. of title page in AbbS I, 422; GaspaC I, 336; KinsP, p. 148; and KuV, pl. 1. The fingering chart for the recorder is repr. in WolfH II, 242.

[2] The Wolfenbüttel copy contains manuscript additions by Ganassi himself: a dedication, and an appendix of 175 diminutions of one six-note figure. GanaOF incl. these interpolations. Both GanaOF and MGG IV, col. 1355, incl. a facs. of the manuscript dedication.

[3] On the back cover of the Washington copy there are manuscript remarks in a modern hand. Copies were in the libraries of Gaetano Gaspari and J. E. Matthew (see SartMS, p. 5).

1535

DOUBTFUL WORKS

1. The title page of Luís Milán. *Libro di musica de vihuela de mano. Intitulado El maestro,* is dated 1535, but the colophon is dated 1536. The volume is listed in this bibliography as 1536$_{5}$.

[1536]$_1$

BAENA, GONÇALO

Uma obra e arte pera tanger.

In 1536 Baena solicited King John III of Portugal for a privilege to print the above-named keyboard tablature. See KastnR, p. 97. The volume, if it was ever printed, is now lost.

[1536]$_2$

BRAYSSINGAR, GUILLAUME DE

Tablature d'Épinette. Lyon, Jacques Moderne, 1536.

This volume, now lost, is listed in Du Verdier IV, 71; FétB II, 62; and DraudiusBE, p. 208. It contained ricercares, fantasias, and variations for solo keyboard.

1536_3

FRANCESCO DA MILANO

INTABOLATURA DI LIUTO DE DIVERSI, CON LA / BATAGLIA, ET ALTRE COSE BELLISSIME, DI M. FRANCESCO DA / MILANO, STAMPATA NUOVAMENTE PER FRANCESCO / MARCOLINI DA FORLI, CON GRATIA E PRIVILEGIO. / [Cut of a lutenist and two auditors][1]

34 fols. Italian lute tablature. On fol. 1^v: preface headed "Francesco Marcolini, Ai Musici," reprinted in SchmidOP, p. 120.[2] Colophon on fol. 34: "In Vinegia per Francesco Marcolini da Forlì, In la Contrà di Santo Apostolo, ne le Case de i Frati di Crosachieri, negli anni del Signore. M D XXXVI. del mese di Magio." Thematic index of the entire volume in WieM II. SlimK II, 454, contains a thematic index of the ricercares. For further information on Francesco and transcriptions of some of his music see NewmM. Contents = 154?$_4$. All of the compositions are for solo lute.

Copy in: A:Wn.

	fol.	
1	2	*Recercare*[3] = 1546_7, no. 4; 1561_3, no. 4; 1563_5, no. 4; 1568_7, no. 12; 1571_6, no. 6
2	3	*Recercar* = 1546_7, no. 5; 1561_3, no. 5; 1563_5, no. 5
3	3^v	*Recercare*[4] = 1546_7, no. 6; 1546_9, no. 73; 1561_3, no. 6; 1562_4, no. 78; 1563_5, no. 6
4	4^v	*Recercar*[5] = 1568_7, no. 18
5	4^v	*Recercar*[6] = 1546_7, no. 7; 1561_3, no. 7; 1563_5, no. 7; 1568_7, no. 14
6	6^v	*Recercar*[7] = 1546_7, no. 8; 1561_3, no. 8; 1563_5, no. 8
7	7^v	*Recercar* = 1546_7, no. 9; 1561_3, no. 9; 1563_5, no. 9; 1568_7, no. 10; 1571_6, no. 15
8	7^v	*Recercar*
9	8^v	*Recercar*
10	9	*Recercar*[8] = 1548_4, no. 4; 1563_4, no. 17
11	9^v	*Recercar*[9]
12	9^v	*Recercar*
13	10^v	*Recercar*[10] = 1547_2, no. 10; 1562_1, no. 10; 1563_6, no. 10, 1566_1, no. 10 (lost)
14	11	*Recercar*
15	11^v	*Recercar* = 1568_7, no. 19; 1571_6, no. 8
16	12	*Recercar*[11] = 1568_7, no. 8; 1571_6, no. 11
17	12^v	*Recercar*
18	13^v	*Recercar*
19	14^v	*Recercar* = 1546_7, no. 3; 1561_3, no. 3; 1563_5, no. 3
20	16	*Mon per si ma marie* (F:Pn, MS nouv. acq. fr. 4599, fol. 3^v: [tenor only])
21	17	*Le plus gorgias du monde* (1533_2, no. 28: lost) = 1546_7, no. 10; 1561_3, no. 10; 1563_5, no. 10
22	17^v	*Chi voleno dir de moy* ["Que voulez vous dire de moy"][12] = 1547_2, no. 23; 1562_1, no. 23; 1563_6, no. 23; 1566_1, no. 23 (lost)
23	18	*Tu dicois* [*que je mourroye*] (RISM 1530_3, no. 3: Sermisy) = 1546_7, no. 11; 1561_3, no. 11; 1563_5, no. 11
24	19	*Fort se lament* (ObrWW, p. 90: "Fors seulement," Josquin or Févin) = 1547_2, no. 22; 1562_1, no. 22; 1563_6, no. 22; 1566_1, no. 22 (lost)

25 20 *Nos bergeres* (RISM 1535_8, no. 9: "Nous bergiers") = 1546_7, no. 13; 1561_3, no. 13; 1563_5, no. 13

26 20ᵛ *Can gieto fu marie* (compare RISM 1535_8, no. 5: "Quand j'estoye à marier," Willaert)

27 21ᵛ *Se la natura* (RISM 1531_2, no. 3: "Si la nature en la diversité")

28 22 *Gentil galans* (compare RISM 1520_6, nos. 11 and 23)

29 22ᵛ *Resionit* (I:Fn, MS Magl. XIX, 117, fol. 45ᵛ: "Resjouissez vous bourgeoises," Mouton)

30 23 *Las ye my plains* (LesAC, no. 1: Sermisy)

31 23ᵛ *Perquoy ale vo soleta* (RISM $[1535]_9$, no. 5: "Pourquoy allez vous") = 1546_7, no. 12; 1561_3, no. 12; 1563_5, no. 12

32 24ᵛ *Pater noster a sey de Josquin* (JosqMT, no. 50) = 1546_7, no. 1; 1561_3, no. 1; 1563_5, no. 1

26ᵛ 2a pars *Ave maria a sey de Josquin*

33 28 *Stabat mater dolorosa* (JosqMT, no. 36: Josquin) = 1546_7, no. 2; 1561_3, no. 2; 1563_5, no. 2

34 29ᵛ *La bataglia*[13] (MMRF VII, 31: Janequin) = 1546_6, no. 2; 1546_8, no. 26; 1547_5, no. 12; 1550_4, no. 10; 1556_3, no. 2; 1563_4, no. 2; 1563_{10}, no. 10; 1571_6, no. 196

35 32ᵛ *O bone Jesu* (SmijO, no. 33: Compère)

[1] Facs. of title page in AbbS I, 424; EF II, 156; EI XXII, 259; and KinsP, p. 134.

[2] Marcolini's privilege to print this work, granted by the Signoria of Venice, is pr. in SchmidOP, p. 121. FétB III, 305, incorrectly lists 1536_3 as two different volumes of music by Francesco da Milano: "Intabulatura di organo, lib. 1," and "Intabolatura di liuto, Milano, 1540"; apparently Fétis misread DoniL, p. 159.

[3] Mod. ed. in NeemAM I, no. 18.

[4] Facs. and mod. ed. in GomRF, pp. 166, 174 (after 1546_7).

[5] Mod. ed. in BruAL I, no. 14; WasG. no. 14; DTO XVIII/37, p. 104 (after A:Wn, MS 18.827).

[6] Mod. ed. in HamC, p. 138 (after S:Uu, MS 87).

[7] Mod. ed. in ChilF, no. 7.

[8] Mod. ed. in SlimK II, 632.

[9] Mod. ed. in SlimK II, 613.

[10] Mod. ed. in ChilF, no. 6 (after 1547_2).

[11] Mod. ed. in MU III, app., p. 91.

[12] Mod. ed. in ChilCI, p. 66.

[13] Mod. ed. in ChilS, p. 37 (after 1563_4). Facs. of a part of fol. 29ᵛ in KinsP, p. 134.

1536_4

LUSCINIUS, OTTOMAR

MUSURGIA / seu praxis MUSICAE. / Illius primo quae Instrumentis agitur certa ratio, ab Ottomaro / Luscinio Argentino duobus Libris absoluta. / Eiusdem Ottomari Luscinii, de Concentus polyphoni, id est, / ex plurifariis vocibus compositi, canonibus, Libri totidem. / Argentorati apud Joannem Schottum, / Anno Christi. 1536. / Cum gratia & privilegio Imperiali, / ad Quinquennium.

56 fols. On fol. a2: dedication to "Magnifico viro Domino Andreae Calvo Mediolanensis. Ottomarus Luscinius, Argentinus, S. D." On fol. a3ᵛ: cut of Andreas Silvanus and Sebastian Virdung.[1] On fol. o3: index. This is a free translation of Virdung's *Musica getutscht* (1511_3). It contains the same musical example as 1511_3 ("O haylige, onbeflecte, zart junckfrawschafft marie") in mensural notation (fol. f3ᵛ), organ tablature (fol. f4ᵛ), and German lute tablature (fol. h2). On Luscinius see NiemOL. Contents = 1542_0.

Copies in: A:Wn, B:Br, CH:Lcortot, D:Bds-Tü, D:Mbs, D:Rp, D:W, DK:Kk, E:Mmc, E:Mn, F:CV, F:Pc, GB:Lbm, I:Bc, I:Rsc, NL:DHgm, US:Cn, US:NYp, US:R, US:Wc.[2]

[1] Facs. of this cut in Maggs 28, p. 71; MagniSM I, 330; and WolffC I, pl. 26. Maggs 28, p. 72, repr. another illustration from the volume.

[2] Copies were in the libraries of A. H. Littleton (see LittC, p. 11, and MLE, 1904, p. 35), Werner Wolffheim (see WolffC I, no. 788), and in CS:Os (see EitO VI, 254).

1536_5

MILÁN, LUÍS

LIBRO DE MU/sica de vihuela de mano. Intitulado El / maestro. El quale trahe el mesmo estilo y orden / que un maestro traheria con un discipulo / principiante: mostrandole ordenadamen/te desde los principios toda cosa que / podria ignorar, para entender la / presente obra. Compuesto por / don Luys Milan. Dirigido / al muy alto & muy pode/roso & invictissimo princi/pe don Juhan: por / la gracia de dios / rey de Portu/gal y de las / yslas. / &c. / Anno. M. D. xxxv. / Con privilegio Real.[1]

102 fols. Italian lute tablature.[2] The title page = fol. A2. On fol. A2v: a woodcut of a seated king, with the coat of arms of King John III of Portugal, and the legend: "Invictissimus Rex Lusitanorum." On fol. A3: dedication to the king.[3] Beginning on fol. A3v: a preface explaining the intentions of the book and giving preliminary instructions for playing the vihuela (cut of a vihuela on fol. A4). On fol. A6: summary of the contents of the book. On fol. A6v: cut of a vihuelist with the heading: "El grande Orpheo, primero inventor. Por quien la vihuela, paresce en el mundo. Si el fue primero, no fue sin segundo. Porque es de todos, de todo hazedor."[4] On fol. B1: introduction to the music. On fol. R5v: a note headed "Intelligencia y declaracion de los tonos que en la musica de canto figurado se usan." Colophon on fol. R6: "A honor y gloria de dios todo poderoso y de la sacratissima virgen Maria madre suya y abogada nuestra. Fue impresso el presente libro de musica de Vihuela de mano intitulado el Maestro: por Francisco Diaz Romano. En la Metropolitana y Coronada Ciudad de Valencia. Acabose a. iiii. dias del mes de Deziembre Año de nuestra reparacion. de Mil y quinientos treynta y seys." On fol. R6v: author's corrections. The fourth gathering has been misbound. The correct order of folios is: D3, D2, D1, D6, D5, D4. In the following inventory the revised order is adopted.

The entire collection is reprinted in MilanM, which includes facsimiles of the title page and fols. A2 and A6v (see also the review by Otto Gombosi in *Zeitschrift für Musikwissenschaft,* XIV [1933], 185). The compositions identified by superior letters are reprinted as follows: ([a]) in BruAL I; ([b]) in MilanSP; ([c]) in MorL I; ([d]) in PedCP III; ([e]) PujBG, nos. 1001–03, 1017, 1045–47, 1055. Three compositions (nos. 41, 48, and 50) are reprinted in JacobsTN, pp. 53–69. SlimK II, 461, contains a thematic index of the ricercares. For a discussion of the volume see TreL. Nos. 29–39 and 62–72 are for voice (written in red ciphers in tablature) and vihuela. The other compositions are for solo vihuela. The music is usually introduced by a paragraph of prose explaining the technical problems set by each piece.

Copies in: D:LEm,[5] E:Bd, E:Mn (two copies), F:Pc, F:Pn, GB:Lbm, I:PAc, NL:DHgm, P:V, US:Cn, US:Wc (imperfect).

VIHUELA SOLO

	fol.	
1	B1v	*Fantasia del primero tono*
2	B2v	*Fantasia del primero tono*
3	B3v	*Fantasia del primero tono*
4	B5	*Fantasia del segundo tono* [6]
5	B6	*Fantasia del segundo tono*[c] [7]
6	C1v	*Fantasia del primero tono*
7	C3	*Fantasia del tercero tono*[c]
8	C4v	[*Fantasia*][c] [8]
9	C5v	*Fantasia del tono mixto*[c]
10	D3v	*Fantasia del primero y segundo tono* [9]
11	D2v	[*Fantasia*]
12	D6	*Fantasia del tercero y quarto tono*
13	D5	*Fantasia del primero tono*
14	D4	*Fantasia del quarto y tercero tono*[c] [10]
15	E1	*Fantasia del quinto y sexto tono*
16	E2v	*Fantasia del quinto y sexto tono*[bce] [11]
17	E4	*Fantasia del quinto y sexto tono* [12]
18	E5v	*Fantasia del septimo y octavo tono*
19	F1v	*Fantasia del quinto tono*[c]
20	F3v	*Fantasia del sexto tono*[c]
21	F6v	*Fantasia del septimo tono*
22	G2	*Fantasia del octavo tono*[e]
23	G3v	*Pavana*[be]
24	G4	*Pavana*[be]
25	G5	*Pavana*[bce] [13]
26	G5v	*Pavana*[abce] [14]
27	G6	*Pavana: Que la bella franceschina*[abce] [15]
28	G6v	*Pavana*[bce] [16]

VOICE AND VIHUELA

29	H1	*Toda mi vida vos ame*[c] [17] Villancico in Spanish
	H1	[Another version]
30	H1v	*Sospiro una señora*[c] [18] Villancico in Spanish
	H1v	[Another version]
31	H2	*Agora viniesse*[c] Villancico in Spanish
32	H2	*Quien amores ten a fin*[acd] Villancico in Portuguese
	H2v	[Another version]

33 H3 *Falai miña amor*[acd 19] Villancico in Portuguese

34 H3 *Poys dezeys que me quereys*[acd] Villancico in Portuguese

H3 [Another version]

35 H3v *Durandarte, durandarte*[cd 20] Romance in Spanish (see QueI, p. 312)

H4 2a pars. *Palabras son lisongeras*

36 H4v *Sospirastes, baldovinos*[c 21] Romance in Spanish (see QueI, p. 312)

H5 2a pars. *Si te vas conmigo en francia*

37 H5v *Amor che nel mio pensier* Soneto in Italian

38 H6v *Porta chiascun nela fronte* Soneto in Italian

39 H7v *Nova angeleta* Soneto in Italian

VIHUELA SOLO

40 J1 *Fantasia del primero tono*

41 J3 *Fantasia del segundo tono*

42 J5 *Fantasia del tono mixto*[c 22]

43 K1v *Fantasia del tercero y quarto tono*[c]

44 K3 *Fantasia del tercero tono*

45 K5 *Fantasia del quarto tono*[c]

46 L1 *Fantasia del tercero y quarto tono*

47 L3v *Fantasia del tercero y quarto tono*[c]

48 L5 *Fantasia del sexto tono*

49 M1 *Fantasia del sexto tono*

50 M2v *Fantasia del sexto tono*[c]

51 M4v [*Fantasia*]

52 N1 *Fantasia del tercero y quarto tono*

53 N3 *Tentos del quinto y sexto tono*

54 N5 *Tentos del septimo y octavo tono*

55 O1 *Fantasia del septimo tono*

56 O2v *Fantasia del octavo tono*

57 O4 *Fantasia del septimo y octavo tono*

58 O6 *Fantasia del septimo y octavo tono*

59 P1 *Fantasia del sexto tono*

60 P3 *Fantasia del septimo y octavo tono*

61 P5 *Fantasia del septimo y octavo tono*

VOICE AND VIHUELA

62 Q1 *Al amor quiero vencer*[c 23] Villancico in Spanish

Q1 [Another version]

63 Q1v *Aquel cavallero*[cd] Villancico in Spanish

Q2 [Another version]

64 Q2v *Amor que tan bien sirviendo*[c] Villancico in Spanish

Q3 [Another version]

65 Q3 *Levayme amor*[cd 24] Villancico in Portugese

Q3v [Another version]

66 Q4 *Un cuydado que mia vida ten*[c] Villancico in Portuguese

Q4 [Another version]

67 Q4v *Perdida tenyo la color*[c 25] Villancico in Portuguese (VasquezVC [1551], no. 12: Vasquez)

Q4v [Another version]

68 Q4v *Con pavor recordo el moro*[cd 26] Romance in Spanish (see QueI, p. 312)

R1v 2a pars. *Mi cama las duras peñas*

69 R2 *Triste estava muy quexosa*[c 27] Romance in Spanish (see QueI, p. 312)

70 R2v *O gelosia damanti* Soneto in Italian

71 R3v *Madonna per voi ardo* Soneto in Italian

72 R4v *Gentil mia donna*[28] Soneto in Italian

[1] Facs. of title page in AbbS I, 431; EF III, 206; MGG V, col. 180, and IX, col. 289; SalvaC II, 345; SchraLM, p. 20; VinS, p. 89.

[2] Unlike all other Italian lute and Spanish vihuela tablatures this one uses the lowest line to represent the lowest string, and the highest line to represent the highest string.

[3] Facs. of fol. A3 in SubHME, p. 207.

[4] Facs. of fol. A6v in AngME (cover); MGG IX, col. 289; VinS, p. 89; WardL, p. 26; and Otto Haas Sales Catalogue, no. 37 (1959), p. 41.

[5] The Leipzig copy was in the Wolffheim library (see WolffC I, no. 1200).

[6] Mod. ed. in MilanF.

[7] Mod. ed. in RieH II/1, p. 445.

[8] Mod. ed. in PujHC, p. 4.

[9] Mod. ed. in PujHC, p. 6.

[10] Mod. ed. in MilanF.

[11] Mod. ed. in AzpiaA, no. 2; MilanFa; MilanSP, no. 7; and TagA I, no. 4.

[12] Mod. ed. in HAM, no. 121.

[13] Mod. ed. in TagA I, no. 5, and TreL, p. 105.

[14] Mod. ed. in ApelM II, 13; NeemAM I, no. 10; OHM III, 17; SteinitA, no. 31; TagA I, no. 6; TapS, p. 16 (incl. quasi-facs.); and WasG, no. 5.

[15] Mod. ed. in *Die Laute* IV (1920–21), 22; NeemAM I, no. 9; and MagniSM I, 349.

[16] Facs. of fol. G6v in ApelN, facs. 18; MorL I, xxxix; and WolfMS, pl. 74. Mod. ed. in ApelM II, 12; EC, pt. I, vol. II, p. 647; and TreL, p. 108.

[17] Mod. ed. in MilanT; MilanT (Puj); TreL, p. 101; and TornCM, p. 58.

[18] Mod. ed. in BruS III, no. 109, and WolfH II, 107 (incl. quasi-facs.).

[19] Mod. ed. in BalR, p. 19 (arr. for voice and piano); ScherG, no. 96b; and TreL, p. 103.

[20] Facs. of fols. $H3^v$–H4 in MorL I, xxxvii. Mod. ed. in BalR, p. 14 (arr. for voice and piano); BruS IV, no. 139 (incl. beg. in tablature on p. 183); EC, pt. I, vol. II, p. 647, and vol. IV, p. 2018; and ScherG, no. 96a.

[21] Mod. ed. (arr. for voice and piano) in BalR, p. 11.

[22] Mod. ed. in TagA I, no. 3.

[23] Mod. ed. in BruS III, no. 89.

[24] Mod. ed. in MilanL (arr. for voice and guitar).

[25] Facs. of fol. $Q4^v$ in SchraLM, p. 21. Mod. ed. in BruS III, no. 119. The model is identified in TreBM, p. 537.

[26] Mod. ed. in MilanC (arr. for voice and guitar).

[27] Mod. ed. (arr. for voice and piano) in BalR, p. 9.

[28] Mod. ed. in BarthaZ, no. 45.

1536_6

NEWSIDLER, HANS

Ein Newgeordent Künstlich Lau/tenbuch, In zwen theyl getheylt. Der erst für die anfahenden / Schuler, die aus rechter kunst und grundt nach der Tabulatur, sich one / einichen Meyster darin zuüben haben, durch ein leicht Exempel dieser / punctlein. . . . . wohin man mit einem yeden finger recht greiffen / sol. Weyter ist angezeigt, wie man die Tabulatur auch die Men/sur, und die gantz Application recht grundtlich lernen und versteen sol. / Im andern theyl sein begriffen, vil ausserlessner kunstreicher stuck, / von Fantaseyen, Preambeln, Psalmen und Muteten, die von den hochberümb/ten, und besten Organisten, als einen schatz gehalten, die sein mit sonderm fleiss auff / die Organistisch art gemacht und colorirt, für die geübten und erfarnen di/ser kunst, auff die Lauten dargeben. Dergleichen vormals nie im / Truck, Aber yetzo durch mich Hansen Newsidler Lutinisten / und Bürger zu Nürnberg, offentlich aussgangen. / Mit Röm. Keys. und Königk. Ma. freyheit, in / funff iaren nit nach zu trucken, begnadet.

87 fols. German lute tablature. On fol. a2: the same printer's privilege as in 1536_7, 1544_2, 1544_3, and 1549_6, headed "Wir Ferdinand von Gottis genaden, Römischer Kunig," and dated "in unser Statt Wien den fünffzehenden tag des monats Maii, im Funffzehenhundert und fuffunddreissigisten unserer Reich des Römischen im Funfften,

Ein Newgeordent Künstlich Lau/
tenbuch/ In zwen theyl getheylt. Der erst für die anfahenden
Schuler/ die aus rechter kunst vnd grundt nach der Tabulatur/ sich one
einichen Meyster darin zuüben haben/ durch ein leicht Exempel dieser
punctlein · ·· ··· ···· wohin man mit einem yedē finger recht greiffen
sol. Weyter ist angezeigt/ wie mā die Tabulatur auch die Men
sur/ vñ die gantz Application recht grundtlich lernen vñ versteen sol.

Im andern theyl sein begriffen/ vil außerleßner kunstreicher stuck/
von Fantaseyen/ Preambeln/ Psalmen vnd Muteten/ die von den hochberümb/
ten vñ besten Organisten/ als einen schatz gehalten/ die sein mit sonderm fleiß auff
die Organistisch art gemacht vnd colorirt/ für die geübten vnd erfarnen di/
ser kunst/ auff die Lauten dargeben. Dergleichen vormals nie im
Truck/ Aber yetzo durch mich Hansen Newsidler Lutinisten
vnd Bürger zu Nürnberg/ offenlich außgangen.

Mit Röm. Keys. vnd Königk. Ma. freyheit/ in
funff iaren nit nach zu trucken/ begnadet.

Title page of 1536_6

und der andern im Neunten Jarn." On fol. a2^v: preface headed "Dem gütigen Leser glück und hayl." Beginning on fol. a3^v: instructions for playing the lute, including a number of musical examples (nos. 1–4 below). Remarks by Newsidler are interpolated at various points throughout the volume (for example, fols. f1^v, k1). On fol. x3^v: list of errata. Colophon on fol. x4: "Getruckt zu Nurmberg bey Johan Petreio, durch angebung und verlegung, Hansen Newsidler Lutinisten, bürtig von Pressburck jetzt bürger zu Nurmberg. Anno Tausent funff hundert und sechs und dreyssig." On fol. x4^v: the same cut of the neck of a lute with an explanation of the tablature as appears in 1536_7, 1544_1, 1544_2, and 1547_4.[1] On the unsigned fol. after fol. x4 (= fol. 86): index of the contents.

The compositions identified by superior letters are reprinted as follows: ([a]) in BruS; ([b]) in ChilLS (including a facsimile of fol. t3^v on p. iii); ([c]) in DTO XVIII/37; ([d]) in DTO XXXVII/72; ([e]) in MolzHN; ([f]) in SenflW VII. There is a modern edition of a preamble and a dance in NeuP (arranged for guitar). SlimK II, 460, contains a thematic index of the preambles. The table of contents is given in MfMG III (1871), 152. For further information see ChilHN, and *Library of Congress. Annual Report*, 1930, p. 196 (which includes facsimiles of the title page and fol. k1). Some of Newsidler's different intabulations of one vocal model are closely related to each other. The versions marked with an equals sign in the following inventory are not always absolutely identical, but the differences are trivial. All of the compositions are for solo lute. Nos. 5–24 are *a2*; all the rest are *a3*.

Copies in: CH:BEsu, CH:ZO, D:Bds-Tü, D:HAu, D:LEm (two copies), D:Mbs (imperfect), D:W, DK:Kk, F:Ssp (imperfect), US:Wc.[2]

	fol.	
1	b3	*Mein fleiss und mü*[f] (SenflW IV, no. 19: Senfl) = 1544_2, no. 1
2	c3	*Die Erst Regel, und ist ein gering fundament der Lauten* = 1540_1, no. 1; 1544_1, no. 1; 1544_2, no. 2; 1545_3, no. 1; 1547_4, no. 1; 1549_6, no. 1
	c3^v	*Die Ander Regel, und ist ein ander art*
	c3^v	*Die drit regel und ist auch eine andere art*
3	c4	*Das klein fundament mit dem einigen pünctlein*[a] = 1544_2, no. 3, and 1549_6, no. 2
	c4^v	*Die ander regel*[a]
	c4^v	*Die drit regel*[a]
4	d1	*Nun volgt ein anders fundament, das vil kunstreycher, ist, aber ein wenig schwerer dann das erst*[e] = 1544_2, no. 4, and 1549_6, no. 3
5	d3^v	*Ich klag den Tag*[d 3] (DTO XXXVII/72, p. 71: Stoltzer; another version of no. 25 below) = 1532_2, no. 18
6	d4	*Mein hertz hat sich mit lieb verpflicht* (MosPH, p. 154: Hofhaimer; another version of no. 38 below) = 1540_1, no. 4
7	d4^v	*Zart schöne fraw gedenck und schaw*[a] (CW XXIX, 28; compare $151?_1$, no. 26; another version of no. 30 below)
8	e1	*Entlaubt ist uns der walde*[ad 4] (EDMR XX, no. 61: Stoltzer) = 1544_1, no. 5; 1544_2, no. 7; 1547_4, no. 5
9	e1^v	*Mag ich unglück nicht widerstan*[f] (SenflW V, no. 13: Senfl) = 1540_1, no. 5
10	e2	*Ein guts hofftentzlein fur ein schüler* (compare 1549_6, no. 7)
	e2^v	*Der hupff auff*
11	e3	*Der vorig tantz auff ein ander art gesetzt* = 1547_4, no. 7
	e4	*Hupff auff*
12	e4^v	*Nach willen dein*[d 5] (MosPH, p. 74: Hofhaimer; another version of no. 34 below; compare $151?_1$, no. 28) = 1544_2, no. 8
13	f1	*Von edler art*[e] (MosPH, p. 180: J. Schönfelder or Hofhaimer; another version of no. 33 below; compare $151?_1$, no. 30) = 1544_2, no. 9)
14	f1^v	*Mein einigs A*[d] (MosPH, p. 66: Hofhaimer; another version of no. 35 below)
15	f2^v	*Zucht ehr und lob*[d] (MosPH, p. 99: Hofhaimer)
16	f3^v	*Tröstlicher lieb*[d] (MosPH, p. 86: Hofhaimer; another version of no. 36 below)

17 f4 *Ach lieb mit leid*[d 6] (MosPH, p. 26: Hofhaimer; another version of no. 31 below)

18 f4[v] *O weiblich art*[7] (EDMR XX, no. 108: Isaac)

19 g1 *Wol kumpt der May*[adf] (EDMR XX, no. 66: W. Grefinger; another version of no. 42 below) = 1523_2, no. 4

20 g2 *Ach hilff mich leid* (MosL, no. 21: Adam von Fulda)

21 g3 *La mora Isaac*[8] (HewO, no. 44: Isaac; another version of no. 48 below)

22 g4[v] *Alexander agricola* (1538_2, no. 27: "Caecox" or "Cecus")

h2[v] *Alexander der ander theyl*

23 h4[v] *Hie folgt der Tannernack*[d] (LenN, p. [14]: Erasmus Lapicida; different from no. 51 below)

24 i3[v] *Ich stund an einem morgen* (SenflW VII, no. 3: Senfl)

25 k1 *Ich klag den tag*[bd 9] (another version of no. 5 above)

26 k2 *Der hund mir vor dem liecht umb gat* (EDMR XX, no. 44) = 1544_1, no. 19, and 1547_4, no. 19

27 k2[v] *In liebes brunst* (EDMR XX, no. 76) = 1540_1, no. 20

28 k3 *Liebs meidlin gut, was hast im mut*

29 k3[v] *Elslein liebstes Elslein mein*[f 10] (SenflW IV, no. 17: Senfl) = 1544_1, no. 22, and 1547_4, no. 18

30 k3[v] *Zart schöne fraw* (another version of no. 7 above)

31 k4[v] *Ach lieb mit leid*[d] (another version of no. 17 above) = 1544_1, no. 28, and 1547_4, no. 22

32 l1 *Nie noch nimmer* (MosL, no. 3)

33 l2 *Von edler art*[e] (another version of no. 13 above)

34 l3 *Nach willen dein*[d] (another version of no. 12 above)

35 l4 *Mein einigs A*[d 11] (another version of no. 14 above)

36 m1 *Tröstlicher lieb*[d] (another version of no. 16 above)

37 m2 *Jetz scheyden pringt mir schwer* (MosL, no. 2)

38 m2[v] *Mein hertz hat sich mit lieb verpflicht*[b] (another version of no. 6 above)

39 m4 *So wunsch ich ir ein gute nacht*[d] (DTO XXXVII/72, p. 74: Stoltzer)

40 n1 *Nur nerrisch sein ist mein monier* (PubAPTM XXIX, 106: Sixt Dietrich)

41 n2 *In rechter lieb und trew* (MosPH, p. 168: Hofhaimer)

42 n3 *Wol kumbt der May*[df] (another version of no. 19 above)

43 n4 *Freundtlicher gruss, mit büss*[12] (PubAPTM IX, 25)

44 o1 *Ach unfall wes zeihest du mich*

45 o2[v] *Was wurt es doch des wunders noch*[f] (SenflW IV, no. 26: Senfl)

46 o3[v] *Ach Gott wem soll ichs klagen, das heimlich leiden mein*[d 13] W. Gräfinger (MosGR II, no. 18)

47 o4[v] *Die prünlein die da fliessen*[14] (DTO XIV/28, p. 69: Isaac)

48 p1[v] *La mora Isaac*[15] (another version of no. 21 above)

49 p3 *Benedictus* (HewO, no. 76: Isaac)

50 p4[v] *Adiu mes amours* (HewO, no. 14: Josquin)

51 q2 *Ander nacken op den Rhin* (different from no. 23 above; compare 1533_1, no. 30)

52 q4[v] *Ach meidlein rein, ich hab allein, mich dir eigen ergeben*[df] (EDMR XX, no. 62: Grefinger)

53 r1[v] *Wan ich lang klag, alle tag, und grüm mich ser, hab nichts dest mer* (RISM $[1536]_8$, no. 26: Huldrich Brätel)

54 r2 *Kunt ich schön reines werdes weyb*[f 16] (SenflW II, 1: Senfl)

55 r2[v] *In diser welt, hab ich kein gelt*[17] (RISM $[1536]_8$, no. 17: Paul Wüst)

56 r3 *On tugent freyd die leng nit wert* (RISM $[1536]_8$, no. 49: Sixt Dietrich)

57 r3[v] *Wer wenig behelt, und vil verthut* (RISM $[1536]_8$, no. 7: Thomas Sporer)

58 r4[v] *Sie ist mein gluck, wenn ich mich schick* (RISM $[1536]_8$, no. 31: Paul Wüst)

59 s1 *Lieb ist subtil, fürt gferlich spil* (RISM $[1536]_8$, no. 40: Thomas Sporer)

60	s1v	*Dis fassnacht solt ich hoch auff springen* (RISM [1536]8, no. 16: Thomas Sporer)
61	s2	*Mir würt untrew getheylet mit* (RISM [1536]8, no. 11)
62	s3	*[Preambel]*[c 18] = 15442, no. 57
63	s3v	*Preambel*[c]
64	s4	*Preambel*[ce 19] = 15474, no. 26
65	s4v	*Preamel* [sic][c 20] = 15474, no. 27
66	t1	*Hie folget ein welscher tantz Wascha mesa*[bc] [= passamezzo]
	t2	*Der hupff auff*[bc]
67	t2v	*Ein guter welscher tantz*[bc 21]
68	t3v	*Hie folget der recht artlich hofftantz im abzug*[b 22] = 15442, no. 24, and 15496, no. 25
	t4v	*Hupff auff*[b]
69	u1	*Ein geringer hoff tantz*[b] = 15401, no. 16, and 15474, no. 14
	u1v	*Der hupff auff*[b 23]
70	u2	*Ein ser guter hoff tantz mit durch straichen*[bc 24]
	u3v	*Hupff auff*[bc]
71	x1	*Gassenhawer*[bc 25]
72	x2	*Ich gieng wol bey der nacht* (compare BöhA, no. 74)
73	x3	*Ein gut Preambel*[ce 26]

[1] Facs. of fol. x4v in ApelN, p. 75, and WolfH II, 40.

[2] At the end of the Washington copy there are two fols. of manuscript music in German lute tablature—fol. 87v: "Salltarelo des passamezo gehört dartzu"; fol. 88v: "Nun gruess dich got." There was a copy in PL:L. The manuscript music bound into one of the Leipzig copies is listed in DieL, p. 101.

[3] Mod. ed. in RaL, p. 333, and StolI. Heading on fol. d3v: "Hie volgen ettliche Lieder auffs aller schlechtest, wie es in Noten oder Gesang steht für die anfahenden Schuler."

[4] Mod. ed. in StolI.

[5] For a comparison of this intabulation with various others, see NowakH.

[6] Beg. pr. in MosPH, p. 28.

[7] Mod. ed. in BruD, no. 17, and DTO XIV/28, p. 160.

[8] Mod. ed. in BruD, no. 20, and DTO XIV/28, p. 151.

[9] Mod. ed. in KlaemM II, no. 1 (arr. for guitar), and RaL, p. 333. Heading on fol. i4v: "Hie enden sich die stuck mit zweyen stymmen." Heading on fol. k1: "Hienach folgen nun die stuck mit drey stymmen."

[10] Mod. ed. in *Die Laute* V (1921–22), 38.

[11] Mod. ed. in ChilHN, p. 58.

[12] Mod. ed. (arr. *a2*) in BruD, no. 19.

[13] Facs. of fol. o3v in MGG V, col. 765.

[14] Mod. ed. in DTO XIV/28, p. 138, and MU III, app., p. 40. Facs. of fol. o4v in KinsP, p. 133, and MGG IX, col. 1409.

[15] Mod. ed. in DTO XIV/28, p. 152.

[16] Mod. ed. in BruD, no. 18 (arr. *a2*); ChilHN, p. 57; and EC, pt. I, vol. II, p. 643 (incl. facs.).

[17] Mod. ed. in ChilHN, p. 59.

[18] Heading on fol. s3: "Hie folgen etlich Preameln."

[19] Mod. ed. in BruAL I, 6; KörL, p. 137; NeemAM I, no. 11; ScherG, no. 93; ValentinTo, no. 2; *Die Laute* IV (1920–21), 22; and ZanG I, 17.

[20] Mod. ed. in BruAL I, 7; MU II, app., p. 8; and WasG, no. 6.

[21] Mod. ed. in ChilB VIII, no. 1; GünthB, 1937; and NeemAM I, no. 13. Manuscript heading in Washington copy: "Paduana."

[22] Mod. ed. and facs. in EC, pt. I, vol. II, p. 644.

[23] Mod. ed. (arr. for guitar) in KlaemM II, no. 2.

[24] Mod. ed. in HAM, no. 105a.

[25] Mod. ed. in BarthaZ, no. 46; GünthB, 1937; WolfME, no. 29; and ZanG II, 6.

[26] Mod. ed. in ZanG I, 18.

1536_7

NEWSIDLER, HANS

Der ander theil des Lautenbuchs. / Darin sind begriffen, vil ausserlesner kunstreycher stuck, von Fanta/seyen, Preambeln, Psalmen und Muteten, die von den Hochberümbten und besten / Organisten, als einen schatz gehalten, die sein mit sonderm fleyss auff die Orga/nistisch art gemacht und coloriert, für die geübten unnd erfarnen di/ser kunst, auff die Lauten dargeben. Dergleichen vormals nie im / Truck, aber yetzo durch mich Hansen Newsidler Lutinisten / und Bürger zu Nürnberg, offenlich aussgangen. / Mit Röm. Keys. und Königk. Ma. freyheit, in / funff jarn nit nach zu trucken, begnadet.

120 fols. German lute tablature. On fols. A1v–A2: the same printer's privilege as in 15366. On fols. A2v–A3: preface headed "Zu dem Leser." On fols. Gg2–Gg3: author's corrections. On fols. Gg3–Gg3v: table of contents. On fol. Gg4: a note to the reader, followed by the colophon: "Getruckt zu Nurnberg beym Petreio, durch verlegung Hansen Newsidlers Lutinisten. Anno 1536." The table of contents is given in MfMG III (1871), 152. All of the compositions are for solo lute.

Copies in: B:Br (imperfect), D:Bds-Tü, D:HAu, D:Ngm, D:W, F:Ssp.

	fol.	
1	A3^v	*Ein seer guter Organistischer Preambel* [1]
2	B1	*Trium Si ascendero* (RISM 1504_3, no. 122: Nicolas Craen)
3	B3	*Disant adiu madame* (HewO, no. 89: Compère)
4	B3^v	*Harraytre amours* (HewO, no. 86: "Ha traitre amours," Stokhem)
5	B4^v	*Mater patris* Trium A. Brumel (HewO, no. 62)
6	C1^v	*Lastangeta* (HewO, no. 49: Weerbecke or Obrecht)
7	C3	*La plus te plus* Jossquin (HewO, no. 64: "La plus des plus")
8	C4^v	*Medobt* Compere (HewO, no. 45: "Ne doibt on prendre")
9	D2	*Tus Biens* Ghiselin (RISM 1502_2, no. 42: "De tous biens")
10	D3^v	*Ein gut trium, mit schönen fugen* [2]
11	E1	*Vostrea Jamais* Ghiselin (RISM 1504_3, no. 130: "Vostre a jamais/J'en ay dueul")
12	E2	*La Bernardina* Jossquin (ScherG, no. 62b)
13	E3	*Jay vien ahur* Alexander Agricola (HewO, no. 82: "Jay bien a huer")
14	E4^v	*Jay pris amors* Ghiselin (DrozT, no. 2)
15	F1^v	*La alfonsina* Jo. Ghiselin (HewO, no. 80)
16	F3	*Mess pensees* Compere (HewO, no. 59)
17	G1	*Favus distillans* Ghiselin (RISM 1504_3, no. 123)
18	G3	*Tartara* [3] Henricus Isaac (DTO XIV/28, p. 107)
19	H1^v	*Juli amors* Ghiselin (RISM 1504_3, no. 115)
20	H4	*Si sumpsero* [4] Jacobus Obrecht (ObrMT, no. 19)
21	I2^v	*Ave sanctissima der erste theil* Alexander agricola
	K1	2a pars
22	K3^v	*Si dormiero. der erste theil* [5] Hainricus Finck (DTO XIV/28, p. 104: Isaac [Agricola or La Rue?])
	L2	2a pars
23	L4^v	*Ecce video celos apertos. der dritt theil* N. Croen [sic] (RISM 1502_1, fol. 24^v: Craen)
24	M4	*Taner nack* Paulus Hoffhamer (compare HewO, no. 69)
25	N3	*Ander nacken up dem Rhin* [6] Ja. Obrecht (HewO, no. 69)
26	O2^v	*Ander nacken up dem Rhin* Alex. agricola (GomO, no. 25)
27	P2	*Alexan. agricola. der erste theil* [7] (1538_2, no. 27: "Caecox" or "Cecus")
	Q3	2a pars
28	R4	*Letatus sum. der erste theil* Andreas de Sylva (RISM 1514_1, fol. 4^v)
	S2	2a pars [*Fiat pax in virtute*]
29	S3	*Memor esto* Jossquin de press (JosqMT, no. 31)
	T2	2a pars [*Portio mea, Domine*]
30	V1	*Laudate dominum de celis. Der erste theyl* Antonius brumel (RISM 1514_1, fol. 15)
	X1	2a pars [*Laudate dominum in sanctis eius*]
31	X3^v	*Adiu mes amours* Joss Quin (HewO, no. 14: Josquin)
32	Y2^v	*Sancta trinitas* Jo. muton (RoksT, no. 8: Févin)
33	Z2	*Plus mültz regres* Joss Quin (JosqWW, no. 29: Josquin)
34	Z4	*Cum sancto spiritu* Joss Quin (JosqMS XVI: "Missa de Beata Virgine," Josquin)
35	Aa1^v	*Hie volget ein sehr kunstreicher Preambel oder Fantasey* [8]
36	Bb4	*Von edler art* (MosPH, p. 180: J. Schönfelder or Hofhaimer)
37	Cc1^v	*Tröstlicher lieb* [9] (MosPH, p. 86: Hofhaimer)
38	Cc3	*Mein fleys und mühe* [10] (SenflW IV, no. 19: Senfl)
39	Cc4	*Ach lieb mit leid* [11] (MosPH, p. 26: Hofhaimer)
40	Dd1	*Mein einigs A* [12] (MosPH, p. 66: Hofhaimer)
41	Dd2^v	*Die prünlein die da fliessen* [13] (DTO XIV/28, p. 69: Isaac)
42	Dd4	*Was wirt es doch des wunders noch* [14] (SenflW IV, no. 26: Senfl)
43	Ee1^v	*Ach unfal wes zeigstu mich*
44	Ee3^v	*Mile regretz* (JosqWW, no. 24: Josquin)

45	Ff1	*Mein hertz alzeyt hat gross verlangen* (ObrWW, no. 21: "Mijn hert heest altijts verlanghen," Obrecht [Pierre de la Rue?])
46	Ff2ᵛ	*Si dedero* Ja. Obrecht (HewO, no. 56: Alexander Agricola)
47	Gg1	*Nach willen dein*[15] (MosPH, p. 74: Hofhaimer)

1 Mod. ed. in DTO XVIII/37, p. 17, and NeemAM I, no. 12.
2 Mod. ed. in DTO XVIII/37, p. 24.
3 Mod. ed. in DTO XIV/28, p. 166.
4 Mod. ed. in ObrMT IV, 194.
5 Facs. of fol. K3ᵛ in WolfH II, 43, and *Handbuch der Bibliothekswissenschaft* II (1931), 499.
6 Mod. ed. in ObrWW, no. 24.
7 Mod. ed. in DTO XVIII/37, p. 26.
8 Mod. ed. in DTO XVIII/37, p. 19, and KörL, no. 6.
9 Mod. ed. in DTO XXXVII/72, p. 87.
10 Mod. ed. in SenflW VII, no. 30c.
11 Mod. ed. in DTO XXXVII/72, p. 80.
12 Mod. ed. in DTO XXXVII/72, p. 83.
13 Mod. ed. in DTO XIV/28, p. 139.
14 Mod. ed. in SenflW VII, no. 32d.
15 Mod. ed. in DTO XXXVII/72, p. 84.

1536_8

VERDELOT, PHILIPPE

INTAVOLATURA DE / LI MADRIGALI DI VERDE/LOTTO DA CANTARE ET SONARE NEL LAUTO, INTA/volati per Messer Adriano, Novamente Stampata. Et / con ogni diligentia Corretta. / M. D. [Cut of angel blowing horn with the motto "Famam extendere factis, est Virtutis opus"] XXXVI. / Con Gratia, & Privilegio.

32 fols. Italian lute tablature and mensural notation. The printer's mark is that of Ottaviano Scotto.[1] On fol. 1ᵛ: table of contents. All of the compositions are for solo voice (written in mensural notation) and lute; the vocal models are all in RISM 1537_9, which names Verdelot as the composer of all but no. 21. Contents = 1540_2.

Copy in: A:Wn.

	fol.	
1	2	*Quanto sia liet'il giorno*
2	3ᵛ	*Quando amor i begli occhi*
3	4ᵛ	*Donna leggiadra, e bella*
4	5ᵛ	*Madonna qual certezza*[2]
5	7ᵛ	*Con lagrime, & sospir*[3]
6	8ᵛ	*Fugi fugi cor mio*
7	10	*Igno soave*
8	11ᵛ	*Amor se d'hor in hor la doglia cresce*
9	12	*Donna che sete tra le belle bella*
10	13ᵛ	*Se mai provasti donna*
11	14ᵛ	*Afflitti spirti mei*
12	16	*Ben che'l misero cor*
13	17ᵛ	*Madonna il tuo bel viso*
14	20	*Divini occhi sereni*
15	21	*Si lieta e grata morte*
16	23	*Vita de la mia vita*
17	24	*Gloriar mi poss'io donne*
18	25ᵛ	*Piove da gli occhi della donna mia*
19	26ᵛ	*Con l'angelico riso*
20	28	*So'o pensasso madonna che mia morte*
21	29ᵛ	*Madonna io sol vorrei* [Andreas de Silva][4]
22	30ᵛ	*Madonna per voi ardo*

1 See SartD, p. 142.
2 Mod. ed. in TagA I, no. 1.
3 Mod. ed. in BruAL I, 20; EinIM III, no. 95; and TapS, p. 18.
4 Verdelot is named as the composer in some later editions (see Vogel: Verdelot 13 [1557]).

1536_9

CASTELIONO, GIOVANNI ANTONIO

INTABOLATURA DE LEU/TO DE DIVERSI AUTORI NOVA/MENTE STAMPATA: ET CON DELIGENTIA / REVISTA: CON GRATIA ET PRIVILEGIO / CHE NIUNO POSSA STAMPARE: NE / FARE STAMPARE PER DIECI ANNI. / SOTTO PENA DE Scutti CENTO: APLI/CATI ALA IMPERIALE CAME/RA: COME NE CAPITOLI / SI CONTENE.

64 fols. Italian lute tablature. On fol. 1: cut of a lutenist playing. On fol. 1ᵛ: the title page proper. On fol. 2: preface by the editor, Raynaldo Dadda, headed "Allo Illu. S. Baptista Vesconte." On fol. 2ᵛ: table of contents.[1] On fol. 63ᵛ: "Stampata Nela Cita De Milano per. Io. Antonio Casteliono al Primo De Magio. M. D. XXXVI." On fol. 64: printer's mark. In the inventory below the information in

brackets is from the table of contents. Modern editions of the compositions identified by the superior letter *a* ([a]) are in MoeDM. SlimK II, 457–460, contains a thematic index of the ricercares. MoeDM contains a thematic index of the dances (p. 357) and some concordances (p. 221). WieM II contains a thematic index of the volume and selected transcriptions. 1563_{11} is a partial reprint of this volume (see there for a modern edition of 1563_{11}). All of the compositions are for solo lute. In the following inventory composers' initials are resolved the first time they appear only.

Copies in: A: Wn, F: Pn (imperfect), I: Fc.

fol.

1 3 *Fantasia del divino Francesco da Milano* = 1552_{11}, no. 11; 1568_7, no. 15; 1571_6, no. 12 (compare 1552_4, no. 6)

2 5 *Fantasia de M. Alberto [Ripa] da Mantua* = 1552_1, no. 27; 1554_7, no. 3; 1562_{11}, no. 9; 1574_7, no. 1

3 7 *Fantasia de M. Marcho da Laquila*[2] = 1552_1, no. 26

4 9 *Pavana chiamata la Milanesa* [P(ietro) Paulo B(orrono) da Milano]

10 *Saltarelo [de la preditta]*

11^v *Saltarelo chiamato Rose [e] Viole*[3]

12^v *Saltarelo chiamato bel Fiore*

13^v *Tochata da sonare nel fine del ballo*

5 14 *Pavana ditta la Malcontenta*[a] P. P. Borono da Mi. = $154?_5$, no. 9

14^v *Saltarelo nel fine del ballo [de la preditta]*

15^v *Saltarelo chiamato Baggino*

17 *Saltarello ditto el Burato*

17^v *Tochata nel fine del Ballo*[a][4]

6 18 *Pavana chiamato Monta su che son de Vella*[a] P. P. B.

20^v *Saltarelo [dela ditta]*

22^v *Saltarelo chiamato la Torgia* (and *Fa la danza. Jo. Petro che la balla ben*)[5]

23^v *Saltarelo chiamato el Mazolo*

24^v *Tochata del Divino Fran. Da Milano*[6]

7 25 *Fantasia del Divino Fran. Da Milano* = 1546_{20}, no. 5; 1552_1, no. 21; 1573_8, no. 5

8 26^v *Fantasia de M. Alberto de Mantua* = 1552_1, no. 28, and 1555_4, no. 1

9 29 *Fantasia de M. Marcho Da Laquila*[7] = 1552_1, no. 31

10 31 *Fantasia de M. Jo. Jacobo Albutio da Milano* = 1552_1, no. 29; 1552_{11}, no. 6; 1563_{12}, no. 3

11 33 *Fantasia de M. Petro Paulo [B.] da Milano*[8] = 1552_1, no. 24; 1552_{11}, no. 19; 1563_{12}, no. 9; 1568_7, no. 4; and 1571_6, no. 2

12 34^v *Pavana Nova [del ditto P. P. B.]*

36 *[Saltarello de la ditta]*

38 *Saltarello [ditto] la traditorella*[a]

39^v *Peschatore che va cantando*[9]

13 40^v *Pavana chiamata la Gombertina*[a] P. P. B. = 1552_1, no. 47a

42^v *Saltarello [de la ditta]* = 1552_1, no. 47b

44^v *Saltarello che glian strazza la socha* = 1552_1, no. 47c

46 *Saltarelo chiamato Antonola* = 1552_1, no. 47d

14 47 *Pavana chiamata la Desperata*[a] P. P. B. = 1552_1, no. 48a, and 1563_{12}, no. 122a

49 *Saltarello [dela ditta]* = 1552_1, no. 48b, and 1563_{12}, no. 122b

50 *Saltarello la Mantuanella* = 1552_1, no. 48c

51^v *Tocha tocha La Canella*[a] = 1552_1, no. 48d

53^v *Thochata*[10] [P. P. B.]

15 54 *Fantasia del divino Francesco da Milano*

16 55 *[Fantasia del ditto]* = 1552_1, no. 22, and 1553_9, no. 2: Albert de Rippe (compare 1547_5, no. 102)

17 57 *Fantasia de M. Marcho da Laquila* = 1552_1, no. 25, and 1552_{11}, no. 8

18 59^v *Fantasia de M. Jo. Jacobo Albutio* = 1552_1, no. 30

19 62 *Fantasia del divino Francisscho da Milano* = 1552_1, no. 23 †

[1] Facs. of fols. 1, 2^v, and 5 in LiuM, p. 84.
[2] Mod. ed. in ScherG, no. 94.
[3] Mod. ed. in TapS, p. 20.
[4] Mod. ed. in FerandM, p. 388.
[5] Mod. ed. in ScherG, no. 95.
[6] Mod. ed. in ValentinTo, no. 1; quasi-facs. and mod. ed. in WolfH II, 55.
[7] Mod. ed. in KörL, no. 7 (after 1552_1).
[8] Mod. ed. in SlimK II, 615.
[9] Mod. ed. in PujBG, no. 1056.
[10] Mod. ed. in FerandM, p. 388.

1536

DOUBTFUL WORKS

1. EitQ I, 32, erroneously dated Julio Abondante, *Intabolatura di Julio Abondante sopra el lauto de ogni sorte de balli...Libro Primo*, ten years too early. The volume is listed in this bibliography as 1546_1.

1537_1

GERLE, HANS

Musica Teutsch, auf die In/strument der grossen und kleinen Geygen auch Lautten, / welcher massen die mit grund und art irer Composicion / auss dem gesang in die Tabulatur zu ordnen / und zu setzen ist, sampt verborgener applica/cion und kunst, / Darinnen ein liebhaber und anfanger berürter Instrument so dazu Lust und ney/gung tregt, on ein sonderlichen Meyster mensürlich durch tegliche ubung leichtlich / begreiffen und lernen mag, vormals im Truck nye und ytzo durch Hans Gerle / Lutinist zu Nurenberg aussgangen. / 1537.

64 fols. German lute and viola da gamba tablature and mensural notation. The title is placed within the same ornamental border containing the initials H. G. and the date 1530, as in 1532_2. On fol. A2: the same preface as in 1532_2. Colophon on fol. Q3v: "Gedruckt zu Nurenbergk durch Jeronimum Formschneyder." On fol. Q4: list of errata. For further information see TapL. Contents = 1532_2.

Copy in: F:Pc (imperfect).[1]

[1] A copy was in D:Bds. The Paris copy is completed in manuscript after the Berlin copy.

1538_1

NARVÁEZ, LUIS DE

Los seys libros del Delphin de musica / de cifras para tañer Vihuela. Hechos por Luys de Narbaez. Dirigi/dos al muy Illustre Señor el Señor don Francisco delos / Covos, Comendador mayor de Leon, Adelantado / de Caçorla, Señor de Saviote, y del Consejo / del estado de su Magestad Cesarea, &c. / y este primer libro tracta de los ocho tonos para tañer por / diversas partes en / la Vihuela. / M. D. xxx. viii. / Con previlegio Imperial para Castilla y / Aragon y Valencia y Cataluña por diez años.

4 + 102 fols. Italian lute tablature with voice parts in red ciphers included in the tablature. On fol. *1v: cut of Arion on a dolphin's back.[1] On fol. *2: preface. On fol. *2v: dedicatory poem in Spanish headed "Coplas al muy Illustre S. el S. comendador mayor de Leon." Beginning on fol. *3: preliminary instructions for playing the vihuela. Fol. *5 = fol. 1. Each of the six books of the volume has its own title page (with the same woodcut as on fol. *1v on the verso), its own table of contents and on the verso of the folio with the contents a cut of an eagle mounted on a pedestal above a poem in praise of music. That part of each title page which summarizes the contents has been included in the inventory below. On fol. 98: table of contents for all six books. On fol. 99: author's corrections. On fol. 100: a poem in Spanish headed "Coplas del auctor en loor de la musica."[2] On fol. 101v: the same cut of an eagle above a poem as at the end of each book. Colophon on fol. 102: "Fue impresa la presente obra de los seys libros del Delphin, Hecho por el excelente musico Luys de Narbaez en la muy noble villa de Valladolid por Diego Hernandez de Cordova impresor. Acabose a treynta dias del mes de Octubre. M. D. xxx. viii," followed by the printer's mark. Each composition is introduced by a statement of its tempo and mode. The entire collection has been reprinted in a critical edition with introduction, concordances, and facsimiles of the title page, the colophon, and fols. *1v and 40v in MME III. The compositions identified by superior letters are reprinted as follows: (a) in MorL I; (b) in TornC. JacobsTN, pp. 70–81, reprints two complete compositions (nos. 8 and 31) and sections from two others (nos. 22 and 23). SlimK II, 469–471, contains a thematic index of the ricercares. Nos. 24–30 are for voice (written in red ciphers in the tablature) and vihuela. The other compositions are for vihuela solo.

Copies in: E:Mn (two copies, one imperfect), E:Tp, GB:Lbm, US:Wc.[3]

VIHUELA SOLO

fol.

1 1 *Primer tono por gesolreut*[b][4] = 1546_{18}, no. 9 (compare 1553_9, no. 1, and 1557_2, no. 56)

2 3^{v} *Segundo tono*[b] = 1546_{18}, no. 10

3 7 *Tercer tono*[b]

4 9^{v} *Quarto tono*[b] (compare 1557_2, no. 62)

5 12 *Quinto tono de consonancia*[b] (compare 1557_2, no. 66)

6 14 *Sesto tono sobre fa ut mi re*[b] (compare 1557_2, no. 67)

7 17 *Setimo tono sobre ut re mi fa mi*[b] (compare 1557_2, no. 69)

8 20 *Octavo tono*[b]

El segundo libro del Delphin de musica... Ay en el fantasias por algunos tonos que no son tan dificultosas de tañer como las del primer libro.

9 26 *Fantasia del primer tono*[b][5] = 1546_{18}, no. 3; 1552_4, no. 3; 1563_{12}, no. 18; 1568_7, no. 21

10 27 *Fantasia del quarto tono*[b] = 1546_{18}, no. 4, and 1552_4, no. 4

11 28^{v} *Fantasia del quinto tono*[b] = 1546_{18}, no. 5, and 1552_4, no. 5

12 31 *Fantasia del quinto tono*[b] = 1546_{18}, no. 6

13 33^{v} *Fantasia del primer tono*[b] = 1546_{18}, no. 7

14 35 *Fantasia del primer tono*[b] = 1546_{18}, no. 8

El tercero libro del Delphin de musica...Ay en el obras compuestas de Josquin y canciones Francesas de diversos auctores.

15 38 *Sanctus dela misa de faisan regres de josquin*[6] (JosqMS, no. 7: *Missa Hercules Dux Ferrariae*)

38^{v} *Ossanna de la misma missa*

16 40 *Sanctus de josquin de la misa de faissan regres* (JosqMS, no. 13: *Missa Faysant regrets*)

41 *Ossanna de la misma missa*

17 42^{v} *Cum sancto spiritu de la missa de la fuga de josquin* (JosqMS, no. 17: *Missa sine nomine*)

18 44^{v} *Mille regres. La cancion del Emperador del quarto tono de Jusquin*[a][7] (JosqWW, no. 24: Josquin)

19 46^{v} *Cancion de niculas Gombert del quinto tono* (RISM 1534_{12}, no. 5: "Jamais je n'euz tant de soulas," Gombert)

20 47^{v} *Cancion del primer Tono* [Gombert]

21 49 *Je veulx laysser melancolie* ricaforte [Richafort]

El quarto libro del Delphin de musica... Ay en el diferencias de contrapuntos sobre el igno de nuestra Señora. O gloriosa domina, y de Pange lingua y Sacris solenniis.

22 54 *O gloriosa domina*[8] (six *diferencias* on the hymn melody)

23 60 *Sacris solenniis* (five *diferencias* on the hymn melody)

VOICE AND VIHUELA

El quinto libro del Delphin de musica...Ay en el romances y villancicos para tañer y cantar y contrapunctos sobre algunos villancicos.

24 69 *Ya se asienta el rey Ramiro*[a][9] Romance (see QueI, p. 308)

25 70 *Paseavase el rey Moro*[a] Romance = 1546_{18}, no. 31 (see QueI, p. 308)

26 71 *Si tantos halcones*[a] (three *diferencias* on the villancico) = 1546_{18}, nos. 32–33.

27 76^{v} *Y la mi cinta dorada*[a] (six *diferencias* on the villancico) = 1546_{18}, no. 34

28 81 *La bella mal maridada*[a][10] Villancico = 1546_{18}, no. 37

29 82 *Con que la lavare*[ab][11] Villancico

30 84 *Ay arde coraçon arde*[ab][12] Villancico

VIHUELA SOLO

El sesto libro del Delphin de musica...Ay en el veynte y dos diferencias de Conde claros para discantar y siete diferencias de guardame las vacas, y una baxa de contrapunto.

31 87 *Conde claros*[13] (22 *diferencias* on the romance)

32 91^{v} *Guardame las vacas*[ab][14] (seven *diferencias* on the villancico)

33 95^{v} *Baxa de contrapunto*[b][15]

[1] Facs. of fol. *1^{v} in EF III, 277; MGG I, cols. 623–624; SubHM I, 488; and VinS, p. 93.

[2] Facs. of poem in SubHME, p. 208.

[3] A copy was in D:Bds (formerly in the Wolffheim library; see WolffC I, no. 1204).
[4] Mod. ed. in SainzF, no. 4.
[5] Mod. ed. in NeemAM I, no. 14, and PujBG, no. 1041.
[6] Facs. of fols. 38 and 38ᵛ in WolfMS, pl. 62; on nos. 15 and 16 see FellJ.
[7] Mod. ed. in PujHC, p. 12.
[8] Mod. ed. in HAM, no. 122.
[9] Mod. ed. in PedCP III, 106.
[10] Mod. ed. in BarbiC, p. 607; EC, pt. I, vol. IV, p. 2020; and SubHM I, 485.
[11] Mod. ed. in NarC.
[12] Mod. ed. in BalR, p. 38.
[13] Mod. ed. in FischV, no. 21; NarV; PujBG, no. 1042.
[14] Mod. ed. in NarG; NarT; and PujHC, p. 15; partly repr. in ApelM II, 14; AzpiaA, no. 3; BehS, p. 5.
[15] Mod. ed. in PedCP III, 101, and PujHC, p. 14.

1538₂

FORMSCHNEIDER, HIERONYMUS, PUBLISHER

TENOR / TRIUM VOCUM CARMINA / A DIVERSIS MUSICIS / COMPOSITA / Cum privilegio Caesareae atque Regiae maiestatis ad sexennium.

Three part books in mensural notation, each of 52 fols. The discantus part book (with title page: "DISCAN/TUS") is signed A1–N4. The bassus part book (with title page: "BASSUS") is signed O1–c4. The tenor part book is signed Aa1–Nn4. Preface on fol. Aa2 of the tenor part book only reads:

CANDIDIS MUSICIS SALUTEM.

Endamus vobis magno numero delecta trium vocum Carmina, á probatissimis Musices professoribus, tum veteribus tum recentioribus composita. Congessimus autem ea singulari studio, non eò solum, ne suavissima summorum in hoc genere ingeniorum monumenta perirent, sed ut etiam iuventutis studia accenderemus ad artem longè omnium suavissimam diligenter complectendam. Notae enim sunt non solum veterum Graecorum Poetarum, Theognidis, Homeri, et aliorum insignes commendationes, quibus Musicam ornarunt, tanquam perpetuam honestatis et eruditionis comitem, sed etiam Philosophorum iudicia non obscura extant, quae testantur ad Rempublicam pertinere, ut iuventus diligenter discat Musica. Quod si nihil haberet haec ars praeter illam suavitatem ac oblectationem, an non satis magna ea commendatio esset: praesertim cum haec vita ob curas et negotiorum varietatem non possit esse iucunda, nisi aliqua docta suavitate condiatur. Existimamus igitur hoc studium nostrum omnibus bonis probatum iri, quod et Reipublicae ac iuventutis commodis consulimus, et suavissimos labores insignium Musicorum ab interitu vindicamus. Quia autem Carmina haec non unius linguae verba habebant, commodius fore iudicavimus, si obmissis verbis, carmina signaremus numeris. Deformitatem enim res habitura videbatur. si nunc Germanica, nunc Gallica, nonnunquam Italica, aut latina commixta essent. Deinde in trium vocum carminibus videntur artifices magis sonorum eruditam mixturam spectasse, quám verba. Hac voluptate eruditus Musicus abunde fruetur, etiam si nulla subiecta verba sint. Neque de Autorum nominibus valde fuimus soliciti, quod singuli suas insignes notas habeant, quibus ab eruditis Musicis facile possint agnosci. Bene valete, et fruimini feliciter laboribus nostris. Nam huius generis alia quoque dabimus. Deo aspirante.

Colophon on fol. Nn3ᵛ of the tenor part book only: "Impressum Nürenberge per Hieronymum Formschneyder. 1538." All of the compositions are without text, title, or composer's name. The tenor part books in Berlin and Jena both contain some of this information, written in by hand. The manuscript additions of the Jena copy are given without brackets in the inventory below. Significantly different manuscript additions in the Berlin copy are footnoted. For further information on the volume see HolzTVC.

Copies in: D:Bhm, D:J.

	fol.	
1	A2	[*Das lang*] L[udwig] S[enfl] (SenflW VII, no. 1)
2	A3	[*Der hund*[1] Heinrich] Isaak (DTO XXXVII/72, p. 75)
	A3ᵛ	2a pars
3	A4ᵛ	*Helas je suis mary* H. Isac (DTO XIV/28, p. 75: "Helas que devera mon cueur")

4 B1 [*Vray dieu d'amours*][2] Anton. Brumel (GiesS II, 64)

5 B1^v [*Pleni sunt coeli* from *Missa Fortuna desperata*] (ObrMS III, 115: Obrecht)

6 B1^v [Unidentified]

7 B2 *Allez regretz* Hayne (HewO, no. 57)

8 B2^v [*Al mein mut* Isaac] (DTO XIV/28, p. 3)

9 B3 [Unidentified]

10 B3 *Pleni sunt celi*[3] [from *Missa Fortuna desperata*] Joskin (JosqMS, no. 4: Josquin des Prez)

11 B3^v *Gabrielem archangelum*

12 B4 *Si sumpsero* Jacobus Obrecht (ObrMT, no. 19)

13 C1 *Si dedero*[4] [Alexander Agricola] (HewO, no. 56)

14 C1^v [*Christe* from *Missa Si dedero* Obrecht] (ObrMS IX, 4)

15 C2 [Unidentified]

16 C2^v *La Bernardina* Joskin (ScherG, no. 62b: Josquin des Prez)

17 C2^v *Naves point veu* [*mal assenée*] [Richafort] (RISM 1536$_1$, fol. 17)

18 C3 *Mes pensees* L. Compère (HewO, no. 59)

19 C3^v [Unidentified]

20 C4 *Die brünlein die do fliessen* [Isaac? Hofhaimer?] (DTO XIV/28, p. 126)

21 C4^v [*Se mai il cielo* Johannes Martini] (I:Fn, MS Magl. XIX, 59 [B. R. 229], fol. 4^v)

22 D1 [Unidentified] H. Finck (DTO XXXVII/72, p. 24)

23 D1 *Tristitia vestra* H. Isaac (RISM 1541$_2$, no. 24)

24 D1^v [Unidentified]

25 D2 *Will nieman singen so sing aber ich*

26 D2^v *Comme femme desconfortee* [Alexander] Agricola (AmbG V, 180)

27 D3^v *Caecox* Alexander Agricola (I:Bc, MS Q 17, fol. 12^v: "Cecus")

D4 2a pars

28 E1 *Een frölic wesen* Jacob Barbireau [Isaac? Obrecht?] (DTO XIV/28, p. 5, and LenN, p. [28])

29 E1^v *La morra* H. Isac (HewO, no. 44)

30 E2 *Benedictus qui venit* H. Isac (HewO, no. 76)

31 E2^v *Fors seulement* Joskin [Févin?] (ObrWW, p. 90)

32 E3 [Unidentified]

33 E3^v [*Adieu fillette de regnon* Isaac] (RISM 1502$_2$, no. 44: anon.; DTO XIV/28, p. 120: "Carmen," Isaac)

34 E4 [Unidentified]

35 E4^v [*La Martinella*] (I:Fn, MS Magl. XIX, 59 [B. R. 229], fol. 141^v)

36 F1 *La martinella* [Johannes Martini] (DTO VII, 223)

37 F1^v [*N*]*il nest plaisir* Isaac (DTO XIV/28, p. 160)

38 F1^v *Mein muterlin, mein muterlin, das fraget aber mich* Johan Buchner

39 F2^v *Peccavi* [*super numerum*] (RISM 1541$_2$, no. 44)

40 F2^v *Da pacem domine / Christ ist erstanden*

41 F3 *Myn hert hefft altyt verlanghen* (GomO, no. 30)

42 F3^v *Myn hert heft alltyt verlanghen* (GomO, no. 31)

43 F4 [*Pleni sunt coeli*[5] from *Missa Narayge*] Joh. Ghyselin (SartP, no. 9, fol. 14^v)

44 F4^v *La stangetta* (HewO, no. 49: Weerbecke or Obrecht)

45 G1 [Unidentified]

46 G1 *Fors seulement* (GB:Lbm, Add. MS 35087, fol. 80^v)

47 G1^v *Fors seulement* [Ockeghem] (GomO, no. 10)

48 G2 [*Een vrouwelic wesen* Johannes Ghiselin alias Verbonnet] (I:Fc, MS Basevi 2439, fol. 49^v)

49 G2^v *La alfonsina* Joh. Ghiselin (HewO, no. 80)

50 G3 [*Tous nobles cueurs* Pierre de la Rue] (I:Fc, MS Basevi 2439, fol. 87^v)

51 G3^v [*Tant est gentil plaisant & gracieulx*] (RISM 1542$_8$, no. 67)

52 G3^v [Unidentified]

53 G4 *Garisses moy* [Compère] (HewO, no. 58)

54 G4^v [*Rendes le moy* Ghiselin] (I:Fc, MS Basevi 2439, fol. 82^v)

55 H1 *Mater patris* Ant. Brumel (HewO, no. 62)
56 H1v *Elslin liebes elselin min wie gern waer ich by dir* Sixtus Dietrich[6]
57 H2 [*Elslin liebes elselin min*]
58 H2v [*Oublier veuil tristesse*] [Alexander] Agric[ola] (I:Fc, MS Basevi 2439, fol. 72v, and WolfME, no. 17: textless)
59 H3 *Weit ghy* (LenN, p. [18])
60 H3v *De tous biens playne* Hayne (GomO, no. 17: anon.)
61 H4 [*C'est donc pour moy*] (RISM 1541_{13}, no. 60)
62 H4v [*Vostre a jamays/J'en ay dueul* Ghiselin] (RISM 1504_3, no. 130)
63 H4v [Unidentified]
64 I1 [*Se jay requis*][7] Jo. Ghiselin (RISM 1504_3, no. 131)
65 I1v *Ecce video celos apertos* Nicolaus Craen (RISM 1502_1, fol. 24v)
66 I2v *Si dormiero* [La Rue? Isaac? Agricola?] (DTO XIV/28, p. 104)
67 I3 *Fantasia*[8] L[udwig] S[enfl] (SenflW VII, no. 2)
68 I4 [Unidentified]
69 I4v [*Sancta maria virgo* Pierre de la Rue] (I:Fc, MS Basevi 2439, fol. 94v)
70 K1 [Unidentified]
71 K1 *Ein schönes weib erfrewet mich*[9] Arnoldus Brugensis [Arnoldus de Bruck] (DTO XXXVII/72, p. 6)
72 K1v *La pris* [*la tient*] Prioris (F:Pn, MS fonds fr. 1596, fol. 4v)
73 K2 [*Jen ay deuil*[10] Agricola]
74 K2v [*Pleni*][11]
75 K2v *En lombre dung buissonet*
76 K3 [*Pleni sunt coeli* from *Missa Malheur me bat*] (ObrMS IV, 173: Obrecht)
77 K3v [*Les bien amore*] [Isaac? Martini?][12] (DTO XVI/31, p. 220)
78 K4 *Es wonet lieb bey liebe*
79 K4v *Petite camusette* [Févin] (GB:Cmc, Pepys MS 1760, fol. 57v)
80 L1 [Unidentified]
81 L1v *Si bibero* (BridgmE, p. 154)
82 L2 *La plus des plus* [Josquin] (HewO, no. 64)
83 L2v [Unidentified]
84 L3 *Belle sur toutes* Agricola (RISM 1504_3, no. 132)
85 L3 [*Christe* from *Missa Malheur me bat*[13] Obrecht] (ObrMS IV, 142)
86 L3v *Ma bouche rit* [Ockeghem] (HewO, no. 54)
87 L4 [Unidentified]
88 L4v *Fortuna desperata* H. Isac (DTO XIV/28, p. 134)
89 M1 *Je suis infortune*[14]
90 M1v *Tota pulchra es amica mea*
91 M2v *Malheur me bat* [Ockeghem] (HewO, no. 63)
92 M2v [*Crucifixus* from *Missa Malheur me bat*[15] Obrecht] (ObrMS IV, 161)
93 M3 [*Agnus II* from *Missa Malheur me bat* Obrecht] (ObrMS IV, 183)
94 M3v [Unidentified]
95 M4 *Ich stund an einem morgen* [Senfl] (SenflW VII, no. 3)
96 N1 *Ich stund an einem morgen* L[udwig] S[enfl] (SenflW VII, no. 4)
97 N1v [Unidentified]
98 N2 *Pater a nullo est factus* Samson (RISM 1541_2, no. 31)
99 N3 *To andernaken up dem Ryn* Alexander Agricola (GomO, no. 25: "Tandernacken")
100 N4 *In gotes namen faren wir* Paul Hofhaimer[16] (ZfMW XV, 137)

[1] Manuscript title in both the Berlin and the Jena copy: "Das kind lag in der wiegen" (in the Jena copy this text appears under mm. 98–108; midway through the 2a pars of the Jena copy appears the text, "Das kind lag in der wiegen, do bissen es die fliegen").

[2] Manuscript title in both copies: "En ung matin."

[3] Manuscript title in Berlin copy only.

[4] Manuscript attribution to Obrecht in the Berlin copy only.

[5] Manuscript title in the Berlin copy: "Narraige." Manuscript title in the Jena copy: "Pleni La narraige." The composer is named in both copies.

[6] Manuscript attribution in the Berlin copy: "Sixtus Dietrich Augustanus."

[7] Manuscript title in both copies: "Vostre a jamais" (see no. 62).

[8] Manuscript title in the Berlin copy only.

[9] Manuscript title in the Berlin copy: "Ich weiss ein schönes weib."
[10] The title and composer are added in the Berlin copy only in a modern hand.
[11] The title is added in the Berlin copy only in a modern hand.
[12] Martini is named as composer in I:Fn, MS Magl. XIX, 178, fol. 44ᵛ (title: "La re"), and in I:Fn, MS Magl. XIX, 59 (B. R. 229), fol. 19ᵛ.
[13] Manuscript title in Jena: "Malheur me bat."
[14] Manuscript title in Berlin: "Cedant."
[15] Manuscript title in Jena: "Malheur me bat."
[16] Manuscript attribution in the Berlin copy only.

[1538]$_3$

ATTAINGNANT, PIERRE, PUBLISHER

Neuf basses dances deux branles vingt et cinq Pavennes avec quinze Gaillardes en musique a quatre parties le tout nouvellement imprime a Paris par Pierre Attaingnant libraire demourant en la rue de la Harpe au bout de la rue des Mathurins pres leglise saint Cosme. 1538.

This volume is listed in EitQ I, 230, as being in A:Wn, and in SchmidOP, p. 228, as being in D:Mbs. Neither library owns it now. If the volume ever existed, it was a second edition of 1530_5.

1539_1

GARDANE, ANTONIO, PUBLISHER

MUSICHE FATTE NELLE NOZZE / DELLO ILLUSTRISSIMO DUCA DI / FIRENZE IL SIGNOR COSIMO DE MEDICI / ET DELLA ILLUSTRISSIMA CONSORTE / SUA MAD. LEONORA DA TOLLETO. / [Printer's mark] / CON GRATIA ET PRIVILEGIO.[1]

Five part books in mensural notation (S, 16 fols.; ATB, each of 12 fols.; 5/6, 8 fols.). On the recto side of the last folio of each part book: table of contents. Printer's mark and colophon on the verso side of the last folio of each part book: "In Venetia nella Stampa d'Antonio Gardane Nellanno del Signore M. D. XXXIX. Nel mese di Agosto. Con gratia et privilegio." The inventory below is taken from the table of contents of the cantus part book; the tables in the other books are simpler. All of the compositions are fully texted.

Copies in: A:Wn, I:Vnm (S wanting).

	fol.	
1	1ᵛ (= p. 2)	*Ingredere* a otto voci di Franc. corteccia cantato sopra l'arco del portone della porta al prato da vinti quatro voci da una banda, et da l'altra da quatro tromboni, et quatro cornetti nella entrata della Illustrissima Duchessa
2	p. 5	*Sacro et santo himeneo* a nove voci di Franc. corteccia cantato dalle muse con le sette seguenti canzonette il giorno del convito
3	10	*Piu che mai vaga* a quatro voci. Constantio festa ["Fiorenza"]
4	12	*Lieta per honorarte* a quatro voci. Ser Mattio rampollini ["Pisa"]
5	14	*Ecco Signor volterra* a cinque voci. Jo. Petrus masaconus ["Volterra"]
6	16	*Come lieta si mostra* a quatro voci. Constantio festa ["Arezzo"]
7	18	*Non men ch'ogn'altra lieta* a quatro voci. Baccio moschini ["Cortona"]
8	20	*Ecco la fida ancella* a quatro voci. Ser Mattio rampollini ["Pistoia"]
9	22	*Ecco Signor il Tebro* a cinque voci. Baccio Moschini ["Il Tevero"]

Musicha della comedia di Franc. Corteccia recitata al secondo convito.

10	24	*Vattene almo riposo* a quatro cantata dall'aurora, et sonata con uno grave cimbalo con organetti et con varii registri per principio della comedia ["Aurora"]

11 25 *Guardane almo pastore*[2] a sei voci cantata alla fine del primo atto da sei pastori, et dipoi ricantata da detti et sonata insieme da sei altri pastori con le storte ["I pastori"]

12 26 *Chi ne l'atolt'oime* a sei voci cantata a la fine del secondo atto da tre sirene, et da tre monstri marini sonata con tre traverse, et da tre Ninfe marine con tre liuti tutti insieme ["Le syrene"]

13 27 *O begli anni del'oro*[3] a quatro voci sonata a la fine del terzo atto da Sileno con un violone sonando tutte le parti, et cantando il soprano ["Sileno"]

14 28 *Hor chi mai cantera*[4] a quatro voci cantata a la fine del quarto atto da otto nimphe cacciatrici ["Le nimphe"]

15 29 *Vientene almo riposo* a cinque voci cantata alla fine del quinto atto dalla notte, et sonata con quatro tromboni ["La notte"]

16 30 *Bacco bacco euoe* a quatro voci cantata et ballata da quatro Baccante et quatro satiri, et sonata da altri otto satiri, con varii strumenti tutti ad un tempo, laquale subito dopo la notte fu la fine della comedia ["Ballo di satiri et baccante"]

[1] Facs. of title page of the altus part book in GhiFM, p. 47.

[2] Mod. ed. in GhiFM, p. 49.

[3] Mod. ed. in ScherG, no. 99, and KiesS, no. 38.

[4] Mod. ed. in GhiFM, p. 58.

1540_1

NEWSIDLER, HANS

Ein newes Lautenbüchlein, mit vil / schonen Liedern, die gantz artlich und lieb/ lich, auch Teütsch und Welsche Tentz, Auch Welsche und Fran/tzösische Stück, mit sondern fleyss verfasst, und zusamen / gebracht, Durch mich Hansen Newsidler Lutten/nisten, und Burger zu Nürnberg, offent/lich aussgegangen, im XL. Jar. / Mit Römischer Kay. und König. May. freyheyt, in / zweyen Jaren, nicht nach zudrücken, begnadet.

32 fols. German lute tablature. On fol. A1v: advertisement for Newsidler's first two books (1536_6 and 1536_7). On fol. A2: table of contents. On fol. H4: a note on the tablature (the same as in 1544_1, and 1547_4) headed "Von den Creutzlein und pünctlein, wie man sie verstehen soll," followed by the colophon: "Gedruckt zu Nürnberg bey Hans Guldenmundt, durch verlegung Hansen Newsidler Lutinisten. Anno M. D. xl Jar." The compositions identified by the superior letter *a* ([a]) are reprinted in DTO XVIII/37. Some of the dances are very similar to but not identical with those in 1562_4. All of the compositions are for solo lute.

Copy in: A:Wn.

	fol.	
1	A2v	*Das erst fundament auf die Lauten, volgen Drey Regel* (another version of no. 8 below) = 1536_6, no. 2
	A3	*Die ander Regel*
	A3	*Die Dritt Regel*[1]
2	A3v	*Unser Köchin kan auss der massen kochen* (compare BöhA, no. 304: "Unser Magd kan auss der massen kochen") = 1544_1, no. 3; 1547_4, no. 3; 1549_6, no. 4
3	A4	*Hast du mich genummen, so mustu mich* (another version of no. 35 below) = 1544_1, no. 2; 1547_4, no. 2; 1549_6, no. 5 (compare $151?_1$, no. 21)
4	A4v	*Mein hertz hat sich mit lieb verpflicht* = 1536_6, no. 6: Hofhaimer
5	B1	*Mag ich unglück nicht widerstehen* = 1536_6, no. 9: Senfl

6 $B1^v$ *Wayss mir ein hüsche Mülnerin*[2] = 1544_1, no. 14, and 1547_4, no. 10: "Ich wais mir ain stoltze Mülnerin" (compare SenflW V, 45: Senfl)

$B1^v$ *Hie volgt der hupff auff*

7 $B2^v$ *Der Ziegler in der hecken* (compare BöhA, no. 473, and PubAPTM XXIX, no. 16: Forster) = 1544_1, no. 15: "Der ziegler in der ave mit seiner hawen"

B3 *Der hupff auff*

8 $B3^v$ *Unser Köchin kan auss der massen* = 1544_1, no. 11 (another version of no. 1 above)

9 B4 *Es reyt ein armes Reuterlein auss*

$B4^v$ *Der hupff auff*

10 C1 *Es ist nit alles Golde* (compare SenflW V, no. 54: Senfl)

$C1^v$ *Hie volgt der hupff auff*

11 C2 *Der Zeuner tantz*[a][3] = 1544_1, no. 17, and 1547_4, no. 12

$C2^v$ *Hupff auff*

12 C3 *Der Nunnen tantz*[a][4] = 1544_1, no. 16, and 1547_4, no. 11

$C3^v$ *Hupff auff*[4]

13 C4 *Ich het mir ein Annelein* (SenflW V, no. 26: Senfl) = 1544_1, no. 25, and 1547_4, no. 16

14 $C4^v$ *Es taget vor dem holtze* (compare EitD II, no. 63: "Es taget vor dem walde") = 1544_1, no. 26

15 D1 *Der Bethler tantz*[a][5] = 1544_1, no. 18, and 1547_4, no. 13

$D1^v$ *Hupff auff*

16 D2 *Der Hoftantz* = 1536_6, no. 69

$D2^v$ [*Hupff auff*]

17 D3 *Lieblich hat sich gesellet*[6] (compare PubAPTM XXIX, no. 14) = 1544_1, no. 13

18 $D3^v$ *Ich klag den tag*[7] (DTO XXXVII/72, p. 71: Stoltzer) = 1544_1, no. 12

19 D4 *Die not sucht weg* (SenflW IV, no. 27: Senfl)

20 $D4^v$ *In liebes prunst* = 1536_6, no. 27

21 E1 *Mein gemüd und blüe* (EDMR XX, no. 85: "Mein gmüt und blüt," Johann Wenck) = 1544_1, no. 20

22 $E1^v$ *Nach willen dein*[8] (MosPH, p. 74: Hofhaimer)

23 E2 *Nun grüss dich Got mein* (EDMR XX, no. 82: Sixt Dietrich) = 1544_1, no. 24, and 1547_4, no. 23

24 $E2^v$ *Auff erd lebt nit ein* (MosL, no. 56) = 1544_1, no. 29

25 E3 *Im abzug ein gütter tantz*[9]

$E3^v$ *Hupff auff*

26 E4 *Ein gütter Venecianer tantz*[a]

$E4^v$ *Hupff auff*

27 F1 *Ein Welscher tantz*[a][10]

$F1^v$ *Hupff auff*

28 F2 *Ein seer guter welscher tantz im abzug*[a]

F3 *Hupff auff* [at end: *Saltarella*]

29 $F3^v$ *Lodesana. Ein Welscher tantz* [gagliarda] = 1544_2, no. 30

30 $F4^v$ *Passa mesa* [= *passamezzo*]. *Ein Welscher tantz*[a][11] = 1544_2, no. 31, and 1549_6, no. 36 (compare 1563_{12}, no. 134)

31 $G1^v$ *Ami sofre. Ein Welscher tantz* (AttainCK III, no. 7: Moulu) = 1544_2, no. 38; 1562_3, no. 23

32 G2 *Du wentzela. Ein Welscher tantz* (AttainCK III, no. 22: "Dont vient cela," Sermisy) = 1544_1, no. 31; 1544_2, no. 35; 1547_4, no. 29

33 $G3^v$ *Cesta grand* [*tort*]. *Ein Welscher tantz* (AttainCK II, no. 18: Sermisy) = 1544_2, no. 40

34 $G4^v$ *Mein fleyss und mühe* (SenflW IV, no. 19: Senfl)

35 H1 *Fors seulament* (ObrWW, p. 90: Josquin or Févin)

36 $H3^v$ *Madunna Katherina* (another version of no. 3 above) = 1547_4, no. 15

[1] Heading on fol. A3: "Hienach volgen etliche schlechte Liedlein, die leycht und kurtz seind, für junge knaben zu lernen."

[2] Mod. ed. in MolzHN, no. 4.

[3] Mod. ed. in ApelM I, 9, and BruS IV, no. 137 (no. 11a only).

[4] Mod. ed. in ZanG II, 6.

[5] Mod. ed. in BruS II, no. 59.

[6] Mod. ed. in MolzHN, no. 5.

[7] Mod. ed. in DTO XXXVII/72, p. 96.

[8] Mod. ed. in DTO XXXVII/72, p. 85; for a comparison of this intabulation with various others see NowakH.

[9] Mod. ed. in BruS II, no. 69, with title: "Der Künigin tantz. Ein Welischer tantz."

[10] Mod. ed. in GomVC, p. lxvii, and MolzHN, no. 13.

[11] Mod. ed. in MolzHN, no. 14.

1540_2

VERDELOT, PHILIPPE

INTAVOLATURA DE LI MADRIGALI / DI VERDELOTTO DA CANTARE ET SONARE NEL / LAUTO, INTAVOLATI PER LO ECCELLENTISSIMO / Musico MESSER ADRIANO Willaert, maestro di Capella / de la Illustrissima Signoria di Venegia. Novamente Stam/pata. Et con ogni diligentia correta. / CUM GRATIA [Cut of an angel blowing a horn] ET PRIVILEGIO. / VENETIIS / APUD HIERONYMUM SCOTUM. / 1540.

32 fols. Italian lute tablature and mensural notation. On fol. 1^v: table of contents. All of the compositions are for solo voice (written in mensural notation) and lute. Contents = 1536_8.

Copy in: GB:Lbm.

1540_3

[ARRIVABENE, ANDREA, PUBLISHER]

MUSICA NOVA / ACCOMMODATA PER CANTAR / ET SONAR SOPRA ORGANI; ET ALTRI / STRUMENTI, COMPOSTA PER DIVERSI / ECCELLENTISSIMI MUSICI. / MD [Cut of figure seated before a well out of which a woman dips water, with motto: SITIENTES VENITE AD AQUAS] XL. / IN VENETIA AL SEGNO DEL POZZO.[1]

Four part books in mensural notation, each of 16 fols. (?). The printer's mark and address are those of Andrea Arrivabene.[2] SlimK II, 471, contains a thematic index of the entire volume. SlimMN is a modern edition of the entire collection, with the upper voices reconstructed after $154?_6$, and facsimiles of the title page and fol. O2^v. For further information see MischR. All of the compositions are for instrumental ensemble *a 4*. Nineteen of the 21 compositions (nos. 1, 3–4, and 6–21) are reprinted in $154?_6$.

Copy in: I:Bc (B).

	fol.	
1	N2	*R[icercare]* ADRIAN WILLAERT
2	N2^v	*R.* JULIO [Segni] DA MODENA
3	N3	*R.* JULIO DA MODENA
4	N3^v	*R.* JULIO DA MODENA
5	N4^v	*R.* JULIO DA MODENA
6	O1	*R.* JULIO DA MODENA
7	O1^v	*R.* NICOLO BENOIST
8	O2^v	*R.* JULIO DA MODENA
9	O3	*R.* JULIO DA MODENA[3] (compare 1546_{10}, no. 4: Giovanni Maria da Crema)
10	O3^v	*R.* ADRIAN WILLAERT
11	O4	JULIO DA MODENA (1557_2, no. 46)
12	O4^v	*R.* JULIO DA MODENA (1557_2, no. 45)
13	P1	*R.* JULIO DA MODENA (1557_2, no. 52)
14	P1^v	*R.* ADRIAN WILLAERT
15	P2^v	*R.* JULIO DA MODENA
16	P3^v	*R.* JULIO DA MODENA
17	P4^v	*R.* GUILIELMO GOLIN [sic]
18	Q2	*R.* Hieronimo parabsco[4] [sic]
19	Q2^v	JULIO DA MODENA
20	Q3^v	*R.* Hieronimo [Cavazzoni] da bologna[5]
21	Q4^v	*Da pacem* Hieronimo parabsco[6]

[1] Facs. of title page in MischR, opp. p. 74.
[2] On Arrivabene see SlimCA, p. 35.
[3] Mod. ed. in SlimK II, 635.
[4] Mod. ed. in ParaC, no. 8.
[5] Mod. ed. in CavazzO II, 54.
[6] Mod. ed. in Para C, no. 9, and SlimK II, 637.

1540

DOUBTFUL WORKS

1. FétB III, 305, lists the following volume of lute music by Francesco da Milano: "Intabolatura di liuto, Milano, 1540." See 1536_3, note 2.

1542_1

AGRICOLA, MARTIN

Musica instru/mentalis deudsch / inn welcher begrif/fen ist: wie man / nach dem gesange auff mancherley / Pfeiffen lernen sol. Auch wie auff / die Orgel, Harffen, Lauten, Gei/gen, und allerley Instrument und / Seitenspiel, nach der recht/gegründten Tabelthur / sey abzusetzen. / Mart. Agric. / Anno. 1542.

60 fols. plus four inserted tables. Contents = 1529_1.

Copies in: CH:Lcortot (imperfect), D:Mbs, D:MZ, US:Wc.[1]

[1] Copies were also in D:LEm and PL:Tm.

1542_2

GANASSI, SILVESTRO DI

REGOLA. RUBERTna / [Cut of four men: three playing viols, the fourth singing]/ Regola che insegna. Sonar de viola darcho Tastada de Silvestro ganasi dal fontego[1]

25 fols. On fol. A2: dedication headed "Allo illustre signor Ruberto Strozzi." On fol. A2v: preface headed "A LI LETTORI." On fol. G1v: table of contents, followed by the colophon: "CON GRATIA ET PRIVILEGIO in Venetia ad instantia de l'autore MDXLII." Ganassi's instruction book for viols contains, besides numerous musical examples, four complete compositions, all ricercari for solo viol. They are printed both in mensural notation and in viola da gamba tablature. GanaR is a facsimile reprint of the entire volume. SartMS, p. 6, prints the dedication and table of contents. SlimK II, 476, contains a thematic index of the ricercares. For further information see ReFS, no. 39. See 1543_2 for a second volume in the same series by Ganassi.

Copies in: B:Bc (imperfect), I:Bc, I:Fc, I:Fn, US:Wc.[2]

	fol.	
1	F2v	*Recerchar primo*[3]
2	F3	*Recerchar Secondo*[4]
3	F4	*Recerchar terzo*[5]
4	F4v	*Recerchar quarto*[6]

[1] Facs. of title page in AbbS I, 423; KinsP, p. 145; and MGG IV, col. 1355. The cut on the title page is repr. in BachV, opp. p. 32. Facs. of fol. E2v (showing the tuning of the bass viol) in DiseC, opp. p. 145.

[2] The Washington copy was in the Landau-Finaly library in Florence.

[3] Mod. ed. in HAM, no. 119a, and RoyM, p. 39. Facs. in WolfH II, 225.

[4] Ed. in tablature and modern notation in BachV, p. 52.

[5] Ed. in tablature and modern notation in BachV, p. 53.

[6] Ed. in tablature and modern notation in BachV, p. 54.

1542_3

LUSCINIUS, OTTOMAR

MUSURGIA / seu Praxis MUSICAE. / Illius primo quae Instrumentis agitur certa ratio, ab Ottomaro / Luscinio Argentin. duobus Libris absoluta. / Eiusdem Ottomari Luscinii, de Concentus polyphoni, id est, / ex plurifariis vocibus compositi, canonibus, / Commentarii duo. / Argentorati apud Joannem Schottum, / Anno Christi M. D. XLII. / Cum gratia & PRIVILEGIO Imperiali, / ad Quinquennium.

56 fols. On fol. a2: the same dedication to Andreas Calvo as in 1536_4. On fol. a3v: the same cut of Andreas Silvanus and Sebastian Virdung as in 1536_4. Beginning on fol. o3: table of contents. Contents = 1536_4.

Copies in: D:Bds-Tü, F:Pn.

1543_1

CAVAZZONI, GIROLAMO

INTAVOLATURA / CIOE RECERCARI CANZONI / HIMNI MAGNIFICATI / COMPOSTI PER HIERONIMO / DE MARCANTONIO DA / BOLOGNA, DETTO / D'URBINO. / LIBRO PRIMO / Co'l Privilegio dell'Illustriss. Senato Veneto, per Anni X.

28 fols. Keyboard score. On fol. A1v: dedication headed "ALL'ILLUSTRISS. ET REVERENDISS. SIGNORE IL CARDINAL BEMBO" and dated "il di XXV. di Novembre. Nel XLII. de Venetia," repr. in SartMS, p. 9, and GaspaC IV, 37. Colophon on fol. G4v: "Stampata in Vinegia Nel Anno del Signor M. D. XLIII," along with the printer's mark: an

ornamented cross with the initials B. V. (Bernardino di Vitali, or Bernardinus Vercelensis?).[1] The entire collection is reprinted in CavazzO I (which includes the dedication); CDMI, quaderni 23–27; and TorA III, 1. SlimK II, 478, contains a thematic index of the ricercares. All of the compositions are for solo keyboard.

Copies in: I:Bc (two copies, one lacking fol. A1, and the other lacking fols. G3 and G4).

	fol.	
1	A2	*RECERCAR PRIMO*[2]
2	B1^v	*RECERGAR* [sic] *.II.*
3	B4^v	[*RECERCAR III*][3]
4	C4	*RECERCAR IIII.*[4]
5	D3	*CANZON SOPRA I LE BEL E BON*[5] (compare RISM 1534_{12}, no. 1: "Il est bel et bon," Passereau)
6	D4^v	*CANZON SOPRA FALT D'ARGENS*[6] (compare HAM, no. 91: "Faulte d'argent," Josquin)
7	E2	*HYMNUS CHRISTI REDEMPTOR OMNIUM*[7]
8	E3	*HYMNUS AD COENAM AGNI PROVIDI*[8]
9	E3^v	*HYMNUS LUCIS CREATOR OPTIME*
10	E4^v	*HYMNUS AVE MARIS STELLA*[9]
11	F1^v	*MAGNIFICAT PRIMI TONI*[10]
	F2	*QUIA RESPEXIT*
	F3	*DEPOSUIT A TRE VOCE*
	F3^v	*SUSCEPIT*
	F4	*GLORIA PATRI*
12	F4^v	*MAGNIFICAT OTTAVO TONI*[11]
	G1	*QUIA RESPEXIT*
	G1^v	*DEPOSUIT*
	G2	*SUSCEPIT A TRE VOCE*
	G2^v	*GLORIA PATRI*

[1] See SartC. Facs. of title page in MGG XI, col. 434.
[2] Mod. ed. in RieM, no. 36, and TagA I, no. 7.
[3] Mod. ed. in FuserC, no. 3, and TagA I, no. 8.
[4] Mod. ed. in CavazzR, and HAM, no. 116.
[5] Mod. ed. in FroideA I, 18, and TagA I, no. 12.
[6] Mod. ed. in HAM, no. 118.
[7] Mod. ed. in DallaLO II, no. 1, and FuserC, no. 4.
[8] Mod. ed. in ScherG, no. 103.
[9] Mod. ed. in DallaLO VI, no. 28.
[10] Mod. ed. of both the "Magnificat" and the "Gloria patri" in KleinO, p. 73; mod. ed. of the "Gloria patri" only in TagA I, no. 11.
[11] Mod. ed. of the "Magnificat" only in DallaL, no. 42, and MFH VII, 9.

1543_2

GANASSI, SILVESTRO DI

Lettione Seconda. / LETTIONE SECONDA PUR / DELLA PRATTICA DI SONARE IL VIOLONE D'AR/CO DA TASTI. COMPOSTA PER SILVESTRO GA/NASSI DAL FONTEGO DESIDEROSO NELLA PI/CTURA, LAQUALE TRATTA DELL'EFFETTO / DELLA CORDA FALSA GIUSTA E MEDIA / ET IL PONERE LI TASTI CON OGNI / RASONE PRATTICA, ET ANCORA LO ACORDAR / DITTO VIOLONE CON LA DILIGENTIA CON/VENIENTE IN DIVERSE MANIERE ET ACCO/MODE ANCORA PER QUELLI CHE SONA/NO LA VIOLA SENZA TASTI CON UNA / NUOVA TABULATURA DE LAUTO ADOTTATA DI MOLTI ET UTILIS/SIMI SECRETI A PROPOSITI NELL'EFFETTO DIL VALENTE DI / TAL STRUMENTO E STRUMENTI ET ANCORA IL MODO DI SO/NARE PIU PARTE CON IL VIOLONE UNITO CON LA VOCE. / OPERA UTILISSIMA A CHI SE DILETTA DE IMPARARE SONARE.

36 fols. Mensural notation and viola da gamba tablature. On fol. A1^v: Cut of a lute and of a viola da gamba. On fol. A2: dedication "Allo Illustre Signor Neri Capon," repr. in SartMS, p. 8. On fol. A3: a preface "Alli Lettori," and on fol. A4: "Prologo." On fol. I4: table of contents, followed by the colophon: "Lettor la diligentia del lezer sera il mezzo del conoscere alcun error si nel intaglio quanto della Stampa per il replicamento. Stampata per Lauttore proprio. Nel M. D. XXXXIII." This is a sequel and companion volume to 1542_2. It contains, besides numerous musical examples, five complete compositions in viola da gamba tablature: four ricercares for solo viol, and one intabulated madrigal for voice and viol.[1] The modern facsimile edition of 1542_2

(GanaR) includes this second volume as well. SlimK II, 478, contains a thematic index of the four ricercares.

Copies in: B:Bc, D:W, F:Pc, I:Bc, I:Fc, US:Wc.[2]

	fol.	
1	E4^v	*Recercar Primo*[3]
2	E4^v	*R[ecercar] S[econdo]*[4]
3	F2^v	*Io vorei Dio d'amor*[5] (Vogel Einstein 1537_3: Giacomo Fogliano)
4	H2^v	*Recercar Primo*[6]
5	H3	*R[ecercar] S[econdo] a sola voce*

[1] The cut of a viola da gamba showing proportions of string length for placing frets (on fol. B4^v of the original) is repr. in facs. in BachV, opp. p. 17.

[2] The Washington copy was in the Landau-Finaly library in Florence.

[3] Ed. in tablature and in modern notation in BachV, p. 56; mod. ed. and quasi-facs. in TapS, p. 22, and WolfH II, 225.

[4] Ed. in tablature and in modern notation in BachV, p. 57; mod. ed. in HAM, no. 119b.

[5] Mod. ed. in EinIM III, 54.

[6] Facs. and partial mod. ed. in WolfH II, 225.

1543_3

GARDANE, ANTONIO, PUBLISHER

MOTETTA TRIUM VOCUM / AB PLURIBUS AUTHORIBUS COMPOSITA. / quorum nomina sunt / JACHETUS GALLICUS. / MORALES HISPANUS. / CONSTANTIUS FESTA. / ADRIANUS WIGLIARDUS. / TRIUM [Cut with printer's mark] VOCUM / Venetiis Apud Antonium Gardane. / M. D. XXXXIII.

Three part books in mensural notation, each of 16 fols. (cantus: A1–D4; tenor: E1–H4; bassus: I1–M4). On the final verso of each book: table of contents. The volume contains 20 vocal pieces *a 3* with Latin text, and four textless pieces (nos. 21–24). These latter (labeled "trium" in the table) are probably for instrumental ensemble. Contents = 1551_7 and 1569_7.

Copies in: A:Wn, GB:Lbm.

	fol.	
1	A2	*Quam pulchra es* Jachet
2	A2^v	*O Pulcherrima* Jachet
3	A3	*In lectulo meo* Jachet
4	A3^v	*Tu es Petrus* Morales
5	A4	*Puer natus est* Morales
6	A4^v	*Virgo ante partum* Jachet
7	B1	*Ave Maria* Jachet
8	B1^v	*O Clemens* Jachet
9	B2	*Cantate domino & benedicite* Jachet
10	B2^v	*Cantate domino canticum novum quia fecit* Jachet
11	B3	*Cantate domino canticum novum laus eius* Jachet
12	B3^v	*Sancta Maria* Constantius Festa
13	B4	*Ave virgo gratiosa* Constantius Festa
14	B4^v	*Quam pulchra es* Constantius Festa
15	C1	*Pleni sunt celi* Jachet
16	C1^v	*Benedictus qui venit* Jachet
17	C2	*Agnus dei* Jachet
18	C2^v	*Surge amica mea* Constantius Festa
	C3	2a pars. *O Pulcherrima*
19	C3^v	*Ave regina celorum* Constantius Festa
	C4	2a pars *Gaude gloriosa*
20	C4^v	*Ave regina celorum* [Constantius Festa]
	D1	2a pars *Gaude gloriosa*
21	D1^v	*Re* Adrianus
22	D2	*Mi* Adrianus
23	D2^v	*Fa*[1] Adrianus
24	D3^v	*Sol* Adrianus

[1] Mod. ed. in KleinO, p. 56; PeetM I, no. 11 (arr. for organ); and ScherG, no. 105 (labeled "Ricercare").

$[1543]_4$

CONSEIL, JEAN

Livre de danceries à six parties, par Consilium. Paris, Pierre Attaingnant, 1543.

This volume, now, lost, is mentioned in FétB I, 161, and in SchmidOP, p. 225.

1544_1

NEWSIDLER, HANS

Das Erst Buch. / Ein Newes Lautenbüchlein mit vil feinen liebli/chen Liedern, für die jungen Schuler, die fein leicht und gantz ring zu lernen / seind, auch etlich feine Tentz, Welisch und Frantzösische Stück, die fein / artlich und lieblich Collerirt, mit sunderm fleys verfast, und / zusamen gebracht, durch mich Hansen Newsidler / Lutennisten und Burger zu Nürnberg, / offentlich aussgangen, im M. D. XLIIII. Jar. / Mit Römischer Kay. und König. May. freyheyt, / inn Fünff Jaren, nicht nach zu drücken / begnadet.

32 fols. German lute tablature. On fol. A1^v: table of contents. On fol. H3^v: instructions on performance (the same as in 1547_4), headed "Wie man die Lauten sol lernen ziehen." On fol. H4: advertisement for Newsidler's first two books (1536_6 and 1536_7), followed by the same notice as in 1540_1, headed "Von dem Creutzlein und pünctlein, wie man sie verstehen soll," followed by the colophon "Gedruckt zu Nürnberg bey Hans Günther, durch verlegung Hansen Newsidler Lutinisten. Anno M. D. xliiii. Jar." The advertisement and notice also appear in 1540_1. On fol. H4^v: the same cut of the neck of a lute with an explanation of the tablature as appears in 1536_6 (see there for concordances). See 1547_4 for a second, revised edition. All of the compositions are for solo lute.

Copy in: D:KA.

	fol.	
1	A2	*Das Erst Fundament auff die Lauten* = 1536_6, no. 2
	A2^v	*Die ander Regel am Fundament*
	A2^v	*Die drit Regel*
2	A3	*Hastu mich genummen* = 1540_1, no. 3
3	A3^v	*Unser köchin kan auss der massen kochen wol* = 1540_1, no. 2
4	A4	*Ein Niderlendisch tentzlein* [1] = 1547_4, no. 4
5	A4^v	*Entlaubet ist der walde* [2] = 1536_6, no. 8
6	B1	*Willig und trew an alle rew* (EDMR XX, no. 42: Georg Forster) = 1544_2, no. 12, and 1549_6, no. 9
7	B1^v	*Ein guter Hofftantz*
	B2	*Der hupff auff zum Hofftantz*
8	B2^v	*Wo gehnd die Bamberger Meidlein hin, wo gehns sie hin nach gras* = 1547_4, no. 8
	B3	*Der hupff auff*
9	B3^v	*Es wolt ein jeger jagen, wolt jagen vor dem holtz* [3] = 1547_4, no. 9
	B4	*Hupff auff*
10	B4^v	*Scaramella* (compare AmbG V, 134: Josquin des Prez)
11	C1	*Unser köchen kan auss der massen kochen wol* = 1540_1, no. 8
12	C1^v	*Ich klag den tag* [4] = 1540_1, no. 18: Stoltzer
13	C2	*Lieblich hat sich gesellet* = 1540_1, no. 17
14	C2^v	*Ich wais mir ain stoltze Mülnerin* = 1540_1, no. 6
	C3	*Hupff auff*
15	C3^v	*Der ziegler in der ave mit seiner hawen* = 1540_1, no. 7: "Der Ziegler in der hecken")
	C4	*Der hupff auff*
16	C4^v	*Der Nunnen tantz* [5] = 1540_1, no. 12
	D1	*Der hupff auff zum Nunnen tantz*
17	D1^v	*Der Zeiner tantz* = 1540_1, no. 11
	D2	*Der hupff auff*
18	D2^v	*Der petler tantz* [6] = 1540_1, no. 15
	D3	*Der hupff auff zum petler tantz*
19	D3^v	*Der hund, mir vor dem licht umbgat* = 1536_6, no. 26
20	D4	*Mein gmüd und plüt* = 1540_1, no. 21: Johann Wenck
21	D4^v	*In liebes prunst* (EDMR XX, no. 76)
22	E1	*Elslein liebstes Elslein mein* = 1536_6, no. 29: Senfl
23	E1^v	*Ein Meidleyn sagt mir freuntlich zu* (EDMR XX, no. 25: Malchinger or Senfl)
24	E2	*Nun grüss dich Gott mein truserlein* = 1540_1, no. 23: Sixt Dietrich
25	E2^v	*Ich het mir ein Annelein für genumen* = 1540_1, no. 13: Senfl
26	E3	*Es taget vor dem holtze* = 1540_1, no. 14
27	E3^v	*Nach willen dein nich dir allein* [7] (MosPH, p. 74: Hofhaimer) = 1547_4, no. 21
28	E4	*Ach lieb mit leid wie hast den bscheyd* = 1536_6, no. 31: Hofhaimer

29 E4^v *Auff erd lebt nit ein schönes weib* = 1540_1, no. 24

30 F1 *Ic seg adiu* [8] (compare BridgmE, p. 162, and LenN, p. [108]) = 1547_4, no. 28, and 1562_3, no. 63

31 F1^v *Du Fiensela* = 1540_1, no. 32: "Dont vient cela," Sermisy

32 F2^v *Je suis ami aux* (compare RISM 1502_2, no. 11: "Je suis amy du forier," Compère) = 1547_4, no. 30

33 F3 *Glori. armi [poss'io donne]* (EinIM III, no. 18: Verdelot)

34 F3^v *In te domine speravi* (CesF, p. 38: Josquin des Prez) = 1547_4, no. 31

35 F4^v *Languir Me fais* (AttainCK II, no. 12: Sermisy) = 1547_4, no. 32

36 G1 *Las sil Covent* (PubAPTM XXIII, no. 16: "Las s'il convient," Certon)

37 G1^v *Fons perte* (PubAPTM XXIII, no. 56: "Vous perdez temps," Sermisy) = 1547_4, no. 33

38 G2^v *O dulx Roueoir* (RISM 1540_{10}, no. 13: "O doulx reveoir," Godard) = 1547_4, no. 34

39 G3^v *En esperant [en ceste longue attente]* (RISM 1536_4, no. 12: Sermisy) = 1547_4, no. 35, and 1562_3, no. 58

40 G4^v *Dame de Beaulte* (PubAPTM XXIII, no. 43: Morel) = 1547_4, no. 36

41 H1^v *Mon petit Nose* (compare RISM 1520_3, fol. 29^v: "Mon petit cueur") = 1547_4, no. 37

42 H2 *Adieu amours de fons suis lus trop* (RISM 1529_4, no. 41: "Adieu amours de vous suys las trop") = 1547_4, no. 38

43 H2^v *Le departir* (ClemensO X, 3: Clemens non Papa) = 1547_4, no. 39

[1] Mod. ed. in DTO XVIII/37, p. 53; MolzHN, no. 1; MU IV, app., p. 11; and ZanG I, 5.
[2] Mod. ed. in DTO XXXVII/72, p. 95.
[3] Mod. ed. in MolzHN, no. 8.
[4] Mod. ed. in DTO XXXVII/72, p. 96.
[5] Mod. ed. of no. 16a in BruS I, no. 22.
[6] Mod. ed. in TapS, p. 24.
[7] Mod. ed. in DTO XXXVII/72, p. 85.
[8] Mod. ed. in MolzHN, no. 7.

1544_2

NEWSIDLER, HANS

Das Ander Buch. / Ein New künstlich Lautten Buch, für die anfa/henden Schuler, die aus rechtem grund und kunst nach der Tabulatur, gantz / leicht und ring zu lernen, durch ein leicht Exempel dieser pünbtlein [*sic*]. . . . ., / Wohin man mit einem yeden finger recht und ordenlich greiffen sol. Weyter / ist angezeygt, wie man die Tabulatur, auch die Mensur, und die gantz appli/cation, recht und grundtlich lernen und verstehn sol. Mit vil schönen liebli/chen stücken, Teutscher und Welischer tentz, auch vil artlicher guter Welischer / und Frantzösischer Stück, auch zwo schlacht, die vor Bafia und die / Frantzösisch, die seind mit allem fleys, mit lieblicher Colloratur / gemacht, die ein yeder zu seinem lust gebrauchen mag. / Durch mich Hansen Newsidler, Lutinisten und / Burger zu Nürnberg zusamen gebracht, / und offenlich aussgangen, im / D. M. XLIIII. Jar. / Mit Römischer Kay. und König. May. freyheyt / inn Fünff Jaren, nicht nach zu drücken / begnadet.

72 fols. German lute tablature. On fol. A2: the same printer's privilege as in 1536_6. On fol. A2^v: preface (same as in 1549_6) beginning "Dem Leser glück und heyl." Beginning on fol. A3^v: instructions for playing the lute, including some musical examples (nos. 1–4 below). On fol. S4: table of contents followed by the colophon: "Gedruckt zu Nürnberg bey Hans Günther, durch angebung und verlegung, Hansen Newsidler Lutinisten, Anno. M. D. XLIIII." On fol. S4^v: the same cut of the neck of a lute with an explanation of the tablature as appears in 1536_6 (see there for concordances). The compositions identified by the superior letter *a* (^{a}) are reprinted in DTO XVIII/37. The table of contents is given in MfMG III (1871), 210. See 1549_6 for a second revised edition. All of the compositions are for solo lute.

Copies in: D:KA, F:Pc (imperfect).

fol.

1 B3 *Mein fleiss und mü* = 1536_6, no. 1: Senfl

2 C3 *Die Erst Regel, und ist ein gering fundament der Lautten* = 1536_6, no. 2

C3^v *Die Ander Regel, und ist ein ander art*

C3^v *Die drit Regel und ist auch ein andere art*

3 C4 *Das klein fundament mit dem einigen pünctlein* = 1536_6, no. 3

C4^v *Die Ander Regel*

C4^v *Die drit regel*

4 D1 *Nun volgt ein anders fundament, dz vil kunstreycher ist, aber ein wenig schwerer dass dz erst* = 1536_6, no. 4

5 D3 *Ich klag den tag und alle stund*[a] (DTO XXXVII/72, p. 71: Stoltzer) = 1549_6, no. 6

6 D3^v *Mag ich unglück nit widerston*[1] (SenflW V, no. 13: Senfl)

7 D4 *Entlaubet ist der walde* = 1536_6, no. 8: Stoltzer

8 D4^v *Nach vilen deim* = 1536_6, no. 12: Hofhaimer

9 E1 *Von Edler art ein frewlen zart* = 1536_6, no. 13: Schönfelder or Hofhaimer

10 E1^v *Ein guter artlicher hoff tantz* (compare 1549_6, no. 24)

E2^v *Der hupff auff zum hoff tantz*

11 E3 *Artlich und schön gantz wol gestalt*[2] (EDMR XX, no. 23: Casparus Bohemus) = 1549_6, no. 8

12 E3^v *Willig und trew ich mich ergib* = 1544_1, no. 6: Georg Forster

13 E4 *Fraw ich bin euch von hertzen holdt* (SenflW VI, no. 16: Senfl or Gregor Peschin)

14 E4^v *Gesell, wis urlaub saumb dich nit umb ein trit* (EDMR XX, no. 20: Matthias Eckel)

15 F1 *Ich schwüng mein horn*[3] (SenflW V, no. 44: Senfl) = 1549_6, no. 10

16 F1^v *Kumbt her ir lieben gesellen, wir haben ein gans*

17 F2^v *Gentil galans [compaignons du resin]* (BrownTC, no. 24)

18 F3 *Lautre Jour Janes* (MMRF V, no. 2: "L'autre jour jouer m'aloie," Conseil)

19 F3^v *Je suis damour deschredite* (CM II, 5: "D'amours je suis desheritée")

20 F4 *Feme du Bien*

21 F4^v *[Der Polnisch Tantz]*[a 4]

G1 *Der hupff auff*

22 G1^v *Der recht alt Hoff Tantz* = 1549_6, no. 23

G2^v *Der hupff auff zum hoff tantz*

23 G3 *Ein Welisch tentzlein clira Cassa*[a 5] ["Cara cossa gagliarda"]

24 G3^v *Hie volget der Hofftantz noch ein mal, auff ein andre art im abzug* = 1536_6, no. 68

G4^v *Der hupff auff*

25 H1 *Ein Welischer tantz*[a 6]

26 H1^v *Ein ander Welischer Tantz*[a]

H2 *Der hupff auff zum tantz*

27 H2^v *Ein gut Welisch tentzlein*[a]

28 H3 *Ameur vault trop* (AttainCK III, no. 5: "Amour vault trop")

29 H3^v *Ein Welischer tantz* [Der Künigin Tantz][a 7]

H4 *Der Hupff auff*

30 H4^v *Lodesana ein Welische tantz* = 1540_1, no. 29

31 J1 *Passa mesa. Ein Welischer tantz* = 1540_1, no. 30

32 J2 *Sula Bataglia*[a]

J3 *Der hupff auff*

33 J4 *Ein guter Welischer tantz*

J4^v *Der hupff auff*

34 K1 *Son Tornato Diolosa*

35 K1^v *Du Wentzela* = 1540_1, no. 32: "Dont vient cela," Sermisy

36 K2^v *Si par son fre* (RISM 1529_4, fol. 7^v: "Si par souffrir") = 1549_6, no. 57

37 K3 *Le vray amor* (RISM 1538_{10}, no. 7: "Le vray amy," Sermisy)

38 K3^v *Ami son fre* = 1540_1, no. 31: "Ami sofre," Moulu

39 K4 *O seul Espoir*[8]

40 K4^v *Testa grant* = 1540_1, no. 33: "Cest a grand [tort]," Sermisy

41 L1^v *Cest faschaux* (AttainCK II, no. 25)

42 L2^v *Lamar Narite* (compare KosackL, p. 99: "La Marguaritt") = 1549_6, no. 52

43 L3^v *Ic sege adiu* (LenN, p. [108]) = 1547_4, no. 29

44 L4ᵛ *Benedetur Welisch*
45 M1ᵛ *Ha quel tourment* (RISM 1540₁₀, no. 16: Godard)
46 M2ᵛ *Disantal*
47 M3ᵛ *Naur acorgete* (RISM 1541₉, p. 24: "Non v'accorgete," Arcadelt)
48 M4ᵛ *Henneur sons plus* (CW XV, no. 8: "Honneur sans plus," Lupus)
49 N1ᵛ *Folpechi* = 1549₆, no. 40
50 N2ᵛ *Petit*
51 N3ᵛ *Hec est dies quam fecit dominus* Archadelt (RISM 1539₁₂, p. 29)
52 N4ᵛ *Hie volget die Schlacht vor Bafia. Der erst Teyl* (MMRF VII, 31: Janequin) = 1549₆, no. 64
O2ᵛ 2a pars [*Fan frere le le lan fan*]
53 P2ᵛ *Nun volget Lalafete*[a] (MMRF VII, 105: "Le chant de l'Alouette," Janequin)
54 Q1 *Hie volget die Frantzösisch Schlacht die heist Singnori*[a]
Q4ᵛ 2a pars
R2ᵛ 3a pars
55 R4ᵛ *Hie volget der Juden Tantz*[a 9]
S1 *Der huff auff*
56 S1ᵛ *Ein guter gassenhauer auff die Welisch art*[a 10]
S2ᵛ *Der hupff auff*
57 S3ᵛ *Preambel* = 1536₆, no. 62

[1] Mod. ed. in MolzHN, no. 15.
[2] Heading on fol. E3: "Hie nach volgen, guter Newer stücklen 10. Teutsch und Frantzösisch, die aus rechten grund und kunst, mit den pünctlen ausspunctirt seind, wie man mit einem yeden finger recht und ordenlich greyffen soll."
[3] Mod. ed. in SenflW VII, no. 49a (after 1549₆, no. 10).
[4] Heading on fol. F4ᵛ: "Nun volgen etlich tentz Welisch und Teutsch."
[5] Mod. ed. in ZanG I, 17.
[6] Heading on fol. H1: "Nun volgen etlich Welisch Tentz." Mod. ed. in ZanG I, 18.
[7] Mod. ed. in MolzHN, no. 12 (as "Im abzug ein gutter tantz"), and ZanG II, 7.
[8] Not related musically to RISM 1540₁₃, no. 11: "Mon seul espoir," Maillard.
[9] Mod. ed. in ApelM I, 10, and HAM, no. 105b. Facs. of fols. R4ᵛ and S1 in ApelN, facs. 22 (incorrectly dated 1536). Mod. ed. and discussion of Apel's transcription in MorrA.
[10] Mod. ed. of no. 56a only in BruS I, no. 35; mod. ed. of no. 56b only in TapS, p. 21; mod. ed. of both in ZanG II, 18.

1544₃

NEWSIDLER, HANS

Das Dritt Buch. / Ein New künstlich Lauten Buch, darin vil treff/licher grosser Maisterlichen kunst stück, vom Psalmen, und Muteten, ein auss/geklaubter kern, die in dieser zeyt die berumbtisten Stück sind, und vor / der keins nye in druck kumen, aber itzo durch mich Hansen Newsi/dler Lutenisten und Burger zu Nürmberg, mit allem fleiss / zusamen gebracht, und offentlich / aussgangen. / Mit Römischer Kay. und Künigk. May. freyheyt, / in Fünff Jarn nit nach zudrucken, Erst hewr / auff ein Newes begnadet. / M. D. XLIIII Jar.

48 fols. German lute tablature. On fols. A1ᵛ–A2: the same printer's privilege as in 1536₆. On fols. A2ᵛ–A3: the same preface headed "Dem Leser Glück und heyl" as in 1536₇. On fol. M4: table of contents followed by the colophon: "Gedruckt zu Nürmberg bey Hans Günther, durch angebung und verlegung Hansen Newsidler Lutinisten, Bürtig von Presspurck, yetzt Burger und Lutenist zu Nürnberg. Anno M. DXLIIII. Jar." On fol. M4ᵛ: the same cut of the neck of a lute as appears in 1536₆ (see there for concordances). All of the compositions are for solo lute.

Copies in: D:Ngm, D:Usche.

fol.
1 A3ᵛ *Dilexi quoniam* (I:BGid, MS 1209, no. 51: Hieronim[o] Maff[onio])
B1 2a pars [*O domine libera animam meam*]
2 B2ᵛ *Beatus vir*
C1 2a pars
3 C2ᵛ *Beati omnes. Der Erste Teyl*
C4ᵛ 2a pars
4 D2ᵛ *Bonitatem fecisti. Der Erste teyl* (RISM 1514₁, no. 3: Carpentras)
E3 2a pars [*Manus tue Domine*]
5 F3ᵛ *Domine ne in furore tuo. Der Erste Teyl*
G4ᵛ 2a pars
6 H2 *Jerusalem luge. Der Erste Teyl* (RISM 1532₉, p. 49: Richafort [or Lupus?])
H4ᵛ 2a pars [*Deduc quasi torrente*]
7 J3ᵛ *Vita in ligno. Der Erste teyl* (RISM 1537₁, no. 20: Senfl)

K2 2a pars [*Qui prophetice*]
K4 3a pars [*Qui expansis*]
8 $L1^v$ *Verbum Iniquum. Der Erste Teyl* (MoralesO II, 122: Morales)
L4 2a pars [*Duo rogavi te*]
9 M3 *Tristicia vestra* (RISM 1541_2, no. 24: Isaac)

1545_1

AGRICOLA, MARTIN

Musica In/strumentalis Deudsch, / darin das fundament / und application der finger und zungen, / auff mancherley Pfeiffen, als Flöten, / Kromphörner, Zincken, Bomhard, Schal/meyen, Sackpfeiffen und Schweitzerpfeif/fen, etc. Darzu von dreierley Geigen, als / Welschen, Polisschen, und kleinen hand/geiglein, und wie die griffe drauff, auch / auff Lauten künstlich abgemessen wer/den, Item vom Monochordo, auch von / Künstlicher stimmung der Orgelpfeiffen, / und zimbeln, etc. kürtzlich begriffen, / und für unser Schulkinder und / andere gmeine Senger, auffs / verstendlichst und ein/feltigst, itzund new/lich zugericht, / Durch / Martinum Agricolam. / Anno Domini, 1545.

83 fols, plus two inserted tables. On fol. $A1^v$ (= fol. 1^v): Cut of lady playing lute with other instruments in background, entitled "Fraw Musica." On fol. 2: dedication "Dem ersamen und weysen herrn Georgio Rhaw, Buchdrücker, vorweser und fürderer der edlen fraw Musices, zu Wittemberg, meinem grossgönstigen lieben herrn und Patron, wündsch ich Martinus Shor odder Agricola, Gnad und fried von Gott," and "Vorrhede" signed (on fol. 6): "Anno Domini, 1545. Um 14. tage Aprilis. Mart. Agricola." The preface is reprinted in RothB, p. 120. Colophon on fol. 83: "Gedruckt zu Wittemberg durch Georgen Rhaw, Anno M. D. XLv." This is a completely revised edition of 1529_1. Agricola does not include any complete compositions among his musical examples. PubAPTM XX is a quasi-facsimile of this volume.

Copies in: D:As, D:Bds-Tü, D:DS, D:G, D:HVl, D:LEm, D:W, GB:Gu, GB: Lbm, NL:DHgm.

1545_2

LICINO, AGOSTINO

AGOSTIN LICINO / PRIMO LIBRO DI DUO CROMATICI DI AGOSTINO / LICINO CREMONESE DA CANTARE ET SONARE / Composti una parte sopra laltra con la sua resolutione da parte / Novamente posti in luce / A DUE [Printer's mark] VOCI / Venetiis Apud Antonium Gardane. / M. D. XXXXV.

Two part books in mensural notation, each of 20 fols. (?). Fol. $A1^v$ = p. 1. For a second volume in the same series see 1546_{12}. All of the compositions in the volume are canons *a 2* without text. Contents = 1586_1.

Copy in: D:Mbs (S).

p.
1 1 *Duo. Canon. In diapente superius, Primi Toni*
2 3 *Duo. Canon. Ad semiditonum superius, Primi Toni*
3 5 *Duo. Canon. In diapente superius, Primi Toni*
4 7 *Duo. Canon. In diapente superius, Primi Toni*
5 9 *Duo. Canon. Ad ditonum inferius, Primi Toni*
6 11 *Duo. Canon. In diapente superius, Secundi Toni*
7 13 *Duo. Canon. In diapente superius, Secundi Toni*
8 15 *Duo. Canon. In diapente superius, Secundi Toni*
9 17 *Duo. Canon. In diapente inferius, Secundi Toni*
10 19 *Duo. Canon. In diatesaron superius, Secundi Toni*
11 21 *Duo. Canon. Ad eptachordum superius, Tertii Toni*
12 23 *Duo. Canon. Ad semiditonum superius, Tertii Toni*
13 25 *Duo. Canon. In diapente superius, Tertii Toni*
14 27 *Duo. Canon. In diapente superius, Tertii Toni*
15 29 *Duo. Canon. In diapente superius, Tertii Toni*
16 31 *Duo. Canon. In diapente superius, Quarti Toni*
17 33 *Duo. Canon. In diapente superius, Quarti Toni*

18 35 *Duo. Canon. In diapente inferius, Quarti Toni*
19 37 *Duo. Canon. In diapente inferius, Quarti Toni*
20 39 *Duo. Canon. In diapente superius, Quarti Toni*

1545_3

PHALÈSE, PIERRE, PUBLISHER

DES CHANSONS RE/duictz en Tabulature de Lut à deux, / TROIS, ET QUATRE PARTIES. / Avecq une briefve & familiare Introduction pour entendre & apprendre par soy / mesmes à jouer dudict Lut. Livre premier. / [Cut of a lute] / Tout nouvellement Imprime / A LOUVAIN / PAR JACQUES BATHEN ET REYNIER VELPEN. / AUX DESPENS DE PIERRE PHALEYS LI/BRAIRE. Lan de Grace M. D. XLV.

48 fols. French lute tablature. On fol. A1^v: preface headed "AU BENING LECTEUR," and dated "De Louvain le 22. de Septembre. Lan 1545." Beginning on fol. A2: instructions for playing the lute.[1] Fol. B1 = p. 1. Some of the pages are incorrectly numbered; in the inventory below the numbers are corrected without comment. SlimK II, 479, contains a thematic index of the abstract pieces. The collection was reprinted in a second, revised edition (1547_7 and 1547_8) and in a third edition (1549_8); all copies of another edition ($[1575]_6$) have been lost.[2] All of the compositions are for solo lute.

Copy in: F:B.[3]

p.
1 1 *Primum Fundamentum* = 1536_6, no. 2
2 2 *Praeludium* = 1575_3, no. 1
3 3 *Praeludium*
4 3 *Aliud Praeludium* = 1533_1, no. 3
5 4 *Fundamentum*
6 6 *Praeludium*
7 7 *Fantasia*
8 8 *Benedictus Isaac*[4]
9 10 *Fantasia* = 1546_{18}, no. 11
10 11 *Fantasia*
11 12 *Fantasia* = 1508_2, no. 7
12 13 *Praeludium*
13 14 *Fantasia*
14 16 *Praeludium*
15 17 *Die Lustelycke Mey* (compare RISM 1572_{11}, no. 25: Clemens non Papa, and DuyL I, 356)
16 18 *Jay mis mon cueur* (AttainCK III, no. 16)
17 19 *Damours ie suis desherite* = 1529_3, no. 35
18 20 *Amour vault trop* = 1529_3, no. 21a
19 21 *Dolent depart* = 1529_3, no. 18a
20 22 *Ces facheux sotz* (AttainCK II, no. 25)
21 23 *Il me souffit* (another version of no. 35 below) = 1529_3, no. 24a: Sermisy
22 24 *Cest grand plaisir* (AttainCK I, no. 17)
23 25 *Dont vient cela* (AttainCK III, no. 22: Sermisy) = 1563_{12}, no. 110
24 26 *Le cueur est bon* (RISM 1531_2, no. 34)
25 27 *Tous mes amis* (RISM $[c. 1528]_5$, no. 4: Sermisy)
26 28 *Languir mi fault* (AttainCK II, no. 12: "Languir me fais," Sermisy; another version of no. 29 below)
27 29 *Amis souffrez* (AttainCK III, no. 7: Moulu)
28 30 *Een vrolic vvesen* (DTO XIV/28, p. 5, and 1538_2, no. 28: Barbireau, Isaac, or Obrecht)
29 32 *Aliud languir* (another version of no. 26 above) = 1552_{11}, no. 34
30 33 *Tant que vivray* (another version of no. 45 below) = 1529_3, no. 33a: Sermisy
31 34 *Cest donc par moy* (RISM 1541_{13}, no. 60)
32 36 *Du bon du cueur*
33 38 *Myn hert heeft altyt verlangen* = 1533_1, no. 17
34 40 *Miins liefkens bruyn oogen* (compare VNM XXX, 6: Susato, and LenN, p. 70)
35 42 *Il me souffit* (AttainCK I, no. 9: Sermisy; another version of no. 21 above)
36 43 *Helas amy* (RISM 1541_8, fol. 4: Sandrin)
37 44 *Aupres de vous* [*secretement*] (AttainCK I, no. 16)

38 46 *Ung gay bergier* (RieH II, 462: Crecquillon) = 1552_{11}, no. 33; 1563_{12}, no. 45; 1568_7, no. 39a
39 48 *Damour me plains. Ad descensum* (PubAPTM XXIII, no. 49: Roger Pathie)
40 50 *Le content est riche* (AttainCK III, no. 9: Sermisy)
41 52 *Plourez mes yeulx* (RISM 1540_{13}, no. 22: Sandrin) = 1574_7, no. 28
42 53 *Jamays naymeray masson* (RISM 1520_6, fol. 6[v]) = 1563_{12}, no. 100
43 54 *Pour ung petit coup*
44 56 *Sur tous regres* (PubAPTM II, no. 78: Richafort)
45 58 *Tant que vivray* (AttainCK II, no. 10: Sermisy; another version of no. 30 above) = 1563_{12}, no. 98
46 60 *Vous perdez temps* (PubAPTM XXIII, no. 56: Sermisy)
47 62 *Je prens en gre la dure mort* (ClemensO X, 14: Clemens non Papa)
48 64 *Or sus a coup* (RISM 1570_8, p. 39)
49 65 *La fiellette* (LesAC, no. 10: "Il estoit une fillette," Janequin)
50 66 *La Bataille. Pars Prima* (MMRF VII, 31: Janequin) = 1546_{18}, no. 55
70 2a pars [*Fan frere le le lan fan*]
51 76 *La Traditora*
52 78 *Galliarde*
53 79 *Gallairde* [sic]
54 80 *Galliarde*
55 81 *Paduana*
56 82 *Paduana* = 1546_{20}, no. 24
57 83 *Paduana*
58 84 *Paduana* = 1546_{20}, no. 21, and 1563_{12}, no. 127
59 85 *Ronde*
60 86 *Ronde*
61 86 *Tripla*

[1] On fol. A2: "BREFVE INTRODUCTION POUR APPRENDRE DE SOY mesme lart & usance du Lutz." On fol. A3: "POUR SCAVOIR TROUVER LES TONS." On fol. A3[v]: "SENSUIT DU TEMPS OU DES MESURES ET PAUSES." On fol. A4[v]: "POUR SCAVOIR METTRE LES DOITZ." On fol. A4[v]: "POUR SCAVOIR TENDRE ET ACCORDER LES CORDES." A Latin version of these instructions is pr. in 1549_8.

[2] The following volumes in the "Des Chansons" series published by Phalèse can be traced: vol. I: 1543_8, 1547_7, 1547_8, 1549_8, $[1575]_6$, II. 1546_{18}, 1546_{19}; III: 1547_9, 1547_{10}, 1573_5; IV: 1546_{20}, 1573_8; V: $[1547]_{11}$, $[1547]_{12}$.

[3] In the unique copy there is some manuscript music without title in French lute tablature on p. 55.

[4] Not related musically to HewO, no. 76: "Benedictus," Isaac.

1546_1

ABONDANTE, JULIO

INTABOLATURA / DI JULIO ABONDANTE / SOPRA EL LAUTO DE OGNI SORTE DE BALLI / NOVAMENTE STAMPATI ET POSTI IN LUCE / LIBRO PRIMO / INTABOLATURA [Cut of a lion and a bear standing on their hind legs facing each other, and holding between them an open rose, in which is a fleur-de-lis, with the motto CONCORDES VIRTUTE ET NATURAE MIRACULIS and the initials A. G.] DE LAUTO / IN VENETIA Apresso di / Antonio Gardane. / M. D. XXXXVI. / CON GRATIA ET PRIVILEGGIO

20 fols. Italian lute tablature. On fol. E4[v]: table of contents. MoeDM contains concordances with similar (but not identical) settings (p. 226) and a thematic index of the entire volume (p. 361). Modern editions of the compositions identified by the superior letter *a* ([a]) are to be found in MoeDM. For further information see EitGA. Contents = 1563_1 (see there for a modern edition of the entire collection). All of the compositions are for solo lute.

Copy in: A:Wn.[1]

fol.
1 A1[v] *Pass'e mezo* [*moderno*]
2 A2[v] *Venetiana gagliarda* (compare 1561_2, no. 12: "La Barcha del mio amor")
3 A3 *El Traditor gagliarda*
4 A3[v] *La Meza notte* [*gagliarda*][a]
5 A4 *El Ciel turchin gagliarda* (compare RISM 1563_6, p. 41: "O Maria Diana Stella")
6 A4[v] *L Herba fresca* [*gagliarda*][a] (compare I:Vnm, MS It. Cl. IV, 1795–1798, II, p. 1: "La via de la fiuma")

7 B1 *El Poverin*[a]
8 B1v *El Pass'e mezo [antico]*[a]
9 B2v *La Traditora*
10 B3v *El Pichardo gagliarda*
11 B4v *Pass'e mezo [moderno]*
12 C1 *La Poverina*
13 C1v *La Chara cossa gagliarda*
14 C2v *El Todesco gagliarda*
15 C3 *Bel fior gagliarda*
16 C3v *La Fornerina gagliarda*
17 C4 *La Inspirita gagliarda*
18 C4v *La Comadrina gagliarda*
19 D1 *Zorzi gagliarda*[a] (compare AzzaiV, no. 8: "Occhio non fu," Azzaiolo)
20 D1v *Quadrelin gagliarda*[a]
21 D2v *La Gasparina gagliarda*
22 D3 *El Burato gagliarda*[a]
23 D3v *La Canella gagliarda*
24 D4 *Corneto gagliarda*
25 D4v *Tu te parti cor mio charo* (compare AzzaiV, no. 12: "Ti parti, cor mio caro," Azzaiolo)
26 E1 *La Ben contenta [pavana]*
27 E1v *L Herba fresca gagliarda*
28 E2 *La Ferarese gagliarda*
29 E2v *Pass'e mezo [antico]*
30 E3 *Gagliarda del dito pass'e mezo*
31 E3v *La Disperata*
32 E4 *Le Forze di Erchole [pavana]*

[1] A copy was in PL:S. EitQ I, 32, erroneously dates this volume 1536.

1546_2

BARBERIIS, MELCHIORE DE

INTABULATURA / DI LAUTO / LIBRO QUARTO / DE LA MESSA DI ANTONIO FEVINO. SOPRA AVE MARIA / Intabulata & accomodata per sonare sopra il Lautto dal Reverendo messer pre / MARCHIORE de barberiis da Padova sonatore eccellentissimo de Lautto, da / lui proprio nuovamente à utilità di virtuosi posta in luce, / con alcuni altri suoi recercari accomodati so/pra il tuono di ditta messa. / Agiontovi il nuovo modo di accordare il Lautto posto in fine. / Con gratia & privilegio. / VENETIA M D XLVI

24 fols. Italian lute tablature. On fol. 1v: dedication "AL REVERENDISSIMO MONSIGNOR M. FRANCESCO Pisani Cardinale di san Marco pre Merchiore Padoano." On fol. 23v: instructions for playing the lute headed "Per dechiarare a quelli che non hanno musicha, & etiam hanno pocca pratica nel sonar de Liuto io li mostrerò qui disotto per ragione, et per pratica," with one musical example on fol. 24, "Tastar daspoi acordato." The same instructions appear in 1546_3 and 1546_4. On fol. 24v: table of contents. SlimK II, 483, contains a thematic index of the ricercares. All of the compositions are for solo lute.[1]

Copy in: GB:Lbm.[2]

fol.
1 2 *La messa di Antonio fevino intitulata Ave maria* (RISM 1516_1: Missa no. 3, Févin)
2 *Chirie*
2v *Christe*
3v *Chirie*
4 *Domine deus in duo*
4v *Et in terra pax*
5v *Qui tolis peccata mundi*
7 *patrem omnipotentem*
8v *Et incarnatus est*
9 *Crucifixus*
9v *Et rexurexit*
10v *Et iterum venturus est*
11 *Et in spiritum sanctum*
12v *Sanctus*
13 *pleni sunt celi in duo*
13v *Osana*
14 *Benedictus qui venit*
15 *Agnus dei*
16 *Agnus dei*
2 17 *Qui tollis peccata* Richafort
3 17v *Benedictus qui venit*
4 18v *Agnus dei* lupus
5 19 *Agnus dei* lehortur [Heurteur or L'Héritier]
6 19v *Duo*
7 20v *Fantasia*
8 21 *Fantasia*
9 22 *Crucifizus in duo* Carpentias [Carpentras]
10 22v *Fantasia*

[1] Five volumes of lute music composed and arranged by Barberiis survive. These five volumes probably formed part of a series published between 1546 and 1549, presumably all by Girolamo Scotto (see MoeDM, p. 8). This series comprises the

following collections: vol. I: Antonio Rotta (1546_{15}); II: Francesco da Milano and Borrono (1546_8); III: Joan Maria da Crema (1546_{11}); IV, V, and VI: Barberiis (1546_2, 1546_3, 1546_4); VII: Francesco da Milano (1548_4); VIII: Borrono (1548_2); IX and X: Barberiis (1549_1, and 1549_2).

[2] A copy was in D:Bds (formerly in D:W).

1546_3

BARBERIIS, MELCHIORE DE

INTABULATURA / DI LAUTTO / LIBRO QUINTO. / DE MADRIGALI, ET CANZON FRANCESE INTABULATI / & accomodati per sonare sopra il Lautto dal Reverendo messer pre MERCHIORE / de barberiis da Padova sonatore eccellentissimo di Lautto da lui proprio / nuovamente à utilità di virtuosi posta in luce. / Agiontovi il nuovo modo di accordare il Lautto posto in fine. / Con gratia & privilegio. / VENETIA M D XLVI

28 fols. Italian lute tablature. Dedication on fol. 1ᵛ headed "ALL'ECCELENTISSIMO DOTTORE M. MARCANTONIO da genova Philosopho Padoano," and signed "Di V. E. Pre Merchiore Padoano." On fol. 27: the same instructions for playing the lute that appear in 1546_2. On fol. 28: table of contents. For other volumes in the same series, see 1546_2, note 1. SlimK II, 484, contains a thematic index of the ricercares. All of the compositions are for solo lute.

Copy in: D:LEm.

	fol.	
1	2	*Si Roi Regret mi complans. Canzon francese* (RISM 1530_5, fol. 4: "Si je regrette et my complains")
2	2ᵛ	*De vos sechur* (RISM 1533_1, no. 1 [= 1533_3 above]: "De vous servir," Sermisy)
3	3ᵛ	*Canzun francese*
4	4	*A bien gran tort* (RISM [c. 1528]$_7$, no. 9)
5	5	*Contra rasun* (AttainCK II, no. 5: "Contre raison," Sermisy)
6	6	*O sio potesse donna* (RISM 1541_9, p. 19: Giachet Berchem)
7	7	*Amor non vede* (RISM 1541_{15}, no. 2: Maître Jan)
8	8	*Canzun Iatens secors* (AttainCK II, no. 11: Sermisy)
9	9	*Canzon francese*
10	9ᵛ	*Fantasia*
11	11	*Fantasia*
12	12	*Fantasia*
13	13ᵛ	*Fantasia*
14	14ᵛ	*Con lacrime & sospiri* (EinIM III, 319: Verdelot)
15	15	*Madonna io sol vorei* (RISM 1537_9, no. 5: Andreas de Silva [Verdelot?])
16	16	*Vitta de la mia vitta* (RISM 1537_9, no. 25: Verdelot)
17	16ᵛ	*Madonna qual certezza* (EinIM III, 21; Verdelot)
18	18	*Si suave*
19	18ᵛ	*Madonna mi consumo* (I:Fc, MS Basevi 2440, no. 33)
20	19ᵛ	*Altro non é el mio amore* (RISM 1534_{15}, fol. 14ᵛ: C. Festa)
21	20ᵛ	*Veramente madonna*
22	22	*Quando vostri belli occhi*
23	23	*Perche bramo morire*
24	24	*A l'umbra al caldo al gello* (I:Vnm, MSS It. Cl. IV. 1795–1798, no. 70)
25	24ᵛ	*La dolce umbra*
26	25ᵛ	*Celis asamplus* (CH:Bu, MSS F.X. 1–4, no. 87: "Cela sans plus," Pope Leo X)

1546_4

BARBERIIS, MELCHIORE DE

INTABULATURA / DI LAUTTO / LIBRO SESTO /DI DIVERSI MOTETTI A QUATTRO VOCE, INTABULATI, / & accomodati per sonare sopra il Lautto dal Reverendo messer pre MERCHIORE / de barberiis da Padova sonatore eccellentissimo di Lautto da lui proprio / nuovamente à utilità di virtuosi posta in luce. / Agiontovi il nuovo modo di accordare il Lautto posto in fine. / Con gratia & privilegio. / VENETIA M D XLVI

32 fols. Italian lute tablature. On fol. Aa1ᵛ: dedication "ALL'ECCELLENTISSIMO DOTTORE M. MARCO MANTOA JURISCONSULATO PADOANO." On fol. 30ᵛ: the same instructions for playing

the lute that appear in 1546_2. On fol. 31v: table of contents. For other volumes in the same series, see 1546_2, note 1. All of the compositions are for solo lute.

Copy in: D:W.

	fol.	
1	2	*Beati omnes qui timet* (RISM 1539_6, p. 21: Gombert)
2	5	*Ave Ancilla trinitatis* (RISM 1520_1, no. 1: Andreas de Silva)
	7	2a pars [*Ave cuius conceptio*]
3	9	*Ave virgo singularis* [La] fage
4	11v	*Postquam consumati sunt* Lupus (RISM 1519_1, no. 5)
5	13	*Salve regina* Jusquino (JosqMS, no. 48)
6	15	*Domine quis habitabit in tabernaculo tuo* (RISM 1532_{10}, p. 50: Jo. Courtois)
7	16v	*Michael arcangelle* Jacotin (RISM 1519_1, no. 6)
	18v	2a pars [*In conspectu angelorum*]
8	20	*Inter natos mulierum* (RISM 1532_{10}, p. 53: F. de Layolle)
	21	2a pars [*Fuit homo missus a deo*]
9	22	*Dignare me laudare te* (GombertO V, 93: Gombert)
	23	2a pars [*O regina poli*]
10	24v	*Elisabet Zacharie* (RISM 1519_1, no. 24: Lafage)
	26	2a pars [*Inter natos mulierum*]
11	27v	*Super flumina babilonis* Gombert (HAM, no. 114)

1546_5

BIANCHINI, DOMINICO

INTABOLATURA / DE LAUTO / DI DOMINICO BIANCHINI / DITTO ROSSETTO DI RECERCARI MOTETTI / MADRIGALI CANZON FRANCESE NAPOLITANE / ET BALLI NOVAMENTE STAMPATI / LIBRO [Cut with the printer's mark of Antonio Gardane] PRIMO / IN VENETIA Apresso di / Antonio Gardane / M. D. XXXXVI.

20 fols. Italian lute tablature. On fol. A1v: dedication "DOMINICO BIANCHINI DITTO ROSSETTO A LI SIGNORI MARCADANTI DI FONTEGO ALLEMANI." On fol. E4v: table of contents. MoeDM contains concordances for the dances (p. 235) and a thematic index of the dances (p. 367). Some of the compositions were probably reprinted in $[1547]_{11}$ (see there for details). SlimK II, 485, contains a thematic index of the ricercares. For further information see MorcouB. The compositions identified by the superior letter *a* ([a]) are reprinted in ChilLI. Contents = 1554_2 and 1563_2. All of the compositions are for solo lute.

Copies in: D:Ngm, GB:Lbm, US:Wc.[1]

	fol.	
1	A2	*Recercar primo*[a] = 1552_1, no. 9
2	A2v	*Recercar segondo*
3	A3v	*Recercar terzo*[a] = 1552_1, no. 11
4	A4	*Recercar quarto*
5	B1	*Con lei fuss'io* (RISM 1543_{17}, p. 36: Arcadelt, Berchem, Corteccia, or Giaches de Ponte)
6	B1v	*Aupres de vous* [*secretement*] (AttainCK I, no. 16: Sermisy or Jacotin)
7	B2v	*Madonna io non lo so* [*napolitane*] (CW VIII, 18: Willaert)
8	B3	*Pass'e mezo* [*antico*][a2] = 1552_1, no. 32a
	B3v	*La sua padoana*[a3] = 1552_1, no. 32b
	B3v	*Il suo saltarello*[a] = 1552_1, no. 32c
9	B4	*Le forze derculle* [passamezzo antico] = 1552_1, no. 33
10	B4v	*Lodesana*[4] = 1552_1, no. 34
11	C1	*Meza notte* = 1552_1, no. 35
12	C1v	*La cara cossa*[a] = 1552_1, no. 36
13	C2	*El Burato*[5] = 1552_1, no. 37
14	C2v	*Ave santissima* (GombertO V, 77: Gombert) = 1547_9, no. 15
15	D1	*Santo erculano*[a 6]
16	D1v	*Cest grand pitie* (SeayFC, p. 8: Certon)
17	D2	*Recercar*[7] = 1552_1, no. 10
18	D2v	*Il me suffit*[8] (AttainCK I, no. 9: Sermisy)
19	D3	*Par ton regard* (RISM 1530_4, fol. 3v: Sermisy)
20	D3v	*Le dur travail* (RISM 1544_{12}, fol. 12: Willaert)
21	D4v	*Recercar*[9]
22	E1	*Torza* [*saltarello*][a]
23	E1v	*O s'io potessi donna* (RISM 1541_9, p. 19: Giachet Berchem)

24 E2^{v} *Tant que vivrai*[a][10] (AttainCK II, no. 10: Sermisy)

25 E3^{v} *Pongente dardo* (RISM 1541_9, p. 3: Giachet Berchem)

[1] A copy was in PL:S, and in the Wolffheim library (see WolffC I, no. 1186). The Sorau copy, bound with various other tablatures pr. in 1546 and 1547 (see TischA), contained also 21 fols. of manuscript music in Italian lute tablature, beginning with instructions for learning tablature headed "Instructio tradens eiusmodi Tabellatura intelligentiam, quoad tactum Testudinis," in Polish and Latin. The following titles were included: Tocada, Ballo Pollacho, Gagliarda, Pass'e mezzo, Psalmus [Polish text], Corente Francese, Almane, Taniez, Praeambulum, and Final by Cavaliero maestro di Roma (see BoettB).

[2] Mod. ed. in WasG, no. 10 (after 1552_1).

[3] Mod. ed. in EitT, no. 39 (after 1552_1).

[4] Mod. ed. in MoeDM, p. 344.

[5] Mod. ed. in EitM, no. 38 (after 1552_1).

[6] Mod. ed. in MoeDM, p. 329.

[7] Mod. ed. in WasG, no. 7 (after 1552_1).

[8] Mod. ed. (along with vocal model) in MorcouB, p. 182.

[9] Mod. ed. in MorcouB, p. 193.

[10] Mod. ed. in ChilB VIII, no. 4; ChilCI, p. 70; EC, pt. I, vol. II, p. 649; and PujBG, no. 1069.

1546_6

FRANCESCO DA MILANO

INTABOLATURA / DE LAUTO / DI FRANCESCO DA MILANO / NOVAMENTE RISTAMPATA / LIBRO PRIMO / INTABOLATURA [Printer's mark] DE LAUTO / IN VENETIA Apresso di / Antonio Gardane / M. D. XXXXVI.

20 fols. Italian lute tablature. On fol. E4^{v}: table of contents. WieM II contains a thematic index of the entire volume. SlimK II, 489, contains a thematic index of the ricercares. Contents = 1556_3 and 1563_4 (which has some additions).[1] All of the compositions are for solo lute.

Copies in: A:Wn, CH:Lcortot, D:Ngm, GB:Lbm, US:Cn, US:NYp.[2]

fol.

1 A1^{v} *La canzon delli ucelli*[3] (MMRF VII, 1: "Le Chant des Oyseaux," beginning "Reveillez vous, cueurs endormis," Janequin) = 1546_8, no. 25; 1546_{18}, no. 54; 1550_4, no. 9

A2^{v} 2a pars [*Vous orrez a mon advis*]

A3^{v} 3a pars [*Rossignol du boys joli*]

B1 4a pars [*Arriere, maistre Cocu*]

2 B2^{v} *La bataglia francesa* = 1536_3, no. 34: Janequin

B4^{v} 2a pars [*Fan frere le le lan fan*]

3 C3^{v} *Hors envieulx retires vous* (EngL, p. 51: Gombert) = 1546_8, no. 19, and 1546_{18}, no. 49

4 C4^{v} *Martin menoit* Janequin (CM II, 79) = 1546_8, no. 24, and 1546_{18}, no. 53

5 D1^{v} *Fortune alors*[4] (RISM 1539_{15}, no. 2: Certon) = 1546_8, no. 22, and 1546_{18}, no. 50

6 D2 *Pour avoir paix* (RISM $[1539]_{20}$, fol. 2: F. de Layolle) = 1546_8, no. 18, and 1546_{18}, no. 29

7 D2^{v} *Sur toutes fleurs jayme la margarite* = 1546_8, no. 20, and 1546_{18}, no. 51

8 D3^{v} *Fantesia di F. da Milano*[5] = 1546_8, no. 15, and 1546_{20}, no. 2

9 D4 *Fantesia di F. da Milano* = 1546_8, no. 13

10 E1 *Fantesia di F. da Milano*[6] = 1546_8, no. 11; 1546_{20}, no. 3; 1568_1, no. 43

11 E2 *Fantesia di F. da Milano*[7] = 1546_8, no. 16; 1552_{11}, no. 7; 1563_{12}, no. 6; 1571_6, no. 33

12 E2^{v} *Pourtant si je suis brunette*[8] (CW LXI, no. 6: Sermisy) = 1546_8, no. 21, and 1546_{18}, no. 45

13 E3^{v} *Reveillez moy*[9] (PubAPTM XXIII, no. 23: Garnier) = 1546_8, no. 17; 1546_{18}, no. 48; 1568_1, no. 36

[1] PiciA, p. 197, lists under Francesco (da Milano): "Lib. I. Intavolatura di liuto. Venet. 1547," probably referring to this volume.

[2] A copy was in PL:S (see 1546_5, n. 1).

[3] Mod. ed. in ChilLS, p. 44 (after 1563_4), and ChilS, p. 37; prima pars only in BossiC, no. 1, and CorteA, no. 58 (after 1563_4); end of 3a pars in BruS IV, no. 132.

[4] Mod. ed. in ChilF, no. 3.

[5] Mod. ed. in BruAL I, no. 16; ChilF, no. 1; and ChilLI, p. 48.

[6] Mod. ed. in ChilF, no. 2; LefL (after 1568_1); and NeemAM I, no. 19.

[7] Mod. ed. in NeemAM I, no. 17.

[8] Mod. ed. in ChilCI, p. 67.

[9] Mod. ed. in ChilF, no. 4, and LefL (after 1568_1).

1546_7

FRANCESCO DA MILANO

INTABOLATURA / DE LAUTO / DI FRANCESCO DA MILANO / De motetti recercari & canzoni francese novamente ristampata. / LIBRO SEGONDO. / [Printer's mark] / In Venetia apresso di / Antonio Gardane. / M. D. XXXXVI.

20 fols. Italian lute tablature. On fol. E4^v: table of contents. WieM II contains a modern edition of the entire volume, as well as a thematic index. Contents = 1561_3 and 1563_5. All of the compositions are for solo lute.

Copies in: A:Wn, CH:Lcortot, D:Ngm, F:Pthibault,[1] GB:Lbm, US:Cn, US:Wc.

	fol.	
1	A1^v	*Pater noster di Jusquin a sei* = 1536_3, no. 32
	A4	[2a pars] *Ave Maria di Jusquin a sei*
2	B1^v	*Stabat mater di Jusquin a 5* = 1536_3, no. 33
3	B4	*Fantesia di F. da Milano* = 1536_3, no. 19
4	C2	*Fantesia di F. da Milano* = 1536_3, no. 1
5	C3	*Fantesia di F. da Milano* = 1536_3, no. 2
6	C4	*Fantesia di F. da Milano*[2] = 1536_3, no. 3
7	D1	*Fantesia di F. da Milano* = 1536_3, no. 5
8	D3	*Fantesia di F. da Milano* = 1536_3, no. 6
9	D4	*Fantesia di F. da Milano* = 1536_3, no. 7
10	D4^v	*Le plus gorgias du monde* = 1536_3, no. 21
11	E1^v	*Tu disois* = 1536_3, no. 23: Sermisy
12	E2^v	*Pourquoy alles vous seullette* = 1536_3, no. 31
13	E3^v	*Nous bergiers* = 1536_3, no. 25

[1] Mme. Thibault's copy was in the Écorcheville library (see ÉcorC, no. 246).

[2] Facs. of fols. C4 and C4^v and mod. ed. of no. 6 in GomRF, pp. 166 and 174.

1546_8

FRANCESCO DA MILANO AND PIETRO PAOLO BORRONO

INTABULATURA / DI LAUTO / DEL DIVINO FRANCESCO DA MILANO, / ET DELL'ECCELLENTE PIETRO PAULO / Borrono da Milano, nuovamente posta in luce, et con ogni / diligentia corretta, opera nuova, & perfettissima / sopra qualunche altra Intavolatura. / LIBRO SECONDO /VENETIIS M D XLVI.

50 fols. Italian lute tablature. On fol. 1^v: instructions for reading lute tablature headed "Regola per quelli che non sanno la Intavolatura," reprinted in HamC, p. 66. On fol. 50^v: table of contents. MoeDM contains a thematic index of the dances (p. 371) and concordances for them (p. 238). SlimK II, 486, contains a thematic index of the ricercares. WieM II contains a thematic index of the entire volume. Parts of this volume were reprinted in 1550_4. For other volumes in the same series, see 1546_2, note 1. The pavane and first saltarello of no. 6 are both supplied with a second lute part; they may be performed either by one or two lutes. All of the other compositions are for solo lute.

Copy in: S:Uu.

	fol.	
1	2	*Pavana detta la Borroncina dell'Eccellente P. Paulo Borrono da Milano*[1] = 1546_{20}, no. 7
	3^v	*Saltarello Primo* = 1546_{20}, no. 27: "Galiarda"
	4^v	*Saltarello secondo della Duchessa* = 1546_{20}, no. 28: "Galiarda"
	6^v	*Saltarello terzo detto la Barbarina* = 1546_{20}, no. 29: "Galiarda"
2	7	*Pavana novissima detta la Moniardina dell'Eccellente P. Paulo Borrono da Milano* = 1546_{20}, no. 9
	8	*Saltarello Primo*[2] = 1546_{20}, no. 30: "Galiarda"
3	8^v	*Pavana detta la rinoldina del- l'Eccellente P. Paulo Borrono* = 1546_{20}, no. 14
	9^v	*Saltarello Primo*

	11	*Saltarello secondo detto la mezza gamba*
	12ᵛ	*Saltarello terzo detto Madonna zanna* = 1546_{20}, no. 40: "Galiarda"
4	13ᵛ	*Pavana novissima detta la centoria dell'Eccellente P. Paulo Borrono da Milano* = 1546_{20}, no. 15
	14	*Saltarello Primo*
	14ᵛ	*Saltarello secondo novissimo detto el Scharavelino* [3]
5	15	*Pavana detta la Pianzolenta dell'Eccellente P. Paulo Borrono da Milano* = 1546_{20}, no. 13
	16ᵛ	*Saltarello Primo* = 1546_{20}, no. 37: "Galiarda"
	17ᵛ	*Saltarello secondo detto la rocha el fuso* = 1546_{20}, no. 38: "Galiarda"
	18ᵛ	*Saltarello terzo novissimo detto che le el martello che tel fa dire* [4] = 1546_{20}, no. 39: "Galiarda"
6	19ᵛ	*Pavana Milanesa dell'Eccellente P. Paulo Borrono da Milano* = 1546_{20}, no. 11
	20	*La detta Pavana a duy Lauti*
	20ᵛ	*Saltarello Primo* = 1546_{20}, no. 32: "Galiarda"
	21	*El detto saltarello a duy Lauti*
	21ᵛ	*Saltarello secondo novissimo detto non dite mai ch'io habbia il torto*
	22	*Saltarello terzo novissimo detto le pur bon o ruschina* = 1546_{20}, no. 33: "Galiarda"
7	22	*Pavana novissima detta la Bella Ugazzotta dell'Eccellente P. Paulo Borrono da Milano* = 1546_{20}, no. 10
	23	*Saltarello Primo* [5] = 1546_{20}, no. 31: "Galiarda"
8	23ᵛ	*Pavana nova detta la bella zudea dell'Eccellente P. Paulo Borrono da Milano* = 1546_{20}, no. 12
	24	*Saltarello Primo* = 1546_{20}, no. 34
	24ᵛ	*Saltarello Secondo detto El Verceleso* = 1546_{20}, no. 35
	26	*Saltarello terzo detto De leva su Brunetta* = 1546_{20}, no. 36
9	26ᵛ	*Fantasia del divino Francescho da Milano* = 1546_{20}, no. 1
10	28	*Fantesia dell'Eccellente P. P. Borrono da Milano* [6] = 1546_{20}, no. 4; 1552_{11}, no. 12; 1563_{12}, no. 2
11	30ᵛ	*Fantesia del divino Francescho da Milano* = 1546_9, no. 10
12	31ᵛ	*Fantesia dell'Eccellente P. Paulo Borrono da Milano*
13	32ᵛ	*Fantesia del divino Francescho da Milano* = 1546_6, no. 9
14	33	*Fantesia dell'Eccellente P. Paulo Borrono da Milano* = 1546_{20}, no. 6
15	34ᵛ	*Fantesia del divino F. da Milano* = 1546_6, no. 8
16	35ᵛ	*Fantesia del divino Francescho da Milano* = 1546_6, no. 11
17	36	*Resvillez moy* = 1546_6, no. 13: Garnier
18	37	*Pour avoir paix* = 1546_6, no. 6: F. de Layolle
19	37ᵛ	*Hors envies retires vous* = 1546_6, no. 3: Gombert
20	38	*Sur toutes Jayme la marguaritte* = 1546_6, no. 7
21	39	*Pour tant si Je suis Brunette* = 1546_6, no. 12: Sermisy
22	39ᵛ	*Fortune alors* = 1546_6, no. 5: Certon
23	39ᵛ	*Martin menuyt de Claudin* (RISM 1535_6, no. 14: Sermisy) = 1546_{18}, no. 52
24	40ᵛ	*Martin menuyt de C. Jannequin* = 1546_6, no. 4
25	41ᵛ	*La Canzone delli Ucelli. Revillez vous cuer* = 1546_6, no. 1: Janequin
	42ᵛ	2a pars *Vous orrez a mon advis*
	43ᵛ	3a pars *Rossignol du boys Jolii*
	44ᵛ	4a pars *Arriere*
26	45ᵛ	*La bataglia Francesca* = 1536_3, no. 34: Janequin
	47ᵛ	2a pars [*Fan frere le le lan fan*]

[1] Mod. ed. in MoeDM, p. 324.

[2] Instructions: "Per il Secondo et Terzo Saltarello toleti quelli de la Borroncina."

[3] Instructions: "Per il terzo saltarello sonate il terzo de la rinoldina."

[4] Instructions: "Volendo sonare le riprese toleti quelli che sono nel secondo Saltarello de la detta Pavana."

[5] Instructions: "Per il secondo & terzo Saltarello toleti quelli de la Milanesa."

[6] Instructions: "Per che ne la detta fantesia li sono alchune battute che alli scholari serano dificile glie fatte le medeme battute in altra forma di tempo piu facile, cioe se redotta la semicroma in croma. Et la croma in semi[mi]nima. Et accio se cognosca dove se hanno a fare glie stato fatto uno tal segno."

1546_9

GERLE, HANS

Musica und Tabulatur, auff die In/strument der kleinen und grossen Gey/gen, auch Lautten, Welcher massen die mit grundt und art irer / composition, aus dem gesang in die Tabulatur zu ordnen und / zu setzen ist, sambt verborgner Application unnd kunst, darin / ein ytlicher liebhaber und anfenger berürter Instrument so / darzu naigung dregt an ein sunderlichen Meyster men/surlich durch Tegliche ubung leychtlich kumen kan, Von newem / Corrigirt und durch auss gebessert, Durch Hansen Gerle / Lautten macher zü Nürnberg. Im / M. D. XXXXvi. Jar. / Gemert mit. 9. Teutscher und 36. Welscher auch Frantzöscher Liedern, Unnd 2. Mudeten, / wie das Register anzeygt. / Mit Rhö. Kayser. May. Auffs New in fünff Jaren nit nach zü drücken / Bey straff fünfzehen Marcklötdigs Goldts.

102 fols. German lute and viola da gamba tablature, and mensural notation. The title is placed within the same ornamental border as in 1532_2. On fol. A1v: table of contents. On fol. A2: the same preface as in 1532_2.[1] This is a revised and augmented version of the first edition of 1532_2; see there for details concerning the organization of this instruction book. Colophon on fol. c4v: "Gedrückt zü Nürnberg Bey Jheronimus Formschneyder." The contents are listed in MfMG IV (1872). See also TapL. Eight of the pieces for Grossgeigen are printed in MonkS, vol. II.

Copies in: A:Wn, D:Bds-Tü, D:Mu, F:Pc.[2]

PIECES FOR FOUR GROSSGEIGEN

	fol.	
1	C2	*Ich klag den tag* = 1532_2, no. 1: Stoltzer
2	C2v	*Ich schwing mein Horn*[3] (SenflW V, no. 44: Senfl; another version of no. 33 below)
3	C3	*Vivrai je [tousjours en soucy]* (AttainCK III, no. 17: Sermisy)
4	C3v	*Hors de plaisir* (RISM 1538_{16}, fol. 23: Richafort; another version of no. 39 below)
5	C4	*Licite [mest endurer]* (RISM 1538_{16}, fol. 19: G. de la Moeulle)
6	C4v	*O Herr ich rueff dein namen an*[4] (SenflW V, no. 29: Senfl)
7	D1v	*Sur tous regres* (PubAPTM II, no. 78: Richafort)
8	D2v	*Dont Vienzela* (AttainCK III, no. 22: Sermisy)
9	D3v	*Lheur et malheur* (RISM 1538_{17}, fol. 24: P. de Villiers)
10	D4v	*Ce fut amour* (RISM 1538_{16}, fol. 13: Passereau)
11	E1v	*Si par sofrir* (RISM 1534_{14}, no. 4: Courtois)
12	E2v	*Jay faict pour vous* (RISM 1530_3, no. 20: Sermisy)
13	E3v	*Si Jay pour vous* (AttainCK III, no. 12: Sermisy)
14	E4v	*Amissofre* (AttainCK III, no. 7: Moulu)
15	F1v	*Damour me plains* (PubAPTM XXIII, no. 49: Roger Pathie)
16	F2v	*Ein gut geselle*
17	F3v	*Ich habs gewagt* (EDMR XX, no. 16: Georg Forster; another version of no. 32 below)
18	F4v	*Elsslein liebes elselein*[5] = 1532_2, no. 12: Senfl
19	G1	*Ich het mir ein Endlein für genommen*[6] (SenflW V, no. 26: Senfl)

PIECES FOR FOUR GROSSGEIGEN PRINTED ALSO IN MENSURAL NOTATION

20	J1v	*Es flug ein kleynes walt vogelein* (compare BöhA, no. 115)
21	J3v	*[Mag ich hertzlieb erwerben dich]* = 1532_2, no. 15: Senfl

PIECES FOR FOUR KLEINGEIGEN

22	L1	*Es ligt ein Hauss im Oberlandt*[7] (PubAPTM I, no. 8: Oswalt Reytter)
23	L1v	*Artlich und schön*[8] (EDMR XX, no. 23: Casparus Bohemus)

PIECES FOR SOLO LUTE

24	M4	*Ich klag den tag* = 1532_2, no. 18: Stoltzer
25	M4	*Pacientia* = 1532_2, no. 19: Senfl
26	M4v	*Nach Willen dein* = 1532_2, no. 20: Hofhaimer

27 N1 *Trostlicher lieb* = 1532_2, no. 21: Hofhaimer
28 N2 *Der heilig herr S. Matheis schleust uns auff dy thür* (PubAPTM XXIX, no. 51)
29 N2v *Willig und Trew* (EDMR XX, no. 42: Georg Forster)
30 N3 *Gesell wiss urlawb* (EDMR XX, no. 20: Mathias Eckel)
31 N3v *Es sout ein meskin holen win* (PubAPTM XXIX, no. 1: Sampson)
32 N4v *Ich habs gewagt* (another version of no. 17 above)
33 O1 *Ich schwing mein horn* (another version of no. 2 above)
34 O1v *Jay le desyr content* (AttainCK III, no. 18: Sermisy)
35 O2v *O felici [pensier]* (RISM 1541_{13}, p. 18: C. Festa)
36 O3v *Le dur travil* (RISM 1544_{12}, fol. 12: Willaert)
37 O4v *Ce nest a vous* (RISM 1540_{10}, no. 26: Certon)
38 P1v *Lass me fault [il tant de mal]* (RISM 1540_{13}, no. 19: Maille)
39 P2 *Hors de Plaisir* (another version of no. 4 above)
40 P2v *Ce me semblent* (RISM 1538_{16}, fol. 4: F. de Layolle)
41 P3v *Une sans plus* (CW LXI, no. 5: Cadéac)
42 P4 *Il est cellui* (RISM $[1538]_{15}$, fol. 25: "Il n'est celuy," Cadéac)
43 Q1 *Sans Ceser ye lamente* (RISM $[1538]_{15}$, fol. 26: "Incessament sans cesser je lamente," Mornable)
44 Q2 *Celle qui fut* (RISM 1540_{13}, no. 18: Sandrin)
45 Q2v *Venons au poinct* (RISM 1540_{13}, no. 10: Maillard)
46 Q3v *Plus nay espoir* (RISM 1540_{13}, no. 16: Certon)
47 Q4v *Venus par tout* (RISM 1538_{16}, fol. 3: Sermisy)
48 R1v *Je ne le croy* (RISM $[1538]_{15}$, fol. 28: P. Sandrin)
49 R2v *Priegi qui muoia* (RISM $[1538]_{15}$, fol. 32: P. de Villiers)
50 R3v *Plus je la vois* (RISM 1539_{15}, no. 8: Mittantier)
51 R4v *En revenant*
52 S1v *Dung amy*
53 S2v *Il nest tresor* (CW XV, no. 3: Lupi)
54 S3 *Si dieu vouloit pour* (RISM 1541_7, fol. 28: A. Mornable)
55 S3v *Ha quel tourmont* (RISM 1540_{10}, no. 16: Godard)
56 T1 *O doulx reveoir* (RISM 1540_{10}, no. 13: Godard)
57 T1v *Qui peche plus luy* (RISM 1540_{13}, no. 17: Sermisy)
58 T2v *Mon seul espoir* (RISM 1540_{13}, no. 11: Maillard)
59 T3v *Si je vous ayme* (RISM 1540_{13}, no. 3: Maillard)
60 T4v *Le vray amy* (RISM 1538_{10}, no. 7: Sermisy)
61 V1v *Languir me faiz* (AttainCK II, no. 12: Sermisy; another version of no. 62 below)
62 V2 *Languir me faiz* (another version of no. 61 above)
63 V3 *Amour est bien* (RISM 1538_{10}, no. 1: Certon)
64 V3v *Le mal que jay* (RISM 1540_{10}, no. 2: Le Moisne)
65 X1 *Vostre beaulte* (PubAPTM II, no. 79: Gombert)
66 X2 *Celui qui fust* (RISM 1542_{13}, no. 22: Mittantier)
67 X3 *Gens qui parlez*
68 X3v *Si mon vouloir* (RISM 1540_{10}, no. 19: Maillard)
69 X4 *Super salutem* (RISM 1546_8, no. 1: Janin)
Y2 2a pars [*Dixi sapientiae*]
70 Y3v *Spes salutis* (RISM 1538_5, fol. 23v: Lupus)
Z1 2a pars *Tu es enim*
71 Z2v *Amour Je suis* (compare CM II, 5: "D'amours je suis déshéritée")
72 Z3v *Bean*
73 a1v *Priambel* = 1536_3, no. 3: Francesco da Milano
74 a2v *Dein freundtlichs gesicht* (PubAPTM VIII, no. 12: Heinrich Finck)
75 a3 *Ich klag den tag* = 1532_2, no. 34: Stoltzer
76 a3v *Saltarelo*
77 a4 *Ich weyss mir ein hübsch Paumgertelein*[9]
78 c1v *Scaramella* = 1532_2, no. 35

[1] Facs. of fol. A4 (from 1546 ed.) in LM I, 389.
[2] A copy was in USSR:K.

[3] Mod. ed. in SenflW VII, app., no. 2.
[4] Mod. ed. in SenflW VII, app., no. 3.
[5] Facs. of fol. F4^{v} in KinsP, p. 133.
[6] Mod. ed. in SenflW VII, app., no. 1.
[7] Mod. ed. in TapS, p. 25.
[8] Mod. ed. in MU IV, app., p. 59.
[9] Mod. ed. in BruS II, no. 68.

1546$_{10}$

GIOVANNI MARIA DA CREMA

JOAN MARIA / INTABOLATURA / DE LAUTO / DI RECERCARI CANZON FRANCESE / Motetti Madrigali padoane é Saltarelli Composti per lo Eccellente / musicho & sonator di Lauto messer Jo. Maria da Crema / novamente ristampata & del medesmo autore corretta / LIBRO [Cut with printer's mark of Antonio Gardane] PRIMO / In Venetia apresso di / Antonio Gardane. / M. D. XXXXVI.

40 fols. Italian lute tablature. On fol. K4^{v}: table of contents. MoeDM contains a thematic index of the dances (p. 369) and concordances for them (p. 237). SlimK II, 487, contains a thematic index of the ricercares. The compositions identified by the superior letter *a* ([a]) are reprinted in ChilLI. CremaI is a modern edition of the entire volume. Contents = 1546$_{11}$. Some of the compositions were probably reprinted in [1547]$_{11}$ (see there for details). All of the compositions are for solo lute.

Copies in: A:Wn, CH:Lcortot, D:Ngm, F:Pthibault, GB:Lbm.[1]

fol.
1 A2 *Recercar primo* = 1552$_{1}$, no. 1 (compare 1548$_{4}$, no. 14)
2 A2^{v} *Recercar segondo* = 1552$_{1}$, no. 2
3 A3^{v} *Recercar terzo*
4 A4 *Recercar quarto* = 1552$_{1}$, no. 3, and 1571$_{6}$, no. 25 (compare 1540$_{3}$, no. 9: Julio da Modena [Giulio Segni])
5 B1 *Recercar quinto*[a] = 1548$_{4}$, no. 15; 1559$_{7}$, no. 23; 1571$_{6}$, no. 13
6 B1^{v} *Recercar sexto*[a 2] = 1549$_{8}$, no. 3, and 1552$_{1}$, no. 4
7 B2 *Recercar settimo* = 1548$_{4}$, no. 20: Julio da Modena [Giulio Segni]
8 B2^{v} *Recercar ottavo* = 1568$_{7}$, no. 11
9 B3 *Recercar nono* = 1549$_{8}$, no. 5
10 B3 *Recercar decimo* = 1552$_{1}$, no. 7
11 B4^{v} *Recercar undecimo*[a 3] = 1549$_{8}$, no. 4, and 1552$_{1}$, no. 6
12 C1 *Recercar duodecimo*
13 C1^{v} *Recercar tredecimo*[4]
14 C2 *Recercar decimoquarto* = 1552$_{1}$, no. 5
15 C2^{v} *Recercar decimoquinto* = 1552$_{1}$, no. 8
16 C4 *Entre mes bras*
17 C4^{v} *Vivre ne puis*[5] (RISM 1536$_{3}$, no. 9: Sermisy)
18 D1 *Jayme le cueur* (CM II, no. 16: Sermisy)
19 D1^{v} *De vous servir* (RISM 1533$_{1}$, no. 1: Sermisy)
20 D2 *Amours ont change* (SeayFC, p. 28: Mahiet)
21 D2^{v} *Le content e riche* (AttainCK III, no. 9: Sermisy)
22 D3^{v} *Je le laray* (compare BrownM, Cat., no. 199)
23 D4 *Amy souffres* (AttainCK III, no. 7: Moulu)
24 D4^{v} *Jamais [je naymeray grant homme]* (CM II, no. 17)
25 E1 *Holla be*[6] (HM, vol. 137, no. 15: "Hola ho par la vertu goy") = 1552$_{11}$, no. 39
26 E1^{v} *Et don bon soir*[7] (RISM [c. 1528]$_{4}$, fol. 7)
27 E2 *Bayses moy [tant tant]*[8]
28 E3 *Mon amy [na plus que faire de venir en ma maison]* (compare F:Pn, MS nouv. acq. fr. 4599, fol. 5^{v} [tenor only]: Gascongne) = 1571$_{6}$, no. 138
29 E3^{v} *Il nest plaisir*[9] (CM II, no. 13: Janequin)
30 E4 *Mais quest ce*[10]
31 F1 *Allons allons [gay gayement]* (BrownTC, no. 2: Willaert)
32 F1^{v} *Queramus [cum pastoribus]*[11] (RISM 1529$_{1}$, fol. 9^{v}: Mouton)
F3 3a pars [*recte* 2a pars] [*Ubi pascas ubi cubes*]
33 F4 *Letare [nova syon]*[12] (RISM 1532$_{10}$, p. 59: Andreas de Silva)
G1^{v} 2a pars [*Cantate canticum*]
34 G2^{v} *Que es ista* [Gombert] (GombertO V, 59)
35 G3^{v} *Si bona suscepimus [a 4]* (MoralesO III, 172: Sermisy)
36 H1^{v} *Lasciar il velo* (RISM 1541$_{9}$, p. 22: Arcadelt)

37 H3 *Con lacrime e sospiri*[a] (EinIM III, 319: Verdelot)
38 H3[v] *Quanto sia liet'el giorno* (RISM 1537_9: Verdelot)
39 H4[v] *O felici occhi miei* (CW V, 19: Arcadelt)
40 I1 *Occhi miei lassi* (RISM 1541_9, p. 8: Arcadelt) = 1552_{11}, no. 37
41 I2[v] *Sal*[*tarello*] *ditto el maton*[13] = 1552_1, no. 38
42 I3 *Sal*[*tarello*] *ditto bel fior*[14] = 1552_1, no. 39
43 I3[v] *Sal*[*tarello*] *ditto la bertoncina*
44 I4 *Sal*[*tarello*] *ditto el giorgio*[15]
45 I4[v] *Pass'e mezo ala bolognesa* = 1552_1, no. 40a
K1 *Saltarello a la bolognesa* = 1552_1, no. 40b
46 K1[v] *Pass'e mezo della louetta* = 1552_1, no. 41a
K2[v] *Saltarel de la louetta* = 1552_1, no. 41b
47 K3[v] *Pass'e mezo de la sasinata*[a]
K4 *Saltarello de la sasinata*

[1] Copies were in PL:S (see 1546_5, n. 1), and the Écorcheville library (see ÉcorC, no. 246).
[2] Mod. ed. in EC, pt. I, vol. II, p. 652.
[3] Mod. ed. in CremaR.
[4] Mod. ed. in CremaR.
[5] Mod. ed. in ChilCI, p. 203.
[6] Mod. ed. in ChilCI, p. 203.
[7] Mod. ed. in ChilCI, p. 204, and EC, pt. I, vol. II, p. 652.
[8] Not identical with the Willaert setting in RISM 1536_1, fol. 15[v], although Crema's version uses the same thematic material. Willaert's other settings of this text (*a 3* and *a 5*) are unrelated to no. 27.
[9] Mod. ed. in ChilCI, p. 205.
[10] Unrelated to "Mais que ce fust le plaisir delle" (monophonic in GéroB, no. 75; and *a 3* in RISM 1520_6, fol. 19[v]), and to "Mais que ce fust secretement" (a setting *a 3* by Compère in HewO, no. 87; and a setting *a 4* by Janequin in RISM 1535_6, fol. 16).
[11] Listed in the table of contents as "de Jusquino."
[12] Listed in the table of contents as "de Jusquino."
[13] Mod. ed. in BruAL, no. 5; FerandM, p. 410; and KörL, no. 10 (all after 1552_1).
[14] Mod. ed. in EitT, no. 41 (after 1552_1), and MoeDM, p. 338.
[15] Mod. ed. in MoeDM, p. 330.

1546_{11}

GIOVANNI MARIA DA CREMA

INTABOLATURA / DI LAUTO / DI RECERCHARI, CANZON FRANCESE, MOTETTI, / MADRIGALI, PADOANE, E SALTARELLI COMPOSTI / per lo Eccellente musicho, & sonator di Lautto / messer JO.MARIA da Crema. / LIBRO TERZO. / Con gratia & Privilegio. / VENETIIS M D XLVI.

39 fols. Italian lute tablature. On fol. 2: instructions for playing the lute headed "Regola alli lettori," reprinted in HamC, p. 67. On fol. 39[v]: table of contents. Contents = 1546_{10}. For other volumes in the same series, see 1546_2, note 1. All of the compositions are for solo lute.

Copies in: A:Wn, S:Uu.

1546_{12}

LICINO, AGOSTINO

AGOSTIN LICINO / IL SECONDO LIBRO DI DUO / CROMATICI DI AGOSTINO / Licino Cremonese da Cantare Et Sonare Composti una parte / sopra l altra con la sua resolutione da parte / Novamente posto in luce / A DUE [Printer's mark] VOCI / In Venetia Apresso di / Antonio Gardane. / M. D. XXXXVI.

Two part books (the second called "Resolutio") in mensural notation, each of 20 fols. For the first volume in this series see 1545_2. On fol. A1[v]: dedication "Al Molto Magnifico Signor Il Signor Benedetto Guarna da salerno patron mio osservandissimo," reprinted in SartMS, p. 12. Fol. A2 = p. 1. All of the compositions in the volume are canons *a 2* without text.

Copy in: D:Mbs.

	p.	
1	1	*Duo. Canon. In diapente inferius. Quinti Toni*
2	2	*Duo. Canon. In diapente superius. Quinti Toni*
3	4	*Duo. Canon. In diapente superius. Quinti Toni*
4	6	*Duo. Canon. Ad ditonum superius. Quinti Toni*
5	7	*Duo. Canon. In diapente superius. Quinti Toni*
6	8	*Duo. Canon. In diapente superius. Quinti Toni*
7	10	*Duo. Canon. In diapente inferius. Sexti Toni*

8	12	*Duo. Canon. Ad eptachordum superius. Sexti Toni*
9	14	*Duo. Canon. Ad endecachordum inferius. Sexti Toni*
10	15	*Duo. Canon. Ad endecachordum superius. Sexti Toni*
11	16	*Duo. Canon. In diapente superius. Sexti Toni*
12	17	*Duo. Canon. In diapente inferius. Sexti Toni*
13	18	*Duo. Canon. In diapente superius. Sexti Toni*
14	20	*Duo. Canon. In diapente superius. Sexti Toni*
15	21	*Duo. Canon. In diapente superius. Sexti Toni*
16	22	*Duo. Canon. In diapente superius. Septimi Toni*
17	23	*Duo. Canon. In diapente superius. Septimi Toni*
18	24	*Duo. Canon. In diapente superius. Septimi Toni*
19	26	*Duo. Canon. Ad eptachordum minus superius. Septimi Toni*
20	28	*Duo. Canon. In diapente inferius. Septimi Toni*
21	30	*Duo. Canon. In diapente superius. Septimi Toni*
22	32	*Duo. Canon. In diapente superius. Octavi Toni*
23	34	*Duo. Canon. In diapente superius. Octavi Toni*
24	36	*Duo. Canon. In diapente superius. Octavi Toni*
25	38	*Duo. Canon. In diapente superius. Octavi Toni*

1546₁₃

MARCANTONIO DEL PIFARO

INTABOLATURA / DE LAUTO / DI MARCANTONIO DEL PIFARO / BOLOGNESE DE OGNI SORTE DE BALLI NOVAMENTE / STAMPATI ET POSTI IN LUCE / LIBRO PRIMO / INTABOLATURA [Cut with the printer's mark of Antonio Gardane] DE LAUTO / IN VENETIA Apresso di / Antonio Gardane / M. D. XXXXVI.

20 fols. Italian lute tablature. On fol. E4v: table of contents. Since the chiarenzana–saltarello pairs are sometimes separated in the volume (for example, nos. 5 and 14 form one unit), each dance has been given a separate number in the inventory below. MoeDM contains a thematic index of the volume (p. 376) and concordances (p. 240). The compositions identified by the superior letter *a* ([a]) are reprinted in ChilLI. All of the compositions are for solo lute.

Copies in: A:Wn, CH:Lcortot, GB:Lbm.[1]

	fol.	
1	A1v	*Ciarenzana de megio*[2]
2	A2	*Il suo saltarello*[3]
3	A3	*Chiarenzana la geometrina*[4]
4	A4	*Sal[tarello] de la giometuna*
5	A4v	*Chiarenzana la ciriolla*
6	B1v	*Saltarello il girotto*
7	B2	*Chiarenzana larcholano*
8	B3	*Il suo sal[tarello]*
9	B3v	*Chiarenzana la bataglia*[a] (compare MMRF VII, 31: "La Bataille," Janequin)
10	B4v	*Chiarenzana G. stampa*
11	C1	*Saltarello de la stamp*
12	C1v	*Saltarello bel fiore*
13	C2v	*Chiarenzana la malveza*[a]
14	C2v	*Saltarello la ciriola*[a]
15	C3v	*Chiarenzana la bianchetta*
16	C4	*Saltarello bianchetto*
17	D1	*Chiarenzana laquila*
18	D1v	*Sal[tarello] de laquila*
19	D2	*Chiarenzana la bolognese*
20	D3	*Sal[tarello] non ti partir da me*[a]
21	D3v	*Chiarenzana la marsilia*
22	D4	*Saltarel[lo] il marsilio*
23	E1	*Chiarenzana la madalena*
24	E1v	*Sal[tarello] laconitano*[a] [5]
25	E2	*Chiarenzana la lambertina*
26	E3	*Sal[tarello] il cremonese*
27	E3v	*Chiarenzana il est bel & bon* (compare RISM 1534₁₂, no. 1: Passereau)

[1] The British Museum copy has an extra folio bound in at the end, with a manuscript explanation and diagram of the musical gamut. A copy was in PL: S (see 1546₅, n. 1).

[2] Mod. ed. in MoeDM, p. 312.

[3] Mod. ed. in MoeDM, p. 313.

[4] Mod. ed. in MoeDM, p. 343.

[5] Mod. ed. in EC, pt. I, vol. II, p. 651.

1546_{14}

MUDARRA, ALONSO

ALONSO, MUDARRA / TRES LIBROS DE MUSICA EN CI/FRAS PARA VIHUELA. EN EL PRIMERO. AY. MUSICA. FACIL Y DIFI/cil en fantasias: y ComPosturas: y Pavanas: y Gallardas: y AlGunas fanta/sias pora guitarra. El segundo trata de los ocho tonos (o modos) / tiene muchas fantasias Por diversas partes: y Com/posturas glosadas. El tercero es de musica / para cantada y tañida. Tiene mo/tetes. Psalmos. Romances. / canciones, Sonettos en / castellano: y Italiano / Versos en latin. Villanzicos. Di/rigidos al muy magni/fico señor el se/ñor don Luys / çapata. / Fue impresso el presente libro en la muy noble y leal ciudad de Sevilla en casa de Juan de Leon. / 1546.

117 fols. Italian lute tablature, harp (or organ) tablature, and mensural notation. On fol. *1^v: dedication headed "Epistola al muy magnifico señor Don Luys Çapata." On fol. *2: table of contents for Book I. On fols. *2^v–*3^v: instructions for learning the tablature and the rudiments of music headed "De como se an de entender estos libros." On fol. *4^v: cut of the god Mercury playing on a lute-like instrument made from a tortoise shell; beneath the cut: two lines from Horace. Fol. *5 – fol. 1. Each of the three books has its own title page (reproduced below) and on the verso its own table of contents. On fol. 58 of Book III: cut of the prophet Elijah praying on the mountainside; in the distance a man singing and playing the vihuela, with the legend: "Cumque caneret Psaltes, facta est / Super eum manus domini." On fol. 58^v of Book III: printer's mark with the motto "Ex bello pax; ex pace concordia; ex concordia musica constat." On fol. 59–59^v: author's corrections. On fol. 60: a note explaining that Mudarra includes one example of a new tablature for harp or organ ("una nueva manera de cifras para Harpa y Organo"). On fol. 60^v: a cut of King David playing the harp with a Latin inscription beneath. On fol. 61: a *tiento* in the new tablature. On fol. 61^v: the same printer's mark as on fol. 58^v, followed by the colophon: "Acabose la presente obra en la muy noble y leal Ciudad de Sevilla por Juan de Leon impressor a sancta Marina en la calle real a siete dias del mes de Deziembre. 154[6]." The entire collection has been reprinted in a critical edition with introduction, concordances, and facsimiles of the title page, the colophon, fol. *4^v, fol. 24 of Book I, and fols. 1, 34, 58, and 61 of Book III in MME VII. SlimK II, 492–498, contains a thematic index of the ricercares. The compositions identified by the superior letter *a* ([a]) are reprinted in MorL II. Two compositions (nos. 30 and 58) are reprinted in JacobsTN, pp. 82–85. Nos. 17–22 are for solo four-course guitar, and nos. 49–75 are for vihuela and voice, written partly in ciphers in the tablature (nos. 49–50) and partly in mensural notation (nos. 51–75). No. 76 is for solo harp or organ. All of the other compositions are for solo vihuela.

Copies in: E:E, E:Mn (imperfect).[1]

VIHUELA SOLO

	fol.	
1	1	*Fantasia de pasos largos para desenboluer las manos*
2	2	*Fantasia pa[ra] desenboluer las manos*
3	3	*Fantasia de pasos pa[ra] desenboluer las manos*
4	4	*Fantasias de pasos de contado*[2]
5	5	*Fantasia facil*
6	5^v	*Fantasia facil*
7	7	*Fantasia facil*
8	8	*Fantasia*
9	9	*Fantasia*
10	10^v	*La segunda parte de la gloria de la misa de faysan regres de Josquin*[3] (JosqMS XIII: *Missa Faysant regrets*)
	12	*Pleni de la misa de faysan regres de Josquin*
11	13	*Fantasia que contrahaze la harpa en la manera de Luduvico*[a 4]
12	15^v	*Conde Claros*[a 5]
13	17	*Romanesca: o guardame las vacas*[a 6]
14	18	*Pavana*[a 7]
15	19^v	*Pavana de Alexandre*[a]
16	20	*Gallarda*[a 8]

GUITAR SOLO

17	21	*Fantasia del primer tono* Guitarra al temple viejo
18	21^v	*Fantasia del quarto tono* Guitarra al temple nuevo

19 22 *Fantasia del quinto tono* Guitarra al temple nuevo
20 23 *Fantasia del primer tono* Guitarra al temple nuevo
21 23^{v} *Pavana*[a] Guitarra al temple nuevo
22 24 *Romanesca: o guardame las vacas*[9] Guitarra al temple nuevo

VIHUELA SOLO

LIBRO SEGUNDO DE MUSICA / EN CIFRAS PARA VIHUELA. EN EL QUAL AY MUCHAS / fantasias y algunas ComPosturas Glosadas / por los ocho tonos que por otro / nombre mas propio / Se llaman mo/dos / Fue impresso el presente libro en la muy noble y leal ciudad de Sevilla en casa de Juan de Leon. / 1546

fol.
1^{v} Table of contents
23 2 *Tiento* [Primer tono] (compare 1557_2, no. 56)
24 2 *Fantasia* [Primer tono]
25 4 *Kyrie primero de la missa de Beata Virgine de Josquin glosado* (compare JosqMS XVI: *Missa De Beata Virgine*) [Primer tono]
26 5 *Fantasia* [Primer tono]
27 6^{v} *Tiento* [Segundo tono] (compare 1557_2, no. 57)
28 6^{v} *Fantasia* [Segundo tono] (compare 1557_2, no. 57)
29 7 *Fantasia de sobre fa mi ut re* [Segundo tono] (compare 1557_2, no. 58)
30 8 *Tiento* [Tercero tono] (compare 1557_2, no. 60)
31 8 *Fantasia* [Tercero tono] (compare 1557_2, no. 59)
32 9^{v} *Glosa sobre un Kyrie postrero de una misa de Josquin que va sobre Pange Lingua* [Tercero tono] (compare CW I: *Missa Pange Lingua*, Josquin, and also 1557_2, no. 60)
33 11 *Tiento* [Quarto tono] (compare 1557_2, no. 62)
34 11^{v} *Fantasia* [Quarto tono] (compare 1557_2, no. 61)
35 12^{v} *Glosa sobre un Benedictus de una missa de Josquin que va sobre la sol fa re mi* [Quarto tono] (compare JosqMS II: *Missa La sol fa re mi*)
36 13^{v} *Tiento* [Quinto tono] (compare 1557_2, no. 65)
37 14 *Fantasia* [Quinto tono] (compare 1557_2, no. 65)
38 15 *Fantasia* [Quinto tono] (compare 1557_2, no. 64)
39 16^{v} *Tiento* [Sexto tono] (compare 1557_2, no. 68)
40 17 *Fantasia* [Sexto tono] (compare 1557_2, no. 68)
41 18 *Glosa sobre el primer Kirie de una missa de Fevin que va sobre Ave Maria* [Sexto tono] (compare RISM 1515_1: *Missa Ave Maria*)
42 20 *Tiento* [Septimo tono] (compare 1557_2, no. 70)
43 20^{v} *Fantasia* [Septimo tono] (compare 1557_2, no. 70)
44 22 *Glosa sobre el Cum Sancto Spiritu de la missa de Beata Virgine de Josquin* [Septimo tono] (compare JosqMS XVI: *Missa De Beata Virgine*)
45 24 *Tiento* [Octavo tono] (compare 1557_2, no. 72)
46 24 *Fantasia* [Octavo tono] (compare 1557_2, no. 72)
47 25^{v} *Fantasia* [Octavo tono] (compare 1557_2, no. 71)
48 27 *Fantasia va sobre fa mi fa re ut sol fa sol mi re* [Octavo tono] (compare 1557_2, no. 73)

VOICE AND VIHUELA

LIBRO TERCERO / DE MUSICA, EN CIFRAS Y CANTO / de organo para tañer y cantar con la Vihuela: en el / qual ay Motetes, Psalmos, Romances, Cancio/nes, Sonetos, Versos en latin, Villan/cicos, como veran en la tabla que a la buelta desta hoja esta. / Fue impresso el presente libro en la muy noble y muy / leal ciudad de Sevilla en casa de Juan de Leon. / 1546

fol.
$*1^{v}$ Table of contents
49 *2 (= fol. 1) *Pater noster a 4* Vuilliart (WillO II, 11)
50 4 *Respice in me Deus* Gombert (JosqWW, no. 31: "Je ne me puis tenir d'aimer," Josquin)
51 6 *Clamabat autem mulier* Motete de la Cananea (compare ElúsA, p. 33: Pedro de Escobar)[10]

52 10ᵛ *Durmiendo yva el señor*[a] Romance (see QueI, p. 318)
11ᵛ 2a pars *El agua, con la tormenta*
53 13 *Triste estava el rey David*[a 11] Romance (see QueI, p. 318)
54 14 *Israel, mira tus montes*[a] Romance (see QueI, p. 318)
55 15ᵛ *Sin dudar* Cancion al milagro de la encarnacion
18 2a pars *Por que arte*
56 20 *Recuerde el alma dormida*[a 12] Cancion (text by Jorge Manrique)
57 21 *Claros y frescos rios*[a] Cancion (text by Juan Boscán)
58 23 *Que llantos son aquestos* Sonetto a la muerte de la serenissima princesa Doña Maria Nuestra Señora. Va a manera de dialogo
59 25ᵛ *Si por amar el hombre* Soneto
60 28 *Por asperos caminos* Soneto (text by Garcilaso)
61 30ᵛ *Regia qui mesto* Versos a la muerte de la Serenissima Princesa Doña Maria nuestra Señora
62 32ᵛ *Dulces exuviae* Versos del quarto de Virgilio
63 34 *Beatus ille* Verso en latin, de Horacio (MosPH, p. 123: Paul Hofhaimer)
64 34ᵛ *Hanc tua Penelope* Verso en latin, de Ovidio
65 36 *La vita fugge* Soneto en italiano (text by Petrarch)
66 39 *Lassato a yl tago* Soneto
67 41ᵛ *O gelosia d'amanti* [Soneto] (text by Sannazaro)
68 44 *I tene al ombra* [Soneto] (text by Sannazaro)
69 45 *Dime a do tienes las mientes*[a 13] Villancico
70 47ᵛ *Si me llaman a mi*[a] Villancico
71 50 *Gentil cavallero*[a] Villancico
72 53 *Isabel, perdiste la tu faxa*[a 14] Villancico
73 55 *Si viesse e me levasse*[a 15] Villancico
74 56 *Nisi Dominus* Psalmo por el septimo tono = 1557_2, no. 74
75 57 *Exurge quare* Psalmo por el primer tono

HARP OR ORGAN SOLO

76 61 *Tiento*[16]

[1] Bound in at the end of the Madrid copy are ten pages of manuscript music in Italian lute tablature: fol. 1: *Duo de flecha que dis os amores me an de matar* = 1554_3, no. 4; 1ᵛ: *Contrapunto sobre este vilancico* = 1554_3, no. 5; 2ᵛ: *Duo de folhana* = 1554_3, no. 9; 4: *duo de morales susepi disrael* = 1554_3, no. 3; 5: *benedictus a tres da misa de guaude* [sic] *barbara de morales* = 1554_3, no 13; 6: *beneditus* [sic] *a quatro da misa dave Regina celorum de morales* = 1554_3, no. 53; 7ᵛ: Blank; 8: *basa e alta* (compare 1581_1, no. 66)

[2] Mod. ed. in PujBG, no. 1012.

[3] For information on this piece see FellJ.

[4] Mod. ed. in MudF; PujHC, p. 10; and SainzF, no. 1.

[5] Mod. ed. in PujHC, p. 8; mod. ed. of beg. in TreM, pp. 226–227.

[6] Mod. ed. in AzpiaA, no. 1, and TagA I, no. 13.

[7] Mod. ed. in TagA I, no. 14.

[8] Mod. ed. in BehS, p. 3; MudG; PujHC, p. 8; and TagA I, no. 15.

[9] Mod. ed. in MudR.

[10] See RibF for a discussion of the relation between the intabulation and the motet.

[11] Mod. ed. in MudT; PedCP III, 116; TreL, p. 113; and VillalbaCE, p. 12.

[12] Mod. ed. in TornCM, p. 61; TreL, p. 111; and VillalbaCE, p. 8.

[13] See BarbiC, p. 192. The piece is pr. and discussed in SchneiderV.

[14] Mod. ed. in MudI, and VillalbaCE, p. 14.

[15] Mod. ed. in TreL, p. 116, and VillalbaCE, p. 10.

[16] Mod. ed. in KastnSI, no. 1. Facs. of fol. 61 in EF III, 265, and MGG V, col. 1567.

1546_{16}

ROTTA, ANTONIO

INTABOLATURA / DE LAUTO / DI LO ECCELLENTISSIMO MUSICHO MESSER / ANTONIO ROTTA DI RECERCARI MOTETTI, BALLI, MADRI/gali, Canzon francese da lui composti, & Intabulati, / & novamente posti in luce. / LIBRO PRIMO / Con gratia e privilegio. / VENETIIS M D XLVI.

52 fols. Italian lute tablature. On fol. 52: table of contents. The numbering of the dances in the inventory below is subject to revision (perhaps nos. 5–8 and 9–10 should each be considered one unit). Some of the compositions were probably reprinted in [1547]$_{11}$ (see there for details). MoeDM contains a thematic index of the dances (p. 381) and concordances for them (p. 242). SlimK II, 491, contains a thematic index of the ricercares. The compositions identified by the superior letter *a* ([a]) are reprinted in

MoeDM. For further information see MalAR and MalR. Contents = 1546_{16}. For other volumes in the same series, see 1546_{2}, note 1. All of the compositions are for solo lute.

Copies in: A:Wn, B:Br, CH:Lcortot, D:Mbs, F:Pthibault, S:Uu.[1]

	fol.	
1	1^{v}	*Pass'e mezo*[2] = 1552_{1}, no. 42
	2^{v}	*Gagiarda*
	3	*Padouana*
2	3^{v}	*Pass'e mezo* [*antico*] = 1552_{1}, no. 43
	4^{v}	*Gagiarda*
	5^{v}	*Padouana*
3	6^{v}	*Pass'e mezo* = 1552_{1}, no. 45
	7^{v}	*Gaiarda*
	8	*Padouana*[3]
	8^{v}	*Gientil madonna*[a]
4	9	*Pass'e mezo* = 1552_{1}, no. 44
	10	*Gaiarda*
	10^{v}	*Padouana*[4]
5	11	*Pass'e mezo* [*moderno*] = 1552_{1}, no. 46
	13	*Gaiarda*
	14^{v}	*Padouana*
6	16^{v}	*Il Sabioncelo: Sal*[*tarello*]
7	17	*Sal*[*tarello*] *dito la fantasia*
8	18	*Rose e viole*[a]
9	18^{v}	*Pass'e mezo a la villana*[a]
	19	*Alio modo*
	19^{v}	*Saltarel cioè gagliarda*[a]
	20	*Padouana gaiarda*
10	20^{v}	*La rocha'l fuso*[a] [5]
11	21^{v}	*Pass'e mezo ditto el de*
	22	*Gaiarda*
	22^{v}	*Gaiarda ditto stradiot*
12	23	*Canzon francese. basso una voce piu basso*
13	24	*Hellas mon dieu*
14	24^{v}	*A qui me doibz ig* [sic] *retirer* (RISM 1542_{13}, fol. 15^{v}: Maille)
15	25^{v}	*Si iay Ayme legierement* (RISM 1540_{12}, fol. 11^{v}: De porta)
16	26^{v}	*Malheur me suit fortune* (RISM 1545_{8}, fol. 14^{v}: Meigret)
17	27^{v}	*Fringotes jeunes filletes* (RISM 1538_{19}, no. 2: Nicolo Payen)
18	29	*Unum cole deum* Jachet (RISM 1540_{6}, no. 2)
	30^{v}	2a pars *Non occisor*
19	31^{v}	*In illo tempore* Jo. monton (RISM 1537_{1}, no. 50: Mouton)
	33	2a pars *Propter hoc dimittet*
20	34^{v}	*Sancte paule* Adr. Vuilgliar (WillO I, 89: Willaert)
21	35^{v}	*Levavi oculos meos* Gomb[ert] (GombertO V, 47)
	37	2a pars *Dominus custodit te*
22	39	*In un boschetto adorno* (RISM 1545_{18}, p. 22: Arcadelt)
23	40	*Bramo morir per non patir piu morte* (RISM 1556_{22}, no. 21: C. Festa)
24	41^{v}	*Tanto piu grat'e charo* (RISM 1543_{18}, p. 23)
25	42^{v}	*In me donna il desio*
26	43^{v}	*Valle*
27	44^{v}	*Se pur ti guardo* (RISM 1570_{8}, p. 46: Roger Pathie) = 1552_{11}, no. 38
28	46	*Reccerchar* A. R. = 1552_{1}, no. 16; 1552_{11}, no. 16; 1563_{12}, no. 4
29	47	*Reccerchar* A. R. = 1552_{1}, no. 17
30	48	*Reccerchar*[6] A. R. = 1552_{1}, no. 19; 1552_{11}, no. 17; 1563_{12}, no. 12; 1568_{7}, no. 20
31	48^{v}	*Reccerchar* A. R. = 1552_{11}, no. 3; 1563_{12}, no. 8; 1568_{7}, no. 3
32	50	*Reccerchar*[7] A. R. = 1552_{1}, no. 18, and 1552_{11}, no. 14
33	51	*Reccerchar* A. R.

[1] A copy was in PL: S (see 1546_{5}, n. 1).

[2] Mod. ed. in EitT, no. 40 (after 1552_{1}), and WasG, no. 11 (after 1552_{1}).

[3] Mod. ed. in BruS II, no. 78.

[4] Mod. ed. in NeemAM I, no. 16.

[5] Mod. ed. in ChilLI, p. 251, and PujBG, no. 1070.

[6] Mod. ed. in WasG, no. 9 (after 1552_{1}).

[7] Mod. ed. in NeemAM I, no. 15.

1546_{16}

ROTTA, ANTONIO

ANTONIO ROTTA / INTABOLATURA / DE LAUTO / DE L'ECCELLENTISSIMO MUSICHO M. / Antonio Rotta di Recercari Motetti, Balli, Madrigali. Canzon francese da Lui / composti & Intaboladi novamente posti in luce. / LIBRO [Cut with printer's mark of Antonio Gardane] PRIMO / In Venetia apresso di / Antonio Gardane. / M. D. XXXXVI.

40 fols. Italian lute tablature. On fol. K4ᵛ: table of contents. Contents = 1546_{15}. All of the compositions are for solo lute.

Copies in: D:Mbs, D:Ngm, GB:Lbm, I:Bc.

1546_{17}

VINDELLA, FRANCESCO

INTAVOLATURA / DI LIUTO / DI FRANCESCO VINDELLA / TRIVIGGIANO D'ALCUNI MADRIALI D'ARCHADELT / NUOVAMENTE POSTA IN LUCE / LIBRO PRIMO / INTAVOLATURA [Cut with the printer's mark of Antonio Gardane] DI LIUTO / IN VENETIA Apresso di / Antonio Gardane / M. D. XXXXVI.

20 fols. Italian lute tablature. On fol. A2: dedication headed "Al molto magnifico Signor Giovanbattista visconte padron & Signor mio osservandissimo," and signed "Gioanfrancesco Vindella. S." On fol. E4ᵛ: table of contents. The contents are listed in MfMG XIX (1887), 145. All of the compositions are for solo lute.

Copies in: A:Wn, D:Mbs, D:Ngm, D:W.[1]

	fol.	
1	A2ᵛ	*Si grand'e la pieta*[2] (RISM 1539_{24}, p. 4: Arcadelt) = 1552_{11}, no. 65
2	A3	*Dolci rime leggiadre* (RISM 1550_{17}, no. 1: Arcadelt)
3	A4ᵛ	*Quand'io penso al martire* (RISM 1541_{9}, p. 54: Arcadelt) = 1552_{4}, no. 16; 1563_{12}, no. 71; 1568_{7}, no. 60
4	B2	*Se'l tuo partir mi spiaque* (RISM 1541_{9}, p. 25: Arcadelt)
5	B3	*Pongente Dardo* (RISM 1541_{9}, p. 3: Giachet Berchem) = 1552_{11}, no. 36
6	B4	*O s'io potessi donna* (RISM 1541_{9}, p. 19: Giachet Berchem)
7	C1	*Nova donna* (RISM 1541_{9}, p. 12: Arcadelt)
8	C2ᵛ	*Non v'accorgete Amanti* (RISM 1541_{9}, p. 24: Arcadelt)
9	C3ᵛ	*Ancidetemi pur* (RISM 1541_{9}, p. 9: Arcadelt)
10	C4ᵛ	*Fra piu bei fiori* (RISM 1541_{9}, p. 26: Arcadelt)
11	D1ᵛ	*Se la dura durezza* (RISM 1541_{9}, p. 20: Arcadelt)
12	D2ᵛ	*Che piu foco* (RISM 1541_{9}, p. 16: Arcadelt)
13	D3ᵛ	*Io mi rivolgo indietro* (Vogel: Arcadelt 31 [1539], no. 2)
14	D4ᵛ	*Florida mia gentil*
15	E1ᵛ	*Fato son esca* (RISM 1550_{17}, no. 13: Arcadelt) = 1552_{4}, no. 15
16	E2ᵛ	*Bella fioreta* (RISM 1541_{9}, p. 45: Arcadelt)
17	E3ᵛ	*Deh fugite o mortali* (Vogel: Arcadelt 31 [1539], no. 4)

[1] A copy was in PL: S (see 1546_{5}, n. 1).

[2] Although the first intabulation is labeled no. 2, the print is complete. FétB VIII, 357, erroneously dates the volume 1556.

1546_{18}

PHALÈSE, PIERRE, PUBLISHER

Des chansons reduictz en Tabulatu/RE DE LUC A TROIS ET QUATRE PAR/TIES LIVRE DEUXIEME. / [Cut of ten performing musicians] / A LOUVAIN / Par Piere Phaleys libraire. Lan de Grace M. D. XLVI.

56 fols. French lute tablature. Fol. a1ᵛ is blank. On fol. a2: preface headed "Au bening lecteur Salut," and dated "A dieu Le dernier de May. 1546"; this is a French version of the preface of 1546_{19}. Fol. a2ᵛ is blank. The music begins on the next page, signed "b." On the two pages after fol. o4ᵛ: table of contents. The following page is blank. Colophon on its verso: "LOVANII. Ex officina Servatii Zasseni Diestensis, Anno M. D. XLVI." SlimK II, 481–482, contains a thematic index of the abstract pieces. Contents = 1546_{19}. All of the compositions are for solo lute.

Copy in: GB:Lbmh.

	fol.	
1	b1	*Praeludium*[1]
2	b1ᵛ	*Praeludium*

Des chanſons reduictz en Tabulatu RE DE LVC A TROIS ET QVATRE PAR TIES LIVRE DEVXIEME.

A LOVVAIN

Par Piere Phaleys libraire, Lan de Grace M. D. XLVI.

Title page of 1546_{18}

3 b2 *Fantasie* = 1538_1, no. 9: Narváez

4 $b2^v$ *Fantasie* = 1538_1, no. 10: Narváez

5 b3 *Fantasie* = 1538_1, no. 11: Narváez

6 b4 *Fantasie* = 1538_1, no. 12: Narváez

7 c1 *Fantasie* = 1538_1, no. 13: Narváez

8 $c1^v$ *Fantasie* = 1538_1, no. 14: Narváez

9 c2 *Fantasie* = 1538_1, no. 1: Narváez

10 c3 *Fantasie* = 1538_1, no. 2: Narváez

11 $c4^v$ *Fantasie* = 1545_3, no. 9

12 $d1^v$ *Fortune lesse moy la vie* = 1529_3, no. 9a

13 $d2^v$ *Si jay pour vous* (AttainCK III, no. 12: Sermisy)

14 $d3^v$ *Jay trop aymez* = 1529_3, no. 11a

15 $d4^v$ *Sebahist on* (RISM 1529_4, no. 15: "Sesbahist on se jay perdu")

16 e1 *Cest a grand tort* (AttainCK II, no. 18: Sermisy)

17 $e1^v$ *Forsseulement* = 1533_1, no. 41: Josquin or Févin

18 e3 *Contre raison* (compare AttainCK II, no. 5: Sermisy, and RISM 1545_{14}, fol. 9^v: Susato)

19 $e3^v$ *Mille regres* = 1533_1, no. 32: Josquin

20 $e4^v$ *Si mon malheur* (RISM 1532_{12}, fol. 10^v: Le peletier)

21 f1 *Joyssance [vous donneray]* (AttainCK III, no. 24: Sermisy)

22 $f1^v$ *Je suys desherite* (CW XV, no. 2: Lupus or Cadéac[2]) = 1562_3, no. 8

23 $f2^v$ *En espoir [d'avoir mieulx]* (KemE, p. 15: Gombert)

24 $f3^v$ *Vray dieu*

25 $f4^v$ *Entre tous viellartz* = 1552_{11}, no. 62, and 1563_{12}, no. 94

26 g1 *Tribulatie en verdriet* (compare DuyL I, 581) = 1563_{12}, no. 95

27 $g1^v$ *Cest une dure partie* (AttainCK II, no. 3: Sermisy)

28 $g2^v$ *Noch weet ic een scoon vroucen*[3] (LenN, p. [101]: "Noch weet ick een schoen ioffrau," Nicolas Liégeois) = 1552_{11}, no. 68

29 g4 *Pour avoir paix* = 1546_6, no. 6: F. de Layolle

30 $g4^v$ *Pour ung plaisir* (ParrishM, no. 20: Crecquillon) = 1552_{11}, no. 57; 1563_{12}, no. 32; 1568_7, no. 41

31 h1 *Pa[s]eavase* = 1538_1, no. 25: Narváez

32 $h1^v$ *Si tantos halcones* = 1538_1, no. 26: Narváez

33 $h2^v$ *Si tantos halcones* = 1538_1, no. 26: Narváez

34 h3 *I la mi cinta* = 1538_1, no. 27: "Y la mi cinta dorada," Narváez

35 h3v *Peysen ende trueren* (compare LenN, pp. 77 and [62])
36 h4v *Il me souffit* (compare AttainCK I, no. 9: Sermisy)
37 i1 *La bella mal maridada* = 1538_1, no. 28: Narváez
38 i1v *Deul dobble duel* (CW XV, no. 1: Lupi)
39 i2v *O combien en madoreus* (ClemensO VII, 156: "O combien est malheureux," Sandrin or Sermisy) = 1562_3, no. 25, (compare 1568_7, no. 22, and 1571_6, no. 166
40 i3v *Le ceueur le corps* (RISM $[1556]_{17}$, p. 7: Crecquillon; "responce" to no. 41)
41 i4v *Je ne desir aymer auter* (RISM $[1556]_{17}$, p. 6: Crecquillon)
42 k1 *Den lustelike mey* (compare RISM 1572_{11}, no. 25: Clemens non Papa, and DuyL I, 356)
43 k1v *Elle le veult donc*
44 k2v *En poursuivant*
45 k3v *Pour tant si je suis brunette* = 1546_6, no. 12: Sermisy)
46 k4 *La bella franciscana*
47 k4v *Toutes les nuyt* (RISM 1570_8, p. 12: Crecquillon)
48 l1v *Revillez moy* = 1546_6, no. 13: "Reveillez moy," Garnier
49 l2v *Hors envies retires vous* = 1546_6, no. 3: Gombert
50 l3 *Fortune alors* = 1546_6, no. 5: Certon
51 l3v *Sur toutes la margarite* = 1546_6, no. 7: "Sur toutes fleurs jayme la margarite"
52 l4v *Mertin menuit* Claudin = 1546_8, no. 23
53 m1v *Martin menuyt* Jennequin = 1546_6, no. 4
54 m2v *Revillez vous cuer endormis* = 1546_6, no. 1: "Le Chant des Oiseaux," Janequin
m3v 2a pars *Vous orres a mon advis*
n1 3a pars *Rossingnoul du boys joly*
n2v 4a pars *Arriere maistre coquu*
55 n3v *Bataille. Descendat uno tono* = 1545_3, no. 50: Janequin
o2 2a pars [*Fan frere le le fan fan*]

[1] Mod. ed. in SlimK II, 609.

[2] The same chanson is pr. in PubAPTM XXIII, no. 11 attributed to Cadéac.

[3] Mod. ed. (with the vocal model) in LenK, no. 26 (after 1552_{11}).

1546_{19}

PHALESE, PIERRE, PUBLISHER

Carminum Quae chely vel testudi/NE CANUNTUR, TRIUM, QUATUOR, ET/ QUINQUE PARTIUM LIBER SECUNDUS. / [Cut of ten performing musicians] / LOVANII. / Apud Petrum Phalesium bibliopolam, anno M. D. XLVI.

56 fols. French lute tablature. On fol. A2: preface headed "Benigno Lectori Salutem," and dated "Pridie cal. Junii. 1546"; this is a Latin version of the preface in 1546_{18}. On the two pages after fol. o4v: table of contents. The following page is blank. Colophon on its verso: "LOVANII. Ex officina Servatii Zasseni Diestensis, Anno M. D. XLVI." Contents = 1546_{18}. All of the compositions are for solo lute.

Copy in: A:Wn.

1546_{20}

PHALÈSE, PIERRE, PUBLISHER

Carminum pro Testudine Liber IIII. / IN QUO CONTINENTUR EXCELLENTISSIMA / carmina, dicta Paduana & Galiarda, composita per Franciscum Mediolanensem: / & Petrum Paulum Mediolanensem, ac alios artifices / in hac arte praestantissimos. / [Cut of ten performing musicians] / LOVANII / Apud PETRUM PHALESIUM Bibliopolam juratum. / Anno Domini M. D. XLVI. / Cum gratia & privilegio ad triennium.

40 fols. French lute tablature. On fol. aa1v: printer's privilege. Colophon on fol. kk4v: "LOVANII EXCUDEBAT JACOBUS BATIUS TYPOGRAPHUS A CAE. MA. ADMISSUS. M. D. XLVI. Men. Decemb. [Cut of a lute]." Contents = 1573_8. Nos. 22 and 48 are for two lutes; the other compositions are for solo lute.

Copies in: A:Wn, GB:Lbmh.

fol.
1 aa2 *Fantasia Francisci Mediolanensis* = 1546_8, no. 9: Francesco da Milano
2 aa3v *Fantasia Francisci Mediolanensis* = 1546_6, no. 8

3	aa4^v	*Fantasie de Francoys de Milan* = 1546_6, no. 10
4	bb1^v	*Fantasia de Petro Paulo da Milano* = 1546_8, no. 10: Pietro Paolo Borrono
5	bb3^v	*Fantasia da Francesco da Milano* = 1536_9, no. 7
6	bb4^v	*Fantasie de Pierre Paule Barron* = 1546_8, no. 12
7	cc2	*Paduana I* = 1546_8, no. 1a
8	cc2^v	*Paduana [II]*
9	cc3^v	*Paduana III* = 1546_8, no. 2a
10	cc4^v	*Paduana [IV]* = 1546_8, no. 7a
11	dd1	*Paduana V* = 1546_8, no. 6a
12	dd1^v	*Paduana VI* = 1546_8, no. 8a
13	dd2^v	*Paduana VII* = 1546_8, no. 5a
14	dd4^v	*Paduana VIII* = 1546_8, no. 3a
15	ee2	*[Paduana IX]* = 1546_8, no. 4a
16	ee2^v	*Paduana X*
17	ee3	*Paduana XI*
18	ee3^v	*Paduana [XII]* = 1530_3, no. 43
19	ee4^v	*Passa mezo a la bataìlla*
20	ff1^v	*Passa mezo de vaccas*
21	ff2	*Paduana* = 1545_3, no. 58
22	ff2^v	*Paduana* [for two lutes]
23	ff3	*Passa mezo* = 1563_{12}, no. 133
24	ff3^v	*Paduana* = 1545_3, no. 56
25	ff4	*Paduana*
26	ff4^v	*Gailliarda I*
27	gg1	*Galiarda II* = 1546_8, no. 1b
28	gg2	*Galiarda III* = 1546_8, no. 1c
29	gg2^v	*Galiarda IIII* = 1546_8, no. 1d
30	gg3^v	*Galiarda V* = 1546_8, no. 2b
31	gg4	*Galiarda VI* = 1546_8, no. 7b
32	gg4^v	*Galiarda VII* = 1546_8, no. 6c
33	hh1^v	*Galiarda VIII* = 1546_8, no. 6f
34	hh2	*Galiarda IX* = 1546_8, no. 8b
35	hh2^v	*Galiarda X* = 1546_8, no. 8c
36	hh3^v	*Galiarda XI* = 1546_8, no. 8d
37	hh4	*Galiarda XII* = 1546_8, no. 5b
38	ii1	*[Galiarda XIII]* = 1546_8, no. 5c
39	ii1^v	*Galiarda [XIV]* = 1546_8, no. 5d
40	ii2^v	*[Galiarda XV]* = 1546_8, no. 3d
41	ii3	*[Galiarda XVI]*
42	ii4	*Galiarda [XVII]*
43	kk1	*Bourata*
44	kk1^v	*Bourata*
45	kk2	*Almanda*[1]
46	kk2^v	*Almanda*
47	kk3	*Quatre branles*
48	kk3^v	*Caracossa* [for two lutes]
49	kk4	*Roman[e]scha*

[1] Mod. ed. in MohrA I, 18 (the beginning is accidentally left out).

1546

DOUBTFUL WORKS

1. MorL I, xliii, lists Antonio di Becchi, *Intavolatura di lauto. Libro 1°* (Venice, 1546), as having been in the library of King John IV of Portugal. The volume is otherwise unknown; it is not mentioned in VasJ. The only volume of music by Becchi that survives is 1568_1.

1547_1

BUUS, JACQUES

SUPERIUS / RECERCARI DI M. JACQUES BUUS / Organista in Santo Marco di Venetia da cantare, & sonare d'Organo / & altri Stromenti Novamente posti in luce. / LIBRO PRIMO / A QUATRO [Printer's mark] VOCI / In Venetia Apresso di / Antonio Gardane. / M. D. XLVII.

Four part books in mensural notation (S, 13 fols.; AT, each of 14 fols.; B, 12 fols.). Fol. A1^v = p. 1. On p. 27 of the tenor part book only: dedication "AL MOLTO MAGNIFICO MESSER HIERONIMO UTINGHER," reprinted in GaspaC IV, 191, and SartMS, p. 13. SlimK II, 509, contains a thematic index of the entire volume. For further information see SutherR and SutherS. All of the compositions are for instrumental ensemble *a 4* (or solo keyboard).

Copies in: D:Mbs, D:Rp, I:Bc (T only).

	p.	
1	1	*Recercar primo*
2	3	*Recercar segondo*[1]
3	5	*Recercar terzo*
4	7	*Recercar quarto*[2]
5	9	*Recercar quinto*
6	12	*Recercar sexto*
7	15	*Recercar septimo*
8	18	*Recercar ottavo*
9	21	*Recercar nono*
10	23	*Recercar decimo*

[1] Mod. ed. in LenK, no. 27.

[2] Mod. ed. in RieM, no. 40, and WasG, no. 18.

1547_2

FRANCESCO DA MILANO AND PERINO FIORENTINO

INTABOLATURA / DE LAUTO / DI M. FRANCESCO MILANESE / ET M. PERINO FIORENTINO / Suo Discipulo Di Recercate Madrigali, & Canzone Francese / Novamente Ristampata & corretta. / LIBRO [Printer's mark] TERZO / In Venetia Apresso di / Antonio Gardane / M. D. XLVII.

24 fols. Italian lute tablature. On fol. 24^v: table of contents. WieM II includes a modern edition and thematic index of the entire volume. SlimK II, 500, contains a thematic index of the ricercares. The compositions identified by the superior letter *a* ([a]) are reprinted in ChilLI. Some of the compositions were probably reprinted in $[1547]_{11}$. For a discussion of Perino's music see WieP. Contents = 1562_1, 1563_6, and 1566_1. All of the compositions are for solo lute.

Copies in: A:Wn, D:Mbs, D:Ngm, F:Pthibault, US:Cn, US:Wc.[1]

	fol.	
1	$A1^v$	*Fantasia di F. Milanese*[2] = 1552_1, no. 20, and 1586_5, no. 1
2	$A2^v$	*Fantasia di F. Milanese*[3] = 1559_7, no. 17
3	A3	*Fantasia di F. Milanese*[a][4] = 1559_7, no. 20
4	$A3^v$	*Fantasia di M. Perino*[5]
5	B1	*Fantasia di F. Milanese*[6] = 1571_6, no. 14
6	$B2^v$	*Fantasia di F. Milanese*[7]
7	$B3^v$	*De mon triste [desplaisir] di F. Milanese*[8] (BrownTC, no. 16: Richafort)
8	B4	*Fan[tasia] de mon triste di F. M.*[a][9]
9	C1	*Fantasia di F. Milanese*[10] (compare 1557_2, no. 27)
10	$C2^v$	*Fantasia di F. Milanese*[11] = 1536_9, no. 13
11	$C3^v$	*Fantasia di F. Milanese*
12	$C4^v$	*Fantasia di F. Milanese*[12]
13	$D1^v$	*F[antasia] di Perino Fiorentino*

INTABOLATVRA
DE LAVTO
DI M. FRANCESCO MILANESE
ET M. PERINO FIORENTINO
Suo Discipulo Di Recercate Madrigali, & Canzone Francese
Nouamente Ristampata & corretta.

LIBRO  *TERZO*

In Venetia Apresso di
Antonio Gardane
M. D. XLVII.

Title page of 1547_2

14 D3 *Quanta belta di F. Milanese* (RISM 1541_{9}, p. 5: Arcadelt)

15 D4 *F[antasia] di Perino Fiorentino*[a]

16 $D4^{v}$ *Fantasia di F. Milanese*[a 13] = 1559_{7}, no. 21

17 $E1^{v}$ *O felici ochi mei de P. F.*[a] (CW V, 19: Arcadelt)

18 E2 *Fantasia di F. Milanese* = 1559_{7}, no. 18

19 $E2^{v}$ *Fantasia di F. Milanese*[a 14]

20 $E3^{v}$ *Quanti travagli di P. F.* (RISM 1541_{9}, p. 35: Arcadelt)

21 $E4^{v}$ *Quand'io penso al martir di F. Milanese* (RISM 1541_{9}, p. 54: Arcadelt)

22 $F1^{v}$ *Fort seulement* = 1536_{3}, no. 24: Josquin or Févin

23 $F2^{v}$ *Que voles vous dire de moy*[15] = 1536_{3}, no. 22

24 $F3^{v}$ *Vignon vignetta F. M.* (AttainCK II, no. 14)

[1] A copy was in PL: S (on this copy see 1546_{5}, n. 1), and the Wolffheim library (see WolffC I, no. 1190). Mme. Thibault's copy was in the Écorcheville library (see ÉcorC, no. 246).

[2] Mod. ed. (after 1586_{5}) in ScherG, no. 138.

[3] Facs. of fol. $A2^{v}$ and mod. ed. of no. 2 in SzmolyanAL, p. 542. Mod. ed. in BruS III, no. 92 (in tablature on p. 181).

[4] Mod. ed. in ChilLS, p. 24 (after 1559_{7}), and FranF, no. 1.

[5] Mod. ed. in ChilPF, and NeemAM I, no. 23.

[6] Mod. ed. in SlimK II, 621.

[7] Mod. ed. in ChilF, no. 7.

[8] Mod. ed. in ChilCI, p. 65, and SlimK II, 624.

[9] Mod. ed. in SlimK II, 626.

[10] Mod. ed. in ÉcorL, p. 149 (after 1566_{1}), and MME II, 20 (after 1557_{2}).

[11] Mod. ed. in ChilF, no. 6.

[12] Mod. ed. in ChilF, no. 5, and ScherG, no. 115.

[13] Mod. ed. and facs. in BlochL, p. 17; mod. ed. only in FranF, no. 2.

[14] Mod. ed. in FranF, no. 3.

[15] Mod. ed. in ChilPF.

1547_{3}

GINTZLER, SIMON

INTABOLATURA / DE LAUTO / DI SIMON GINTZLER MUSICO / Del Reverendissimo Cardinale di Trento, De Recercari Motetti Madrigali / Et Canzon Francese Novamente posta in luce. / LIBRO [Cut with printer's mark of Antonio Gardane] PRIMO / In Venetia Apresso di / Antonio Gardane. / M. D. XLVII.

60 fols. Italian lute tablature. On fol. $A1^{v}$: dedication headed "ILLUSTRISSIMO AC REVERENDISSIMO Domino Domino Christophoro Madrucio Cardinali ac Principi Tridenti Et administratori Briximen. Domino meo Colendissimo," and signed "Simon Gintzler." On fol. A2: table of contents. The attributions in brackets are from the table of contents. The compositions identified by the superior letter *a* ([a]) are reprinted in DTO XVIII/37, pp. 60–67, which includes a facsimile of fol. $B2^{v}$ (p. viii). SlimK II, 499, contains a thematic index of the ricercares. All of the compositions are for solo lute.

Copies in: A:Wn, D:Ngm, GB:Lbm,[1] and I:Gu.[2]

fol.

1 $A2^{v}$ *Recercar primo*[a] = 1552_{1}, no. 12

2 $A3^{v}$ *Recercar segondo*[a 3] [Simon gintzler] = 1552_{1}, no. 13

3 B1 *Recercar Terzo*[a] = 1552_{11}, no. 13; 1563_{12}, no. 7; 1568_{7}, no. 2

4 $B2^{v}$ *Recercar Quarto*[a 4] = 1552_{1}, no. 14; 1552_{11}, no. 10; 1563_{12}, no. 10

5 $B3^{v}$ *Recercar Quinto*[a] = 1552_{11}, no. 4

6 $B4^{v}$ *Recercar Sexto*[a 5] = 1552_{1}, no. 15, and 1552_{11}, no. 15

7 $C1^{v}$ *Pater noster* [Josquin] (JosqMT, no. 50) = 1552_{11}, no. 81, and 1563_{12}, no. 106

C3 2a pars *Ave maria* = 1563_{12}, no. 108

8 $C4^{v}$ *Benedicta es [coelorum Regina]* [Josquin] (JosqMT, no. 46) = 1552_{11}, no. 84; 1563_{12}, no. 111; 1568_{7}, no. 114

$D2^{v}$ 2a pars *[Per illud ave] DUO*

$D3^{v}$ 3a pars *Nunc mater*

9 D4 *Sancta maria* [Verdelot] (RISM 1538_{2}, p. 52)

10 E2 *Preter rerum* [Josquin] (JosqMT, no. 33)

$E3^{v}$ 2a pars *Virtus sancti spiritus*

11 F1 *Circundederunt me* [Josquin] (JosqWW, no. 21: "Nimphes, nappés")

12 F3 *Descendi in ortum meum* [Jachet (Berchem)] (RISM 1539_{3}, p. 21)

13 G1 *Stabat mater* [Josquin] (JosqMT, no. 36) = 1552_{11}, no. 77; 1563_{12}, no. 105; 1568_7, no. 113; 1571_6, no. 158

G2v 2a pars [*Eya mater*]

14 G4v *Vita in ligno moritur*[a] [Ludo. Senfl] (RISM 1537_1, no. 20)

15 H2 *Aspice domine* [Jachet] (MonteO XXVI, app., p. 1)

16 H4 *Tua est potentia* [Moton] (RISM 1521_3, no. 14) = 1552_{11}, no. 78

17 I1v *Ne proiicias nos* [Adriano (Willaert)] (RISM 1538_3, no. 18)

18 I3 *Gaudent in celis* [Archadelt] (RISM 1538_2, p. 49)

19 K1 *Magnum hereditatis* [Adriano (Willaert)] (WillO II, 32) = 1552_{11}, no. 72

20 K2v *Benedictus dominus deus israel* [Lupus] (RISM 1539_{13}, p. 16) = 1552_{11}, no. 74

K3v 2a pars *Honor virtus*

21 K4v *Puer qui natus est* [Jachet (Berchem)] (RISM 1538_5, fol. 32v) = 1552_{11}, no. 73

22 L2 *Sancte paule apostole* [Adriano (Willaert)] (WillO I, 89)

23 L3v *Deus canticum novum* [Lupus] (RISM 1538_5, fol. 9) = 1552_{11}, no. 75

24 L4v *Domine deus omnipotens* [Archadelt] (RISM 1538_5, fol. 33v) = 1552_{11}, no. 76

25 M3 *Madonna s'il morire* [Verdelot] (Vogel: Verdelot 4 [ca. 1535], p. 10)

26 M4 *Donna si fiera stella* [Verdelot] (RISM 1540_{18}, p. 15)

27 N1 *Occhi miei lassi* [Archadelt] (RISM 1541_9, p. 8) = 1563_{12}, no. 67

28 N2v *O s'io potessi donna* [Jachet Berchem] (RISM 1541_9, p. 19) = 1563_{12}, no. 70

29 N4 *Lasciar il velo* [Archadelt] (RISM 1541_9, p. 22)

30 N4v *Il ciel che rado* [Archadelt] (RISM 1541_9, p. 49)

31 O3 *Jay veu que jestois* [*franc*][6] [Sandrin] (RISM 1543_7, no. 4)

32 O3v *Ce qui est plus en ce monde* [Sandrin] (RISM 1543_7, no. 3) = 1563_{12}, no. 77

33 O4v *Veu le grief mal* [Villiers] (RISM 1540_{12}, fol. 8v) = 1552_{11}, no. 48

34 P2 *Mais pourquoy* [*noze lon prendre le bien*][7] [Sandrin] (RISM 1543_{11}, no. 4) = 1552_{11}, no. 35

35 P3 *Si de beau*[*coup*][8] [Sandrin] (RISM 1543_{11}, no. 3)

36 P4 *Dames* [*dhonneur voyez*] [Sandrin] (RISM 1543_{11}, no. 17)

[1] The British Museum copy has manuscript remarks scattered throughout the volume.

[2] A copy was in PL: S (see 1546_5, n. 1).

[3] Mod. ed. in ChilLS, p. 18; EnI, app., p. 8; and NeemAM I, no. 20.

[4] Mod. ed. in ChilLS, p. 20, and NeemAM I, no. 22.

[5] Mod. ed. in BarthaZ, no. 44; NeemAM I, no. 21; WasG, no. 8 (after 1552_1); WolfHM, p. 524 (after 1552_1); and WolfME, no. 32 (after 1552_1).

[6] Mod. ed. in ChilCI, p. 68.

[7] Mod. ed. in ChilCI, p. 69.

[8] Mod. ed. of the chanson (reconstructed from the intabulation) in ChilS, p. 23.

1547_4

NEWSIDLER, HANS

Das Erst Buch. / Ein Newes Lautenbüchlein mit vil feiner lieblichen Liedern, / für die jungen Schuler, die fein leicht unnd gantz ring zu lernen seind, auch etlich / feine Tentz, Welisch unnd Frantzösische Stück, die fein artlich unnd lieb/lich Collerirt, mit sündern fleys verfast, unnd zusamen gebracht, / durch mich Hansen Neusidler Lutennisten unnd Burger / zü Nürnberg, offentlich aussgangen, im / M. D. XLVII. / Mit Römischer Kay. unnd König. May. freyheyt, / inn Fünff Jaren nicht nach zu drücken / begnadet.

32 fols. German lute tablature. On fol. A1v: table of contents. On fol. H3v: the same notice as in 1547_4 headed "Wie man die Lauten sol lernen ziehen." On fol. H4: a note advertising Newsidler's other volumes of lute music (the same as in 1549_6), followed by the same notice as in 1540_1 headed "Von den Creutzlein und pünctlein, wie man sie verstehen sol," followed by the colophon: "Gedruckt zü Nürmberg bey Christoff Gutknecht durch verlegung Hansen

Newsidler Lutinisten Anno M. D. XLVII." On fol. H4v: the same cut of the neck of a lute with a brief explanation of the tablature as appears in 1536_6 and later volumes by Newsidler. The three "Regeln" at the beginning of the volume are unnumbered; the compositions are numbered beginning with "Hastu mich genummen." This is a revised second edition of 1544_1. For further information see DorfS. All of the compositions are for solo lute.

Copy in: D:Ngm.

	fol.	
1	A2	*Das Erst Fundament auff die Lauten* = 1536_6, no. 2
	A2v	*Die ander Regel am Fundament*
	A2v	*Die drit Regel*
2	A3	*Hastu mich genumen* (another version of no. 15 below) = 1540_1, no. 3
3	A3v	*Unser köchin kan auss der massen kochen wol* = 1540_1, no. 2
4	A4	*Ein niderlendisch tentzlein* = 1544_1, no. 4
5	A4v	*Entlaubet ist der walde* = 1536_6, no. 8: Stoltzer
6	B1	*Willig und trew on alle rew* (EDMR XX, no. 42: Georg Forster)
7	B1v	*Ein guter Hofftantz* = 1536_6, no. 11
	B2	*Der hupff auff*
8	B2v	*Wo gehnd die Bamberger Meidlein hin, wo gehn sie hin nach gras*[1] = 1544_1, no. 8
	B3	*Der hupff auff*
9	B3v	*Es wolt ein jeger jagen, wolt jagen vor dem holtz* = 1544_1, no. 9
	B4	*Hupff auff*
10	B4v	*Ich wais mir ain stoltze Mülnerin* = 1540_1, no. 6: "Wayss mir ein hüsche Mülnerin"
	C1	*Hupff auff*
11	C1v	*Der Nunnen tantz* = 1540_1, no. 12
	C2	*Der hupff auff zum Nunnen tantz*
12	C2v	*Der Zeiner tantz* = 1540_1, no. 11
	C3	*Der hupff auff*
13	C3v	*Der petler tantz* = 1540_1, no. 15
	C4	*Der hupff auff zum petler tantz*
14	C4v	*Der Hofftantz mit drey stimmen* = 1536_6, no. 69
	D1	*Der hupff auff*
15	D2	*Madunna Katherina*[2] = 1540_1, no. 36 (another version of no. 2 above)
16	D2v	*Ich het mir ein Annelein für genumen* = 1540_1, no. 13: Senfl
17	D3	*Es taget vor dem holtze* = 1540_1, no. 14
18	D3v	*Elslein liebstes Elslein mein* = 1536_6, no. 29: Senfl
19	D4	*Der hund, mir vor dem licht umbgat* = 1536_6, no. 26
20	D4v	*Ich klag den tag*[3] (DTO XXXVII/72, p. 71: Stoltzer)
21	E1	*Nach willen dein mich dir allein* = 1544_1, no. 27: Hofhaimer
22	E1v	*Ach lieb mit leid wie hast den bscheid* = 1536_6, no. 31: Hofhaimer
23	E2	*Nun gruss dich Gott mein truserlein* = 1540_1, no. 23: Dietrich
24	E2v	*Ein guter welscher gassenhawer* = 1549_6, no. 68
	E3v	*Den hupff auff muss man gar behend schlagen*
25	E4	*Ein guter gassenhawer für die jungen*
	E4v	*Der hupff auff*
26	F1	*Ein gut Preambulum*[4] = 1536_6, no. 64
27	F1v	*Ein guter Preambulum* = 1536_6, no. 65
28	F2	*Ic seg adiu*[5] = 1544_1, no. 30
29	F2v	*Du Fiensela* = 1540_1, no. 32: "Dont vient cela," Sermisy
30	F3v	*Je suis ami aux* = 1544_1, no. 32
31	F4	*In te domine speravi* = 1544_1, no. 34: Josquin des Prez
32	G1	*Languir Me fais* = 1544_1, no. 35: Sermisy
33	G1v	*Fons perte*[6] = 1544_1, no. 37: "Vous perdez temps," Sermisy
34	G2v	*O dulx Roveoir* = 1544_1, no. 38: Godard
35	G3v	*En esperant* = 1544_1, no. 39: Sermisy
36	G4v	*Dame de Beaulte* = 1544_1, no. 40: Morel
37	H1v	*Mon petit Nose* = 1544_1, no. 41: "Mon petit [cueur]"
38	H2	*Adieu amours de fons suis lus trop* = 1544_1, no. 42

39 H2[v] *Le departir* = 1544_1, no. 43: Clemens non Papa

[1] Heading on fol. B2[v]: "Hie volgend feine ringe liedlein mit drey stymmen."
[2] Heading on fol. D2: "Hie volgend feine ringe liedlein mit drey stymmen."
[3] Mod. ed. in MolzHN, no. 6.
[4] Mod. ed. in MolzHN, no. 4.
[5] Heading on fol. F2: "Hie nach volgen etliche Frantzösische Stück."
[6] Heading on fol. G1[v]: "Hienach volgen etliche Frantzösische und Welische Stück, die fein artlich colerirt seind."

1547_5

VALDERRÁBANO, ENRIQUEZ DE

[Cut of the coat of arms of the Conde de Miranda] / LIBRO DE MUSICA / DE VIHUELA, INTITULADO SILVA DE / sirenas. En el qual se hallara toda diversidad de musica. Compuesto por Enrriquez / de Valderravano. Dirigido al Illustrissimo señor don Francisco de Çuñiga Con/de de Miranda. Señor de las casas de Avellaneda y Baçan, &c. / CON PRIVILEGIO IMPERIAL

8 + 104 fols. Italian lute tablature and mensural notation. On fol. *2: printing privilege granted by Prince Philip (later Philip II), dated "Fecha en Madrid, a seys dias de Mayo de mill y quinientos y quarenta y siete años. Va escripto sobre raydo, o diz diez vale. Yo el Principe. Por mandado de su alteza Francisco de Ledesma." On fol. *2[v]: dedication headed "Al Illustrisimo Sennor Don Francisco de Çuñiga Conde de Miranda." On fols. *3–*3[v]: preface headed "Prologo." On fols. *3[v]–*5: a note in praise of music headed "Musice laus, Nullo authore." On fol. *5: two poems in Latin, the first headed "In Henrrici summi musici syrenas Epigramma, Nullo Authore," and the second headed "Eiusdem Nulli Tetrastichon." On fols. *5–*6: a note explaining the tablature headed "Relacion de la obra." On fols. *6[v]–*8[v]: table of contents. On fol. *8[v]: a note headed "Aviso para que la musica deste libro sea bien tañida," explaining that the fingers of the left hand should stay on the frets until the music or another fingering requires that they be raised, followed by a note headed "De los tonos," explaining that the modes were not associated with fixed positions on the vihuela; mode is determined by the intabulated music and is identified by means of solfa. Fol. *9 = fol. 1. Colophon on fol. 104[v]: "A Gloria y alabança de Nuestro Redemptor y Maestro Jesu Christo, y de su gloriosa madre. Fenesce el libro Llamado Silva de sirenas. Compuesto por el excelente musico Anrriquez de Valderavano. Dirigido al Illustrissimo señor don Francisco de Çuñiga Conde de Miranda, &c. Fue impresso en la muy insigne y noble villa de Valladolid Pincia otro tiempo llamada Por Francisco Fernandez de Cordovo impresor. Junto a las Escuelas Mayores. Acabose a veynte y ocho dias del mes de Julio Deste Año de 1547," followed by the printer's mark with the motto "Ne ingenium volitet, Paupertas de primit ipsum." SlimK II, 503–508, contains a thematic index of the ricercares. The compositions identified by the superior letter *a* ([a]) are reprinted in MorL II; those identified by ([b]) are reprinted in JacobsTN, pp. 86–100. For a discussion of Valderrábano's parody fantasias, see WardP, p. 226. For further information see WardV II, 389. The volume is divided into seven books, each of which has its own title, reproduced in the inventory below. The compositions in Books I, V, VI, and VII are for solo vihuela; those in Book II for voice (notated in red ciphers in the tablature) and vihuela; those in Book III for voice (notated in mensural notation) and vihuela; and those in Book IV for two vihuelas.[1]

Copies in: A:Wn,[2] E:Bu, E:Mn (two copies), E:VAc (imperfect), GB:Lbm, I:MOe, US:NYhs (imperfect).

	fol.	
1	1	*Fuga*[b 3] *a 3*
2	1[v]	*Fuga a 3*
3	1[v]	*Agnus dei sobre mi fa re sol fa mi a 3*
4	2	*Benedictus a 3* = 1552_{11}, no. 82
5	2	*Osanna sobre el dicho mi fa re sol fa mi a 3*
6	2[v]	*Agnus dei a 4*
7	3[v]	*Agnus dei* Josquin *a 4* (JosqMS, no. 1: *Missa L'homme armé super voces musicales*)

Comiença el Segundo libro de motetes y otras cosas para cantar y tañer contrabaxo y en otras partes tenor.

8 5 *Laudate dominum omnes gentes* Layole *a4* (I:Fn, MS Magl. XIX, 117, no. 33)

5^v 2a pars *Gloria patri et filio*

9 5^v *O gloriosa dei genitrix* Gombert (SmijT I, 167)

10 6^v *Beata quorum agmina* *a4*

11 6^v *Si bona suscepimus*[4] *a4*

12 7^v *Infirmitatem nostram* Verdelot *a4* (SmijT IV, no. 17) = 1552_{11}, no. 79

13 8 *Repleti sunt quidem spiritu sancto* Verdelot *a4*

14 8^v *Panis quem ego dabo* Lupus *a4* (KJ XXV [1930], Notenbeilagen, p. 2)

15 9^v *Hic precursor et dilectus* Gombert *a4* (GombertMT I [1539], no. 19b: 2a pars of "Fuit homo missus")

16 10^v *Exultet celum laudibus* Sepulveda *a4*

17 10^v *Ave Maria*[5] Loyset *a5*

18 11^v *Jesum queritis*[5] Loyset *a4*

19 12 *Tibi soli peccavi* Jaquet *a4* (JachetMT I [1539], no. 12)

20 13 *Aparens Christus discipulis suis* Gombert *a5*

21 14 *Veni in altitudinem maris* Jaquet *a5* (RISM 1538_2, fol. 9^v: 2a pars of "Salvum me fac Domine")

22 15 *Nomine disimulavi* Morales *a4* (MME XIII, 42: 2a pars of "Antequam comedam")

23 15^v *Virgo prudentissima* Pieton *a4* (compare SmijT III, no. 10: Penet)

24 16^v *Peccavi supra numerum* Adriano [Willaert] *a5* (WillO III, 61)

25 17 *Augustine lux doctorum*[6] Adriano [Willaert] *a5* (WillO III, 43: 2a pars of "Laetare sancta mater")

26 17^v *Ave Maria* Josquin *a6* (JosqMT, no. 50b)

27 18^v *Antequam comedam* Vicencio rufo *a5*

28 19^v *Ay de mi dize el buen padre*[7] *a4* "Historia de come Matatias llora la destruycion de Hierusalem . . . a sonada de romance viejo" (see QueI, p. 318)

29 20 *Adormido se a el buen viejo* (2 *diferencias*) "Historia de como el propheta Helias huyo por el disierto . . . a sonada de romance viejo" (see QueI, p. 318)

30 20^v *En la ciudad de betulia* "Historia de Judith quando siendo biuda degollo a Holofernes . . . a sonada de romance viejo" (see QueI, p. 318)

31 21 *Laudate dominum deum nostrum*

32 21^v *De hazer lo que jure*[a] Proverbio

33 21^v *Auchelina vel auchlina*[a] Soneto (in table: Villancico)

34 22 *Eulalia de tarpeya vernan*[a] Soneto (in table: "Eulalia borgonela")

35 22 *O que en la cumbre*[a] Villancico

36 22^v *Muera en las hondas* Villancico

37 22^v *Corten espadas afiladas*[a] Soneto a manera de ensalada contrahecho al de Cepeda (compare MME VIII, 131: Cepeda)

38 23 *A monte sale el amor*[a] Soneto (in table: Villancico)

23^v 2a pars *A los montes de diana*[8]

39 23^v *De donde venis amore*[a 9] Juan Vasquez Villancico (MME IV, 207)

40 24 *Corona de mas hermosas*[a 10] Villancico

41 24 *Desposose te tu amiga juan pastor*[a] Villancico

42 24 *Rugier qual sempre fui tal*[10] Soneto (compare EinAR)

43 24 *Con que la lavare*[a] Villancico (compare MME IV, 209: Juan Vásquez) = 1552_{11}, no. 5

44 24^v *Como puedo yo bivir que el remedio*[a] Villancico

45 25 *Las tristes lagrimas mias* Villancico

46 25 *Sea quando recordares*[a] "Proverbio sacado de la sagrada escriptura"

47 25[v] *Los braços traygo*[a] Romance (see QueI, p. 47; compare MME IV, 193)

48 26 *Y arded coraçon arded*[a] Villancico

49 26 *Ya cavalga calaynos*[a 11] Romance (see QueI, p. 312)

50 26[v] *La bella mal maridada*[a 12] Villancico

51 26[v] *Donde son estas serranas*[a 12] Villancico (see QueI, p. 316)

SIGUESE EL TERCE/RO LIBRO, EL QUAL TRATA DE MOTETES / Canciones, Villancicos, y otras cosas para cantar en falsete. Lo qual es muy provechoso.

52 27 *Vita dulcedo* Lupus
27[v] 2a pars *Et Jesum*
28 3a pars *O dulcis virgo*

53 28 *In te domine speravi* Lupus (RISM 1535_1, fol. 6[v]) = 1553_{10}, no. 22

54 29[v] *O quam suavis*

55 30[v] *Hierusalem luge* Verdelot (RISM 1532_9, p. 49: Richafort [or Lupus?])

56 31 *Cum invocarem* Verdelot (anon. in 1557_2, no. 93)

57 31[v] *Ut fidelium propagatione* Miguel Ortiz

58 32[v] *Hierusalem convertere ad dominum* Miguel Ortiz Lamentacion

59 33 *Se pur te guardo* (RISM 1570_8, p. 46: Pathie)

60 34 *Quid prodest* "Ovidi carmen"

61 34 *Se in me exstremo*[b] (compare 1558_6, no. 6: "Si come estremo ardore")

62 35 *Gloriarmi poss'io* Verdelot (EinIM III, 26)

63 35[v] *Madonna qual certezza*[a] Verdelot (EinIM III, 21)

64 36[v] *Qui la dira* Verdelot (RISM 1572_2, fol. 2: Willaert)

65 37[v] *Madonna non so dir* Verdelot (CW V, 13)

66 38 *Dormendo un giorno* Verdelot (WagMP, p. 461) = 1568_7, no. 106

67 39 *Vita de la mia vita* Verdelot (RISM 1537_8, no. 25)
39[v] 2a pars *Quel foco che*

68 40 *Amor tu say* Archadelt (MaldP XXVI [1890], 27)

69 41 *Ytalia mia* Verdelot (RISM 1540_{18}, p. 7)

70 42[v] *Quien me otorgase señora*[a] Cancion Juan Vasquez (MME IV, 76)
43 2a pars *Aunque mill años turases*

71 43[v] *Argimina nombre le dio*[a] Anrriquez [Valderrábano] "Cancion de las reynas que fueron en españa . . . contrahecha a otra francesa"

72 44 *Señora si te olvidare*[a] Anrriquez [Valderrábano]

73 44[v] *Jamas cosa que quisiesse*[a 13] Anrriquez [Valderrábano]

[Within an ornamental border:] **1547** / COMI/ençan las obras com/puestas del quarto Libro para ta/ñer dos juntos en dos vihuelas, en / quatro maneras de temples, en uniso/nus, en tercera, en quarta, en quin/ta, lo qual es muy util y provecho/so para gozar de la musica, y / orden de las bozes, ay gu/ardas, y haspiraciones, / las quales se aguarda/ran, como es uso / en el canto de / organo.

74 45[v] *Assiste parata* Gombert (RISM 1538_2, p. 12: 2a pars of "O beata Maria") = 1552_{11}, no. 86

75 46[v] *Et in spiritum sanctum de la missa sobre la cancion mille regres* Morales (MME XI, 238: *Missa Mille regrets*) = 1552_{11}, no. 87

76 47[v] *Petite camusete*[a] Adriano [Willaert] (RISM 1572_2, fol. 57)

77 48[v] *Conde Claros* Anrriquez [Valderrábano]

78 49[v] *Andreas Christi Sancte Andrea** Morales (MME XIII, 157)

79 50[v] *Quanti mercenarii* Morales (MME XIII, 166)

80 51[v] *La primera parte del Credo de la missa de Josquin de beata virgine* (JosqMS, no. 16: *Missa de Beata Virgine*)

81 52v *Cum sancto spiritu* Morales (MME XI, 1: *Missa de Beata Virgine*)

82 53v *Pater noster** Adriano [Willaert] (WillO II, 11)

83 54v *Payne trabel* Mouton Cancion

84 55v *Cancion de sibivit* Adriano [Willaert] (RISM 1572$_2$, fol. 54v: "Or suis-je bien au pire") = 1552$_{11}$, no. 104

85 57v *Obsecro te domina** Josquin

86 58v *Contrapunto sobre el tenor de la baxa* Anrriquez [Valderrábano] = 1552$_{11}$, no. 105

87 60v *Inviolata* Josquin (JosqMT, no. 42)

61v 2a pars *O benigna*[14]

88 61v *Jubilate* [*deo*][14] Morales (MoralesO II, 184)

AQUI COMIENÇA EL / QUINTO LIBRO, EL QUAL TRATA DE FANTA/ sias, assi sueltas como acomposturadas. Las primeras que se / siguen son del primero grado, y por esto no / ternan tanta musica como las / de adelante.

89 63v *Fantasia. Quarto tono*[15] Anrriquez [Valderrábano] = 1552$_{11}$, no. 1

90 63v *Fantasia* = 1552$_{11}$, no. 2

91 64 *Fantasia sobre un Benedictus. Primero tono*

92 64 *Fantasia sobre entrada de una baxa. Tono mixto*

93 65 *Fantasia de tañer algo despacio. Tercero tono*

94 65v *Fantasia. Primero tono*

95 66v *Fantasia remedando en algunos pasos al aspice de Gombert* (compare SmijT II, 147: "Aspice Domine," Gombert)

96 67v *Fantasia remedando a una magnificat de Morales, que es al primer verso, y al tercero. Primero tono*

97 68 *Fantasia* [*contrahecha a otra estrangera*] *Otavo tono*[16] (compare 1536$_9$, no. 2: "Fantasia de M. Alberto [Ripa] da Mantua")

98 68v *Fantasia sobre un pleni de contrapunto*

99 69 *Fantasia contrahecha a una entrada de una ave maristella. Quinto tono*

100 69v *Fantasia. Quinto tono* = 1552$_{11}$, no. 9

101 70 *Fantasia de tañer conforme al tiempo, por que es de contrapunto. Quinto tono*[b]

102 70 [*Fantasia contrahecha a la del milanes*] *Quinto tono*[b] ("En esta fantasia se hallaran redobles") (compare 1536$_9$, no. 16: "Fantasia del divino Francesco da Milano")

103 71 *Fantasia remedando al motete de Gombert Inviolata. Quinto tono* (compare RISM 1539$_7$, no. 1: "Inviolata," Gombert)

104 71v *Fantasia sobre un benedictus de la misa de Mouton tua est potentia. Septimo tono* (compare RISM 1532$_2$: Mass no. 1)

105 72 *Fantasia sobre la entrada de la gloria de la misa de panis quem ego dabo. Septimo tono* (compare RISM 1532$_5$: Mass no. 3: Lupus)

106 73 *Fantasia. Primero tono*

107 73v *Fantasia remedada al chirie postrero de la misa de Josquin, de beata virgine. Primero tono* (compare JosqMS, no. 16)

108 74 *Fantasia sobre un Pleni* [*de una misa de Bauldoin*] *Primero tono*

109 74v *Fantasia hecha sobre una cancion. Primero tono*[b]

110 75v *Fantasia acomposturada de cierta parte de la missa de Ave maristella de Josquin. Primero tono* (JosqMS, no. 6)

111 76v *Fantasia. Primero tono*

112 77 *Fantasia sobre un quia fecit. Otavo tono* [Magnificat verse]

113 77v *Fantasia. Otavo tono*

114 78 *Fantasia. Quinto tono*

115 78v *Fantasia contrahecha a otra de Francisco milanes. Quinto tono*

116 79v *Fantasia remedando al motete de queramus cum pastoribus. Quinto tono* (compare RISM 1529$_1$, fol. 9v: "Queramus cum pastoribus," Mouton; see no. 117 below)

117 80 *Fantasia sobre la segunda parte del dicho motete, queramus cum pastoribus. Quinto tono* (see no. 116 above)
118 80^v *Fantasia de tañer espacio, por que es consonancia. Sexto tono*
119 81 *Fantasia. Tono mixto*
120 81^v *Fantasia. Quarto tono* (compare 1557_2, no. 63)
121 82 *Fantasia. Tono mixto*

LIBRO SEXTO EL / QUAL TRATA DE PARTES DE MISAS, DUOS, / CANCIONES, Y SONETOS, ALGUNOS FA/CILES DE TAÑER, EN EL PRIMERO / GRADO, A DONDE EL QUE / NO TOVIERE MANO HA/LLARA MAS FACILI/DAD QUE EN / OTRA PARTE DEL LIBRO, SALVO ALGUNAS PAR/TES DE MISAS QUE SON MAS DIFICULTO/SAS, QUE ES LO PRIMERO QUE / SE SIGUE.

122 83 *Qui tollis de la misa de pange lingua* Josquin (JosqMS, no. 18)
123 83^v *Osana* Mouton (CW LXX: *Missa Alleluya*, Mouton)
124 83^v *Agnus dei* Morales *a 3*
125 84 *Agnus dei de la misa de gaudeamus* Josquin (JosqMS, no. 3)
126 84^v *Cum sancto spiritu de la misa de ad fugam* Josquin (JosqMS, no. 14)
127 85 *Cum sancto spiritu de beata virgine* Josquin (JosqMS, no. 16)
128 85^v *Et incarnatus est de la misa de faysan regres* Josquin (JosqMS, no. 13)
129 85^v *Otra parte del credo de la dicha misa* Josquin (see preceding piece)
130 86 *Crucifixus de la misa de quem dicunt homines* (RISM 1540_1, no. 4: Mouton)
131 86^v *Et resurrexit Duo*
132 86^v *Benedictus Duo* (JosqMS, no. 6: *Missa Ave Maris Stella*) = 1552_{11}, no. 80
133 86^v *Pleni sunt Duo*
134 87 *Agnus dei Duo* (RISM 1532_2, Mass no. 1: *Missa Tua est potentia*, Mouton)
135 87 *Pleni sunt Duo*
136 87^v *Per illud ave Duo* Josquin (SmijO V, 146–154: 2a pars of "Benedicta es regina coelorum")
137 87^v *Et misericordia eius Duo* [Magnificat verse]
138 88 *Si tantos monteros* ("Soneto contrahecho ala sonada que dizen si tantos monteros")
139 88 *Adiu mes amours* Cancion (BerH, p. 66: Mouton)
140 88^v *Diviencela* (AttainCK III, no. 22: "Dont vient cela," Sermisy)
141 89 *Teresica hermana* (MitU, p. 91: Mateo Flecha)
142 89 *Ami sufle* (AttainCK III, no. 7: "Amy souffrez," Moulu)
143 89^v *Soneto lombardo a manera de dança*
144 90 *Soneto*[17]
145 90^v *Soneto*[17]
146 90^v *Soneto*
147 90^v *Soneto*
148 90^v *Soneto*
149 91 *Soneto* = 1552_{11}, no. 18
150 91 *Dichosa fue mi ventura* Soneto (in table: Villancico)
151 91^v *Soneto*
152 91^v *Soneto*
153 92 *Soneto*
154 92 *Soneto*
155 92^v *Soneto*
156 92^v *Soneto*
157 92^v *Omni mal de amor procedi* Morales (compare $152?_1$, no. 21: "Ogni mal d'amor procede," B[artolomeo] T[romboncino])
158 93 *Lo que queda es lo seguro* Soneto
159 93 *Soneto*
160 93^v *Soneto*
161 93^v *Gentil galans* Soneto
162 93^v *Soneto contrahecho a la sonada de benedicto sea el iorno*
163 94 *Soneto*
164 94 *Viva la Margarita* Soneto

LIBRO SEPTIMO / EL qual tracta de pavanas, y diferencias sobre guardame / las vacas, y para discantar sobre el conde claros, por / dos partes con otro discante facil.

165 94ᵛ *Pavana*[a 18] ("Quatro diferencias sobre la pavana por grados")

166 95ᵛ [*Pavana*] ("Tres diferencias sobre la dicha pavana por otro tono")

167 96ᵛ *Guardame las vacas*[19] (seven *diferencias*)

168 97ᵛ *Conde claros* (a set of *diferencias*) (compare 1552₁₁, no. 100)

169 99ᵛ *Conde claros* ("Otras diferentes diferencias") (compare 1552₁₁, no. 100)

170 103 *Sobre la pavana real*[a]

171 103ᵛ *Musica para discantar sobre un punto* [Two vihuelas]

[1] The compositions in Book IV marked with an asterisk are those for which the complete text is given in the intabulation.

[2] The Vienna copy has a variant title page, but is in all other respects identical with the other copies. The title page, within an ornamental border, reads: MUSIS DICATUM / Libro llamado / Silva de Sirenas. / Compuesto por el ex/celente musico Anriquez / de Valderavano. / Dirigido al ilustrissimo / senor don Francisco de / Çuñiga conde de / Miranda &c. / Con privilegio. / 1547 / NUNC REVIVISCO. The Vienna copy has manuscript music in Italian lute tablature (from the seventeenth century?) added at the end of the volume: fol. 105: [*19*] *Differencias de la çarabanda*; 105ᵛ: *Folias* (13 *diferencias*); 107: *Saltarello* (13 *diferencias*).

One of the Madrid copies (R. 14018) contains four pages of manuscript music in Italian lute tablature: fol. I (glued to the front cover): *Tiento de los Tonos. Fuenllana. Primero tono* = 1554₃, no. 174; I: *Segundo tono* = 1554₃, no. 175; I: *tercero tono* = 1554₃, no. 176; II (guard leaf at end of volume): *Fuenllana. Ave maris stella* = 1554₃, no. 170 (texted voice part in mensural notation; vihuela accompaniment in tablature); IIᵛ: fragments of music in mensural notation; III (glued to the back cover): fragments of music in mensural notation and in tablature.

[3] Most pieces in the volume are introduced by several sentences explaining the mode, the degree of difficulty, or how the solfa of the music can be located. These comments are omitted in the inventory. The preliminary remarks for no. 1, unusually full, are given here as an example: "Aqui se siguen dos fugas para principio de entender la musica deste libro, y son a tres, esta primera se señala desta manera para entender la solfa. tercera en primero traste se señala la clave de ce sol fa ut. para saber que la primera cifra colorada es alamire, cantando y tañendo la sol. sol. la. re. con las cifras negras. Y para mejor gustar estando tres juntos el que tañere cantara juntamente la dicha cifra colorada, y entonara al segundo en segunda en vazio, aguardando dos compases, como se vera en la primera señal, y el segundo entonara al tercero en prima en vazio, aguardando el dicho tercero un compas al segundo."

[4] Neither the setting by Verdelot, nor that by Sermisy (see Index V, below, for details).

[5] Loyset is probably not Compère (see FinschC, p. 141), but Pieton.

[6] Mod. ed. and quasi-facs. in WolfH II, 109–112.

[7] Mod. ed. in PedCP III, 121, and ValdeA (arr. for voice and guitar).

[8] Mod. ed. in BruAL I, 34.

[9] Mod. ed. in BalR, p. 18 (arr. for voice and piano), and PedCP III, 124.

[10] Mod. ed. of no. 40 in BruS II, no. 55; mod. ed. of no. 42 in WardM, p. 171.

[11] Mod. ed. in PedCP III, 118, and ValdeY (arr. for voice and guitar).

[12] Facs. of fol. 26ᵛ in AngME, pl. 30.

[13] Mod. ed. in PedCP III, 127.

[14] Facs. of fol. 61ᵛ in SubHME, p. 210. Facs. of fol. 63 (incl. the title for Book V) in SubHM I, 490, and SubHME, p. 221.

[15] Mod. ed. in ApelM II, 15, and SainzF, no. 2.

[16] Facs. in LiuM I, 84.

[17] Mod. ed. in PujHC, p. 3.

[18] Mod. ed. of first *diferencia* in BehS, p. 6.

[19] Mod. ed. in HAM, no. 124; first *diferencia* only in ApelL, p. 434.

1547₆

ATTAINGNANT, PIERRE, PUBLISHER

Second livre contenant trois Gaillardes, / TROIS PAVANES, VINGT TROIS BRANLES, / Tant gays, Simples, Que doubles, Douze basses dances, & Neuf tourdions, / En somme Cinquante, Le tout ordonne selon les huict tons. Et / nouvellement imprime en Musique a quatre parties, en ung / livre seul, par Pierre Attaingnant, Imprimeur / de musique du Roy, demourant a Paris / en la Rue de la Harpe, pres / leglise sainct Cosme. / 1547. / Avec prorogation du privilege du Roy, De nouvel obtenu par ledit attaingnant / Pour les livres Ia par luy imprimez & quil Imprimera cy apres jusques a six ans.[1]

32 fols. (signed I1–Q4ᵛ). Fol. I1ᵛ = fol. 1ᵛ. Mensural notation. The compositions identified by the superior letter *a* ([a]) are reprinted in MMRF XXIII, which includes a facsimile of the title page. For further information see CombDF and HeartzSF (which includes concordances). All of the compositions are for instrumental ensemble *a 4* except for no. 50, which is *a 5*.[2]

Copy in: F:Pn.

fol.

1 1^v *Basse dance*
2 1^v *Basse dance* = 154?$_6$, no. 25
3 2^v *Basse dance*
4 3^v *Basse dance*
5 4^v *Basse dance. Celle qui ma le nom damy donne*[a] (compare RISM 1543$_7$, no. 2: Sandrin)
6 5^v *Basse dance. La volunte*[a][3] (compare RISM 1543$_{11}$, no. 9: Sandrin)
7 6^v *Tourdion* = 154?$_6$, no. 28
8 6^v *Tourdion* = 154?$_6$, no. 26
9 7^v *Tourdion*[a][4]
10 7^v *Tourdion*
11 8^v *Branle*[a] = 1557$_3$, no. 8: "Bransle simple"
12 8^v *Branle* [*simple*] = 1559$_1$, no. 10: "Bransle commun"
13 9^v *Tourdion*
14 9^v *Branle* [*simple*]
15 10^v *Branle* [*simple*]
16 10^v *Branle* [*simple*]
17 11^v *Branle*[a] (compare 1530$_5$, no. 11, and 154?$_6$, no. 43: "Branle simple")
18 11^v *Branle* [*simple*]
19 12^v *Basse dance*
20 12^v *Branle* [*simple*]. *Lespoir que jay* (compare AttainCK III, no. 20)
21 13^v *Branle* [*simple*]
22 13^v *Branle* [*gay*]. *Mari je songeois laultre jour*[a] (compare RISM 1532$_{12}$, no. 18: Jacotin)
23 14^v *Branle* [*gay*][a]
24 14^v *Branle* [*double*][a] = 154?$_6$, no. 47: "Branle de bourgoigne," and 1550$_6$, no. 43: "Bransle de champaigne"
25 15^v *Branle* [*double*][a][5]
26 15^v *Branle*[a] = 1555$_5$, no. 12: "Bransle de champaigne"
27 16^v *Branle* = 1555$_5$, no. 13: "Bransle de champaigne"
28 16^v *Branle* (compare 1564$_5$, no. 33: "Branle courant")
29 17^v *Basse dance. Aupres de vous* (compare AttainCK I, no. 16: Sermisy or Jacotin)
30 18^v *Tourdion. Cest grand plaisir*[a] (compare AttainCK I, no. 17)
31 19^v *Tourdion. Vous aurez tout ce qui est myen*[a][6] (compare RISM 1532$_{12}$, no. 28)
32 20^v *Basse dance*
33 21^v *Basse dance. Content desir* (compare BrownTC, no. 13: Sermisy)
34 22^v *Basse dance. Par fin despit*[a] (compare RISM 1534$_{14}$, no. 8: Sermisy)
35 23^v *Branle* [*simple*][a]
36 24^v *Branle gay. Que je chatoulle ta fossette*[a][7]
37 25^v *Branle*[a] = 154?$_6$, no. 42: "Branle simple"
38 25^v *Basse dance. Trop de regretz*[a] (compare RISM 1530$_5$, no. 2: [Hesdin])
39 26^v *Tourdion*[a]
40 26^v *Tourdion*
41 27^v *Branle* (compare 1557$_3$, no. 12: "Bransle simple")
42 27^v *Branle gay*
43 28^v *Branle*[a] = 1555$_5$, no. 15: "Bransle de champaigne"
44 28^v *Branle* = 1555$_5$, no. 14: "Bransle de champaigne" (compare 1559$_1$, no. 46)
45 29^v *Pavane*
46 29^v *Pavane*
47 30^v *Pavane* = 1555$_2$, no. 202
48 31^v *Gaillarde*
49 31^v *Gaillarde*
50 32^v *Gaillarde* [*a 5*]

[1] Facs. of title page in EF II, 252.

[2] The following volumes from the same series survive: III (1557$_3$), IV (1550$_5$), V (1550$_6$), VI (1555$_5$), and VII (1557$_4$).

[3] Mod. ed. in BarthaZ, no. 49a; HAM, no. 137a; and TwittT II, no. 1.

[4] Mod. ed. in TwittT I, no. 3.

[5] Mod. ed. in BarthaZ, no. 50c.

[6] Mod. ed. in BarthaZ, no. 49b, and TwittT I, no. 2.

[7] Mod. ed. in BS, vol. 51.

1547$_7$

PHALÈSE, PIERRE, PUBLISHER

Des Chansons Reduictz en Tabulature de / LUT A DEUX, TROIS, ET QUATRE PARTIES. / Avec une briefve & familiaire Introduction pour entendre & apprendre par / soy mesmes a jouer dudict Lut. / Livre premier. / [Cut of ten performing musicians] / A Louvain par Pierre de

Phaleys libraire jure / Lan M. D. XLVII. / Avec Grace & Privilege.[1]

32 fols. French lute tablature. Printer's privilege on fol. A1^v: "Il est defendu a tous libraires & imprimeurs de nenprimer les Tabulatures de Lut, si non du consentement de Pierre Phaleys libraire jure, sur la peine de la confiscation des toutes les libres & lamende de 25. Carolus comme plus amplement est declaire en les lettres par Limperialle Ma. a luy donnez. Nel an 1546. En soubsigne P. de Lens." Beginning on fol. A2: the same instructions for playing the lute that appear in 1545_3. Colophon on fol. H4^v: "LOVANII Ex officina Jacobi Batii typographi jurati, & à Caes. Ma. admiss. Anno Domini M. D. XLVII. [Cut of a lute]." The volume is a revised edition of 1545_3. All compositions appearing in the 1545 edition are marked with an asterisk. Attributions in brackets are from that edition. See 1545_3 for the sources of the intabulations. Contents = 1547_8. All of the compositions are for solo lute.

Copy in: GB:Lbmh.

	fol.	
1	B1	_Praeludium_*
2	B1^v	_Praeludium_*
3	B1^v	_Praeludium_*
4	B2	_Praeludium_[2]
5	B2^v	_Praeludium_*
6	B3	_Praeludium_*
7	B3^v	_Die lustelycke Mey_*
8	B4	_Jay mis mon cueur_*
9	B4^v	_Damour je suis desherite_*
10	C1	_Amour vault trop_*
11	C1^v	_Dolent depart_*
12	C2	_Ces facheux sotz_*
13	C2^v	_Il me souffit_* [Sermisy]
14	C3	_Dont vient cela_* [Sermisy]
15	C3^v	_Le cueur est bon_*
16	C4	_Tous mes amys_* [Sermisy]
17	C4^v	_Languir mi_* [Sermisy]
18	D1	_Amys souffrez_* [Moulu]
19	D1^v	_Een vrolick Wesen_* [Barbireau, Isaac, or Obrecht]
20	D2^v	_Languir mi fault_* [Sermisy]
21	D3	_Tant que vivray_* [Sermisy]
22	D3^v	_Cest donc par moy_*
23	D4^v	_Du bon du cueur_*
24	E1^v	_Miin hert heeft altiit verlangen_*
25	E2^v	_Miins liefkens bruyn ooghen_*
26	E3^v	_Il me souffit_* [Sermisy]
27	E4	_Helas amy_* [Sandrin]
28	E4^v	_Aupres de vous_*
29	F1	_Ick seg adieu_ = 1544_2, no. 43
30	F1^v	_Ung gay bergier_* [Crecquillon]
31	F2^v	_Le content est riche_* [Sermisy]
32	F3^v	_Plourez mes yeulx_* [Sandrin]
33	F4	_Jamais naymeray masson_*
34	F4^v	_Pour ung petit coup_*
35	G1	_Sur tous regres_* [Richafort]
36	G2^v	_Tant que vivray_* [Sermisy]
37	G3	_Het is soe goeden dinck_
38	G3^v	_Or sus a coup_*
39	G4	_Grace & vertu_ (RISM [c. 1528]$_5$, no. 7: [Roquelay])
40	G4^v	_De mon triste_[3] (compare BrownTC, no. 16: Richafort)
41	H1	_Cest grand plaisir_*
42	H1^v	_Gequest ben ick_ (compare DuyL I, 541, and III, 2731; and LenN, p. 84) = 1563_{12}, no. 93
43	H2^v	_Quant je cogneu. la responce de helas amy_ (RISM [1539]$_{20}$, fol. 20: Sandrin)
44	H3^v	_Roude_* [sic]
45	H4	_Ronde_*

[1] Facs. of the title page in HirK III, pl. 13; KommaM, p. 93; MGG II, col. 1075; and ZurM, p. 28.

[2] Incipit in SlimK II, 499.

[3] Mod. ed. in WardLM, p. 124.

1547_8

PHALÈSE, PIERRE, PUBLISHER

Carminum quae Chely vel Testudine ca/NUNTUR, DUARUM, TRIUM, ET QUATUOR PARTIUM, / Liber Primus. / Cum brevi Introductione in usum Testudinis. / Omnia recens & elegantius quàm antea unquàm impressa. / [Cut of ten performing musicians] / LOVANII, / Apud Petrum Phalesium bibliopolam iuratum, Anno Domini / M. D. XLVII. / Cum gratia & privilegio Caes. Ma. ad triennium.

32 fols. French lute tablature. Printer's privilege on fol. A2^v: "Caesaris privilegio cantum est ne quis haec exemplaria excudat aut distrahere tentet, nisi de consensu Petri Phalesii bibliopolae iurati, sub poena confiscationis omnium librorum, ac mulctae aurariae 25. florenorum, uti latius patet in literis illi à Cae. Ma. concessis. Subsignavit

Philippus de Lens," followed by the table of contents. Beginning on fol. A3: the same instructions for playing the lute as in 1545_{3}, here translated into Latin. Colophon on fol. H4v: "LOVANII Ex officina Iacobi Batii typographi iurati, & à Caes. Ma. admis. Anno Domini M. D. XLVII. [Cut of a lute]." Contents = 1547_{7}. All of the compositions are for solo lute.

Copy in: A:Wn.

1547_{9}

PHALÈSE, PIERRE, PUBLISHER

Des Chansons & Motets Reduicts en / TABULATURE DE LUC, A QUATRE, CINQUE ET / SIX PARTIES, LIVRE TROIXIESME. / Composees par lexcellent maistre PIERRE DI TEGHI Paduan. / La table vous trouverez au dernier feullet. / [Cut of ten performing musicians] / A LOUVAIN. / Par Piere Phaleys libraire jure, nel an de Grace / M. D. XLVII. / Avec Grace & privilege a troix ans

36 fols. French lute tablature. On fol. Aa1v: same printer's privilege as in 1547_{7}. On fol. Ii3: table of contents. Colophon on fol. Ii3v: "LOVANII. Excudebat Jacobus Batius, typographus juratus, & à Caes. Maies. admissus. M. D. XLVII. [Cut of a lute]." WieM II contains a thematic index of the volume and selected transcriptions. Contents = 1547_{10} and 1573_{5}. All of the compositions are for solo lute.

Copies in: A:Wn, GB:Lbmh.

fol.

1 Aa2 *Je prens en gre* (ClemensO X, 14: Clemens non Papa) = 1552_{11}, no. 25; 1563_{12}, no. 25; 1568_{7}, no. 38; 1573_{3}, no. 18

2 Aa3v *Damour me plains. Descendat uno tono maior nervus*[1] (PubAPTM XXIII, no. 49; Pathie) = 1552_{11}, no. 30; 1563_{12}, no. 34; 1568_{7}, no. 45; 1571_{6}, no. 49

3 Aa4v *Vous perdez tamps* (PubAPTM XXIII, no. 56: Sermisy) = 1552_{11}, no. 43, and 1563_{12}, no. 21

4 Bb1v *Tel en mesdict* ("Responce" to no. 3) (RISM 1540_{10}, no. 15: Mittantier) = 1552_{11}, no. 44; 1563_{12}, no. 22; 1568_{7}, no. 25; 1571_{6}, no. 38

5 Bb2v *Si mon travail* (PubAPTM XXIII, no. 52: Sandrin) = 1552_{11}, no. 27; 1563_{12}, no. 26; 1568_{7}, no. 30; 1571_{6}, no. 43

6 Bb3 *Le deul yssu* ("Response" to no. 5) (RISM 1540_{9}, no. 14: Villiers) = 1552_{11}, no. 28

7 Bb4 *Il estoit une fiellette* (LesAC, no. 10: Janequin) = 1563_{12}, no. 101

8 Bb4v *Ung gay bergiere* (RieH II, 462, Crecquillon) = 1568_{1}, no. 33; 1568_{7}, no. 39b; 1571_{6}, no. 51

9 Cc1v *Jay veu que jestois franc* (RISM 1543_{7}, no. 4: Sandrin)

10 Cc2v *Je ne puis bonnement penser* (RISM 1541_{5}, no. 6: Sandrin)

11 Cc3 *Doulce memoire. Descendat bassus uno tono* (PubAPTM XXIII, no. 50: Sandrin) = 1552_{11}, no. 60

12 Cc4 *Fini le bien. Descendat bassus uno tono* ("Responce" to no. 11) (RISM 1540_{11}, no. 8: Certon) = 1552_{11}, no. 61; 1563_{12}, no. 29; 1568_{7}, no. 27; 1571_{6}, no. 40

13 Dd1 *Aime aime* (RISM 1541_{9}, p. 53: "Ahime, ahime dov'e'l bel viso," Arcadelt)

14 Dd2v *Queramus cum pastoribus* (RISM 1529_{1}, fol. 9v: Mouton)

Dd4 2a pars *Ubi pascas ubi cubes*

15 Ee1v *Ave sanctissima a 4* = 1546_{5}, no. 14: Gombert

16 Ee4 *Si bona suscepimus a 5* (MoralesO I, 274: Verdelot)

17 Ff2v *Hierusalem luge a 5* (RISM 1532_{9}, p. 49: Richafort [or Lupus?])

Ff3v 2a pars *Deduc quasi torrente a 5 Descendat bassus*

18 Gg1v *Pater noster a 6* (JosqMT, no. 50: Josquin)

Gg4 2a pars *Ave Maria a 6*

19 Hh2 *Benedicta [es caelorum regina] a 6* (JosqMT, no. 46: Josquin)

Ii1	2a pars	*Per illud ave*
Ii2	3a pars	*Nunc mater*

[1] Mod. ed. in KosackL, app. III.

1547_{10}

PHALÈSE, PIERRE, PUBLISHER

Carminum ad Testudinis usum composi/ TORUM LIBER TERTIUS. / Ab excellentissimo artifice PETRO TEGHIO Patavino elegantissime concinnatus. / Tabulam Carminum habes ultima pagella. / [Cut of ten performing musicians] / LOVANII. / Apud Petrum Phalesium bibliopolam iuratum, Anno Domini / M. D. XLVII. / Cum gratia & privilegio Caes. Ma. ad triennium.

36 fols. French lute tablature. On fol. Aa1^{v}: the same printer's privilege as in 1547_{8}. On fol. Ii3: table of contents. Colophon on fol. Ii3^{v}: "LOVANII. Excudebat Iacobus Batius, typographus iuratus, & à Caes. Maies. admissus. M.D.XLVII. [Cut of a lute]." Contents = 1547_{9}. All of the compositions are for solo lute.

Copy in: A:Wn.

[1547]$_{11}$

PHALÈSE, PIERRE, PUBLISHER

DES Chansons Gaillardes, Paduanes & Mo/TETZ, REDUITZ EN TABULATURE DE LUC, / Par les excellentz Maistres Francoys, de Milan, A. à Rota, & Jean Maria / de Crema & autres, / LIVRE CINQUIESME. / [Cut of ten performing musicians] / A LOUVAIN / Par PIERE PHALEYS Libraire Jure. Nel an de grace / M. D. XLVII. / Avec Grace & Privilege.

32 fols. French lute tabulature. On fol. H4: table of contents and printer's privilege. On fol. H4^{v}: colophon and printer's mark. This volume, now lost, was in D:Bds. Mme. la comtesse de Chambure made an inventory of the contents from the Berlin copy. I am grateful to her for granting me permission to reproduce her inventory, and to Arthur Ness and Brigadier Michael W. Prynne for making it available to me. The concordances in the inventory below are all conjectural. Contents = [1547]$_{12}$. All of the compositions were for solo lute.

	fol.	
1	A1	*Fantasie*
2	A2	*Fantasie*
3	A3^{v}	*Fantasie*
4	A4^{v}	*Fantasie de mon triste de F. de Milan* = 1547_{2}, no. 8
5	B1^{v}	*De mon triste* F. de Milan = 1547_{2}, no. 7: Richafort
6	B2	*Vivre ne puis content* = 1546_{10}, no. 17: Sermisy
7	B3	*Jay mis le cuer* = 1546_{10}, no. 18: "Jayme le cueur," Sermisy (?)
8	B3^{v}	*De vous servir* = 1546_{10}, no. 19: Sermisy
9	B4	*Amours ont changes* = 1546_{10}, no. 20: Mahiet
10	B4^{v}	*Elle lara* = 1546_{10}, no. 22: "Je le laray" (?)
11	C1^{v}	*Ho la he* = 1546_{10}, no. 25
12	C2	*Et don bon soir* = 1546_{10}, no. 26
13	C3	*Bayse moy tant* = 1546_{10}, no. 27
14	C4	*Mon amy* = 1546_{10}, no. 28
15	C4^{v}	*El neye plaisir* [in table: "El nye plaisir"] = 1546_{10}, no. 29: "Il nest plaisir," Janequin (?)
16	D1	*Puis ce que* = 1546_{10}, no. 30 = "Mais quest ce" (?)
17	D2	*Allons, allons* = 1546_{10}, no. 31: Willaert
18	D3	*Helas mon dieu* = 1546_{15}, no. 13
19	D3^{v}	*A qui me doit je retirer* = 1546_{15}, no. 14: Maille
20	D4^{v}	*Malheureux suis fortune* = 1546_{15}, no. 16: Meigret
21	E1^{v}	*Fringotes uenes filettes* = 1546_{15}, no. 17: Payen
22	E2^{v}	*Le dur travail* = 1546_{5}, no. 20: Willaert
23	E3^{v}	*Que voules vous dire de moy* = 1547_{2}, no. 23
24	E4^{v}	*Par ton regard* = 1546_{5}, no. 19: Sermisy
25	F1	*Cest grand pitie* = 1546_{5}, no. 16: Certon
26	F1^{v}	*Amour crainte & esperance sont ensamble*

27 F2v *A demy mort*
28 F3v *A dieu vous dit*
29 F4v *In illo tempore* = 1546_{15}, no. 19: Mouton
G2 2a pars *Propter hoc relinquet*
30 G3 *Si bona suscepimus* (*a4*) = 1546_{10}, no. 35: Sermisy
31 H1 *Gaiarda*
32 H1v *Passa mezo*
33 H2 *Gaiarda*
34 H2v *Gaiarda*
35 H3 *Passe e mezo a la Bolognese* = 1546_{10}, no. 45
H3v *Saltarello a la Bolognesa*

[1547]$_{12}$

PHALÈSE, PIERRE, PUBLISHER

Carminum pro Testudine, in quo conti/ NENTUR EXCELLENTISSIMA CARMINA, / Galliarda, Paduana, ac Moteta: Composita per Franciscum Mediolanensem, / A. Rota & Joannem Maria Cremens. ac alios in hac arte / praestantissimos, / LIBER QUINTUS. / [Cut of ten performing musicians] / LOVANII / Apud PETRUM PHALESIUM Bibliopolam Iuratum. / ANNO M. D. XLVII. / Cum Gratia & Privilegio.

32 fols. French lute tablature. This volume, now lost, was in D: Bds. Contents = [1547]$_{11}$. See there for further details. All of the compositions were for solo lute.

1547

DOUBTFUL WORKS

1. PiciA, p. 197, lists the following volume of lute music by Francesco da Milano: "Lib. I. Intavolatura di liuto. Venet. 1547." He probably refers to 1546_6.

2. WolfH II, 256, mistakenly lists a 1547 edition of *Jacques Buus, Intabolatura d'Organo di Ricercari . . . Libro Primo*. The volume is listed in this bibliography as 1549_4.

1548_1

ABONDANTE, JULIO

INTABOLATURA / DI LAUTTO LIBRO SECONDO. / Madrigali a cinque & a quattro. / Canzoni Franzese a cinque & a quattro / Motetti a cinque, & a quattro. / Recercari di fantasia, / Napolitane a quattro / Intabulati & accomodati per sonar di Lautto per lo Excellentissimo M. / Julio abondante. Novamente poste in luce, & per / lui medemo corretti. / In Venetia appresso Hieronimo Scotto. / M. D. XLVIII.

4 + 28 fols. Italian lute tablature. Dedication on fol. *1v headed "AL NOBILE ET GENEROSO S. Allessandro Ramuino del Nobilissimo S.or Gian Antonio Genovese .S. mio osservandis." Fol. *5 = fol. A1. SlimK II, 511, contains a thematic index of the ricercares. All of the compositions are for solo lute.

Copies in: A: Wn, CH: Lcortot.

fol.
1 *2 *Qual dolcezza giamai* m. Adriano Vilaert (WagMP, p. 449)
*3 2a pars [*E la dolc'armonia si fa serena l'aria*]
2 *4v *Amor che vedi ogni pensiero aperto* m. Cipriano Rore (Vogel: Rore 2 [1544], nos. 31 and 32)
A2 2a pars *Ben veggio di lontano il dolce lume*
3 A3 *La pastorella mia che m'inamora* Pre Nicola Vicentino (Vogel: Vicentino 1 [1546], no. 1)
4 A4 *Se l'alto duol m'ancide* M. Leonardus Barre (RISM 1540_{18}, p. 5)
A4 2a pars [*Ond'all'estremo passo pianto*]
5 B1 *Cantai mentre ch io arsi del mio fuoco* (Vogel: Rore 2 [1544], no. 5: Rore)
6 B2v *Qual anima ignorante* (RISM 1543_{17}, p. 3: Nollet)
7 B3v *Cosi mi guida amor* (RISM 1543_{17}, p. 9: Arcadelt)
8 B4v *Da bei rami scendea* (RISM 1543_{17}, p. 5: Arcadelt)

9 C1v *Con lei fusio* (RISM 1543_{17}, p. 36: Arcadelt, Berchem, Corteccia, or Giaches de Ponte)
10 C2v *Helas mamert* (RISM 1572_2, fol. 1v: "Helas ma mère helas maman," Willaert)
11 C4 *Mia de lognon* (RISM 1538_{19}, no. 24: "Il y a de longnon," Payen)
12 D1v *Fringotes [jeunes fillettes]* (RISM 1538_{19}, no. 2: Payen)
13 D2v *Mais ma mignone* (RISM 1538_{19}, no. 16: Janequin)
14 D3v *Prenes le galan* (RISM 1538_{19}, no. 9: Janequin or Sohier)
15 E1 *Si dum pet de vetre bien* (RISM 1538_{19}, no. 1: "Si dung petit de votre bien," Janequin)
16 E2 *Cantantibus organis* M. Cipriano Rorre (RoreO I, no. 16)
E3 2a pars *Biduanis ac triduanis*
17 E4v *Pater noster*[1] M. Adriano [Willaert] (WillO II, 11)
18 F2v *Fantasia* Julio abondante
19 F3 *Fantasia* Julio abondante
20 F4 *Fantasia*[2] Julio abondante
21 G1 *Fantasia* Julio abondante
22 G1v *Fantasia* Julio abondante
23 G2v *Madonna mia fami bona offerta*[3] (RISM 1545_{20}, no. 6: Willaert)
24 G3 *A quando a quando havea*[4] (RISM 1545_{20}, no. 11: Willaert)
25 G3v *Vechie retrose* (RISM 1545_{20}, no. 5: Willaert)
26 G4 *Madonna io non lo so perche lo sai* (CW VIII, 18: Willaert)

[1] Mod. ed. in ChilP, p. 469.
[2] Mod. ed. in ChilLI, p. 247.
[3] Mod. ed. in ChilLI, p. 249, and EC, pt. I, vol. II, p. 654 (with title "Napolitana").
[4] Mod. ed. in ChilLI, p. 250.

1548_2

BORRONO, PIETRO PAOLO

INTAVOLATURA / DI LAUTO / DELL'ECCELLENTE PIETRO PAOLO BORRONO / DA MILANO, NUOVAMENTE POSTA IN LUCE, ET CON OGNI / diligentia corretta, opera perfettissima sopra qualunche altra Intavolatura / che da qua indrieto [sic] sia stampata. / LIBRO [Printer's mark] OTTAVO / Venetiis apud Hieronymum Scotum. / M. D. XLVIII.

36 fols. Italian lute tablature. Contents are almost identical with 1548_3 (see there for details). See 1563_3 (which is available in a modern edition) for a partial reprint of 1548_2. MoeDM contains a thematic index of the dances (p. 386) and concordances for them (p. 248). SlimK II, 517, contains a thematic index of the ricercares. For other volumes in the same series, see 1546_2, note 1. All of the compositions are for solo lute.

Copy in: I:Vnm.[1]

fol.
1 A1v *Pavana detto la bella Andronica dell'eccell. P. P. Borrono*
A3 *Saltarello primo*
A4 *Saltarello Secondo*
A4v *Saltarello*
2 B1v *Pavana detta la Lacrimosa* [P. P. Borrono]
B2v *Saltarello primo*
B3v *Saltarello secondo detto la Laurina*
B4v *Saltarello terzo detto il Penono*
3 C1v *Pavana novissima detta la Lucretia* [P. P. Borrono]
C2v *Saltarello primo*
C4 *Saltarello secondo detto la bella Bianca ha hauto torto*
D1 *Saltarello terzo detto O chel me tira il brazo*
4 D2 *Saltarello secondo detto [recte: Pavana chiamata] la bella Bianca Margarita*[2]
D3 *Saltarello primo*
D4 *Saltarello secondo detto Se la passasse*
E1 *Saltarello terzo dell Duchessa*[3]
5 E2 *Fantasia* Francesco da Milano
6 E4v *Fantasia* Francesco di Milano
7 F1v *Fantasia* Francesco da Milano
8 F2 *Fantasia*[4] Francesco da Milano
9 F3 *Fantasia* Francesco da Milano
10 F3v *Fantasia*[5] Francesco da Milano
11 F4 *Fantasia* Francesco da Milano
12 F4v *Fantasia* Francesco da Milano
13 G1 *Fantasia* Francesco da Milano = 1563_{11}, no. 12

14 G1v *Fantasia*[6] P. Paolo Borrono = 1563_{11}, no. 13

15 G2v *Fantasia* Francesco da Milano = 1563_{11}, no. 14

16 G3 *Fantasia*[7] Francesco da Milano

17 G4v *Fantasia* P. Paolo Borrono

18 H2 *Le content est riche* Canzon Franzese (AttainCK III, no. 9: Sermisy)

19 H2v *Gemi mon cur* Canzon Francese (AttainCK III, no. 16: "J'ay mis mon cuer")

20 H3 *Ale venture* Canzon Francese (CM II, no. 5: "A l'aventure," Willaert)

21 H4 *Mala Se nea* Canzon Francese Josquino *a 5*

22 I1 *Bon Juor mamye* (RISM 1531_1, no. 18)

23 I1v *Noe noe noe psallite noe Hierusalem* Jo. Moton *a 4* (SmijT II, 8)

24 I3v *Noe noe noe puer nobis nascetur* Jo. Moton *a 4*

[1] A copy was in the Wolffheim library (see WolffC I, no. 1187).
[2] Mod. ed. of no. 4a in ChilLI, p. 260.
[3] Mod. ed. in MoeDM, p. 342.
[4] Mod. ed. in ChilF, no. 9.
[5] Mod. ed. in SlimK II, 628.
[6] Mod. ed. in SlimK II, 618.
[7] Mod. ed. in ChilF, no. 8.

1548_3

FRANCESCO DA MILANO AND PIETRO PAOLO BORRONO

INTAVOLATURA DI / LAUTO DEL DIVI/NO FRANCESCO DA MILANO, ET DELL'/ECCELLENTE PIETRO PAULO BOR/rono da Milano nuovamente posta in luce: & con ogni diligentia cor/retta, opera novissima & perfettissima sopra qualunche altra In/tavolatura che da qua indreto sia stampata facendo certo a / tutto il mondo che piu non si poter a imprimere de meglio. / CON GRATIA ET PRIVILEGII CONCESSI DAL / SANTISSIMO PAPA PAULO .III. DAL SE/renissimo Imperatore, Et Illustrissima Signoria di Venetia che niuno / possa Imprimere tale opera, ne Impressa vendere fino ad / anni dieci sotto pena como in esst Privilegii si contene. / M. D. XLVIII. / LIBRO SECONDO.

40 fols. Italian lute tablature. On fol. A1v: dedication "ALL'ILLUSTRE ET GENEROSO S. IL S. CONTE HIPPOLITO DEL MAYNO. Jo: Battista Borrono." On fol. A2: "Regola per quelli che non sanno la Intavolatura." On fol. A2v: table of contents. On fol. 40v: colophon, "Stampato nella Inclita Citta de Milano per Gio: Antonio da Castilliono ad Instantia de .M. Gio: Bap. Borrono." Contents = 1548_2, with the addition of one more fantasia by Francesco da Milano between 1548_2, nos. 17 and 18. This fantasia is reprinted in 1574_1, no. 2. All of the compositions are for solo lute.

Copy in: F:Pthibault (imperfect).

1548_4

FRANCESCO DA MILANO

INTABOLATURA / DE LAUTTO LIBRO SETTIMO. / Recercari novi del Divino M. Francesco da Milano. Estratti da li soi / proprii Esemplari li quali non sono mai piu stati / visti ne stampati. / AGGIONTOVI ALCUNI ALTRI RECERCA/ri di Julio da Modena intabulati & acomodati per so/nar sopra il Lautto da M. Jo. Maria da Crema so/natore Excelentissimo opera veramente di/vina como a quelli che la sonarano & / udiranosara palese / Apresso di Hieronimo Schotto. / M. D. XLVIII.

23 fols. Italian lute tablature. SlimK II, 512, and WieM II both contain a thematic index of the volume. The compositions followed by an asterisk are headed by a plus sign printed in red. For other volumes in the same series, see 1546_2, note 1. All of the compositions are for solo lute.

Copies in: A:Wn, GB:Lbmh.

fol.

1 A2 *Recercario primo*[1] Francesco da Milan = 1563_4, no. 14

2 A2v *Recercar secondo* Francesco da Milan = 1563_4, no. 15

3	A3	*Recercar terzo* Francesco da Milan = 1563_4, no. 16
4	A3ᵛ	*Recercar quarto* [2] Francesco da Milan (compare 1536_3, no. 10) = 1563_4, no. 17
5	A4	*Recercar quinto* Francesco da Milan
6	A4ᵛ	*Recercar sesto* Francesco da Milan
7	B1	*Recercar settimo* Francesco da Milan
8	B1ᵛ	*Recercar ottavo* Francesco da Milan
9	B2ᵛ	*Recercario nono* Francesco da Milan
10	B3ᵛ	*Recercario decimo* [3] Francesco da Milan
11	B4ᵛ	*Recercario undecimo* Francesco da Milan
12	C1	*Recercario duodecimo* Francesco da Milan
13	C1ᵛ	*Recercar terzo decimo* Francesco da Milan
14	C4	*Recercar primo* Julio da Modena [Giulio Segni] (compare 1546_{10}, no. 1)
15	C4ᵛ	*Recercar secondo* [Julio da Modena] = 1546_{10}, no. 5
16	D1	*Recercar terzo* [4] [Julio da Modena]
17	D2	*Recercario quarto* [Julio da Modena] = 1552_4, no. 1
18	D3ᵛ	*Recercar quinto* [Julio da Modena]
19	D4ᵛ	*Recercar sesto* [Julio da Modena]
20	E1	*Recercar setimo** [Julio da Modena] = 1546_{10}, no. 7
21	E2ᵛ	*Recercar ottavo* [Julio da Modena]
22	E3ᵛ	*Recercar nono* [Julio da Modena]
23	F1	*Recercar decimo** [Julio da Modena]
24	F2	*Recercario undecimo** [Julio da Modena]
25	F3	*Recercar duodecimo* [Julio da Modena]

[1] Mod. ed. in ChilB VIII, no. 2; ChilLS, p. 53 (after 1563_4); and EC, pt. I, vol. II, p. 646.
[2] Mod. ed. in SlimK II, 632.
[3] Mod. ed. in SlimK II, 630.
[4] Mod. ed. in SlimK II, 611.

1549_1

BARBERIIS, MELCHIORE DE

INTABOLATURA DI LAUTO / LIBRO NONO INTITOLATO IL BEMBO, / DI FANTASIE, BALLI, PASSI E MEZI, E PADOANE GAGLIARDE, / Composte per il Reverendo M. pre Melchioro de Barberis Padoano, Musico, & sonator / di Lauto eccellentissimo. Dedicato al Signor Torquato Bembo. / LIBRO [Printer's mark: an anchor decorated with the motto "IN TENEBRIS FULGET," and the initials "S O S"] NONO / Venetiis apud Hieronymum Scotum. / M. D. XLIX.

22 fols. Italian lute tablature. Dedication on fol. a1ᵛ headed "AL REVERENDISSIMO SIGNOR MIO IL SIGNOR TORQUATO BEMBO." MoeDM contains a thematic index of the dances (p. 389) and concordances for them (p. 248). SlimK II, 519, contains a thematic index of the ricercares. The compositions identified by superior letters are reprinted as follows: ([a]) in ChilLI, pp. 242–245; ([b]) in MoeDM. Modern editions of a pavane and a saltarello are in PujBG, no. 1061. The second dance in each of the paired dances except no. 24 is related to the first thematically. For other volumes in the same series, see 1546_2, note 1. All of the compositions are for solo lute.

Copies in: A:Wn, US:Wc.

	fol.	
1	a2	*Passo e mezo*
2	a2ᵛ	*Passo e mezo*
3	a3	*Gagliarda*
4	a3ᵛ	*Saltarello*
5	a4	*Saltarello*
6	a4ᵛ	*La pavana del Duca*[b]
	b1	*Saltarello*[b]
7	b1	*Pass'e mezo* [*antico*]
	b2	*Saltarello*
8	b2ᵛ	*Pass'e mezo*
	b3	*Saltarello*
9	b4	*Saltarello*[a]
10	b4ᵛ	*Piva*
11	c1ᵛ	*Pass'e mezo* [*antico*]
12	c2ᵛ	*La Bertonzina*[a]
13	c3	*Brando Franzese*
14	c3	*Vesentino*[b]
15	c3ᵛ	*Saltarello gagliardo*
16	c3ᵛ	*Pavana*
	c4ᵛ	*Saltarello*

17 d1 *Pavana*[a 1]
d1[v] *Saltarello*[a 1]
18 d1[v] *Pass'e mezo della Battaia*
d2 *Saltarello del Pass'e mezo della Battaia*
19 d3 *Saltarello*[a]
20 d3[v] *Pavana gagliarda*
d4 *Seconda parte*
e1 *Saltarello*
21 e1[v] *La cara cosa*[b]
22 e2 *Il vecchio da Conegian*
23 e2[v] *Saltarello La vilanella*
24 e3 *Il Formigoto*
e3[v] *Saltarello del Formigoto: Madonna Tenerina*
25 e4 *Il traditore*
26 e4[v] *Mia mare e anda al merco per comprarme un pignolo*[b] (compare RISM 1569_{24}, no. 10: Azzaiolo)
27 f1 *Fantasia*[2]
28 f1[v] *Fantasia*
29 f2[v] *Piangete occhi miei lassi*
30 f3 *Fantasia*
31 f4 *Vray dieu damors* Josquin (GB:Lbm, Add. MS 35087, fol. 84[v]: "Vray dieu damours confortez moy," anon.)
32 g1 *Fantasia*

[1] Mod. ed. in EC, pt. I, vol. II, p. 654.

1549_2

BARBERIIS, MELCHIORE DE

OPERA INTITOLATA CONTINA, / INTABOLATURA DI LAUTO DI FANTASIE, MOTETTI, / CANZONI, DISCORDATE A VARII MODI, FANTASIE PER SONAR / uno solo con uno Lauto, & farsi tenore & soprano: Madrigali per sonar a dui Lauti: Fantasie per / sonar a dui Lauti: Fantasie per sonar sopra la Chitara da sette corde. / COMPOSTA PER IL REVERENDO M. PRE MELCHIORO / de Barberis Padoano, Musico, & sonator di Lauto eccellentissimo. / LIBRO [Cut of printer's mark of Girolamo Scotto] DECIMO. / Venetiis apud Hieronymum Scotum / M. D. XLIX.

30 fols. Italian lute and guitar tablature. Dedication on fol. Aa1[v] headed "IMPERATORIAE MAJESTATIS COMITI FIDELISSIMO AC CANONICO PATAVINO RELIGIOSISSIMO HERCULI A SANCTO Bonifacio patrono suo observandiss. Melchior Barberius Sacerdos Patavinus, & humillimus servus S. P. D.," and dated "VI. Kal. Januarii. M. D. XLIX." On fol. Hh2: table of contents. SlimK II, 520, contains a thematic index of the ricercares. For other volumes in the same series, see 1546_2, note 1. Nos. 1–15, 17, and 19–24 are for solo lute; nos. 16 and 18 are for two lutes; and nos. 25–28 are for solo seven-course guitar.

Copies in: A:Wn, CH:Lcortot, D:W, F:Pthibault.

	fol.	
1	Aa2[v]	*Recercada Prima parte*
	Aa3	*Fantasia Seconda parte*
2	Aa4	*Deul double deul* (CW XV, no. 1: Lupi)
3	Aa4[v]	*Il est bel & bon* (RISM 1534_{12}, no. 1: Passereau)
4	Bb2	*Queramus cum pastoribus* (RISM 1529_1, fol. 9[v]: Mouton)
	Bb3	2a pars [*Ubi pascas ubi cubes*]
5	Bb4[v]	*Christi Corpus Ave*
6	Cc2	*Fantasia*
7	Cc2[v]	*Fantasia*
8	Cc3[v]	*Fantasia*
9	Cc4[v]	*La volunte* Canzon (RISM 1549_{18}, no. 15: Sandrin)
10	Dd1	*Fantasia*
11	Dd1	*Fantasia Discorda*
12	Dd2	*Canzon Francese*
13	Dd2[v]	*Canzon* (AttainCK III, no. 9: "Le content est riche," Sermisy)
14	Dd3[v]	*Se mai provasti donna* Madrigale (RISM 1537_9, no. 8: Verdelot)
15	Dd4	*Fantasia sopra Se mai provasti donna*
16	Ee1[v]	*Madonna qual certezza Soprano per sonare a dui Lauti* (EinIM III, 21: Verdelot)
	Ee3	*Tenor di Madonna qual certezza*
17	Ee3[v]	*Pas de mi bon compagni*[1]
18	Ee4[v]	*Fantasia per sonar con dui Lauti in ottava. Soprano* = 1552_{11}, no. 85, and 1563_{12}, no. 112
	Ff1	*Fantasia ante scritta per sonare con dui Lauti in ottava. Tenor*

19	Ff1v	*Fantasia*
20	Ff2v	*Fantasia per sonar un Lauto, & farsi Tenor & Soprano*[2]
21	Ff3	*Fantasia discordata per sonare solo uno*
22	Ff3v	*Fantasia discordata*
23	Ff4v	*Fantasia. Prima parte*
	Gg1v	*Fantasia. Seconda parte*
	Gg3	*Fantasia. Terza parte*
24	Gg3v	*Canzon*
25	Gg4v	*Fantasia prima per sonar sopra la Chitara da sette corde. Canto*[3] = 1553₄, no. 23: "Branle"
26	Gg4v	*Fantasia seconda per sonar sopra la Chitara da sette corde. Canto*[3]
27	Hh1	*Fantasia terza per sonare sopra la Chitara da sette corde. Canto*[3]
28	Hh1v	*Fantasia quarta per sonar sopra la Chitara da sette corde. Canto*[3]

[1] Marked "Canzone" in table of contents.
[2] Facs. of fol. Ff2v in EF I, 343, and MGG I, col. 1233.
[3] Mod. ed. of the four guitar fantasias in KoczM, p. 16. See there, pp. 11–15, for further information about this volume.

1549₃

BERMUDO, JUAN

Comiença el libro / primero de la declaracion de instrumentos, / dirigido al clementissimo y muy podero/so don Joan tercero deste nombre, Rey / de Portugal, &c. / [Coat of arms of the king and the inscription "Abjiciamus opera tenebrarum, et induamur arma lucis, ad ro. 13. d."]

12 + 145 fols. The title is placed within an ornamental border. On fol. *1v: royal printing privilege dated "Dado en Cigales a diez y ocho dias de noviembre año de el señor de mil y quinientos y quarenta y nueve" (November 18, 1549); this privilege is repr. in 1550₁. On fol. *2: license from the ecclesiastical authorities allowing Juan Bermudo to publish his book, headed "Licencia. Fray Gómez de llanos de la orden de los frayles menores de observancia, Ministro Provincial en la provincia del Andaluzía: a vos el venerando padre fray Joan Bermudo de la mesma orden," and dated "Dada en el convento de madre de Dios de Ossuna primero de Agosto de. 1549. Años"; this license is reprinted in 1550₁. On fols. *2v–*3: letter from [Bernardino de] Figueroa, master of the Royal Chapel of Granada and official examiner of the book, to the King of Portugal giving Figueroa's approval headed "Esta es una epistola que Figueroa maestro dignissimo de capilla de la Real de Granada, examinador de este libro embio al clementissimo Rey de Portugal." On fols. *3–*7v: dedication to King John III of Portugal. On fols. *7v–*11v: preface explaining the purpose of the book headed "Prologo general de toda la obra para el lector." On fols. *11v–*12: a letter from Figueroa to Fray Gómez de Llanos in praise of the book, headed "Esta es una carta de el excellente musico el maestro Figueroa, examinador de este libro, embiada al muy reverendo padre, el padre fray Gómez de llanos ministro provincial de la provincia del Andaluzía . . . " On fol. *12v: a list of authors cited by Bermudo. Fol. *13 = fol. 1. Colophon on fol. 145v: "Fue impressa la presente obra en la villa de Ossuna por el honrrado varon Juan de Leon impressor dela Universidad del illustrissimo señor don Juan Tellez Giron, Conde de Urveña, &c., Acabose a diez y siepte dias del mes de Setiembre Año del señor de mil y quinientos y quarenta y nueve. Y fue la primera impression esta," followed by the printer's mark and his initials, J. L. This treatise begins with a general discussion of the merits of music, and continues with a study of plainsong and polyphony. Bermudo explains that since instrumentalists will have to intabulate music written in mensural notation, they should understand this notation thoroughly. The treatise is listed in this bibliography since it was a preliminary study for 1555₁; most of the material in it was reprinted in 1555₁ (for detailed concordances see StevnsnJB, especially p. 4).[1]

Copies in: D:Bds-Tü, D:Mbs, E:Mn (two copies), NL:DHgm, US:Cn, US:NYhs.[2]

[1] Facs. of fol. a2 in Otto Haas Sales Catalogue no. 37: "A Selection of Rare Music from Boethius to Webern," London, 1959, p. 8; facs. of fols. *4 and

c4 in SubHME, p. 282; and facs. of fol. 106 (02) in SubHM I, 501.

[2] The volume was once in the Fugger library (see SeligG, p. 65).

1549₄

BUUS, JACQUES

INTABOLATURA D'ORGANO / DI RECERCARI DI M. GIACHES / Buus Organista Dell'illustrissima Signoria di Venetia in San Marco / Novamente stampata Con Carateri di stagno. / LIBRO [Printer's mark] PRIMO / In Venetia Apresso di / Antonio Gardane. / 1549 / CUM GRATIA ET PRIVILEGIO

32 fols. Keyboard score. Dedication on fol. A1^{v} headed "Al molto Nobile. & Vertuoso Giovane. M. Paolo di Hanna," reprinted in SartMS, p. 14. Printer's mark on fol. H4^{v}. SlimK II, 526, contains a thematic index of the volume. All of the compositions are for solo keyboard.

Copy in: GB:Lbm.[1]

fol.			
1	A2	*Recercar Primo*[2]	(1549₅, no. 1)
2	D1	*Recercar Secondo*	
3	F1^{v}	*Recercar Terzo*[3]	
4	G2^{v}	*Recercar Quarto*[3]	

[1] WolfH II, 256, mistakenly lists a 1547 edition of this volume.

[2] Mod. ed. in KinO, p. 245, and SchlechtG, no. 55. Facs. of fol. A2 in MGG XI, col. 435.

[3] Mod. ed. in BuusR.

1549₅

BUUS, JACQUES

SUPERIUS / IL SECONDO LIBRO DI RECERCARI / DI M. JAQUES BUUS ORGANISTA / In San Marco di Venetia da Cantare, & sonare d'Organo / & altri Stromenti Novamente Posti in Luce. / A QUATRO [Printer's mark] VOCI / In Venetia Apresso di / Antonio Gardane. / 1549

Four part books in mensural notation (SAT, each of 16 fols.; B, 14 fols.). Dedication on fol. 1^{v} of each part book headed "AL MOLTO MAGNIFICO MESSER HIERONIMO UTINGHER," reprinted in SartMS, p. 14. On the verso of the last folio of soprano and bassus: printer's mark. SlimK II, 524, contains a thematic index of the volume. All of the compositions are for instrumental ensemble *a 4* (or for keyboard).

Copies in: D:Rp (SAT), and GB:Lbm (SAB).

fol.			
1	A2	*Recercar Primo*[1]	(1549₄, no. 1)
2	A4	*Recercar Secondo*	
3	B2	*Recercar terzo*	
4	B3^{v}	*Recercar quarto*	
5	C2	*Recercar quinto*	
6	C3	*Recercar sesto*	
7	C4	*Recercar settimo*	
8	C5^{v}	*Recercar ottavo*	

[1] Incomplete mod. ed. in KinO, p. 245, and SchlechtG, no. 55.

1549₆

NEWSIDLER, HANS

Das Ander Buch / Ein new künstlich Lauten Buch, erst yetzo von newem ge/ macht, für junge und alte Schüler, die auss rechtem grund und kunst, nach der Ta/ bulatur, gantz leicht und ring zu lernen, durch ein leicht Exempel diser pünctlein / . .. ., wohin man mit einem yeden finger recht und ordenlich greyffen soll, und / wie man die Tabulatur unnd die Mensur gantz leichtlich lernen unnd verstehen / soll, mit vil schönen lieblichen Teutschen, Welschen, Frantzösischen unnd La/teynischen Stücken, Tentzen, und Preambeln, unnd die Schlacht vor Pavia, die seind mit allem fleyss gemacht, durch mich Hansen / Newsidler Lutinisten und Burger zu Nürnberg / zusamen gebracht und offenlich / aussgangen. / M. D. XLIX. / Mit Römischer Key. und König. May. freyheit, / inn Fünff Jaren nicht nach zu drucken, / begnadet.

100 fols.[1] German lute tablature. On fols. a2–a2^{v}: the same printer's privilege as in 1536₆. On fols. a3–a3^{v}: preface (same as in 1544₂) headed "Dem Leser glück und heyl."

On fol. a3^v: the same note advertising Newsidler's other books as in 1547_4. On fols. a4–c2: instructions for playing the lute; the subdivisions are headed:

fol. a4	"Wie sich erstlich einer zur Lauten schicken, und die bezeycheten Buchstaben darauss lernen soll."
b1	"Wie man die Tabulatur lernen sol."
b1^v	"Wie man die Lauten sol lernen ziehen."
b2	"Wie man applicieren und recht greyffen sol."
b3^v	"Von der Mensur."
c1	"Von dem einigen pünctlein über den buchstaben."
c2	"Hie volget das erst Fundament der Lauten."

On fol. b1^v: an untitled musical example. On fols. 9–3^v and 9–4: table of contents. Colophon on fol. 9–4: "Zu Nürnberg truckts Jul. Paulus Fabritius Laub. durch verlegung Hansen Newsidlers Lutinisten. M. D. XLIX." On fol. 9–4^v: the same cut of the neck of a lute with a brief explanation of the tablature as appears in 1536_6 and later volumes by Newsidler. SlimK II, 527, contains a thematic index of the preambles. This is a revised second edition of 1544_2. All of the compositions are for solo lute.

Copy in: D:Ngm.

	fol.	
1	c3	*Die Erst Regel, und ist ein gering Fundament der Lauten* = 1536_6, no. 2
	c3^v	*Die Ander Regel und ist ein ander art*
	c3^v	*Die Drit Regel, und ist auch ein andere art*
2	c4^v	*Das klein Fundament mit dem einigen pünctlein* = 1536_6, no. 3
	d1	*Die Ander Regel*
	d1	*Die Drit Regel*
3	d1^v	*Nun volgt ein anders fundament, dz vil kunstreycher ist, aber ein wenig schwerer dann dz erst* = 1536_6, no. 4
4	d3	*Unser Köchin kan wol kochen* = 1540_1, no. 2
5	d3^v	*Maduna Katherina* = 1540_1, no. 3
6	d4	*Ich klag den tag und alle stundt* = 1544_2, no. 5: Stoltzer
7	d4^v	*Der recht alt Hofftantz mit zweyen stymmen* (compare 1536_6, no. 10)
	e1	*Volgt der Hupff auff*
8	e1^v	*Artlich und schön gantz wol gestalt* = 1544_2, no. 11: Casparus Bohemus
9	e2	*Willig unnd trew ich mich ergib* = 1544_1, no. 6: Forster
10	e2^v	*Ich schwing mein horn*[2] = 1544_2, no. 15: Senfl
11	e3	*Sant Merten bringt der gesellschafft vil*[3] (SenflW V, no. 39: "Jetz bringt Sankt Marten Gsellschaft viel," Senfl)
12	e3^v	*Ich het mir ein feines beumelein*
13	e4	*Dein hübsch und schön*
14	e4^v	*Ich bin ein fischer auff einem see*
15	f1	*Ein gut Preambl für junge Schüler*
16	f1^v	*Mein freud allein in aller welt* (DTO XIV/28, p. 17: Isaac)
17	f2^v	*Was unfals qual*
18	f3^v	*Untrew ist yetz gewachsen* (compare RISM [c. 1550]$_{22}$, no. 24)
19	f4	*Volgt ein gut Preambl*[4]
20	f4^v	*Nach willen dein* (MosPH, p. 74: Hofhaimer)
21	g1^v	*Von edler art ein frewlein zart* (MosPH, p. 180: Schönfelder or Hofhaimer)
22	g2^v	*Tröstlicher lieb ich mich stets üb* (MosPH, p. 86: Hofhaimer)
23	g3^v	*Ein guter geringer Hoff tantz*[5] = 1544_2, no. 22
	g4^v	*Volgt der Hupff auff*
24	h1	*Der Hoff tantz auff ein andere art* (compare 1544_2, no. 10)
	h1^v	*Volget der Hupff auff*
25	h2^v	*Hie volget der recht artlich Hoff tantz, wie man an den Fürsten Höfen pflegt. Im abzug* = 1536_6, no. 68
	h3	*Der Hupff auff*
26	h4	*Der recht Studenten Tantz*
	h4^v	*Der Hupff auff*
27	i1	*Wie möcht ich frölich werden, Tantz weyss*
	i1^v	*Volgt der Hupff auff*
28	i2^v	*Der Bentzenawer, Tantz weyss*
	i3^v	*Volgt der Hupff auff*

29 i4^v *Der Beyrisch Bot, Tantz weyss*
k1^v *Volgt der Hupff auff*
30 k2^v *Ich stund an einem morgen, Tantz weyss* (compare BridgmE, p. 160, and SenflW VII, nos. 3, 4)
k3^v *Volgt der Hupff auff*
31 k4^v *Ein artlicher rechter Fürstlicher Hofftantz, wie an Fürsten Höfen der gebrauch ist*
l1^v *Volgt der Hupff auff*
32 l2^v *Ein geringer welscher tantz* [6]
l3 *Hupff auff*
33 l3^v *Königs Ferdinandus Tantz*
l4 *Volgt der Hupff auff*
34 l4^v *Sospiri amorosi*
35 m1^v *Saltarela*
36 m2^v *Passa mesa* [*Ein Welscher tantz*] = 1540_1, no. 30
37 m3^v *Passa mesa mit vier stimmen*
38 n1 *Ein gut Proambel* [7]
39 n1^v *Laiarosa*
40 n2^v *Folpechi* [8] = 1544_2, no. 49
41 n3^v *Con lachrime sospir* (EinIM III, 319: Verdelot)
42 n4^v *Lodar voi*
43 o1^v *Quando cor dolce*
44 o2^v *La bella Donna*
45 o3^v *Benedetur*
46 o4^v *Questa piagha*
47 p1^v *O voi che sospicai*
48 p2^v *Signor de amor*
49 p3^v *Alma perche*
50 q1 *Vous mi faictes* [*tant rire*] [9] (RISM 1535_8, no. 21)
51 q2^v *Plus je la vois* (RISM 1539_{15}, no. 8: Mittantier)
52 q3^v *Lamar narite* = 1544_2, no. 42: "La Marguaritt"
53 q4^v *Rosignolet*
54 r2 *Mon cuor* [*mon*] *corps* (RISM [c. $1528]_9$, fol. 5: Willaert)
55 r3^v *Vostre beautle* [sic] (PubAPTM II, no. 79: Gombert)
56 r4^v *O dulcis memorie* (PubAPTM XXIII, no. 50: "Doulce memoire," Sandrin)
57 s2 *Si par son fre* = 1544_2, no. 36: "Si par souffrir"
58 s2^v *Fors seulement* (ObrWW, p. 90: Josquin or Févin)
59 s4^v *Le content* [*est riche*] (AttainCK III, no. 9: Sermisy)
60 t1^v *Ami son fre* (AttainCK III, no. 7: "Amy souffrez," Moulu)
61 t2^v *Amour lassio*
62 t3^v *Cest a grant* [*tort*] (AttainCK II, no. 18: Sermisy)
63 t4^v *Cest faschaux* (AttainCK II, no. 25: "Ces fascheux sotz")
64 v1^v *Hie volget die Schlacht vor Pavia. Der Erste Teyl* = 1544_2, no. 52: "La Bataille," Janequin
v3^v 2a pars [*Fan frere le le lan fan*]
65 x3^v *Apparens Christi* [10] (RISM 1539_8, no. 12: "Apparens Christus post passionem," Joan. Lupi)
y2^v 2a pars [*Et convescens precepit*]
66 y4^v *Vita in ligno* (RISM 1537_1 no. 20: Senfl)
z3 2a pars [*Qui prophetice*]
7–1 3a pars [*Qui expansis*]
67 7 3 *Wass will doch drauss werden*
68 7–4^v *Ein guter Welscher Gassenhawer* = 1547_4, no. 24
9–1^v *Hupff auff*
69 9–2^v *Ein gut Preambel mit fugen*

[1] The signatures run from a to z (23 gatherings), plus two gatherings signed with symbols that resemble "7" and "9," which are used in this inventory.
[2] Mod. ed. in SenflW VII, no. 49a.
[3] Mod. ed. in SenflW VII, no. 48a.
[4] Mod. ed. in MolzHN, no. 11.
[5] Heading on fol. g3^v: "Nun volgen die Teutschen Tentz."
[6] Heading on fol. l2^v: "Hienach volgen etlich Welsch Tentz."
[7] Mod. ed. in MolzHN, no. 16.
[8] Heading on fol. n2^v: "Nun volgen die Welschen Stück."
[9] Heading on fol. q1: "Nun volgen die Frantzsösichen Stück."
[10] Heading on fol. x3^v: "Hienach volgen die Lateynischen Stück."

1549_7

TIBURTINO, GIULIANO

FANTASIE, ET RECERCHARI / A TRE VOCI, ACCOMODATE / DA CANTARE ET SONARE PER OGNI IN/strumento, Composte da M. Giuliano

Tiburtino / da Tievoli, Musico Eccellentiss. / CON LA GIUNTA DI ALCUNI / altri Recerchari, & Madrigali a tre Voce, Composti / da lo Eccellentiss. Adriano Vuigliart, / Et Cipriano Rore suo / Discepolo. / CON SOMMA DILIGENTIA STAMPATI, / Et da gli proprii exemplari estratti, / Novamente posti in luce. / BAS [Printer's mark] SUS / VENETIIS, APUD / Hieronymum Scottum. / M D XLIX.

Three part books in mensural notation, each of 20 fols. On the last verso of each part book: table of contents. The volume was partly reprinted in 1551 and later (see 1551_6 for details).[1] The Willaert ricercares are reprinted in WillR (after 1559_8; see there for details). SlimK II, 528, contains a thematic index of the ricercares (nos. 1–12, 22–29). The titles of nos. 1–12 in the inventory below are taken from the table of contents; the compositions are labeled with slightly different solmization syllables in each part book. The foliation is from the bass part book. Nos. 14–21 are vocal music; each voice is fully texted. The other compositions are for instrumental ensemble *a 3*.

Copies in: E:Bim (B), E:Mmc (T), GB:Lbm, I:Bc (S).

	fol.	
1	A1^v	*Ut re mi fa sol la* [Tiburtino]
2	A2	*La sol fa mi fa re la* [Tiburtino]
3	A2^v	*Fa re mi re sol mi fa mi* [Tiburtino]
4	A2^v	*Fa mi fa re ut* [Tiburtino]
5	A3	*Sol sol sol ut* [Tiburtino]
6	A3^v	*Ut mi fa ut fa mi re ut* [Tiburtino]
7	A3^v	*Re ut fa re fa sol la* [Tiburtino]
8	A4	*Re ut re fa mi re* [Tiburtino]
9	A4^v	*Ut fa mi ut mi re ut* [Tiburtino]
10	B1	*Re fa mi re la* [Tiburtino]
11	B1	*Ut re mi ut fa mi re ut* [Tiburtino]
12	B1^v	*La sol fa re mi* [Tiburtino]
13	B2	*Fantasia* [Tiburtino]
14	B2^v	*O felice colui* Baldesar Donato
15	B3	*Grave pen'in Amor* Cipriano Rore
16	B3^v	*Se'l veder voi* Adriano Vuigliart
17	B4^v	*Io dico & dissi* Cipriano Rore
18	C1	*Sur le joly joly jonc* Adriano Vuigliart
19	C1^v	*Tutt'il di piango* Cipriano Rore
	C2	2a pars *Lasso che pur*
20	C2^v	*Ite caldi sospiri* Nadal
	C3	2a pars *Dir si puo ben*
21	C3^v	*Amor che ved'ogni pensier aperto* Nadal
22	C4^v	[*Ricercar*] Adriano Vuigliart (see no. 29 below)
23	D1^v	[*Ricercar*][2] Adriano Vuigliart = 1551_6, no. 8
24	D2^v	[*Ricercar*] Adriano Vuigliart = 1551_6, no. 6
25	D3^v	[*Ricercar*] Adriano Vuigliart = 1551_6, no. 10
26	D4^v	[*Ricercar*] Adriano Vuigliart = 1551_6, no. 5
27	E1^v	[*Ricercar*] Adriano Vuigliart = 1551_6, no. 4
28	E2^v	[*Ricercar*] Adriano Vuigliart = 1551_6, no. 9
29	E3^v	[*Ricercar*] Adriano Vuigliart (= no. 22 above, transposed) = 1551_6, no. 7

[1] FétB IV, 17, erroneously dates this volume 1579.
[2] Mod. ed. in PeetM I, no. 10 (arr. for organ).

1549_8

PHALÈSE, PIERRE, PUBLISHER

CARMINUM QUAE / CHELY VEL TESTUDINE CANUNTUR, / Liber primus. / Cum brevi Introductione in usum Testudinis. / [Cut of ten performing musicians] / LOVANII / Apud PETRUM PHALYSIUM Bibliopolam iuratum, Anno M. D. XLIX. / Cum gratia & Privilegio.

36 fols. French lute tablature. On fol. A1^v: cut of a lute. On fols. A2–A4: a Latin version of the instructions for playing the lute printed in 1545_3. On fol. I4^v: cut of a lute. This is a third, revised edition of 1545_3. All compositions reprinted from the first edition are followed by an asterisk in the inventory below. See there for the sources of the intabulations. In almost every case the ornamentation has been slightly modified for this edition. Titles in brackets have been trimmed off the unique copy. Attributions

in brackets are from 1545₃. All of the compositions are for solo lute.

Copy in: GB:Lbm.[1]

	fol.	
1	B1	*Fantasie**
2	B1ᵛ	*Fantasie**
3	B1ᵛ	*Fantasie* = 1546₁₀, no. 6: Giovanni Maria da Crema
4	B2	*Fantasie* = 1546₁₀, no. 11: Giovanni Maria da Crema
5	B2ᵛ	*Fantasie* = 1546₁₀, no. 9: Giovanni Maria da Crema
6	B3	*Si vous estes belle*
7	B3	*Ryckgodt* (compare LenN, p. 79: "Rick God wien sal ick clagen")
8	B3ᵛ	*[Die lustelycke Muy]**
9	B4	*Il me souffit** [Sermisy]
10	B4ᵛ	*Fortune helas*
11	C1	*[Dont vient cela]** [Sermisy]
12	C1ᵛ	*Languir** [Sermisy]
13	C2	*[Amis souffrez]** [Moulu]
14	C2ᵛ	*Du bon du cueur**
15	C3ᵛ	*Cest doncq pour moy**
16	C4ᵛ	*Tant que vivray** [Sermisy]
17	D1	*[Ces fascheux sotz]**
18	D1ᵛ	*Vivray je tousjours en soucy* = 1529₃, no. 15a: Sermisy
19	D2	*[Destre amoureux]* = 1529₃, no. 32a
20	D2ᵛ	*Si vostre cueur* (RISM [c. 1528]₅, no. 30)
21	D3	*[Le dur regret]* = 1529₃, no. 27
22	D3ᵛ	*Si mon travail* (PubAPTM XXIII, no. 52: Sandrin)
23	D4ᵛ	*Vous perdez tamps** [Sermisy]
24	E1	*[Aupres de vous]**
25	E1ᵛ	*Je prens en gre** [Clemens non Papa]
26	E2ᵛ	*Damour me plains** [Pathie]
27	E3ᵛ	*Toutte le nuict* (RISM 1570₈, p. 12: "Toutes les nuycts," Crecquillon)
28	E4ᵛ	*Or combien est [malheureux]* (ClemensO VII, 156: Sandrin or Sermisy)
29	F1ᵛ	*Vivray je tousjours en soucy* (RISM 1554₂₂, p. 21: "Vivray je tout jour en telle peyne," Petit Jehan de Latre)
30	F2ᵛ	*Doulce memoire* (PubAPTM XXIII, no. 50: Sandrin)
31	F3ᵛ	*Faict on failly* (compare 1533₂, no. 20: Bridam)
32	F4	[Unidentified]
33	F4ᵛ	*Jamays jaymera** ["Jamais n'aymeray masson"]
34	G1	*[Aupres de vous]**
35	G1ᵛ	*Helas amy** [Sandrin]
36	G2	*Amy helas* (RISM 1540₁₂, fol. 2ᵛ) = 1552₁₁, no. 42
37	G2ᵛ	*Tant que vivray** [Sermisy]
38	G3	*[Il me suffit]** [Sermisy]
39	G3ᵛ	*Ung gay bergier** [Crecquillon]
40	G4ᵛ	*Ronde*
41	H1ᵛ	*Currendo*
42	H1ᵛ	*Quatre brañt*
43	H2ᵛ	*Fago*
44	H2ᵛ	*Brant de champaigne*
45	H2ᵛ	*Six brant*
46	H3	*[Le pied cheval]*
47	H3ᵛ	*Passemeso [d'Anglotorro]* (compare 1571₅, no. 14)
48	H3ᵛ	*Gallarde*
49	H4	*[Gaillarde?]*
50	H4ᵛ	*Alemaigne*
51	I1	*Paduana**
52	I1ᵛ	*Gaillarde**
53	I2	*Paduana**
54	I2ᵛ	*Gallairde**
55	I3	*Gallairde**
56	I3ᵛ	*[Traditora]* (compare 1545₃, no. 51)
57	I3ᵛ	*La bella franciskina*
58	I4	*Factie*[2]
59	I4	*Si vous estes belle*

†

[1] Manuscript addition on fol. I4: "Lovanii Excudebat Jacobus Bathenus M. D. XLIX." Manuscript addition on fol. I4ᵛ: "J. S. S. 1.5.51," and "B:. D. Lan. 5.51."

[2] Mod. ed. in BrownM, p. 154.

154?₁

BIANCHINI, FRANCESCO

TABULATURE DE LUTZ, / En diverses formes. / de / Fantasie, Bassedances, /Chansons, Pavanes, / Pseaulmes, Gaillardes. / Composées par divers Musiciens, & / Entablées, selon le Jeu du Lutz. / par / M. FRANCESCHO Bianchini / Venetiano. / [Cut of a lute] / Imprimées nouvellement a Lyon, par Jacques Moderne.

16 fols. Italian lute tablature. On fol. A1ᵛ (= p. 2): table of contents.[1] Dedication on p. 3 headed "A Illustre, & reverendissime

Seigneur Francois GOUFFIER Evesque de Beziers," and signed "Francois Blanchin présente humble Salut." MoeDM contains a thematic index of the dances (p. 395) and concordances for them (p. 254). All of the compositions are for solo lute.

Copy in: D:Mbs.

	p.	
1	4	*Fantasia* F. Bianchini[2]
2	6	*Quant tu vouldras* Isaac Lheritier
3	8	*Est il regret* G. Bichenet
4	10	*Si jay lamour* Croquillon (RISM [1552]$_9$, fol. 16: Crecquillon)
5	12	*Ung grand desir* Maillard
6	14	*Dame sante* Entaygues
7	16	*Vous semble t il* G. de la Moeulle
8	18	*In domino confido* [*Psalme XI: Veu que du tout*] A. Mornable (MornableP II, fol. 4)[3]
9	20	*Domini est terra* [*Psalme XXIV: La terre au Seigneur*] A. Mornable (MornableP II, fol. 2v)[3]
10	22	*Benedic anima mea dominum* [*Psalme CIII: Sus, louez Dieu, mon cueur*] [Certon] (LesLRB, no. 17bis, fol. 26v)
11	24	*Bassedance. Quand je congneu* (compare RISM 1539$_{20}$, no. 18: Sandrin)
12	25	*Bassedance. La mestresse*
13	26	*Pavane. La Millanese*
14	28	*Pavane. La favorita*
15	30	*Gaillarde. El Peschadore*
16	31	*Gaillarde. El mulinaro*

[1] The table of contents lists a "Bassedance. Fortuna alors" as being on p. 16 and omits no. 12.

[2] Incipit in SlimK II, 509.

[3] On MornableP see PidP. I have been unable to check these concordances.

154?2

CAVAZZONI, GIROLAMO

INTABULATURA / DORGANO, / CIOE MISSE HIMNI MAGNIFICAT / COMPOSTI PER HIERONIMO / DE MARCANTONIO DA / BOLOGNA DETTO / D'URBINO. / LIBRO SECONDO. / Col privillegio dell'Illustrisimo Senato Veneto, Per anni .X.

40 fols. Keyboard score. On fol. A1v: table of contents. Dedication on fol. A2 headed "ALLO ILIUSTRISSIMO ET REVERENDISSIMO MONSIGNOR, IL CARDINAL DI RAVENNA ETC. SIGNORE ET PATRONE COLENDISSIMO," reprinted in GaspaC IV, 37, and SartMS, p. 11. There is a modern edition of the entire volume in CavazzO II (which includes the dedication), and CDMI, quaderni 23–27. The three Masses (nos. 1–3) are reprinted in 154?$_3$. All of the compositions are for solo keyboard.

Copy in: I:Bc (imperfect).

	fol.	
1	A2v	*MISSA APOSTOLORUM*[1]
	A2v	*Chirie primus. Iterum repetitur*
	A3	*Christe*
	A4	*Christe Quartus. Iterum repetitur*
	A4v	*Et in terra pax*
	B1	*Benedicimus te*
	B1v	*Glorificamus te*
	B1v	*Domine deus rex*
	B2v	*Domine deus agnus dei*
	B3	*Qui tollis*
	B3v	*Quoniam tu solus sanctus*
	B3v	*Tu sol[u]s altis. a tre voce*
	B3v	*Amen*
	B4	*CREDO CARDINALIS. Patrem*
	B4v	*Et ex patre natum*
	C1	*Genitum non factum*
	C1v	*Crucifixus a tre voci*
	C2	*Et ascendit in celum*
	C2v	*Et in spiritum sanctum*
	C3	*Et unam sanctam catholicam*
	C3	*Et expecto*
	C3v	*Amen*
	C3v	*Sanctus primus*
	C4	*Sanctus secundus*
	C4	*Agnus Dei*
2	C4v	*MISSA DOMINICALIS*
	C4v	*Chirie primus. Iterum repetitur*
	D1	*Christe eleyson*
	D1v	*Chirie eleyson*
	D2v	*Et in terra pax*
	D3	*Benedicimus te*
	D3	*Glorificamus te*
	D3	*Domine deus rex*
	D3v	*Domine deus agnus dei*

D4 *Qui tollis a tre voce*
D4^{v} *Quoniam tu solus sanctus*
E1 *Tu solus altissimus*
E1 *Amen*
E1^{v} *CREDO DOMINICAL. Patrem*
E2 *Et ex patre natum*
E2 *Genitum non factum*
E2^{v} *Crucifixus*
E3 *Et ascendit in celum*
E3^{v} *Et in spiritum sanctum*
E4 *Et unam sanctam catholicam*
E4^{v} *Et expecto*
E4^{v} *Amen*
F1 *Sanctus primus*
F1 *Sanctus secundus a tre voce*
F1 *Agnus dei*
3 F1^{v} *MISSA DE BEATA VIR.*
F1^{v} *Chirie primus. Iterum repetitur*
F2 *Christe leyson*
F2^{v} *Chirie eleyson*
F3 *Et in terra pax*
F3^{v} *Benedicimus te*
F3^{v} *Glorificamus te*
F3^{v} *Domine deus rex*
F4^{v} *Spiritus & alme*
G1 *Primo genitus*
G1 *Qui tollis a tre voce*
G1^{v} *Qui sedes*
G2 *Mariam sanctificans*
G2 *Mariam gubernans*
G2 *Mariam coronans*
G2^{v} *Amen*
G2^{v} *Sanctus primus*
G3 *Sanctus secundus a tre voce*
G3 *Agnus dei*
G3^{v} *In hac missa dicitur Credo Cardinalis*
4 G4 *IN DIE PENTHECOSTES. Hymnus Veni creator spiritus*
5 G4^{v} *IN DIE APOSTOLORUM. Hymnus Exultet caelum laudibus*
6 H1^{v} *IN FESTO CORPORIS CHRISTI. Hymnus Pange Lingua gloriosi* [2]
7 H2^{v} *IN FESTO CONFESSORUM: Hymnus Iste confessor*
8 H3^{v} *IN ASCENSIONE DOMINI. Hym. Jesu nostra redemptio* [3]
9 H4 *IN SOLIMNITATE VIRGINUM. Hymnus Jesu corona virginum*
10 I1 *IN FESTO UNIUS MAR. Hymnus Deus tuorum militum* [4]
11 I2 *IN EPIPHANIA DOMINI. Hym. Hostis Herodes impie*
12 I3 *Magnificat. Quarti Toni*
I3 *Quia respexit*
I4 *Deposuit*
I4^{v} *Suscepit a tre voce*
I4^{v} *Gloria patri*
13 K1^{v} *Magnificat Sexti Toni*
K2 *Quia respexit*
K2^{v} *DePosuit*
K3 *Suscepit DUO*

[1] Mod. ed. of a part of the "Gloria" in ApelM I, 21; mod. ed. of the "Kyrie" in ApelMK, p. 52; mod. ed. of the "Patrem," "Et unam sanctam catholicam," and "Et expecto" in DallaL, no. 71; mod. ed. of the "Kyrie" in DallaLO I, no. 1, and FuserC, no. 5; and mod. ed. of the "Kyrie" and "Gloria" in HAM, no. 117.

[2] Mod. ed. in DallaLO I, no. 2, and TagA I, no. 10.

[3] Mod. ed. in DallaLO VI, no. 29.

[4] Mod. ed. in TagA I, no. 9.

154?3

CAVAZZONI, GIROLAMO

DI HIERONIMO D'URBINO / IL PRIMO LIBRO DE INTABOLATURA / D'organo dove si contiene tre Messe Novamente da Antonio Gardano / Ristampato & da molti errori emendato. / MISSA Apostolorum / MISSA Dominicalis / MISSA De Beata Virgine / LIBRO [Printer's mark] PRIMO / In Venetia apresso di / Antonio Gardano [1]

29 fols. Keyboard score. Contents = 154?2, nos. 1–3. All of the compositions are for solo keyboard.

Copy in: I:Bc.

[1] Antonio Gardane called himself Gardano from about 1557 on. Thus this volume was more apt to have been printed after 1557 than in the 1540's.

154?4

FRANCESCO DA MILANO

INTABOLATURA DA LEUTO / DEL DIVINO FRANCISCO / DA MILANO NOVAME/NTE STANPATA / [Cut of a crown]

36 fols. Italian lute tablature. WieM II contains a thematic index of this volume.

Contents = 1536_3. All of the compositions are for solo lute.[1]

Copy in: A:Wn.

[1] There is no evidence to suggest that this volume was printed during the 1540's. It is included here only because the majority of volumes devoted to Francesco da Milano's music were brought out during that decade.

154?5

PALADIN, JEAN PAUL

TABULATURE DE LUTZ / En diverses Sortes. / COMME / Chansons, Pavanes. / Fantaisies. Gaillardes. / ET / LA BATAILLE / Le tout Compose Par M. Jean Paulo Paladin Milanoys. / [Cut of a lute] / Imprimées nouvellement a Lyon, par Jacques Moderne.

16 fols. Italian lute tablature. The title is placed within an ornamental border. MoeDM contains a thematic index of the dances (p. 400) and concordances for them (p. 256). SlimK II, 532, contains a thematic index of the ricercares. All of the compositions are for solo lute.

Copy in: D:Mbs.[1]

	p.	
1	3	*De trop penser* (RISM 1532_{12}, no. 24: Jacotin)
2	4	*Vous perdez temps* (RISM 1538_{17}, fol. 31: Arcadelt)
3	6	*Le content est riche* (AttainCK III, no. 9: Sermisy)
4	8	*Si mon travail* (PubAPTM XXIII, no. 52: Sandrin)
5	9	*Fantasia*
6	11	*Fantasia*
7	13	*Pavane*
8	15	*Pavane*
9	17	*Pavane* = 1536_9, no. 5a: "Pavana ditta la Malcontenta"
10	18	*Gaillarde*
	19	*La Reprise*
11	21	*Gaillarde*
	21	*La Reprise*
12	23	*La Bataille* = 1536_3, no. 34: Janequin (intab. Francesco da Milano)
	27	2a pars [*Fan frere le le lan fan*]

[1] There is a manuscript date, 1549, on the parchment cover of this volume.

154?6

MODERNE, JACQUES, PUBLISHER

MUSICQUE DE JOYE. / Appropriée tant a la voix humaine, que pour apprendre a sonner Espinetes, / Violons, & fleustes. Avec Basses Danses, eleves Pavanes, Gail/lardes, & Branles, ou lon pourra apprendre, & scavoir / les mesures, & cadences de la Musicque, / & de toutes danses. / Composées par divers aucteurs Musiciens tresparfaictz / & excellents, en leur siecle. / [Cut of a fleur-de-lis] / On les vend à Lyon chez Jacques Moderne dict grand Jacques.[1]

Four part books in mensural notation, each of 20 fols. On fol. A1^v of each part book: table of contents listing nos. 1–22 only. Each composition is numbered beginning with no. 3; the dances are numbered in a separate series, no. 26 being omitted. The compositions identified by superior letters are reprinted as follows: ([a]) in GiesIF; ([b]) in BS, vols. 6, 8, 19, 27, and 38. SlimMN, pp. xxvi and xxxi, contains facsimiles of the title page and fol. C4^v. All of the dances are reprinted in ModF. Eighteen of the ricercares (nos. 1–4, 6–11, and 13–21) and the cantus firmus setting (no. 12) are reprinted in 1540_3 (see 1540_3 for further details). All of the compositions are for instrumental ensemble *a 4*, except no. 8 which is *a 3*.

Copy in: D:Mu.

	fol.	
1	A2	*R*[*icercare*] Adrianus Willart
2	A2^v	*R* Adrianus Willart
3	A3	*R*[a] Julius de Modena [= Giulio Segni] (1557_2, no. 46)
4	A3^v	*R* Julius de Modena
5	A4^v	*R*[ab] [2] Adrianus Willart
6	B1	*R* Julius de Modena
7	B1^v	*R*[b] Julius de Modena
8	B2	*R* Julius de Modena
9	B2^v	*R*[ab] Guilielmus Colin
10	B4	*R*[3] Hieronimus Parabosco
11	B4^v	*R*[a] Julius de Modena
12	C1	*R. Da pacem domine*[4] Hieronimus Parabosco
13	C1^v	*R* Julius de Modena
14	C2^v	*R*[ab] Julius de Modena (1557_2, no. 45)

15 C3 *R*^{ab}[5] Julius de Modena (1557_2, no. 52: Antonio [de Cabezón?])
16 C3^v *R* Nicolaus Benoist
17 C4^v *R* Julius de Modena
18 D1 *R*[5] Adrian Willart
19 D1^v *R*^{ab} Adrian Willart
20 D2^v *R*^{ab} Julius de Modena
21 D3^v *R* Hieronimus de Bononia [= Girolamo Cavazzoni?]
22 D4^v *R*[6] G. Coste
23 E1 *Bassedance. Ta bone grace* (compare SeayFC, p. 16: Roquelay)
24 E1 *Tordion*
25 E1 *Bassedance* = 1547_6, no. 2
26 E1 *Tordion* = 1547_6, no. 8
27 E1^v *Bassedance. Hellas Amy* (compare RISM 1541_8, fol. 4: Sandrin)
28 E1^v *Tordion* = 1547_6, no. 7
29 E1^v *Bassedance*
30 E1^v *Tordion*
31 E2 *Moytie de Bassedance. Il me suffit* (compare AttainCK I, no. 9: Sermisy)
32 E2 *Tordion* (compare 1547_6, no. 9)
33 E2 *Pavane. La Bataille* (compare 1557_3, no. 4) = 1555_2, no. 63
34 E2^v *Pavane*
35 E2^v *Pavane. La Gaiette* (compare LesAC, no. 10: "Il estoit une fillette," Janequin) = 1555_2, no. 111
36 E2^v *Pavane*
37 E3 *Gailarde*
38 E3 *Gailarde*
39 E3 *Branle de bourgoigne* = 1555_5, no. 17: "Branle de champaigne"
40 E3 *Branle de bourgoigne*
41 E3 *Branle de bourgoigne*
42 E3^v *Branle simple* = 1547_6, no. 37
43 E3^v *Branle simple* (compare 1530_5, no. 11, and 1547_6, no. 17)
44 E3^v *Branle simple*
45 E4 *Branle de bourgoigne*
46 E4 *Branle de bourgoigne*
47 E4 *Branle de bourgoigne* = 1547_6, no. 24
48 E4^v *Branle gay nouveau*
49 E4^v *Branle gay* (compare 1552_3, no. 21: "Bransle gay Je ne serais jamais bergere")
50 E4^v *Branle nouveau*
51 E4^v [Unidentified]

[1] Facs. of title page in MischR, opp. p. 74.
[2] Incipit in SlimK II, 477.
[3] Mod. ed. in ParaC, no. 8.
[4] Mod. ed. in ParaC, no. 9.
[5] Nos. 15 and 18 are identical.
[6] Incipit in SlimK II, 477; mod. ed. *ibid.*, p. 639. Heading on fol. D4^v: "Fin de Phantaisies Instrumentales. Et Commencent Dances Musicales."

1550_1

BERMUDO, JUAN

Comiença el arte Tripharia dirigida / a la ylustre y muy reverenda señora / Doña ysabel pacheco, abadessa en el mo/nesterio de sancta Clara de Montilla, / compuesta por el Reverendo padre Fray / Juan Bermudo, religioso de la orden de / los frayles menores de observancia en la / provincia del Andaluzia. / [Cut of two saints: "Sancta Clara" and "Sancta Ynes"][1]

40 fols. On fol. 1^v: the same printing privilege as in 1549_3. On fol. 2: the same ecclesiastical license as in 1549_3. On fol. 2^v: a letter from Francisco Cervantes de Salazar addressed to the dedicatee in praise of Bermudo's book; the letter is headed "Carta. A la yllustre y muy reverenda señora doña Ysabel Pacheco abadessa del monasterio de sancta Clara de montilla, Francisco cevantes de Salazar, Cathedrático de rethórica de la Universidad de Ossuna," and dated "de ossuna. a 4. de febrero. 1550." On fol. 3: dedication headed "Prólogo epistolar del autor." On fol. 4: preface headed "Prólogo al Lector." Colophon on fol. 40^v: "Fué impresso en la villa de Ossuna en casa de Juan de León, impresor. Siendo primeramente visto y examinado por el consejo real. Acabose el dia del bienaventurado sanct Bernardino el mes de mayo año de .1550.," followed by the printer's mark with the motto "Soli Deo Honor et Gloria," and, at the bottom of the page, "Sola fides sufficit." This treatise is an introduction to plainsong (*canto llano*), polyphony (*canto de órgano*), and keyboard performance. Most of the material in the volume is reprinted in 1555_1 (for detailed concordances see StevnsnJB, especially p. 5). On fol. 38^v Bermudo includes one short composition *a 2*, the romance *Donde son estas serranas* in mensural

notation and in a number tablature for keyboard (reprinted in StevnsnJB, p. 83).

Copy in: E:Mn.[2]

[1] Facs. of title page in VinS, p. 95.

[2] Fifteen copies of a facs. ed. of this volume were prepared by Francisco Asenjo Barbieri (see AngCM II, 222, and KinO, p. 9).

$[1550]_2$

MORLAYE, GUILLAUME

Guillaume Morlaye. Tabulature de guiterne où sont chansons, gaillardes, pavanes, bransles, allemandes, fantaisies, etc. Paris, Michel Fezandat, 1550.

This volume, now lost, is mentioned in FétB VI, 205. It is probably a first edition of one of the series of guitar books published by Fezandat between 1551 and 1553 (for further information see 1552_5).

$[1550]_3$

SEGNI, GIULIO

Giulio Segni da Modena. Ricercari, intabulature da organi et da tocco.

A volume of Segni ricercares is listed in DoniL, 1550 edition, fol. 66. The above title is taken from CafS I, 105. For further information, see SlimK I, 139. The volume does not survive.

1550_4

WYSSENBACH, RUDOLF, PUBLISHER

Tabulaturbüch uff die Lut/ten, von mancherley Lieplicher Italianischer / Dantzliedern mitsampt dem Vogelgsang und einer Fäld/schlacht, uss Wälhscher [*sic*] Tabulatur, flyssig / in Thütsche gesetzt. / Getruckt zü Zürych by Rüdolff Wyssenbach / Formschnyder, Im M. D. L. Jar.

47 fols. German lute tablature. The title is placed within an ornamental border. On fol. 2: preface headed "Rüdolff Wyssenbach dem günstigen Läser." On fol. 2ᵛ: instructions for the lute headed "Erklärung der Mensur und anderer hierin gebruchten zeychen." On fol. 3: cut of a lute with the heading "Der ussgerissen Luttenkragen mit der Tabulatur." On fol. 47ᵛ: table of contents. All of the compositions in this volume are transcriptions of those in 1546_8; they were originally in Italian lute tabulature, and Wyssenbach here prints them in German tablature. Contents = 1563_{10}. All of the compositions are for solo lute except no. 6, which is for two lutes.

Copies in: A:Wn, D:LEm.[1]

	fol.	
1	4	*Pavana genant La Barroncina* = 1546_8, no. 1a
	5ᵛ	*Der erst Sprynngerdanntz. Saltarello Primo* = 1546_8, no. 1b
	7	*Der annder Sprynngerdanntz* [*Saltarello della Duchessa*] = 1546_8, no. 1c
	10	*Der dritt Springerdanntz genannt La Barbarina* = 1546_8, no. 1d
2	10ᵛ	*Pavana genannt Moniardina* P[ietro] P[aolo] B[orrono] = 1546_8, no. 2a
	11ᵛ	*Der erst Sprynngerdanntz*[2] = 1546_8, no. 2b
3	12ᵛ	*Pavana genant La Rinoldina* = 1546_8, no. 3a
	14	*Der erst Springerdanntz* = 1546_8, no. 3b
	15	*Der ander genant La meza gamba* = 1546_8, no. 3c
	17ᵛ	*Der dritt Springerdanntz genant Madonna Zoanna* = 1546_8, no. 3d
4	18	*Pavana genannt La Centoria* = 1546_8, no. 4a
	18ᵛ	*Der erst Spryngerdanntz volgt hernach* = 1546_8, no. 4b
	19ᵛ	*Der annder Spryngerdanntz el Scaravelino gennant*[3] = 1546_8, no. 4c
5	20	*Pavana genannt La Pianzolenta* P[ietro] P[aolo] B[orrono] = 1546_8, no. 5a
	22	*Der erst Spryngerdanntz* = 1546_8, no. 5b
	23	*Der annder Springerdantz genant La Rocha el fuso ec.* = 1546_8, no. 5c

24ᵛ *Der dritt Sprynngerdantz genant Le el Martello che tel fa dire* = 1546_8, no. 5d

6 25ᵛ *Pavana Milanesa* P[ietro] P[aolo] B[orrono] = 1546_8, no. 6a

26 [A second lute part for the preceding pavane]

27 *Der erst Spryngerdanntz* = 1546_8, no. 6b

27ᵛ [A second lute part for the preceding saltarello]

28 *Der annder Sprynngerdantz genant Non dite mai ch'io habia il torto* = 1546_8, no. 6c

28ᵛ *Der dritt Spryngerdanntz genant Le pur bon o Ruschina* = 1546_8, no. 6d

7 29 *Pavana genannt La bella Ugazzota* = 1546_8, no. 7a

30 *Der erst Springerdanntz*[4] = 1546_8, no. 7b

8 30ᵛ *Pavana genannt La bella Judea &c.* = 1546_8, no. 8a

31ᵛ *Der erst Spryngerdanntz* = 1546_8, no. 8b

32 *Der annder Sprynngerdanntz genant el Vercelese* = 1546_8, no. 8c

33ᵛ *Der dritt Sprynngerdanntz genannt Deh Leva su Bruneta* = 1546_8, no. 8d

9 34ᵛ *Revillez vous ceur. Das vogelgesang* ("Le chant des oiseaux," Janequin) = 1546_8, no. 25

35ᵛ 2a pars *Vous orrez a mon advis. &c.*

37 3a pars *Rossignol du boys. Joly. &c.*

39 4a pars *Arriere Maystre coque*

10 40ᵛ *Ein Franntzösische fäldschlacht. Im abtzug* ("La Bataille," Janequin) = 1546_8, no. 26

43 2a pars [*Fan frere le le lan fan*]

[1] A copy was in D:Bds (formerly owned by Wilhelm Tappert). At the end of this copy were 29 fols. of manuscript music in German lute tablature (for a description of the contents see BoettB, art. "Be 510" and DieL, pp. 89–91), including German, Italian, and French dances, and intabulations of secular compositions. The following compositions from this manuscript appendix are pr. in TapS: p. 26: *Issbruck ich muss dich lassen*; 32: *Les Bouffons*; 33: *Der Bockstanz*; 54: *Der Prinzen-Tanz* (with *Proporz*; repr. in ParrishM, no. 22); 56: *Aus tiefer Not schrei'ich zu dir*, Conrad Neusidler. A facs. page from the manuscript is pr. in WolfMS, no. 59 (with one dance, "Chorea").

[2] Note on fol. 12: "Für den anndern unnd dritternn Sprynngerdanntz mag man nämen die zwen so fornen stand nechst nach der Pavana genannt die Barroncina."

[3] Note on fol. 20: "Für den drittenn Sprynngerdanntz nim den. 3. uss der Pavana Rinoldina."

[4] Note on fol. 30ᵛ: "Für den andern unnd 3. spring dantz nim die uss der Pavana Milanesa."

1550_5

GERVAISE, CLAUDE, EDITOR

Quart livre de danceries, A quatre parties / Contenant xix pavanes & xxxi gaillardes / EN UNG LIVRE SEUL, VEU ET CORRIGE PAR / Claude gervaise scavant Musicien. Et imprimez par Pierre Attaingnant / Imprimeur du Roy en musique. Demeurant á Paris En / la Rue de la Harpe pres lesglise S. cosme. / 19. Augusti 1550. / Avec privilege du Roy pour six ans

32 fols. Mensural notation. Fol. 1ᵛ = fol. A1ᵛ. The compositions identified by the superior letter *a* ([a]) are reprinted in MMRF XXIII, which includes a facsimile of the title page. There are modern editions of some of the dances in this volume and in 1550_6 in BFS, 1931 (no. 8); BFS, 1932 (nos. 2, 8); and BS, vol. 51. For further concordances see HeartzSF, p. 337. For other volumes in the same series, see 1547_6, note 2. All of the compositions are for instrumental ensemble *a 4* except nos. 2, 3, 6, and 11–13, which are *a 5*.

Copy in F:Pn.

fol.

1 1ᵛ *Pavane. La venissienne*

2 2ᵛ *Pavane a 5*

2ᵛ *Gaillarde a 5*

3 3ᵛ *Pavane a 5*

3ᵛ *Gaillarde a 5*

4 4ᵛ *Pavane. Loeil pres & loing* (compare RISM 1549_{20}, no. 6: Certon)

4ᵛ *Gaillarde*

5 5ᵛ *Pavane. Vous qui voulez*[1]

5ᵛ *Gaillarde*

6 6ᵛ *Pavane a 5*

6ᵛ *Gaillarde*

7 7v *Pavane. Qui souhaitez* (compare RISM 1549_{25}, p. 24: Janequin)
7v *Gaillarde*
8 8v *Pavane. Plus revenir* [2]
8v *Gaillarde. Plus revenir*
9 9v *Pavane. Mamye est tant honneste & saige*[a] (compare RISM 1549_{21}, no. 10: Sandrin)
9v *Gaillarde*
10 10v *Pavane. O foyble esprit*[a] (compare RISM 1549_{22}, no. 22: Gentian)
11 11v *Pavane. Le bon vouloir*[a] [3] *a5*
12 12v *Pavane*[a] [4] *a5*
13 13v *Pavane. Pour mon plaisir* *a5*
14 14v *Pavane*
15 15v *Pavane*
16 16v *Pavane*[a]
17 17v *Pavane*
18 18v *Pavane DELLESTARPE* = 1555_2, no. 204
19 19v *Pavane*[a]
20 20v *Gaillarde I*
21 21v *Gaillarde II*
22 22v *Gaillarde III*
23 23v *Gaillarde IIII*
24 24v *Gaillarde V*
25 24v *Gaillarde VI* (compare 1568_6, no. 82: "Gaillarde Si pour t'aymer")
26 25v *Gaillarde VII*
27 25v *Gaillarde VIII*
28 26v *Gaillarde I*[a] [5] (compare LesLRB, art. 3, fol. 9: "L'Ennuy qui me tourmente," Certon)
29 26v *Gaillarde II*[a]
30 27v *Gaillarde III* (Manuscript addition: "Si congneu")
31 27v *Gaillarde IIII*[a]
32 27v *Gaillarde V*[a]
33 28v *Gaillarde VI*
34 28v *Gaillarde VII*
35 28v *Gaillarde VIII*
36 29v *Gaillarde IX*
37 29v *Gaillarde X*
38 29v *Gaillarde XI*
39 30v *Gaillarde XII*
40 30v *Gaillarde XIII* (compare 1571_5, no. 45: "Gaillarde. Mon plaisir")
41 31v *Gaillarde XIIII*
42 31v *Gaillarde XV*

[1] Not related musically to RISM 1534_{11}, no. 10: "Vous qui voulez scavoir mon nom," Sermisy, nor to RISM 1549_{19}, no. 4: "Vous qui voulez avoir contentement," Mornable.

[2] Not related musically to PubAPTM XXIII, no. 37: Lupi.

[3] Facs. of fols. 11v and 12 in MMRF XXIII; mod. ed. of no. 11 in TwittT III, no. 3.

[4] Mod. ed. in TwittT III, no. 2.

[5] Mod. ed. in ZfSM XI, no. 3.

1550_6

GERVAISE, CLAUDE, EDITOR

Cinquiesme livre de danceries, A quatre / PARTIES, CONTENANT DIX BRANSLES GAYS, / Huict bransles de poictou, Trentecinq bransles de Champaigne, Le tout / en ung livre seul, Veu & corrige par Claude gervaise scavant / Musicien. Nouvellement imprimez par Pierre / Attaingnant Imprimeur du Roy en mu/sique. Demeurant á Paris En la / Rue de la Harpe pres / lesglise S. cosme. / 28. Augusti / 1550. / [Table of contents] / Avec privilege du Roy pour six ans

32 fols. Mensural notation. Fol. 1v = fol. I1v. The compositions identified by the superior letter *a* ([a]) are reprinted in MMRF XXIII, which includes a facsimile of the title page. For other modern editions see 1550_5. For further concordances see HeartzSF, p. 340. For other volumes in the same series, see 1547_6, note 2. All of the compositions are for instrumental ensemble *a4*.

Copy in: F:Pn.

fol.
1 1v *Bransle gay I*
2 1v *Bransle gay II*
3 2v *Bransle gay III*
4 2v *Bransle gay IIII* = 1555_5, no. 33
5 3v *Bransle gay V*
6 3v *Bransle gay VI*
7 4v *Bransle gay VII*
8 4v *Bransle gay VIII*
9 5v *Bransle gay IX*
10 5v *Bransle gay X*
11 6v *Bransle de poictou I*[a] = 1583_7, no. 72
12 6v *Bransle de poictou II*[a] = 1583_7, no. 73
13 7v *Bransle de poictou III*[a] = 1583_7, no. 74

14 7^v *Bransle de poictou IIII*^{a} = 1583$_7$, no. 75
15 8^v *Bransle de poitou V*^{a} = 1583$_7$, no. 76
16 9^v *Bransle de poictou VI* = 1583$_7$, no. 77
17 10^v *Bransle de poictou VII* = 1583$_7$, no. 78
18 10^v *Bransle de poictou VIII* = 1583$_7$, no. 79
19 11^v *Bransle de champaigne I* = 1583$_7$, no. 80
20 12^v *Bransle II* = 1583$_7$, no. 81
21 12^v *Bransle III* = 1583$_7$, no. 82
22 13^v *Bransle IIII* = 1583$_7$, no. 83
23 13^v *Bransle V* = 1583$_7$, no. 84
24 14^v *Bransle VI* = 1583$_7$, no. 85
25 15^v *Bransle VII* = 1583$_7$, no. 86
26 15^v *Bransle VIII* = 1583$_7$, no. 87
27 16^v *Bransle IX* = 1583$_7$, no. 88
28 17^v *Bransle X*
29 17^v *Bransle XI*
30 18^v *Bransle de champaigne*
31 19^v *Bransle II*
32 19^v *Bransle III*
33 20^v *Bransle IIII*
34 21^v *Bransle V*
35 21^v *Bransle VI*
36 22^v *Bransle VII*
37 23^v *Bransle VIII*
38 24^v *Bransle IX*
39 24^v *Bransle X*
40 25^v *Bransle XI*
41 25^v *Bransle XII*^{a}
42 26^v *Bransle XIII*^{a} [1]
43 26^v *Bransle XIIII*^{a} = 1547$_6$, no. 24: [Branle de bourgoigne]
44 27^v *Bransle de champaigne*
45 28^v *Branlse II*
46 28^v *Bransle III*^{a} [2]
47 29^v *Bransle IIII*
48 29^v *Bransle V*
49 30^v *Bransle VI*
50 30^v *Bransle VII*
51 31^v *Bransle VIII*
52 31^v *Bransle IX*
53 31^v *Bransle X*

[1] Mod. ed. in BarthaZ, no. 50e.
[2] Mod. ed. in ZfSM XI, no. 9.

1551$_1$

GORLIER, SIMON

LE / TROYSIEME LIVRE / CONTENANT PLUSIEURS DUOS, ET / Trios, avec la bataille de Jancquin a trois, nouvellement / mis en tabulature de Guiterne, par Simon / Gorlier, excellent joueur. / [Cut of a guitar lying on an open book] / A PARIS. / De l'Imprimerie de Robert GranJon & Michel Fezandat, au Mont / S. Hylaire, à l'Enseigne des Grandz Jons. / 1551. / Avec privilege du Roy.[1]

26 fols. French guitar tablature. Dedication on fol. a1^v headed "Simon Gorlier, a Francoys Pournas Lyonnois, seigneur de la Pimente son singulier amy, Salut." On fol. 26^v: excerpt from the royal privilege granting Robert Granjon permission to print music for six years, signed and dated "Paris le 12. jour de Febvrier 1549. & signees Bassourdi." The same excerpt is printed in 1552$_5$. The foliation given here follows the manuscript foliation in the unique copy (fol. 1 = fol. a2). For other volumes in the same series, see 1552$_5$, note 2. For further information see HeartzP. All of the compositions are for solo four-course guitar.

Copy in: CH:SGv.[2]

fol.

1 1 *Mamie un jour* (RISM 1549$_{18}$, no. 1: Certon)
2 2^v *Qui souhaitez* (compare RISM 1549$_{20}$, no. 1: Sandrin, and RISM [c. 1555]$_{24}$, fol. 5: Gardane)
3 4 *Ce qui est plus en ce monde amy* (RISM 1543$_7$, no. 3: Sandrin)
4 5^v *Sy jay du bien* (compare RISM 1547$_9$, no. 10: Sandrin)
5 7^v *Il ne se treuve en amytié* (RISM 1548$_3$, no. 14: Sandrin)
6 9^v *Je suis desheritée* Jacotin (RISM 1545$_7$, no. 22: anon.)
7 10^v *Le duo de Benedicta. Per illud Ave prol.* (JosqMT, no. 46: from Josquin, "Benedicta es coelorum regina")
8 12 *Je n'ay point plus d'affection* (LesAC, no. 14: Sermisy)

9 13 *La voulonté* (RISM 1549_{18}, no. 15: Sandrin)
10 14 *Estantz assis aux rives aquatiques* (Psalm 137; compare LesLRB, art. 17 *bis*, no. 14; and MornableP I, fol. 6)
15 *Celuy mesme en duo*
11 15^{v} *Pourquoy font bruit & s'assemblent les gens* (Psalm 2; compare LesLRB, art. 17 *bis*, no. 11)
12 16^{v} *Canon. In subdyapenté*
13 17 *Autre Canon*
14 18^{v} *Duo*
15 20 *La premiere partie de la Bataille de Janequin à trois* (MMRF VII, 31)
21^{v} 2a pars [*Fan frere le le lan fan*]

[1] Facs. of title page in HeartzP, opp. p. 452.
[2] Preceding the title page in the unique copy is a manuscript table of contents and two manuscript compositions in keyboard tablature: "Fuga in subdiapason di Fabricio Facciola," and "Fantasia: Giovanni di Antiquis."

1551_2

LE ROY, ADRIAN

PREMIER LIVRE DE / TABULATURE DE LUTH, CONTENANT / plusieurs Motetz, Chansons, Fantasies, Pavanes, Gaillardes, / Almandes, Branles, tant simples qu'autres: / Le tout composé / Par / ADRIAN LE ROY. / [Table of contents] / A PARIS, / De l'imprimerie, d'Adrian le Roy, & Robert Ballard, rue Saint Jean de / Beauvais, à l'enseigne Sainte Genevieve. / 29. d'Aoust. 1551. / Avec privilege du Roy, pour neuf ans.

40 fols. French lute tablature. On fol. 1^{v}: excerpt from the royal privilege granting Le Roy and Ballard permission to print music for nine years, signed and dated: "Données à Fontainebleau. Le quatorziesme jour d'Aoust. L'an de grace Mil cinq cens cinquante & un. Et de nostre regne le cinqyesme. Signées Par le Roy en son conseil. Robillart." The same excerpt appears in 1551_3, 1553_3, 1553_9, 1554_4, and 1556_8. LeRoyF is a modern edition of the entire volume, and includes concordances. See also HeartzSF, p. 385. All of the dances except no. 14 are modeled on the ensemble dances in 1550_5 and 1557_3. All of the compositions are for solo lute.

Copy in: D:Mbs.

fol.
1 2 *Fantasie premiere*[1]
2 4 *Fantasie seconde*[2]
3 6^{v} *Domine si tu es* Maillard (LesLRB, art. 16, fol. 11)
4 8^{v} *Dignare me laudare* Maillard (RISM 1553_7, fol. 19)
5 10 *Preparate corda vestra domino* Maillard (RISM 1553_7, fol. 4)
6 13 *Helas mon dieu ton yre s'est tournee* Maillard (RISM 1553_{19}, fol. 6)
7 15^{v} *Voulant honneur* Sandrin (RISM 1545_{12}, no. 8)
8 17^{v} *Je n'ay point plus d'affection* Claudin [de Sermisy] (LesAC, no. 14) = 1563_{12}, no. 79
9 19 *N'ayant le souvenir* (RISM 1554_{26}, no. 1: Entraigues)
19^{v} *N'ayant le souvenir plus diminuee*
10 21 *Pavane sy je m'en vois* (compare LesLRB, art. 3, fol. 9: "L'Ennuy qui me tourmente," Certon)
21^{v} *La pavane precedente plus diminuee*
22^{v} *Gaillarde sy je m'en vois*
23 *La gaillarde precedente plus diminuee*
11 24 *Pavane est il conclud* (compare LeRoyF, p. xix)
25 *La pavane precedente plus diminuee*
26^{v} *Gaillarde est il conclud*
27 *La precedente gaillarde plus diminuee*
12 28 *Gaillarde*
28^{v} *La precedente gaillarde plus diminuee*
13 29 *Gaillarde*
29^{v} *La gaillarde precedente plus diminuee*
14 30^{v} *Gaillarde* (compare 1536_9, no. 4d: "Saltarelo chiamato bel Fiore")
31 *La gaillarde precedente plus diminuee*
15 31^{v} *Almande*
31^{v} *L'almande precedente plus diminuee*

16 32^v *Almande*
33 *L'almande precedente plus diminuee*
17 34 *Branle simple*
34^v *Le branle precedent plus diminué*
18 35 *Branle gay*
19 35^v *Branle gay la ceinture que je porte*
20 36 *Premier Branle de bourgongne* = 1568_7, no. 154, and 1571_6, no. 187
21 36^v *Second branle* = 1568_7, no. 155, and 1571_6, no. 188
22 37 *Tiers branle* = 1563_{12}, no. 139; 1568_7, no. 156; 1571_6, no. 189
23 37^v *Quatreyesme branle* = 1563_{12}, no. 140; 1568_7, no. 157; 1571_6, no. 190
24 38 *Cinquiesme branle* = 1568_7, no. 158, and 1571_6, no. 191
25 38^v *Sixiesme branle* = 1568_7, no. 159, and 1571_6, no. 192
26 39 *Septiesme branle*[3] = 1563_{12}, no. 138; 1568_7, no. 160; 1571_6, no. 193
27 39^v *Huictiesme branle* = 1568_7, no. 161, and 1571_6, no. 194
28 40 *Neufiesme branle* = 1568_7, no. 162, and 1571_6, no. 195

[1] The thematic material of this fantasia resembles that in "Le content est riche" (AttainCK III, no. 9: Sermisy).
[2] Mod. ed. in NeemAM II, no. 1.
[3] Mod. ed. in NeemAM II, no. 2.

1551_3

LE ROY, ADRIAN

PREMIER LIVRE DE / TABULATURE DE GUITERRE, CONTE/nant plusieurs Chansons, Fantasies, Pavanes, Gaillardes, Alman/des, Branles, tant simples qu'autres: / Le tout composé. / Par / ADRIAN LE ROY. / [Table of contents] / A PARIS, / De l'imprimerie, d'Adrian le Roy, & Robert Ballard, rue Saint Jean de / Beauvais, à l'enseigne Sainte Genevieve. / 12. Septembre. 1551. / Avec privilege du Roy, pour neuf ans.

24 fols. French guitar tablature. On fol. 1^v: the same excerpt from the printer's privilege as in 1551_2. On fol. 24^v: diagram for tuning the guitar. For some dance concordances see HeartzSF, p. 392. All of the compositions are for solo four-course guitar.[1]

Copies in: F:Pm, GB:Lbm.

fol.
1 2 *Fantasie premiere*
2 3^v *Fantasie seconde*
3 4^v *Helas mon dieu* Maillard (RISM 1553_{19}, fol. 6)
4 6 *Je sens l'affection* Boyvin (RISM 1544_7, no. 28)
5 7^v *Je cherche autant amour* Boyvin (RISM 1545_{12}, no. 2) = 1570_4, no. 47
8 *La Chanson precedente plus diminuée*
6 8^v *Pavane si je m'en vois*[2] (compare LesLRB, art. 3, fol. 9: "L'Ennuy qui me tourmente," Certon) = 1570_4, no. 55a
8^v *La Pavane precedente plus diminuée*
9^v *Gaillarde Si je m'en vois* = 1570_4, no. 55b
10 *La Gaillarde precedente plus diminuée*
7 10^v *Pavane de la gambe* = 1570_4, no. 56a
11 *La Pavane precedente plus diminuee* = 1570_4, no. 56b
12 *Gaillarde de la gambe* = 1570_4, no. 56c
12^v *La Gaillarde precedente plus diminuee*
8 13^v *Gaillarde* = 1570_4, no. 81a
14 *La Gaillarde precedente plus diminuee* = 1570_4, no. 81b
9 14^v *Gaillarde par deppit* (compare JanT, no. 12: "Par fin depit," Janequin) = 1570_4, no. 85
15 *La Gaillarde precedente plus diminuee*
10 15^v *Gaillarde la rocquo el fuzo*
16 *La Gaillarde precedente plus diminuee*
11 16^v *Gaillarde la peronnelle* (compare ParisC, no. 39: "Av'ous point veu la Perronnelle") = 1570_4, no. 80
17 *La Gaillarde precedente plus diminuee*

12 17^v *Branle simple. N'aurez vous point de moy pitié*
18 *Le Branle precedent plus diminué*
13 18^v *Branle gay*[3]
18^v *Le Branle precedent plus diminué*
14 19 *Branle gay*
19^v *Le Branle precedent plus diminué*
15 19^v *Almande*[4] = 1570_4, no. 68
20 *L'Almande precedente plus diminuee*
16 20^v *Almande. La mon amy la* = 1570_4, no. 69
17 21 *Premier Branle de Bourgongne*[5] = 1570_4, no. 87
18 21^v *Second Branle*[5] = 1570_4, no. 88
19 22 *Troisieme Branle*[5] = 1570_4, no. 89
20 22 *Quatriesme Branle*[5] = 1570_4, no. 90
21 22^v *Cinquiesme Branle*[5] = 1570_4, no. 91
22 23 *Sixiesme Branle*[5] = 1570_4, no. 92
23 23 *Septiesme Branle*[5] = 1570_4, no. 93
24 23^v *Huitiesme Branle*[5] = 1570_4, no. 94
25 24 *Neufyesme Branle*[5] = 1570_4, no. 95
26 24^v *La Muniere de Vernon* (compare RISM 1554_{26}, no. 18: Maillard)

[1] Five volumes of guitar music survive in this series: I (1551_3), II (1556_8), III (1552_3), IV (1553_3), and V (1554_4). Vol. IV was compiled by Gregoire Brayssing, the others by Adrian le Roy. This 1551 volume is probably the one mentioned in FétB I, 231, as being from 1561.

[2] Mod. ed. in PujBG, no. 1060.

[3] Mod. ed. in PujBG, no. 1066.

[4] Mod. ed. in PujBG, no. 1065.

[5] Mod. ed. in PujBG, no. 1071.

$[1551]_4$

LE ROY, ADRIAN

Briefve et facile instruction pour apprendre la tabulature a bien accorder, conduire et disposer la main sur la guiterne.

This volume, now lost, is listed in F:Pn, MS fonds fr. 22.103, fol. 102 (notes of La Caille), and mentioned in Pierre Trichet, "Traité des instruments," *Annales musicologiques*, IV (1956), 218. See also LesLRB, art. 2 *bis*. For notice of another edition, see $[1578]_7$. This volume may have been translated into English (see $[1568]_9$), and Latin (see 1570_4, note 1).

1551_5 †

GARDANE, ANTONIO, PUBLISHER

INTABOLATURA NOVA / DI VARIE SORTE DE BALLI DA / Sonare Per arpichordi, Claviciembali, Spinette, & Manachordi, Raccolti Da / diversi Eccellentissimi Autori, Novamente data In Luce, & per / Antonio Gardane Con ogni diligentia stampata. / LIBRO [Printer's mark] PRIMO / In Venetia Apresso di / Antonio Gardane. / 1551

23 fols. Keyboard score. On fol. 23^v: table of contents. The compositions identified by the superior letter *a* ([a]) are reprinted in SchraTI. All of the compositions are for solo keyboard.

Copy in: I:Bc.

fol.
1 1^v *Pass'e mezo nuovo [primo]*[a][1] (1571_1, no. 62)
2 2^v *Pass'e mezo nuovo segondo* (1571_1, no. 63)
3 3^v *Pass'e mezo nuovo [terzo]* (1571_1, no. 64)
4 4^v *Cathacchio Gagliarda* (1571_1, no. 65)
5 5^v *L'herba fresca Gagliarda*
6 6^v *Gamba Gagliarda*
7 7^v *Le forze d'hercole*[2]
8 8 *Tu te parti Gagliarda*
9 8^v *A la ho*
10 9^v *Lodesana Gagliarda*[a]
11 10^v *Meza notte Gagliarda*
12 11^v *Fusi pavana piana*
13 12 *La vien dal porto Gagliarda*
14 12^v *Pass'e mezo antico primo*[a]
15 13^v *Pass'e mezo antico secondo*[a]
16 14^v *Pass'e mezo antico terzo*[a]
17 15^v *Moneghina Gagliarda*
18 16^v *La Canella Gagliarda*
19 17^v *Venetiana Gagliarda*[3]
20 18^v *Saltarello del Re*
21 19 *El Poverin Gagliarda*[a]

22	19v	*Gonella Gagliarda*
23	20v	*Fantina gagliarda*
24	21v	*Comadrina Gagliarda*
25	22v	*Fornerina gagliarda*

[1] Mod. ed. in WasG, no. 29.
[2] Mod. ed. in ApelM I, 23.
[3] Mod. ed. in ScherG, no. 112, and WasG, no. 30.

1551_6

GARDANE, ANTONIO, PUBLISHER

FANTASIE RECERCARI / CONTRAPUNTI A TRE VOCI DI / M. adriano & de altri Autori appropriati per Cantare & Sonare d'ogni / sorte di Stromenti, Con dui Regina celi, l'uno di M. adriano & l'altro / di M. cipriano, Sopra uno medesimo Canto Fermo, Novamente / dati In Luce, & per Antonio Gardane / Con ogni diligentia stampati. / LIBRO [Printer's mark] PRIMO / In Venetia Apresso di / Antonio Gardane. / 1551

Three part books in mensural notation, each of 20 fols. On fol. 20v of each part book: table of contents. The compositions identified by the superior letter *a* ([a]) are reprinted in WillR after 1559_8. SlimK II, 533, contains a thematic index of the volume. Contents = 1559_8 and 1593_8. Nos. 1 and 2 are fully texted; the other compositions are for instrumental ensemble *a 3*.

Copy in: I:Fm (S).

	p.	
1	1	*Regina celi* Adriano [Willaert]
2	3	*Regina celi* Cipriano [de Rore]
3	5	*Recercar primo*[a 1] Adriano
4	7	*Recercar segondo*[a] Adriano = 1549_7, no. 27
5	9	*Recercar Terzo*[a] Adriano = 1549_7, no. 26
6	11	*Recercar Quarto*[a] Adriano = 1549_7, no. 24
7	13	*Recercar quinto*[a] Adriano = 1549_7, no. 29
8	15	*Recercar sesto*[a] Adriano = 1549_7, no. 23
9	17	*Recercar Settimo*[a] Adriano = 1549_7, no. 28
10	19	*Recercar Ottavo*[a] Adriano = 1549_7, no. 25
11	21	*Recercar Nono* Incerto Autore
12	23	*Recercar Decimo*[2] Adriano
13	24	*Recercar Undecimo* Incerto Autore
14	25	*Recercar Duodecimo* Antonino Barges
15	27	*Recercar Tertio Decimo* Antonino Barges
16	29	*Recercar Quartodecimo* Antonino Barges
17	30	*Recercar Quintodecimo*[3] Jeronimo da Bologna [Girolamo Cavazzoni]

[1] Mod. ed. in RieH, vol. II, pt. 1, p. 450; RieM, no. 42; and TagA I, no. 2.
[2] Mod. ed. in BarthaZ, no. 56; BedbK, p. 53; HAM, no. 115; KatzF, no. 3; PeetM I, no. 9; and WasG, no. 17.
[3] Mod. ed. in CavazzO II, 58.

1551_7

GARDANE, ANTONIO, PUBLISHER

MOTETTA TRIUM VOCUM / Ab pluribus Authoribus Composita Quorum nomina sunt. / JACHETUS GALICUS / MORALES HISPANUS / CONSTANTIUS FESTA / ADRIANUS WILGLIARDUS / TRIUM [Printer's mark] VOCUM / Venetiis Apud / Antonium Gardane. / 1551

Three part books in mensural notation, each of 16 fols. The tenor part book is dated 1551, the two others 1552. On the final verso of each book: table of contents. Contents = 1543_3 and 1569_7. Contains 20 vocal compositions *a 3* with Latin text, and four textless compositions for instrumental ensemble *a 3*.

Copies in: D:Mbs, F:Ameyer (ST).

1551_8

SUSATO, TIELMAN, PUBLISHER

Het derde musyck boexken begre/PEN INT GHET AL VAN ONSER / neder duytscher spraken, daer inne begrepen syn alderhande / danserye, te vuetens Basse dansen, Ronden, Allemain/gien, Pavanen ende meer andere, mits oeck vyfthien / nieuwe gaillarden, zeer lustich ende bequaem om / spelen op alle musicale Instrumenten, Ghecom/poneert ende naer dinstrumenten ghestelt / duer Tielman Susato, Int iaer ons / heeren, M. D. LI. / TENOR. / Ghedruckt Tantwerpen by Tielman Susato wonende voer / die niewe waghe In den Cromhorn. / CUM GRATIA ET PRIVI-LEGIO

Four part books in mensural notation, each of 16 fols. On fol. 1^v: table of contents. SusaD is a modern edition of the entire volume. The compositions identified by superior letters are reprinted as follows: ([a]) in BlumeS; ([b]) in EitT; ([c]) in MohrA; ([d]) in ZfSM I. All of the compositions are for instrumental ensemble *a 4*.

Copies in: E:Mmc (T), NL:DHgm (S).[1]

	fol.	
1	2	*Bergerette Dont vient cela*[a] (compare AttainCK III, no. 22: Sermisy)
	2	*Reprise*
2	2^v	*Bergeret [sans roch]*[a 2]
	3	*Reprise*
	3	*Reprise aliud*
3	3^v	*Reprise Cest une dure despartie*[3] (compare AttainCK II, no. 3: Sermisy)
4	4	*Bergerette*[a] (compare 1530_3, no. 4: "La brosse. Basse dance")
5	4	*La morisque*
6	4^v	*Les grands douleurs. Bergerette*
7	5	*Entre du fol*
8	5^v	*Danse du Roy*
9	5^v	*Le joly boys*
10	6	*Mon desir. Basse danse*[a]
11	6^v	*Reprise Le cueur est bon*[a] (compare AttainCK I, no. 11)
12	7	*Reprise Cest a grant tort* (compare AttainCK II, no. 18: Sermisy)
13	7^v	*Den iersten ronde. Pourquoy*[bd] (compare LesAC, no. 4: "Pourquoy donc ne fringuerons," Passereau) = 1571_5, no. 64, and 1583_7, no. 89
14	7^v	*Den II. ronde. Mon amy* = 1571_5, no. 65, and 1583_7, no. 90
15	8	*Den III. ronde*
16	8	*Den IIII. ronde*[bd]
17	8^v	*Den V. ronde. Wo bistu* = 1571_5, no. 66
18	8^v	*Den VI. ronde*[bd 4] (compare no. 22 below) = 1571_5, no. 67
19	9	*Den VII. ronde. Il estoit une fillette* (compare LesAC, no. 10: Janequin)
20	9	*Den VIII. ronde. Mille ducas en vostre bource* (compare nos. 39 and 52 below)
21	9^v	*Den IX. ronde*[b] = 1571_5, no. 68, and 1583_7, no. 91
	9^v	*Aliud*
22	9^v	*Saltarelle*[bd 4] (compare no. 18 above)
23	10	*Les quatre branles* = 1571_5, no. 61, and 1583_7, no. 94
24	10	*Fagot* = 1571_5, no. 62, and 1583_7, no. 95
25	10	*Den hoboecken dans* = 1571_5, no. 63, and 1583_7, no. 96
26	10^v	*De post*[5] = 1571_5, no. 4a
	10^v	*Reprise* = 1571_5, no. 4b
27	10^v	*De matrigale*
28	10^v	*Danse de Hercules oft maticine*[b] = 1571_5, no. 5
29	11	*Den iersten Allemaingne*[c] = 1571_5, no. 21, and 1583_7, no. 31
	11	*Recoupe*[c]
30	11	*Den tweeden Allemaingne*[bcd]
31	11^v	*Den III. Allemaingne*[c]
32	11^v	*Den IIII. Allemaingne*[c]
33	12	*Den V. Allemaingne*[bd] = 1571_5, no. 20
34	12	*Den VI. Allemaingne*[c] (compare 1551_3, no. 16: "Almande. La mon amy la")
35	12^v	*Den VII. Allemaingne*[c] (compare WardDVM, p. 49) = 1571_5, no. 19: "Almande smedelijn"
36	12^v	*Den VIII. Allemaingne*[c] (compare WardDVM, p. 47) = 1571_5, no. 18: "Almande prince"
	12^v	*Recoupe*[c]
	12^v	*Recoupe aliud*[c]
37	13	*Pavane. Mille regretz*[6] (compare JosqWW, no. 24: Josquin)
38	13	*Pavane. La dona* (compare no. 50 below)
39	13	*Pavane. Mille ducas*[bd] (compare no. 20 above and no. 52 below)
40	13^v	*Pavane. Si par souffrir*[b] (compare RISM 1534_{14}, no. 4: "Si par souffrir," Courtois)

41 13v *Pavane. La battaille*[bd] = 1571_5, no. 12a, and 1583_7, no. 10
42 14 *Passe & medio*[b]
14 *Reprinse le pingue*[b]
43 14 *1. Gaillarde*
44 14 *2. Gaillarde*
45 14v *3. Gaillarde*
46 14v *4. Gaillarde*[b]
47 14v *5. Gaillarde Ghequest bin ick* (compare DuyL I, 541; DuyL III, 2731; and LenN, p. 84)
48 15 *6. Gaillarde*
49 15 *7. Gaillarde*
50 15 *8. Gaillarde La dona* (compare no. 38 above)
51 15v *9. Gaillarde*
52 15v *10. Gaillarde Mille ducas*[b] (compare nos. 20 and 39 above)
53 16 *11. Gaillarde*
54 16 *12. Gaillarde*[b]
55 16 *13. Gaillarde*[b]
56 16v *14. Gaillarde*
57 16v *15. Gaillarde Le tout*

[1] A complete set of part books was in D:Bds.
[2] Mod. ed. in ARC 16, no. 4.
[3] Mod. ed. in OppelF, p. 217.
[4] Mod. ed. in FroideA I, 26; MUB, vol. 22; RehA I, 21; and ScherG, no. 119.
[5] Mod. ed. in MGG IV, col. 1291.
[6] Mod. ed. in TwittT I, no. 1.

1552_1

GERLE, HANS

Eyn Newes sehr Künstlichs / Lautenbuch, darinen etliche Preambel, unnd / Welsche Tentz, mit vier stimmen, von den berumbsten / Lutenisten, Francisco Milaneso. Anthoni Rotta. Joan Maria. Rosseto / Simon Gintzler und andern mehr gemacht, und zu samen getra/gen, aus welscher ihn teusche Tabulatur versetzt, durch / Hanssen Gerle den Eltern, Burger zu Nüren/berg vormals nie gesehen, noch im / Truck aussgangen. / M. D. LII

85 fols. German lute tablature. The title is placed within the same ornamental border containing the initials H. G. and the date 1530 as in 1532_2. Dedication on fol. A2 headed "Dem Ersamen, und achbarn, Frantzen Lederer, Burger zu Nürenberg meinnem besundern günstigen guten günner, und wolverwanten freunde," and signed on fol. A4, "Gegeben zu Nürenberg den 14 Octobris Anno 15 51. E E williger guter günner und freunde Hans Gerle der Elter Burger zu Nürenberg." On fols. A4v–A5v: instructions for playing the lute headed "Nun volgt ein unterricht von ettlichen griffen wie man die greiffen sol." On fol. A6: table of contents including attributions to composers. Colophon on fol. X3v: "Gedruckt zu Nürenberg bey Jeronimus Formschneyder." The contents of the volume are listed in MfMG IV (1872), 39. See also TapL. All of the compositions are for solo lute.

Copies in: A:Wn, D:LEm (two copies), D:Usche.[1]

fol.
1 A6v *Das 1. Preambel* Joan maria [da Crema] = 1546_{10}, no. 1
2 B1 *Das 2. Preambel* Jo. Maria = 1546_{10}, no. 2
3 B2v *Das 3. Preambel* = 1546_{10}, no. 4: Giovanni Maria da Crema
4 B3v *Das 4. Preambel* = 1546_{10}, no. 6: Giovanni Maria da Crema
5 B4 *Das 5. Preambel* = 1546_{10}, no. 14: Giovanni Maria da Crema
6 C1 *Das 6. Preambel* = 1546_{10}, no. 11: Giovanni Maria da Crema
7 C1v *Das 7. Preambel* = 1546_{10}, no. 10: Giovanni Maria da Crema
8 C3 *Das 8. Preambel* = 1546_{10}, no. 15: Giovanni Maria da Crema
9 C4v *Das 9. Preambel* Rossetto = 1546_5, no. 1: Dominico Bianchini
10 D1v *Das 10. Preambel*[2] = 1546_5, no. 17: Bianchini
11 D2 *Das 11. Preambel* = 1546_5, no. 3: Bianchini
12 D3 *Das 12. Preambel* Simon Gintzler = 1547_3, no. 1
13 D4 *Das 13. Preambel* = 1547_3, no. 2: Gintzler
14 E1v *Das 14. Preambel* = 1547_3, no. 4: Gintzler
15 E3 *Das 15. Preambel*[3] = 1547_3, no. 6: Gintzler

16 E4 *Das 16. Preambel* Anthoni Rotta = 1546_{15}, no. 28

17 E4^{v} *Das 17. Preambel* = 1546_{15}, no. 29: Rotta

18 F1^{v} *Das 18. Preambel* = 1546_{15}, no. 32: Rotta

19 F2^{v} *Das 19. Preambel*[4] = 1546_{15}, no. 30: Rotta

20 F3^{v} *Das 20. Preambel* Franciscus von Maylandt = 1547_2, no. 1

21 F4^{v} *Das 21. Preambel* = 1536_9, no. 7: Francesco da Milano

22 G2 *Das 22. Preambel* = 1536_9, no. 16: Francesco da Milano

23 G4 *Das 23. Preambel* = 1536_9, no. 19: Francesco da Milano

24 H2 *Das 24. Preambel* Petter Paul [Borrono] von Mailandt = 1536_9, no. 11

25 H3^{v} *Das 25. Preambel* Marx vom Adler [Marco d'Aquila] = 1536_9, no. 17

26 J1^{v} *Das 26. Preambel* = 1536_9, no. 3: Marco d'Aquila

27 J3 *Das 27. Preambel* Albrecht von Mantua [Albert de Rippe] = 1536_9, no. 2

28 K1 *Das 28. Preambel* = 1536_9, no. 8: Albert de Rippe

29 K3^{v} *Das 29. Preambel* Hans Jacob von Mailandt [Johannes Jacobo Albutio] = 1536_9, no. 10

30 L1^{v} *Das 30. Preambel* = 1536_9, no. 18: Albutio

31 L4 *Das 31. Preambel*[5] Marx vom Adler [Marco D'Aquila] = 1536_9, no. 9

32 M2 *Der 1. Passemeso*[6] Rosseto = 1546_5, no. 8a: Dominico Bianchini

M2^{v} *Der 2. Padoana*[7] = 1546_5, no. 8b: Bianchini

M3 *Der 3. Saltarello* = 1546_5, no. 8c: Bianchini

33 M3^{v} *Der 4. Elfortze dercule* = 1546_5, no. 9: Bianchini

34 M4 *Der 5. Lodesano* = 1546_5, no. 10: Bianchini

35 M4^{v} *Der 6. Mesa note* = 1546_5, no. 11: Bianchini

36 N1 *Der 7. Lacara Cossa* = 1546_5, no. 12: Bianchini

37 N1^{v} *Der 8. Elburato*[8] = 1546_5, no. 13: Bianchini

38 N2 *Der 9. Saltarelo*[9] Johann Maria [da Crema] = 1546_{10}, no. 41: "Saltarello ditto el maton"

39 N2^{v} *Der 10. Saltarelo*[10] = 1546_{10}, no. 42: "Saltarello ditto bel fior," Giovanni Maria da Crema

40 N3 *Der 11. Passe Messo* = 1546_{10}, no. 45a: "Pass'e mezo ala bolognesa," Giovanni Maria da Crema

N3^{v} *Der 12. Saltarelo* = 1546_{10}, no. 45b: "Saltarello a la bolognesa," Giovanni Maria da Crema

41 N4 *Der 13. Passemeso* = 1546_{10}, no. 46a: "Pass'e mezo della louetta," Giovanni Maria da Crema

O1 *Der 14. Saltarello* = 1546_{10}, no. 46b: "Saltarel de la louetta," Giovanni Maria da Crema

42 O2 *Der 15. Passe Messo*[11] Anthoni Rotta = 1546_{15}, no. 1a

O3 *Der 16. Gagliarda* = 1546_{15}, no. 1b: Rotta

O3^{v} *Der 17. Padoana* = 1546_{15}, no. 1c: Rotta

43 O4^{v} *Der 18. Passemesso* = 1546_{15}, no. 2a: Rotta

P1^{v} *Der 19. Gagliarda* = 1546_{15}, no. 2b: Rotta

P2^{v} *Der 20. Padoana* = 1546_{15}, no. 2c: Rotta

44 P3^{v} *Der 21. Passemesso* = 1546_{15}, no. 4a: Rotta

P4^{v} *Der 22. Gagliarda* = 1546_{15}, no. 4b: Rotta

Q1 *Der 23. Padoana* = 1546_{15}, no. 4c: Rotta

45 Q2 *Der 24. Passemesso* = 1546_{15}, no. 3a: Rotta

Q2^{v} *Alio Modo*

Q3 *Der 25. Gagliarda*[12] = 1546_{15}, no. 3b: Rotta

Q3^{v} *Der 26. Gentil madonna* = 1546_{15}, no. 3d: Rotta

Q4 *Der 27. Padoana* = 1546_{15}, no. 3c: Rotta

46 R1 *Der 28. Passemesso* = 1546_{15}, no. 5a: Rotta

R3 *Der 29. Gagliarda* = 1546_{15}, no. 5b: Rotta

	R4[v]	*Der 30. Padoana* = 1546_{15}, no. 5c: Rotta
47	S2	*Der 31. Pavana chiamata Petter Paul von Maylandt* = 1536_9, no. 13a: "Pavana chiamata la Gombertina," Pietro Paolo Borrono
	S4	*Der 32. Saltarello* = 1536_9, no. 13b: Borrono
	T2[v]	*Der 33. Saltarello* = 1536_9, no. 13c: "Saltarello che glian strazza la socha," Borrono
	T4	*Der 34. Saltarello* = 1536_9, no. 13d: "Saltarello chiamato Antonola"
48	V1	*Der 35. Pavana chiamata La desperata* = 1536_9, no. 14a: Borrono
	V3	*Der 36. Saltarello* = 1536_9, no. 14b: "Saltarello de la Desperata"
	V4	*Der 37. Saltarello la mantuanello* = 1536_9, no. 14c
	X1[v]	*Der 38. Tochatocha La canella* = 1536_9, no. 14d

1 A copy was in D:Bds.
2 Mod. ed. in WasG, no. 7.
3 Mod. ed. in WasG, no. 8; WolfHM, p. 524; and WolfME, no. 32.
4 Mod. ed. in WasG, no. 9.
5 Mod. ed. in KörL, no. 7.
6 Heading on fol. M2: "Volgen hernach die welschen Tentze." Mod. ed. in WasG, no. 10.
7 Mod. ed. in EitT, no. 39.
8 Mod. ed. in EitT, no. 38.
9 Mod. ed. in BruAL, no. 5; FerandM, p. 410; and KörL, no. 10.
10 Mod. ed. in EitT, no. 41.
11 Mod. ed. in EitT, no. 40, and WasG, no. 11.
12 Facs. in WolfH II, 47.

1552_2

LE ROY, ADRIAN

TIERS LIVRE DE TA/BULATURE DE LUTH, CON/tenant vingt & un Pseaulmes, Le tout mis / selon le subjet par / ADRIAN LE ROY. / [Printer's mark] / A PARIS. / De l'imprimerie, d'Adrian le Roy, & Robert Ballard, Imprimeurs du Roy, rue / saint Jean de Beauvais, à l'enseigne sainte Genevieve. / 1552. / Avec privilege du Roy, pour neuf ans.

24 fols. Superius (called "subject") in mensural notation; accompaniment in French lute tablature. The "subjects" are related to the monophonic melodies in *Pseaulmes cinquante de David, mis en vers francois par Clement Marot* (Lyons, Godefroy et Marcelin Beringen frères, 1549), but the settings are apparently new. The entire collection is reprinted in a modern edition in Le RoyP. For information on this volume and for modern editions of nos. 2, 5, 18, and 19, see MorcouA. All of the compositions are for solo voice and lute.

Copy in: D:Mbs.

	fol.	
1	1[v]	*Pseaulme III. Domine quid multiplicati sunt* (*O Seigneur que de gens*)
2	3[v]	*Pseau. XXXIII. Exultate justi in domino* (*Resveillez vous chascun fidelle*)
3	4[v]	*Pseau. CXXXVII. Super fl[u]mina babylonis* (*Estans assis*)
4	5[v]	*Pseaulme CXXVIII. Beati omnes qui timent dominum* (*Bien heureux*)
5	6[v]	*Pseaul. XXX. De profundis clamavi* (*Du fond de ma pensée*)
6	7[v]	*Pseau. L. Deus Deorum do.* (*Le Dieu le fort*)[1]
7	8[v]	*Pseau. LXXII. Deus judicium tuum regi* (*Tes jugementz*)
8	9[v]	*Pseaul. V. Verba mea auribus per* (*Aux parolles que je veulx dire*)
9	10[v]	*Pseaul. XIX. Coeli en arrant glo* (*Les cieulx en chascun lieu*)
10	11[v]	*Pseaul. XIIII. Dixit insipiens in corde* (*Le fol maling*)
11	12[v]	*Pseaul. IX. Confiteor tibi domine* (*De tout mon coeur*)
12	13[v]	*Pseaul. CXIII. Laudate pueri dominum* (*Enfans qui le Seigneur servez*)
13	14[v]	*Pseaul. XLIII. Deus deus meus ad te* (*Revenge moy*)
14	15[v]	*Pseaul. XXIIII. Domini est terra, et plen.* (*La terre au Seigneur*)
15	16[v]	*Pseaul. CXLIII. Domine exaudi orationem* (*Seigneur Dieu, oy l'oraison mienne*)
16	17[v]	*Psealume CIIII. Benedic anima mea domino, domine* (*Sus, sus mon ame*)

17 19^v *Pseaul. XCI. Qui habitat in adjutorio* (*Qui en la garde*)

18 20^v *Pseaul. I. O Beatus vir qui non abiit* (*Qui au conseil*)

19 21^v *Pseaulme CI. Misericordiam et judicium cantabo* (*Vouloir m'est*)

20 22^v *Pseaul. XLVI. Deus noster refugium et* (*Des qu'adversité*)

21 23^v *Pseaul. CXIIII. In exitu Israel de Aegypto* (*Quand Israel*) [2]

[1] Mod. ed. in BruS II, no. 45.

[2] Mod. ed. in BruS IV, no. 127.

1552_3

LE ROY, ADRIAN

TIERS LIVRE DE TABU/LATURE DE GUITERRE, CONTE/nant plusieurs Préludes, Chansons, Basse-dances, Tour/dions, Pavanes, Gaillardes, Almandes, Bransles, tant / doubles que simples. Le tout composé par / ADRIAN LE ROY. / [Printer's mark] / A PARIS. / De l'imprimerie, d'Adrian le Roy, & Robert Ballard, Imprimeurs du Roy, rue / saint Jean de Beauvais, à l'enseigne sainte Genevieve. / 1552. / Avec privilege du Roy, pour neuf ans.

24 fols. French guitar tablature. On fol. 24^v: table of contents. For some dance concordances see HeartzSF, p. 397. For other volumes in the same series, see 1551_3, note 1. All of the compositions are for solo guitar.

Copies in: F:Pm, GB:Lbm.

fol.

1 1^v *Prelude*

2 2 *Autre prelude* = 1570_4, no. 6

3 2^v *Un advocat* [*dit à sa femme*] = 1570_4, no. 41

4 3^v *La la la je ne* [*l'ose dire*] (PubAPTM XXIII, no. 15: Certon) = 1570_4, no. 18

5 4 *Jean de Lagny* (PubAPTM XXIII, no. 6: Berchem) = 1570_4, no. 19

6 4^v *Pour un plaisir que si peu dure* (SeayFC, no. 5: Sermisy) = 1570_4, no. 20

7 5^v *Il estoit une fillette en basse dance* (LesAC, no. 10: Janequin)

6 *Demie basse-dance*

8 6^v *Tourdion* [1] = 1570_4, no. 58

9 7 *Pavane J'ay du mal tant tant* (compare LesAC, no. 18: "J'ay le rebours," Certon) = 1570_4, no. 57a

8^v *Gaillarde de la precedente pavane* = 1570_4, no. 57b

10 9^v *Pavane de la guerre* = 1570_4, no. 59a

10^v *Gaillarde de la precedente pavane* = 1570_4, no. 59b

11 11^v *La toulouzane gaillarde* = 1570_4, no. 70

12 12^v *La lionnoyse gaillarde* = 1570_4, no. 71

13 13^v *Gaillarde* = 1570_4, no. 83

14 14^v *Gaillarde* = 1570_4, no. 73

15 15 *La Romanesque Gaillarde* = 1570_4, no. 79

16 15^v *Almande le Pied de cheval* [2] = 1570_4, no. 65

17 16 *Almande tournée* = 1570_4, no. 64: "Almande. Loreyne"

18 17 *Bransle simple*

19 18 *Bransle gay*

20 18^v *Bransle gay la ceinture que je porte*

21 19^v *Bransle gay Je ne seray jamais bergere* = 1570_4, no. 100 (compare $154?_6$, no. 49)

22 20 *Bransle de Champaigne*

23 20^v *Bransle de Champaigne*

24 21 *Bransle de Champaigne*

25 21 *Bransle de Champaigne*

26 21^v *Bransle Haulbaroys*

27 22 *Pimontoyse*

28 22^v *Bransle de Poictou* [3]

29 23 *Bransle de Poictou* [*en mode de cornemuse*]

30 23^v *Bransle de Poictou* [*en mode de cornemuse*]

31 24 *Autre bransle de Poictou grand bonnet large* [*en mode de cornemuse*]

32 24 *Autre Bransle de Poictou* [*en mode de cornemuse*]

[1] Facs. of fols. 6^v and 7 in MGG III, col. 711. Mod. ed. of no. 8 in FischV, no. 3.

[2] Mod. ed. in WardDVM, p. 48.

[3] Quasi-facs. and mod. ed. in WolfH II, 169; mod. ed. in PujBG, no. 1060.

1552_4

MORLAYE, GUILLAUME

PREMIER LIVRE DE / TABULATURE DE LEUT, CONTE/nant plusieurs Chansons, Fantasies, Pavanes & Gaillardes, / Composées par maistre Guillaume Morlaye joueur de / Leut, & autres bons Autheurs. / [Printer's mark with the motto "NE LA MORT NE LE VENIM"]/A PARIS, / De l'imprimerie de Michel Fezandat, au mont sainct Hilaire, a l'hostel d'Albret. / Et en la rue de Bievre, en la maison de maistre Guillaume Morlaye. / 1552. / Avec privilege du Roy, pour dix ans.

44 fols. French lute tablature. Fol. A2 = fol. 1.[1] On fol. 42^v: table of contents. On fol. 43: excerpt from the royal privilege granting Morlaye permission to print the works of Albert de Rippe and other composers, valid for ten years, signed "Ainsi signé par le Roy en son conseil, Coignet. Et seelé de cire jaulne, sur simple queue." The same excerpt appears in 1552_6, 1554_6, 1554_7, and 1554_8; a shortened version of the privilege appears in 1555_4, 1558_3, 1558_4, and 1558_6; a fuller version of the privilege appears in 1552_8 and 1553_8. For information on Morlaye see ProdM.[2] For some dance concordances see HeartzSF, p. 390. All of the compositions are for solo lute.

Copies in: B:Br, D:Mbs, F:Pthibault.

	fol.	
1	1	*Fantasie* = 1548_4, no. 17: Julio da Modena [Segni]
2	3^v	*Fantasie*
3	4^v	*Fantasie* = 1538_1, no. 9: Narváez
4	5^v	*Fantasie* = 1538_1, no. 10: Narváez
5	6^v	*Fantasie* = 1538_1, no. 11: Narváez
6	8	*F[antasie]* = 1563_{12}, no. 1; 1568_7, no. 5; 1571_6, no. 31 (compare 1536_9, no. 1: Francesco da Milano)
7	9^v	*Las on peut juger* Janequin (RISM 1544_7, no. 21) = 1563_{12}, no. 66
8	11	*Auparavant [que jeusse congnoissance]* Megret (RISM 1547_{11}, no. 3: Olivier)
9	13^v	*Tristes pensees*
10	14^v	*Sortes mes [pleurs]* Mornable (RISM 1544_7, no. 3)
11	15^v	*Sans liberté* Magdelain (RISM 1546_{11}, no. 19) = 1563_{12}, no. 55
12	18^v	*O Foible esprit*[3] Gentian = 1563_{12}, no. 50
13	19^v	*O Seigneur Dieu pere des orphelins* Mithou = 1563_{12}, no. 51
14	20	*Susanne un jour* Mithou (RISM 1552_3, p. 6)
15	21^v	*Fato son esca* Archadelt (RISM 1550_{17}, no. 13) = 1546_{17}, no. 15
16	22^v	*Quando io penso al martire* Archadelt (RISM 1541_9, p. 54) = 1546_{17}, no. 3
17	24^v	*Non at* [sic] *suo amante* (RISM 1526_6, no. 8: B[artolomeo] T[romboncino]) = 1563_{12}, no. 87, and 1568_7, no. 103
18	25^v	*Lasso la speme*
19	27^v	*Paduane* (compare "Pavana la pianzolenta," 1546_8, no. 14)
	28^v	*Gaillarde*
	29^v	*Gaillarde*
20	30	*Paduane*
	31	*Gaillarde*
21	32^v	*Paduane* (compare LesAC, no. 18: "J'ay le rebours," Certon, and also 1552_3, no. 9: "Pavane J'ay du mal tant tant")
	33^v	*Gaillarde* †
22	34^v	*Paduane*
	35^v	*Gaillarde*
23	36^v	*Paduane* (compare 1548_2, no. 1: "Pavana detto la bella Andronica")
	37^v	*Gaillarde*
24	38^v	*Paduane* = 1563_{12}, no. 130a
	40^v	*Gaillarde* = 1563_{12}, no. 130b
	41^v	*Gaillarde* = 1563_{12}, no. 130c

[1] There are two folios marked 30, and two marked 31, as well as other typographical errors in the foliation.

[2] Three volumes of lute music by Guillaume Morlaye survive: I (1552_4), II (1558_3) and III (1558_4).

[3] Not related musically to RISM 1549_{22}, no. 22.

1552_5

MORLAYE, GUILLAUME

LE / PREMIER LIVRE DE / CHANSONS, GAILLARDES, PAVANNES, / Bransles, Almandes, Fantaisies, reduictz en tabulature de Guiterne / par Maistre Guillaume Morlaye joueur de Lut. / [Cut of a guitar lying on an open book] / A PARIS. / De l'Imprimerie de Robert GranJon & Michel Fezandat, au Mont / S. Hylaire, à l'Enseigne des Grandz Jons. / 1552. / Avec privilege du Roy.[1]

30 fols. French guitar tablature. On fol. *A1^v: the same excerpt from the printer's privilege as in 1551_1. Preceding title page: manuscript table of contents. The foliation given here follows the manuscript foliation in the unique copy: fol. *A2 = fol. 1. For further information see HeartzP. All of the compositions are for solo guitar.[2]

Copy in: CH:SGv.

	fol.	
1	1	*Fantaisie*
2	3	*Fantaisie*
3	4	*Je cherche autant amour* (RISM 1545_{12}, no. 2: Boyvin)
4	5	*Plus le voy de beaucoup estimé* (RISM 1549_{18}, no. 11: "Plus je le voy," Belin)
5	5^v	*Elle a bien ce ris gratieuls* (RISM 1542_{14}, no. 25: Sermisy)
6	7	*Il estoit une fillette* (LesAC, no. 10: Janequin)
7	7^v	*Ce qui est plus* (RISM 1543_7, no. 3: Sandrin)
8	9^v	*Plourez mes yeuls* (RISM 1540_{13}, no. 22: Sandrin)
9	11	*La voulonté* (RISM 1549_{18}, no. 15: Sandrin)
10	12^v	*Jay veu que j'estoys franc & maistre* (RISM 1543_7, no. 4: Sandrin)
11	13^v	*Pavanne*
	14^v	*Gaillarde*
12	15^v	*Pavanne*
	16^v	*Gaillarde*
13	17^v	*Gaillarde. Puis que nouvelle affection* (compare RISM 1554_{26}, no. 2: Certon)
14	18	*Gaillarde*
15	18^v	*Gaillarde*
16	19	*Gaillarde*
17	19^v	*Gaillarde. Les cinq pas* (compare 1546_{15}, no. 10: "La rocha'l fuso")
18	21	*Gaillarde*
19	21^v	*Gaillarde*
20	22^v	*Gaillarde* (compare LesLRB, art. 3, no. 16: "O combien est heureuse," Certon)
21	23^v	*Buffons*
22	24^v	*Conte clare*
23	26	*Bransle [double]*
24	26^v	*Bransle [simple]*
25	27	*Bransle [de Bourgongne]*
26	27^v	*Bransle [double]*
27	28^v	*Allemande*
28	29	*Allemande*

[1] Facs. of title page in HeartzP, opp. p. 452.

[2] Four volumes of guitar music published by Fezandat survive: I (1552_5), II (1553_4), III (1551_1), and IV (1552_6), three of them edited by Guillaume Morlaye, and one (vol. III) by Simon Gorlier. All survive as unique copies, bound together, in St. Gall.

1552_6

MORLAYE, GUILLAUME

QUATRIESME LIVRE / CONTENANT PLUSIEURS FANTASIES, / Chansons, Gaillardes, Paduanes, Bransles, reduictes en Tabulature de Guyterne, / & au jeu de la Cistre, par Maistre Guillaume Morlaye, / & autres bons autheurs. / [Cut of a guitar lying on an open book] / A PARIS, / De l'imprimerie de Michel Fezandat, au mont sainct Hylaire, a l'hostel d'Albret, / 1552. / Avec privilege du Roy, pour dix ans.[1]

30 fols. French guitar tablature and, for nos. 22–30, French cittern tablature. On fol. A2: the same excerpt from the printer's privilege as in 1552_4. Fol. A3 = fol. 1. Preceding title page in unique copy: manuscript table of contents. SlimK II, 562, contains a thematic index of the ricercares. For further information see HeartzP. For other volumes in the same series, see 1552_5, note 2. Nos. 1–21 are for solo guitar, nos. 22–30 for solo cittern.

Copy in: CH:SGv.

MUSIC FOR SOLO GUITAR

	fol.	
1	1	*Fantasie d'Albert* [*de Rippe*]
2	4^v	*Fantasie d'Albert*
3	8^v	*La volunté* (RISM 1549_{18}, no. 15: Sandrin)
4	9^v	*Si jay du bien* (RISM 1547_9, no. 10: Sandrin)
5	11	*Si son esperit*
6	13^v	*Non é pieu fedé* Villanesche
7	14	*Chi dira mai* Villanesche (Vogel: Giovane da Nola 8 [1545], no. 4)
8	14^v	*Oy mé dolente* Villanesche (CW VIII, 11: Giovane da Nola)
9	15^v	*La Seraphine*
10	18^v	*Contreclare*
11	19^v	*Paduane*
12	20	*Paduane au joly bois*
13	21	*Paduane*
14	21^v	*Paduane. Chant d'Orlande* [2]
15	22	*Gaillarde* [2]
16	23	*Gaillarde*
17	24	*Gaillarde*
18	24^v	*Gaillarde*
19	25^v	*Gaillarde* (compare LesLRB, art. 3, no. 8: "L'Ennuy qui me tourmente," Certon)
20	26	*Branle*
21	26^v	*Branle*

MUSIC FOR SOLO CITTERN

22	27	*Paduane*
23	27^v	*Contreclare*
24	27^v	*Gaillarde*
25	28	*Matasins*
26	28^v	*Boufons*
27	29	*Gaillarde*
28	29^v	*Gaillarde*
29	30	*Gaillarde*
30	30^v	*Gaillarde*

[1] Facs. of title page in HeartzP, opp. p. 452.
[2] Facs. of fols. 21^v and 22 in HeartzP, opp. p. 453. Mod. ed. of no. 14 *ibid.*, p. 463.

1552_7

PISADOR, DIEGO

LIBRO DE MUSICA DE / VIHUELA, AGORA NUEVA/mente compuesto por Diego Pisador, ve/zino dela ciudad de Salamanca, dirigi/do al muy alto y muy poderoso/señor don Philippe princi/pe de España nue/stro Señor. / [The coat of arms of the royal family of Spain] / CON PRIVILEGIO. / Esta tassado en [blank] maravedis. / 1552 [1]

112 fols. Italian lute tablature and mensural notation. On fol. $*1^v$: royal printing privilege signed: "Fecha en Aranda a. xviii. de Mayo de mil y quinientos y cinquenta años. Maximiliano. La Reyna. Por mandado de su Magestad, sus Altezas en su nombre. Juan Vazquez," followed by the dedication headed "Muy alto y muy poderoso Señor." On fol. *2: preface headed "Prologo al lector prefacio." On fols. $*2^v$–*3: preliminary instructions in reading the tablature. On fols. $*3^v$–$*4^v$: table of contents. Fol. *5 = fol. 1. Colophon on fol. 98^v: "A Gloria y alabanca de nuestro Redemptor Jesu Christo, y de su gloriosa madre. Fenesce el presente libro de Cifra para tañer Vihuela, Hecho por Diego Pisador vezino de Salamanca y impresso en su casa, Acabose año del nascimiento de nuestro redemptor Jesu Christo. De mil & quinientos y cinquenta y dos Años," followed by the coat of arms of Guillermo Millis, Spanish printer and bookseller.[2] The volume is divided into seven books; the headings at the beginnings of each book are reproduced in the inventory below. The compositions identified by the superior letter *a* ([a]) are reprinted in MorL II, 176–193. For further information see CortP and HutchV. All of the pieces followed by an asterisk are for voice (notated either in mensural notation or in red ciphers in the tablature) and vihuela. The other compositions are for solo vihuela.

Copies in: E:E, E:Mn (two copies, one imperfect), F:Pn, GB:Lbm, NL:DHgm, US:BE, US:R.

	fol.	
1	1	*Conde claros* Romance with *diferencias*
2	2^v	*Las bacas* [*Guárdame las vacas*] Villancico with *diferencias*
3	4	*Pavana muy llana para tañer*[a] [3]
4	4	*Dezilde al cavallero que* [4] Villancico
5	4^v	*A las armas moriscote**[a] Romance

6 4v *Guarte, guarte el rey don Sancho**a[5] Romance

7 5 *Quien hu viesse tal ventura**a Romance

8 5v *La mañana de sant Juan**a[6] Romance

9 5v *Passeavase el rey moro**a[7] Romance

10 6v *Paraqu'es dama tanto quereros**a[8] *Endechas de canaria*

11 7 *Passando el mar leandro** Soneto (text by Garcilaso)

12 7v *Flerida para mi dulce y sabrosa**a[9] *Otra sonada de otras endechas* (text by Garcilaso)

13 7v *Fantasia sobre la, sol, fa, re, mi, a tres bozes*

14 8 *Fantasia a tres*

Comienca el Segundo Libro que trata de villancicos a tres para cantar el que quisiere, y sino tañerlos, y son para principiantes. Y otros a quatro bozes, tambien para tañer. Y otros que se cantan las tres bozes, y se canta el tiple que va apuntado encima.

15 9 *Si la noche haze escura**a[10] *a3*

16 9 *Y con que la lavare**a[11] *a3*

17 9v *Quien tuviesse tal poder**a *a3*

18 10 *Partense partiendo yo**a *a3*

19 10v *Pues te partes y te vas** *a4*

20 10v *No me llames sega la erva**a *a4* Juan Vasquez (MME IV, 223)

21 11 *Si te quitasse los hierros** *a4*

22 11v *Si me llaman a mi llaman** *a4* Juan Vasquez (MME IV, 198)

23 12 *En la fuente del rosel**[12] *a4* Juan Vasquez (MME IV, 221)

24 12 *Por una vez** *a4* (MME IV, 211: Juan Vásquez)

25 12v *Aquellas sierras madre** *a4*

26 13 *Gentil cavallero**[13] *a4*

27 14 *Mal ferida va la Garça** *a4*

28 14v *Si te vas a banar, Juanica**a *a4*

29 15 *Pange lingua** *a3*

30 15v *Sacris solempniis** *a3*

31 16 *Dixit dominus domino** *a4*

32 16v *Dixit dominus domino** *a4* = 1557_2, no. 75

33 16v *In exitu Israel a4**

Libro Tercero de fantasias, por todos los tonos sobre passos remedados, ansi de a quatro bozes como de a tres. Y canta se la boz que va asseñalada de colorado.[14]

34 17 [*Fantasia del primer tono sobre*] *la fa sol la re mi re**

35 17v *Fantasia del segundo tono sobre el seculorum: ut re ut fa mi ut re mi re**

36 18 *Fantasia del tercero tono sobre mi la sol mi fa sol mi**

37 18v *Fantasia del quarto tono sobre la sol fa re mi**

38 19v [*Fantasia del*] *quinto tono sobre fa fa sol mi fa re**

39 20 *Fantasia del sesto tono sobre fa mi re fa sol fa**

40 20v *Fantasia del septimo tono sobre ut sol mi sol la sol**

41 21 *Fantasia del octavo tono sobre sol mi fa sol mi re**

42 21v [*Fantasia del*] *primer tono sobre re mi fa sol mi re**

43 22 *Fantasia* [*del quarto tono*] *sobre la sol la mi fa mi**

44 23 *Fantasia del quarto tono sobre mi la sol mi fa mi** *a3*

45 23v *Fantasia del primer tono sobre re la fa sol la re** *a3*

46 24 *Fantasia sin paso ninguno a3*

47 24v *Fantasia del primer tono a4*

48 25 *Fantasia del primer tono a4*

49 26 *Fantasia del quarto tono a4*

50 26v *Fantasia del sesto tono a4*

51 27 *Fantasia del sesto tono a4*

52 27v *Fantasia del sesto tono a4*

53 28 *Fantasia del septimo tono a4*

54 28v *Fantasia del segundo tono a4*

55 29 *Fantasia del otavo tono a4*

56 29v *Fantasia del otavo tono a4*

57 30 *Fantasia del otavo tono a4*

Libro Quarto donde van quatro missas de Jusquin y algunas cantadas, y a donde va la letra colorada es el canto llano que se ha de cantar, que es sobre que van las missas.

58 31 *Missa de Jusquin, de Ercules dux ferrarie**[15] (JosqMS, no. 7)

59 36 *Missa de Jusquin que va sobre fa re mi re**[16] JosqMS, no. 13: *Missa Faysant regrets*)

60 41 *Missa de Jusquin de la fuga**[17] (JosqMS, no. 14: *Missa ad fugam*)

61 46 *Missa de super bozes musicales**[18] Jusquin (JosqMS, no. 1: *Missa L'homme armé super voces musicales*)

62 52 *Benedictus de Jusquin de la missa de fortuna desesperata* (JosqMS, no. 4)

Libro Quinto con otras quatro missas de Jusquin

63 53 *Missa sobre la sol fa re mi*[19] Josquin (JosqMS, no. 2)
64 57v *Missa de Jusquin de gaudeamus*[20] (JosqMS, no. 3)
65 63v *Missa de Jusquin de ave maristella*[21] (JosqMS, no. 6)
66 68 *Missa de Jusquin de beata virgen*[22] (JosqMS, no. 16)
67 73v *Pleni de Jusquin de la missa de fortuna desesperata* *a 3* (JosqMS, no. 4)

Libro Sexto que tracta de motetes, a quatro y a cinco y a ocho bozes, de famosissimos authores. Dellos van cantados y va la letra que se canta la boz va asseñalada de colorado.

68 75 *In principio erat verbum** Josquin *a 4* (CW XXIII, 4)
69 75v *Fuit homo missus** Gombert *a 4* (GombertO V, 81)
70 76 *Ave maria** Adrianus de vilart *a 4* (WillO II, 14) 2a pars of *Pater noster* (no. 71)
71 77 *Pater noster** Adrianus de villart *a 4* (WillO II, 11)
72 78 *Tota pulchra** Jusquin *a 4* (JosqMT, no. 30: "Ecce, tu pulchra es")
73 79 *Dum complerentur** Basurtu[23] *a 4*
74 79v *Qui seminant in lachrymis** Gombert *a 4* (RISM 1539_{13}, no. 2)
75 80 *Queramus cum pastoribus** Juan Monton *a 4* (RISM 1529_1, fol. 9v)
76 81 *Miserere mei deus** Jusquin *a 5* (JosqMT, no. 37)
77 82 *Decendid angelus* Morales *a 4*
78 83 *Angelus domini* Basurto *a 4*
83v 2a pars
79 84 *Salve [Regina]* Jusquin *a 5* (JosqMS, no. 48)
80 85 *Tulerunt dominum** Gombert *a 8* (CW XXIII, 22: Josquin)

Libro Septimo que trata de villanescas a tres y a quatro bozes, y dellas las tres tañidas, y la otra boz cantada por de fuera, y canciones Francesas.

81 87 *O dulce vita mea* *a 3* (Vogel: Fontana [1545], no. 12: Vincenzo Fontana)
82 87 *Toti voria contar* *a 3* (Vogel: Fontana [1545], no. 18: "Io ti vorria contare")
83 87v *Quanto de vele* *a 3* (Vogel: Fontana [1545], no. 20: "Quanto debbe allegrarse")
84 87v *Ma dona mala vostra* *a 3* (Vogel: Fontana [1545], no. 15: "Madonna mia la vostra")
85 88 *La cortesia*[24] *a 3* (Vogel: Fontana [1545], no. 16)
86 88 *Tutta tutta sarissi* *a 3* (Vogel: Fontana [1545], no. 19)
87 88v *Sempre me fingo** *a 4*
88 89 *A quand'a quand'haveva** *a 4* (RISM 1545_{20}, no. 11: Adrian Willaert)
89 89v *Lagrime mesti & voi sospir dolenti** *a 4* (Vogel: Willaert 5 [1563], no. 3: Adrian Willaert)
90 90 *Madonna mia fa[mi bona offerta]**[25] *a 4* (RISM 1545_{20}, no. 6: Adrian Willaert)
91 90v *O bene mio fa famm'uno favore** *a 4* (CW V, 12: Adrian Willaert)
92 91 *Mon pere aussi ma mere ma voulu marier*[26] *a 4* (F:Pn, MS nouv. acq. fr. 4599, fol. 3v [tenor only]: "Mon pere si ma marie")
93 91v *Que faran del pobre Jan* *a 4* [Flecha]
94 92v *Cancion Francesa Sparsi sparcium* *a 4* (RISM 1526_6, no. 4: "O passi sparsi," Sebastian Festa)
95 93 *Vostra fui* *a 4* Madrigal (RISM 1541_9, p. 36: Arcadelt)

[1] Facs. of title page of the Berkeley copy in MLI, pl. 1 (with the price of the volume given in manuscript as 629 maravedis). The dance, "Alta," pr. in PedCP III, 140, supposedly by Pisador, does not in fact appear in 1552_7 (BukMR, p. 204, is therefore incorrect). The dance is a polyphonic arrangement of the tenor "La Spagna" (see $148?_1$, no. 10) by Francisco de la Torre (repr. in MME X, 84).
[2] See SalvaC II, 350.
[3] Mod. ed. in PedCP III, 138, and PujHC, p. 2.
[4] Mod. ed. in StaakS, p. 3.
[5] Mod. ed. in PedCP III, 143, and PisG.
[6] Mod. ed. in PedCP III, 146, and PisM.
[7] Quasi-fac. in WolfH II, 108; facs. of fol. 5v in MorL I, xl.

[8] On the meaning of the term *endecha* see StevensnJB.
[9] Mod. ed. in BruS II, no. 71.
[10] Mod. ed. in BalR, p. 39, and PisS.
[11] Mod. ed. in PisQ.
[12] Mod. ed. in BalR, p. 26.
[13] Facs. of fols. 13 and 13ᵛ, and mod. ed. of no. 26 in NoskeS, pp. 12 and 23.
[14] Facs. of fol. 17 in SubHME, p. 211.
[15] Lacking the "Pleni sunt coeli" and "Agnus dei."
[16] Lacking the "Pleni sunt coeli" and the second and third "Agnus dei."
[17] Lacking the second "Agnus dei."
[18] Lacking the "Hosanna," "Benedictus," and first and second "Agnus dei."
[19] Lacking the "Pleni sunt coeli," the second "Hosanna," and the second "Agnus dei."
[20] Lacking the "Hosanna," "Benedictus," and the second and third "Agnus dei."
[21] Lacking the "Benedictus," and the second and third "Agnus dei."
[22] Lacking the "Hosanna," "Benedictus," and the second and third "Agnus dei."
[23] On this composer see MME I, 125, 121; *ibid.* II, 92, 95, 100, etc.
[24] Mod. ed. in PujHC, p. 2.
[25] Mod. ed. in PisMA.
[26] Mod. ed. in PujBG, no. 1013.

1552_8

RIPPE, ALBERT DE

PREMIER LIVRE DE / TABULATURE DE LEUT, / contenant plusieurs Chansons & Fantasies, / Composées par feu messire Albert de Rippe de Mantoue, Seigneur du Carois, / joueur de Leut, & varlet de chambre du Roy nostre sire. / [Printer's mark with motto "NE LA MORT, NE LE VENIM"] / A PARIS, / De l'imprimerie de Michel Fezandat, au mont sainct Hilaire, a l'hostel d'Albret. / Et en la rue de Bievre, en la maison de maistre Guillaume Morlaye. / 1552. / Avec privilege du Roy pour dix ans.

48 fols. French lute tablature. Dedication on fol. A2 headed "Au Roy treschrestien, Henry deuxiesme de ce nom," and signed "Vostre subject & tres obeissant serviteur, Guillaume Morlaye," repr. in ProdM, p. 163. On fol. A3: an expanded version of the printer's privilege that appears in 1552_4. This version is signed and dated "Donné à Paris le treiziesme jour de Febvrier, L'an de grace mil cinq cens cinquante ung: Et de nostre regne le cinqiesme. Ainsi signé: Par le Roy en son conseil, Coignet. Et seellé de cire jaulne sur simple queue." On fol. A4: table of contents. Fol. B1 = fol. 1. There is a modern edition of the entire volume in BuggR. SlimK II, 562, contains a thematic index of the ricercares. Contents = 1553_8. All of the compositions are for solo lute.[1]

Copies in: F:Pc, F:Pthibault.

	fol.	
1	1	*Fantasie*[2] = 1562_8, no. 1
2	6ᵛ	*Fantasie* = 1562_8, no. 2
3	8ᵛ	*Fantasie* = 1562_8, no. 3
4	11	*F[antasie]*
5	17	*Fantasie* = 1562_{11}, no. 8 (compare 1574_7, no. 3)
6	18	*F[antasie]*
7	20ᵛ	*Je suis desheritée*[3] (CW XV, no. 2: Lupus or Cadéac) = 1562_9, no. 2; 1568_7, no. 44; 1571_6, no. 52; 1574_7, no. 14
8	21ᵛ	*Loeil grat[ieux]*
9	23ᵛ	*D'un seul Soleil* (RISM 1550_{12}, no. 8: Janequin) = 1562_9, no. 14, and 1574_7, no. 23
10	26	*Si comme [espoir]* (RISM 1540_{12}, no. 13: Maillard) = 1562_9, no. 1, and 1574_7, no. 13
11	28ᵛ	*Un jour [le temps]*
12	30ᵛ	*Plus n'est mon bien*
13	32ᵛ	*Il ne se treuve en amytié* (RISM 1548_3, no. 14: Sandrin) = 1562_9, no. 3, and 1574_7, no. 16
14	35	*Mons & vaulx* (RISM 1548_3, no. 21: Sandrin) = 1562_9, no. 15, and 1574_7, no. 24
15	36ᵛ	*Quel bien parler* (RISM 1545_{12}, no. 9: Sandrin)
16	37ᵛ	*Voulant honneur* (RISM 1545_{12}, no. 8: Sandrin) = 1562_9, no. 4, and 1574_7, no. 17
17	39ᵛ	*L'aveugle Dieu* (JanT, no. 22: Janequin)
18	41ᵛ	*Celle qui ha le coeur haultain*
19	43ᵛ	*Plus ne peut [mon coeur] estre* = 1562_9, no. 13

[1] Six volumes of lute music by Albert de Rippe were edited by Guillaume Morlaye, and published by Michel Fezandat: I (1552_8 and 1553_8); II (1554_6); III (1554_7); IV (1554_8); V (1555_4); and VI (1558_6). See 1562_8 for the series of volumes of music by De Rippe published by Le Roy and Ballard.
[2] Facs. of fol. 1 in EF III, 577.
[3] Facs. of fols. 20ᵛ and 21 in LiuM, p. 82, incorrectly dated 1554.

[1552]$_9$

WECKER, HANS JACOB

Discant Lautenbuch vonn mancherley schönen und lieblichen stucken mitt zwey lauten zusamen zu schlagen. Basel, Ludwig Lück, 1552.

This volume, now lost, must have existed, since the tenor book is known (see 1552_{10}).

[1552]$_{10}$

WECKER, HANS JACOB

Tenor/Lautenbuch vonn mancherley schönen / und lieblichen stucken mit zweyen lauten zusamen zu schlagen, Italienische lieder, Pass'emezi, Saltarelli, Paduane. Weiter Frantzösische, Teütsche, / mit sampt / mancherley däntzen, durch Hans Jacob Wecker von Basel auffs aller fleissigest auff zwo lauten / züsamen gesetzt. Gedruckt zu Basel, durch Ludwig Lück, im MDLII. Jar.

German lute tablature. This volume, now lost, was in D:Bds (formerly in D:WEs). It contained 34 compositions. The dances listed below are cited in DieL, p. 115, with concordances. Nos. 15 and 16 listed below are cited in RaL (nos. 19 and 403). The title is taken from RaL, p. 289. Since nos. 15 and 16 also appear in 1562_3 (nos. 18 and 27) perhaps the later volume contains other Wecker intabulations. For a companion volume see [1552]$_9$. All of the compositions were for two lutes.

	no.	
1	5	*Pass'emezo Comun*
	6	*Il suo saltarello*
	7	*Padouana comun*
2	10	*Pass'emezo antiquo*
3	12	*Gentil madonna, Padouana*
4	13	*Santo Herculano, Padouana*
5	14	*La traditora, Saltarello*
6	18	*Pass'emezo* = 1562_3, no. 32a
	19	*Il suo saltarello* = 1562_3, no. 32b
7	20	*Pass'emezo* = 1562_3, no. 33a
	21	*Il suo saltarello* = 1562_3, no. 33b
8	22	*La gamba* = 1562_3, no. 34
9	23	*Le forze de Ercule* = 1562_3, no. 35
10	27	*Der Bentzenawer dantz*
11	28	*Der schwartz knab dantz* = 1562_4, no. 60
12	29	*Dantz* = 1562_3, no. 36a: "Hofftantz"
	30	*Hupff auff* = 1562_3, no. 36b
13	33	*Paduana* = 1562_3, no. 37
14	34	*Les Buffons* = 1562_3, no. 38
15	?	*Ach Jupiter* (MosL, no. 38: Fulda)
16	?	*Was würt es doch des wunders noch* Senfl (SenflW IV, no. 26)

1552_{11}

PHALÈSE, PIERRE, PUBLISHER

HORTUS MUSARUM / IN QUO TANQUAM FLOSCULI / quidam selectissimorum carminum collecti sunt ex optimis / quibusque autoribus. / Et primo ordine continentur αὐτόματα, quae Fantasiae dicuntur. / Deinde cantica quatuor vocum. / Post, carmina graviora, quae Muteta appellantur, eaque quatuor, / quinque, ac sex vocum. / Demum addita sunt carmina longe elegantissima duabus testudinibus / canenda, hactenus nunquam impressa. / COLLECTORE / Petro Phalesio. / [Cut of ten performing musicians] / Concessum est Petro Phalesio Cae. Ma. privilegio ad triennium, ne quis hunc librum imprimat, / aut alibi impressum divendat, sub poena vigintiquinque florenorum, / ut latius patet in literis illi concessis. / Signato à Philippo de Lens. / LOVANII / apud Petrum Phale/sium bibliopolam iuratum. / M. D. LII.[1]

56 fols. French lute tablature. On p. 2: table of contents. Fol. A1 = p. 3. On p. 112: cut of a lute and the colophon, "LOVANII Sub praelo Reyneri Velpii Diestensis, An. M. D. LII." For further information see QuittM and WotqHM. Nos. 1–84 are for solo lute; nos. 85–105 are for two lutes.

Copy in: B:Bc.[2]

MUSIC FOR SOLO LUTE

	p.	
1	3	*Fantasia*[3] = 1547_5, no. 89: Valderrábano

2 3 *Fantasia* = 1547_5, no. 90: Valderrábano

3 4 *Fantasia* Rota = 1546_{15}, no. 31: Rotta

4 4 *Fantasia* Simon Sentlerus = 1547_3, no. 5: Gintzler

5 5 *Conque la lavare* = 1547_5, no. 43: Valderrábano

6 6 *Fantasia* Jo. Jacobi Albutti = 1536_9, no. 10: Albutio

7 7 *Fantasia*[4] = 1546_6, no. 11: Francesco da Milano

8 8 *Fantasia* = 1536_9, no. 17: Marco d'Aquila

9 9 *Fantasia* = 1547_5, no. 100: Valderrábano

10 10 *Fantasia* Simon Sentler = 1547_3, no. 4: Gintzler

11 10 *Fan[tasia]* Francisci Mediola. = 1536_9, no. 1: Francesco da Milano

12 12 *Fantasia* Pauli Baroni = 1546_8, no. 10: Borrono

13 14 *Fantasia* Simon Sentler = 1547_3, no. 3: Gintzler

14 15 *Fantasia* Rota = 1546_{15}, no. 32: Rotta

15 16 *Fantasia* Simon Sentler = 1547_3, no. 6: Gintzler

16 16 *Fantasia* Rota = 1546_{15}, no. 28: Rotta

17 17 *Fantasia* Rota = 1546_{15}, no. 30: Rotta

18 17 *Soneto* = 1547_5, no. 149: Valderrábano

19 18 *Fantasia* Pauli Baroni = 1536_9, no. 11: Borrono

20 19 *Toute la nuyt* Thomas Crequillon (RISM 1570_8, p. 12: "Toutes les nuycts")

21 20 *Quest il besoingne* (*Response*) (RISM 1570_8, p. 13)

22 21 *Vivray je tout jour en telle peyne*[5] Petit Jehan de Latre (RISM 1554_{22}, p. 21) = 1563_{12}, no. 39

23 22 *Sans plourer* (*Response*) (RISM 1554_{22}, p. 22: Latre) = 1563_{12}, no. 40

24 22 *Oncques amour me fut* Thomas Crequillon

25 23 *Je prens en grez* = 1547_9, no. 1: Clemens non Papa

26 24 *Morir mi fault* (RISM 1570_8, p. 11: "Response de Je prens en gre")

27 24 *S[i] mon Travail* = 1547_9, no. 5: Sandrin

28 25 *Le duel yssu* (*Response*) = 1547_9, no. 6: Villiers

29 26 *Si mon languir* (*Response de morir me fault*) (RISM 1543_{16}, fol. 13^v: Jo. Baston)

30 27 *Damour me plains* = 1547_9, no. 2: Pathie

31 28 *Comme la Rosa [se pied]*[6] Petit Jan [de Latre] (RISM 1570_8, p. 34) = 1563_{12}, no. 48

32 29 *En languissant* = 1563_{12}, no. 54

33 30 *Ung gay bergiere* = 1545_3, no. 38: Crecquillon

34 30 *Languir me fault* = 1545_3, no. 29: Sermisy

35 31 *Mais pourquoy [noze lon prendre le bien]* = 1547_3, no. 34: Sandrin

36 32 *Pongente Dardo* = 1546_{17}, no. 5: Berchem

37 33 *Ochi mei lassi* = 1546_{10}, no. 40: Arcadelt

38 34 *Si pur ti guardo* = 1546_{15}, no. 27: Pathie

39 34 *Ho la he* = 1546_{10}, no. 25: "Ho la he par la vertu goy"

40 35 *Aupres de vous* (AttainCK I, no. 16: Sermisy or Jacotin)

41 35 *Helas amy* (RISM 1541_8, fol. 4: Sandrin)

42 36 *Amy helas* = 1549_8, no. 36

43 36 *Vous perdez tamps* = 1547_9, no. 3: Sermisy

44 37 *Tel en mesdit* (*Response de vous perdez temps*) = 1547_9, no. 4: Mittantier

45 38 *Or combien est [malheureux]* (ClemensO VII, 156: Sandrin or Sermisy)

46 39 *Le mal que sent* (*Response*)[7]

47 39 *Il me souffit* (AttainCK I, no. 9: Sermisy)

48 40 *Veu le grief mal* = 1547_3, no. 33: Villiers

49 41 *Duel double duel* (CW XV, no. 1: Lupi) = 1563_{12}, no. 47

50 42 *Cessez mes yeulx* Criquillon (RISM 1554_{22}, p. 1)

51 42 *Las si je nay autre secours* (RISM 1545_{16}, fol. 8: Clemens non Papa)

52 43 *O triste adieu* Jehan Loys

53 44 *Revenez vers moy* Criquillon (PubAPTM XXIII, no. 35: "Reviens vers moy," Lupi)

54 45 *P[l]us revenir (Response)* (PubAPTM XXIII, no. 37: Lupi)

55 46 *Mais languiray je touttesjours* (ClemensO X, 77: Clemens non Papa) = 1563_{12}, no. 46, and 1568_{7}, no. 33

56 46 *En attendant* (compare no. 98 below)

57 47 *Pour ung plaisir* = 1546_{18}, no. 30: Crecquillon

58 48 *Ung jour passe bien ascoutez* (ClemensO X, 10: Clemens non Papa)

59 49 *Les yeulx ficez* Thom. Criquillon

60 50 *Doulce memoire* = 1547_{9}, no. 11: Sandrin

61 50 *Fine le bien (Response)* = 1547_{9}, no. 12: Certon

62 51 *Entre tous viellart* = 1546_{18}, no. 25

63 52 *Sur tous regres* (PubAPTM II, no. 78: Richafort) = 1563_{12}, no. 43

64 52 *Mille regrez* (JosqWW, no. 24: Josquin) = 1563_{12}, no. 44

65 53 *Si grande la pieta* = 1546_{17}, no. 1: Arcadelt

66 54 *Incessament [mon povre coeur lamente]* (RISM 1572_{2}, fol. 52^{v}: De La Rue)

67 55 *Pour quoy languir*

68 56 *Noch weet ick een schoon vrouken* = 1546_{18}, no. 28: Nicolas Liégois

69 57 *Cum sancto spiritu* (JosqMS, no. 16: *Missa de Beata Virgine*, Josquin)

70 58 *Cuidez de dieu nous faille* (RISM $[1543]_{15}$, fol. 9^{v}: "Cuidez vous que dieu," Richafort)

71 59 *Quam pulchra es*[8] (RISM 1519_{2}, no. 12: Mouton) = 1563_{12}, no. 102a

60 2a pars *Labia tua* = 1563_{12}, no. 102b

72 60 *Magnum haereditaris* = 1547_{3}, no. 19: Willaert

73 62 *Puer qui natus est* = 1547_{3}, no. 21: Berchem

74 63 *Benedictus dominus Deus israel* = 1547_{3}, no. 20: Lupus

64 2a pars *Honor virtus*

75 65 *Deus canticum novum* = 1547_{3}, no. 23: Lupus

76 66 *Domine Deus omnipotens* = 1547_{3}, no. 24: Arcadelt

77 68 *Stabat mater dolorosa* = 1547_{3}, no. 13: Josquin

70 2a pars *Eya mater*[9]

78 72 *Tua est potentia* = 1547_{3}, no. 16: Mouton

79 73 *Infirmitatem nostram* = 1547_{5}, no. 12: Verdelot

80 73 *Benedictus. Duo* = 1547_{5}, no. 132: *Missa Ave Maris Stella*, Josquin

81 74 *Pater noster* = 1547_{3}, no. 7: Josquin

82 75 *Benedictus* = 1547_{5}, no. 4

76 2a pars of *Pater noster* (no. 81) *Ave Maria* = 1547_{3}, no. 7b

83 77 *Tribulatio & angustia* (JosqMT, no. 54: Josquin)

84 78 *Benedicta es [coelorum Regina]* = 1547_{3}, no. 8: Josquin

80 2a pars *Per illud ave. Duo*

80 3a pars *Nunc mater*

MUSIC FOR TWO LUTES[10]

85 81 *Fantasia* = 1549_{2}, no. 18: Barberiis

86 82 *Assiste parata* = 1547_{5}, no. 74: Gombert

87 84 *Et in spiritum sanctum* = 1547_{5}, no. 75: *Missa Mille regrets*, Morales

88 86 *Damour me plains* (PubAPTM XXIII, no. 49: Pathie)

89 88 *Languir me fault*

90 90 *Filles orsus*

91 92 *Plus oultre*[11] Gombert

92 92 *Galliarde*

93 94 *Alleges moy* (JosqWW, no. 14: Josquin)

94 94 *La lodisana*
95 96 *Adieu mon esperance* (RISM 1553₂₄, fol. 13: Clemens non Papa)
96 96 *Caracosa*
97 98 *Je prens en gre* (RISM 1544₁₃, fol. 12: Jo. Baston)
98 100 *En attendant* (RISM 1545₁₄, fol. 5: Gombert) (compare no. 56 above)
99 100 *Grace et vertu* (RISM [c. 1528]₅, fol. 5) = 1563₁₂ no. 114
100 102 *Conde claros*[12] = 1547₅, nos. 168, 169: Valderrábano
101 104 *Pis ne me peult venir* (RISM 1572₂, fol. 25: Crecquillon) = 1563₁₂, no. 113
102 104 *En espoir [d'avoir mieulx]* (KemE, p. 15: Gombert)
103 106 *Arousez [voz violier]* Benedictus (RISM 1544₁₃, fol. 14ᵛ)
104 108 *Or suis je bien [au pire]* = 1547₅, no. 84: Willaert
105 110 *Baxa* = 1547₅, no. 86: Valderrábano

[1] Facs. of title page in CollaerAH, p. 66.
[2] Copies were in F:CA and F:DU. On F:DU see CouN, p. 162.
[3] Heading on p. 3: "HORTUS MUSARUM VARIIS ELEGANTISSIMISQUE Carminibus refertus."
[4] Manuscript attribution to Francesco da Milano in the unique copy.
[5] Facs. of p. 21 in MGG III, col. 123.
[6] Facs. of p. 28 in AudaL, pl. 9; mod. ed. in AudaL, p. 280.
[7] In RISM 1570₈, p. 5, a chanson beginning "Le mal que sent" follows "Or combien est" and is called a "response." However it is unrelated musically to this intabulation.
[8] Heading on p. 58: "SEQUUNTUR MOTETA ALIQUOT, EXCELLENTIORA QUATUOR, quinque, & sex vocum."
[9] Mod. ed. in QuittM, p. 276.
[10] Heading on p. 81: "SEQUUNTUR DEINCEPS CARMINA DUABUS TESTUDINIBUS ACCOMMODA. Atque inter haec prima requirunt testudines ad unisonum compositas, quae proxima sunt ad diatesseram hoc est quartam: postrema ad diapente sive ad quintam."
[11] Mod. ed. in LenK, no. 19.
[12] This a composite work composed of the first 22 variations of two separate sets of *diferencias* on "Conde claros," each of which was originally inended for solo performance. The superius lute part has the first 23 variations of 1547₅, no. 169. The tenor lute part has the first 21 variations of 1547₅, no. 168.

1553₁

BAKFARK, VALENTIN

INTABULATURA VALEN/TINI BACFARC TRANSILVANI CORONENSIS. / LIBER PRIMUS. / [Cut of Bakfark playing a large lute; to the left, the arms of the archbishop of Lyons, the Count of Tournon; to the right, the arms of Bakfark] / Lugduni apud Jacobum Modernum. / Cum privilegio ad triennium.[1]

40 fols. Italian lute tablature. On fol. A1ᵛ: table of contents followed by the printer's privilege: "Il est defendu à tous Imprimeurs & Libraires, de ceste ville, de non imprimer, ou faire imprimer, ny exposer en vente, ce present Livre, intitule la Iutabulature [*sic*] de Luch composee par Maistre Valentin Bacfarc Transilvain Coronensis, jusques au terme de troys ans, commencant du jour & date des presentes, sinon par le congé & permission de Jacques Moderne imprimeur & libraire de Lyon, & ce sur peine de confiscation desdicts livres, & d'amende arbitraire, Faict a Lyon, le xviii. de Janvier Mil cinq cens cinquante deux. I. Tignac." Dedication on fol. A2 headed "Reverendiss. ac S. S. Apost. digniss. Card. Turnonio Archiepiscopo & Comiti Lugdunensis," and dated "Lugduni. 23. Calendas Januarii," reprinted in GomVB, p. 91. The compositions identified by the superior letter *a* ([a]) are reprinted in DTO XVIII/37, pp. 68–82, which also includes (pl. VIII) a facsimile of the title page. GomVB, app., pp. 1–13, reprints the four ricercari. See there, pp. 71–73, for a bibliography of studies of Bakfark. A selection of pieces from this volume was reprinted as 1564₁. All of the compositions are for solo lute.

Copy in: US:CA.[2]

fol.
1 A2ᵛ *Recercate Valentini Bacfarc transilvani Coronensis*[a] = 1574₇, no. 7
2 A4 *Recercate Valentini. Bacfarc. Transilvani Coronensis*[a] = 1568₇, no. 17
3 B2ᵛ *Recercate Valentini Bacfarc. transilvanus Coronensis*[a]
4 B4ᵛ *Recercate Valentini Bacfarc. transilvanus Coronensis*

5 C2^v *Aspice domine, quatuor vocum* Nicolaus Gombert. per Valentinum Bacfarc (GombertO V, 86)

D1 2a pars *Muro tuo inexpugnabili. Quatuor vocum*

6 D3 *Aspice domine. Quinque vocum* Jacquet de Mantua (MonteO XXVI, app., p. 1)

7 E1 *Benedicta es celorum. Sex vocum. Prima pars*[a] Loyset pieton. per Valentinum Bacfarc (RISM 1539_3, p. 18) = 1574_7, no. 54

E3 2a pars *Per illud Ave*

8 E4^v *Hierusalem* [*luge*]. *Quinque vocum. Prima pars* Johanes Richafort par Valentni [*sic*] Bacfarc (RISM 1532_9, p. 49: Richafort [or Lupus?])

F1^v 2a pars *Deduc quasi torrentum lachrsmas* [sic]

9 F3 *Le corps absent cause en amoureux. Quatuor vocum* T. Criquillon

10 F4 *Or vien sa vien ma mia Perretta. Quatuor vocum*[a] Jenequin (RISM 1540_{17}, fol. 6^v)

11 G1 *Damour me plains. 4. vocum*[a 3] Rogier (PubAPTM XXIII, no. 49: Pathie) = 1571_6, no. 72

12 G4 *O combien* [*est malheureux*] *4. Vocum* Tomas Criquilon (ClemensO VII, 156: Sandrin or Sermisy)

13 H1 *Martin menoit son porceau au marche. 4. Vocum* Jenequin (CM II, 79)

14 H2^v *Un gay bergier. 4. Vocum* Jenequin (RieH II, 462: Crecquillon)

15 H4 *Si grande la pieta. 4. Vocum* Archadelt (RISM 1539_{24}, p. 4) = 1574_7, no. 33

16 I1 *Il ciel che, rado. 4. Vocum* Archadelt (RISM 1541_9, p. 49) = 1574_7, no. 34

17 I2 *Che piu foc'al mio foco. 4. Vocum*[4] Archadelt (RISM 1541_9, p. 16) = 1571_6, no. 115

18 I3 *Quand'io pens'al martire. 4. Vocum* Archadelt (RISM 1541_9, p. 54) = 1556_2, no. 20

19 K1 *Dormend'un giorno. 5. Vocum* Verdelot (WagMP, p. 461)

20 K2^v *Ultimi mei suspiri. 6. Vocum* Verdelot (MonteO V, app.)

[1] Facs. of title page in EF II, 489.
[2] A copy was in F:VE.
[3] Mod. ed. in KosackL, app., III.
[4] Facs. of fol. I2 in EC, pt. I, vol. V, p. 2572.

1553_2

BENDUSI, FRANCESCO

OPERA NOVA DE BALLI / Di Francesco Bendusi A quatro Accommodati da cantare & sonare / d'ogni sorte de Stromenti Novamente dati in luce. / A QUATRO [Printer's mark] VOCI / In Venetia Appresso di / Antonio Gardane. / 1553

Four part books in mensural notation, each of 6 fols. Fol. 1^v = p. 1. On the last page of each part book except the bass: table of contents. All of the compositions except no. 16 are reprinted in 1555_2. See there for details. The compositions identified by the superior letter *a* ([a]) are reprinted in BlumeS, app. B. All of the compositions are for instrumental ensemble *a 4*.

Copies in: A:Wgm, D:Mbs, GB:Lbm (AT).

	p.	
1	1	*Pass'e mezo ditto il Romano*[1]
2	1	*Moschetta*[a]
3	2	*Desiderata*[2]
4	2	*Pietoso*[a]
5	3	*Speranza*[3]
6	3	*La mala vecchia*[4]
7	4	*Il stocco*
8	4	*Doi stanchi*
9	5	*La falilela*
10	5	*La Bruna*
11	5	*E Dove vastu o bon solda*
12	6	*Chi non ha martello*
13	6	*Incognita*
14	7	*Bella foresta*
15	7	*Galante*
16	8	*Fusta*[a]
17	8	*Animoso*
18	8	*Cortesa Padoana*[5]
19	9	*Bandera*[a]
20	9	*Gioia*
21	9	*La Giovenetta*

22 10 *Il ben ti vegna*[a]
23 10 *Pass'e mezo ditto il Compasso*
24 11 *Violla*

[1] Mod. ed. in WasG, no. 30a.
[2] Mod. ed. in ApelM I, 23, and SachsPM, pp. 13–14.
[3] Mod. ed. in BarthaZ, no. 51, and WolfME, no. 33.
[4] Mod. ed. in WasG, no. 30b.
[5] Mod. ed. in ApelM I, 24.

1553_3

BRAYSSING, GREGOIRE

QUART LIVRE DE TABU/LATURE DE GUITERRE, CONTENANT / plusieurs Fantasies, Pseaulmes, & Chansons: avec L'alouette, & la Guerre, / Composées par M. Gregoire Brayssing deaugusta. / [Table of contents] / A PARIS. / De l'imprimerie, d'Adrian le Roy, & Robert Balard, Imprimeurs du Roy, rue / saint Jean de Beauvais, à l'enseigne sainte Genevieve. / 26. Novembre. / 1553. / Avec privilege du Roy, pour neuf ans.

28 fols. French guitar tablature. On fol. 1^v: the same excerpt from the printer's privilege as in 1551_2. On fol. 28^v: printer's mark. For other volumes in the same series, see 1551_3, note 1. All of the compositions are for solo guitar.

Copies in: F:Pm, GB:Lbm.

fol.
1 2 *Fantasie, des Grues*[1] = 1570_4, no. 3a
2 3 *Fantasie* = 1570_4, no. 2
3 3^v *Fantasie* = 1570_4, no. 1
4 4 *Fantasie* = 1570_4, no. 4
3 5^v *Fantasie*[1] = 1570_4, no. 3b
6 5^v *Fantasie*[1] = 1570_4, no. 5
7 6^v *Verba mea* [*Aux parolles que je veux dire*][2] = 1570_4, no. 48
8 7 *In exitu Israel de Aegypto* [*Quand Israel hors d'Egypte*] (JosqMT, no. 51: Josquin) = 1570_4, no. 49
9 10^v *Cum invocarem* [*Quand je t'invoque*][2] = 1570_4, no. 50
10 11^v *Beati quorum* [*O bienheureux*][2] = 1570_4, no. 51
11 12^v *Super flumina* [*Estant assis aux rives aquatiques*][2] = 1570_4, no. 52
12 13^v *Helas mon Dieu, ton ire s'est tournée* (RISM 1553_{19}, fol. 6: Maillard) = 1570_4, no. 7
13 15 *O Passi sparsy* (RISM 1526_6, no. 4: S. Festa) = 1570_4, no. 8
14 16^v *Voulant honneur* (RISM 1545_{12}, no. 8: Sandrin) = 1570_4, no. 9
15 17^v *Je cherche autant amour* (RISM 1545_{12}, no. 2: Boyvin) = 1570_4, no. 10
16 18^v *Au temps heureux* (SCMA V, no. 1: Arcadelt) = 1570_4, no. 11
17 19^v *Qui souhaitez*[3] (RISM 1549_{20}, no. 1: Sandrin) = 1570_4, no. 12
18 21 *Un mesnagier vieillard recru d'ahan* (RISM 1542_{14}, no. 22: Sohier) = 1570_4, no. 13
19 22^v *L'Alouette* (MMRF VII, 105: Janequin) = 1570_4, no. 53
20 25^v *La guerre, faitte à plaisir*[4] = 1570_4, no. 54

[1] Mod. ed. in BrayF.
[2] The vocal models of the four psalms, nos. 7 and 9–11, may probably be found in [*Livre premier contenant XXXI. pseaulmes*] (Paris, Attaingnant, 1546), of which only a defective superius is extant, and in *Cinquante Pseaulmes . . . par M. Pierre Certon* (Paris, Le Roy and Ballard, 1555), of which only the tenor is extant; see 1554_5, and PidP for further information.
[3] In RISM 1554_{25}, no. 10, this chanson is attributed to De Bussy.
[4] Pr. in the margin: "Veldt schlacht Wieder loblicher Churfurst herzogk Johans Friderich Von sachsen Vor Mulberg gefangen ist Worden."

1553_4

MORLAYE, GUILLAUME

LE / SECOND LIVRE DE / CHANSONS, GAILLARDES, PADUANES, / Bransles, Almandes, Fantasies, reduictz en tabulature de Guiterne, / par Maistre Guillaume Morlaye joueur de Leut. / [Cut of a guitar lying on an open book] / A PARIS. / De l'imprimerie de Michel Fezandat, au mont sainct Hilaire en l'hostel d'Albret. / 1553. / Avec privilege du Roy, pour dix ans.[1]

31 fols. French guitar tablature. On fol. 31: excerpt from the royal privilege granting

Michel Fezandat permission for ten years to print music, signed "Signé par le Roy en son conseil, Et seelé du grand sel, en cire jaune. Coignet." The same excerpt appears in 1554_5. Preceding title page: manuscript table of contents. The foliation given here follows the manuscript foliation in the unique copy. Fol. a2 = fol. 1. For other volumes in the same series, see 1552_5, note 2. All of the compositions are for solo guitar.

Copy in: CH:SGv.

	fol.	
1	1	*Fantasie*
2	3^v	*Fantasie*
3	5^v	*Robin* (RISM 1550_5, no. 12: Certon)
4	6^v	*Regretz soucy & peine* (RISM 1541_{13}, p. 38: Janequin [?])
5	7^v	*Ce qui m'est deu & ordonné* (RISM 1543_{11}, no. 18: Sandrin)
6	9	*Au temps heureux* (SCMA V, no. 1: Arcadelt)
7	10^v	*Je ne sçay pas comment* (AttainCK I, no. 7)
8	11^v	*Mais pourquoy* (RISM 1543_{11}, no. 4: Sandrin)
9	12^v	*Vous estes la personne* (LesLRB, art. 3, no. 12: Certon)
10	13	*Ma bouche rit* (AttainCK III, no. 21: Duboys)
11	14	*Branle. Tin que tin tin* (compare 1559_3, no. 11: "Tintelore")
12	14	*Tin que tin tin*
13	14^v	*Pavanne*
	15^v	*Gaillarde*
14	16^v	*Paduanne*
	18^v	*Gaillarde*
15	20	*Gaillarde*
16	21	*Gaillarde*
17	21^v	*Gaillarde*
18	22	*Gaillarde*
19	22^v	*Gaillarde*
20	23	*Gaillarde*
21	23^v	*Gaillarde*
22	24^v	*Bransle*
23	24^v	*Bransle* = 1549_2, no. 25: "Fantasia"
24	25	*Bransle*
	25^v	*Ce mesme a corde avallée*
25	25^v	*Bransle*
26	26^v	*Bransle* (compare 1551_3, no. 12: "Branle simple. N'aurez vous point de moy pitié")
27	27^v	*Hornepipe d'Angleterre* [2]
28	28^v	*Villanesque*
29	29	*Conteclare* [3]
30	29^v	*Conte clare*
31	30^v	*Allemande*

[1] Facs. of title page in HeartzP, opp. p. 452.
[2] Mod. ed. in HeartzP, p. 465.
[3] Mod. ed. in HeartzP, p. 464.

1553_5

ORTIZ, DIEGO

DE DIEGO / ORTIZ / TOLLE/DANO / LIBRO / PRIMERO / [Portrait of the author] / TRATTADO / de Glosas sobre / Clausulas y otros / generos de puntos / en la Musica de / Violones nueva/mente puestos / en luz.[1]

62 fols. Mensural notation. The title is placed within an ornamental border. On fol. 2: printing privilege from Pope Julius III. Dedication on fol. 2^v headed "Al Illustriss. Senor Don Pedro D'Urries Comendador de Santyago Señor d'Ayerbe y Baron de Riesi, &c. Diego Ortiz Toledano," and dated "De Napoles. X. de Diziembre. 1553." On fol. 3: preface headed "A Los Lectores." Colophon on fol. 62^v: printer's mark with the motto "Nulla est via invia virtuti," followed by the legend "En Roma por Valerio Dorico, y Luis su hermano a x. de Dezemb. 1553." This volume is divided into two books. Book I is designed for the performer of consort music for viols; it presents systematically various ways of ornamenting cadences and of filling in ascending and descending intervals from a second to a fifth.[2] Book II presents several different kinds of compositions for one viol and keyboard ("cimbalo").[3] On fol. 3, after the preface: a note headed "El modo que se ha de tener para glosar," explaining that each individual player must choose his ornaments according to his ability. On fol. 3^v: a note headed "Modo de glosar sobre el Libro," explaining several ways of ornamenting a given part. On fol. 4: a note headed "Regla de como se ha de glosar una boz para tañer, o cantar," explaining how to use this volume in order to ornament a given composition. On fol. 4^v: table of

contents for Book I. On fol. 25: title page of Book II within the same ornamental border as the first title page: "DE DIEGO / ORTIZ / TOLEDANO / LIBRO SEGUNDO." On fol. 25ᵛ: table of contents for Book II. On fol. 26: a note headed "Declarationi de las maneras que ay de tañer el Violon y el Cimbalo," explaining various ways to play the viol with a keyboard instrument, followed by a note headed "El Orden que se ha de tener en templar el Violon con el Cymbalo," explaining how to tune a viol to a keyboard instrument. Ortiz gives three ways for a viol player to perform with a keyboard player (fol. 26: "la primera es fantasia la segunda sobre canto llano la tercera sobre compostura"). The first way is to play fantasias, that is, for both players to improvise. Ortiz gives no examples of this technique. On fol. 30: a note headed "De la seconda manera de tañer el Violon con el Cymbalo que es sobre canto llano," explaining the second way: the viol plays over a cantus firmus. On fol. 35: a note headed "La tercera manera de tañer el Violon con el Cymbalo que es sobre cosas compuestas," explaining the third way: the viol player adds an ornamented line to a polyphonic composition. Following fol. 47 are further examples of the second way of playing (over a cantus firmus). OrtizT is a modern edition (partly in facsimile) of the entire volume. In the inventory below page numbers for Book II are taken from OrtizT. Contents = 1553₆.

Copy in: D:Bds-Tü.

Book I: Method of adding diminutions to a given part for viol players

fol.	
5	Examples of ornamented cadences
20ᵛ	Examples of filled-in intervals (ascending and descending seconds to fifths)

Book II: Compositions for viol and keyboard

RICERCARES FOR SOLO VIOL

	p.	
1	52	*Recercada primera*
2	53	*Recercada segunda* [4]
3	54	*Recercada tercera*
4	55	*Recercada quarta*

RICERCARES FOR VIOL AND KEYBOARD ON "LA SPAGNA" (COMPARE [148?]₁, NO. 10)

5	56	*Recercada primera* [5]
6	57	*Recercada segunda* [6]
7	59	*Recercada tercera*
8	62	*Recercada quarta*
9	65	*Recercada quinta*
10	67	*Recercada sesta*

RICERCARES FOR VIOL AND KEYBOARD ON JACQUES ARCADELT'S "O FELICI OCCHI MIEI"

11	69	[Original version *a 4*] [7]
12	73	*Recercada primera sobre O felici occhi miei* [7]
13	76	*Recercada segunda sobre el mismo madrigal* [7]
14	79	*Recercada tercera sobre el mismo madrigal*
15	83	*Recercada quarta que es quinta boz sobre el mismo madrigal*

RICERCARES FOR VIOL AND KEYBOARD ON PIERRE SANDRIN'S "DOULCE MEMOIRE" [8]

16	86	[Original version *a 4*]
17	90	*Recercada prima sobre Doulce memoire*
18	94	*Recercada segonda sobre la misma cancion* [9]
19	98	*Recercada tercera sobre la misma cancion*
20	103	*Recercada quarta que es una quinta boz sobre la misma cancion*

RICERCARES FOR VIOL AND KEYBOARD ON VARIOUS GROUNDS [10]

21	107	*Recercada primera* [11] (= passamezzo antico)
22	110	*Recercada segunda* [12] (= passamezzo moderno)
23	113	*Recercada tercera* (= passamezzo moderno)
24	117	*Recercada quarta* [13] (= folia)
25	120	*Recercada quinta* [14] (= passamezzo antico)
26	124	*Recercada sesta* (= romanesca)
27	126	*Recercada settima* (= romanesca)
28	130	*Recercada ottava* (= folia)
29	134	*Quinta pars* [15] (= Ruggiero)

[1] Facs. of title page in KinsP, p. 145, and MGG X, col. 422.

[2] Some of these examples are repr. in KuV, p. 92.

[3] The viol parts are notated mostly in the bass clef, although there are several examples using treble or tenor clefs.

[4] Mod. ed. in EinZ, no. 1b.

[5] Mod. ed. in EC, pt. I, vol. IV, p. 1966. The beginnings of nos. 5–10 are printed, one above the other, in BukMR, p. 208, and the recercadas are discussed there, pp. 207–209.

[6] Beginning pr. in SchneidA, p. 47.

[7] The vocal model and the first two ricercares are repr. in KuV, p. 94. The first ricercare is repr. in RoyM, p. 40.

[8] All four ricercares on "Doulce memoire" are repr. in FerandIM, no. 11, along with the chanson *a 4*.

[9] Mod. ed. in OrtizR.

[10] Nos. 20–26 and 28 have a written-out chordal keyboard accompaniment. The identification of the Italian tenors was made with the help of the table in ReMR, p. 524; almost all of the Ortiz basses differ in details from the prototypes listed by Reese. See also BukMB, p. 41; GomF; and ReR.

[11] Mod. ed. in SchneidA, p. 110.

[12] Mod. ed. in EC, pt. I, vol. IV, p. 1967. Partial transcription in SubHME, p. 220.

[13] Mod. ed. in FischV, no. 4.

[14] Mod. ed. in BarthaZ, no. 52.

[15] Mod. ed. in SchneidA, p. 113.

1553_6

ORTIZ, DIEGO

EL PRIMO / LIBRO / DE DIEGO / ORTIZ / TOLLE/TANO / [Portrait of the author] / Nel qual si tratta / delle Glose sopra / le Cadenze & al/tre sorte de punti / in la Musica del / Violone novamen/te posti in luce.[1]

62 fols. Mensural notation. Contents = 1553_5, except that here all of the prefatory material and textual commentary has been translated into Italian.

† Copy in: E:Mn.

[1] Facs. of title page in SubM, pl. III.

$[1553]_7$

PALADIN, JEAN PAUL

Premier livre de tablature de luth de M. Jean Paule Paladin.

The colophon of 1560_3 reads: "Stampato in Lione per Giovan Pullon de Trino, à l'instantia di M. Giovan Paulo Paladino, l'Anno 1553." Evidently Gorlier reissued the volume in 1560 simply by adding a new title page. See 1560_3 for contents; all of the compositions are for solo lute, in Italian lute tablature.

1553_8

RIPPE, ALBERT DE

PREMIER LIVRE DE / TABULATURE DE LEUT, / contenant plusieurs Chansons & Fantasies, / Composées par feu messire Albert de Rippe de Mantoue, Seigneur du Carois, / joueur de Leut, & varlet de chambre du Roy nostre sire. / [Printer's mark with motto "NE LA MORT, NE LE VENIM"] / A PARIS, / De l'imprimerie de Michel Fezandat, au mont sainct Hilaire, a l'hostel d'Albret. / Et en la rue de Bievre, en la maison de maistre Guillaume Morlaye. / 1553. / Avec privilege du Roy pour dix ans.

48 fols. French lute tablature. Contents = 1552_8. The two volumes are identical except for the date on the title page. For other volumes in the same series, see 1552_8, note 1. All of the compositions are for solo lute.

Copy in: B:Br.[1]

[1] A copy was in F:VE.

1553_9

RIPPE, ALBERT DE

QUART LIVRE DE TABU/LATURE DE LUTH, CONTENANT / plusieurs Fantasies, Chansons, & Pavanes: / Composées par feu Maistre Albert de Rippe de Mantoue, Seigneur du Carois, / joueur de Luth, & varlet de chambre du Roy nostre sire. / [Table of contents] / A PARIS. / De l'imprimerie, d'Adrian le Roy, & Robert Balard, Imprimeurs du Roy, rue / saint Jean de Beauvaus, à l'enseigne sainte Genevieve. / 4. Novembre. / 1553. / Avec privilege du Roy, pour neuf ans.

24 fols. French lute tablature. On fol. 1v: printer's mark. On fol. 24: diagrams for "Accordz au commun" and for "Accordz à corde avalée" (lute in normal tuning and scordatura). On fol. 24v: the same excerpt from the printer's privilege as in 1551_2. BuggR contains a modern edition of the entire collection. SlimK II, 563, contains a thematic index of the ricercares. For other volumes in the same series, see 1562_8, note 1. All of the compositions are for solo lute.

Copies in: B:Br, D:Mbs, D:ROu.

	fol.	
1	2	*Fantasie* = 1574_7, no. 4 (compare 1538_1, no. 1)
2	5	*Fantasie* = 1536_9, no. 16: Francesco da Milano
3	8	*Fantasie* = 1574_7, no. 5
4	10v	*Fantasie* = 1574_7, no. 6
5	13v	*Fantasie*
6	15v	*Quando pens'io el martir* (RISM 1541_9, p. 54: Arcadelt) = 1571_6, no. 144
7	18	*Elle voyant* (LesLRB, art. 17, fol. 14: Certon)
8	19v	*Pavane La romanesque* = 1574_7, no. 55
9	22	*Pavane, Est il conclud*
10	23	*Pavane, J'ay du mal tant tant* (compare LesAC, no. 18: "J'ay le rebours," Certon)

1553₁₀

PHALÈSE, PIERRE, PUBLISHER

HORTI MUSARUM SE/CUNDA PARS, CONTINENS SELECTISSIMA / QUAEDAM AC IUCUNDISSIMA CARMINA / TESTUDINE SIMUL ET VOCE HUMANA, VEL / alterius instrumenti Musici admmiculo modulanda. / Iam recens collecta & impressa. / AD LECTOREM. / Praefiximus unicuique carmini literam nervuque / secundum cuius in Testudine tonum, seu soni in/tentionem, erit prima nota partis canende, id te / ignorare nolebam lector candide, Vale. / [Cut of ten performing musicians] / LOVANII. / Apud Petrum Phalesium bibliopolam iuratum. / Anno. M. D. LIII. / Cum gratia & Privilegio. C.M.

16 fols. Superius in mensural notation, and lute accompaniment in French lute tablature. On fol. A1v: table of contents. The compositions identified by the superior letter *a* ([a]) are reprinted in LauC, pp. 52–131. For further information see WotqHM. All of the compositions except no. 24b are for solo voice and lute.

Copy in: B:Bc.[1]

	fol.	
1	A2	*Cessez mes yeulx*[a] Crequillon (RISM 1558_{10}, no. 1)
2	A2v	*En esperant*[a] Cauleray (RISM 1555_{20}, no. 17)
3	A3	*Quand me souvient*[a 2] Crequillon (RISM 1558_{10}, no. 17)
4	A3v	*Ung triste coeur* (*Response*)[a] Crequillon (RISM 1558_{10}, no. 18)
5	A4	*Or puis quil est*[a 3] Clemens non Papa (ClemensO X, 173)
6	A4v	*Misericorde*[a 4] Clemens non Papa (ClemensO X, 140)
7	B1	*Cesses mon yeul*[a] Rogier [Pathie] (RISM 1558_{10}, no. 23)
8	B1v	*Cest a grant tort*[a] Crequillon (RISM 1558_{10}, no. 24)
9	B2	*Venes mes serfs*[a] Clemens non Papa (ClemensO X, 149)
10	B2v	*Puis que voulez*[a] Clemens non Papa (ClemensO X, 152)
11	B3	*Puis que malheur*[a] Crequillon (RISM 1555_{21}, no. 10)
12	B3v	*Lardant amour*[a] Crequillon (RISM 1555_{21}, no. 22)
13	B4	*Si purte guardo* Rogier [Pathie] (RISM 1570_8, p. 46)
14	B4v	*A vous en est*[a] Crequillon (RISM 1555_{20}, no. 1)
15	C1	*Je suis ayme de la plus belle*[a 5] Crequillon (RISM 1545_{14}, fol. 3)
16	C1v	*Je ne desire que la mort*[a] Chastelain (RISM 1553_{24}, fol. 8)
17	C2	*Le bon espoir*[a] Josquin baston (RISM 1553_{24}, fol. 9)
18	C2v	*Aymer est ma vie*[a 6] Clemens non Papa (RISM 1553_{24}, fol. 3)
19	C3	*Le souvenir que jay de ma maistresse*[a]

20	C3[v]	*Plaisir nay plus*[a] Crequillon (RISM [1543]₁₅, fol. 9: anon.)
21	C4	*Incessament mon povre cueur lamente*[a] (RISM 1572₂, fol. 52[v]: De La Rue)
22	C4[v]	*In te domine speravi* = 1547₅, no. 53: Lupus
23	D1[v]	*Stabat mater* (JosqMT, no. 36: Josquin)
	D2[v]	2a pars *Eya mater*
24	D3[v]	*Benedicta es celorum Regina* (JosqMT, no. 46: Josquin)
	D4[v]	2a pars *Per illud ave* [for solo lute]
	D4[v]	3a pars *Nunc mater*

[1] A copy was in F:DU (see CouN, p. 162).
[2] Mod. ed. in BruS III, no. 101, QuittM, p. 280, and ScherG, no. 118.
[3] Mod. ed. in QuittM, p. 283.
[4] Mod. ed. in WotqHM, opp. p. 70.
[5] Facs. of fol. C1 in CollaerAH, p. 66.
[6] Mod. ed. in NoskeS, p. 20.

1553

DOUBTFUL WORKS

1. MGG IV, col. 561, erroneously dates Hans Gerle, *Tabulatur auff die Laudten*, 1553. The volume is listed in this bibliography as 1533₁.

1554₁

BALLETTI, BERNARDINO

INTABOLATURA / DE LAUTO / DI BERNARDINO BALLETTI / Di varie sorte de Balli Novamente data in Luce. / LIBRO [Printer's mark] PRIMO / In Venetia Apresso di / Antonio Gardane. / 1554

20 fols. Italian lute tablature. Dedication on fol. 1[v] headed "All'Illustre Signore Il Conte Honorio Scotto," and signed "Di Piacenza alli 24 di Decembrio 1554 Di V. S. servidor Bernardino Balletti." On fol. 20[v]: table of contents. MoeDM contains a thematic index of the volume (p. 396) and concordances (p. 255). The entire volume is reprinted in LefL. All of the compositions are for solo lute.

Copies in: A:Wn, US:Wc.[1]

	fol.	
1	2	*Padoana* [*prima*]
	3	*Saltarelo primo*
2	4	*Il sgazotto*
3	6	*Non ti partir da me*[2] (compare AzzaiV, no. 12: "Ti parti, cor mio caro," Filippo Azzaiolo)
4	7	*La meza gamba*[3]
5	7[v]	*La Favorita* (= romanesca) (1568₁, no. 6)
6	8[v]	*La Rocha il Fuso*
7	10	*La moretta*
	12[v]	*Repr*[*e*]*se*
8	16	*Tocata*
9	16	*Padoana* [*seconda*]
	17	*Saltarello secondo*
10	18	*La Gamba*
11	19[v]	*Ciel turchino*

[1] The Washington copy was in the Landau–Finaly library in Florence (see HillM, pp. 14–16).
[2] Mod. ed. in MoeDM, p. 335.
[3] Mod. ed. in MoeDM, p. 345.

1554₂

BIANCHINI, DOMINICO

INTABOLATURA / DE LAUTO / DI DOMINICO BIANCHINI / Ditto Rossetto Di Recercari Mottetti Madrigali Canzon Francese Napolitane / Et Balli Novamente Ristampati. / LIBRO [Printer's mark] PRIMO / In Venetia Apresso di / Antonio Gardane. / 1554.

20 fols. Italian lute tablature. On fol. E4[v]: table of contents. Contents = 1546₅. All of the compositions are for solo lute.

Copies in: A:Wn, F:Pn, F:Pthibault.

1554₃

FUENLLANA, MIGUEL DE

[The royal coat of arms of Spain] / LIBRO DE MUSICA PARA / Vihuela, intitulado Orphenica lyra. En el / qual se contienen muchas y diversas obras. / Compuesto por Miguel de Fuenllana. / Dirigido al muy alto y muy poderoso se/ñor don Philippe principe de España, / Rey de Ynglaterra, de Napoles &c. nuestro señor. / CON PRIVILLEGIO REAL. / 1554 / Tassado en veynte y ocho reales.[1]

10 + 175 fols. The title is placed within an ornamental border. Italian lute tablature, Italian guitar tablature, and mensural notation. On fol. *2: royal printing privilege signed "Fecha en Valladolid a onze de Agosto de mil y quinientos y cincuenta y tres años. Yo el principe. Por mandado de su alteza, Juan Vazquez." On fol. *2ᵛ: dedication "Al Muy Alto Y Muy Poderoso señor don Philippe principe de España, Rey de Inglaterra, y de Napoles. &c. Nuestro señor." On fols. *3–*4: preface headed "Prologo al lector." On fols. *4ᵛ–*8: an introduction to the volume headed "Siguense los avisos y documentos que en este libro se contienen," including an explanation of the organization and contents of the volume, and of the tablature used. The headings of the various parts of this introduction follow:

fol.	
*5	"Del orden y fantasias que en este libro se ponen."
*5ᵛ	"De los redobles."
*6	"Del tañer con limpieza."
*6ᵛ	"De los tonos."
*7	"Al lector."

On fols. *8ᵛ–*9ᵛ: table of contents for the entire volume. On fols. *10–*10ᵛ: five poems, the first in Spanish, the others in Latin, headed "Sonetto de Benedito Arias Montano," "Martini a Montesdoca carmen in laudem Michaelis a Fuenllana artis musicae, & lyrae peritissimi, qui Divinam potius, quam Orphaeam condidit lyram," "Aliud eiusdem ad musicos," "Joannis Chirosii prasbyteris Carmen," and "Joannis çumetae patricii Hispalensis. Carmen."[2] Fol. *11 = fol. 1. The volume is divided into six books, each of which has its own title page, reproduced below. Colophon on fol. 175ᵛ: printer's mark with the initials ".M. .D. .M.," followed by "Fue impresso en Sevilla, en casa de Martin de Montesdoca. Acabose a dos dias del mes de Octubre de mill y quinientos y cincuenta y quatro años."

The compositions identified by superior letters are reprinted as follows: (a) in BalR, pp. 16–37; (b) in MorL II, 196–225; (c) in PedC II, 132–190; (d) in PedCP III, 148–181. For a possible later edition of this volume see 1564₃. For further information see AngMF, BalF, and RieMF. The compositions marked with an asterisk are for solo voice (notated either in mensural notation or in red ciphers in the tablature) and vihuela. Nos. 151–158 are for five-course vihuela. Nos. 159–167 are for four-course guitar. All of the other compositions are for solo six-course vihuela.

Copies in: A:Iu, A:Wn, D:WI, E:Bd, E:E, E:Mn (four copies in various states),[3] F:Pc, F:Pn, GB:Lbm, US:Cn, US:Wc.[4]

	fol.	
1	1	*Pleni sunt celi. Duo de la missa de Hercules* Josquin (JosqMS, no. 7: *Missa Hercules Dux Ferrariae*)
2	1ᵛ	*Benedictus. Duo de la missa pange lingua* Josquin (JosqMS, no. 18: *Missa Pange Lingua*)
3	2	*Suscepit Israel* Duo. Morales (P:C, MS M.M. 9, fol. 120ᵛ)
4	2	*Si amores me han de matar*[c 5] Duo de flecha (MitU, no. 51)
5	2ᵛ	*Duo contrapunto del author sobre el tiple deste villancico* Fuenllana
6	3	*Suscepit Israel* Duo de Guerrero
7	3ᵛ	*Fecit potentiam* Duo de Francisco Guerrero
8	4	*Fecit potentiam*[6] Duo de Josquin
9	4	*Duo de Fuenllana*[7]
10	5	*Fecit potentiam* Duo de Morales (MoralesO IV, 43)
11	5ᵛ	*Et ascendit in celum de la Missa Benedicta es coelorum regina** Morales *a 3* (MoralesO III, 15)
12	6	*Fantasia del author*[8] Fuenllana *a 3*
13	7	*Benedictus de la missa de gaude barbara** Morales *a 3* (MoralesMS II [1551])
14	7ᵛ	*Fantasia del author* Fuenllana *a 3*

15 8ᵛ *Et resurrexit de la missa de lomme arme** Morales *a 3* (MoralesMS II [1551])

16 9 *Fantasia del author*[9] Fuenllana *a 3*

17 10 *Crucifixus de la missa tu es vas electionis**[10] Morales *a 3* (MoralesMS II [1551])

18 10ᵛ *Fantasia del author*[11] Fuenllana *a 3*

19 11ᵛ *Agnus dei de la missa de ave maria** Morales *a 3* (MoralesO III, 61)

20 12 *Fantasia del author* Fuenllana *a 3*

21 13 *Deposuit** Morales *a 3* (MoralesO IV, 4)

22 13 *Fantasia del author* Fuenllana *a 3*

ORPHENICA LYRA / LIBRO SEGUNDO, / en que se ponen motetes a / quatro, de famosos autho/res. Assi mismo, fantasias a / quatro de el author, por / el orden ya dicho. / Labor omnia vincit. (fol. 14)

23 14ᵛ *Hodierna lux** Lupus [Hellinck] *a 4* (RISM 1553₁₀, fol. 3) D[12]

15ᵛ 2a pars *Ave domina coelurum*

24 17 *Fantasia del author* Fuenllana *a 4* D

25 18ᵛ *Qui confidunt in domino** Lirithier *a 4* (RISM 1532₁₀, no. 21: anon.)

20 2a pars *Benefac domine*

26 21ᵛ *Fantasia del author* Fuenllana *a 4* D

27 23 *Letentur omnes** Lupus *a 4* (RISM 1532₁₁, no. 6: "Letetur omne seculum")

24 2a pars *Hec maria fuit*

28 24ᵛ *Fantasia del author* Fuenllana *a 4* D

29 25ᵛ *Cum appropinquasset**[13] Gascon [Mathieu Gascongne?] *a 4* F

30 26ᵛ *Fantasia del author* Fuenllana *a 4* F

31 27ᵛ *Parce domine** Gombert *a 4* D (GombertO V, 6: 2a pars of "Miserere pie Jesu")

32 29 *Fantasia del author* Fuenllana *a 4* D

33 30ᵛ *Inter natos mulierum** Morales *a 4* D (MoralesO II, 69)

34 31ᵛ *Fantasia del author* Fuenllana *a 4* D

35 32ᵛ *O regem coeli** Andres de silva *a 4* F (RISM 1532₁₀, no. 1)

33ᵛ 2a pars *Salvator qui est Christus* (RISM 1532₁₀: "Natus est nobis")

36 34 *Fantasia del author* Fuenllana *a 4* F

37 35 *Ave maria** Adrian villar. *a 4* D (WillO II, 14: 2a pars of "Pater noster")

38 36 *Fantasia del author remedando esta ave maria* Fuenllana *a 4* D

39 37 *Super flumina babilonis** Gombert *a 4* D (HAM, no. 118)

40 39 *Fantasia del author* Fuenllana *a 4* D

41 40ᵛ *Benedictus de la missa de Lome arme** Morales *a 4* F (MoralesMS II [1551])

42 41ᵛ *Fantasia del author* Fuenllana *a 4* F

43 42 *Ave sanctissima Maria** Gombert *a 4* F (GombertO V, 77)

44 44 *Fantasia del author* Fuenllana *a 4* D

45 45 *O quam pulchra es** Gombert *a 4* F (GombertO V, 73)

46 46ᵛ *Fantasia del author* Fuenllana *a 4* F

47 47ᵛ *Sancta et inmaculata** Morales *a 4* F MoralesO II, 17)

48ᵛ 2a pars *Benedicta tu*

48 49ᵛ *Fantasia del author* Fuenllana *a 4* F

49 50 *Domine pater** Gombert *a 4* F (GombertO V, 1)

50 51ᵛ *Fantasia del author* Fuenllana *a 4* F

51 52ᵛ *Sancte Alfonse** Gombert *a 4* F (GombertMT II [1541], no. 8)

52 54 *Fantasia del author*[14] Fuenllana *a 4* F

53 55 *Benedictus de la missa Benedicta es coelorum regina** Morales *a4* D (MoralesO III, 24)
54 55^v *Fantasia del author* Fuenllana *a4* F
55 57 *Veni domine** Morales *a4* D
56 58 *Fantasia del author va remedado a este motete* Fuenllana *a4*

LIBRO TERCERO. / En el qual se contienen mote/tes a cinco y seys bozes / de muy excellen/tes authores. / [Woodcut] / Laudate Deum in cithara: / laudate Deum chordis, & organo. (fol. 59)

57 59^v *Aspice domine** Jaquet [da Mantua] *a5* D (MonteO XXVI, app.)
58 61^v *Si bona suscepimus** Verdelot *a5* D (MoralesO I, 274: Verdelot)
59 63 *Verbum inicuum** Morales *a5* D (MoralesO II, 122)
60 64 *Lamentabatur Jacob** Morales *a5* D (MoralesO II, 102)
61 65^v *Lauda syon** Gombert *a5* F
62 67 *Virgo Maria** Morales *a5* D
68^v 2a pars *Virgo Maria*
63 70 *O beata Maria** Gombert *a5* D (RISM 1538₂, fol. 18)
64 71 *Germinavit radix Jesse** Gombert *a5* D
65 72 *O felix Anna** Gombert *a5* F (GombertMT II a 5 [1541], no. 15)
66 73^v *Credo [de la missa] de beata virgine** Josquin *a5* D (JosqMS, no. 16)
76 *Crucifixus (ibid.)*
67 77 *Lamentacion** Morales *a5*
68 81^v *Jubilate deo** Morales *a6* D (MoralesO II, 184)
82^v 2a pars *O felix etas*
69 83^v *Agnus dei de la missa de si bona suscepimus** Jaquet *a6* (I:Rvat, Cappella Sistina MS 13, fol. 79^v)
70 85 *Benedicta es coelorum regina** Josquin *a6* D (JosqMT, no. 46)
71 86^v *Manus tue domine** Morales *a6* (E:E, MS Plut. 53, fol. 73)
72 88 *Preter rerum** Josquin *a6* D (JosqMT, no. 33)

LIBRO QUARTO / en el qual se ponen algunas / partes de Missas, Hym/nos, Fantasias, Favor/dones con otras / obras compue/stas. / Delphinas mulsit vocalis Arion in undis. / Hec Orphea chelys pectora nostra rapit.[15] (fol. 89^v)

73 90 *Qui tollis peccata. Segunda parte de la gloria de [la missa de] la sol fa re mi** Josquin *a4* F (JosqMS, no. 2)
74 91 *Agnus dei de la missa Lomme Arme** Morales *a4* D (MoralesMS II [1551])
75 91^v *Et in terra. Primera parte de la gloria de la missa de Faysan regres** Josquin *a4* D (JosqMS, no. 13)
92 *Primero kyrie de la missa de Faisan regres* Josquin *a4* D
92^v *Postrero kyrie de la missa de Faysan regres* Josquin *a4* F
76 93 *Primero kyrie de la missa de la sol fa re mi** Josquin *a4* D (JosqMS, no. 2)
93 *Christe de la missa de la sol fa re mi* Josquin *a4* F
93^v *Postrero kyrie [de la misma missa]* Josquin *a4* F
77 94 *Pange lingua** Guerrero *a4* D
78 94^v *Pange lingua** Guerrero *a3* F
79 95^v *Sacris solemniis** Guerrero *a3* F
80 96 *Sacris solenniis. Una boz de contrapunto sobre el canto llano** Fuenllana
81 96^v *Pater noster** [Francisco] Guerrero *a4* D (GuerrM, no. 1)
82 98^v *Fantasia* Fuenllana D
83 99 *Fantasia*[16] Fuenllana D
84 99^v *Fantasia* Fuenllana D
85 100^v *Fantasia* Fuenllana F
86 101^v *Fantasia* Fuenllana F
87 102 *Fantasia*[17] Fuenllana F
88 102^v *Fantasia* Fuenllana F

89 103 *Fantasia* Fuenllana F
90 103^v *Fantasia* Fuenllana F
91 104^v *Fantasia* Fuenllana
92 105 *Fantasia sobre un passo forçado ut re mi fa sol la*[18] Fuenllana D
93 106 *Fantasia*
94 106^v *Fantasia* Fuenllana D
95 107^v *Ave maris stella** Fuenllana *a4* D
96 108 *Benedictus de la missa de Mila regres** Morales *a3* (MoralesO I, 266)
97 108^v *Donec ponam inimicos tuos. Los ochos tonos en fabordon. Primero tono** Francisco Guerrero *a4*
98 109 *Donec ponam. Segundo tono** Guerrero *a4*
99 109 *Donec ponam. Tercero tono** Guerrero *a4*
100 109^v *Donec ponam. Quarto tono** Guerrero *a4*
101 109^v *Donec ponam. Quinto tono** Guerrero *a4*
102 110 *Donec ponam. Sexto tono** Guerrero *a4*
103 110^v *Sicut erat in principio. Este verso es a cinco** Guerrero
104 111 *Magna opera domine. Setimo tono** Guerrero *a4*
105 111 *Quoniam confortavit. Octavo tono** Guerrero *a4*

ORPHENICA LYRA / LIBRO QUINTO / en el qual se contienen estram/botes a cinco y a quatro. / Sonetos y Madrigales, en lengua Ca/stellana: villancicos a tres y a / quatro. Villanescas: y Ro/mances viejos. (fol. 111^v)

106 112 *Come havro dunque** Verdeloth Strambote *a5* D (RISM 1542_{16}, p. 16: Denis Brumen)
112 2a pars *Deh deh vi faise sin notta*
107 113 *Se le interna mia** Archadelt Strambote *a5* (RISM 1542_{16}, p. 17: Arnoldo [de Bruck?])
108 114 *Amor far me** Strambote *a5* Con. Festa (RISM 1540_{18}, p. 23: "Amor ben puoi tu hormai")
109 114^v *Signora Julia** Verdelot Strambote *a5* D (RISM 1542_{16}, p. 13: Jean Conseil)
110 116 *Madonna per voi ardo** Laurus Strambote *a4* D (ScherG, no. 98: Verdelot)
111 116^v *Liete madonne** Laurus Strambote *a4* D (RISM 1537_{10}, no. 1: Verdelot)
112 117^v *Quanto sia liet'il giorno** Verdeloth Strambote *a5* D (RISM 1537_9, no. 27)
113 118 *Tan que vivray**[19] Strambote *a4* F (AttainCK II, no. 10: Sermisy)
118^v *Glosa sobre la misma cancion*
114 119 *O sio potessi dona** Archadelt Strambote *a4* F (RISM 1541_9, p. 19: Berchem)
115 119^v *Bella fioretta** Archadelt Strambote *a4* F (RISM 1541_9, p. 45)
116 120^v *O felici occhi miei** Archadelt Strambote *a4* (CW V, 19)
117 121 *Il bianco e dolce cigno** Archadelt Strambote *a4* D (BuH II, 244)
118 121^v *Occhi miei lassi** Archadelt Strambote *a4* F (RISM 1541_9, p. 8)
122 2a pars *Morte puo chiuder*
119 122^v *O io mi pensai** Arcadelt Strambote *a4* D (RISM 1541_9, p. 46: "Io mi pensai")
120 123^v *O mas dura que marmol**[b] Pedro Guerrero Soneto *a4* F (MME VIII, 112)
124^v 2a pars *Tu dulce habla*
121 125^v *Quien podra creer** Pedro Guerrero Soneto *a3* F
122 126 *Passando el mar leandro** Pedro Guerrero Soneto *a4* D (MME IX, 96: anon.)
123 127 *Por do començare mi triste** Pedro Guerrero Soneto *a4* F (MME VIII, 100)
124 128 *Dun spiritu triste** Pedro Guerrero Soneto *a4* F
125 128^v *Amor es voluntad** Pedro Guerrero Soneto *a4* F
126 129^v *Mi coraçon fatigado** Pedro Guerrero Madrigal *a4* F
130 2a pars *Agora cobrando acuerdo*

127 131 *Oyme oyme dolente** Villanesca *a3* (CW VIII, 11: Nola)

128 131 *Quando ti vegio** Villanesca *a3*

129 131ᵛ *Madona mia la vostra** Villanesca *a3* (Vogel: Fontana [1545], no. 15: Vincenzo Fontana)

130 132 *Como quereys madre**abcd [20] Juan Vasquez Villancico *a3* (VasquezVC [1551], no. 15)

131 133 *Morenica dame un beso**cd Juan Vasquez Villancico *a3* (VasquezVC [1551], no. 16)

132 133ᵛ *Vos me matastes niña**abcd Juan Vasquez Villancico *a3* (VasquezVC [1551], no. 11)

133 134 *Ay que non oso**bcd Juan Vasquez Villancico *a3* (VasquezVC [1551], no. 3)

134 134ᵛ *No se que me bulle**cd Juan Vasquez Villancico *a3* (VasquezVC [1551], no. 4)

135 135ᵛ *Duelete de mi señora**bcd Juan Vasquez Villancico *a3* (VasquezVC [1551], no. 1)

136 136 *No me hableys conde**b Juan Vasquez Villancico *a3* (VasquezVC [1551], no. 5)

137 137 *Quiero dormir**ab Juan Vasquez Villancico *a3* (VasquezVC [1551], no. 14)

138 138 *Con que la lavare**ab Juan Vasquez Villancico *a4* (MME IV, 209)

139 138ᵛ *Que faran del pobre Juan**cd [21] Flecha Villancico *a4*

140 139ᵛ *Teresica hermana** Flecha Villancico *a4* (MitU, no. 36: anon.)

141 140 *Mal aya quien a vos caso**c [22] Flecha *a4*

142 141ᵛ *Puse mis amores**b [23] Raveneda Villancico *a4* F

143 142 *De los alamos vengo madre**abd Juan Vasquez Villancico *a4* (MME IV, 153)

144 143 *Ojos claros**cd [Francisco] Guerrero Villancico *a4* (GuerrO I, 121)

145 144 *Guarda fuera** [24] Guerrero Villancico *a4* D

146 145 *De antequera sale el moro**ab [25] Morales Romance *a4*

147 145 *A las armas moriscote**b Bernal Romance *a4*

Accipe divinam, que venit ab aethere musam. / LIBRO SEXTO / en el qual se ponen ensaladas: musica compuesta / y fantasias, para vihuela de cinco ordenes. Assi / mismo musica compuesta y fantasias para / guitarra. Tambien se ponen algunas / fantasias y pedaços de contrapun/to, para vihuela de seys, con / ocho tientos para los ochos tonos: con / los quales / acaba / el presente libro. / Hac poteris curas artenuare Lyra. (fol. 145ᵛ)

148 146 *Jubilate deo** Ensalada de Flecha D (FlechaE, no. 1)

149 149 *Bomba bomba** [26] Ensalada de Flecha D (FlechaE, no. 6)

150 153 *Oyd oyd los bivientes [La Justa]** Ensalada de Flecha (FlechaE, no. 3)

MUSIC FOR THE FIVE-COURSE VIHUELA

151 158 *Et resurrexit de la missa de ave Maria** Morales (MoralesO III, 48)

158ᵛ *Osanna de la misma Missa*

152 159 *La mi sola** Juan Vasquez Villancico (VasquezVC [1551], no. 10)

153 159ᵛ [*Fantasia*] Fuenllana D

154 160 *Fantasia* Fuenllana F

155 160ᵛ *Fantasia* Fuenllana F

156 161 *Fantasia* Fuenllana F

157 161ᵛ *Fantasia* Fuenllana F

158 162 *Fantasia* Fuenllana D

MUSIC FOR THE FOUR-COURSE GUITAR [27]

159 162ᵛ *Crucifixus* *a3* D

160 162ᵛ *Covarde cavallero** [28] Juan Vasquez Villancico (VasquezVC [1551], no. 5)

161 163ᵛ *Passeavase el Rey moro**bcd [29] Fuenllana "sobre el canto llano de este romance" F

162 163ᵛ [*Fantasia*] Fuenllana D

163 164ᵛ *Fantasia* Fuenllana D

164 164ᵛ *Fantasia* Fuenllana F

165 165 *Fantasia* [30] Fuenllana D

166 165 *Fantasia* Fuenllana F

167 165ᵛ *Fantasia* Fuenllana F

MUSIC FOR THE SIX-COURSE VIHUELA

168 166 *Fantasia de consonancias* Fuenllana D

169 167 *Fantasia sobre un passo forçado: ut sol sol la sol* Fuenllana F

170 168 *Una compostura con dos canto llanos: Ave maris stella y Gaudeamus** Fuenllana

171 168v *El que sin ti bivir: primero llana, y luego de contrapunto**[31] Fuenllana (text by Boscan)

172 169 *Si los delfines mueren de amores** Fuenllana Las endechas *a 3* F

173 169v *Una fantasia de redobles*[32] Fuenllana

174 170v *Tiento del primero tono*[33] Fuenllana

175 170v [*Tiento del*] *segundo tono* Fuenllana

176 171 [*Tiento del*] *tercero tono* Fuenllana

177 171 [*Tiento del*] *quarto tono* Fuenllana

178 171v [*Tiento del*] *quinto tono* Fuenllana

179 172 [*Tiento del*] *sexto tono* Fuenllana

180 172v [*Tiento del*] *septimo tono* Fuenllana

181 172v [*Tiento del*] *octavo tono* Fuenllana

182 173 *Benedicamus patrem** Fuenllana Motete F

[1] Facs. of title page in AbbS I, 482; EF II, 184; KinsP, p. 115; MGG IV, col. 1090; PedC II, 126; VinS, p. 97; and ZurM, p. 27. PedC II also repr. parts of the prefatory matter.

[2] Two of the copies in E:Mn, evidently from different printings of the same edition, have slightly different laudatory poems. In these copies there are only four poems on fols. *10–*10v: the two by Martin a Montesdoca, the one by Joannis Çumetae, and a fourth that does not appear in the other copies, a soneto by Juan Iranço. See AngCM III, 97, for further information.

[3] See AngCM III, 95–98, for descriptions of all four copies. This catalogue describes the one of the four copies that has a manuscript title page dated 1564 (see 1564_3).

[4] A copy was in D:Bds (formerly in the Wolffheim library; see WolffC I, no. 1191). A copy is in a private library in Morelia, Mexico (M:M).

[5] Only the two lowest voices of Flecha's original appear in Fuenllana's intabulation.

[6] See OsM, p. 230, for a discussion of this composition.

[7] Mod. ed. in ApelM II, 16.

[8] Mod. ed. in PujBG, no. 1016.

[9] Mod. ed. in PujBG, no. 1015.

[10] Facs. of fol. 10 in WolfH II, 13, showing the use of red ciphers.

[11] Mod. ed. in PujBG, no. 1014.

[12] Fuenllana has marked many of the pieces in this volume *D* (for difficult: "dificil") or *F* (for easy: "facil").

[13] Facs. of a part of fol. 26 in PN, p. 72.

[14] Facs. of fol. 54 in MGG III, col. 1763, and SubHM I, 491.

[15] Facs. of title page of Book IV in SubHME, p. 214.

[16] Mod. ed. in BruS IV, no. 143, and RieMF, p. 89.

[17] Mod. ed. in NeemAM II, no. 4.

[18] Mod. ed. in HawkeO V, 12; RieM, no. 41; and TagA I, no. 16.

[19] Mod. ed. in TapS, p. 27.

[20] Facs. of fol. 132 in BalR, frontispiece. Concordances with VasquezVC [1551] are listed in TreBM, p. 535ff.

[21] Facs. of fol. 138v in EF II, 76, and MGG IV, col. 295.

[22] SaliM, p. 318, quotes the tune incipit.

[23] Different from the anon. setting in MME VIII, 11, and from the setting by Juan Vásquez in VasquezVC [1551].

[24] Called "Torna Mingo" in the table of contents.

[25] Mod. ed. in FuenD, and ScherG, no. 114. Facs. of fol. 145 in MorL I, xli.

[26] Mod. ed. in EC, pt. I, vol. IV, p. 2013. Facs. of fol. 149 in PedC II, 151.

[27] All of the pieces for four-course guitar (nos. 159–167) are repr. in KoczD.

[28] Mod. ed. in GR, no. 12 (1951), p. 6.

[29] Mod. ed. in EC, pt. I, vol. IV, p. 2022; HAM, no. 123; TreL, p. 114; and WolfH II, 161 (with quasi-facs.).

[30] Mod. ed. in FuenF; MU I, app., p. 48; and TapS, p. 28.

[31] Facs. of fol. 168v in SubHME, p. 215. Mod. ed. in HeartzSM, p. 62.

[32] Partial transcription in KoczD, p. 246. Facs. of a part of fol. 169v in MGG III, col. 1763.

[33] Mod. ed. in PujBG, no. 1009.

1554_4

LE ROY, ADRIAN

CINQIESME LIVRE DE GUI/TERRE, CONTENANT PLUSIEURS CHANSONS A TROIS / & quatre parties, par bons & excelens Musiciens: Reduites en Tabu/lature par Adrian le Roy. / [Table of contents] / A PARIS. / De l'imprimerie, d'Adrian le Roy, & Robert Balard, Imprimeurs du Roy, rue / saint Jean de Beauvais, à l'enseigne sainte Genevieve. / 6. Decembre. / 1554. / Avec privilege du Roy, pour neuf ans.

24 fols. Superius in mensural notation; accompaniment in French guitar tablature. On fol. 24^v: the same excerpt from the printer's privilege as in 1551_2. For other volumes in the same series, see 1551_3, note 1. All of the compositions are for solo voice and guitar.

Copies in: F:Pm, GB:Lbm.

fol.

1 1^v *Escoutez ma complainte* De Bussi (RISM 1554_{26}, no. 17) = 1570_4, no. 44

2 2^v *Lesté chault bouilloit* Trio Adr. le Roy (RISM 1569_{12}, no. 5: Nicolas) = 1570_4, no. 46

3 3^v *Je ne me confesseray point* Trio Arcadet (LesLRB, art. 169, no. 6) = 1570_4, no. 43

4 4^v *Au jour au jour au jour* Bonard = 1570_4, no. 21

5 5^v *Quand viendra la clarté* Trio Arcadet (LesLRB, art. 169, no. 5) = 1570_4, no. 22

6 6^v *Je ne sçay que c'est qu'il me faut* Trio Arcadet (LesLRB, art. 169, no. 4) = 1570_4, no. 24

7 7^v *Que te sert amy d'estre ainsi* Trio Arcadet (LesLRB, art. 169, no. 2) = 1570_4, no. 23

8 9^v *J'ay tant bon credit qu'on voudra* Arcadet (LesLRB, art. 169, no. 1) = 1570_4, no. 26

9 10^v *Dieu inconstant* Trio Arcadet (SCMA V, no. 3)

10 12^v *Ce n'est bien ne plaisir* Arcadet (SCMA V, no. 7) = 1570_4, no. 25

11 13^v *Amour ha pouvoir sur les dieus* Trio Arcadet (SCMA V, no. 14) = 1570_4, no. 28

12 14^v *Qui pourra dire la douleur* Trio Arcadet (SCMA V, no. 4) = 1570_4, no. 45

13 15^v *Si ce n'est amour qu'est-ce* Trio Arcadet (SCMA V, no. 10) = 1570_4, no. 27

14 16^v *Si j'ayme ou non* Adr. le Roy (LesLRB, art. 171, fol. 3) = 1570_4, no. 29

15 17^v *Nous voyons que les hommes* Trio Arcadet (SCMA V, no. 11) = 1570_4, no. 30

16 19^v *La pastorella mia* Trio Arcadet (SCMA V, no. 5) = 1570_4, no. 31

17 20^v *Margot labourez les vignes* Arcadet (SCMA V, no. 9) = 1570_4, no. 32

18 21^v *Jamais femme ne sera* Certon = 1570_4, no. 33

19 22^v *Amour me sçauriez vous aprendre* Trio Arcadet (SCMA V, no. 12) = 1570_4, no. 34

20 23^v *Je sonne la retraitte* Certon = 1570_4, no. 35

1554_5

MORLAYE, GUILLAUME

PREMIER LIVRE DE PSAL/MES MIS EN MUSIQUE PAR MAISTRE PIERRE / Certon, maistre des enfans de la saincte Chapelle à Paris. / Reduitz en Tabulature de Leut par maistre Guillaume Morlaye, reservé la partie du / Dessus, qui est notée pour chanter en jouant. / [Printer's mark with motto "NEQUE MORS, NEQUE VENENUM"] / A PARIS. / De l'Imprimerie de Michel Fezandat, au mont Sainct Hilaire, à l'hostel d'Albret. / 1554. / AVEC PRIVILEGE DU ROY.

24 fols. Superius in mensural notation; accompaniment in French lute tablature. On fol. 23^v: table of contents. On fol. 24: the same excerpt from the printer's privilege as in 1553_4. The vocal models may probably be found in [*Livre premier contenant xxxi. pseaulmes*] (Paris, Attaingnant, 1546), of which only a defective superius is extant, and in *Cinquante Pseaulmes . . . par M. Pierre Certon* (Paris, Le Roy and Ballard, 1555), with only the tenor extant; see PidP for a discussion of the two volumes and their relation with Morlaye's intabulations. MorlayeC is a modern edition of the entire volume. All of the compositions are for solo voice and lute.

Copies in: B:Br, D:Mbs.[1]

fol.

1 2 *Pseaulme VI. Domine ne in furore tuo* (*Je te supplie o Sire*)

2 3 *Pseaulme XXXII. Beati quorum* (*O bienheureux celuy*)

3	4ᵛ	*Pseaulme XXXIII. Exultate justi in domino* (*Reveillez vous chascun fidelle*)
4	6ᵛ	*Pseaulme V. Verba mea* (*Aux parolles que je veulx dire*)
5	8	*Pseaulme II. Quare fremuerunt gentes* (*Pourquoy font bruit*)
6	10	*Pseaulme XIII. Usquequo Domine* (*Jusques à quand as establi*)
7	11ᵛ	*Pseaulme CXXX. De profundis* (*Du fons de ma pensée*)[2]
8	13	*Pseaulme CXIIII. In exitu Israel* (*Quand Israel hors d'Egypte sortit*)
9	14ᵛ	*Pseaulme CXLIII. Domine exaudi orationem meam* (*Seigneur Dieu oy l'oraison mienne*)
10	16ᵛ	*Pseaulme CXXXVII. Super flumina Babylonis* (*Estans assis aux rives aquatiques*)
11	18	*Pseaulme XLV. Deus noster refugium, et virtus* (*Des qu'adversité nous offense*)
12	20	*Pseaulme CLII. Nunc dimittis.* [*Cantique de Siméon*] (*Or laisse createur En paix ton serviteur*)
13	21ᵛ	*Pseaulme III. Domine quid multiplicati sunt* (*O seigneur que de gens*)

[1] A copy was in PL:S. Bound in with this copy were six pages of manuscript music in French lute tablature containing Italian and German dances and "Schlacht für pavia." On the cover of the volume was the date 1566, the name "Andreas Belenczki," and a portrait of "Joannes Fridericus elector dux saxo." A manuscript dedicatory poem headed "Testudine Joannis Kosmvsky" was included in the volume. For further details see BoettB.

[2] Mod. ed. in BruS III, no. 91.

1554₆

RIPPE, ALBERT DE

SECOND LIVRE DE / TABULATURE DE LEUT, CONTENANT / plusieurs Chansons, Motetz & Fantasies, / Composées par feu Messire Albert de Rippe de Mantoue, Seigneur du Carois, / joueur de Leut, & varlet de chambre du Roy nostre sire. / [Printer's mark] / A PARIS, / De l'imprimerie de Michel Fezandat, au mont sainct Hilaire, à l'hostel d'Albret. / 1554. / Avec privilege du Roy, pour dix ans.[1]

24 fols. French lute tablature. On fol. A1ᵛ: table of contents. Fol. A2 = fol. 1. On fol. 23ᵛ: the same excerpt from the printer's privilege as in 1552₄. For other volumes in the same series, see 1552₈, note 1. All of the compositions are for solo lute.

Copy in: F:Pthibault.

	fol.	
1	1	*Fantasie d'Albert* = 1562₈, no. 4
2	3ᵛ	*Fantasie* [*d'Albert*] = 1562₈, no. 5
3	6	*Fantasie* [*d'Albert*] = 1562₈, no. 6
4	9ᵛ	*Regi seculorum* Claudin [de Sermisy] (SermM, no. 24)
	10ᵛ	2a pars [*Et beata viscera Marie*]
5	11ᵛ	*Ave sanctissima* Claudin (RISM 1565₃, fol. 10)
6	13ᵛ	*Fors seulement* Fevin (ObrWW, p. 90: Josquin or Févin)
7	15ᵛ	*Adieu qui par façon honneste*
8	17	*De qui plus tost* Sandrin (RISM 1549₂₀, no. 29)
9	19ᵛ	*L'Eccho* Gentian
10	21	*Mamie est tant honneste & sage* Sandrin (RISM 1549₂₁, no. 10)
11	22ᵛ	*Or vien ça vien mamie Perrette* Janequin (RISM 1540₁₇, fol. 6ᵛ)

[1] Facs. of title page in MLI, pl. 36.

1554₇

RIPPE, ALBERT DE

TROISIESME LIVRE DE / TABULATURE DE LEUT, CONTENANT / plusieurs Chansons, Motetz & Fantasies, / Composées par feu Messire Albert de Rippe, de Mantoue, Seigneur du Carois, / joueur, de Leut, & varlet de chambre du Roy nostre sire. / [Printer's mark with motto "NE LA MORT, NE LE VENIM"] / A PARIS, / De l'imprimerie de Michel Fezandat, au mont sainct Hilaire, à l'hostel d'Albret. / Et par maistre Guillaume

Morlaye, en la rue de Bievre. 1554. / Avec privilege du Roy.[1]

24 fols. French lute tablature. On fol. 1^{v}: the same excerpt from the printer's privilege as in 1552_{4}. On fol. 23^{v}: table of contents. On fol. 24: Printer's mark with the initials "M. F." BuggR contains a modern edition of the entire volume. SlimK II, 564, contains a thematic index of the ricercares. For other volumes in the same series, see 1552_{8}, note 1. All of the compositions are for solo lute.

Copies in: B:Br, F:Pthibault.

	fol.	
1	2	*Fantasie* = 1562_{8}, no. 7
2	4	*Fantasie* = 1562_{8}, no. 8
3	7^{v}	*Fantasie* = 1536_{9}, no. 2
4	10^{v}	*Damours me plains* Roger Patie (PubAPTM XXIII, no. 49) = 1562_{9}, no. 6, and 1574_{7}, no. 19
5	11^{v}	*Mon pensement* Gombert (RISM 1550_{5}, no. 21) = 1562_{9}, no. 7, and 1574_{7}, no. 20
6	13^{v}	*Si quelque fois* Gentian (RISM 1545_{12}, no. 28) = 1562_{9}, no. 8
7	14^{v}	*Si vous voulez* (RISM 1567_{6}, fol. 15: Arcadelt)
8	15^{v}	*La volunté si long temps endormie* Sandrin (RISM 1549_{18}, no. 15) = 1562_{9}, no. 9
9	17^{v}	*Se qui m'est deu & ordonné* Sandrin (RISM 1543_{11}, no. 18) = 1562_{9}, no. 10
10	19	*Adiuva me domine* Consilium (RISM 1535_{3}, no. 6) = 1562_{11}, no. 2, and 1574_{7}, no. 53
	21	2a pars *Servus tuus ego sum*

[1] Facs. of title page in LiuM, p. 81.

1554_{8}

RIPPE, ALBERT DE

QUATRIESME LIVRE DE / TABULATURE DE LEUT, CONTENANT / plusieurs Chansons, Motetz & Fantasies, / Composées par feu Messire Albert de Rippe, de Mantoue, Seigneur du Carois, / joueur, de Leut, & varlet de chambre du Roy nostre sire. / [Printer's mark with motto "NE LA MORT, NE LE VENIM"] / A PARIS, / De l'imprimerie de Michel Fezandat, au mont sainct Hilaire, à l'hostel d'Albret. / Et en la rue de Bievre, par Maistre Guillaume Morlaye. 1554. / Avec privilege du Roy.

24 fols. French lute tablature. On fol. 1^{v}: the same excerpt from the printer's privilege as in 1552_{4}. On fol. 24: table of contents. BuggR contains a modern edition of the entire volume. SlimK II, 565, contains a thematic index of the ricercares. For other volumes in the same series, see 1552_{8}, note 1. All of the compositions are for solo lute.

Copies in: B:Br, F:Pthibault.

	fol.	
1	2	*Fantasie*
2	5^{v}	*Fantasie pour jouer sans chanterelle*
3	8	*Fantasie* = 1562_{8}, no. 9
4	10^{v}	*Te o virgo virginum mater & filia*
5	14	*Verbum iniquum* (MoralesO II, 122: Morales)
6	16^{v}	*N'as tu point veu mal assenée* (RISM 1572_{2}, fol. 41: "N'avons point veu mal assenée," Le Brun) = 1562_{10}, no. 12, and 1574_{7}, no. 30
7	18^{v}	*Au temps heureux* (SCMA V, no. 1: Arcadelt)
8	20^{v}	*O verdémont* (MB XVIII, no. 42)
9	21^{v}	*Soleil qui tout voit* (RISM 1549_{21}, no. 2: Certon)
10	23	*Trop plus penser* (RISM 1547_{9}, no. 20: Sandrin)

1554_{9}

VAN GHELEN, JAN

Dit is een zeer schoon / Boecxken, om te leeren maken alderhande tabulatueren / wten Discante. Daer duer men lichtelijck mach / leeren spelen opt Clavecordium luyte ende Fluyte. / [Cut of a man playing the lute, with two recorders and a clavichord forming the border]

42 fols. This is a Flemish translation by Jan van Ghelen of Vorsterman's French translation (1529_2) of Virdung's *Musica getutscht* (1511_3). For further details see the description of the second edition (1568_8). Contents = 1568_8.

Copy in: F:Pn.

1555_1

BERMUDO, JUAN

Comiença el libro llamado de/claracion de inst[r]umentos musicales dirigido al illustrissimo señor el se/ñor don Francisco de çuniga Conde de Miranda, señor de las ca/sas de avellaneda y baçan &c. compuesto por el muy reverendo pa/dre fray Juan Bermudo de la orden de los menores: en el qual halla/ran todo lo que en musica dessearen, y contiene seys libros: segun en la / pagina siguiente se vera: examinado y aprovado por los egregios / musicos Bernardino de figueroa, y Christoval de morales. 1555 / Con privilegio.[1]

150 fols. The title is placed within an ornamental border; above the title is the coat of arms of Francisco de Zuniga y Avellaneda, with verses from Psalm 150 and Proverbs 23 on either side. On fol. $*1^v$: a summary of the contents of the volume headed "Cathalogo de los libros contenidos en el presente volumen, y de que tracta cada uno dellos." On fol. *2: a summary of the royal printing privilege. On fol. $*2^v$: a poem in Spanish headed "Sonetos. En alabança de la Musica y deste libro de un amigo del author." On fol. *3: the dedication headed (on fol. $*2^v$): "Al illustrissimo señor el señor don Francisco de çuniga Conde de Miranda, &c, mi señor."[2] On fol. *4: an open letter from Bernardino de Figueroa, master of the Royal Chapel at Granada, in praise of Bermudo's book, headed "Epistola recomendatoria de la presente obra del señor Bernardino de figueroa. El maestro de capilla real de Granada a los desseosos de saber el arte de la musica practica y especulativa." On fols. $*4^v$–*6: the first preface headed "Prologo primero para el piadoso lector"; this is a revised version of the preface of 1549_3. On fols. $*6^v$–$*8^v$: the second preface headed "Prologo segundo para el piadoso lector." Fol. *9 = fol. 1. On fol. 120^v (incorrectly printed as 128^v): a letter from Christobal de Morales in praise of Bermudo's book, headed "Epistola del egregio musico Morales. Christoval de Morales maestro de capilla del señor Duque de arcos al prudente lector. S," and dated "Vale de marchena año de. M. D. L. a veynte dias del mes de octubre." On fol. 142: a note explaining that Book VI, promised in the summary on fol. $*1^v$, has not been printed, followed by the author's corrections. Colophon on fol. 142^v: "Fin de los cinco libros de la declaracion de los instrumento[s] musicales los quales compuso el muy reverendo padre fray Juan Bermudo de la orden de los menores de observancia, de la provincia del andaluzia, natural de la muy noble y leal cibdad [*sic*] de Ecija en el Arçobispado de Sevilla, y fueron impressos en la villa de Ossuna por Juan de Leon impressor de libros de la insigne Universidad del Illustrissimo señor don Juan Tellez Giron conde de Urvena &c. Y acabaronse de imprimir a treze dias del mes de Julio siendo bispera de sanct Buenaventura Año de. M. D. L. v."

The treatise is divided into five books. The sixth book, summarized on fol. $*1^v$, and a seventh book mentioned on fol. 142, were never printed. Most of the material in Bermudo's first two treatises (1549_3 and 1550_1) is included in the present volume (see StevnsnJB for details). The five books may be summarized as follows:

Book I, fols. 1–20 (incorporating chaps. 3–19 and 49 of 1549_3), is given over to praises of music.[3]

Book II, fols. 20^v–30^v (incorporating chap. 2 of 1549_3, and chaps. 1–12 and 14–28 of 1550_1) is an introduction to plainsong, polyphony, and to performance on keyboard and plucked string instruments (vihuela, guitar, bandore, and rebec).

Book III, fols. 31–59^v (incorporating chaps. 20–29 and 33–48 of 1549_3, and chap. 13 of 1550_1) is devoted to more advanced instruction in the theory and practice of plainsong and polyphony.

Book IV, fols. 60–120^v (incorporating chaps. 30–37 and 39–40 of 1550_1) offers advanced instruction in keyboard performance and in the playing of the vihuela, the guitar, the bandore, and the harp. Bermudo explains how to intabulate, discusses various tablatures and tuning problems, shows how modes affect instrumental music, and offers much practical advice, such as how to expand one's repertoire. (Much of Book IV is summarized in German in KinO, pp. 9–25).[4]

Book V, fols. 121–141ᵛ, is an introduction to the art of composition. Bermudo explains how to compose single lines as well as polyphony, how to improvise, and how to write counterpoint over a cantus firmus.

Book VI was to have listed the musical errors of the Spanish theorists who preceded Bermudo.

BermuD is a facsimile edition of the entire treatise except for the prefatory matter (fols. *1ᵛ–*8ᵛ). For further information see StevnsnJB, KinO, and ReFS, no. 41. The treatise contains numerous diagrams and short musical examples (some of them reprinted in StevnsnJB).[5] The inventory below lists only the longer, complete compositions. The compositions identified by the superior letter *a* ([a]) are reprinted in BermuOO and PedB. No. 5 is notated in a number tablature for keyboard, with the beginning only printed in mensural notation. No. 6 is for six-course vihuela (notated in Italian lute tablature) and voice (in mensural notation). No. 7 is for seven-course vihuela (in Italian lute tablature) and voice (in mensural notation). All of the other examples are for keyboard performance, with the separate voice parts being printed in mensural notation and arranged in choirbook format.

Copies in: A:Wn, CH:Lcortot, D:Bds–Tü,[6] E:Bd, E:Mn, E:V, F:Pn, GB:Lbm, US:CA, US:NYhs, US:Wc.

	fol.	
1	61ᵛ	[*Tiento*][a 7] *a 4*
2	77ᵛ	[*Modo*] *primero por Elami*[a] *a 4*
3	78	[*Modo*] *primero por ♮ mi*[a] *a 4*
4	78ᵛ	[*Modo*] *octavo por Elami*[a] *a 4*
5	83	*Aunque me veys en tierra agena*[8] Endecha [lament]
6	101	*Mira Nero de tarpea*[9] Romance
7	101ᵛ	*Mira Nero de tarpea* Romance
8	114	*Ave maris stella*[a 10] Hymn *a 4*
9	114ᵛ	[*Tiento*] *Modo primero con resabios de quarto*[a] *a 4*
10	115ᵛ	[*Tiento*] *modo quarto*[a 11] *a 4*
11	116ᵛ	[*Tiento*] *modo sexto verdadero*[a 12] *a 4*
12	117ᵛ	[*Tiento*] *modo octavo*[a] *a 4*
13	118ᵛ	*Conditor alme siderum*[a 13] Hymn *a 4*
14	119	*Vexilla regis prodeunt a cinco bozes*[a 14] Hymn *a 5*
15	119ᵛ	*Veni creator spiritus*[a 15] Hymn *a 4*
16	120	*Pange lingua*[a 16] Hymn *a 4*

[1] Facs. of title page in PedC I, 127, and MGG XI, col. 254.
[2] Facs. of fol. *3 in SubHME, p. 284.
[3] Facs. of fol. 9 in SubHME, p. 205.
[4] Facs. of fol. 110 (a cut of a vihuela) in EF III, 858, and SubHM I, 487.
[5] The puzzle canon on "Ave maris stella" repr. in DavB, p. 15; EF I, 702; and MGG I, col. 1763, is taken from Domenico Pietro Cerone, *El melopeo y maestro* (1613), and not from Bermudo. The page is also repr. in AudaL, pl. 7; CollaerAH, p. 177; MagniSM I, 218; and SubHM I, 502.
[6] Formerly in the Wolffheim library (see WolffC I, no. 809).
[7] Mod. ed. in HawkeO V, 10; KinO, p. 228; PedOL, no. 1; StevnsnJB, p. 49; and TagA I, no. 17.
[8] Mod. ed. in StevnsnJB, p. 83; beginning pr. in KinO, p. 227; a section pr. in tablature and modern notation in TapS, p. 30, and in WolfH II, 265; facs. of fol. 83 in MGG IX, col. 1649, and partly in ApelN, p. 48.
[9] Mod. ed. in BalR, p. 17; BermuM; and PedCP III, 135.
[10] Mod. ed. in StevnsnJB, p. 78.
[11] Mod. ed. in KinO, p. 229.
[12] Mod. ed. in KinO, p. 231.
[13] Mod. ed. in StevnsnJB, p. 80.
[14] Mod. ed. in KinO, p. 233.
[15] Mod. ed. in KinO, p. 234.
[16] Mod. ed. in DallaLO IV, no. 1; FroideA I, 72 (as "Tantum ergo"); and KinO, p. 235.

1555₂

HESSEN, PAUL AND BARTHOLOMEUS

Viel Feiner Lieblicher Stuck/lein, Spanischer, Welscher, Englischer, Frantzösisch/er composition und tentz, Uber drey hundert, mit / Sechsen, Fünffen, und Vieren, auff alle In/strument dienstlich, mit sonderm fleis / zusamen bracht, vor nie in druck kommen. / Gedruckt zu Breslaw, Durch / Crispinum Scharffenberg.

Five part books in mensural notation (S wanting; AB, each of 72 fols.; T, 76 fols.; 5/6, 38 fols.). The title page and prefatory material appear only in the tenor part book; the other part books have as title simply the name of the voice part and the coat of arms of the dedicatee. Dedication on fols. *2–*3 of the tenor part book headed "Dem Durchlauchtigisten, Grosmechtigisten Fürsten und Herren, Herrn Maximiliano, Königen zu Behem, Ertzhertzogen zu Osterreich, Margraffen in Merhern, Hertzogen zu Lücemburg und in Slesien, Margraffen zu Lausatz, &c. unserm Gnedigsten Herren und König," and signed "Datum Breslaw, An dem Heiligen Ostertag, des 1555. Jahrs. Ewr Kön. Wyrde Underthenigste diener Paulus und Bartholomeus Hessen gebrüder, besolte Instrumentisten der Königlichen Stadt Breslaw." Preface on fols. *3ᵛ–*4ᵛ of the tenor part book:

> Gottes Güt, Gnad und Barmhertzigkeit, So wol unsern Freundlichen Grus, auch gehorsame unnd Willige dienst, sindt von uns gebrüdern, Paulo unnd Bartholomeo Hessen besolten Musicis, und mitbürgern der Königlichen und Loblichen Stat Breslaw, allen liebhabern und ehrlichen nachforschern, der Edlen, Freien und Hochlöblichen kunst Musica. Dieweil wir Kön. Wyrden zu Behem &c. Unserm aller gnedigsten Herrn zu underthenigster schuldiger dienstbarkeit, diese nachvolgende Composition frembder landt art, in druck gefertiget, Haben wir fur unerfarne derer Nation einen kleinen underricht fur notwendig geacht, und hiernach gestelt. Erstlich, weil dise noten und Composition ohne namen und Text verlassen ist, das jere Carmen dicke verkeret, auch solchs wenig zum singen, allein auff die instrument lieblich und dienstlich. Derwegen nichts daran gelegen wie sie jeder taufft, Zum andern, die vielfaltigen bezeichneten kreutzlein, bedeuten die Semitonien, so wider den gebrauch deutscher Musica befunden, wirdt darmit ihres landes gebrauch angezeigt, zu viel angenemer lieblicheit, wo sie recht gemacht werden. Auch werden an etlichen orten vitia gespürt, weil aber solches bein ihrer nation also componiert und zum theil nit fur unrecht geacht, Auch nicht fur deutsche compositz ausgeben, haben wir nichts endern wollen, damit ihr art und das sprichwort bleibe und erhalten, Jedes land fürt seinen eignen brauch und weise. Auch sind etliche anfangende stücklen, mit fünffer unnd sechster stimmen gemehrt, wegen volkommenheit und viler geselschafft, und mügen auch wider ausgelassen werden. Denn wo zu end einer stimmen ein Klebletlein befunden wird, das sind die zu gefürten stimmen, Und wo solche ausgelassen werden, und im Bass zu ende ein sternlein verzeichnet ist, So sol derselbe Bass entgegen ein octava höher als es claviert genomen werden. Auch ist dieser stücklen art und gebrauch alles und jedes von einer repetition zu der andern, unter einer durchgehenden mensur, ohne stilhalten zurepitieren, Wo aber zwerch liny zwischen den noten befunden werden, so solle man bey der nechstfolgenden repetition bey solche linien die repetierung wider holen. Auch sindt solche stück von uns nit allein zum tantzen vermaint. Sonder wegen ihrer frembden lieblichen unnd aller Nation annemblichen art, vor unserer landtsgebrauch und Compositionen darinnen auch wunderliche unergründte freud, und von himel entleihender gaben Gottes auff erden wenig mit geschmeckt, unnd manigfeldtiglich under allen nationen wunderlicher weis zerteilt, vermerckt zu seinem Götlichen lob und ehren, nachmals zu aufflösung und erquickung vieler Gotseliger und fromer, doch etlicher massen beladener und betrübter gemüter. Damit wir auch der heiligen unnd unerforschlichen Trinitet, ohne auffhören mit triumphieren, fur alle seine Allmechtige wundergaben, nicht allein lob und dancksagung thüen, sondern auch von hertzen nach den rechten unnd ewigen freuden trachten sollen, die unaussprechlich sind, und welcher dise irdische und zergengliche freude, nichts oder ja gar wenig zuvergleichen ist. Allweil wir aber uns der Röm. Kön. Maiestet, Unserm aller gnedigsten Herrn, So wol ihren hoch adelichsten Erben alles schnidigen gehorsams und underthenigkeit underworffen erkennen, Und denselben nach höchstem vermügen mit Lein unnd gut sonderlich zudienen verpflichtet. So haben wir ihrer Röm. Kön. Maiestet, und derselben Erben zu ehren, auch aufspieler ehrlicher leut und liebhaber der Musica, anlangen, solch lieblich und schön composition in druck geben und

verlegt, Und so viel wir der aus fleissiger samlung diser zeit gehabt. Demnach wir einen jeden nach seinem standt dienstlich unnd freundtlich wollen gebetten haben, wolte ihm solchen unsern fleis nicht allein dencklich gefallen, Sonder die Musica und uns der selben liebhaber zu forderung und Freundtschafft lassen entpfolhen sein. Sich auch enthalten inner sechs jahren dieses nachzudrucken, Bey der Röm. Kön. Maiestet schweren ungnaden, Und in unserm Privilegio austrucklicher straffe, nemblich bey verlust zehen marcklötiges golds und der bücher. Des sich meniglich wirt zurichten haben.

Fol. *5 (= fol. A1) of the tenor part book has the word: "Tenor" and the coat of arms of the dedicatee. On the verso of the last folio of each part book except for the Quinta-Sexta part book: the coat of arms of the city of Breslau. On the verso of the last folio of the Quinta-Sexta part book: an insignia with the legend: "PAULUS BARTOLOMEUS HESSI. CIVITATIS VRATISLAVIEN: MUSICI. 1554." The volume contains 322 compositions for instrumental ensemble *a4*, *a5*, and *a6*, without text or title. The compositions identified in the inventory below were found by searching for concordances only in printed volumes of dances for instrumental ensemble.[1]

Copy in: D:As (S wanting).[2]

	fol.	
6	A3	[*Pavane*] = 1530_5, no. 29
23	B4	[*Passamezzo antico*]
28	C2	[*Pavane d'Angleterre*] = 1555_5, no. 3a
30	C2^v	[*Basse dance*] = 1530_5, no. 1
60	E3	[*Passamezzo antico*]
63	E3^v	[*Pavane La Bataille*] = $154?_6$, no. 33
64	E3^v	[*Jamais n'aymeray masson*] (RISM 1520_6, fol. 6^v)
65	E4	[*Pavane J'ay le rebours*] = 1530_4, no. 9
94	G3^v	[*Quando ritrovo la mia pastorella*] (HAM, no. 129: C. Festa)
111	H3^v	[*Pavane La Gaiette* ("Il estoit une fillette")] = $154?_6$, no. 35
126	I3^v	[*Romanesca*] (compare no. 241 below)
156	L2^v	[*Pavane*] (compare no. 197 below)
158	L2^v	[*Pavane*] = 1530_4, no. 10
159	L2^v	[*Passamezzo antico*]
175	M2	[*Pavane*] = 1530_5, no. 24
184	M3^v	[*Pavane*] = 1530_5, no. 28
191	M4^v	[*Gaillarde*] = 1530_4, no. 6
194	N1^v	[*Pavane*] = 1530_5, no. 16
197	N2	[*Pavane*] = 1530_4, no. 7 (compare no. 156 above)
202	N3^v	[*Pavane*] = 1547_6, no. 47
204	N4^v	[*Pavane Dellestarpe*] = 1550_5, no. 18
218	O3	[*Pavane*] = 1530_5, no. 23
239	P2	[*Basse dance*] = 1530_5, no. 2
241	P2^v	[*Romanesca*] (compare no. 126 above)
248	P3^v	[*Pavane*] = 1530_5, no. 19
249	P4	[*Basse dance La Magdalena*] = 1530_5, no. 6
250	P4	[*Tourdion*] = 1530_5, no. 7
254	P4^v	[*Pavane*] = 1530_5, no. 18
258	Q1^v	[*Pavane*] = 1530_5, no. 49
268	Q3	[*Pavane*] = 1530_5, no. 20
270	Q3^v	[*Gaillarde*] = 1530_5, no. 34
271	Q3^v	[*Gaillarde*] = 1530_5, no. 45
276	Q4^v	[*Pavane*] = 1530_5, no. 12
277	R1	[*Gaillarde*] = 1530_5, nos. 32 and 44
290	R3	[*Gaillarde*] = 1530_4, no. 1
291	R3	[*Gaillarde*] = 1530_4, no. 2
292	R3^v	[*Pass'e mezo ditto il Romano*] = 1553_2, no. 1
293	R3^v	[*Moschetta*] = 1553_2, no. 2
294	R3^v	[*Il ben ti vegna*] = 1553_2, no. 22
295	R4	[*La Giovenetta*] = 1553_2, no. 21
296	R4	[*Bandera*] = 1553_2, no. 19
297	R4	[*Galante*] = 1553_2, no. 15
298	R4^v	[*E dove vastu o bon solda*] = 1553_2, no. 11
299	R4^v	[*Incognita*] = 1553_2, no. 13
300	R4^v	[*Gioia*] = 1553_2, no. 20
301	S1	[*Pietoso*] = 1553_2, no. 4
302	S1	[*Desiderata*] = 1553_2, no. 3
303	S1	[*La mala vecchia*] = 1553_2, no. 6
304	S1^v	[*Doi stanchi*] = 1553_2, no. 8
305	S1^v	[*Il stocco*] = 1553_2, no. 7
306	S1^v	[*Speranza*] = 1553_2, no. 5
307	S2	[*La falilela*] = 1553_2, no. 9
308	S2	[*La Bruna*] = 1553_2, no. 10

309 S2 [*Chi non ha martello*] = 1553_2, no. 12
310 S2^v [*Bella foresta*] = 1553_2, no. 14
311 S2^v [*Animoso*] = 1553_2, no. 17
312 S2^v [*Violla*] = 1553_2, no. 24
313 S3 [*Pavane*] = 1530_5, no. 15
314 S3 [*Basse dance La gatta en italien*] = 1530_5, no. 4
315 S3 [*Pass'e mezo ditto il Compasso*] = 1553_2, no. 23
319 S3^v [*Pavane*] = 1530_5, no. 23
320 S4 [*Gaillarde*] = 1530_4, no. 3
321 S4 [*Gaillarde*] = 1530_5, no. 36
322 S4 [*Cortesa Padoana*] = 1553_2, no. 18

[1] That is, 1530_4, 1530_5, 1532_2, 1547_6, $154?_6$, 1550_5, 1550_6, 1551_8, 1553_2, 1555_5, 1557_3, 1557_4, 1559_1, 1559_2, 1559_3, 1564_2, 1571_5, 1583_7.

[2] A copy of the altus part book was in PL:WRu.

1555_3

HESSEN, PAUL AND BARTHOLOMEUS

Etlicher gutter Teutscher und / Polnischer Tentz, biss in die anderthalbhundert / mit fünff und vier Stimmen, zugebrauchen, / auff allerley Instrument dinstlich, mit sonderm / vleis zusamen getragen, dermassen vor nie in Druck komen. / Mit Römischer, Ungrischer, Böhmischer / Kön. Maiestat &c. freiheit begnadet und begabet, / innerhalb sechs jaren nicht nach/zudrucken. / Gedruckt zu Breslaw, Durch / Crispinum Scharffenberg. / M. D. LV.

Five part books in mensural notation (S wanting; T, 62 fols.; B, 63 fols.; A5, each of 64 fols.). The title page and prefatory material appear only in the tenor part book; the other part books have as title simply the name of the voice part and the coat of arms of the dedicatee. Dedication on fols. *2–*2^v of the tenor part book headed "Dem durchlauchtigisten hochgebornen Fürsten und Herrn Ferdinando Ertzhertzogen zu Osterreich, Hertzogen in Kernten, Steir, Krain, Wirtenwerg, Grafen zu Tiroll, Obristen Statthalter der Kron Behem," and signed "Bresslaw, 14 Aprilis 1555. Paulus und Bartholomeus Hessen, gebrüder, besolte Instrumentisten der Königlichen Stadt Breslaw." Fol. *3 (= fol. A1) of the tenor part book has the word "Tenor" and the coat of arms of the dedicatee. The volume contains 155 compositions for instrumental ensemble *a4* and *a5* without texts or titles.

Copy in: D:As (S wanting).[1]

[1] A copy of the altus part book was in PL:WRu.

1555_4

RIPPE, ALBERT DE

CINQUIESME LIVRE DE / TABULATURE DE LEUT, CONTENANT / plusieurs Chansons, Fantasies, Motetz, Pavanes, & Gaillardes. / Composées par feu Messire Albert de Rippe, de Mantoue, Seigneur du Carois, / joueur de Leut, & varlet de chambre du Roy nostre sire. / [Printer's mark with motto "NE LA MORT, NE LE VENIN"] / A PARIS, / De l'imprimerie de Michel Fezandat, au mont sainct Hilaire, à l'hostel d'Albret. / 1555. / Avec privilege du Roy.

24 fols. French lute tablature. On fol. 24: table of contents followed by a shortened version of the printer's privilege that appears in 1552_4. The entire collection is transcribed in BuggR. For other volumes in the same series, see 1552_8, note 1. All of the compositions are for solo lute.

Copies in: B:Br, F:Pthibault.

fol.
1 2 *Fantasie* = 1536_9, no. 8
2 5 *Fantasie*[1]
3 8 *Praeter rerum seriem* Josquin (JosqMT, no. 33)
10^v 2a pars [*Virtus sancti spiritus*]
4 13 *O Passi sparsi* Constantius festa (RISM 1526_6, no. 4: S. Festa) = 1562_{10}, no. 1, and 1574_7, no. 25
5 16^v *Qui souhaitez* Sandrin (RISM 1549_{20}, no. 1)
6 19 *Ma belle porée*
7 20^v *Pavane* (compare 1557_3, no. 3a: "Pavanne l'Admiral")
21^v *Gaillarde* (compare 1557_3, no. 3b: "Gaillarde [l'Admiral]")
8 22^v *Pavane* (compare 1557_3, no. 1a: "Pavanne. Si je m'en vois")

	23^v	*Gaillarde* (compare 1557_3, no. 1b: "Gaillarde. Si je m'en vois")

[1] Incipit in SlimK II, 566.

1555_5

GERVAISE, CLAUDE

SIXIEME LIVRE DE DANCERIES, / MIS EN MUSIQUE A QUATRE PARTIES PAR / Claude Gervaise, nouvellement imprimé à Paris par la vefve de Pierre Attaingnant, / demourant en la Rue de la Harpe, pres leglise sainct Cosme. / [Table of contents] / 1555. / Avec privilege du Roy, pour neuf ans.

32 fols. Mensural notation. Fol. $A1^v$ = fol. 1^v. Colophon on fol. 32^v: "FIN DU SIXIEME LIVRE de danceries, nouvellement imprimé à Paris le ii. jour d'Octobre, 1555. Avec privilege du Roy, pour neuf ans." The compositions identified by the superior letter *a* ([a]) are reprinted in MMRF XXIII, which includes a facsimile of the title page. For further concordances see HeartzSF, p. 343. For other volumes in the same series, see 1547_6, note 2. All of the compositions are for instrumental ensemble *a 4*, except no. 3, which is *a 5*.

Copy in: F:Pn.

	fol.	
1	1^v	*Pavanne passemaize*[a][1]
	1^v	*Gaillarde*[a]
2	2^v	*Pavanne des dieux*[2] (manuscript addition: "qui est fort bonne pour les violons")
	2^v	*Gaillarde*
3	3^v	*Pavanne d'Angleterre*[a][3] *a 5* = 1555_2, no. 28
	3^v	*Gaillarde*[3] *a 5*
4	4^v	*II. Gaillarde*
5	4^v	*III. Gaillarde*
6	4^v	*IIII. Gaillarde*
7	5^v	*V. Gaillarde*
8	5^v	*VI. Gaillarde*
9	6^v	*Fin de Gaillarde*
10	7^v	*Bransle simple I*[a]
11	8^v	*Bransle simple II*[a][4] = 1557_3, no. 11
12	9^v	*Bransle de Champaigne I* = 1547_6, no. 26
13	9^v	*Bransle de Champaigne II* = 1547_6, no. 27
14	10^v	*Bransle de Champaigne III* = 1547_6, no. 44
15	10^v	*Bransle de Champaigne IIII* = 1547_6, no. 43
16	11^v	*Bransle de Champaigne V*
17	11^v	*Bransle de Champaigne VI* = $154?_6$, no. 39: "Branle de bourgoigne"
18	12^v	*Bransle de Champaigne VII*
19	12^v	*Bransle de Champaigne VIII*
20	13^v	*Bransle de Champaigne IX*
21	13^v	*Bransle de Champaigne X*
22	14^v	*Bransle de Champaigne XI*
23	14^v	*Bransle de Champaigne XII*
24	15^v	*Bransle courant I*[a][5]
25	16^v	*Bransle courant II*[a][5]
26	17^v	*Bransle gay I*
27	18^v	*Bransle gay II*
28	18^v	*Bransle gay III*
29	19^v	*Bransle simple I*
30	20^v	*Bransle simple II*
31	21^v	*Bransle simple III*
32	21^v	*Bransle simple IIII*
33	22^v	*Bransle gay I*[a] = 1550_6, no. 4
34	23^v	*Bransle gay II*[a]
35	24^v	*Bransle de Champaigne I*[a]
36	24^v	*Bransle de Champaigne II*[a]
37	25^v	*Bransle de Champaigne III*[a][6]
38	25^v	*Bransle de Champaigne IIII*[a]
39	26^v	*Bransle de Champaigne V*
40	26^v	*Bransle de Champaigne VI*
41	27^v	*Bransle de Champaigne VII*
42	27^v	*Bransle de Champaigne VIII*[7]
43	28^v	*Bransle de Champaigne IX*[a]
44	28^v	*Bransle de Champaigne X*[a][8]
45	29^v	*Bransle de Champaigne XI*[a]
46	29^v	*Bransle de Champaigne XII*[a]
47	30^v	*Bransle gay I* (compare 1556_8, no. 14: "A mes peines & ennuiz")
48	30^v	*Bransle gay II*
49	31^v	*Bransle gay III* (compare 1552_3, no. 31: "Autre bransle de Poictou grand bonnet large")
50	31^v	*Bransle gay IIII*

[1] Mod. ed. in BarthaZ, no. 50a; MFH IX, 5; and ZfSM XI, no. 2.

[2] Facs. of fol. 2^v in EF III, 401.

[3] Mod. ed. in EC, pt. I, vol. III, p. 1206, and HAM, no. 137b.

[4] Mod. ed. in TwittT I, no. 5.

[5] Mod. ed. in BS, vol. 51.

[6] Mod. ed. in ZfSM XI, no. 7.

[7] Mod. ed. in ZfSM XI, no. 8.

[8] Mod. ed. in ZfSM XI, no. 10.

1556_1

BELIN, JULIEN

PREMIER LIVRE CONTE/NANT PLUSIEURS MOTETZ, CHANSONS, / & Fantasies: reduictz en Tabulature de Leut, par / Maistre Julien Belin. / Nouvellement Imprimé a Paris, le 18. Jour de Juing. / 1556. / [Printer's mark] / De l'imprimerie de Nicolas du Chemin, à l'enseigne du Gryphon / d'argent, rue S. Jean de Latran. / Avec privilege du Roy, pour dix ans.

24 fols. French lute tablature. On fol. A1ᵛ: excerpt from the royal privilege granting Du Chemin permission for ten years to publish music, signed "Donné à Fontainebell'eaue le treziesme jour de Mars, Mil cinq cens cinquante quatre. Par le Roy. M. Martin fumée, maistre des requestes ordinaire de l'hostel present. Signé de la Ruë: et séele du grand seau, en Cire jaulne, en simple queuë." The same excerpt was printed in 1559_1, 1559_2, 1559_3, and 1564_2. The dedication on fol. A2, headed "A Monseigneur, Monsieur Rene de Saint Françoys, grand Archydiacre du Mans," is reprinted in LesDC, p. 283. On fol. F4: table of contents. All of the compositions are for solo lute.

Copy in: D:Mbs.

	fol.	
1	A2ᵛ	*Fantasie*[1]
2	A3ᵛ	*Cantate Domino*
3	A4ᵛ	*Qui souhaittez* Gentian (RISM 1549_{20}, no. 1: Sandrin)
4	B3	*Fantasie* = 1574_7, no. 8
5	B4	*De mes ennuys* Archadelt (RISM 1561_3, fol. 3)
6	C2ᵛ	*D'amour me plains* Rogier [Pathie] (PubAPTM XXIII, no. 49)
7	D1	*Fantasie* = 1547_7, no. 9
8	D2	*En vous voyant* Rogier [Pathie] (RISM 1538_{17}, no. 11)
9	D3ᵛ	*Fantasie* = 1574_7, no. 10
10	D4ᵛ	*Trio*
11	E1	*Trio*[2]
12	E2	*Fantasie*
13	E3	*Les Bourguignons*
14	E3ᵛ	*Elle voyant* Certon (LesLRB, art. 17, fol. 14)
15	F1ᵛ	*Voulant honneur* Sandrin (RISM 1545_{12}, no. 8)

[1] Mod. ed. in NeemAM II, no. 5.
[2] Mod. ed. in NeemAM II, no. 6.

1556_2

DRUSINA, BENEDIKT DE

TABULATURA / CONTINENS INSIGNES ET / SELECTISSIMAS QUASDAM FANTASIAS: / cantiones Germanicas, Italicas, ac Gallicas: Passemezo: / Choreas: & Mutetas, Iam primum in / lucem aeditas / PER BENEDICTUM DE DRU/SINA ELBINGENSEM. / Quarum ordinem ac numerum sequens / pagina indicabit. / 15 [Printer's mark] 56. / FRANCOFORTI AD VIADRUM IN OFFICINA / JOAN. EICHORN.

56 fols. German lute tablature. On fol. a1ᵛ: table of contents. Dedication on fols. a2–a3, headed "INCLYTO ET ILLUSTRISS. PRINCIPI ERICO GUSTAVI ELECTO REGI SUECORUM GOTTHORUM ET VANDALORUM. S. D.," and signed "Francoforti, cis Viadrum pridie Calend. April. Anno 1556. Maiest. T. Addictiss. Benedictus de Drusina Elbingensis," followed by a Latin poem headed "Epigramma," and signed "C. Pannon." KosackL, p. 100, contains a thematic index of the entire volume. GrimmM, pp. 95–97, describes the volume and lists the contents. All of the compositions are for solo lute.

Copy in: D:LEm.[1]

	fol.	
1	a3ᵛ	*Fantasia 1*
2	a4	*Fantasia 2*
3	b1	*Fantasia 3*
4	b2ᵛ	*Fantas. 4*
5	b3ᵛ	*Ich rew und klag* (EDMR XX, no. 121: Jörg Brack)
6	b4ᵛ	*So wunsch ich ihr* (DTO XXXVII/72, p. 74: Stoltzer)
7	c1ᵛ	*Wer wolt ihr in ehren nicht sein holt* H. Hofman

TABVLATVRA

CONTINENS INSIGNES ET
SELECTISSIMAS QVASDAM FANTASIAS:
cantiones Germanicas, Italicas, ac Gallicas: Passemezo:
Choreas: & Mutetas, Iam primum in
lucem æditas.

PER BENEDICTVM DE DRV-
SINA ELBINGENSEM.

Quarum ordinem ac numerum sequens
pagina indicabit.

1 5  5 6.

FRANCOFORTI AD VIADRVM IN OFFICINA
IOAN. EICHORN.

Title page of 1556_2

8 c2^{v} *Le content* [*est riche*] (AttainCK III, no. 9: Sermisy) = 1573_3, no. 9

9 c3^{v} *Adiu mes amours* (HewO, no. 14: Josquin)

10 d1 *O sio potessi donna* (RISM 1541_9, p. 19: Berchem)

11 d2^{v} *Je prens en gre* ClemensO X, 14: Clemens non Papa)

12 d4^{v} *Deul deuble deul* (CW XV, no. 1: Lupi)

13 e1^{v} *Damour me plains*[2] (PubAPTM XXIII, no. 49: Pathie)

14 e3^{v} *Madonna ardo per voi* (RISM 1537_9, no. 4: Verdelot)

15 e4^{v} *Je cherche autant amour* (RISM 1545_{12}, no. 2: Boyvin)

16 f1 *De vostre amours*

17 f2^{v} *Reviens vers moy* (PubAPTM XXIII, no. 35: Lupi)

18 f3^{v} *Se dire laso*

19 f4^{v} *Fille qui prend* [*facieux mary*] = 1563_{12}, no. 82

20 g1^{v} *Quando io pens'al martire Ex Gallico transl: V*[*alentin*] *B*[*akfark*] = 1553_1, no. 18: Arcadelt

21 g3^{v} *Quanto o Madonna*

22 g4^{v} *Fraus & galliard* (ClemensO X, 17: "Frisque et gaillard," Clemens non Papa)

23 h2 *Doulce memoire, en plaisir* (PubAPTM XXIII, no. 50: Sandrin)

24 h3 *Passe, mezo 1*[3] = 1591_{13}, no. 85a: "Passemezo anticho"

h4^{v} *Saltarello* = 1591_{13}, no. 85b

25 i1^{v} *Passe, mezo 2* = 1591_{13}, no. 87a: "Passemezo anticho"

i2^{v} *Saltarello* = 1591_{13}, no. 87b

26 i3^{v} *Passe, mezo 3* = 1591_{13}, no. 86a: "Passemezo anticho"

i4^{v} *Saltarello* = 1591_{13}, no. 86b

27 k1^{v} *Passe, mezo 4* = 1591_{13}, no. 88a: "Passemezo anticho"

k2^{v} *Saltarello* = 1591_{13}, no. 88b

28 k3 *Bel Fiore*

29 k3v *Non dite mai*
30 k4v *La rocha el fuso*
31 l1v *Tantz*[4]
l1v *Sprunck*
32 l2 *Tantz*
l2 *Sprunck*
33 l2v *Tantz*[5]
l3 *Sprunck*
34 l3v *Tantz*
l4 *Sprunck*
35 l4v *Tristitia [vestra]*[6] (RISM 1541_2, no. 24: Isaac) = 1568_7, no. 110
36 m1v *Per illud ave a2* (JosqMT, no. 46: 2a pars of "Benedicta es coelorum regina," Josquin)
37 m2v *Domine Miserere a4* H[ans] W[ilde]
38 m4v *Pater peccavi a4* (ClemensO IX, no. 1: Clemens non Papa)
n1v 2a pars *Quanti mercenarii*
39 n3 *Dilexi quoniam a4* (I:BGid, MS 1209, no. 51: Hieronim[o] Maff[onio])
o1 2a pars [*O domine libera animam meam*]
40 o2v *Dum complerentur a5* (RISM 1538_2, fol. 23: Arcadelt)

[1] A copy was in D:Bhm.
[2] Mod. ed. in KosackL, pp. 122–137 (with vocal model).
[3] Heading on fol. h3: "Sequuntur Passe.Mezo aliquot et Choreae Italicae."
[4] Heading on fol. l1: "Sequuntur Choreae Germanicae."
[5] Mod. ed. of the "Tantz" (without the "Sprunck") in TapS, p. 31, headed "Chorea Germanica."
[6] Heading on fol. 14v: "Sequuntur Mutetae Quatuor et Quinque Vocum."

1556_3

FRANCESCO DA MILANO

INTABOLATURA / DE LAUTO / DI FRANCESCO DA MILANO / NOVAMENTE RISTAMPATA / LIBRO PRIMO / [Printer's mark] / In Venetia apresso di / Antonio Gardano / 1556

20 fols. Italian lute tablature. On fol. E4v: table of contents. Contents = 1546_6 and 1563_4 (which has some additions). All of the compositions are for solo lute.

Copy in: F:Pthibault.[1]

[1] This copy was in the Écorcheville library (see ÉcorC, no. 246).

$[1556]_4$

GERVAISE, CLAUDE

Premier livre de violle contenant dix chansons avec l'introduction de l'accorder et apliquer les doigts selon la maniere qu'on a accoutumé de jouer, le tout de la composition de Claude Gervaise, Paris, 14. Febr. 1555, Veuve Attaingnant.

This volume, now lost, is listed in the manuscript catalogue of Sébastien de Brossard, which is now in F:Pn (see MGG, IV, col. 1846). The *Second livre*, 1547, listed there probably refers to 1547_6.

1556_5

HECKEL, WOLFF

Discant/Lautten Buch, von mancherley / schönen und lieblichen stucken, mit zweyen Lautten / zusamen zuschlagen, und auch sonst das mehrer theyl / allein für sich selbst. Gute Teutsche, Lateinische, Frantzösische, Itallianische Stuck oder lieder. Auch / vilfaltige Newe Tentz, sampt mancherley Fantaseyen, / Recercari, Pavana, Saltarelli, Unnd Gassenhawer, / etc. Durch Wolffen Heckel von München, Bur/ger zu Strassburg Auff das aller lieblichst in / ein verstendige Tabulatur nach geschribner art / aussgesetzt und zusamengebracht, welisches vor nie also ge/sehen worden. / Getruckt zu Strassburg durch Urban / Wyss Rechenmeister. Im Jar M. D. L. VI.

120 fols. German lute tablature. This volume and its companion ($[1556]_6$) are discussed in DieL. The title is taken from RaL, p. 289.[1] Contents = 1562_3. The first 40 compositions are for two lutes; the remaining 40 compositions are for solo lute.

Copy in: F:Pthibault.[2]

[1] The title as given in DTO XIV/28, p. 178, is slightly different.
[2] A copy was in D:Bds.

[1556]6

HECKEL, WOLFF

Tenor/Lautten Buch, von mancherley / / schönen und lieblichen stucken, mit zweyen Lautten / zusamen zuschlagen, und auch sonst das mehrer theyl / allein für sich selbst. Gute Teutsche, Lateinische, Frantzösische, Itallianische Stuck oder lieder. Auch / vilfaltige Newe Tentz, sampt mancherley Fantaseyen, / Recercari, Pavana, Saltarelli, Unnd Gassenhawer, / etc. Durch Wolffen Heckel von München, Bur/ger zu Strassburg Auff das aller lieblichst in / ein verstendige Tabulatur nach geschribner art / aussgesetzt und zusamengebracht, welisches vor nie also ge/sehen worden. / Getruckt zu Strassburg durch Urban / Wyss Rechenmeister. Im Jar M. D. L. VI.

This volume, now lost, was in D:Hs. It and its companion (1556_5) are discussed in DieL. The title is taken from RaL, p. 289.[1] Contents = 1562_4. It was in German lute tablature. The first 40 compositions were for two lutes; the remaining 38 compositions were for solo lute.

[1] The title as given in DTO XIV/28, p. 178, is slightly different.

1556_7

JAMBE DE FER, PHILIBERT

EPITOME MUSICAL / DES TONS, SONS / ET ACCORDZ, ES VOIX / HUMAINES, FLEUSTES / d'Alleman, Fleustes a neuf trous, / Violes, & Violons. / ITEM. / Un petit devis des accordz de Musique; par forme de dialogue interro/gatoire & responsif entre deux interlocuteurs. P. & I. / A LYON, Par Michel du Bois. M. D. LVI. / Avec privilege du Roy.

35 fols., plus several oversize tables inserted at the end. Colophon on p. 70: "Imprime a Lyon. Par Michel du Boys. M. D. LVI." On p. 2: excerpt from the royal privilege granting Michel du Bois permission to print and sell this volume for six years beginning April 28, 1556, signed, "Donné à Blois le troisiesme jour de Fevrier. 1555. avant Pasques. Par le Roy maistre Geoffroy de haute clerc: maistre des requestes ordinaire de l'hostel present. De la Rue." Dedication on pp. 3–6, headed "A vertueux et honorables Jehan Darud marchant es franchises de Lyon, [par] Philibert Jambe de fer," and dated "De Lyon ce 10[e], Apuril, 1556."

Jambe de Fer's instruction book contains six sections: (1) beginning on p. 7, an exposition of the elements of music; (2) beginning on p. 47, instructions for playing the transverse flute ("fleuste d'alleman"); (3) beginning on p. 53, instructions for playing the recorder ("fleuste a neuf trous appellée par les Italiens Flauto"); (4) beginning on p. 56, instructions for playing the viola da gamba; (5) beginning on p. 61, instructions for playing the violin; and (6) beginning on p. 65, a dialogue on the intervals ("accordz") of music.[1] Inserted at the end are several tables. Only the first three tables survive in the unique copy: (1) cut of a viola da gamba with its fingering (incomplete in unique copy); (2) fingering chart for the transverse flute; and (3) fingering chart for the recorder. LesE is a facsimile of the complete volume.

Copy in: F:Pc (some tables missing).

[1] Facs. of a page in EF II, 597; GreuB, p. 28, and MGG VI, col. 1676.

1556_8

LE ROY, ADRIAN

SECOND LIVRE DE GUI/TERRE, CONTENANT PLUSIEURS CHANSONS EN / forme de voix de ville: nouvellement remises en tabulature, / par Adrian le Roy. / [Table of contents] / A PARIS. / De l'imprimerie, d'Adrian le Roy, & Robert Balard, Imprimeurs du Roy, rue / saint Jean de Beauvais, à l'enseigne sainte Genevieve. / 5. Janvier. / 1555. / Avec privilege du Roy, pour neuf ans.

24 fols. Superius in mensural notation; accompaniment in French guitar tablature. On fol. 24[v]: the same excerpt from the printer's privilege as in 1551_2. All of the compositions except nos. 9, 16, and 20 are based on those by Adrian le Roy in LesLRB,

art. 171. The categories ("Chanson a plaisir," "Pavanne," and so on) are taken from the running heads. For some concordances see HeartzSF, p. 394. For other volumes in the same series, see 1551_3, note 1. All of the compositions are for solo voice and guitar.

Copies in: F:Pm, GB:Lbm

fol.

1 1ᵛ *Laissez la verte couleur* Chanson a plaisir = 1570_4, no. 42

2 2ᵛ *J'ay le rebours* Pavanne = 1570_4, no. 14

3 3ᵛ *Puisque vivre en servitude* Gaillarde

4 4ᵛ *Pour m'eslongner* Chanson a plaisir = 1570_4, no. 36

5 *Autrement*

5 5ᵛ *O combien est heureuse* Branle gay

6 6ᵛ *Je ne suis moins aimable* Branle gay

7 7ᵛ *Mes pas semez* Chanson a plaisir = 1570_4, no. 37

8 8ᵛ *Quand j'entens le perdu temps* Branle gay

9 *Autrement*

9 9ᵛ *Je ne veux plus à mon mal consentir* Trio (compare Les LRB, art. 3, no. 13: Certon) = 1570_4, no. 15

10 10ᵛ *Plus ne veux estre à la suite* Branle gay = 1570_4, no. 38

11 *Autrement*

11 11ᵛ *L'ennuy qui me tourmente* Gaillarde = 1570_4, no. 75

12 12ᵛ *C'est de la peine dure* Branle gay

13 13ᵛ *Helas mon dieu y ha il en ce monde* Branle gay

14 *Autrement*

14 14ᵛ *A mes peines & ennuiz* Branle gay

15 15ᵛ *Puis que nouvelle affection* Gaillarde

16 16ᵛ *J'ay cherché la science* Chanson a plaisir (compare LesLRB, art. 3, no. 4: Certon) = 1570_4, no. 16

17 17ᵛ *Vous estes la personne* Chanson a plaisir = 1570_4, no. 17

18 18ᵛ *Une m'avoit promis* Paduane (compare LesLRB, art. 3, no. 6: Certon)

19 *Autrement*

19 19ᵛ *O la mal assignée* Gaillarde

20 20ᵛ *Oyez tous amoureux* Chanson a plaisir (compare RISM 1554_{26}, no. 9: Mithou) = 1570_4, no. 39

21 21ᵛ *Maintenant c'est un cas estrange* Branle gay

22 *Autrement*

22 22ᵛ *O ma dame per-je mon temps* Bransle de Poitou

23 23ᵛ *Mon dieu vostre pitié* Chanson a plaisir = 1570_4 no. 40

24 *Autrement*

1556_9

PADOVANO, ANNIBALE

DI ANNIBALE / PADOVANO, ORGANISTA / Della Illustrissima .S. di Venetia in San Marco, Il Primo / Libro de Ricercari a quattro voci, Nuovamente da / lui composti, & dati in luce. / A QUATTRO [Printer's mark] VOCI / In Venetia apresso di / Antonio Gardano / 1556[1]

Four part books in mensural notation (S, 14 fols.; A, 15 fols.; T, 13 fols.; B, 11 fols.). On fol. A1ᵛ of each part: dedication headed "Allo Illustre Cavalliero et Dignissimo Procurator di San Marco il Clarissimo M. Giovanni da Legge del Clar. M. Priamo Signor Mio Osservandissimo," reprinted in SartMS, p. 21. Fol. A2 = p. 1. On p. 28 of the altus part only: table of contents; on p. 29: printer's mark. Page numbers below refer to cantus part book. For a later edition see 1588_7. The entire collection is reprinted in PadovanoR (which includes facsimiles of the title page, fol. A1ᵛ, fol. A2 of the cantus part book, and p. 22 of the bass part book). All of the compositions are for instrumental ensemble *a 4* (or for organ).

Copy in: GB:Lcm. †

p.

1 1 *Ricercar del Terzo Tono* = 1591_4, no. 5

2 3 *Ricercar del Settimo Tono* (1584_5, no. 2)

3 5 *Ricercar del Sesto tono*
4 6 *Ricercar del Primo Tono* (compare LU, p. 25: "Kyrie cunctipotens") = 1591_4, no. 4
5 9 *Ricercar del secondo tono*
6 11 *Ricercar del Ottavo tono*
7 13 *Ricercar del Primo Tono* (compare PadovanoR, p. 18: "Salve Regina")
8 14 *Ricercar del Ottavo Tono* (1584_3, no. 42)
9 16 *Ricercar del Primo tono*
10 18 *Ricercar del Quinto Tono* (compare LU, p. 957: "Qui pacem")
11 20 *Ricercar del Terzo Tono* (1584_3, no. 41)
12 21 *Ricercar del Terzo tono*
13 24 *Ricercar del Sesto Tono*

[1] Facs. of title page in SartUD, p. 178. This entire volume is transcribed into keyboard partitura in B:Bc, MS 26661; for a discussion of this manuscript, see LowE, p. 134. The manuscript dedication (the same as that in 1556_9) is reproduced in LowE, pl. 6.

1556

DOUBTFUL WORKS

1. FétB VIII, 357, erroneously dates Francesco Vindella, *Intavolatura di liuto . . . Libro Primo*, 1556. The volume is listed in this bibliography as 1546_{17}.

$[1557]_1$

LE ROY, ADRIAN

Adrian le Roy. Instruction de partir toute musique des huits divers tons en tablature de luth. Paris, Adrian le Roy et Robert Ballard, 1557.

This volume, now lost, is mentioned in FétB V, 280. LesLRB, art. 130, gives reasons for supposing 1567 to be a more probable date (see $[1567]_3$). For later editions see $[1570]_2$ and $[1583]_3$. For English translations see 1568_3 and 1574_2.

1557_2

HENESTROSA, LUIS VENEGAS DE

LIBRO DE CIFRA NUEVA / PARA TECLA, HARPA, Y VIHUELA, EN EL / qual se enseña brevemente cantar canto llano, y canto de orga/no, y algunos avisos para contrapunto. / Compuesto por Luys Venegas de Henestrosa. Dirigido al / Illustrissimo señor don Diego Tavera, / obispo de Jaen. / [Cut with a bishop's hat and coat of arms] / En Alcala. / En casa de Joan de Brocar. / 1557.

78 fols. Spanish keyboard tablature (using ciphers; see ApelN, pp. 49–52). Dedication on fol. *1v headed "Al muy illustre y reverendissimo senor, el señor don Diego Tavera, obispo de Jaen." On fol. *2: a shield held by a figure representing Death; on the shield is a composition *a 3* with text beginning "Recuerde el alma dormida"; beneath the shield are several biblical verses in Latin (see the facsimile of fol. *2 and the modern edition of the piece in MME II, 151). On fol. *2v: two poems in Latin headed "In commendationem operis clarissimi viri Ludovici Henestrosa, Didaci Carrili presbiteri Complutensis Epigramma," and "Eiusdem." Fol. *3 = fol. 1.[1] On fols. *2v–10 (numbered 7, see note 1): introductory essay on the rudiments of music and on the tablature used in this volume. On fol. 74: the text of three villancicos, beginning "Por las mas altas montañas," "Tiembla de frio el calor," and "El abismo del peccado." On fols. 74v–75v: table of contents. On fol. 76: author's corrections followed by the colophon: "Fue impresso el presente libro de cifra nueva, en la muy noble y florentissima villa de Alcala de Henares, en casa de Joan de Brocar, que sancta gloria aya. Año mil y quinientos y cinquenta y siete." On fol. 76v: printer's mark with the initials "J. B." MME II is a modern edition of the entire collection, including facsimiles of the title page and fols. *2 and 20v. The compositions identified by superior letters are reprinted as follows: (a) in FroideA I; (b) in OL XXX; (c) in PedH III; (d) in PedH VIII; (e) in PedAO I; (f) in JacobsTN, pp. 101–109. The compositions followed by an asterisk are supplied with complete text. Information in brackets

is from the table of contents. For further information about concordances with other volumes see WardVH. For further information on Henestrosa see MollM. All of the compositions are for solo keyboard, except no. 111, which is for two keyboards.

Copies in: E:Mn (two copies).

	fol.	
1	9[1]	*Pange lingua* Antonio [de Cabezón?] (see MME II, 169)
2	9	*Sacris solemnis*
3	9v	*Primer tres*
4	9v	[*Tres II*]
5	10	[*Tres III*] *sobre el canto llano de la alta* Antonio (compare 148?$_1$, no. 10: "La Spagna")
6	11	[*Fabordon llano.*] *Primus tonus*[a 2]
7	11	[*Fabordon llano.*] *Secundus tonus*
8	11	[*Fabordon llano.*] *Tertius tonus*[a]
9	11	[*Fabordon llano.*] *Quartus tonus*
10	11	[*Fabordon llano.*] *Quintus tonus*[a]
11	11	[*Fabordon llano.*] *Sextus tonus*
12	11v	[*Fabordon llano.*] *Septimus tonus*[a]
13	11v	[*Fabordon llano.*] *Octavus tonus*[a]
14	11v	[*Fabordon llano.*] *Septimus tonus*[a]
15	11v	[*Fabordon llano.*] *Primero tono de Gombert*
16	11v	[*Tiento.*] *Primer tono*[bc] Antonio
17	12v	*Dixit dominus.* [*Fabordon glosado.*] *Primus tonus*
18	12v	*Dixit dominus.* [*Fabordon glosado.*] *Secundus tonus*
19	12v	[*Fabordon glosado.*] *Tertius tonus*
20	13	[*Fabordon glosado.*] *Quartus tonus*
21	13	[*Fabordon glosado.*] *Quintus tonus*
22	13	[*Fabordon glosado.*] *Sextus tonus*
23	13	[*Fabordon glosado.*] *Septimus tonus*
24	13v	*Dixit dominus.* [*Fabordon glosado.*] *Octavus tonus*
25	13v	[*Fabordon glosado.*] *Otro octavo*
26	13v	[*Tiento*][bd] Antonio
27	14	*Tiento de vihuela* (compare 1547_2, no. 9)
28	15[1]	*Dic nobis Maria.* [*Fabordon glosado*][bd 3] Antonio
29	15[1]	*Tiento*[bd 4] Antonio
30	15v[1]	[*Tiento*][d 5] [Antonio]
31	18v	*Tiento*[bd 6] [Antonio]
32	19v	*Sesto tiento*[e 7] [Antonio]
33	20	*Septimo tiento* Antonio
34	20v	*Tiento. Primer tono*[8] Antonio
35	21v	[*Tiento.*] *Primer tono* [Antonio]
36	22	[*Tiento. Primer tono* Antonio]
37	22v	[*Tiento. Primer tono* Antonio]
38	23	*Otro tiento* [Vila]
39	23v	*Otro tiento.* [*Primero tono*] [Vila]
40	24	[*Tiento. Primer tono* Antonio]
41	25	[*Tiento.*] *Segundo tono*
42	25	[*Tiento.*] *Tercero tono*
43	26	[*Tiento.*] *Quarto tono sobre Malheur me bat* [Antonio] (compare HewO, no. 63: Ockeghem?) (see WardP, p. 215)
44	26v	[*Tiento.*] *Quarto tono*
45	27v	[*Tiento.*] *Quarto tono* [Julius de Modena] = Giulio Segni (1540_3, no. 12, and 154?$_6$, no. 14)
46	28	*Otro* [*tiento.*] *Quarto tono* [Julius de Modena] (1540_3, no. 11, and 154?$_6$, no. 3)
47	28v	[*Tiento.*] *Quinto tono*
48	29	[*Verso de Morales del quinto tono glosado de Palero*][c]
49	29v	[*Tiento.*] *Sesto tono*[e 9]
50	30	[*Tiento.*] *Sesto tono*[e 10] [Francisco de] Soto
51	31	[*Tiento.*] *Sesto tono* [Antonio]
52	31v	*Otro* [*tiento.*] *Sesto tono* [Antonio] (1540_3, no. 13: Julio da Modena; 154?$_6$, no. 15: Julio da Modena; and 154?$_6$, no. 18: Adrian Willaert)
53	32	[*Tiento*] *super Philomena. Septimo tono* [Francisco Fernandez Palero] (compare LesLRB, art. 18, fol. 4: Richafort)
54	33	[*Tiento.*] *Septimo tono sobre cum sancto Spiritu, de Jusquin, de beata virgine* [glosado de Palero] (compare JosqMS, no. 16)
55	33v	[*Tiento.*] *Octavo tono*[ef] [Palero]
56	34	[*Fantesia de vihuela.*] *Primer tono* (compare 1538_1, no. 1, and 1546_{14}, no. 23)
57	34v	[*Fantasia de vihuela.*] *Segundo tono* (compare 1546_{14}, nos. 27 and 28)
58	35	*Otra fantesia* [*de vihuela.*] *Segundo tono, sobre fa mi ut re* (compare 1546_{14}, no. 29)

59 35^v *Primera fantesia* [*de vihuela.*] *Tercero tono* (compare 1546_{14}, no. 31)

60 36 *Segunda fantesia* [*de vihuela.*] *Tercero tono* (compare 1546_{14}, nos. 30 and 32: "Glosa sobre un Kyrie . . . de Josquin que va sobre Pange Lingua")

61 36^v *Primera fantesia* [*de vihuela.*] *Quarto tono* (compare 1546_{14}, no. 34)

62 37 *Segunda fantesia* [*de vihuela.*] *Quarto tono* (compare 1538_1, no. 4, and 1546_{14}, no. 33)

63 37 *Tercera fantesia* [*de vihuela.*] *Quarto tono* (compare 1547_5, no. 120)

64 37^v *Primera fantesia* [*de vihuela.*] *Quinto tono* (compare 1546_{14}, no. 38)

65 38 *Segunda fantesia* [*de vihuela.*] *Quinto tono* (compare 1546_{14}, no. 37 and no. 36)

66 39 *Tercera fantesia* [*de vihuela.*] *Fantesia de consonancia, del quinto tono* (compare 1538_1, no. 5)

67 39^v *Primera fantesia* [*de vihuela.*] *Sesto tono* (compare 1538_1, no. 6)

68 40 *Segunda fantesia* [*de vihuela.*] *Sesto tono* (compare 1546_{14}, nos. 40 and 39)

69 40^v *Primera fantesia* [*de vihuela.*] *Septimo tono, sobre ut re mi fa mi* (compare 1538_1, no. 7)

70 41^v *Segunda fantesia* [*de vihuela.*] *Septimo tono* (compare 1546_{14}, no. 43 and 42)

71 42 *Primera fantesia* [*de vihuela.*] *Octavo tono* (compare 1546_{14}, no. 47)

72 42^v *Segunda fantesia* [*de vihuela.*] *Octavo tono* (compare 1546_{14}, nos. 46 and 45)

73 43 *Tercera fantesia* [*de vihuela.*] *Octavo tono* (compare 1546_{14}, no. 48)

74 43^v *Fabordon de vihuela. Septimo tono* = 1546_{14}, no. 74: "Nisi Dominus" (Venegas omits the voice part)

75 43^v [*Fabordon de vihuela.*] *In exitu Israel de Egipto* = 1552_7, no. 32: "Dixit dominus domino"

76 43^v *Pange lingua* [*I*] [Antonio]

77 44 *Pange lingua* [*II*] [Antonio]

78 44^v *Pange lingua* [*III*][c] [Antonio] = 1578_3, no. 15

79 45 *Pange lingua* [*IV*] [Antonio]

80 45^v *Pange lingua* [*V*] *de Urreda glosado de Antonio*[11]

81 46^v *Ave maristella* [*I*][f] [Antonio] (three *diferencias*)

82 46^v *Ave maristella* [*II*][f] [Antonio]

83 47 *Ave maristella* [*III*] [Antonio]

84 47^v *Ave maristella* [*IV*] [Antonio]

85 48 *Ave maristella* [*V*][bc] [Antonio] = 1578_3, no. 36

86 49 [*Ave maristella VI*] [Antonio]

87 49 *Ave maristella* [*VII*] Palero

88 49^v *O gloriosa*

89 50 *O lux beata trinitas* [Antonio]

90 50 *Jesu Christo hombre y Dios**[d 12]

91 50 *Veni redemptor quaesumus* [Palero]

92 50^v *Sacris solemniis** Para la fiesta del sanctissimo virgen Joseph [Morales]

93 51 *Cum invocarem**[13] Para las completas de quaresma

94 51 *Non accedet ad te malum** [Luys Alberto]

95 51^v *In pace in idipsum** [Alberto]

96 52 *Te lucis ante terminum*[bd] Antonio

97 52^v *Secundum verbum tuum**[bde] (in table of contents as "Nunc dimittis servum tuum")

98 52^v *Salve regina**[bd 14] Antonio

99 53^v *O gloriosa domina**

100 54 *Primer Kyrie de Jusquin glosado* [*de Palero*] (compare JosqMS, no. 16: *Missa de Beata Virgine*, and no. 101 below)

101 54^v *Tercer Kyrie* (compare no. 100 above)

102 55 *Quem terra pontus* [Antonio]

103 55^v *Pues no me quereys hablar* [Antonio]

104 55^v *Mira Nero* [*de Tarpeya*] [Palero]

105 56 *Passeavase el rey moro* [Palero]

106 56 [*Un tres glosado*] [Luys Alberto]

107 56^v *Conditor alme* [Gracia Baptista, monja]

108 56^v *Final* Antonio

109 56^v [*Final*] [Antonio]

110	56^{v}	*Sacris solemnis* Antonio
111	57^{v}	*Belle sans pere* [Crecquillon; "A doze para dos instrumentos] [two keyboards]
112	59^{v}	*Unum colle deum ne iures vana per eum* Fuga a quarenta
113	60^{v}	*Miralo como llora** [Chansoneta]
114	60^{v}	*Aspice Domine** [Jaquet, glosado de Palero] (MonteO XXVI, app., p. 1)
115	62^{v}	*Si bona suscepimus** [Verdelot, glosado de Palero] (MoralesO I, 274: Verdelot)
116	64	*Queramus a quatro glosado* [Mouton, glosado de Palero] (RISM 1529$_{1}$, fol. 9^{v}: "Queramus cum pastoribus")
	64^{v}	[2a pars *Ubi pascas ubi cubes*]
117	65^{v}	*Conde Claros* (five *diferencias*)
118	65^{v}	*Las vacas*[f] ["Guardame las vacas"] (five *diferencias*)
119	66^{v}	*Para quien crie yo cabellos* Antonio
120	67	*Rugier Glosado De Antonio* [15]
121	67	*Pavana* [Antonio]
122	67^{v}	*De la virgen que pario**[d] [16]
123	68	*Revellebu* ("Primera Parte De la Cancion de los pajaritos"; compare MMRF VII, 1: "Le Chant des Oyseaux," beginning "Reveillez vous, cueurs endormis," Janequin)
124	68	*Alix* [*avoit aux dens*] (RISM 1545$_{16}$, fol. 12^{v}: Crecquillon)
125	68^{v}	*Jeprens Engrei* (ClemensO X, 14: "Je prens en gre," Clemens non Papa)
126	69	*Un gai bergier* (RieH II, 462: Crecquillon)
127	69^{v}	*Ade mi mort* (ClemensO X, 32: "A demy mort," Clemens non Papa)
128	70	*Demandes vous* (RISM 1543$_{16}$, fol. 3: Crecquillon)
129	70^{v}	*Io vous*
130	71	*Pour un Plaiser* (ParrishM, no. 20: Crecquillon)
131	71^{v}	*Frasqui gallard* (ClemensO X, 17: "Frisque et gaillard," Clemens non Papa)
132	72	[*Mort ma prive*] [glosado por Palero]
133	73^{v}	*Mundo que me puedes dar**
134	73^{v}	*Primera entrada* [17]
135	73^{v}	*Segunda* [*entrada*] [17]
136	73^{v}	*Tercera* [*entrada*] [17]
137	73^{v}	*Al rebuelo de una garça** [Villancico]
138	74	*Te matrem Dei laudamus**

[1] The foliation at the beginning of the volume contains a number of errors. The printer began numbering at the third folio, but there are many duplications and omissions to fol. 18. To avoid confusion the numbers given in the inventory are those actually printed in the original. The following list should make the relation between correct number and actual number clear:

Correct fol. nos.	Nos. pr. in vol.
*1	
*2	
1	1
2	2
3	3
4	4
5	2
6	3
7	[4]
8	4
9	6
10	7
11	9
12	10
13	11
14	12
15	13
16	14
17	13 (called 15 in the inventory; see nos. 28–30)
18	18

Occasional errors later in the volume have been corrected without comment.

[2] Heading on fol. 11: "Siguense ocho favordones llanos y glosados."

[3] Mod. ed. in MusetS, p. 1.

[4] Mod. ed. in CabezonF, no. 2.

[5] Mod. ed. in PedOL, no. 2, and TagA I, no. 22.

[6] Mod. ed. in CabezonF, no. 3.

[7] Mod. ed. in MusetS, p. 12 (attributed to Vila). PedAO also attributes it to Vila.

[8] Facs. of. fol. 20^{v} in AngME, pl. 29, and MGG II, col. 599.

[9] PedAO attributes this to Pedro de Soto.

[10] Mod. ed. in MusetS, p. 3.

[11] GerbH, p. 182, gives the incipit of the vocal model by Urrede after a manuscript in Taragona. The entire vocal model is pr. in GerbS, p. 17. See also AngPL.

[12] Mod. ed. in RubioP I, 17 (written *a 4*).

[13] This work is attributed to Verdelot in 1547$_{5}$, no. 56.

[14] Mod. ed. in OLI XXI, 15.

[15] Another version is in 1547$_{5}$, no. 42, with the text "Rugier qual sempre fui tal" (see Ariosto, *Orlando Furioso* XLIV, 61; and also EinAR).

[16] Mod. ed. in BonnA VI (attributed to Cabezon), and RubioP I, 11 (written *a 4*).

[17] Mod. ed. in PedOL, p. 8.

1557_3

GERVAISE, CLAUDE

TROISIEME LIVRE DE DANCERIES / A QUATRE ET CINQ PARTIES, VEU PAR CLAUDE / Gervaise (le tout en un volume) nouvellement imprimé à Paris par la vefve de Pierre / Attaingnant, demourant en la Rue de la Harpe, pres leglise S. Cosme. / [Table of contents] / 15. cal. Feb. 1556. / Avec privilege du Roy, pour neuf ans.

32 fols. Mensural notation. Fol. R1^v = fol. 1^v. The compositions identified by superior letters are reprinted as follows: ([a]) in MMRF XXIII, which includes a facsimile of the title page; ([b]) in MohrA, pt. II, p. 6. For some concordances see HeartzSF, p. 331. For other volumes in the same series, see 1547_6, note 2. All of the compositions are for instrumental ensemble *a 4*, except nos. 1 and 3, which are *a 5*.

Copy in: F:Pn.

fol.

1 1^v *Pavanne. Si je m'en vois a 5* (compare LesLRB, art. 3, fol. 9: "L'Ennuy qui me tourmente," Certon)

1^v *Gaillarde. Si je m'en vois a 5*

2 2^v *Pavanne. Est il conclud*

3^v *Gaillarde. Est il conclud*

3 4^v *Pavanne l'Admiral a 5*

4^v *Gaillarde a 5*

4 5^v *Pavanne de la guerre* (compare $154?_6$, no. 33)

7^v *Gaillarde [de la guerre]*

5 8^v *Gaillarde [du ton de la guerre]* = 1583_7, no. 12

6 8^v *Gaillarde [du ton de la guerre]*

7 9^v *Bransle simple I* = 1583_7, no. 50

8 10^v *Bransle simple II* = 1547_6, no. 11, and 1583_7, no. 51

9 10^v *Bransle simple III* (compare 1551_3, no. 12: "Branle simple. N'aurez vous point de moy pitié") = 1583_7, no. 52

10 11^v *Bransle simple IIII* = 1583_7, no. 53

11 12^v *Bransle simple V*[1] = 1555_5, no. 11, and 1583_7, no. 54

12 12^v *Bransle simple VI*[2] (compare 1547_6, no. 41) = 1583_7, no. 55

13 13^v *Bransle gay I* = 1583_7, no. 56

14 13^v *Bransle gay II* = 1583_7, no. 57

15 14^v *Bransle gay III* = 1583_7, no. 58

16 14^v *Bransle gay IIII* = 1583_7, no. 59

17 15^v *Bransle gay V* = 1583_7, no. 60

18 15^v *Bransle gay VI* (compare 1551_2, no. 19: "Branle gay la ceinture que je porte") = 1583_7, no. 61

19 16^v *Almande I*[a 3] (compare 1552_3, no. 17: ["Almande Loreyne"])

20 17^v *Almande II*[a 4]

21 18^v *Almande III*[a]

22 18^v *Almande IIII*[a 4]

23 19^v *Almande V*[b]

24 19^v *Almande VI*[b]

25 20^v *Almande VII*[b]

26 20^v *Et d'ou venez vous madame Lucette. Almande VIII*[b] (compare BrownTC, no. 21: Moulu)

27 21^v *Bransle [de Bourgongne] I*[a 5] = 1583_7, no. 62

28 22^v *Bransle II*[a 6] = 1583_7, no. 63

29 23^v *Bransle III*[a 7] = 1583_7, no. 64

30 24^v *Bransle IIII*[a 8] = 1583_7, no. 65

31 24^v *Bransle V* = 1583_7, no. 66

32 25^v *Bransle VI* = 1583_7, no. 67

33 26^v *Bransle VII*[a 9] = 1583_7, no. 68

34 27^v *Bransle VIII*[a] = 1583_7, no. 69

35 27^v *Bransle IX*[a 10] = 1583_7, no. 70

36 28^v *Bransle X* = 1583_7, no. 71

37 29^v *Bransle [de Bourgongne] I*

38 29^v *Bransle II*

39 30^v *Bransle III*

40 30^v *Bransle IIII*

41 31^v *Bransle V*

42 31^v *Bransle VI*

[1] Mod. ed. in MFH IX, 5.

[2] Mod. ed. in BarthaZ, no. 50b.

[3] Mod. ed. in MFH IX, 6.

[4] Mod. ed. of no. 20 in BarthaZ, no. 49c; HAM, no. 137c; and ZfSM XI, no. 1. Mod. ed. of no. 22 in BS, vol. 51.

[5] Mod. ed. in BarthaZ, no. 50d, and TwittT I, no. 7.

[6] Mod. ed. in ZfSM XI, no. 4.

[7] Mod. ed. in ZfSM XI, no. 5.

[8] Mod. ed. in TwittT I, no. 8.

[9] Mod. ed. in MFH IX, 6, and ZfSM XI, no. 6.

[10] Mod. ed. in TwittT I, no. 6.

1557₄

DU TERTRE, ETIENNE

SEPTIEME LIVRE DE DANCERIES, / MIS EN MUSIQUE A QUATRE PARTIES / par Estienne du Tertre, nouvellement imprimé à Paris par la vefve de / Pierre Attaingnant, demourant en la Rue de la / Harpe, pres l'eglise sainct Cosme. / [Table of contents] / 1557. / Avec privilege du Roy, pour neuf ans.

32 fols. (?) Mensural notation. Fol. I1ᵛ = fol. 1ᵛ. The compositions identified by the superior letter *a* ([a]) are reprinted in MMRF XXIII, which includes a facsimile of the title page. For some concordances see HeartzSF, p. 347. For other volumes in this series, see 1547₆, note 2. All of the compositions are for instrumental ensemble *a4*, except nos. 3 and 6, which are *a5*.

Copy in: F:Pn (fols. 1–19).

	fol.	
1	1ᵛ	*Pavane premiere*
	1ᵛ	*Gaillarde premiere* (compare 1564₇, no. 42: "Gaiarda de la Royne de Eschosse")
2	2ᵛ	*Pavane 2*
	2ᵛ	*Gaillarde 2*
3	3ᵛ	*Pavane 3*[a] *a5*
	4ᵛ	*Gaillarde 3* *a5*
4	5ᵛ	*Pavane 4*
	5ᵛ	*Gaillarde 4*
5	6ᵛ	*Pavane 5*[a]
	6ᵛ	*Gaillarde 5*
6	7ᵛ	*Pavane 6* *a5*
	8ᵛ	*Gaillarde 6* *a5*
7	9ᵛ	*Premiere suytte de Bransles. Bransle 1*
8	10ᵛ	*Bransle 2*
9	10ᵛ	*Bransle 3*
10	11ᵛ	*Bransle 4*
11	11ᵛ	*Bransle 5*
12	12ᵛ	*Seconde suytte de Bransles. Bransle 1*
13	12ᵛ	*Bransle 2*
14	13ᵛ	*Bransle 3*
15	13ᵛ	*Bransle 4*
16	14ᵛ	*Bransle 5*
17	14ᵛ	*Bransle 6*
18	15ᵛ	*Troisieme suytte de Bransles. Bransle 1*
19	15ᵛ	*Bransle 2*
20	16ᵛ	*Bransle 3*
21	16ᵛ	*Bransle 4*
22	17ᵛ	*Bransle 5*
23	17ᵛ	*Bransle 6*
24	18ᵛ	*Premiere suytte de Bransles d'Escosse. Premier Bransle d'Escosse*[a 1]
25	18ᵛ	*Bransle 2*[a]
26	19ᵛ	*Bransle 3*
27	19ᵛ	*Bransle 4*
	[21ff	*Seconde suytte de bransles d'Escosse*]
	[23ff	*Six bransles de Poictou*]
	[26ff	*Huict branles gays*]
	[29ff	*Cinq Gaillardes*]

[1] Mod. ed. in TwittT I, no. 9.

1558₁

CONFORTI, GIOVANNI BATTISTA

DI GIO. BATTISTA CONFORTI. / IL PRIMO LIBRO DE RICERCARI / à quattro Voci, Nuovamente da lui Composti, / & dati in luce. / CAN [Printer's mark] TUS / In Roma per Valerio Dorico l'Anno / M. D. LVIII.

Four part books in mensural notation, each of 17 fols. On fol. 1ᵛ (= A1ᵛ): coat of arms. Dedication on fol. 2 headed "Al REVERENDIS. ET ILLUSTRIS. MONSIgnor Reverendissimo Il Cardinale Sermoneta," reprinted in GaspaC IV, 195, and SartMS, p. 22. All of the compositions are for instrumental ensemble *a4* except no. 13, which is *a3*.

Copies in: F:Psg (ATB), GB:Lbm, GB:Lcm, I:Bc.[1]

	fol.	
1	2ᵛ	*Ricercar del ottavo tono*
2	3ᵛ	*Ricercar del ottavo ton.*
3	4ᵛ	*Ricercar del ottavo tono*
4	5ᵛ	*Ricercar del quinto tono*
5	6ᵛ	*Ricercar del sesto tono*
6	7ᵛ	*Ricercar del Sesto tono*
7	8ᵛ	*Ricercar del Terzo tono*
8	9ᵛ	*Ricercar del Quarto tono*
9	10ᵛ	*Ricercar del Primo tono*
10	11ᵛ	*Ricercar del Secondo tono*
11	12ᵛ	*Ricercar del Secondo tono*
12	13ᵛ	*Ricercar del Secondo tono*

13 14v *Ricercar del Secondo tono a 3*
14 15v *Ricercar del Secondo tono*
15 16v *Ricercar del Settimo tono*

[1] A copy was in the library of Gaetano Gaspari.

[1558]$_2$

GORLIER, SIMON

Livre de Tabulature de flûtes d'Allemand. Lyon, Simon Gorlier.

This volume, now lost, is listed in MGG V, col. 533, and Du Verdier III, 473.

1558_3

MORLAYE, GUILLAUME

SECOND LIVRE DE / TABULATURE DE LEUT, CONTENANT / plusieurs Chansons, Fantasies, Motetz, Pavanes, & Gaillardes. / Composées par maistre Guillaume Morlaye, joueur de / Leut, & autres bons Autheurs. / [Printer's mark with motto "NE LA MORT, NE LE VENIN"] / A PARIS, / De l'imprimerie de Michel Fezandat, au mont sainct Hilaire, à l'hostel d'Albret. / 1558. / Avec privilege du Roy, pour dix ans.[1]

24 fols. French lute tablature. On fol. 24: table of contents, followed by a shortened version of the printer's privilege that appears in 1552_4. On fol. 24v: printer's mark with the initials "M. F." For some concordances see HeartzSF, p. 390. For other volumes in the same series, see 1552_4, note 2. All of the compositions are for solo lute.

Copies in: B:Br, D:Mbs, F:Pthibault.

fol.
1 2 *Fantasie*
2 3v *Fantasie*
3 5 *Virgo prudentissima* Pieton (compare SmijT III, no. 10: Penet)
4 7 *Infirmitatem* [*nostram*] Verdelot (SmijT IV, no. 17)
5 8v *Pour heur en amour demander* Arcadet (SCMA V, no. 28)
6 10 *Quand un chacun sert & commande* (*Responce*) Ebram (RISM 1565_5, fol. 15: Nicolas)
7 11v *Est il douleur cruelle* Arcadet (SCMA V, no. 36)
8 13 *Laffection si long temps prisonniere* Arcadet (SCMA V, no. 39)
9 14v *Ta privaulté* Arcadet (RISM 1567_6, fol. 2)
10 16 *Amour tu le scais bien* Arcadet (RISM 1565_5, fol. 14)
11 17 *Pavana des Dieux*
18 *Gaillarde*
12 19 *Pavane la Milanoise*
20 *Gaillarde*
13 21 *Gaillarde* [*piemontoise*]
14 22 *Gaillarde piemontoise*
15 22v *Gaillarde*
16 23v *Gaillarde*

[1] Facs of title page in MGG IV, col. 149.

1558_4

MORLAYE, GUILLAUME

TROISIESME LIVRE DE / TABULATURE DE LEUT, CONTENANT / plusieurs Chansons, Fantasies, Motetz, Pavanes, & Gaillardes. / Composées par maistre Guillaume Morlaye, joueur de / Leut, & autres bons Autheurs. / [Printer's mark with motto "NE LA MORT, NE LE VENIN"] / A PARIS, / De l'imprimerie de Michel Fezandat, au mont sainct Hilaire, à l'hostel d'Albret. / 1558. / Avec privilege du Roy, pour dix ans.

24 fols. French lute tablature. On fol. 24v: table of contents followed by a shortened version of the printer's privilege that appears in 1552_4. For some concordances, see HeartzSF, p. 391. For other volumes in the same series, see 1552_4, note 2. All of the compositions are for solo lute.

Copies in: B:Br, D:Mbs.

fol.
1 2 *Fantasie*
2 4 *Fantasie* = 1563_{12}, no. 11; 1568_7, no. 7; 1571_6, no. 4 (compare 1560_3, no. 2)
3 5v *Fantasie* = 1568_7, no. 13, and 1571_6, no. 9

4 7 *Hierusalem luge* (RISM 1532_9, p. 49: Richafort or Lupus)

8v 2a pars [*Deduc quasi torrentem*]

5 11 *Laudate dominum omnes gentes* Arcadet

6 13v *Reviens vers moy, qui suis tant desolée* Lupi (PubAPTM XXIII, no. 35)

7 15v *Plus revenir ne puis vers toy madame* (PubAPTM XXIII, no. 37: Lupi)

8 17v *Mon pere ma tant batu* Janequin

9 19 *Je me repute bien heureux* Arcadet (RISM 1567_4, fol. 7)

10 20v *Mais de quoy sert le desirer* Arcadet (SCMA V, no. 38)

11 21v *Pavane* (compare 1548_2, no. 4a: "La bella Bianca Margarita")

22v *Gaillarde*

12 24 *Gaillarde* (compare 1569_6, no. 79: "Gailliarde o ma gente brunette")

1558_5

OCHSENKUN, SEBASTIAN

Tabulatur/buch auff die Lauten, von Moteten, / Frantzösischen, Welschen und Teütschen Geystlichen und / Weltlichen Liedern, sampt etlichen iren Texten, mit Vieren, Fünffen, / und Sechs stimmen, dergleichen vor nie im Truck aussgangen, zu sondern / hohen Ehren, und undertenigstem wolgefallen, dem Durchleuch/tigsten Hochgebornen Fürsten und Herren, Herren Otthein/richen Pfaltzgraven bey Rhein, des heyligen Römischen / Reichs Ertzdruchsessen und Churfürsten, Hertzogen / in Nidern und Obern Bairn, &c. Durch Seba/stian Ochsenkhun irer Churfürstlichen / Gnaden Luttinisten zusamen / ordinirt und gelesen. / Hab Gott für augen. / Sebastian Ochsenkun. / Mit Kaiser. Maiest. Freyheit begnad, / nit nachzutrucken. / Gedruckt in der Churfürstlichen Stat Heydelberg / durch Johann Kholen.[1]

92 fols. German lute tablature. On fol. *1v: portrait and coat of arms of Pfalzgraf Ottheinrich with the heading "Mit Der Zeyt." Dedication on fol. *2 headed "Dem Durchleuchtigsten Hochgebornen Fürsten und Herrn, Herrn Otthainrichen, Pfaltzgraven bey Rhein, des heyligen Römischen Reichs Ertztruchsessen unnd Churfürsten, Hertzogen in Nidern und Obern Bairn &c. meinem genedigsten Herrn," and signed on fol. *4 (= fol. 1) "Datum Haidelberg den 26. Julii. Anno &c. Lviii. E. Churf. G. Underthenigster und Gehorsamer Sebastian Ochsenkhun Luttinist." On fols. 56v–57: table of contents for the motets (nos. 1–29). On fols. 87v–88: table of contents for the second part of the tablature (no. 30 to the end). On fol. 88v: cut of Ochsenkun[2] with the motto "Hab Gott für Augen, Sebastian Ochsenkun," and the heading: "Seines Alters Im XXXVIII. Jar. Den VI. Februarii. M. D. LVIII." Colophon on fol. 89: the printer's mark with the legend "INSIGNIA JOANNIS CARBONIS TYPOGRAPHI ELECTORII HEYDELBERGENSIS." The contents are listed in MfMG IV (1872), 52. For a possible second edition see $[1564]_6$. The compositions identified by superior letters are reprinted as follows: ([a]) in DTO XXXVII/72; ([b]) in SenflW VII. All of the compositions are for solo lute, but the intabulations of German lieder include several stanzas of text for each piece.

Copies in: D:DO, D:KA,[3] D:LEm (fragment),[4] D:Mbs, D:W, GB:Lbm (imperfect), US:NYp.[5]

fol.

1 1v *Pater Noster a6* Josquin de Pres (JosqMT, no. 50)

3 2a pars *Ave Maria*

2 4v *Praeter rerum seriem a6* Josquin de Pres (JosqMT, no. 33)

5v 2a pars *Virtus Sancti Spiritus*

3 7 *Benedicta es coelorum a6* Josquin de Pres (JosqMT, no. 46)

8v 2a pars *Per illud ave a2*

9 3a pars *Nunc mater exora natum a6*

4 9v *Stabat mater dolorosa a5* Josquin de Pres (JosqMT, no. 36)

10v 2a pars *Eya mater fons amoris me*

5 12 *Inviolata integra a5* Josquin de Pres (JosqMT, no. 42)
13 2a pars *Nostra ut pura pectora*
13ᵛ 3a pars *O Benigna O Regina O Maria*
6 14ᵛ *Jerusalem luge a5* Adrianus Caen (RISM 1532_9, p. 49: Richafort [or Lupus?])
15 2a pars *Deduc quasi torrentum lachrymas*
7 16ᵛ *Tua est potentia a5* Johan Mouton (RISM 1521_3, no. 14)
8 17ᵛ *Si bona suscepimus a5* Verdelot (MoralesO I, 274: Verdelot)
9 19 *Date siceram morentibus a5* Claudin (D:Rp, MSS B. 211–215, no. 30; see MohrH)
10 20 *Vita in ligno a5* Ludovicus Senffel (RISM 1537_1, no. 20)
11 21 *Oppressit reducem a5* Jobst Vom Brandt
12 22ᵛ *In exitu Israel de Egipto*[6] *a4* Josquin de Pres (JosqMT, no. 51)
24 2a pars [*Deus autem noster*]
26 3a pars [*Dominus memor fuit*]
13 27 *Qui habitat a4* Josquin de Pres (JosqMT, no. 52)
14 30 *Absolon fili mi a4* Josquin de Pres (PubAPTM VI, 57)
15 31ᵛ *Cum Sancto spiritu a4* Josquin de Pres (JosqMS, no. 16: *Missa de Beata Virgine*)
16 32 *Spiritus Domini a4* Joann Mouton (D:Rp, MSS B. 211–215, no. 74; see MohrH)
17 33ᵛ *Sancta Trinitas a4* Antoni Fevin (RoksT, no. 8)
18 35 *Laudate dominum omnes gentes a4* Joann Kilian
19 36 *Alleluia Confitemini a4* Joann Mouton (I:Bc, MS Q 19, fol. 185ᵛ)
37 2a pars [*Stetit Jesus in medio*]
20 38 *Invocabat autem Samson a4* Gregorius Peschin (D:Rp, MSS B. 211–215, no. 52 = anon.; see MohrH)
38ᵛ 2a pars [*Et Calumnias quibus*]
21 39ᵛ *Si bona suscepimus a4* Claudin (MoralesO III, 172: Sermisy)
22 41 *In illo tempore a4* Benedictus
42ᵛ 2a pars [*Dicebant ergo*]
23 43ᵛ *Beati omnes a4* Benedictus (RISM 1532_{11}, no. 14)
44ᵛ 2a pars [*Ecce sic benedicetur*]
24 46 *De profundis a4* Joann Mouton
46ᵛ 2a pars [*Sustinuit anima mea*]
25 48 *Sancta Maria a4* Gombert (RISM 1539_{13}, fol. 28: Verdelot)
26 49 *Dilexi quoniam exaudiet a4* Incertus Autor (SmijT IX, no. 1: Denis Briant)
50ᵛ 2a pars [*O Domine libera animam meam*]
27 51ᵛ *Aspice domine a4* Claudin (RoksT, no. 1: Lafage)
28 52ᵛ *Impetum Inimicorum a4* Joann Mouton (RISM $[1528]_2$, no. 4)
29 54 *Nisi dominus a4* Lupus (SmijT IX, no. 18: Le Heurteur)
55 2a pars *Cum dederit dilectis*
30 58 *Gott alls in allem wesentlich*[b 7] Ludwig Senffel (SenflW V, no. 7)
31 58ᵛ *Herr Gott lass dich erbarmen*[8] Heinrich Isaac (DTO XIV/28, p. 15: "Innsbruck ich muss dich lassen")
32 59 *Im friede dein, O Herre mein* Gregor. Petschin
33 59ᵛ *Es wöll uns Gott genedig sein* Gregor. Petschin
34 60ᵛ *Erhalt uns Herr bey deinem wort* Wilh. Braitengrasser
35 61 *Mein Seel erhebt den Herren mein* Gregor. Petschin
36 61ᵛ *O Herr, nit ferr, sey dein genad*[9] Gregor. Petschin
37 62 *Wol dem die ubertrettung gross*[9] Gregor. Petschin
38 62ᵛ *Herr das du mich so gstürtzet hast* Gregor. Petschin
39 63ᵛ *All ding auff erd zergencklich ist* Caspar Glanner
40 64ᵛ *Freüd und muet het mich verlassen*[9] Gregor. Petschin
41 65ᵛ *Herr durch Barmhertzigkeyt und Gnad* Gregor Petschin
42 66ᵛ *Glück mit der zeit* Caspar Otmair
43 67ᵛ *Mancher wünschet im grosses gut* Jobst vom Brand
44 69 *Jetzt bringt Sanct Martin*[b] Ludwig Senffel (SenflW V, no. 39)

45 68^v *Der Ehelich stand ist billich gnant*[b] Ludwig Senffel (SenflW V, no. 23)

46 69^v *Mag ich hertz lieb erwerben dich*[b] Ludwig Senffel (SenflW IV, no. 28)

47 70 *Mein selbs bin ich nit gwaltig mehr* Steffan Zirler (CW LXIII, no. 4)

48 70^v *Freundlicher Held, ich hab erwelt*[b] Ludwig Senffel (SenflW V, no. 20)

49 71 *Ach lieb mit leyd, wie hast dein bscheyd*[a][10] (MosPH, app., p. 26: Hofhaimer)

50 71^v *Tröstlicher lieb*[a][11] Paulus Hoffhamer (MosPH, app., p. 86)

51 72 *Ich weiss nit wie es komen mag* Martin Zilte Organist

52 72^v *Mein freüd allein*[12] Heinrich Isaac (DTO XIV/28, p. 17)

53 73^v *Mein selbs bin ich nit gwaltig mehr*[b] Ludwig Senffel (SenflW VI, no. 6)

54 74 *Die aller holdseligst auff erden*[a] Gregor Petschin

55 74^v *Ich armes Meydlein klag mich sehr*[b] Ludwig Senffel (SenflW VI, no. 8)

56 75 *Sih lieb ich muss dich lassen* Hans Kilian

57 75^v *Fraw ich bin euch von hertzen hold*[b] Ludwig Senffel (SenflW VI, no. 16: Peschin or Senfl)

58 76 *Die weyber mit den flöhen*[b][13] Ludwig Senffel (SenflW VI, no. 18)

59 76^v *Ein Abt den wöll wir weyhen*[b][14] Ludwig Senffel (SenflW V, no. 27)

60 77 *Ich schwing mein horn ins jamer*[b][15] Ludwig Senffel (SenflW V, no. 44)

61 77^v *Was seltzam ist, man ausserlist*[b] Ludwig Senffel (SenflW VI, no. 12)

62 78 *Sih Paurenknecht lass Tröslein stahn*[b][16] Ludwig Senffel (SenflW V, no. 28)

78 2a pars *Das Nessel kraut*

78^v 3a pars *Es rewet mich sehr*

63 78^v *Ich armes keützlein kleine*[ab][17] Steffan Mahu (SenflW V, no. 46: Senfl?)

64 79 *Dort niden an dem Rheyne*[a][18] Gregor Petschin

65 79^v *So wünsch ich ir ein gute nacht*[a] Thomas Stoltzer (DTO XXXVII/72, p. 74)

66 80 *Und wer der Winter noch so kalt*[a] Gregor Petschin

67 80^v *Bewar mich Herr*[19] Steffan Zirler (D:Rp, MS A. R. 855, no. 19)

68 82 *Non Come fisti* Incertus Autor

69 82^v *Quand Io pens ala martire* Archadelt (RISM 1541$_9$, p. 54)

70 83 *Ahime [dov'e'l bel viso]* Archadelt (RISM 1541$_9$, p. 53)

71 84 *Petite fleur* Crequillon (RISM 1549$_{29}$, no. 28)

72 84^v *Occhi miei Lassi* Archadelt (RISM 1541$_9$, p. 8)

73 85^v *Se purti guardo* Incertus Autor (RISM 1570$_8$, p. 46: [Pathie])

74 86 *Pour Ung Helas* Crequillon (RISM 1554$_{23}$, p. 10)

75 86^v *Ung gay bergiere* Crequillon (RieH II, 462)

76 87 *Pour Ung plaisir* Crequillon (ParrishM, no. 20)

[1] Facs. of title page and of fol. 88^v in KinsP, p. 132.

[2] The portrait is repr. in KinsP, p. 130; LauLL, p. 49; MGG IX, col. 1825; ReissmA, p. 206; and WolfH II, 37.

[3] This copy is bound with 1572$_1$. See there for information about manuscript additions containing music in German lute tablature.

[4] This copy has manuscript additions in German lute tablature dated 1569 and 1570, and including "Ich hab mein Sachen," "Dixit dominus," and "Tanntz." The volume has the call number II. 2. 45; it was once in the library of C. F. Becker. See BoettB.

[5] A copy was in D:Bds; an imperfect copy was in PL:WRu.

[6] Facs. of a part of fol. 22^v in PN, p. 78.

[7] Heading on fol. 57^v: "Volgen hernach Teütsche, Geystliche, Weltliche und Frantzösische Lieder sampt etlichen iren Texten."

[8] Mod. ed. in BruAL, no. 16c; DTO XIV/28, p. 147; and *Die Laute* IV (1920–21), 20.

[9] Nos. 36, 37, and 40 are repr. in BS, vol. 31.

[10] Mod. ed. in MosPH, app., p. 28.

[11] Beginning pr. in MosPH, app., p. 92.

[12] Mod. ed. in DTO XIV/28, p. 158.

[13] Facs. and mod. ed. in WolfH II, 44; mod. ed. in NeemL, no. 3.

[14] Mod. ed. in BruS II, no. 80.

[15] Mod. ed. in BruAL, no. 16a.

[16] Mod. ed. in BruAL, no. 16b.

[17] Mod. ed. in NeemL, no. 2; RaL, p. 334; and *Die Laute* IV (1920–21), 21.

[18] Mod. ed. in BruS IV, no. 138; KörL, no. 15; TapS, p. 34; and WolfME, no. 34.
[19] Heading on fol. 81ᵛ: "Volgen hernach etliche Wellsche und Frantzösische Lieder."

8	21	*Gaillarde* (compare 1578_8, no. 10: "La Lavandera Gagliarda"
9	21ᵛ	*Pavane La rosignolle*
10	22ᵛ	*Gaillarde l'amirale*

[1] Incipits in SlimK II, 566.

1558_6

RIPPE, ALBERT DE

SIXIESME LIVRE DE / TABULATURE DE LEUT, CONTENANT / plusieurs Chansons, Fantasies, Motetz, Pavanes, & Gaillardes. / Composées par feu Messire Albert de Rippe, de Mantoue, Seigneur du Carois, / joueur de Leut, & varlet de chambre du Roy nostre sire. / [Printer's mark with motto "NE LA MORT, NE LE VENIN"] / A PARIS, / De l'imprimerie de Michel Fezandat, au mont sainct Hilaire, à l'hostel d'Albret. / 1558. / Avec privilege du Roy, pour dix ans.

24 fols. French lute tablature. On fol. 23ᵛ: table of contents. On fol. 24: a shortened version of the printer's privilege that appears in 1552_4. On fol. 24ᵛ: printer's mark with the initials "M. F." BuggR contains a modern edition of the entire collection. For other volumes in the same series, see 1552_8, note 1, All of the compositions are for solo lute.

Copy in: B:Br.

	fol.	
1	2	*Fantasie* [1]
2	5	*Fantasie* [1] = 1562_{11}, no. 6
3	7ᵛ	*Benedicta* Josquin = 1562_{11}, no. 1a: "Benedicta es coelorum Regina"
	10ᵛ	2a pars [*Per illud ave*] = 1562_{11}, no. 1b
	12	3a pars [*Nunc Mater exora natum*] = 1562_{11}, no. 1c
4	13	*Si bona suscepimus* Claudin (MoralesO III, 172: Sermisy)
5	16	*O comme heureux* (RISM 1542_{13}, no. 1: Certon) = 1562_{10}, no. 2
6	18	*Si come estremo lardore* (compare 1547_5, no. 61: "Se in me exstremo")
7	20	*Je sens l'affection* (RISM 1544_7, no. 28: Boyvin) = 1562_9, no. 12

1559_1

ESTRÉES, JEAN D'

PREMIER LIVRE DE DANSERIES, / Contenant / 14 Bransles Communs. / 16 Bransles Gays. / 20 Bransles de Champaigne. / 6 Autres Bransles de Champaigne legiers. / 1 Autre Bransle appellé le petit gentilhomme. / 1 Autre Bransle des Lavandieres. / Le tout mis en Musique à quatre parties (appropriés tant à la voix humaine, / que pour jouer sur tous instruments musicalz) Par Jean d'Estrée, / joueur de Hautbois du Roy. / De l'imprimerie de Nicolas du Chemin, à l'enseigne du Griffon / d'argent, rue Saint Jean de Latran, à Paris. / 1559. / Avec privilege du Roy pour dix ans.

Four part books in mensural notation, each of 16 fols. (?). On fol. 1ᵛ: the same excerpt from the printer's privilege as in 1556_1. On fol. 16ᵛ: printer's mark. For some concordances see HeartzSF, p. 358. For further information see NettlE. All of the compositions are for instrumental ensemble *a4*.

Copies in: F:Psg (S), GB:Lbm (B).

	fol.	
1	2	*Premier Bransle Commun*
2	2	*2*
3	2ᵛ	*3*
4	2ᵛ	*4*
5	3	*5*
6	3	*6*
7	3ᵛ	*7* = 1571_5, no. 69
8	3ᵛ	*8*
9	4	*9* = 1571_5, no. 70
10	4	*10* = 1547_6, no. 12
11	4ᵛ	*11*
12	4ᵛ	*12*
13	5	*13*
14	5	*14*

15 5^v *Premier Bransle Gay*
16 5^v *2*
17 6 *3*
18 6 *4*
19 6^v *5* (compare ParisC, no. 30: "Trop penser") = 1571_5, no. 71
20 6^v *6*
21 7 *7*
22 7 *8*
23 7^v *9*
24 7^v *10*
25 8 *11*
26 8 *12*
27 8^v *13*
28 8^v *14* = 1571_5, no. 72
29 9^v *15* (compare 1552_3, no. 31: "Autre bransle de Poictou grand bonnet large")
30 9 *16*
31 9^v *Premier Bransle de Champaigne* = 1571_5, no. 75
32 9^v *2* = 1571_5, no. 76
33 10 *3* = 1571_5, no. 77
34 10 *4* = 1571_5, no. 78
35 10^v *5* = 1571_5, no. 79
36 10^v *6* = 1571_5, no. 80
37 11 *7* = 1571_5, no. 81
38 11 *8* = 1571_5, no. 82
39 11^v *9*
40 11^v *10*
41 12 *11*
42 12 *12*
43 12^v *13*
44 12^v *14*
45 13 *15*
46 13 *16* (compare 1547_6, no. 44)
47 13^v *17*
48 13^v *18*
49 14 *19*
50 14 *20*
51 14^v *Premier Bransle de Champaigne legier*
52 14^v *2*
53 15 *3*
54 15 *4*
55 15^v *5*
56 15^v *6*
57 16 *Bransle legier, appellé le petit gentilhomme*
58 16 *Bransle des Lavandieres* = 1571_5, no. 101

1559_2

ESTRÉES, JEAN D'

SECOND LIVRE DE DANSERIES, / Contenant / 18 Bransles de Bourgongne. / 1 Bransle de Bourgongne legier. / 18 Bransles de Poitou. / 7 Bransles d'Escosse. / 1 Bransle appellé le Bransle des Sabots. / 9 Bransles de la Guerre. / 1 Bransle appellé la Tireteinne. / 1 Autre Bransle appellé le petit Velours. / Le tout mis en Musique à quatre parties (appropriés tant à la voix humaine, / que pour jouer sur tous instruments musicalz) Par Jean d'Estrée, / joueur de Hautbois du Roy. / De l'imprimerie de Nicolas du Chemin, à l'enseigne du Griffon / d'argent, rue saint Jean de Latran, à Paris. / 1559. / Avec privilege du Roy pour dix ans.

Four part books in mensural notation, each of 16 fols. (?). On fol. 1^v: the same excerpt from the printer's privilege as in 1556_1. On fol. 16^v: printer's mark. For some concordances see HeartzSF, p. 363. For further information see NettlE. All of the compositions are for instrumental ensemble *a4*.

Copies in: F:Psg (S), GB:Lbm (B).

fol.
1 2 *Premier Bransle de Bourgongne* = 1571_5, no. 83
2 2 *2* = 1571_5, no. 84
3 2^v *3* = 1571_5, no. 85
4 2^v *4* = 1571_5, no. 86
5 3 *5* = 1571_5, no. 87
6 3 *6* = 1571_5, no. 88
7 3^v *7* = 1571_5, no. 89
8 3^v *8* = 1571_5, no. 90
9 4 *9* = 1571_5, no. 91
10 4 *10* = 1571_5, no. 92
11 4^v *11* = 1571_5, no. 93
12 4^v *12* = 1571_5, no. 94
13 5 *13* = 1571_5, no. 95
14 5 *14* = 1571_5, no. 96
15 5^v *15* = 1571_5, no. 97
16 5^v *16* = 1571_5, no. 98
17 6 *17* = 1571_5, no. 99
18 6^v *18* = 1571_5, no. 100
19 6^v *Bransle de Bourgongne legier*
20 7 *Premier Bransle de Poitou*
21 7 *2*
22 7^v *3*
23 7^v *4*

24	8	*5*
25	8	*6*
26	8^v	*7*
27	8^v	*8*
28	9	*9*
29	9	*10*
30	9^v	*11*
31	9^v	*12*
32	10	*13*
33	10	*14*
34	10^v	*15*
35	10^v	*16*
36	11	*17*
37	11	*18*
38	11^v	*Premier Bransle d'Escosse*
39	11^v	*2*
40	12	*3*
41	12	*4*
42	12^v	*5*
43	12^v	*6*
44	13	*7* = 1571_5, no. 59, and 1583_7, no. 101
45	13	*Bransle des Sabots* = 1571_5, no. 60, and 1583_7, no. 102
46	13^v	*Premier Bransle de la Guerre* = 1571_5, no. 73, and 1583_7, no. 92
47	13^v	*2* = 1571_5, no. 74, and 1583_7, no. 93
48	14	*3*
49	14	*4*
50	14^v	*5*
51	14^v	*6*
52	15	*7*
53	15	*8*
54	15^v	*9*
55	15^v	*La Tireteinne*
56	16	*Le petit velours*

1559_3

ESTRÉES, JEAN D'

TIERS LIVRE DE DANSERIES, / Contenant

5 Bransles de Malthe.
1 Le pas meige.
1 La Padouenne.
4 Tintelores.
1 Les Bouffons.
10 Allemandes.
1 Bransle de la torche.
1 Bransle de Montirandé.
3 Ballets du Canat.
1 La volte de Prouvence.
3 Pavanes à 4, & à 6.
8 Gaillardes à 4, & à 5.
5 Basse danses.
1 Hauberrois.

Le tout mis en Musique à quatre parties (appropriés tant à la voix humaine, / que pour jouer sur tous instruments musicalz) Par Jean d'Estrée, / joueur de Hautbois du Roy. / De l'imprimerie de Nicolas du Chemin, à l'enseigne du Griffon / d'argent, rue Saint Jean de Latran, à Paris. / 1559. / Avec privilege du Roy, pour dix ans.

Four part books in mensural notation, each of 16 fols. (?). On fol. 1^v: the same excerpt from the printer's privilege as in 1556_1. On fol. 16^v: printer's mark. For some concordances see HeartzSF, p. 367. For further information see NettlE. All of the compositions are for instrumental ensemble *a4* except nos. 29 and 30, which are *a6*, and no. 37, which is *a5*.

Copies in: F:Psg (S), GB:Lbm (B).

	fol.	
1	2	*Premier Bransle de Malthe*
2	2	*2*
3	2^v	*3*
4	2^v	*4*
5	3	*5 Bransle de Malthe, dit furieux*
6	3	*Le pas meige*
7	3^v	*La Padouenne* (compare 1556_8, no. 18: "[Paduane] Une m'avoit promis")
8	3^v	*Premiere Tintelore de Milan*
9	4	*2 Tintelore d'Angleterre* [1]
10	4	*3*
11	4^v	*4*
12	4^v	*Les Bouffons* = 1571_5, no. 3
13	5	*Premiere Allemande*
14	5	*2*
15	5^v	*3*
16	5^v	*4*
17	6	*5* = 1571_5, no. 29, and 1583_7, no. 37
18	6	*6*
19	6^v	*7*
20	6^v	*8*
21	7	*9 Allemande courante*
22	7	*10 Allemande courante*
23	7^v	*Bransle de la torche*
24	7^v	*Bransle de montirandé*
25	8	*Premier Ballet du Canat*
26	8^v	*2 Le petit Ballet* [2]
27	8^v	*3 [Ballet]* [2]
28	9	*La volte de Prouvence*
29	9^v	*Pavane Si j'ay du bien à6* (compare RISM 1547_9, no. 10: Sandrin)

30 10v *Pavane de la Guerre à6*
31 11v *Pavane Lesquercarde* = 1571_5, no. 11
32 12 *Premiere Gaillarde* = 1571_5, no. 48, and 1583_7, no. 26
33 12 *2*
34 12v *3* = 1571_5, no. 50
35 12v *4* (compare 1550_5, no. 25: "Gaillarde [Si pour t'aimer]") = 1571_5, no. 37, and 1583_7, no. 17
36 13 *5 Gaillarde, La Brune* (compare 1569_6, no. 79: "Gailliarde o ma gente brunette") = 1571_5, no. 49, and 1583_7, no. 27
37 13 *6 Gaillarde, Les cinq pas à 5* (compare 1546_{15}, no. 10: "La rocha'l fuso")
38 13v *7 Gaillarde, La mirande*
39 13v *8 Gaillarde, La fatigue*
40 14 *Premiere Bassedanse, Si j'ay du mal, & du bien* (compare RISM 1532_{12}, no. 19: "Si j'ay eu du mal," Sermisy)
41 14 *2 Bassedanse, Amy je ny veulx plus aymer*
42 14v *3 Bassedanse, Benardine*
43 15 *4 Bassedanse, L'Amour premiere* (compare RISM 1540_{12}, no. 1: Sandrin)
44 15v *5 Bassedanse, Ce qui est plus* (compare RISM 1549_{18}, no. 8: Sandrin)
45 16 *Hauberrois, Jean de Lagny*[3] = 1571_5, no. 102

[1] Mod. ed. in WardDVM, p. 44.
[2] Facs. of fol. 8v, superius, in MGG III, col. 1580.
[3] Not related musically to PubAPTM XXIII, no. 6: Berchem.

1559_4

LE ROY, ADRIAN

SIXIESME LIVRE DE / LUTH, CONTENANT PLU/sieurs chansons nouvellement mises en Tabulature / PAR / ADRIAN LE ROY. / [Table of contents] / A PARIS. / De l'Imprimerie d'Adrian le Roy, & Robert Ballard, Imprimeurs du Roy, / ruë saint Jean de Beauvais, à l'enseigne sainte Genevieve. / 1559. / Avec privilege du Roy, pour dix ans.

24 fols. French lute tablature. All of the compositions are for solo lute.
Copies in: D:Mbs, D:ROu.

fol.
1 1v *Tout ce qu'on peut* Ciprian Rore (RISM 1557_{15}, no. 2) = 1571_6, no. 89
2 3 *Soupirs ardans* Arcadet (SCMA V, no. 30)
3 5 *Qui souhaittés* De Bussy (RISM 1549_{20}, no. 1: Sandrin)
4 7v *Il ne se trouve en amytié* Sandrin (RISM 1548_3, no. 14)
5 10 *Mamie un jour* Certon (RISM 1549_{18}, no. 1)
6 12 *Je cerche autant amour* Boyvin (RISM 1545_{12}, no. 2)
7 13v *Si j'ay du bien* Sandrin (RISM 1547_9, no. 10)
8 15 *M'amie est tant* Sandrin (RISM 1549_{21}, no. 10)
9 16v *De qui plus tost* Sandrin (RISM 1549_{20}, no. 29)
10 19v *Les yeux qui me sceurent prendre* Arcadet (RISM 1554_{26}, no. 16)
11 21v *L'yver sera* Arcadet (SCMA V, no. 19)
12 23 *Au temps heureux* Arcadet (SCMA V, no. 1)

1559_5

LIETO PANHORMITANO, DON BARTHOLOMEO

DIALOGO QUARTO DI MUSICA / Dove si ragiona sotto un piacevole discorso delle cose pertinenti per / intavolare le opere di Musica esercitarle con viola a mano / over Liuto con sue tavole ordinate per diversi / gradi alti e bassi Del Reverendo Don / Bartholomeo lieto Panhormitano / Theorico secondo i filosofi et / Prattici Eccelentissimo / Compositore. / [Printer's mark with motto "Discedite Oscuratores Qui Clariorsum"][1]

20 fols. Dedication on fol. A1v, headed "Allo Eccelente Signor Giovan Michele Bocca Signor Mio Osservandissimo," and signed, "Di Napoli à 4. d'Ottobre del M. D. LVIII. Di V. S. Eccellente Humilissimo

servitore Don Bartolomeo Lieto." On fol. E1^v (and again on fol. E3^v): "Conclusione delli circoli et Semicircoli con punti & senza punti, con linee & senza linee, & altri segni de Pause, & ancho qual si voglia segno de Numeri, similmente i, b, molli & Diesis, come segni vani, disutili, capricciosi, & oscuration di Prattica, & non se ne puo disputare, ne per quelli si puo conoscere un perfetto Musico, ne un perfetto & buon Cantore. Alli Theorici Secondo La Prattica Capricciosa." These "Conclusione" have a separate dedication on fol. E3 to "Eccellente S. Ascanio Bocca." Colophon on fol. E2^v (and again on fol. E4^v): "Stampato in Napoli per Matthio Cancer dil mese d'Aprile. M. D. LIX." As the title suggests, this elementary instruction book, in the form of a dialogue, describes how to intabulate a vocal composition for the viol or lute using Italian tablature. It includes (on fols. B3–D1^v) tables for those who cannot read mensural notation. There is one complete musical example, in mensural notation and in tablature, without text or title, on fols. B1–B1^v. For further information see WardH (including one page in quasi-facsimile), and WolfH II, 64.

Copy in: GB:Lbmh.[2]

[1] Facs. of title page in HirK IV, pl. 28.

[2] This copy was in the Wolffheim library (see WolffC I, no. 770). Another copy was in D:Bds.

1559_6

LUPACCHINO, BERNARDINO, AND JOAN MARIA TASSO

DI BERNARDINO LUPACCHINO / Et di Joan Maria Tasso, Il Primo libro a Due voci Novamente con ogni / diligentia ristampato & da molti errori emendato. / Aggiontovi ancora alcuni canti a due voci de diversi autori. / A DUE [Printer's mark] VOCI / In Venetia Apresso di / Antonio Gardano. / 1559.

Two part books in mensural notation, each of 20 fols. For later editions, see 1560_2, 1562_6, 1568_4, 1584_9, 1587_4, 1590_4, 1591_8, and 1594_8. See also 1565_4, and, for editions after 1600, RISM and SartMS. The compositions identified by the superior letter *a* ([a]) are reprinted in DoflS. All of the compositions are *a2* and are without text or title.

Copy in: I:Bc (T).

	fol.	
1	1^v	Lupacchino
2	2	[Anon.][a]
3	2^v	Joan Maria Tasso
4	3	Lupacchino
5	3^v	Lupacchino
6	4	[Anon.][a][1]
7	4^v	Joan Maria Tasso
8	5	Joan Maria Tasso[a]
9	5^v	Lupacchino
10	6	[Anon.]
11	6^v	Lupacchino
12	7	[Anon.]
13	7^v	Lupacchino
14	8	[Anon.]
15	8^v	Joan Maria Tasso
16	9	Joan Maria Tasso
17	9^v	Lupacchino
18	10	Joan Maria Tasso
19	10^v	Lupacchino
20	11	[Anon.][2]
21	11^v	Joan Maria Tasso
22	12	[Anon.][3]
23	12^v	Lupacchino
24	13	Joan Maria Tasso
25	13^v	Joan Maria Tasso
26	14	Lupacchino = 1590_{12}, no. 46
27	14^v	Joan Maria Tasso
28	15	[Anon.]
29	15^v	Joan Maria Tasso
30	16	Joan Maria Tasso
31	16^v	Joan Maria Tasso
32	17	Lupacchino
33	17^v	Lupacchino[4]
34	18	[Anon.][a]
35	18^v	Joan Maria Tasso
36	19	[Anon.]
37	19^v	Lupacchino *sopra la battaglia*[5]
38	20	[Anon.][a]
39	20^v	Joan Maria Tasso *sopra la battaglia*

[1] Mod. ed. in MI IV, 12.

[2] Mod. ed. in HM V, no. 3.

[3] Mod. ed. in HM V, no. 2.

[4] Mod. ed. in HM IV, no. 10.

[5] Mod. ed. in HM V, no. 10.

1559₇

MATELART, JEAN

INTAVOLATURA / DE LEUTO / DE IOANNE MATELART / FIAMENGO MUSICO / Libro Primo novamente da lui composto intabulato & corretto / & posto in luce, con gratia & privilegio de li Superiori. / [Cut of a winged horse] / IN ROMA / Per Valerio Dorico, L'anno M. D. LIX.[1]

12 fols. Italian lute tablature. Dedication on fol. 1ᵛ headed "Al Molto Reverendo et Virtuoso Signor Sulpitio Gallo Nobile Romano Suo Oss." On fol. 12ᵛ: table of contents. Nos. 1–16 are for solo lute. The seven fantasias for two lutes (nos. 17–23) each consist of a previously composed independent solo composition to which Matelart has added music for a second lute. Concordances therefore refer only to the first lute.

Copies in: F:Pthibault,[2] I:Bc.

MUSIC FOR SOLO LUTE

	fol.	
1	2	*Fantasia Prima*[3]
2	2ᵛ	*Fantasia Secunda*
3	3	*Fantasia Terza*
4	3ᵛ	*Fantasia Quarta*
5	3ᵛ	*Fantasia Quinta*
6	4	*Fantasia Sesta*
7	4ᵛ	*Fantasia Settima*
8	5	*Fantasia Ottava*
9	5	*Fantasia Nona*
10	5ᵛ	*Fantasia Decima*
11	6	*Fantasia Undecima*
12	6	*Fantasia Duodecima*
13	6ᵛ	*Fantasia Tertiadecima*
14	7ᵛ	*Fantasia Quatuordecima*
15	7ᵛ	*Fantasia Quinquedecima*
16	8	*Il Benedictus de la missa de Benedicta de Morales* (MoralesO III, 22–26)
	8	*L'Osanna de la medesima missa*[4]

MUSIC FOR TWO LUTES

17	8ᵛ	*Seguens le R[ecercate concertate]*[5] *Di M. Francesco Milanese la prima* = 1547₂, no. 2 [two lutes; second part by Matelart on facing page]
18	8ᵛ	*La seconda* = 1547₂, no. 18 [same as for no. 17]
19	8ᵛ	*La terza*[6] [same as for no. 17]
20	9ᵛ	*Fantasia di M. Francesco Milanese la quarta*[7] = 1547₂, no. 3 [same as for no. 17]
21	9ᵛ	*Fantasia di M. Francesco Milanese la quinta* = 1547₂, no. 16 [same as for no. 17]
22	10ᵛ	*Fantasia Sexta*[8] [same as for no. 17]
23	11ᵛ	*[Fantasia 7ª.]*[9] = 1546₁₀, no. 5: Giovanni Maria da Crema [same as for no. 17]

[1] Facs. of title page in HeyerV II, pl. 4; KinsP, p. 135; and MGG VIII, col. 1784.

[2] This copy was in the library of Wilhelm Heyer (see HeyerV II, 41).

[3] Mod. ed. in ChilLS, p. 22.

[4] Mod. ed. in EC, pt. I, vol. II, p. 655.

[5] In the Bologna copy the heading has been trimmed. It is supplied here from the table of contents.

[6] Incipit in SlimK II, 543.

[7] Mod. ed. in ChilLS, p. 24.

[8] Mod. ed. in ChilF, no. 10; incipit in SlimK II, 543.

[9] Manuscript title.

1559₈

GARDANE, ANTONIO, PUBLISHER

FANTASIE RECERCARI / CONTRAPUNTI A TRE VOCI DI / M. adriano & de altri Autori appropriati per Cantare & Sonare d'ogni / sorte di Stromenti, Con dui Regina celi, l'uno di M. adriano & l'altro / di M. cipriano, Sopra uno medesimo Canto Fermo, Novamente / per Antonio Gardane ristampati. / LIBRO [Printer's mark] PRIMO / In Venetia Apresso di / Antonio Gardane. / 1559.

Three part books in mensural notation (SB, each of 16 fols.; T, 14 fols.). On the title page verso of each part book: table of contents. Contents = 1551₆, 1593₈. Nos. 1 and 2 are fully texted; the other compositions are for instrumental ensemble *a 3*.

Copies in: D:Mbs, E:Mmc (T), I:Msartori (SB), I:Pu (B).

1559

DOUBTFUL WORKS

1. DraudiusBC, p. 1651, dates a volume of lute music by Valentin Bakfark 1559. Draudius probably refers to 1569_1.

$[155?]_1$

VILA, PEDRO ALBERCH

Tentos de Organo. De Petro Villa Doctor.

This volume, now lost, was in the library of King John IV of Portugal; see VasJ, p. 110, no. 443. For further information on the composer see ReMR, p. 615.

$[1560]_1$

GORLIER, SIMON

Premier Livre de Tabulature d'Espinette, contenant Motets, Fantasies, Chansons, Madrigales & Gaillardes. Lyon, Simon Gorlier.

This volume, now lost, is listed in Du Verdier III, 473. A copy of this work was once in the library of Raimund Fugger the Younger (see SchaalM, art. 113: "Livre de Tabalature d'Espinette, Contenant, Mutettor., Fantasies, Chansons, Madrigales et Galliardes Imprimes, a, Lion A 1560."). See also MGG V, col. 533.

1560_2

LUPACCHINO, BERNARDINO, AND JOAN MARIA TASSO

DI BERNARDINO LUPACCHINO / ET DI JOAN MARIA TASSO, / IL PRIMO LIBRO / A DUE VOCI. / Novamente con ogni diligentia ristampato, & da molti errori emendato. / Aggiontovi ancora alcuni canti a Due voci de diversi auttori. / [Printer's mark] / In Venegia, Appresso Girolamo Scotto. 1560.

Two part books in mensural notation, each of 20 fols. Contents = 1559_6. All of the compositions are for instrumental ensemble *a 2*.

Copy in: I:Bc.

1560_3

PALADIN, JEAN PAUL

PREMIER / LIVRE DE TABLATURE DE / LUTH DE M. JEAN PAULE PALADIN, / contenant Fantasies, Motetz, Madrigales, Chansons / Françoises, Pavanes & Gaillardes: avec une brié/ve instruction de la Tablature dudit instru/ment, de nouveau adjoutee. / A LYON, / De l'Imprimerie de Simon Gorlier. / Avec Privilege / du Roy pour dix ans. / 1560.

4 + 40 fols. Italian lute tablature. Colophon on fol. 40ᵛ: "Stampato in Lione per Giovan Pullon de Trino, à l'instantia di M. Giovan Paulo Paladino, l'Anno 1553" (see $[1553]_7$). On fol. *1ᵛ: excerpt from the royal privilege granting Simon Gorlier permission to print music and books on music for ten years, signed and dated "à Paris le dixseptieme jour de Fevrier, 1557. PAR LE ROY. Moyen. Le Seigneur de Royssy maistre des requestes ordinaire de l'hostel, present." On fol. *2: instructions for reading lute tablature headed "Instruction de la tablature de luth." On fol. *4ᵛ: table of contents. Fol. *5 = fol. 1. MoeDM contains a thematic index of the dances (p. 399) and concordances for them (p. 255). For further information see LesP. All of the compositions are for solo lute.

Copies in: A:Wn, CH:Zz.

	fol.	
1	1	*Fantasia* = 1563_{12}, no. 17; 1568_7, no. 9; 1571_6, no. 10
2	2ᵛ	*Fantasia* = 1558_5, no. 2: Morlaye
3	4	*Fantasia* = 1568_7, no. 6, and 1571_6, no. 23
4	6	*Fantasia* = 1563_{12}, no. 15
5	7	*Fantasia* = 1563_{12}, no. 13

6 8v *Fantasia senza canto*
7 10 *Madrigal primo. Qual anim'ignorante* (RISM 1543_{17}, p. 3: Nollet) = 1563_{12}, no. 73, and 1568_7, no. 102
8 11v *Anchor che col partir* (SCMA VI, no. 13: Rore) = 1563_{12}, no. 90
9 12v *Alcun'non po saper'* (RISM 1543_{17}, p. 37)
10 13 *Fantasia sopra al detto Madrigal*
11 14v *Quan'io penso al martir'* (RISM 1541_9, p. 54: Arcadelt)
12 16 *Fantasia sopra al detto Madrigal*
13 17v *S'io credesse per morte essere scarcho* (RISM 1543_{17}, p. 16: Anselmo de Reulx) = 1563_{12}, no. 89
14 18v *Ver'inferno al mio petto* (Vogel: Arcadelt 15 [1566], no. 43: Arcadelt) = 1563_{12}, no. 86
15 20 *M'amye un jour* (RISM 1549_{18}, no. 1: Certon)
16 21 *La palme doulce* (RISM 1544_7, no. 17: Gardane) = 1563_{12}, no. 57
17 22 *Un jour passé avec Collete* (RISM 1540_{17}, fol. 29: Le Hugier) = 1563_{12}, no. 64
18 23 *Las on peut susier clerement* (RISM 1544_7, no. 21: "Las on peut juger clerement," Janequin)
19 24 *Or vien sa vien m'amye* (RISM 1540_{17}, fol. 7: Janequin) = 1562_{10}, no. 5; 1568_7, no. 100; 1574_7, no. 26
20 25 *Si jay du bien* (RISM 1547_9, no. 10: Sandrin)
21 26v *Ave sanctissima* (RISM 1565_3, fol. 10: Sermisy)
22 27v *Fantasia sopra al detto*
23 30 *Proba me Domine* (RISM 1535_1, fol. 8: Jacotin)
24 31v *Fantasia sopra al detto*
25 33v *Pavana chiamata la Milanesa*
35 *Gagliarda sopra la detta*
26 36v *Gagliarda [Gaillarde Italienne]* [1]
27 37v *Pavana chiamata la Paladina*
38 *Gagliarda sopra la detta*
28 39v *Gagliarda [Gaillarde nouvelle]*

[1] Mod. ed. in MoeDM, p. 327.

1560_4

VINCI, PIETRO

DI PIETRO VINCI / SICULO / IL PRIMO LIBRO DELLA MUSICA / a Due Voce, / Nuovamente stampato & dato in luce. / [Printer's mark] / In Venegia, Appresso Girolamo Scotto. 1560

Two part books in mensural notation, each of 16 fols. Dedication on fol. 1v headed "ALL'ILLUSTRISS. SIGNOR DON FRANCISCO SANCTA PAR." and signed "Pietro Vinci de Nicosia," reprinted in SartMS, p. 23. On fol. 16v: table of contents. For a later edition see 1586_9. All of the compositions are for instrumental ensemble *a 2*.

Copy in: I:Bc.

	fol.	
1	2	*La marencha*
2	2v	*Lo canallotto*
3	3	*Vinci*
4	3v	*Castro Joanni & muxa*
5	4	*Fontana di chiazza*
6	4v	*Xumo sanzo Con Mastro Joanni & Mastro Antoni* [1]
7	5	*Piro con lo furno*
8	5v	*Barressi* [2]
9	6	*Coccocino*
10	6v	*Chiucia*
11	7	*Lo cayordo*
12	7v	*Spinello cundo Antonino d'allena* [3]
13	8	*Panuso*
14	8v	*Le gorre con lo paschiero*
15	9	*Mal portuso*
16	9v	*Paravola*
17	10	*Pe Martino*
18	10v	*Gallina ratto rattonis* [4]
19	11	*La vaccarra con le buscaglie* [5]
20	11v	*Spatta folco con lo gobbetto* [6]
21	12	*La murada*
22	12v	*Sper lingua E presti paulo Bono*
23	13	*San Basilli*
24	13v	*Senza octava*
25	14	*Planzuni*
26	14v	*Il gambaro con denaretto* (= "La Spagna"; see $148?_1$, no. 10)
27	15	*Xiri che senza Xiri stamo male*
28	15v	*La danzulina E luchia peri*
29	16	*Le poletine*

[1] Title in tenor part book: "Xumo sanzo Con li garbi."
[2] Title in tenor part book: "Barressi e scalisi."
[3] Title in tenor part book: "Spinello e Don Antonino d'allena."
[4] Title in tenor part book: "Gallina con lo corvo."
[5] Title in tenor part book: "La vaccarra."
[6] Title in tenor part book: "Spatta soleo."

1561_1

AGRICOLA, MARTIN

DUO LIBRI / MUSICES, CON/ TINENTES COM/pendium artis, & illustria / exempla. / SCRIPTI A MARTI / NO AGRICOLA SILE/sio Soraviensi, in gratiam eorum, / qui in Schola Magdeburgensi / prima elementa artis disce/re incipiunt. / WITEBERGAE / Ex Officina Haeredum Georgii / Rhaw. / Anno salutis 1561.

112 fols. Mensural notation. Dedication on fols. A2–A4^v headed "ORNATISSIMIS VIRIS PRUDENTIA & pietate praestantibus D. Ebelingo Alemanno Consuli, M. Gregorio Willichio Scabino, Matthaeo Baur, & Petro Backmeister Senatoribus, Martini Agricolae testamentariis S. D.," and signed "Datae Magdeburgi 10. Junii, anno 1559. quo die ante annos tres Martinus Agricola vesperi ante noctem intempestam ex hac mortali vita ad coelestem consuetudinem evocatus est. Siegfridus Sacus." Colophon on fol. O7^v: "WITEBERGAE HAEREDES GEORGII Rhaw excudebant. ANNO M. D. LXI." The volume is an introduction to music theory written for classroom use. On fols. E8 to the end are 54 textless pieces (mostly *a3* and some *a4*) for use in connection with instrumental instruction. There is one piece for each week of the year, except for two weeks, which have two pieces each. All of them are two- or three-voiced canons each with a free voice. AgricolaIG is a mod. ed. of all of these instrumental compositions. The compositions identified by the superior letter *a* ([a]) are reprinted in ZfSM II. The following inventory includes chapter and division headings of the theoretical part and all of the complete compositions included as examples. Other examples (tables, graphs, and incomplete pieces) in the theoretical part are not listed here.

Copies in: D:Bds-Tü, D:HB, D:HVl.

	fol.	
	A5	Caput Primum. De Musices Descriptione
	A5^v	De Divisione Musicae
*1	A5^v	*Fuga in subdiapent. post 2. Tactus* (canon *a2* over "Veni sancte Spiritus")
*2	A6	*Fuga post Tempus unisonans* (canon *a2* over a bass)
	A6	De Figurali Musica
*3	A6^v	*Fuga post Tempus unisonans* (canon *a2* over a bass)
	A7	De Musica Instrumentali
	B1	Caput II. De Clavibus Vocibusque Musicalibus
	B1^v	De Scala
	B1^v	De Characteristicis Clavibus
	B3	De Sex Vocibus Musicalibus
	B3	De Vocum Divisione
*4	B3^v	*Fuga unisonans post Tempus* (canon *a2* over a bass)
	B4	Caput Tertium. De Vocum Mutatione & Solmisatione
*5	B4^v	*Fuga in Epidiapa. post tempus unum* (canon *a2* over a bass)
	B4^v	De Solmisatione
	B5	De Cantus Divisione [De Cantu bmollis]
	B6^v	De Cantu ♮ Duro
	B7^v	De Ficto Cantu
	C1	Caput IIII. De Transpositione Clavium
	C1	De Elevatione
	C1^v	De Submissione
*6	C1^v	*Fuga in Epidiapa. post 4. Tactus* (canon *a2* over a bass)
	C2	De Modis Musicalibus
	C3^v	De Intervallis prohibitis
	C3^v	Caput VI. De Tonis
	C4	De Quatuor Tonorum Sedibus
	C4^v	De Tonorum Repercussionibus & Tenoribus
	C5^v	De Tono Imperfecto
	C6	De Mixto Tono
	C6	De Tonorum Transpositione
	C7^v	De Certa Cantionum inceptione
	C8	SEQUITUR SE/CUNDUS HUIUS COM/pendii Liber, omnium praeceptorum / hactenus traditorum exempla, & pro / primis Tyronibus

exercitia composita, / quae in singulas quae totius anni Sep/timanas digesta sunt, / complectens. / Per / MART. SOREN MUSI/cum & Symphonistam Magde/burgensis Scholae. / PLINIUS. / Et quatenus negatur nobis diu vivere, relin/quamus aliquid, quo, nos vixisse testemur.

C8 Caput I. Breve, ad cantum mensuratum, introductorium

C8ᵛ De Notulis Simplicibus mensurati concentus

D1ᵛ De Pausis

D2 Caput II. De Notularum colligatione

*7 D3ᵛ *Paradigma omnium regularum rationem explicans* [textless composition *a 4*]

D6ᵛ Caput III. De Punctis et Colore

D6ᵛ De Perfectionis Puncto

D7 De Alterationis Punctulo

D7 De Puncto Additionis

*8 D7ᵛ *De Additionis Puncto aliud, quatuor vocum, Exemplum* [textless composition *a 4*]

E1 De Colore

E2 Caput IIII. De Tribus Tactibus

E2ᵛ De Tactu Maiore

E2ᵛ De Semitactu

E3 De Tactu Proportionato

*9 E3ᵛ *De Integro et Semitactu Exemplum. Fuga in Epidiapas. post 2. Temp.* (canon *a 2* over a bass)

E4 Caput V. De Tribus Gradibus generalis institutio

E4ᵛ De Modo Minore

E5 De Tempore

E5 De Prolatione

*10 E7 *Fuga, post tres Breves, unisonans* (canon *a 2* over a bass)

E8 De VI. Vocibus Musicalibus, ut, re, mi, fa, sol, la.

1 E8 *Fuga unisonans post Tempus unum* [*a 3*] In Septimana Paschatis, exercitium ♮ durum

2 E8 *Fuga duum ex Epidiapent. post Tempus* [*a 3*] In Sept. prima post Pasch. de tertiis exemplum [1]

3 F1 *Fuga post Semib: in Epidiapen.* [*a 3*] In 2. Sept. post Pasch. de tertiis aliud Paradigma

4 F1ᵛ *Fuga in Epidiapent. post Temp.* [*a 3*] In 3. Sept. post Pasch. de Quartarum nomenclatione exercitium

5 F2 *Fuga in Subdiapent. post Tempus* [*a 3*] In 4. Sept. post Pasch. de Quartis aliud exemplum

6 F2ᵛ *Fuga post 3. Temp. unisonans* [*a 3*] In 5. Sept. post Pasch. *Christ ist erstanden* (compare ZahnM, no. 8584)

7 F3ᵛ *Fuga in Epidiapent. post Temp.* [*a 3*] In 6. Sept. post Pasch. [2] *Jhesus Christus unser Hei*[*land*] (compare ZahnM, no. 1576)

8 F5 *Fuga in Epidiatess. post Semibrevem* [*a 3*] In Sept. Pentecos. de Cantu bmol, exercitium

9 F6ᵛ *Fuga ex eadem Clave post 2. Temp.* [*a 3*] In Sept. Trinitatis exercitium bmolle

10 F7ᵛ *Fuga duorum Temp. unisonans* [*a 3*] In prima Sept. post Trinitatis exemplum bmolle

11 F8ᵛ *Fuga in eadem Clave post 2. Temp.* [*a 3*] In secunda Sept. post Trinitatis

12 G2 *Fuga post Temp. unisonans*[a] [3] [*a 3*] In 3. Sept. post Trinit. exemplum bmolle. *Wol dem der in Gottes furchten steht* (compare ZahnM, no. 305)

13 G3 *Fuga ex eadem clave post Tem. unum.* [*a 3*] In 4. Sept. post Tri. exerci. bmol. [4]

14 G4ᵛ *Fuga in Epidiapent. post Temp. unum.* [*a 3*] In 5. Sept. post Trinit. exemplum bmolle

15 G5ᵛ *Cancrissat vox altera* [*a 3*] In 6. Sept. post Trinit. exercitium bmolle

16 G6ᵛ *Fuga in eadem clave. post 3 Temp.*[a] [*a 3*] In 7. Sept. post Trinitatis. *Vater unser* (compare ZahnM, no. 2561)

17 G8 *Fuga trium Temp. unisonans* [*a3*] In 8. Sept. post Trinit. *Wir gleuben* [*all an einem Gott*] (compare ZahnM, no. 7971)

18 H1v *Fuga, post Temp. unum, unisonans* [*a3*] In 9. Sept. post Trinit. exemplum ♮ durum

19 H3 *Fuga post Temp. unum in subdiapente* [*a4*] In 10. Sept. post Trinit. ♮ duri cantus paradigma

20 H4v *Fuga ex eadem Clave post 2. Temp.* [*a3*] In 11. Sept. post Trinit. ♮ dur. exercitium

21 H6v *Fuga 2. Temp. in Subdiapent.* [*a3*] In 12. Sept. post Trinit. exercitium ♮ durum

22 H8v *Fuga in Epidiapent. post Temp. unum* [*a3*] In 13. Sept. post Trinit. paradigma ♮ dur

23 I2 *Fuga in eadem Clave post 2. Temp.* [*a3*] In 14. Sept. post Trinit. exercitium ♮ duri cantus

24 I3 *Fuga, post 3. Temp. unisonans* [*a3*] In 15. Sept. post Trinit. ♮ dur. paradigma

25 I4v *Fuga duum Epitono post Temp. unum* [*a3*] In 16. Sept. post Trinit. exercitium ♮ durae cantionis[5]

26 I5v *Fuga, post Temp. unum unisonans* [*a3*] In 17. Sept. post Trinit. ♮ dur. exercitium

27 I7v *Fuga post Temp. unum in Epidiapente* [*a3*] In 18. Sept. post Trinit. paradigma ♮ durum

28 I8v *Fuga in eadem clave post Brevem* [*a3*] In 19. Sept. post Trinit. ♮ duri Systematis exemplum

29 K1 *Fuga, 2. Temp. unisonans* [*a4*] In 20. Sept. post Trinit. ♮ durae Scalae exercitium

30 K2v *Fuga unisonans post duo Tempora* [*a3*] In 21. Sept. post Trinit. exemplum ♮ durum

31 K4 *Fuga post brevem unisonans* [*a3*] In 22. Sept. post Trinit. exercitium Prolationis perfectae

32 K5 *Fuga in Epidiatess. post Temp.* [*a3*] In 23. Sept. post Trinit. exemplum ♮ durum

33 K6v *Fuga, trium vocum, unisonans* [*a3*] In 24. Sept. post Trinit. exercitium ♮ duri concentus

34 K7 *Fuga ex eadem Clave post 3. Temp.* [*a3*] In 25. Sept. post Trinit. *Mit fried und freud* (compare ZahnM, no. 3986)

35 L1 *Fuga duorum Temp. unisonans* [*a4*] In prima Sept. Adventus, *Veni redemptor gentium* (compare ZahnM, no. 307)

36 L2v *Fuga ex eadem Clave post 2. breves*[a] [*a3*] In 2. Sept. Adventus, *Mag ich nicht unglück widerstan* (compare ZahnM, no. 8113)

37 L4 *Fuga unisonans post Tempus unum*[a] [*a3*][6] In 3. Sept. Adventus. *Aus tieffer not* (compare ZahnM, no. 4437)

38 L5 *Fuga, post duas breves, unisonans*[a] [*a3*] In 4. Sept. Adventus. *Christum wir sollen loben schon* (compare ZahnM, no. 297)

39 L6 *Fuga in subdiatess. post Tempus* [*a4*] In prima Sept. post Nativitatis. *Dies est laetitiae* (compare ZahnM, no. 7869)

40 L8v *Fuga post brevem in Epidiapente* [*a3*] In 2. Sept. post Nativitatis, exercitium ♮ durum

41 M2v *Fuga post 2. Temp. unisonans*[a] [*a3*][7] In 3. Sept. post Nativitatis. *Gelobet seistu Jhesu Christ* (compare ZahnM, no. 1947)

42 M3v *Fuga in eadem Clave post 2. Te*[*mp.*] [*a3*] In 4. Sept. post Nativita, ♮ durum Paradigma

43 M5 *Fuga unisonans post Tempus unum*[a] [*a3*] In 5. Sept. post Nativi. exercitium ♮ duri concentus. *Ein feste burg* (compare ZahnM, no. 7737)

44 M6 *Fuga, post Tempus unum, unisonans* [*a 4*] In Sept. Septuagesimae exemplum bmolle. *Christe qui lux es* (compare ZahnM, no. 343)
45 M8 *Fuga unisonans post duas breves* [*a 3*] In Sept. Sexagesimae exercitium ♮ durum
46 N1 *Fuga ex eadem Clave, post Brevem* [*a 3*] In Sept. Quinquagesimae exercitium
47 N2ᵛ *Fuga post duo Tempora unisonans* [*a 3*] In Sept. Invocavit, exercitium
48 N3 *Fuga in eadem clave, post 4. breves* [*a 3*] In Sept. Reminiscere, exercitium
49 N4 *Duo in unum* [*a 3*] Aliud, praecedentis Septimanae, exercitium
50 N5 *Fuga in Epidiapente post 2. breves* [*a 3*] In Sept. Oculi exercitatio bmollaris
51 N7ᵛ In Sept. Laetare, exercitium bmollis Cantus[8] [*a 3*]
52 O1ᵛ *Fuga in Epidiapent. post brevem* [*a 3*] In Sept. Judica exercitium prolationis perfectae
53 O3ᵛ *Fuga ex eadem Clave, post Brevem* [*a 3*] In Septimana Palmarum exercitium bmollis concentus
54 O5ᵛ *Fuga unisonans post duo Tempora* [*a 4*] Aliud ♮ duri cantus exercitium. *Gott sey gelobet und gebenedeiet*[9] (compare ZahnM, no. 8078)

[1] Note on fol. E8ᵛ: "Omnis cantus in fa exiens est 5. vel 6. Tonorum."
[2] Note on fol. F3: "Omnis cantus exiens in Re, est 1. nel 2. Toni."
[3] Note on fol. G2ᵛ: "Cantus in fa terminatus, est 5. vel 6. tonorum."
[4] Note on fol. G3ᵛ: "Omnis cantus in Sol desinens, est 7. vel 8. To."
[5] The lowest voice of no. 25 is marked "Baritonae."
[6] Note on fol. L4ᵛ: "Mi finis est tertii & quarti Tonorum."
[7] Note on fol. M3: "Sol, 7. vel 8. Toni finis est."
[8] The lowest voice of no. 51 is marked "Baritonans."
[9] Note on fol. o7: "ANNOTATIONCULA. Omnis Cantus in Sol exiens, hoc est, in Clave ubi accinitur Ut sursum, Solque deorsum, est Septimi vel octavi Toni."

1561₂

GORZANIS, GIACOMO DE

INTABOLATURA DI LIUTO / DI MESSER JACOMO GORZANIS CIECO / PUGLIESE, HABITANTE NELLA CITTA DI / TRIESTE. Novamente da lui composto & per Antonio Gardano / stampato & dato in Luce. / LIBRO [Printer's mark] PRIMO / In Venetia Appresso di / Antonio Gardano. / 1561

36 fols. Italian lute tablature. Dedication on fol. A1ᵛ headed "AL MOLTO MAGNIFICO ET GENEROSO SIGNO[R] IL SIGNOR GIOVANNE KHISL DETTO DA KOLTEN PRUEN Della CESAREA M. Dignissimo Conseglier & Supremo Pagator alle Frontere & confini de Croatia." On fol. I4ᵛ: table of contents. MoeDM contains a thematic index of the volume (p. 401) and concordances (p. 256). All of the compositions are for solo lute.[1]

Copies in: F: Pthibault, I: Gu.[2]

	fol.	
1	A2	*Pasamezo antico primo*
	A4ᵛ	*Padoana del ditto*
	B2ᵛ	*Saltarelo del ditto*
2	B4ᵛ	*Pass'e mezo moderno Primo*
	C3ᵛ	*Padoana del ditto prima*
	D1ᵛ	*Saltarello del ditto*
3	D2ᵛ	*Pass'e mezo detto il Gorzanis Primo*
	D4ᵛ	*Saltarello del ditto*
4	E2ᵛ	*Il Todischino*[3]
	E4ᵛ	*Padoana del ditto*
5	F1ᵛ	*Pass'e mezo ditto La dura partita*[4]
	F2	*Padoana del ditto*[4]
6	F2ᵛ	*Pass'e mezo de la Roca el Fuso*
	F3ᵛ	*Padoana del ditto*
7	G1	*Saltarello detto il zorzi*
8	G2	*Saltarello ditto el Teteme*[5]
9	G3ᵛ	*Saltarelo detto il Poverin*
10	G4ᵛ	*Saltarelo detto Sona Baloni*[5]
11	H1	*Saltarello ditto Ciel Turchin*
12	H2	*La Barcha del mio amor*
13	H2ᵛ	*Te parti cor mio caro*[6] (compare AzzaiV, no. 12: "Tu te parti cor mio caro," Azzaiolo)
14	H3	*Bal Todescho*[7]
	H3ᵛ	*Il suo Salto*[7]

15 H4 *Occhi lucenti assai piu che le stelle* [Napolitana]

16 H4v *Ricercar primo*

17 I1v *Ricercar Secondo*

18 I3 *Ricercar Terzo*

19 I4 *Ricercar Quarto*

[1] Four volumes of solo lute music and one volume of lute songs by Gorzanis survive: I (1561_2), II (1563_8, 1565_2, and see $[1562]_2$), III (1564_4), and IV ($156?_3$ and 1579_1); and *Il Primo Libro di Napolitane* (1570_1).

[2] A copy was in the Landau-Finaly library in Florence (see RoedigC I, 526).

[3] Mod. ed. in ChilS, p. 17 (headed "Pass'e mezo"), and CorteA, no. 57.

[4] Mod. ed. in BruAL, no. 17, and ChilLS, p. 26; mod. ed. of the padoana only in MagniSM I, 277.

[5] Mod. ed. in MoeDM, p. 312.

[6] Mod. ed. in ChilLS, p. 28.

[7] Mod. ed. in ChilLS, p. 29.

1561_3

FRANCESCO DA MILANO

INTABOLATURA DI LIUTO / DI FRANCESCO DA MILANO / De Motetti Recercari & Canzoni Francese Novamente ristampata. / LIBRO [Printer's mark] SECONDO / In Venetia Appresso di / Antonio Gardano. / 1561

20 fols. Italian lute tablature. On fol. 20v: table of contents. Contents = 1546_7 and 1563_5. WieM II contains a thematic index of the entire volume. All of the compositions are for solo lute.

Copies in: A:Wn, F:Pc.

1561

DOUBTFUL WORKS

1. FétB I, 387, erroneously dates Sperindio Bertoldo, *Tocate Ricercari et Canzoni Francesci Intavolate per sonar d'organo,* 1561. The volume is listed in this bibliography as 1591_4.

2. FétB I, 231, erroneously dates Adrian le Roy, *Premier Livre de Tabulature de Guiterre,* 1561. The volume is listed in this bibliography as 1551_3.

1562_1

FRANCESCO DA MILANO AND PERINO FIORENTINO

INTABOLATURA DI LIUTO / DI M. FRANCESCO DA MILANO / ET PERINO FIORENTINO SUO DISCI/pulo. Di Recercari, Mardigali [*sic*], & Canzoni Francese. / Novamente Ristampata & Corretta. / LIBRO [Printer's mark] TERZO / In Venetia appresso di / Antonio Gardano. / 1562.

24 fols. Italian lute tablature. On fol. 24v: table of contents. Contents = 1547_2, 1563_6, and 1566_1. All of the compositions are for solo lute.

Copies in: A:Wn, F:Pn, GB:Lbm.

$[1562]_2$

GORZANIS, GIACOMO DE

IL SECONDO LIBRO DE INTABULATURA DI LIUTO, NOVAMENTE COMPOSTO PER MESSER JACOMO DE GORZANIS.

The colophon of 1563_8 (p. 62) reads: "IN VINEGIA Appresso Gyrolamo Scotto. 1562," suggesting that Scotto reprinted Gorzanis' second book in 1563 from the same type used in a first edition, now lost, one year earlier. All of the compositions in 1563_8 are in Italian lute tablature, for solo lute. For other volumes in the same series, see 1561_2, note 1.

1562_3

HECKEL, WOLFF

DISCANT. / Lautten Buch, von mancherley / schönen und lieblichen stucken, mit zweyen Lautten / zusamen zu schlagen, und auch sonst das mehrer theyl allein für sich selbst. Gu/te Teutsche, Lateinische, Frantzösische, Italienische Stuck oder lieder. Auch / vilfaltige Newe Tentz, sampt

DISCANT
Lautten Bůch / von mancherley
schönen vnd lieblichen stucken / mit zweyen Lautten
zůsamen zůschlagē / vnd auch sonst das mehrer theyl allein für sich selbst. Gůte Teutsche / Lateinische / Frantzösische / Italienische Stuck oder lieder. Auch
vilfaltige Newe Tentz / sampt mancherley Fantaseyen / Recercari / Pauana
Saltarelli / vnd Gassenhawer / &c. Durch Wolffen Heckel von München / Burger zů Strasburg. Auff das aller lieblichst in ein
verstendige Tabulatur / nach geschribner art / aufge-
setzt / vnd zůsamen gebracht.
Getruckt zů Straßburg am Kornmarckt
bey Christian Müller / Im Jar /
M. D. LXII.

Title page of 1562_3

mancherley Fantaseyen, Recercari, Pavana, / Saltarelli, und Gassenhawer, &c. Durch Wolffen Heckel von Mün/chen, Burger zu Strassburg. Auff das aller lieblichst in ein / verstendiger Tabulatur, nach geschribner art, aussge/setzt, und zusamen gebracht. / Getruckt zu Strassburg am Kornmarckt / bey Christian Müller, Im Jar, / M. D. LXII.

120 fols. German lute tablature. On fol. *1^v: instructions for using the tablature, headed "Ein kleyner bericht diser Tabulatur halben, wie man die selbig applicìern solle." On fol. *2: instructions in the rudiments of music, headed "Die Mensur, wie du sie verstehn solt." Beginning on fol. *3^v: table of contents. Fol. *5 = p. 1. The compositions identified by the superior letter *a* ([a]) are reprinted in SenflW VII. For an earlier edition see 1556_5. Some of the lied intabulations are similar but not identical to those in 1540_1. Nos. 1–40 are for two lutes; the second lute part is printed in 1562_4. All of the other compositions are for solo lute.

Copies in: A:Wn, D:Dl, D:TR, F:Pthibault,[1] GB:Lbmh (imperfect), GB:Lcm (imperfect).

MUSIC FOR TWO LUTES

	p.	
1	1	*Nun bitten wir den heyligen Geyst* (compare BaümK, no. 337, and ZahnM, no. 2029)
2	3	*Ich klag den tag und alle stund*[2] (DTO XXXVII/72, p. 71: Stoltzer)
3	5	*Tröstlicher Lieb, ich mich stets üb*[3] (MosPH, p. 86: Hofhaimer)
4	7	*Mein gmüt und blüt* (EDMR XX, no. 85: Johann Wenck)
5	8	*Patientia* [*muss ich han*][a] (SenflW IV, no. 64: Senfl)
6	10	*Per illud ave, ein Duo* (JosqMT, no. 46: 2a pars of "Benedicta es coelorum Regina," Josquin)
7	12	*Cest a grand tort* (AttainCK II, no. 18: Sermisy)
8	14	*Je suis desheritee* (CW XV, no. 2: Lupus [or Cadéac]) = 1546_{18}, no. 22

9 17 *Plus mille regres* (JosqWW, no. 29: "Plus nulz regretz," Josquin) = 1533_1, no. 33

10 23 *Ein frölich wesen*[4] (DTO XIV/28, p. 5, and LenN, p. [28]: Barbireau, Isaac, or Obrecht)

11 28 *Mein hertz hat sich mit lieb verpflicht* (MosPH, p. 154: Hofhaimer)

12 30 *Dismonta del cavallo saltarello*

13 32 *La fantina saltarello*

14 33 *Je suis ayme* (compare RISM 1502_2, no. 11: "Je suis amy du forier," Compère)

15 35 *Zart schöne fraw* (CW XXIX, 28)

16 37 *Nach willen dein*[5] (MosPH, p. 74: Hofhaimer)

17 39 *Von Edler art, ein Frewlin zart* (MosPH, p. 180: J. Schönfelder or Hofhaimer)

18 42 *Was wurt es doch, des wunders noch*[a] (SenflW IV, no. 26: Senfl) = $[1552]_{10}$, no. 16 (?)

19 46 *Benedictus* (HewO, no. 76: Isaac)

20 49 *Amica mea*[a] (SenflW IV, no. 4: Senfl)

21 53 *Veillez vo'* [in tenor: "Voules vous"]

22 57 *Languir me fais* (AttainCK II, no. 12: Sermisy)

23 59 *Amy souffres* = 1540_1, no. 31: "Ami sofre," Moulu

24 61 *Il estoit une fillete* (LesAC, no. 10: Janequin)

25 62 *Or combien est [malheureux]* = 1546_{18}, no. 39: Sandrin or Sermisy

26 66 *Mille Regres* (JosqWW, no. 24: Josquin)

27 69 *Ach Juppiter* (MosL, no. 38: Fulda) = $[1552]_{10}$, no. 15 (?)

28 72 *Hilff Herre Gott* (compare ZahnM, no. 8304)

29 76 *Il bianco e dulce cigno* (BuH II, 244: Arcadelt)[6]

30 79 *Non chi non voglio*

31 82 *Pongente Dardo* (RISM 1541_9, p. 3: Berchem)

32 85 *Pass e mezo* = $[1552]_{10}$, no. 6a

89 *Il suo saltarello* = $[1552]_{10}$, no. 6b

33 92 *Pass e mezo* = $[1552]_{10}$, no. 7a

95 *Il suo saltarello* = $[1552]_{10}$, no. 7b

34 100 *La gamba*[7] = $[1552]_{10}$, no. 8

35 101 *Le forze d'Ercule* = $[1552]_{10}$, no. 9

36 103 *Ein güter Hofftantz* = $[1552]_{10}$, no. 12a

104 *Proportz darauff* = $[1552]_{10}$, no. 12b

37 105 *Pavana* = $[1552]_{10}$, no. 13

38 107 *Les Bouffon* = $[1552]_{10}$, no. 14

39 109 *Ein kunstreicher Gassenhawer*

111 2a pars

116 3a pars *Proportz*

40 118 *Ein schöner [Baierscher] hoff tantz* G. Heynreich

119 *Gassenhawer uff den Tantz*

MUSIC FOR SOLO LUTE[8]

41 121 *Ave gloriosa*

42 125 *Gelobet seist du Jesu Christ*

43 127 *Pour ung plasier*[9]

44 131 *Cest a Faux* (AttainCK II, no. 25: "Ces fascheux sotz")

45 133 *Quando io penso alli martirio* (RISM 1541_9, p. 54: Arcadelt)

46 137 *Je prens en gre* (ClemensO X, 14: Clemens non Papa)

47 139 *Doeul double doeul* (CW XV, no. 1: Lupi)

48 142 *Si par souffrir* (RISM 1534_{14}, no. 4: Courtois)

49 144 *Contre raison* (AttainCK II, no. 5: Sermisy)

50 146 *Aupres de vous* (AttainCK I, no. 16: Sermisy or Jacotin)

51 148 *Mauldit soye [la mondaine richesse]* (AttainCK I, no. 14: Sermisy)

52 150 *Vivre ne puis* (RISM 1536_3, no. 9: Sermisy)

53 152 *Doulce memoire* (PubAPTM XXIII, no. 50: Sandrin)

54 156 *Vous perdes Temps* (PubAPTM XXIII, no. 56: Sermisy)

55 159 *Dilectus meus*

56 162 *Si la fortune, Künigs von Franckreichs Lied*

57 164 *Le departir* (ClemensO X, 3: Clemens non Papa)

58 166 *En esperant* = 1544_1, no. 39: Sermisy

59 168 *Il ont mesdit*

60 171 *Mon petit [cueur]* (compare RISM 1520_3, fol. 29^v)
61 172 *Damour me plais* (PubAPTM XXIII, no. 49: Roger [Pathie])
62 177 *Et factus est. Mutet*
181 2a pars
63 185 *Ick sege adieu* = 1544_1, no. 30
64 186 *Incessament [mon pauvre cueur]* (RISM 1572_2, fol. 52^v: De La Rue)
65 189 *Qui son heritier* (RISM 1549_{20}, no. 1: "Qui souhaittez," Sandrin)
66 191 *Preambulum*
67 193 *O sia potesi Tanna* (RISM 1541_9, p. 19: Berchem).
68 196 *Date syceram merentibus* [Sermisy][10] (D:Rp, MSS B. 211–215, no. 30; see MohrH)
69 200 *He he, das neüw jar, Gott geb der aller Liebsten*
70 205 *Helas [amy]* (RISM 1541_8, fol. 4: Sandrin)
71 207 *Cum sancto spiritu* Josquin (JosqMS, no. 16: *Missa de Beata Virgine*)
72 210 *Bewar mich Herr* (D:Rp, MS A. R. 855, no. 19: Zirler)
73 212 *Die brünlin die da fliessen*[a] (PubAPTM I, no. 44: Senfl)
74 215 *Unfall wann ist deins wesen gnug*[a] (PubAPTM I, no. 50: Senfl)
75 218 *Sie ist die sich heldt*[a] (SenflW V, no. 21: Senfl)
76 220 *Man spricht waz gott zusamen fügt*[a] (SenflW IV, no. 52: Senfl)
77 222 *Kein ding uff erden* (SenflW II, no. 64: Senfl)
78 224 *Mein freud allein*[11] (DTO XIV/28, p. 17: Isaac)
79 227 *Freündtlicher Helde*[a] (PubAPTM II, no. 46: Senfl)
80 229 *Alde*

[1] This copy was in the Écorcheville library (see ÉcorC, no. 39).
[2] Mod. ed. in DTO XXXVII/72, p. 97, and RaL, p. 335.
[3] Mod. ed. in DTO XXXVII/72, p. 87.
[4] Mod. ed. in DTO XIV/28, p. 141.
[5] Mod. ed. in DTO XXXVII/72, p. 85; for a comparison of this intabulation with various others see NowakH.
[6] Page numbering of BuH is after the new Dover reprint.
[7] Mod. ed. in StaakS, p. 1 (arr. for guitar after a manuscript source).
[8] Heading on p. 121: "Hie enden sich die stuck so zusamen gangen auff zwo lauten, und gehn dise nachfolgenden stuck, so auff das aller lieblichst und kunstlichst auszgesetzt allein für sich selbs bis zum end."
[9] Not related musically to ParrishM, no. 20: Crecquillon, nor to SeayFC, no. 5: Sermisy.
[10] Attributed to Sermisy in 1558_5, no. 9.
[11] Mod. ed. in DTO XIV/28, p. 157.

1562_4

HECKEL, WOLFF

TENOR. / Lautten Buch, von mancherley / schönen und lieblichen stucken, mit zwey Lautten / zusamen zu schlagen, und auch sonst das mehrer theyl allein für sich selbst. Gu/te Teutsche, Lateinische, Frantzösische, Italienische Stuck oder lieder. Auch / vilfaltige Newe Tentz, sampt mancherley Fantaseyen, Recercari, Pavana, / Saltarelli, und Gassenhawer, &c. Durch Wolffen Heckel von Mün/chen, Burger zu Strassburg. Auff das aller lieblichst in ein / verstendiger Tabulatur, nach geschribner art, aussge/setzt, und zusamen gebracht. / Getruckt zu Strassburg am Kornmarckt / bey Christian Müller, Im Jar, / M. D. LXII.

112 fols. German lute tablature. Dedication on fol. *1^v headed "Den Wolgebornen Herrn, Herrn Johan, Graven zu Nassaw, Katzenellenbogen, Vianden und Dietz, Herrn Heinrichen von Eyssenburg, Graven zu Budingen, Herrn Philipsen, dem Jüngern, Graven zu Hanaw, und Herrn zu Liechtenberg, &c. meinen gnedigen Herrn," and signed "Datum zu Strassburg an Sanct Johannis des heyligen Teuffers tag, Nach Christi unsers Erlösers geburt M. D. Lvi. Jare. E. G. Undertheniger gehorsamer Diener Wolff Heckel." On fol. *2^v: a note about the instrumentation headed "Wie man die Lautten soll zusamen richten." Beginning on fol. *3: table of contents. On fol. *4^v: cut of the neck of a lute with the heading "Der auffgerissen Lautenkragen." The music begins on fol. *5 (= p. 1). For an earlier edition see $[1556]_6$. Some of the dances are similar but not identical to those by Hans Newsidler. The first 40 compositions are second lute parts for 1562_3, nos. 1–40.

The compositions in the following list are all for solo lute.

Copies in: A:Wn, B:Br,[1] CH:Bu, D:Bds, D:Dl.

p.

41 100 *Graff Johan von Nassaw dantz, Wie kan ich frölich werden*[2]

102 *Proportz darauff*

42 104 *Wider ein schöner Hofftantz mit lieblicher Colleratur*[2]

106 *Proportz auff den Tantz*

43 107 *Ein schöner Tantz in Höffen zu gebrauchen*

108 *Proportz auff den Tantz*

44 109 *Wider ein guter Tantz, mit vier stymmen*

110 *Proportz darauff*

45 111 *Ein schöner schwäbischer Tantz*

113 *Proportz auff den Tantz*

46 115 *Ein Bocks Tantz*

116 *Proportz auff den Tantz*

47 117 *Wider ein Sechsisch täntzlin*

118 *Proportz*

48 119 *Ein schöner Burger Tantz*

120 *Proportz auff den Tantz*

49 121 *Der Künigin Tantz*

122 *Proportz auff der Künigin Tantz*

50 123 *Ein schöner gemeyner Tantz*

125 *Proportz darauff*

51 126 *Ein schöner Tantz, mit lieblicher Colleratur, d'Müller genant*

128 *Proportz auff den Tantz*

52 129 *Wider ein schöner Tantz, Ich weysz mir ein schöne Müllerin*

131 *Proportz auff die Müllerin*

53 132 *Des Printzen Tantz* (compare 1571_1, no. 46: "Wer das Töchterlein haben wil")

133 *Proportz auff den tantz*

54 135 *Der Westfäler Tantz*

136 *Proportz darauff*

55 138 *Der Züner Tantz*

140 *Proportz auff den Züner*

56 141 *Der welsch scharrer*

143 *Proportz auff den scharrer*

57 146 *Der Pissepot, ein welscher Tantz genant allein im tripel für sich selbs gaht*

58 147 *Der Maruscat Tantz*

149 *Proportz auff den Maruscat Tantz*

59 151 *Der Betler Tantz*

152 *Proportz auff den Betler*

60 153 *Der schwartz Knab* = $[1552]_{10}$, no. 12

155 *Proportz auff den schwartzen Knaben*

61 157 *Helena Tantz sehr lieblich*

158 *Proportz darauff*

62 159 *Ein Ungerischer Tantz*[3]

160 *Proportz auff den Ungerischen Tantz*

63 162 *Ein guter Bayrischer Bauren Tantz*[4]

164 *Proportz daruff den Bauren Tantz*

64 165 *Ein springendter Tantz für sich selbst*[5]

65 167 *Ein ander springendter Tantz für sich selbst*

66 169 *Der Juden Tantz*

172 *Proportz auff den Juden Tantz*

67 174 *Der Kochelsperger Tantz*

176 *Proportz auff den Kochelsperger Tantz*

68 177 *Ein Schweitzer Tantz der sibentaler genandt.* Urban Weiss

179 *Proportz auff den Sibentaler*

69 180 *Der Lauffer Tantz*[6]

182 *Proportz auff den Lauffer tantz*

70 185 *Der Frantzösisch Tantz für sich selbs*

71 187 *Ein schöner welscher Tantz für sich selbst*

72 189 *Ein guter Paduaner*

191 *Saltarelli auff den Paduener*

73 193 *Pasemezo, sehr gut*

74 198 *Recercari de milla new*[7] [Francesco da Milano ?]

75 200 *Ein Fantasey mit fugen*

76 204 *Ein ander fantasey auff Welsch auszgesetzt*

77 208 *Ein fast schöner Paduaner*[8]

209 *Saltarello auff den Paduaner*

78 211 *Ein sehr lieblich Fantasey durch Wolff Heckel* = 1536_3, no. 3: Francesco da Milano

[1] MorL I, xliii, lists an anon. *Lautenbuch* (Strasbourg: Christian Müller, 1567), as being in B:Br. Morphy probably refers to 1562_4. A copy of 1562_4 was in D:WEs.

[2] Facs. of fols. 98 (including no. 40b), 99, 100, and 104 in EF II, 449, and MGG VI, col. 15 (both after the 1556 ed.). Mod. ed. of no. 41 in StaakF, no. 4 (arr. for guitar from a manuscript source).

[3] Mod. ed. of no. 62a in FerandM, p. 405.

[4] Melody only pr. in BruD, no. 1.

[5] Mod. ed. in BöhT II, no. 132.

[6] Mod. ed. in TapS, p. 35.
[7] Mod. ed. in EnI, app., p. 11.
[8] Mod. ed. in SteinitA, no. 34.

$[1562]_5$

LE ROY, ADRIAN

Livre de Tabulature sur le luth par Adrian le Roy D'Octante Trois pseaumes de David . . . composés à quatre parties par Cl. Goudimel, mis en rime françoise par Cl. Marot et Th. de Besze. Paris, Le Roy et Ballard, 1562.

This volume was in PL:S (see TischA, art. 538, and LesLRB, art. 79 *bis*).

1562_6

LUPACCHINO, BERNARDINO, AND JOAN MARIA TASSO

DI BERNARDINO LUPACCHINO / ET DI JOAN MARIA TASSO. / IL PRIMO LIBRO / A DUE VOCI. / Novamente con ogni / diligentia ristampato, & da molti errori emendato. / Aggiontovi ancora alcuni canti a Due voci de diversi autori. / [Printer's mark] / In Venegia, Appresso Girolamo Scotto. 1562

Two part books in mensural notation, each of 20 fols. Contents = 1559_6. All of the compositions are for instrumental ensemble *a2*.

Copy in: I:Msartori (S).

$[1562]_7$

PALADIN, ANTOINE FRANÇOIS

Ant. Franc. Paladin. Tablature de Luth, ou sont contenus plusieurs Psalmes & Chansons spirituelles, à Lyon, Simon Gorlier. 1562.

This volume, now lost, is listed in DraudiusBE, p. 210, and in Du Verdier I, 132. The reference may be to 1560_3.

1562_8

RIPPE, ALBERT DE

PREMIER LIVRE DE TABELATU/RE DE LUTH CONTENANT / plusieurs fantasies. / Par Maistre Albert de Rippe / Mantouan. / [Cut of goddesses with musical instruments] / A PARIS. / De l'Imprimerie d'Adrian le Roy, & Robert Ballard, Imprimeurs du Roy, ruë / saint Jean de Beauvais, à l'enseigne du mont Pernasse. / 1562. / Avec privilege du Roy, pour dix ans.

24 fols. French lute tablature. On fol. 1^v: portrait of Henry II. On fol. 24^v: table of contents followed by the printer's mark with the motto "VIRTUTI FORTUNA CEDIT" and intertwined initials. SlimK II, 567–568, contains a thematic index of this volume. All of the compositions are for solo lute.[1]

Copies in: D:Mbs, D:ROu.

	fol.	
1	2	*Fantasie premiere* = 1552_8, no. 1
2	6^v	*Fantasie seconde* = 1552_8, no. 2
3	8^v	*Fantasie troisiesme* = 1552_8, no. 3
4	10^v	*Fantasie quatriesme* = 1554_6, no. 1
5	12^v	*Fantasie cinquiesme* = 1554_6, no. 2
6	14^v	*Fantasie sixiesme* = 1554_6, no. 3
7	17^v	*Fantasie septtiesme* = 1554_7, no. 1
8	19^v	*Fantasie huitiesme* = 1554_7, no. 2
9	22^v	*Fantasie neufiesme* = 1554_8, no. 3

[1] Five volumes of lute music by Albert de Rippe, published by Le Roy and Ballard, survive: I (1562_8), II (1562_9), III (1562_{10}), IV (1553_9), and V (1562_{11}). See 1552_8, note 1, for the series of volumes of music by De Rippe published by Michel Fezandat.

1562_9

RIPPE, ALBERT DE

SECOND LIVRE DE TABELATU/RE DE LUTH CONTENANT / plusieurs chansons. / Par Maistre Albert de Rippe / Mantouan. / [Cut of goddesses with musical instruments] / A PARIS. / De l'Imprimerie d'Adrian le Roy, & Robert Ballard, Imprimeurs du Roy, ruë / saint Jean de Beauvais, à l'enseigne du mont Pernasse. / 1562. / Avec privilege du Roy, pour dix ans.

24 fols. French lute tablature. On fol. 1v: portrait of Henry II. On fol. 24v: table of contents followed by the printer's mark. For other volumes in the same series, see 1562_8, note 1. All of the compositions are for solo lute.

Copies in: D:Mbs, D:ROu.

	fol.	
1	2	*Si comme espoir* = 1552_8, no. 10: Maillard
2	3v	*Je suis desheritée* = 1552_8, no. 7: Lupus or Cadéac
3	5	*Il ne se trouve en amytyé* = 1552_8, no. 13: Sandrin
4	7	*Voulant honneur* = 1552_8, no. 16: Sandrin
5	9	*Fors seullement* (ObrWW, p. 90: Josquin or Févin) = 1574_7, no. 18
6	11	*D'amour me plains* = 1554_7, no. 4: Pathie
7	12	*Mon pensement* = 1554_7, no. 5: Gombert
8	13v	*Si quelque fois* = 1554_7, no. 6: Gentian
9	14v	*La volonté* = 1554_7, no. 8: Sandrin
10	16	*Ce qu'il m'est deu* = 1554_7, no. 9: Sandrin
11	17	*Mais pourquoy* (RISM 1543_{11}, no. 4: Sandrin) = 1574_7, no. 22
12	18v	*Je sents l'affect*[*ion*] = 1558_6, no. 7: Boyvin
13	20v	*Plus ne peult mon coeur estre* = 1552_8, no. 19
14	21	*Dun seul soleil* = 1552_8, no. 9: Janequin
15	23	*Montz & vaux* = 1552_8, no. 14: Sandrin

1562_{10}

RIPPE, ALBERT DE

TIERS LIVRE DE TABELATU/RE DE LUTH CONTENANT / plusieurs chansons. / Par Maistre Albert de Rippe / Mantouan. / [Cut of goddesses with musical instruments] / A PARIS. / De l'Imprimerie d'Adrian le Roy, & Robert Ballard, Imprimeurs du Roy, ruë / saint Jean de Beauvais, à l'enseigne du mont Pernasse. / 1562. / Avec privilege du Roy, pour dix ans.

24 fols. French lute tablature. On fol. 1v: portrait of Henry II. On fol. 24v: table of contents followed by the printer's mark. For other volumes in the same series, see 1562_8, note 1. All of the compositions are for solo lute.

Copies in: D:Mbs, D:ROu.

	fol.	
1	2	*O passi sparsi* = 1555_4, no. 4: S. Festa
2	3v	*O comme heureux* = 1558_6, no. 5: Certon
3	4v	*Celle qui m'a le nom donné* (RISM 1543_7, no. 2: Sandrin)
4	6v	*Dieu qui conduis* (RISM 1549_{24}, no. 16: Gentian) = 1574_7, no. 39
5	7v	*Or vien ça vien* = 1560_3, no. 19: Janequin
6	8v	*Douce memoire* (PubAPTM XXIII, no. 50: Sandrin) = 1574_7, no. 15
7	10	*Ayant cognu* (RISM 1546_{14}, no. 13: Certon) = 1574_7, no. 27
8	12	*Pleurés mes yeux* (RISM 1540_{13}, no. 22: Sandrin)
9	13	*Dueil double dueil* (CW XV, no. 1: Lupi)
10	14v	*Corps s'esloigant* (RISM 1546_{12}, no. 17: Certon)
11	16	*Martin menoit* (CM II, 79: Janequin) = 1574_7, no. 29
12	17v	*Navous point veu* = 1554_8, no. 6: "Navez point veu mal assenée," Richafort
13	19v	*Au temps heureux* (SCMA V, no. 1: Arcadelt) = 1574_7, no. 31
14	20v	*Dames d'honneur* (RISM 1543_{11}, no. 17: Sandrin)
15	22	*On en dira ce qu'on voudra* (RISM 1578_{14}, no. 5: Sermisy) = 1574_7, no. 32
16	23	*De qui plus tost* (RISM 1549_{20}, no. 29: Sandrin)

1562_{11}

RIPPE, ALBERT DE

CINQIESME LIVRE DE TABELATU/RE DE LUTH CONTENANT / plusieurs motetz, & fantasies. / Par Maistre Albert de

Rippe / Mantouan. / [Cut of goddesses with musical instruments] / A PARIS, / De l'Imprimerie d'Adrian le Roy, & Robert Ballard, Imprimeurs du Roy, ruë / saint Jean de Beauvais, à l'enseigne du mont Pernasse. / 1562. / Avec privilege du Roy, pour dix ans.

24 fols. French lute tablature. On fol. 1v: portrait of Henry II. On fol. 24v: table of contents. For other volumes in the same series, see 1562_8, note 1. All of the compositions are for solo lute.

Copies in: D:Mbs, D:ROu.

	fol.	
1	2	*Benedicta* = 1558_6, no. 3a: Josquin
	4v	2a pars [*Per illud ave*] = 1558_6, no. 3b
	5	3a pars [*Nunc Mater exora natum*] = 1558_6, no. 3c
2	6	*Adiuva me* = 1554_7, no. 10a: Conseil
	8	2a pars [*Servus tuus ego sum*] = 1554_7, no. 10b
3	9v	*Ave* [*sanctissima*] (RISM 1565_3, fol. 10: Sermisy)
4	11	*Pater pecavi* (SmijT II, 141: Conseil) = 1574_7, no. 52a
	12	2a pars [*Quanti mercenarii*] = 1574_7, no. 52b
5	13v	*Noe noe psallité* (SmijT II, 8: Mouton)
6	16v	*Fantasie* = 1558_6, no. 2
7	18v	*Fantasie*[1] = 1574_7, no. 2
8	20	*Fantasie*[1] = 1552_8, no. 5
9	22	*Fantasie* = 1536_9, no. 2

[1] Incipits in SlimK II, 568.

$[1562]_{12}$

SCOTTO, GIROLAMO

IL TERZO LIBRO / DELLI MADRIGALI A DUE VOCI, / DI GIROLAMO SCOTTO, / NUOVAMENTE RISTAMPATI / Et da lui proprio con Nuova gionta / ampliati, & con ogni dili/gentia coretti. / [Printer's mark] / In Vinegia, Appresso Girolamo Scotto, / M D LXII.

Two part books in mensural notation, each of 12 fols. According to Vogel: Scotto 14 (1562), this collection contained six instrumental pieces *a2*. A complete set of part books was in D:C; they were moved to D:Bds and are now lost (see SartMS, pp. 24–25). Vogel: Scotto 14 and Sartori list the pieces with Italian text included in the collection.

1563_1

ABONDANTE, JULIO

INTABOLATURA DI LIUTO / DI JULIO ABUNDANTE. / DE OGNI SORTE DE BALLI, NOVAMENTE / Ristampati. / LIBRO [Printer's mark] PRIMO / In Venetia appresso di / Antonio Gardano. / 1563.

20 fols. Italian lute tablature. On fol. E4v: table of contents. LefL contains a modern edition of the entire volume. Contents = 1546_1. All of the compositions are for solo lute.

Copy in: US:Wc.[1]

[1] This copy was in the Landau-Finaly library in Florence (see RoedigC I, 491).

1563_2

BIANCHINI, DOMINICO

LA / INTABOLATURA DE LAUTO / DI DOMINICO BIANCHINI / DETTO ROSSETTO. / DI RECERCARI, MOTETTI, MADRIGALI, / Canzon Francese, Napolitane, Et Balli. / Novamente ristampata & corretta. / LIBRO PRIMO./ [Printer's mark] / IN VINEGIA Appresso Girolamo Scotto. / 1563.

20 fols. Italian lute tablature. On fol. 20v: table of contents followed by the colophon: "IN VINEGIA Appresso Girolamo Scotto. 1563." Contents = 1546_5 and 1554_2. All of the compositions are for solo lute.

Copy in: A:Wn.

1563_3

BORRONO, PIETRO PAOLO

LA / INTABOLATURA DE LAUTO / DELL'ECCELLENTE P. PAUOLO / BORRONO DA MILANO. / DI SALTARELLI, PADOUANE, BALLI, / FANTASIE, ET CANZON FRANCESE, / NOVAMENTE POSTA IN LUCE. / Con ogni diligentia ristampata & corretta. / [Printer's mark] / IN VINEGIA Appresso Girolamo Scotto. / 1563.

24 fols. Italian lute tablature. On p. 48: table of contents followed by the colophon: "In Vinegia Appresso Girolamo Scotto. 1563." This is a partial reprint of 1548_2 (see there for complete list of contents). LefL contains a modern edition of the entire volume. All of the compositions are for solo lute.

Copies in: A:Wn, US:Wc.[1]

1–4 = 1548_2, nos. 1–4
5–10 = 1548_2, nos. 17–22
11 = 1548_2, no. 24

[1] This copy was in the Landau-Finaly library in Florence (see RoedigC I, 500).

1563_4

FRANCESCO DA MILANO

LA / INTABOLATURA DE LAUTO / DI FRANCESCO DA MILANO / CON LA CANZON DELI UCCELLI / LA BATAGLIA FRANCESE. ET ALTRE COSE / COME NELLE TAVOLA NEL FIN APARE. / Novamente ristampata / LIBRO PRIMO. / [Printer's mark] / IN VINEGIA Appresso Gyrolamo Scotto. / 1563.

20 fols. Italian lute tablature. On fol. 20v: table of contents followed by the colophon: "In Vinegia Appresso Gyrolamo Scotto. 1563." Contents = 1546_6 and 1556_3 with some additions. All of the compositions are for solo lute.

Copy in: I:Gu.

	fol.	
1–13	1vff	Contents identical to 1546_6 and 1556_3
	p.	
14	36	*Recercar I de F[rancesco] da M[ilano]* = 1548_4, no. 1
15	36	*Recercar II de F. da M.* = 1548_4, no. 2
16	38	*Recercar III de F. da M.* = 1548_4, no. 3
17	38	*Recercar IIII de F. da M.* = 1548_4, no. 4

1563_5

FRANCESCO DA MILANO

LA / INTABOLATURA DE LAUTO / DI FRANCESCO DA MILANO / DE MOTETTI RECERCARI / ET CANZONE FRANCESE. / Novamente ristampata & coretta. / LIBRO SECONDO. / [Printer's mark] / IN VINEGIA Appresso Gyrolamo Scotto. / 1563.

20 fols. Italian lute tablature. On fol. 20v: table of contents. Contents = 1546_7 and 1561_3. WieM II contains a thematic index of the entire volume. All of the compositions are for solo lute.

Copy in: A:Wn.

1563_6

FRANCESCO DA MILANO AND PERINO FIORENTINO

LA / INTABOLATURA DE LAUTO / DI FRANCESCO DA MILANO / ET M. PERINO FIORENTINO SUO DISCEPOLO / Di Recercate Madrigali, & canzone Francese. / Novamente ristampata & corretta. / LIBRO TERZO. / [Printer's mark] / IN VINEGIA Appresso Girolamo Scotto. / 1563.

24 fols. Italian lute tablature. On fol. 24v: table of contents. Contents = 1547_2, 1562_1, and 1566_1. All of the compositions are for solo lute.

Copies in: A:Wn, I:Gu.

1563_7

GALILEI, VINCENZO

INTAVOLATURE / DE LAUTO / DI VINCENZO GALILEO FIORENTINO / MADRIGALI, E RICERCATE / LIBRO [Printer's mark] PRIMO. / In Roma per .M. Valerio Dorico, l'Anno M. LXIII. / con privilegio per Anni .X.[1]

28 fols. Italian lute tablature. Dedication on fol. 2 headed "AL MOLTO ILL.re. S. IL SIGNOR ALESSANDRO DE MEDICI. S. mio sempre osservandissimo," and signed "Di Pisa il di vii. di Aprile. M. D. LXIII. Di V. S. Ill.re. Humilis. Servitore. Vincentio Galilei," reprinted in IMAMI IV, lxxxiv (facsimile opposite p. lxxxv). Fol. 2v = p. 1. On p. 52: table of contents. For further information see ChilLV. All of the compositions are for solo lute.

Copy in: A:Wn.

p.

1 1 *Ahi bella liberte* Alessandro Romano

2 2 *Pur mi consola* Alessandro Romano

3 3 *Cl'occhi in vaghiro al'hor'* Alessandro Romano

4 3 *Ne mi lece ascoltar* Alessandro Romano

5 5 *Pur mi consola* [Alessandro Romano] (compare no. 2)

6 6 *Com'havra vit'Amor* Vincentio Ruffo *a 5* (Vogel: Ruffo 16 [1556], p. 21)

7 7 *Ahi chi mi da consiglio* Alessandro Romano (Vogel: Romano 2 [1577], p. 5)

8 9 *Bacia mi vita mia* [Domenico] Ferabosco (RISM 1554_{28}, p. 10)

10 2a pars [*Baciami mille volt'e mille anchora*]

9 11 *Mordimi questa lingua* Giovanni del Cartolaio

10 13 *Vel puo giurar Amor* Jan Gero *a3* (RISM 1551_{10}, p. 21: Vincenzo Ferro)

11 15 *Chiare fresche e dolci acque* Arcadelt *a 5* (EinIM III, no. 52)

17 2a pars *Segli e per mio destino* *a 4*

19 3a pars *Tempo verra ancor forse*[2] *a 3*

21 4a pars *Da bei rami* *a 4*

22 5a pars *Quante volte dissi io* *a 5*

12 25 *Signor mio caro* Vincentio Galilei

13 27 *Alcun non può saper* Vincentio Galilei (Vogel: Galilei 2 [1587], p. 7)

14 28 *Nasce la gioia mia* Giovan Nasco (Vogel: Nasco 5 [1554], p. 16)

15 30 *Dove tocca costei* Giovan Nasco (Vogel: Nasco 5 [1554], p. 17)

16 32 *Dapoi che sotto il ciel* Vincentio Galilei *a 5*

17 33 *Questo leggiadra* Vincentio Galilei

18 34 *Io mi son giovinetta*[3] [Domenico] Ferabosco (EinIM III, no. 30)

34 2a pars [*Io vo per verdi prati*]

19 35 *Deh non fuggir* Hippolita Cera

20 37 *O famelice inique* Vincentio Galilei

21 38 *Cosi nel mio cantar* Vincentio Galilei

22 39 *Giunto m'ha amor* Orlando di lassus (RISM 1583_{15}, fol. 4: anon.)

23 40 *Nella piu verde piaggia* Hippolito Cera

41 2a pars

24 43 *Zeffiro torna* Vincentio Galilei

25 44 *Ricercare primo* [Francesco da Milano][4]

26 45 *Ricercare Secondo* [Francesco da Milano]

27 47 *Ricercare terzo* [Francesco da Milano]

28 48 *Ricercare quarto* [Francesco da Milano]

29 49 *Ricercare quinto* [Francesco da Milano]

30 50 *Ricercare sesto* [Francesco da Milano]

[1] Facs. of title page in MGG IV, col. 1267, and IMAMI IV, opp. p. lxxxiv.

[2] Mod. ed. in ChilLV, pp. 756–758, wrongly attributed to Verdelot.

[3] The beginning of this composition is labeled "Seconda parte." The section headed "Io mi son giovinetta" on p. 34 is actually the second part of the composition.

[4] The ricercares are attributed to Francesco in Galilei's dedication.

1563_8

GORZANIS, GIACOMO DE

IL / SECONDO LIBRO DE INTABULATURA / DI LIUTO, / NOVAMENTE COMPOSTO PER MESSER JACOMO / DE GORZANIS PUGLIESE HABITANTE / NELLA CITTA DE TRIESTE. / Da lui diligentemente Revisto & Coretto. / [Printer's mark] / IN VINEGIA, Appresso Girolamo Scotto. / M D LXIII.

32 fols. Italian lute tablature. Dedication on fol. A1v headed "AL MOLTO MAGNIFICO: ET GENEROmo. Sor. MAURITIO de Metriehstain detto da pizelsteten hereditario coppiero de l'Archiducato de Carintia, possessore della Signoria: de Ballnberg, Signor mio gratiosissimo." Fol. A2 = p. 1. On p. 62: table of contents followed by the colophon: "IN VINEGIA Appresso Gyrolamo Scotto. 1562" (see $[1562]_2$). The compositions identified by the superior letter *a* ([a]) are reprinted in ChilLS, pp. 30–43. MoeDM contains a thematic index of the volume (p. 405) and concordances (p. 257). Contents = 1565_2. For other volumes in the same series, see 1561_2, note 1. All of the compositions are for solo lute.

Copies in: F:Pthibault, I:Gu.

	p.	
1	1	*Passo e mezzo anticho primo*
	3	*Padouana del detto*
	5	*Saltarel del detto*
2	8	*Passo e mezo moderno* = 1591_{13}, no. 92a
	10	*Padouana del detto*
	12	*Saltarel del detto* = 1591_{13}, no. 92b
3	14	*Passo e mezzo detto il Gorzanis*
	16	*Saltarel del detto* [= padovana]
	17	*Saltarel del detto*
4	19	*Passo e mezo detto o Perfida che sei*[a] (compare AzzaiV, no. 2: "Chi passa per questa strada," Azzaiolo, and no. 16 below)
	20	*Padoana del detto*[a]
	20	*Saltarel del detto*[a]
5	21	*Passo e mezzo detto il Todeschin*[a]
	23	*Padouana del detto*[a]
	24	*Saltarel del detto*[a]
6	27	*Passo e mezzo della cara cosa*
	29	*Padoana del detto*
	31	*Saltarel del detto*
7	33	*Passo e mezzo della Pigna*
	35	*Padoana del detto*
	36	*Saltarel del detto*
8	37	*Passo e mezo detto caro fier homo*
	38	*Saltarel del detto*
9	40	*Passo e mezo bellissimo*
10	41	*Passo e mezzo bellisimo sopra i soprani*[a]
11	42	*Passo e mezo bellissimo sopra i contralti*
	45	*Saltarel del detto*
12	46	*Passo e mezo bellissimo sopra il quarto tuono*[1]
13	48	*La barca del mio Amore*
14	50	*Saltarel detto il Philipin*[a]
15	52	*Bal Todesco*[2]
	52	*La sua padoana*[2]
16	53	*Padoana detta chi passa per questa strada*[a][3] (compare AzzaiV, no. 2: Azzaiolo, and no. 4a above)
17	54	*Recercar .i. de j. Gor*[*zanis*]
18	55	*Recercar .ii. de j. Gor*[*zanis*]
19	57	*Recercar .iii. de j. Gor*[*zanis*]
20	58	*Recercar .iiii. de j. Gor*[*zanis*]
21	60	*Se pur ti guardo* [Napolitana] (RISM 1570_8, p. 46: [Rogier Pathie])

[1] Mod. ed. in ChilJ, p. 94.

[2] Mod. ed. in MoeDM, p. 323.

[3] Mod. ed. in EC, pt. I, vol. II, p. 656; MoeDM, p. 333; and WardDVM, p. 54.

$[1563]_9$

VREEDMAN, SEBASTIAN

Carmina quae cythara pulsantur Sebast. Vreedman. Louvain, Pierre Phalèse, 1563.

This volume of music for the cittern, now lost, is listed in an inventory of the firm of Plantin in Antwerp; see StellMB, p. 24. The contents were probably the same as 1569_6.

1563_{10}

WYSSENBACH, RUDOLF

Ein schön Tabulaturbuch / auff die Lauten, von mancherley Lieplicher Ita/

lianischer Dantzliedern, mit sampt dem Vogelgsang und einer / Feldschlacht, erst neuwlich durch einen kunstlichen / Lautenisten auss Welscher Tabulatur, / fleyssig in Teutsche gesetzt. / Getruckt zu Zürych bey / Jacobo Gessner.

47 fols. German lute tablature. On fol. 2: preface headed "Rudolf Wyssenbach dem günstigen Läser." On fol. 2^v: instructions for the lute headed "Erklärung der Mensur und anderer zeychen so hierinn gebraucht werdend." On fol. 3: cut of a lute with the heading "Der aufgerissen Lautenkragen mit der Tabulatur." On fol. 47^v: table of contents. Contents = 1550_4. All of the compositions are for solo lute.

Copies in: D:Dl, D:W.

1563_{11}

SCOTTO, GIROLAMO, PUBLISHER

LA / INTABOLATURA DE LAUTO. / DE DIVERSI AUTORI. / Di Francesco da Milano. / Di Alberto da Mantoa. / Di Marco da Laquila. / Di Jo. Jacomo Albutio da Milano. / Di Pietro Pauolo Borono da Milano. / Con alcune padouane. Et saltarelli novi. / NOVAMENTE RISTAMPATA. / Con ogni diligentia revista. / [Printer's mark] / IN VINEGIA Appresso Girolamo Scotto. / 1563.

24 fols. Italian lute tablature. On p. 47^v: table of contents followed by the colophon: "IN VINEGIA Appresso Girolamo Scotto. 1563." Fol. 1^v = p. 2. LefL contains a modern edition of the entire collection. WieM II contains a thematic index of the entire collection. For some concordances see MoeDM, p. 261. All of the compositions are for solo lute.

Copies in: A:Wn, and US:Wc.[1]

p.

1 2 *Fantasia del divino F. da Milano* = 1536_9, no. 7

2 4 *Fantasia di Alberto da Mantoua* = 1536_9, no. 8

3 8 *Fantasia di Marco da Laquila* = 1536_9, no. 9

4 11 *Fantasia di Jo. Jacomo Albutio da Milano* = 1536_9, no. 10

5 14 *Fantasia di P. Pa. Borono da Milano* = 1536_9, no. 11

6 16 *Pavana nova* = 1536_9, no. 12a

18 *[Il suo saltarello]* = 1536_9, no. 12b

20 *Saltarello detto la traditorella* = 1536_9, no. 12c

22 *Peschatore che va cantando* = 1536_9, no. 12d

7 23 *Pavana detta la Gombertina di P. Pauolo Bor.* = 1536_9, no. 13a

26 *Saltarello* = 1536_9, no. 13b

28 *Saltarello detto che glian strazza la socha* = 1536_9, no. 13c

30 *Saltarello detto Antonola* = 1536_9, no. 13d

8 32 *Pavana detta la Despetata* = 1536_9, no. 14a

9 35 *Fantasia di Marco da Laquila* = 1536_9, no. 17

10 38 *Fantasia di Jo. Jacomo Albu.* = 1536_9, no. 18

11 41 *Fantasia di F. da Milano* = 1536_9, no. 19

12 43 *Fantasia di F. da Milano* = 1548_2, no. 13

13 44 *Fantasia di P. Pa. Borono* = 1548_2, no. 14

14 46 *Fantasia di F. da Milano* = 1548_2, no. 15

[1] This copy was in the Landau-Finaly library in Florence (see RoedigC I, 531).

1563_{12}

PHALÈSE, PIERRE, PUBLISHER

THEATRUM MUSICUM / in quo selectissima optimorum quorumlibet auto/ RUM AC EXCELLENTISSIMORUM ARTI/ficum cum veterum tum etiam novorum Carmina summa dili/gentia ac industria expressa oculis proponuntur. / Et primo ordine continentur αὐτόματα que Fantasiae dicuntur, / Secundo Cantilenae quatuor & quinque Vocum. / Postea Carmina difficiliora quae Muteta appellantur, eaque quatuor / quinque & sex Vocum. / Deinde succedunt Carmina longa elegantissima duabus Testudinibus / Canenda. / Postremo habes & eius generis Carmina quae tum festivitate / tum facilitate sui discentibus primo maxime satissfacient ut sunt /

Passemezo Gaillarde Branles, & caet: / [Cut of Melpomene] / LOVANII. / Ex Typographia Petri Phalesii Bibliopolae Jurati, Anno. M. D. LXIII. / Cum Gratia & Privilegio.

70 fols. French lute tablature. On fol. A1^v: preface in Latin headed "Musices Candidatis," followed by the same poem in Latin as in 1568_7 headed "IN LAUDEM THEATRI Musici Frederici vidrae [sic] Frisii Carmen." Fol. A2 = fol. 1. On fol. 69: table of contents. Colophon on fol. 69^v beneath a cut of ten performing musicians: "Impressum Lovanii apud Petrum Phalesium Bibliopol. Jurat. Anno M. D. LXIII. Sub Liberaria Aurea." All of the compositions are for solo lute except nos. 112–118, which are for two lutes.

Copy in: GB:Ob.[1]

MUSIC FOR SOLO LUTE

	fol.	
1	1	*Fantasia*[2] = 1552_4, no. 6: Morlaye
2	1^v	*Fantasia Pauli Baroni* = 1546_8, no. 10: Borrono
3	2^v	*Fantasia Jo. Jacobi Albutii* = 1536_9, no. 10: Albutio
4	3	*Fantasia a Rota* = 1546_{15}, no. 28: Rotta
5	3^v	*Fan[tasia] Francisci Mediola.* = 1536_9, no. 1: Francesco da Milano
6	4	*Fantasia* = 1546_6, no. 11: Francesco da Milano
7	4^v	*Fantasia Simon Sentler* = 1547_3, no. 3: Gintzler
8	5	*Fantasia a Rota* = 1546_{15}, no. 31: Rotta
9	5^v	*Fantasia Pauli Baroni* = 1536_9, no. 11: Borrono
10	6	*Fantasia Simon Sentler* = 1547_3, no. 4: Gintzler
11	6^v	*Fantasia* = 1558_4, no. 2: Morlaye
12	7	*Fantasia a Rota* = 1546_{15}, no. 30: Rotta
13	7^v	*Fantasia* = 1560_3, no. 5: Paladin
14	8	*Fantasia*
15	8^v	*Fantasia* = 1560_3, no. 4: Paladin
16	9	*Fantasia Raphael viola* = 1568_7, no. 1
17	9^v	*Fantasia* = 1560_3, no. 1: Paladin
18	10	*Fantasia* = 1538_1, no. 9: Narváez
19	10^v	*Or combien est* (ClemensO VII, 156: Sandrin or Sermisy)
20	11	*Le mal qui sent* ("Response") = 1568_7, no. 23
21	11^v	*Vous perdez temps* = 1547_9, no. 3: Sermisy
22	12	*Telz en mesdict* ("Response") = 1547_9, no. 4: Mittantier
23	12^v	*Toutes les nuyct* = 1568_7, no. 32: Crecquillon
24	13	*Quest il besoing* ("Response") (RISM 1570_8, p. 13)
25	13^v	*Je prens en gre* = 1547_9, no. 1: Clemens non Papa
26	14	*Si mon traveil* = 1547_9, no. 5: Sandrin
27	14^v	*Le deul yssu* ("Response") = 1568_7, no. 31: Villiers
28	15	*Doulce memoire* = 1568_7, no. 26: Sandrin
29	15^v	*Finii le bien* ("Response") = 1547_9, no. 12: Certon
30	16	*Languir me fais* = 1568_7, no. 29: Sermisy
31	16^v	*Cessez mes yeulx* = 1568_7, no. 36: Crecquillon
32	17	*Pour ung plaisir* = 1546_{18}, no. 30: Crecquillon
33	17	*De mon triste* (compare 1547_7, no. 40)
34	17^v	*Damour me plains* = 1547_9, no. 2: Pathie
35	18	*Amour au coeur* = 1568_7, no. 70: Crecquillon
36	18^v	*Cest a grand tort* = 1568_7, no. 28: Crecquillon
37	19	*Dung seul regard*
38	19^v	*O combien je suis*
39	20	*Vivray je tout jour en telle peine* = 1552_{11}, no. 22: Latre
40	20^v	*Sans plourer* ("Response") = 1552_{11}, no. 23: Latre
41	20^v	*Den lustelycken mey* (compare RISM 1572_{11}, no. 25: Clemens non Papa, and DuyL I, 356)
42	21	*Mais languiraige* = 1552_{11}, no. 55: Clemens non Papa
43	21^v	*Sur tous regres* = 1552_{11}, no. 63: Richafort
44	22	*Mille regres* = 1552_{11}, no. 64: Josquin

45 22^v *Ung gay bergier* = 1545_3, no. 38: Crecquillon
46 23 *Fortune helas*
47 23^v *Duel double deul* = 1552_{11}, no. 49: Lupi
48 24 *Comme la rose* = 1552_{11}, no. 31: Latre
49 24^v *Le content est riche* (AttainCK III, no. 9: Sermisy)
50 25 *O foible esprit* = 1552_4, no. 12: Gentian
51 25^v *O Seigneur Dieu* = 1552_4, no. 13: Mithou
52 26 *Puisque voules* (ClemensO X, 152: Clemens non Papa)
53 26^v *Si dire je losoye*
54 27 *En languissant* = 1552_{11}, no. 32
55 27^v *Sans liberte* = 1552_4, no. 11: Magdelain
56 27^v *Een aerdich trommelaerken* C. G. (ClemensO II: Psalm XXIII, "Domini est terra," Clemens non Papa)
57 28 *La palme doulce* = 1560_3, no. 16: Antonio Gardane
58 28^v *Venez venez mon bel amy* = 1568_7, no. 43
59 29 *Ung doulx nenni* = 1568_7, no. 82: Lasso
60 29^v *Tout bellement*
61 30 *Vray dieu disoit* Orlando di Lassus (LassoW XII, 72)
62 30^v *Sur la verdure* = 1568_7, no. 48
63 30^v *Contente vous amy*
64 31 *Ung jour passe* = 1560_3, no. 17: Le Hugier
65 31^v *Ce mois de may* = 1568_7, no. 46: Godard
66 32 *Las on peult [juger]* = 1552_4, no. 7: Janequin
67 32^v *Ochi mei lassi* = 1547_3, no. 27: Arcadelt
68 33 *Misericorde* = 1568_7, no. 73: Clemens non Papa
69 33^v *Adieu lespoir* ("Response")
70 33^v *O scio potessi dona* = 1547_3, no. 28: Berchem
71 34^v *Quando ie penso al martire* = 1546_{17}, no. 3: Arcadelt
72 35 *Oncques amour*
73 35^v *Qual anima [ignorante]* = 1560_3, no. 7: Nollet
74 36 *Godt es mijn licht* = 1568_7, no. 52: Clemens non Papa
75 36^v *Mamye ung jour* = 1568_7, no. 50: Certon
76 37 *Si por ti guardo* = 1568_7, no. 51: Pathie
77 37^v *Ce qui est plus en ce monde* = 1547_3, no. 32: Sandrin
78 37^v *Recipe assis*
79 38 *Je n'ay point plus d'affection* = 1551_2, no. 8: Sermisy
80 38^v *Frisque et Gallard* (ClemensO X, 17: Clemens non Papa)
81 39 *Fault il qui soit ma doulce amye*
82 39^v *Fille qui prend facieux mary* C. G.[3] = 1556_2, no. 19
83 39^v *Or puis quil est* C. G.[3] (ClemensO X, 173: Clemens non Papa)
84 40 *Si mon amour*
85 40 *Or demourez* C. G.[3] = 1568_7, no. 49
86 40^v *Ver inferno al mio petto* = 1560_3, no. 14: Arcadelt
87 41 *Non at suo amante* = 1552_4, no. 17: Tromboncino
88 41^v *Vostre par heritage*
89 42 *Sio credesse* = 1560_3, no. 13: Reulx
90 42^v *Anchor che col partir* = 1560_3, no. 8: Rore
91 43 *Je suis desheritee* (CW XV, no. 2: Lupus)
92 43^v *Ung triste ceur* (RISM 1558_{10}, no. 18: Crecquillon)
93 44 *Gequest ben ick* = 1547_7, no. 42
94 44^v *Entre tous viellartz* = 1546_{18}, no. 25
95 44^v *Tribulatie en verdriet* = 1546_{18}, no. 26
96 45 *Las je cognois*
97 45 *Susanne ung jour* (LassoW XIV, 29: Lasso)
98 46 *Tant que vivray* = 1545_3, no. 45: Sermisy
99 46^v *Pis ne me peult venir* (RISM 1572_2, fol. 25: Crecquillon)
100 47 *Jamais naymeray masson* = 1545_3, no. 42
101 47 *Il estoit une filette* = 1547_9, no. 7: Janequin
102 47^v *Quam pulchra es* = 1552_{11}, no. 71a: Mouton
48 2a pars *Labia tua* = 1552_{11}, no. 71b
103 48^v *Pater peccavi* = 1568_7, no. 112a: Clemens non Papa

104 49 *Quam dilecta tabernacula* (ClemensCS VI, no. 1: Clemens non Papa)
105 49ᵛ *Stabat mater dolorosa* = 1547_3, no. 13a: Josquin
50ᵛ 2a pars *Eya mater* = 1547_3, no. 13b
106 51ᵛ *Pater noster* = 1547_3, no. 7a: Josquin (see no. 108 below)
107 52 *Aupres de vous* (AttainCK I, no. 16: Jacotin or Sermisy)
108 52ᵛ *Ave Maria* = 1547_3, no. 7b: Josquin (2a pars of "Pater noster," no. 106 above)
109 53 *Il me souffit* = 1529_3, no. 24a: Sermisy
110 53 *D'ou vient cela* = 1545_3, no. 23: Sermisy
111 53ᵛ *Benedicta es* = 1547_3, no. 8a: Josquin
54ᵛ 2a pars *Per illud ave* = 1547_3, no. 8b
54ᵛ 3a pars *Nunc mater* = 1547_3, no. 8c

MUSIC FOR TWO LUTES

112 55 *Fantasia*[4] = 1549_2, no. 18: Barberiis
113 55ᵛ *Pis ne me peult venir* = 1552_{11} no. 101: Crecquillon
114 55ᵛ *Grace & vertu* = 1552_{11}, no. 99
115 56ᵛ *Bataglia* = 1568_7, no. 118: Janequin
116 57ᵛ *Amor e gratioso* = 1568_7, no. 116
117 58ᵛ *Passomezo* = 1568_7, no. 119
118 59ᵛ *Or combien est* = 1568_7, no. 121

MUSIC FOR SOLO LUTE

119 60ᵛ *Passomezo d'ytalye* = 1568_7, no. 123
120 61 *Galliarde* [*Royne d'ecosse*] = 1568_3, no. 25
121 61 *Si pour t'aymer* [*Gaillarde*] = 1568_3, no. 27
122 61ᵛ *Pavana desperata* = 1536_9, no. 14a
62 *Galliarde* = 1536_9, no. 14b: "Saltarello"
123 62ᵛ [*Passomezo*] *La Milaneza*
62ᵛ *Gaillarde*
124 63 *Passomezo vaccas*
63 *Salterello*
125 63 *Gepeis ghij doet mij trueren* (compare DuyL II, 1685)
126 63ᵛ *Passomezo*
63ᵛ *Galliarde*
127 64 *Paduana* = 1545_3, no. 58
128 64 *Passomezo* [*d'Angleterre*] (compare 1571_5, no. 14)
129 64 *Gaillarde*
130 64ᵛ *Pavana* = 1552_4, no. 24a
65 *Gaillarde* = 1552_4, no. 24b
65 *Gaillarde* = 1552_4, no. 24c
131 65 *Verjubileert ghij Venus dierkens* (compare DuyL III, 2574)
132 65ᵛ *Passemezo Italiana*
133 66 *Passomezo* = 1546_{20}, no. 23
134 66ᵛ *Passemezo* (compare 1540_1, no. 30)
135 67ᵛ *Almande*
136 67ᵛ *Almande* [*Loreyne*] (compare 1552_3, no. 17)
137 67ᵛ *Almande* [*de Ungrie*] = 1568_7, no. 144
138 68 *Brandt de Bourgoinge* = 1551_2, no. 26
139 68 *Branle* = 1551_2, no. 22
140 68 *Branle* = 1551_2, no. 23
141 68ᵛ *Brant Champaigne* = 1568_7, no. 153
142 68ᵛ *Linkens hoven*

[1] The unique copy has a manuscript note on the title page reading: "Vaute 6 pataxes Le 17 de Novembre en Amiens 1569." Bound in at the end of this copy are two pages of manuscript music in French lute tablature: p. 1: *Almande D'egmont, Almande poussinge, Almande Nonette,* and *Almande baviere;* 2: *Aultre Almande* and *Almande court.*

[2] Heading on fol. 1: "THEATRUM MUSICUM Selectissimis optimorum artificum Carminibus instructum atque exornatum."

[3] The initials C. G. may stand for Claude Gervaise (but see no. 56).

[4] Heading on fol. 55: "SEQUUNTUR DEINCEPS CARMINA DUABUS TESTUDInibus Accommoda."

1563

DOUBTFUL WORKS

1. MorL I, xliii, lists "Antonio di Becchi. *Intavolatura di lauto. Libro 1⁰.* Venetia, 1563," as having been in the library of King John IV of Portugal. The volume is otherwise unknown The only volume of music by Becchi that survives is 1568_1

2. DraudiusBC, p. 1651, lists "Petri Teghii. *Cantionum Gallicarum & mutetorum liber*. Lov. 1563. 4." He probably refers to 1573_5.

3. LumS, p. 22, and SteeleE, p. 101, list an otherwise unknown 1563 edition of Adrian le Roy's lute instruction book, translated into English by John Alford. The volume is listed in this bibliography as 1568_3.

1564_1

BAKFARK, VALENTIN •

PREMIER LIVRE DE TABELATURE /DE LUTH CONTENANT PLUSIEURS / fantasies, motetz, chansons françoises, et madrigalz. / Par Vallentin bacfarc / [Printer's mark] / A PARIS. / De l'Imprimerie d'Adrian le Roy, & Robert Ballard, Imprimeurs du Roy, ruë / saint Jean de Beauvais, à l'enseigne du mont Parnasse. / 1564. / Avec privilege du Roy, pour dix ans.

24 fols. French lute tablature. On fol. $A1^v$: portrait of Henry II. On fol. $F4^v$: table of contents. All of the compositions are reprinted from 1553_1. See there for the sources of the intabulations. All of the compositions are for solo lute.

Copies in: B:Br, D:Mbs.

	fol.	
1	A2	*Fantasie*[1] = 1553_1, no. 1
2	$A3^v$	*Fantasie* = 1553_1, no. 2
3	B2	*Aspice domine* N. Gombert *a 4*
	$B4^v$	2a pars [*Muro tuo*]
4	C3	*Benedicta* L. Pieton *a 6*
	$D1^v$	2a pars [*Per illud ave*]
5	D3	*Le cors absent* T. Crepuillon [sic] *a 4*
6	D4	*Or vien ça vien* C. Janequin
7	E1	*D'amour me plains*[2] Roger [Pathie]
8	$E4^v$	*Si grande la pieta* Archadet
9	F2	*Il ciel che rado* Arcadet
10	F3	*Che pui foe al mio feco* [sic] Arcadet

[1] Facs. of fol. A2 in DTO XVIII/37, pl. ix. Mod. ed. in NeemAM II, no. 7.

[2] Mod. ed. in KosackL, app. III.

1564_2

ESTRÉES, JEAN D'

QUART LIVRE DE DANSERIES, / Contenant

5 Pavanes, avec leurs Gaillardes a 4. & a 5. parties	3 Bransles des contrainctz
1 Gaillarde ditte la Visdame	4 Bransles de Poictou, simples & legeirs
1 Autre a 5. ditte la Milannoise	1 Le Bransle de Guillemette
1 Autre Gaillarde a 5.	1 Le Bransle du petit homme
1 Le Bal de Calais a 5. parties	1 Bransle legeir double du p. h.
1 La basse Gaillarde a 4.	4 Alemandes

Le tout mis en Musique à 4. à 5. & à 6. parties (appropriés tant à la voix humaine, / que pour jouer sur tous instruments musicaulz) Par Jean d'Estrée, / joueur de Hautbois du Roy. / De l'imprimerie de Nicolas du Chemin, a l'enseigne du Griffon / d'argent, rue Sainct Jean de Latran à Paris. 1564. / Avec privilege du Roy, pour dix ans.

Four part books in mensural notation, each of 22 fols. (?). On fol. 1^v: the same excerpt from the printer's privilege as in 1556_1. Colophon on fol. 22^v: "Fin du Quatriesme Livre de Danserie, achevé d'imprimer le 15. Juillet. 1564," followed by the printer's mark. For some concordances see HeartzSF, p. 372. All of the compositions are for instrumental ensemble, *a 4*, *a 5*, or *a 6*.

Copy in: GB:Lbm (imperfect B).

	fol.	
1	2	*1. Pavane a 5*
2	2^v	*1. Gaillarde a 5*
3	3	*2. Gaillarde a 5*
4	3^v	*3. Gaillarde a 5*
5	4	*2. Pavane la Mignonne a 5*
6	4^v	*4. Gaillarde a 5*
7	5^v	*5. Gaillarde a 5*
8	6^v	*6. Gaillarde La Millannoise a 5*
9	7^v	*3. Pavane a 5*
10	8	*7. Gaillarde a 5*
11	8^v	*8. Gaillarde a 5*
12	9^v	*9. Gaillarde a 5*

13	10^v	*4. Pavane a6*
14	11	*10. Gaillarde a6*
15	11^v	*11. Gaillarde a5*
16	12	*12. Gaillarde a5*
17	12^v	*5. Pavane a5*
18	13^v	*13. Gaillarde a5*
19	14	*14. Gaillarde a5*
20	14^v	*15. Gaillarde a4*
21	14^v	*16. Gaillarde la Visdame a4* = 1571_5, no. 51
22	15	*17. Gaillarde a5*
23	15^v	*18. Gaillarde la Milannoise a5*
24	16^v	*Le Bal de Calais*
25	17	*La basse Gaillarde a4* = 1571_5, no. 52
26	17^v	*1. Bransle du contraint* = 1571_5, no. 57, and 1583_7, no. 99
27	18	*2. Bransle de la suitte du contraint*
28	18^v	*3. Bransle legeir de la suitte du contraint* = 1571_5, no. 58, and 1583_7, no. 100
29	19	*1. Bransle de Poictou, simple* = 1571_5, no. 53, and 1583_7, no. 103
30	19^v	*2. Bransle de Poictou simple*
31	20	*3. Bransle de Poictou, legeir* = 1571_5, no. 54, and 1583_7, no. 104
32	20	*4. Bransle de Poictou, legeir*
33	20^v	*Bransle de Guillemette* = 1571_5, no. 103
34	20^v	*Bransle Le petit homme* = 1571_5, no. 55, and 1583_7, no. 98a
35	20^v	*Bransle legeir double, du petit homme* = 1571_5, no. 56, and 1583_7, no. 98b
36–38 [fol. 21]		[*Alemandes 1–3*] [1]
39	22	*4. Alemande courante* = 1571_5, no. 32

[1] Probably these three allemandes are among the five pr. in 1571_5, nos. 27–31.

[1564]$_3$

FUENLLANA, MIGUEL DE

Libro de música pa/ra Vihuela intitulado Orphe/nica Lira: en el qual se contienen / muchas y diversas obras, comp. [to] / por Miguel de Fuenllana, diri/gido al mui alto y mui poderoso / Sr. D. Phelipe Príncipe de Espana / Rei de Inglaterra / de / Nápoles, &c. / Con Privilegio Real. / En Madrid por Francisco / Sánchez. Ano de 1564.

One of the four copies of Miguel de Fuenllana's *Orphenica Lyra* (1554_3) in E:Mn is lacking the original title page. A manuscript title page added at an unknown date is reproduced above (after AngCM III, 97). Before this can be taken as proof that there was a second edition of Fuenllana's tablature, corroboration is necessary. Francisco Sánchez is not known to have been active as a printer in Madrid before 1572. Furthermore according to Professor Robert Stevenson (quoted in WardV, p. 365) the "1564" edition is identical with that of 1554.

1564_4

GORZANIS, GIACOMO DE

IL TERZO LIBRO / DE INTABOLATURA DI LIUTO / DI MESSER GIACOMO GORZANIS / Pugliese, Hab[i]tante nella Citta di Trieste. Novamente / da lui composto & per Antonio Gardano stampato. / [Printer's mark] / In Venetia Apresso / di Antonio Gardano. / 1564.

40 fols. Italian lute tablature. Dedication on fol. A1^v headed "AL MOLTO MAGNIFICO ET CLARISSIMO SIGNOR IL SIGNOR VITO DE DORIMBERGO BENEMERITO Cavalliero Aureato, & de sua Cesarea Maesta Consigliero & dignissimo Logotenente dello Illustrissimo Contado di Goritia. Signor mio Gratiosissimo." On fol. K4^v: table of contents. MoeDM contains a thematic index of the volume (p. 410) and concordances (p. 261). For other volumes in the same series, see 1561_2, note 1. All of the compositions are for solo lute.

Copies in: A:Wn, F:Pthibault.

	fol.	
1	A2	*Pass'e mezo anticho primo*
	A4^v	*Padouana del ditto prima*
	B2^v	*Saltarello ditto primo*

2 B3v *Pass'e mezo moderno primo*
C2v *Padoana del ditto*
C3v *Saltarello ditto*
3 D1 *Galiarda alla Milanesa*
4 D1v *L'herba fresca* (compare I:Vnm, MSS It. Cl. IV, 1795–98, no. 92: "La via de la fiumera")
5 D2 *Saltarello dito il palvelo*
6 D3v *Saltarello dito Dimel su presto*
7 D4v *Saltarello dito Il mal contento*
8 E1 *Saltarello dito Il bergamasco*
9 E2v *Caccia la vechia fuora del campo*
10 E3v *Saltarello dito L'imperial*
11 E4 *Pass'e mezo della bataglia*
F2v *Padoana del ditto*
F3 *Saltarello del dito*
12 F4 *Pass'e mezo del Imperator* [1]
13 G1 *Pass'e mezo moderno*
G2 *Padoana del dito*
14 G2v *Pass'e mezo dito il Cavalier*
G3v *Saltarello del ditto*
15 G4v *Pass'e mezo del Todeschin*
H2 *Padoana del dito*
16 H2v *Pass'e mezo Antico*
H3 *Padoana del dito*
H3v *Saltarello del ditto*
17 H4 *Saltarello ditto amor mio bello*
18 H4v *Pass'e mezo antico sul quarto ton*
I1v *Padoana del ditto*
I2v *Saltarello ditto*
19 I3 *Pass'e mezo del Gorzanis*
20 I4 *Saltarello ditto Tantara*
21 K1 *Pass'e mezo ditto il Giordano*
22 K1v *Bal Boemo dito la Filippina*
K2 *Padoana del dito*
23 K2 *Bal Todescho* [2]
K2v *Padoana del dito* [2]
24 K2v *Bal Todescho*
K3 *Padoana del dito*
25 K3 *Recercar Primo*
26 K4 *Recercar secondo*

[1] Mod. ed. in MoeDM, p. 326.
[2] Mod. ed. in MoeDM, p. 346.

1564_5

LE ROY, ADRIAN

SECOND LIVRE DE CISTRE, / CONTENANT LES COMMANDEMENS / de DIEU: Six Pseaumes de DAVID, & autres oeuvres faciles, avec / l'intelligence de la tabulature, & accords, dudict instrument / PAR ADRIAN LE ROY. / [Printer's mark] / A PARIS. / Par Adrian le Roy, & Robert Ballard / Imprimeurs du Roy. / 1564. / Avec privilege dudit Seigneur.

24 fols. French cittern tablature. On fol. 1v: instructions for reading the tablature, headed "Briefve et facile introduction pour l'intelligence de la tabulature, & accord du Cistre"; these instructions include some musical examples. On fol. 24v: table of contents. For some concordances see HeartzSF, p. 402. The compositions followed by an asterisk are based on the monophonic melodies in *Pseaulmes de David* (Paris, Le Roy and Ballard, 1562); see MorcouA and PraM. All of the compositions are for solo cittern.

Copy in: D:TR.

fol.
1 2 *Les commandemens de Dieu. Leve le cueur**
2 2v *Psaume [CXXXVIII] Il faut que de tous mes esprits**
3 3 *Psaume [XXXIII] Reveillés vous chacun fidelle**
4 3v *Psaume [I] Qui au conseil**
5 4 *Psaume [III] O Seigneur que de gens**
6 5 *Psaume [LXXIX] Les gens entrés**
7 6 *Psaume [LXXII] Tes jugemens**
8 6v *Pavane J'ay du mal tant tant* (compare LesAC, no. 18: "J'ay le rebours," Certon)
7 *Gaillarde de la precedente pavane*
9 7v *Pavane Si je m'en vois* (compare LesLRB, art. 3, fol. 9: "L'ennuy qui me tourmente," Certon)
8v *Gaillarde de la precedente pavane*
10 9 *Gaillarde la Morette* = 1570_3, no. 53; 1578_4, no. 68; and 1582_5, no. 81
11 9v *Gaillarde la Lionnoise* = 1570_3, no. 56; 1578_4, no. 66; and 1582_5, no. 78
12 10 *Gaillarde la Burate* = 1564_7, no. 19, and 1569_8, no. 84: "Marchese de Gasto Gaiarda"

13	10v	*Gaillarde Puisque vivre en servitude* (compare LesLRB, art. 3, no. 10: Certon, and LesLRB, art. 171, fol. 2: Le Roy)
14	11	*Gaillarde Puisque nouvelle affection* (compare RISM 1554_{26}, no. 2: Certon) = 1570_3, no. 55; 1578_4, no. 65; 1582_5, no. 88
15	11v	*Gaillarde de la Gaye* = 1570_3, no. 57, and 1582_5, no. 83
16	12	*Gaillarde O combien est heureuse* (compare LesLRB, art. 3, no. 16: Certon) = 1570_3, no. 58
17	12v	*Gaillarde Romanesque* = 1570_3, no. 37, and 1582_5, no. 52
	12v	*Plus diminuée*
18	13v	*Gaillarde J'aymeroys myeulx dormir seulette*[1] (compare 1589_1, no. 12)
	13v	*La precedente Gaillarde plus diminuée*
19	14v	*Les Bouffons* = 1578_4, no. 56
	14v	*Plus diminuée*
20	15v	*Les Matachins*[2] = 1570_3, no. 130, and 1582_5, no. 140
21	16	*Les forces d'Hercules* = 1570_3, no. 131
22	16v	*Branle simple N'aurés vous point de moy pitié* = 1570_3, no. 108
23	17	*Branle gay* = 1570_3, no. 109
24	17v	*Branle gay* = 1582_5, no. 129
25	18	*Branle gay* (compare 1547_6, no. 22: "Branle [gay]. Mari je songeois laultre jour")
26	18v	*Branle de Champagne* = 1570_3, no. 100
27	19	*Branle de Champagne* = 1570_3 no. 101
28	19v	*Branle de Champagne* = 1570_3, no. 102
29	20	*Branle de Champagne* = 1570_3, no. 103
30	20v	*Branle de poictou* = 1570_3, no. 111, and 1582_5, no. 139
31	21	*Branle de poictou*
32	21v	*Branle de Poictou*
33	22	*Branle [courant]* (compare 1547_6, no. 28)
34	22v	*Branle des Cordeliers*
35	23	*Passepied [Branle d'Escosse]*
36	23v	*Almande*
37	24	*Almande* = 1570_3, no. 68: "Almande de Loraine"

[1] Not related musically to RISM 1554_{26}, no. 11: Certon.

[2] Mod. ed. in TapS, p. 38.

$[1564]_6$

OCHSENKUN, SEBASTIAN

Sebastian Ochsenkun. Tabulaturen auff die Lauten inhaltendt Moteten, welsche und teutsche geystliche und weltlich Lieder, sampt iren Texten, mit vier, fünff und sechs Stimmen, &c. ordinirt durch Sebastian Ochsenkun irer Churfürstlichen Gnaden Musicum und Lautenisten. Gedruckt in der Churfürstlichen Statt Heidelberg durch Joannem Maier, inn verlegung und kosten Matthaei Harnisch. M.DLXIIII.

88 fols. This volume of solo lute music, in German lute tablature, once owned by the Pfarrbibliothek in Bingen (D:BIN), is now lost. The contents were probably the same as those in 1558_5. See RothGH, p. 235, and MGG IX, col. 1824.

1564_7

VIAERA, FREDERIC

NOVA ET ELEGANTISSIMA / IN CYTHARA LUDENDA CARMINA QUAE / VIDELICET IN SOLA CYTHARA VEL ETIAM CUM / tribus Testudinibus exhibita, mira dulcedine auditorum possunt / oblectare, eaque omnia facilitate quam fieri potuit / summa in tyronum usum composita. / Et Primo quidem libro Passomezi, Padoani, Saltarelli, ad Joannis Pacoloni tabulaturas / (ut vocant) trium Testudinum, apprime congruentes, ut etiam sola Cythara ex/hibendi. Deinde etiam Alemandae Branles & similia. Et Secundo quidem / libro habes Cantiones Musicales quantum Cythara rei admittit / Musicae habes & iam non minus jucundas. / AUTORE FREDERICO VIAERA FRISIO. / [Fleuret] / LOVANII. / Apud Petrum Phalesium Bibliopol. Jurat. Anno 1564. / Cum Gratia & Privilegio.

36 fols. French cittern tablature. Dedicatory poem in Latin on fol. *1[v] headed "NATALIUM SPLENDORE AC MORUM INTEGRITATE PRESTANTI VIRO D. JOANNI A ZULEN METROPOLITANAE ECCLESIAE APUD VITRAJECTINOS CANONICO. Fredericus Viaera Frisius. S. D." Fol. *2 = fol. 1. For information about Pacolini's [*sic*] music for three lutes mentioned on the title page see $[1587]_6$. All of the compositions are for solo cittern.

Copy in: US:Cn.[1]

	fol.	
1	1	*Passemezo Milanese* = 1570_3, no. 36a
	1[v]	*Padoana Milanese*
	1[v]	*Il suo Saltarello* = 1570_3, no. 36b: "Gaillarde"
2	2	*Passemezo Commune* = 1570_3, no. 40a, and 1582_5, no. 45a
	2[v]	*Padoana Commune*
	3[v]	*Saltarello Commune* = 1570_3, no. 40c, and 1582_5, no. 45b: "Gailliarde Commune"
3	4	*Passemezo de Zorzi* = 1570_3, no. 41a
	4[v]	*Padoana de Zorzi* = 1570_3, no. 41b
	5	*Saltarello de Zorzi* = 1570_3, no. 41c
4	5[v]	*Passemezo Ungaro* = 1570_3, no. 42a
	6	*Il suo Saltarello* = 1570_3, no. 42b
5	6[v]	*Passemezo de la Rocha el Fuso*
	7[v]	*Padoana de la Rocha el Fuso*
	8[v]	*Il suo Saltarello*
6	9	*Passemezo Tuti por ti core mio caro* (compare AzzaiV, no. 12: "Ti parti, cor mio caro," Azzaiolo)
	9[v]	*Padoana*
	10	*Il suo Saltarello*
7	10[v]	*Passemezo Desperata*
	11[v]	*Padoana Desperata*
	12[v]	*Il suo Saltarello*
8	13[v]	*Passemezo Ducessa*
	14[v]	*Padoana*
	15	*Il suo Saltarello*
9	15[v]	*Passemezo Il est jour* (compare RISM 1531_2, no. 14: Sermisy)
10	16	*Passemezo Batalgia* [sic] = 1570_3, no. 44a, and 1582_5, no. 49a
11	16[v]	*Madona Zohanna*
12	17	*Passemezo D'Italic* = 1570_3, no. 39a
	17[v]	*Gaiarda* = 1570_3, no. 39b
13	17[v]	*Gaiarda*
14	18	*La forza de Hercule*
15	18[v]	*Galiarda* = 1570_3, no. 48
16	19	*Chi passa per questa strada* (compare AzzaiV, no. 2: Azzaiolo) = 1570_3, no. 47
17	19[v]	*La Caracossa* = 1570_3, no. 66 (compare 1570_3, no. 170)
18	20	*Gaiarda L. Milleri*
19	20[v]	*Marchese de Gasto Gaiarda* = 1564_5, no. 12: "Gaillarde la Burate"
20	21	*Gaiarda*[2]
21	21[v]	*Gaiarda* = 1570_3, no. 50, and 1582_5, no. 89
22	22	*Gaiarda*
23	22[v]	*Gaiarda* = 1569_6, no. 85; 1570_3, no. 51; 1582_5, no. 80
24	23	*La Milanesa* = 1570_3, no. 49
	23[v]	*Alio modo*
25	24	*Era di Maggio* = 1582_5, no. 151a
26	24[v]	*Languir me fault* (AttainCK II, no. 12: Sermisy)
27	25[v]	*Den lustelijcken mey* (compare RISM 1572_{11}, no. 25: Clemens non Papa, and DuyL I, 356) = 1570_3, no. 132, and 1582_5, no. 142
28	26	*Jamais n'aymeray*
29	26[v]	*D'ont vient cela* (AttainCK III, no. 22: Sermisy)
30	27[v]	*La pastorella mia* (SCMA V, no. 5: Arcadelt)
31	28	*O bella sopra tutte altre bella*
32	28[v]	*Susanne ung jour* (LevyS, p. 403: Didier Lupi Second)
33	29[v]	*Jay acquis ung serviteur*
34	29[v]	*Te mey als alle die voghelen singen* (compare DuyL II, 1024)
35	30	*Het vvas een aerdich vrauken*
36	30	*Ick had een gestraedich minneken* (ClemensO II, 11: "Psalm XVIII," Clemens non Papa) = 1570_3, no. 133, and 1582_5, no. 143
37	30[v]	*Branle* = 1570_3, no. 116
38	31	*Branle* = 1570_3, no. 115: "Branle tu disois"
39	31[v]	*Quatrebrant* = 1570_3, no. 117
40	32	*Gaiarda du Roy* = 1570_3, no. 52
41	32[v]	*Almande d'amours*

42	33	*Gaiarda de la Royne de Eschosse* (compare 1557_4, no. 1b) = 1569_6, no. 81; 1570_3, no. 63; 1582_5, no. 77
43	33^v	*Almande du Prince* = 1570_3, no. 71a
	33^v	*Reprinse* = 1570_3, no. 71b
44	33^v	*Almande* = 1570_3, no. 70a
	33^v	*Reprinse* = 1570_3, no. 70b
45	34	*Gaiarda La Moretta* = 1569_6, no. 82
46	34^v	*Almande du Court*
47	35	*La brunette* (compare 1569_6, no. 79: "Gailliarde o ma gente brunette")

[1] A copy was in D:TR.

[2] A series of solmization syllables is added in manuscript on fol. 21 of the unique copy.

1564_8

RUFFO, VICENZO

CAPRICCI IN MUSICA / A TRE VOCI, / DI VICENZO RUFFO MASTRO / DI CAPELLA NEL DOMO / DI MILANO. / Nuovamente dati in luce, à commodo de virtuosi. / [Cut of two figures.] / Formati da Francesco Moscheni / IN MELANO [*sic*]. / MDLXIIII.

Three part books in mensural notation, each of 16 fols. Dedication on title page verso headed "ALL'ILLUSTRE S.or IL S.or CONTE MARC'ANTONIO MARTINENGO, DE VILLA CHIARA, S. mio singularissimo," and dated "Di Milano alli 24, di Marzo. 1564." Table of contents on the last page of each part book. All of the compositions are for instrumental ensemble *a 3*.

Copies in: I:PS (imperfect Tenor only), and I:Rvat.[1]

	fol.	
1	1	*La, Sol, Fa, Re, Mi*
2	1^v	*Quand'io penso al martire* (compare 1541_9, p. 54: Arcadelt)
3	2	*El Chiocho*
4	3	*La Brava*
5	3^v	*La Gamba in Tenor*
6	4	*Ut, Re, Mi, Fa, Sol, La*
7	4^v	*Il Capriccioso*
8	5	*O Felici occhi mei* (compare CW V, 19: Arcadelt)
9	6	*La disperata*
10	6^v	*Martin minoit son portiau au marche* (compare CM II, 79: Janequin)
11	8	*Dormendo un giorno* (compare WagMP, p. 461: Verdelot)
12	9^v	*El Travagliato*
13	10^v	*La Gamba in Basso, & Soprano*
14	11	*Hor ch'l cielo e la terra* (compare Vogel Rore 6 [1562], no. 2: Rore)
15	11^v	*La Danza*
16	12^v	*El Perfidioso*
17	13	*Da bei rami scendea* (compare RISM 1543_{17}, p. 5: Arcadelt)
18	13^v	*El Pietoso*
19	14	*El Malenconico*
20	14^v	*Trinitas in unitate* (Headed "Resolutione")
21	15	*El Trapolato*
22	15^v	*El Cromato*
23	16	*La Piva*

[1] SartMS, p. 105, lists the Pistoia copy (the only one known to him), under "1600?" DonaSM, p. 47, lists the volume under 1566. Earlier, Kroyer, in KrI, p. 77, n. 2, had called attention to a complete copy of the work in the Biblioteca Rossiana, Vienna, but for some reason had dated it 1589. LockVR, p. 357, properly dates the work and points out that the copy Kroyer saw is now in I: Rvat. I am indebted to Professor John Ward for telling me about the existence of this volume.

1565_1

BAKFARK, VALENTIN

VALENTINI GREFFI / BAKFARCI PANNONII, HARMONIARUM / MUSICARUM IN USUM TESTUDI/NIS FACTARUM, / TOMUS PRIMUS. / Ad Potentissimum totius Sarmatiae Principem, ac Dominum SIGIS/MUNDUM AUGUSTUM, Poloniae Regem, et caet. Patrem / Patriae, et omnium Musicorum Patronum beneficentissimum, / Dominum suum clementissimum. / [Latin quatrain, followed by: ΑΓΑΘΗ ΤΥΧΗ] / Cautum est Privilegiis Imperatoriae Majestatis, et Serenissimi POLoniae Regis, ne quis / intra decursum duodecim annorum, hoc opus invito Authore recudere audeat. / CRACOVIAE, / Impensis Authoris LAZARUS ANDREAE

VALENTINI GREFFI
BAKFARCI PANNONII, HARMONIARVM
MVSICARVM IN VSVM TESTVDI-
NIS FACTARVM,

TOMVS PRIMVS.

Ad potentißimum totius Sarmatiæ Principem, ac Dominum SIGIS-
MVNDVM AVGVSTVM, Poloniæ Regem, etcæt. Patrem
Patriæ, et omnium Musicorum Patronum beneficentißimum,
Dominum suum clementißimum.

AVGVSTI pietas toto cantabitur orbe,
Donec erunt nitidis flammea signa polis.
Omnia cùm poßit longæua abolere vetustas,
Virtutis famam nunquam abolere potest.
ΑΓΑΘΗ ΤΥΧΗ.

Cautum est Priuilegijs Imperatoriæ Maiestatis, & Serenißimi POLoniæ Regis, ne quis intra decursum duodecim annorum, hoc opus inuito Authore recudere audeat.

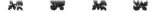

CRACOVIÆ,
Impensis Authoris LAZARVS ANDREÆ excudit.
Anno à virgineo partu, M. D. LXV.
Mense Octobri.

Σὺν θεῷ, καὶ εὐτυχῶς.

Title page of 1565_1

excudit. / Anno à virgineo partu, M. D. LXV / Mense Octobri. / Συμ Θεῷ, και ευτυχῶζ.

4 + 24 fols. Italian lute tablature. On fol. a1^v: arms of Sigismund August II, king of Poland, with the motto "Armiger adversos Jovis iste ut proterit hostes, Subjectos placido sic regit imperio. A. T." Dedication on fol. a2 headed "SERENISSIMO AC POTENTISSIMO PRINCIPI, AC DOMINO, DOMINO SIGISMUNDO AUGUSTO, DEI GRATIA REGI POLONIAE, MAGNO DUCI LITWANIAE, RUSSIAE, PRUSSIAE, MAZOVIAE, SAMOGITIAE, LIVONIAE, & caet. DOMINO AC HAEREDI, DOMINO CLEMENTISSIMO," and signed on fol. a3^v "CRACOVIAE, die XV. Octobris, Anno à restis tuta salute humano generi, post sesquimilles simum sexagesimo quinto. SERENISSIMAE MAJESTATIS VESTRAE, Perpetuus & fidelis Cliens, & subditus. VALENTINUS BAKFARK PANNO-

NIUS," printed in GaspaC IV, 166. On fol. a4: the arms of Bakfark with the motto "VIRTUTI CEDUNT OMNIA" and a Latin device headed "SYMBOLUM EIUSDEM" (facsimile in DTO XVIII/37, pl. ix), followed by a Latin poem headed "DE INSIGNIBUS EIUSDEM, CARMEN ANDREAE TRICESII EQUITIS POLONI." On fol. a4^v: two Latin poems, headed "AD EUNDEM" and "AD SODALES MUSICOS." Fol. b1 = fol. 1. On fol. 24: Psalm 118, verse 105, followed by the printer's mark. For further information, see GomVB (which reprints all of the prefatory matter) and DTO XVIII/37. For a later edition, see 1569_1.[1] All of the compositions are for solo lute.

Copies in: D:Mbs, I:Bc.[2]

	fol.	
1	1	*Fantasia*[3] *a3* = 1574_7, no. 12
2	1^v	*Fantasia*[4] *a4*
3	3	*Fantasia*[5] *a4*
4	5	*Jesu nomen sanctissimum* Clemens non Papa *a4* (ClemensCS V, no. 14) = 1571_6, no. 145
	6	2a pars *Sit nomen Domini benedictum*
5	6^v	*Erravi sicut Ovis quae periit* Cle. non Papa *a4* (RISM 1553_8, fol. 7) = 1571_6, no. 146
	7	2a pars *Delicta iuventutis meae*
6	8	*Circumdederunt me viri mendaces* Clem. non Papa *a4* (RISM 1553_9, fol. 4) = 1571_6, no. 147
	9	2a pars *Quoniam tribulatio proxima est*
7	9^v	*Cantibus Organicis, Christi Cecilia sponsa* Nicol. Gomberth *a4* (RISM 1553_{11}, fol. 5^v)
	11^v	2a pars *Fundite Cantores dulci*
8	12^v	*Domine si tu es, jube me venire ad te* Nicolaus Gomberth *a4* (GombertO V, 101)
	13^v	2a pars *Cumque vidisset ventum*
9	14^v	*Venite filii audite me* Nic. G[ombert] *a4* (GombertO V, 10)
	16	2a pars *Servite Domino cum timore*
10	17	*Exaltabo te Domine* Archadelth *a4*
	18	2a pars *Domine in voluntae tua praestitisti decori meo*
11	19	*Qui habitat in adjutorio altissimi* Josquin Depres *a4* (JosqMT, no. 52)
	21	2a pars *Non accedat ad te malum*
12	23	*Faulte dargent Cest douleur non pareille* Josquin De Pres *a5* (JosqWW, no. 15) = 1574_7, no. 51

[1] FétB I, 184, says that a second volume in this series was published in Cracow in 1568, but this volume does not survive.

[2] A copy was in D:Bds.

[3] Mod. ed. in DTO XVIII/37, p. 83, and in GomVB, no. 5; facs. of fol. 5 in DTO XVIII/37, pl. x.

[4] Mod. ed. in DTO XVIII/37, p. 84, and GomVB, no. 6.

[5] Mod. ed. in DTO XVIII/37, p. 87, and GomVB, no. 7.

1565_2

GORZANIS, GIACOMO DE

IL SECONDO LIBRO / DE INTABOLATURA DI LIUTO / DI MESSER GIACOMO GORZANIS / Pugliese, Habitante nella Citta di Trieste. Novamente / da lui revisto & per Antonio Gardano ristampato. / [Printer's mark] / In Venetia appresso di / Antonio Gardano / 1565.

38 fols. Italian lute tablature. On fol. K2^v: table of contents. Contents = 1563_8. For other volumes in the same series, see 1561_2, note 1. All of the compositions are for solo lute.

Copy in: A:Wn.

1565_3

LE ROY, ADRIAN, AND ROBERT BALLARD

BREVE ET FACILE INSTRUCTION / POUR APPRENDRE LA TABLATURE, / A BIEN ACCORDER, CONDUIRE, ET / DISPOSER LA MAIN SUR / LE CISTRE. / [Printer's mark] / A PARIS. / Par Adrian le Roy, & Robert Ballard, / Imprimeurs du

Roy / 1565. / Avec privilege de sa magesté pour dix ans.

24 fols. French cittern tablature. On fol. 1^v: cut of a cittern. Beginning on fol. 2: instructions for playing the cittern, including tuning diagram, and other musical examples. On fol. 24^v: table of contents. For some concordances see HeartzSF, p. 401. All of the compositions are for solo cittern.

Copy in: D:TR.

	fol.	
1	8	*Prelude* = 1570_3, no. 2
2	8^v	*Les Bouffons*[1] = 1570_3, no. 32c; 1578_4, no. 57; 1582_5, no. 90
	9	*Bouffons plus diminuée*
3	9^v	*Pavane des Bouffons* = 1570_3, no. 32e, and 1578_4, no. 55a
	10^v	*Gaillarde des Bouffons* = 1570_3, no. 32g, and 1578_4, no. 55b
4	11^v	*Pavane Romanesque* = 1570_3, no. 38a, and 1578_4, no. 45a: "Passemezo"
	12	*Plus diminuée*
	12^v	*Gaillarde Romanesque* = 1570_3, no. 38b, and 1578_4, no. 45b: "Saltarello"
	12^v	*Autrement*
	13	*Autrement*
5	13^v	*Gaillarde J'aymeroys mieux dormir seullette*[2] (compare 1589_1, no. 12) = 1570_3, no. 46c; 1578_4, no. 60; and 1582_5, no. 72c: "Gaillarde Caracossa Bassus"
6	14^v	*L'espagnolle* = 1570_3, no. 34; 1578_4, no. 49: "Pavane L'espagnolle"; 1582_5, no. 50
	14^v	*Autrement*
7	15	*Gaillarde Hely* = 1570_3, no. 54
8	15^v	*Gaillarde des cornus*
9	16	*Premier Bransle de bourgongne* = 1570_3, no. 88, and 1582_5, no. 130
10	16^v	*Second Branle De Bourgongne* = 1570_3, no. 89, and 1582_5, no. 131
11	17	*Troisieme Branle de Bourgongne* = 1570_3, no. 90, and 1582_5, no. 132
12	17^v	*Quatriéme Branle de Bourgongne* = 1570_3, no. 91, and 1582_5, no. 133
13	18	*Cincquieme Branle de bourgongne* = 1570_3, no. 92, and 1582_5, no. 134
14	18^v	*Sisieme Branle de Bourgongne* = 1570_3, no. 93, and 1582_5, no. 135
15	19	*Setieme Branle de Bourgongne* = 1570_3, no. 94, and 1582_5, no. 136
16	19^v	*Huitieme Branle de Bourgongne* = 1570_3 no. 95, and 1582_5, no. 137
17	20	*Neuviéme Branle de bourgongne* = 1570_3, no. 96, and 1582_5, no. 138
18	20^v	*Branle le beau Robert* = 1582_5, no. 123
19	21	*Branle de la becasse*
20	21^v	*Branle sont des poix*
21	22	*La muniere de vernon* (compare RISM 1554_{26}, no. 18: Maillard)
22	22^v	*Branle & tant plus* = 1570_3, no. 110
23	23	*Branlle de la nonnette*
24	23^v	*Il a brule la hotte*[3]
25	24	*Une m'avoit promis* (compare LesLRB, art. 3, no. 6: Certon)

[1] Mod. ed. in TapS, p. 36.

[2] Unrelated musically to RISM 1554_{26}, no. 11: Certon.

[3] Unrelated musically to RISM 1554_{26}, no. 7: Mithou.

1565_4

LUPACCHINO, BERNARDINO, AND JOAN MARIA TASSO

IL PRIMO LIBRO A NOTE NEGRE / A DUE VOCI, COMPOSTO PER BERNARDIN / LUPACHINO DAL VASTO, CON ALCUNI / DI GIAN MARIA TASSO. / Con la nuova giunta di alcuni Canti di nuovo ristampati. / [Printer's mark] / In Venetia appresso Girolamo Scotto. / M D L X V.

Two part books in mensural notation, each of 16 fols. Fol. 1^v = p. 2. The six pieces followed by an asterisk are fully texted; the others are without text or title; all are *a 2*.

Copy in: I:Bc (T).[1]

	p.	
1	2	Lupacchino[2] = 1559_6, no. 1
2	3	*Ancidetemi pur** (compare RISM 1541_9, p. 9: Arcadelt)
3	3	[Joan Maria Tasso] = 1559_6, no. 3

4	4	[Lupacchino] = 1559_6, no. 4
5	5	Lupacchino = 1559_6, no. 5
6	6	*Pungente dardo** (compare RISM 1541_9, p. 3: Berchem)
7	7	[Joan Maria Tasso] = 1559_6, no. 7
8	7	[Joan Maria Tasso] = 1559_6, no. 8
9	8	Gian Maria Tasso = 1559_6, no. 15
10	9	Gian Maria Tasso = 1559_6, no. 9: Lupacchino
11	10	Gian Maria Tasso = 1559_6, no. 16
12	11	*Ragion'e ben** (compare RISM 1541_9, p. 4: Berchem)
13	12	Lupacchino = 1559_6, no. 13
14	12	*Il bianch' & dolce Cigno** (compare BuH II, 244: Arcadelt)
15	13	Lupacchino
16	14	Lupacchino = 1559_6, no. 17
17	15	Lupacchino = 1559_6, no. 11
18	16	[Anon.]
19	17	Gian Maria Tasso = 1559_6, no. 18
20	17	[Lupacchino] = 1559_6, no. 19
21	18	Lupacchino = 1559_6, no. 23
22	19	Gian Maria Tasso = 1559_6, no. 24
23	20	*Voi ven'andat'al Cielo** (compare CW V, no. 4: Arcadelt)
24	21	*Occhi miei lassi** (compare RISM 1541_9, p. 8: Arcadelt)
25	22	Gian Maria Tasso = 1559_6, no. 21
26	23	Lupacchino = 1559_6, no. 25: Joan Maria Tasso
27	24	Lupacchino = 1559_6, no. 26
28	24	Lupacchino = 1559_6, no. 27: Joan Maria Tasso
29	26	Gian Maria Tasso = 1559_6, no. 29
30	27	Gian Maria Tasso = 1559_6, no. 30
31	28	Gian Maria Tasso = 1559_6, no. 31
32	28	Lupacchino = 1559_6, no. 32
33	29	Lupacchino = 1559_6, no. 33
34	31	Lupacchino *Sopra la battaglia* = 1559_6, no. 37
35	32	Gian Maria Tasso *Sopra la battaglia* = 1559_6, no. 39

[1] A copy was in D:Bds.

[2] The compositions are numbered beginning with no. 2 (that is, no. 1 of this inventory = no. 2 of the original).

1565_5

SANCTA MARIA, TOMÁS DE

Libro llamado / Arte de tañer Fantasia, assi para Tecla / como para Vihuela, y todo instrumento, en que se pudiere / tañer a tres, y a quatro vozes, y a mas. Por el qual en breve tiempo, y / con poco trabajo, facilmente se podria tañer Fantasia. El qual / por mandado del muy alto consejo Real fue examina/do, y aprovado por el eminente musico de su / Magestad Antonio de Cabeçon, y / por Juan de Cabeçon, / su hermano. / Compuesto por el muy Reverendo padre Fray Thomas de Sancta / Maria, de la Orden de los Predicadores. Natu/ral de la villa de Madrid. / Dirigido al Illustrissimo Señor don Fray BERNARDO de Fresneda, / Obispo de Cuenca. Comissario general, y Confessor de su Magestad, &c. / [Coat of arms of the dedicatee] / Impresso en Valladolid, por Francisco Fernandez de / Cordova, Impressor de su Magestad. Con licencia, / y privilegio Real, por diez años. / En este año, de 1565. / Tassado por los Señores del Consejo Real, a veynte reales, cada cuerpo en papel.[1]

218 fols. (94 in Book I and 124 in Book II). On fol. *1^v: royal printing privilege signed "Fecha en el monasterio de Guisando a onze dias del mes de Abril de mill y quinientos y sesenta, y tres Años. Yo El Rey. Por mandado de su Magestad, Francisco de Erasso." Dedication on fol. *2 headed "Al Illustrissimo y Reverendissimo. S. Don F. Bernardo de Fresneda, Obispo de Cuenca, Comissario general, y Confessor de su Magestad, &c. Fray Thomas de sancta Maria, de la orden de sancto Domingo. S. P. D." On fols. *2^v–*3: preface headed "Prologo. Al pio Lector." On fols. *3^v–*4: table of contents for both books. Fol. *5 = fol. 1. Fol. 91 = fol. 1 of Book II. Title page of Book II: "Comien/ça la segunda parte de/sta Obra, la qual tra/cta del arte de / tañer fan/tasia." The title is placed within an ornamental border. On fol. 1^v of Book II: preface headed "El Auctor al pio Lector." On fols. 123–124^v of Book II: author's corrections. Colophon on fol. 124^v of Book II: "A gloria y alabança de Dios, y augmento de su culto divino. Fenesce el libro llamado, Arte de tañer fantasia. Compuesto, por el

muy reverendo padre, fray Thomas de sancta Maria, de la orden de los predicadores. Impresso en Valladolid con licencia de su Magestad, por Francisco Fernandez de Cordova su impressor. Acabose a veynte dias del mes de Mayo, de este año de mil y quinientos y sesenta y cinco. Laus Deo."

Book I of this treatise (containing 27 chapters) begins with an introduction to the rudiments of music. The main part of this book, however, is a detailed discussion of the technique of playing a keyboard instrument. Sancta Maria explains such things as hand position, fingering, ornaments, and the qualities of good performance (for example, playing cleanly, with steady rhythm, and with taste).

Book II (containing 53 chapters) is concerned with the technical knowledge required to be able to improvise. Among other things Sancta Maria treats intervals, counterpoint in two, three, and four voices, how to write imitative entries, how to play fantasias, and how to tune keyboard instruments and the vihuela.

The table of contents of both books and a detailed summary of much of Book I is given in KinO, pp. 25–55. The table of contents of Book II is given in SchneidA, pp. 31–33. Chapters 13–20 of Book I (those chapters especially concerned with the details of performance) are translated into German in SaV. See also HarZ and ReFS, no. 45. The treatise is copiously supplied with musical examples (most of them are headed "Exemplo"); some of them are reprinted in DallaL, nos. 9 and 43 (two fantasias); DallaLO IV, no. 2, and VI, no. 21 (two fantasias); FerandIM, no. 19; FroideA I, 44–55; KallLO III, 44–51 (eight fantasias from Book I, fol. 67ff.); KinO, pp. 236–244; KleinO, p. 121; MusetS, p. 8; PedH VI, xii; PeetA, no. 4; RiessO, p. 2ff.; RitZ II, 91; SaA; SainzF, no. 3; and SchneidA, pp. 37–38 and 110. All of the examples are in mensural notation; some are for solo keyboard and others are included to make some theoretical point without reference to actual performance.

Copies in: CH:Lcortot, E:Bu, E:E, E:Mmc, E:V, GB:Ge, GB:Lbm, US:Cn, US:R, US:Wc.[2]

[1] Facs. of title page and fol. K2 in Maggs28, p. 88; SubHM I, 633; and SubHME, p. 216; facs. of title page only in VinS, p. 99. Facs. of fol. 56 of Book I in AngME, pl. 47; BonnO VI, 16; and SubHM I, 499.

[2] A copy was in D:Bds, and one was in the Écorcheville library (see ÉcorC, no. 82).

$[1565]_6$

ALDE, JOHN

The Sequence of lutynge.

Licensed to John Alde (see ArberT I, 298). This volume, now lost, is listed in DeakinMB, p. 4; DeakinO, p. 35; and SteeleE, p. 99. DartHL, p. 14, lists the title as "Science of Lutyng."

1566_1

FRANCESCO DA MILANO AND PERINO FIORENTINO

INTABOLATURA / DE LAUTO / DI .M. FRANCESCO MILANESE ET .M. PERINO / FIORENTINO / Ricercate Madrigali, & Canzone Franzese: / LIBRO [Printer's mark] PRIMO. / In Roma per .M. Valerio Dorico, & Lodovico / Fratello. / M. D. LXVI. / Cum privilegio summi Pontificis ad quinquenium.

Unknown number of fols. Italian lute tablature. On fol. A1v: preface headed "Valerio Dorico a quelli se dilettano de la musica de lauto," reprinted in OsG, p. 6, and translated in WieP, p. 3. The preface is followed by the table of contents:

Fantasia di M. Francesco Milanese — Numero XII
Fantasia di .M. Pierino Fiorentino — Numero IIII

MADRIGALI

Quanta belta di — M. Francesco
Quando io penso al martir di — M. Francesco
O felici ochi mei di — M. Pierino
Quanti travagli di — M. Pierino

CANZONI FRANCIESE

De mon triste di — M. Francesco
Vignon vignetta di — M. Francesco.

The volume was apparently a new edition of 1547$_2$. All of the compositions were for solo lute.

Copy in: F:CV (fols. 1–4).[1]

fol.

1 A2 *Fantasia di M. Francesco Milanese* = 1547$_2$, no. 2

2 A2^v *Fantasia di M. Francesco Milanese* = 1547$_2$, no. 1

3 A3^v *Fantasia di M. Francesco Milanese* = 1547$_2$, no. 5

[1] A copy was in D: Bds (formerly in the Wolffheim library; see WolffC I, no. 1189).

1566$_2$

NEWSIDLER, MELCHIOR

IL / PRIMO / LIBRO / INTABOLATURA / DI LIUTO / DI MELCHIOR NEYSIDLER / Alemano, Sonatore di Liuto in Augusta, / ove sono Madrigali, Canzon Francesi, / Pass'e mezi, Saltarelli & alcuni / suoi Ricercari, Novamente / da lui posti in luce. / [Printer's mark] / In Venetia appresso di Antonio Gardano. / 1566.

20 fols. Italian lute tablature. Dedication on fol. *1^v headed "AL MOLTO MAGNIFICO ET GENEROSO SIGNOR, IL SIGNOR GIOVANNI LANGNAUER Patritio Augustano, mio Signor osservandissimo," and signed "Melchior Neysidler." The music begins on fol. *2 = p. 1. On p. 38: table of contents. The contents are listed in MfMG III (1871), 152. For a later edition of the same music see 1573$_1$. MoeDM contains a thematic index of the dances (p. 417) and concordances for them (p. 263). All of the compositions are for solo lute.

Copies in: D:Mbs, GB:Lbm, S:Uu.[1]

p.

1 1 *Deh ferma amor* [*costui*] [Lasso] (CW LVIII, no. 6: D. Ferabosco) = 1571$_6$, no. 99

2 2 *O s'io potessi donna* (RISM 1541$_9$, p. 19: Berchem) = 1571$_6$, no. 101

3 4 *Io mi son giovinetta* (EinIM III, no. 30: Domenico Ferabosco) = 1571$_6$, no. 100

4 5 *Con lei fuss'io* (RISM 1543$_{17}$, p. 36: Arcadelt, Berchem, Corteccia, or Giaches de Ponte) = 1571$_6$, no. 107

5 7 *Vita de la mia vita* (RISM 1537$_9$, no. 25: Verdelot) = 1571$_6$, no. 104, and 1572$_1$, no. 9

6 8 *Perche la vita breve* = 1571$_6$, no. 113

7 9 *Signor mio caro* (SCMA VI, p. 25: Cipriano da Rore) = 1571$_6$, no. 110, and 1572$_1$, no. 8

8 11 *Ca[r]ità di Signore* (SCMA VI, p. 28: Rore) = 1571$_6$, no. 112

9 12 *Avecq[u]e vous* (LassoW XII, 37: Lasso) (compare 1571$_6$, no. 77)

10 14 *Suspirs ardans* (SCMA V, p. 70: Arcadelt) = 1571$_6$, no. 73

11 15 *Mo[n]sieur Labe* (RISM 1570$_5$, p. 18: "Maistre Robin," Lasso) = 1571$_6$, no. 81

12 17 *Hellas quel jour* (LassoW XII, 47: Lasso)

13 18 *Un doulx nenny* (LassoW XII, 45: Lasso) = 1571$_6$, no. 78; 1572$_1$, no. 19; 1573$_2$, no. 12

14 19 *Content ou non* = 1571$_6$, no. 62

15 20 *Vray dieu disois* (LassoW XII, 72: Lasso) = 1571$_6$, no. 74

16 22 *Petite folle* (LassoW XII, 78: Lasso) = 1571$_6$, no. 80

17 23 *Pass'e mezo antico* = 1571$_6$, no. 173a: "Passomezo la Milanese"

25 *Il suo saltarello con la ripresa* = 1571$_6$, no. 173b

18 27 *Pass'e mezo la Milanese* = 1574$_7$, no. 56a

28 *Il suo saltarello con la ripresa* = 1574$_7$, no. 56b

19 31 *Ricercar Primo*[2] = 1571$_6$, no. 28

20 33 *Ricercar Secondo* = 1571$_6$, no. 29

21 35 *Ricercar Terzo* = 1571$_6$, no. 30

22 37 *Ricercar Quarto* = 1571$_6$, no. 32

[1] A copy was in D: Bds.

[2] Mod. ed. in NeemAM II, no. 8.

1566$_3$

NEWSIDLER, MELCHIOR

IL / SECONDO / LIBRO / INTABOLATURA / DI LIUTO / DI MEL-

CHIOR NEYSIDLER / Alemano, Sonatore di Liuto in Augusta, / ove sono Motetti, Canzon Francesi, / Pass'e mezi, Saltarelli & alcuni / suoi Ricercari, Novamente / da lui posti in luce. / [Printer's mark] / In Venetia appresso di Antonio Gardano. / 1566

26 fols. Italian lute tablature. Dedication on fol. *1ᵛ headed "AL MOLTO MAGNIFICO ET GENEROSO SIGNOR, IL SIGNOR MELCHIOR LINCK Patritio Augustano, mio Signor & compadre mio osservandiss.," and signed "Melchior Neysidler." The music begins on fol. *2 = p. 1. On p. 49: table of contents. The contents are listed in MfMG III (1871), 152. For a later edition of the same music see 1573_1. MoeDM contains a thematic index of the dances (p. 418) and concordances for them (p. 263). All of the compositions are for solo lute.

Copies in: D:Mbs, GB:Lbm, S:Uu.[1]

	p.	
1	1	*Deus canticum novum* (LassoW VII, 164: Lasso) = 1571_6, no. 149a, and 1586_5, no. 15a
	2	2a pars *Quia delectasti* = 1571_6, no. 149b, and 1586_5, no. 15b
2	3	*Omnia que fecisti* (LassoW VII, 127: Lasso) = 1571_6, no. 150, and 1586_5, no. 10
3	6	*In me transierunt* (LassoW IX, 49: Lasso) = 1571_6, no. 151
4	8	*Surrexit Pastor bonus* (LassoW V, 57: Lasso) = 1571_6, no. 152, and 1586_5, no. 13
5	10	*Benedicam Dominum* (LassoW IX, 174: Lasso) = 1571_6, no. 155a, and 1586_5, no. 17a
	12	2a pars *In domino* = 1571_6, no. 155b, and 1586_5, no. 17b
6	14	*Gustate & videte* (LassoW V, 73: Lasso) = 1571_6, no. 153a, and 1586_5, no. 20a
	16	2a pars *Divites eguerunt* = 1571_6, no. 153b, and 1586_5, no. 20b
7	18	*Susanne ung jour* (LassoW XIV, 29: Lasso) = 1571_6, no. 132
8	21	*Secoures moy* (LassoW XVI, 163: Lasso) = 1571_6, no. 120
9	22	*Jouissance* [*vous donneray*] (RISM 1545_{14}, fol. 2: Willaert) = 1572_1, no. 18
10	24	*Oncques amour* (RISM $[1544]_{11}$, fol. 16: Crecquillon) = 1571_6, no. 116
11	26	*Dung petit* [*mot*] = 1571_6, no. 143
12	28	*Le departir* (LassoW XIV, 116: Lasso) = 1571_6, no. 133, and 1572_1, no. 17
13	29	*Pass'e mezo* = 1571_6, no. 172a
	32	*El suo saltarello* = 1571_6, no. 172b
14	34	*Pass'e mezo La paranzino* = 1571_6, no. 175a
	37	*El suo saltarello*[2] = 1571_6, no. 175b
15	39	*Recercar primo* = 1571_6, no. 24
16	40	*Recercar secundo* = 1571_6, no. 26
17	43	*Recercar Terzo* = 1571_6, no. 34
18	46	*Recercar quarto* = 1571_6, no. 27

[1] A copy was in D: Bds.
[2] Mod. ed. in NeemAM II, no. 9.

$[1567]_1$

BALLARD, ROBERT

An Exortation to all Kynde of Men how they shulde learn to play of the lute. Printed by Robert Balla[r]de.

This volume, now lost, is listed in ArberT I, 343; DartHL, p. 14; DeakinMB, p. 4; and SteeleE, p. 99.

$[1567]_2$

MERULO, CLAUDIO

RICERCARI / D'INTAVOLATURA / D'ORGANO DI CLAUDIO / MERULO DA CORREGGIO / ORGANISTA DELL'ILLUSTRISS. / SIGNORIA DI VENETIA / Nella Chiesa di S. Marco: / Nuovamente da lui dati in luce, & con ogni diligentia corretti / AL MOLTO ILLUSTRE SIGNORE / IL S. CONTE MARCANTONIO / Martinengo Villachiara. / LIBRO [Fleuret] PRIMO. / IN VENETIA, / 1567.

This volume, now lost, was in D:Bds. The title and description are taken from SartMS, p. 26. 42 fols. Keyboard score.

Dedication on fol. 2 headed "Al Molto Illustre et Magnanimo Signore Il Signor Conte Marcantonio Martinengo Villachiara," and signed "Di Venetia il primo di Luglio 1567," reprinted in SartMS. On fol. 2^v: printer's privilege. On fol. 42: table of contents. The volume also contained a list of works announced for publication by Merulo. This list is reprinted in IMAMI II, xliii–xliv. A second edition of this volume, in 1605, is described in SartMS, p. 134. Transcriptions of the 1567 edition may be found in the Alfred Einstein Collection at Smith College in Northampton, Massachusetts, Instrumental Music, vol. VIII (US:Nf, Einstein MSS). All of the compositions are for solo keyboard.

	fol.	
1	3	*Ricercar del primo tuono*
2	9	*Ricercar del secondo tuono* [1]
3	13^v	*Ricercar del terzo tuono*
4	19	*Ricercar del quarto tuono*
5	22^v	*Ricercar dell'undecimo tuono*
6	26	*Ricercar del duodecimo tuono*
7	31^v	*Ricercar del settimo tuono*
8	37^v	*Ricercar dell'ottavo tuono* [2]

[1] Mod. ed. in FrotOI, no. 2.
[2] Mod. ed. in EinSH, app., no. 22.

[1567]$_3$

LE ROY, ADRIAN

Instruction d'asseoir toute musique facilement en tablature de luth. Paris, Adrian le Roy et Robert Ballard.

This volume, now lost, is mentioned in Dom Caffiaux's notes for a history of music (F:Pn, MS fonds fr. 22537, fol. 137). For other editions, see [1557]$_1$, [1570]$_2$, and [1583]$_3$. For English translations, see 1568$_3$ and 1574$_2$. For further information see LesLRB, art. 130.

1567

DOUBTFUL WORKS

1. MorL, xliii, lists an anonymous *Lautenbuch*, published by Christian Müller in Strasbourg in 1567 as being in B:Br. Morphy probably refers to 1562$_4$ (see 1562$_4$, note 1).

1568$_1$

BECCHI, ANTONIO DI

LIBRO PRIMO / D'INTABULATURA DA LEUTO, / DI M. ANTONIO DI BECCHI PARMEGIANO. / COMPOSTA DA LUI NOVAMENTE, ET DATA IN LUCE, CON ALCUNI / Balli, Napolitane, Madrigali, Canzon Francese, Fantasie, Recercari / [Printer's mark] / IN VINEGIA, / APPRESSO GIROLAMO SCOTTO. / M D LXVIII.

46 fols. Italian lute tablature. Fol. 1^v = p. 2. LefL contains a modern edition of the entire volume. MoeDM contains a thematic index of the dances (p. 419) and concordances for them (p. 264). On Becchi see also Doubtful Works for 1546 and 1563. All of the compositions are for solo lute.

Copies in: A:Wn, US:Wc.[1]

	p.	
1	2	*Pass'e mezzo alla Millanesa*
	5	*Il suo saltarello*
2	8	*Pass'e mezzo alla Millanesa*
	11	*Il suo saltarello*
3	14	*Pass'e mezzo alla Millanesa*
	19	*Il suo saltarello*
4	22	*Pass'e mezzo alla Millanesa*
	30	*Il suo saltarello*
5	35	*Romanesca*
6	38	*Favorita* (= romanesca) (1554$_1$, no. 5)
	39	*La sua Rotta*
7	40	*Madama mi domanda*
8	41	[*Aria*] *Da cantar*
9	42	*Tre damme alla Francesa*
10	43	*Fantinella aria da cantar*
11	44	*Pavana*
	45	*La sua gagliarda*
12	46	*Pavana*
	48	*La sua gagliarda*
13	49	*Pass'e mezzo dalla Saracena*
	50	*Il suo saltarello*
14	51	*Pass'e mezzo della bella donna*
	52	*La sua gagliarda*

15	54	*Pavana della Francesa*
	56	*La sua gagliarda*
16	57	*Moresca*
17	58	*La Moretta*
18	60	*Seguit'amor donna gentil'e bella* (RISM 1566_9, no. 7: Nola)
19	61	*Occhi che date al sole & alle stelle*
20	61	*Nicola mia gentil*
21	62	*Poiche pietà non ha di me pietade*
22	62	*O voi che in mille in mille pene sete*
23	63	*Questa questa crudel*
24	63	*Madonne se volete doi sorti de lemosine farete*
25	64	*Le cortegiane se ne vane via*
26	64	*Gratiosa se mai*
27	65	*Non mi pensava mai* (RISM 1566_{10}, no. 10: Don Francesco Celano)
28	65	*Faccia mia bella* (RISM 1566_{10}, no. 11: Giov. Domenico da Nola)
29	66	*Madrigale Nasce la pena mia* (MonteO XVI, app.: Striggio)
30	68	*O d'amarissim'onde* (LassoW VIII, 97: Lassus)
31	70	*Occhi facci d'amor*
32	71	*Ancor che col partire* (CCMA VI, no. 13: Rore) = 1568_7, no. 63
33	72	*Un gai bergier* = 1547_9, no. 8: Crecquillon
34	74	*Pour quoi voles vous [cousturier]* (RISM 1534_{12}: Janequin [Passereau?])
35	76	*Une bergere*
36	77	*Reveiles* = 1546_6, no. 13: "Reveillez moy," Garnier
37	77	*Fantasia*
38	80	*Fantasia* = 1571_6, no. 18
39	81	*Fantasia*
40	82	*Fantasia per accordar il lauto in altro modo*
41	82	*Recercare* = 1507_2, no. 42: Spinacino
42	84	*Recercare* = 1507_2, no. 41: Spinacino
43	85	*Recercare* = 1546_6, no. 10: Francesco da Milano
44	87	*Recercare accorda il lauto in altro modo* = 1507_2, no. 39: Spinacino
45	88	*Recercare*

[1] This copy was in the Landau-Finaly library in Florence (see RoedigC I, 497).

1568_2

GALILEI, VINCENZO

FRONIMO DIALOGO / DI VINCENTIO GALILEI FIORENTINO, / NEL QUALE SI CONTENGONO LE VERE, / Et necessarie regole del Intavolare la Musica nel Liuto, / Posto nuovamente in luce, & da ogni errore emmendato. / [Printer's mark] / IN VINEGIA, / APPRESSO GIROLAMO SCOTTO. / M D LXVIII.

82 fols. Italian lute tablature. Dedication on p. 3 headed "ALL'ILLUSTRISS.mo ET ECCELLENTISS. S. PRINCIPE IL S. GULIELMO CONTE PALATINO DEL RENO, ET DUCA DELL'UNA ET l'altra Baviera, signor mio semper osservandiss.," and signed "Di Venetia il di 20. Ottobre 1568. Di V. Illustriss. & Eccellentiss. signoria Humiliss. & devotiss. servitor Vincentio Galilei," printed in SartMS, p. 28, and IMAMI IV, lxxxiv–lxxxv. On p. 5: preface headed "L'Autore ai lettori," printed in IMAMI IV, lxxxv. On p. 6: poem in Italian headed "M. Gasparo Torello All'Auttore." On p. 161: table of contents. On p. 163: table of composers and colophon: "In Vinegia, Appresso Girolamo Scotto. M D LXIX [*sic*]."[1] This treatise on playing the lute is in the form of a dialogue with musical examples. In the following inventory only complete pieces with titles are given. Certain of the shorter untitled examples are printed in ChilLS, p. 54, and IMAMI IV, 19.[2] Nos. 65–95 are reprinted in 1569_8. 1584_5 is a revised and expanded edition. Attributions to composers and number of voices in the vocal model are given here in brackets after the table of contents of the 1584 edition. All of the compositions are for solo lute unless otherwise noted.

Copies in: GB:Lbmh, I:Fn,[3] I:Fr, I:PAc, I:Rsc.[4] †

	p.	
1	7	*Si puor bivir ardiendo*[5] [Pedro Guerrero *a 4*]
2	8	*Biviendo sin amar*[5] [P. Guerrero *a 4*]
3	13	*Dun spiritu triste* [P. Guerrero *a 4*] (compare 1554_3, no. 124)

FRONIMO DIALOGO

DI VINCENTIO GALILEI FIORENTINO,

NEL QVALE SI CONTENGONO LE VERE,

Et necessarie regole del Intauolare la Musica nel Liuto,

Posto nuouamente in luce, & da ogni errore emmendato.

IN VINEGIA,

APPRESSO GIROLAMO SCOTTO.

M D LXVIII.

Title page of 1568_2

4 15 *Vestiva i colli*[6] [Palestrina *a5*] (PalO IX, 117)

16 2a pars *Cosi le chiome mie*

5 23 *Questi ch'inditio fan del mio tormento* [Alessandro Striggio *a6*] (Vogel: Striggio 12 [1579], no. 2)

6 24 *Nasce la pena mia* [Striggio *a6*] (MonteO XVI, app.)

7 26 *Nasce la gioia mia* [Giovanni Animuccia *a6*]

8 27 *Io mi son Giovinetta*[7] [Domenico Ferabosco *a4*] (EinIM III, no. 30)

9 29 *Lieti felici spirti*[8] [Vincenzo Ruffo *a3*] (RISM 1561_{11}, p. 14)

10 29 *Il vostro gran valore*[9] [Ruffo *a3*] (RISM 1561_{11}, p. 15)

11 31 *Se tra quest'herb'è fiore*[10] [Palestrina *a5*] (IMAMI IV, 49)

12 34 *Io mi son Giovinetta*[11] (another version of no. 8 above)

13 50 *Duo tutto di fantasia*[12] (mensural notation) = 1584_4, no. 4, and 1584_5, no. 20

14 54 [*O envieulx qui de mon infortune*] (mensural notation and lute tablature; PhalCh VI [1555], no. 14: Latre)

15 55 *Crainte & spoir*[13] [P. Guerrero *a4*] (mensural notation and lute tablature; RISM 1555_{20}, no. 22: "Crainte & espoir," Baston)

16 59 *Ricercar primo*

17 62 *Alla dolc'ombra* Cipriano de Rore *a4* (SCMA VI, 12)

63 2a pars *Non vide il mondo*

64 3a pars *Un lauro mi difese*

64 4a pars *Però piu ferm'ogn'hor*

65 5a pars *Selve sassi campagne*

66 6a pars *Tante mi piacque*

18 66 *Anchor che col partir*[14] (SCMA VI, 45: Rore)

19 67 *Come ha[v]ran fin le dolorose tempre* [Rore *a4*] (SCMA VI, 51)

20 68 *Spesso in parte del ciel* [Marc'Antonio Ingegneri *a4*] (Vogel: Ingegneri 6 [1578], no. 6)

21 68 *Non mi tolga il ben mio* [Ingegneri *a4*] (Vogel: Rore 33 [1569], p. 5: Rore)

22 69 *Appariran per me le stelle in cielo* Orlando [Lasso] (LassoW VIII, 27)

23 70 *Ma di che debbo lamentarmi hai lassa* [Vincenzo] Ruffo (Vogel: Ruffo 16 [1556], no. 29)

24 71 *A qualunque Animale*[15] Annibale Padovano (IMAMI IV, 65)

72 2a pars *Et io da che comincia*

73 3a pars *Quando la sera*

73 4a pars *Non credo che pascesse*

74 5a pars *Prima ch'io torni a voi*

74 6a pars *Con lei fuss'io*

25 75 *Dal laccio d'oro* Constanzo Porta (Vogel: Porta 4 [1555], no. 1)

26 76 *Regal donna cortese* (Vogel: Porta 4 [1555], nos. 2–3: Porta)

76 2a pars *O virtute, o beltate*

27 77 *Il chiaro sol* (Vogel: Porta 4 [1555], no. 6: Porta)

28 78 *Spontando lieto fuora* (Vogel: Porta 4 [1555], no. 12: Porta)

29 79 *Viva fiamma d'amor* (Vogel: Porta 4 [1555], no. 16: Porta)

30 79 *In bianco letto* Gian Nasco (Vogel: Nasco 5 [1554], no. 22)

31 80 *Nel'odorato e lucido oriente* Giaches de Ponte (Vogel: Ponte 2 [1554], no. 1)

32 81 *A cui piu ch'altri mai* [Ponte *a4*] (Vogel: Ponte 2 [1554], no. 2)

33 82 *La qual in somma e questa* [Ponte *a4*] (Vogel: Ponte 2 [1554], no. 3)

34 82 *A questo confortando* (Vogel: Ponte 2 [1554], no. 4: Ponte)

35 83 *Fedeli miei* [Ponte *a4*] (Vogel: Ponte 2 [1554], no. 5)

36 84 *Non scorse occhio giamai* Vincenzo Galilei

37 84 *Ricercar Secondo*

38 85 *Ricercar Terzo*

39 87 *Ricercar Quarto*

40 88 *Ricercar Quinto*

41 89 *Ricercar Sesto*

42 90 *Ricercar settimo*

43 91 *Ricercar ottavo, & ultimo*

44 92 *Fantasia Prima. Sopra, Nasse la pena mia* (compare no. 6 above)

45 94 *Fantasia Seconda. Sopra, Anchor che col partire* (compare no. 18 above)

46 96 *Fantasia Terza*

47 96 *Fantasia Quarta*

48 97 *Fantasia Quinta*

49 98 *Fantasia sesta*

50 98 *Fantasia Settima*

51 99 *Fantasia ottava, & ultima*[16]

52 100 *I begli occhi ond'io fui* Adriano Villahert *a5* (Vogel: Willaert 1 [1559], nos. 56–57)

101 2a pars *Questi son que begli occhi*

53 102 *Quando fra l'altre donne* (Vogel: Willaert 1 [1559], nos. 46–47: Willaert)

102 2a pars *Da lei ti vien*

54 103 *Madonna s'io v'amai* (RISM 1559_{16}, no. 1: Willaert)

55 104 *Cantai mentre ch'io arsi* Cipriano de Rore (Vogel: Rore 2 [1544], no. 5)

56 105 *Hor ch'il cielo e la terra* (Vogel: Rore 6 [1562], nos. 2–3: Rore)

106 2a pars *Cosi sol d'una chiara*

57 107 *Se voi potessi per turbati segni* (RoreO III, 60: Rore)

108 2a pars *Che gentil pianta*

58 108 *S'amor la viva fiamma* (RoreO III, 84: Rore)

109 2a pars *Novo consiglio*

59 110 *Quando fra l'altre donne* (RoreO III, 64: Rore)

110 2a pars *Da lei ti vien* (= "Io benedico'l loco")

60 111 *Scarco di doglia* (RoreO III, 88: Rore)

112 2a pars *Ma'l bel pensier*

61 113 *Ite rime dolenti* (RoreO III, 80: Rore)

113 2a pars *E se qualche pietà*

62 114 *Alma Susanna*

63 115 *Deh hor foss'io*

64 116 *Standomi un giorno* Canzone d'Orlando [Lasso] (LassoW II, 89)

117 2a pars *Indi per alto man*

118 3a pars *In un boschetto novo*

118 4a pars *Chiara fontana*

119 5a pars *Una strania fenice*

120 6a pars *Al fin ud'io*

65 122 *Là ver l'aurora* (LassoW IV, 65: Lasso)

122 2a pars *Temprar potess'io in si*

123 3a pars *Quante lagrime*

123 4a pars *Huomini, & Dei*

124 5a pars *A l'ultimo bisogno*

125 6a pars *Ridon hor per le piagge*

125 7a pars *In rete accolgo l'aura*

66 126 *La notte che segui l'horribil caso* (LassoW VIII, 88: Lasso)

126 2a pars *Riconosce colei*

127 3a pars *Come non conosco io*

67 128 *Pon freno al gran dolor* (LassoW II, 46: Lasso)

68 129 *Fiera stella* (LassoW II, 50: Lasso)

129 2a pars *Ma tu prendi a diletto*

69 130 *Amor mi strugge il cor* (LassoW IV, 26: Lasso)

70 130 *Mentre che il cor* (LassoW II, 27: Lasso)

131 2a pars *Quel fuoco è morto*

71 132 *Da quei bei crini* Baldassar Donato (Vogel: Donato 2[1557], p. 12)

72 133 *Candid'e richa vela* Francesco Portinaro (Vogel: Portinaro 5 [1557], no. 9)

133 2a pars *Piacciati com'i tuoi*

73 134 *Chi puo fuggir amor* [Alessandro] Striggio (Vogel: Striggio 22 [1571], no. 26)

74 135 *Caro dolce ben mio* (Vogel: Striggio 20 [1585], no. 6: Striggio)

75 136 *Invidioso amor* (Vogel: Striggio 20 [1585], no. 4: Striggio)

76 137 *Alla dolc'ombra* Annibale Padovano (Vogel: Padovano [1564], nos. 19–20)

137 2a pars *Non vid'il mondo*

77 138 *Io piango*

78 139 *Solo, e pensoso* Gioan Nasco (RISM 1559_{16}, p. 9)

140 2a pars *Si ch'io mi credo homai*

79 141 *Dhe porgi mano alla mia fragil barca* [Vincenzo] Ruffo (Vogel: Ruffo 3 [1555], p. 24)

141 2a pars *Sdegno regge il timon*

80 142 *O dolci sguardi* [Ruffo *a 5*]

81 143 *Tanto co'lieti suoni* Claudio da Coreggio [= Merulo] (Vogel: Merulo 1 [1566], nos. 4–5)

144 2a pars *Che vaghi suoni*

82 144 *Guidommi in parte il ciel* [Francesco] Rosello (RISM 1561_{10}, p. 10)

145 2a pars *Da indi in qua*

83 146 *Io son ferito hai lasso*[17] Giannetto da Palestrina (PalW XXVIII, 179)

84 147 *Se ben non veggion gl'occhi* (PalW XXVIII, 215: Palestrina)

85 148 *Voi caduci ligustri* Vincenzo Galilei (IMAMI IV, 215)

86 149 *Aspro core e selvaggio* Adriano Villahert *a 6* (Vogel: Willaert 1 [1559], p. 96)

150 2a pars *Vivo sol di speranza*

87 151 *I dolci colli* [Alessandro] Striggio (Vogel: Striggio 3 [1566], nos. 1–2)

152 2a pars *E qual cervo ferito*

88 152 *Se ogni mio bene havete* (Vogel: Striggio 3 [1556], no. 20: Striggio)

89 153 *Anchor ch'io possa dire* (Vogel: Striggio 3 [1566], no. 3: Striggio)
90 154 *Là ver l'aurora* (Vogel: Striggio 3 [1566], no. 14: Striggio)
91 155 *Quando vede'il pastor* (Vogel: Striggio 3 [1566], no. 10: Striggio)
92 156 *Dolce ritorno amor* (Vogel: Striggio 12 [1579], no. 6: Striggio)
93 157 *Voglia mi sprova* (Vogel: Striggio 3 [1566], no. 13: Striggio)
94 158 *Ultimi miei sospiri* [Philippe] Verdelotto (MonteO V, app.)
95 159 *Beltà si com'in mente* [Francesco] Rosello (RISM 1561_{10}, p. 27)
96 160 *Pien d'un vago pensier* Orlando Lasso

[1] DraudiusBC, p. 1650, and DraudiusBE, p. 267, both date this volume 1569.
[2] One composition repr. after Chilesotti in KlaemM II, no. 7.
[3] The copy now in Florence was formerly in the Landau-Finaly library; see RoedigC I, 522. The manuscript appendix to this copy is inventoried in BecherC, p. 132.
[4] A copy was in D:Bds (formerly in the Wolffheim library; see WolffC I, no. 656). A copy was also in the Écorcheville library (see ÉcorC, no. 33).
[5] Incipits pr. in IMAMI IV, lix.
[6] Mod. ed. in ChilLS, p. 58; both the vocal model and the intabulation are repr. in IMAMI IV, 33; facs. of no. 4 after 1584_5 in PalW XXXIII, 71.
[7] Mod. ed. in IMAMI IV, 89.
[8] Mod. ed. in ChilLS, p. 92.
[9] Mod. ed. in ChiLS, p. 56.
[10] Mod. ed. in IMAMI IV, 49; facs. of no. 11 after 1584_5 in PalW XXXIII, 73.
[11] Mod. ed. in ChilLS, p. 90.
[12] There are four counterpoints *a 2* against a cantus firmus on p. 49 in mensural notation.
[13] Mod. ed. in ChilS, no. 12.
[14] Mod. ed. in ChilLS, p. 60.
[15] Mod. ed. in IMAMI IV, 65.
[16] Mod. ed. in ChilLS, p. 62.
[17] Facs. of no. 83 after 1584_5 in PalW XXXIII, 74.

1568_3

LE ROY, ADRIAN

A Briefe and easye instru[c]tion to learne the tableture / to conducte and dispose thy hande unto the Lute / englished by J. Alford Londenor. / [Cut of a lute] / Imprinted at London by Jhon Kyngston for James / Roubothum and are to be solde at hys shop in paternoster rowe / Lycensed accordynge to the order apoynted in the queenes maiestes iniuntions / 1568

39 fols. French lute tablature. On fol. 2: author's preface headed "The Author to the Reader." On fol. 2v: translator's preface headed "The Transllatour to the Reader," and dated "Farewell this .xxiiij. Daye of Septembre. M. ccccc. lxviii." Fols. 3–14 contain instructions for playing the lute, an English translation of Adrian Le Roy's lost volume (see $[1557]_1$ and $[1567]_3$; see 1574_2 for a more complete translation).[1] Nos. 1–5 below are musical examples illustrating the text. Beginning on fol. 14v: tuning diagrams. All of the compositions except nos. 1–5 are reprinted in Le RoyFD. For further information see CaseyP. All of the compositions are for solo lute.

Copy in: GB:Lbm.

	fol.	
1	7	*The x. Commaundementes* [*Leve le cueur*] (compare PraM, no. 140) = 1574_2, no. 13
2	7v	*Je ne veux plus a mon mal consentir* (compare LesLRB, art. 3, no. 13: Certon) = 1574_2, no. 14
3	8	[*Musical example*] = 1574_2, no. 15
4	11	[*Musical example*] = 1574_2, no. 16
5	12v	*Ce n'est bien ne plaisir* (SCMA V, no. 7: Arcadelt) = 1574_2, no. 17
6	16	*Petite fantasie dessus l'accord du Leut* = 1574_2, no. 18
7	17	[*Fantasie*]
8	17v	*Passemeze*
	18v	*Passameze more shorter*
9	19v	*The Paduane* (compare 1556_8, no. 18: "Une m'avoit promis [Paduane]")
	20	*Otherwise*
10	20v	*Passe velours*
11	21	*La tintalore*
12	21v	*La souris*
13	22v	*La tirantine*
14	23	*Le petit gentilhomme*
15	23v	*La volte de Provence*

16	24^v	*First Branle of Malte*
	24^v	*Otherwise*
17	25^v	*The seconde Branle of Malte*
	26	*Otherwise*
18	26^v	*The third Branle of Malte*
19	27^v	*The fowerth Branle of Malte*
20	28^v	*Pavane si je m'en voy* (compare LesLRB, art. 3, fol. 9: "L'Ennuy qui me tourmente," Certon)
	29^v	*Shorter tyme*
	30^v	*Gaillarde of the precedent Pavane*
21	31^v	*Gaillarde Romanesque*
	32^v	*Fredon sur la Romanesque*
22	33^v	*J'aymeroye mieux dor[mir seulette]* [2] (compare 1589_1, no. 12)
23	34^v	*The first Gaillarde Milanoise*
24	35^v	*The seconde Milanoise*
25	36^v	*The thirde Milanoise* (compare 1564_7, no. 42: "Gaiarda de la Royne de Eschosse") = 1563_{12}, no. 120
26	37^v	*Fowerth Milano* (compare 1564_2, no. 21: "Gaillarde la Visdame")
27	38^v	*The fift Milanoise* (compare 1571_5, no. 37: "Gaillarde Si pour t'aymer") = 1563_{12}, no. 121
28	39^v	*Branle de Poictou*

[1] LumS, p. 22, and SteeleE, p. 101, list a 1563 edition of this volume, a dating probably based on a misreading (see DartHL, p. 14).

[2] Unrelated to RISM 1554_{26}, no. 11: Certon.

1568_4

LUPACCHINO, BERNARDINO, AND JOAN MARIA TASSO

DI BERNARDINO / LUPACCHINO ET DI / GIO: MARIA TASSO, IL / PRIMO LIBRO A DUE VOCI. / NUOVAMENTE RISTAMPATO / ET AGIONTOVI ANCHOR ALCUNI / CANTI A DUE VOCI DE / diversi Auttori. / A DUE [Printer's mark] VOCI / IN VENETIA, Appresso Claudio da Correggio. / MDLXVIII.

Two part books in mensural notation, each of 20 fols. Contents = 1559_6. All of the compositions are *a2* and without text or title.

Copy in: S:Uu (T).

1568_5

MERULO, CLAUDIO

MESSE / D'INTAVOLATURA / D'ORGANO DI CLAUDIO / MERULO DA CORREGGIO / ORGANISTA DELL'ILLUSTRISS. / SIGNORIA DI VINETIA / Nella Chiesa Di San Marco: / Nuovamente da lui date in luce, et con ogni diligentia corrette. / AL REVERENDISS. MONS. IL S. ANTONIO / ALTOVITI ARCIESCOVO DI FIORENZA, / CON GRATIA, ET PRIVILEGIO. / LIBRO [Printer's mark] QUARTO / IN VINETIA, / 1568.

74 fols. Keyboard score. Dedication on fol. $A1^v$ headed "Al Reverendiss. Mons. il S. Antonio Altoviti Arciescovo di Fiorenza," and dated "Di Vinetia il primo d'Aprile. M D LXVIII," reprinted in SartMS, p. 27. Fol. A2 = p. 1. On p. 146: table of contents. MeruO is a modern edition of the entire volume. All of the compositions are for solo keyboard.

Copies in: B:Br, I:Bc, I:Rsc.

	p.	
1	1	*Missae Apostolorum*
	1	*Kyrie*
	2	*Kyrie*
	4	*Christe*
	5	*Kyrie*
	7	*Kyrie*
	11	*Et in terra pax*
	13	*Benedicimus te*
	15	*Glorificamus te*
	16	*Domine deus rex celestis*
	18	*Domine deus agnus dei*
	20	*Qui tollis*
	21	*Quoniam tu solus sanctus*
	23	*Tu solus altissimus*
	25	*Amen*
	26	*Sanctus*
	28	*Sanctus*
	31	*Agnus dei*
2	33	*Missae In Dominicis Diebus*
	33	*Kyrie*
	34	*Kyrie*
	35	*Christe*
	36	*Kyrie*
	39	*Kyrie*
	41	*Et in terra pax*
	42	*Benedicimus te*

43 *Glorificamus te*
45 *Domine deus rex celestis*
46 *Domine deus agnus dei*
47 *Qui tollis*
49 *Quoniam tu solus sanctus*
50 *Tu solus altissimus*
51 *Amen*
53 *Sanctus*
54 *Sanctus*
55 *Agnus dei*
3 57 *Missae Virginis Mariae*
57 *Kyrie*[1]
59 *Kyrie*
60 *Christe*
61 *Kyrie*
63 *Kyrie*
64 *Et in terra pax*
66 *Benedicimus te*
67 *Glorificamus te*
68 *Domine deus rex celestis*
70 *Spiritus et alme*
73 *Primo genitus*
75 *Qui tollis*
77 *Qui sedes*
79 *Mariam sanctificans*
80 *Mariam gubernans*
82 *Mariam coronans*
83 *In gloria*
86 *Sanctus*
87 *Sanctus*
89 *Agnus dei*
4 92 [*Patrem*] *In Dominicis Diebus*
92 *Patrem*
93 *Et ex patre*
94 *Genitum non factum*
96 *Crucifixus*
98 *Et ascendit*
100 *Et in spiritum*
103 *Et unam sanctam*
105 *Et expecto*
107 *Amen*
5 109 [*Patrem*] *Angelorum*
109 *Patrem*
111 *Et ex patre*
113 *Genitum non factum*
116 *Crucifixus*
118 *Et ascendit*
120 *Et in spiritum*
122 *Et unam sanctam*
123 *Et expecto*
125 *Amen*
6 127 [*Patrem*] *Cardinalium*
127 *Patrem*
128 *Et ex patre*
130 *Genitum non factum*
132 *Crucifixus*
134 *Et ascendit*
136 *Et in spiritum*
138 *Et unam sanctam*
140 *Et expecto*
143 *Amen*

[1] Mod. ed. of four versets of the Kyrie in OL XII, 11, and of three versets in DallaL, no. 40.

1568_6

VREEDMAN, SEBASTIAN

NOVA / LONGEQUE ELEGANTIS/ SIMA CITHARA LUDENDA CARMINA, / CUM GALLICA TUM ETIAM GERMANICA: FANTASIAE ITEM, / Passomezi, Gailliarde, Branles Almandes etc. Nunc primum ex Musica in usum Ci/tharae traducta per Sebastianum Vreedman / Mechliniensem. / His accessit luculenta quadam & perutilis institutio qua quisque citra alicuius / subsidium artem Citharisandi facillimè percipiet. / [Fleuret] / LOVANII. / Excudebat Petrus Phalesius Bibliographus Iuratus. / Anno 1568.

56 fols. French cittern tablature. On fol. A1^v: a poem in Latin headed "AD LECTOREM CARMEN." On fols. A2–A4: instructions for playing the cittern headed "IN USUM CITHARAE INTRODUCTIO." The instructions include a cut of the neck of a cittern and two subdivisions in the text: "DE TEMPORE ET PAUSIS" (on fol. A3) and "MODUS TENDENDI NERVOS IN CITHARA" (on fol. A4). The same instructions appear in 1570_3 and 1582_5. Fol. A4^v is blank. Fol. B1 = fol. 1. All of the compositions are for solo cittern.

Copy in: A:Wn.

	fol.	
1	1	*Fantasia* = 1570_3, no. 3, and 1582_5, no. 4
2	1^v	*Fantasia* = 1570_3, no. 1, and 1582_5, no. 3
3	2	*Les Bouffons*
	2	*Autrement*
4	2^v	*Era di magio* = 1570_3, no. 135a
	2^v	*Autrement* = 1570_3, no. 135b

5 3 *Een venus dierken* (compare DuyL I, 556) = 1570_3, no. 136, and 1582_5, no. 145

6 3^v *Een amoureux fiereghelate* = 1570_3, no. 137, and 1582_5, no. 146

7 3^v *Het wasser te nacht* (compare DuyL I, 292, and 490) = 1570_3, no. 138, and 1582_5, no. 147

8 4 *Vreucht es ons toeghecomen*

9 4^v *Ick segge adieu*[1] (compare BridgmE, p. 162, and LenN, p. [108])

10 5 *Ick hadde een ghestadich minneken* (ClemensO II, 11: "Psalm XVIII," Clemens non Papa)

11 5^v *Te mey als alle die voghelkens singhen* (compare DuyL II, 1024)

12 6 *Een schilderken fraey*

13 6 *En het was een aerdich vrouken* (compare LenN, p. 58: "Ic sach een aerdich vrouken")

14 6^v *Het sadt een schipperken op sijn schip*

15 6^v *Een meysken op een ryuierken sadt*

16 7 *Wijsheyt edel vrouwe*

17 7 *O edel bloem der vrouwen*

18 7^v *La bella franciskina*

19 7^v *Le souffre passion*[2] (= "Je souffre passion"?)

20 8 *Robin c'est un galland* = 1570_3, no. 141

21 8 *Valla de la roma*

22 8^v *Si pay me ou non* (LesLRB, art. 171, fol. 3: "Si j'ayme ou non," Le Roy)

23 9 *Je sonne la retraicte* [Certon]

24 9^v *En fut il oncque* (RISM 1545_8, no. 4: Certon) = 1570_3, no. 21, and 1578_4, no. 20

25 10 *Un advocat dist a sa femme* (RISM 1545_{10}, no. 19: Delafont) = 1570_3, no. 12, and 1582_5, no. 10

26 10^v *Ick sach vrou venus burseken*

27 11 *Den lusteleken mey* (compare RISM 1572_{11}, no. 25: Clemens non Papa, and DuyL I, 356)

28 11^v *Voor ia qui tu me canta* (RISM 1557_{18}, no. 12: "Vorrei che tu cantassi," Azzaiolo)

29 12 *Ma man ia*

30 12^v *La pastorella mia* (SCMA V, no. 5: Arcadelt) = 1570_3, no. 10, and 1578_4, no. 19

31 13^v *Languyr me fais* (AttainCK II, no. 12: Sermisy)

32 14^v *Tant que vivray* (AttainCK II, no. 10: Sermisy) = 1570_3, no. 8, and 1582_5, no. 9

33 15 *Pis ne me peult venir* (compare RISM 1572_2, fol. 25: Crecquillon) = 1570_3, no. 9, and 1582_5, no. 25

34 15^v *D'ou vient cela* (AttainCK III, no. 22: Sermisy; another version of no. 39 below) = 1570_3, no. 6, and 1582_5, no. 7

35 16 *J'ay veu le cerf* (compare ClemensO VI, 140: Manchicourt)

16 *Autrement*

36 16^v *J'ay trop aymer* (AttainCK I, no. 12) = 1570_3, no. 11; 1578_4, no. 21; 1582_5, no. 20

37 17 *Jamais n'aymeray*

38 17^v *Ick hebbe wel alsoo langhen tijt*

39 17^v *D'ou vient cela autrement* (another version of no. 34 above)

40 18^v *Sur le pont* (compare ClemensO II, 61: Clemens non Papa)

41 19 *Een vrolijck beelt* (compare ClemensO II, 55: Clemens non Papa)

42 19^v *Meisken wildiv*

43 20 *Het soude een proper meisken* (compare DuyL I, 780)

44 20^v *Het was een aerdisch vrouken* = 1570_3, no. 140

45 20^v *Edel bloem bouen alle vrouwen*

46 20^v *Het was een macht* = 1570_3, no. 139

47 21 *Cupido triumphant* (compare DuyL II, 899)

48 21^v *Le petit Bataille*

49 22^v *Vous perdez temps* (PubAPTM XXIII, no. 56: Sermisy)

50 23^v *Aupres de vous* (AttainCK I, no. 16: Sermisy or Jacotin)

51 24 *N'oseroit on dire* (compare DuyL II, 1090)

52 24^v *Si parti guardo* (RISM 1570_8, p. 46: "Si pur ti guardo," Pathie)

53 25^v *Or puis qu'amour*

54 26 *Ghepeis ghij doet mij trueren* (compare DuyL II, 1685)

55 26^v *Niet dan druck en lijden* (compare LenN, p. 75)

56 27 *Sloef sloef waer hebdi gheweest* = 1570_3, no. 134, and 1582_5, no. 144

57 27^v *Allegez moy* (BrownTC, no. 1) = 1570_3, no. 4, and 1582_5, no. 5

58 28^v *Misericorde* (ClemensO X, 140: Clemens non Papa)

59 29^v *Vivre ne puis* (RISM 1536_3, no. 9: Sermisy)

60 30^v *Content desir* ("*Response*") (BrownTC, no. 13: Sermisy)

61 31^v *Susanne ung jour* (LevyS, p. 403: Didier Lupi Second)

62 32^v *Dames qui au plaisant* ("*Response*") (LesDC, art. 69, fol. 22: Didier Lupi Second)

63 33 *Un doulx nenny* (LassoW XII, 45: Lasso)

64 34^v *Doulce memoire* (PubAPTM XXIII, no. 50: Sandrin) = 1570_3, no. 16, and 1582_5, no. 12

65 35^v *Finy le bien* ("*Response*") (RISM 1540_9, no. 8: Certon) = 1570_3, no. 17

66 36^v *O combien est* [*malheureux*] (ClemensO VII, 156: Sandrin or Sermisy) = 1570_3, no. 14, and 1578_4, no. 27

67 37^v *Le mal* [*qui sent*] (RISM 1570_8, p. 5: "Response" to "O combien est") = 1570_3, no. 15

68 38 *Je prens en gré* (ClemensO X, 14: Clemens non Papa)

69 39^v *Morir me fault* ("*Response*") (RISM 1570_8, p. 11)

70 40^v *Si mon traveil* (PubAPTM XXIII, no. 52: Sandrin) = 1570_3, no. 19, and 1582_5, no. 16

71 41^v *Le dueil yssu* ("*Response*") (RISM 1540_9, no. 14: Villiers) = 1570_3, no. 20, and 1582_5, no. 17

72 42^v *Je suis desheritée* (CW XV, no. 2: Lupus or Cadéac)

73 43^v *Hors envieulx* (EngL, p. 51: Gombert)

74 44^v *Godt es mijn licht* (VNM XXVI, 51: Clemens non Papa) = 1570_3, no. 18; 1578_4, no. 40; and 1582_5, no. 24 (?)

75 45^v *Toutes les nuyct* (RISM 1570_8, p. 12: Crecquillon)

76 46^v *Ce mois de may* (PubAPTM XXIII, no. 25: Godard) = 1570_3, no. 13; 1578_4, no. 22; and 1582_5, no. 11

77 47^v *Ne pense plus* M. Simon Levrart = 1570_3, no. 29, and 1578_4, no. 17

78 48^v *Angelus Domini*

79 49^v *Chorea Dianae*[3] M. Simon Levrart

80 50 *Passomezo d'ytalye*

81 50^v *Gaill*[*arde*] *Wij sal mij troetelen* (compare 1568_7, no. 132: "Gaillarda la Royne d'escosse")

82 50^v *Gaill*[*arde*] *Si pour t'aymer*

83 51 *Almande damours*

84 51^v *Almande de lignes* = 1570_3, no. 86

85 51^v *Almande a deux pas* = 1570_3, no. 87

86 52 *Brande d'artois*

87 52 *Brande de Bataille* = 1570_3, no. 118

[1] Mod. ed. in TapS, p. 37.

[2] Not related musically to RISM 1549_{20}, fol. 9^v: Gentian.

[3] Heading on fol. 49^v: "Huiusmodi e [that is, an *e* with a diagonal slash through it] denotat istum semitonium quod est inter d & e."

1568_7

PHALÈSE, PIERRE, PUBLISHER

LUCULENTUM / THEATRUM MUSICUM, / IN QUO (DEMPTIS VETUSTA/TE TRITIS CANTIONIBUS) SELECTISSIMA OPTIMO/RUM QUORUMLIBET AUTORUM, AC EXCELLEN/tissimorum artificum tum veterum, tum praecipuè recentio/rum carmina, maiore quam unquam diligentia & / industria expressa, oculis / proponuntur. / Et primo ordine continentur αὐτόματα quae Fantasiae dicuntur, / Secundo Cantilenae quatuor & quinque Vocum. / Postea Carmina difficiliora quae Muteta appellantur, eaque quatuor, / quinque & sex Vocum. / Deinde succedunt Carmina longe elegantissima duabus Testu/dinibus ludenda. / Postremo habes & eius generis Carmina quae tum festivitate, / tum facilitate sui discentibus, primo maximè satisfacient ut sunt / Passomezo, Gailliardes, Branles etc. / [Cut of ten performing musicians] / LOVANII. / Ex Typographia Petri Phalesii Bibliopolae Iurati. / ANNO M. D. LXVIII.

92 fols. French lute tablature. On fol. A1v: a poem in Latin headed "IN LAUDEM THEATRI Musici, Frederici Viaere Frisii Carmen." Fol. A2 = fol. 1. At the bottom of each page from fol. 1 to fol. 12v appears an epigram from a classical author in Greek or Latin. On fol. 91: table of contents. SlimK II, 550, contains a thematic index of the ricercares. Nos. 115–122 are for two lutes; the other compositions are for solo lute.

Copies in: A:Wn, D:ROu, GB:Ob, NL:DHgm.

MUSIC FOR SOLO LUTE

	fol.	
1	1	*Fantasia prima*[1] = 1563_{12}, no. 16: Raphael Viola, and 1571_6, no. 22
2	1v	*Fantasia Simon Sentler* = 1547_3, no. 3: Gintzler
3	2	*Fantasia a Rota* = 1546_{15}, no. 31: Rotta
4	2v	*Fantasia Pauli Baroni* = 1536_9, no. 11: Borrono
5	3	*Fantasia* = 1552_4, no. 6: Morlaye
6	3v	*Fantasia* = 1560_3, no. 3: Paladin
7	4v	*Fantasia* = 1558_4, no. 2: Morlaye
8	5	*Fantasia* = 1536_3, no. 16: Francesco da Milano
9	5v	*Fantasia* = 1560_3, no. 1: Paladin
10	6	*Fantasia* = 1536_3, no. 7: Francesco da Milano
11	6	*Fantasia* = 1546_{10}, no. 8: Giovanni Maria da Crema
12	6v	*Fantasia* = 1536_3, no. 1: Francesco da Milano
13	7	*Fantasia* = 1558_4, no. 3: Morlaye
14	7v	*Fantasia* = 1536_3, no. 5: Francesco da Milano
15	8v	*Fantasia Francisci Milan* = 1536_9, no. 1: Francesco da Milano
16	9	*Fantasia* = 1571_6, no. 20
17	9v	*Fantasia* = 1553_1, no. 2: Bakfark
18	10	*Fantasia* = 1536_3, no. 4: Francesco da Milano
19	10v	*Fantasia* = 1536_3, no. 15: Francesco da Milano
20	11	*Fantasia* = 1546_{15}, no. 30: Rotta
21	11	*Fantasia* = 1538_1, no. 9: Narváez
22	11v	*O combien est* [*malheureux*] (ClemensO VII, 156: Sandrin or Sermisy)
23	12	*Le mal qui sent* ("*Response*")[2] = 1563_{12}, no. 20, and 1571_6, no. 36
24	12v	*Vous perdés temps* (PubAPTM XXIII, no. 56: Sermisy) = 1571_6, no. 37
25	13	*Telz en mesdict* ("*Response*") = 1547_9, no. 4: Mittantier
26	13v	*Doulce memoire* (PubAPTM XXIII, no. 50: Sandrin) = 1563_{12}, no. 28, and 1571_6, no. 39
27	14	*Finy le bien* ("*Response*") = 1547_9, no. 12: Certon
28	14v	*C'est a grand tort* (RISM 1558_{10}, no. 24: Crecquillon) = 1563_{12}, no. 36, and 1571_6, no. 41
29	15	*Languyr me fais* (AttainCK II, no. 12: Sermisy) = 1563_{12}, no. 30, and 1571_6, no. 42
30	15v	*Si mon traveil* = 1547_9, no. 30: Sandrin
31	16	*Le dueil yssu* ("*Response*") (RISM 1540_9, no. 14: Villiers) = 1563_{12}, no. 27, and 1571_6, no. 44
32	16v	*Toutes les nuyct* (RISM 1570_8, p. 12: Crecquillon) = 1563_{12}, no. 23, and 1571_6, no. 45
33	17	*Mais languyray-je* = 1552_{11}, no. 55: Clemens non Papa
34	17v	*Qu'est il besoing* ("*Response*") (RISM 1570_8, p. 13)
35	18	*Fault il qu'il soit*
36	18v	*Cessez mes yeux* (RISM 1554_{22}, p. 1: Crecquillon) = 1563_{12}, no. 31
37	19	*Le content est riche* (AttainCK III, no. 9: Sermisy) = 1571_6, no. 69
38	19v	*Je prens en gré* = 1547_9, no. 1: Clemens non Papa

39 20 *Un gay bergier* = 1545_{3}, no. 38: Crecquillon

20^{v} *Un gay bergier. Alio modo* = 1547_{9}, no. 8

40 21 *Dolci suspiri*

41 21 *Pour un plaisir* = 1546_{18}, no. 30: Crecquillon

21^{v} *Pour un plaisir. Alio modo* = 1571_{6}, no. 46

42 21^{v} *Si de present* ("*Response*") (RISM 1545_{14}, fol. 16^{v}: Susato)

43 22^{v} *Venez venez[mon bel amy]* = 1563_{12}, no. 58

44 23 *Je suis desheritée* = 1552_{8}, no. 7: Lupus or Cadéac

45 23^{v} *Damour me plains* [3] = 1547_{9}, no. 2: Pathie

46 24 *Ce mois de may* (PubAPTM XXIII, no. 25: Godard) = 1563_{12}, no. 65

24^{v} *Ce mois de may. alio modo* = 1571_{6}, no. 65b

47 24^{v} *Canzon Mapolitano* [sic] *in tolledo* (RISM 1566_{5}, p. 6: "In Toledo una donzella")

48 25 *Sur la verdure* (RISM 1570_{8}, p. 29) = 1563_{12}, no. 62

49 25 *Or demourez* = 1563_{12}, no. 85

50 25^{v} *Mamye un jour* (RISM 1549_{18}, no. 1: Certon) = 1563_{12}, no. 75

51 26 *Si purti guardo* (RISM 1570_{8}, p. 46: Pathie) = 1563_{12}, no. 76; 1571_{6}, no. 105; 1574_{7}, no. 36

52 26^{v} *Godt es mijn licht* (VNM XXVI, 51: Clemens non Papa) = 1563_{12}, no. 74, and 1571_{6}, no. 54

53 26^{v} *Responce*

54 27^{v} *Susanne ung jour* *a4* (LevyS, p. 403: Didier Lupi Second) = 1571_{6}, no. 53

55 28 *Que pleust a dieu* Verius (RISM 1578_{6}, fol. 8) = 1571_{6}, no. 64

56 28^{v} *Si de nouveau* Verius

57 28^{v} *Fortune allors* (RISM 1539_{15}, no. 2: Certon) = 1571_{6}, no. 117

58 29 *Pour une helas* Cricquillon *a4* = 1571_{6}, no. 56

59 29 *Tutta tutta saressa* = 1571_{6}, no. 97

60 29^{v} *Quando ie penso al martire* = 1546_{17}, no. 3: Arcadelt

61 30 *O faccia puita mia*

62 30^{v} *Martin menoit* Clemens non Papa = 1571_{6}, no. 58

63 31 *Anchor che col partire* = 1568_{1}, no. 32: Rore

64 31 *Si tu non mi voi*

65 31^{v} *O sio potessi donna* (RISM 1541_{9}, p. 19: Berchem)

66 32 *La pastorella mia* (SCMA V, no. 5: Arcadelt) = 1571_{6}, no. 111

67 32^{v} *Frisque et gaillard* (ClemensO X, 17: Clemens non Papa) = 1571_{6}, no. 55

68 33 *Adieu madame par amour*

69 33^{v} *A demy mort* (ClemensO X, 32: Clemens non Papa)

70 34 *Amour au ceur* (RISM $[1552]_{7}$, no. 25: Crecquillon) = 1563_{12}, no. 35, and 1571_{6}, no. 67

71 34^{v} *Si me tenez* *a3* (compare RISM 1545_{14}, fol. 14: Crecquillon, *a6*) = 1571_{6}, no. 61

72 35 *Or il ne m'est possible* (RISM 1553_{24}, fol. 9^{v}: Clemens non Papa) = 1571_{6}, no. 50

73 35^{v} *Misericorde* (ClemensO X, 140: Clemens non Papa) = 1563_{12}, no. 68

74 36 *Avecque vous* Orlando [Lasso] (LassoW XII, 37)

75 36^{v} *Ardant amour* Orlando [Lasso] (LassoW XIII, 25) = 1571_{6}, no. 83

76 37 *Vray dieu disoit* Orlando [Lasso] (LassoW XII, 72) = 1571_{6}, no. 74b

77 37^{v} *Du corps absent* Orlando [Lasso] (LassoW XII, 55)

78 37^{v} *En espoir vis* Orlando [Lasso] (LassoW XII, 52) = 1571_{6}, no. 88

79 38 *En un lieu* Orlando [Lasso] (LassoW XII, 83) = 1571_{6}, no. 79

80 38 *Bon jour mon ceur* (LassoW XII, 100: Lasso)

81 38^{v} *Las voulez vous* Orlando [Lasso] (LassoW XII, 3) = 1571_{6}, no. 76a

39 *Las voulez vous. Alio modo* Orlando [Lasso]

82 39^v *Un doulx nenny* Orlando [Lasso] (LassoW XII, 45) = 1563_{12}, no. 59

83 40 *Ce faux amour* Orlando [Lasso] (LassoW XII, 103) = 1574_2, no. 11

84 40^v *O comme heureux* ("La Responce d'un doux nenny") Orlando [Lasso] (LassoW XVI, 160)

85 41 *La giustitia immortate* (SCMA VI, 41: "La giustitia immortale," Rore)

86 41^v *Donna ch'ornata sete* (SCMA VI, 63: Rore)

87 42 *L'inconstantia channo* (SCMA VI, 60: "L'inconstantia che seco han le mortali cose," Rore)

88 42^v *Se'l mio sempre per voi* (SCMA VI, 72: Rore)

89 43 *Non gemme non fin oro* Cypriano [de Rore] (SCMA VI, 75)

90 43^v *Souspirs ardans* Arcadet (SCMA V, no. 30)

91 44 *Si la dureza* Orlando (Vogel: Arcadelt 7 [1544], p. 36: "Se la dura durezza," Arcadelt)

92 44^v *Carita di signore* (SCMA VI, 28: Rore)

93 44^v *Per pianto la mia carne* Orlando [Lasso] (LassoW VIII, 13)

94 45 *Io cantarei d'amor* (SCMA VI, 31: Rore)

95 45^v *Di tempo in tempo* (SCMA VI, 67: Rore)

96 46 *Signor mio caro* (SCMA VI, 25: Rore)

97 46^v *Qual e piu grand'o amore* (SCMA VI, 78: Rore)

98 47 *Non e ch'il duol mi scena* (SCMA VI, 34: Rore)

99 47^v *A'i trepida* (SCMA V, no. 21: Arcadelt)

100 48^v *Or vien sa mamye* = 1560_3, no. 19: "Or vien sa vien m'amye," Janequin)

101 49 *La bella mita* (SCMA VI, 38: "La bella netta ignuda," Rore) = 1574_1, no. 16

102 49^v *Qual anima [ignorante]* = 1560_3, no. 7: Nollet

103 50 *Non at sua amante* = 1552_4, no. 17: "Non al sua amante," Tromboncino

104 50^v *Vita della mia vita* (RISM 1537_9, no. 25: Verdelot)

105 51 *Pensa domi quel giorno*

106 51^v *Dormiendo i giorno* = 1547_5, no. 66: Verdelot

107 52 *Pis ne me peult venir* (RISM 1572_2, fol. 25: Crecquillon)

108 52^v *Susanne un jour* Orlando [Lasso] *a 5* (LassoW XIV, 29)

53 *Susanne un jour. [Alio modo] a 5*

53^v *Susanne un jour. a 5. plus diminuée* Orlando [Lasso] = 1571_6, no. 130, and 1572_1, no. 13

109 54 *Je ne desire aymer* (RISM $[1556]_{17}$, p. 6: Crecquillon)

110 54^v *Tristitia obsedit me* = 1556_2, no. 35: "Tristitia [vestra]," Isaac

111 55 *Descendit angelus*

112 55^v *Pater peccavi* = 1563_{12}, no. 103: Clemens non Papa

56 2a pars *Quanti mercenarii*

113 56^v *Stabat mater dolorosa* = 1547_3, no. 13: Josquin

114 57^v *Benedicta es* = 1547_3, no. 8a: Josquin

58^v 2a pars *Per illud ave* = 1547_3, no. 8b

58^v 3a pars *Nunc mater* = 1547_3, no. 8c

MUSIC FOR TWO LUTES

115 59 *Canti di voi le ladi*[4] (RISM 1543_{17}, p. 12: Naich) = 1571_6, no. 160

116 59^v *Amor e gratioso* = 1563_{12}, no. 116, and 1571_6, no. 161

117 59^v *Burato* = 1571^6, no. 162

118 60^v *La Bataille* (MMRF VII, 31: Janequin) = 1563_{12}, no. 115, and 1571_6, no. 163

119 61^v *Passomezo* = 1563_{12}, no. 117; 1571_6, no. 164a; 1573_3, no. 32a

62^v *Il suo saltarello* = 1571_6, no. 164b, and 1573_3, no. 32c

120 62^v *Chi passa* (AzzaiV, no. 2: Azzaiolo) = 1571_6, no. 165

121 63^v *O combien est* [*malheureux*] (ClemensO VII, 156: Sandrin or Sermisy) = 1563_{12}, no. 118, and 1571_6, no. 166 (compare 1546_{18}, no. 39)

122 64^v *Passomezo d'ytalye*

MUSIC FOR SOLO LUTE

123 65^v *Passomezo D'italye* = 1563_{12}, no. 119

124 66^v *Passomezo*

125 67^v *Passomezo* [*Nicolas*] *Rans*

70 *Gailliarda de N. de Rans*

126 72^v *Passomeso de Marck Antoine*

127 76 *Passomezo D'italye*

76^v *Gailliarda*

77^v *Gailliarda*

128 78^v *Passemezo d'ytalye*

78^v *La Gailliarde*

129 79 *Passomezo D'italye. Contratenor*

79^v *Gailliarda*

130 79^v *Passemezo. Bassus*

80 *La Gailliarda*

131 80^v *Padoana Romanisca*

81 *La Gailliarda*

132 82 *Gailliarda la Royne d'escosse* (compare no. 142 below)

133 82 *Gailliarda de Meller*

134 82^v *Chi passa*

135 83 *Gailliarda la Massengiere*[5]

136 83^v *Gailliarda*

137 83^v *Gailliarda La Vergiliana*

138 84 *Gailliarda Si pour t'aymer*

139 84^v *Gaillar*[*da*] *Morette*

140 84^v *Gailliarda la Varionessa* = 1573_2, no. 11

141 85 *Gailliarda Brunette* (compare 1569_6, no. 79: "Gailliarde o ma gente brunette") = 1573_2, no. 10

142 85^v *Gaill*[*arda*] *Wij sal mij troe telen* (compare no. 132 above)

143 85^v *Gailliarda Baisons nous belle* = 1571_6, no. 185

144 86 *Almande* [*de Ungrie*][6] = 1563_{12}, no. 137

145 86 *Almande de Spiers*

146 86^v *Almande Noseroit on dire*

86^v *Reprinse*

147 86^v *Almande Philippine*

87 *Reprinse*

148 87 *Almande de la rocha el fuso*

149 87^v *Almande smeechdelijn*

87^v *Reprinse*

150 87^v *Almande*

151 88 *Almande Nonette*

152 88 *Almande Pouloingne*

88 *Reprinse*

153 88^v *Brandt Champaigne* = 1563_{12}, no. 141; 1573_2, no. 16; 1591_{13}, no. 131

154–162 89 *Branles des Bourgoignes* = 1551_2, nos. 20–28

163 90 *Branles de N. Rans* = 1573_2, no. 17

[1] Heading on fol. 1: "THEATRUM MUSICUM, SELECTISSIMIS OPTIMORUM ARTIFICUM CARMInibus instructum atque exornatum."

[2] In RISM 1570_8, p. 5, a chanson beginning "Le mal que sent" follows "O combien est" and is called a "response." However it is unrelated musically to this intabulation.

[3] Mod. ed. in KosackL, app. III.

[4] Heading on fol. 59: "SEQUUNTUR DEINCIPS CARMINA DUABUS TESTUDINIBUS ACCOMMODA."

[5] Mod. ed. in StaakS, p. 7.

[6] The information in brackets is a manuscript addition.

1568_8

VAN GHELEN, JAN

Dit is een seer Schoon / Boecxken, om te leeren maken alderhande tabulatueren / wten Discante. Daer duer men lichtelijck mach / leeren spelen opt Clavecordium Luyte end Fluyte. / [Cut of a man playing the lute, with two recorders and a clavichord forming a border][1]

42 fols. Colophon on fol. L3: "Gheprint Thantwerpen op die Lombaerde veste inden witten Hasewint, by Jan van Ghelen Ghesworen Boeckprinter der C. M. Anno .M. CCCCC. LXVIII." On fol. $L4^v$: printer's mark with two dogs and a hare, an elaborate monogram, and the motto "Frangitres pontio mollis cauda canis hominem." This is a Flemish translation of Vorsterman's French translation (1529_2) of Virdung's *Musica getutscht* (1511_3). The same musical examples occur here as in Vorsterman.[2] Contents = 1554_9.

Copy in: NL:DHk.

[1] Facs. of title page in CesM and StraM II, opp. p. 110.

[2] Vorsterman repeats the superius only of "Een vrolic wesen" at the end of the volume. Van Ghelen omits this.

$[1568]_9$

ROWBOTHAM, JAMES, PUBLISHER

The breffe and playne instruction to lerne to play on the gyttron and also the Cetterne. London, James Rowbotham.

This volume, now lost, is listed in ArberT I, 380, and DeakinMB, p. 4. This may have been a translation of one of the treatises by Adrian le Roy, either $[1551]_4$, or 1565_3. MaunC, p. 18, lists "A briefe & plaine instruction for to learne the Tablature, to Conduct & dispose the hand unto the Gitterne. Pri. for James Rowbotham," which may be identical with this. See also DartHL, p. 14; LesLRB, art. 2 *bis*; and SteeleE, p. 99.

1568

DOUBTFUL WORKS

1. MorL I, xliii, lists: "Flecha, Mateo. *Il 1⁰ libro di madrigali . . . novamente da liuto composti*. Ven. Antonio Gardane. 1568." This is probably the volume listed in EitQ III, 475, as "Flecha, Mateo. *Il 1⁰ libro de Madrigali a 4 et 5 voci con uno sesto & un dialogo a 8 novamente da lui composti & per Ant. Gardano stampati & dati in luce. Primo libro*. Ven. 1568 Gardane."

2. FétB I, 184, lists a 1568 volume of lute music by Valentin Bakfark published in Cracow. The volume, otherwise unknown, is supposed to be a second volume to 1565_1.

1569_1

BAKFARK, VALENTIN

VALENTINI GREFFI / BAKFARCI PANNONII, HAR/MONIARUM MUSICARUM IN / USUM TESTUDINIS / FACTARUM / TOMUS PRIMUS. / [Fleuret] / ANTVERPIAE, / Apud Viduam Joannis Latii, sub, intersignio Agricolae. / 1569.

51 fols. Italian lute tablature. Fol. 1ᵛ: blank. On fol. 2: the same dedication to Sigismund August II, King of Poland as in 1565_1. On fol. 4: arms of Bakfark with Latin couplet below. On fol. 4ᵛ: poem in Latin headed "De Insignibus Eiusdem, Carmen Andreae Tricesii Equitis Poloni." On fol. 5: two Latin poems, one headed "Ad Eundem," and the other "Ad Sodales Musicos." Colophon on fol. 51ᵛ: "Typis Viduae Latii." DraudiusBC, p. 1651, lists this for 1559. Contents = 1565_1. All of the compositions are for solo lute.

Copy in: A:Wn.

1569_2

BARBETTA, GIULIO CESARE

IL PRIMO LIBRO / DELL'INTAVOLATURA / DE LIUTO DE JULIO / CESARE BARBETTA PADOVANO / NUOVAMENTE DA LUI COMPOSTO, / ET DATTO IN LUCE. / [Printer's mark] / IN VINEGIA, / Appresso Girolamo Scotto. / M D LXIX.

16 fols. Italian lute tablature. Dedication on fol. 1ᵛ (= p. 2) headed "NOBILISS. AC GENEROSO, DOMINO JOANNI HUGOLDO A SCHLEINITZ MISNENSI." On p. 32: table of contents. MoeDM contains a thematic index of the dances (p. 424) and concordances for them (p. 265). The compositions identified by the superior letter *a* ([a]) are reprinted in ChilLS, pp. 64–81. All of the compositions are for solo lute.

Copies in: F:Pthibault, GB:Lbm, I:Vnm.

	p.	
1	3	*Pavana prima Detta la Barbarina*
2	3	*Pavana Seconda Detta la Borgognona* [1]
3	3	*Pavana Terza Detta la Porcelina*
4	4	*Pavana Quinta* [sic] *Detta la Fiamengina*

5	4	*Pavana Quinta Detta la Beloncina*
6	5	*Pavana Sesta Detta la Schiavonetta*
7	5	*Pavana Settima Detta la Todeschina*[a]
8	6	*Pavana Ottava Detta la Favorita*
9	7	*Galgiarda prima detta ol Zacarii* = 1571_6, no. 179
10	7	*Gagliarda seconda Detto il Barbetino* = 1571_6, no. 180
11	8	*Galgiarda terza Detta li Mazocho* = 1571_6, no. 178
12	8	*Galgiarda quarta Detta la Franctia*[a] = 1571_6, no. 182
13	9	*Gagliarda quinta detta la Imperiale*[a] = 1571_6, no. 181
14	9	*Gagliarda Sesta detta la Grave*
15	10	*Settima Gagliarda di Franctia*[a] = 1571_6, no. 183
16	11	*Gagliarda ottava De Franctia* = 1571_6, no. 186
17	12	*Passo e mezo, ficto* = 1571_6, no. 169, and 1586_5, no. 51
18	13	*Passo e mezo, Sopra la Battaglia*[a] [2] = 1571_6, no. 170
19	15	*Passo e mezo, detto il Nobile*[a] [3] = 1571_6, no. 168
20	16	*Passo e mezo, detto il Bachiglione*[a] [4]
21	17	*Pass'e mezo, detto il moderno* [5] = 1571_6, no. 167a, and 1586_5, no. 49a
	19	*Gagliarda de Passo e mezo antescritto*[a] = 1571_6, no. 167b, and 1586_5, no. 49b
22	20	*Passo e mezo, detto l'anticho* = 1571_6, no. 171a
	23	*Gagliarda del Passo e mezo antescritto* = 1571_6, no. 171b
23	24	*Fantasia Prima* a 3
24	25	*Fantasia seconda* a 4
25	26	*Fantasia Terza* a 4
26	27	*Fantasia quarta* a 4 [6]
27	29	*Fantasia Quinta, ficta* a 4
28	30	*Fantasia Sesta, ficta*

[1] Mod. ed. in MoeDM, p. 332.

[2] Heading on p. 13: "Al Molto Magnifico et Prudentissimo Signor, il Signor Melchioro Adiebes, dignissimo Consigliero della Illustre nation Alemana."

[3] Heading on p. 15: "Al Valoroso Signor Constantino Mal'ombra."

[4] Heading on p. 16: "Al molto magnifico, & Eccellentissimo Dottor di legie, il Signor Sicheo Salietr."

[5] Heading on p. 17: "Al molto magnifico & generoso Signor, il Signor Giovanni Hugoldo Ascleinitz."

[6] Heading on p. 27: "Al molto Magnifico & Illustrissimo Signor, il S. Contramtonio de Hortemburgi."

$[1569]_3$

KARGEL, SIXT

Carmina Italica, Gallica & Germanica ludenda cythara, Moguntiae, 69.

This volume, now lost, is listed in DraudiusBC, p. 1622. This may be a first edition of 1575_6

$[1569]_4$

KARGEL, SIXT

Nova & elegantiss. Italica & Gallica carmina pro testudine, Moguntiae, 69.

This volume, now lost, is listed in DraudiusBC, p. 1622. Probably the contents = 1574_1.

$[1569]_5$

KARGEL, SIXT

Renovata Cythara . . . Moguntiae, 1569. in fol.

This volume, now lost, is listed in DraudiusBC, p. 1622. Probably the contents = 1578_4. The dedication of 1578_4 is dated 1575, however, suggesting that year as the date of the first edition. Perhaps this entry for 1569 was a mistake by Draudius.

1569_6

VREEDMAN, SEBASTIAN

CARMINUM QUAE CY/THARA PULSANTUR LIBER SECUNDUS: /

IN QUO SELECTISSIMA QUAEQUE ET JUCUNDA CARMI/na continentur: ut Passomezi, Gailliardes, Branles, Alemande & alia eius generis per/multa quae sua dulcedine auditorum animos mire oblectant. / Nunc primum summa qua fieri potuit facilitate in tyronum usum / per Sebastianum Vreedman Mechliniensem / composita. / [Fleuret] / LOVANII. / Excudebat Petrus Phalesius Typographus Juratus. / Anno M. D. LXIX.

47 fols. French cittern tablature. Fol. *2 = fol. 1. The compositions identified by the superior letter *a* ([a]) are reprinted in WardDVM, pp. 46–51. See $[1563]_9$ for a possible earlier edition. All of the compositions are for solo cittern.

Copies in: A:Wn, US:SM (fol. 44 only, laid into a copy of 1596_4).

	fol.	
1	1	*Almande du Prince*[a]
	1	*Le Reprinse*
2	1^v	*Almande Frison* = 1570_3, no. 78
	1^v	*Le reprinse*
3	2	*Almande bruynsmedelijn*[a] = 1570_3, no. 69
	2	*Le reprinse*
4	2^v	*Almande hertoch Mauritius*
5	3	*Almande Malines* = 1570_3, no. 79
6	3^v	*Almande des Oosterlings*
	4	*Le Reprinse*
7	4^v	*Almande de worms*
	5	*Le Reprinse*
8	5^v	*Almande switsers*
9	6	*Almande gerre gerre*[a] = 1570_3, no. 76
10	6	*Almande Bruynswijck* = 1570_3, no. 77
11	6^v	*Almande Jolie*
12	7	*Almande de Spiers* = 1570_3, no. 74: "Almande de Philippine"
13	7	*Almande deux trois aes* = 1570_3, no. 75
14	7^v	*Almande* = 1570_3, no. 72a: "Almande Poussinghe," and 1582_5, no. 102
	8	*Le reprinse* = 1570_3, no. 72b
15	8	*Almande bisarde* = 1570_3, no. 73, and 1582_5, no. 108
16	8^v	*Almande dambrugghes* = 1570_3, no. 81
17	8^v	*Almande dousame*
	9	*Le reprinse*
18	9	*Almande la tour* = 1570_3, no. 80
19	9^v	*Almande de deux dames*
20	10	*Almande rouwane*
21	10	*Almande nivelle* = 1570_3, no. 82
22	10^v	*Almande Brusselles* = 1570_3, no. 83
23	10^v	*Almande Coloigne*
24	11	*Almande Loreyne* = 1582_5, no. 92
25	11	*Almande* = 1570_3, no. 85: "Almande Lieve gheburen"
26	11^v	*Almande d'anvers*
27	11^v	*Almande de Spaigne* = 1570_3, no. 84
28	12	*Branle Berghes* = 1570_3, no. 121
29	12^v	*Branle del duc* = 1570_3, no. 120a
	12^v	*Le saltarelle* = 1570_3, no. 120b
	13	*Le courante* = 1570_3, no. 120c
	13^v	*Le reprinse* = 1570_3, no. 120d
30	13^v	*Branle d'anvers*
31	14	*Branle troij*
32	14^v	*Branle damours* = 1582_5, no. 122
33	15^v	*Branle hoboken*[a] = 1570_3, no. 122
34	16	*Den reij* = 1570_3, no. 123
35	16	*Coucquelecock*
36	16^v	*L'homarmé*[a] = 1570_3, no. 127
37	17	*Branle Loreyne*
38	17^v	*Branle de bourgoingne*
39	18	*Le courante* (unrelated thematically to no. 38)
40	18	*Branle coupe* = 1570_3, no. 124 (compare 1547_6, no. 11: "Branle simple")
41	18^v	*Branle Champaigne* = 1570_3, no. 125
42	19	*Branle de coloingne*
	19^v	*Le saltarelle*
43	20	*Les 6. branles de bourgoinne* = 1582_5, no. 125
44	20	*Branle 2* = 1582_5, no. 126
45	20^v	*Branle 3* = 1582_5, no. 127
46	20^v	*Branle 4* = 1582_5, no. 128
47	21	*Branle 5*
48	21^v	*Branle 6*
49	21^v	*Branle d'angleterre*
50	22	*Branle de Brusselles*
	22	*Le saltarelle*
51	22^v	*Quaterbrant*
52	23	*Le fagot*
53	23^v	*Branle rebecca* = 1570_3, no. 126a, and 1582_5, no. 124a
	23^v	*Le saltarelle* = 1570_3, no. 126b, and 1582_5, no. 124b

54	24	*Branle toutes les nuyct* (compare RISM 1570_9, p. 12: Crecquillon)
55	24^v	*Branle simple*
56	24^v	*Branle de Spiers* = 1570_3, no. 119
57	25	*Calleken van nieupoorte* = 1570_3, no. 128, and 1582_5, no. 141
58	25^v	*Passomezo de haultbois*
	26	*La gailliarde*
59	26	*Passomezo d'angleterre* = 1570_3, no. 43a, and 1582_5, no. 47a
	27	*Le reprinse* = 1570_3, no. 43b, and 1582_5, no. 47b
60	27^v	*La gailliarde* (unrelated thematically to no. 59)
61	28	*Padoana de vaecas*
	28	*La gailliarde*
62	28^v	*Passomezo Padua*
	29	*La gailliarde*
63	29^v	*Passomezo Loreyne*
	30	*Le reprinse*
64	30^v	*Passomezo Jolye*
	31	*Le reprinse*
65	31^v	*Passomezo la douce* = 1570_3 no. 45a, and 1582_5, no. 48a
	32	*Le reprinse* = 1570_3, no. 45b, and 1582_5, no. 48b
	32	*La gailliarde*
66	32^v	*Padoana de esperance* = 1570_3, no. 33a
	33	*La gailliarde* = 1570_3, no. 33b
67	33^v	*Padoana de Prince*
	34	*Le gailliarde*
68	34^v	*Passomezo Cologne*
	35	*Le gailliarde*
69	35^v	*Padoana le brave*
	36	*La gailliarde*
70	36^v	*Passomezo d'Italye*
	37	*La gailliarde* = 1582_5, no. 67
71	37^v	*Paduana damours*
	38	*Le gailliarde*
72	38^v	*Passomezo de Bruynswijck*
	39	*Le gailliarde*
73	39^v	*Passomezo Frison*
	40	*La gailliarde*
74	40^v	*Caracossa*[1]
	41	*Autrement*
75	41^v	*Chi passa* (compare AzzaiV, no. 2: Azzaiolo)
76	42	*Gailliarde elle ma faict ceste grace* = 1570_3, no. 65
77	42^v	*Gailliarde Berghentine*
78	43	*Gailliarde Botert v koecxkens wel*
79	43^v	*Gailliarde o ma gente brunette*
80	44	*La gailliarde del duc*
81	44^v	*Gaiarda la royne d'Escosse* = 1564_7, no. 42
82	45	*Gaiarda la Moretta* = 1564_7, no. 45
83	45^v	*Gailliarde de Battaille* = 1570_3, no. 44b, and 1582_5, no. 49c
84	46	*Marchese de gasto gailliarda* = 1564_5, no. 12: "Gaillarde la Burate"
85	46^v	*Gailliarda* = 1564_7, no. 23

[1] Quasi-facs. and mod. ed. in WolfH II, 133.

1569_7

CARDANE, ANTONIO, PUBLISHER

MOTECTA TRIUM VOCUM / AB PLURIBUS AUTHORIBUS COMPOSITA / QUORUM NOMINA SUNT / Jachetus Gallicus Morales Hispanus Costantius Festa Adrianus Wigliardus. / TRIUM [Printer's mark] VOCUM / Venetiis Apud / Antonium Gardanum. / 1569

Three part books in mensural notation, each of 16 fols. (?). On fol. 16^v: table of contents. Contents = 1543_3 and 1551_7. The volume contains 20 vocal pieces with Latin text, and four textless pieces, presumably for instrumental ensemble; all are *a 3*.

Copy in: I:Pu (B).[1]

[1] The unique copy has a name, "Franciscus Murraninus," in manuscript on the title page.

1569_8

GALILEI, VINCENZO

LA SECONDA PARTE / DEL DIALOGO / DI VINCENTIO GALILEI FIORENTINO, / DELLA INTAVOLATURA DI LIUTO. / Posto nuovamente in luce, & corretto. / [Printer's mark] / IN VINEGIA, / APPRESSO GIROLAMO SCOTTO. / M D LXIX.

20 fols. Italian lute tablature. Fol. 1^v = p. 122. On p. 160: table of contents. Contents = 1568_2, nos. 65–95. All of the compositions are for solo lute.

Copy in: I:Bc.

[156?]$_1$

GORLIER, SIMON

Livre de Tabulature de Cistre. Lyon, Simon Gorlier, n.d.

This volume, now lost, is listed in Du Verdier III, 473. See also MGG V, col. 533.

[156?]$_2$

GORLIER, SIMON

Livre de Tabulature de Guiterne. Lyon, Simon Gorlier, n.d.

This volume, now lost, is listed in Du Verdier III, 473. See also MGG V, col. 533.

156?$_3$

GORZANIS, GIACOMO DE

OPERA NOVA DE LAUTO / COMPOSTA DA MISIER JACOMO GORZANIS CITADINO / Della Magnifica Città di Trieste messa in Luce da suo Figliolo Massimiliano. / LIBRO [Printer's mark] QUARTO / IN VENETIA Apresso Alessandro Gardane.

40 fols. Italian lute tablature. Dedication on fol. A1^v headed "ALLA ILLUSTRISSIMA SIGNORA LA SIGNORA RACHEL MALVASIA BARONESSA DE DORINBEG ADORNECH AMBASCIATRICE CESAREA ET CAPITANIA DI TRIESTE SIGNORA ET PATRONA MIA SEMPRE COLENDISSIMA." On fol. K4^v: table of contents. MoeDM contains a thematic index of the dances (p. 429) and concordances for them (p. 266). Contents = 1579$_1$. For other volumes in the same series, see 1561$_2$, note 1. All of the compositions are for solo lute.

Copy in: A:Wn.

	fol.	
1	A2	*Fantasia Prima di Misier Jacomo Gorzanis*
2	A3	*Fantasia Seconda del ditto*
3	A4	*Fantasia Terza del ditto*
4	B1	*Fantasia Quarta del ditto*
5	B2	*Fantasia Quinta del ditto*
6	B2^v	*Fantasia Sesta del ditto*
7	B3^v	*Pass'e mezo Anticho Primo*
	D2^v	*Padoana del Ditto*
	D4	*Saltarelo del Dito*
8	E2^v	*Pass'e mezo antico primo Tenori*
	F2	*Saltarello del ditto*
9	F3^v	*Saltarello detto il Bors*
10	F4^v	*Pass'e mezo antico*
	G1^v	*Padoana del deto*
	G2	*Saltarello del detto*
11	G3^v	*Saltarello detto tu me dai pena*
12	H1	*Saltarello detto porgi aiuto al mio core*
13	H2	*Saltarello detto quando sara Madonna*
14	H2^v	*Saltarello ditto cavame ormai daffani*
15	H3^v	*Saltarello detto dona mi fai morire*
16	H4^v	*Pass'e mezo sopra Je presigne del Gorzanis* (compare ClemensO X, 14: "Je prens en gré," Clemens non Papa)
17	I1	*Pass'e mezo sopra gie vo deser d'un bois ah. del Gorzanis*
18	I1^v	*Pas'e mezo sopra una Canzon Francese*
19	I2	*Pas'e mezo Moderno*
	I4	*Saltarello del ditto primo*
20	K1	*Saltarello detto varia picca*
21	K1^v	*Pas'e mezo detto loisa core per el mondo*
	K2	*Padoana del ditto*
	K2^v	*Saltarello del detto*
22	K2^v	*Balo Todesco*
	K3	*La sua galiarda*
23	K3	*Balo Todesco*
	K3^v	*La sua galiarda*
24	K3^v	*Balo Todesco*[1]
	K4	*La sua gagliarda*
25	K4^v	*Balo Todesco*

[1] Mod. ed. in MohrA II, no. 61.

[156?]$_4$

LE ROY, ADRIAN

[Troisième livre de cistre par Adrian le Roy.]

This volume, now lost, is listed in an inventory of the firm of Plantin in Antwerp. See StellMB, p. 24.

[156?]₅

RODRIGUEZ DE MESA, GREGORIO SILVESTRE

Libro de cifra para tecla.

This volume, now lost, is mentioned in PedH III, v, and in AngO, p. 24.

1570_1

GORZANIS, GIACOMO DE

IL PRIMO LIBRO DI NAPOLITANE / CHE SI CANTANO ET SONANO / IN LEUTO. / Nuovamente composte da Jacomo Gorzanis Leutanista / Cittadino della Magnifica Città di Trieste. / [Printer's mark] / IN VINEGIA, / APPRESSO GIROLAMO SCOTTO, / M D LXX.

14 fols. Superius in mensural notation; accompaniment in Italian lute tablature. Dedication on fol. 1^v (= p. 2) headed "AL MOLTO MAGNIFICO SIGNORE IL S. GIORGIO KIS DE KOLTEMPRUN, Figliuolo del Clariss. & Generoso S. Gio. Kisl benemerito Cavalliero aureato Hereditario epifaro dell'Illustre Contado de Goritio, & Cesareo Arciducale consegliero, & vicecapitanio della provincia del Cragno, Patron, & Signor mio osservandissimo." On p. 28: table of contents. For other volumes in the same series, see 1561_2, note 1. All of the compositions are for solo voice and lute.

Copy in: I:Fn.

	p.	
1	3	*Da che si part'il sol*
2	4	*Guerra non hò da far*
3	5	*Questi capelli d'or'e*
4	6	*Donna gentil non so*
5	7	*Di berettino*
6	8	*Lo fio lo fior che mi donasti*
7	9	*Duca vi voglio dir* [1]
8	10	*Lasso dal primo giorno*
9	11	*Lassai d'amar un tempo*
10	12	*Amor tu m'hai ferito*
11	13	*Che giova far morir*
12	14	*Tu m'hai gabbato*
13	15	*S'io veglio dormo*
14	16	*Alma perche t'affliggi*
15	17	*Sta vecchia canaruta*
16	18	*Non fu mai donna*
17	19	*Chiara piu che'l chiar sol*
18	20	*Tu m'amast'un temp'affe*
19	21	*Se ben mi parto donna*
20	22	*Ti parti e qui mi lasci*
21	23	*O quant'affann'o quanti aspri*
22	24	*La manza mia*
23	25	*La turturella*
24	26	*Se scior si ved'il laccio* Pitio Santucci
25	27	*S'aprest'indovinar* Anon.

[1] Facs. of p. 9 in MGG V, col. 535.

[1570]₂

LE ROY, ADRIAN

Instruction de partir toute musique des huits divers tons en tablature de luth. Paris, Adrian le Roy et Robert Ballard.

This volume, now lost, is mentioned in FétB V, 280, as a later edition of [1557]₁.

1570_3

PHALÈSE, PIERRE, AND JEAN BELLÈRE, PUBLISHERS

HORTULUS CYTHARAE, IN / DUOS DISTINCTUS LIBROS, QUORUM PRIOR / CANTIONES MUSICAS LONGE PULCHERRIMAS, PASSOMEZO, / Paduanas, Galliardes, Alemandes, Branles, ad Usum vulgaris Cythara: Posterior similiter / Cantiones Musicas Passomezo, Almandes aliaque non nulla in tabulaturam / Cytharae, Italicae vulgò dicta, convenientem re/dacta, continet. / Quaedam denique inserta sunt passim carmina, pulsanda tribus Cytharisita inter se / coaptatis, ut Tenor, diatessaron, id est per quartam, Bassus vero diapen/te id est per quintam à Superiore distet. / Accessit praeterea brevis

& dilucida in Cytharam Isagoge, qua sua marte quilibet / artem pulsanda Cytharae addiscere possit facilime. / [Fleuret] / Lovanii apud Petrum Phalesium, Antwerpia apud Joannem Bellerum. Anno M.D.LXX.

4 + 110 fols. French tablature for a four-course cittern (nos. 1–147 in French tuning and nos. 148–182 in Italian tuning). On fol. $A1^v$: the same poem in Latin as in 1568_6 headed "IN LAUDEM HORTULI CYTHARAE, CARMEN." On fols. A2–A4: the same instructions for playing the cittern as in 1568_6. Fol. B1 = fol. 1. For a later edition see $[1575]_7$. All of the compositions are for solo cittern.

Copy in: D:ROu.

	fol.	
1	1	*Fantasia* = 1568_6, no. 2
2	1^v	*Fantasia* = 1565_3, no. 1
3	2	*Fantasia* = 1568_6, no. 1
4	2^v	*Allegez moy* = 1568_6, no. 57
5	3^v	*Susanne ung jour* (LevyS, p. 403: Didier Lupi Second) = 1582_5, no. 6
6	4^v	*D'ou vient cela* = 1568_6, no. 34: Sermisy
7	5^v	*Languyr me fais* (AttainCK II, no. 12: Sermisy) = 1582_5, no. 8
8	6^v	*Tant que vivray* = 1568_6, no. 32: Sermisy
9	7	*Pis ne me peult venir* = 1568_6, no. 33
10	7^v	*La pastorella mia* = 1568_6, no. 30: Arcadelt
11	8^v	*J'ay trop aymer* = 1568_6, no. 36
12	9	*Un advocat dist a sa femme* = 1568_6, no. 25
13	9^v	*Ce mois de may* = 1568_6, no. 76: Godard
14	10^v	*O combien est [malheureux]* = 1568_6, no. 66: Sandrin or Sermisy
15	11^v	*Le mal [qui sent]* ("*Response*") = 1568_6, no. 67
16	12^v	*Doulce memoire* = 1568_6, no. 64: Sandrin
17	13^v	*Finy le bien* ("*Response*") = 1568_6, no. 65: Certon
18	14^v	*Godt es mijn licht* = 1568_6, no. 74: Clemens non Papa
19	15^v	*Si mon traveil* = 1568_6, no. 70: Sandrin
20	16^v	*Le dueil yssu* ("*Response*") = 1568_6, no. 71: Villiers
21	17	*En fut il oncque* = 1568_6, no. 24: Certon
22	17^v	*Dames qui au plaisant son* (LesDC, art. 69, fol. 22: Didier Lupi Second) = 1578_4, no. 14, and 1582_5, no. 26
23	18	*Je ne veux plus* (compare LesLRB, art. 3, no. 13: Certon) = 1578_4, no. 5, and 1582_5, no. 27
24	18^v	*Helas mon Dieu [ton yre s'est tournée]* (RISM 1553_{19}, fol. 6: Maillard)
25	19^v	*J'ay bien mal choisi* (RISM 1564_8, fol. 7: Nicolas) = 1582_5, no. 29
26	20	*Bon jour mon coeur* (LassoW XII, 100: Lasso) = 1578_4, no. 16, and 1582_5, no. 28
27	20^v	*Quand mon mary vient de dehors* (LassoW XII, 23: Lasso) = 1578_4, no. 15, and 1582_5, no. 30
28	21	*Amour est un grand maistre* (RISM 1557_{13}, fol. 16: Arcadelt; another version of no. 164 below) = 1582_5, no. 31
29	21^v	*Ne pense plus* M. Simon Levrart = 1568_6, no. 77
30	22	*Si ce n'est amour qu'est-ce* (SCMA V, no. 20: Arcadelt)
31	22^v	*Si purti guardo* (RISM 1570_8, p. 46: Pathie) = 1578_4, no. 30, and 1582_5, no. 14
32	23^v	*Les Bouffons. Superius*
	23^v	*Plus diminuee*
	24^v	*Les Bouffons. Bassus* = 1565_3, no. 2
	24^v	*Plus diminuee*
	25	*Pavane des Bouffons* = 1565_3, no. 3a
	25^v	*Autrement*
	25^v	*Gaillarde des bouffons* = 1565_3, no. 3b
	26	*Autrement*
33	26^v	*Padoana de esperance* = 1569_6, no. 66a
	27	*La gaillarde* = 1569_6, no. 66b

34 27^v *Pavane L'espagnolle* = 1565_3, no. 6
27^v *Autrement*
35 28 *Passemezo ditalye. Super*[*ius*] = 1582_5, no. 57
36 28^v *Passemezo milanese. Superius* = 1564_7, no. 1a
29 *Gaillarde de la precedente* = 1564_7, no. 1c: "Il suo Saltarello"
29^v *Autrement*
37 29^v *Gaillarde Romanesque* = 1564_5, no. 17
30 *Plus diminuée*
38 30^v *Passemezo. Bassus* = 1565_3, no. 4a: "Pavane Romanesque"
30^v *Gaillarde de la precedente* = 1565_3, no. 4b
31 *Autrement*
39 31^v *Passemezo D'Italie. Tenor* = 1564_7, no. 12a
32 *Gaillarde. Tenor* = 1564_7, no. 12b
32 *Autrement*
40 32^v *Passemezo commune* = 1564_7, no. 2a
33^v *Gaillarde Commune* = 1564_7, no. 2c: "Saltarello Commune"
41 34 *Passemezo de Zorzi* = 1564_7, no. 3a
34 *Padoana de Zorzi* = 1564_7, no. 3b
34^v *Saltarello de Zorzi* = 1546_7, no. 3c
42 35 *Passemezo Ungaro* = 1564_7, no. 4a
35^v *Gaillarde Ungaro* = 1564_7, no. 4b: "Il suo Saltarello"
43 36 *Passemezo d'angleterre* = 1569_6, no. 59a
36^v *Le reprinse* = 1569_6, no. 59b
44 36^v *Passemezo Bataglia* = 1564_7, no. 10
37^v *Gaillarde de Bataille* = 1569_6, no. 83
45 38 *Passemezo la douce* = 1569_6, no. 65a
38^v *Reprinse* = 1569_6, no. 65b
46 39 *Gaillarde Caracossa. Sup*[*erius*] = 1582_5, no. 72a
39^v *Plus diminuée* = 1582_5, no. 72b
40 *Gaillarde Caracossa Bassus* = 1565_3, no. 5: "Gaillarde J'aymeroys mieux dormir seulette"
40^v *Autrement* = 1582_5, no. 72d
47 41 *Chi passa per questa strada* (another version of no. 171 below) = 1564_7, no. 16: Azzaiolo
48 41^v *Gaillarde* = 1564_7, no. 15
49 41^v *La Milanesa* = 1564_7, no. 24
50 42 *Gaillarde* = 1564_7, no. 21
51 42^v *Gaillarde* = 1564_7, no. 23
52 43 *Gaillarda du Roy* = 1564_7, no. 40
53 43^v *Gaillarde la Morette* = 1564_5, no. 10
54 43^v *Gaillarde Hely* = 1565_3, no. 7
55 44 *Gaillarde Puisque nouvelle affection* = 1564_5, no. 14
56 44^v *Gaillarde la Lionnoise* = 1564_5, no. 11
57 45 *Gaillarde de la Gaye* = 1564_5, no. 15
58 45^v *Gaillarde O combien est heureuse* = 1564_5, no. 16
59 46 *Gaillarde Baisons nous belles* = 1578_4, no. 67, and 1582_5, no. 79
60 46^v *Premiere milanoise*
61 47 *Seconde milanoise*
62 47^v *Troisieme milanoise*
63 48 *Quatrieme milanoise* = 1564_7, no. 42: "Gaiarda de la Royne de Eschosse"
64 48^v *Cinquieme milanoise La brunette* (compare 1569_6, no. 79: "Gaillarde O ma gente brunette") = 1582_5, no. 87
65 49 *Gaillarde elle ma faict ceste grace* = 1569_6, no. 76
66 49^v *Gaillarde Caracossa diminuee Superius* = 1564_7, no. 17
67 50^v *Passe pied*
68 51 *Almande de Loraine* = 1564_5, no. 37
69 51^v *Almande bruynsmedelijn* = 1569_6, no. 3
70 51^v *Almande* = 1564_7, no. 44a
51^v *Reprinse* = 1564_7, no. 44b
71 52 *Almande du Prince* = 1564_7, no. 43a
52 *Reprinse* = 1564_7, no. 43b
72 52^v *Almande Poussinghe* = 1569_6, no. 14a
53 *La reprinse* = 1569_6, no. 14b
73 53 *Almande de Bisarde* = 1569_6, no. 15

74 53^v *Almande de Philippine* = 1569_6, no. 12: "Almande de Spiers"

75 53^v *Almande deux trois aes* = 1569_6, no. 13

76 54 *Almande guerre guerre* = 1569_6, no. 9

77 54 *Almande Bruijnswijck* = 1569_6, no. 10

78 54^v *Almande Frison* = 1569_6, no. 2

79 54^v *Almande Malines* = 1569_6, no. 5

80 55 *Almande la tour* = 1569_6, no. 18

81 55 *Almande dambrugghes* = 1569_6, no. 16

82 55^v *Almande nivelle* = 1569_6, no. 21

83 55^v *Almande Brusselles* = 1569_6, no. 22

84 56 *Almande de Spainge* = 1569_6, no. 27

85 56 *Almande Lieve gheburen* = 1569_6, no. 25

86 56^v *Almande de lignes* = 1568_6, no. 84

87 56^v *Almande a deux pas* = 1568_6, no. 85

88 57 *Premier Branle de Bourgongne* = 1565_3, no. 9

89 57^v *Seconde Branle de Bourgongne* = 1565_3, no. 10

90 57^v *Troisiéme Branle de Bourgongne* = 1565_3, no. 11

91 58 *Quatriéme Branle de Bourgongne* = 1565_3, no. 12

92 58^v *Cinquiéme Branle de Bourgongne* = 1565_3, no. 13

93 59 *Sisiéme Branle de Bourgongne* = 1565_3, no. 14

94 59^v *Setiéme Branle de Bourgongne* = 1565_3, no. 15

95 60 *Huitiéme Branle de Bourgongne* = 1565_3, no. 16

96 60^v *Neufiéme Branle de Bourgongne* = 1565_3, no. 17

97 61 *Premier Branle de malte*

61 *Plus diminuee*

98 61^v *Seconde Branle de malte* (compare 1564_5, no. 22: "Branle simple N'aurés vous point de moy pitié")

99 62 *Troisieme Branle de malte*

100 62^v *Branle de Champagne* = 1564_5, no. 26

101 62^v *2. Branle de Champagne* = 1564_5, no. 27

102 63 *3. Branle de Champagne* = 1564_5, no. 28

103 63^v *4. Branle de Champagne* = 1564_5, no. 29

104 63^v *5. Branle de Champagne*

105 64 *Sisiéme Branle de Champagne*

106 64^v *7. Branle de Champagne*

107 64^v *8. Branle de Champagne*

108 65 *Branle simple N'aures vous point de moy pitie* = 1564_5, no. 22

109 65^v *Branle gay* = 1564_5, no. 23

110 65^v *Branle & tant plus* = 1565_3, no. 22

111 66 *Branle de Poictou* = 1564_5, no. 30

112 66 *Branle cent escus*

113 66^v *Branle des Bergers*

114 67 *Branle Las il n'a nul mal* (compare LesAC, no. 19: De Bussy)

115 67^v *Branle tu disois* = 1564_7, no. 38

116 68 *Branle* = 1564_7, no. 37

117 68^v *Quatrebrant* = 1564_7, no. 39

118 69 *Branle de Bataille* = 1568_6, no. 87

119 69 *Branle de Spiers* = 1569_6, no. 56

120 69^v *Branle del duc* = 1569_6, no. 29a

69^v *La saltarelle* = 1569_6, no. 29b

70^v *La courante* = 1569_6, no. 29c

70^v *La reprinse* = 1569_6, no. 29d

121 71 *Branle de Berghes* = 1569_6, no. 28

122 71^v *Branle hoboken* = 1569_6, no. 33

123 72 *Den raij* = 1569_6, no. 34

124 72 *Branle coupe* = 1569_6, no. 40

125 72^v *Branle* = 1569_6, no. 41: "Branle Champaigne"

126 73 *Branle rebecca* = 1569_6, no. 53a

73 *Le saltarelle* = 1569_6, no. 53b

127 73^v *L'homarmé* = 1569_6, no. 36

128 74 *Calleken van nieupoorte* = 1569_6, no. 57

129 74^v *Tant vous alez doux guillemette* (RISM 1571_1, fol. 11: Abran)

130 75 *Les Matachins* = 1564_5, no. 20
131 75^v *Les forces d'Hercules* = 1564_5, no. 21
132 76 *Den lustelijcken mey* = 1564_7, no. 27
133 76^v *Ick had een gestadich minneken* = 1564_7, no. 36: Clemens non Papa
134 76^v *Sloefst ef waer hebdi gheweest* = 1568_6, no. 56
135 77 *Era di magio* = 1568_6, no. 4a
77 *Autrement* = 1568_6, no. 4b
136 77^v *Een venus dierken* = 1568_6, no. 5
137 77^v *Een amoureux fireghelate* = 1568_6, no. 6
138 78 *Het wasser te nacht* = 1568_7, no. 7
139 78^v *Het was een macht* = 1568_6, no. 46
140 78^v *Het was een ardich vrauken* = 1568_6, no. 44
141 79 *Robin c'est un galland* = 1568_6, no. 20
142 79^v *Linkens houen es bestouen* = 1582_5, no. 148
143 79^v *Thyenette venestost*
144 80^v *Veriubileert ghij venus dierkens* (compare DuyL III, 2574) = 1582_5, no. 149
145 80 *Entre vous gentilz galans*
146 80^v *Il estoit ung lourdault*
147 80^v *La veille des roys*
148 81^v *Si purti guardo*[1] (RISM 1570_8, p. 46: Pathie)
149 82^v *Madona mia pieta* (LassoW X, 61: Lasso) = 1578_4, no. 32, and 1582_5, no. 38
150 83 *Tu traditora* (LassoW X, 68: Lasso)
151 83^v *Mia mari ando al maria* (compare RISM 1569_{24}, no. 10: "Mia mari andò al marco," Azzaiolo) = 1578_4, no. 35
152 84 *La Cortesia* (LassoW X, 66: Lasso) = 1578_4, no. 33, and 1582_5, no. 36
153 84^v *Sto Core mio* (LassoW X, 69: Lasso) = 1578_4, no. 34, and 1582_5, no. 37
154 85 *Le vechie per invidia*
155 85^v *Sia sia maladetta* = 1578_4, no. 37, and 1582_5, no. 35
156 86 *Era di maggio*
157 86^v *Chy vol vedere*
158 87 *Vita mia bella*
159 87^v *E me levai* (RISM 1557_{18}, no. 8: Azzaiolo) = 1578_4, no. 31
160 88^v *Tribulatje ende verdriet* (compare DuyL I, 581)
161 89^v *De mesa nui* (RISM 1567_5, fol. 10: "De mes ennuis," Arcadelt) = 1578_4, no. 11
162 90 *Amour partez*
163 90^v *Gross lieb hat mich umbfangen* (compare ScanL, no. 5: Scandello) = 1578_4, no. 41, and 1582_5, no. 43
164 91 *Die liebe ist meisterin* (another version of no. 28 above) = 1578_4, no. 42, and 1582_5, no. 40
165 91^v *Passemezo Bataglia* = 1578_4, no. 58, and 1582_5, no. 49b
166 92^v *Nun fahr hin alle mein trauren* = 1578_4, no. 39, and 1582_5, no. 42
167 93^v *Passemezo Commune* = 1578_4, no. 53a, and 1582_5, no. 51c: "Passomezo de Haubois"
94^v *Saltarello Commune* = 1578_4, no. 53b, and 1582_5, no. 51d: "Saltarello de Haubois"
168 95^v *Passemezo dytalye* = 1578_4, no. 51a, and 1582_5, no. 54a
96^v *Gaillarde dytalie* = 1578_4, no. 51b: "Saltarello," and 1582_5, no. 54c
169 97^v *Passemezo dytalye Superius* = 1578_4, no. 52a: "Passomezo Milanese," and 1582_5, no. 44a
98 *Padoana milanese* = 1578_4, no. 52b, and 1582_5, no. 44b
98^v *Gaillarde dytalye* = 1578_4, no. 52c: "Saltarello Milanese," and 1582_5, no. 44c
170 99 *La Caracossa Superius* (compare 1564_7, no. 17)
171 99^v *Chy passa* (another version of no. 47 above) = 1578_4, no. 61b
172 100^v *Gaillarde*
173 101 *Gaillarde*
174 101^v *Gaillarde*
175 102 *Branle del duc* = 1578_4, no. 81a, and 1582_5, no. 111a

	102^v	*La Courante* = 1578_4, no. 81b: "La Saltarelle," and 1582_5, no. 111b
	103	*Le saltarelle* = 1578_4, no. 81c: "La courante," and 1582_5, no. 111c
176	103^v	*Branle*
	104	*La courrante*
	104^v	*La reprise*
177	105	*Almande*
	105^v	*La reprinse*
178	106	*Almande* = 1578_4, no. 71
	106^v	*La reprinse*
179	107	*Almande*
	107^v	*Reprinse*
180	108	*Almande* = 1578_4, no. 72
	108^v	*La reprinse*
181	109	*Almande*
	109^v	*Reprinse*
182	110	*Gheloost sy Codt*

[1] Heading on fol. 81: "Liber Secundus. Continens cantiones musicas, Passomezo. Gailliardas, Almandes aliaque non nulla in tabulaturam Cythare Italicae vulgò dictae redacta. Cytharum autem hoc modo aptabis [Table of tuning]." The compositions following are for four-course cittern with Italian tuning.

1570_4

PHALÈSE, PIERRE, AND JEAN BELLÈRE, PUBLISHERS

SELECTISSIMA ELEGANTIS/SIMAQUE, GALLICA, ITALICA ET LATI/NA IN GUITERNA LUDENDA CARMINA, QUIBUS ADDUN/tur & Fantasie, Passomezzi, Saltarelli, Galliardi, Almandes, Branles & similia, ex optima / elegantissimaque collecta, & iam cum omni diligentia recens impressa. / His abcessit luculenta quaedem & perutilis Institutio qua quisque citra / alicuius subsidium artem facillimè percipiet. / [Fleuret] / Lovanii apud Petrum Phalesium, Antwerpiae apud Joannem / Bellerum. Anno M.D. LXX.

84 fols. French guitar tablature. On fol. *1^v: cut of a guitar. Beginning on fol. *2: instructions for playing the guitar headed "BREVIS AC PERUTILIS INSTITUTIO QUA QUISQUE FACILE EA PERCIPIET QUA AD USUM Guiternae cognoscendum spectant." The instructions have two subdivisions: "De Tempore & Pausis" (on fol. *3^v), and "Modus tendendi nervos in Guiterna" (on fol. *4^v).[1] Fol. *5 = fol. 1. For a second edition see $[1573]_7$. All of the compositions are for solo guitar.

Copy in: D:ROu (two copies).

	fol.	
1	1	*Fantasie* = 1553_3, no. 3
2	1^v	*Fantasie* = 1553_3, no. 2
3a	2^v	*Fantasie, des Grues* = 1553_3, no. 1
3b	3^v	*Fantasie* = 1553_3, no. 5
4	4	*Fantasie* = 1553_3, no. 4
5	5	*Fantasie* = 1553_3, no. 6
6	6	*Fantasie* = 1552_3, no. 2
7	6^v	*Helas mon Dieu [ton ire s'est tournée]* = 1553_3, no. 12: Maillard
8	8	*O passi sparsy* = 1553_3, no. 13: S. Festa
9	9^v	*Voulant honneur* = 1553_3, no. 14: Sandrin
10	10^v	*Je cherche [autant amour]* = 1553_3, no. 15: Boyvin
11	11^v	*Au temps heureux* = 1553_3, no. 16: Arcadelt
12	13	*Qui souhaitez* = 1553_3, no. 17: Sandrin
13	14^v	*Un mesnagier viellard* = 1553_3, no. 18: Sohier
14	16	*J'ay le rebours* = 1556_8, no. 2: "Pavanne," Le Roy
15	16^v	*Je ne veux plus a mon mal consentir* = 1556_8, no. 9
16	17	*J'ay cherché la science* = 1556_8, no. 16
17	17^v	*Vous estes la personne* = 1556_8, no. 17: Le Roy
18	18	*La la je ne l'ose dire* = 1552_3, no. 4: Certon
19	18^v	*Jean de lagni* = 1552_3, no. 5: Berchem
20	19^v	*Pour un plaisir* = 1552_3, no. 6: Sermisy
21	20^v	*Au jour au jour* = 1554_4, no. 4: Bonard
22	21	*Quand viendra la clarté* = 1554_4, no. 5: Arcadelt
23	21^v	*Que te sert amy d'estre ainsi* = 1554_4, no. 7: Arcadelt
24	22^v	*Je ne sçay que c'est qu'il me faut* = 1554_4, no. 6: Arcadelt
25	23	*Ce n'est bien ny plaisir* = 1554_4, no. 10: Arcadelt

26 23^v *J'ay tant bon credit qu'on voudra* = 1554_4, no. 8: Arcadelt
27 24 *Si ce n'est amour qu'est se* = 1554_4, no. 13: Arcadelt
28 24^v *Amour ha povoir sur les dieus* = 1554_4, no. 11: Arcadelt
29 25 *Si j'ayme ou non* = 1554_4, no. 14: Le Roy
30 25^v *Nous voyons que les hommes* = 1554_4, no. 15: Arcadelt
31 26^v *La pastorella mia* = 1554_4, no. 16: Arcadelt
32 27 *Margot labourez les vignes* = 1554_4, no. 17: Arcadelt
33 27^v *Jamais femme ne sera* = 1554_4, no. 18: Certon
34 28 *Amour ne sçauriez vous aprendre* = 1554_4, no. 19: Arcadelt
35 28^v *Je sonne la retraitte* = 1554_4, no. 20: Certon
36 29 *Pour m'eslongner* = 1556_8, no. 4a: Le Roy
29 *Autrement* = 1556_8, no. 4b
37 29^v *Mes pas semez* = 1556_8, no. 7: Le Roy
38 30 *Plus neulx estre a la suite* = 1556_8, no. 10a: "Branle gay," Le Roy
30 *Autrement* = 1556_8, no. 10b
39 30^v *Oyez tous amoureux* = 1556_8, no. 20
40 31 *Mon dieu vostre pitié* = 1556_8, no. 23a
31 *Autrement* = 1556_8, no. 23b
41 31^v *Un advocat* = 1552_3, no. 3: Delafont
42 32^v *Laissez la verte couleur* = 1556_8, no. 1
43 33 *Je ne me confesseray point d'avoir aymé* = 1554_4, no. 3: Arcadelt
44 33^v *Escoutez ma complainte* = 1554_4, no. 1: De Bussy
45 34^v *Qui pourra dire la douleur* = 1554_4, no. 12: Arcadelt
46 35 *Lesté chault bouilloit* = 1554_4, no. 2: Le Roy
47 35^v *Je cherche autant amour* = 1551_3, no. 5a: Boyvin
36 *La chanson precedente plus diminuée* = 1551_3, no. 5b
48 36^v *Verba mea* ("Motet") = 1553_3, no. 7
49 37^v *In exitu Israel de Aegypto* = 1553_3, no. 8: Josquin
50 41 *Cum invocarem* = 1553_3, no. 9
51 42^v *Beati quorum* = 1553_3, no. 10
52 43^v *Super flumina* = 1553_3, no. 11
53 44^v *L'alouette* = 1553_3, no. 19: Janequin
54 47^v *La guerre, faitte a plaisir* = 1553_3, no. 20
55 51 *Pavane si je m'envois* = 1551_3, no. 6a
51^v *Gaillarde si je m'envois* = 1551_3, no. 6c
56 52 *Pavane de la gambe* = 1551_3, no. 7a
52^v *La Pavane predecente plus diminuée* = 1551_3, no. 7b
53^v *Gaillarde de la gambe* = 1551_3, no. 7c
57 54 *Pavane J'ay du mal tant tant* = 1552_3, no. 9a
54^v *Gaillarde de la precedente pavane* = 1552_3, no. 9b
58 55 *Tourdion* = 1552_3, no. 8
59 55^v *Pavane de la guerre* = 1552_3, no. 10a
56^v *Gaillarde de la precedente pavane* = 1552_3, no. 10b
60 57^v *Pavane des Bouffons*
58 *Gaillarde des Bouffons*
61 58 *Pavane Romanesque*
58^v *Gaillarde de la precedente pavane*
62 59 *Passemese*
63 59^v *Almande. Les Bouffons*
59^v *Plus diminuée*
64 60 *Almande. Loreyne* = 1552_3, no. 17: "Almande tournée"
65 60^v *Almande. Le pied de cheval*[2] = 1552_3, no. 16
66 61 *Almande*
67 61^v *Almande*
68 61^v *Almande*[3] = 1551_3, no. 15
69 62 *Almande. La mon amy la* = 1551_3, no. 16
70 62^v *La toulouzane gaillarde* = 1552_3, no. 11
71 63 *Gaillarde la Lionnoyse* = 1552_3, no. 12
72 63^v *Caracossa gaillarda*
63^v *Plus diminuée*
73 64^v *Gaillarde* = 1552_3, no. 14
74 65 *Gaillarde la Roque el fuze*
75 65^v *L'ennuy qui me tourmente. Gaillarde* = 1556_8, no. 11

76 66 *Premiere gaillarde milanoise*
77 66v *Seconde gaillarde milanoise*
78 67 *Troisieme gaillarde milanoise* (compare 1564_7, no. 42: "Gaiarda de la Royne de Eschosse")
79 67v *Gaillarde la Romanesque* = 1552_3, no. 15
67v *Plus diminuée*
80 68 *Gaillarde La Peronnelle* = 1551_3, no. 11
81 68v *Gaillarde* = 1551_3, no. 8a
68v *Autrement* = 1551_3, no. 8b
82 69 *Gaillarde Milanoise* (compare 1568_6, no. 82: "Gaill[arde] Si pour t'aymer")
83 69v *Gaillarde* = 1552_3, no. 13
69v *Plus diminuée*
84 70 *Gaillarde Milanoise* (compare 1571_5, no. 33: "Gaillarde Au joly bois")
85 70v *Gaillarde par deppit* = 1551_3, no. 9
86 71 *Gaillarde* (compare no. 84 above)
87 71v *Premier Branle de Bourgongne* = 1551_3, no. 17
88 72 *Seconde Branle de Bourgongne* = 1551_3, no. 18
89 72v *Troisieme Branle de Bourgongne* = 1551_3, no. 19
90 73 *Quatriesme Branle de Bourgongne* = 1551_3, no. 20
91 73 *Cinquiesme Branle de Bourgongne* = 1551_3, no. 21
92 73v *Sixiesme Branle de Bourgongne* = 1551_3, no. 22
93 74 *Septiesme Branle de Bourgongne* = 1551_3, no. 23
94 74v *Huitiesme Branle de Bourgongne* = 1551_3, no. 24
95 75 *Neufyesme Branle de Bourgongne* = 1551_3, no. 25
96 75v *Branle de la nonneste*
97 76 *Branle des Lavendieres*
98 76 *Branle de la Bergerre*
99 76v *Branle d'ecosse*
100 77 *Branle gay* = 1552_3, no. 21: "Bransle gay Je ne seray jamais bergere"
77 *Plus diminuée*
101 77v *Branle moresque*
102 77v *Branle à la fontaine du pré* (compare ClemensO VII, 43: Willaert)
103 78 *Branle de la torche*
104 78v *Branle du beau Robert*
105 79 *Branle. Tenez vos amours secrettes*
106 79v *Matachins*[4]
107 79v *Branle*
108 80 *Branle des Bergers*

[1] These instructions are reproduced in facsimile and translated into English in HeartzE, where the suggestion is made that they are by Adrian le Roy and were originally printed in [$1551]_4$.

[2] Mod. ed. in MohrA II, no. 35.

[3] Mod. ed. in MohrA II, no. 34.

[4] Mod. ed. and quasi-facs. in TapS, p. 38.

1570_5

ANTONELLI, CORNELIO

IL TURTURINO / IL PRIMO LIBRO DELLE / NAPOLITANE ARIOSE DA CANTARE / ET SONARE NEL LEUTO, / Composte da diversi Eccellentissimi Musici, & novamente / per il Rever. P. F. Cornellio Antonelli da Rimino / detto il Turturino, acomodate sul leuto. / [Printer's mark] / IN VINEGIA, / APPRESSO GIROLAMO SCOTTO / M D LXX.

18 fols. Solo voice in mensural notation and accompaniment in Italian lute tablature. Dedication on p. 2 headed "ALL'ECCELLENTE ET ILLUSTRE SIGNOR MIO OSSERVANDISSIMO, IL S. GASPARO PIGNATTA DA RAVENNA DOTTORE ET CAVALLIERE," and signed "Da Venetia il 20. di Maggio. M D LXX. D. V. S. Illustre & Eccellente, Devotissimo Servitore, Frate Cornelio Antonelli da Rimino Eremitano." On p. 36: table of contents. All of the compositions are for solo voice and lute.

Copy in: I:Fn.

p.

1 3 *All'apparir dell'alba* (RISM 1571_9, p. 17: Anselmo Perugino)
2 4 *S'io dormo haggio gran male* (RISM 1570_{19}, p. 4: Meo)
3 5 *Poi che pietà non trov'al mio* (RISM 1570_{19}, p. 6: Anselmo Perugino)
4 6 *Sospira core sospira core* (RISM 1570_{18}, p. 18: Nola)

5 7 *Da poi ch'io viddi* (RISM 1570_{18}, p. 32: Mazzone)
6 8 *Correte tutti quanti* (RISM 1570_{18}, p. 26: Arpa)
7 9 *Andand'un giorn'a spasso*
8 10 *Date la strad'o voi*
9 11 *Gioia ch'avanzi tanto* (RISM 1570_{31}, p. 28: anon.)
10 12 *Come farò cor mio* (RISM 1569_{30}, no. 5: Nola)
11 13 *Tutta sei bella donna*
12 14 *Io vo cercando* (RISM 1570_{31}, p. 27: anon.)
13 15 *Cosi vuol mia chiara stella*
14 16 *Le donne belle ch'a Venetia stanno*
15 17 *Dolci colli fioriti* (compare Vogel: Ferretti 4 [1575], p. 5)
16 18 *Tanto v'ha fatt'il ciel*
17 19 *Quando miro'i capelli* (RISM 1570_{31}, p. 2: Primavera)
18 20 *Amor sia benedetto* (RISM 1570_{31}, p. 5: Primavera)
19 21 *Bella che tieni li capigli d'oro* (RISM 1566_{6}, p. 29: Scotto)
20 22 *Gli occhi la bocc'e la tua leggiadria* (RISM 1570_{31}, p. 11: Primavera)
21 23 *Non mi date tormento* (compare Vogel: Ferretti 11 [1569], p. 6)
22 24 *Pascomi sol di pianto* (RISM 1570_{18}, p. 12: Mazzone)
23 25 *Dolc'amorose e leggia* (RISM 1565_{17}, p. 13: anon.)
24 26 *Bellezza ch'emp'il ciel* (RISM 1565_{17}, p. 8: Arpa)
25 27 *Ditemi o diva mia* (Vogel: Trojano 4 [1569], p. 25: Trojano)
26 28 *Donne leggiadr'e voi vaghe citelle* (RISM 1565_{17}, p. 6: Primavera)
27 29 *Deh lasciatemi star tanti* (RISM 1565_{17}, p. 7: Primavera)
28 30 *Cassandra mia gentil*
29 31 *Amor lasciami stare* (RISM 1565_{17}, p. 15: Arpa)
30 32 *Quando mirai sa bella faccia d'oro* (RISM 1570_{18}, p. 6: Mazzone)
31 33 *Se scior si ved'il laccio* (RISM 1570_{19}, p. 12: anon.)
32 34 *O core di diamante* (RISM 1570_{18}, p. 40: Arpa)
33 35 *Credeva che la fiamma* (RISM 1570_{18}, p. 46: Arpa)

1571_1

AMMERBACH, ELIAS NICOLAUS

Orgel oder In/strument Tabulatur. / Ein nützlichs Büchlein, in welchem notwendige erklerung der / Orgel oder Instrument Tabulatur, sampt der Application, Auch froliche / deutsche Stücklein unnd Muteten, etliche mit Coloraturn abgefasst, Desgleichen schöne / deutsche Tentze, Galliarden unnd Welsche Passometzen zubefinden, etc. Desglei/chen zuvor in offenem Druck nicht ausgangen. / Jetzundt aber der Jugend und anfahenden dieser / Kunst zum besten in Druck vor/fertiget, Durch / Eliam Nicolaum, sonst Ammerbach genandt, Orga/nisten zu Leipzig in S. Thomas Kirchen. / Mit fleis vom Autore selbs ubersehen und Corrigirt. / Anno, 1571.[1]

111 fols. German keyboard tablature. On fol. 1^v: cut of musicians performing, with the legend: "Psal. 150. Laudate Dominum in tympano & choro: laudate eum in chordis & organo." Preface and dedication on fol. 2 headed "Den Hochgelarten und Achtbarn, hoch und wolweisen Herrn, Bürgermeister unnd Rath der Churfürstlichen Stadt Leipzig, Meinen grosgünstigen gebietenden lieben Herren," and signed on fol. 5^v: "Datum Leipzig, den 20. Septemb. nach Christi unsers Erlösers und Seligmachers Geburt, nu 1571. Jahr. E. A. h. und w. W. Gehorsamer und Dienstwilliger Elias Nicolaus, sonst Ammerbach genandt, Bürger daselbst und Organista zu S. Thomas." On fol. 6: instructions for playing the organ headed "Kurtze anleitung und Instruction für die anfahenden Discipel der Orgelkunst."[2] On fol. 12^v: poem in Latin headed "Lectori Musices Organicae Studiosos," and signed "Gregorius Bersmanus." Colophon on fol. 111^v: "Gedruckt zu Leipzig, Durch Jacob Berwalds Erben. [Printer's mark] Anno, 1571."

The compositions identified by superior letters are reproduced as follows: (^{a}) in AntoniK, pp. 5–13; (^{b}) in BöhT II, nos. 143–146; (^{c}) in DTO XXXVII/72; (^{d}) in EhmL, nos. 6, 9, 10, and 14; (^{e}) HalbK, pp. 9–10; (^{f}) in MerT, pp. 76–78; (^{g}) in WustM, pp. 239–262. For further information see RitZ, p. 113, and WustA. The second edition, 1583_2, is revised and expanded. The compositions followed by an asterisk in the following inventory are identical with those in 1583_2. All of the compositions are for solo keyboard.

Copies in: D:HAu, D:LEm, D:ROu, DK:Kk, GB:Cu, GB:Lbm (imperfect).[3]

	fol.	
1	13	*Wo Gott der Herr nicht bey uns helt* (compare BäumK II, 276, and ZahnM III, no. 4441a)
2	13ᵛ	*Herr Gott nu sey gepreiset* (Le MaiG, no. 33: Le Maistre)
3	13ᵛ	*Ein ander Herr Gott nu sey gepreiset* (Le MaiG, no. 34: Le Maistre)
4	14ᵛ	*Also sehr jammert Gott des Sünders grosse not* (compare BraunS, p. 49, no. 81)
5	15ᵛ	*Aller augen warten auff dich* Matthias Le Maistre
6	15ᵛ	*Alio modo* [*Aller augen*]
7	16ᵛ	*Dancket dem Herren denn er ist sehr freundlich** (AmeH, vol. I, pt. 2, p. 236: anon.)
8	17	*Dancket dem Herren inn Ewigkeit*
9	17ᵛ	*Ehr lob und Danck mit hohem fleis**
10	17ᵛ	*Gantz sehr betrübt ist mir mein Hertz*
11	18ᵛ	*Dieweil umbsonst jetzo alle kunst* (EDMR XX, no. 120: Forster)
12	19ᵛ	*Allein nach dir Herr Jhesu Christ verlanget** (RISM 1570_8, p. 46: "Si pur ti guardo," [Pathie])
13	20ᵛ	*Ein Henlein weis mit grossen fleis** (compare ScanL, no. 14: Scandello)
14	21ᵛ	*Ich habs gewagt**
15	22	*Ich setze dahin** (EDMR XX, no. 88)
16	22ᵛ	*Gros lieb hat mich umbfangen**[4] (compare ScanL, no. 5: Scandello)
17	23	*Frisch auff gut Geselle, las dz Gleslein**[d] (compare BöhA, no. 321)
18	23ᵛ	*Zart freuntlichs M.**
19	24ᵛ	*Ach du edler Rebensafft**
20	25ᵛ	*Sophia spanne das Füllein inn den wagen** (RISM c. 1550_{23}, no. 58: Buchner)
21	26ᵛ	*Schön unnd zart von edler art* (RISM c. $[1550]_{22}$, no. 8)
22	26ᵛ	*Ich bitt dich Megdelein hab mich hold** (PubAPTM XXIX, no. 53: anon.)
23	28ᵛ	*Mit lust thet ich ausreiten** (PubAPTM I, no. 25: Senfl)
24	29ᵛ	*Ich armes Megdlein klag mich sehr**[d 5] (SenflW VI, no. 8: Senfl)
25	30ᵛ	*Vergangen ist mir glück und heil** (EDMR XX, no. 15: Forster)
26	31ᵛ	*Ach unfahls neid** (EDMR XX, no. 39: Wolff)
27	32ᵛ	*Fuchswilde bin ich**
28	33ᵛ	*Ian Ian Iadrian*
29	34ᵛ	*Elend ich rieff und seuffs so tieff**
30	35ᵛ	*Gehabt euch wol zu diesen zeiten**
31	36ᵛ	*Mein fleis und mühe* (SenflW IV, no. 19: Senfl)
32	37	*Ein Meidlein sprach mir freundlich zu** (SenflW VII, no. 15: Malchinger or Senfl)
33	37ᵛ	*Tröstlicher lieb stets ich mich ube**[c 6] (MosPH, no. 19: Hofhaimer)
34	38ᵛ	*Ich sage Ade**[d] (LenN, p. [108])
35	39ᵛ	*Ich bin vorsagt* (EDMR XX, no. 40)
36	39ᵛ	*Paule lieber Stallbruder mein**
37	40ᵛ	*Vor zeiten war ich lieb unnd werth** (RISM [c. $1550]_{22}$, no. 42)
38	41	*Wenn wir in höchsten nöten sind*[7] Johan. Baptista
39	41ᵛ	*Ich rew und klag** (another version of no. 33 above)
40	42ᵛ	*Mein gemüth unnd gblüt** (EDMR XX, no. 85: Wenck)
41	43ᵛ	*Ispruck ich mus dich lassen**[8] (DTO XIV/28, p. 15: Isaac)
42	55	*Mein Man der ist in Krieg gezogen* (compare BöhA, no. 235)
43	44ᵛ	*Ach edler Hort*[c] (DTO XXXVII/72, p. 31: Hofhaimer)
44	45ᵛ	*So wünsch ich ir ein gute nacht**[cd] (DTO XXXVII/72, p. 74: Stoltzer)

45 46v [*1. Bruder Cunrads Tanzmaass*]*abf 9 (= 1583_2, no. 121)
47 *Proportio**ab
46 46v *2. Wer das Töchterlein haben wil** abf(= 1583_2, no. 122: "Heckerling unnd Haberstro") (compare 1562_4, no. 53: "Des Printzen Tantz")
46v *Proportio**abef
47 47v *3. Der Allmeyer Dantz*g
48v *Proportio, Tripla, oder Nachtantz*g
48 50 *3* [*sic*]. *Hertzog Moritz dantz**bfg 10
50 *Proportio**bfg
49 50v *4. Pastorum Dantz**abef (= 1583_2, no. 127)
50v *Proportio**abef
50 50v *5. Ein kurtzer Dantz** (= 1583_2, no. 118)
50v *Proportio**
51 51v *6. Sol ich denn nu sterben**c
51v *Proportio**e
52 51v *7. Die Megdlein sind von Flandern**abef 11 (= 1583_2, no. 120)
52v *Proportio**abef
53 52v *8. Ein ander Dantz** (= 1583_2, no. 116: "Ein kurtz Schlesisch Dentzlein")
52v *Proportio**
54 53v *9. Ein sehr guter Dantz* (compare 1583_2, no. 124)
54v *Proportio*
55 54v *10. Ein kurtzer Dantz*
55v *Proportio*
56 55v *11. Ein ander hübscher Dantz** (= 1583_2, no. 119)
56v *Proportio**
57 56v *12. Ein ander Dantz** (= 1583_2 no. 115: "Salve puella, Gott grüs")
56v *Proportio**
58 57v *13. Ein ander hübscher Dantz*
58v *Proportio*
59 58v *14. Ein ander Dantz** (= 1583_2, no. 114: "Sind denn die Bürgers Söhne so leiden wol gehort")
59v *Proportio**
60 59v *15. Ein ander Dantz*
59v *Proportio*
61 60v *Passametzo I**g 12 (= 1583_2, no. 98a)
60v *La Reprisa**g (= 1583_2, no. 98b)
61v *Gaillarde**g (= 1583_2, no. 98c: "Saltarella")
62 61v *2. Passametzo** (= 1583_2, no. 94: "Passamezo antico") (1551_5, no. 1)
63 62v *3. Passametzo** (= 1583_2, no. 95: "Passamezo antico") (1551_5, no. 2)
64 62v *4. Passametzo**g (= 1583_2, no. 96: "Passamezo antico") (1551_5, no. 3)
65 63v *Catachio Gaillarde* (1551_5, no. 4)
66 64 *Gaillarde**g (= 1583_2, no. 111)
67 64v *Gaillarde** (= 1583_2, no. 106)
68 64v *Gaillarde** (= 1583_2, no. 110; compare 1568_6, no. 82: "Gaill[arde] Si pour t'aymer")
69 66 *Passametzo Dangleterre**e 13 (= 1583_2, no. 99a: "Der Englische Passamezo")
66v *La Reprisa*e
67 *Proportio Oder Gaillard**e (= 1583_2, no. 99b: "Saltarella")
70 67v *Passametzo** (= 1583_2, no. 97: "Passamezo nova")
68v *La Gaillarde*
71 69v *Passametzo Itali, auff den langen duplen Tact*
70v *La Reprisa*
71v *Saltarella altera cum Reprisa*
72 72v *1. Gott ist mein Liecht und mein Seligkeit*[14] (VNM XXVI, no. 16: Clemens non Papa)
73 74v *2. Bewar mich Herr, und sey nicht ferrn von mir* (D:Rp, MS AR 855, no. 19: Zirler)
74 76v *3. Mag ich Hertzlieb erwerben dich* (SenflW IV, no. 28: Senfl)
75 77v *4. Petercken sprack tho Peterchen, Ick hebbe so ein schon Kammirken*
76 79v *5. Die mich erfrewet ist lobenswerth*
77 81v *6. Ich schwing mein Horn ins Jamerthal* (SenflW V, no. 44: Senfl)
78 82v *7. Dich als mich selbst* (EDMR XX, no. 1)
79 84 *8. Ich rith mir einmal spatzieren* (RISM [c. 1550]$_{22}$, no. 18)

80 84v 9. *Gar hoch auff einem Berge* Wolff Heintz (PubAPTM XXIX, no. 21)
81 86v 10. *Der Frisische Tritt, oder Galliard*
82 88v 11. *Hertzliebstes Büd*c [15] (MosPH, no. 9: Hofhaimer)
83 90v 12. *Verlorner dienst der sind gar viel* (RISM c. 1550_{23}, no. 51: Buchner)
84 91v 1. *Susanna* [16] (LassoW XIV, 29: Lasso)
85 94v 2. *Ich weis mir ein festes gebawtes Haus* Antonius Scandel[lus] (ScanL, no. 6) = 1575_1, no. 35
86 97v 3. *Ich weis mir gar ein schönes Reis*
87 98v 4. *Ich ruff zu dir Herr Jhesu Christ* Orlandus [Lasso] (LassoW XVIII, 4)
88 101v 5. *Im Meyen hört man die Hanen krehen* (LassoW XVIII, 21: Lasso)
89 103v 6. *Ach Gott was sol ich singen* Ivo de Vento (VentoN, no. 1)
106v 2a pars *Auff dich setz ich mein grund und all mein zuversicht* (VentoN, no. 2)
90 110 *Fraw ich bin euch von hertzen hold* Orlandus [Lasso] (LassoW XVIII, 31)

[1] Facs. of title page in GodB, opp. p. 22, and MGG I, col. 428. Facs. of title page and fols. 1v and 43v in KinsP, p. 77.

[2] Three of Ammerbach's 12 "Exempla Applicationis in beiden Henden durch die Ziffern erkleret" are pr. in WustM, p. 227.

[3] The Cambridge copy was a gift from C. P. E. Bach to Charles Burney; it had come from the library of J. S. Bach, as did the Leipzig copy. The British Museum copy was also associated with the Bach family at one time; see GodB.

[4] Mod. ed. in SenflW VII, no. 25c.

[5] Mod. ed. of the first half in GottA, no. 50.

[6] Mod. ed. in MosPH, p. 94.

[7] Mod. ed. in RitZ, no. 64.

[8] Mod. ed. in DTO XIV/28, p. 15. Facs. of fol. 43v in KinsP, p. 77, and SubHM I, 434.

[9] Mod. ed. in BeckH, app., no. 15; heading on fol. 46v: "Allhie folgen gemeine gute deutsche Dentze."

[10] Mod. ed. in BeckH, app., no. 16, and SteinitA, no. 17.

[11] Mod. ed. in ScherG, no. 135.

[12] Mod. ed. in ApelM I, 12 (after the 1583 ed.); HAM, no. 154; and ZfSM CXCII, no. 1 (*a4*); heading on fol. 59v: "Folgen etliche Passametzen, Reprisen, und Galliarden."

[13] Mod. ed. in ApelM I, 11 (after the 1583 ed.) and ZfSM CXCII, no. 2 (*a4*).

[14] Heading on fol. 72v: "Folgen die Gecolorirten Stücklein."

[15] Mod. ed. in BeckH, app., no. 17, and MosPH, p. 54.

[16] Mod. ed. in KinO, p. 264; heading on fol. 91v: "Folgen hernach etliche Stücklein Quincque Vocum."

[1571]₂

GABRIELI, ANDREA

CANZONI ALLA FRANCESE / PER SONAR SOPRA STROMENTI DA TASTI; / Tabulate dall'Eccellentiss. Andrea Gabrieli; Già Organista in S. Marco di Venetia. Con uno Madrigale / nel fine & uno Capricio a imitatione beliss. / Novamente date in luce. / LIBRO SESTO & Ultimo. / [Printer's mark] / In Venetia. / Appresso Angelo Gardano, 1571.

This edition is mentioned in WasG, p. 141, but a copy has never been found. The second edition of 1605 is described, and its contents are listed in SartMS, p. 133, and in IMAMI I, p. cviii. The title page is taken from this latter source. There is a modern edition of two pieces from this collection in WasG, nos. 24 and 25. Gabri(A)CF is a modern edition of the 1605 edition. For other volumes in the same series, see 1593_4.

1571₃

LE ROY, ADRIAN

LIVRE / D'AIRS DE COUR / MIZ SUR LE LUTH, / PAR ADRIAN LE ROY / A PARIS. / Par Adrian le Roy & Robert Ballard, / Imprimeurs du Roy. / 1571. / Avec privilege de sa majesté.

24 fols. Superius in mensural notation, accompaniment in French lute tablature. The title is placed within an ornamental border. Dedication on fol. A1v (= fol. 1v) headed "A TRESEXCELLENTE DAME CATERINE DE CLERMONT, CONTESSE DE RETZ," and signed "A Paris

le 15 jour de Fevrier 1571. Votre treshumble serviteur, Adrian le Roy," reprinted in LauC, xxv–xxvi. On fol. 2: portrait of Adrian le Roy.[1] On fol. 24v: table of contents. The compositions followed by an asterisk are missing from the unique copy; the compositions followed by a dagger are furnished with alternative lute accompaniments. The poets' names following the titles in the present index are supplied in the original. The entire collection is reproduced in LauC, including facsimiles of the title page and fols. 2, 5v, and 6. The compositions identified by the superior letter *a* ([a]) are reprinted in DoA. Almost all of the chansons were intabulated for solo lute in 1574_2. All of the compositions are for solo voice and lute.

Copy in: B:Br (imperfect).

	fol.	
1	2v	*Le ciel qui fut* Sillac (LesLRB, art. 140, fol. 10: La Grotte)
2	3v	*Quand ce beau printemps*[a] Ronsard (ExF, p. 60: La Grotte)
3	4v	*Las que nous sommes misérables* Des Portes (LesLRB, art. 140, fol. 7: La Grotte)
4	5v	*Quand j'estoys libre* Ronsard (LesLRB, art. 140, fol. 2v: La Grotte)
5	6v	*Mais voyez, mon cher esmoy*†[a] Ronsard (LesLRB, art. 140, fol. 8: La Grotte)
6	7v	*Quand le gril chante*[a] (LesLRB, art. 140, fol. 9: La Grotte)
7	8v	*Or voy je bien* De Baif (LesLRB, art. 140, fol. 5v: La Grotte)
8	9	*Has-tu point veu ce grand vilain*† (LesLRB, art. 171, fol. 17: Le Roy)
9	10v	*La terre n'agueres*[a] Desportes (LesLRB, art. 140, fol. 4: La Grotte)
10	11v	*Ah Dieu que c'est un estrange* [Desportes] (LesLRB, art. 140, fol. 17v: La Grotte)
11	12v	*Las je n'eusse jamais pensé*[a] Ronsard (LesLRB, art. 140, fol. 15: La Grotte)
12	13v	*Autant qu'on voit* Ronsard (LesLRB, art. 140, fol. 14v: La Grotte)
13	14v	*Tant que j'estoys*† [Ronsard] (LesLRB, art. 132, fol. 19: La Grotte)
14	15v	*Je suis amour*[a] [2] Ronsard (ExF, p. 62: La Grotte)
15	16v	*Demandes-tu*† [lute part only] (ExF, p. 52: La Grotte)
16	17v	*Ma maistresse est toute angelette** [Ronsard] (ExF, p. 58: La Grotte)
17	18v	*Douce maistresse touche** [3] [Ronsard]
18	19v	*J'estoys pres de ma maistresse**
19	20v	*J'ay bien mal choisi* [superius only] (RISM 1564_8, fol. 7: Nicolas)
20	21v	*Ce n'est point pour t'estrener* Pagnier
21	22v	*D'un gosier machelaurier* [Ronsard] (LesLRB, art. 56, fol. 10: Clereau)
22	23v	*Mon coeur, ma chère vie* Ronsard (LesLRB, art. 254, fol. 27: Thessier)

[1] Facs. of portrait in LauLL, p. 49.

[2] Mod. ed. in *Revue musicale*, Supplement: *Ronsard et la musique*, May 1924, p. 36.

[3] Unrelated musically to ExF, p. 54: La Grotte.

1571_4

FIORINO, GASPARO

LA NOBILTÀ DI ROMA. / VERSI IN LODE DI CENTO / GENTILDONNE ROMANE, / Et le vilanelle à tre voci di Gasparo Fiorino, della Città di Rossano, / Musico dell'Illustrissimo & Reverendissimo Signore / Cardinale di Ferrara. / Intavolate dal Magnifico M. FRANCESCO di Parise, / Musico eccellentissimo in Roma. / [Fleuret] / NUOVAMENTE POSTE IN LUCE. / [Printer's mark] / IN VINEGIA, / APPRESSO GIROLAMO SCOTTO, / M D LXXI.

44 fols. Each piece is written in mensural notation and, on the facing page in a version for solo lute, in Italian lute tablature. Dedication on fol. A2 (= p. 3) headed "ALL'ILLUSTRIS.mo ET ECCELLENT.mo SIGNOR D. HORATIO DELLA NOIIA PRENCIPE DI SULMONA," and signed "Di Roma a di 25.

Genaro. M D LXXI. Di V. Eccellenza Illustrissima, Humilissimo & devotissimo Servitore. Gasparo Fiorino della città di Rossano," printed in GaspaC III, 229. On pp. 6–25: 99 quatrains, each dedicated to a different lady. On p. 86: "Due ottave sopra la Illustrissima Signora Donna Beatrice della Noiia." On p. 86: table of contents. Contents = 1573$_{4}$. All of the vocal versions are *a3*.

Copies in: GB:Lbm, I:Bc, I:Fn, I:FEc, US:Wc.

p.

1 4 *Come'l Sol fra le nuvole* ("Sopra quest'aria s'hanno da cantarei versi seguenti")

2 26 *Romane belle*

3 28 *Acendi pur tutte le faci* ("Alla Illustrissima Signora Donna Vittoria della Noiia Aqua viva, Contessa di Caserta")

4 30 *Con tue lusingh'Amore* ("All'Illustrissimo Signor Filippo da Este, mio signore")

5 32 *Non vad'affrica* ("Sopra l'arme dell'Illustriss. S. Federico Sforza, & la Illustris. S. Beatrice Orsina sua Consorte")

6 34 *Amor l'aspre catene* ("All'Illustrissimo Signor Cesare Doria, mio Signore")

7 36 *Ogn'un me dice* ("Vilanella a soggetto della felice memoria dell'Illustriss. S. Agnolo da Cesi. C. M.")

8 38 *Se tua beltà infinita* ("All'Illustre Signor Fabio Mattei. T. C.")

9 40 *Come da set'oppresso* ("All'Illustre Signor Carlo Mezza barba")

10 42 *Dal dì ch'io fei partita* ("All'Illustre Signor Lodovico Busca, Signor mio")

11 44 *Vivo sol contemplando* ("All'Illustre Signor Camillo Fantuccio, mio Signore")

12 46 *Cedano le Piramide* ("Sopra l'arme dell'Illustre Sig. Giacomo Marieri, & la Signora Isabella Priorata sua consorte")

13 48 *Amor s'io mai sprezzai* ("Al mio Signore Aggapito Grillo Gentil'huomo Genovese")

14 50 *Na volta m'hai gabbato* ("Al mio Signore & padrone, Il S. Andrea l'Arcaro, Gentil'huomo Genovese")

15 52 *Ancor che co'l partir* (1584$_{3}$, no. 46)

16 54 *Non arse cosi* ("Al Molto Magnifico. M.F.B.V.A.G.V.")

17 56 *O la O la chi mi sa dar*

18 58 *Io vo morir*

19 60 *Io son ferito e fuggo*

20 62 *Madonna tu mi fingi*

21 64 *Se si vedessi fuore* (1574$_{6}$, no. 18)

22 66 *Angelica tua mano* D'incerto

23 68 *L'alma ch'errando*

24 70 *Voi altre donn'havete*

25 72 *Se quel Turco crudel*

26 74 *Affaciati uno poco*

27 76 *Fra quante faccie ho visto* Del mio Signor Giovan Leonardo dell'Arpa, musico Eccellentissimo

28 78 *Con quesse labra* Di Sulpicio Santuccio Romano, virtuosissimo, & mio caro amico

29 80 *Quant'han già detto*

30 82 *Siamo voi donn'et io*

31 84 *Ne tempesta giamai* ("Sopra l'Accademia della nobile Città di Rossano")

32 86 *Piange'l Thebro* ("Sopra la morte dell'Illustrissima & Eccellen. S. Donna Isabella Colonna, Principessa di Sulmona")

1571$_{5}$

PHALÈSE, PIERRE, AND JEAN BELLÈRE, PUBLISHERS

LIBER PRIMUS / LEVIORUM CARMINUM, OMNIS / FERE GENERIS TRIPUDIA COMPLECTENS, / PADOANAS NIMIRUM, PASSOMEZO, ALEMANDAS, GAIL/lardas, Branles & similia, omnibus Instrumentis Musicis apprimè convenientia, iam / demùm summa cura è variis libris collecta. / Premier Livre de Danseries, contenant plusieurs Pavanes, / PASSOMEZO, ALMANDES, GAILLIARDES, / BRANLES &c. LE TOUT CONVENABLE SUR / tous Instrumens

Musicalz, nouvellement amassé hors / de plusieurs livres. / Supe[Fleuret]rius. / LOVANII. / Apud Petrum Phalesium Bibliopol. Jurat. Antwerpiae apud Joannem Bellerum / ANNO M. D. LXXI.

Four part books in mensural notation, each of 28 fols. On fol. 1^v of each part book: table of contents. For a description of the volume see OppelF, p. 220. The compositions identified by superior letters are reproduced as follows: ([a]) in BlumeS, nos. 2a, 3b, 5, 6, and 23c; ([b]) in MohrA, nos. 12–20; ([c]) in SchmidT; ([d]) in TwittT II–III; ([e]) in PhalLT. Some of the dances are arranged for piano, four hands, in VNM XXVII. All of the compositions are for instrumental ensemble *a 4*.

Copy in: D:HB.

	fol.	
1	2	*Fantasia*[ce]
2	2	*Autre*[ce]
3	2^v	*Les Bouffons*[e] = 1559_3, no. 12
4	2^v	*De Post* = 1551_8, no. 26a
	2^v	*Reprinse* = 1551_8, no. 26b
5	2^v	*Dans de Hercules* = 1551_8, no. 28
6	3	*Pavane Ferrareze*[e][1] (1591_{13}, no. 125a) = 1583_7, no. 8a
	3^v	*Gaillarde Ferrareze*[e][1] (1591_{13}, no. 125b) = 1583_7, no. 8b
7	4	*Pavane des Dieux*[ce] (1591_{13}, no. 126a)
	4	*Gaillarde des dieux*[ce] (1591_{13}, no. 126b)
8	4^v	*Pavane La garde*[ae][2] (1591_{13}, no. 127a)
	4^v	*La Gaillarde de La garde*[ade][2] (1591_{13}, no. 127b)
9	5	*Volte. Pour jouer a la fin de toutes gaillardes de ce ton*
10	5^v	*Pavane j'ay du mal tant tant*[e] (compare LesAC, no. 18: "J'ay le rebours," Certon) = 1583_7, no. 9a
	5^v	*La gaillarde*[e] = 1583_7, no. 9b
11	6	*Pavane Lesquercarde*[ce] = 1559_3, no. 31
12	6^v	*Pavane sur la battaille* = 1551_8, no. 41
	6^v	*Gaillarde sur la battaille*[d]
13	7	*Passomezo d'italye*[e]
	7	*Reprinse*[e]
	7	*La gaillarde* [*d'italye*]
14	7^v	*Passomezo dangleterre*[e] (1571_1, no. 69) = 1583_7, no. 4a
	7^v	*La Reprinse*[e] = 1583_7, no. 4b
15	7^v	*Passomezo danvers*[c] = 1583_7, no. 5
16	8	*Passomeso la doulce*[ce] = 1583_7, no. 6a
	8	*La Reprinse*[ce] = 1583_7, no. 6b
17	8^v	*Passemezo du roy*
	8^v	*Reprinse*
18	9	*Almande prince* = 1551_8, no. 36
19	9	*Almande smedelijn*[a][3] = 1551_8, no. 35
20	9	*Almande* = 1551_8, no. 33
21	9^v	*Almande* = 1551_8, no. 29a
	9^v	*La Reprinse* = 1551_8, no. 29b
22	9^v	*Almande Savoye*[be]
23	10	*Almande de liege*[b] = 1583_7, no. 35
24	10	*Almande danvers*[b]
25	10^v	*Almande Lorayne*[bc]
26	10^v	*Almande damours*[b] = 1583_7, no. 33
27	10^v	*Almande*
28	11	*Almande*[b]
29	11	*Almande*[be] = 1559_3, no. 17
30	11^v	*Almande*[be] = 1564_2, nos. 36–38 (?), and 1583_7, no. 38
31	11^v	*Almande*[be] = 1564_2, nos. 36–38 (?)
32	11^v	*Almande, courrante*[e] = 1564_2, no. 39
33	12	*Gaillarde Au joly boys*[de] = 1583_7, no. 11
34	12	*Gaillarde La Peronnelle* (compare ParisC, no. 39: "Av'ous point veu la Perronnelle") = 1583_7, no. 14
35	12^v	*Gaillarde Mais pourquoy* (compare RISM 1543_{11}, no. 4: Sandrin) = 1583_7, no. 15
36	12^v	*Gaillarde Traditore* (1592_{12}, no. 23) (compare 1589_1, no. 6: "La Traditore my fa morire") = 1583_7, no. 16
37	13	*Gaillarde Si pour t'aymer*[e] = 1559_3, no. 35
38	13^v	*Gaillarde L'esmerillonne*[e] = 1583_7, no. 18
39	13^v	*Puisque vivre en servitude Gaillarde*[e] (compare LesLRB, art. 3, no. 10: Certon) = 1583_7, no. 19
40	14	*Gaillarde La fanfare* = 1583_7, no. 20

41 14^v *Ce qui m'est deu & ordonné. Gaillarde*[a] (compare RISM 1543$_{11}$, no. 18: Sandrin) = 1583$_7$, no. 13

42 14^v *Burate*[e]

43 15 *La rocque Gaillarde*[e] (1592$_{12}$, no. 22) = 1583$_7$, no. 21

44 15^v *Gaillarde, françoise*[e] = 1583$_7$, no. 22

45 15^v *Gaillarde. mon plaisir*[e] (compare 1550$_5$, no. 40) = 1583$_7$, no. 23

46 15 *L'Admiralle Gaillarde* (compare 1577$_6$, no. 54) = 1583$_7$, no. 24

47 16^v *Gaillarde d'escosse*[e] = 1583$_7$, no. 25

48 16^v *Gaillarde*[d] = 1559$_3$, no. 32

49 17 *Gaillarde, La Brune* = 1559$_3$, no. 36

50 17 *Gaillarde*[a] = 1559$_3$, no. 34

51 17^v *Gaillarde la Vidasme* = 1564$_2$, no. 21

52 17^v *La basse gaillarde* = 1564$_2$, no. 25

53 18 *Bransle de poytou simple*[c] = 1564$_2$, no. 29

54 18 *Bransle de poytou legier*[c] = 1564$_2$, no. 31

55 18^v *Bransle du petit homme* = 1564$_2$, no. 34

56 18^v *Bransle legier double du petit homme* = 1564$_2$, no. 35

57 18^v *Le bransle du contraint* = 1564$_2$, no. 26

58 19 *Bransle de la suitte du contraint legier* = 1564$_2$, no. 28

59 19 *Bransle D'escosse*[a 4] = 1559$_2$, no. 44

60 19 *Bransle des Sabots* = 1559$_2$, no. 45

61 19^v *Quatre branles* = 1551$_8$, no. 23

62 19^v *Fagot* = 1551$_8$, no. 24

63 20 *Den Hoboken dans* = 1551$_8$, no. 25

64 20 *Ronde pourquoy* = 1551$_8$, no. 13

65 20^v *Bransle mon amy* = 1551$_8$, no. 14

66 20^v *Bransle* = 1551$_8$, no. 17: "Ronde. Wo bistu"

67 21 *Bransle* = 1551$_8$, no. 18

68 21 *Bransle* = 1551$_8$, no. 21

69 21^v *Premier Bransle Commune*[e] = 1559$_1$, no. 7

70 21^v *2. Bransle*[e] = 1559$_1$, no. 9

71 21^v *Premiere Bransle Gay*[e] = 1559$_1$, no. 19

72 22 *2. Bransle Gay*[e] = 1559$_1$, no. 28

73 22 *Premier Bransle de la guerre*[e] = 1559$_2$, no. 46

74 22 *2. Bransle*[e] = 1559$_2$, no. 47

75 22^v *Premier bransle de Champaigne* = 1559$_1$, no. 31

76 22^v *2. Bransle* = 1559$_1$, no. 32

77 22^v *3. Bransle* = 1559$_1$, no. 33

78 23 *4. Bransle* = 1559$_1$, no. 34

79 23 *5. Bransle* = 1559$_1$, no. 35

80 23^v *6. Bransle* = 1559$_1$, no. 36

81 23^v *7. Bransle* = 1559$_1$, no. 37

82 23^v *8. Bransle* = 1559$_1$, no. 38

83 24 *Premier Bransle de Bourgoigne* = 1559$_2$, no. 1

84 24 *2. Bransle* = 1559$_2$, no. 2

85 24^v *3. Bransle* = 1559$_2$, no. 3

86 24^v *4. Bransle* = 1559$_2$, no. 4

87 24^v *5. Bransle* = 1559$_2$, no. 5

88 25 *6. Bransle* = 1559$_2$, no. 6

89 25 *7. Bransle* = 1559$_2$, no. 7

90 25^v *8. Bransle* = 1559$_2$, no. 8

91 25^v *9. Bransle* = 1559$_2$, no. 9

92 25^v *10. Bransle* = 1559$_2$, no. 10

93 26 *11. Bransle* = 1559$_2$, no. 11

94 26 *12. Bransle* = 1559$_2$, no. 12

95 26^v *13. Bransle* = 1559$_2$, no. 13

96 26^v *14. Bransle* = 1559$_2$, no. 14

97 26^v *15. Bransle* = 1559$_2$, no. 15

98 27 *16. Bransle* = 1559$_2$, no. 16

99 27^v *17. Bransle* = 1559$_2$, no. 17

100 27^v *18. Bransle* = 1559$_2$, no. 18

101 28 *Bransle des Lavandieres*[d] = 1559$_1$, no. 58

102 28 *Bransle Hauberrois* = 1559$_3$, no. 45

103 28 *Bransle Guillemette*[d] = 1564$_2$, no. 33

[1] Mod. ed. in ScherG, no. 134.

[2] Mod. ed. in MFH II, 9.

[3] Mod. ed. in WolfHM, p. 529, and WolfME, no. 39.

[4] Mod. ed. in WolfHM, p. 529, and WolfME, no. 40.

1571$_6$

PHALÈSE, PIERRE, AND JEAN BELLÈRE, PUBLISHERS

THEATRUM / MUSICUM, LONGE AM/PLISSIMUM CUI (DEMPTIS QUAE / VETUSTATE VILVERANT) AUTHOREM PRAE/STANTISS. TUM

VETERUM, TUM RECENTIORUM CARMINA SE/LECTISSIMA SUNT INSERTA, MAIORI QUAM ANTE/ HAC FIDE ET DILIGENTIA IN USUM PUBLI/CUM COMPARATA. / Et Primo quidem ordine αὐτόματα quae Fantasiae, vel Praeludia nuncupantur. / Secundo Cantilenae vulgares, sed exquisitae tum 4. tum 5. vocum. / Tertia classis eorum Carminum quae ex lingua Gal: Italica Latina à praestan/tissima artificibus instituta (ut Clemente non papa, Orlandoque di Lasso, / & pluribus aliis) Moteti nomen 4. 5. aut 6. vocum promerentur. / Quibus succedunt alia quae duabus Testudinibus concini solent. / Postremò & eius generis Carmina, quae tum facilitate tum lepore discentes, / pariter ac audientes rapiunt, ut sunt Passomezo, Gaill. Branles etc. / Universa propemodum nunc recenter à peritissimis quibusque; translata in Testudinis usum, velut / Julio Cesare Paduano, Melchiore Nenslyder Germano, & Sixto Kargl / ac nonnullis aliis quorum industria prae cateris / hodiè celebratur. / [Cut of ten performing musicians] / LOVANII. / Excudebat Petrum Phalesius sibi & Joanni Bellero Bibliopolae Antverpiensi. / ANNO M.D. LXXI.

126 fols. French lute tablature. On fol. $A1^v$: table of contents. Fol. A2 = fol. 1. SlimK II, 553, contains a thematic index of the ricercares. Nos. 160–166 are for two lutes; the other compositions are for solo lute.

Copies in: D:Mbs, GB:Ob, PL:Kj.[1]

MUSIC FOR SOLO LUTE

fol.

1 1 *Fantasia Prima*[2] = 1573_3, no. 3, and 1586_5, no. 6

2 1^v *Fantasia Pauli Baroni* = 1536_9, no. 11: Borrono

3 2 *Fantasia*

4 2^v *Fantasia* = 1558_4, no. 2: Morlaye

5 3 *Fantasia* = 1573_3, no. 1

6 3^v *Fantasia* = 1536_3, no. 1: Francesco da Milano

7 4 *Fantasia*

8 4^v *Fantasia* = 1536_3, no. 15: Francesco da Milano

9 5 *Fantasia* = 1558_4, no. 3: Morlaye

10 5^v *Fantasia* = 1560_3, no. 1: Paladin

11 6 *Fantasia* = 1536_3, no. 16: Francesco da Milano

12 6^v *Fantasia Francisci Milan* = 1536_9, no. 1: Francesco da Milano

13 7 *Fantasia* = 1546_{10}, no. 5: Giovanni Maria da Crema

14 7^v *Fantasia Francisco da Milan* = 1547_2, no. 5

15 8 *Fantasia* = 1536_3, no. 7: Francesco da Milano

16 8^v *Fantasia Prima Sixti Kargl*

17 9^v *Fantasia 2* = 1574_1, no. 3: Kargel

18 10 *Fantasia* = 1568_1, no. 38

19 10^v *Fantasia 3*

20 11 *Fantasia* = 1568_7, no. 16

21 11^v *Fantasia 4*

22 12 *Fantasia* = 1568_7, no. 1: Raphael Viola

23 12^v *Fantasia* = 1560_3, no. 3: Paladin

24 13^v *Fantasia 1. Melchior* [*Newsidler*] = 1566_3, no. 15

25 14 *Fantasia* = 1546_{10}, no. 4: Giovanni Maria da Crema

26 14^v *Fantasia 2* = 1566_3, no. 16: M. Newsidler

27 15^v *Fantasia* = 1566_3, no. 18: M. Newsidler

28 16^v *Fantasia 4* = 1566_2, no. 19: M. Newsidler

29 17^v *Fantasia 5* = 1566_2, no. 20: M. Newsidler

30 18^v *Fantasia 6* = 1566_2, no. 21: M. Newsidler

31 19 *Fantasia* = 1552_4, no. 6: Morlaye

32 19^v *Fantasia 7* = 1566_2, no. 22: M. Newsidler

33 20 *Fantasia* = 1546_6, no. 11: Francesco da Milano

34 20^v *Fantasia 8* = 1566_3, no. 17: M. Newsidler

35 21^v *O combien est* [*malheureux*] (ClemensO VII, 156: Sandrin or Sermisy)

36 22 *Le mal qui sent* ("*Response*") = 1568_7, no. 23

37 22^v *Vous perdés temps* = 1568_7, no. 24: Sermisy

38 23 *Telz en mesdict* ("*Response*") = 1547_9, no. 4: Mittantier

39 23^v *Doulce memoire* = 1568_7, no. 26: Sandrin

40 24 *Finy le bien* ("*Response*") = 1547_9, no. 12: Certon

41 24^v *C'est à grand tort* = 1568_7, no. 28: Crecquillon

42 25 *Languir me fais* = 1568_7, no. 29: Sermisy

43 25^v *Si mon traveil* = 1547_9, no. 5: Sandrin

44 26 *Le deuil yssu* ("*Response*") = 1568_7, no. 31

45 26^v *Toutes les muyct* = 1568_7, no. 32: Crecquillon

46 27 *Pour un plaisir* = 1568_7, no. 41b: Crecquillon

47 27^v *Je prens en gre* (ClemensO X, 14: Clemens non Papa)

48 28 *Mon cueur chante joyeusement* *a 4*

49 28^v *Damour me plains* = 1547_9, no. 2: Pathie

50 29 *Or il ne m'[e]st possible* = 1568_7, no. 72: Clemens non Papa

51 30^v *Ung gay bergier. Alio modo* = 1547_9, no. 8: Crecquillon

52 31 *Je suis desheritée* = 1552_8, no. 7: Lupus or Cadéac

53 31^v *Susanne ung jour* *a 4* = 1568_7, no. 54: Didier Lupi Second

54 32 *Godt es mijn licht* = 1568_7, no. 52: Clemens non Papa

55 32^v *Frisque & gaillard* = 1568_7, no. 67: Clemens non Papa

56 33 *Pour une helas* *a 4* = 1568_7, no. 58: Crecquillon

57 33^v *A demy mort* *a 4* (ClemensO X, 32: Clemens non Papa)

58 34 *Martin menoit* Clemens non Papa = 1568_7, no. 62

59 34^v *Un doulx nenny* Cricquillon *a 4* (LassoW XII, 45: Lasso)

60 35 *Tant vous allez doux guillemette* (RISM 1564_{11}, fol. 11: Abran) = 1574_7, no. 42

61 35^v *Si me tenez* = 1568_7, no. 71

62 36 *Content ou non* = 1566_2, no. 14

63 36^v *En regardant la beaulté* Verius

64 37 *Que pleust à dieu* Verius = 1568_7, no. 55

65 37^v *Ce mois de may* (PubAPTM XXIII, no. 25: Godard)

38 *Ce mois de may. Alio modo* = 1568_7, no. 46b

66 38^v *Alix avoir* (RISM 1545_{16}, fol. 12^v: "Alix avoit aux dens la malerage," Crecquillon)

67 39 *Amour au cueur* = 1568_7, no. 70: Crecquillon)

68 39^v *Amour partez* (compare 1586_5, no. 25)

69 40 *Le content est riche* = 1568_7, no. 37: Sermisy

70 40^v *Rossignollet qui chantez* Clemens [non Papa] *a 4* (ClemensO X, 41)

71 41 *Au fait damour* *a 4*

72 41^v *D'amour me plains* Vallentin Bacfarc = 1553_1, no. 11: Pathie

73 42^v *Souspiers ardans* = 1566_2, no. 10: Arcadelt

74 43^v *Vray dieu disoit* Orlando [Lasso] = 1566_2, no. 15

44 *Vray dieu disoit. Alio modo* Orlando [Lasso] = 1568_7, no. 76

75 44^v *Je l'ayme bien* Orlando [Lasso] (LassoW XII, 41)

76 45 *Las voulez vous* Orlando [Lasso] = 1568_7, no. 81

45^v *Las voulez vous. Alio modo* = 1574_1, no. 5

77 46 *Avecque vous* Orlando [Lasso] (LassoW XII, 37) (compare 1566_2, no. 9)

78 46^v *Ung doulx nenny* Orlando [Lasso] = 1566_2, no. 13

79 47 *En un lieu* = 1568_7, no. 79: Lasso

80 47^v *Petite folle* Orlando [Lasso] = 1566_2, no. 16

81 48 *Monsieur Robbin* Orlando [Lasso] = 1566_2, no. 11

82 48^v *Je ne veux riens* Orlando [Lasso] *a 4* (LassoW XII, 98) (compare 1574_2, no. 10)

83 49 *Ardant amour* Orlando [Lasso] = 1568_7, no. 75

84 49^v *Ce faux amour* Orlando [Lasso] *a 4* (LassoW XII, 103)

85 50 *Helas quel jour* Orlando [Lasso] (LassoW XII, 47)

86 50^v *Bon jour mon coeur* Orlando [Lasso] (LassoW XII, 100)

87 51 *Quand mon mary* Orlando [Lasso] (LassoW XII, 23)

88 51 *En espoir vis* Orlando [Lasso] = 1568_7, no. 78

89 51^v *Tout ce qu'on peut* Cyprian Rore = 1559_4, no. 1

90 52 *Madonna mia pieta* Orlando [Lasso] (LassoW X, 61)

91 52 *Tu sai madona* (LassoW X, 63: Lasso)

92 52^v *La cortesia* Orlando [Lasso] (LassoW X, 66) = 1574_1, no. 21

93 52^v *Sto core mio* Orlando [Lasso] (LassoW X, 69)

94 53 *Tu traditore* Orlando [Lasso] (LassoW X, 68)

95 53 *Bem para che dame* ("Vilanesche")

96 53^v *Sife Cristallo* (LassoW VIII, 7: 4a pars of "Del freddo rheno," Lasso) = 1586_5, no. 40

97 53^v *Tutta saressi* = 1568_7, no. 59

98 54 *Chilcre il sole* (LassoW VIII, 4: 2a pars of "Del freddo rheno," Lasso) = 1572_1, no. 12

99 54^v *Deh ferma amor* Orlando [Lasso] = 1566_2, no. 1: D. Ferabosco

100 55 *Io mi son giovenetta* Orlando = 1566_2, no. 3: D. Ferabosco

101 55^v *O sio potessi donna* = 1566_2, no. 2: Berchem

102 56^v *Se ben lempia mia sorte* (LassoW VIII, 17: Lasso) = 1586_5, no. 39

103 57 *Per pianto* Orlando [Lasso] (LassoW VIII, 13) = 1586_5, no. 37

104 57^v *Vite della mia vita* = 1566_2, no. 5: Verdelot

105 58 *Si purti guardo* = 1568_7, no. 105: Pathie

106 58^v *Del freddo rhenno* ("Madrigali") (LassoW VIII, 3: Lasso) = 1572_1, no. 11

107 59 *Con lei fussio* Orlando = 1566_2, no. 4: Arcadelt, Berchem, Corteccia, or Giaches de Ponte

108 59^v *Et io qual fui* (LassoW VIII, 9: Lasso) = 1574_1, no. 18

109 60 *Vatena lieta homani* (LassoW VIII, 21: Lasso)

110 60^v *Signor mio caro* = 1566_2, no. 7: Rore

111 61 *La pastorella mia* = 1568_7, no. 66: Arcadelt

112 61^v *Carita di signore* = 1566_2, no. 8: Rore

113 62 *Perche la vita breve* = 1566_2 no. 6

114 62^v *Anchor quel partir* (SCMA VI, 45: Rore)

115 63 *Che piu foco* Bacfarc = 1553_1, no. 17: Arcadelt

116 63^v *Oncques amour* Cricquillon = 1566_3, no. 10

117 64 *Fortune allors* = 1568_7, no. 57: Certon

118 64^v *Le rossignol* Orlando [Lasso] *a 5* (LassoW XIV, 107) = 1572_1, no. 22

119 65 *Vous qui aymez les dames* Orlando [Lasso] (LassoW XIV, 45)

120 65^v *Secourez moy* Orlando [Lasso] *a 5* = 1566_3, no. 8

121 66 *Jattens le temps* Orlando [Lasso] (LassoW XIV, 48)

122 66^v *Ardant amour* Orlando [Lasso] *a 5* (LassoW XIV, 84)

123 67 *Un triste cueur* Orlando [Lasso] *a 5* (LassoW XIV, 80)

124 67^v *Mon cueur ravi d'amour* Orlando [Lasso] (LassoW XIV, 22)

125 68 *De tout mon cueur* Orlando [Lasso] (LassoW XIV, 33)

126 68^v *Veulx tu ton mal* Orlando [Lasso] (LassoW XIV, 71)

127 68^v *Le voulez vous* ("*Response*") Orlando [Lasso] (LassoW XIV, 74)

128 69 *Mon cueur se recommand*[3] Orlando [Lasso] (LassoW XIV, 15)

69^v *Mon cueur se recommand. Alio modo* Orlando

129 70 *Sur tous regrez* Orlando [Lasso] *a5* (LassoW XIV, 26)

130 70^v *Susanne un jour* Orlando [Lasso] = 1568_7, no. 108c

131 71 *Est il possible* *a5* (LassoW XIV, 112: Lasso)

132 71^v *Susanne un jour. Alio modo* = 1566_3, no. 7: Lasso

133 72^v *Le departir* Orlando [Lasso] = 1566_3, no. 12: Lasso

134 73 *Elle s'en va* Orlando [Lasso] (LassoW XIV, 105)

135 73^v *Et d'ou venez vous* Orlando [Lasso] *a5* (LassoW XIV, 68)

136 74 *Las me fault il* Orlando [Lasso] *a5* (LassoW XIV, 76)

137 74^v *La vita fuge* Orlando [Lasso] (LassoW IV, 44)

138 75 *Mon amy. Alio modo* = 1546_{10}, no. 28: Gascongne

139 75^v *Pis ne me peult venir* *a5* (RISM 1572_2, fol. 25: Crecquillon)

140 76 *Aymer est ma vie* Clemens non Papa *a5* (RISM 1553_{24}, fol. 3)

141 76^v *Musiciens regardez devant vous* Clemens non Papa *a5*

142 77 *Adieu mon esperance* Clemens non Papa *a6* (RISM 1553_{24}, fol. 13)

143 77^v *Dung petit mot* *a5* = 1566_3, no. 11

144 78^v *Quando pens'io el martir'* = 1553_9, no. 6: Arcadelt

145 79^v *Jesu nomen sanctissimum* Clemens non Papa *a4* = 1565_1, no. 4a

80 2a pars *Sit nomen domini benedictum* Clemens non Papa *a4* = 1565_1, no. 4b

146 80^v *Eravi sicut ovis* Clemens non Papa *a4* = 1565_1, no. 5a

81 2a pars *Delicta juventutis meae* = 1565_1, no. 5b

147 81^v *Circundederunt me viri mendaces* Clemens non Papa *a4* = 1565_1, no. 6a

82 2a pars *Quoniam tribulatio proxima est* = 1565_1, no. 6b

148 82^v *Heu mihi domine* Orlando [Lasso] *a5* (LassoW IX, 6)

149 83^v *Deus canticum novum* Orlando [Lasso] *a5* = 1566_3, no. 1a

84 2a pars *Quia delectasti* = 1566_3, no. 1b

150 84^v *Omnia quae fecisti* Orlando [Lasso] *a5* = 1566_3, no. 2

151 85^v *In me transierunt* Orlando [Lasso] *a5* = 1566_3, no. 3

152 86^v *Surrexit pastor bonus* Orlando [Lasso] *a5* = 1566_3, no. 4

153 87^v *Gustate & videte* Orlando [Lasso] *a5* = 1566_3, no. 6a

88^v 2a pars *Divites eguerunt* = 1566_3, no. 6b

154 89 *Veni in hortum meum* Orlando [Lasso] (LassoW V, 120)

155 89^v *Benedicam Dominum* *a5* = 1566_3, no. 5: Lasso

90^v 2a pars *In Domino* = 1566_3, no. 5b

156 91^v *Aspice Domine* *a5* (MonteO XXVI, app., p. 1: Jachet)

157 92^v *In te Domine speravi* (RISM 1535_1, fol. 6^v: Lupus)

93^v 2a pars [*Quoniam fortitudo mea*]

158 94^v *Stabat mater dolorosa* *a5* = 1547_3, no. 13: Josquin

159 95^v *Benedicta* *a6* (JosqMT, no. 46: Josquin)

96^v 2a pars *Per illud ave*

96^v 3a pars *Nunc mater*

MUSIC FOR TWO LUTES

160 97 *Canti di voi le ladi*[4] = 1568_7, no. 115: Naich

161 97^v *Amour e gratioso* = 1568_7, no. 116

162 97^v *Burato* = 1568_7, no. 117

163 98^v *La Bataille* = 1568_7, no. 118: Janequin

164 99^v *Passomezo* = 1568_7, no. 119a

100^v *Il suo saltarello* = 1568_7, no. 119b

165 100^v *Chi passa* = 1568_7, no. 120: Azzaiolo

166 101^v *O combien est* = 1568_7, no. 121: Sandrin or Sermisy

MUSIC FOR SOLO LUTE

167 102^v *Passomezo il Moderno* = 1569_2, no. 21a

103^v *Gaillarde del Moderno* = 1569_2, no. 21b

168 104 *Passomezo detta il nobile* = 1569_2, no. 19

169 104^v *Passomezo ficta* = 1569_2, no. 17

170 105^v *Passomezo de la Bataille* = 1569_2, no. 18

171 106 *Passomezo antico* = 1569_2, no. 22a

107^v *Gaillarde antico* = 1569_2, no. 22b

172 108^v *Passomezo* = 1566_3, no. 13a

109^v *Il suo saltarello* = 1566_3, no. 13b

173 110^v *Passomezo la Milanese* = 1566_2, no. 17a: "Pass'e mezo antico"

111^v *Il suo saltarello con la represa* = 1566_2, no. 17b

174 112^v *Passemezo Marck Antoine*

175 115^v *Passemezo La paruzino* = 1566_3, no. 14a

116^v *Il suo saltarello* = 1566_3, no. 14b

176 117^v *Gailliarde Milanese*

177 117^v *Gailliarde de la battaille*

178 118 *Gailliarde Marocho* = 1569_2, no. 11

179 118^v *Gailliarde il zacarii* = 1569_2, no. 9

180 118^v *Gailliarde il barbetino* = 1569_2, no. 10

181 119 *Gailliarde la Imperale* = 1569_2, no. 13

182 119^v *Gaillarde la Francia* = 1569_2, no. 12

183 120 *Gaillirade* [*sic*] *2. frantia* = 1569_2, no. 15

184 120^v *Chi passa*

185 120^v *Gaillarde Baisons nous* = 1568_7, no. 143

186 121 *Gailliarde 3. frantia* = 1569_2, no. 16

187–195 121^v *Branles des Bourgoignes* [nos. 1–9] = 1551_2, nos. 20–28

196 123 *La Bataille* = 1536_3, no. 34: Janequin

124 2a pars [*Fan frere le le lan fan*]

[1] Copies were in D:Bds and D:KA.

[2] Heading on fol. 1: "THEATRUM MUSICUM, SELECTISSIMIS OPTIMORUM ARTIFICUM CARMINIBUS INSTRUCTUM ATQUE EXORNATUM."

[3] Facs. of fol. 69 in MGG VII, col. 689.

[4] Heading on fol. 97: "SEQUUNTUR DEINCEPS CARMINA DUABUS TESTUDINIBUS ACCOMMODA."

1572_1

JOBIN, BERNHART, PUBLISHER

Das Erste Büch / Newerlessner / Fleissiger ettlicher viel / Schöner Lautenstück, von artlichen / Fantaseyen, lieblichen Teütschen, Frantzösischen / unnd Italiänischen Liedern / künstlichen Lateini/schen Muteten, mit vier und fünff stimmen, Auch / lustigen allerhand Passomezen: in die Teutsche / Tabulatur, zü nutz und gefallen allen diser Kunst / lehrbegirigen, fürnämlich den jenigen, so der fremb/den Welschen Tabulatur etwas unerfahr/ner, auff das verständtlichest und rich/tigest zusamen getragen, geord/net, und auch selber / getruckt, / Durch Bernhard Jobin, / Burger zü Strassburg. / M. D. LXXII.[1]

50 fols. German lute tablature. The title is placed within an ornamental border (the same border as in 1577_6). Dedication on fol. *2 headed "Dem Ehrenhafften, Wolgeachten, und Kunstreichen Herr Thobie Stimmer von Schaffhausen, meinem lieben Gevattern, und besonders günstigen freündt," and signed "Geben in Strassburg den 17. Martii, Anno 72. E.Gütwilliger Compere Bernhard Jobin, Burger zü Strassburg," partly reprinted in EitK, p. 93. Beginning on fol. *2^v: a poem in German headed "Ein Artliches lob der Lauten," and signed on fol. *6 "J. F. G. Mentzer," a pseudonym for Johann Fischart.[2] On fol. *6: "Ein kurtze Verwarnung vom verstand diser Tabulatur." On fol. *6^v: table of contents. Fol. *7 = fol. A1. All of the compositions are for solo lute.[3]

Copies in: A:Wgm, A:Wn, CH:Zz, D:Dl, D:KA,[4] D:Ngm (imperfect), D:ZW, GB:Lbm, PL:WRu.[5]

fol.

1 A1 *Fantasia 1*

2 A2^v *Fantasia 2*

3 $A3^v$ *Fantasia 3*
4 A4 *Fantasia 4*
5 $B1^v$ *1. Si pur ti guardo* Ferrabosco (RISM 1570_8, p. 46: Pathie)
6 $B2^v$ *2. O sio potessi donna* Arcadelt (RISM 1541_9, p. 19: Berchem)
7 $B3^v$ *3. Quand Io pens a la martire* Arcadelt (RISM 1541_9, p. 54)
8 $B4^v$ *4. Signor mio Caro* Orland. = 1566_2, no. 7: Rore
9 $C1^v$ *5. Vita de la mia vita* Verdelot = 1566_2, no. 5
10 $C2^v$ *6. Io mi son giovinetta* Ferrabosco (EinIM III, no. 30: D. Ferabosco)
11 $C3^v$ *7. Del freddo rhenno* Orland[o Lasso] = 1571_6, no. 106
12 C4 *8. Chil cre il sole* Orland[o Lasso] = 1571_6, no. 98
13 $C4^v$ *1. Susanne ung Jour* Orland[o Lasso] = 1568_7, no. 108c
14 D2 *2. Je prens en gre* Crecquillon (ClemensO X, 14: Clemens non Papa)
15 D3 *3. Pour parvenir* Crecquillon
16 D4 *4. Puis ne me peult venir* Crecquillon (RISM 1572_2, fol. 25: "Pis ne me peult venir")
17 E1 *5. Le departir* Orland[o Lasso] = 1566_3, no. 12
18 $E2^v$ *6. Joyssance [vous donneray]* Adrian Villart = 1566_3, no. 9
19 $E3^v$ *7. Un doulx nenny* Orland[o Lasso] (LassoW XII, 45)
20 $E4^v$ *8. Vray dieu disoit une fillette* Orland[o Lasso] (LassoW XII, 72)
21 F1 *9. Helas quel jour* Orland[o Lasso] (LassoW XII, 47)
22 F2 *10. Le rossignol* Orland[o Lasso] = 1571_6, no. 118
23 F3 *11. De plusieurs choses* Orland[o Lasso] (LassoW XVI, 72)
24 $F3^v$ *1. Bewar mich Herr* Steffan Zirler (D:Rp, MS AR 855, no. 19)
25 G1 *2. Ich weiss mir ein vest gebautes Hauss* Scandell[o] (ScanL, no. 6)
26 G2 *3. Der wein der schmackt mir also wol* Orland[o Lasso] (LassoW XVIII, 11)
27 G3 *4. Ist keiner hie der spricht zu mir* Orland[o Lasso] (LassoW XVIII, 8)
28 G4 *5. Im Meyen* Orland[o Lasso] (LassoW XVIII, 24)
29 G4 *1. Legem pone mihi Domine* Orlando [Lasso] (LassoW IX, 73)
$H1^v$ 2a pars *Da mihi intellectum*
30 $H2^v$ *2. Sicut mater consolatur* Orland[o Lasso] (LassoW VII, 97)
31 $H3^v$ *3. Confundantur* Orland[o Lasso] (LassoW IX, 155)
$H4^v$ 2a pars *Fiat cor meum*
32 $I1^v$ *4. Confitemini Domino* Orland[o Lasso] (LassoW VII, 131)
$I2^v$ 2a pars *Narrate*
33 $I3^v$ *5. Veni in hortum* Orland[o Lasso] (LassoW V, 120)
34 K1 *6. Nuncium vobis fero* Orland[o Lasso] (LassoW V, 9)
$K1^v$ 2a pars *Thus do myrrham*
35 $K2^v$ *1. Passemezo*
K4 *Saltarello*
36 L1 *2. Passemezo*
L2 *Saltarello*
37 $L2^v$ *3. Passemezo [Zorzy]*[6]
$L3^v$ *Saltarello*

[1] Facs. of title page in KinsP, p. 134.
[2] For a discussion of the poem see PeterM.
[3] The copy of 1573_2 (the second volume of this series) in A:Wn is defective. 1572_1, fols. $E2^v$–$E3^v$ and $E4^v$–$L3^v$ are pr. there in place of 1573_2, fols. $E2^v$–$E3^v$ and $E4^v$–H4.
[4] The Karlsruhe copy (which is bound with 1558_5 and 1573_2) contains 43 fols. of manuscript music in German lute tablature including dances ("Pavan," "Galliarde," "Allmandt," "Passamezo") and intabulations of German lieder. See DieL, pp. 95–96, for a full list of the contents with concordances.
[5] Copies were in D:Bds and the Wotquenne library (see ThibaultC). The Berlin copy contained an appendix of manuscript dances in German lute tablature, including "Passametzo," "Saltarello," "Intrada," and "Matazina."
[6] Manuscript addition in British Museum copy: "Zorzy" after Passemezo.

1572_2

VICENTINO, NICOLÒ

MADRIGALI A CINQUE VOCI. / DI L'ARCIMUSICO / DON NICOLA

VICENTINO / PRATICO ET THEORICO ET / INVENTORE DELLE NUOVE ARMONIE. / Nuovamente posti in luce, da Ottavio Resino / suo Discepolo. / LIBRO QUINTO. / IN MILANO. / Appresso Paolo Gottardo Pontio. M D LXXII.

Five part books in mensural notation, each of 12 fols. Dedication on p. 2 of each part book headed "AL MOLTO MAGNIFICO ET HONORATO Signor il S. Lucilio Cavenago. S. mio osservandissimo," and signed "Ottavio Resino." On p. 24 of each part book: table of contents. Vogel: Vicentino 2 gives a complete list of the contents. Contains Italian madrigals and one instrumental piece *a 5*.

† Copy in: I:MOe.

	p.	
1	22	*La bella. Canzone da sonare*[1]

[1] Mod. ed. in IMAMI II, xlvi, and VicenO, pp. 119–122.

1573₁

NEWSIDLER, MELCHIOR

TABULATURA / CONTINENS / PRAESTANTISSIMAS ET / SELECTISSIMAS QUASQUE CAN/tiones, in usum Testudinis, à Melchiore Neusydler Italicè / invulgatas, Nunc typis germanicis redditas: / PER / Benedictum de Drusina. / [Cut of a lutenist] / FRANCOFORDIAE CIS VIADRUM, IN / OFFICINA JOANNIS EICHORNI: / M. D. LXXIII. / Cum gratia & Privilegio Caesareae Maiestatis.[1]

47 fols. German lute tablature. On fol. A2: printer's privilege from the Emperor Maximilian II, dated from Prague, April 29, 1571. Dedication on fol. A3 headed "Illustrissimo Illustrissimique Generis Principi ac Domino, D. Augusto Electori, Duci Saxoniae, Lantgravio Turingiae, Marchioni Misniae, Sacri Romani Imperii Archimarschalco, Domino suo clementissimo," and signed "Datum Wittebergae in die Pentecostes, Anno 1573. Illustriss. Celsitud. subjectis. Benedictus de Drusina." A thematic index of this volume is pr. in KosackL, pp. 102–104. The volume is described in GrimmM, pp. 97–98. Contents = 1566₂ and 1566₃. Drusina has transcribed Newsidler's pieces from Italian into German tablature. On fol. F2ᵛ: table of contents for the first half of the volume (= 1566₂). On fol. M3: table of contents for the second half of the volume (= 1566₃). All of the compositions are for solo lute.

Copies in: B:Br, D:DO.[2]

[1] Facs. of title page in MGG III, col. 1190.
[2] A copy was in D:Bds (formerly in the Wolffheim library; see WolffC I, no. 1205).

1573₂

JOBIN, BERNHART, PUBLISHER

Das Ander Buch / Newerlessner / Kunstlicher Lauten/stück, von allerhand Musicartlichen / Passomezo, Gailliarden, Branlen, und ange/nemen Teutschen Däntzen, zü dienst unnd ge/fallen den diser Kunst übenden, inn die / Teutsche gebräuchliche Tabulatur / gericht und zůsammen ge/truckt durch / Bernhard Jobin, Burger / zü Strassburg. / M. D. LXXIII.

30 fols. German lute tablature. The title is placed within an ornamental border (the same border as in 1577₆). On fol. *2: preface and dedication headed "Dem Ehrenhafften, Wolachtbarn und Fürnemmen Herrn Samson Liechtensteigern, meinem viel günstigen Herrn, und geliebten Gevattern," and signed "Actum Strassburg, den ersten Martii. Anno 1573. E. A. Dienstwilliger Compere, Bernhard Jobin, Burger daselbest," partly reprinted in EitK, p. 93. Fol. *3 = fol. B1. All of the compositions are for solo lute.

Copies in: A:Wgm, A:Wn,[1] CH:Zz, D:Dl, D:KA,[2] D:Ngm (imperfect), D:ZW, PL:WRu.[3]

	fol.	
1	B1	*Passemezo Antiquo*
	B2ᵛ	*Saltarello Antiquo*
2	B4	*Passemezo Ungaro*
	C1	*Saltarello Ungaro*
3	C1ᵛ	*Passemezo comun*
	C2ᵛ	*Saltarello comun*

4	C3v	*Passemezo zorzy*
	C4v	*Saltarello zorzy*
5	D1v	*Passemezo*
	D2v	*Saltarello*
6	D3	*Gailliarde Chi passa*
7	D4	*Gailliarde* (compare 1568_7, no. 132: "Gailliarda la Royne d'escosse")
8	D4v	*Gailliarde*
9	E1	*Gailliarde*
10	E1v	*Gailliarde brunette* = 1568_7, no. 141
11	E2	*Gailliarde la Varionessa* = 1568_7, no. 140
12	E2v	*Gailliarde*
13	E3	*Branle de Bourgoingne* = 1591_{13}, no. 129
14	E3v	*Branle 2*
15	E4	*Branle 3* = 1591_{13}, no. 130: "Branle de Bourgoigne"
16	E4	*Branle de Champaigne* = 1568_7, no. 153
17	E4v	*Branles de N. Rans* = 1568_7, no. 163
18	F1v	*Les quatres Branles* = 1591_{13}, no. 134
19	F2	*Teutscher Dantz*
	F2v	*Nach dantz*
20	F3	*Teutscher Dantz*
	F3v	*Nach dantz*
21	F4	*Dantz Proficiat*
	F4v	*Nach dantz*
22	G1	*Deutscher Dantz*
	G1v	*Nach dantz*
23	G1v	*Dantz*
	G2	*Nach dantz*
24	G2v	*Dantz*
	G2v	*Nach dantz*
25	G3	*Dantz*
	G3v	*Nach dantz*
26	G3v	*Dantz*
	G4	*Nach dantz*
27	G4v	*Dantz*
	G4v	*Nach dantz*
28	H1	*Dantz*
	H1	*Nach dantz*
29	H1v	*Dantz* (compare 1540_1, no. 6: "Ich weiss mir ein stoltze Müllerin")
	H2	*Nach dantz*
30	H2	*Dantz*
	H2v	*Nach dantz*
31	H3	*Dantz*
	H3	*Nach dantz*
32	H3	*Dantz*
	H3v	*Nach dantz*
33	H4	*Dantz*
	H4	*Nach dantz*

[1] The copy in the Österreichische Nationalbibliothek is defective. Fols. E2v–E3v and E4v–L3v of 1572_1 are pr. in place of 1573_2, fols. E2v–E3v and E4v–H4.

[2] For information about a manuscript appendix in the Karlsruhe copy see 1572_1, note 4.

[3] A copy was in D:Bds.

1573_3

WAISSEL, MATTHÄUS

TABULATURA / CONTINENS INSIGNES ET / SELECTISSIMAS QUASQUE / Cantiones, quatuor, quinque, et sex Vo/cum, Testudini aptatas, ut sunt: Praeambula: Phan/tasiae: Cantiones Germanicae, Italicae, Gallicae, & / Latinae: Passemesi: Gagliardae: & Choreae. / In lucem aedita / PER / MATTHAEUM WAISSELIUM / BARTSTEINENSEM BORUSSUM. / [Cut of a lutenist] / FRANCOFORDIAE AD VIADRUM, IN OFFICINA / JOANNIS EICHORN. ANNO M. D. LXXIII. / Cum gratia, & Privilegio Caesareae Majestatis.

48 fols. German lute tablature. On fol. A1v: table of contents. Dedication on fol. A2 headed "ILLUSTRISSIMO PRINCIPI AC DOMINO, DOMINO ALBERTO FRIDERICO, MARCHIONI BRANDENBURgensi, Prussiae, Stetinensi, Pomeraniae, Cassubiorum, Wandalorumque Duci, Burggravio Norinbergensi, ac Principi Rugiae: Principi, & Domino suo clementissimo," and signed "Matthaeus Waissel, Scholae Schippenbellensis moderator." On fol. A3: poem in Latin headed "In Gratiam Matthaei Waisselii Elegia," and signed "M. Valentinus Schreckius." A thematic index of the volume is printed in KosackL, pp. 104–107. The volume is described in GrimmM, pp. 98–100, which includes a facsimile of the title page. There are modern editions of several compositions in WaissT. All of the compositions are for solo lute.

Copies in: B:Br, D:Mbs, D:W, H:Bn.[1]

	fol.	
1	A4	*Praeambulum* = 1571_6, no. 5
2	A4^v	*Praeambulum*
3	B1	*Phantasia* = 1571_6, no. 1
4	B1^v	*Phantasia*
5	B2	*Beware mich Herr* (D:Rp, MS AR 855, no. 19: Zirler)
6	B2^v	*Gott ist mein licht* (VNM XXVI, 51: "Godt es mijn licht," Clemens non Papa)
7	B3^v	*Was wird es doch* [2] (SenflW IV, no. 26: Senfl)
8	B4	*Zarth freundtlichs M*
9	B4^v	*Le content est riche* B[enedikt] D[e] D[rusina] = 1556_2, no. 8: Sermisy
10	C1	*Cest à grand tort* (AttainCK II, no. 18: Sermisy)
11	C1^v	*La battaglia* (compare 1544_2, no. 32)
12	C2	*Languir me fais* (AttainCK II, no. 12: Sermisy)
13	C2^v	*Doulce memoire* (PubAPTM XXIII, no. 50: Sandrin)
14	C3^v	*Quanto è madonna mia*
15	C4	*Si pourti guardo* (RISM 1570_8, p. 46: Pathie)
16	C4^v	*Dumour me plains* [3] (PubAPTM XXIII, no. 49: Pathie)
17	D1^v	*Ung gay bergier* G[uillaume] M[orlaye] (?) (RieH II, 462: Crecquillon)
18	D2	*Je prens engrè* = 1547_9, no. 1: Clemens non Papa
19	D2^v	*O sio potessi donna* (RISM 1541_9, p. 19: Berchem)
20	D3^v	*Frisque & gailliard* (ClemensO X, 17: Clemens non Papa)
21	D4^v	*Quand, io pense* (RISM 1541_9, p. 54: Arcadelt)
22	E1^v	*Susanne ung jour* ["Orlandi" in table] (LassoW XIV, 29: Lasso)
23	E3	*Dum transisset Sabbathum* Christian: Plate ["Hollandi" in table] (RISM 1555_8, fol. 8: Christian Hollander)
	E4^v	2a pars *Et valde mane*
24	F2	*Non est bonum hominem esse solum* ["Dressleri" in table] (DressSC, no. 2: Dressler)
25	F3^v	*Veni in hortum meum soror mea* Valentin: Backvart ["Orlandi" in table] (LassoW V, 120: Lasso)
26	G1	*Ave Jesu Christe rex regum* ["Verdelot" in table]
27	G3	*Pass e, mezo*
	G3^v	*La sua Padoana*
	G4	*El suo Saltarello*
	G4^v	*Le Represe*
28	H1	*Pass e, mezo*
	H1^v	*La sua Padoana*
	H2	*El suo Saltarello*
	H2^v	*Le Represe*
29	H3	*Pass e, mezo*
	H3^v	*La sua Padoana*
	H4	*El suo Saltarello*
	H4^v	*Le Represe*
30	I1	*Pass e, mezo*
	I1^v	*La sua Padoana*
	I2	*El suo Saltarello*
	I2^v	*Le Represe*
31	I3	*Passe, mezo*
	I4	*La sua Padoana*
	I4^v	*El suo Saltarello*
32	K1	*Passe, mezo* = 1568_7, no. 119a
	K2	*La sua Padoana*
	K2^v	*El suo Saltarello* = 1568_7, no. 119b
33	K3	*Pass e, mezo*
	K3^v	*La sua Padoana*
	K4	*El suo Saltarello*
34	L1	*Pass e, mezo*
	L1^v	*La sua Padoana*
	L2	*El suo Saltarello*
35	L2^v	*La Gamba. Gagliarda* [4]
36	L2^v	*La Rocha el fuso. Gagliarda*
37	L3	*La Traditora. Gagliarda*
38	L3	*Chi passa. Gagliarda*
39	L3^v	*Bel fiore. Gagliarda*
40	L4	*Non dite mai. Gagliarda*
41	L4^v	*Val cerca. Gagliarda* (compare 1568_7, no. 132: "Gailliarda la Royne d'escosse")
42	L4^v	*Il Ciel turchino. Gagliarda*
43	M1	*Gagliarda Cypriana* [5]
44	M1	*Gagliarda Todesca* (compare 1550_5, no. 28: "Gaillarde L'ennuy qui me tourmente")
45	M1^v	*Tantz*
	M1^v	*Sprunck*
46	M2	*Tantz* (compare 1574_5, no. 29: "Ich gieng ein mal spacieren")
	M2	*Sprunck*
47	M2^v	*Tantz* = 1591_{13}, no. 22a
	M2^v	*Sprunck* = 1591_{13}, no. 22b
48	M2^v	*Tantz* = 1591_{13}, no. 41a
	M2^v	*Sprunck* = 1591_{13}, no. 41b

49	M3	*Tantz*
	M3	*Sprunck*
50	M3	*Tantz* = 1591_{13}, no. 32a
	M3	*Sprunck* = 1591_{13}, no. 32b
51	M3^{v}	*Tantz. Almande damour*
52	M4	*Tantz. Matazina*

[1] This copy was in H:BA (see GomM, p. 38).
[2] Mod. ed. in SenflW VII, no. 32h.
[3] Mod. ed. in KosackL, app. III.
[4] Tablature and transcription in SchlechtG, no. 67.
[5] Mod. ed. in DieL, p. 37; on this piece see SchraG.

1573_{4}

FIORINO, GASPARO

LA NOBILTA DI ROMA. / VERSI IN LODE DI CENTO / GENTILDONNE ROMANE / Et le vilanelle à tre voci di Gasparo Fiorino, della Città di Rossano, / Musico dell'Illustrissimo & Reverendissimo Signore / Cardinale di Ferrara. / Intavolate dal Magnifico M. FRANCESCO di Parise / Musico eccellentissimo in Roma. / [Fleuret] / NUOVAMENTE RISTAMPATE. / [Printer's mark] / IN VINEGIA, / APPRESSO GIROLAMO SCOTTO, / M D LXXIII.

44 fols. Each piece is written in mensural notation and, on the facing page in a version for solo lute, in Italian lute tablature. Contents = 1571_{4}.[1]

Copies in: GB:Lcm, I:Fn, I:Rc.

[1] The single difference between this volume and 1571_{4} (aside from minor changes in the title page) is the deletion of the qualifying "mio Signore" after the dedications to nos. 6, 10, and 11.

1573_{5}

TEGHI, PIERRE DE

CANTIONUM GALLICARUM, / ET MOTETTARUM LIBER, AB EXCELLEN/TISSIMO MUSICO PETRO TEGHIO PATAVINO / Ad usum Testudinis elegantissimo concinnatus. / Indicem pagina sequens exhibet. / [Cut of ten performing musicians] / LOVANII. / Excudebat Petrus Phalesius, sibi & Joanni Bellero Bibliopolae Antverpiensi. / M. D. LXXIII.

36 fols. French lute tablature. On fol. Aa1^{v}: table of contents. DraudiusBC, p. 1651, dates this 1563. In the unique copy fols. Dd2 and Dd3, and all folios after Ee4 are missing. Contents = 1547_{9}. All of the compositions are for solo lute.

Copy in: F:T (imperfect).

$[1573]_{6}$

PHALÈSE, PIERRE, PUBLISHER

Petit trésor des danses et branles à quatre et cinq parties des meilleurs autheurs propres à jouer sur tous les estrumenz. A Louvain, chez Pierre Phalèse, libraire juré, l'an 1573.

This volume, now lost, is mentioned in GoovH, no. 221. FétB I, 241, names Maître Antoine Barbe as composer of the pavanes and courantes. The volume contained music for instrumental ensemble *a4* and *a5*.

$[1573]_{7}$

PHALÈSE, PIERRE, AND JEAN BELLÈRE, PUBLISHERS

Selectissima carmina ludenda in Quinterna, cum tripudis & institutione ad arte in eandem. Lovanii apud Petrum Pha[lesiu]s & Antverp. apud Bellerum. 70. & 73.

These two volumes of music for guitar are listed in DraudiusBC, p. 1625; the later volume, presumably a second edition of 1570_{4}, is now lost if it ever existed. Draudius may have been confused by the similarity between the titles of 1570_{4} and 1573_{8}.

1573_{8}

PHALÈSE, PIERRE, AND JEAN BELLÈRE, PUBLISHERS

SELECTISSIMORUM PRO / TESTUDINE CARMINUM LIBER. / Continens optimus aliquot Fantasias, Paduanas, Passomezos & Gaillardas, a Francisco & / Petro Paulo Mediolanensibus, aliique praestantissimis divine Musices / auctoribus, compositas. / [Cut of ten performing musicians] / LOVANII. / Excudebat Petrus Phalesius, sibi & Joanni Bellero Bibliopolae Antverpiensi. / M. D. LXXIII.[1]

40 fols. French lute tablature. Contents = 1546_{20}. This is probably the volume listed in DraudiusBC, p. 1651, as "Petri Pauli pro testud. Lovanii 73." Two of the compositions are for two lutes; the others are for solo lute.

Copies in: F:T, GB:Lbmh.

[1] Facs. of title page in LiuM, p. 90.

$[1573]_9$

PHALÈSE, PIERRE, AND JEAN BELLÈRE, PUBLISHERS

THESAURUS MUSICUS CONTINENS SELECTISSIMA ALBERTI RIPAE, VALENTINI BACFARCI, ET ALIORUM Praestantissimorum Carmina, ad usum Chelys, vel Testudinis accommodata. Quibus adjecta sunt ingeniosae quaedam Fantasiae, Passomezi, Alemandes, Galliardae, Branles, atque id genus caetera, recens in lucem edita. Lovanii. Excudebat Petrum Phalesius, sibi & Joanni Bellero, Bibliopolae Antverpiensi M. D. LXXIII.

GoovH, no. 223, lists this as a first edition of 1574_7 (in French lute tablature, for solo lute). No copies of the volume are known to exist.

1574_1

KARGEL, SIXT

NOVAE, ELE/GANTISSIMAE, GALLICAE, / ITEM ET ITALICAE CANTILENAE, / Mutetae & Passomezo, adjunctis suis Sal/tarellis, mira dulcedine in Testudine ca/nendae: in Tabulaturam per M. Six/tum Kaergel Lautenistam, in no/bilissimae huius artis Ama/toribus gratiam, trans/latae, & typis ex/cusae. / Newe, schöne, und / liebliche Tabulatur auff der Lau/ten zu spilen, von Fantasien, Frantzösi/schen, auch Italianischen stucken, Muteten, Passome/zen: mit ihren angehenckten Saltarellen: durch / M. Sixtum Kärgil Lautenisten, allen di/ser edlen Kunst liebhabenden zu eh/ren und gefallen, in truck / gegeben. / Getruckt zu Strassburg durch Bernhard / Jobin. Anno 1574.

30 fols. Italian lute tablature. The title is placed within an ornamental border. Dedication on fol. *2 headed "Dem Hochwürdigen Fürsten und Herren, Herrn Johan, Erwölten Bischoven zu Strassburg, und Landgraven im Elsass, ec. Meinem gnädigen Fürsten und Herren," and signed "Geben Elsass Zabern, den ersten Januarii, Anno 1574. E. F. G., Underthäniger gehorsamer Diener Sixtus Kargel Lautenist." On fol. $*2^v$: a coat of arms with the heading "INSIGNIA REVERENDISSIMI PRINCIPIS AC DOMINI, D. JOHANNIS, EPISCOPI ARGENTOretensis, ac Landgravii in Alsatia, &c. Mecoenatis mei clementissimi." Fol. *3 = fol. A1. On fol. $G3^v$: cut of a lutenist. On fol. G4: table of contents. MoeDM contains a thematic index of the dances (p. 428) and concordances for them (p. 266). For a possible earlier edition, see $[1569]_4$. All of the compositions are for solo lute.

Copies in: D:Mbs, D:TR, S:Uu.

	fol.	
1	A1	*Fantasia*
2	A2	*Fantasia* (compare 1548_3, no. 18)
3	A3	*Fantasia* = 1571_6, no. 17
4	$A4^v$	*Fantasia*
5	$B1^v$	*Las Voulez Vous* = 1571_6, no. 76b: Lasso
6	B2	*Fleur de quinze ans* (LassoW XII, 43: Lasso)
7	$B2^v$	*Je ne Veulx rien* (LassoW XII, 98: Lasso)
8	$B3^v$	*Bon Jour mon Ceur* (LassoW XII, 100: Lasso)
9	B4	*Le temps pult bien* (LassoW XII, 76: Lasso)
10	$B4^v$	*Quant mon mary* (LassoW XII, 23: Lasso)
11	C1	*Jay Un mary*
12	$C1^v$	*Susann Ung Jour* (LassoW XIV, 29: Lasso)
13	$C2^v$	*Jattens le temps* (LassoW XIV, 48: Lasso)

14 C3 *Est il possibile* (LassoW XIV, 112: Lasso)
15 C3ᵛ *Non e lasso martire* (CW V, no. 8: Rore)
16 D1 *La bella netta [ignuda e bianca mano]* = 1568_7, no. 101: Rore
17 D2 *Si grande la pieta* (RISM 1539_{24}, p. 4: Arcadelt)
18 D3 *Et io qual fui* = 1571_6, no. 108: Lasso
19 D3ᵛ *Napoletanae, Sio Canto*
20 D4 *Madonna mia pieta* (LassoW X, 61: Lasso)
21 D4ᵛ *La cortesia* = 1571_6, no. 92: Lasso
22 E1 *Quanto debbe allegrasse* (compare Vogel: Fontana [1545], no. 20: Fontana)
23 E1 *Letaentur Coeli* (LassoW III, 76: Lasso)
E2 2a pars *Tunc Exultabunt*
24 E3 *Tu deus noster*
25 E3ᵛ *Nuncium vobis fero de supernis* (LassoW V, 9: Lasso)
E4ᵛ 2a pars *Thus Deo mirrham*
26 F1 *Titire tu patulae* (LassoW XIX, 68: Lasso)
27 F2ᵛ *Pasemezo la bella donsella*
F3 *Il suo saltarello*
28 F3ᵛ *Passemezo Zorzy*
F4ᵛ *Il suo saltarello*
29 G1ᵛ *Pasemezo*
G2 *Il suo saltarello*

1574_2

LE ROY, ADRIAN

A briefe and plaine Instruction to set all Musicke of eight / divers tunes in Tableture for the Lute. / With a briefe Instruction how to play on the Lute by Tablature, to conduct and dispose thy / hand unto the Lute, with certaine easie lessons for that purpose. / And also a third Booke containing divers new / excellent tunes. / ALL FIRST WRITTEN IN FRENCH BY / ADRIAN LE ROY, AND NOW TRANS/LATED INTO ENGLISH BY I. Ki. / GENTEL-MAN. / Imprinted at London by James Rowbothome, and are to be / sold in Paternoster row at the signe of the Lute. / ANNO. 1574.[1]

90 fols. French lute tablature and mensural notation. On fol. 1ᵛ: poem entitled "The Bookes verdict." Dedication on fol. 2 headed "To the Right Honorable and my very good Lord the Lord Edward Seamour, Viscount Beauchamp, Erle of Hertford. I. R. wisheth long lyfe, perfect helth, encrease of honour, and endles Felicitie." Dedication on fol. 2ᵛ headed "To my very good Ladie my Ladie the Countesse of Retz," and signed "Your humble servant, Adrian le Roy," reprinted in LauC, p. lvi. On fol. 3: "The Preface of Jacques Gohory. unto the curteous Reader," reprinted in LesLRB, p. 33. On fol. 3ᵛ: "The Preface of the Author." Colophon on fol. 90ᵛ: "Imprinted at London by Jhon Kyngston, for James Robothome. Anno. 1574." This is an English translation of Adrian le Roy's lost instruction book for the lute (see $[1557]_1$ and $[1567]_3$). It is divided into three parts: (1) fols. 1–61, explaining how to set all music of the eight modes in tablature[2]; (2) fols. 62–74, explaining how to play the lute by tablature (part 2 = 1568_3); and (3) fols. 75–90, a collection of compositions in lute tablature (nos. 19–36 and 44 are arranged as songs for solo voice and lute in 1571_2). See below, fols. 62 and 75, for the title pages of the second and third parts. The compositions identified by the superior letter *a* ([a]) are reproduced in Le RoyP. For further information on the volume see CaseyP. Nos. 1–4 are discussed at length in the volume. First the "reche or compass" of each of the voices of the vocal model is given. Then the treble alone is printed in mensural notation and in tablature, followed by the treble with the countertenor, the treble and countertenor with the tenor, and finally all four voices together. Each example concludes with an intabulation "more finelier handeled." Nos. 5–12 are given in tablature only, first in a simpler version, then in a version "more finelier handeled." All of the other compositions are for solo lute.

Copies in: F:Pn, GB:Lbm (imperfect), GB:Ob.

fol.

1 4ᵛ *Quand mon mary* Orlande [Lasso] (LassoW XII, 23)
2 14 *Si le bien qui au plus grand bien* (RISM 1571_1, fol. 2: Arcadelt)

3 22^{v} *Je l'ayme bien* Orlande (LassoW XII, 41)

4 29^{v} *Un doux nennin* Orlande (LassoW XII, 45)

5 38^{v} *En espoir vy* Orlande (LassoW XII, 52)

6 41 *Du corps absent* Orlande (LassoW XII, 55)

7 43^{v} *Trop endurer* Orlande (LassoW XII, 70)

8 46 *Vray dieu disoit* Orlande (LassoW XII, 72)

9 49 *En un lieu* Orlande (LassoW XII, 83)

10 52 *Je ne veux rien* Orlande (LassoW XII, 98) (compare 1571_6, no. 82)

11 55 *Ce faux amour* Orlande (LassoW XII, 103) = 1568_7, no. 83

12 57 *Las voulez vous* Orlande (Lasso XII, 3)

62 Title page: "A brief instruction how to plaie on the Lute by Tablatorie, with / certaine easie lessons for the purpose: gathered together: to the greate commoditie / and pleasure of the learner of the same. By A[drian le] R[oy] [Cut of a lute]"

62^{v} [Cut of Le Roy playing the lute.]

13 66^{v} *The x. Commaundementes [Leve le cueur]* = 1568_3, no. 1

14 67 *Je ne veux plus a mon mal consentir* = 1568_3, no. 2

15 67^{v} [*Musical example*] = 1568_3, no. 3

16 70 [*Musical example*] = 1568_3, no. 4

17 71 *Ce n'est bien ne plaisir* = 1568_3, no. 5: Arcadelt

72^{v} [Tuning diagrams]

18 74 *A little fantesie for the tunyng of the Lute* = 1568_3, no. 6

75 Title page: "The thirde booke for the Lute, conteinyng diverse Psalmes, / and many fine excellente Tunes, sette forthe by A[drian le] R[oy] the aucthour thereof. [Cut of a lute]"

19 76 *Le ciel qui fut* (LesLRB, art. 140, fol. 10: La Grotte)

20 76^{v} *Quand ce beau [printems je voy]* (ExF, p. 60: La Grotte)

21 77 *Las que nous [sommes misérables]* (LesLRB, art. 140, fol. 7: La Grotte)

22 77^{v} *Quand j'esto [libre]* (LesLRB, art. 140, fol. 2^{v}: La Grotte)

23 78 *Mais voyez [mon cher esmoy]* (LesLRB, art. 140, fol. 8: La Grotte)

24 78^{v} *Quand le [gril chante]* (LesLRB, art. 140, fol. 9: La Grotte)

25 79 *Or voy je bien* (LesLRB, art. 140, fol. 5^{v}: La Grotte)

26 79^{v} *Has tu [point veu ce grand vilain]* (LesLRB, art. 171, fol. 17: Le Roy)

27 80 *La terre [nagueres glacée]* (LesLRB, art. 140, fol. 4: La Grotte)

28 80^{v} *Ah dieu [que c'est un estrange]* (LesLRB, art. 140, fol. 17^{v}: La Grotte)

29 81 *Las je neusse [jamais pensé]* (LesLRB, art. 140, fol. 15: La Grotte)

30 81^{v} *Autant qu'on void [aux cieux]* (LesLRB, art. 140, fol. 14^{v}: La Grotte)

31 82 *Tant que j'estoys* (LesLRB, art. 132, fol. 19: La Grotte)

32 82^{v} *Demandes tu [douce ennemie]*[3] (ExF, p. 52: La Grotte)

33 83 *Douce maitresse touche*[4]

34 83^{v} *J'estoys [pres de ma maistresse]*[5]

35 84 *J'ay bien mal choisi*[6] (RISM 1564_8, fol. 7: Nicolas)

36 84^{v} *Ce n'est point [pour t'estrener]*

37 85 *D'un grosier [machelaurier]* (LesLRB, art. 56, fol. 10: Cléreau)

38 85^{v} *The xi. Psalme. I truste in God*[a] (compare PraM, no. 11)

39 86 *The xvii. Psalme. O Lorde give eare to*[a] (compare PraM, no. 17)

40 86^{v} *The xxv. Psalme. I lift my harte to thee*[a] (compare PraM, no. 25)

41 87 *The xxxvi. Psalme. The wicked with his*[a] (compare PraM, no. 36)

42 87^{v} *The Cvii. Psalme. Give thankes*[a] (compare PraM, no. 107)

43 88 *The Cxxx. Psalme. Lorde to thee*[a] (compare PraM, no. 130)

44 88^{v} *Mon coeur, [ma chère vie]* (LesLRB, art. 254, fol. 27: Thessier)

45 89 *Harte opprest*

46	89ᵛ	*The Cxxxvi. Psalme. Praise ye the lorde*[a] (compare PraM, no. 136)
47	90	*The Cxxxvii. Psalme. When as we sat in Babilon*[a] (compare PraM, no. 137)

[1] Facs. of title page in LM I, 541.
[2] Facs. of fol. 8 in SteeleE, fig. 24.
[3] Mod. ed. in LauC, p. lxvi.
[4] Mod. ed. in LauC, p. lxvii.
[5] Mod. ed. in LauC, p. lxviii.
[6] Mod. ed. in LauC, p. lxxi.

1574₃

MERULO, CLAUDIO

IL PRIMO LIBRO / DE RICERCARI DA CANTARE, A QUATTRO VOCI / DI CLAUDIO MERULO DA CORREGGIO / Organista in San Marco dell'Illustrissima Signoria di Venetia. / Novamente composti & dati in Luce. / CON PRIVILEGIO. / LIBRO [Printer's mark] PRIMO / In Venetia Appresso li Figliuoli / di Antonio Gardano. / 1574

Four part books in mensural notation, each of 16 fols. Dedication on fol. A1ᵛ of each part book headed "ILLUSTRIBUS WOLFGANGO BARONI A STUBMBERG, ET GEORGIO KHISL A KHALTEMPRUN," and dated "Venetiis X. Kl. Decembris. MDLXXIIII," reprinted in SartMS, p. 31. Fol. A2 = p. 1. On p. 30: printer's mark. All of the compositions are for instrumental ensemble *a 4*.

Copies in: F:Pn (SAB), I:A (T), I:VEaf (B).

	p.	
1	1	*Ricercar primo*
2	3	*Ricercar secondo*
3	4	*Ricercar Terzo*
4	6	*Ricercar Quinto*[1]
5	8	*Ricercar sesto*
6	9	*Ricercar septimo*
7	11	*Ricercar Octavo*
8	12	*Ricercar Nono*
9	13	*Ricercar Decimo*
10	15	*Ricercar Undecimo*
11	16	*Ricercar Duodecimo*
12	18	*Ricercar Terzodecimo*
13	19	*Ricercar Quartodecimo*
14	20	*Ricercar Quintodecimo*
15	22	*Ricercar Sestodecimo*
16	23	*Ricercar Septimo decimo*
17	24	*Ricercar Octavodecimo*
18	26	*Ricercar Nonodecimo*
19	28	*Ricercar Vigesimo*

[1] There is no "Ricercar Quarto."

[1574]₄

METZLER, BARTHEL

Galliarden.

In 1574 Barthel Metzler received a three-year privilege from Duke Albrecht of Prussia, for whom he was court lutenist. This privilege (see FedM, p. 111) stated that Metzler wanted "etzliche Galiarda so er selbst Componirt, auch neben andern unsern Musicis ein Zeit hern für uns geubet und gebraucht auf anhalten etzlicher gutter leutte den Musicis zum besten uf seinen unkosten in druck verfertigen." The volume, if it was ever printed, has been lost.

1574₅

NEWSIDLER, MELCHIOR

Teutsch Lauten/buch / Darinnenn / kunstliche Muteten, lieb/liche Italianische, Frantzösische, Teüt/sche Stuck, fröliche Teütsche Täntz, Passo e / mezo, Saltarelle, und drei Fantaseien Alles mit / fleiss aussgesetzt, auch artlich und / zierlich Coloriert, / durch / Melchior Newsidler, Bur/ger und Lautenist in / Augspurg. / Getruckt zü Strassburg, durch / Bernhart Jobin, Im Jar. / 1574. / Mit Röm. Key. May. Freyheit, / auff zehen Jar.

56 fols. German lute tablature. The title is placed within an ornamental border (the same border as in 1577₆). Dedication on fol. *2 headed "Der Durchleuchtigsten Hochgebornen Fürstin und Frawen, Frawen Dorothea, Pfalzgräfin bei Rein, Hertzogin in Beiern, Wittiben, der Königreich Denmarck, Schweden und Norwegen, geborne Princessin und Erbin, meiner Genedigsten

Fürstin und Frawen," and signed "Unterthänigst Dienstwilliger, Melchior Newsidler," partly reprinted in EitK, p. 102. On fol. *2v: preface headed "Vorred an den Günstigen Leser," and signed on fol. *3: "Geben und in Truck verfertigt, auch durch mich selbsten Corrigicrt, inn der hochlöblichen Keyserlicher Reichs und Freystat Strassburg, Den 20. Julii, Im Jar nach Christi Jesu unsers lieben Herrn und Heylands Geburt gezelet. 1574., Melchior Newsidler." On fol. *3v: table of contents. On fol. *4v: portrait of Newsidler, with the legend: "Melchior Newsidler. Aetatis suae XXXXIII," and beneath, "Lautenschlagen du edle Kunst, Erfröwest s Hertz und machest gunst."[1] Fol. *5 = fol. A1. For later editions see $[1576]_2$, $[1593]_7$, and $[1596]_{10}$. All of the compositions are for solo lute.

Copies in: A:Wn, D:Dl, D:HEu (imperfect), D:Mbs, D:W, US:Bp.

	fol.	
1	A1	*Benedicta es coelorum* Josquin de pres *a6* (JosqMT, no. 46)
	A3	2a pars *Per illud ave* *a2*
	A4	3a pars *Nunc Mater exora natum*
2	A4v	*Tua est potentia* Joannes Mouton *a5* (RISM 1521_3, no. 14)
3	B1v	*Vita in ligno moritur* Ludwig Senfel *a5* (RISM 1537_1, no. 20)
	B2v	2a pars *Qui prophetice*
	B3	3a pars *Qui Expansis*
4	B4	*Creator omnium* Adrianus Willart *a5* (RISM 1557_3, no. 15)
5	C1	*In te domine speravi* Johan Lupus *a5* (RISM 1535_1, fol. 6v)
	C2v	2a pars *Et propter nomen tuum* (compare 1571_6, no. 157b: "[Quoniam fortitudo mea]")
6	C4	*Si bona suscepimus* Verdalot *a5* (MoralesO I, 274)
7	D2v	*Aspice Domine* Jacquet *a5* (MonteO XXVI, app.)
8	D4v	*Hierusalem luge* Adrianus Kein *a5* (RISM 1532_9, p. 49: Richafort or Lupus)
	E1v	2a pars *Deduc quasi torrentem*
9	E3	*Maria Magdalenae* Clemens non Papa *a5* (RISM 1546_6, fol. 15)
	F1	2a pars *Cito euntes*
10	F2v	*Domine quinque talenta tradidisti mihi* Orlando Lassus *a5*
11	F3v	*Du fond de ma pensee* Orlando di Lassus *a4* (LassoW XVI, 159)
12	F4	*Damour me plauis* [sic][3] Rogier [Pathie] *a4* (PubAPTM XXIII, no. 49)
13	G1	*Frais & galiarte* Clemens non Papa *a4* (ClemensO X, 17)
14	G2	*Ung gai Bergier* Tomas Qriquilon *a4* (RieH II, 462: Crecquillon)
15	G3	*Si natem presces* Thomas Quequilon *a4* (RISM 1554_{22}, no. 25: "Si nattem pres ces yeulx": Crecquillon)
16	G4	*Bon Juor mon Cour* Orlando Lassus *a4* (LassoW XII, 100)
17	G4v	*Quando io Penso al martire* Archadelt *a4* (RISM 1541_9, p. 54)
18	H1v	*Non so per qual cagion* Archadelt *a4* (Vogel: Arcadelt 31 [1539], p. 19)
19	H3	*Il ciel che rado virtu* Archedelt *a4* (RISM 1541_9, p. 49)
20	H3v	*O felici oichi miei* Archadelt *a4* (CW V, 19)
21	H4	*Anchor che col partire* Cipriano Rore *a4* (SCMA VI, 45)
22	I1	*Quanto il mio duol senza conforto sia* Orlando Lassus *a4* (LassoW VIII, 31)
23	I1v	*Bewar mich Herr* Steffan Zirler (D:Rp, MS AR 855, no. 19)
24	I2v	*Was wirt es doch des wunders noch*[4] Ludwig Senfel *a4* (SenflW IV, no. 26)
25	I3v	*Mein fleiss und müh*[5] Ludwig Senfel *a4* (SenflW IV, no. 19)
26	I3v	*Tröstlicher lieb, ich mich stets yeb*[6] Paulus Hoffhamer *a4* (MosPH, p. 86)
27	I4v	*Ich reüw und klag, das ich mein tag* Gregorius Brack *a4* (EDMR XX, no. 121)

28 K1v *Wo Gott der Herr nicht bey uns helt* Orlando Lassus *a4*
29 K1v *Ich gieng ein mal spacieren*[7]
K2 *Volget der Hupffauff*
30 K2 *Ein lieblicher und sehr güter Tantz*
K2v *Volget der Hupffauff*
31 K3 *Der Fuggerin Dantz*[8]
K3 *Volget der Hupffauff*
32 K3 *Die alt Schwiger*
K3v *Volget der Hupffauff*
33 K3v *Wann ich des morgens frü auffsteh*[9]
K3v *Volget der Hupffauff*
34 K4 *Der alten Weiber Tantz*[10]
K4 *Volget der Hupffauff*
35 K4 *Wie möcht ich frölich werden*
K4v *Volget der Hupffauff*
36 K4v *Proficiat ir lieben herren*
L1 *Volget der Hupffauff*
37 L1v *Mein hertz ist frisch, mein gmüt ist frey*
L1v *Volget der Hupffauff*
38 L2 *Beschaffens glück ist unversammpt*
L2 *Volget der Hupffauff*
39 L2v *Der Dorisanen Dantz*[11]
L2v *Volget der Hupffauff*
40 L3 *Mir ist ein feins brauns mägetlin gefallen in meinen sin*
L3 *Volget der Hupffauff*
41 L3v *Passa é mezo La millanesa*[12]
L4 *Il saltarelle*
42 M1 *Passa é mezo Anticho*
M2 *Il saltarelle*
43 M3 *Passa é mezo comune*
M4v *Il saltrelle*
44 N2 *Fantasia* M[elchior] N[ewsidler]
45 N2v *Fantasia* M[elchior] N[ewsidler]
46 N3v *Fantasia super anchor che col partire* M[elchior] N[ewsidler] (compare SCMA VI, 45: Rore)

[1] Facs. of cut in KinsP, p. 134; MGG IX, col. 1407; and ReissmA, p. 205.

[2] The Wolfenbüttel copy once belonged to the organist Christian Erbach (1573–1635). His signature appears on the title page. Bound in with this copy is a manuscript appendix of 33 fols. in German keyboard tablature containing music for solo keyboard: 14 ricercares, five introits (each with a Versus) and one toccata, all by Erbach.

[3] Mod. ed. in KosackL, app. III.

[4] Mod. ed. in SenflW VII, no. 32i.

[5] Mod. ed. in SenflW VII, no. 30g.

[6] Mod. ed. in DTO XXXVII/72, p. 88, and MosPH, p. 89.

[7] Mod. ed. in LB, no. 12, and *Die Laute* V (1921–22), p. 38. Heading on fol. K1v: "Hernach volgen etliche Teutsche Täntz."

[8] Mod. ed. in BruAL, no. 7, and TapS, p. 40.

[9] Mod. ed. in BruS III, no. 103.

[10] Mod. ed. in AntoniK, p. 21, and BöhT II, no. 133.

[11] Mod. ed. in BöhT II, no. 134; melody only in BruD, no. 2.

[12] Heading on fol. L3v: "Hernach volgen Passa è mezo."

1574₆

VIRCHI, PAOLO

IL PRIMO LIBRO DI TABOLATURA / DI CITTHARA DI RICERCATI MADRIGALI / CANZONI NAPOLITANE ET SALTARELLI. / DI PAOLO VIRCHI ORGANISTA BRESCIANO, / All'Illustrissimo & Eccellentissimo Signore, il Signor Ottavio Farnese / Duca di Parma, & di Piacenza. / NOVAMENTE POSTA IN LUCE. / [Printer's mark] / IN VINEGGIA, / Appresso l'Herede di Girolamo Scotto. / M D LXXIIII.

22 fols. Italian tablature for the six-course cittern,[1] and mensural notation. Dedication on fol. 1v (= p. 2) headed "ALL'ILLUSTRISS.mo ET ECCELLENTISS.mo SIGNORE IL SIGNOR OTTAVIO FARNESE Duca di Parma & di Piacenza," and signed "Di Brescia il dì 20. Agosto. 1574. D. V. Eccellenza Illustrissima. devotissimo servitore, Paolo Virchi." On p. 4: preface headed "AI LETTORI." On p. 44: table of contents. The compositions followed by an asterisk are for solo voice (notated in mensural notation) and cittern. No. 12 is for a cittern with 14 strings. The other compositions are for solo six-course cittern.

Copy in: A:Wn.

	p.	
1	5	*Fantasia del primo Tono*
2	7	*Fantasia del quinto Tuono*
3	9	*Non mi tolga il ben mio* Cipriano [de Rore] *a4* (Vogel: Rore 33 [1569], p. 5)
4	10	*Dolce Signoria mia* Lelio Bertani *a4*

5 12 *Appariran per me* Orlando lasso *a4* (LassoW VIII, 27)
6 13 *Quale piu grand'amore* Cipriano Rore *a4* (SCMA VI, 78)
7 15 *Io mi son giovinetta* Ferabosco *a4* (EinIM III, no. 30)
15 2a pars [*Io vo per verdi prati*]
8 16 *Io son ferit'hai lasso* Gianetto da Palestina *a5* (PalW XXVIII, 179)
9 18 *S'ogni mio ben havete* Striggio *a6* (Vogel: Striggio 3 [1566], no. 20)
10 20 *Canzone di Florentio Maschera* *a4* (1584_{10}, no. 2: "Canzon seconda La Martinenga")
11 23 *Canzone di Florentio Maschera* *a4* (1584_{10}, no. 4)
12 26 *Ma tu prendi a diletto* Orlando di lassus ("Per sonar con la citthara da quattordeci corde") (LassoW II, 52: 2a pars of "Fiera stella")
13 28 *Amor mi sforza amar una crudela** Lelio Bertani
14 29 *Come son vivo oime** Paolo Virchi
15 30 *Io vidi solo il fare trato Amore** Lelio Bertani
16 31 *Donna non trovo pace in alcun loco** Lelio Bertani
17 32 *Claudia gentil col tuo si dolce riso** Lelio Bertani
18 33 *Se si vedesse fuore** Paolo Virchi (1571_4, no. 21: Fiorino)
19 34 *Chi vuol veder gigli rose e viole** Lelio Bertani
20 36 *Padouana de la Milanesa*
38 *Saltarello de la Milanesa*
21 39 *Saltarello novo*
22 41 *Saltarello del Mangiavino*
42 *La volta in tenore*

[1] This cittern is tuned D F b g d e.

1574_7

PHALÈSE, PIERRE, AND JEAN BELLÈRE, PUBLISHERS

THESAURUS MUSICUS / CONTINENS SELECTISSIMA ALBERTI / RIPAE, VALENTINI BACFARCI, ET ALIO/rum Praestantissimorum Carmina, ad usum Chelys, vel / Testudinis accommodata. / Quibus adiecta sunt ingeniosae quaedam Fantasiae, Passomezi, Alemandes, Galliardae, Branles, / atque id genus caetera, recens in lucem edita. / [Cut of ten performing musicians] / LOVANII. / Excudebat Petrum Phalesius, sibi & Joanni Bellero, Bibliopolae Antverpiensi / M. D. LXXIIII.[1]

84 fols. French lute tablature. On fol. 1^v: table of contents. For an earlier edition see [$1573]_9$. All of the compositions are for solo lute.

Copies in: F:T, GB:Lbm.

fol.

1 2 *Fantasie* = 1536_9, no. 2: Rippe
2 4 *Fantasie 2* = 1562_{11}, no. 7: Rippe
3 5 *Fantasie 3* (compare 1552_8, no. 5: Rippe)
4 6^v *Fantasie 4* = 1553_9, no. 1: Rippe
5 9 *Fantasie 5* = 1553_9, no. 3: Rippe
6 11 *Fantasie 6* = 1553_9, no. 4: Rippe
7 13 *Fantasie Bacfarc* = 1553_1, no. 1: Bakfark
8 14 *Fantasie* = 1556_1, no. 4: Belin
9 15 *Fantasie* = 1556_1, no. 7: Belin
10 15^v *Fantasie* = 1556_1, no. 9: Belin
11 16^v *Fantasie*[2]
12 18 *Fantasie a3* = 1565_1, no. 1: Bakfark
13 19^v *Si comme espoir* = 1552_8, no. 10: Maillard
14 21 *Je suis desheritée* = 1552_8, no. 7: Lupus or Cadéac
15 22 *Douce memoire* = 1562_{10}, no. 6: Sandrin
16 23 *Il ne se trouve en amytyé* = 1552_8, no. 13: Sandrin
17 25 *Voulant honneur* = 1552_8, no. 16: Sandrin
18 26^v *Fors seullement* = 1562_9, no. 5: Josquin or Févin
19 28 *Damour me plains* = 1554_7, no. 4: Pathie
20 29 *Mon pensement* = 1554_7, no. 5: Gombert

21 30 *La volonté* (RISM 1549_{18}, no. 15: Sandrin)
22 31^v *Mais pourquoy* = 1562_9, no. 11: Sandrin
23 32^v *D'un seul soleil* = 1552_8, no. 9: Janequin
24 34 *Mons & vaux* = 1552_8, no. 14: Sandrin
25 35 *O passi sparsi* = 1555_4, no. 4: S. Festa
26 36 *Or vien ça vien* = 1560_3, no. 19: Janequin
27 37 *Ayant cognu* = 1562_{10}, no. 7: Certon
28 38 *Pleurés mes yeux* = 1545_3, no. 41: Sandrin
29 39 *Martin menoit* = 1562_{10}, no. 11: Janequin
30 40^v *Na vous point veu* = 1554_8, no. 6: "N'avons point veu mal assenée," Le Brun
31 42 *Au temps heureux* = 1562_{10}, no. 13: Arcadelt
32 43 *On en dira ce qu'on voudra* = 1562_{10}, no. 15: Sermisy
33 44 *Si grande la pieta* Archadet = 1553_1, no. 15
34 45 *Il ciel che rado* Arcadet = 1553_1, no. 16
35 46 *L'homme qui n'est point amoureux*
36 46^v *Si purti guardo*[3] = 1568_7, no. 51: Pathie
37 47^v *Soyons yoieulx* Orlando [Lasso] (LassoW XII, 20)
38 48^v *Le temps peult bien* Orlando [Lasso] *a 4* (LassoW XII, 76)
39 49^v *Dieu qui conduis* = 1562_{10}, no. 4: Gentian
40 50^v *Soyons plaisans* *a 4*
41 51 *Cest de vous ô ma valentine*
42 51^v *Tant vous alles douce guillemette* = 1571_6, no. 60: Abran
43 52^v *Tout doulcement*
44 53 *Bon jour mon coeur* (LassoW XII, 100: Lasso)
45 53^v *Un doux nenny* (LassoW XII, 45: Lasso)
46 54^v *Sus prens ton lut*
47 55^v *Quant mon mari* (LassoW XII, 23: Lasso)
48 56 *Pis ne me peult* (RISM 1572_2, fol. 25: Crecquillon)
49 57 *Adieu Anvers*
50 58 *Adieu celle*
51 59 *Faulte d'argent* *a 5* = 1565_1, no. 12: Josquin
52 60^v *Pater peccavi* = 1562_{11}, no. 4: Conseil
61^v 2a pars [*Quanti mercenarii*]
53 62^v *Adiuva me* = 1554_7, no. 10a: Conseil
64 2a pars [*Servus tuus ego sum*] = 1554_7, no. 10b
54 65^v *Benedicta* L. Pieton *a 6* = 1553_1, no. 7a
67^v 2a pars [*Per illud ave*] = 1553_1, no. 7b
55 69 *Pavane La romanesque* = 1553_9, no. 8
56 70^v *Passomezo La milanese. Bassus* = 1566_2, no. 18a
72 *Il suo saltarello con la reprinse* = 1566_2, no. 18b
57 74 *Passomezo Superius*
76 *Gaillarde*
77^v *La Reprinse*
58 78^v *Almande*
59 78^v *Almande*
60 79 *Almande d'Egmont*
61 79 *Almande Bavier*
62 79^v *Almande de Spiers*
63 79^v *Almande Poussinghe*
64 80 *Almande la nonette*
65 80^v *Galliarda Caracossa*
66 81 *Gailliarde Chi passa*
67 81^v *Gailliarde d'Angolesmes*
68 82 *Gaillarde*
69 82^v *Branle d'Arras*
70 82^v *2. Branle*
71 82^v *3. Branle*
72 83 *4. Branle*
73 83 *5. Branle*
74 83 *6. Branle*
75 83^v *Premier Branle de Bourgoinge*
76 83^v *2. Branle*
77 83^v *3. Branle*
78 84 *4. Branle*
79 84 *5. Branle*
80 84 *6. Branle*

[1] Facs. of part of title page in LiuM, p. 86.
[2] Fols. 16^v and 17 are missing from the Troyes copy.
[3] Facs. of fols. 46^v and 47 in LiuM, p. 93 (incorrectly labeled as from 1573_8).

1575_1

AMMERBACH, ELIAS NICOLAUS

Ein New / Kunstlich Tabu/laturbuch, darin sehr gute Mo/teten und lieblich Deutsche Tenores jetziger zeit / vornehmer Componisten auff die Orgel unnd Instrument / abgesetzt, beydes den Organisten unnd der / Jugendt dienstlich. / Mit gantzem fleis zusammen gebracht, / auffs beste colorirt, uberschlagen, corrigirt / und in Druck vorfertiget, Durch / Eliam Nicolaum Ammorbach, / Bürger und Organist in Leip/zig zu Sanct Thomas. / Mit Römischer Keyserlicher• Mayestet / Freyheit auff sechs Jar. / Gedruckt zu Leipzig durch Johan. / Beyer, in verlegung Dietrich Ger/lachs zu Nürmberg. / Im Jar, 1575. / [Cut of performing musicians] [1]

90 fols. German keyboard tablature. The title is placed within an ornamental border. Dedication on fol. *2 headed "Dem Durchleuchtigsten, Hochgebornen Fürsten und Herrn, Herrn Augusto, Hertzogen zu Sachsen, des Heiligen Römischen Reichs Ertzmarschall und Churfürsten, Landgraven in Düringen, Marggraven zu Meissen, unnd Burggraven zu Magdeburg, etc. meinem Gnedigsten Churfürsten und Herrn," and signed on fol. *4 "Geben zu Leipzig den 22. Aprilis, Anno 1575. Ewer Churf. Gnaden unterthenigster Diener Elias Nicolaus Amerbachius Bürger und Organist in Leipzig zu Sanct Thomas." On fol. *4^v: a list of the symbols used to designate the notes, covering the entire gamut of the keyboard, headed "Folget alhie die ordnung des gantzen Claviers, wie es auff Orgeln und Instrumenten gebraucht wird," followed by an explanation of the rhythmic signs, headed "Nun wollen wir ferner anzeigen was die Caracteres für bedeutung, und wie sie in diesem Buch gebraucht werden." On fol. *5 (= fol. 1): Latin poem headed "Lectori Musices Organicae Studioso Sal.," and signed "M. Gregorius Bersmanus F." On fol. 85^v: table of contents. Colophon on fol. 86: "Gedruckt zu Leipzig, durch Johan. Beyer, in verlegung Dietrich Gerlatzen zu Nürmberg. Im Jar, M. D. Lxxv." In the following inventory, the composer's initials or abbreviated names are resolved the first time they appear only. All of the compositions are for solo keyboard.

Copies in: A:Wgm, D:Mbs, GB:Lbm.[2]

	fol.	
1	1^v	*In principio erat Verbum*[3] Orlandi [Lasso] (LassoW XV, 8)
	4	2a pars *Fuit homo missus à DEO a4*
	5^v	3a pars *In propria venit a6*
2	8^v	*Angelus ad Pastores ait* Orlandi *a5* (LassoW III, 139)
3	9^v	*Oculi omnium in te sperant domine* Orlandi (LassoW VII, 122)
	11^v	2a pars *Justus dominus in omnibus*
4	12^v	*Confitemini domino* Orlandi (LassoW VII, 131)
	13^v	2a pars *Narrate omnia mirabilia*
5	15^v	*In me transierunt irae tuae* Orlandi (LassoW IX, 49)
6	17^v	*Surexit pastor bonus* Orlandi *a4* (LassoW V, 57)
7	19^v	*Amen dico vobis* Orlandi *a4* (LassoW I, 119)
8	21	*Si quis me diligit sermonem meum servabit*[4] (RISM 1555_{10}, no. 37: Ville Font)
9	22^v	*Maria Magdalena* Cl[emens] non pa[pa] (RISM 1546_6, fol. 15)
	25^v	2a pars *Cito euntes*
10	27^v	*Adesto dolori meo* Cl. non pa. (RISM 1553_{13}, fol. 7)
	28^v	2a pars *Interiora mea*
11	31	*Beati omnes qui timent dominum* Orl. (LassoW VII, 136)
	32^v	2a pars *Ecce sic benedicetur homo*
12	33^v	*Omnia quae fecisti nobis domine* Orlan. (LassoW VII, 127)
13	35^v	*Ego dormio & cor meum vigilat*
	38	2a pars *Anima mea liquefacta est*
14	39^v	*Non auferetur sceptrum, &c.* Jacob. Meiland (RISM 1564_3, no. 38)
	41^v	2a pars *Lavabit in vino stolam suam a6*
15	43	*Gaudete filiae Jerusalem* Jacob. Meiland (MeiC, no. 17)

16 46 *Pater noster qui es in coelis* *a6* (RISM 1568_3, p. 205: Formellis)

17 48v *Si me tenes* Thomas Crequil[lon] *a6* (RISM 1545_{14}, fol. 14)

18 51 *Divitias & paupertatem ne dederis mihi* Jachet (RISM 1558_4, no. 15)

19 53 *Nos autem gloriari oportet* *a6* (RISM 1568_4, p. 267: Wilhelmus Formellis)

20 56 *Sussanna [se videns]* *a6* (compare CH:Bu, MS F.X. 21, fol. 73)

21 59 *Sequitur praeambulum primi thoni in G b molle*[5]

22 59v *Justus non conturbabitur* Mathias Gastritz *a5* (GastN, no. 2)

60v 2a pars *Noli aemulari in malignantibus* *a5*

23 62 *Non est bonum* Dresleri (DressSC, no. 2)

24 64 *Dum complerentur dies Pentecostes* (RISM 1538_2, fol. 23: Arcadelt)

25 66 *Cum sancto spiritu in gloria DEI patris, Amen*

26 66v *Venit vox de coelo* Cle. non pa. (RISM 1559_1, no. 49)

69 2a pars *Respondit miles*

27 70v *Vater unser im Himelreich* Orlan. (LassoW XVIII, 1)

28 71v *Frölich zu sein* Orlandi (LassoW XVIII, 38)

29 72v *Im Meyen hört man die Hanen kröen* Orlan. (LassoW XVIII, 24)

30 74 *Der Mey bringt uns die Blümlein viel* Orlan. (LassoW XVIII, 75)

31 74v *Vor zeiten war ich lieb und werd* Orlan. (LassoW XVIII, 16)

32 74v *Willig und trew* Orlan. (LassoW XVIII, 80)

33 75v *Ich weis ein hübsches Frewlein* Orlan. (LassoW XVIII, 91)

34 76v *Es jagt ein Jeger vor dem Holtz* Orlan. Di las. (LassoW XVIII, 88)

35 77v *Ich weis mir ein festes gebawtes Hauss* [Antonio] Scandel[lo] = 1571_1, no. 85

36 78v *Den liebsten Buhlen den ich hab* Scan. (ScanL, no. 2)

37 80 *Gros lieb hat mich umbfangen* Scandel. (ScanL, no. 5)

38 80v *Kein lieb ohn leid, mag mir nicht wiederfahren* Antho. Scandelli (ScanL, no. 7)

39 82 *Von deinet wegen bin ich hie* Scan. (ScanL, no. 12)

40 83 *Ich stund an einem Morgan* Ivonis de vento (VentoN, no. 26)

41 83v *Es flog ein kleines Waldvögelein* Ivo de vent. (VentoN, no. 25)

[1] Facs. of title page in FrotO, after p. 144.

[2] A copy was in D:Bds.

[3] Most of the prima pars is pr. with the vocal model in WustM, p. 370.

[4] Composer named in table of contents as "Orlan[do di Lasso]."

[5] Mod. ed. in WustM, p. 220. No. 21 is not numbered in the original; therefore nos. 22–41 in this inventory do not correspond with the original numeration.

$[1575]_2$

KARGEL, SIXT.

Renovata Cythara . . . Argentorati 1575.

This volume, now lost, is listed in DraudiusBC, p. 1622. Probably the contents = 1578_4 (for solo cittern).

1575_3

KARGEL, SIXT, AND JOHAN DOMINICO LAIS

Toppel Cythar. / NOVA EAQUE ARTIFICIOSA ET VALDE / COMMODA RATIO LUDENDAE CYTHARAE, / quam inventores sive compilatores Duplam Cytharam vocant: aliquot ele/gantissimis, Italicis, Germanicis, & Gallicis cantionibus & sal/tationibus, exempli vice ornata. / Neue und Künstliche, und noch nie vil ersehene oder ubliche / Tabulatur auf die Lautengemäse Toppel Cythar mit sechs Cohren, von etlichen / Italianischen, Teutschen und Frantzösischen Lidern und Tänzen: baides für sich selbs volkommen/lich, und auch zu andern Instrumenten dinstlich zuspilen und / zugebrauchen:

Toppel Cythar.

NOVA EAQVE ARTIFICIOSA ET VALDE COMMODA RATIO LVDENDÆ CYTHARÆ, quam inventores sive compilatores Duplam Cytharam vocant: aliquot ele-gantissimis, Italicis, Germanicis, & Gallicis cantionibus & sal-tationibus, exempli vice ornata.

Neue vnd Künstliche / vnd noch nie vil ersehene oder vbliche Tabulatur auf die Lautengemäse Toppel Cythar mit sechs Cohren / von etliche Italianischen / Teutschen vnd Französischen Lidern vnd Tänzen: baides für sich selbs volkommenlich / vnd auch zu andern Instrumenten dinstlich zuspilen vnd zugebrauchen: gestelt

Durch

Sixtum Kärgel Lautenisten /

Vnd

Johan Dominico Lais.

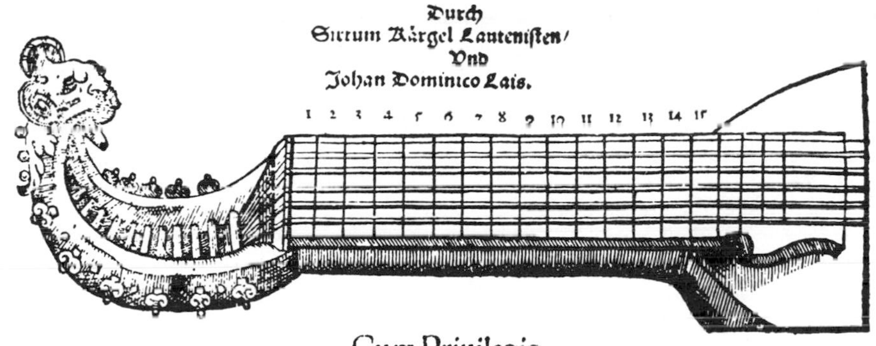

Cum Priuilegio.

Bei Bernhard Jobin zu Strasburg/ Anno 1575.

Title page of 1575_3

gestelt / Durch / Sixtum Kärgel Lautenisten, / Und / Johan Dominico Lais. / [Cut of the neck of a cittern] / Cum Privilegio. / Bei Bernhard Jobin zu Strasburg, Anno 1575.

36 fols. Italian tablature for the six-course cittern.[1] Dedication on fol. 2 headed "Den Wolgebornen Herrn, Herrn Eberharden und Arnolden, baiden Gebrüdern, Graven zu Manderschaid und Blankenhaim, Herrn zu Jungkerrot, unsern Gnädigen Herrn," and signed "Geben zu Strasburg den 3. Martii.: Anno, 1575. Unterthänige Williggeflissene Diner. Sixt Kärgel Lautenist, Und Johan Dominico Lais." On fol. 2ᵛ: rules for tuning the instrument, in Latin and German. On fol. 3 (= fol. A1): two "exempla," illustrating the tuning. On fol. I2ᵛ: table of contents. For an earlier edition, see $[1569]_3$; for a later edition, see 1578_5. All of the compositions are for solo cittern.

Copy in: CH:Zz.

	fol.	
1	A1	*Fantasia* = 1545_3, no. 2 (for lute solo)
2	A1ᵛ	*Fantasia*
3	A2	*Oyes aman*[2]
4	A2ᵛ	*Quand je Cogneu* (compare RISM $[1539]_{20}$, fol. 20: Sandrin)
5	A3	*Par bien Servir*[3]
6	A3ᵛ	*Les yeux [qui me sceurent]* (RISM 1554_{26}, no. 16: Arcadelt)
7	A4	*De tant de peine* (RISM 1567_4, fol. 14: Arcadelt)
8	A4ᵛ	*Qui Veult du ciel* (RISM 1569_{13}, no. 5: Arcadelt)
9	B1ᵛ	*Susan ung Jour* (LevyS, p. 403: Didier Lupi Second)
10	B2ᵛ	*Bon Jour mon coeur* (LassoW XII, 100: Lasso)
11	B3	*Mon coeur se recomande a Vous* (LassoW XIV, 15: Lasso)

12 B4 *Pis ne me peult venir* (RISM 1572_2, fol. 25: Crecquillon)
13 B4v *Susan ung Jour* Orlando [Lasso] (LassoW XIV, 29)
14 C2 *Non e lasso Martire* (CW V, no. 8: Rore)
15 C3 *Os, io potessi donna* (RISM 1541_9, p. 19: Berchem)
16 C4v *Se pur ti guardo* (RISM 1570_8, p. 46: Pathie)
17 D1 *Bona sera*
18 D1v *Audieu singnora*
19 D2 *Madonna mia pieta* (LassoW X, 61: Lasso)
20 D3 *Tu sai madonna* (LassoW X, 63: Lasso)
21 D3v *La Cortesia*[4] (LassoW X, 66: Lasso)
22 D4 *Chi Vol vedere*
23 D4v *Bewar mich Herr* (D:Rp, MS AR 855, no. 19: Zirler)
24 E1v *Ach Herre Got, meins Heils ein Horn*
25 E2v *Ich schwing mein horn ins Jamerthal* (SenflW V, no. 44: Senfl)
26 E3 *Gelobet sei Gott*
27 E4 *Pass e mezo milanese*
E4 *Il suo saltarello*
28 E4v *Passemezo Italiae*
F1 *Il suo saltarello*
29 F1v *Pass e mezo altra modo*
F2v *Il suo saltarello*
30 F3 *Pass e mezo Zorzy*
F3v *Il suo saltarello*
31 F4 *Pass e mezo comune*
F4v *Il suo saltarello*
32 G1 *Gaiarde chi passa per questa strada* (compare AzzaiV, no. 2: Azzaiolo)
G1 *Chi Passa altra modo*
33 G1v *Gaiarda Era di magio*
34 G2 *Gaiarda la Caracossa*
35 G2v *Gaiarda Milanessa*
36 G3 *Secunda milanesse*
37 G3v *Tertia milanessa*[5]
38 G4 *Quarta Milanessa*
39 G4v *Quinta milanesa*
40 H1 *Almanda Teutscher Tanz*
H1 *Reprinse. Der nach Tanz*
41 H1v *Almanda Teutscher Tanz*
H1v *RePrinse. Der nach Tanz*
42 H2 *Almanda Teutscher Tanz*
H2v *Reprinse. Der nach Tanz*
43 H3 *Almanda Imperiala*
H3 *RePrinse. Der nach Tanz*
44 H3 *Almanda Teutscher Tanz*
H3v *Reprinse. Der nach Tanz*
45 H4 *Almanda Teutscher Tanz*
H4v *Reprinse. Der nach Tanz*
46 H4v *Almanda Teutscher Tanz*
I1 *Reprinse. Der nach Tanz*
47 I1v *Almanda Teutscher Tanz*
I1v *Reprinse. Der nach Tanz*
48 I1v *Almanda Teutscher Tanz*
I2 *Reprinsa. Der nach tanz*

1 This cittern is tuned B G D g d e.

2 Not related to RISM 1554_{27}, fol. 7: "Oyez amants," Entraigues.

3 Not related to RISM 1545_{12}, no. 11.

4 Facs. of fol. D3v in WolfMS, no. 71.

5 Pseudo-facs. and mod. ed. in WolfHN II 141–142, after 1578 ed.

[1575]₄

VIOLA, RAPHAEL

Raphaelis Violae Carminum pro Testudine liber, continens fantasia mutetas, Gallicas & Italicas Cantiones. Lovanii. 1575.

This volume of music for solo lute, now lost, is listed in BasseC; DraudiusBC, p. 1651; and GoovH, no. 257. See also [1580]₄.

1575₅

RODIO, ROCCO

LIBRO / DI RICERCATE A / QUATTRO VOCI DI ROCCO RODIO / CON ALCUNE FANTASIE SOPRA / VARII CANTI FERMI NOVAMENTE / POSTI IN LUCE. / [Printer's mark] / IN NAPOLI, Con Privilegio, Appresso Gioseppe Cacchio / dall'Aquila. M D LXXV.

49 fols. Keyboard partitura. Dedication on fol. 1v (= p. 2) headed "MOLTO MAGNIFICO SIGNOR IL SIGNOR GIO Battista Turbolo da Napoli." The compositions identified by the superior

letter *a* ([a]) are reprinted in RodioR. All of the compositions are for solo keyboard.

Copy in: I:Fc.

	p.	
1	3	*Ricercata prima*[a]
2	16	*Seconda ricercata*[a]
3	29	*Terza ricercata*[a]
4	47	*Quarta ricercata*[a]
5	57	*Quinta ricercata*[a]
6	64	*Iste confessor* (compare LU, p. 1177)
7	75	*Ave maris Stella* (compare LU, p. 1259)
8	83	*Salve Regina* (compare LU, p. 276)
9	90	*La mi re fa mi re*[a] (compare $148?_1$, no. 10: "La Spagna")

$[1575]_6$

PHALÈSE, PIERRE, AND JEAN BELLÈRE, PUBLISHERS

Des chansons réduitz en tabulature de lut à deux, trois et quatre parties avecq une briève et familière introduction pour entendre et apprendre par soy-mesmes à jouer dudict lut. Livre premier. A Louvain chez Pierre Phalèse libraire juré. Et en Anvers chez Jean Bellere. L'an MDLXXV.

This volume of music for solo lute (in French lute tablature), now lost, is listed in GoovH, no. 237. DraudiusBE, p. 212, dates it 1576. Probably the contents = 1545_3.

$[1575]_7$

PHALÈSE, PIERRE, PUBLISHER

Hortulus cytharae. Louvain, Pierre Phalèse.

This volume of music for solo cittern (in French cittern tablature), now lost, is listed in an inventory of the firm of Plantin in Antwerp. See StellMB, p. 24. The contents were probably the same as 1570_3. The same inventory enters for this year a "Jardinet de cistre" which is apparently a different work, perhaps the same as $[1592]_{15}$.

1575

DOUBTFUL WORKS

1. SeiffG, p. 35, erroneously dates Andrea Gabrieli, *Ricercari . . . Composti & Tabulati per ogni sorte di Stromenti da Tasti . . . Libro Secondo*, 1575. The volume is listed in this bibliography as 1595_3.

1576_1

DAZA, ESTEBAN

LIBRO DE MUSICA / en cifras para Vihuela, intitulado el / Parnasso, en el qual se hallara toda diversidad de Musica, assi Mo/tetes, Sonetos, Villanescas, en lengua Castellana, y otras cosas, / como Fantasias del Autor, hecho por Estevan Daça, ve/zino de la muy insigne villa de Valladolid, diri/gido al muy Illustre señor Licenciado / Hernando de Habalos de Soto / mayor del Consejo su/premo de su Ma/gestad, &c. / Impresso por Diego Fernandez de Cordova, Impressor / de su Magestad. Año de M. D. Lxxvii. / Esta tassado en [in manuscript in Madrid copy: 130] Maravedis.

120 fols. Italian lute tablature. On fol. *1[v]: royal printing privilege signed "Fecha en S. Lorenço a xxix. dias del mes de Junio, de mil y quinientos y setenta y cinco años. Yo el Rey. Por mandado de su Magestad Antonio de Erasso." Dedication on fol. *2 headed "Al muy Illustre Señor, el Señor Licenciado Hernando de Habalos de Soto mayor del Consejo supremo Estevan Daça su servidor. P. F. & S. desea." On fol. *2[v]: poem in Latin headed "De Stephano Dazza Colloquium inter Mussas & Appollinem," followed by a note stating that the easy pieces will be marked with an *F* (*facil*), and the difficult ones with a *D* (*dificil*). On fols. *3–*4: instructions for reading the tablature. On fols. *4–*4[v]: author's corrections. Fol. *5 = fol. 1. On fols. 114[v]–115[v]: table of contents. Colophon on fol. 116: "Fue impresso el presente Libro hecho por Estevan Daça en la muy Noble villa de Valladolid por Diego Fernandez de Cordova Impressor de su Magestad, acabose a doze dias del mes de Abril año de mil y quinientos

y setenta y seys." The volume is divided into three books, each of which has its own title page, reproduced in the inventory below. The compositions identified by the superior letter *a* ([a]) are reprinted in MorL II, 230–251. The compositions in Book I and the last two compositions in Book III are for solo vihuela. The compositions in Book II and all but the last two in Book III are for voice (notated in ciphers in the tablature) and vihuela.

Copies in: D:Mbs, E:Mn (two copies), P:Pm.[1]

Comiença el libro primero, el qual / trata de muchas Fantasias de Estevan Daça, / a tres y a quatro. Van al principio los ochos tonos a quatro, por su or/den, y despues van otras fantasias por differentes tonos, y en to/das las de a quatro va señalada la voz del Tenor con / unos puntillos, para que si quisieren la can/ten: y en las de a tres va señalada la voz del Contra alto.

	fol.	
1	1	[*Fantasia por el primer tono*]
2	2v	*Fantasia por el segundo tono*
3	4	*Fantasia por el tercero tono*
4	6	*Fantasia por el quarto tono*
5	7	*Fantasia por el quinto tono*
6	9	*Fantasia por el sexto tono*
7	10	*Fantasia por el septimo tono*
8	11	*Fantasia por el octavo tono*
9	12v	*Fantasia a tres, por el primer tono*[2]
10	14	*Fantasia a tres, por el quinto tono*
11	15v	*Fantasia a tres, por el septimo tono*
12	16v	*Fantasia a tres, por el octavo tono*
13	18v	*Fantasia por el primer tono a quatro*[3]
14	20	*Fantasia por el primero tono, por Gsolreut a quatro*
15	21v	*Fantasia por el segundo tono a quatro por G sol re ut*
16	23	*Fantasia a quatro por el quarto tono por a la mi re*
17	24v	*Fantasia por el sexto tono* [*a quatro*]
18	26	*Fantasia por el primero tono a quatro*
19	27	*Siguense unas fantasias que llevan ciertos passajes para desemvoluer las manas.* [*por el primer tono*][4]
20	29v	*Fantasia de passos largos para desemvoluer las manos.* [*por el mismo tono*]
21	31	*Fantasias de passos largos, para desemvoluer las manos.* [*por el quinto tono*]
22	33	*Fantasias de passos largos, para desemvoluer las manos.* [*por el octavo tono*]

Comiença el segundo Libro de Mu/sica en Cifras para Vihuela, el qual contiene / Motetes a quatro y a cinco, de diversos Autores, en todos los quales / se canta la voz que se señala con unos puntillos, y tambien / se señalan las Claves en los trastes que se re/quiere conforme al termino. / M. D. LXXVI. (fol. 35)

23	35v	*Nigra sum sed formosa* Crecquillon *a 5* (RISM 1555_8, fol. 6)
24	38	*Dum deambularet dominus* Crecquillon *a 4* (RISM 1564_5, no. 11)
	40v	2a pars *Vocem tuam audivi*
25	43	*In me transierunt* Maillard *a 4* (RISM 1559_2, no. 26)
26	45v	*O beata Maria* Pedro Guerrero *a 4* (ElúsA, p. 83)
	47	2a pars *Accipe quod*
27	49	*Ave Maria*[5] Francisco Guerrero *a 4* (GuerrM)
28	52	*Deus Deus meus* Simon Buleau *a 4* 2a pars of "Domine ne longe facias" (BoylM, no. 1b)
29	54v	*Genuit puerpera* Simon Buleau *a 4* 2a pars of "O magnum mysterium" (BoylM, no. 2b)
30	57	*Absterget Deus* Simon Buleau *a 4* (BoylM, no. 7)
	59v	2a pars *Non esurient*
31	62	*Turba multa* Simon Buleau *a 4* (BoylM, no. 8b: 2a pars of "Occurrunt turbe")
32	64v	*Respexit Helias* Simon Buleau *a 4* (BoylM, no. 10)
33	66v	*Tulerunt ergo fratres* Simon Buleau *a 4* (BoylM, no. 4b: 2a pars of "Videns Jacob")
34	69	*Angelus domini* Vasurto (= Basurto) *a 4*
35	71	*Quem dicunt homines* Richafort *a 4* (RISM 1532_{10}, no. 19)

Comiença el Libro tercero de Mu/sica en cifras para Vihuela, el qual con/tiene un Romance, y algunos Sonetos y Villanescas en letra / Castellana, y Villancicos, en todo lo qual se señala / la voz con unos puntillos: y al cabo del / ay dos canciones Francesa: / tañidas sin can/tar. / M. D. LXXVI. (fol. 74)

36 74v *Enfermo estaba Antioco*[6] Romance *a 4*
37 75 *Ay mudo soy hablar no puedo* Pedro Ordonez Soneto *a 4*
38 77v *Ay fortuna crudel* Pedro Ordonez Soneto *a 4*
78 2a pars *Lebantaron muy alto*
39 79 *Escrito esta en mi alma* Soneto *a 4* (text by Garcilaso)
80v 2a pars *Yo no nasci sino para querer*
40 81v *Quan bienaventurado* Cancion *a 4* (MME IX, 54: Rodrigo de Cevallos; text by Garcilaso)
41 83 *Prado verde*[a][7] Francisco Guerrero Villanesca *a 4* (MME VIII, 104)
42 84 *Pues ya las claras fuentes*[a] Zaballos (= Cevallos) Villanesca *a 4*
43 85v *Ay de mi sin ventura*[a] Nabarro (= Juan Navarro) Villanesca *a 4* (MME VIII, 83)
44 87v *Adios verde ribera*[a] [Francisco] Guerrero Villanesca *a 4* (GuerrO II, no. 37)
45 89 *Nos vez amor* Nabarro (= Juan Navarro) Villanesca *a 4* (MME VIII, 83: anon.)
46 90v *Esclareçida Juana* Villalar Villanesca *a 4* (MME IX, 121: Francesco Guerrero)
47 91v *Duro mal terrible llanto* Caballos (= Cevallos) Villanesca *a 4* (MME IX, 72: anon.)
93 *Dime manso viento*[a] Caballos (= Cevallos) Villanesca *a 4* (MME IX, 75: anon.)
49 94 *Callese ya Mercurio* Villanesca *a 4*
50 95v *Nunca mas veran mis ojos* Villancico *a 3*
51 96v *Dame acogida en tu hato*[a] Villancico viejo *a 3*
52 97 *A tierras agenas* Villancico *a 3*
53 99 *Que razon podeys vos tener* Nabarro (= Juan Navarro) Villancico *a 4*
54 100v *Alegrias alegrias* Villancico *a 4*
55 102v *Gritos dava la morenica*[a] Villancico *a 4*
56 103v *Serrana donde dormistes*[a] Villancico *a 4*
57 104v *Zagaleja la de lo verde*[a] Villancico *a 4*
58 107v *Quien te hizo Juan pastor*[a] Villancico *a 4*
59 108v *Quando las desdichas mias* Villancico *a 4*
60 109v *Mira Juan lo que te dixe*[a] Villancico *a 4*
61 110 *Vostre rigueur* Crecquillon Cancion Francesa *a 3* (RISM 1569_{11}, p. 9)
62 112 *Je prens en gre* Cancion Francessa *a 4* (ClemensO X, 14: Clemens non Papa)

[1] One of the Madrid copies is defective. WolfH II, 114, lists a copy in E:E, and Professor John Ward reports that a copy was in the Biblioteca nacional in Lisbon, but I have been unable to verify either copy.

[2] Heading on fol. 12v: "Siguense ciertas Fantasias a tres, y señalase la voz de en medio con unos puntillos que es el alto y esta primera es del primer tono, señalase la clave de fefaut tercera en primer Traste."

[3] The complete title of no. 13 is "Fantasia por el primero tono a quatro, señalase la clave de Fefaut quarta en vacio, y señalase la voz del Tenor con unos puntillos, y en todas las demas que se siguen."

[4] Mod. ed. in PujBG, no. 1067.

[5] Facs. of fol. 49 in SubHME, p. 213.

[6] Mod. ed. in DazaE; EC, pt. I, vol. IV, p. 2024 and PedCP III, 182.

[7] Mod. ed. in EC, pt. I, vol. IV, p. 2004.

$[1576]_2$

NEWSIDLER, MELCHIOR

Il primo libro intabulatura di liuto, ove sono Madrigali, Motetti, canzon francesi, &c. in Venetia, appresso di Antonio Gardano.

This volume of music for solo lute, now lost, is mentioned in FétB VI, 307, as a later edition, in Italian tablature of 1574_5. See also $[1595]_7$ and $[1596]_{10}$.

1576_3

VALENTE, ANTONIO

INTAVOLATURA DE CIMBALO / RECERCATE / FANTASIE ET CANZONI / FRANCESE DESMINUITE / CON ALCUNI TENORI BALLI ET VARIE / SORTE DE CONTRAPONTI. / LIBRO PRIMO. / De M. Antonio Valente Cieco, Organista della Venerabile Chiesa / Di Sant'Angelo à Nido, di Napoli. / DA LUI COMPOSTE, INTAVOLATE, ET POSTE IN LUCE. / [Printer's mark] / Con Licenza, & Privileggio, per Anni diece. / IN NAPOLI. / Appresso Giose ppe Cacchio dall'Aquila, / M. D. LXXVI.

46 fols. Spanish keyboard tablature using numbers. On fol. $*1^v$: dedication to Gio. Geronimo Capece. On fol. *2: letter to the reader from Frat'Alberto Mazza. On fol. $*2^v$: explanation of the notation with a cut of a harpsichord. On fol. $*3^v$: instructions in the rudiments of music. Fol. *5 = p. 1. On fol. 46^v: table of contents followed by the register of signatures, imprimatur, and colophon: "REGISTRO. ABCDEFGHIKL. Tutti sono duerni eccetto L, che è Terno. Imprimatur. Laelius Sessa. Io Franciscus Lombardus. NEAPOLI Apud Giosephum Cacchium. 1575." A facsimile of one page is printed in CollaerAH, p. 62. For further information see BurnsAV and CaravI, which includes the complete dedication, letter to the reader and explanation of the notation, and a facsimile of the title page and p. 6. All of the compositions are for keyboard solo.

Copy in: I:Nn.

	p.	
1	1	*Fantasia del primo tono*[1]
2	6	*Recercata del primo tono a cinque con la quinta parte in canone al unisono del tenore*[2]
3	11	*Recercata del primo tono*
4	15	*Recercata del terzo tono*
5	20	*Recercata del sesto tono a quattro voce con lo basso in canone a l'ottava del contralto*
6	23	*Recercata del septimo tono*
7	27	*Recercata dell'ottavo tono*
8	31	*Salve Regina*
9	34	*Pisne disminuita* (RISM 1572_2, fol. 25: "Pis ne me peult venir," Crecquillon)
10	43	*Chi la dirra* (RISM 1572_2, fol. 2: "Qui la dira," Willaert)
11	47	*Sortemeplus de Filippo de Monto con alcuni fioretti d'Antonio Valente*
	49	*Sortemeplus disminuita*
12	54	*Tenore de zefiro con dodeci mutanze* [Passamezzo moderno]
13	62	*Tenore del passo e mezo* [*antico*] *con sei mutanze*
14	67	*Lo ballo dell'intorcia con sette mutanze* [Passamezzo antico]
15	70	*Bascia Flammignia*[3] (compare $148?_1$, no. 10: "La Spagna")
16	71	*Tenore grande alla Napolitana con sei mutanze*
17	75	*La Romanesca con cinque mutanze*[4]
18	78	*Gagliarda Napolitana con molte mutanze*
19	82	*Gagliarda Lombarda*
20	82	*Ballo Lombardo*[5]

[1] Facs. of p. 4 in ApelN, pl. 16, and MGG IX, col. 1654.

[2] Facs. of p. 6 and mod. ed. of no. 2 in CaravI, p. 506.

[3] In the original the pages are incorrectly numbered beginning with p. 70, which reads "80." The pagination is corrected in this inventory.

[4] Mod. ed. in KastnSI, no. 3.

[5] Mod. ed. in CaravI, p. 505.

1576

DOUBTFUL WORKS

1. DraudiusBE, p. 212, dates *Des chansons réduitz en tabulature lut . . . Livre premier* (Louvain, Pierre Phalèse, and Antwerp, Jean Bellère), 1576. The volume is listed in this bibliography as $[1575]_6$.

2. The Leipzig copy of 1577_7 (Bernhard Schmid, *Zwey Bücher. Ein Neuen Kunstlichen Tabulatur auff Orgel und Instrument*) is dated 1576.

3. DraudiusBC, p. 1621, dates Giorgio Mainerio, *Il Primo Libro de Balli a Quatro Voci*, 1576. The volume is listed in this bibliography as 1578_8.

[1577]₁

FABRICIUS, BERNHARD

Bernhard Fabricii tabulaturae organis & instrumentis inservientes, Argent. apud Jobin. 77.

This volume of solo keyboard music, now lost, is listed in DraudiusBC, p. 1647, and in FétB III, 174.

1577₂

LASSO, ORLANDO DI

NOVAE ALIQUOT ET ANTE / HAC NON ITA USITATAE AD DUAS VO/ces Cantiones suavissimae, omnibus Musicis summè uti/les: nec non Tyronibus quàm ejus artis pe/ritioribus summopere in/servientes. / Authore / ORLANDO DI LASSO, / Illustrissimi Bavariae Ducis ALBERTI Mu/sici Chori Magistro. / Summa diligentia compositae, correctae, et nunc primùm in lucem aeditae. / Monachii excudebat Adamus Berg. / Cum gratia & privilegio Caes: Maiestatis. / M. D. LXXVII.

Two part books in mensural notation, each of 20 fols. Dedication on fol. 1ᵛ headed "SERENISSIMO ET ILLUSTRISSSIMO PRINCIPI AC DOMINO, DOMINO WILHELMO, COMITI Palatino Rheni, utriusque Bavariae Duci, &c. Domino meo clementissimo," and signed "Monaci 2 Januarii. Anno 1577. Serenissimae ac Illust: Cels: Tuae Perpetuus & addictissimus Orlandus de Lasso," reprinted in LassoW I, x. On fol. 20ᵛ of each part book: table of contents. For later editions see [1577]₃, 1578₆, 1579₄, 1585₆, [1586]₆, 1589₄, [1590]₃, and 1598₈. For editions after 1600 see BoettL. The entire collection is reprinted in HM XVIII–XIX; LassoF; LassoW I; and LassoCDV.[1] Contains 24 compositions *a2*; nos. 1–12 have Latin text; nos. 13–24 are without text and title.

Copy in: D:Mbs.[2]

[1] Eight of the duos are repr. in ZfSM XVIII; nos. 13 and 16 are repr. in DoflS as nos. 14 and 15; no. 13 is repr. in FortI, I, 4; no. 14 is repr. in MU III, app., p. 33; and no. 15 is repr. in MI IV, 8.

[2] A copy was in PL:L.

[1577]₃

LASSO, ORLANDO DI

ORLANDI NOVAE ALIQUOT SUAVISSIMAE CANTIONES 2 VOCUM. Louvain, Pierre Phalèse, 1577.

This volume, now lost, is listed in BoettL, p. 779, after a manuscript catalogue in the Plantin Archives, Antwerp. Contents = 1577₂. The volume contained 24 compositions *a2* in mensural notation; 12 had Latin text, and 12 were without text or title.

1577₄

MALVEZZI, CRISTOFANO

DI CRISTOFANO / MALVEZZI DA LUCCA, MAESTRO / DI CAPPELLA DEL SERENISSIMO / GRAN DUCA DI TOSCANA. / IL PRIMO LIBRO DE RECERCARI / à Quattro Voci, Nuovamente da lui / Composti, & dati in luce. / CAN [Printer's mark] TUS. / IN PERUGIA, / Appresso Pietroiacomo Petrucci, l'Anno, 1577.

Four part books in mensural notation, each of 10 fols. (?). Dedication on fol. 2 headed "Al Molto Illustre Signore Giovanni de Bardi De Conti di Vernio," and signed "Christofano Malvezzi," reprinted in GaspaC IV, 207, and SartMS, p. 32. Fol. 2ᵛ = p. 1. On p. 17: table of contents. The page numbers in the following inventory are taken from the altus part book. All of the ricercares are complete in score in I:Fn, MS Magl. XIX, 107, fols. 38ᵛ–50 (see BecherC, p. 42). All of the compositions are for instrumental ensemble *a4*.

Copy in: I:Bc (A and imperfect ST).

	p.	
1	1	*Ricercar del Terzo Tuono*
2	2	*Ricercar del Secondo Tuono*
3	4	*Ricercar del Secondo Tuono*

4 5 *Ricercar del Primo Tuono*
5 7 *Ricercar del Ottavo Tuono*
6 8 *Ricercar senza unisoni del Duodecimo Tuono*
7 10 *Ricercar del Settimo Tuono*
8 12 *Ricercar del Undecimo Tuono*
9 13 *Ricercar del Primo Tuono* Zazzerino
10 15 *Ricercar del Terzo Tuono*

1577_5

RORE, CIPRIANO DE

TUTTI I MADRIGALI / DI CIPRIANO DI RORE / A QUATTRO VOCI. / SPARTITI ET ACCOMMODATI PER / sonar d'ogni sorte d'Instrumento perfetto, & per / Qualunque studioso di Contrapunti. / Novamente posti alle stampe. / [Printer's mark] / In Venetia Apresso di Angelo Gardano. / 1577.

32 fols. Keyboard partitura. The title is placed within an ornamental border. The texts of the madrigals are not included in this edition. All of the compositions are for solo keyboard.

Copy in: I:A, I:Bc.[1]

fol.
1 1^v *Alla dolc'ombra. Prima stanza* (SCMA VI, 12)
1^v *Non vide'l mondo. Seconda stanza*
2^v *Un lauro. Terza stanza*
2^v *Però [più fermo]. Quarta stanza*
3^v *Selve sassi. Quinta stanza*
3^v *Tanto mi piacque. Sesta stanza*
2 4^v *Signor mio caro* (SCMA VI, 25)
3 4^v *Carita di Signore* (SCMA VI, 28)
4 5^v *Io canterei d'amor* (SCMA VI, 31)
5 6^v *Non è ch'il duol mi scema* (SCMA VI, 34)
6 7^v *La bella netta ignuda* (SCMA VI, 38)
7 7^v *La giustitia immortale* (SCMA VI, 41)
8 8^v *Anchor che co'l partire* (SCMA VI, 45)
9 9^v *Amor ben mi credevo* (SCMA VI, 47)
10 9^v *Come havran fin* (SCMA VI, 51)
11 10^v *Io credea che'l morire* (SCMA VI, 54)
12 11^v *Quel foco* (SCMA VI, 57)
13 11^v *La inconstantia* (SCMA VI, 60)
14 12^v *Donna ch'ornata sete* (SCMA VI, 63)
15 13^v *Di tempo in tempo* (SCMA VI, 67)
16 14^v *Se'l mio sempre* (SCMA VI, 71)
17 14^v *Non gemme non fin oro* (SCMA VI, 75)
18 15^v *Qual'è più grand'o amore* (SCMA VI, 78)
19 16^v *Chi con eterna legge* (SCMA VI, 88)
20 16^v *Un'altra volta* (SCMA VI, 90)
21 17^v *Chi non sa* (SCMA VI, 95)
22 18^v *Schiett'arbuscel* (SCMA VI, 97)
23 19^v *Beato me direi* (SCMA VI, 102)
24 19^v *O sonno* (SCMA VI, 106)
20^v 2a pars *Ove'l silentio*
25 21^v *Fontana di dolore* (SCMA VI, 110)
26 22^v *Datemi pace* (SCMA VI, 115)
27 23^v *Mentre la prima mia* (SCMA VI, 119)
28 23^v *Mia benigna fortuna* (SCMA VI, 124)
24^v 2a pars *Crudele acerba*
29 25^v *Ben qui si mostra'l Ciel* (RISM 1561_{15}, no. 1)
30 25^v *Nel'aria in questi di* (RISM 1575_{15}, no. 1)
31 26^v *Era il bel viso suo* (RISM 1561_{15}, no. 2)
26^v 2a pars *E ne la face*
32 28 *Chi vol veder tutta* (RISM 1575_{15}, no. 2)
27^v 2a pars *Vedrai biondi capei*
33 28^v *Se qual e'l mio dolore* (RISM 1575_{15}, no. 3)
34 29^v *Felice sei Trevigi* (RISM 1575_{15}, no. 4)
35 30^v *Musica dulci sono* (RISM 1575_{15}, no. 5)
36 30^v *Calami sonum ferentes* (RISM 1561_{15}, no. 3)

[1] An imperfect copy was in D:Bds.

1577₆

SCHMID, BERNHARD

Zwey Bücher. / Einer Neu/en Kunstlichen Tabu/latur auff Orgel und Instrument. / Deren das Erste ausserlesne Moteten und Stuck / zu sechs, fünff und vier Stimmen, auss den Kunstreichesten und / weitberümbtesten Musicis und Componisten diser unser zeit / abgesetzt. Das ander Allerley schöne Teutsche, Italienische, / Frantzösische, Geistliche und Weltliche Lieder, mit fünff / und vier Stimmen, Passamezo, Galliardo / und Täntze in sich begreifft. / Alles inn ein richtige bequemliche und artliche ord/nung, deren dergleichen vormals nie im Truck aussgangen, / Allen organisten und angehenden Instrumentisten zu nutz, / und der Hochloblichen Kunst zu Ehren, auffs / Neue zusamen gebracht, colloriret / und ubersehen. / Durch Bernhart Schmid, Bur/ger und Organisten zu Strassburg. / Getruckt zu Strassburg, bei Bernhart Jobin. / M. D. LXX vii.[1]

98 fols. German keyboard tablature. The title, printed in red and black, is placed within an ornamental border (the same border as in 1572_1, 1573_2, 1574_5, 1582_1, 1586_5, and 1589_6). Dedication on fol. *2 headed "Dem Ehrwirdigen Wolgebornen Herren, Herrn Christoffen Ladisslao, Graven zu Nellenburg, Herren zu Thengen, Hoher Stifft Strassburg Dohm Brobst, der Dohmkirchen zu Cöllen Affter Dechant, und Churfürstlichem Rhat daselbst, meinem gnädigen Herren," and signed on fol. *3 "Datum Strassburg. Den 12. Martii, Anno. 77. E. Gnaden. Untertäniger Dienstwilliger. Bernhart Schmid Organist und Burger daselbs." On fol. *3ᵛ: poem in Latin headed "In honorem et commendationem musicae. Carmen," and signed "Sigis. Sultzpergerus, Argentorati p. Vigilia Epiphaniae anni MD. lxxiiix" (reprinted in 1586_5). Also on fol. *3ᵛ: a cut of Phoebus and the three Charities with lyra, tibia, and syrinx (reprinted in 1589_6). On fols. *3ᵛ–*4: a brief instruction on the tablature headed "Kurtzer Bericht an den Günstigen Leser." On fol. *4: table of contents. On fol. *4ᵛ: cut of Bernhard Schmid with a quatrain in Latin signed "Sultzpergerus. p."[2] Fol. *5 = fol. A1.

The title page of Book II (on fol N1) reads: "Das Ander Buch. / Einer Neu/en Tabulatur auff / Orgeln und Instrumenten / Innhaltend / Allerlei schöne Teutsche, Italiä/nische, Frantzösische, Geistliche und / Weltliche Lieder, mit fünff und vier / Stimmen, Passomezo, Gal/liardo und Täntz. / Durch Bernhart Schmid, Burger und / Organisten zu Strassburg, zusamen / geordnet und ubersehen. / Mit Rö: Kai: Mai: Befreiung. / M. D. LXXVII."

Thematic incipits of the compositions followed by an asterisk are printed in MerT, pp. 82–93. The compositions identified by superior letters are reprinted as follows: ([a]) in BöhT II, nos. 148–152; ([b]) EitT, nos. 42–47; ([c]) MerT, pp. 94–113. For further information see YoungBS. In the following inventory, composers' initials or abbreviated names are resolved the first time they appear only. All of the compositions are for solo keyboard.

Copies in: B:Br, CH:Bu, D:KNu, D:LEm,[3] D:Mbs, D:PA, D:Rp, D:W, F:G, GB:Lbmh, US:Wc.[4]

Book One

	fol.	
1	A1	*Pater noster* Orlandi [Lasso] *a6* (LassoW XIII, 81)
2	A4	*Iam non Dicam* Orlandi *a6* (LassoW XIII, 38)
	B1ᵛ	2a pars *Accipite Spiritum Sanctum*
3	B3	*Surge propera* Orlandi *a6* (LassoW XIII, 158)
	B4ᵛ	2a pars *Surge amica mea*
4	C2	*Ego sum qui sum* Orlandi *a6* (LassoW XIII, 4)
	C3	2a pars *Ego dormivi*
5	C4ᵛ	*In te Domine Speravi* Orlandi *a6* (LassoW XVII, 87)
	D2	2a pars *Quoniam fortitudo mea*
6	D4ᵛ	*Si me tenes** Crequillon *a6* (RISM 1545_{14}, fol. 14)
7	E3	*Confitemini Domino* Orlandi *a5* (LassoW VII, 131)
	E4	2a pars *Narrate omnia*
8	F1ᵛ	*Deus noster refugium* Orlandi *a5* (LassoW IX, 131)
9	F2ᵛ	*Surrexit Pastor bonus* Orlandi *a5* (LassoW V, 57)

10 $F4^v$ *Non vos me elegistis* Orlandi *a5* (LassoW V, 141)

11 G2 *Benedicam Dominum* Orlandi *a5* (LassoW IX, 174)

$G3^v$ 2a pars *In Domino Laudabitur anima mea*

12 H1 *Hierusalem Luge** Richafurt *a5* (RISM 1532_9, p. 49: Richafort or Lupus)

$H2^v$ 2a pars* *Deduc quasi*

13 $H4^v$ *Veni in hortum meum* Orlandi *a5* (LassoW V, 120)

14 $J2^v$ *In me transierunt irae tuae* Orlandi *a5* (LassoW IX, 49)

15 K1 *Tribus miraculis*[5] Orlandi *a5* (LassoW V, 25)

16 K3 *Legem Pone mihi Domine* Orlandi *a5* (LassoW IX, 73)

K4 2a pars *Da mihi intellectum*

17 L1 *Gustate et videte* Orlandi *a5* (LassoW V, 73)

L3 2a pars *Divites eguerunt*

18 $L4^v$ *Sicut mater consolatur* Orlandi *a5* (LassoW VII, 97)

19 $M1^v$ *Angelus ad Pastores ait* Orlandi *a5* (LassoW III, 139)

20 $M3^v$ *Quia vidisti meThoma* Orlandi *a4* (LassoW I, 137)

Book Two

21 N2 *Vater unser im Himelreich*[c] Orlandi *a5* (LassoW XVIII, 1)

22 $N3^v$ *Ich Rüf zu dir Herr Jesu Christ** Orlandi *a4* (recte: *a5*) (LassoW XVIII, 4)

23 $N4^v$ *Susanne ung Jour** Orlandi *a5* (LassoW XIV, 29)

24 $O2^v$ *Frölich zu sein** Orlandi *a4* (recte: *a5*) (LassoW XVIII, 38)

O4 2a pars *Wer frisch will sein, der sing mit mir**

25 P1 *Im Meyen hört man die Hanen krehen** Orlandi *a5* (LassoW XVIII, 24)

26 $P1^v$ *Trit auff den Rigel von der Thür*[c] Orlandi *a5* (LassoW XVIII, 35)

27 $P2^v$ *Ein guter Wein ist lobenswerdt** Orlandi *a5* (LassoW XVIII, 44)

28 P3 *Der Wein der schmackt mir also wol** Orlandi *a5* (LassoW XVIII, 11)

29 $P4^v$ *Puis ne me peult venir** Crequillon *a5* (RISM 1572_2, fol. 25: "Pis ne me peult venir")

30 Q2 *Bewar mich Herr** Zirlerus *a4* (D:Rp, MS AR 855, no. 19)

31 Q3 *Hertzlich lieb hab ich dich O Herr**[6] *a4* (compare ZahnM, no. 8326)

32 $Q3^v$ *Vray dieu disoit une fillette** Orlandi *a4* (LassoW XII, 72)

33 $Q4^v$ *Damours me Plains** Roger [Pathie] *a4* (PubAPTM XXIII, no. 49)

34 $R1^v$ *Je prens en gre** Clemens non Papa *a4* (ClemensO X, 14)

35 R3 *Quand io pens al martire** *a4* (RISM 1541_9, p. 54: Arcadelt)

36 S1 *Osio Potessi Donna** Giachet Berhem *a4* (RISM 1541_9, p. 19)

37 $S2^v$ *Io mi son giovanetta** Fr. à Bosco *a4* (EinIM III, no. 30: D. Ferabosco)

38 S3 *Avecque vous Amour finira** Orlandi *a4* (LassoW XII, 37)

39 S4 *Ung gaii bergier** Crequillon *a4* (RieH II, 462)

40 T1 *Pour ung plaisier** Claudin *a4* (ParrishM, no. 20: Crecquillon)

41 T2 *Bon Jour mon cuer** Orlandi *a4* (LassoW XII, 100)

42 $T2^v$ *Ce moys de may** Godardum *a4* (PubAPTM XXIII, no. 25: Godard)

43 $T3^v$ *Anchor che col partir** Ciprianus de Rore *a4* (SCMA VI, 45)

44 $T4^v$ *Las voules vous** Orlandi *a4* (LassoW XII, 3)

45 $V1^v$ *Monsieur labbe** Orlandi *a4* (LassoW XII, 16)

46 $V2^v$ *Allein nach dir Herr, oder Si Purti Quarto** *a4* (RISM 1560_6, p. 46: Pathie)

47 $V3^v$ *Wol auf gut Gesel von hinnen** Meilandus *a4* (RISM 1597_7, no. 52)

48 V4 *Wie schön Blüet uns der Maye*[c][7] Jacobus Meiland *a 4* (RISM 1597_7, no. 50)
49 V4[v] *Passomezo 1**
X1[v] *Ill suo saltarello**
50 X2 *Passomezo*[c][8]
X3 *Ill suo saltarello*[c]
51 X3 *Passomezo Comun 3**[ab]
X3[v] *Ill suo Saltarello**
52 X3[v] *Passomezo Ungaro** *a 4*[9]
Y1 *Saltarello suo**
53 Y1[v] *Passomezo Anticho**
Y3[v] *Ill suo Saltarello**
54 Z1 *Galliarde Des Admirals auss Franckreich*[c][10] (compare 1571_5, no. 46)
55 Z1[v] *Galliarda Francoise*[bc]
56 Z1[v] *Ein schöner Englischer Dantz*[ac][11]
57 Z2 *Ein Fürstlicher schöner Hofdantz I*[c][12]
Z2[v] *Hupfauff*[c]
58 Z2[v] *Ein guter Hofdantz II*[abc]
Z3 *Nachdantz*[abc]
59 Z3 *Bruder Cunrad Dantzmass IIII*[c][13]
Z3 *Proportz darauf*[c]
60 Z3[v] *Der Imperial. Ein Fürstlicher Hofdantz IIII*[c]
Z3[v] *Der Hupfauf*[c]
61 Z4 *Ein guter Dantz. Man ledt uns zu der Hochzeit freud V*[c][14]
Z4 *Volget der Hopeldantz darauf*[c]
62 Z4[v] *Marggraf Caroli Dantz VI*[c]
Z4[v] *Hupfauff*[c]
63 Z5 *Alemando novelle. Ein guter neuer Dantz VII*[bc][15]
Z5 *Proportz darauf*[bc]
64 Z5[v] *La volte du roy VIII*[c]
Z5[v] *La corante du roy*[abc][16]
65 Z6 *Ein guter neuer Dantz. Du hast mich wöllen nemmen*[abc][17] I[acob] P[aix] O[rganista] (compare 1583_4, no. 75)
Z6 *Hopeldantz darauf*[abc]

[1] Facs. of title page in EF III, 657; KinsP, p. 83; and ZurM, p. 19.
[2] On this portrait see EnglertBS and HirthK.
[3] This copy is dated 1576.
[4] Copies were in D:Bds and F:Pm. The Washington copy was in the Landau–Finaly library in Florence (see HillM, pp. 14–16).
[5] Mod. ed. in KrausCO I, no. 18.
[6] Mod. ed. in FaisstH, *Beilage*, and Ritz II, 103. On the vocal model see BodeH and FaisstH.
[7] Mod. ed. in EhmL, no. 18.
[8] Mod. ed. in AulerS I, 10.
[9] Mod. ed. in HalbK, p. 12.
[10] Mod. ed. in ScherG, no. 136.
[11] Mod. ed. in AntoniK, p. 10, and BeckH, app., no. 18.
[12] Superius in BöhT II, 39; hupfauff in ForkA II, 753. Compare the allemande in MGG I, col. 351.
[13] No. 59a has no musical relation to 1571_1, no. 45.
[14] Mod. ed. in GeorgK, p. 13.
[15] Mod. ed. in DolDE, p. 157; MohrA I, 15; and TapS, p. 42.
[16] Mod. ed. in AntoniK, p. 6.
[17] Mod. ed. in KriegerME, p. 134.

1577_7

GARDANO, ANGELO, PUBLISHER

MUSICA / DE DIVERSI / AUTORI / LA BATAGLIA / FRANCESE / ET CANZON DELLI UCELLI / Insieme alcune Canzoni Francese, / Partite in Caselle per sonar d'in/stromento perfetto: Nova/mente Ristampate. / [Printer's mark] / In Venetia apresso di Angelo Gardano. / 1577.

27 fols. Keyboard partitura. The title is placed within an ornamental border. The texts of the chansons are not included in this edition. Fol. *2 = fol. 1. On fol. 27[v]: table of contents. All of the compositions are for keyboard solo.

Copy in: I:Bc.

fol.
1 *1[v] *Bataglia Francese di Clemens Janecquin. Prima parte* (MMRF VII, 31)
2[v] 2a pars [*Fan frere le le lan fan*]
2 6[v] *Canzon delli Uccelli* [*di Clemens Janequin*]. *Prima parte* (MMRF VII, 1)
8[v] 2a pars [*Vous orrez a mon advis*]
9[v] 3a pars [*Rossignol du boys joli*]
11[v] 4a pars [*Arriere maistre coqu*]
3 12[v] *Ung gay bergier* ("Canzon Francese") Crequillon (RieH II, 462)
4 13[v] *Petite Fleur coincte* Crequillon (RISM 1549_{29}, no. 28)
5 15[v] *Mais languiraige* Clemens non Papa (ClemensO X, 77)
6 16[v] *Frais & gaillart* Clemens non Papa (ClemensO X, 17)
7 18[v] *Petit jacquet* Curtois (I:Bc, MS Q 26, no. 27: Courtois)

8 19v *Rossignolet que cantes* Clemens non Papa (ClemensO X, 41)
9 20v *Je prens en gre* Clemens non Papa (ClemensO X, 14)
10 22v *Doulce memoire* Rogier (PubAPTM XXIII, no. 50: Sandrin)
11 23v *Martin Menoit* C[lement] Janecquin (CM II, 79)
25v *Je layme bien* Orlando di Lassus (LassoW XII, 41)
13 26v *Avecque vous* Orlando di Lassus (LassoW XII, 37)

[1578]₁

BESSON, JACQUES

THEATRUM / INSTRUMEN/TORUM ET MA/chinarum Jacobi Bessoni / Delphinatis, Mathemati/ci ingeniosissimi. / Cum FRANC. BEROALDI / Figuram declaratione de/monstrativa. / LUGDUNI, / Apud Barth. Vincentium / Cum Privilegio Regis. / M. D. LXXVIII.

According to FétB I, 397, this volume deals with percussion instruments, with special emphasis on bells. In fact the copy in US:Cn contains a number of plates illustrating various mechanical devices (a screw-cutting lathe,[1] a machine for fighting fires, designs for fountains and carriages, and so forth), with descriptions of them by François Béroald. The only musical instrument reproduced is a bowed stringed instrument (pl. 29). The volume belongs not in a bibliography of instrumental music, but in one dealing with the mechanical arts. For further information, including notices of later editions, see BU IV, s.v. "Besson," and GE VI, s.v. "Besson."

[1] Reproduced in CromM I, pl. xxxv (where the volume is incorrectly dated 1568).

[1578]₂

BRUNET, PIERRE

Tablature de Mandorre. A Paris, Adrian le Roy et Robert Ballard, 1578.

This volume of mandora music, now lost, is listed in BrunetML, Supplément, col. 178; DraudiusBE, p. 208; and Du Verdier III, 256. See also LesLRB, art. 228.

1578₃

CABEZÓN, ANTONIO DE

OBRAS DE MUSI/CA PARA TECLA ARPA Y / vihuela, de Antonio de Cabeçon, Musico de / la camara [*sic*] y capilla del Rey Don Phi/lippe nuestro Señor. / RECOPILADAS Y PUESTAS EN CIFRA POR HERNANDO / de Cabecọn su hijo. Ansi mesmo Musico de camara y capilla de su Magestad. / DIRIGIDAS ALA S. C. R. M. DEL REY DON / Philippe nuestro Señor. / [Coat of arms of the royal family of Spain] / CON PRIVILEGIO. / Impressas en Madrid en casa de Francisco Sanchez. Año de M. D. LXXVIII.[1]

213 fols. Spanish keyboard tablature using numbers. Dedication on fol. *2 headed "ALA S. C. R. M. EL REY DON PHILIPPE NUESTRO SEÑOR. Hernando de Cabeçon su criado." On fol. *2v: excerpt from the royal printing privilege signed "Fecha en el Pardo a veynte y un dias del mes de Septiembre, de mil y quinientos y setenta y cinco años. Yo El Rey. Por mandado de su Magestad. Antonio de Erasso." On fols. *3–*6: preface in praise of music headed "Proemio al lector en loor de la musica," ending with some biographical information about the editor's father (and composer of the music), Antonio de Cabezón. On fols. *6v–*7: a poem in Latin headed "Joan. Christophori Calveti Stellae. De Antonio Cabeçone Musico Regio. Encomium." On fol. *7: a poem in Spanish headed "De Pedro Laynez. Soneto." On fol. *7v: two poems in Spanish, the first headed "A Antonio Cabeçon, El Licenciado Juan de Vergara," the other headed "Alonso de Morales Ṣalado, en alavança del author. Soneto." On fols. *8–*8v: table of contents. On fols. *9–*11v: an explanation of the tablature used in the volume headed "Declaracion de la cifra que en este libro se usa." On fols. *11v–*12: a note on fingering headed "El orden que se ha de tener para

subir y baxar en la tecla." On fol. *13: a note on editorial practices headed "Advertimientos." Some of the prefatory material is reprinted in PedH III, xxi. Fol. *12 = fol. 1. All of the compositions except those followed by an asterisk are reprinted in PedH III, IV, VII, and VIII. The compositions identified by superior letters are reprinted as follows: ([a]) in ApelM II, 17–20; ([b]) in CabezonC; ([c]) in CabezonT; ([d]) in KallLO III, 5–43; ([e]) in OL XXX and XXXIV; ([f]) in PedAO I (selected versos only); ([g]) in Jacobs TN, pp. 110–121. The contract between Hernando de Cabezón and Francisco Sanchez for printing this volume is printed in full in PastorE and in part in PedH VIII, xvi. For further information on the volume see CarpAC, which includes English translations of the prefatory material. All of the compositions are for solo keyboard.

Copies in: B:Br, D:Bds, D:Rp, E:Bu, E:E, E:Mn, GB:Lbm (imperfect), I:Nc, US:Wc.[2]

Los duos para principiantes[3]

	fol.	
1	1	*Duo*[4]
2	1ᵛ	*Duo*[a]
3	1ᵛ	*Duo*[a]
4	2	*Ave Maristella*
5	2ᵛ	*Ave Maristella. Duo*
6	3	*Ave Maristella. Duo*
7	3ᵛ	*Ave Maristella. Duo*
8	4	*Te Lucis Ante Terminum. Duo* ("Creator alme siderum")
9	4ᵛ	*Duo*

Las obras de a tres para principiantes

10	5	*Kyrie de Nuestra Señora [sobre el canto llano de rex virginum]*[5]
11	5ᵛ	*Segundo Kyrie*
12	5ᵛ	*Tercer Kyrie*
13	6	*Ave Maristela* Hernando de Cabeçon
14	6ᵛ	*Ave Maristella*
15	7	*Pange lingua* = 1557_2, no. 78
16	8	*Pange lingua*

Las obras de a quatro

17	9	*Quatro versos del primer tono [sobre el seculorum]*[df 6]
18	9ᵛ	*Versos del segundo tono*[d 7]
19	10	*Versos del tercero tono*[d]
20	10ᵛ	*Versos del sexto tono*[d]
21	11	*Versos del VII tono*[d 8]
22	11ᵛ	*Versos del quarto tono*[ad]
23	12	*Versos del quinto tono*[d]
24	12ᵛ	*Versos del octavo tono*[d]

Los favordones de todos los ocho tonos

25	13	*Quatro fabordones del primero tono*
26	14	*Fabordones del segundo tono*
27	15	*Fabordones del tercer tono*
28	16	*Fabordones del quarto tono*[9]
29	16ᵛ	*Fabordones del quinto tono*
30	17ᵛ	*Fabordones del sexto tono*
31	19	*Fabordones del septimo tono*
32	19ᵛ	*Fabordones del octavo tono*[a]

Los Hymnos

33	21	*Ave maris stella*
34	21	*Ave maris stella*
35	21ᵛ	*Ave maris stella*
36	22	*Ave maris stella*[f] = 1557_2, no. 85
37	23	*Veni creator*[e]
38	23ᵛ	*Christe redemptor*
39	24	*Ut queant laxis*[c 10] ("Iste confessor")
40	25	*Christe redemptor*[g]
41	26	*Pange lingua*
42	26ᵛ	*Pange lingua*[11]
43	28	*Pange lingua*[12] Urreda (E:TZ, MS 2, fol. 9ᵛ)

Los versos de magnificat sobre todos los ochos tonos

44	29	*Versos del primer tono*[de 13]
45	30	*Versos del segundo tono*[de]
46	31ᵛ	*Versos del tercero tono*[de]
47	33	*Versos del quarto tono*[de 14]
48	34ᵛ	*Versos del quinto tono*[deg]
49	35ᵛ	*Versos del sexto Tono*[deg 15]
50	37ᵛ	*Versos del septimo tono*[ade 16]
51	39	*Versos del octavo Tono*[de]

Quatro Kiries de cada tono

52	40ᵛ	*Quatro Kyries de nuestra señora. Rex virginum*[e]
53	42ᵛ	*Quatro Kyries del primero Tono*
54	43ᵛ	*Kyries del segundo tono*[f]
55	45	*Kyries del tercero tono*[e]
56	46	*Kyries del quarto tono*[eg 17]
57	47	*Kyries del sexto tono*
58	48	*Kiries del septimo tono*[eg]
59	49ᵛ	*Kyries del quinto tono*

Los tientos

60 50^v *Tiento. Segundo tono*

61 52 *Tiento. Quarto tono*

62 53 *Tiento. Primer tono*

63 55 *Tiento sobre qui la dira* (compare RISM 1572_2, fol. 2: "Qui la dira la peine," Willaert)

64 56 *Tiento del segundo tono*[cef 18]

65 57 *Tiento del tercero Tono. [Fugas al contrario]*[c 19]

66 59 *[Tiento del] quarto tono*[cefg 20]

67 61 *Tiento del octavo [tono]*[cf 21]

68 62^v *Tiento del quinto tono*[c 22]

69 64 *Tiento del primer tono*[cef 23]

70 64^v *Tiento del sexto tono*[bc]

66^v *Segunda parte*[c]

71 68 *Tiento sobre Cum Sancto Spiritu [de beata virgine de Jusquin]*[c 24] (compare JosqMS, no. 16: *Missa de Beata Virgine*)

Las canciones glosadas y motetes a quatro

72 69 *Prenes pitie** Criquillon (RISM $[1544]_{11}$, fol. 9^v)

73 70^v *Ye pres en grey** Criquillon (ClemensO X, 14: "Je prens en gré," Clemens non Papa)

74 72^v *Ye pres en grey* glossado de Hernando de Cabeçon (another version of no. 73)

75 74^v *Si par suffrir** Criquillon

76 76^v *Cancion Francesa** Clemens non Papa

77 77^v *Ancol que col partire*[25] (SCMA VI, 45: Rore)

78 79 *Por un plasir** Criquillon (ParrishM, no. 20)

79 80 *Un gay bergeir** Criquillon (RieH II, 462)

80 82 *Dulce memoriae*[f] Hernando de Cabeçon (PubAPTM XXIII, no. 50: Sandrin)

81 84 *Fuga a quatro todas las bozes por una sexto tono*[c 26]

82 85 *Quaeramus [cum pastoribus]** Moton (RISM 1529_1, fol. 9^v; another version of no. 83 below)

86 2a pars *[Ubi pascas ubi cubes]*

87 3a pars

83 89 *Quaeramus [cum pastoribus]* Moton. con differente glossa (another version of no. 82 above)

90 2a pars *[Ubi pascas ubi cubes]*

84 91^v *Clama ne cesses** Jusquin (JosqMS, no. 1: *Missa L'homme armé super voces musicales*, "Agnus Dei III")

85 96^v *Osanna de la missa de lome arme** (JosqMS, no. 1)

86 98^v *Benedictus de la missa de lome arme** Jusquin (JosqMS, no. 1)

87 99^v *Ave maris stella a 3*

88 102 *Beata viscera mariae a 3*

89 103 *Cum sancto Spiritu** Jusquin (JosqMS, no. 16: *Missa de Beata Virgine*)

Los motetes y canciones de a cinco glosados

90 105 *Stabat mater dolorosa** Jusquin (JosqMT, no. 36; another version of 98 below)

107^v 2a pars *[Eya mater]*

91 110^v *Inviolata [integra]** Jusquin (JosqMT, no. 42; another version of no. 99 below)

112 2a pars *[Nostra ut pura]*

113^v 3a pars *[O benigna]*

92 114^v *Si bona suscepimus** Verdelot (MoralesO I, 274: Verdelot)

93 118 *Aspice Domine** Jaquet (MonteO XXVI, app.)

94 121 *Sana me Domine** Clemens non Papa (RISM 1556_1, no. 2)

95 123^v *In te Domine speravi** Lupus (RISM 1535_1, fol. 6^v)

126 2a pars *[Quoniam fortitudo mea]*

96 128^v *Tercera parte de virgo salutifera**[27] Jusquin (JosqMT, no. 35: "Ave Maria")

97 129 *Hierusalem luget**[27] Ricafort (RISM 1532_9, p. 49: Richafort or Lupus)

98 131 *Stabat mater dolorosa** Jusquin (another version of no. 90 above)

99 134 *Inviolata** Jusquin (another version of no. 91 above)

100 136 *Ye fille qua ni le me dona de que** Adrian Villarte (BrownTC, no. 34: "Je fille quant Dieu me donne de quoy," Vuildre)

101 137 *Pis ne me pulvenir** Criquillon (RISM 1572_2, fol. 25; another version of no. 109 below)

102 138^v *Aiuli vous sola verdura** Lupus (RISM 1544_{13}, fol. 3: "Au joly bois sur la verdure," Jo. Lupi)

103 140^v *Ayme qui voldra** Gombert (RISM 1544_{13}, fol. 5^v)

104 142^v *Durmendo un jorno** Verdelot (WagMP, p. 423)

105 144^v *Triste de par** Gombert (RISM 1544_{13}, fol. 5: "Triste depart")

106 146 *Je suis ayme** Criquillon (RISM 1545_{14}, fol. 3)

107 148 *Susana un jur* glossada de Hernando de Cabeçon (LassoW XIV, 29: Lasso another version of no. 108 below)

108 149^v *Susana* (another version of no. 107 above)

109 151^v *Pis ne me pulvenir* glossado de Hernando de Cabeçon (another version of no. 101 above)

110 153 *Qui la dira** Adrian Villart (RISM 1572_2, fol. 2)

111 155 *Ad Dominum cum tribularer. Fuga en .4. con el tiple*[ce]

112 156^v *Pues ami desconsolado tantos males me rodean*[f 28] Juan de Cabeçon

113 157^v *Quien llamo al partir partir*

Los motetes y canciones a seys

114 159 *Benedicta es regina celorum** [Jusquin] (JosqMT, no. 46; another version of no. 115 below)

115 164 *Benedicta es caelorum Regina* (another version of no. 114 above)

168 2a pars *Duo* [*Per illud ave*]

170 3a pars [*Nunc mater*]

116 171 *Sancta Maria** Verdelot (RISM 1538_2, p. 30)

117 175^v *Ave Maria**[b] Jusquin (JosqMT, no. 50b: 2a pars of "Pater noster")

118 178^v *Ultimi mei suspiri**[b29] Verdelot (MonteO V, app.)

119 181^v *Ardenti mei suspiri**[b] Verdelot (RISM 1541_{16}, no. 4)

Discantes

120 185 *Diferencias sobre las Vacas.* = [*Guardame las vacas*]

121 186^v [*Discante sobre*] *Pavana Italiana*[bf 30]

122 188 *Diferencias sobre la Gallarda Milanesa*[g 31]

123 189 *Diferencias sobre el canto llano del Cavallero*[bf 32]

124 190^v *Diferencias sobre la Pavana Italiana*[33]

125 192 *Diferencias sobre el canto de la dama le demanda*

126 193^v *Diferencias sobre el Villancico, de quien te me enojo Isabe.*

127 197 *Diferencias sobre las Vacas.* [*Guardame las vacas*][b]

128 199 *Otras diferencias de Vacas*

129 200 *Duviensela*[h] (compare AttainCK III, no. 22: "Dont vient cela," Sermisy)

[1] Facs. of title page in ApelSM, p. 294; MGG II, col. 597; and SubHME, p. 262.
[2] A copy was in D:W.
[3] The headings in the inventory are taken from the table of contents of the volume. Seven of the duos are repr. in PierO, p. 42.
[4] Facs. of fol. 1 in Maggs28, p. 95.
[5] Facs. of fol. 5 and mod. ed. of no. 10 in WolfH II, 268.
[6] Mod. ed. of a section in DallaL, no. 19.
[7] Facs. of fol. 9^v in ApelSM, opp. p. 295.
[8] Mod. ed. of a section in DallaL, no. 58.
[9] Mod. ed. of the first fabordon in PujBG, no. 1072, and TapS, p. 44.
[10] Mod. ed. in BonnO VI, 14.
[11] Mod. ed. in TagA I, no. 23.
[12] On the vocal model see AngPL, and GerbH, p. 182. The identification of the model is made after StevnsnS, p. 203.
[13] Mod. ed. in PeetA, no. 5.
[14] Mod. ed. in FroideA I, 67.
[15] Facs. of fol. 37 in ApelN, pl. 17. Mod. ed. of no. 49 in ApelMK, p. 50, and HAM, no. 133.
[16] Mod. ed. in KleinO, p. 80.
[17] Mod. ed. in RauQ, p. 9.
[18] Mod. ed. in DallaLO V, no. 4.
[19] Mod. ed. in ScherG, no. 113.

[20] Mod. ed. in DallaLO V, no. 6; EC, pt. I, vol. IV, p. 1990; HawkeO V, 1; and StraubeM I, no. 9.
[21] Mod. ed. in CabezonF, no. 4.
[22] Mod. ed. in CabezonF, no. 1.
[23] Facs. of fol. 64 in KinsP, p. 115; SubHM I, 494; and SubHME, p. 222. Mod. ed. of no. 69 in FroideA I, 38.
[24] Mod. ed. in OLI XIV, 16.
[25] Mod. ed. in TagA I, no. 24.
[26] Mod. ed. in BonnO VI, 11, and TagA I, no. 25.
[27] Facs. of fols. 128v and 129 in WolfMS, pls. 63 and 64.
[28] Facs. of fol. 156v in KommaM, p. 102, and MGG II, col. 603.
[29] Facs. of fol. 178v in WolfH II, opp. p. 268.
[30] Mod. ed. in AulerS I, 6, and CabezonP. On this dance see PoulN.
[31] Mod. ed. in AulerS I, 4; BonnO VI, 6; and PedCP III, 57.
[32] Facs. of fol. 189 in LliuQ, opp. p. 606, and SubHME, p. 263. Mod. ed. of no. 123 in AulerS I, 1; BonnO I, 5; DallaLO V, no. 5; HAM, no. 134; OL II, 7; and PedCP III, 61.
[33] Mod. ed. in ApelMK, p. 46 (who compares it with 1589_1, no. 3), and HalbK, p. 16.

1578_4

KARGEL, SIXT

RENOVATA CYTHARA: / Hoc est / NOVI ET COMMODISSIMI EXER/ CENDAE CYTHARAE MODI: CONSTANTES / CANTIONIBUS MUSICIS, PASSOMEZO, PADOANIS, / Gaillardis, Allemanicis, & aliis eiusmodi pulchris exemplis: / ad Tabulaturam communem redactis. / QUIBUS ACCESSIT DI LUCIDA IN CYTHARAM ISA/GOGE, QUO SUO MARTE QUILIBET EAM LUDERE DISCAT. / Neugestalt Cytharbuch. / Darinn vilerlai art Gesäng, Lider, Passomezo, Padoana, / Gaillarde, Branle und Teutsche Täntz, nach gemainer Tabulatur, auf / die Teutsch Cythar, sehr bekömmlich: Samt ainem unterricht, wie solche / leichtlich zu lernen, begriffen sind: / Durch Sixt Kärgel, Lautenisten. / [Cut of the neck of a cittern] / GRATIA PRIVILEGIOQUE. / Bei Bernhart Jobin / zu Strassburg, Anno M. D. LXXVIII.

50 fols. Tablature for the four-course cittern with French tuning (the tablature uses numbers; the highest line represents the highest string). Dedication on fol. 2 headed "Den Edelen und Ehrnvesten, Philips Böcklin, und Hans Waldraf Zugmantel von Brummat, baiden Schwägern, meinen Grosgönstigen Jungherrn," and signed on fol. 2v "Geben inn Strasburg, den ersten Septembris. Anno M. D. LXXV. E. E. Veste. Willig geflissener Diner. Sixt Kärgel, Lautenist." Beginning on fol. 3: instructions in Latin and German for playing the cittern. Fol. 5 = fol. A1. For other editions see $[1569]_5$, $[1575]_2$, and 1580_2. All of the compositions are for solo cittern.

Copy in: D:Bds-Tü.[1]

	fol.	
1	A1	*Plus que jamais* = 1582_5, no. 22
2	A1v	*Oye saman*
3	A2	*Quand je cogneu* (compare RISM $[1539]_{20}$, fol. 20: Sandrin)
4	A2v	*En esperance j'endure* = 1582_5, no. 19
5	A3	*Je ne veux plus* = 1570_3, no. 23
6	A3v	*Par bien servir*
7	A4	*Lennuy qui me tourmente* (compare LesLRB, art. 3, fol. 9: Certon) = 1582_5, no. 23
8	A4v	*Est il possible*
9	A4v	*Puisqu'une mort* (RISM 1550_8, fol. 31: Sohier)
10	B1	*Susan ung jour* (LevyS, p. 403: Didier Lupi Second)
11	B1v	*De me sanui* = 1570_3, no. 161: "De mes ennuis," Arcadelt
12	B2v	*J'ay bien mal*
13	B3	*Allegez moy* (BrownTC, no. 1)
14	B4	*Dames qui au plaisant son* = 1570_3, no. 22: Didier Lupi Second
15	B4v	*Quand mon mary* = 1570_3, no. 27: Lasso
16	C1	*Bon jour mon coeur* = 1570_3, no. 26: Lasso
17	C1v	*Ne pense plus*[2] = 1568_6, no. 77: M. Simon Levrart
18	C2	*Entre vos gentils galans*
19	C2v	*La Pastorella mia* = 1568_6, no. 30: Arcadelt
20	C3	*En fut il oncques* = 1568_6, no. 24: Certon
21	C3v	*J'ay trop ayme* = 1568_6, no. 36
22	C4	*Ce mois de may* = 1568_6, no. 76: Godard

23 C4^{v} *Un Advocat dist à sa femme* (RISM 1545$_{10}$, no. 19: Delafont)

24 D1^{v} *La Jeune dame*

25 D2 *Le coeur l'esprit* = 1582$_{5}$, no. 33

26 D2^{v} *C'est a grand tort* = 1582$_{5}$, no. 18

27 D3^{v} *Or combien est [malheureux]* = 1568$_{6}$, no. 66: Sandrin or Sermisy

28 D4^{v} *Doulce memoire* (PubAPTM XXIII, no. 50: Sandrin)

29 E1^{v} *Helas mon Dieu* (RISM 1553$_{19}$, fol. 6: Maillard)

30 E2^{v} *Se purti guardo* = 1570$_{3}$, no. 31: Pathie

31 E3^{v} *E me levai* = 1570$_{3}$, no. 159: Azzaiolo

32 E4^{v} *Madona mia pieta* = 1570$_{3}$, no. 149: Lasso

33 F1 *La Cortesia* = 1570$_{3}$, no. 152: Lasso

34 F1^{v} *Sto core mio* = 1570$_{3}$, no. 153: Lasso

35 F2 *Mia mari andò al Marco* = 1570$_{3}$, no. 151: Azzaiolo

36 F2^{v} *Le vecchie per invidia* = 1582$_{5}$, no. 39

37 F3 *Sia sia maladetta* = 1570$_{3}$, no. 155

38 F3^{v} *Donna Crudell* = 1582$_{5}$, no. 34

39 F4 *Nun fahr hin alle mein trauren* = 1570$_{3}$, no. 166

40 F4^{v} *Got ist mein Licht* = 1568$_{6}$, no. 74: Clemens non Papa

41 G1^{v} *Gros lib hat mich umfangen* = 1570$_{3}$, no. 163

42 G2 *Die Lib die ist ain Maister* = 1570$_{3}$, no. 164

43 G2^{v} *So wunsch ich dir ain gute Nacht* (compare BöhA, no. 435) = 1582$_{5}$, no. 41

44 G3 *Passomezo Italye*

G3^{v} *Il suo saltarello*

45 G4 *Passomezo Bassus* = 1565$_{3}$, no. 4a: "Pavane Romanesque"

G4^{v} *Il suo saltarello* = 1565$_{3}$, no. 4c: "Gaillarde Romanesque"

46 G4^{v} *Gaillarde autrement*

47 H1 *Passomezo commune* = 1582$_{5}$, no. 51a

H1^{v} *Gaillarde commune* = 1582$_{5}$, no. 51b

48 H1^{v} *Pavane*

H2 *Gaillarde la precedente pavane*

49 H2^{v} *Pavane L'espagnolle* = 1565$_{3}$, no. 6: "L'espagnolle"

50 H2^{v} *Passomezo Zorzi* = 1582$_{5}$, no. 46a

H3 *Saltarello de Zorzi* = 1582$_{5}$, no. 46b

51 H3^{v} *Passomezo Italye altro modo* = 1570$_{3}$, no. 168a

H4 *Il suo saltarello* = 1570$_{3}$, no. 168b: "Gaillarde"

52 H4^{v} *Passomezo Milanese*[3] = 1570$_{3}$, no. 169a: "Passemezo dytalye Superius"

I1 *Padoana Milanese*[3] = 1570$_{3}$, no. 169b

I1 *Saltarello Milanese*[3] = 1570$_{3}$, no. 169c: "Gaillarde dytalye"

53 I2 *Passomezo commune plus diminue* = 1570$_{3}$, no. 167a

I2^{v} *Il suo saltarello* = 1570$_{3}$, no. 167b

54 I3 *Passomezo Mit Lib bin ich umfangen*

I4 *Il suo saltarello Mit Lib bin ich umfangen*

55 I4^{v} *Pavane des Bouffons* = 1565$_{3}$, no. 3a

I4^{v} *Gaillarde des Bouffons* = 1565$_{3}$, no. 3b

56 K1 *Les Bouffons superius* = 1564$_{5}$, no. 19

57 K1 *Les Bouffons Bassus* = 1565$_{3}$, no. 2

58 K1^{v} *Passomezo Bataglia* = 1570$_{3}$, no. 165

59 K2 *Gaillarde La Caracossa superius*

60 K2^{v} *La Caracossa Bassus* = 1565$_{3}$, no. 5: "Gaillarde J'aymeroys mieux dormir seullette"

61 K2^{v} *Chi passa per questa strada* (AzzaiV, no. 2: Azzaiolo)

K3 *Chi passa altra modo* = 1570$_{3}$, no. 171

62 K3^{v} *Gaillarde Era di magio* = 1582$_{5}$, no. 84

63 K3^{v} *Gaillarde* = 1582$_{5}$, no. 85

64 K4 *Gaillarde Ich kan und mag nicht frölich sein* = 1582$_{5}$, no. 82

65 K4 *Gaillarde puisque nouvelle affection* = 1564$_{5}$, no. 14

66 K4^{v} *Gaillarde la Lionnoise* = 1564$_{5}$, no. 11

67 L1 *Gaillarde Baisons nous belles* = 1570$_{3}$, no. 59

68 L1 *Gaillarde la Morette* = 1564_5, no. 10
69 L1v *Gaillarde M. Sixto* = 1582_5, no. 73
70 L1v *Almande Teutscher Tanz* = 1582_5, no. 99
L2 *Reprinse. Der Nachtantz*
71 L2 *Almande Teutscher Danz* = 1570_3, no. 178
L2v *Reprinse. Der nach Tantz*
72 L2v *Almande* = 1570_3, no. 180
L2v *Reprinse*
73 L3 *Almande nova* = 1582_5, no. 109
L3 *Reprinse*
74 L3v *Almande* = 1582_5, no. 103: "Almande de lignes"
L3v *Reprinse*
75 L3v *Almande nova*
L4 *Reprinse*
76 L4 *Almande nova*
L4 *Reprinse*
77 L4v *Almande nova*
L4v *Reprinse*
78 M1 *Almande Ich ging ainmal spaciren* = 1582_5, no. 93: "Almande de la Nonette"
M1 *Reprinse*
79 M1 *Almande du Prince* = 1582_5, no. 110
M1v *Reprinse*
80 M1v *Almande nova*
M1v *Reprinse*
81 M2 *Branle del duc* = 1570_3, no. 175a
M2 *La Saltarelle* = 1570_3, no. 175b: "La Courante"
M2v *La courante* = 1570_3, no. 175c: "Le saltarelle"

[1] This copy was in the Wolffheim library (see WolffC I, no. 1195). A copy was in the Wotquenne-Plattel library (see ThibaultC, p. 55).
[2] Facs. of fol. C1v in WolfMS, no. 72.
[3] Quasi-facs. and partial transcription in WolfH II, 136.

1578_5

KARGEL, SIXT, AND JOHAN DOMINICO LAIS

Toppel Cythar. / NOVA EAQUE ARTIFICIOSA RA/TIO LUDENDAE CY THARAE, QUAM COMPI/LATORES DUPLAM CYTHARAM VOCANT: ALIQUOT / ELEGANTISSIMIS, ITALICIS, GERMANICIS, ET GALLICIS / cantionibus & saltationibus, exempli vice ornata. / Neue, Künstliche Tabulatur, auf die Lautengemäse Toppel / Cythar mit sechs Cohren, von etlichen Italiänischen, Teutschen und Fran/zösischen Lidern und Täntzen: baides für sich selbs volkommenlich, und auch zu andern / Instrumenten dinstlich zuspilen und zugebrauchen: gestellet / Durch / Sixt Kargel Lautenist, Und Johan Dominico Lais. / [Cut of the neck of a cittern] / Cum Privilegio. / Bei Bernhart Jobin zu Strasburg, Anno M. D. lxxviii.[1]

36 fols. Italian tablature for the six-course cittern. On fol. 2: the same dedication to "Herrn Eberharden und Arnolden, baiden Gebrüdern, Graven zu Manderschaid und Blankenhaim" as in 1575_3. On fol. 2v: the same rules for tuning as in 1575_3. On fol. 36v: table of contents. Contents = 1575_3. All of the compositions are for solo cittern.

Copies in: D:Bds-Tü, F:Ssc, PL:WRu.[2]

[1] Facs. of title page in EF II, 659.
[2] A copy was in the Wotquenne-Plattel library (see ThibaultC, p. 55). GolosT, p. 127, refers to a copy in PL: Tm.

1578_6

LASSO, ORLANDO DI

MODULI / DUARUM VOCUM / NUNQUAM HACTENUS EDITI / MONACHII BOIOARIAE COMPOSITI / ORLANDO LASSO / AUCTORE. / LUTETIAE PARISIORUM. / Apud Adrianum le Roy, & Robertum Ballard, / Regis Typographòs sub signo / montis Parnassi. / M D LXXVIII. / Cum privilegio Regis ad decennium.

Two part books in mensural notation, each of 20 fols. On fol. 1v of each part book: the coat of arms of William V, Duke of Bavaria, with the motto "VINCI TUIM VIRTUS" and the initials "W H I B." On fol. 2 of each part book: the same dedication as in 1577_2, but dated "Monaci 2. Januarii. Anno 1578." The music begins on fol. 2v of each part book. On fol. 20v of each part book: table of contents. Contents = 1577_2. Nos.

1–12 have Latin text; nos. 13–24 are without text (labeled "fantasies"); all of the compositions are *a 2*.

Copies in: F:O (imperfect T), I:Bc.[1]

[1] In the Bologna copy the last folio is missing in the tenor part book, and the first and last folios of the superius part book are damaged.

[1578]$_7$

LE ROY, ADRIAN

Briefve & facile instruction pour apprendre la tabulature à bien accorder, conduire & disposer la main sur la Guiterne. Paris, Adrian le Roy et Robert Ballard.

This volume, an instruction book for the guitar, is now lost; it is listed in Du Verdier I, 25. For an earlier edition, see [1551]$_4$. For a possible English translation, see [1568]$_9$.

1578_8

MAINERIO, GIORGIO

IL PRIMO LIBRO DE BALLI / A QUATRO VOCI, / ACCOMMODATI PER CANTAR ET SONAR D'OGNI / Sorte de Istromenti. Di D. Giorgio Mainerio Parmeggiano / Maestro di Capella della S. Chiesa d'Aquilegia, / Novamente stampati & dati in luce. / [Printer's mark] / In Venetia Appresso / Angelo Gardano / 1578.

Four part books in mensural notation, each of 12 fols. Dedication on fol. 1^v headed "ALLI MOLTO MAG.^{ci} SIG.^{ri} ACCADEMICI PHILARMONICI DEL NOBIL CASIN DEL REVERENDO MONSIGNOR ORATIO BILLIARDO DIGNISSIMO CANONICO DI PARMA," reprinted in SartMS, p. 34. Fol. 2 = p. 1. On p. 23: table of contents. MainB is a modern edition of the entire collection. DraudiusBC, p. 1621, dates this 1576. All of the compositions are for instrumental ensemble *a 4*.

Copies in: GB:Lbm (AT), I:Bc (T), I:Tn.

	p.	
1	1	*La Billiarda* = 1583_7, no. 32a: "Almande"
	1	*Saltarello* = 1583_7, no. 32b
2	2	*Pass'e mezzo antico in cinque modi* = 1583_7, no. 2a (1583_4, no. 57a)
	3	*Represa in tre modi* = 1583_7, no. 2b
	4	*Saltarello in quattro modi* = 1583_7, no. 2c (1583_4, no. 57b)
	4	*Represa* = 1583_7, no. 2d
3	5	*Pass'e mezzo della Paganina* = 1583_7, no. 7a
	5	*Saltarello* = 1583_7, no. 7b
4	6	*Caro Ortolano* = 1583_7, no. 1a
	6	*Saltarello* = 1583_7, no. 1b
5	6	*Gagliarda*
6	7	*Putta Nera Ballo Furlano* = 1583_7, no. 48
7	8	*La Zanetta Padoana*
8	9	*La Saporita Padoana*
9	10	*Todescha* = 1583_7, no. 34a: "Almande Bruynsmedelijn"
	10	*Saltarello* = 1583_7, no. 34b
10	11	*La Lavandara Gagliarda* = 1583_7, no. 29
11	12	*Pass'e mezzo Moderno in cinque modi* = 1583_7, no. 3a
	13	*Represa in quattro modi* = 1583_7, no. 3b
	14	*Saltarello in tre modi* = 1583_7, no. 3c
	14	*Represa* = 1583_7, no. 3d
12	14	*Schiarazula Marazula* = 1583_7, no. 49 (1583_4, no. 88)
13	15	*Tedescha* = 1583_7, no. 36a: "Almande"
	15	*Saltarello* = 1583_7, no. 36b
14	16	*Ungaresca* = 1583_7, no. 46a (1583_4, no. 74a)
	16	*Saltarello* = 1583_7, no. 46b (1583_4, no. 74b)
15	17	*L'arboscello ballo Furlano* = 1583_7, no. 44 (1583_4, no. 86)
16	17	*Ballo Millanese* = 1583_7, no. 28 (1583_4, no. 87)
17	18	*La Parma* = 1583_7, no. 47a
	18	*Saltarello* = 1583_7, no. 47b
18	19	*Ballo Francese in doi modi* = 1583_7, no. 39a: "Almande Loreyne" (1583_4, no. 82a)
	19	*Saltarello* = 1583_7, no. 39b (1583_4, no. 82b)

19 20 *Ballo Anglese* = 1583_7, no. 45a (1583_4, no. 83a)
20 *Saltarello* = 1583_7, no. 45b (1583_4, no. 83b)
20 21 *Todescha* = 1583_7, no. 30a: "Almande Poussinghe"
21 *Saltarello* = 1583_7, no. 30b
21 22 *La fiamenga* = 1583_7, no. 97

[$1578]_9$

PHALÈSE, PIERRE, PUBLISHER

Carmina in Testudine. Louvain, Pierre Phalèse.

This volume of lute music, now lost, is listed in an inventory of the firm of Plantin in Antwerp. See StellMB, p. 24.

1579_1

GORZANIS, GIACOMO DE

OPERA NOVA DE LAUTO / COMPOSTA DA MISIER JACOMO GORZANIS CITADINO / Della Magnifica Città di Trieste messa in Luce da suo Figliolo Massimiliano. / LIBRO [Printer's mark] QUARTO / IN VENETIA Apresso Alessandro Gardane 1579.

40 fols. Italian lute tablature. On fol. $A1^v$: same dedication as in $156?_3$. On fol. $K4^v$: table of contents. MoeDM contains a thematic index of the dances (p. 429) and concordances for them (p. 266). Contents = $156?_3$. For other volumes in the same series, see 1561_2, note 1. All of the compositions are for solo lute.

Copy in: I:Bc.

1579_2

LAS INFANTAS, FERNANDO DE

NON LIBERA MUSIS NON HIC / AB APOLLINE, NON A FLORE, / SED A SANCTO FLAMINE / NOMEN HABET. / [Cut depicting the Holy Ghost encircled by a canon *a 2* on the text "Veni creator spiritus"] / DON FERDINANDI DE LAS INFANTAS / Patritii Cordubensis / PLURA MODULATIONUM GENERA / quae vulgò contrapuncta appellantur / SUPER EXCELSO GREGORIANO CANTU, / omnibus musicam profitentibus utilissima. / Venetiis Apud heredemi Hieronimi Scoti. / M D LXXIX

74 fols. Mensural notation. The title is placed within an ornamental border. Dedication on fol. $A1^v$ headed "FOELICISSIMO PUBLICAE LAETITIAE AUCTORI. D. N. JACOBO, PHILIPPI .II. REGIS .F. HISPANIARUM POTENTISSIMO PRINCIPI," and signed "Venetiis Klendis [sic] Aprilis. 1579. Tuae Altitudini deditissimus cliens, Don Ferdinandus de las Infantas." The volume contains 100 canons over the cantus firmus "Laudate Dominum omnes gentes."[1] Nos. 1–47 (pp. 3–37) are *a3*; nos. 48–57 (pp. 38–41) are *a2*; nos. 58–91 (pp. 42–103) are *a4*; nos. 92–95 (pp. 104–105) are *a5*; nos. 96–98 (pp. 116–131) are *a6*; no. 99 (pp. 132–137) is *a7*; and no. 100 (pp. 138–147) is *a8*. All of the canons are without text except for nos. 75–84 and 100.[2]

Copy in: US:BE.[3]

[1] On the last page (p. 148) Las Infantas has added three additional canons: *Ave Maria* ("Canon super Excelso Gregoriano Cantu"); *Tu es Petrus* ("Canon super Excelso Gregoriano Cantu"); and *Duo* (without text).

[2] The fully texted canons are: no. 75, p. 70: *Veni sancte spiritus;* no. 76, p. 72: *Veni pater pauperum;* no. 77, p. 74: *Consolator optime;* no. 78, p. 76: *In labore requies;* no. 79, p. 78: *O lux beatissima;* no. 80, p. 80: *Sine tuo nomine;* no. 81, p. 82: *Lava quod est sordidum;* no. 82, p. 84: *Flecte quod est rigidum;* no. 83, p. 86: *Da tuis fidelibus;* no. 84, p. 88: *Da virtutis meritum;* no. 100, p. 138: *Laudate Dominum omnes gentes.* The text for the cantus firmus is given only for no. 1 and for the fully texted canons.

[3] I am grateful to Vincent Duckles, music librarian of the University of California at Berkeley, for telling me of the existence of this volume. A manuscript copy by Ephraim Kellner, amanuensis to Dr. Pepusch, of this volume is listed in the *Catalogue of the Library of the Sacred Harmonic Society*, revised ed. (1872), item 1936.

1579_3

INGEGNIERI, MARC'ANTONIO

IL SECONDO LIBRO DE' MADRIGALI / DI MARC'ANTONIO IN-

GEGNIERI A QUATTRO / VOCI, CON DUE ARIE DI CANZON FRAN/cese per sonare. Novamente composti, & dati in luce. / [Printer's mark] / In Venetia Appresso / Angelo Gardano. / 1579.

Four part books in mensural notation, each of 12 fols. Dedication on fol. 1^v of each part book headed "ALL'ILLUSTRISSIMO SIGNOR ET PADRON MIO OSSERVANDISSIMO, Il Signor Barone Sfondrato," and signed "Di Cremona il di 25. Genaro. 1579. D. V. Sig. Illustriss. Obligatissimo Ser. Marc'Antonio Ingegnieri," reprinted in SartMS, p. 35. Fol. 2 = p. 1. On p. 22 of each part book: table of contents. Vogel: Ingegnieri 8 gives a complete list of the contents. Contents = 1584_7. Nineteen of the 21 compositions have Italian text; two are for instrumental ensemble *a 4*.

Copies in: D:Mbs, GB:Lbm (T), I:Bc (T and imperfect S), I:Fn, and I:Vnm AB).[1]

	p.	
1	20	*Aria di Canzon Francese per sonar del primo tono*[2] (1583_4, no. 84)
2	21	*Aria di Canzon Francese per sonar del ottavo tono*[2] (1583_4, no. 85)

[1] Copies were in D:Bds, D:C, and PL:L.

[2] Mod. ed. in IMAMI II, l and lii. Mod. ed. of no. 1 in DallaA, no. 11. See EinN for the thesis that these compositions are not instrumental but are intended as models to which various narrative chanson texts might be set.

1579_4

LASSO, ORLANDO DI

MOTETTI ET RICERCARI / D'ORLANDO LASSO A DUE VOCI, / Novamente Composti & dati in luce. / LIBRO [Printer's mark] PRIMO. / In Venetia Appresso / Angelo Gardano / 1579

Two part books in mensural notation, each of 12 fols. Contents = 1577_2. Nos. 1–12 have Latin text; nos. 13–24 are without text (labeled "ricercares"); all of the compositions are *a 2*.

Copy in: F:Pc (S).

1579

DOUBTFUL WORKS

1. FétB IV, 17, erroneously dates Giuliano Tiburtino, *Fantasie, et Recerchari a tre voci*, 1579. The volume is listed in this bibliography as 1549_7.

$[157?]_1$

TROMBONCINO, IPPOLITO

Intabolatura de Trombоncino da Cantar in Liuto. Venezia, Angelo Gardano.

This volume of music for solo voice and lute, now lost, is listed in GardI, fol. 8^v (see ThibaultD). The composer is probably Ippolito Tromboncino (see EitQ IX, 461, and MacC, p. 181).

$[1580]_1$

CROCE, GIOVANNI DALLA, DETTO IL CHIOZZOTTO

Sonate a cinque. Venzia. 1580.

This volume of music for instrumental ensemble, now lost if it ever existed, is listed in FétB II, 393. The volume is not mentioned in TorriC, which includes a list of Croce's works.

1580_2

KARGEL, SIXT

RENOVATA CYTHARA: / Hoc est / NOVI ET COMMODISSIMI EXER/CENDAE CYTHARAE MODI: CONSTANTES / CANTIONIBUS MUSICIS, PASSOMEZO, PADOANIS, / Gaillardis, Allemanicis, & aliis eiusmodi pulchris exemplis: / ad Tabulaturam communem redactis. / QUIBUS ACCESSIT DILUCIDA IN CYTHARAM ISA/GOGE, QUO SUO MARTE QUILIBET EAM LUDERE DISCAT. / Neugestalt Cytharbuch. / Darinn vilerley art Gesäng, Lider, Passomezo, Padoana, / Gaillarde, Branle und Teutsche Täntz, nach gemeyner Tabulatur, auf / die Teutsch Cythar, sehr bekömlich: Sampt eynem unterricht, wie solche / leichtlich zu lernen, begriffen sind: / Durch Sixt Kärgel, Lautenisten. / [Cut of the neck of a cittern] / GRATIA PRIVILEGIOQUE. / Bei Bernhart Jobin zu Strassburg, Anno M. D. L XXX.

50 fols. Tabulature for the four-course cittern with French tuning (the tablature uses numbers; the highest line represents the highest string). The same dedication on fol. 2 as in 1578_4. Beginning on fol. 3: the same instructions for playing the cittern as in 1578_4. Contents = 1578_4. All of the compositions are for solo cittern.

Copy in: F:Ssc.

1580_3

VALENTE, ANTONIO

VERSI SPI/RITUALI SOPRA / TUTTE LE NOTE, CON DIVERSI CA/NONI SPARTITI PER SONAR NE / GLI ORGANI, MESSE, / VESPERE, ET ALTRI OF/FICII DIVINI. / Di. M. ANTONIO Valente Cieco, Libro secondo, Novamente da lui / composto, & posto in luce. / [Printer's mark] / IN NAPOLI. / Appresso gli Eredi di Mattio Cancer. / M. D. LXXX.

56 fols. Keyboard partitura. Dedication on fol. *1ᵛ headed "ALLA ILLUSTRE SIGNORA MIA OSSERVANDISSIMA la Sig. Donna Elionora Palmiera," and signed "Di Napoli, il dì .10. di Settembre. 1580. Di V. S. Ill. Divotissimo & affettionatissimo Servitore, Antonio Valente," reprinted in GaspaC IV, 38, and SartMS, p. 36. On fol. *1ᵛ: "Sonetto del Signor Angelo di Costanzo all'Autore," repr. in GaspaC IV, 68, and SartMS, p. 37. The music begins on fol. *2(= p. 1). On p. 109: the imprimatur and colophon: "Paulus Regius vidit. Idem. f. 27. Imprimatur. V. Quatrimanus Vic. Ge. Neap. NEAPOLI. Apud Haeredes Matthiae Cancri. 1580." The entire volume is reprinted in ValVS, which includes a facsimile of the title page and of p. 41. There is a modern edition of one verso in MFH VII, 10. The compositions identified by the superior letter *a* ([a]) are reprinted in FuserC, nos. 13–17. All of the compositions are for solo keyboard.

Copies in: GB:Lcm,[1] I:Bc. †

	p.	
1	1	*Verso primo sopra dell'Ut*
2	3	*Verso Secondo*
3	5	*Verso Terzo*
4	7	*Verso Quarto*
5	9	*Verso Quinto*
6	11	*Verso Sesto. Canon in Diapente superius*
7	14	*Sopra il Re verso primo*[a]
8	17	*Verso Secondo*
9	20	*Verso Terzo*[a]
10	23	*Verso Quarto*[a]
11	27	*Verso Quinto*[a]
12	30[2]	*Verso Sesto. Canon in diapente superius*
13	33	*Sopra il Mi verso primo*[3]
14	36	*Verso sesto* [recte: secondo]
15	37	*Verso Terzo*
16	41	*Verso Quarto*
17	44	*Verso Quinto*
18	47	*Verso Sesto. Canon in diatesaron inferius*
19	50	*Sopra il Fa verso primo*
20	53	*Verso Secondo*[4]
21	54	*Verso Terzo*
22	56	*Verso Quarto*
23	60	*Verso Quinto*
24	63	*Verso Sesto. Canon in diatesaron inferius*
25	67	*Sopra il Sol verso primo*
26	69	*Verso Secondo*
27	71	*Verso Terzo*
28	74	*Verso Quarto*
29	76	*Verso Quinto*
30	78	*Verso Sesto. Canon in diatesaron superius*
31	82	*Sopra il La verso primo*
32	84	*Verso Secondo*
33	86	*Verso Terzo*[5]
34	88	*Verso Quarto*
35	90	*Verso Quinto*[a]
36	94	*Verso Sesto. Canon in Diapente superius*
37	97	*Verso primo sopra il fa di be fa be mi*
38	98	*Verso Secondo*
39	100	*Verso Terzo*

40	101	*Verso Quarto*
41	103	*Verso Quinto*
42	105	*Verso Sesto*
43	107	*Verso sopra il .b. molle di e la mi*

[1] This copy has manuscript Italian verses between the staves on the first 14 pages.

[2] Page 29 is incorrectly numbered "17," so that all subsequent page numbers are consequently one number too low. The incorrect pagination is maintained in this inventory.

[3] Mod. ed. in TorA III, 45.

[4] Mod. ed. in TorA III, 46.

[5] Mod. ed. in TorA III, 48.

[1580]₄

VIOLA, [RAPHAEL]

Lautenbuch. Leuven. 1580.

This volume of music for solo lute, now lost, is listed in GoovH, no. 257. It may be the same as [1575]₄.

1581₁

CAROSO, FABRITIO

IL BALLARINO / DI M. FABRITIO CAROSO / DA SERMONETA, / Diviso in due Trattati; / Nel primo de' quali si dimostra la diversità de i nomi, che si danno à gli / atti, & movimenti, che intervengono nei Balli: & con / molte Regole si dichiara come debbano farsi. / Nel secondo d'insegnano diverse sorti di Balli, & Balletti sì / all'uso d'Italia, come à quello di Francia, & Spagna. / Ornato di molte Figure. / Et con l'Intavolatura di Liuto nella Sonata di ciascun Ballo, & / il Soprano della Musica alla maggior parte di essi. / Opera nuovamente mandata in luce. / ALLA SEREN.MA S.RA BIANCA CAPPELLO DE MEDICI, / GRAN DUCHESSA DI TOSCANA. / CON PRIVILEGIO. / [Printer's mark] / IN VENETIA, / Appresso Francesco Ziletti. M D LXXXI.[1]

24 + 188 fols. Italian lute tablature and mensural notation. Dedication on fol. *2 headed "ALLA SERENISS.MA SIG.RA LA SIG.RA BIANCA CAPELLO DE MEDICI, Gran Duchessa di Toscana," and signed on fol. *3 "Di Venetia, a 16. d'Ottobre, M. D. LXXXI. Di V. Altezza Sereniss. Humilissimo, & Devotissimo Servitore Fabritio Caroso da Sermoneta." On fol. *3v: poem in Italian headed "Alla Seren.ma Sig.ra La Sig.ra Bianca Capello de Medici, Gran Duchessa di Toscana." On fol. *4: poem in Italian headed "Alla Medesima Sereniss. Signora Gran Duchessa." On fol. *4v: preface headed "Ai Lettori." On fol. *5v: poem in Italian headed "Sonetto in Lode dell'Autore. Del Sig. Quintilio Romoli." On fol. *6: poem in Italian headed "Al Medesimo. Di. M. Marco Sofronio." On fol. *6v: poem in Italian headed "Al Medesimo. Di M. Francesco Guglia." On fol. *7: poem in Italian headed "Al Medesimo. Di M. Vincenzo Mucci." On fol. *7v: poem in Italian headed "Al Medesimo." Fol. *8 is blank. On fol. *8v: portrait of Caroso with legend "Fabritio Caroso da Sermoneta nell'eta sua d'anni XXXXVI." The *trattato primo*, containing instructions for dancing, comprises fol. *9 (numbered fol. 1) to fol. *24v. On fol. *25: a second title page that reads:

> TRATTATO SECONDO / DEL BALLARINO / DI M. FABRITIO CAROSO / DA SERMONETA, / Nel quale s'insegnano varie sorti di Balletti, Cascarde, Tordiglione, / Passo e mezo, Pavaniglia, Canario, & Gagliarde all'uso / d'Italia, Francia, & Spagna. / Con molte Figure, & con l'Intavolatura di Liuto, & il / Soprano della Musica à ciascuno di essi Balli. / Nuovamente mandato in luce. / ALLA SERENISS. SIG.RA LA SIG.RA / BIANCA CAPPELLO DE' MEDICI / Gran Duchessa di Toscana. / CON PRIVILEGIO. / [Printer's mark] / IN VENETIA, Appresso Francesco Ziletti. / M. D. LXXXI.

Fol. *26 = fol. 2. On fol. 185: table of contents for the *trattato primo* headed "Tavola delle Regole, Che si contengono nel primo Trattato." Beginning on fol. 185v: table of contents for the *trattato secondo* headed "Tavola dei Balli, del Secondo Trattato, coi nomi delli persone, à chi sono dedicati." On fol. 188v: a list of errata followed by the table of signatures and the colophon: "In Venetia, Appresso Francesco Ziletti, M D LXXXI." Later editions appeared in 1600, 1605 (selections are reprinted in ChilB I), and 1630. These later editions, revised and expanded, have the title *Nobiltà di Dame*. MoeDM contains a thematic index of the volume (p. 434) and concordances (p. 270). For a discussion of several of the dances and a selection of cuts and music from the volume see DolDS. For most of the dances Caroso includes a dedicatory poem, a cut of a couple dancing,[2] choreography, and the music. In this inventory the complete heading over the music is given only for nos. 1–5. Nos. 1–22 are arranged for an instrument capable of playing a single line (printed in mensural notation) and lute; nos. 23–83 are arranged for solo lute.

Copies in: A:Wn, A:Wu, CH:Lcortot, D:Bds-Tü, D:Mbs, E:Mmc, F:Pc, F:Pn, F:Pthibault, GB:Gu, GB:Lbm, I:Bc, I:FEc, I:Rsc, NL:DHgm, US:Bp, US:CA (three copies, one of them imperfect), US:NYhs, US:Wc, US:Ws.[3]

	fol.	
1	2	*Alba Novella*, Balletto; In Lode Della Sereniss. Sig. La Sig. Bianca Cappello De' Medici, Gran Duchessa di Toscana: four dedicatory poems (two called "madrigale"), cut of a couple dancing, and choreography
	5v	"Intavolatura di Liuto con la Musica della Sonata del Balletto Alba Novella."
	6	[La sua sciolta]
2	6v	*Alta Regina*, Cascarda; In Lode Della Sereniss. Sig. La Sig. Bianca Cappello De' Medici, Gran Duchessa di Toscana: two dedicatory poems (one called "madrigale"), cut of a couple dancing, and choreography
	9	"Intavolatura di Liuto con la Musica, della Sonata della Cascarda Alta Regina, fatta in sei Tempi." = nos. 14, 60, and 64
	9	[La sua sciolta]
3	9v	*Este Gonzaga*, Balletto; In Lode Della Sereniss. Sig. [Margarita Gonzaga de Este], Duchessa di Ferrara: dedicatory poem, cut of a couple dancing, and choreography
	11v	"Intavolatura di Liuto, con la Musica, della Sonata del Balletto Este Gonzaga, fatta in quattro Tempi."
	12	La Sciolta della Sonata, farassi à un Tempo solo
4	13	*Austria Gonzaga*, Balletto; In Lode Della Sereniss.ma Sig.ra [Leonora d'Austria Gonzaga], Duchessa di Mantova: dedicatory poem, cut of a couple dancing, and choreography
	15	"Intavolatura di Liuto, con la Musica, della Sonata del Balletto Austria Gonzaga, fatta in quattro Tempi."
	15	La Sciolta della Sonata, farassi à un Tempo solo
	15v	Sonata del Canario = no. 22c
5	16	*Ardente Sole*, Balletto; In Lode Dell'Illustr.ma et Ecc.ma Sig.ra [Lucretia da Este], Duchessa di Urbino: dedicatory poem, cut of a couple dancing, and choreography
	18	"Intavolatura di Liuto, con la Musica della Sonata del Balletto Ardente Sole, fatta in cinque Tempi." = no. 15
6	19	*Bassa Colonna*, Balletto; Di. M. Andrea da Gaeta. In Lode Dell'Illustr.ma et Ecc.ma Sig. [Felice Orsina Colonna], Duchessa di Tagliacozzo, et di Paliano, [Vice Regina di Sicilia]: dedicatory poem, cut of a couple dancing, and choreography
	21	Music for lute and one instrument
	21	La Sciolta della Sonata
7	21v	*Gagliarda di Spagna*, Balletto; In Lode dell'Illustr.ma et Ecc.ma Signora [Donna Anna de Mendozza], Duchessa di Medina Cidonia, Governatrice di Milano: dedicatory poem, cut of a couple dancing, and choreography
	24	Music for lute and one instrument
8	24v	*Amor Costante*, Balletto; In Lode dell'Illustr.ma et Ecc.ma Sig.ra [Costanza Sgorza Buoncompagni], Duchessa di Sora: two dedicatory poems, cut of a couple dancing,[4] and choreography

27 Music for lute and one instrument

27v La Sciolta della Sonata = no. 56

9 28 *Fulgente Stella*, Cascarda; In Lode della Sereniss.ma Sig.ra La Sig. Leonora de Medici, Principessa di Toscana: dedicatory poem, cut of a couple dancing, and choreography

30 Music for lute and one instrument

10 30v *Florido Giglio*, Cascarda; In Lode della Principessa di Mantova [Margherita Farnese Gonzaga]: dedicatory poem, cut of a couple dancing, and choreography

32v Music for lute and one instrument = no. 39c

11 33 *Occhi Leggiadri*, Balletto; In Lode della Illustrissima, et Eccellentiss. Signora [Lavinia della Rovere], Principessa d'Urbino: dedicatory poem, cut of a couple dancing, and choreography

35 Music for lute and one instrument

35v La sua Sciolta

12 36 *Pavaniglia*, Balletto d'Incerto; In Lode dell'Illustr.ma et Ecc.ma Signora [Isabella della Rovere Sanseverina], Principessa di Bisignano: dedicatory poem, cut of a couple dancing, and choreography

39v Music for lute and one instrument[5]

13 40 *Villanella*, Balletto d'Incerto; In Lode dell'Illustrissima et Eccellentissima Signora Principessa di Selmona: dedicatory poem, cut of a couple dancing, and choreography

42 Music for lute and one instrument[6] = no. 45

14 42v *Squilina*, Cascarda; In Lode dell'Illustrissima et Eccelentissima Signora Principessa di Squillace: dedicatory poem, cut of a couple dancing, and choreography

44v Music for lute and one instrument = nos. 2, 60, and 64

15 45 *Passo e mezo* d'Incerto; Con le Mutanze, & Passeggio nuovo, dell'Autore dell'Opera: In Lode della Illustrissima, et Eccellentiss.ma Signora [Donna Hieronima Colonna], Duchessa di Monte Lione: dedicatory poem, cut of a couple dancing, and choreography

49 Music for lute and one instrument = no. 5

16 49v *Il Conto dell'Orco*, Balletto D'incerto; In Lode della Illustrissima et Eccellentiss.ma Signora Duchessa di Traetto: dedicatory poem, cut of a couple dancing, and choreography

51 Music for lute and one instrument

17 51v *Bassa Ducale*, Balletto; In Lode dell'Illustr.ma et Ecc.ma Signora La Signora [Madama Dorothea], Duchessa di Branswich, [& Luneburc, nativa Duchessa di Lorena, & Bar, Contessa di Cleremonte]: dedicatory poem, cut of a couple dancing, and choreography

53 Music for lute and one instrument

53v La sua Sciolta

18 54 *Se Pensand'al Partire*, Balletto di M. Bastinao; In Lode della Signora Costanza Colonna Sforza, Marchese di Caravaggio: dedicatory poem, cut of a couple dancing, and choreography

56 Music for lute and one instrument

19 56v *Copia Felice*, Balletto; In Lode dell'Illustrissima Signora Clelia Farnese Cesarina, Marchese di Cività Nuova: dedicatory poem, cut of a couple dancing, and choreography

58v Music for lute and one instrument

59 La sua Sciolta

20 59v *Contentezza d'Amore*, Balletto di M. Battistino; In Lode della Illustrissima Signora Portia Ceri dell'Anguilara Cesi, Marchesa di Riano: dedicatory poem, cut of a couple dancing, and choreography

61^{v} Music for lute and one instrument

62 La sua Sciolta

21 62^{v} *Le Bellezze d'Olimpia*, Balletto; In Lode della Illustriss. Sig. Padrona et Benefattrice mia, sempre osservandissima, la Signora Olimpia Orsina Cesi, Marchesa di Monticelli: three dedicatory poems, cut of a couple dancing, and choreography

66 Music for lute and one instrument = no. 32

22 66^{v} *Cesia Orsina*, Balletto; In Lode della Medesima Illustrissima Signora Olimpia Orsina Cesi, Marchesa di Monticelli: two dedicatory poems, cut of a couple dancing, and choreography

69^{v} Music for lute and one instrument

70 La Sciolta in Saltarello

70 Il Canario = no. 4c

23 70^{v} *Alta Orsina*, Balletto; In Lode dell'Illustrissima Signora Donna Cornelia Orsina Altemps, Marchese di Gallese: dedicatory poem and choreography

72 Music for lute

72 La sua Sciolta

24 72^{v} *Bassa Savella*, Balletto; In Lode dell'Illustrissima S.^{ra} la Signora Virginia Savella Vitella, Marchesa d'Andridoca: dedicatory poem and choreography

74 Music for lute

25 74^{v} *Bassa Honorata*, Balletto di M. Battistino; In Lode dell'Illustrissima Signora Donna Agnesina Colonna Caetana: dedicatory poem and choreography

76 Music for lute = no. 49

76 La Sua Sciolta

26 76^{v} *Barriera*, Balletto di M. Battistino; In Lode dell'Illustr.^{ma} Sig.^{ra} Mia et Patrona Osservand.^{ma} la Signora Beatrice Caetana Cesi: two dedicatory poems and choreography

78^{v} Music for lute ["Questo farassi sette volte"]

79 La rotta grave farassi due volte

79^{v} La rotta in Saltarello farassi una volta

79^{v} La rotta in Gagliarda

27 80 *Bassa Romana*, Balletto di M. Battistino; In Lode dell'Illustr.^{ma} Signora et Patrona Mia Osservand.^{ma} la Signora Giovanna Caetana Orsina: dedicatory poem and choreography

81 Music for lute

81^{v} La sua Sciolta in Gagliarda

28 82 *Gratia d'Amore*, Balletto; In Lode dell'Illustr.^{ma} Signora, la Signora Beatrice Orsina Sforza Conti: dedicatory poem and choreography

83^{v} Music for lute = no. 79a

83^{v} [La sua sciolta] = no. 79b

29 84 *Lucretia Favorita*, Balletto di M. Battistino; In Lode dell'Illustr.^{ma} Signora, la Signora Lucretia Salviati Orsina: dedicatory poem and choreography

85^{v} Music for lute

86 La sua Sciolta in Gagliarda, farassi due volte

30 86^{v} *Bentivoglio*, Cascarda; In Lode dell'Illustr.^{ma} Signora la Signora Pellegrina Cappello Bentivogli: dedicatory poem and choreography

87^{v} Music for lute

87^{v} Riprese due

31 88 *Pungente Dardo*, Balletto; In Lode dell'Illustr.^{ma} Signora la Signora Costanza Conte Cuppis: dedicatory poem and choreography

89^{v} Music for lute

89^{v} La Sciolta va due volte

32 90 *Coppia Cappelli*, Balletto; In Lode dell'Illustr.^{ma} Signora la Signora Elena Cappello Cappelli: dedicatory poem and choreography

91 Music for lute = no. 21

33 91^{v} *Amor Felice*, Balletto d'Incerto; In Lode dell'Illustr.^{ma} Signora la Signora Virginia dell'Anguillara Bordugiera: dedicatory poem and choreography

93 Music for lute ["Questo primo tempo farassi dieci volte"]

93^{v} La sua Sciolta

34 94 *Bella Gioiosa*, Cascarda; In Lode dell'Illustr.^{ma} Signora la Signora Giulia Savella Orsina: dedicatory poem and choreography

95v Music for lute ["farassi duoi Tempi senza li Ritornelli"]

95v Questo ritornello farassi tre volte

35 96 *Nobiltà*, Balletto; In Lode dell'Illustrissima Signora, la Signora Giulia Nobile Ricci: dedicatory poem and choreography

97 Music for lute

36 97v *Fiamma d'Amore*, Cascarda; In Lode dell'Illustr.ma Signora la Signora Cornelia Teodola Orsina: dedicatory poem and choreography

98v Music for lute

37 99 *Saporita*, Balletto; In Lode dell'Illustrissima Signora, la Signora Portia Orsina Celsi: dedicatory poem and choreography

100 Music for lute

100 [La sua sciolta]

38 100v *Leggiadria d'Amore*, Balletto; In Lode dell'Illustre Signora la Signora Lucretia Crescenza Frangipane, Gentildonna Romana: dedicatory poem and choreography

102 Music for lute

39 102v *Alta Vittoria*, Balletto di M. Oratio Martire; In Lode dell'Illustre Signora, la Sig. Vittoria Accorambona, Gentildonna Romana: dedicatory poem and choreography

104v Music for lute

104v La sua Gagliarda

105 La Sciolta = no. 10

105 Il Canario

40 105v *Amor Mio*, Balletto di M. Paolo Arnandes; In Lode dell'Illustre Signora la Signora Giulia Matthei de Torres: dedicatory poem and choreography

107 Music for lute

41 107v *Allegrezza d'Amore*, Cascarda di M. Oratio Martire fatta in terzo; In Lode dell'Illustre Signora la Signora Lavinia Cavalieri Carducci, Gentildonna Romana: dedicatory poem and choreography

109 Music for lute

42 109v *Coppia Matthei*, Balletto di M. Battistino; In Lode dell'Illustre Signora la Signora Claudia Matthea Matthei, Gentildonna Romana: dedicatory poem and choreography

110v Music for lute

111 La sua Sciolta in Gagliarda

43 111v *Pavana Matthei*, Balletto di M. Battistino; In Lode dell'Illustre Signora, la Signora Giulia Bandina Matthei, Gentildonna Romana: dedicatory poem and choreography

113v Music for lute[7]

113v La sua Sciolta[7]

44 114 *Chiara Stella*, Cascarda; In Lode dell'Illustre Signora la Signora Olimpia Cuppis de' Massimi, Gentildonna Romana: dedicatory poem and choreography

115v Music for lute[8]

45 116 *Gentilezza d'Amore*, Cascarda; In Lode dell'Illustre Signora, la Signora Costanza Castra Scalinci, Gentildonna Romana: dedicatory poem and choreography

117v Music for lute = no. 13

46 118 *Rustica Palina*, Balletto di M. Battistino; In Lode dell'Illustre Signora, la Signora Laura Palina Rustici, Gentildonna Romana: dedicatory poem and choreography

119v Music for lute

119v La Rotta

120 [La sua sciolta] = no. 57

47 120v *Alta Sergarda*, Cascarda; In Lode dell'Illustre Signora, la Signora Martia Rustici Sergardi, Gentildonna Romana: dedicatory poem and choreography

121v Music for lute

48 122 *Gloria d'Amore*, Cascarda; In Lode dell'Illustre Signora, La Sig. Virginia Mancina Glorieri, Gentildonna Romana: dedicatory poem and choreography

123 Music for lute

49 123v *Candida Luna*, Cascarda; In Lode dell'Illustre Signora la Sig. Laura Lanti Cenci, Gentildonna Romana: dedicatory poem and choreography

125 Music for lute = no. 25

50 125v *Rustica Amorosa*, Balletto di M. Battistino; In Lode dell'Illustre Signora la Signora Vittoria Rustici della Corvara, Gentildonna Romana: dedicatory poem and choreography

127 Music for lute

127 La sua Sciolta

51 127v *Ombrosa Valle*, Balletto; In Lode dell'Illustre Signora la Signora Clelia Pontana della Valle, Gentildonna Romana: dedicatory poem and choreography

129 Music for lute

52 129v *Alta Ragonia*, Balletto di M. Battistino; In Lode dell'Illustre Signora la S. Giulia Stalla Ragonia, Gentildonna Romana: dedicatory poem and choreography

130v Music for lute

131 La Sciolta in Gagliarda

53 131v *Gracca Amorosa*, Cascarda; In Lode dell'Illustre Signora, la Sig. Margherita Gracca Boccamazzi, Gentildonna Romana: dedicatory poem and choreography

133 Music for lute

54 133v *Alta Morona*, Balletto; In Lode dell'Illustre Signora la Signora Angela Morona Palazzuola Gentildonna Romana: dedicatory poem and choreography

135 Music for lute

135 La sua Sciolta

55 135v *Giunto m'ha amore*, Cascarda; In Lode dell'Illustre Signora la Signora Quintilia Gloriera Ferreri, Gentildonna Romana: dedicatory poem and choreography

136v Music for lute

56 137 *Maraviglia d'Amore*, Cascarda; In Lode dell'Illustre Signora, la Sig. Francesca Turini Bufalini: dedicatory poem and choreography

138v Music for lute = no. 8b

57 139 *La Castellana*, Cascarda; In Lode dell'Illustre Signora, la Sig. Isabella Castella Malvasia, Gentildonna Bolognose: dedicatory poem and choreography

140v Music for lute = no. 46c

58 141 *Laccio d'Amore*, Cascarda; In Lode dell'Illustre Signora la Sig.ra Giulia Colloreta di Valvasone: dedicatory poem and choreography

142 Music for lute

59 142v *Nuova Fenice*, Balletto; In Lode dell'Illustre Signora la Signora Flaminia Americi Giacomelli, Gentildonna Romana: dedicatory poem and choreography

144 Music for lute

60 144v *Leggiadra Ninfa*, Cascarda; In Lode della Molto Mag.ca Madonna Margherita della Torre, Gentildonna di Saravezza in Toscana: dedicatory poem and choreography

146 Music for lute = nos. 2, 14, and 64

61 146v *Fedeltà*, Cascarda; In Lode dell'Illustre Sig.ra La Sig. Artemitia Ruberti Binzona, Gentildonna Romana: choreography

147 Music for lute

147 Ritornello farassi due volte

62 147v *Contrapasso nuovo*, Balletto in sesto; In Lode dell'Illustre Signora la Signora Silvia Crispi Cardana: choreography

148v Music for lute

63 149 *Furioso*, Balletto d'Incerto, da farsi in sesto: choreography

150 Music for lute ["farassi in dieci tempi gravi"]

150v La Sciolta farassi in tre Tempi

150v In questa Sonata si faranno le due Riverenze gravi

150v Fatto questo, faranno un'altro Tempo della Rotta

64 151 *Cesarina*, Balletto d'Incerto: choreography

151v Music for lute = nos. 2, 14, and 60

65 152 *Felice Vittoria*, Balletto di M. Ippolito Ghidotti da Crema; In Lode dell'Illust.ma et Ecc.ma Sig.ra la Sig.ra Vittoria D'Oria Gonzaga: dedicatory poem and choreography

153v Music for lute

154 La sua Sciolta

66 154v *Bassa et Alta*, Balletto d'Incerto: choreography

155v Music for lute

67 157 *Ballo del Fiore*, Da farsi in due; In Lode della Clarissima Sig.ra la Sig.ra Laura Moro Contarini, Gentildonna Venetiana: dedicatory poem and choreography

159 Music for lute

68 159v *Torneo Amoroso*, Balletto di M. Battistino; In Lode dell'Illustre Signora, la Sig. Lilia Crescenza Frangipane: choreography

160v Music for lute

161 [La sua sciolta]

161 [La sua sciolta]

69 161v *Bassa Toscana*, Balletto di M. Battistino; In Lode dell'Illustre Signora la Sig. Panta Crescenza Patritii, Gentildonna Romana: choreography

162v Music for lute

162v Sciolta della Sonata

70 163 *Spagnoletta:* choreography

163v Music for lute

71 164v *Spagnoletta Nuova*, da farsi in terzo; In Lode della Molto Mag.ca Madonna Giulia Paulina de' Rossi: choreography but no music (at end: "Farassi la medesima Sonata della Spagnoletta")

72 165v *Bassa Pompilia*, Balletto d'Incerto: choreography

166 Music for lute

166v La sua Gagliarda

73 167 *Tordiglione*, Con la Mutanze nuove dell'Auttore: choreography

169v Music for lute

74 170 *Vita, e quanto haggio*, Cascarda; In Lode dell'Illustre Signora la Signora Virginia Bruna Donati, Gentildonna Romana: choreography

171 Music for lute

171v *Barriera*, Balletto Da farsi in sesto; In Lode dell'Illustre Signora la Sig. Francesca Giunta Mannucci: choreography but no music

76 173 *Contrapasso*, Balletto d'Incerto, da farsi in due; In Lode della Molto Mag.ca Madonna Felicita Ziletti: choreography but no music (at end: "Farassi la medesima Sonata del Contrapasso")

77 174 *Dolce Amoroso Foco*, Balletto da farsi in sesto; In Lode della Molto Mag.ca Madonna Marta Rampazetti: choreography but no music (at end: "Farassi la medesima Sonata del Passo e mezo")

78 175 *Alta Ruissa*, Balletto; In Lode dell'Illustre Signora la Signora Virginia Crivella Ruissa, Gentildonna Romana

176 Music for lute

176 La sua Sciolta

176 Canario = nos. 80, 81

79 176v *Chiaranzana:* choreography

178v Music for lute[9] = no. 28a

178v La sua Sciolta[9] = no. 28b

80 179 *Il Canario;* In Lode dell'Illustre Sig.ra la Sig. Vittoria Santacroce Borghese, Gentildonna Romana: choreography

180v Music for lute = nos. 78, 81

81 181 *Ballo del Piantone;* In Lode della Molto Mag.ca Madonna Gratiosa Bembo, Gentildonna Venetiana: dedicatory poem and choreography

183v Music for lute = nos. 78, 80

82 183v *La Gagliarda detta Cesarina*

83 184 *La Gagliarda detta Meza notte*

[1] Facs. of title page in MagB, p. 42.

[2] Some of these cuts are repr. in HeyerV II, no. 11; KinsP, p. 116; RossiM, pp. 27, 43, and 51; and ZontaS, vol. II, pt. 2, p. 319.

[3] Copies were in the libraries of W. H. Cummings (see CummC, no. 409), Jules Écorcheville (see ÉcorC, no. 367), Wilhelm Heyer (see HeyerV II, no. 11), Horace Landau-Finaly (see RoedigC I, 122), and A. H. Littleton (see LittC, p. 22, and MLE, 1904, p. 17), and in PL:WRu.

[4] Facs. in MagniSM I, 259.

[5] On this dance, sometimes called the Spanish Pavan, see PoulN. Facs. of fols. 36v and 39v in ZontaS, vol. II, pt. 2, pp. 321–322.

[6] Mod. ed. in BehI, p. 5; ChilLS, p. 82; and KlaemM II, no. 10.

[7] Mod. ed. in StaakS, p. 4.

[8] Mod. ed. in BehI, p. 5; ChilLS, p. 82; and KlaemM II, no. 11.

[9] Mod. ed. in ChilLS, p. 83.

1582_1

BARBETTA, GIULIO CESARE

NOVAE / TABULAE MU/SICAE TESTUDINA/RIAE HEXACHORDAE / ET HEPTACHORDAE. / Julii Caesaris

Barbetti Paduani. / Neu / Lautenbuch auff sechs / und Siben Chorseyten gestellt / Durch / Julium Caesarem Barbettum / von Padua. / Getruckt zu Strassburg, durch Bern/hart Jobin, Im Jar. 1582.[1]

42 fols. Italian lute tablature. The title is placed within an ornamental border (the same border as in 1577_6). On fol. *1^v: cut of a man holding a lute with the legend "Haud Libenter Testudinem Ignaris Aut Invidis, Sed Flammis Satius Commisero. Id Quod Nec Invidia Neque Ignorantia Praestare Poterit." On fol. *2: coat of arms and dedication to "ILLUSTRISSIMO PRINCIPI AC DOMINO, DOMINO PHILIPPO MARCHIONI BADENSI, Comiti Spanheimensi, &c. Domino suo Clementissimo," signed "Devotissimus, addictissimus & humilis Servitor. Julius Caesar Barbetta Patavinus." On fol. *2^v: table of contents. Fol. *3 = fol. A1. MoeDM contains a thematic index of the dances (p. 454) and concordances for them (p. 278). All of the compositions are for solo lute.

Copies in: D:DO, PL:WRu, US:Wc.

	fol.	
1	A1	*Pavana Prima ditta la Molinara*
2	A1^v	*Pavana seconda detta la bella ragazzona*
3	A1^v	*Pavana tercia detta la Contarina*
4	A2^v	*Pavana quarta detta la reale*
5	A3	*Galgiarda prima detta il toscanelo*
6	A3^v	*Galgiarda seconda detto il mato*
7	A4	*Galgiarda terctia detto Aria de Comedia*
8	A4^v	*Galgiardo quarto ditto salta Marino*
9	B1	*Preambulo Primo*
10	B1^v	*Preambulo secondo*
11	B1^v	*Preambulo tertio*
12	B2	*Preambulo quarto*
13	B2^v	*Preambulo quinto*
14	B2^v	*Preambulo sesto*
15	B3	*Passo'e mezo Primo detto il bachffart*
16	B4	*Passo'e mezo secondo musicale detto il milanese*[2]
17	C1^v	*Passo'e mezo tertio detto il Comune in 4. modi*[3] = 1592_{12}, no. 20a
	C3	*Galgiarda del Passo e mezo ut supra*[3] = 1592_{12}, no. 20c
18	C4^v	*Passo'e mezo detto la paganina*
	D1^v	*Galgiarda del Passo'e mexo ut supra*
19	D2^v	*Passo e mezo detto il .N.*
20	D3^v	*Passo e mezo deto il ponderoso*
21	D4	*Gioveneta real* Archadelt *a 4* (RISM 1541_9, p. 19)
22	D4^v	*Non mi duol il morir*[4] Barbetta padoan *a 4*
23	E1^v	*Amar un solo amante* Jachet Berchen *a 4* (RISM 1546_{15}, no. 29)
24	E2^v	*In dubio de mio stato* Orland de laso *a 4* (LassoW VIII, 35)
25	E3	*Liquide perle* Luca merentio *a 5* (MarenW I, 1)
26	E3^v	*Piangi Cor mio* Sabino *a 5* (Vogel: Hippolito Sabino 3 [1570], no. 24)
27	E4^v	*Che giova posseder* Giacohes Wert *a 4* (Vogel: Wert 31 [1564], no. 1–4)
	F1	2a pars *Mache non giov'haver*
	F1	3a pars *Quant esser Vid'car*
	F1^v	4a pars *Pero che voi vosete*
28	F2	*Basiami vita mia* B[aldesar] donato (Vogel: Donato 6 [n.d.], p. 24)
29	F3	*Dolce Fial mortir* P. A. penesstrina *a 5*
30	F3^v	*Fantasia 1*
31	F4^v	*Fantasia 2*
32	G1^v	*Fantasia 3 a 4*
33	G2	*Fantasia 4 a 4*
34	G3	*Fantasia 5 a 4*
35	G3^v	*Fantasia 6*[5] *a 4*
36	G4^v	*Fantasia 7*
37	H1^v	*Fantasia lesti 8*[6] *a 4*
38	H2^v	*Un gay Bergier* C. Janequin *a 4* (RieH II, 462: Crecquillon)
39	H3^v	*Martin menoit* C. Janequin *a 4* (CM II, 79)
40	H4	*Il nest plaisir* C. Janequin *a 4* (CM II, 51)
41	H4^v	*Il me conviet* paserau *a 4*
42	I1	*Je cherche autant Amour* Boyvin *a 4* (RISM 1545_{12}, no. 2)
43	I2	*Du moy de may* Rogier *a 4* (PubAPTM, no. 25: "Ce mois de may," Godard)
44	I2^v	*Petit giachet* Crequillon *a 4* (compare I:Bc, MS Q 26, no. 27: Courtois)

45 I3[v] *Susanne ung jour* Orlando [Lasso] *a 5* (LassoW XIV, 29)
46 I4[v] *Domine Jesu Christe* P. demonte *a 4*
47 K1[v] *Quasi Cedrus Exaltata Sum* Orlando [Lasso] *a 4* (LassoW I, 93)
48 K2[v] *Bewar mich Herr* C. non Papa *a 4* (D:Rp, MS AR 855, no. 19: Zirler)
49 K3[v] *Tua est Potentia* Joh. mouton *a 5* (RISM 1521_3, no. 14)

[1] Facs. of title page in MGG I, col. 1239.
[2] Heading on fol. B4: "Nobilissimo ac Praeclarissimo Domino Nicasio Magensreuter à Tensing, &c. Illustrissimi Principis Philippi Marchionis Badensis ac Comitis Spanheimensis aulae praefecto, &c. Domino meo colendissimo."
[3] Mod. ed. in MoeDM, p. 313.
[4] Heading on fol. D4[v]: "Admodum Reverendo ac Excellentissimo Domino Francisco Bornio a Madrigal Hispano S. S. Theologiae Licentiato Illustrissimi Principis Philippi Marchionis Badensis ac Comitis Spanhaimensis &c. Concionatori aulico ac in Spiritualibus à consiliis fautori meo amantissimo."
[5] Heading on fol. G3[v]: "Magnifico ac Excelentissimo Domino Wolfgango Hungeroi. V. D. Peritissimo, Illustrissimi Principis Philippi Marchionis Badensis ac Comitis Spanheimensis consiliario intimo & Domino meo summo amoris studio prosequendo."
[6] Heading on fol. H1: "Ala Molto Magnifica et Virtuosissima Amatrice de Vertuosi La Magnifica Signora Chiara Pisani Gientildona padona."

[1582]$_2$

BRAMBILLA, AMBROSIUS

Anleitung die Zither zu spielen, nebst Noten eines Psalmes. Ambrosius Brambilla fecit 1582, gr. qu. fol.

This work, now lost, is listed in NagM I, no. 946. It was probably a set of instructions for playing the cittern similar in scope and format to 1585_5 (instructions for playing the lute).

1582_3

BEAUJOYEULX, BALTHASAR DE

BALET COMIQUE / DE LA ROYNE, FAICT / AUX NOPCES DE MON/sieur le Duc de Joyeuse & / madamoyselle de Vau/demont sa soeur. / PAR / BALTASAR DE

BEAUJOYEULX, / VALET DE CHAMBRE DU / Roy, & de la Royne sa mere. / [Printer's mark] / A PARIS, / Par Adrian le Roy, Robert Ballard, & Mamert / Patisson, Imprimeurs du Roy. / M. D. LXXXII. / AVEC PRIVILEGE.

84 fols. Mensural notation. Dedication on fol. *2 headed "AU ROY DE FRANCE ET DE POLONGNE." On fol. *4[v]: a poem in Latin headed "Henrico III. Regi Francorum et Polonorum Christianissimo," and signed "A. Pogoesaeus." On fol. *5: a poem in French headed "Au Sieur de Beaujoyeux, sur le Balet Comique de la Royne," and signed "Billard." On fol. *5[v]: a poem in French signed "August. Costé, Dunoisien." Beginning on fol. *5[v]: a poem in French signed (on fol. *7): "Volusian." Beginning on fol. *7[v]: preface. On fol. *8[v]: the coat of arms of the king. The libretto begins on fol. *9 (= fol. 1). On fol. 76: printer's privilege. The volume contains a description of, and excerpts from, the theatrical entertainments for the wedding of the Duke de Joyeuse. Illustrations of scenes from the first performance are included, as well as some but not all of the music.[1] Instruments are specified for some of the pieces printed with text (and consequently omitted from the following list). The music from the volume is reprinted in a modern edition with piano accompaniments in WeckB. BeauB is a facsimile of the entire volume. For further information see CellerO; PruB, pp. 82–94; and YaF. All of the compositions listed below are for instrumental ensemble *a 5* except no 3, which is *a 12*.

Copies in: A:Wn, CH:Lcortot, F:Ameyer, F:B, F:Nd, F:Pa, F:Pc, F:Pm, F:Pn (seven copies), F:Po, F:Pthibault, F:RO, GB:Lbm, GB:Lbmh, I:Tn, NL:DHgm, US:CA, US:NYp,[2] US:SM, US:U, US:Wc.[3]

fol.
1 27[v] *La premiere entrée*[4]
2 30[v] *Le son de la clochete, auquel Circé sortie de son Jardin*[5]
3 42[v] *Response* [to the "Chant des quatre vertus" on fol. 41[v]] *de la voute dorée aux vertus: à chaque couplet c'estoit une Musique de douze instrumens sans voix*[6]

4	56ᵛ	*La petite entrée du grand balet a5*
5	56ᵛ	*La grand'entrée*

[1] Some of the cuts illustrating the performance are repr. in EF I, 362; HarmM, pl. 18; LiuM, p. 120 (including title page and fol. *5) and pls. 9–11; MagB, p. 138 (title page); Maggs28, p. 101 (title page) and pls. 14 and 15; MGG I, pl. 42 and col. 1166; PinchIH, p. 42; PruB, pl. 3; SharpD, pl. 25; and SubHM I, 533.

[2] This copy once belonged to Ben Jonson.

[3] Copies once belonged to J. E. Matthew (see MLE, 1904, p. 105), and Henry Prunières (see ThibaultC).

[4] Mod. ed. of the beginning in AmbG IV, 173, and EC, pt. I, vol. III, p. 1208.

[5] Mod. ed. in AmbG IV, 175.

[6] Mod. ed. in AmbG IV, 180, and EC, pt. I, vol. III, p. 1209; facs. of a part of fol. 42ᵛ in PN, p. 76.

$[1582]_4$

MASCHERA, FIORENZO

LIBRO PRIMO DE CANZONI DA SONARE, A QUATTRO VOCI, DI FLORENTIO MASCHERA ORGANISTA NEL DUOMO DI BRESCIA.

The 1584 edition of this volume "con diligenza ristampate" has a dedication dated March 2, 1582. It therefore seems likely that the first edition was printed in that year. The entire collection is transcribed into keyboard partitura in B:Bc, MS 26660 (dated 1582); for a discussion of the manuscript see LowE, p. 135.[1] Contents = 1584_{10}.

[1] Facs. of one page of the manuscript in LowE. pl. 7.

1582_5

PHALÈSE, PIERRE, AND JEAN BELLÈRE, PUBLISHERS

HORTULUS CITHARAE / VULGARIS CONTINENS OPTIMAS / FANTASIAS, CANTIONES QUE MUSICAS PULCHER/RIMAS, ET PASSOMEZOS IN VARIOS TONOS CON/cinné variatos atque deductos: Paduanas, Gailliardas, Almandes, Branles: / aliaque nonnulla jucundissima in Tabulaturam Citharae conve/nienter redacta, nunc primum in lucem elegan/tiore modo ac ordine edita. / Accessit praeterea brevis & dilucida in Citharam Introductio, qua suo marte / quilibet artem pulsanda Citharae addiscere possit facillime. / ANTVERPIAE / Excudebat Petrus Phalesius sibi & Joanni Bellero. / 1582.

4 + 100 fols. French cittern tablature. The title is placed within an ornamental border. On fol. A1ᵛ: a poem in Latin beginning "Forte parens Citharae, Citharam pulsabat Apollo," and signed "LUCAE BELLERI I. F." Beginning on fol. A2: the same instructions for playing the cittern as in 1568_6, headed "In usum citharae brevis introductio." Fol. B1 = fol. 1. On fols. 99ᵛ–100: table of contents. All of the compositions are for solo cittern.

Copy in: PL:WRu.

	fol.	
1	1	*Fantasia Prima*
2	1ᵛ	*Fantasia 2*
3	2ᵛ	*Fantasia 3* = 1568_6, no. 2
4	3	*Fantasia 4* = 1568_6, no. 1
5	3ᵛ	*Allegez moy* = 1568_6, no. 57
6	4ᵛ	*Susanne un jour a4* = 1570_3, no. 5: Didier Lupi Second
7	5ᵛ	*D'ou vient cela* = 1568_6, no. 34: Sermisy
8	6ᵛ	*Languir me faut* = 1570_3, no. 7: Sermisy
9	7ᵛ	*Tant que vivray* = 1568_6, no. 32: Sermisy
10	8	*Un Advocat dict à sa femme* = 1568_6, no. 25: Delafont
11	8ᵛ	*Ce mois de may* = 1568_6, no. 76: Godard
12	9ᵛ	*Douce memoire* = 1568_6, no. 64: Sandrin
13	10ᵛ	*Damour me plains* (PubAPTM XXIII, no. 49: Pathie)
14	11ᵛ	*Si pur ti guardo* = 1570_3, no. 31: Pathie
15	12ᵛ	*Je prens en gré* (ClemensO X, 14: Clemens non Papa)
16	13ᵛ	*Si mon traveil* = 1568_6, no. 70: Sandrin
17	14ᵛ	*Le dueil yssu* ("*Response*") = 1568_6, no. 71: Villiers
18	15	*C'est à grand tort* = 1578_4, no. 26
19	16ᵛ	*En esperance j'endure* = 1578_4, no. 4

20 17 *J'ay trop aymer* = 1568$_6$, no. 36
21 17^v *Si me tenez* (RISM 1545$_{13}$, fol. 14: Crecquillon)
22 19 *Plus que jamais* = 1578$_4$, no. 1
23 19^v *L'ennuy qui me tourmente* = 1578$_4$, no. 7
24 20 *Godt es mijn licht*[1]
25 21 *Pis ne me peult venir* = 1568$_6$, no. 33: Crecquillon
26 21^v *Dames qui au plaisant* = 1570$_3$, no. 22: Didier Lupi Second
27 22 *Je ne veux plus* = 1570$_3$, no. 23
28 22^v *Bon jour mon coeur* = 1570$_3$, no. 26: Lasso
29 23 *J'ay bien mal choisi* = 1570$_3$, no. 25: Nicolas
30 23^v *Quand mon mury* = 1570$_3$, no. 27: Lasso
31 24 *Amour est un grand maistre* = 1570$_3$, no. 28: Arcadelt (compare no. 40 below)
32 24^v *Susanne un jour* Orlando [Lasso] (LassoW XIV, 29)
33 26 *Le coeur l'esprit* = 1578$_4$, no. 25
34 26^v *Donna crudel* = 1578$_4$, no. 38
35 27 *Sia sia maladetta* = 1570$_3$, no. 155
36 27^v *La cortesia* = 1570$_3$, no. 152: Lasso
37 28 *Sto core mio* = 1570$_3$, no. 153: Lasso
38 28^v *Madonna mia pieta* = 1570$_3$, no. 149: Lasso
39 29 *Le vecchie per invidia* = 1578$_4$, no. 36
40 29^v *Die lieb ist ein maister* = 1570$_3$, no. 164 (compare no. 31 above)
41 30 *So wunsch ich dir gute nacht* = 1578$_4$, no. 43
42 30^v *Nun fahr hin alle mein trauren* = 1570$_3$, no. 166
43 31^v *Gros lieb hat mich ombfanghen* = 1570$_3$, no. 163
44 32 *Passomezo Milanese* = 1570$_3$, no. 169a: "Passomezo dytalye Superius"
32^v *Padoana Milanese* = 1570$_3$, no. 169b
32^v *Saltarello Milanese* = 1570$_3$, no. 169c: "Gaillarde dytalye"
45 33^v *Passomezo Commune* = 1564$_7$, no. 2a
34^v *Gailliarde Commune* = 1564$_7$, no. 2c: "Saltarello Commune"
46 35 *Passomezo de Zorsi* = 1578$_4$, no. 50a
35^v *Gailliarde de Zorsi* = 1578$_4$, no. 50b
47 36^v *Passomezo d'Angleterre* = 1569$_6$, no. 59a
36^v *Reprinse* = 1569$_6$, no. 59b
48 37 *Passomezo la douce* = 1569$_6$, no. 65a
37^v *Reprinse* = 1569$_6$, no. 65b
49 37^v *Passomezo de la Bataille* = 1564$_7$, no. 10
38^v *La precedente diminuée* = 1570$_3$, no. 165
39^v *Gailliarde de la Battaille* = 1569$_6$, no. 83
50 40 *Padoana Espanolle* = 1565$_2$, no. 6
51 40^v *Passomezo de Haubois* = 1578$_4$, no. 47a: "Passomezo commune"
41 *Gailliarde de Haubois* = 1578$_4$, no. 47b
41^v *Passomezo de Haubois, diminuée* = 1570$_3$, no. 167a: "Passemezo Commune"
42^v *Saltarello de Haubois diminuée* = 1570$_3$, no. 167b: "Saltarello Commune"
52 43^v *Gailliarde Romanesque* = 1564$_5$, no. 17
53 44 *Bassus de Passomezo d'Italye*
44^v *Gailliarde d'Italye. Bassus*
44^v *Autre [gailliarde d'Italye]*
54 45 *Passomezo d'Italye. Tenor* = 1570$_3$, no. 168a
45^v *Plus diminuée*
46^v *Gailliarde de Passomezo. Tenor* = 1570$_3$, no. 168b
55 47^v *Passomezo d'Italye. Contratenor*
47^v *La Gailliarde*
56 48 *Prima Passomezo d'Italie. Superius*
57 48^v *Secunda Passomezo* = 1570$_3$, no. 35
58 49 *Tertia Passomezo*
59 49^v *Quarta Passomezo*
60 50 *Quinta Passomezo*
61 50^v *Sexta Passomezo*
62 51^v *Septima Passomezo*
63 52 *Octava Passomezo*
64 52^v *Nona Passomezo*
53 *Reprinse de la Passomeze*
65 53^v *La Premiere Gailliarde de Passomezo*
66 54 *Gailliarde 2*

67 54^v *Gailliarda Tertia* = 1569_6, no. 70b

68 55 *Gailliarde Quarta*

69 55^v *Quinta Gailliarda*

70 56 *Sexta Gailliarda*

71 56^v *Chy Passa Superius*

57 *Autre*

57^v *Gailliarde Chy Passa autrement*

58^v *Plus diminuée*

59 *Tenor eiusdem*

59^v *Bassus eiusdem*

72 60 *Caracossa Superius* = 1570_3, no. 46a

60^v *Caracossa Gailliarde diminuée* = 1570_3, no. 46b

61 *Caracossa Bassus* = 1565_3, no. 5: "Gaillarde J'aymeroys mieux dormir seulette"

61^v *Caracossa Contratenor* = 1570_3, no. 46d

73 61^v *Gailliarde* = 1578_4, no. 69: "Gaillarde M. Sixto"

74 62 *Si pour t'aymer Gailliarde*

75 62^v *Gailliarde*

76 63 *La Gailliarde roche el fuso*

77 63^v *Gailliarde de la Royne d'Ecosse* = 1564_7, no. 42

78 64 *Gailliarde la Lionnoyse* = 1564_5, no. 11

79 64^v *Gailliarde Baisons nous* = 1570_3, no. 59

80 65 *Gailliarde* = 1564_7, no. 23

81 65^v *La Morette gailliarde* = 1564_5, no. 10

82 65^v *Gailliarde* = 1578_4, no. 64: "Gaillarde Ich kan und mag nicht frölich sein"

83 66 *Gailliarde la Gaye* = 1564_5, no. 15

84 66^v *Era di maio Gailliarde* = 1578_4, no. 62

85 66^v *Gailliarde* = 1578_4, no. 63

86 67 *Volte*

87 67^v *Gailliarde Brunette* (compare 1569_6, no. 79: "Gaillarde O ma gente brunette") = 1570_3, no. 64

88 68 *Gailliarde Puisque nouvelle affection* = 1564_5, no. 14

89 68^v *Gailliarde* = 1564_7, no. 21

90 69 *Bouffons Bassus* = 1565_3, no. 2

91 69^v *Si vous estes belle Almande*

92 70 *Almande Loreyne* = 1569_6, no. 24

93 70^v *Almande de la Nonette* = 1578_4, no. 78: "Almande Ich ging ainmal spaciren"

71 *Reprinse*

94 71 *Almande Philippine*

95 71^v *Almande Fleur*

96 72 *Almande d'Amour*

97 72 *Almande guerre guerre*

98 72^v *Almande Bruynswyck*

72^v *Reprinse*

99 73 *Almande* = 1578_4, no. 70

100 73^v *Almande en truert nyet meer*

101 73^v *Almande d'Anvers*

102 74 *Almande Poussinghe* = 1569_6, no. 14

103 74^v *Almande de lignes* = 1578_4, no. 74

74^v *Reprinse*

104 75 *Almande Guillemette*

105 75^v *Almande d'Egmont*

106 75^v *Almande de don Frederico*

107 76 *Almande France*

108 76^v *Almande Bisarde* = 1569_6, no. 15

109 76^v *Almande* = 1578_4, no. 73: "Almande nova"

110 77 *Almande Prince* = 1578_4, no. 79

77 *Reprinse*

111 77^v *Branle de Lovain* = 1570_3, no. 175a: "Branle del duc"

77^v *Autrement*

78^v *Le Saltarelle* = 1570_3, no. 175b: "La Courante"

78^v *La Couraante* = 1570_3, no. 175c: "Le saltarelle"

112 79 *Hoboken*

113 79^v *Den boerendans*

114 80 *Branle Bombirole*

115 80^v *Branle de Champagne*

116 81 *Branle de Malta*

117 81^v *Branle de Berghes*

118 82 *Branle de Battaille*

119 82 *Branle d'Angleterre*

120 82^v *L'Homme armé*

82^v *Autrement*

121 83 *Branle duecht en iuecht*

122 83^v *Branle d'amour* = 1569_6, no. 32

123 84^v *Branle le beau Robert* = 1565_3, no. 18

124 85 *Branle de Rebecca* = 1569_6, no. 53a

85 *Autre* = 1569_6, no. 53b

125 85^{v} *Branle de Bourgoigne* = 1569_6, no. 43
126 86 *2. Branle* = 1569_6, no. 44
127 86 *3. Branle* = 1569_6, no. 45
128 86^{v} *Quatriesme branle* = 1569_6, no. 46
129 87 *Branle le Gay* = 1564_5, no. 24
87 *Autre*
130 87^{v} *Premier Branle de Bourgoigne* = 1565_3, no. 9
131 87^{v} *2. Branle* = 1565_3, no. 10
132 88 *Troisiesme branle* = 1565_3, no. 11
133 88^{v} *Quatrieme branle* = 1565_3, no. 12
134 88^{v} *Cinquiesme branle* = 1565_3, no. 13
135 89 *6. Branle* = 1565_3, no. 14
136 89^{v} *Setiesme branle* = 1565_3, no. 15
137 89^{v} *Huitiesme branle* = 1565_3, no. 16
138 90 *Neufiesme branle* = 1565_3, no. 17
139 90^{v} *Branle de Poictou* = 1564_5, no. 30
140 90^{v} *Les Matachins* = 1564_5, no. 20
141 91 *Calleken van nieu poorte* = 1569_6, no. 57
142 91^{v} *Den lustelycken mey* = 1564_7, no. 27
143 92 *Ick had een ghestadich minneken* = 1564_7, no. 36: Clemens non Papa
144 92 *Slouf slouf* [*waer hebdi gheweest*] = 1568_6, no. 56
145 92^{v} *Een venus dierken* = 1568_6, no. 5
146 96^{v} *Een amoureux fiereghelaete* = 1568_6, no. 6
147 93 *Het wasser te nacht* = 1568_6, no. 7
148 93^{v} *Linkens hoven* = 1570_3, no. 142
149 93^{v} *Verjubileert* = 1570_3, no. 144
150 94 *Int soetste vanden mey* (compare DuyL I, 149 [different melody])
151 94^{v} *Era di maggio. Superius* = 1564_7, no. 25
94^{v} *Tenor eiusdem*
95 *Bassus eiusdem*
95 *Contratenor eiusdem*
152 95^{v} *Battaille*
97^{v} *Victoire*
97^{v} *La Gailliarde de la bataille*

[1] Fol. 20 is missing from the unique copy of the volume. The title is taken from the table of contents. The piece may have been identical with 1568_6, no. 74.

1583_1

AGOSTINI, LODOVICO

IL NUOVO ECHO / A' cinque voci / DEL R.^{DO} MONS.^{OR} DON / LODOVICO AGOSTINI / FERRARESE, / Protonotario Apostolico, Capellano, & Musico / Del Sereniss. & Invittissimo Signor / DUCA DI FERRARA. / Libro Terzo. Opera Decima. / A CINQUE [Cut of the coat of arms of Ferrara] VOCI. / IN FERRARA, / Nella Stamperia di Vittorio Baldini, / Con Licentia de' Superiori. / MDLXXXIII.

Five part books in mensural notation, each of 14 fols. The title is placed within an ornamental border. Dedication on fol. 1^{v} (= p. 2) of each part book headed "AL SERENISS.^{MO} ET INVITTISS.^{MO} PRENCIPE SIGNOR, IL SIGNOR DONNO ALFONSO DA ESTE DUCA DI FERRARA MIO SOMMO, ET SOLO SIGNORE COLENDISSIMO." On p. 28 of each part book: two anonymous sonnets to Agostini, the table of contents, and the colophon: "In Ferrara, Nella Stamperia di Vittorio Baldini, Con licentia de' Superiori, M DL XXXII [*sic*]." The dedication and the sonnets are reprinted in SartMS, pp. 38–39. All of the contents are listed in SartMS, p. 39, and Vogel: Agostini 5 (1583), which includes a part of the dedication. Contains 25 compositions with Italian text, and two pieces for instrumental ensemble *a 5*.

Copies in: I:MOe, I:Tn.

p.
1 11 *FANTASIA da Sonar con gli Istromenti. Ad imitatione del Sig. Alessandro Striggio* (compare Vogel: Striggio 3 [1566], no. 20: "S'ogni mio ben havete")
2 13 *INTRAMEZZO*

1583_2

AMMERBACH, ELIAS NICOLAUS

Orgel oder In/strument Tabulaturbuch, in sich / begreiffende eine notwendige unnd kurtze anlai/tung, die Tabulatur unnd application zuverstehen, / auch dieselbige auss gutem grunde recht zu lernen. / Darnach folgen auffs allerleichtest gute Deutsche La/teinische, Welsche und Frantzösische stücklein, neben etlichen Pas/somezen, Galliarden, Repressen, unnd deutschen Dentzen, dessglei/chen zuvor in offnem druck nie aussgangen. / Jetzund aber, der Jugend und anfahenden diser kunst zu gutem, / mit fleiss zusammen gebracht, und in druck verfertigt, / Durch / Eliam Nicolaum Ammerbach, Burgern und Orga/ nisten inn Leipzig, zu S. Thomas. / Mit Röm: Kei: Maiestat Freiheit, nit nachzudrucken. / Nürmberg.

116 fols. German keyboard tablature. Dedication and preface ("Vorrede") on fol. A2 headed "Dem Durchleuchtigen, Hochgebornen Fürsten und Herrn, Herrn Joachim Ernst, Fürsten zu Anhalt, Grafen zu Ascanien, Herrn zu Zerbst und Bernburgk &c. Meinem genedigen Fürsten und Herrn," and signed on fol. A4^v "Datum Leipzig den 21. Martii, nach Christi unsers Erlösers und Seligmachers geburt, im 1583 Jar. E. F. G. Untertheniger gehorsamer Elias Nicolaus Ammerbach inn Leipzig, Burger und Organist zu S. Thomas." On fol. B1: instructions for playing the organ headed "Kurtze anleitung oder Instruction für die anfahenden Discipel der Orgelkunst." On fol. B1: poem in Latin headed "Epigramma," and signed "M. Michaël Schumlerus, Misnens." Fol. B4^v = p. 1. On p. 214: table of contents. Colophon on p. 216: "Typis Gerlachianis." This is a second revised and expanded edition of 1571_1. Pieces followed by an asterisk are identical with those in 1571_1. See there for concordances. All of the compositions are for solo keyboard.

Copies in: D:Mbs, D:W, PL:WRu, S:Sk.

	p.	
1	1	*Allmechtiger gütiger Gott* (AmeH, vol. I, pt. 2, p. 235: Le Maistre)
2	1	*Dancket dem Herren denn er ist**
3	1	*Herr Gott nu sey gepreyset* (compare 1571_1, no. 2, and nos. 4–6 below)
4	3	[*Herr Gott*] *Aliud Idem in Altu* (compare no. 3 above)
5	3	[*Herr Gott*] *Aliud idem in Tenore* (compare no. 3 above)
6	3	[*Herr Gott*] *Aliud idem & ultimum in Bassu* (compare no. 3 above)
7	5	*Danck sagen wir alle* (compare BäumK I, no. 31, and ZahnM V, no. 8619b–d)
	6	2a pars *Den sollen wir alle*
8	7	*Lobet den Herren* (ScanN, no. 5: Scandello)
9	7	*Ehr lob und danck**
10	9	*Gelobet seistu Jesu Christ* (compare BäumK I, no. 30, and ZahnM I, no. 1947)
11	9	*Puer natus in Bethlehem* (compare BäumK I, no. 52, and ZahnM I, no. 192b)
12	11	*Joseph lieber Joseph mein* (compare BäumK I, 303, and ZahnM I, no. 8573a)
13	13	*Moisi Ex legis observantia*
14	15	*Surrexit Christus hodie*
15	15	*Spiritus sancti gratia* (compare BäumK, 657, and ZahnM I, no. 370)
16	18	*Ich bin zu lang gewesen*
17	17	*Zart freundlichs M.**
18	19	*Schönes lieb was hab ich dir*
19	21	*Schein uns du liebe sonne* (ScanL: Scandello)
20	23	*Scheiden von der lieb das thut wehe*
21	24	*Wie schön blüt uns der Meye* (RISM 1597_7, no. 50: Meiland)
22	25	*Mir liebet im grünen Meyen*
23	25	*Gros lieb hat mich**
24	25	*Venus du unnd dein Kindt* (compare PubAPTM XIX, no. 8: Regnart)
25	27	*Viel strick und Seil*
26	28	*Paule lieber Stalbruder**
27	29	*Elend ich rieff**
28	31	*Stannote, oder Cantate*
29	33	*Sio Canto*
30	33	*Die schöne Sommerzeit*
31	35	*Mit lust thet ich ausreiten** [Senfl]
32	37	*Gehabt euch wol zu diesen**
33	39	*Die mich erfrewet*
34	41	*Ecce Maria genuit*
35	43	*Gott ist mein liecht* (VNM XXVI, 51: "Godt is mijn licht," Clemens non Papa)
36	46	*Tröstlicher liebe** [Hofhaimer]
37	48	*Petercken* [*sprack tho Petercken*]

38 50 *Mein fleis und müh* (SenflW IV, no. 19: Senfl)
39 50 *Ein Megdlein sprach mir** [Malchinger or Senfl]
40 52 *Dantz Megdelein dantz*
52 *Proportio tripla*
41 53 *Mit lieb bin ich umbfangen*[1] (SenflW VI, no. 25: Senfl)
42 53 *Isspruck ich mus dich lassen** [Isaac]
43 55 *Ich rewe und klage** ["Tröstlicher lieb," Hofhaimer]
44 57 *Fuchs wild bin ich**
45 59 *Ach unfals neid** [Wolff]
46 61 *Vergangen ist mir glück und heil** [Forster]
47 63 *Ach du edler Rebensafft**
48 63 *Sophia spanne das füllein** [Buchner]
49 65 *Ich bitte dich Megdlein hab mich holdt**
50 67 *Ich armes Megdlein** [Senfl]
51 69 *Ich sag ade**
52 71 *Ein Henlein weis**
53 73 *Allein nach dir Herr** ["Si pur ti guardo," Pathie]
54 75 *Ich habs gewagt**
55 76 *Ich setz dahin hertz**
56 77 *Mein gemüht unnd blüt** [Wenck]
57 77 *Ich schwing mein hertz*[2] (SenflW V, no. 44: "Ich schwing mein Horn," Senfl)
58 79 *Frisch auff gut Gesel**
59 81 *So wündsche ich ir eine gute nacht** [Stoltzer]
60 83 *Gar hoch auff jenem berge* (PubAPTM XIX, no. 21: Heintz)
61 84 *Was wird es doch*[3] (SenflW IV, no. 26: Senfl)
62 85 *Von Edeler art* (MosPH, p. 180: Schönfelder or Hofhaimer)
63 88 *Vor zeiten war ich lieb**
64 89 *Wenn ich des Morgens frü auff steh*[4] (SenflW IV, no. 47: Senfl)
65 92 *Wolauff gut Gesell* (RISM 1597_7, no. 52: Meiland)
66 93 *Das nessel kraut* (compare SenflW V, no. 28b)
67 93 *Contingat illis*
68 96 *Bewar mich Herr* (D:Rp, MS AR 855, no. 19: Zirler)
69 97 *Frais & galiart* (ClemensO X, 17: Clemens non Papa)
70 101 *Cum sancto spiritu* (JosqMS, no. 16: *Missa de Beata Virgine*, Josquin)
71 103 *Dulce Memoriae* (PubAPTM XXIII, no. 50: "Doulce memoire," Sandrin)
72 105 *Ade mi mort* (ClemensO X, 32: "A demy mort," Clemens non Papa)
73 107 *Anchor che col partier* (SCMA VI, 45: Rore)
74 109 *Dame par ta Rudesse*
75 111 *Alix Avvos* (RISM 1545_{16}, fol. 12^v: "Alix avoit aux dens," Crecquillon)
76 114 *Panoino languir damour*
77 116 *Ces faux* (AttainCK II, no. 25: "Ces fascheux sotz")
78 117 *Ge prens* (ClemensO X, 14: "Je prens en gre," Clemens non Papa)
119 2a pars *More me fult* (RISM 1570_8, p. 11: "Mourir me fault," response to "Je prens en gre")
79 122 *Damour me plain* (PubAPTM XXIII, no. 49: Pathie)
124 2a pars *De vous me plain*
80 125 *Ung jour advint*
81 129 *Blanque clairet*
82 132 *Gemois de mai* (PubAPTM XXIII, no. 25: "Ce mois de may," Godard)
83 134 *Jo Mison jovenette* (EinIM III, no. 30: "Io mi son giovenetta," D. Ferabosco)
84 135 *Ossiu potessi donu* (RISM 1541_9, p. 19: Berchem)
85 138 *Quiso gramin questo*
86 138 *Lecetur*
87 142 *Amour & moii*
88 144 *Orsus a cop* (RISM 1570_8, p. 39)
89 145 *Ochi lucent*
90 145 *Le departier* (ClemensO X, 3: Clemens non Papa)
91 147 *Ung hug de ugs*
92 149 *Vivous Io jeu*
93 151 *Quantio pens* (RISM 1541_9, p. 54: "Quando io penso al martire," Arcadelt)
94 155 *Passamezo antico primo** (= 1571_1, no. 62)

95 155 _Passamezo antico Secundo_* (= 1571_1, no. 63)
96 156 _Passamezo antico Tertio_* (= 1571_1, no. 64)
157 _Saltarella cum Reprisa_
97 159 _Passamezo nova_* (= 1571_1, no. 70)
98 161 _Alia passamezo_*[5] (= 1571_1, no. 61a)
161 _La Reprisa_* (= 1571_1, no. 61b)
161 _Saltarella vel tripla proportio_* (= 1571_1, no. 61c: "Gaillarde")
99 164 _Der Englische Passamezo_*[6] (= 1571_1, no. 69a)
164 _Saltarella_* (= 1571_1, no. 69c: "Proportio Oder Gaillard")
100 165 _Alia Passamezo_
167 _Saltarella ut proportio_
101 168 _Alia Passamezo italica_
102 169 _Aliud Passamezo_
103 169 _Alia & ultima Passamezo_
170 _La Reprisa prima_
171 _Secunda & ultima Reprisa_
104 173 _Chi passa per quaesta strada_ [_Galliarde_][7] (compare AzzaiV, no. 2: Azzaiolo)
105 176 _Ein ander Galliart_ (compare 1564_5, no. 18: "Gaillarde J'aymeroys myeulx dormir seulette")
106 176 _Ein ander Galliarth_* (= 1571_1, no. 67)
177 _Eben derselbige Galliart auff ein ander art_
107 177 _Ein ander Galliarth_ (compare 1568_7, no. 132: "Gaillarda la Royne d'escosse")
108 178 _Ein ander Galliart_ (compare 1550_5, no. 28: "Gaillarde L'ennuy qui me tourmente")
109 180 _Ein ander Galliarth_ (compare 1571_5, no. 39: "Puisque vivre en servitude Gaillarde")
110 179 _Ein ander Galliart_* (= 1571_1, no. 68: compare 1568_6, no. 82: "Gaill[arde] Si pour t'aymer")
111 181 _Ein ander Galliarth_* (= 1571_1, no. 66)
112 181 _Der Wittembergische Galliart mit folgendem nachtantz_
183 _Proportio oder nachtantz_
113 185 _Studenden Dantz_
186 _Proportio tripla_
114 185 _Sind denn die Bürgers Söhne so leiden wol gehort_* (= 1571_1, no. 59)
185 _Proportio tripla_*
115 187 _Salve puella, Gott grüs_ (= 1571_1, no. 57)
188 _Proportio_
116 187 _Ein kurtz Schlesisch Dentzlein_* (= 1571_1, no. 53)
187 _Proportio_*
117 189 _Hertzog Moritz Dantz_* = 1571_1, no. 48
189 _Proportio tripla_*
118 189 _Ein ander kurtzer Dantz_* (= 1571_1, no. 50)
189 _Proportio_*
119 191 _Ein ander lustiges Dentzlein_* (= 1571_1, no. 56)
192 _Proportio_*
120 191 _Aber ein ander Dentzlein_* (= 1571_1, no. 52: "Die Megdlein sind von Flandern")
191 _Proportio_*
121 193 _Ein ander kurtz Dentzlein_* (= 1571_1, no. 45: "[Bruder Cunrads Tanzmaass]")
194 _Proportio_*
122 193 _Heckerling unnd Haberstro_* (= 1571_1, no. 46: "Wer das Töchterlein haben wil")
193 _Proportio tripla_*
123 194 _Sol ich denn nu sterben_* (= 1571_1, no. 51)
196 _Proportio tripla_*
124 196 _Ein ander kurtz Dentzlein_ (compare 1571_1, no. 54)
195 _Proportio tripla_
125 197 _Ein Schlesier Dantz_
197 _Proportio_
126 197 _Margrefische Dantz_
199 _Proportio tripla_
127 200 _Ein ander Dantz_* (= 1571_1, no. 49: "Pastorum Dantz")
200 _Proportio tripla_*
128 201 _Ein österreichischer Dantz_
202 _Der nachtantz_
129 202 _Ein Pollnischer Dantz, pator_
202 _Der nachtantz_
130 203 _Gut gsell du muss wandern_
203 _Proportio tripla_
131 206 _Des Käysers Dantz_
205 _Proportio tripla_
132 207 _Der Magister Dantz_
208 _Proportio tripla_

133	208	*Augustus Dantz*
	210	*Proportio tripla*
134	209	*Ennelein von Torgau*
	210	*Proportio tripla*
135	209	*Proficiat Ir lieben Herren*
	212	*Proportio tripla*

[1] Mod. ed. in SenflW VII, no. 25a.
[2] Mod. ed. in SenflW VII, no. 23.
[3] Mod. ed. in SenflW VII, no. 19.
[4] Mod. ed. in SenflW VII, no. 20.
[5] Mod. ed. in ApelM I, 12.
[6] Mod. ed. in ApelM I, 11, and SachsPM, p. 15.
[7] Mod. ed. in ChilJ, p. 91.

[1583]₃

LE ROY, ADRIAN

Instruction de partir toute musique des huits divers tons en tablature de luth. Paris, Adrian le Roy et Robert Ballard, 1583.

This volume, now lost, is mentioned in FétB V, 280, as a later edition of [1557]₁.

1583₄

PAIX, JAKOB

Ein Schön / Nutz unnd Ge/breüchlich Orgel Tablaturbuch. / Darinnen etlich der berümbten Componi/sten, beste Moteten, mit 12. 8. 7. 6. 5. / und 4. Stimmen ausserlesen, dieselben auff / alle fürneme Festa des gantzen Jars, und zü / dem Chormas gesetzt. Zü letzt auch aller/hand der schönsten Lieder, Pass'è mezzo / und Täntz, Alle mit grossem fleiss Coloriert. / Zü trewem dienst den liebhabern diser / Kunst, selb Corrigiert und in / Truck verwilligt. / Von / Jacobo Paix Augustano, diser zeit / Organist zu Laugingen. / In verlegung Georgen Willers. / Getruckt bey Leonhart Reinmichel, / Fürst: Pfaltz: Büchtrucker zü Laugingen. / Cum gratia & Privilegio. / M. D. XXCIII.[1]

176 fols. German keyboard tablature. The title is placed within an ornamental border. Dedication on fol. 2 headed "CLARISSIMO DOCTISSIMOQUE VIRO, D. JOHANNI LOBBETIO I. V.

DOCTORI CELEBERRIMO, DOMINO ET PATRONO SUO," and signed on fol. 3ᵛ "Lauingae secunda Dominica post Pascha, quae nomen habet ex Psalmo XXXIII. Misericordia Domini plena est terra: Anno partae salutis M. D. XXCIII." On fol. 4: preface headed "An den Käuffer," signed (on fol. 4ᵛ) "Geben zü Laugingen den 22. Februarii Anno 1583. Auff welchen Tag vor 16. Jaren, mein lieber Vatter Peter Paix, Organist zü Augspurg bey S. Anna in Gott seligklich entschlaffen," followed by a poem in Latin headed "In Zoilum." On fol. 5: Latin poem headed "In laudem Musicae Johan. Ortelius Cycnocomaeus." On fol. 5ᵛ: Latin poem by the same man headed "In librum D. Jacobi Paixi," followed by another headed "In eundem librum epigramma Michaëlis Fendii Monhem." On fol. 6: table of contents. On fol. 176: list of printing errors. Attributions to composers are taken from the table of contents. The prefatory material and thematic incipits for all of the pieces from no. 30 to the end are printed in MerT, pp. 114–129. The compositions identified by superior letters are reprinted as follows: ([a]) in EitT, nos. 48–52; ([b]) in KrausCO I, nos. 4, 10, 15, and 20, and II, no. 10; ([c]) in MerT, pp. 130–166. In the following inventory composers' initials or abbreviated names are resolved the first time they appear only. All of the compositions are for solo keyboard.[2]

Copies in: A:Wgm, B:Bc, CH:Lcortot, D:HEu, D:Mbs, D:ROu, D:W, F:Pn (imperfect), GB:Lbmh.[3]

	fol.	
1	7	*Certa fortiter, ora ferventer* Orlandus [Lasso] *a6* (LassoW XV, 82)
2	8ᵛ	*Congratulamini mihi omnes* Orlandus *a6* (LassoW XIII, 10)
	11	2a pars *Tulerunt Dominum meum*
3	13ᵛ	*Angelus Domini* Aloysius [Palestrina] *a5* (PalO VIII, no. 5)
	16ᵛ	2a pars *Et introeuntes*
4	19ᵛ	*Surgens Jesus* Orlandus *a5* (LassoW V, 60)
5	21ᵛ	*Viri Galilei* Aloysius *a6* (PalO V, no. 25)

23^{v} 2a pars *Ascendit Deus in Jubilatione*

6 25^{v} *Jubilate Domino* Gilis Paix *a5*

7 27^{v} *Veni sancte Spiritus*[4] Josquin *a6* (JosqMT, no. 49)

30^{v} 2a pars *O Lux beatissima*

8 33^{v} *Dum complerentur* Aloysius *a6* (PalO, no. 26)

35^{v} 2a pars *Dum ergo essent*

9 37^{v} *O beata et gloriosa Trinitas*[5] Aloysius *a5* (PalO V, no. 8)

40 2a pars *O vera summa sempiterna Trinitas*

10 42^{v} *Jerusalem plantabis vineam*[b] Orland. *a5* (LassoW III, 134)

44 2a pars *Gaude et Laetare Jacob*[b]

11 46 *Hodie Christus natus est*[b] Aloysius *a8* (PalO VIII, no. 32)

12 49 *Laudate Dominum omnes gentes* Orlandus *a12* (LassoW XXI, 152)

13 53 *Haec dies quam fecit Dominus* Aloysius *a6* (PalO VIII, no. 22)

14 54^{v} *Nuncium vobis* Orlandus *a5* (LassoW V, 9)

55^{v} 2a pars *Thus Deo mirrham*

15 56^{v} *Lapidabant Stephanum*[b] Aloysius *a5* (PalO V, no. 19)

16 59^{v} *Valde honorandus est* Aloysius *a4* (PalO III, no. 3)

17 61^{v} *Senex puerum*[b] Aloysius *a5* (PalO V, no. 4)

64 2a pars *Hodie Beata virgo Maria*[b]

18 66^{v} *Tribus miraculis* Aloysius *a4* (PalO III, no. 5)

19 69 *Ave Maria* Riccius *a6*

20 70^{v} *Vita in Ligno* Senflius *a5* (RISM 1559_1, no. 31)

72^{v} 2a pars *Qui Prophetice*

74 3a pars *Qui expansis*

21 75^{v} *Cantantibus Organis* Aloysius *a5* (PalO VIII, no. 3)

77^{v} 2a pars *Biduanis ac triduanis*

22 79^{v} *Beati omnes* Orlandus *a5* (LassoW VII, 136)

82 2a pars *Ecce sic benedicetur*

23 83^{v} *Decantabat populus in Israel* Clemens *a5* (RISM 1554_5, fol. 11)

24 86 *Da pacem Domine*[b] Orlandus *a6* (LassoW XIII, 72)

25 87^{v} *Domine quid multiplicati sunt* Jac. Paix *a5*

26 88^{v} *Pater noster* Aloysius *a5* (PalO VIII, no. 1)

27 91 *Phantasia primi toni*[6] [*a4*]

28 93 *Phantasia septimi toni* [*a4*]

29 95 *Benedictio, et Claritas, et Sapientia*[7] Orland. *a6* (LassoW XI, 139)

30 97 *Alma de amor* Phil. de monte *a7* (Vogel: Monte 14 [1580], no. 7)

31 99 *Nasce la pena mia* Strigio *a6* (MonteO XVI, app.)

32 101 *Le departir* Orlandus *a5* (LassoW XIV, 116)

33 103 *Resonet in laudibus* Waltherus *a5*

34 104^{v} *Erhalt uns Herr* Jacobus Paix *a4* (compare BöhA, no. 632; BraunS, p. 64, nos. 314–315; and ZahnM, no. 350)

35 105 *Susanna frumm* Orlandus *a5* (LassoW XVIII, 109)

36 107 *Non elasso martire* Cyprianus [de Rore] *a5* (CW V, no. 8)

37 108^{v} *Onques amour* Crequilon *a5* (RISM $[1544]_{11}$, fol. 16)

38 110 *La battaille. Escoutez* Janequin *a4* (MMRF VII, 31)

112^{v} 2a pars *Fan Fan Feyne*

39 116 *Ist keiner hie* Orlandus *a5* (LassoW XVIII, 8)

40 117^{v} *Im Mayen* Orlandus *a5* (LassoW XVIII, 24)

41 118^{v} *Mein Man der ist in Krieg zogen.* [*Die alte Schwiger*] Utentaler *a8* (UtenF, no. 13)

120 2a pars *In welchs Hauss wölt ir dann ziehen*

42 122^{v} *Elle s'en va de moy* Orlandus *a5* (LassoW XIV, 105)

43 123^{v} *Der Liendel alle tag, trat zü der* Ivo [de Vento] *a5* (VentoN, no. 10)

124^{v} 2a pars *Lauff mein lieber Liendel lauff* (VentoN, no. 11)

44 125^{v} *Es was ein mal eins Baurn Dö*[*chterlein*] Uten [taler] *a4* (UtenF, no. 5)

45 126 *Der Liendel alle tag, der war* Jac. Paix *a4* (PaixZ)

46 127 *Auff gnad so wil ichs heben an* Jac. Paix *a4* (compare BraunS, p. 50, no. 99)

47 128 *Recht so man acht unnd wol* Jac. Paix *a4* (PaixZ)

48 128[v] *Je ne veulx rien* Orlandus *a4* (LassoW XII, 98)

49 130 *Monsieur Labbè* Orlandus *a4* (LassoW XII, 16)

50 131 *Bon jour mon* [*coeur*] Orlandus *a4* (LassoW XII, 100)

51 132 *Alix avoit* Crequilon *a4* (RISM 1545_{16}, fol. 12)

52 133 *Ich armes Medlein klag mich*[8] Senflius *a4* (SenflW VI, no. 8)

53 134 *Da bei rami* Clem. de Bourges *a4* (RISM 1543_{18}, p. 31: Arcadelt)

54 135 *Schöne zucht* Jac. Paix *a4*

55 136 *Bewar mich Herr, und sey* Cirlerus *a4* (D:Rp, MS AR 855, no. 19: Zirler)

56 137[v] *Zucht Ehr unnd Lob ir wohnet*[c 9] Hofheimer *a4* (PubAPTM IX, 61: Hofhaimer)

57 139 *Pass'è mezzo Antico in Cinque modi*[c] (1578_8, no. 2a)

140[v] *Saltarello*[c] (1578_8, no. 2c)

58 141[v] *Der Pass'è mezzo Coloriert* (compare no. 57)

144[v] *Saltarello*

59 146[v] *Pass'è mezzo novo*

147 *Saltarello*

60 148 *Pass'è mezzo La parenzina*

149 *Saltarello*

61 149[v] *Un altro Pass'è mezzo novo*

151 *Saltarello*[a]

62 152 *Padoana Venetiana*[a 10]

63 153 *Galliarda nova*

64 153[v] *Branle commune*

65 154 *Branle*

66 154[v] *Galliarda*

67 155 *Branle gay*[11] (compare 1564_5, no. 24)

68 156 *Ein güter gar Newer T*[*eutscher*] *Tantz*[c] I[acobo] P[aix] O[rganista]

156[v] *Nachtantz*

69 157 *Ein güter newer Teu. Tantz*[c] A[egidius] P[aix] O[rganista]

157[v] *Nachtantz*[c]

70 158 *Ein güter newer Teu. Tantz*[c] E. M[ertel] O[rganista]

159 *Nachtantz*[c]

71 159[v] *Der Keyserin Tantz*[ac]

160 *Nachtantz*

72 160[v] *Ein güter newer Teu. Tantz*[c] I. P. O.

161 *Nachtantz*[c]

73 162 *Auss frischem freyem müth*[c]

162[v] *Nachtantz*[c]

74 163 *Ungarescha*[ac 12] (1578_8, no. 14a)

163 *Saltarello*[ac] (1578_8, no. 14b)

75 163[v] *Du hast mich wöllen nemmen*[c] I. P. O.

164 *Nachtantz*[c]

76 164[v] *Ein güter newer Teu. Tantz*[c]

165 *Nachtantz*[c]

77 165[v] *Ein güter newer Teu. Tantz*[c] A. P. O.

166 *Nachtantz*[c]

78 166[v] *Ein gar güter newen T. Tantz*[c] A. P. O.

167 *Nachtantz*[c]

79 168 *Ein güter newer Teu. Tantz*[c]

168[v] *Nachtantz*[c]

80 169 *Ist mir ein fein braun Meg*[c 13]

169[v] *Nachtantz*[c]

81 170 *Es wolt ein Med. ein Schr.*[c]

170[v] *Nachtantz*[c]

171 *Proportio invers.*[c]

82 171[v] *Ballo Francese* (1578_8, no. 18a: "Almande Loreyne")

172 *Saltarello* (1578_8, no. 18b)

83 172[v] *Ballo Anglese*[c] (1578_8, no. 19a)

173 *Saltarello*[c] (1578_8, no. 19b)

84 173[v] *Aria di Canzon francese per sonar del' primo tono*[14] (1579_3, no. 1: Ingegnieri)

85 174 *Aria di Canzon francese per sonar del'ottavo tono* (1579_3, no. 2: Ingegnieri)

86 175 *L'arboscello ballo Furlano*[c] (1578_8, no. 15)

87 175 *Ballo Millanese*[c] (1578_8, no. 16)

88 175[v] *Schirazula Marazula*[ac 15] (1578_8, no. 12)

[1] Facs. of the title page in KinsP, p. 83, and ZurM, p. 20.

[2] DraudiusBC, p. 1651, lists "Jacobi Paix Tabulatura organi fistularum, Lauing. 87. fol." He probably refers either to this volume or to an otherwise unknown second edition of 1587.

[3] Copies were in D:Bds and D:KZg.

[4] Quasi-facs. and mod. ed. in ForkA II, 731.

[5] Mod. ed. in SchlechtG, no. 63.

[6] Mod. ed. in SchlechtG, no. 64.

[7] Facs. of fol. 95 in HirK III, pl. 12.
[8] Mod. ed. in EhmL, no. 8, and SenflW VII, no. 24.
[9] Mod. ed. in DTO XXXVII/72, p. 90.
[10] Mod. ed. in HalbK, p. 19.
[11] Mod. ed. in HalbK, p. 20.
[12] Mod. ed. in LeiH, p. 102.
[13] Mod. ed. in EhmL, no. 12.
[14] Mod. ed. in AulerS I, 12.
[15] Mod. ed. in BöhT II, no. 153.

1583[5]

PEETRINO, JACOBO

DI JACOBO PEETRINO / DE MALINES / IL PRIMO LIBRO DE MADRIGALI A QUATRO VOCI / Novamente composti, & dati in luce. / [Printer's mark] / In Venetia Appresso Angelo Gardano / M D LXXXIII.

Four part books in mensural notation, each of 12 fols. Dedication on fol. 1^v (= p. 2) of each part book headed "ALL'ILLUSTRISSIMO SIGNORE IL SIGNOR CONTE DE BOSSU' ETC. Signor mio sempre osservandissimo," and signed "Di Milano l'ultimo d'Aprile 1583. Di V. S. Illustrissima Devotissimo Servitore Jacobo Peetrino de Malines," reprinted in SartMS, p. 38. All of the contents are listed in SartMS, p. 38, and Vogel: Peetrino 1 (1583). Contains 20 compositions with Italian text, and one piece for instrumental ensemble *a 4*.

Copy in: I:Vnm (STB).

	p.	
1	21	*Aria Francese per sonare*

1583[6]

RÜHLING, JOHANNES

Tabulaturbuch, / Auff / Orgeln und Instrument / Darinne auff alle Sontage / und hohen Fest durchs gantze Jhar auserlesene, liebliche und künst/liche Moteten so mit den Evangeliis, Episteln, Introitibus, Responsoriis, Antiphonis, / Oder derselben Historien uberein kommen unnd eintreffen, der Fürnembsten unnd be/rümbsten Componisten, verfasset, und also geordnet, wie dieselben von den / Autoribus im Gesang ohne Coloraturen gesetzt worden, damit ein / jeglicher Organist solche Tabulatur auff seine Applica/tion bringen, und füglich brauchen kan. / Mit sonderlichem fleiss auserlesen, in eine richtige Ordnung / bracht, abgesatzt, und in Druck vorfertiget, / Durch / Johannem Rühling, von Born, Organist / zu Döbeln. / Der Erste Theil. / [Printer's mark] / PSALMUS CL. / Laudate Dominum in tympano & Choro, / Laudate eum in Chordis & Organo. / Gedruckt zu Leipzig, bey Johan: Beyer, / Im Jahr unserer Erlösung, / M. D. Lxxxiii.

143 fols. German keyboard tablature. Preface ("Vorrede") and dedication on fol. *2 headed "Den Durchlauchtigen, Hochgebornen Fürsten und Herrn, Herrn Fridrich Wilhelm, Herrn Johansen, Herrn Johan Casimirn, und Herrn Johan Ernsten, Gebrüdern und Vettern, Hertzogen zu Sachssen, Landgrafen in Düringen, und Marggrafen zu Meissen, etc. Meinen genedigen Fürsten und Herrn.," and signed on fol. *3^v "Datum Döbeln den 10. Decemb. Anno 1582. E. F. G. Unterthenigster Johannes Rüling, Organist daselbst." On fol. *4: a note on performance practice headed "Ad Organistam." On fol. *4^v: poem in Latin headed "Ad Juventutem Organicae Musices studiosam. Petrus Albinus Nivemontius. Profess. Publ. in academia Witebergensi." Fol. *5 = fol. 1. On fol. 1: poem in Latin headed "In Analysin Harmoniarum Ecclesiasticarum Organicam, ut vocant: ab Johanne Rulingo Bornensi editam: M. Martinus Hayneccius Bor. ad Lectorem," and signed "Ad Muldam Faciebat. VI. Decemb: 82," followed by another poem in Latin signed "A. Siberus." On fol. 138^v: table of contents. Colophon on fol. 139^v: "Gedruckt zu Leipzig, bey Johan: Beyer. Anno M. D. LXXXIII." In the following inventory composers' initials or abbreviated names are resolved the first time they appear only. All of the compositions are for solo keyboard.

Copies in: CH:Bu, D:Mbs, D:W.[1]

Dominica Prima Adventus

	fol.	
1	1^v	*Intuemini quantus sit istae* Jacobus Regnart *a 6* (RegnS, no. 1)
	2^v	2a pars *Occurrite illi*

2 3v *Hierusalem surge* Clemens Non Papa *a5* (RISM 1559_1, no. 69)
4v 2a pars *Leva in Circuitu oculos tuos*
3 5v *Ecce Dominus veniet* *a5* (D:Rp, MSS B. 211–215, no. 42; see MohrH)

Dominica Secunda Adventus
4 6v *Ecce apparebit Dominus* Jacobus Vâet *a5* (RISM 1564_4, no. 12)
7v 2a pars *Jerusalem gaude*

Dominica III. Adventus
5 8v *Populus qu ambulat in tenebris* Joseph Schlegel *a5*

Dominica IIII. Adventus
6 9v *Vox Clamantis in deserto* Clemens N. P. *a5* (RISM 1559_1, no. 41)
10v 2a pars *Vox dicentis*

In Die Nativitatis Jesu Christi
7 11v *Castae parentis viscera* Cornelius Canis *a6* (RISM 1564_3, no. 45)
13 2a pars *Enixa est Puerpera*
8 14 *In Principio erat Verbum* Orlandus [Lasso] *a6* (LassoW XV, 8)
15 2a pars *Consulto omismus* [2]
15v 3a pars *In propria venit & sui eum*
9 16v *Verbum Caro Factum est* Orlandus *a6* (LassoW XI, 158)
10 18v *Angelus ad Pastores ait* Orlandus *a5* (LassoW III, 139)
11 19v *Ecce Maria genuit nobis Salvatorem* Orlandus *a5* (LassoW V, 15)
19v 2a pars *Ecce Agnus Dei*
12 20v *Nascitur in mundi promissus gaudia Christus* M. Wolffg. Thalman *a5*
13 21v *Ein Kindelein so löbelich* M. Wolffgangus Thalman *a5* (compare BraunS, p. 63, no. 293)

In Die Circumcisionis Domini
14 22v *Postquam consummati* Joachi: a Burgk *a5*

De Innocentibus Ab Herode Trucidatis
15 23v *In Bethlehem Herodes iratus* Joach: a Burgk *a5*
24v 2a pars *O mira novitas facinoris*

Trium Regum
16 25v *Ab oriente Venerunt magi* Clemens Non papa *a5* (RISM 1559_1, no. 58)
26v 2a pars *Videntes autem Stellam*

De Baptismo Christi
17 27v *Super ripam Jordanis* Clemens non Papa *a5* (RISM 1555_8, fol. 3)
28v 2a pars *Vox de coelo sonuit*

Dominica Prima Post Epiphaniorum
18 29v *Deus qui sedes* Orlandi *a5* (LassoW IX, 12)

Dominica II. Epiphaniorum
19 30v *Nuptiae factae sunt in Cana Galilaeae* Orlandus *a6* (LassoW XV, 30)
31v 2a pars *Dixit mater eius ministris*
31v 3a pars *Trium: Et dicit ei Jesus*
32v 4a pars *Omnis homo Primum bonum vinum ponit*

Dominica III. Post Epiphaniorum
20 33v *Nolite esse prudentes apud vos met ipsos* Jaches Werth *a5* (WertM, no. 6)
33v 2a pars *Non vos met ipsos defendentes charissimi fratres*
35 3a pars *Sed si esurierit inimicus tuus ciba illum da*

Dominica IIII. Post Epiphaniorum
21 35v *Ingressus erat Jesus navim* Paulus Schedius *a4*
36 2a pars *Domine serva nos perimus*

Dominica V. Post Epiphaniorum
22 36v *Domine nonne bonum semen seminasti in agro tuo* Homero Herpols *a5* (HerpN, no. 11)
37v 2a pars *Colligite primum Zizania*

Dominica Septuagesima

23 38v *Deus Virtutum convertere* Crequillonis *a 5* (RISM 1554_{11}, no. 23)

39v 2a pars *Et perfice eam quam plantavit dextera tua*

Dominica Sexagesima

24 40v *Servus tuus ego sum* Clemens non Papa *a 5* (RISM 1554_{11}, no. 4)

41v 2a pars *Ego vero egenus & pauper sum*

Dominica Quinquagesima

25 42v *Transeunte Domino Clamat ad eum* Jaches Werth *a 5* (RISM 1568_3, p. 193)

43v 2a pars *Et ait illi Jesus*

Dominica Quadragesima

26 44v *Adiuva nos Deus Salutaris noster* Crequillonis *a 5* (RISM 1554_{11}, no. 14)

Dominica Reminiscere

27 45v *Dixit Jesus Mulieri Cananeae* Gallus Dreslerus *a 5* (DressSC, no. 25)

Dominica Oculi

28 46v *Dixit Joseph Undecem fratribus suis* Orlandus *a 6* (LassoW V, 76)

47v 2a pars *Nunciaverunt Jacob*

Dominica Letare

29 48v *Dancket dem Herren denn er ist freundtlich* David Köler *a 5* (KölZ, no. 2)

48v 2a pars *Der Herr hat nicht lust an der stercke des Rosses*

50 3a pars *Der Herr hat gefallen an denen die ihn fürchten*

Dominica Judica

30 50v *Cerne meos esse gemitus* Dominicus Finoth *a 6* (RISM $[1556]_9$, no. 39)

50v 2a pars *Non licet afflictas*

Dominica Palmarum

31 52v *Fremuit Spiritu Jesus* Clemens non Papa *a 6* (RISM 1554_2, fol. 15)

53v 2a pars *Videns Dominus flentes Sorores Lazari*

De Passione Christi

32 54v *Vita in ligno moritur a 5* (RISM 1537_1, no. 20: Senfl)

55 2a pars *Qui Prophetice*

55v 3a pars *Qui Expansis*

33 56v *Nos autem gloriari oportet a 5*

34 57v *O Jesu Christ dein Nahm der ist a 5*

35 58v *Tristis est anima mea* Matth: Lemais[tre] *a 4*

59 2a pars *Ecce appropinquabit hora*

36 59v *In nomine Jesu omne genuflectatum a 4*

60v 2a pars *Rogamus te o clementissime Jesu*

De Resurrectione Christi

37 61v *Maria Magdalena* Clemens N. P. *a 5* (RISM 1546_6, fol. 15)

62v 2a pars *Cito euntes dicite discipulis suis*

38 63v *Dum transisset Sabbathum* Joan de Cleve *a 6* (MaldR XIV, 8)

64v 2a pars *Et valde mane una Sabbathorum*

39 65v *Congratulamini mihi omnes* Orlandus *a 6* (LassoW XIII, 10)

66v 2a pars *Tulerunt Dominum meum*

40 68 *Dum Transisset Sabbathum* Michael Tonsor

68v 2a pars *Et valde mane*

41 69v *Mane nobiscum Domine* Meilandus *a 5* (MeiC, no. 11)

42 70 *Christus excitatus est a mortuis* Joachimus á Burgk *a 5*

71v 2a pars *Christus traditus est proper delicta nostra*

43 72v *Domine quid multiplicati sunt qui tribulant me* Binellus *a 5*

44 73v *Christ lag in Todesbanden* M. Wolffgangus Thalman *a 5* (compare ZahnM, no. 7012)

Quasimodo Geniti

45 74v *Surgens Jesus* Orlandus *a 5* (LassoW V, 60)

Misericordias Domini

46 75v *Oves mea vocem meam audiunt* Gallus Dreslerus *a 4* (DressSC, no. 67)

76 2a pars *Pater meus qui dedit mihi*

Jubilate

47 76v *Jubilate Deo omnis terra* Petri Colin *a 5* (ColinM II, no. 7)

77v 2a pars *Populus eius & oves pascuae*

Cantate

48 78v *Cantate Domino canticum novum* Michael Tonsor *a 4* (RISM 1580_4, no. 10)

Domini Cunditatis

49 79v *Domus mea domus orationis vocabitur* *a 4*

De Ascensione Domini

50 80v *Ascendit Deus in Jubilatione* Leonhardt Panninger *a 6* (RISM 1558_4, no. 42)

81 2a pars *Et Dominus in voce Tubae*

81v 3a pars *Gloria Patri & filio & Spiritui sancto*

51 82v *Tempus est ut revertar* Orlandus *a 6* (LassoW XIII, 25)

83v 2a pars *Nisi ego abiero*

Exaudi

52 84v *Paracletus autem Spiritus Sanctus* Jaches Werth *a 5* (WertM, no. 18)

85v 2a pars *Non Turbetur, cor vestrum*

In Die Pentecostes

53 86v *Veni sancte Spiritus* Josquin de pres *a 6* (JosqMT, no. 49)

88 2a pars *O lux beatissima*

54 89v *Dum complerentur dies pentecostes* Archadelt *a 5* (RISM 1538_2, fol. 23)

55 90v *Also hat Gott* Paulus Prescherus *a 5* (PL:L MS)[3]

91v 2a pars *Gleiche wie Moises eine Schlange erhöhet hat*

56 92v *Sic deus dilexit Mundum* Scheifler *a 6* (RISM 1564_3, no. 22: Franciscus de Rivulo)

93v 2a pars *Venite ad me omnes qui laboratis*

De Sancta Trinitate

57 94v *Te Deum patrem in genitum* Holland *a 6* (RISM 1558_4, no. 53)

95v 2a pars *Quoniam magnus es tu*

58 96v *Tibi laus tibi gloria* Orlandus *a 5* (LassoW III, 130)

97 2a pars *Da gaudiorum praemia*

Dominica I. Post Trinitatis

59 97v *Homo quidam erat dives* Leonhardus Schröter *a 5* (D:LO, MS s.n.)[4]

98v 2a pars *Accidit autem dum moreretur Lazarus*

Dominica II. Post Trinitatis

60 99v *Homo quidam fecit coenam magnam* Jacobus Bultel *a 6* (RISM 1554_2, fol. 3)

100v 2a pars *Venite & comedite*

Dominica III. Post Trinitatis

61 101v *Pater peccavi in coelum & coram te* *a 4* (ClemensO IX, no. 1: Clemens non Papa)

101v 2a pars *Quanti mercenarii in domo patris mei*

Dominica IIII. Post Trinitatis

62 102v *Estote misericordes* Herpolensis *a 5* (HerpN, no. 33)

103v 2a pars *Nolite Judicare*

Dominica V. Post Trinitatis

63 104v *Mirabilia testimonia tua Domine* Joan de Cleve *a 6* (RISM 1558_4, no. 47)

Dominica VI. Post Trinitatis

64 105v *Legem pone mihi Domine* Orlandus *a 5* (LassoW IX, 73)

106 2a pars *Da mihi intellectum*

Dominica VII. Post Trinitatis

65 106v *Gustate & videte* Orlandus *a 5* (LassoW V, 73)

107v 2a pars *Divites eguerunt*

Dominica VIII. Post Trinitatis

66 108v *Non vos me elegistis* Orlandus *a5* (LassoW V, 141)

Dominica IX. Post Trinitatis

67 109v *Divitias & paupertatem* Jaches Werth *a6* (RISM 1558_4, no. 15: Jachet)

Dominica X. Post Trinitatis

68 110v *Hierusalem luge* Richafort *a5* (RISM 1532_9, p. 49: Richafort or Lupus)

111v 2a pars *Deduc quasi torrentem lachrimas*

Dominica XI. Post Trinitatis

69 112v *Emendemus in melius* Arnoldus Feisius *a5* (MaldR XXVIII, 1: A. Feys)

113v 2a pars *Peccavimus cum patribus nostris*

Dominica XII. Post Trinitatis

70 114v *Deus in adiutorium meum intende* Clemens non Papa *a6* (RISM 1555_7, fol. 26)

115v 2a pars *Ecce in tenebris sedeo*

Dominica XIII. Post Trinitatis

71 116v *Tua est Potentia* Crequillonis *a5*

116v 2a pars *Creator omnium Deus terribilis & fortis*

Dominica XIIII. Post Trinitatis

72 117v *Cum transiret Jesus quoddam castellum* Gombert *a5*

Dominica XV. Post Trinitatis

73 118v *Nolite quaerere* Gallus Dreslerius *a4* (DressSC, no. 44)

119 2a pars *Quia potius quarito regnum Dei*

Dominica XVI. Post Trinitatis

74 119v *Si bona suscepimus* Verdeloth *a5* (MoralesO I, 274)

Dominica XVII. Post Trinitatis

75 120v *Discite à me cuia mitu sum* Clemens N. P. *a5* (RISM 1553_{12}, fol. 2)

121v 2a pars *Quia qui se exaltat humiliabitur*

Dominica XVIII. Post Trinitatis

76 122v *Congregati sunt inimici nostri* Crequillonis *a6* (RISM 1555_4, fol. 12)

123v 2a pars *Tua est potentia*

Dominica XIX. Post Trinitatis

77 124v *Salus populi ego sum* Joan Walther *a5* (WalthW, no. 47)

Dominica XX. Post Trinitatis

78 125v *Omnia quae fecisti nobis Domine* Orlandus [Lasso] *a5* (LassoW VII, 127)

Dominica XXI. Post Trinitatis

79 126v *O bone Jesu* Clemens non Papa *a5* (RISM 1554_3, fol. 4)

127v 2a pars *Eya dulcissime Jesu*

Dominica XXII. Post Trinitatis

80 128v *De profundis Clamavi* Ludovicus Senffel *a5* (SenflW III, no. 11)

129v 2a pars *A custodia matutina uscque ad noctem*

Dominica XXIII. Post Trinitatis

81 130v *Magister scimus quia verax ea* Herpolensis *a5* (HerpN, no. 52)

131v 2a pars *Reddite ergo quae sunt Caesaris Caesari*

Dominica XXIIII. Post Trinitatis

82 132v *Si bona suscepimus* *a6* (RISM 1549_3, p. 6)

Dominica XXV. Post Trinitatis

83 133v *Virgines prudentes ornate Lampades vestras* *a4* (ClemensCS V, no. 11: Clemens non Papa)

134 2a pars *Media autem nocte Clamor factus est*

Dominica XXVI. Post Trinitatis

84 134v *Sint lumbi vestri precincti* Crequillon *a5* (RISM 1554_5, fol. 9)

135v 2a pars *Vigilate ergo*

Dominica XXVII. Post Trinitatis. De clarificatione Christi

85 136v *Assumpsit Jesus Petrum & Jacobum* Clemens N. P. *a5* (RISM 1555_{12}, no. 7)

137v 2a pars *Et ecce vox de nube dicens*

[1] A copy was in D:Bds.
[2] Only the title appears in this volume, not the music.
[3] See EitQ VIII, 62.
[4] See EitQ IX, 74.

1583_7

PHALÈSE, PIERRE, AND JEAN BELLÈRE, PUBLISHERS

CHOREARUM / MOLLIORUM COLLECTANEA, / OMNIS FERE GENERIS TRIPUDIA COMPLECTENS: / UTPOTE PADOANAS, PASS'E MEZOS, ALEMANDAS, GALLIARDAS, / Branles: atque id genus quaecunque alia, tam vivac Voci, quam Instrumentis Musicis / accommoda: nunc demum ex variis Philoharmonicorum / libris accuratè collecta. / RECUEIL DE DANSERIES, / CONTENANT PRESQUE TOUTES SORTES DE DANSES, / comme Pavanes, Pass'e mezes, Allemandes, Gaillardes, Branles, & plusieurs autres, accommodées / aussi bien a la Voix, comme à tous Instrumens Musicaux, nouvellement amassé d'aucuns / sçavans maistres Musiciens, & autres amateurs de toute sorte d'Harmonie. / SUPERIUS. / EN ANVERS. / Chez Pierre Phalese au Lyon Rouge, & chez Jean Bellere à l'Aigle d'Or. / 1583.

Four part books in mensural notation, each of 35 fols. On fol. 1v of each part book: table of contents. The compositions identified by superior letters are reprinted as follows: ([a]) in BlumeS, app. B; ([b]) in MohrA, nos. 21–26; ([c]) in ReyD; ([d]) in PhalAT. All of the compositions are for instrumental ensemble *a4*.

Copies in: D:KNu, D:Mbs, S:Uu (STB).

	fol.	
1	2	*Caro Ortolano* = 1578_8, no. 4a
	2	*Saltarello* = 1578_8, no. 4b
2	2v	*Pass'e mezzo d'Italie*[ac 1] = 1578_8, no. 1a
	3v	*Represa* = 1578_8, no. 2b
	3v	*Saltarello* = 1578_8, no. 2c
	4	*Represa* = 1578_8, no. 2d
3	4v	*Pass'e mezzo Moderno*[ac] = 1578_8, no. 11a
	5v	*Represa* = 1578_8, no. 11b
	6	*Salterello* = 1578_8, no. 11c
	6	*Represa* = 1578_8, no. 11d
4	6v	*Passomezo d'Angleterre*[c] = 1571_5, no. 14a
	6v	*La Reprinse* = 1571_5, no. 14b
5	6v	*Passomezo d'Anvers* = 1571_5, no. 15
6	7	*Passomeso la doulce*[c] = 1571_5, no. 16a
	7	*La Reprinse* = 1571_5, no. 16b
7	7v	*Pass'e mezzo della Paganina*[c] = 1578_8, no. 3a
	7v	*Salterello* = 1578_8, no. 3b
8	8	*Pavane Ferrareze* = 1571_5, no. 6a
	8v	*Gaillarde Ferrareze* = 1571_5, no. 6b
9	9	*Pavane J'ay du mal*[c] = 1571_5, no. 10a
	9	*La Gaillarde* = 1571_5, no. 10b
10	9v	*Pavane de la Bataille* = 1551_8, no. 41
	10	*Gaillarde de la Battaille*[c]
11	10v	*Gaillarde Au joly bois* = 1571_5, no. 33
12	10v	*Gaillarde [du ton de la guerre]*[d] = 1557_3, no. 5
13	11	*Gaillarde Ce qui m'est deu* = 1571_5, no. 41
14	11	*Gaillarde La Peronelle* = 1571_5, no. 34
15	11v	*Gaillarde Mais pourquoy*[d] = 1571_5, no. 35
16	11v	*Gaillarde Traditore* = 1571_5, no. 36
17	12	*Gaillarde Si pour t'aymer* = 1559_3, no. 35
18	12v	*Gaillarde L'esmerillonne* = 1571_5, no. 38
19	12v	*Gaillarde Puisque vivre* = 1571_5, no. 39
20	13	*Gaillarde La fanfare* = 1571_5, no. 40
21	13v	*Gaillarde La roque el fuso* = 1571_5, no. 43
22	14	*Gaillarde Francoise* = 1571_5, no. 44

23 14 *Gaillarde Mon plaisir* = 1571_5, no. 45

24 14v *Gaillarde l'Admiralle* = 1571_5, no. 46

25 15 *Gaillarde d'Escosse* = 1571_5, no. 47

26 15 *Gaillarde* = 1559_3, no. 32

27 15v *Gaillarde Brunette* = 1559_3, no. 36: "Gaillarde o ma gente brunette"

28 15v *Ballo Milanese*[d] = 1578_8, no. 16

29 16 *Gaillarde la Lavandara*[d] = 1578_8, no. 10

30 16v *Almande Poussinghe*[bd 2] = 1578_8, no. 20a: "Todescha"

16v *Saltarello*[d] = 1578_8, no. 20b

31 17 *Almande* = 1551_8, no. 29a

17 *La Reprinse* = 1551_8, no. 29b

32 17v *Almande*[d] = 1578_8, no. 1a: "La Billiarda"

17v *Saltarello*[d] = 1578_8, no. 1b

33 18 *Almande d'Amour* = 1571_5, no. 26

34 18v *Almande Bruynsmedelijn*[ad] = 1578_8, no. 9a: "Todescha"

18v *Saltarello*[ad] = 1578_8, no. 9b

35 19 *Almande de Liege* = 1571_5, no. 23

36 19v *Almande*[bd] = 1578_8, no. 13a: "Tedescha"

19v *Saltarello*[d] = 1578_8, no. 13b

37 20 *Almande* = 1559_3, no. 17

38 20 *Almande* = 1571_5, no. 30

39 20v *Almande Loreyne*[a] = 1578_8, no. 18a: "Ballo Francese"

20v *Saltarello* = 1578_8, no. 18b

40 21 *Almande Bisarde*[bd 3]

41 21v *Almande Fortune helas pourquoy*[b]

42 22 *Almande de Don Frederico*[b]

43 22v *Almande Spiers*[b]

44 23 *L'arboscello ballo Furlano*[d 4] = 1578_8, no. 15

45 23v *Ballo Anglese*[d] = 1578_8, no. 19a

23v *Saltarello*[d] = 1578_8, no. 19b

46 24 *Ungaresca*[d] = 1578_8, no. 14a

24 *Saltarello*[d] = 1578_8, no. 14b

47 24v *La Parma* = 1578_8, no. 17a

24v *Saltarello* = 1578_8, no. 17b

48 25 *Putta Nera Ballo Furlano* = 1578_8, no. 6

49 25 *Schiarazula Marazula*[d] = 1578_8, no. 12

50 25v *Branle simple*[d] = 1557_3, no. 7

51 25v *Branle 2*[d] = 1557_3, no. 8

52 25v *Branle 3*[d] = 1557_3, no. 9

53 25v *Branle 4* = 1557_3, no. 10

54 26 *Branle 5*[d] = 1557_3, no. 11

55 26 *Branle 6* = 1557_3, no. 12

56 26v *Premier Branle de Gay*[d] = 1557_3, no. 13

57 26v *Branle 2*[d] = 1557_3, no. 14

58 26v *Branle 3* = 1557_3, no. 15

59 27 *Branle 4* = 1557_3, no. 16

60 27 *Branle 5* = 1557_3, no. 17

61 27 *Branle 6* = 1557_3, no. 18

62 27v *Branle [commun]*[d] = 1557_3, no. 27: "Bransle [de Bourgongne]"

63 27v *Branle 2*[d] = 1557_3, no. 28

64 27v *Branle 3*[d] = 1557_3, no. 29

65 28 *Branle 4* = 1557_3, no. 30

66 28 *Branle 5*[d] = 1557_3, no. 31

67 28v *Branle 6*[d] = 1557_3, no. 32

68 28v *Branle 7*[d] = 1557_3, no. 33

69 28v *Branle 8* = 1557_3, no. 34

70 29 *Branle 9* = 1557_3, no. 35

71 29 *Branle 10* = 1557_3, no. 36

72 29v *Branle de Poictou*[d] = 1550_6, no. 11

73 29v *Branle 2* = 1550_6, no. 12

74 29v *Branle 3*[d] = 1550_6, no. 13

75 30 *Branle 4*[d] = 1550_6, no. 14

76 30 *Branle 5* = 1550_6, no. 15

77 30 *Branle 6*[ad] = 1550_6, no. 16

78 30v *Branle 7*[ad] = 1550_6, no. 17

79 30v *Branle 8*[d] = 1550_6, no. 18

80 31 *Branle de Champaigne*[d] = 1550_6, no. 19

81 31 *Branle 2*[d] = 1550_6, no. 20

82 31 *Branle 3* = 1550_6, no. 21

83 31v *Branle 4*[d] = 1550_6, no. 22

84 31v *Branle 5* = 1550_6, no. 23

85 31v *Branle 6*[d] = 1550_6, no. 24

86 32 *Branle 7*[d] = 1550_6, no. 25

87 32 *Branle 8*[d] = 1550_6, no. 26

88 32 *Branle 9*[d] = 1550_6, no. 27

89 32v *Branle pourquoy* = 1551_8, no. 13

90 32v *Branle mon amy* = 1551_8, no. 14

91 33 *Branle 2* = 1551_8, no. 21

92 33 *Premier Branle de la guerre* = 1559_2, no. 46

93 33 *Branle 2* = 1559_2, no. 47

94 33v *Quatre branles* = 1551_8, no. 23

95 33v *Les Fagots* = 1551_8, no. 24

96 34 *Hoboken dans* = 1551_8, no. 25

97 34 *Autre* = 1578_8, no. 21: "La fiamenga"

98	34[v]	*Branle de petit homme*[d] = 1564_2, no. 34
	34[v]	*Branle legier*[d] = 1564_2, no. 35
99	34[v]	*Branle du contraint* = 1564_2, no. 26
100	35	*Branle de la suite du contraint legier*[d] = 1564_2, no. 28
101	35	*Branle d'Escosse* = 1559_2, no. 44
102	35	*Branle des Sabots* = 1559_2, no. 45
103	35[v]	*Branle de Poitou simple* = 1564_2, no. 29
104	35[v]	*Branle de poitou legier* = 1564_2, no. 31

[1] Mod. ed. in ParrishT, no. 35.
[2] Mod. ed. in MU IV, app., p. 49, and TwittT III, no. 4.
[3] Mod. ed. in TwittT II, no. 7.
[4] Mod. ed. in TwittT I, no. 4.

1584_1

DALLA CASA, GIROLAMO

IL VERO MODO / DI DIMINUIR, CON TUTTE / LE SORTI DI STROMENTI / Di fiato, & corda, & di voce humana. / DI GIROLAMO DALLA CASA / DETTO DA UDENE / Capo de Concerti delli Stromenti di fiato, / della Illustriss. Signoria di Venetia. / LIBRO PRIMO. / AL MOLTO ILLUSTRE / Sig. Conte Mario Bevilacqua. / CON PRIVILEGGIO. / [Printer's mark] / In Venetia Appresso Angelo Gardano. / M D LXXXIIII.

26 fols. Mensural notation. The title is placed within an ornamental border. Dedication on fol. 1[v] headed "AL MOLTO ILLUSTRE SIGNOR IL SIGNOR CONTE MARIO BEVILACQUA MIO SIGNORE OSSERVANDISSIMO," and signed "Servitore Girolamo dalla Casa detto da Udene," reprinted in GaspaC I, 331, and SartMS, p. 49. On fol. 2: preface headed "Ai Lettori," reprinted in GaspaC I, 331. On fol. 2[v]: rules for tonguing ("Delle Tre Lingue Principali"), followed by a short notice on the cornetto. Fol. 3 = p. 1. On p. 48: table of contents. Pp. 1–7 contain examples of ornaments and schemes for filling in various intervals with *passaggi*. Beginning on p. 7 Dalla Casa presents excerpts from compositions, with elaborate ornamentation added. Only sections of the superius parts of these compositions are included. For the second volume in this series, see 1584_2. For a discussion of this work see HorsS. In the following inventory, short forms of composers' names are expanded the first time they appear only.

Copy in: I:Bc.

Essempii de Crome & Semplici

	p.	
1	7	*Io canterei d'Amor* Cipriano [da Rore] *a4* (SCMA VI, 31)
2	8	*Non e ch'el duol* Cipriano *a4* (SCMA VI, 34)

Essempii de Crome

3	9	*La bella netta ignuda & bianca mano* Cipriano *a4* (SCMA VI, 38)

Essempii de Semicrome

4	11	*Signor mio caro*[1] Cipriano *a4* (SCMA VI, 25)
5	12	*Carita di Signore* Cipriano *a4* (SCMA VI, 28)

Passi & cadenze de Croma & semicroma

6	13	*Nasce la pena mia* Striggio *a6* (MonteO XVI, app.)
7	14	*I dolci colli* Striggio *a6* (Vogel: Striggio 3 [1566], nos. 1–2)
	14	2a pars [*Et qual cervo ferito*]
8	15	*La prima vergine* Cipriano *a5* (RoreO III, 1: "Vergine bella")
9	15	*Cantai un tempo* Filippo de Monte *a6* (Vogel: Monte 10 [1576], no. 1)
10	16	*La nona Vergine* Cipriano *a5* (RoreO III, 25: "Vergine, in cui ho")
11	16	*Se la gratia divina* Adriano [Willaert] *a5* (Vogel: Rore 17 [1548], p. 26)
12	16	*La ver l'aurora* Striggio *a6* (Vogel: Striggio 3 [1566], p. 11)
13	17	*La quarta vergine* Cipriano *a5* (RoreO III, 10: "Vergine santa")
14	18	*La quinta vergine* Cipriano *a5* (RoreO III, 12: "Vergine sol'al mondo")
15	19	*Di tempo in tempo* Cipriano *a4* (SCMA VI, 67)
16	20	*Dall'estremo Orizonte* Cipriano *a5* (Vogel: Rore 31 [1574], p. 23)

17 20 *La sesta vergine* Cipriano *a5* (RoreO III, 16: "Vergine chiara")
18 21 *S'amor la viva fiamma* Cipriano *a5* (RoreO III, 84)
19 21 *Dale belle contrade* Cipriano *a5* (HAM, no. 131)
20 22 *Alla dolc'ombra* Cipriano *a4* (SCMA VI, 12)
22 3a pars [*Un lauro mi diffese*]
22 4a pars [*Però più ferm'ogn'hor*]
23 5a pars [*Selve, sassi, campagne*]
23 6a pars [*Tanto mi piacque*] [2]
21 23 *La seconda vergine* Cipriano *a5* (RoreO III, 4: "Vergine saggia")
22 24 *La terza vergine* Cipriano *a5* (RoreO III, 7: "Vergine pura")
23 25 *La seconda parte De quando fra l'altre donne* [= "Io benedico'l loco"] Cipriano *a5* (RoreO III, 64)
24 25 *Dolce ritorn'amor* Striggio *a6* (Vogel: Striggio 12 [1579], p. 6)

Passe & cadenze de semicrome & de treplicate
25 27 [*Il n'est plaisir*] Canzon a 6 di Martin Peu d'Argent (RISM 1553_{25}, no. 24)
26 29 *Helas ma mere* Adriano *a5* (RISM 1572_2, fol. 1^v)

Passi & cadenze de le treplicate sole
27 32 *Si me tenez* *a6* (RISM 1545_{14}, fol. 14: Crecquillon)

Passi & cadenze delle quadruplicate sole
28 34 *Rossignolet* Clemens non Papa *a4* (ClemensO X, 41)

Passi & cadenze delle treplicate & quadruplicate
29 36 *Voules ouiir* Adriano *a5* (RISM 1572_2, fol. 27)

Passi & cadenze de le quattro figure
30 39 *Ancor ch'io possa dire* Striggio *a6* (Vogel: Striggio 3 [1566], no. 3)
31 40 *Amor mi struggie il cor* Andrea Gabrieli *a6* (Vogel: Gabrieli 3 [1587], p. 12)
32 40 *Ringratto & lodo il ciel* Andrea Gabrieli *a6* (Vogel: Gabrieli 3 [1587], p. 1)
41 2a pars [*Amor rimanti in pace*]
33 42 *Alla fontaine* Adriano *a6* (RISM 1572_2, fol. 53)
34 44 *Larose* Gombert *a6* (compare BrownM, p. 198, art. 49: "La rousée du moys de may")
35 46 *Di virtu di costumi* Cipriano *a5*

[1] Mod. ed. in FerandIM, no. 14.
[2] Mod. ed. in FerandIM, no. 13.

1584_2

DALLA CASA, GIROLAMO

IL VERO MODO / DI DIMINUIR, CON TUTTE / LE SORTE DI STROMENTI / Di fiato, & corda, & di voce humana. / DI GIROLAMO DALLA CASA / DETTO DA UDENE / Capo de Concerti delli Stromenti di fiato, / dalla Illustriss. Signoria di Venetia. / LIBRO SECONDO. / AL MOLTO ILLUSTRE / Sig. Conte Mario Bevilacqua. / CON PRIVILEGGIO. / [Printer's mark] / In Venetia Appresso Angelo Gardano. / M D LXXXIIII.

26 fols. Mensural notation. The title is placed within an ornamental border. On fol. 1^v: preface headed "Alli Lettori," reprinted in GaspaC I, 332, and SartMS, p. 50, followed by a notice on the importance of playing *passaggi* in time ("Del Portar La Minuta a Tempo") and notices on the "viola bastarda" and the human voice. Fol. 2 = p. 1. On p. 50: table of contents. Nos. 1–9 present an ornamented version of the superius part only of the compositions listed. Nos. 10–19 present a single ornamented line for "viola bastarda" taken from the various voices of each of the compositions listed. Nos. 20–24 present an ornamented version of the superius part only of the compositions listed, with the text included. No. 25 presents all four voices of the Rore madrigal with ornamentation added. For the first volume in the series see 1584_1. In the following inventory short forms of composers' names are expanded the first time they appear only.

Copy in: I:Bc.

p.
1 1 *Canzon delli Ucelli* Clemens Janequin (MMRF VII, 1: "Le Chant des Oiseaux")

2 2a pars [*Vous orrez*]
3 3a pars [*Rossignol*]
4 4a pars [*Arriere*]
2 5 *Frais & gaillart* Clemens non Papa *a4* (ClemensO X, 17)
6 *Frais & gaillart. Alio modo*
3 7 *Petite fleur coincte* Tomas Crequillon *a4* (RISM 1549_{29}, no. 28)
4 8 *Alix avoit* Tomas Crequillon *a4* (RISM 1545_{16}, fol. 12^v)
5 9 *Petit Jacquet* Curtois *a4* (I:Bc, MS Q 26, no. 27: Courtois)
6 10 *Oncques amour* Tomas Crequillon *a5* (RISM $[1544]_{11}$, fol. 16)
11 *Oncques amour. Alio modo*
7 12 *Susana un giur* Orlando Lasso *a5* (LassoW XIV, 29)
13 *Susanna un giur. Alio modo*
8 14 *Joyssance* Adriano [Willaert] *a5* (RISM 1545_{14}, fol. 2)
9 16 *Content* Tomas Crequillon *a4*

Canzoni & Madrigali da Sonar con la Viola Bastarda
10 17 *Mais languiraige* Clemens non Papa *a4* (ClemensO X, 77)
11 18 *Qual e piu grand'o amore* Cipriano [da Rore] *a4* (SCMA VI, 78)
12 19 *Ung gay bergier* Tomas Crequillon *a4* (RieH II, 462)
13 20 *Ancor che co'l partire* Cipriano *a4* (SCMA VI, 45)
14 22 *Petit Jacquet* D'incerto *a4* (compare I:Bc, MS Q 26, no. 27: Courtois)
15 24 *Ben qui si mostra'l ciel* Cipriano *a4* (RISM 1561_{15}, no. 1)
16 25 *Martin Menoit* Clemens Janecquin *a4* (CM II, 79)
17 26 *Non gemme non fin oro* Cipriano *a4* (SCMA VI, 75)
18 28 *Doulce Memoire* Rogier *a4* [Delle Treplicate sole] (PubAPTM XXIII, no. 50: Sandrin)
19 29 *Come havran fin* Cipriano *a4* [Delle Quadruplicate sole] (SCMA VI, 51)

Madrigali da cantar in compagnia, & anco co'l Liuto solo
20 30 *Beato a me direi* Cipriano *a4* (SCMA VI, 102)
31 2a pars *Datemi pace*
21 32 *O sonno* Cipriano *a4* (SCMA VI, 106)
33 2a pars *Ove'l silentio*
22 34 *Non gemme non fin oro* Cipriano *a4* (SCMA VI, 75)
23 35 *Ancor che co'l partire* Cipriano *a4* (SCMA VI, 45)
24 36 *Vestiva i colli*[1] Palestina *a5* (PalO IX, 117)
37 2a pars *Cosi le chiome*

Canzon di Cipriano tutte le quattro parte diminuite
25 38 *Alla dolc'ombra* Cipriano *a4* (SCMA VI, 12)
40 2a pars *Non vidde'l mondo*
42 3a pars *Un lauro mi diffese*
44 4a pars *Pero piu ferm'ogn'hor*
46 5a pars *Selve sassi campagne*
48 6a pars *Tanto mi piacque*[2]

[1] Mod. ed. in PalW XXXIII, 70.
[2] Mod. ed. in FerandIM, no. 13.

1584_4

FALLAMERO, GABRIEL

IL PRIMO LIBRO DE INTAVOLATURA / DA LIUTO, DE MOTETTI RICERCATE MADRIGALI, / ET CANZONETTE ALLA NAPOLITANA, / A TRE, ET QUATTRO VOCI, PER CANTARE, ET / Sonare composte per Gabriel Fallamero Gentilhuomo Allessandrino, / NOVAMENTE POSTO IN LUCE. / [Printer's mark] / IN VINEGIA. / Appresso l'Herede di Girolamo Scotto. / M D LXXXIIII.[1]

40 fols. Italian lute tablature and mensural notation. Dedication on p. 2 headed "ALLA MOLTO ILLUSTRE SIGNORA LIVIA GUASCA POZZA DAMMA NOBILISSIMA ALESSANDRINA Signora mia Osservandissima," and signed "D'Alessandria il dì primo di Febraro. M D LXXXIIII. V. S. M. Illustre. Affectionnatissimo Servitore. Gabriello Fallamero." On p. 80: table of contents. All of the

compositions are for solo lute except nos. 17–36, which are for solo voice (in mensural notation) and lute (in tablature).

Copies in: A:Wn, GB:Lbmh (imperfect), I:Gu (imperfect), US:Bp.

MUSIC FOR SOLO LUTE

p.

1 4 *In me tanto l'ardore* Filippo de Monte *a4* (Vogel: Monte 7 [1592], no. 1)

2 5 *Apariran per me le stelle in cielo* Rolando [Lasso] *a4* (LassoW VIII, 27)

3 7 *La Ver l'aurora* Rolando [Lasso] *a5*

4 8 *Tirsi morir volea* Luca Marentio *a5* (MarenW I, 12)

5 9 *Madona mia gentile* Marentio *a5* (MarenW I, 25)

6 10 *Ma di chi debo lamentarmi* [Vincenzo] Rufo *a4* (Vogel: Ruffo 16 [1556], p. 29)

7 12 *Sapi Signor che Lilia son io* [Pietro] Vinci *a5* (Vogel: Vinci 10 [1579], p. 10)

8 13 *Per pianto la mia carne* Rolando [Lasso] *a4* (LassoW VIII, 13)

9 14 *Quando la sera scai a il chiaro giorno* Rolando [Lasso] *a5* (LassoW II, 55)

10 15 *Liquide perle amor* Luca Marentio *a5* (MarenW I, 1)

11 17 *Partiro donque* Marentio *a5* (MarenW I, 31)

12 18 *Fera Gentil* Cipriano [da Rore] *a5* (Vogel: Rore 31 [1574], p. 15)

19 2a pars *Per che si streto il nodo*

13 20 *Cantati hor piango* Rolando [Lasso] *a5* (LassoW II, 1)

22 2a pars *Tengan donque ver me*

14 23 *Mentre la bella Dori* Andrea Gabrieli *a6* (Vogel: A. Gabrieli 4 [1580], no. 16)

15 25 *Non ti sdegnar* Andrea Gabrielli *a6* (Vogel: A. Gabrieli 4 [1580], no. 17)

16 26 *Io mi son giovenetta* Ferraboscho *a4* (EinIM III, no. 30)

MUSIC FOR LUTE AND SOLO VOICE

17 28 *Livia gentil*

18 29 *Poi che sei cosi sorte* (IISM I, 28: anon.)

19 30 *Preso son io*

20 31 *Canzonete d'amore* (Vogel: Orazio Vecchi 21 [1591], no. 1)

21 32 *S'all'aparir*

22 33 *Voria madonna fare*[2] (RISM 1562_{13}, and RISM 1567_{17}, p. 33: anon.)

23 34 *O faccia che rallegri* (RISM 1562_{13} and RISM 1567_{17}, p. 1: anon.)

24 35 *Siate avertiti*[3] (Vogel Einstein 1565_2, fol. 22^v: anon.)

25 36 *Occhi leggiadri e cari* (IISM I, 27: Antiquis)

26 37 *Amanti miei*

27 38 *Io son bell'e delicata* (compare Vogel: Ferretti 22 [1585], p. 12: Ferretti)

28 39 *Vorria saper*

29 40 *Chi mira gl'occhi tuoi* (Vogel: Vecchi 21 [1591], no. 6)

30 41 *Io son fenice*[4]

31 42 *Nel vago lume*

32 43 *Viver non posso*

33 44 *Gridate gridate guerra guer'inamorati*[5]

34 45 *Amor se giusto*

35 46 *Io vo morir* (1571_4, no. 18: Fiorino)

36 47 *Mentr'io campai*[6] (Vogel: Vecchi 21 [1591], no. 2: Vecchi)

MUSIC FOR SOLO LUTE

37 48 *Standomi un giorno solo alla finestra* Rolando [Lasso] *a5* (LassoW II, 89)

49 2a pars *Indi per alto mar*

51 3a pars *In un boscheto*

53 4a pars *Chiara fontana*

55 5a pars *Una strana Fenice*

56 6a pars *Al fin vid io* *a6*

38 59 *Si dolce damar voi* [Alessandro] Strigio *a5* (Vogel: Striggio 20 [1585], p. 29)

39 60 *Dolce mio ben amor mio caro* Strigio *a6* (Vogel: Striggio 12 {1579], p. 11)

40 62 *Animam meam dilectam* Rolando [Lasso] *a5* (LassoW V, 29)

64 2a pars *Congregamini*

41 65 *Recercar del terzo tono di Anibal Padovano* (1556_9, no. 11)

42 69 *Recercar del ottavo tono di Anibal Padovano* (1556_9, no. 8)

43 72 *I dolci coli* Strigio *a6* (Vogel: Striggio 3 [1566], nos. 1–2)

74 2a pars *Et qual Cervo ferito di saeta*

44 75 *Anchor ch'io possa* Strigio *a6* (Vogel: Striggio 3 [1566], no. 3)

45 77 *Nasce la pena mia* Strigio *a6* (MonteO XVI, app.)

46 79 *Anchor che col partir* (1571_4, no. 15)

[1] Facs. of title page in MolmS II, 319.
[2] Mod. ed. in ChilCS, no. 3, and ChilS, no. 17.
[3] Mod. ed. in ChilCS, no. 1; ChilS, no. 18; and EC, pt. I, vol. II, p 662.
[4] Mod. ed. in ChilLS, p. 84.
[5] Mod. ed. in ChilCS, no. 6, and ChilLS, p. 86.
[6] Mod. ed. in ChilCS, no. 4, and ChilS, no. 19.

1584_4

GALILEI, VINCENZO

CANTO [TENORE] / DE CONTRAPUNTI / A DUE VOCI / Di Vincenzio Galilei Nobile Fiorentino. / [Cut of three ladies playing lute and viola da braccio and singing from an open book] / IN FIORENZA, M. D. LXXXIIII. / Appresso Giorgio Marescotti.

Two part books in mensural notation, each of 16 fols. On fol. 1^v (= p. 2): a composition headed "DELL'AUTORE Fuga a cinque voci all'unisono dopo tre tempi," on the text "Hor che'l cielo." Dedication on p. 3 headed "AL MOLTO MAGNIFICO M. FEDERIGO TEDALDI PARENTE OSSERVANDIS.," and signed "Michelangnolo Galilei," reprinted in SartMS, p. 48. The volume contains 29 compositions *a2* without text or titles, one on each page beginning with p. 4. No. 4 is reprinted from 1568_2, no. 13. The entire collection is reprinted in SCMA VIII. For further information see EinVG, which includes the dedication and a modern edition of no. 17.

Copy in: I:Fn.[1]

[1] This copy was in the Landau-Finaly library in Florence (see RoedigC I, 523).

1584_5

GALILEI, VINCENZO

FRONIMO / DIALOGO / DI VINCENTIO GALILEI / NOBILE FIORENTINO, / SOPRA L'ARTE DEL BENE INTAVOLARE, / ET RETTAMENTE SONARE LA MUSICA / Negli strumenti artificiali si di corde come di fia/to, & in particulare nel Liuto. / Nuovamente ristampato, & dall'Autore istesso arrichito, / & ornato di novità di concetti, & d'essempi. / [Printer's mark] / IN VINEGGIA, / Appresso l'Herede di Girolamo Scotto, / M. D. LXXXIIII.[1]

99 fols. Italian lute tablature and mensural notation. Dedication on fol. *A2 headed "AL MOLTO MAGNIFICO SIG ET MIO PADRONE OSSERVANDISSIMO IL SIGNORE JACOPO CORSI," and signed "Di Fiorenza a il di ultimo di Aprile. 1584. D. V. S. Affetionatissimo et obligatissimo servidore: Vincentio Galilei," reprinted in GaspaC I, 334; IMAMI IV, lxxxvii; and SartMS, p. 42. On fol. *A3: table of contents for the text. On fol. *A3^v: table of compositions. On fol. *A4: table of composers. On fol. *A5 (= p. 1): preface headed "L'Autore ai lettori," reprinted in GaspaC I, 334. On p. 182: register of signatures and colophon: "[Printer's mark] IN VINEGIA, M D LXXXIIII." Attributions to composers and number of voices in the vocal original are taken from the table of contents; they do not appear in the body of the text. The compositions identified by the superior letter *a* ([a]) are reprinted in IMAMI IV, 5–85. Twelve of the ricercares, arranged for instrumental ensemble *a4*, are reprinted in GalR. This treatise on playing the lute, in the form of a dialogue, is a second revised and enlarged edition of 1568_2. All of the compositions are for solo lute, except nos. 1 and 20, which are printed in mensural notation; nos. 5 and 6, which are printed in a version for solo lute and in a version in mensural notation; and nos 9–11, 107, and 108, which are for two lutes.

Copies in: B:Br, CH:Lcortot, D:Bds-Tü, D:LEm, F:Pc (two copies), F:Pn (two copies), F:Pthibault, GB:Ge, †

GB:Lbm (two copies), I:Bc, I:Fr, I:Mb, I:MOe, I:PIu, I:Rsc, US:R, US:Wc.[2]

fol.

1 *A3 *Fuga à cinque voci dopo quattro tempi, all'Unisono*[a 3] (mensural notation)

2 p. 4 *Ricerca[re]* Annibale [Padovano] *a4* (1556_9, no. 2)

3 6 *Si pour bivir ardiendo* Pedro Guerrero *a4* = 1568_2, no. 1

4 7 *Biviendo sin amar* Pedro Guerrero *a4* = 1568_2, no. 2

4a 12 *Duo*

5 14 *Qual miracolo Amore*[a 4] Vincenzo Galilei *a3* (also printed in mensural notation) (IMAMI IV, 21)

6 17 *In exitu Israel*[a 5] Vincenzo Galilei *a4* (also printed in mensural notation) (IMAMI IV, 25)

7 23 *Dun spiritu triste* Pedro Guerrero *a4* = 1568_2, no. 3

8 26 *Vestiva i colli* Palestrina *a5* = 1568_2, no. 4a

27 2a pars *Cosi le chiome mie* = 1568_2, no. 4b

9 31 *Alle fiorite sponde* (for two lutes)

10 33 *Questi che la città* (for two lutes)

11 37 *Fuga a l'unisono, dopo sei tempi*[a] (for two lutes)

12 43 *Questi ch'inditio fan del mio tormento* Alessandro Striggio *a6* = 1568_2, no. 5

13 44 *Nasce la pena mia* Striggio *a6* = 1568_2, no. 6

14 45 *Nasce la gioia mia* Giovanni Animuccia *a6* = 1568_2, no. 7

15 47 *Io mi son giovinetta*[6] Domenico Ferabosco *a4* = 1568_2, no. 8

16 49 *Liete felici spiriti*[7] Vincenzo Ruffo *a3* = 1568_2, no. 9

17 49 *Il vostro gran valore* Ruffo *a3* = 1568_2, no. 10

18 53 *Se tra quest'herbe e fiore* Palestrina *a5* = 1568_2, no. 11

19 56 *Io mi son giovinetta* (another version of no. 15) = 1568_2, no. 12

20 78 *Duo tutto di fantasia*[8] (mensural notation) = 1568_2, no. 13

21 80 *Ricercar del primo Tuono per* ♮[a 9]

22 80 *Ricercare del secondo tuono per* ♮[a]

23 80 *Ricercare del terzo tuono per* ♮

24 81 *Ricercare del quarto tuono per* ♮

25 81 *Ricercare del quinto tuono per* ♮

26 81 *Ricercare del sesto tuono per* ♮[10]

27 82 *Ricercare del settimo tuono per* ♮[11]

28 82 *Ricercare del ottavo tuono per* ♮[a]

29 82 *Ricercare del nono tuono per* ♮

30 83 *Ricercare del decimo tuono per* ♮

31 83 *Ricercare dell'undecimo tuono per* ♮

32 83 *Ricercare de l'undecimo tuono & ultimo per* ♮

33 84 *Ricercare del primo tuono per b*

34 84 *Ricercare del secondo tuono per b*

35 85 *Ricercare del terzo tuono per b*[12]

36 85 *Ricercare del quarto tuono per b*[13]

37 85 *Ricercare del quinto tuono per b*

38 86 *Ricercare del sesto tuono per b*

39 86 *Ricercare del settimo tuono per b*[14]

40 87 *Ricercare del ottavo tuono per b*

41 87 *Ricercare del nono tuono per b*

42 87 *Ricercare del decimo tuono per b*

43 88 *Ricercare dell'undecimo tuono per b*

44 88 *Ricercare del duodecimo, & ultimo tuono per b*

45 88 *Altro Ricercare del primo tuono per* ♮[15]

46 89 [*Altro Ricercare del duodecimo tuono per b molle*][a]

47 112 *Crai[n]te & Sospir*[16] Pedro Guerrero *a4* = 1568_2, no. 15: Baston

48 116 [*Ricercare a4. voci di B. M.*][a 17]

49 119 *Ben sapevo io* Spontone *a5*

119 2a pars *Io fuggia le tue mani*

50 120 *Se di penne gia mai* Pietro Taglia *a5* (RISM 1570_{14}, p. 12)

51 121 *Io son ferito hai lasso* Palestrina *a5* = 1568_2, no. 83

52 122 *Il dolce sonno in cui sepolto giace*[18] Palestrina

53 122 *O vago Endimione*

54 123 *Chi salira per me* Giaches Wert *a4* (Vogel: Wert 31 [1564], no. 25)

55 124 *A qualunque animal* Annibale Padovano *a4* = 1568_2, no. 24a

125 2a pars *Et io da che comincia* = 1568_2, no. 24b

126 3a pars *Quando la sera* = 1568_2, no. 24c

126 4a pars *Non credo che pascesse* = 1568_2, no. 24d

127 5a pars *Prima ch'io torni* = 1568_2, no. 24e

128 6a pars *Con lei fuss'io* = 1568_2, no. 24f

56 128 *Si traviato* [*e'l folle*] Annibale Padovano *a 4* (Vogel: Rore 50a [1561])

57 129 *Cantai hor piango* Annibale Padovano *a 4* (Vogel: Padovano [1564], nos. 21–22)

130 2a pars *Tenga dunque ver me*

58 131 *Dal piu bel viso* Annibale Padovano *a 4* (Vogel: Padovano [1564], nos. 23–24)

131 2a pars *Dalle soavi*

59 132 *La notte che segui* Orlando Lasso *a 5* = 1568_2, no. 66a

133 2a pars *Riconosci colei* = 1568_2, no. 66b

133 3a pars *Come non conosco io* = 1568_2, no. 66c

60 134 *Amor m'ha posto* Pietro Vinci *a 5* (Vogel: Vinci 6 [1563], nos. 5–6)

135 2a pars *I pensier son saette*

61 136 *Deh lascia l'antro ombroso* Baldissera Donato *a 4* (Vogel: Donato 11 [1568], p. 21)

62 137 *Dolor se'l mio dolor* Donato *a 4* (Vogel: Donato 11 [1568], p. 5)

63 138 *Da quei bei crini* Donato *a 5* = 1568_2, no. 71

64 138 *Come havran fin* Cipriano de Rore *a 4* = 1568_2, no. 19

65 139 *Fuggi speme mia fuggi* Alessandro Striggio *a 5* (compare SonnD, p. 50)

66 140 *Ma di che debbo lamentarmi* Vincenzo Ruffo *a 4* = 1568_2, no. 23

67 140 *Beltà* [*si come in mente*] Francesco Rossello *a 6* = 1568_2, no. 95

68 141 *O del mio navigar* Costanzo Porta *a 4*

69 142 *Qual'anima ignorante* Adrian Willaert *a 5* (Vogel: Willaert 5 [1563], no. 9)

70 144 *Deh porgi mano* Vincenzo Ruffo *a 5* = 1568_2, no. 79a

145 2a pars *Sdegno regge il timor* = 1568_2, no. 79b

71 145 *Ben mio chi mi ti toglie* Ruffo *a 5* (Vogel: Ruffo 7 [1554], no. 11)

72 147 *O dolci sguardi* Ruffo *a 5* = 1568_2, no. 80

73 147 *Donna gentil* Giovanni Maria Nanino *a 5* (RISM 1574_4)

74 148 *Scoprirò l'ardor mio* Nanino *a 5* (RISM 1576_5, p. 5)

149 2a pars *Se voi sete'l mio ben*

75 150 *In qual parte del Cielo*[19] Philippe de Monte *a 5* (MonteO XXV, 38)

150 2a pars *Per divina bellezza*

76 151 *Candida e ricca vela* Francesco Portinaro *a 5* = 1568_2, no. 72a

151 2a pars *Piacciati come i tuoi* = 1568_2, no. 72b

77 152 *Chi per voi non sospira*[a] Annibale Zoilo *a 5* (IMAMI IV, 59)

78 153 *Io piango* = 1568_2, no. 77

79 153 *Ma folle io spargo* Giacomini *a 5*

80 154 *La bella mano* Giacomini *a 6*

81 154 *Alla dolc'ombra* Animuccia *a 5* (RISM 1566_3)

155 2a pars *Non ved'il mondo*

82 156 *I dolci colli* Marco Antonio Pordenone *a 5* (Vogel: Pordenone 3 [1571], nos. 1–2)

156 2a pars *E qual cervo ferito*

83 157 *O dolorosi amanti* Giovanni Dragoni *a 5* (Vogel: Dragoni 2 [1575], p. 4)

84 158 *Eran si chiari* Dragoni *a 5* (Vogel: Dragoni 2 [1575], p. 5)

85 158 *Per pianto la mia carne* Hippolito Baccusi *a 5* (Vogel: Baccusi 1 [1570], nos. 1–4)

159 2a pars *Hor pensate al mio mal*

159 3a pars *Si m'è dolce il morire*

160 4a pars *Cosi vuol mia ventura*

86 160 *Quando lieta sperai* Morales *a 5* (RoreO III, 34: Rore)

87 162 *Caronte* [*chi sei? Sono una anima dannata*][20] Morales *a 5*

88 162 *Mentre di pioggia* Giovanni Primavera *a 6*

89 163 *Ecco che pur dopo l'assentia amara* Antonio del Pace *a 6* (Vogel: Pace 1 [1575], no. 3)

90 164 *Ultimi miei sospiri* Philippe Verdelot *a6* = 1568_2, no. 94
91 165 *Nell'odorato & lucido oriente* Giaches de Ponte *a4* = 1568_2, no. 31
92 166 *A cui piu ch'altri mai* Ponte *a4* = 1568_2, no. 32
93 167 *La quale in somma è questa* Ponte *a4* = 1568_2, no. 33
94 167 *A questo confortando* = 1568_2, no. 34: Ponte
95 168 *Fedeli miei* Ponte *a4* = 1568_2, no. 35
96 169 *Spesso in parte del ciel* Marc'Antonio Ingegneri *a4* = 1568_2, no. 20
97 170 *Non mi tolga'l ben mio* Ingegneri *a4* = 1568_2, no. 21: Rore
98 170 *A casa un giorno* Giaches Wert *a5* (Vogel: Wert 13 [1567], no. 25)
99 171 *Di men stupor saria* Giovanni Contino *a4*
100 172 *Chi vuol veder* Contino *a5*
101 173 *Da mille gravi affanni* Contino *a4* (RISM 1569_{20}, p. 33)
102 173 *Sapete amanti* Contino *a4* (RISM 1589_{12})
103 174 *In qual giardin* Contino *a4*
104 175 *Se voi sete cor mio* (RISM 1569_{20}, p. 35: Contino)
105 175 *In dubio di mio stato*[a] Lasso (IMAMI IV, 82)
106 176 *In dubio di mio stato*[a] Lasso (IMAMI IV, 85)
107 178 [*Contrapunto primo di B. M.*][a] [21] (for two lutes)
108 180 [*Contrapunto secondo del medesimo*] [22] (for two lutes)

[1] Facs. of title page in AbbS I, 407, and KinsP, p 110. Facs. of title page, dedication, and p. 14 in IMAMI IV, following p. 2; see also p. lv for information on this volume.
[2] A copy was in the Heyer library (see HeyerV II, no. 24).
[3] Mod. ed. in ChilS, p. 22.
[4] Mod. ed. in ChilS, p. 31.
[5] Mod. ed. in ChilLS, p. 88.
[6] Mod. ed. in ChilLS, p. 90.
[7] Mod. ed. in ChilLS, p. 92.
[8] On p. 77 are four counterpoints *a2* against a cantus firmus, in mensural notation.
[9] Mod. ed. in KinO, p. 283.
[10] Mod. ed. in KinO, p. 284.
[11] Mod. ed. in KinO, p. 285.
[12] Mod. ed. in NeemAM II, no. 11.
[13] Mod. ed. in WasG, no. 15.
[14] Mod. ed. in NeemAM II, no. 10.
[15] Mod. ed. in NeemAM II, no. 12.
[16] Mod. ed. in ChilS, p. 28.
[17] Galilei says that B. M. is a Florentine gentleman. He is otherwise unidentified.
[18] Facs. in PalW XXXIII, 75.
[19] Mod. ed. in MonteO XXV, 1.
[20] The bracketed information has been taken from a late sixteenth-century manuscript of keyboard music, now in a private library in Florence, which contains an intabulation of the same composition. I am grateful to Professor Frank A. D'Accone for making this information available to me.
[21] See note 17 above.
[22] Mod. ed. in ChilLS, p. 93.

1584_6

ADRIANSEN, EMANUEL

PRATUM MUSICUM / LONGE AMOENISSIMUM, / CUIUS SPATIOSISSIMO, EOQUE / JUCUNDISSIMO AMBITU, (PRAETER VARII / GENERIS AUTOMATA SEU PHANTASIAS) / COMPREHENDUNTUR / Selectissima diversorum idiomatum Carmina 4. 5. & 6. Vocum. / Nonnulla Duarum, Trium, & Quatuor Testudinum Symphoniae aptissima. / Cantiones Trium Vocum, quas Neapolitanas vulgò appellant. / Variae ad animorum hilaritatem (praesertim inter symposia) provocantes, / auribusque gratissimae modulationes. / Omnis generis Choreae, Passomezo cum suis Saltarellis, Gailliardae, / Alemandae, Branslae, Courantae, Voltae, etc: / Postremò Tripudia aliquot Anglicana. / Omnia ad Testudinis Tabulaturam fideliter redacta, per id genus Musices / Experientissimum Artificem / EMANUELEM HADRIANIUM ANTVERPIENSEM. / Adjuncta est singulis Carminibus, in gratiam eorum, qui vivae Vocis concentu / oblectantur, distincta Vocibus aliquot Notularum / Descriptio. / Quorum omnium versa Pagina accuratissimum Indicem (qui & Musicorum, è quorum / hac fontibus hausta sunt, Nomina prodet) exhibebit. / OPUS NOVUM. / [Printer's mark] / ANTVERPIAE. / Ex Typographia Musica Petri Phalesii, / ad intersigne Rubri Leonis. / M. D. LXXXIIII.

92 fols. French lute tablature and mensural notation. On fol. 1^v: table of contents. Dedication on fol. 2 headed "MAGNIFICO AC LITERARUM SCIENTIA, PRAE-

STANTISSIMO VIRO, D. BALTASARO DI ROBIANO, CIVI AC MERCATORI ANTVERPIENSI PATRONO SUO OPTIMI MERITO.," and signed "Vale Antverpiae pridie Pentecostes. Anno M. D. LXXXIIII. Tuus ad obsequia omnia paratissimus, Emanuel Hadriani F." Colophon on fol. 92^{v}: "Imprime par Pierre Phalese, L'An M. D. LXXXIIII." This volume is dated 1585 in BasseC and DraudiusBC, p. 1650. For a possible later edition see [1592]$_5$. There was a later edition in 1600. For a discussion of Adriansen and his lute books see SpiessA. Attributions to composers are taken from the table of contents; they do not appear in the body of the text. Two dances are reprinted in AdrT. Nos. 1–5 and 61–95 are for solo lute. Nos. 6–32, 41–52, and 54–58 are for solo lute but include as well two or more voices of the vocal model in mensural notation on the page facing the intabulation (these voices are indicated in the inventory by S, A, T, and B). Nos. 33–40, 53, 59, and 60 are for two, three, or four lutes with and without two or more voices of the vocal model in mensural notation.

Copies in: D:HEu, D:KNu, F:MD, NL:DHgm.[1]

MUSIC FOR SOLO LUTE

fol.

1 2^{v} *Fantasia Prima*

2 3^{v} *Fantasia 2*

3 4 *Fantasia 3*

4 4^{v} *Fantasia 4*[2]

5 5 *Fantasia* [5]

MUSIC FOR LUTE AND SEVERAL VOICES

6 5^{v} *Io mi son giovenetta* (SB) Alfonso Ferabosco (EinIM III, no. 30: D. Ferabosco)

7 6^{v} *Poi ch'el mio largo pianto* (SB) Orlando di Lasso (LassoW VIII, 84)

8 7^{v} *Anchor che col partire* (SB) Cypriano de Rore (SCMA VI, 45)

9 8^{v} *D'un coeur loyal* (SB)

10 9^{v} *La terre les eaux* (SB) Costeley (MMRF III, no. 6)

11 10^{v} *Appariran per me* (SB) Orlando di Lasso (LassoW VIII, 27)

12 11^{v} *Quel lamp'esser vorei* (SB)

13 12^{v} *Os'io potessi donna* (SB) Giachet Berchem (RISM 1541_9, p. 19)

14 13^{v} *Madonna mia pieta* (SB) Orlando di Lasso (LassoW X, 61)

15 14^{v} *Tant vous allez doux Guillemette* (SB) Abrahan (RISM 1564_{11}, fol. 11)

16 15^{v} *Avecques vous* [*mon amour finera*] (SB) Orlando di Lasso (LassoW XII, 37)

17 16^{v} *Ghevaere Ghevaere* [*hoe staet*]

18 17^{v} *Donna crudel* (SB) Giovanni Ferretti (Vogel: Ferretti 7 [1568], no. 2)

19 18^{v} *Io cantero* [*di quel'almo splendore*] (SB) Gironi: Conversi (Vogel: Conversi 2 [1572], p. 22)

19^{v} 2a pars *Ben poss'amor*

20 20^{v} *Io vò gridando*[3] (SB) Giro. Conversi (Vogel: Conversi 2 [1572], p. 3)

21 21^{v} *Veni in hortum meum* (SB) Orlando di Lasso (LassoW V, 120) = 1592_6, no. 52

22 23^{v} *Cara la vita mia* (SB) Giaches de Wert (Vogel: Wert 3 [1564], p. 13)

23^{v} 2a pars *Poiche con* [*gl'occhi*]

23 25^{v} *Primum potum* [*bibe*] (SB) Noë Faignient

24 26^{v} *Et d'ou venez vous* [*madame Lucette*] (SB) Orlando di Lasso (LassoW XIV, 68)

25 27^{v} *Le Rossignol* [*plaisant*] (SB) Orlando di Lasso (LassoW XIV, 107) = 1592_6, no. 38

26 28^{v} *Tu dolc'anima mia* (SB) Alfonso Ferabosco (RISM 1583_{14}, fol. 17^{v})

27 29^{v} *Susanne un jour* (SB) Orlando di Lasso (LassoW XIV, 29)

28 31^{v} *Comme la tourterelle*[4] (SB) Filippo de Monte (MonteO XXV, no. 46)

29 32^{v} *D'un si bel foco* (SB) Giaches de Wert (RISM 1583_{14}, fol. 10^{v}) = 1593_7, no. 29

33^{v} 2a pars *Scorgo tant'alto illume*

30 34^{v} *Vestiv'i colli* (SB) Gian' Palestrino (PalO IX, 117)

35^{v} 2a pars *Cosi le chiome*

31 37v *Nasce la pena mia* (SB) Alessand: Striggio (MonteO XVI, app.)
32 39v *Corrette tutti quanti* (SB) Giovanni Ferretti (Vogel: Ferretti 2 [1576], p. 15)

MUSIC FOR TWO LUTES AND SEVERAL VOICES [5]

33 40v *Chi per voi non sospira* (SSB) Noë Faignient (RISM 1588_{29}, no. 21)
34 42v *Ecco ch'io lass'il core* (SSB) Alessand: Striggio (Vogel: Ferretti 4 [1575], p. 10: anon.)
35 44v *Tre gratiosi Amanti* ("Dialogo à 6") (SSB) Gio. de Macque (RISM 1583_{14}, fol. 34)

MUSIC FOR THREE AND FOUR LUTES [6]

36 46v *Io vo gridando* (three lutes) Gironi: Conversi (another version of no. 20 above)
37 47v *Donna crudel* (three lutes) Gio. Ferretti (another version of no. 18 above)
38 58v *Madonna mia pieta* (three lutes) Orlando di Lasso (another version of no. 14 above)
39 49v *O Vilanella* (four lutes; SATB) Hubertus Walrant
40 50v *Als ick winde* [7] (four lutes; SATB) Hubertus Walrant

MUSIC FOR LUTE AND SEVERAL VOICES [8]

41 51v *Se la mia longa fede* (STB)
42 52 *Dimmi donna crudel* (STB) (compare Vogel: Ferretti 17 [1575], p. 13)
43 52v *Amanti miei* (STB)
44 53 *Stella crudel* (STB) (compare Vogel: Ferretti 11 [1569], p. 4)
45 53v *Venga quel bel narciso* (STB)
46 54 *Sel dolce sguardo* (STB) (compare Vogel: Ferretti 7 [1568], p. 4)
47 54v *Del crud'amor* (STB) (compare 1584_8, no. 2: Regnart)
48 55 *Io son bell'e delicata* (STB) (compare Vogel: Ferretti 22 [1585], p. 12: Ferretti)
49 55v *Fuggit'amore* (STB) (compare Vogel: Nola 4 [1569], no. 15: Nola)
50 *Se ben io vo lontan* (STB)
51 56v *Vostro raro valor* (STB)
52 57 *Ben mio [de dove sei n'ascolti]* (SATB)
53 57v *Fiamenga freda* (two lutes; STB)
54 58v *Vola vola pensier* [Aeria à la Italiana] (SB)
55 59 *Amar donna che bella* (SB)
56 59v *Het soude een meysken gaen om wijn* [9] (SATB) (RISM 1553_{30}, no. 1: Sampson)
57 60 *Het soude een meysken gaen om wijn* (SATB)
58 60v *Het voer een cuyper cuypen* (SATB)

MUSIC FOR TWO LUTES AND SEVERAL VOICES

59 61 *J'ay veu le cerf* (two lutes; SATB) (compare ClemensO VI, 140: Manchicourt)
60 61 *Chantons buvons* (two lutes; SATB)

MUSIC FOR SOLO LUTE

61 61v *Passomeso in Basso*
66 *Gailliarda in Basso*
62 68v *Passomezo in Contratenore*
70 *Gailliarda in Contratenore*
63 70v *Passomezo in Basso. à longue mesure*
64 72 *Passomezo de Haubois. Superius*
74v *Galliarde du precedente*
65 77v *Passomezo in Tenore*
79v *Galliarde in Tenor*
66 81 *Gailliarda*
81 *La mesme autrement*
67 81v *Gaillarda* [10]
81v *La mesme plus diminuée*
68 82 *Galliarda*
69 82v *Galliarda*
70 82v *Chi passa [Gailliarde]* (compare AzzaiV, no. 2)
71 83v *Galliarda*
72 83v *Galliarda*
84 *La precedente plus diminuée*
73 84v *Almande Prince*
74 85 *Almande [de la] Court* [11]
75 85 *L'Almande Slaepen gaen* [12]
76 85v *Almande*
86 *Reprinse*
77 86 *Almande de Duc Mathias*
78 86v *Almande de don Frederico*
79 87 *Almande Fortune helas [pourquoy]*
80 87v *Almande [de Poussinghe]*
88 *Reprinse*
81 88 *Almande Nonnette*

82	88^v	*Almande Bisarde*
	88^v	*Reprinse*
83	89	*Branles* [*commune*]
84	89^v	*Courrante*
85	90	*Branles*
86	90^v	*Courrante*
87	90^v	*Courrante 2*
88	91	*Courrante 3*
89	91	*Volte de France*
90	91	*Volte 2*
91	91^v	*Branle de Poictou*
92	92	*Pavane à l'Englesa*
93	92^v	*Canson Englesa*
94	92^v	*Altra Canson Englesa*
95	92^v	*Saltarello Englesa*

[1] Copies were in D:Bds and the Cummings library (see CummC, no. 768).
[2] Mod. ed. in MFII VII, 0.
[3] Facs. of fol. 21 in BergT, p. 19, and GoovH, opp. p. 60.
[4] Mod. ed. in MonteO, XXV, 4.
[5] Heading on fol. 40^v: "SEQUUNTUR DEINCEPS CARMINA DUABUS TESTUDINIBUS ACCOMMODA."
[6] Heading on fol. 46^v: "SEQUUNTUR MADRIGALES ET CANTIONES NAPOLITANAE TRIBUS ET QUATUOR TESTUDINIBUS LUDENDAE."
[7] Mod. ed. in NoskeL, p. 188.
[8] Heading on fol. 51^v: "CANTIONES NAPOLIT: *a3*."
[9] Facs. of fol. 59^v in KinsP, p. 135.
[10] Mod. ed. in BruAL I, no. 25; SteinitA, no. 32; and WasG, no. 16.
[11] Mod. ed. in NeemAM II, no. 13.
[12] Mod. ed. in MohrA II, no. 36.

1584_7

INGEGNIERI, MARC'ANTONIO

DI MARC'ANTONIO INGEGNIERI / IL SECONDO LIBRO DE MADRIGALI / A QUATTRO VOCI, / Con due Arie di Canzon Francese per sonare. / Novamente Ristampato. / [Printer's mark] / In Venetia Appresso Angelo Gardano / M D LXXXIIII.

Four part books in mensural notation, each of 12 fols. On fol. 12^v (= p. 22): table of contents. Contents = 1579_3. Nineteen of the 21 compositions have Italian text; two are for instrumental ensemble *a4*.

Copy in: D:As.[1]

[1] A copy was in PL:GD.

1584_8

KRENGEL, GREGORIUS

TABULATURA / NOVA / CONTINENS SELECTIS/SIMAS QUASQUE CANTIONES UT / SUNT MADRIGALIA, MUTETAE, PADUANAE ET / Vilanellae, testudini sic aptatas, ut quilibet singulas duplici modo / ludere & concinere possit iam recens edita / PER / GREGORIUM KRENGEL Francostenensem Silesium. / [Cut of a lutenist] / FRANCOFORDIAE CIS VIADRUM, IN OFFI/CINA ANDREAE EICHORN / ANNO / M. D. LXXXIIII. / CUM GRATIA ET PRIVILEGIO CAESAREAE MAIESTATIS.

30 fols. German lute tablature. On fol. A1^v: table of contents. Dedication on fol. A2 headed "EPISTOLA DEDICATORIA MAGNIFICIS VIRIS NOBILITATE GENERIS AC SPLENDORE, DOCTRINA, RERUM PLURIMARUM COGNItione, Virtutibusque ornatissimis Dominis: DOMINO JOHANNI A ZIRN: DOMINO IN KATschkewitz & Detzdorff, &c. & DOMINO BERNHARDO AB AXLEBEN. MAGNO cognominato Illustriss: principis in Ducatu Lignicensi Consiliario Dominis & Moecentib: suis omni observantia colendis.," and signed "Francophordiae ad Viadrum è Musaeo meo. Anno 1584. Magnificentias vestras, Observantia perpetua colens, Gregorius Krengel, Francosteinensis, S." On fol. B1: preface headed "An den guthertzigen Leser." The volume is described in GrimmM, pp. 100–103. Attributions to composers are taken from the table of contents. All of the compositions are for two lutes, each with seven courses. The second lute part is on the recto side of each opening.

Copy in: D:Mbs.[1]

	fol.	
1	B1^v	*Tutto lo giorno* Jakob Regnart (RegnC I, no. 1)
2	B2^v	*Del crud amor* Regnart (RegnC I, no. 2)
3	C1^v	*Non è dolor* Regnart (RegnC I, no. 3)
4	C2^v	*Amor Lasciami stare* Regnart (RegnC I, no. 4)
5	D1^v	*Io voglio* Regnart (RegnC I, no. 5)

6 D2^v *Dolsi sospir* Regnart (RegnC I, no. 14)
7 E1^v *Di pensire* Regnart (RegnC I, no. 10)
8 E2^v *Se not è giorno* Regnart (RegnC I, no. 12)
9 F1^v *Servite fedelment* Regnart (RegnC I, no. 13)
10 F2^v *A lerm à lerm* Regnart (RegnC I, no. 15)
11 G1^v *Mirate che mi fa crudel* Regnart (RegnC II, no. 1)
12 G2^v *Donna ben posso* Regnart (RegnC II, no. 2)
13 H1^v *Alleluia* [*vox laeta*] Orl[ando Lasso] *a5* (LassoW III, 141)
H2^v 2a pars [*Alleluia prae gaudio*]
14 J1^v *Credidi propter quod loquilut* Lasso *a5* (LassoW IX, 21)
J2^v 2a pars *Vota mea*
15 K1^v *Tota pulchra es* Gregorius Langius *a5* (PubAPTM XXV, no. 9)
16 K2^v *Vina parant animos* Langius *a5* (PubAPTM XXV, no. 10)
17 L1^v *Offt wünsch ich Ihr* Langius (PL:B, MS 11)[2]
18 L2^v *Ist keiner hie der spricht zu mir* Henningii Winsiman Hamb.
19 M1^v *Paduana 1*[3]
20 M1^v *Ohn dich mus ich mich aller freuden massen* Regnart (PubAPTM XIX, no. 1)
21 M2^v [*Paduana*] *2*
22 M2^v *Wann ich gedencke der stundt* Regnart (PubAPTM XIX, no. 2)
23 N1^v [*Paduana*] *3*
24 N1^v *Glaube nicht das ich köndt ein* Regnart (PubAPTM XIX, no. 14)
25 N1^v *Kein grösser freud* Regnart (PubAPTM XIX, no. 21)
26 N2^v [*Paduana*] *4*
27 N2^v *Jungfraw ewer wanckelmuth* Regnart (PubAPTM XIX, no. 26)
28 N2^v *Ich bin gen Baden zogen* Regnart (PubAPTM XIX, no. 29)
29 O1^v [*Paduana*] *5*
30 O1^v *Nach meiner lieb viel hundert Knaben trachten* Regnart (PubAPTM XIX, no. 43)
31 O1^v *Sagt mir Jungfraw rechter* Regnart (PubAPTM XIX, no. 44)
32 O2^v [*Paduana*] *6*
33 O2^v *Jungfraw von ewrent wegen* Langius (LangL, no. 13)
34 O2^v *Ich hört ein Jungfraw klagen* Langius (LangL, no. 19)
35 P1^v [*Paduana*] *7*
36 P1^v *Ach möcht es doch gesein* Langius (LangL, no. 20)
P1^v *Alio modo*

[1] A copy was in PL:WRu.
[2] See StarkeHGL, p. 123.
[3] Heading on fol. M1^v: "Sequuntur Cantiones nonnullae quas vulgo Paduanas vocant quibus omnis generis Textus applicari possunt tam Italici Germanici, nec non Polonici, &c. his quoque adjecimus vilanellas nonnullas."

1584_9

LUPACCHINO, BERNARDINO, AND JOAN MARIA TASSO

DI BERNARDINO LUPACCHINO / ET DI GIOAN MARIA TASSO, IL PRIMO LIBRO / A Due Voci: Novamente ristampato. / [Printer's mark] / In Venetia Presso Giacomo Vincenci: & Ricciardo Amadino compagni: / MDLXXXIIII.

Two part books in mensural notation, each of 20 fols. Contents = 1559_6. All of the compositions are *a2* and without text or title.

Copy in: I:Bc (S).

1584_{10}

MASCHERA, FIORENZO

LIBRO PRIMO / DE CANZONI / DA SONARE, / A QUATTRO VOCI, / DI FLORENTIO MASCHERA / ORGANISTA NEL DUOMO / DI BRESCIA. / Di nuovo con diligenza ristampate. / [Printer's mark] / IN BRESCIA, Appresso Vincenzo Sabbio / M. D. LXXXIIII.

Four part books in mensural notation, each of 12 fols. Dedication on fol. 1^v headed "AL MOLTO MAGNIFICO SIG.

MIO OSSERVANDISS. IL SIG. ANTONIO MARIA UGGIERO," and signed "Di Brescia li 2. Marzo. 1582. Di V. S. molto Magnifica obligatiss. Servitore Florentio Maschera," reprinted in GaspaC IV, 126, and SartMS, p. 41. The music begins on fol. 2(= p. 1). On p. 22: table of contents. Thematic incipits for the entire volume are printed in IMAMI II, lvi–lx. The entire collection is transcribed and discussed in McKeeM. For other editions see $[1582]_4$, 1588_6, 1590_5, 1593_5, and 1596_8. All of the compositions are for instrumental ensemble *a 4*.

Copies in: I:Bc, I:Bsp.[1]

	p.	
1	1	*Canzon prima La Capriola*[2] (1593_7, no. 17)
2	2	*Canzon Seconda* [*La Martinenga*][3] (1574_6, no. 10, and 1593_7, no. 18)
3	3	*Canzon Terza*
4	4	*Canzon Quarta*[4] (1574_6, no. 11, and 1593_7, no. 19)
5	5	*Canzon quinta La Maggia* (1593_7, no. 20; compare 1598_4, no. 1)
6	6	*Canzon Sesta* (1593_7, no. 21)
7	7	*Canzon Settima* [*Al S. Pompeo Coradello*]
8	8	*Canzon Ottava* (1593_7, no. 22)
9	9	*Canzon Nona* [*La Duranda*]
10	10	*Canzon Decima* [*La Rosa*] (1593_7, no. 23)
11	11	*Canzon Undecima* [*L'Averolda*] (1593_7, no. 24)
12	12	*Canzon Duodecima* [*L'Uggiera*]
13	13	*Canzon Decimaterza* [*La Girella*] (1593_7, no. 25)
14	14	*Canzon Decimaquarta*[5]
15	15	*Canzon Decimaquinta* (1593_7, no. 26)
16	16	*Canzon Decimasesta*
17	17	*Canzon Decimasettima* (1593_7, no. 27)
18	18	*Canzon Decimottava La Villachiara*
19	19	*Canzon Decimanona*
20	20	*Canzon Vigesima La Foresta*[6]
21	21	*Canzon Vigesimaprima*[7]

[1] A copy was in I:Ma.

[2] Mod. ed. in AulerS I, 16; IMAMI II, lxix; KosI; and WasI, no. 1.

[3] Mod. ed. in ARC 73, and KosI.

[4] Mod. ed. in ARC 74.

[5] Mod. ed. in DallaA, no. 12, and HAM, no. 175.

[6] An arrangement for keyboard is pr. in MerT, p. 216 after an anon. manuscript of 1593 (D:Bds, Mus. MS 40115).

[7] Mod. ed. in FuserC, no. 18; RieM, no. 49; and WasI, no. 2.

1584

DOUBTFUL WORKS

1. HawkH II, 497, and DeakinMB, p. 6, list a 1584 edition of William Bathe, *A Briefe Introduction to the skill of Song*. Their source of information about this volume was probably Thomas East's application for a license to reprint the work, dated October 31, 1597. The entry in ArberT III, 95, reads: "Entred for his [East's] copie under th[e h]andes of the Wardens, *A briefe Introduction to the true arte of musick*, sett forth by WILLIAM BATHE Student at Oxford. yt was a former copie printed by Abell Jeffes *anno* 1584 And is by him sett over to master East as appeareth by his letter written to the wardens to have it nowe entred for Master Eastes copye." The volume is listed in this bibliography as $158?_2$.

1585_1

BARBETTA, GIULIO CESARE

INTAVOLA/TURA DI LIUTO / DI JULIO CESARE / BARBETTA PADOANO / Dove si contiene Padoane Arie Baletti / Pass'e mezi Saltarelli per Ballar / à la Italiana, & altre cose / dilettevoli secondo / l'uso di questi / tempi, / Accommodato per Sonar con Sei / e Sette ordeni de corde. / [Printer's mark] / In Venetia Appresso Angelo Gardano / M. D. LXXXV.

25 fols. Italian lute tablature. The title is placed within an ornamental border. Dedication on fol. 1^v headed "AL MOLTO MAGNIFICO ET GENEROSO SIGNOR IL SIGNOR JERONIMO OTTO MIO SEMPRE SIGNORE OSSERVANDISSIMO," and signed "Di Venetia il dì 12. Ottobre 1585. Di V. Sig. molto Mag. Affettionatiss. Servitore Julio Cesare Barbetta." Fol. 2 = p. 1. On p. 48: table of

contents. MoeDM contains a thematic index of the dances (p. 457) and concordances for them (p. 279). All of the compositions are for solo lute except nos. 32–33, which are for two lutes.

Copies in: GB:Lbm, US:Wc (imperfect).[1]

MUSIC FOR SOLO LUTE

	p.	
1	1	*Padoana Prima, Deta la Dispettosa*[2]
2	2	*Padoana Seconda, Deta la bella dorotea*
3	3	*Padoana Terza, Deta la Lubiana*
4	4	*Padoana Quarta, Deta la Squillitria*
5	4	*Padoana Quinta, Deta Chi mira gl'occhi tuoi*
6	5	*Padoana Sesta, Deta [Mentre] Campai contento* (compare Vogel: Piccioli [1588], no. 1)
7	6	*Padoana Settima, Deta La Farfarella*
8	7	*Padoana Ottava, Deta Zo per la Brenta*
9	8	*Aria Prima*[3]
10	8	*Aria Seconda*
11	9	*Aria Terza*
12	9	*Aria Quarta*
13	10	*Aria Quinta*
14	10	*Aria Sesta*
15	11	*Moresca Prima, Deta le Canarie*[4]
16	12	*Moresca seconda, Deta le forze*
17	13	*Moresca Terza, Deta Il Mattacino*
18	14	*Moresca Quarta, Deta la Bergamasca*
19	17	*Moresca Quinta, Deta L'orsa*
20	18	*Baletto de Rusia deto L'orso*[5]
21	18	*Baletto d'Inghilterra deto il Bufon*
22	19	*Baletto Francese detto la volta*
23	19	*Baletto Francese detto la Corante*[6]
24	20	*Baletto Francese detto Alemande*
25	20	*Baletto detto del Capello Cinganesco*
26	21	*Baletto de Contadini Lombardi*
27	21	*Baletto Borgognese deto il bizaro*
28	22	*Baletto Todesco*
	22	*Gagliarda del baletto Todesco*
29	22	*Baletto Todesco ditto il Terzo*
	23	*Gagliarda del baletto Terzo*
30	24	*Baletto Polaco*
	24	*Gagliarda del Baletto Polaco*
31	25	*Baletto de Ruscia deto Duda*

MUSIC FOR TWO LUTES

32	26	*Passo e mezzo Antico in Tenore*[7]
	27	*Soprano del passo e mezo antico in Tenore*
	30	*Gagliarda del Passo e mezzo antico in Tenor*
	31	*Soprano de la gagliarda antica in Tenor*
33	34	*Passo e mezo Moderno in Tenore*[8]
	35	*Soprano del Passo e mezo Moderno in Tenore*
	38	*Galgiarda del Passo e mezzo moderno in Tenor*
	39	*Soprano de la galgiarda moderna in Tenor*

MUSIC FOR SOLO LUTE

34	42	*Saltarello 1. detto Io vo cogliendo*[9]
35	42	*Saltarello 2. detto Erbe oliose*
36	43	*Saltarello 3. detto Ravanello*
37	44	*Saltarello 4. detto O la val cerca* (compare 1564_7, no. 42: "Gaiarda de la Royne de Eschosse")
38	45	*Saltarello 5. detto Non mi toccare*
39	46	*Saltarello 6. detto Io voglio el Tisis*
40	47	*Saltarello detto Mai non lo trovo*
41	48	*Saltarello 8. detto O che deoni*

[1] The Washington copy was in the Landau–Finaly library in Florence (see HillM, pp. 14–16).

[2] Heading on p. 1: "Padoane per Ballare Secondo L'Uso di Venetia & d'altri lochi."

[3] Heading on p. 8: "Arie con le quale si puo cantare Stanze, e Versi d'ogni sorte, Secondo l'uso di Venetia, & anco de altri Paesi."

[4] Heading on p. 11: "Moresche usitate per Diversi Paesi."

[5] Heading on p. 18: "Baletti de Diverse Nationi Secondo il costume loro."

[6] Mod. ed. in MoeDM, p. 328.

[7] Heading on p. 26: "Pass'e mezzi, e Gagliarde per sonar in compagnia, Secondo l'uso Antico."

[8] Heading on p. 34: "Pass'e mezzi e Gagliarde per sonar in compagnia, Secondo l'uso Moderno."

[9] Heading on p. 42: "Nova Inventione et Modo di Saltarelli Italiani, Acomodati per Ballare A la Gagliarda secondo il Moderno costume."

[1585]$_2$

BARIOLLA, OTTAVIO

Ricercate per suonar l'organo. Milano, 1585.

This volume of music for organ, now lost, is cited in FétB I, 247, and in PiciA, p. 540.

1585_3

BASSANO, GIOVANNI

FANTASIE / A TRE VOCI, / PER CANTAR ET SONAR / con ogni sorte d'Istrumenti: / DI GIOVANNI BASSANO / Musico dell'Illustrissima Signoria di Venetia, / novamente composte & date in luce. / [Printer's mark] / IN VENETIA / Presso Giacomo Vincenzi, & Ricciardo Amadino, compagni. / M D LXXXV

Three part books in mensural notation, each of 12 fols. The title is placed within an ornamental border. Dedication on fol. 1ᵛ headed "AL MOLTO ILLUSTRE SIGNOR CONTE MARIO BEVILACQUA Signor mio Colendissimo," and signed "Di Venetia il dì primo d'Agosto 1585. Di V. S. Molto Illustre Affettionatissimo Servitore Giovanni Bassano," reprinted in SartMS, p. 53. The music begins on fol. 2 (= p. 1). On p. 21: printer's mark. The compositions identified by superior letters are reprinted as follows: ([a]) in HM XVI; ([b]) in HM LXIV. The basso title page is reprinted in facsimile in MGG I, col. 1398. All of the compositions are for instrumental ensemble *a3*.

Copy in: GB:Lbm (B).[1]

	p.	
1	1	[*Fantasia 1*][a]
2	2	[*Fantasia 2*][b]
3	3	[*Fantasia 3*]
4	4	[*Fantasia 4*][b]
5	5	[*Fantasia 5*]
6	6	[*Fantasia 6*][b]
7	7	[*Fantasia 7*][b]
8	8	[*Fantasia 8*][a 2]
9	9	[*Fantasia 9*]
10	10	[*Fantasia 10*][a]
11	11	[*Fantasia 11*]
12	12	[*Fantasia 12*][a]
13	13	[*Fantasia 13*][a]
14	14	[*Fantasia 14*]
15	15	[*Fantasia 15*][a]
16	16	[*Fantasia 16*]
17	17	[*Fantasia 17*]
18	18	[*Fantasia 18*][a]
19	19	[*Fantasia 19*]
20	20	[*Fantasia 20*]

[1] A copy was in D:Bds.
[2] Mod. ed. in KatzF, no. 6.

1585_4

BASSANO, GIOVANNI

RICERCATE / PASSAGGI ET / CADENTIE, / Per potersi essercitar nel diminuir terminatamente con ogni sorte / d'Istrumento: & anco diversi passaggi per / la semplice voce. / DI GIOVANNI BASSANO / Musico Dell'Illustrissima Signoria di Venetia, / novamente composte, et date in luce. / CON PRIVILEGGIO. / [Printer's mark] / IN VENETIA / Appresso Giacomo Vincenzi, & Ricciardo Amadino, compagni. / M D LXXXV.

12 fols. Mensural notation. The title is placed within an ornamental border. Dedication on fol. 2 headed "AL MOLTO MAGNIFICO ET ECCELLENTISSIMO MIO SIGNOR OSSERVANDISSIMO, IL SIGNOR LUIGI BALBI Orator eloquentissimo," and signed "Di Venetia il dì primo di Febraro. 1585. Di V. S. M. Magnifica, & Eccellentiss. Humilissimo servitore Giovanni Bassano," reprinted in GaspaC IV, 79, and SartMS, p. 52. On fol. 2ᵛ: preface headed "Ai Lettori Giovanni Bassano," reprinted in GaspaC IV, 79, and SartMS, p. 52. Fol. 3 = p. 1. For a discussion of this work see HorsS. Contents = 1598_1. Contains highly decorated monophonic ricercares, a series of formulas for ornamenting a given melodic line, and the superius of a madrigal supplied with *passaggi*.

Copy in: I:Bc.

	fol.	
1	2ᵛ	*Ricercata Prima*
2	p. 2	*Ricercata Seconda*
3	3	*Ricercata Terza*
4	4	*Ricercata quarta*
5	5	*Ricercata Quinta*
6	6	*Ricercata Sesta*
7	7	*Ricercata Settima*

8	8	*Ricercata Ottava*
9	9	*Passaggi diminuiti*
10	15	*Cadentie diminuite*[1]
11	19	*Signor mio caro*[2] Cipriano [da Rore] *a4*
	20	*Diverso modo*

[1] Some of the ornamented cadences are repr. in KuV, p. 130.
[2] Mod. ed. of the madrigal and of Bassano's diminutions in FerandIM, no. 14. Facs. of pp. 19 and 20 in MGG VI, col. 1101.

1585_5

CARRARA, MICHELE

[Intavolatura di liuto.]

This set of instructions for the lute is printed on one large folio. In the upper right corner: dedication "All'Ill.mo Sig.re Il S. Vincenzo Tuffavilla. Conte di Sarno," signed "Di Roma a 9. di sett.re 1585. Di V. S. Ill.ma Humiliss.mo Ser.re Michele Carrara." A cut of an eight-course lute is placed diagonally across the page with a Guidonian hand on the belly below the sound hole. Below, to the right of the lute, and on the belly above the sound hole are instructions for tuning and playing the lute, beginning "Regola ferma e vera." In the lower right corner is a comparative chart of Italian, Neapolitan, and French tablatures, and of transpositions, headed "Regola Universale." In the upper left corner are settings of Psalm CL: "Laudate eum" *a2*, *a3*, *a4*, *a5*, and *a6*, in score (in mensural notation), and in the various tablatures.[1] At the bottom of the page: "Ambrosius. Bramb.e [Brambilla]. 1585."[2] On the belly of the lute: "Cum Privilegio e cum licentia de Superiori." FétB II, 195, dates this work 1586. The page is reprinted in facsimile with the musical examples in modern notation in CarraI.[3] For a later edition see 1594_4.

Copy in: I:Fn.[4]

[1] BranR, pl. 4, repr. "Laudate eum" in Italian and French tablature, ostensibly from the 1594 ed.
[2] See $[1582]_2$ for a similar work by Brambilla, a set of instructions for playing the cittern.
[3] The page is repr. in facs. also in TBI, pl. 18.
[4] This copy was in the Landau-Finaly library in Florence.

1585_6

LASSO, ORLANDO DI

MOTETTI ET RICERCARI / DI ORLANDO LASSO / A DUE VOCI. / Novamente con ogni diligenza Ristampati. / LIBRO PRIMO. / [Printer's mark] / In Venetia Appresso Angelo Gardano / M. D. LXXXV.

Two part books in mensural notation, each of 12 fols. Contents = 1577_2. The volume contains 24 compositions *a2*, 12 with Latin text, and 12 without text, called "ricercars."

Copies in: F:Pn, GB:Lbm (imperfect S).

$[1585]_7$

LE ROY, ADRIAN

L'Instruction pour la mandorre.

This volume of mandora music, now lost, is mentioned in TrichT, p. 214. For mention of another mandora tablature published by the firm of Le Roy and Ballard, see $[1578]_2$.

1585

DOUBTFUL WORKS

1. BasseC and DraudiusBC, p. 1650, list a 1585 edition of Emanuel Adriansen, *Pratum Musicum*. The volume is listed in this bibliography as 1584_6.

2. SeiffG, p. 35, erroneously dates Andrea Gabrieli, *Ricercari . . . Composti & Tabulati per ogni sorte di Stromenti da Tasti . . . Libro Secondo*, 1585. The volume is listed in this bibliography as 1595_3.

3. FétB II, 223, lists the following volume by Giovanni Cavaccio: "Musica a 5 da sonare. Venezia. 1585." He probably refers to Vogel: Cavaccio 3 (1585), which contains no instrumental music. See 1597_2.

$[1586]_1$

AMAT, JUAN CARLOS

Guitarra Española, Y Vandola en dos maneras de Guitarra, Castellana, y Cathalana de cinco Ordenes, la qual enseña de templar, y tañer rasgado, todos los puntos naturales, y b, mollados, con estilo maravilloso. Y para poner en ella qualquier tono, se pone una tabla, con la qual podrà qualquier sin dificultad cifrar el tono, y despues tañer, y cantarle por doze modos. Y se haze mencion tambien de la Guitarra de quatro ordenes. Barcelona, 1586.

This instruction book for the Spanish guitar, now lost, is mentioned in a letter from Fray Leonardo de San Martin to Amat, printed in the 1639 edition of the work. On the contents of the later editions see MGG I, cols. 401–402; PedC I, 181–187; and PujA.

$[1586]_2$

FACOLI, MARCO

[Il Primo Libro d'Intavolatura d'arpicordo.]

Facoli's second book of keyboard music was printed in 1588 (= 1588_3). No copies of a first book have ever been found. At least one composition from this lost first book may appear in GB:Lcm, MS 2088 (22 fols. in keyboard score).[1] Fol. *1 of the manuscript is headed "Laus Deus M. D. LXXXVI. / Libro de Intavoladura di arpicordo. / F. A. P." The music begins on fol. *2 = fol. 1. The first composition (on fol. 1) is headed "Passmezo di nome anticho di marcho facoli veneto."

The remaining ten compositions in the manuscript, listed below, are superius and basso seguente parts from vocal music (nos. 4, 5, 7, and 8), dances (nos. 2, 3, and 9–11), and one canzona (no. 6). In one case (no. 9) the upper set of staves contains two superius parts, for the most part in parallel thirds. Presumably the manuscript was arranged for a keyboard player to accompany a vocal or instrumental ensemble. This abbreviated score might also have served the player as the basis for a semi-improvised solo performance of the dances, and perhaps of the other compositions as well.

	fol.	
2	10^v	*Pavana detta la Paganina*
3	12	*Balletto detto il Fantino*
4	13	*Vestiva i colli* (PalO IX, 117: Palestrina)
5	14	*S'hai tu*
6	15	*La Capriola* (1584_{10}, no. 1: Maschera)
7	16^v	*Ung gay bergier* (RieH II, 462: Crecquillon)
8	18	*Dilectus meus loquitur*
9	19^v	*Corrente vesta*
10	21	*Baleto favorita*
11	21^v	*Baletto detto il Marino*

[1] I am grateful to Alan Curtis of the University of California at Berkeley and to H. Colin Slim of the University of Chicago for having brought this manuscript to my attention. The manuscript is briefly described in HuskC, p. 257.

$[1586]_3$

FRANCESCO DA MILANO

Intabolatura de lauto. Antonio Gardane.

This volume of solo lute music, now lost, was in F:VE (see ChaillFM, p. 154).

$[1586]_4$

GABRIELI, ANDREA

Sonate a cinque per istromenti. In Venetia, appresso Ang. Gardano. 1586.

This volume of music for instrumental ensemble, now lost, is listed in BeckT, col. 287, and IMAMI I, lxxx.

1586_5

KARGEL, SIXT

Lautenbuch, / viler / Newerlessner / fleissiger, schöner Lau/tenstück von artlichen Fantaseien, künst/lichen Musicartlichen Lateinischen Muteten, mit / fünff und sechs stimmen allerhand lieblichen Teutschen, Fran/tzösischen und Italienischen Liedern, auch lustigen Passomezen in / die Teutsch Tabulatur, zu nutz und gefallen aller diser Kunst / lehrbegirigen, und besonders denen, so der Italieni/schen und Frantzösischen Tabulaturn uner/faren, auffs verständlichst und rich/tigst zusammen getragen und / geordnet, / Auff sechs und siben Chor/seiten gericht, / Durch / Sixtum Kargel, Fürstlichen Bischoff/lichen, Strassburgischen Lautenisten. / Getruckt zu Strassburg, bey Bernhart / Jobin, ANNO M. D. LXXXVI.

62 fols. German lute tablature. The title is placed within an ornamental border (the same border as in 1577_6). Dedication on fol. 2 headed "Dem Hochwürdigen Fürsten und Herrn, Herrn Johann Bischoffen zu Strassburg und Landgraffen im Elsass, u. meinem gnädigen Fürsten und Herrn.," and signed "Datum inn deren Statt Elsass Zabern, am Zinstag den zweiten Septembris, Anno 1586. E. H. F. G. underthäniger und gehorsamer Diener Sixtus Kargel Lautenist." On fol. 3: coat of arms headed "INSIGNIA REVERENDISSIMI ET ILLUSTRISSIMI PRINCIPIS AC DOMINI, DOMINI JOANNIS EPISCOPI Argentinensis & Landgravii Alsatiae &c." On fol. 3^v: the same poem in Latin as in 1577_6 (fol. *3^v), headed "In Honorem et Commendationem Musicae. Carmen," and signed "Sigis. Sultzpergerus, Argentorati p. Vigilia Epiphaniae anni clɔ. lɔ. lxxiiix." On fol. 4^v: cut of a lutenist headed "IMAGO SIXTI CARGELII MUSICI ET CITHAROEDI EXCELLENTIS IN Aula Episcopali Argentinensi," followed by a poem in Latin signed "N. Reusnerus." On fol. 61^v: table of contents. Colophon on fol. 62: "Ende dises Buchs. [Printer's mark] Getruckt zu Strassburg, bey Bernhard Jobin. Anno M. D. LXXXVI." All of the compositions are for solo lute.

Copies in: A:Wn, B:Br, D:DO, D:DT, PL:WRu, US:Wc.[1]

	fol.	
1	5	*Fantasia I*[2] = 1547_2, no. 1: Francesco da Milano
2	5^v	*Fantasia II*
3	6	*Fantasia III*
4	7^v	*Fantasia IIII*
5	8^v	*Fantasia V*
6	9^v	*Fantasia 6*[3] = 1571_6, no. 1
7	10	*In te Domine speravi* Orlando Lassus *a6* (LassoW XVII, 87)
	11^v	2a pars *Quoniam fortitudo*
8	13^v	*In te Domine speravi* Orlando Lassus *a6* (= no. 7 transposed)
	15	2a pars *Quoniam fortitudo*
9	17	*Gaudete Filiae Jerusalem* Meilandus *a6* (MeiC, no. 17)
10	18^v	*Omnia quae fecisti* Orlando di Lassus *a5* = 1566_3, no. 2
11	20^v	*De ore prudentis* Orlando Lassus *a5* (LassoW VII, 38)
12	21^v	*Angelus ad Pastores* Orlandus Lassus *a5* (LassoW III, 139)
13	22^v	*Surrexit Pastor bonus* Orlando Lassus *a5* = 1566_3, no. 4
14	24	*Surrexit Pastor bonus auff einen andern thon* (= no. 13 transposed)
15	25^v	*Deus Canticum novum* Orlando Lassus *a5* = 1566_3, no. 1a
	26^v	2a pars *Quia delectasti* = 1566_3, no. 1b
16	27	*Exultent et Letentur* Meilandus (MeiC, no. 4)
	27^v	2a pars *Ego vero egenus*
17	28^v	*Benedicam Dominum* Orlando Lassus *a5* = 1566_3, no. 5a
	29^v	2a pars *In Domino Laudabitur* = 1566_3, no. 5b
18	30^v	*Benedicam Dominum auss einem andern thon* (= no. 17 transposed)
	32	2a pars *In Domino laudabitur*
19	33	*Expurgate* Crequilon *a5*
20	34^v	*Gustate et Videta* Orlando Lassus *a5* = 1566_3, no. 6a
	36	2a pars *Divites Eguerunt* = 1566_3, no. 6b
21	37^v	*Fili Honora Dominum* Melchior Schram *a5*
22	38^v	*Ille Dies Redit* Bernhart Klingaensteyn *a4*
23	39	*Confitemini Domino* Orlando Lassus *a5* (LassoW VII, 131)
	40	2a pars *Narrate* [*omnia mirabilia*]
24	41	*Surge Propera* Jacobo Gallo *a4*
	41	2a pars *Surge propera amica mea*
25	41^v	*Amour partes* *a4* (compare 1571_6, no. 68)

26	42^v	*Les Yeux qui me sceurent* Harcadelt (RISM 1554_{20}, no. 16)
27	43	*Qui veult du ciel* Harcadelt *a4* (RISM 1569_{13}, no. 5)
28	43^v	*De qui plus tost* Sandrin *a4* (RISM 1549_{20}, no. 29)
29	44	*Qui souhaites* Gentian *a4* (RISM 1549_{20}, no. 1: Sandrin)
30	44^v	*Ce faux amour* Orlando di Lassus *a4* (LassoW XII, 103)
31	45	*A Dieu de Lion* *a5*
32	46	*Esperant davoir* *a5*
33	47	*Mon cocur se recommande a Vous* Orland. Lass. *a5* (LassoW XIV, 15)
34	48	*Susan ung Jour* Lupi *a4* (LevyS, p. 403: Didier Lupi Second)
35	48^v	*Queste non son piu Lagrime* Orlando Lassus *a4* (LassoW VIII, 15)
36	49	*Io Cantarei d'amor* Cipriano de Rore *a4* (SCMA VI, 31)
37	50	*Per pianto* Orlandus [Lasso] *a4* = 1571_6, no. 103
38	50^v	*Con lei fussio* *a4* (RISM 1543_{17}, p. 36: Arcadelt, Berchem, Corteccia, or Ponte)
39	51	*Se ben l'empia mia sorte* Orlandus [Lasso] *a4* = 1571_6, no. 102
40	51^v	*Si fe Cristalo* Orlandus [Lasso] *a4* = 1571_6, no. 96
41	52	*Se tu pensasti* *a4*
42	52^v	*Sio Fusse* *a4*
43	52^v	*Ich ruff zu dir, hilff mir O trewer Gott* *a4*
44	53^v	*Gott ist mein Schutz*
45	53^v	*HERR Jesu Christ* *a4*
46	54	*Mein hoffnung stehet zu dir allein* *a4*
47	54^v	*Ach HERRE Gott* *a4*
48	55	*Gelobt sey Gott in Himmelsthron* *a4*
49	55^v	*Pass'mezo detto il moderno* = 1569_2, no. 21a
	57	*Saltarello* = 1569_2, no. 21b: "Gagliarda"
50	58	*Passo è mezo*
	59	*Saltarello*
51	60	*Passo e mezo ficto* = 1569_2, no. 17

[1] A copy was in D:Bds.
[2] Mod. ed. in ScherG, no. 138.
[3] Mod. ed. in BruAL I, no. 8, and EnI, app., p. 12.

$[1586]_6$

LASSO, ORLANDO DI

Motetti et ricercari a due voci di Orlando Lasso, novamente ristampati. Libro primo. Venezia, Giacomo Vincenzi & Ricciardo Amadino Compagni, 1586.

This volume, now lost, is listed in BoettL, p. 792. Contents = 1577_2. It contained 24 compositions *a2*, 12 with Latin text, and 12 without text called "ricercares." †

1586_7

LICINO, AGOSTINO

DI AGOSTINO LICINO / CREMONESE / IL PRIMO LIBRO / DI DUO CROMATICI, / DA CANTARE, ET SONARE. / Composti una parte sopra l'altra con la sua resolutione da parte. / Novamente ristampati. / [Printer's mark] / IN VINEGIA Appresso l'Herede di Girolamo Scotto. / M D LXXXVI.

Two part books in mensural notation, each of 20 fols. (?) The music begins on p. 2. Contents = $1545_?$. All of the compositions are canons *a2* without text.
Copy in: I:Bc (S).

1586_8

VEROVIO, SIMONE

DILETTO / SPIRITUALE / CANZONETTE / A tre et a quattro voci / composte da diver/si ecc.^mi Musici. / Raccolte da Simon Verovio / Intagliate / et stampate dal medesimo. / Con L'intavolatura del Cimbalo / Et Liuto / Roma / 1586. / Martin van Buyten incidit.[1]

24 fols. Mensural notation, keyboard score, and Italian lute tablature. The title

page is placed within an ornamental border; at the top is "Te Deum laudamus." On fol. 2: the same dedication as in 1592_{11} (except that this is dated November 10, 1586), reprinted in CasSV, p. 193, and SartMS, p. 54. On fol. 23^v: table of contents. Contents = 1592_{11}, except that no. 15 is missing here.[2] See also $[1590]_9$. The vocal setting of each piece appears on the left page of each opening, keyboard and lute intabulations on the right page. The same canons as in 1592_{11} appear at the bottoms of the right-hand pages.

† Copies in: B:Br, D:Bds, D:LEm,[3] D:Mbs, GB:Lbm, I:Bc, I:Pca, I:Rc.

[1] Facs. of title page in AbbS I, 380; GrandT, p. 19; and PalW XXX, after p. xix.

[2] Verovio published another edition of this same collection in 1586, but without the tablatures for lute and harpsichord. Sartori mistakenly prints the title page after the all-vocal edition. See Vogel Einstein 1586_{10a} and 1586_{11} for the correct title pages.

[3] This copy was in the Wolffheim library (see WolffC I, no. 1212).

1586_9

VINCI, PIETRO

DI PIETRO VINCI / SICILIANO / IL PRIMO LIBRO DELLA MUSICA / a Due Voce, / Novamente ristampato. / [Printer's mark] / IN VINEGIA Appresso l'Herede di Girolamo Scotto. / M D LXXXVI.

Two part books in mensural notation, each of 16 fols. On fol. 16^v of each part book: table of contents. Contents = 1560_4. All of the compositions are for instrumental ensemble *a2*.

Copy in: A:Wn.

1586

DOUBTFUL WORKS

1. FétB II, 195, dates Michele Carrara, [*Intavolatura di liuto*], 1586. This set of instructions for the lute is listed in this bibliography as 1585_5.

1587_1

ABONDANTE, JULIO

IL QUINTO LIBRO / DE TABOLATURA DA LIUTO / DE M. GIULIO ABUNDANTE, / DETTO DAL PESTRINO / Nella qual si contiene Fantasie diverse, Pass'e mezi & Padoane. / Novamente Composte & date in luce. / [Printer's mark] / In Venetia Appresso Angelo Gardano. / M. D. LXXXVII.

32 fols. Italian lute tablature. Dedication on fol. A1^v headed "AL MOLTO MAGNIFICO SIGNOR MIO OSSERVANDISS. IL SIGNOR SCIPION ZILIOLO." Fol. A2 = p. 1. On p. 62: table of contents. MoeDM contains a thematic index of the dances (p. 465) and concordances for them (p. 281). All of the compositions are for solo lute.

Copies in: A:Wn, I:Bc.

	p.	
1	1	*Fantasia Prima* Giulio dal Pestrino
2	2	*Fantasia Seconda del ditto*
3	3	*Fantasia Terza del ditto*
4	4	*Fantasia Quarta del ditto*
5	5	*Fantasia Quinta del ditto*
6	6	*Fantasia Sesta del ditto*
7	7	*Fantasia Settima del detto*
8	9	*Fantasia Ottava del detto*
9	10	[*F*]*antasia Nona del detto*
10	12	*Fantasia Decima del detto*
11	13	*Fantasia Undecima del detto*
12	14	*Fantasia Duodecima del detto*
13	16	*Fantasia decimaterza del detto*
14	17	*Pass'e mezo Moderno in diversi modi* Giulio dal Pestrino [11 *partes*]
	27	*Gagliardo del ditto Moderno* [four *partes*]
	29	*La su Ripresa*
15	30	*Pass'e mezo Antico. in diversi modi* Giulio dal Pestrino [12 *partes*]
	40	*Gagliardo del ditto* [four *partes*]
	42	*La sua Ripresa*
16	43	*Padoana dita la Ziliola* Giulio dal Pestrino
17	44	*Padoana dita la Ferara*[1]
18	46	*Padoana dita la Fondi*
19	46	*Padoana dita la Picona*

20 48 *Padoana dita la Vincenti*
21 48 *Padoana dita la Vica*
22 50 *Padoana dita la Badoera*
23 51 *Padoana dita la Mazzona*
24 52 *Padoana dita la Floriana*
25 53 *Pass'e mezo de la Bataglia* Giulio dal Pestrino [four *partes*]
56 *La sua Ripresa*
26 57 *Padoana dita la Graciosa*
27 58 *Bergamasca*
28 60 *Padoana dita la Costante*
29 61 *Pad[oana] ditta la Fulvia*

[1] Mod. ed. in LowT, p. 67.

[1587]$_2$

BARGAGLIA, SCIPION

Trattenimenti ossia divertimenti da suonare. Venezia, 1587.

This volume of instrumental music, now lost, is mentioned in FétB I, 246. Fétis says that the word "concerto" is used for the first time in this work to mean a composition with a solo instrument. See also EitQ I, 342.

1587$_3$

GABRIELI, ANDREA AND GIOVANNI

CONCERTI / DI ANDREA, / ET DI GIO: GABRIELI / ORGANISTI / DELLA SERENISS. SIG. DI VENETIA. / Continenti Musica DI CHIESA, Madrigali, / & altro, per voci, & stromenti Musi/cali; à 6. 7. 8. 10. 12. & 16. / Novamente con ogni diligentia dati in luce. / LIBRO PRIMO ET SECONDO. / CON PRIVILEGIO. / [Coat of arms of the Fugger family] / IN VENETIA. / Appresso Angelo Gardano. 1587.[1]

Twelve part books in mensural notation (SAB56, each of 40 fols; T, 39 fols.; 7, 31 fols.; 8, 24 fols.; 9 and 10, 10 fols.; 11, 5 fols.; 12, 6 fols.). Dedication on fol. A1^v of the first six part books headed "ALL'ILLUSTRISS. SIGNOR IL SIG. GIACOMO FUCCARI, SENIORI, BARON DE CHIRCHBERG, ET WEISSENHORN, &c. Mio Signore, & Padrone Colendissimo," and signed "Di V. S. Illustriss. Humiliss. Servitore Gioanni Gabrieli," reprinted in SartMS, p. 56. On fol. 40^v of the first five part books: table of contents. Vogel: Gabrieli 1 (1587) and SartMS, p. 55, give a complete list of the contents. Contains compositions with Latin and Italian text, and one piece for instrumental ensemble *a8*.[2]

Copies in: A:Wn, D:As (S wanting), D:F, D:Mbs (SATB56), D:Rp (four imperfect copies), GB:Lbm (5), I:Bc, I:Bsp, I:BRd, I:FEc (9–12 wanting), I:MOd (AB69,11,12), I:Sd, I:TVcap I:Vnm (12 wanting), and US:Cn (T).

fol.
1 I4^v (= p. 70) *Ricercar per sonar a8* Andrea Gabrieli[3]

[1] Facs. of title page in CollaerAH, p. 59; KinsP, p. 106; KommaM, p. 108; MGG IV, col. 1186; and SubHM I, 398. Facs. of canto title page, dedication, fol. I4^v, and table of contents in IMAMI I, after p. 24.

[2] Giovanni Gabrieli's "Lieto godea" on fol. K1 (repr. in IMAMI I, no. 4) is marked "Per cantar & sonar."

[3] Mod. ed. in IMAMI I, no. 3.

1587$_4$

LUPACCHINO, BERNARDINO, AND JOAN MARIA TASSO

DI BERNARDINO LUPACCHINO / ET DI GIOAN MARIA TASSO / IL PRIMO LIBRO A DUE VOCI / Novamente ristampato. / [Printer's mark] / IN VENETIA, MDLXXXVII. / Appresso Ricciardo Amadino.

Two part books in mensural notation, each of 20 fols. Contents = 1559$_6$. All of the compositions are *a2* and without text or title.

Copies in: I: Bc (T), I:Fn.

[1587]$_5$

NEWSIDLER, MELCHIOR

Six motets *a6* by Josquin des Prez intabulated for the lute. Venice, 1587.

This volume, now lost if it ever existed, is mentioned in FétB VI, 307.

[1587]6

PACOLINI, GIOVANNI

Tabulatura tribus testudinibus. Milano, Francesco Tini ed eredi di Simon Tini, 1587.

This volume of music for three lutes, now lost, is mentioned in FétB VI, 401. Fétis says that a second edition appeared in 1591 (see $[1591]_{10}$). Some of the music was arranged for solo cittern according to the title page of 1564_7. See also DonaSM, p. 79.

[1587]7

PAIX, JAKOB

SELECTAE, ARTIFICIOSAE ET ELEGANTES FUGAE DUARUM, TRIUM, QUATUOR, ET PLURIUM VOCUM, pattim ex veteribus & recentibus Musicis summa diligentia & accurato judicio collectae, partim Compositae à JACOBO PAIX, Organico Palatino Lauingano.

This volume of canons in mensural notation, now lost, is listed in BasseC and FétB VI, 427. For later editions see 1590_6 and 1594_{10}.

1587

DOUBTFUL WORKS

1. MorL I, xliii, lists the following volume of lute music by various composers: "Fantasie, Padovane, etc. Liber III. Venezia, Angelo Gardano, 1587," as being in A:Wn. The volume is otherwise unknown.

2. DraudiusBC, p. 1651, lists the following volume of keyboard music by Jakob Paix: "Jacobi Paix Tabulatura organi fistularum, Lauing. 87. fol." He refers either to 1583_4 or to an otherwise unknown second edition of 1583_4.

15881

BASSANO, GIOVANNI

IL FIORE DE / CAPRICI MUSICALI / A QUATRO VOCI / Per sonar con ogni sorte di stromenti. / DI GIOVANNI BASSANO / MUSICO DELLA SERENISSIMA / Signoria Di Venetia. / Novamente Composti, & dati in luce. / CON PRIVILEGIO. / [Printer's mark] / In Venetia, Presso Giacomo Vincenzi. / M D LXXXVIII.

Four part books in mensural notation, each of 21 fols. (?). The title is placed within an ornamental border. Dedication on fol. 1^v headed "AL ILLUSTRE ET MOLTO REVERENDO SIGNOR MIO OSSERVANDISSIMO IL SIGNOR GIROLAMO BONARELLI AUDITOR DELL'ILLUSTRISSIMO Arcivescovo di Capua. NUNTIO DI NOSTRO SIGNORE Appresso l'Illustrissimo Dominio Veneto," and signed "Di Venetia il dì 16. Novemb. 1587. Di Vostra Signoria. Affettionatissimo Servitor Giovanne Bassano," reprinted in SartMS, p. 58. Contains 20 compositions for instrumental ensemble *a 4*, without text or title, one on each folio, beginning with fol. 2.

Copy in: I:Bc (T).

15882

BYRD, WILLIAM

Psalmes, Sonets, & songs of sadnes and / pietie, made into Musicke of five parts: whereof, / some of them going abroade among divers, in untrue coppies, / are heere truely corrected, and th'other being Songs / very rare and newly composed, are heere published, for the recreation / of all such as delight in Musicke: By William Byrd, / one of the Gent. of the Queenes Maiesties / honorable Chappell. / [Cut of the coat of arms of Sir Christopher Hatton] / Printed by Thomas East, the assigne of W. Byrd, / and are to be sold at the dwelling house of the said T. East, by Paules wharfe. / 1588. / Cum privilegio Regiae Maiestatis.

Five part books in mensural notation, each of 24 fols. On fol. 1^v: "Reasons briefely set downne by th'auctor, to perswade every one to learne to sing." Dedication on fol. 2 headed "To The Right Honorable Sir Christopher Hatton knight, Lord Chancellor of England, William Byrd wisheth long lyfe, and the same to be most healthie and happie." On fol. 2ᵛ: "The Epistle to the Reader," followed by a list headed "The names and number of those songs which are of the highest compasse," followed by a list of errata. On fol. 24ᵛ: table of contents. Even though the 35 compositions in the collection are all fully texted Byrd explains in his epistle to the reader that some of them, "being originally made for Instruments to expresse the harmonie, and one voyce to pronounce the dittie, are now framed in all parts for voyces to sing the same." Only those compositions are listed in the inventory below that were originally conceived for solo voice with four instruments (probably viols); Byrd indicates these by labeling the voice part "The first singing part." ByrdW XII is a modern edition of the entire collection, and includes facsimiles of the title page and all of the prefatory matter. EMS XIV is a modern edition of the entire collection and reprints all of the prefatory matter. A facsimile of the title page appears in FelWB, pl. 8; the "Reasons . . . to perswade" are reprinted in FelWB, p. 155. For further information about the volume see AndrewsP. For a later edition see $159?_2$.

Copies in: GB:Ctc (SAT5), GB:Cu (imperfect SB), GB:Ge, GB:Lbm, GB:Lu, GB:Ll, GB:Mp (S5), GB:Ob,[1] GB:Y (imperfect).

PSALMS

	fol.	
2	4	*Mine eyes with fervencie*
3	5	*My Soule opprest with care*
4	6	*How shall a young man?*
5	7	*O Lord, how long wilt thou forget*
6	8	*O Lord, who in thy sacred tent*
7	9	*Help, Lord, for wasted are those men*
8	10	*Blessed is he that feares the Lord*
9	10ᵛ	*Lord, in thy wrath*
10	10ᵛ	*Even from the depth*

12*

SONNETS AND PASTORALS

11	11	*I joy not in no earthly blisse*
12	11ᵛ	*Though Amarillis daunce in greene*
13	12	*Who lykes to love*
14	12ᵛ	*My minde to me a kingdome is*
15	13	*Where fancy fond*
16	13ᵛ	*O you that heare this voice*
19	15	*What pleasure have great princes?*
22	16ᵛ	*In fields abrode*
23	17	*Constant Penelope*
25	18	*Farewell, false love*

SONGS OF SADNESS AND PIETY

27	19	*Prostrate, O Lord, I lie*
28	19ᵛ	*All as a sea*
29	20	*Susanna faire*
30	20ᵛ	*If that a sinner sighes*
31	21	*Care for thy soule*
32	21ᵛ	*Lullaby, my sweet little baby*
33	22ᵛ	*Why do I use my paper, inck and pen?*

[1] The authorities of the Bodleian Library inform me that the library owns a composite set of the 1588 and 1589 [*sic*] editions. I am grateful to Mrs. Geoffrey Wilson of Cambridge, England, for checking my description of this volume against the Cambridge copies.

1588_3

FACOLI, MARCO

IL SECONDO LIBRO / D'INTAVOLATURA, DI BALLI / D'ARPICORDO, PASS'E MEZZI / Saltarelli, Padouane, & alcuni Aeri / Novi dilettevoli, da Cantar, / ogni sorte de Rima, / DI MARCO FACOLI VENETIANO. / Novamente posto in luce. / [Printer's mark] / In Venetia Appresso Angelo Gardano. / M. D. LXXXVIII.

34 fols. Keyboard score. The title is placed within an ornamental border. On fol. 34ᵛ: table of contents. The entire collection is reprinted in a modern edition in CEK II. For a discussion of the contents of this volume see ApelTA. For the first volume in this series see 1586_2. All of the compositions are for solo keyboard.

Copy in: I:Rsc.

	fol.	
1	1v	*Pass'e mezo Moderno*
	10	*Saltarello del Pass'e mezo Ditto*
2	14	*Padoana Prima dita Marucina*
3	16	*Padoana Seconda Dita la Chiareta*
4	18	*Padoana Terza Dita la Finetta*
5	20	*Padoana quarta dita Marchetta. a doi modi*
6	24	*Aria della Signora Livia* [1]
7	24v	*Aria della Comedia*
8	25v	*Aria della Signora Cinthia*
9	26	*Aria della Signora Lucilla*
10	26v	*Aria della Marcheta Saporita* [2]
11	27	*Aria della Signora Moretta*
12	27v	*Aria della Signora Ortensia*
13	28v	*Aria della Marcheta Schiavonetta*
14	29	*Aria della Comedia Novo*
15	30	*Hor ch'io son gionto quivi*
16	30v	*Aria della Signora Michiela*
17	31	*Aria della Signora Fior d'Amor*
18	31v	*Aria da Cantar Terza Rima* [3]
19	32	*S'io m'accorgo ben mio* [4] Napolitana
20	32v	*Deh Pastorella cara* [4] Napolitana
21	33	*Tedesca dita La Proficia* (compare 1583_2, no. 135: "Proficiat Ir lieben Herren")
22	34	*Tedesca dita L'Austria* (compare 1583_7, no. 30a: "Almande Poussinghe")

[1] Mod. ed. in ApelTA, p. 58.
[2] Mod. ed. in ApelTA, p. 57.
[3] Mod. ed. in ApelTA, p. 59.
[4] Complete text is given beneath the upper stave.

1588_5

MANCINUS, THOMAS

Das Erste Buch / Newer Lustiger, und / Höfflicher Weltlicher Lieder, mit vier / und fünff Stimmen, / THOMAE MANCINI Megapolitani, / Fürstlichen Braunschweigischen / Cappelmeisters. / CANTUS. / Helmstadt, Gedruckt durch Jacobum Lucium. 1588.

Five part books in mensural notation (SATB, each of 28 fols.; 5, 12 fols.). The title is placed within an ornamental border. On fol. A1v: cut of the coat of arms of the dedicatees. Dedication on fol. A2 headed "Den Durchleuchtigen, Hochgebornen Fursten, und Herren, Hern Wolffgangen, und Hern Philippo, Hertzogen zu Braunschweig, und Leuneburgk," and signed "Thomas Mancinus." On fol. G4: table of contents. On fol. G4v of the tenor part book: portrait of the composer with the caption: "THOMAS. MANCINUS. AETATIS. SUAE. 35. ANNO. 1585." The collection contains 31 vocal compositions *a4* and *a5* with Italian, Latin and German texts, and one composition for instrumental ensemble *a4*.

Copies in: D:G (SAT5), D:Mbs, PL:WRu (STB).[1]

	fol.	
1	G2v	*Fantasia duarum & quatuor vocum*

[1] A copy (AT only) was in D:Bds.

1588_4

GUAMI, FRANCESCO

RICERCARI A DUE VOCI / DI FRANCESCO GUAMI LUCCHESE / NOVAMENTE POSTI IN LUCE. / [Printer's mark] / In Venetia Appresso Angelo Gardano / M. D. LXXXVIII.

Two part books in mensural notation, each of 12 fols. Contains 23 compositions for instrumental ensemble *a2* without text or title, one on each page beginning with fol. 1v.

Copy in: A:Wn.

1588_6

MASCHERA, FIORENZO

LIBRO PRIMO / DE CANZONI / DA SONARE, / A QUATRO VOCI, / DI FLORENTIO MASCHERA / Organista nel Duomo di Brescia. / Novamente con diligentia ristampate. / [Printer's mark] / IN VENETIA, M D LXXXVIII. / Appresso Ricciardo Amadino.[1]

Four part books in mensural notation, each of 12 fols. The title is placed within an ornamental border. On fol. 1v: same dedication as in 1584_{10}. On p. 22 (= fol. 12v): table of contents. Contents = 1584_{10}. See there for other editions. All of the compositions are for instrumental ensemble *a4*.

Copy in: GB:Lbm.

[1] Facs. of title page in MGG VIII, col. 1750.

1588_7

PADOVANO, ANNIBALE

DI ANNIBALE PADOVANO / ORGANISTA DELLA SERENISS. SIG. DI VENETIA. / IL PRIMO LIBRO DE RICERCARI / A QUATTRO VOCI, / Novamente Ristampato. / [Printer's mark] / In Venezia, Appresso Angelo Gardano. / M. D. LXXXVIII.

Four part books in mensural notation, each of 14 fols. (?). Contents = 1556_9. All of the compositions are for instrumental ensemble *a4*.

Copy in: I:Bc (AT).

1588_8

VINCENTI, GIACOMO, PUBLISHER

CANZON / DI DIVERSI / PER SONAR / CON OGNI SORTE DI STROMENTI / A Quatro Cinque, & Sei Voci. / Novamente Stampate. / LIBRO PRIMO. / CON PRIVILEGIO. / [Printer's mark] / In Venetia, Presso Giacomo Vincenzi. / M D LXXXVIII.

Six part books in mensural notation (SATB, 8 fols.; 5, 6 fols.; 6, 3 fols.). The title is placed within an ornamental border. Dedication on fol. 1v headed "AL MOLTO MAGNIFICO SIGNOR PIETRO ANTONIO DIEDO Signor, & Patron mio osservandissimo," and signed "Di Venetia li 20. Decembre 1587. Di V. S. Molto Magnifica. Servitore affettionatissimo Iacomo Vincenci," reprinted in SartMS, p. 59. Fol. 2 = p. 1. On p. 14: table of contents. All of the compositions are for instrumental ensemble *a4*, *a5*, or *a6*.

Copy in: CH:Bu.

	p.	
1	1	*L'olica* Claudio [Merulo] da Coreggio *a4*
2	2	*Torna*[1] Crequilon *a4*
3	2	Giosefo Guami *a4* (1599_{11}, no. 12: "Fantasia in modo di Canzon Francese")
4	4	Giosefo Guami *a4* (1599_{11}, no. 11: "Fantasia in modo di Canzon Francesa")
5	5	*Las voules* *a5*
6	6	*On ques Amor* *a5* (RISM $[1544]_{11}$, fol. 16: Crecquillon)
7	7	*Viver ne puis* *a5*
8	8	*Io visans* *a5* (RISM 1545_{14}, fol. 2: "Jouissance vous donneray," Willaert)
9	9	*Content* *a5* [Crecquillon]
10	10	*Sine tenez* *a6* (compare RISM 1545_{14}, fol. 14: "Si me tenez," Crecquillon)
11	11	*Sire* *a6*
12	12	*A la fontaine* *a6* (ClemensO VII, 43: Willaert)
13	13	*La rose* *a6* [Gombert] (compare BrownM, p. 198, art. 49: "La rousée du moys de may")

[1] No. 2 has the heading "Claudio da Correggio A4," in the body of the text. The title listed here is taken from the table of contents.

1589_1

ARBEAU, THOINOT

ORCHESOGRAPHIE. / ET TRAICTE EN FORME DE DIALOGUE, / PAR LEQUEL TOUTES PERSONNES PEUVENT / facilement apprendre & practiquer l'honneste / exercice des dances. / Par Thoinot arbeau demeurant a Lengres. / Eccle. 3 / Tempus plangendi, & tempus saltandi. / [Printer's mark with legend: "TELLE EST LA GLOIRE DES HOMMES"] / Imprimé audict Lengres par Jehan des preyz Imprimeur / & Libraire, tenant sa boutique proche l'Eglise / Sainct Mammes dudict Lengres. / M. D. LXXXIX

104 fols. Mensural notation. Dedication on fol. 1v headed "A maistre Guillaume Tabourot, filz de noble homme & sage

Title page of 1588_8

maistre Estienne Tabourot, Conseillier du Roy nostre sire & son Procureur au Bailliage de Dijon, sieur des Accordz," and signed "Vostre humble serviteur Jehan des preyz." On fol. 104ᵛ: excerpt from the printing privilege dated "donné à Bloys le 22. Novembre 1588." The pseudonym Thoinot Arbeau is an anagram for the author's real name, Jehan Tabourot. This treatise on dancing, in the form of a dialogue, gives detailed information on the choreography and music for a large number of sixteenth-century dances. All of the complete musical examples, listed below, are notated as single voices (unless otherwise marked) in mensural notation. ArbOF is a modern edition of the complete treatise. ArbOB and ArbOE are English translations. CzerT is a partial German translation. There are facsimiles of fols. 33ᵛ, 34, 40ᵛ, and 41 in MGG I, pl. xxiii, and facsimiles of other pages in EF I, 290; KinsP, p. 116; and ScheurCM I, opp. pp. 368 and 376. Some of the monophonic dance tunes are reprinted in BöhT II. For further information see BarkT and MaryO, both of which include some facsimile pages. For later editions see 1596_1 and 1597_1.

Copies in: CH:Lcortot, F:Pc,[1] F:Pn, GB:Lbm (two copies, one of which is imperfect),[1] NL:DHgm,[2] US:SM.[3]

	fol.	
1	18v	*Tabulature du Fifre, ou Arigot du troisiesme ton*
2	20v	*Tabulature pour jouer du Fifre ou Arigot en mesure ternaire*
3	30	*Pavane à quatre parties: avec les mesures & battemens du tambour* [*Belle qui tiens ma vie: a 4*][4]
4	33v	*Basse-dance appellee: Jouyssance vous donneray: avec les mesures & battemens du tabourin*[5] (compare AttainCK III, no. 24: Sermisy)
5	49v	[*Air du tourdion*]
6	52v	*Air de la gaillarde appelle, La traditore my fa morire*
7	52v	*Air de la gaillarde appellee Anthoinette*
8	54	*Air de la gaillarde appellee Baisons nous belle. &c.*
9	55v	*Air de la gaillarde appelle Si j'ayme ou non, &c.* (compare LesLRB, art. 171, fol. 3: Le Roy)
10	57v	*Air de la gaillarde appellee La fatigue*
11	59	*Air de la gaillarde appellee la Milannoise*
12	60	*Air de la gaillarde appellee J'aymerois mieulx dormir seulette, &c.* (compare 1564_5, no. 18)
13	61	*Air de la gaillarde appellee L'ennuy qui me tourmente, &c.*
14	65	*Air d'une volte*
15	66v	*Air de la Courante*
16	67v	*Air de l'Allemande*
17	69v	*Air d'un branle double*
18	71	*Air d'un branle simple*
19	72	*Air du branle gay*
20	72v	*Air du branle de Bourgoigne*
21	73v	*Air d'un branle hault Barrois*
22	74v	*Air du branle couppé nommé Cassandre*
23	75	*Air du branle Pinagay*
24	76	*Air du branle couppé appellé Charlotte*
25	77	*Air du branle couppé de la guerre*
26	78	*Air du branle couppé appellé Aridan*
27	79	*Air du branle de Poictou*
28	80	*Air du premier branle d'Escosse*
29	80v	*Air du second branle d'Escosse*
30	81v	[*Le Triory de Bretaigne*]
31	82v	*Air du branle de Malte*
32	83v	[*Branle des Lavandieres*]
33	84v	[*Branle des Pois*]
34	85v	[*Branle des Hermites*]
35	86v	[*Branle de la torche*]
36	87v	[*Branle des Sabots*]
37	88v	[*Branle des Chevaulx*]
38	89v	[*Branle de la Montarde*]
39	90v	*Tabulature de la dance de la haye*
40	92	[*Branle de l'Official*]
41	93v	*Air de la Gavotte*[6]
42	94v	*Air de Morisques*
43	96	*Air des Canaries*
44	96v	*Air & mouvements de la pavane d'Espagne*
45	99	*Air des Bouffons*

[1] These two copies do not carry the date 1589 on the title page.

[2] This copy once belonged to D. F. Scheurleer (see ScheurCM I, 383).

[3] A copy was in the library of J. E. Matthew (see MLE, 1904, p. 105).

[4] Mod. ed. in ApelMK, p. 45 (where it is compared with 1570_3, no. 124); ARC 16, no. 1; BohT II, no. 131; and DolDE, p. 88.

[5] Mod. ed. in BlumeS, app. B, no. 11.

[6] Mod. ed. in CzerG, p. 96.

1589_2

BYRD, WILLIAM

Songs of sundrie natures, some of / gravitie, and others of myrth, fit for all compa/nies and voyces. Lately made and composed in/to Musicke of 3. 4. 5. and 6. parts: and pub/lished for the delight of all such as take plea/sure in the exercise of / that Art. / By William Byrd, one of the Gentlemen / of the Queenes Maiesties honorable / Chappell. / Imprinted at London by Thomas / East, the assigne of William Byrd, and are to be / sold at the house of the sayd T. East, being in / Aldergate streete, at the signe of the / blacke Horse. 1589. / Cum privilegio Regiae Maiestatis.[1]

Six part books in mensural notation, each of 30 fols. Dedication on fol. 2 headed "To the right honorable my very good Lord, Sir Henry Carye, Baron of Hunsdon, knight of the most noble order of the Garter, Lord Chamberlen to the Queenes most excelent Maiestie, Lord Warden of the East Marches towards Scotland, governor of Barwycke and the Castle of Norham, Captaine of the Gentlemen Pencioners, Justice in Oyer, over all her Maiesties Forrests and Chases, on this side the River of Trent, & one of her Maiesties most honorable privie councell, William Byrd wisheth increase of honor, with all true felicitie." On fol. 2^v: preface headed "To the curteous Reader." On fol. 30^v: table of contents. Each of the four compositions listed in the inventory below contains untexted sections for instrumental ensemble with solo voices (for similar compositions see 1588_2). The remainder of the 47 compositions in the collection are fully texted. ByrdW XIII is a modern edition of the entire collection, and includes facsimiles of the title page and all of the prefatory matter. EMS XV is a modern edition of the entire collection and reprints all of the prefatory matter.

Copies in: GB:Ctc (S and imperfect AT56), GB:Cu (S), GB:Ge, GB:Lam, GB:Lbm, GB:Lcm, GB:Lk, GB:Lu, GB:Ob,[2] GB:Och, GB:T, US:SM.[3]

	fol.	
35	23^v	*From Virgins wombe this day did spring*[4]
40	26	*An earthly tree*[5]
41	26^v	*Who made thee Hob?*[6]
46	29^v	*Christ rising agayne*[7]
47	30	2a pars *Christ is risen againe*

[1] Facs. of title page in EF I, 469, and MGG II, col. 576.

[2] The copy in the Bodleian Library is another issue of the same year.

[3] A copy was in the library of Alfred Littleton (see LittC, p. 31). I am grateful to Mrs. Geoffrey Wilson of Cambridge, England, for checking my description of this volume against the Cambridge copies.

[4] No. 35 is scored for solo voice and four instruments (probably viols); it has as chorus no. 24: "Rejoice, rejoice," for four voices, all fully texted.

[5] No. 40 is scored for two solo voices and four instruments (probably viols); it has as chorus no. 25: "Cast off all doubtful care," for four voices, all fully texted.

[6] No. 41 is scored for two solo voices and four instruments (probably viols).

[7] Nos. 46 and 47 are scored for two solo voices and four instruments (probably viols), and include also sections for five and six voices, all fully texted. Mod. ed. in HAM, no. 151.

1589_3

GABRIELI, ANDREA

MADRIGALI / ET RICERCARI / Di Andrea Gabrieli / A Quattro voci, / Novamente Stampati & dati in luce. / CON PRIVILEGIO. / [Printer's mark] / IN VENETIA, / Apresso Angelo Gardano. / 1589.[1]

Four part books in mensural notation, each of 16 fols. The title is placed within an ornamental border. On fol. 16^v (= p. 32) of each part book: table of contents. Contents = 1590_1. Vogel: Gabrieli 14 (1589) gives a list of the vocal pieces; SartMS, p. 63, gives a complete list of the contents. All of the instrumental pieces are reprinted in IMAMI I, nos. 5–11. Contains compositions with Italian text, and seven pieces for instrumental ensemble *a 4*.

Copies in: CH:Bu, D:W (SAT),[2] †
GB:Lbm (B), GB:Lk (imperfect), I:Bc (AB).[3]

	p.	
1	22	*Ricercar del Primo Tuono*
2	24	*Ricercar del Secondo Tuono*
3	26	*Ricercar del Secondo Tuono*[4]
4	27	*Ricercar del Settimo Tuono*
5	28	*Ricercar del Sesto Tuono*[5]
6	30	*Ricercar del Nono Tuono*
7	31	*Ricercar del Duodecimo Tuono*[6]

[1] Facs. of canto title page in MGG IV, col. 1187. Facs. of alto title page and of p. 31 in IMAMI I, following p. 44.

[2] The bass part book in D:W is dated 1590 (= 1590_1).

[3] A copy of the canto part book was in D:Bds.

[4] Mod. ed. in Gabri(A)R, no. 2.

[5] Mod. ed. in Gabri(A)R, no. 1, and in Gabri(A)RST.

[6] Mod. ed. in ARS 13; FuserC, no. 9; Gabri(A)R, no. 3; Gabri(A)RDT; and HAM, no. 136.

1589_4

LASSO, ORLANDO DI

MOTETTI ET RICERCARI / D'ORLANDO LASSO A DUE VOCI, / LIBRO PRIMO. / Novamente Ristampati, & corretti. / [Printer's mark] / IN VENETIA, Appresso Giacomo Vincenti. / M D LXXXIX.

Two part books in mensural notation, each of 12 fols. Contents = 1577_2. The volume contains 24 compositions *a2*, 12 with Latin text, and 12 without text called "ricercares."

Copy in: I:Bc.

1589_5

LINDNER, FRIDERICH

LIBER SECUNDUS / GEMMAE MU/SICALIS: / SELECTISSIMAS VARII STILI / CANTIONES, QUAE MADRIGALI ET NAPO/litane Italis dicuntur, Quatuor, Quinque, Sex & / plurium vocum, continens. / Quarum omnium versa pagina accuratissimum Indicem (qui & Musicorum, è quorum monumentis sumtae sunt, / nomina prodet) exhibebit. Editae studio & ópera FRIDERICI LINDNERI, S. P. Q. NO/RIBERGENSI à cantionibus. / CANTO. / NORIBERGAE, / EX TYPOGRAPHIA MUSICA CATHA/RINAE GERLACHIAE. / M. D. LXXXIX.

Six part books in mensural notation (SAT, each of 60 fols.; B5, each of 56 fols.; 6, 44, fols.). Dedication on fols. a2–a3 of each part book headed "MAGNIFICO VIRO, NOBILITATE GENERIS, OMNISBUSQUE VIRTUTUM ORNAMEN TIS ET multiplici rerum usu & experientia praedito, Domino CAROLO ALBERTINELLO Florentino, Domino & fautori suo suspiciendo, S. P. D.," and signed "Noribergae Calendis Februarii, Anno à Christo nato 1589. Tuam Magnificent: observans & colens, Fridericus Lindenerus," reprinted in SartMS, p. 61. On fols. a3ᵛ–a4 of each part book: table of contents. SartMS, p. 60, gives a complete list of the contents. The volume contains compositions with Italian text, and one piece for instrumental ensemble *a4*.

Copies in: A:Gu (AB), A:Wn (SAT5), D:As (two copies), D:Dl, D:FLs (S), D:FR (SA5), D:Hs, D:Kl (three copies in various states), D:Mbs (one complete copy, and a second copy of T), D:Rp, D:Z, GB:Lbm (S), PL:GD, PL:Wn (SA5), S:Uu.[1]

	fol.	
1	p4	*LXXII. Fantasia Capriccio. 2. Toni a4*

[1] Copies were in D:Bds (ATB5), D:DS, and PL:L.

1589_6

PAIX, JAKOB

THESAURUS / MOTETARUM. / Newerlessner / zwey und zweintzig herz/licher Moteten, Rechte Kunst Stück: der / aller berhümbsten Componisten, in der Ordnung / wie sie nach einander gelebt: Und jede / Moteten zu ihrem gewissen / Modo gesetzt. / Mit sonderm hohen fleiss und müh / zusamen getragen, und in diese / breuchige Tabulatur / gebracht, / Von / JACOBO PAIX AUGUSTANO, / ORGANICO LAUINGANO. / Getruckt zu Strassburg, bei Bern/hart Jobin. / Anno M. D. LXXXIX.

59 fols. German keyboard tablature. The title is placed within an ornamental border (the same border as in 1577_6). On fol. 1ᵛ: portrait of Paix in an ornamental frame; around the frame: "Jacobus Paix Augustanus. Organicus et Symphonetes. Ann. Aeta. Suae XXXIII. Christi CI CIↃ XIC"; at the top: "Estrae 4. Cap. 2. Ego Testor Palam Salvatorem Meum"; at the bottom: "Felix Qui Potuit Rerum Cognoscere Causas."[1] Dedication on fol. 2 headed "NOBILISSIMO AC OMNIBUS VIRTUTIBUS ORNATISSIMO VIRO D. WILHELMO A ROTENHAN, DOMINO RENTWEINSDORFII ET VISCHBACHII, PATRONO suo colendiss: Jacobus Paix Organicus Lauinganus. S. P. D.," and dated "Lauingae VI. Id Jun. Anno M. D. LXXXIX." On fol. 2ᵛ: table of contents, followed by the same cut as in

1577_6, fol. *3ᵛ, including musicians, followed by comments on editorial technique entitled "Observatio." Almost every composition is followed by a brief notice on the mode in which it is written. On fol. 59ᵛ: a statement about the modes headed "De Omnibus Modis Musicis Scribit Joh. Pontifen. Cap. 12. Et 16. Item Franchinus. Lib. 5. Cap. VII.," followed by a quotation ("Qui Modos Musicos ignorat: pro Musico non reputatur") signed "Holandrinus Ait," followed by a poem in Latin headed "Epigramma Michaelis Fendii Monh. Profess. Lauing.," followed by the date "Anno M. D. LXXXVIIII." Attributions to composers are taken from the table of contents. All of the compositions are for solo keyboard.

Copies in: D:Mbs, D:S, F:MD.

	fol.	
1	3	*Benedicta es Coelorum Regina* [Hypomyxolydi] Josquin à prato & Joh. Castileti (JosqMT, no. 46, and RISM 1568_4, p. 339)
	7ᵛ	2a pars *Per illud ave*
	8	3a pars *Nunc mater exocanatum*
2	9	*Nesciens mater* [Hypoionici] Joh. Mouton (RISM 1540_7, no. 17)
3	11ᵛ	*Si bona suscepimus* [Phrygii] Phil. Verdeloth *a 5* (MoralesO I, 274)
4	13ᵛ	*Oculi omnium* [Hypolydii] Nic. Gombert *a 5* (RISM 1554_2, fol. 12)
	14ᵛ	2a pars *Qui edunt a 6*
5	16	*Je prens en gre* [Hypolydii] Eustach. Barbion *a 6*
	17ᵛ	2a pars *Morir mi fault*
6	18ᵛ	*Virgo prudentissima* [Dorii] Hen. Isaac *a 6* (AmbG V, 314)
	21ᵛ	2a pars *Nos Michael*
7	24ᵛ	*O sacrum Convivium* [Lydii] Lud. Senfl *a 5*
8	26ᵛ	*Fratres Cito* [Hypolydii] Cyprianus de Rore *a 5*
9	28ᵛ	*Fremuit spiritus* [Hypolydii] Clem. non Papa *a 6* (RISM 1554_2, fol. 15)
	30	2a pars *Videns Jesus*
10	31ᵛ	*Celle qui matant* [Hypoaeolii] Christ. Hollander *a 6* (RISM 1553_{25}, fol. 26)
11	33	*Domine da Nobis Auxilium* [Dorii] Thom. Crequilon *a 6* (RISM 1554_{11}, no. 18)
	34ᵛ	2a pars *Tibi Subsecta sit*
12	36	*Egressus Jesus* [Dorii] Jach. de Wert *a 7* (RISM 1568_6, p. 456)
13	39	*Ecce quam bonum* [Hypolydii] Lud. Daser *a 12*
14	41ᵛ	*O altitudo divitiarum* [Aeolii] Orland. Lassus *a 6* (LassoW XI, 133)
	42ᵛ	2a pars *Quis enim*
15	44	*Deus deus meus* [Dorii] Phil. de Monte *a 6* (RISM 1583_2, no. 23)
16	45	*Nos autem gloriari oportet* [Dorii] Wil. Formelius *a 6* (RISM 1568_4, p. 267)
17	47	*Beati omnes* a voce pari [Hypodorii] Ivo de Vento *a 4* (VentoM, no. 6)
	47ᵛ	2a pars *Ecce sic benedicetur homo*
18	48ᵛ	*O sacrum convivium* [Hypolydii] Joh. Petraloysius *a 5* (PalW II, 23)
19	50	*Salve summe Pater* [Dorii] V. R. *a 5*
20	53	*Mortalium preces* [Hypoaeolii] Alex. Utentaler *a 6* (RISM 1568_3, p. 201)
	54ᵛ	2a pars *Qui non meretur*
21	55ᵛ	*Memor esto* [Hypodorii] Leon. Lechner *a 6* (LechM, no. 25)
22	56ᵛ	*O quam gloriosum* [Hypolydii] Theod. Riccius *a 5* (RiccS I, no. 15)
23	57ᵛ	Τριάδος *in Choralem, Ave maris Stella, ad Dorium sub* Διαπίντι, Jacobus Paix [headed "Chor"]
24	58ᵛ	*Ecce quam bonum* [Mixolydii] Jacob: Paix *a 5*

[1] Facs. of fol. 1ᵛ in MGG X, col. 648.

1589_7

STIVORI, FRANCESCO

RICERCARI / A QUATRO VOCI, / DI M. FRANCESCO STIVORI / ORGANISTA DELLA MAGNIFICA / Com-

CANTRO

RICERCARI
A QVATRO VOCI,
DI M. FRANCESCO. STIVORI
ORGANISTA DELLA MAGNIFICA
Communità di Montagnana.

Nouamente posti in luce.

A L'ECCELLENTE M. CLAUDIO MERULO
DA CORREGGIO.

IN VENETIA, M D LXXXIX.

Appresso Ricciardo Amadino.

Title page of 1589_7

munità di Montagnana. / Novamente posti in luce. / A L'ECCELLENTE M. CLAUDIO MERULO / DA CORREGGIO, / [Printer's mark] / IN VENETIA, M D LXXXIX. / Appresso Ricciardo Amadino.

Four part books in mensural notation, each of 12 fols. (?). Dedication on fol. *1^{v} headed "AL MOLTO MAGNIFICO SIGNORE, PATRONE, PRECETTORE, & Protettor mio singularissimo. IL SIGNOR CLAUDIO MERULO, Organista del Serenissimo Duca di Parma, & di Piacenza," and signed "Di Montagnana il dì 15 di Giugno 1589. Di V. S. M. Magnifica, Scolare, et Servitore perpetuamente ubligato. Francesco Stivori," reprinted in SartMS, p. 62. The music begins on fol. *2 = p. 1.[1] All of the compositions are for instrumental ensemble *a 4*.

Copy in: I:Bc (SA).

	p.	
1	1	*Recercar Primo*
2	2	*Recercar Secondo*
3	3	*Recercar Terzo*
4	4	*Recercar Quarto*
5	5	*Recercar Quinto*
6	6	*Recercar Sesto*
7	7	*Recercar Settimo*
8	8	*Recercar Ottavo*
9	9	*Recercar Nono*
10	10	*Recercar Decimo*
11	11	*Recercar Undecimo*
12	12	*Recercar Duodecimo*
13	13	*Recercar Terzodecimo*
14	14	*Recercar Quartodecimo*
15	15	*Recercar Quintodecimo*
16	16	*Recercar Sestodecimo*
17	16	*Recercar Decimosettimo*
18	18	*Recercar Decimoottavo*
19	19	*Recercar Decimonono*
20	20	*Recercar Vigesimo*
21	22	*Recercar Vigesimoprimo*

[1] Three volumes of music by Stivori are known: I (1589_7), II ($[1594]_{12}$), and III (1599_{10}).

1589_8

VEROVIO, SIMONE

GHIRLANDA / DI FIORETTI / MUSICALI / [Cut of Orpheus playing to animals] / Composta da diversi Ecc[tl] Musici a 3. voci / Con Lintavolatura del Cimbalo, et / LIUTO / Raccolte et stampate da Simone Verovio[1] / [Cut of a lute and virginals] / In Roma 1589. Con licentia de superiori.

27 fols. Mensural notation, keyboard score, and Italian lute tablature. Dedication on fol. 2 headed "All'Ill[e] s[e] p[ad]ron mio oss[mo] il s[e] Capuan Vincenzo Stella," and signed "Di Roma a di 10. d'Agosto 1589. D. V. S[ia] & Ill[e], oblig[mo] serv[e], Simone Verovio," reprinted in CasSV, p. 195, and GaspaC III, 43. Fol. 2[v] = p. 1. The vocal setting of each piece appears on the left page of each opening, keyboard and lute intabulations on the right page. The contents of this volume were reprinted in three volumes in 1591 ($1591_{14, 15, \text{ and } 16}$). See there for details.

Copies in: B:Br, D:Bds, D:Mbs, F:Pc, GB:Lbm (imperfect), I:Bc, I:Pca, I:Rsc.[2]

	p.	
1	1	*Ahi che quest'occhi miei*[3] Gio. Palestina
2	3	*Da cosi dotta man*[4] Gio. Palestina
3	5	*Ameni colli, vaghi monticelli* Francesco Soriano
4	7	*Mentre l'aguila sta mirando* Gio. Battista Zucchelli
5	9	*Donna, donna tue chiome d'oro* Annibal Stabile
6	11	*Ardenti, miei sospiri*[5] Jacomo Peetrino
7	13	*Vermiglio e vago fiore* Ruggiero Giovanelli
8	15	*Io me n'avedo Amore* Archangelo Crivello
9	17	*Poiche mesto e dolente* Jacomo Peetrino
10	19	*Tutta gentile e bella* Gio. Mario Nanino
11	21	*Ohime partito è'l mio bel sol*[6] Annibal Stabile
12	23	*Fugge da gl'occhi il sonno* Ruggiero Giovanelli
13	25	*Ohime crudele Amore*[7] Gio. Battista Zucchelli
14	27	*Si vaga è la mia fiamma* Ruggiero Giovanelli
15	29	*Al suon non posa il core*[8] Felice Anerio
16	31	*Io ardo o Filli* Jacomo Ricordi
17	33	*Ingiustissimo Amore* Antonio Orlandino
18	35	*Ancora che tu m'odii* Paolo Quagliato
19	37	*Fiamme che da begl'occhi*[9] Felice Anerio
20	39	*Se fredda è la mia donna* Gasparo Costa
21	41	*Vedo ogni selva*[10] Francesco Soriano
22	43	*Donna gentil voi siete* Gio. Battista Locatello
23	45	*Donna se'l cor legasti* Felice Anerio
24	47	*Donna se nel tuo volto* Luca Marentio
25	49	*Mentre il mio miser core* Felice Anerio

[1] This line of the title page, present in the incomplete copy in the British Museum, is missing from the Bologna copy. There must have been at least two printings of the volume during the same year. Facs. of title page in AbbS I, 336, and GrandT, p. 11.

[2] A copy was in PL:L.
[3] Mod. ed. in DehnC, supp. I, and PalW XVIII, 135.
[4] Mod. ed. in PalW XVIII, 136.
[5] Mod. ed. in DehnC, supp. III.
[6] Mod. ed. in WeckC, p. 338.
[7] Mod. ed. in DehnC, supp. II.
[8] Mod. ed. in HAM, no. 160.
[9] Mod. ed. in TebAP, p. 124.
[10] Facs. of pp. 41 and 42 in WolfMS, pls. 69 and 70.

[158?]1

ABONDANTE, JULIO

Intavolatura di Liuto del Pestrin lib. 7. Venezia, Giacomo Vincenti.

This volume of solo lute music, now lost, is listed in VincenI, fol. 6 (see ThibaultD). According to 1587₁, "Pestrin" is the sobriquet of Julio Abondante.

158?2

BATHE, WILLIAM

A BRIEFE INTRO/duction to the skill of / SONG: / Concerning the practise, set forth / by William Bathe / Gentleman. / In which work is set downe X. sundry wayes of 2. parts / in one upon the plaine song. Also a Table newly ad/ded of the comparisons of Cleves, how one followeth / another for the naming of Notes: with other neces/sarie examples, to further the learner. / FABIUS. / Musica est honestum et iucundum oblectamen/tum, liberalibus ingeniis maxime dignum. / LONDON / Printed by Thomas Este.[1]

24 fols. plus one table. Mensural notation. Beginning on fol. A2: preface headed "To the Reader." Beginning on fol. A4: "The ante rules of Song." Beginning on fol. A4ᵛ: "Rules of Song." Beginning on fol. B4ᵛ: "The post rules of Song." On fol. C5: a poem in Latin headed "De Inventione." On fol. C5ᵛ: a composition *a4* by "G. K." headed "O Lord in thee is all my trust." Beginning on fol. C6ᵛ: ten canons *a2* over a cantus firmus headed "10. sundry waies of 2. parts in one upon the plain song."[2] After fol. C8: "A Table of the comparisons of Cliffe, how one followeth another for the naming of Notes: changing (Ut) into (Sol) and (Re) into (La)." HawkH II (1875 ed.), 497, discusses the volume in some detail; he says that it was first published in 1584. DeakinMB, pp. 6 and 8, lists a 1584 edition as well as a 1596 edition. No copies of either are known.

Copies in: GB:Lbm (two copies, of which one is imperfect), US:CA.[3]

[1] Facs. of title page in MLE, 1904, p. 39.
[2] Facs. of nos. 7 and 8 in SteeleE, fig. 31.
[3] Copies were in GB:Lsc and the T. W. Taphouse library (see MLE, 1904, p. 39).

[158?]3

GIULIANI, [GIROLAMO]

Intavolatura de Chitara del Giuliani. Venezia, Giacomo Vincenti.

This volume of music for the guitar, now lost, is listed in VincenI, fol. 6 (see ThibaultD). The composer may be Girolamo Giuliani (see EitQ IV, 271).

[158?]4

LUZZASCHI, LUZZASCHO

Ricercari di Luzzascho Luzzaschi a 4. Venezia, Angelo Gardano.

This volume of music for instrumental ensemble *a4*, now lost, is listed in GardI, fol. 5 (see ThibaultD).

[158?]5

VINCENTI, GIACOMO, PUBLISHER

Musica spartita per Sonar. Venezia, Giacomo Vincenti.

This volume of instrumental music in score, now lost, is listed in VincenI, fol. 5ᵛ (see ThibaultD).

1590_1

GABRIELI, ANDREA

MADRIGALI / ET RICERCARI / di Andrea Gabrieli / A Quattro voci, / Novamente Stampati & dati in luce. / CON PRIVILEGIO. / [Printer's mark] / IN VENETIA, / Apresso Angelo Gardano. / 1590.

Four part books in mensural notation, each of 16 fols. The title is placed within an ornamental border. On fol. 16^v of the bass part book: table of contents. Contents = 1589_3. Contains compositions with Italian text, and seven pieces for instrumental ensemble *a4*.

Copy in: D:W (B).

1590_2

GABRIELI, ANDREA, AND ANNIBALE PADOVANO

DIALOGHI MUSICALI / DE DIVERSI ECCELLEN/TISSIMI AUTORI, / A Sette, Otto, Nove, Dieci, Undeci & Dodeci voci, / Novamente posti in luce. / CON DUE BATTAGLIE A OTTO VOCI, / Per sonar de Istrumenti da Fiato, di Annibale Podoana / & di Andrea Gabrieli, già Organisti della / Serenissima Signoria di Venetia / in San Marco. / CON PRIVILEGIO. / [Printer's mark] / In Venetia Appresso Angelo Gardano / M. D. LXXXX.

Twelve part books in mensural notation (SATB567, 36 fols.; 8, 24 fols.; 9, 9 fols.; 10, 8 fols.; 11, 5 fols.; 12, 4 fols.). On fol. 36^v (= p. 72): table of contents. For later editions, see 1592_3 and $[1594]_6$. Vogel 1590_1 gives a complete list of the contents. The volume contains compositions with Italian text,[1] and two pieces for instrumental ensemble *a8*, both of which are reprinted in IMAMI I, nos. 12 and 15.

Copies in: B:Br, I:VEaf (9).

	p.	
1	49	*Aria della Battaglia per sonar d'Istrumenti da fiato a8* Annibale Padoano
	50	2a pars
2	52	*Aria della Battaglia per sonar d'Istrumenti da fiato a8* Andrea Gabrieli
	53	2a pars

[1] Giovanni Gabrieli's "Chiar'Angioletta" on p. 48 (repr. in IMAMI I, no. 14) is marked "Aria per sonar." This is the same as 1597_{12}, fol. $I1^v$.

$[1590]_3$

LASSO, ORLANDO DI

Novae aliquot et ante hac non ita usitate ad duas voces Cantiones suavissimae omnibus musicis summe utiles: nec non tyronibus quàm ejus artis peritioribus summopere inservientes authore Orlando di Lasso . . . München, Adam Berg, 1590.

This volume, now lost, is listed in BoettL, p. 799. A copy was in D:EL. Contents = 1577_2. The volume contained 24 compositions *a2* in mensural notation; 12 had Latin text and 12 were without text or title.

1590_4

LUPACCHINO, BERNARDINO, AND JOAN MARIA TASSO

DI BERNARDINO / LUPACHINO, / ET DI GIO. MARIA / TASSO, / Il Primo Libro à due voci, / Nuovamente ristampato. / [Printer's mark] / IN MILANO, / Appresso Francesco, & gl'heredi di Simon Tini. / M. D. LXXXX.

Two part books in mensural notation, each of 20 fols. The title is placed within an ornamental border. Contents = 1559_6. All of the compositions are *a2* and without text or title.

Copy in: I:Fr (T).

1590_5

MASCHERA, FIORENZO

Canzoni di Florentio / Maschera à 4 voci / novamente ristampate / per i professori / d'Organo / LIBRO [Cut of St. Cecilia] PRIMO. / In Venetia, àpresso Giacomo Vincenti. / M D LXXXX

26 fols. Keyboard partitura. Dedication on p. *2 headed "Osservandissimo il Padre Cipriano da Venetia dell Ordine delli Cremitani di S. Agostino: dignissimo Organista nella Chiesa di S. Stefano di Venetia," and signed "Giacomo Vincenti." The music begins on p. *5 (= p. 1). Contents = 1584_{10}. This manuscript was either prepared for a printer, or else copied from a now lost edition. An edition of Maschera canzonas by Vincenti is listed in an index of that publisher's output; see ThibaultD. All of the compositions are for solo keyboard.

Copy in: US:Wc (manuscript).

1590_6

PAIX, JAKOB

SELECTAE, AR/TIFICIOSAE ET ELEGAN/TES FUGAE DUARUM, TRI/UM, QUATUOR, ET PLURIUM VOCUM, / partim ex veteribus & recentibus Musicis summa diligen/tia & accurato judicio collectae, partim Compositae / à JACOBO PAIX, Organico / Palatino Lauingano. / Auctae, & denuò in lucem aeditae. / M. D. [Printer's mark] XC. / LAUINGAE / Imprimebat Leonardus Reinmichaelius.

20 fols. Mensural notation. The title is placed within an ornamental border. On fol. 1^v: cut of Jacob Paix; around the frame: "JACOBUS PAIX AUGUSTANUS. ORGANICUS ET SYMPHONETES. ANN. AETA. SUAE XXXIII. [Christi] CI CIↃ XIC"; underneath: "Non artifex artem, sed ars artificem decorat." [1] Dedication on fol. 2 headed "NOBILI ET MAGNIFICO VIRO, D. JOHANNI WEITMOSEro, Domino in Wienbiz, Ramseiden & Grueb &c. Domino suo observando, S. P.," and signed "Vale Lauingae Calend. Sextilibus, Anno M. D. XC. Dignitatis tuae observantissimus Jacobus Paix Organicen Palatinus." On fol. 2^v: table headed "Scala Systematis Mollis, Duri & Anomali." On fol. 19^v: table headed "Tabula Signorum Resolutoria." On fol. 20: a note on proportions headed "De Proportionibus Musicis." For other editions see $[1587]_7$ and 1594_{10}. The volume contains canons. For most of the canons only one voice is written out, without text. In the following inventory texted canons are followed by an asterisk, and the number of written-out voices is included in parentheses when it exceeds one. The examples reprinted by Paix from Glareanus, *Dodecachordon* (1547), and cited in the inventory after GlarDE, are also reprinted in PubAPTM XVI.

Copy in: D:DS.

	fol.	
1	3	*Fuga in epidiapente* D. Jodoci Pratensis vulgo Jusquin de pres (GlarDE, ex. 30: "Pleni" from *Missa Hercules Dux Ferrariae* [JosqMS, no. 7])
2	3	*Trio in homophonia** (the text begins "Non tam profunda") J[akob] P[aix]
3	3^v	*Fuga in subdiapente* Petri Platensis (GlarDE, ex. 31: "Pleni" from *Missa O Salutaris* Pierre de la Rue)
4	3^v	*Fuga in diapente gravi* Georgii Maieri (GlarDE, ex. 57)
5	4	*Fuga in homophonia* Antonii Brumelii (GlarDE, ex. 79)
6	4^v	*Fuga in unisono* [2] Jacobi Hobrechti (GlarDE, ex. 37)
7	5	*Fuga in Hexatono acuto*
8	5	*Fuga in ditono supernè*
9	5^v	*Fuga in diapente gravi*
10	5^v	*Fuga contraria in septima acuta*
11	5^v	*Alia in unisono*
12	6	*Alia in sesquitonio acuto*
13	6	*Triados ex unica* [3] D. Jodoci Pratensis (GlarDE, ex. 101: "Agnus dei" from *Missa L'homme armé*, Josquin)
14	6^v	*Omne trinum perfectum* Senflius (GlarDE, ex. 102)
15	6^v	*Fuga trium vocum in epidiatessaron post perfectum tempus* Okenhemii (GlarDE, ex. 112)
	7	*Resolutio* Iac. Paix
16	7^v	*Fuga in homophonia, trium vocum* Gilis Paix
17	7^v	*Alia Quatuor vocum, in unisono*

18 8 *4. vocum fuga ex unica* Petri Plat. (GlarDE, ex. 103: La Rue)
19 8 *Fuga quatuor vocum in homoph.** Jac. Paix (the text begins "Levavi oculos meos")
20 8ᵛ *Cantus, Altitonans & Basis in fuga 4. vocum, singuli post singula*
21 8ᵛ *Fuga 4. voc. in unisono** Jac. Paix (the text begins "Vive pius")
22 9 *Fuga quinis vocibus in homophonia* D. Lud. Daseri
23 9 *Fuga Quinque vocum in unisono* D. Orland. de Lasso
24 9 *Fuga in unisono senis vocibus* Jac. Paix
25 9ᵛ *Alia in unisono octonis vocibus** Jac. Paix (the text begins "Mich plagt ungluck")
26 9ᵛ *Fuga novem vocum** Jac. Paix (the text, from Psal. XLVII, begins "Psallite Deo nostro")
27 10 *Monas, in diapente infernè*
28 10ᵛ *Trio in Choralem Ave maris stella** Jacobo Paix Org. (the text begins "Ave mundi stella"; three parts written out)
29 11ᵛ *Trio* Jac. Paix ("Canon in sesquitonio acuto"; two parts written out)
30 12 *Monas, in qua Altitonans supra tenorem post sesqui tempus in diapente incedit*
31 12ᵛ *Fuga, in ditono infima chorda*
32 13 *Fuga contraria 4. vocum. Basis ex cantu sub nona. Tenor ex alto in sesquitonio infernè* (two parts written out)
33 13 *Fuga in unisono*
34 13ᵛ *Fuga trium vocum, superius in epidiapente, Basis sub diatessaron incipit* Jodoci Pratensis (GlarDE, ex. 15: "Agnus dei" from *Missa Hercules Dux Ferrariae* [JosqMS, no. 7])
35 14 [*Trio*] (three parts written out)
36 14ᵛ *Dyas in diapente gravi* (three parts written out)
37 15 *Dyas* (two parts written out)
38 15ᵛ *Quatuor sub tribus, in sesquitonio acuto** (the text, from Psalm XXXI, begins "In dich hab ich gehoffet Herr"; four parts written out)
39 16ᵛ *Welt hin, Welt her** Jac. Paix Org. (four parts written out)
40 17ᵛ *Vatter unser** Jac. Paix (four parts written out)
41 18ᵛ *Agimus tibi gratias** ("ad aequalis") Jac. Paix (four parts written out)

[1] Facs. of portrait in ReissmA, p. 210.
[2] Mod. ed. in ObrWW, no. 17.
[3] Facs. from Glareanus in ApelN, p. 181; mod. ed. in HAM, no. 89.

1590₇

SCALETTA, ORAZIO

AMOROSI PENSIERI / IL SECONDO LIBRO / De Madrigaletti A Cinque voci. / DI HORATIO SCALETTA DA CREMA / Maestro di Capella nel Domo di Lodi. / CON UNA CANZONE FRANCESE / A quattro, & uno Dialogo à Sette nel fine. / Novamente Composti, & dati in Luce. / [Printer's mark] / IN VENETIA / Appresso l'herede di Girolamo Scotto, 1590.

Four part books in mensural notation, each of 12 fols. (?). Dedication on fol. 1ᵛ (= p. 2) headed "AL ILLUSTRE MIO SIGNOR ET PATRON CORDIALISSIMO IL SIGNOR BERNARDINO SCOTTO Dottore del Colegio di Millano," and signed "di Lodi il di ultimo d'Aprile. MDXC. Di V. S. Illustre Divotissimo Servitore Horatio Scaletta," reprinted in SartMS, p. 64. On p. 24: table of contents. SartMS, p. 64, gives a complete list of the contents. The volume contains compositions with Italian text and one piece for instrumental ensemble *a 4*.

Copies in: GB:Lbm (imperfect), GB:Lk (B).

p.
1 21 *La Quiricia Canzon Francese*[1] *a 4*

[1] "Al Magnifico Signor Quiricio Rizzi."

1590₈

VECCHI, ORAZIO

SELVA / DI VARIA RICREA/TIONE / DI HORATIO VECCHI, / Nella quale si contengono Varii Soggetti, / A 3. à 4. à 5. à 6. à 7. à 8 à 9 & à 10 voci, / Cioè Madrigali, Capricci, Balli, Arie, Justiniane, Canzo/nette, Fantasie, Serenate, Dialoghi, un Lotto amo/roso, Con una Battaglia à Diece nel fine, / & accommodatevi la Intavolatura di / Liuto alle Arie, ai Balli, & / alle Canzonette. / Novamente Composta, e data in luce. / CON PRIVILEGIO. / [Printer's mark] / In Venetia Appresso Angelo Gardano. / M. D. LXXXX.[1]

Ten part books (S, 30 fols.; AT, each of 24 fols.; B, 28 fols.; 5, 20 fols.; 67, each of 14 fols.; 8, 8 fols.; 9, 5 fols.; 10, 6 fols.) in mensural notation and Italian lute tablature. The title is placed within an ornamental border. Dedication on fol. 1ᵛ headed "ALL'ILLUSTRISSIMI SIGNORI GLI SIGNORI GIACOMO SENIORI ET GIOVANNI FUCCARI, Baroni de Chirchberg, & Weissenhorn, &c. Signori miei, & Padroni Osservandiss.," and signed "Di Venetia il dì 26. Ottobre 1590. Delle SS. W. Illustrissime Servitore Devotiss. Horatio Vecchi," reprinted in SartMS, p. 65. On fol. 30ᵛ: table of contents. Contents = 1595_9. An edition of 1611 is listed in RISM (1611_{18}). SartMS, p. 65, and Vogel: Vecchi 4 (1590) give a complete list of the contents. The volume contains compositions with Italian text (one with French text), and 13 pieces using instruments. Eleven of the 13 are printed as part songs (with texts), and with lute accompaniment. Nos. 3 and 13 are for instrumental ensemble (no. 3 includes a lute part as well). All of the pieces listed below except no. 13 are reprinted in ChilB V, which includes a facsimile of the title page.

† Copies in: B:Br, D:Kl, F:Pc (A), I:Bc, I:Bsp, I:Fn, I:Rsc (SAB56).[2]

	fol.	
1	7ᵛ	*Gitene Ninfe. Pass'e mezo* *a5* [Per sonare e cantare insieme]
2	8ᵛ	*Gioite tutti in suoni. Saltarello detto il Vecchi* *a5*
3	9ᵛ	*Saltarello detto Trivella*[3]
4	10	*Mostrav'in ciel. Tedesca* *a5*
5	10ᵛ	*Segliè vero. Aria*[4] *a3*
6	11	*Amor opra che piu. Aria*[4] *a3*
7	11ᵛ	*Io sper'e tem' & ard'. Aria*[4] *a3*
8	12	*Non vuò pregare. Aria*[4] *a3*
9	14ᵛ	*Damon e Filli insieme. Canzonetta*[5] *a4*
10	15	*Che fai Dori. Canzonetta*[5] *a4*
11	15ᵛ	*Deh prega Amor. Canzonetta*[5] *a4*
12	16	*So ben mi c'hà bon tempo. Aria*[5] *a4*
13	16ᵛ	*Fantasia*[6] *a4*

[1] Facs. of title page in EF III, 844.
[2] Copies were in D:Bds, and in the Landau-Finaly library in Florence (see RoedigC I, 572).
[3] The altus part book reads: "Per Sonare con gli Stromenti da corde. A 5."
[4] The lute part is pr. in SB and 7 part books.
[5] The lute part is pr. in SAT and B part books. Mod. ed. of no. 12 in EC, pt. I, vol. II, p. 663.
[6] Mod. ed. in RieM, no. 55, and WasG, no. 26.

$[1590]_9$

VEROVIO, SIMONE

DILETTO SPIRITUALE CANZONETTE A tre et a quattro voci composte da diversi ecc.ᵐⁱ Musici. Raccolto da Simon Verovio Intagliato et stampate dal medesimo. Con L'intavolatura del Cimbalo Et Liuto Roma. 1590

24 fols. Mensural notation, keyboard score, and Italian lute tablature. The volume had the same dedication as in 1586_8. Contents = 1586_8. The vocal settings of each piece appeared on the left page of each opening, keyboard and lute intabulations on the right page. A copy was in PL:L.

1590_{10}

VIADANA, LUDOVICO GROSSI DA

CANZONETTE / A QUATRO VOCI / DI LODOVICO VIADANA / CON UN DIALOGO A OTTO / di Ninfe e Pastori, & un'aria di Canzon / Francese per sonare. / LIBRO PRIMO. / Novamente composte, & date in luce. / CON PRIVILEGIO. / [Printer's mark] / IN VENETIA, M D XC. / Appresso Ricciardo Amadino.

Four part books in mensural notation, each of 12 fols. (?). The title is placed within an ornamental border. Dedication on fol. 1ᵛ headed "ALL ILLUSTRISSIMO SIGNORE E PADRONE OSSERVANDISSIMO, IL SIGNOR ALESSANDRO PICO," and signed "Di Vinegia il dì 15 di Decembre 1589. Di V. S. Illustrissima Affettionatissimo servitore Lodovico Viadana," followed by the table of contents; both are repr. in SartMS, p. 67. Vogel: Viadana 1 (1590) also gives a complete list of the contents. The volume contains 20 compositions with Italian text and one piece for instrumental ensemble *a 4*.

Copy in: I:Bc (S).

	fol.	
1	12v	*Aria di Canzon Francese per sonar del primo tono a 4*

1590₁₁

WHYTHORNE, THOMAS

CANTUS. / Of Duos, or Songs for two voi/ces, composed and made by Thomas Whythorne / Gent. Of the which, some be playne and easie to / be sung, or played on Musicall Instruments, & be made / for yong beginners of both those sorts. And the / rest of these Duos be made and set foorth / for those that be more perfect in sing/ing or playing as aforesaid, all the / which be devided into three parts. / That is to say: / The first, which doth begin at the first song, are made for a man / and a childe to sing, or otherwise for voices or Instruments / of Musicke, that be of the like compasse or distance in sound. / The second, which doth begin at the XXIII. song, are made for / two children to sing. Also they be aptly made for two treble / Cornets to play or sound: or otherwise for voices or Musicall / Instruments, that be of the lyke compasse or distance in sound. / And the third part which doth begin at the XXXVIII. song, (be/ing all Canons of two parts in one) be of divers compasses / or distances, and therefore are to be used with voices or In/struments of Musicke accordingly. / Now newly published in An. Do. 1590. / Imprinted at London by Tho/mas Este, the assigné of William / Byrd. 1590.[1]

Two part books in mensural notation, each of 26 fols. The title is placed within an ornamental border. On fol. A1v of each part book: a coat of arms with the motto "IN VERITATE VICTORIA." Dedication on fol. A2 of each part book headed "To the right worshipfull, master Francis Hastings, brother to the right honorable, and most noble Erle of Huntington, Thomas Whythorne wisheth all godly felicitie, and life everlasting, in Jesus Christ our onely Saviour," and signed "From London the 19. of November. 1590. By your worships during lyfe to commaund, Thomas Whythorne." On fol. G2 of each part book: table of contents and colophon: "Imprinted at London by Thomas Este, dwelling in Aldersgate street at the signe of the black Horse. 1590." On fol. G2v of each part book: cut of Thomas Whythorne with the legend "THOMAS WHITHORN ANNO AETATIS SUAE XL," and the motto "ASPRA, MA NON TROPPO."[2] The compositions identified by the superior letter *a* ([a]) are reprinted in WhythFD, which includes facsimiles of the title page, the dedication, and the cut of Whythorne. All of the compositions are *a 2*; nos. 1–12 are fully texted; nos. 13–52 have only text incipits in both voices. Nos. 38–52 are canons.

Copies in: GB:Lbm, GB:Ob (B).

	fol.	
1	A2v	*Blessed are those, that are undefiled*
2	A3	*O that my wayes were made so direct*
3	A3v	*Wherewithall shall a yong man*
4	A4	*With my lips have I beene telling*
5	A4v	*O do well unto thy servant*
6	B1	*Thou hast rebuked the proud*
7	B1v	*My soule cleaveth*
8	B2	*Take from mee the waie of lying*
9	B2v	*Teach me O Lord the way of thy statutes*
10	B3	*O turne away mine eyes*
11	B3v	*Let thy loving mercie come*
12	B4	*And I will walke at libertie*
13	B4v	*To God all honour give*
14	C1	*Thy Parents reverence*
15	C1v	*Love thou thy neighbour*
16	C2	*Thy Master feare*
17	C2v	*Be faithfull to thy friend*
18	C3	*In counsell be thou close*
19	C3v	*Accompany the good*
20	C4	*The ill doe thou flye*
21	C4v	*Preace not to heare others secrets*

22 D1v *O Lux beata trinitas*
23 D2v *To use good for ill*
24 D3 *As haughtie pryde oppresseth love*
25 D3v *In over comming appetite*
26 D4 *Who speakes thee fayer unto thy face*
27 D4v *Of all the things that we find best*
28 E1 *When speeches to much and out of frame*
29 E1v *If thou wouldst know the swyftest thing*
30 E2 *No exercise can have*
31 E2v *Though many judge and give sentence*
32 E3 *Of needefull things that oft disgrace*
33 E3v *To give counsell to others is ryfe*
34 E4 *Auctoritie most doe desier*
35 E4v *The great desire to get riches*
36 F1 *Affections strong that doe move us*
37 F1v *Who doth not much esteeme of health*
38 F2 *What makes yong folkes simple in shew*[a]
39 F2v *The mind of man [doth change hourely]*[a]
40 F2v *His mortall lyfe* [*doth lyttle see*][a]
41 F3 *For to be borne as Infants be*[a]
42 F3 *Lament we should at childrens birth*[a]
43 F3v *The worldlings judge that man happie*[a]
44 F3v *But Solon sayd*[a]
45 F4 *Lyke as the birds that Swallows hight*[a]
46 F4 *So fayned friends*[a]
47 F4v *This oft is found for to be true*[a]
48 F4v *The conditions of man* [*doth change*][a]
49 G1 *A tirannie not lasting long*[a]
50 G1 *Acceptable is nothing more*[a]
51 G1v *Two comforts hath the unhappie man*[a]
52 G1v *The other if he to mynde can call*[a]

[1] Facs. of title page in WhythA, opp. p. 1.
[2] The cut is repr. in BoydE, p. 102.

1590_{12}

PHALÈSE, PIERRE, AND JEAN BELLÈRE, PUBLISHERS

BICINIA, SIVE / CANTIONES SUAVISSIMAE / DUARUM VOCUM, TAM DIVINAE MUSICES / TYRONIBUS, QUAM EIUSDEM ARTIS PERITIORIBUS / magno usui futurae, nec non & quibusuis Instrumentis accommoda: ex / praeclaris huius aetatis Auctoribus collectae: quarum Cata/logum pagella sequens explicat. / SUPERIUS. / ANTVERPIAE. / Excudebat Petrus Phalesius sibi & Joanni Bellero. / 1590.

Two part books in mensural notation, each of 35 fols. On fol. A1v (= fol. 1v): table of contents. A complete list of the contents is printed in DavC III, 96. A second edition appeared in 1609. The volume contains 47 compositions *a2*; nos. 1–29 are fully texted (with French, Italian, or Latin texts); nos. 30–47 are without text.

Copies in: D:As, F:Pc (imperfect S), S:Uu.

	fol.	
30	19v	Orlando Lassusio = 1577_2, no. 13
31	20v	B. Lupacchino = 1559_5, no. 1
32	21v	Orlando Lassusio = 1577_2, no. 14
33	22v	Terquinio Papa = 1591_7, no. 3
34	23v	Jean Maria Tasso = 1559_5, no. 3
35	24v	Fabritio Facciola
36	25v	Oratio di Martino
37	26v	B. Lupachino = 1559_5, no. 5
38	27v	Orlando Lassusio = 1577_2, no. 17
39	28v	*Sopra la Battaglia* Joan Maria Tasso = 1559_5, no. 39
40	29v	Giovanni de Antiquis
41	30v	B. Lupachino = 1559_5, no. 23
42	31v	Simon de Baldis
43	32v	Giovanni de Antiquis = 1591_7, no. 8
44	33	Dominico dello Mansaro
45	33v	Pomponio Nenna = 1595_4, no. 1
46	34v	B. Lupachino = 1559_6, no. 26
47	35v	Stefano Felis = 1591_7, no. 6

1590

DOUBTFUL WORKS

1. BrunetML, item 10156, lists a 1590 edition of Ercole Bottrigari, *Il Desiderio*. The volume is listed in this bibliography as 1594_2.

[1591]$_1$

BANCHIERI, ADRIANO

Conclusioni per organo. Lucca, Silvestre Marchetti, 1591.

This volume, now lost, is mentioned in FétB I, 233. Other editions of it were made in 1609 and later. BanchC is a facsimile reprint of the 1609 edition. For a summary of the contents see ReFS, no. 51.

1591_2

BASSANO, GIOVANNI

MOTETTI, MADRIGALI / ET CANZONI / FRANCESE, / Di diversi Eccellentissimi Auttori / à Quattro Cinque, & Sei Voci. / DIMINUITI PER SONAR CON OGNI SORTE / di Stromenti, & anco per cantar con semplice Voce / DA GIOVANNI BASSANO / MUSICO DELLA SERENISSIMA / Signoria di Venetia. / NOVAMENTE DATI IN LUCE. / [Printer's mark] / IN VENETIA, / APPRESSO GIACOMO VINCENTI. / M. D. XCI.

35 fols. Mensural notation. Dedication on p. 3 headed "ALL'ILLUSTRISSIMO ET REVERENDISSIMO S. D. MARCELLO ACQUAVIVA ARCIVESCOVO D'OTTRANTO, & Nuntio Apostolico in Venetia, Patrone mio Colendiss.," and signed "Di Venetia il dì X. di Febraro. M. D. XCI. Di V. S. Illustriss. & Reverndiss. Humilissimo Servitore, Gio. Bassano." On p. 4: table of contents. On p. 5: preface headed "AI LETTORI." The volume, now lost, was in D:Bgk. A manuscript copy in the hand of Friedrich Chrysander is now in D:Hs. The compositions identified by the superior letter *a* ([a]) are reprinted in PalW XXXIII, 45–62. For further information see FerandB. The volume contains parts from polyphonic compositions with *passaggi* added by Bassano. The entries followed by an asterisk are ornamented bass parts; those followed by a dagger include both superius and bass parts ornamented; and those followed by a double dagger are composite lines derived from more than one part of the vocal model. All of the other entries are ornamented superius parts.

p.

1 6 *Benedicta sit sancta Trinitas*[a] [1] Palestina *a4* (PalW V, 33)

2 8 *Ave Maria*[a] Palestina *a4* (PalW V, 20)

3 9 *Hodie beata virgo Maria*[a] Palestina *a4* (PalW V, 17)

4 10 *Ancor che col partire* Rore *a4* (SCMA VI, 45)

5 11 *Io canterei d'amor di novamente* Rore *a4* (SCMA VI, 31)

6 12 *Non è chi'l duol mi scemi* Rore *a4* (SCMA VI, 34)

7 13 *Non gemme, non fin'oro* Rore *a4* (SCMA VI, 75)

8 14 *Era il bel viso suo* Rore *a4* (RISM 1561_{15}, no. 2)

15 2a pars *E nella face*

9 16 *Vaghi leggiadri lumi* Giulio Renaldi *a4* (Vogel: Renaldi 3 [1569], p. 8)

17 2a pars *Chi fia che dal mio cor*

10 18 *Madonna, il mio desio* Giulio Renaldi *a4* (Vogel: Renaldi 3 [1569], p. 11)

11 19 *Dolci rosate labbia* Giulio Renaldi *a4* (Vogel: Renaldi 3 [1569], p. 10)

12 20 *Amor io sento* Giulio Renaldi *a4* (Vogel: Renaldi 3 [1569], p. 20)

13 21 *Legò questo mio core* Gio. Maria Nanino *a4* (RISM 1585_{29}, p. 4)

14 22 *Ahi che farò ben mio* Ruggiero Giovanelli *a4* (RISM 1585_{29}, p. 16)

15 23 *Dissi a l'amata mia* Marenzio *a4* (Vogel: Marenzio 74 [1587], no. 2)

16 24 *La bella bianca mano* Annibal Stabile *a4* (RISM 1585_{28}, p. 7)

17 25 *Fuit homo missus a Dei*[a] Palestina *a4* (PalW V, 38)

18 26 *Benedicta sit sancta Trinitas**[1] Palestina *a4* (the same vocal model as no. 1 above)

19 27 *Anchor che col partire* Rore *a4* (another version of no. 4 above)

20 28 *Anchor che col partire*‡ ("Per sonar più parti") Rore *a4* (the same vocal model as no. 4 above)

21 30 *La bella, netta, ignuda e bianca mano*‡ ("Per più parti") Rore *a4* (SCMA VI, 38)

22 32 *Ung gay berger* Crecquilon *a4* (RieH II, 462)

23 33 *Susanna un giur*[2] Lasso *a5* (LassoW XIV, 29)

24 34 *Onques amour* Clemens non Papa *a5* (RISM $[1544]_{11}$, fol. 16: Crecquillon)

25 35 *[F]rais e gaillart* Clemens non Papa *a4* (ClemensO X, 17)

26 36 *Vestiva i colli*[a 3] Palestina *a5* (PalW XXVIII, 239)

37 2a pars *Così le chiome*[a 3]

27 38 *Io son ferito ahi lasso*[d] Palestina *a5* (PalW XXVIII, 179)

28 39 *Mirami vita mia* Claudio [Merulo] da Corregio *a5* (RISM 1589_8, no. 47)

29 40 *Tirsi morir volea* Marentio *a5* (MarenW I, 12)

41 2a pars *Freni Tirsi il desio*

42 3a pars *Così morire*

30 43 *Amor deh dimmi come* Gio. Maria Nanino *a5* (RISM 1587_{10}, p. 8)

31 44 *Madonna mia gentil* Marentio *a5* (MarenW I, 25)

32 45 *Soavissimi baci* Gios. Guammi da Luca *a5* (Vogel: Guami 2 [1584], p. 6)

33 46 *Quando i vostri ombrando copre*‡ ("Per più parti") Marentio *a5*

34 48 *Caro dolce ben mio* Andrea Gabrielli *a5* (RISM 1576_5, p. 28)

35 49 *Individioso Amor* Alessandro Striggio *a6* (Vogel: Striggio 20 [1585], no. 4)

36 50 *Liquide perle Amor*‡ ("Per più parti") Marentio *a5* (MarenW I, 1)

37 52 *Quando Signor Lasciaste*‡[4] ("Per piu parti") Rore *a5* (RISM 1580_{12}, p. 9)

38 54 *Ma poichè vostr'altezza*‡ ("Per piu parti") Ciprian [da Rore] *a5* (RISM 1580_{12}, p. 10)

39 56 *Nasce la pena mia*‡ ("Per più parti") Strigio (MonteO XVI, app.)

40 58 *Ancor ch'io possa dire* Strigio *a6* (Vogel: Striggio 3 [1566], no. 3)

41 59 *Questi che indizio fan* Striggio *a6* (Vogel: Striggio 12 [1579], no. 2)

42 60 *A la fontana* Adrian [Willaert] *a6* (RISM 1572_9, fol. 53)

43 62 *Le rose* Adrian [Willaert] *a6* (compare BrownM, p. 198, art. 49: "La rousée du moys de may")

44 64 *Tota pulchra es amica mea*†[a] Palestina *a5* (PalW IV, 25)

45 66 *Introduxit me*†[a] Palestina *a5* (PalW IV, 34)

46 66 *Pulchra es amica mea*†[a] Palestina *a5* (PalW IV, 61)

47 68 *Veni dilecte mi*†[a] Palestina *a5* (PalW IV, 81)

[1] Mod. ed. of nos. 1 and 18 (ornamented superius and bass parts of the same motet) in HaasA, p. 115, and KuV, p. 100.

[2] Mod. ed. in HaasA, p. 117.

[3] Mod. ed. in HaasA, p. 117.

[4] Mod. ed. (with vocal model) in KuV, p. 110.

1591_3

BERTOLDO, SPERINDIO

CANZONI FRANCESE / INTAVOLATE / PER SONAR D'ORGANO / DA SPERINDIO BERTOLDO. / Nuovamente date in luce. / [Printer's mark] / IN VENETIA, Appresso Giacomo Vincenti. M. D. XCI.

16 fols. Keyboard score. Dedication on p. 2 headed "A'VIRTUOSI PROFESSORI D'ORGANO. JACOMO VINCENTI," printed in SartMS, p. 72. On p. 31: table of contents. For information on this volume see CarrB. All of the compositions are for solo keyboard.

Copy in: CH:Bu.

	p.	
1	3	*Un gai berger* (RieH II, 462: Crecquillon)
2	10	*Hor vien za vien* (RISM 1540_{17}, fol. 6[v]: "Or vien ça vien mamie Perrette," Janequin)
3	17	*Petit fleur* (RISM 1549_{29}, no. 28: Crecquillon)
4	23	*Frais e gagliard* (ClemensO X, 17: Clemens non Papa)

1591_4

BERTOLDO, SPERINDIO

TOCATE RICERCARI / ET CANZONI FRANCESE / INTAVOLATE PER SONAR DORGANO, / DA SPERINDIO BERTOLDO. / Nuovamente Stampati. / [Printer's mark] / IN VENETIA, Appresso Giacomo Vincenti. / M. D. XCI.

16 fols. Keyboard score.[1] Fol. 2 = p. 1. For information on this volume see CarrB. All of the compositions are for solo keyboard.

Copies in: CH:Bu, I:Bc.

	p.	
1	1	*Tocata prima*
2	6	*Tocata seconda*[2]
3	11	*Ricercar del Sesto Tuono*
4	15	*Ricercar del Primo Tuono*[3] = 1556_9, no. 4: Padovano
5	20	*Ricercar del Terzo Tuono*[4] = 1556_9, no. 5: Padovano
6	24	*Canzon Francese*

[1] FétB I, 387, mistakenly dates this work 1561 (probably a printing error for 1591).

[2] Mod. ed. in ValentinTo, no. 3.

[3] Mod. ed. in TorA III, 55.

[4] Mod. ed. in TorA III, 58.

1591_5

FARMER, JOHN

[Divers and sundry waies of two parts in one, to the number of fortie, uppon one playn song. Imprinted by Thomas Este . . . 1591]

24 fols. (?). Title page and all fols. after D3 are missing from the unique copy. Mensural notation. Dedication on fol. A2 headed "To the right honorable my very good lord & master Edward de Vere Earle of Oxenford, vicount Bulbecke, lord of Escales & Badlesmere, & Lord great Chamberlayne of England, John Farmer wisheth long and happie life with encrease of honor," and signed on fol. A2[v] "John Farmer." On fol. A3: preface headed "Philomusicis," and signed on fol. A3[v] "John Farmer." On fol. A4: poem beginning "Who so delights in Musickes skill," and signed "Richard Wilkinson." On fol. A4[v]: poem beginning "Whether in Musickes prayse to wright," and signed "Francis Yomans." The volume contains forty canons *a2*, each over the same plainsong cantus firmus. One composition appears on each page beginning with fol. B1 (the B and C gatherings are signed 1 to 8). There are two canons on p. 19. The cantus firmus is printed first, followed by the two canonic voices and directions for adding the voices together. No text is given for any of the pieces. In the unique copy nos. 39 and 40 are missing. The title is taken from SteeleE, p. 71.

Copy in: GB:Ob (imperfect).

1591_6

GUMPELZHAIMER, ADAM, EDITOR

COMPEN/DIUM MU/sicae, pro / illius artis tironibus. / A / M. Heinrico Fabro Latinè con/scriptum, & à M. Christophoro Rid / in vernaculum sermonem con/versum, nunc praeceptis / & exemplis / auctum / Studio & operâ Adami / Gumpelzhaimeri, T. / AUGUSTAE / Excusum typis Valentini Schönigii. / Anno M. D. XCI.[1]

64 fols. Mensural notation. The title page is placed within an ornamental border depicting musicians playing various instruments. Dedication on fol. A2 headed

SPLENDORE GENERIS ORNATIS, PIETATIS, VIRTUTIS ET DOCTRINAE STUDIOSIS ADOLESCENTIBUS JOHAN: Georgio Hoermanno, Hieronymo Herwarto, Paulo Rämo, Johan: Huldarico Linckio, Friderico & Johan: Friderico Saliceis Grisonibus, Matthaeo Menharto; Nec non optimae spei pueris Georgio Sigismundo Fabricio, Matthaeo Stürzelio, Hieremiae Puraunero, Philippo Henischio, Danieli Oppenridero Reinhartshofensi, Matthaeo Henningo, Joachimo Prinnero, Johanni Leüchsnero Franco, Hieronymo & Tobiae Zähiis, Marcello Theodorico Neoburgensi, Georgio Knophio Dantiscano, Christophoro Hafnero, Lucae Fischero, Antonio & Magno Jacobo Seitziis, Henrico Schot Tyrolensi, Friderico Davidi & Marco Antonio Schalleris, Magno Widemanno, discipulis percharis S. P. Adamus Gumpelzhaimerus T[rospergii],

and dated on fol. A2v "Mense Novemb: 1590. Augustae Vindelicorum." Following the dedication, on fol. A2v, is a two-line Latin epigraph headed "Ad Zoilum." The A gathering and the R gathering each consist of two folios only. The other gatherings contain four folios apiece. The text of this introduction to the rudiments of music begins on fol. B1. The text is printed in Latin on the left side of each page, and in German on the right side. This is a revision, expansion and translation of Heinrich Faber's *Compendiolum musicae pro incipientibus* (Braunschweig, 1548). Gumpelzhaimer made a new, enlarged edition of his version in 1595. See 1595_4 for further details.

Gumpelzhaimer's exposition of the rudiments of music is shorter than and different from that in his enlarged second edition (see 1595_4 for a summary of the chapters in the enlarged edition). Following the text there are a great many musical examples. On fols. E1–L3v: canons *a2* to *a8*, with Italian, Latin, or German texts, or without texts. Canons without text appear on fols. E1v, F4v, G3v, H1 ("Fuga à 5"), H1v ("Fuga à 4"), H2 ("Fuga à 3"), I2 (two canons), I2v (two canons), I3 ("Fuga di un tempo, una ottava piu passo [sic]" by Matth: Asola), I3v ("Fuga diver tempo, una ottava piu basso" by Matt: Asola), K2, K3, K4, L1, L2 (two canons), L2v (two canons), L2v (two canons), L3 (two canons), and L3v. On fols. L4v–P3v: pieces *a2* with Italian, Latin, or German texts. These duos are preceded by a separate title page (on fol. L4) beginning: "Sequuntur Bicinia Sacra, in usum juventutis Scholasticae collecta." On fols. P4v–R2: pieces *a4* by Gumpelzhaimer with German text. On fol. R2v: table of contents for all of the pieces from fol. L4v to the end. Some but not all of these musical examples are identical with those in the second edition, 1595_4.

Copies in: D:Dl, CH:E, D:MMs, GB:Lbm.

[1] Title page and one other page in facs. in MGG III, cols. 1685 and 1687.

1591_7

LINDNER, FRIDERICH

BICINIA SACRA, / EX VARIIS AUTORIBUS / IN USUM IUVENTUTIS SCHOLASTICAE / collecta: Quibus adjuncta est compendiaria in artem canendi Introductio: / unde brevissimo tempore & labore facilimo, non solum necessaria huius / artis praecepta (quae nec multa nec difficilia adeò sunt) sed & artem / ipsam canendi, pueri addiscere possunt. Edita à / FRID: LINDNERO. / Zweystimmige Gesänglein, sampt einem kurtzen / unterricht, wie man soll lernen singen, für die jungen / Schuler neulich im druck aussgangen. / VOX INFERIOR. / NORIBERGAE, / In officina typographica Catharinae Gerlachiae. M. D. XCI.[1]

Two part books in mensural notation, each of 48 fols. (?). Dedication on fol. a2 headed "Primariis optimaeque spei pueris NICOLAO HIERONYMO Baumgartnero, GEORGIO Im Hofio, JOANNI SIGISMUNDO Furero, ANDREAE, CHRISTOPHORO, BARTHOLOMAEO Harsdorferis fratribus, HIERONYMO Tuchero, PAULO Colero, WILHELMO & BARTHOLOMAEO Halleris fratribus, JACOBO

Welsero, PAULO Stockamero &c. Duum virûm Septem virûmque ac Senatorum Reipub: Noribergens: filiis, discipulis suis dilectissimis, Fridericus Lindnerus S. D.," and dated on fol. a2[v] "Calend: Januarii, anno 1591." The volume contains duos with Latin text, and duos without text. Since the texted duos are not inventoried in any other bibliography, a complete list of the contents is given below.

Copy in: GB:Lbm (vox inferior).

	fol.	
1	a3	*Cantate Domino* Orlan. di Lassus
2	a3[v]	*Scribantur haec in generatione* Orlan. di Lassus
3	a4	*Aegra currit ad medicum* Orlan. di Lassus
4	a4[v]	*Te Prophetarum* Orlan. di Lassus
5	a5	*Non avertas faciem tuam* Orlan. di Lassus
6	a5[v]	*Expectatio justorum* Orlan. di Lassus
7	a6	*Et resurrexit* Lupi
8	a6[v]	*Crucifixus* Anton. Scandellus
9	a7	*Sicut locutus est* Orlan. di Lassus
10	a7[v]	*Et resurrexit* Lupi
11	a8	*Tota die* Orlan. di Lassus
12	a8[v]	*Amici mei & proximi mei* Jacobi Reineri
13	b1[v]	*Putruerunt & corruptae sunt* Orlan. di Lassus
14	b1[v]	*Expandi manus meas ad te* Jacobi Reineri
15	b2[v]	*Oculus non vidit* Orlandus di Lassus
16	b3	*Justus cor suum* Orlan. di Lassus
17	b3[v]	*Dirige nos Domine* Orlan. di Lassus
18	b4	*Expandi manus meas ad te* Orlan. di Lassus
19	b4[v]	*Crucifixus* Jachet Berchem
20	b5	*Pleni sunt coeli* Finot
21	b5[v]	*Crucifixus* Certon
22	b6	*Benedictus qui venit* Vicent. Ruffi
23	b6[v]	*Crucifixus* Tiburt. Massaino
24	b7	*Intellectum tibi dabo* Orlan. di Lassus
25	b7[v]	*Ipsa te cogat pietas* Orlan. di Lassus
26	b8	*Te deprecamur* Orlan. di Lasso
27	b8[v]	*Qui sequitur me* Orlan. di Lassus
28	c1	*Benedictus qui venit* Gomberth
29	c1[v]	*Foelix est puerpera* Jacobi Handel
30	c2	*Pleni sunt coeli* Jachet
31	c2[v]	*Quoniam qui talia agunt* Orlan. di Lassus
32	c3	*Pleni sunt coeli* Anton. Goswinus
33	c3[v]	*Domine Deus, agnus Dei* Orlan. di Lassus
34	c4	*Beata, beata cuius brachiis* Orlan. di Lassus
35	c4[v]	*Beatus vir* Orland. di Lassus
36	c5	*Beatus, beatus homo qui invenit* Orlan. di Lassus
37	c5[v]	*Discedite à me* Orlan. di Lassus
38	c6	*Audi tui meo dabis* Orlan. di Lassus
39	c6[v]	*Per illud ave* Josquin
40	c7	*Pleni sunt coeli* Jachet Berchem
41	c7[v]	*Ego autem semper sperabo* Jacob. Handel
42	c8	*Eripe me Domine* ("Canon duarum") Jac. Handel
43	c8[v]	*Etiam si oportuerit* Jouan Nasco
44	c8[v]	*Benedictus qui venit* Anton. Scandel.
45	d1	*Domine Deus* Certon
46	d1[v]	*Pleni sunt coeli* Certon
47	d2	*Eripe me, Domine* Jacobi Handel
48	d2[v]	*Pleni sunt coeli* Anton. Scandel.
49	d3	*Et si omnes* Jouan Nasco
50	d3	*Benedictus qui venit* Rodolph. di Lasso
51	d3[v]	*Fecit potentiam* Orlan. di Lassus
52	d4	*Justi tulerunt spolia* Orlan. di Lassus
53	d4[v]	*Serve bone & fidelis* Orlan. di Lassus
54	d5	*Et resurrexit* Gomberth
55	d5[v]	*Pleni sunt coeli* Jachet Berchem
56	d6	*Et resurrexit* Certon
57	d6[v]	*Benedictus qui venit* Anton. Scandel.
58	d7	*Benedictus qui venit* Melchior Schram.
59	d7[v]	*Sancti mei* Orlan. di Lassus
60	d8	*Qui vult venire* Orlan. di Lassus

61 d8v *In memoria aeterna erit justus* Orlan. di Lassus
62 e1 *Fulgebunt justi sicut Lilium* Orlan. di Lassus
63 e1v *Benedictus qui venit* Vincentii Ruffi
64 e2 *Crucifixus* Josepho Guami
65 e2v *Crucifixus* Orlan. di Lassus
66 e3 *Et iterum venturus est* Melchior Schram
67 e3v *Benedictus qui venit* Incerti Autoris
68 e4 *Sed & lingua mea* Jacobi Handel
69 e4v Giovanni di Antiquis [1]
70 e5v Gio: Battista Pace
71 e6v Tarquinio Papa = 1590_{12}, no. 33
72 e7v Gio: Francesco Palumbo
73 e8v Resolutio. Fabritio Facciola
74 f1v Stefano Felis = 1590_{12}, no. 47
75 f2v Cola Maria Pizziolis
76 f3v Giovanni de Antiquis = 1590_{12}, no. 43
77 f4v Incertus Autor
78 f5v Gio: Francesco Capoani
79 f6v Di Incerto = 1595_4, no. 6
80 f7v Cola Vincenzo Fanelli = 1595_4, no. 5

[1] Facs. of title page and fol. e4v in MGG VIII, col. 896. Heading on fol. e4v: "RICERCARI, SIVE FANTASIAE ALIQUOT ELEGANTES DIversorum Autorum."

1591_8

LUPACCHINO, BERNARDINO, AND JOAN MARIA TASSO

DI BERNARDINO LUPACCHINO / ET DI GIO. MARIA TASSO. / Il primo Libro A Due Voci: Novamente ristampato. / [Printer's mark] / IN VENETIA, Presso Giacomo Vincenti. / M. D. XCI.

Two part books in mensural notation, each of 20 fols. Contents = 1559_6. All of the compositions are *a2* and without text or title.

Copies in: I:Bc, US:BE (T).

1591_9

MALVEZZI, CRISTOFANO, EDITOR

INTERMEDII / ET CONCERTI, / Fatti per la Commedia rappresentata in / FIRENZE / Nelle Nozze del Serenissimo / DON FERDINANDO MEDICI, / E MADAMA CHRISTIANA DI LORENO, / Gran Duchi di Toscana. / [Printer's mark] / IN VENETIA, / Appresso Giacomo Vincenti. / M. D. XCI.

Fourteen part books in mensural notation (S, 20 fols.; T, 18 fols.; AB7, each of 16 fols.; 5, 14 fols.; 6, 10 fols.; 8, 8 fols.; 9, 12 fols.; 10–14, each of 2 fols.). Dedication on p. 2 headed "ALLA SERENISSIMA CRISTIANA Gran Duchessa di Toscana," and signed "Di Venetia, il dì primo di Luglio. M. D. XCI. Di V. A. Serenissima Devotissimo, & obligatissimo Servitore Cristofano Malvezzi," reprinted in SartMS, p. 71, and SolA II, 16. On p. 3: preface, reprinted in SartMS, p. 71, and SolA II, 17. On p. 40: table of contents. Contains all of the music for the theatrical entertainments at the wedding of Ferdinand de' Medici and Christine of Lorraine in 1589 (for a bibliography of other works describing the festivities, see SolMus, pp. 12–18). All four of the compositions for instrumental ensemble are reprinted in SchneidA, p. 149. Besides these four compositions, listed below, the set of part books contains fully texted compositions that were performed with instrumental accompaniment. The ninth part book includes texts, detailed descriptions of the musical performances (including the instrumentations used in the madrigals),[1] and scores *a4* of the following pieces:

p. 4 *Delle celeste sfere* [2] from the first *intermedio*
13 *Dunque fra* [3] by Jacopo Peri from the fifth *intermedio*
16 *Godi turba* [4] by Emilio de' Cavalieri from the sixth *intermedio*

WalkerI is a modern edition of the entire collection. For further information see GhiA; NaglerT, pp. 70–92, pls. 42–65; SolA II, 16–42; and WalkerM. Pagination in the following list is taken from the superius part book.

Copies in: A:Wn, I:Fn (58, 11, and imperfect 6).

p.
7 *Primo Intermedio* Cristofano Malvezzi
1 8 *Sinfonia a6*
13 *Secondo Intermedio* Luca Marenzio
2 13 *Sinfonia a5*[5]
20 *Terzo Intermedio* Luca Marenzio
24 *Quarto Intermedio* Cristofano Malvezzi
3 24 *Sinfonia a6*
27 *Quinto Intermedio* Christofano Malvezzi
4 30 *Sinfonia a6*
32 *Sesto Intermedio* Christofano Malvezzi

[1] Excerpts from these descriptions and from the dedication and preface are repr. in Vogel: Malvezzi 3 (1591). SolMus, p. 17, repr. in facs. pp. 21 and 22 of the ninth part book, describing the dances at the end of the sixth *intermedio*. ReynaB, p. 160, contains facs. of several pages from the ninth part book, along with a French translation.

[2] Mod. ed. in KiesS, no. 41, and SchneidA, p. 116.

[3] Mod. ed. in KiesS, no. 39, and SchneidA, p. 134.

[4] Mod. ed. in KiesS, no. 40; KinO, p. 306; and SchneidA, p. 147.

[5] Mod. ed. in KinO, p. 312.

$[1591]_{10}$

PACOLINI, GIOVANNI

Tabulatura tribus testudinibus. Anvers, Pierre Phalèse, 1591.

This volume, now lost, contained music for three lutes. It is mentioned in FétB VI, 401, as a second edition of $[1587]_6$.

1591_{11}

VEROVIO, SIMONE

CANZONETTE / A quattro Voci, Composte da diversi / Ecc[tl] Musici, CON / L'intavolatura del Cimbalo / et del LIUTO / Raccolte et stampate da Simone Verovio / In Roma 1591 Con Licentia di sup[rl]

22 fols. Mensural notation, keyboard score, and Italian lute tablature. The title is placed within a border consisting of various cuts including musicians. Dedication on fol. 2 headed "All'Ill[mo] et R[mo] sig[e] et P[ad]ron mio col[mo] Il sig[e] Card. di Lorena," and signed "Di Roma a 20 di Marzo 1591 D V S Ill[ma] et Rev[ma], Devotiss. et Humiliss. Serv[e], Simone Verovio," reprinted in CasSV, p. 196, and GaspaC III, 208. On fol. 21[v]: table of contents. For a second edition without intabulations see Vogel 1597_5 (= RISM 1597_{14}). The collection arranged for piano is reprinted in WotC. The vocal setting of each piece is printed across the top of each opening; the keyboard intabulation appears on the lower left-hand page, and the lute intabulation on the lower right-hand page.

Copies in: D:LEm, D:Mbs, GB:Lbm (imperfect), I:Bc, I:Pca, US:CA, US:R.[1]

fol.
1 2[v] *Hor che vezzosa e bella* Felice Anerio
2 3[v] *Cosi soave stile* Felice Anerio
3 4[v] *Questi capelli d'oro* Paolo Bellasio
4 5[v] *Io non sò come vivo* Annibale Stabile
5 6[v] *Fuggite amanti Amor* Annibale Stabile
6 7[v] *Mentr'io fuggivo* Gio. Andrea Dragoni
7 8[v] *Spesso il canto ad amare* Horatio Griffi
8 9[v] *Pose un gran foco*[2] Gio. da Pellestrina
9 10[v] *Ohime crudele Amore* Rhrodiano Barera
10 11[v] *Vedrassi prima senza luce*[3] Gio. da Pellestrina
11 12[v] *Di che cor mio* Gio. Maria Nanino
12 13[v] *Se dal tuo foco altiero* Francesco Soriano
13 14[v] *Bella d'Amor guerriera* Ruggiero Giovanelli
14 15[v] *Quando miro il bel volto* Paulo Quagliato
15 16[v] *Tal da vostri occhi* Paulo Quagliato
16 17[v] *O mio soave foco* Pompeo Stabile
17 18[v] *Se'l raggio de vostr'occhi* Luca Marentio
18 19[v] *O miser quel che spera* Paulo Bellasio

19 20v *Donna nel vostro volto* Paulo Bellasio

20 21v *La Verginella è simile a la rosa* [vocal setting only]

[1] Copies were in PL:L and the Heyer library (see HeyerV II, no. 210).
[2] Facs. of fols. 9v and 10 in PN, p. 109.
[3] Mod. ed. of the vocal setting and the lute intabulation in BruAL I, 24.

1591₁₂

VINCI, PIETRO, AND ANTONIO IL VERSO

DI PIETRO VINCI / SICILIANO / Della Citta di Nicosia / IL SECONDO LIBRO DE MOTETTI, / E RICERCARI A TRE VOCI, / Con alcuni Ricercari Di Antonio Il Verso suo Discepolo. / Novamente dati in luce. / [Printer's mark] / IN VENETIA, M D XCI. / Appresso lHerede di Gierolamo Scotto.

Three part books in mensural notation, each of 14 fols. Dedication on fol. 1v of each part book headed "ALL'ILLUSTRISSIMO ET ECCELLENTISSIMO SIGNOR DON FRANCESCO MONCADA Principe di Paterno e Duca di Mont'alto &c. Mio Signor Collendissimo," and signed "Da Palermo Il di 20. April 1591. Di V. E. Humilissimo Servitore Antonio il Verso." The volume contains compositions with Latin text,[1] and 14 ricercares for instrumental ensemble *a3*.

Copy in: I:Vnm.

	p.	
1	14	*Ricercar Primo* Pietro Vinci
2	15	*Ricercar Secondo* Pietro Vinci
3	16	*Ricercar Terzo* Antonio il Verso
4	17	*Ricercar quarto* Antonio il Verso
5	18	*Ricercar Quinto* Pietro Vinci
6	19	*Ricercar Sesto* Pietro Vinci
7	20	*Ricercar Settimo* Antonio il Verso
8	21	*Ricercar Ottavo* Pietro Vinci
9	22	*Ricercar Nono* Antonio il Verso
10	23	*Ricercar Decimo* Pietro Vinci
11	24	*Ricercar Undecimo* Antonio il Verso
12	25	*Fa mi la mi sol la* Pietro Vinci
13	26	*Ricercar Terzodecimo* Antonio il Verso
14	27	[*Ricercar Quartodecimo*] Antonio il Verso

[1] Since this volume is not indexed by Sartori, Vogel, or Einstein, the motets are included here: p. 3: *O Patriarcha pauperum;* 4: *Beata es Virgo Maria* (2a pars: *Ave Maria gratia plena*); 6: *Angelus ad Pastores ait;* 7: *Surrexit Pastor bonus;* 8: *O admirabile commercium;* 9: *Quem vidistis;* 10: *Tanto tempore;* 11: *Agnus dei;* 12: *Benedictus;* 13: *Gaude Barbara.*

1591₁₃

WAISSEL, MATTHÄUS

TABULATURA / Allerley künstlicher Preambulen, aus/erlesener Deudtscher und Polnischer Tentze, Passemezen, Gailliar/den Padoanen, Pavanen, und Branlen: / Auff der Lauten zu schlagen gantz fleissig zugerichtet, und al/len Liebhabern dieser Kunst zu nutz, und gefallen, in den / Druck gegeben / Durch / MATTHAEUM WAISSELIUM / Bartensteinensem, Borussum. / [Cut of a lutenist] / Gedruckt zu Franckfurt an der Oder, durch Andream / Eichorn. Im Jahr: 1591. / Cum gratia, & Privilegio.

48 fols. (?) German lute tablature. On fol. A1v: table of contents. Dedication on fol. A2 headed "Den Gestrengen, Ehrnuesten, Achtbaren, Ehrbaren, Hoch, unnd Wolweisen Herrn: Königlichem Burggraven, Bürgermeistern und Raht, der löblichen Königlichen Stadt Elbing: meinen grosgönstigen Herrn," and signed "Gegeben zu Franckfurt an der Oder, am tage Matthei, des Apostels und Evangelisten. Anno. 1591. E. G. A. und Hochw. williger Diener Mattheus Waissel, von Bartenstein, weiland Pfarrer zu Lanckheim." On fol. A3: poem in Latin headed "In Chelyn Matthaei Waisselii Epigramma, M. Nicolai Martini Rectoris Scholae Bartensteinensis." On fol. A3v: preface "An den Leser," reprinted in KosackL, p. 69. A thematic index of this collection (made from [1592]₁₃) is printed in KosackL, p. 111. The volume is described in GrimmM, pp. 103–104. Contents = [1592]₁₃. All of the compositions are for solo lute.

Copy in: D:Ngm (imperfect).

	fol.	
1	A4	*1. Praeambulum*[1]
2	A4	*2. Praeambulum*
3	A4^{v}	*3. Praeambulum*
4	A4^{v}	*4. Praeambulum*
5	B1	*5. Praeambulum*
6	B1	*6. Praeambulum*
7	B1^{v}	*7. Praeambulum*
8	B1^{v}	*8. Praeambulum*
9	B2	*1. Tantz*[2]
	B2	*Sprung*[2]
10	B2	*2. Tantz*
	B2	*Sprung*
11	B2^{v}	*3. Tantz*
	B2^{v}	*Sprung*
12	B2^{v}	*4. Tantz*[3]
	B2^{v}	*Sprung*
13	B3	*5. Tantz*[4]
	B3	*Sprung*
14	B3	*6. Tantz*
	B3	*Sprung*
15	B3^{v}	*7. Tantz*[5]
	B3^{v}	*Sprung*
16	B3^{v}	*8. Tantz*
	B3^{v}	*Sprung*
17	B4	*9. Tantz*
	B4	*Sprung*
18	B4	*10. Tantz*
	B4	*Sprung*
19	B4^{v}	*11. Tantz*
	B4^{v}	*Sprung*
20	B4^{v}	*12. Tantz*
	B4^{v}	*Sprung*
21	C1	*13. Tantz*
	C1	*Sprung*
22	C1	*14. Tantz* = 1573_3, no. 47a
	C1	*Sprung* = 1573_3, no. 47b
23	C1^{v}	*15. Tantz*
	C1^{v}	*Sprung*
24	C1^{v}	*16. Tantz*
	C1^{v}	*Sprung*
25	C2	*17. Tantz*
	C2	*Sprung*
26	C2	*18. Tantz*[6]
	C2	*Sprung*[6]
27	C2^{v}	*19. Tantz*
	C2^{v}	*Sprung*
28	C2^{v}	*20. Tantz*
	C2^{v}	*Sprung*
29	C3	*21. Tantz*
	C3	*Sprung*
30	C3	*22. Tantz*
	C3	*Sprung*
31	C3^{v}	*23. Tantz*
	C3^{v}	*Sprung*
32	C3^{v}	*24. Tantz* = 1573_3, no. 50a
	C3^{v}	*Sprung* = 1573_3, no. 50b
33	C4	*25. Tantz*
	C4	*Sprung*
34	C4	*26. Tantz*
	C4	*Sprung*
35	C4^{v}	*27. Tantz*
	C4^{v}	*Sprung*
36	C4^{v}	*28. Tantz*
	C4^{v}	*Sprung*
37	D1	*29. Tantz*
	D1	*Sprung*
38	D1	*30. Tantz*
	D1	*Sprung*
39	D1^{v}	*31. Tantz*
	D1^{v}	*Sprung*
40	D1^{v}	*32. Tantz*
	D1^{v}	*Sprung*
41	D2	*33. Tantz* = 1573_3, no. 48a
	D2	*Sprung* = 1573_3, no. 48b
42	D2	*34. Tantz*
	D2	*Sprung*
43	D2^{v}	*35. Tantz*
	D2^{v}	*Sprung*
44	D2^{v}	*36. Tantz*
	D2^{v}	*Sprung*
45	D3	*37. Tantz*
	D3	*Sprung*
46	D3	*38. Tantz*
	D3	*Sprung*
47	D3^{v}	*39. Tantz*
	D3^{v}	*Sprung*
48	D4	*40. Tantz*
	D4	*Sprung*
49	D4^{v}	*1. Tantz*[7]
50	D4^{v}	*2. Tantz*
51	D4^{v}	*3. Tantz*
52	D4^{v}	*4. Tantz*
53	E1	*5. Tantz*
54	E1	*6. Tantz*
55	E1	*7. Tantz*
56	E1	*8. Tantz*
57	E1^{v}	*9. Tantz*
58	E1^{v}	*10. Tantz*
59	E1^{v}	*11. Tantz*
60	E1^{v}	*12. Tantz*
61	E2	*13. Tantz*
62	E2	*14. Tantz*
63	E2	*15. Tantz*
64	E2	*16. Tantz*
65	E2^{v}	*17. Tantz*
66	E2^{v}	*18. Tantz*
67	E2^{v}	*19. Tantz*
68	E2^{v}	*20. Tantz*
69	E3	*21. Tantz*

70 E3 *22. Tantz*
71 E3 *23. Tantz*
72 E3 *24. Tantz*
73 E3^v *25. Tantz*
74 E3^v *26. Tantz*
75 E3^v *27. Tantz*
76 E3^v *28. Tantz*
77 E4 *29. Tantz*
78 E4 *30. Tantz*
79 E4 *31. Tantz*
80 E4 *32. Tantz*
81 E4^v *33. Tantz*
82 E4^v *34. Tantz*
83 F1 *35. Tantz*
84 F1 *36. Tantz*[8]
85 F1^v *1. Passemezo anticho*[9] = 1556$_2$, no. 24a
F3 *El suo Saltarello* = 1556$_2$, no. 24b
F4 *Le Represe*
86 F4^v *2. Passemezo anticho* = 1556$_2$, no. 26a
G1^v *El suo Saltarello* = 1556$_2$, no. 26b
G1^v *Le Represe*
87 G2 *3. Passemezo anticho* = 1556$_2$, no. 27a
G2^v *El suo Saltarello* = 1556$_2$, no. 27b
G3 *Le Represe*
88 G3^v *4. Passemezo anticho* = 1556$_2$, no. 28a
H1 *El suo Saltarello* = 1556$_2$, no. 28b
H1^v *Le Represe*
89 H2 *5. Passemezzo commune*
H1^v *Le Represe*
H3 *El suo Saltarello*
H3^v *Le Represe*
90 H3^v *6. Passemezo commune*
H4^v *Le Represe*
H4^v *El suo Saltarello*
I1 *Le Represe*
91 I1^v *7. Passemezo commune*
I2 *El suo Saltarello*
92 I2^v *8. Passemezo commune* = 1563$_8$, no. 2a: "Passo e mezo moderno"
I3 *El suo Salterello* = 1563$_8$, no. 2c
93 I3^v *1. Gailliarda*[10]
94 I3^v *2. Gailliarda*
95 I4 *3. Gailliarda*
96 I4 *4. Gailliarda*
97 I4^v *5. Gailliarda*
98 I4^v *6. Gailliarda*
99 K1 *7. Gailliarda*
100 K1 *8. Gailliarda*
101 K1^v *9. Galliarda*
102 K1^v *10. Gaillarda*
103 K2 *11. Gailliarda*
104 K2 *12. Gailliarda*
105 K2^v *13. Gailliarda*
106 K2^v *14. Gailliarda*
107 K3 *15. Gailliarda*
108 K3 *16. Gailliarda*
109 K3^v *17. Gailliarda*
110 K3^v *18. Gailliarda*
111 K4 *19. Gailliarda*
112 K4 *20. Gailliarda*
113 K4^v *21. Gailliarda*
114 K4^v *22. Galliarda*
115 L1 *23. Gailliarda*
116 L1^v *24. Gailliarda*
117 L2 *1. Padoana*[11]
118 L2^v *2. Padoana*
119 L3 *3. Padoana*[12]
120 L3^v *4. Padoana*
121 L4 *5. Padoana*
122 L4 *6. Padoana*
123 L4^v *7. Padoana*
124 L4^v *8. Padoana*
125 *1. Pavana Ferrareza*[13] (1571$_5$, no. 6a)
Gailliarda Ferrareza (1571$_5$, no. 6b)
126 *2. Pavana des dieux* (1571$_5$, no. 7a)
Gailliarda des dieux (1571$_5$, no. 7b)
127 *3. Pavana la Garde* (1571$_5$, no. 8a)
Gailliarda la Garda (1571$_5$, no. 8b)
128 *4. Pavana sur la Battaglia*
Gailliarda sur la Battaglia
129 *1. Branle de Bourgoigne*[14] = 1573$_2$, no. 13
130 *2. Branle de Bourgoigne* = 1573$_2$, no. 15
131 *3. Branle de Champaigne* = 1568$_7$, no. 153
132 *4. Branle de Champaigne*
133 *5. Branle de Poictou simple*
134 *6. Quatres Branles* = 1573$_2$, no. 18
135 *7. Branle de Angleterre*
136 *8. Branle commune*

[1] Heading on fol. 4: "Folgen erstlich Praeambulen."

[2] Heading on fol. B2: "Folgen Deudtsche Tentze." Facs. of fol. B2 and mod. ed. of no. 9 in SzmolyanAL, p. 540. Mod. ed. also in GiesK, p. 16, and ZanG II, 25.
[3] Mod. ed. in WaissP, no. 2.
[4] Mod. ed. in GiesK, p. 18, and ZanG II, 15.
[5] Mod. ed. in TapS, p. 49.
[6] Mod. ed. in BruS III, no. 114; FerandM, p. 408; and TapS, p. 50.
[7] Heading on fol. D4v: "Folgen Polnische Tentze."
[8] Mod. ed. in OpieD, no. 2.
[9] Heading on fol. F1v: "Folgen Passemezen."
[10] Heading on fol. I3v: "Folgen Gailliarden."
[11] Heading on fol. L2: "Folgen Padoanen."
[12] Mod. ed. in GiesK, p. 16.
[13] Heading: "Folgen Pavanen."
[14] Heading: "Folgen Branlen."

1591_{14}

VINCENTI, GIACOMO, PUBLISHER

CANZONETTE / PER CANTAR / ET SONAR DI LIUTO / A TRE VOCI. / COMPOSTE / DA DIVERSI AUTTORI, / & nouvamente date in luce. / LIBRO PRIMO. / [Printer's mark] / IN VENETIA, / APPRESSO GIACOMO VINCENTI, / M. D. XCI.

6 fols. Mensural notation and Italian lute tablature. The title is placed within an ornamental border. The intabulation for lute appears beneath the vocal setting of each piece. For other volumes in this series see 1591_{15} and 1591_{16}. Later revised editions of all three volumes are listed in Vogel as 1601_4, 1607_2, and 1608_1. Compare also 1589_8 above.

Copy in: I:Fn.

fol.

1 2 *Tutta gentile e bella* Gio. Mario Nanino = 1589_8, no. 10
2 2v *Ohime partito è'l mio* Annibal Stabile = 1589_8, no. 11
3 3 *Io me n'avedo Amore* Archangelo Crivello = 1589_8, no. 8
5 3v *Ardenti miei sospiri* Jacomo Peetrino = 1589_8, no. 6
5 4 *Donna donna tue chiome* Annibal Stabile = 1589_8, no. 5
6 4v *Vermiglio e vago fiore* Ruggiero Giovanelli = 1589_8, no. 7
7 5 *Fugge da gl'occhi il sonno* Ruggiero Giovanelli = 1589_8, no. 12
8 5v *Poi che mesto e dolente* Jacomo Peetrino = 1589_8, no. 9
9 6 *Da cosi dotta man* Gioan Pier Luigi Palestina = 1589_8, no. 2
10 6v *Ahi che quest'occhi miei* Gioan Pier Luigi Palestina = 1589_8, no. 1

1591_{15}

VINCENTI, GIACOMO, PUBLISHER

CANZONETTE / PER CANTAR / ET SONAR DI LIUTO / A TRE VOCI. / COMPOSTE / DA DIVERSI AUTTORI, / & nuovamente date in luce. / LIBRO SECONDO. / [Printer's mark] / IN VENETIA, / APPRESSO GIACOMO VINCENTI, / M. D. XCI.

6 fols. Mensural notation and Italian lute tablature. The title is placed within an ornamental border. The intabulation for lute appears beneath the vocal setting of each piece. For other volumes in this series see 1591_{14} and 1591_{16}. Later revised editions of all three volumes are listed in Vogel as 1601_4, 1607_2, and 1608_1. Compare also 1589_8 above.

Copy in: I:Fn.

fol.

1 2 *Si vaga è la fiamma* Ruggiero Giovanelli = 1589_8, no. 14
2 2v *Al suon non posa il core* Felice Anerio = 1589_8, no. 15
3 3 *Ancora che tu m'odii* Paolo Quagliato = 1589_8, no. 18
4 3v *Fiamme che da begl'occhi* Felice Anerio = 1589_8, no. 19
5 4 *Vedo ogni selva* Francesco Soriano = 1589_8, no. 21
6 4v *Ingiustissimo Amore* Antonio Orlandino = 1589_8, no. 17
7 5 *Io ardo ò Filli* Jacomo Ricordi = 1589_8, no. 16
8 5v *Ohime crudele Amore* Gio. Battista Zucchelli = 1589_8, no. 13
9 6 *Ameni colli vaghi* Francesco Soriano = 1589_8, no. 3
10 6v *Se freda e la mia donna* Gasparo Costa = 1589_8, no. 20

1591_{16}

VINCENTI, GIACOMO, PUBLISHER

CANZONETTE / PER CANTAR / ET SONAR DI LIUTO / A TRE VOCI. / COMPOSTE / DA DIVERSI AUTTORI, / & nuovamente date in luce. / LIBRO TERZO / [Printer's mark] / IN VENETIA, / APPRESSO GIACOMO VINCENTI, / M. D. XCI.

6 fols. Mensural notation and Italian lute tablature. The title is placed within an ornamental border. The intabulation for lute appears beneath the vocal settings of each piece. For other volumes in this series see 1591_{14} and 1591_{15}. Later revised editions of all three volumes are listed in Vogel as 1601_4, 1607_2, and 1608_1. Compare also 1589_8 above.
Copy in: I:Fn.

	fol.	
1	2	*Donna se'l cor legasti* Felice Anerio = 1589_8, no. 23
2	2v	*Perche Barbara sia* Oratio S[c]aletta
3	3	*Donna s'io vi son lunge* Oratio Scaletta
4	3v	*Amor tutto lo leggi* Oratio Scaletta
5	4	*Di che ti lagni Amante* Oratio Scaletta
6	4v	*Ahi Filli, anima mia* Oratio Scaletta
7	5	*Donna se nel tuo volto* Luca Marentio = 1589_8, no. 24
8	5v	*Donna gentil voi siete* Gio. Battista Locatello = 1589_8, no. 22
9	6	*Mentre l'Aquila stà mirando il sole* Gio. Battista Zuccheli = 1589_8, no. 4
10	6v	*Mentre il mio miser core* Felice Anerio = 1589_8, no. 25

1591

DOUBTFUL WORKS

1. The first edition of Grammatico Metallo, *Ricercari a canto e tenore*, may have been issued in 1591 or earlier, since the volume is listed in the trade catalogue of the firm of Vincenti for that year (see VincenI, fol. 2). A lost second edition is listed in this bibliography as $[1595]_5$.

1592_1

BELLASIO, PAOLO

DI PAOLO / BELLASIO / MAESTRO DELLA MUSICA / Nella Accademia degl'Illustriss. / Signori Filarmonici, / VILLANELLE A TRE VOCI, / Con la Intavolatura del Liuto, / Novamente Composte & date in luce. / CON PRIVILEGIO. / [Printer's mark] / In Venetia Appresso Angelo Gardano / M. D. LXXXXII.

Three part books in Italian lute tablature and mensural notation (S of 18 fols.; TB, each of 10 fols.). The title is placed within an ornamental border. Dedication on fol. 2 of each part book headed "AL MOLTO MAGNIFICO SIG: ET PATRON MIO OSSERVANDISSIMO IL SIGNOR GIACOMO VANLEMENS," and signed "Di Venetia il dì 15. Genaro 1592. Di V. Sig. Molto Mag. Servitore Affettionatiss. Paolo Bellasio." On the verso of the last fol. of each part book: table of contents. In the inventory below the foliation is taken from the superius part book. The volume contains villanelle for three voices, with a lute intabulation of each piece. In the superius part book the top voice of the vocal setting appears on the left page of each opening, and the lute intabulation on the right page.
Copies in: GB:Lbm (B), I:Bc.

	fol.	
1	2v	*Una fiamella viva*
2	3v	*Ahi quanti passi*
3	4v	*Questi tuoi occhi*
4	5v	*Mai non vuò pianger piu*
5	6v	*Donna leggiadr'e bella*
6	7v	*Scese dal ciel volando*
7	8v	*Folti boschetti*
8	9v	*Quel tristarel d'Amore*
9	10v	*Libero mentr'io fui*
10	11v	*Che farà Donna*
11	12v	*Non piu lacci d'Amore*
12	13v	*Amor fa quanto sai*
13	14v	*Perche fuggi anima mia*
14	15v	*Tutta sete gentil*
15	16v	*Stillava perle*
16	17v	*Sette del mondo son*

1592_2

BUONA, VALERIO

IL SECONDO LIBRO / DELLE CANZONETTE A TRE VOCI / con l'aggionta di dodeci Tercetti a note. / DI VALERIO BUONA DA BRESCIA / Maestro di Capella nel Duomo di Vercelli. / Novamente poste in luce. / All'Illustre Signor Cavaglier Galeazzo Crotto, / Conte di Vinzaglio. / [Printer's mark] / IN VENETIA, Appresso Ricciardo Amadino. / M D XCII.

Three part books in mensural notation, each of 16 fols. The title is placed within an ornamental border. Dedication on fol. 1^v of each part book headed "ILLUSTRE SIGNOR MIO" and signed "Di Vercelli il dì primo d'Aprile 1592. Di V. S. Illustre Humilissimo servitore Giulio Cesare Carelli," reprinted in SartMS, p. 74. Fol. 2 = p. 1. On p. 30 of each part book: table of contents. SartMS, p. 74, gives a complete list of the contents. The volume contains 18 canzonets with Italian texts, and 12 compositions *a3* for instrumental ensemble.

Copy in: A:Wn.

	p.	
1	19	*Ut*
2	20	*Re*
3	21	*Mi*
4	22	*Fa*
5	23	*Sol*
6	24	*La*
7	25	*La*
8	26	*Sol*
9	27	*Fa*
10	28	*Mi*
11	29	*Re*
12	30	*Ut*

1592_3

GABRIELI, ANDREA, AND ANNIBALE PADOVANO

DIALOGHI MUSICALI / DE DIVERSI ECCELLEN/TISSIMI AUTORI. / A Sette, Otto, Nove, Dieci, Undeci, & Dodeci voci, / Novamente posti in luce. / CON DUE BATTAGLIE A OTTO VOCI, / Per sonar de Istrumenti da Fiato, di Annibale Podoano, / & di Andrea Gabrieli, già Organisti della / Serenissima Signoria di Venetia / in San Marco. / CON PRIVILEGIO. / [Printer's mark] / In Venetia Appresso Angelo Gardano. / M. D. LXXXXII.

Twelve part books in mensural notation (SATB5678, each of 36 fols.; 9 and 10, each of 8 fols.; 11, 12, each of 4 fols.). On fol. 36^v: table of contents. Facs. of title page, pp. 52 and 53, and table of contents in IMAMI I, after p. 92. Contents = 1590_2. The volume contains compositions with Italian text, and two compositions for instrumental ensemble *a8*.

Copies in: A:Wn (T wanting), B:Br (S wanting), D:As (S wanting), GB:Lbm (A5), I:VEaf (10).[1]

[1] A copy was in I:TVcap.

$[1592]_4$

GIOVANELLI, RUGGIERO

Canzon Giovanelli Intavolate per Liuto. Venezia, Giacomo Vincenti.

This volume, now lost, is listed in VincenI, fol. 6 (see ThibaultD). VasJ, p. 479, lists the volume as having been in the library of King John IV of Portugal. FétB IV, 12, lists the title as "Canzonette a tre voci con l'intavolatura del liuto, Rome, Coattino, 1592." The composer is probably Ruggiero Giovanelli (see EitQ IV, 260).

$[1592]_5$

ADRIANSEN, EMANUEL

Pratum musicum longe amoenissimum, cuius spatiosissimo eoque jucundissimo ambitu (praeter varii generis Axiomata seu Phantasias) comprehenduntur. Selectissima diversorum idiomatum Carmina quatuor, quinque et sex Vocum. Nonnulla duarum, trium et quatuor Testudinum Symphoniae aptissima. Cantiones trium vocum, quas neapolitanas vulgo appellant. Variae ad animarum hilaritatem (praesertim inter symposia) provocantes auribusque gratissimae modulationes. Omnis generis choreae, Passomezo cum suis Saltarellis, Gaillardae, Alemandae, Branslae, Courantae, Voltae, etc. Postremo Tripudia aliquot Anglicana. Omnia ad Testudinis Tabulaturam fideliter redacta, per id genus musices experientissimum artificem Emanuelem Hadrianium Antverpiensem. Adjuncta est singulis carminibus, in gratiam eorum, qui vivae vocis concentu oblectantur, distincta vocibus aliquot notularum descriptio. Antverpiae, apud Petrum Phalesium. 1592.

This volume of lute music, now lost if it ever existed, is listed in GoovH, p. 273. This is presumed to be a later edition of 1584_6 (but see 1592_6).

1592_6

ADRIANSEN, EMANUEL

NOVUM / PRATUM MUSICUM / LONGE AMOENISSIMUM, CUIUS / SPATIOSISSIMO, EOQUE JUCUNDISSIMO / AMBITU (PRAETER VARII GENERIS AYTOMATA, / SEU PHANTASIAS) COMPREHENDUNTUR / Selectissimi diversorum Authorum & Idiomatum Madrigales, Cantiones, & Moduli 4. 5. & 6. Vocum. / Cantiones Trium vocum, quas vulgo Neapolitanas aut Villaneschas appellant. / Variae Cantiones Gallicae, quas vulgò Aierosas, vel Airs, nempe sonoras vocant: ad animorum / hilaritatens provocantes, auribus longè gratissimae. / Omnis generis Choreae, Passomezi, cum suis vulgo Gaillardis, Alemandis, Courrantis, Branlis, &c. / Omnia ad Testudinis Tabulaturam fideliter redacta, per id genus Musices / experientissimum Artificem / EMANUELEM HADRIANUM, ANTVERPIENSEM. / Adjuncta est singulis Carminibus in gratiam eorum qui vivae Vocis concentu oblectantur / distincta Vocibus aliquot Notularum descriptio. Tum etiam Methodus ad omnes omnium Tonorum Cantiones, in gratiam illorum, qui in hac arte mediocriter versati, Musicam ad / unguem non callent, ex harmonico concentu in Scalam Testudinis, facili compendio, proprio ferè ductu redigendas. / Quorum omnium Indicem, & Musicorum unde sumpta sunt Nomina / versa pagina exhibebit. / OPUS PLANE NOVUM, NEC HACTENUS EDITUM. / [Printer's mark] / ANTVERPIAE, / Excudebat Petrus Phalesius sibi & Joanni Bellero, / Anno M. D. XCII.

98 fols. French lute tablature and mensural notation. On fol. $*1^v$: table of contents. Dedication on fol. *2 headed "ORNATISSIMO SPECTABILIQUE VIRO CAESARI CINI, APUD ANTVERPIANOS MERCATORI, DOMINO ET AMICO SUO OPTIMO MERITO," and signed "Antverpiae, X. KAL. JANUARII. 1591. Tuae Humanitati deditissimus Emanuel Adriani." On fols. $*2^v$–*12: instructions for playing the lute interspersed with preludes. Fol. *13 = fol. 1. Attributions to composers are taken from the table of contents. For some of the intabulations two or more voices of the vocal model in mensural notation are included on the page facing the lute arrangement. These voices are indicated in the following inventory by S, A, T, and B, nos. 23–66. All of the other compositions are for solo lute. Beginning with no. 67, S, A, T, and B following dance titles indicate clefs of the instrumental parts written in mensural notation and meant to be played with the lute. For a discussion of Adriansen and his lute books see SpiessA.

Copies in: D:W, F:Pm, F:Pn, GB:Lbm.[1]

	fol.	
1	*4	*Praeludium Primi Toni*
2	$*4^v$	*Praeludium Primi Toni ex Ffaut* (a transposed version of no. 1)
3	*5	*Preludium Secundi Toni ex Gsolreut*
4	$*5^v$	*Praeludium Tertii Toni* (compare no. 22 below)
5	*6	*Praeludium Quarti Toni ex Elami*
6	$*6^v$	*Praeludium Quinti Toni*
7	$*6^v$	*Praeludium Sexti Toni ex Ffaut*
8	*7	*Praeludium Septimi Toni ex Dlasolre*
9	$*7^v$	*Praeludium Octavi Toni ex Gsolreut*
10	*8	*Praeludium Noni Toni ex Dlasolre* (compare no. 18 below)

11 *8^v *Praeludium eiusdem Toni ex Ffaut* (a transposed version of no. 10 above)

12 *9 *Praeludium Decimi Toni ex Gsolreut*

13 *9^v *Praeludium Undecimi Toni ex Csolfaut*

14 *10 *Preludium Duodecimi Toni ex Gsolreut* (a transposed version of no. 13 above)

15 *10^v *Preludium Duodecimi Toni ex Ffaut*

16 *11 [*Phantasia*] *Primi Toni in Dlasolre*

17 *12 *Venga quel bel narciso* (STB)

fol.

18 1 *Fantasia Prima* (compare no. 10 above)

19 1^v *Fantasia 2*

20 2 *Fantasia 3*

21 2^v *Fantasia 4*

22 3 *Fantasia 5* (compare no. 4 above)

23 3^v *Quella che gl'occhi* (SB) Gio. Ferretti (Vogel: Ferretti 19 [1573], no. 1)

24 4^v *Qual vive Salamandra* (SB) Luca Marenzio (Vogel: Marenzio 2 [1584], no. 5)

25 5^v *Piangea filli* (SB) Luca Marenzio (Vogel: Marenzio 9 [1589], p. 20)

26 6^v *Anchor che col partire* (SB) Cypriano de Rore (SCMA VI, 45)

27 7^v *Ogni belta* (SB) Gio. Palestrina (Vogel: Palestrina 12 [1586], p. 26)

28 8^v *Su su su su ch'el giorno* (SB) Claudin le Jeusne (Vogel: Le Jeune [1585], p. 85)

29 9^v *Dolce fiamella* (SB) Gio. Maria Nanino (Vogel: Gio. Maria Nanino 5 [1587], no. 4)

30 10^v *Hor va canzona mia* (SB) Gio. Ferretti (Vogel: Ferretti 7 [1568], p. 2)

31 11^v *M'e forza* (SB) Gio. Ferretti (Vogel: Ferretti 22 [1585], p. 23)

32 12^v *Io che tropp'alt'amor* (SB) Gio. Ferretti (Vogel: Ferretti 7 [1568], p. 6)

33 13^v *Sei tanto gratiosa* (SB) Gio. Ferretti (Vogel: Ferretti 7 [1568], p. 5)

34 14^v *Non al suo amante* (SB) Noë Faignient *a 4*

35 15^v *Cantai mentre ch'arsi* (SB) Cypriano de Rore *a 5* (Vogel: Rore 2 [1544], no. 5)

36 16^v *Susann'un jour* (SB) Orlando de Lasso *a 5* (LassoW XIV, 29)

37 18^v *Donna crudel* (SB) Gio. Ferretti (Vogel: Ferretti 7 [1568], no. 2)

38 19^v *Le Rossignol plaisant* (SB) Orlando di Lasso = 1584_6, no. 25

39 20^v *Sola solette* (SB) Giro. Conversi (Vogel: Conversi 2 [1572], p. 9)

40 21^v *Vestiva i colli* (SB) Gio. Palestrina (PalO IX, 117)

22^v 2a pars *Cosi le chiome*

41 23^v *Susann'un Jour* (SB) Claudin le Jeusne (RISM 1572_2, fol. 73)

42 25^v *Tirsi morir volea* (SB) Luca Marenzio (MarenW I, 12)

26^v 2a pars *Frenò Tirsi*

26^v 3a pars *Cosi morirò*

43 27^v *Dolce amorose* (SB) Gio. Ferretti (Vogel: Ferretti 2 [1576], p. 4)

44 28^v *Non mi togl'ben mio* (SB) Marc'Antonio Ingegneri (Vogel: Rore 33 [1569], p. 5: Rore)

45 29^v *Gionto m'hamor* (SB) (RISM 1583_{15}, fol. 4) d'Incerto

46 30^v *Come poss'io morir* (SB) Gio. Ferretti (Vogel: Ferretti 7 [1568], p. 4)

47 31^v *Che fa hogg'il mio sole* (SB) Luca Marenzio (MarenW I, 18)

48 32^v *Un tempo sospirava* (SB) Gio. Ferretti (Vogel: Ferretti 2 [1576], p. 20)

49 33^v *Quando mirai* (SB) Gio. Ferretti (Vogel: Ferretti 2 [1576], p. 21)

50 34^v *La nuict le jour* (SB) Andrea Pevernage

35^v 2a pars *Hasté le pas*

51 36^v *Sonno scendesti in terra* (SB) Stefano Felis (Vogel: Felis 4 [1585], p. 6)

37^v 2a pars *Tu la ritorn'a riva*

52 38^v *Veni in hortum meum* (SB) Orlando de Lasso = 1584_6, no. 21

53 40^v *In te Domine speravi* (SSB) Lupus Hellinc *a5* (RISM 1537_1, no. 16)

42^v 2a pars *Quoniam fortitudo*

54 43^v *In te Domine speravi* (SSB) Orlando de Lasso *a6* (LassoW XVII, 87)

46^v 2a pars *Quoniam fortitudo*

55 49^v *Tulerunt Dominum meum* (SB) N. Gombert *a6* (CW XXIII, 22: Josquin)

56 51^v *Pater noster* (SB) Andrea Pevernage

57 52^v *Chamberiere allez tost* (SB) (LesLRB, art. 306, fol. 21: Planson)

58 53 *Nous estions trois jeunes filles* (SATB) (LesLRB, art. 306, fol. 7)

59 53^v *Dibedibedon la la la laissons melancolie* (SATB)

60 54 *La rousée du joly mois de May* [2] (SATB) (LesLRB, art. 306, fol. 38: Planson)

61 54^v *Par un matin la belle s'est levée* (SATB) (LesLRB, art. 306, fol. 28: Planson)

62 55 *Chi mira gl'occhi* (SB) (Vogel: Vecchi 21 [1591], no. 6: Vecchi)

63 55^v *Tutto lo tempo* (SB) Giacomo Celano (Vogel: Celano [1582], p. 8)

64 56 *La fiera vist'a* (STB) Luca Marenzio *a3*

65 56^v *Fuggirò tant'Amore* (STB) Luca Marenzio *a3* (Vogel: Marenzio 84 [1589], p. 4)

66 57 *Belle bergere* (SB) (RISM 1597_{11}, fol. 6)

67 57^v *Galiarda Prima* (SB)

68 58^v *Galiarda 2* (SB)

69 59^v *Galiarda Englesa 3* (SB)

70 60^v *Galiarda 4* (SB)

71 61^v *Galiarda 5* (SB) (1599_6, no. 20)

72 62^v *Passomezo in b mol ex Dlasolre*

63^v *Galiarda in b mol ex Dlasolre*

73 64^v *Passomezo in b mol ex Csolfaut*

66 *Galiarda per b mol in Csolfaut*

74 67^v *Passomezo per b mol in Ffaut*

68^v *Galiarda per b mol in Ffaut*

75 69^v *Passomezo per b mol in Gsolreut*

71 *Reprinse de Passomezo in Gsolreut*

71 *Galiarda per b mol in Gsolreut*

76 72^v *Passomezo per b dur in Ffaut*

74 *Galiarda per B dure in Ffaut*

77 75^v *Passomezo per B dure in Gsolreut*

76^v *Galiarda per B dure in Gsolreut*

78 77 *Passomezo per B dure in Csolfaut*

78 *Galiarda per B dure in Csolfaut*

79 79 *Passomezo per B dure in Bfabemi*

79^v *Galiarda per B dure in Bfabemi*

80 80 *Passomezo per B dure in Dlasolre*

80 *Galiarda per B dure in Dlasolre*

81 80^v *Almande de Court*

80^v *Reprinse*

82 81 *Almande de son Altezze*

83 81^v *Almande*

82 *Reprinse*

84 82 *Courante*

85 82^v *Branles*

86 83^v *Branle del Campo*

87 84 *Le grand Ballo du Court*

88 85 *Branle double*

89 86 *Fit porta Christi pervia* (SB)

[1] Copies were in D:Bds (formerly in the Wolffheim library; see WolffC I, 1183), D:Hs, and F:AS.

[2] Mod. ed. of the vocal model and the intabulation in VerA, no. 1.

1592_7

MERULO, CLAUDIO

CANZONI. / D'INTAVOLATURA D'ORGANO / DI CLAUDIO MERULO DA CORREGGIO / A QUATTRO VOCI, FATTE ALLA FRANCESE. / Novamente da lui date in luce, & con ogni diligentia corrette. / LIBRO PRIMO. / AL SERENISSIMO PRENCIPE DI PARMA, ET PIACENZA / IL SIGNOR RANUCCIO FARNESE. / [Printer's mark] / In Venetia Appresso Angelo Gardano. / M. D. LXXXXII.

43 fols. Keyboard score. Dedication on fol. $A1^v$ headed "Al Serenissimo Prencipe

di Parma, et Piacenza, il Sig. Ranuccio Farnese," and signed "Di Parma il di 27. Maggio 1592," reprinted in KrebsD, p. 378, and SartMS, p. 75. Fol. A2 = fol. 1. On fol. 43: table of contents. The entire collection is reprinted in MeruC. The four pieces followed by an asterisk are reprinted in versions for instrumental ensemble in MeruCan after I:VEcap, Cod. MCXXVIII. For further information see DiseM. All of the compositions are for solo keyboard.

Copy in: CH:Bu.

	fol.	
1	1	*Canzon a 4 dita la Bovia**
2	7	*Canzon a 4 dita La Zambeccara**[1]
3	12v	*Canzon a 4 dita La Gratiosa**[2]
4	17v	*Canzon a 4 dita La Cortese**[3] (compare 1598_4, no. 2)
5	21v	*Canzon a 4 dita La Benvenuta* (compare 1598_4, no. 3)
6	26	*Canzon a 4 dita La Leonora*[4]
7	28v	*Canzon a 4 dita L'Albergata*
8	33	*Canzon a 4 dita La Rolanda*[5]
9	36	*Canzoǹ a 4 dita Petit Jacquet* (compare I:Bc, MS Q 26, no. 27: Courtois)

[1] Mod. ed. in DiseM, p. 317; FerandIM, no. 20; and KinO, p. 296.

[2] MeruCan, no. 6, is headed "Canzon dita La Zerata."

[3] MeruCan, no. 5, is headed "Canzon dita la Jussona."

[4] Mod. ed. in WolfME, no. 43.

[5] Mod. ed. in DallaA, no. 10, and KinO, p. 300.

1592_8

RADINO, GIOVANNI MARIA

IL PRIMO LIBRO / D'INTAVOLATURA / DI BALLI D'ARPICORDO / DI GIO. MARIA RADINO / ORGANISTA IN S. GIO. DI VERDARA / IN PADOVA. / Nuovamente Composti, & con ogni diligenza Stampati. / [Printer's mark] / IN VENETIA, Appresso Giacomo Vincenti. M. D. XCII.

26 fols. Keyboard score. Dedication on fol. 1v headed "A I MOLTO ILLUSTRI SIG. IL SIG. ADOLFO WOLFGANGO, TETERICO, QUINTINO, FRATELLI: ET GIOVANNI WOLFGANGO, GIORGIO, CUGINI. Baroni d'Altan in Goldburgo, & Mursterlen, &c. Sig. & Patroni miei Colendiss.," and signed "Di Padova li XX. Marzo. M. D. XCII. Delle VV. SS. Molto Illustri Devotissimo Servitore Gio. Maria Radino Organista di San Gio. di Verdara," reprinted in SartMS, p. 73. Fol. 2 = p. 1. The entire volume is reprinted in facsimile and in a modern edition in RadiA. MoeDM contains a thematic index of the volume (p. 468) and concordances (p. 282). Radino arranged the same pieces for solo lute (= 1592_9). All of the compositions are for solo keyboard.

Copy in: B:Br.

	p.	
1	1	*Pass'e mezo*
	14	*Gagliarda del ditto Pass'e mezo*
2	24	*Padoana p[rima]*
3	31	*Padoana Seconda*
4	39	*Gagliarda Prima*
5	41	*Gagliarda Seconda*
6	45	*Gagliarda Terza*
7	48	*Gagliarda Quarta*

1592_9

RADINO, GIOVANNI MARIA

INTAVOLATURA / DI BALLI / PER SONAR DI LIUTO / DI GIO. MARIA RADINO / [Printer's mark] / IN VENETIA M D XCII / Appresso Giacomo Vincenti.

26 fols. Italian lute tablature. The entire volume is reprinted in a modern edition in RadiL. These are the same pieces as in 1592_8, arranged for solo lute.[1]

Copy in: I:Fc.

[1] Mod. ed. of "Gagliarda prima" in EC, pt. I, vol. II, p. 664.

1592_{10}

ROGNIONO, RICHARDO

PASSAGGI / PER POTERSI / ESSERCITARE / Nel Diminuire terminatamente con ogni sorte / d'Instromenti. / ET ANCO DIVERSI PASSAGGI / Per la semplice voce humana. / DI RICHARDO ROGNIONO / ESPULSO DI VAL TAVEGIA, / Musico dell'Eccellentissimo Duca di Terranova Governator Generale / nelle Stato di Milano per Sua Maestà Cattolica. / CON PRIVILEGIO. / [Printer's mark] / IN VENETIA, / Appresso Giacomo Vincenti. M. D. XCII.

35 fols. Mensural notation. The title is placed within an ornamental border. Dedication on fol. A2 headed "SERENISS. GUILIELMO COMITI PALATINO RHENI, UTRIUSQUE BAVARIAE DUCI, Domino meo colendiss.," and signed "Mediolani, Die x. April. M. D. XCII. Richardus Rognionus." On fol. A2ᵛ: preface headed "AI VIRTUOSI LETTORI L' AUTTORE." The second part of the volume begins on fol. C1 with a new title page, placed within an ornamental border:

> IL VERO MODO / DI DIMINUIRE / Con tutte le sorte di Stromenti da corde, da fiato, / & anco per la voce humana. / DI RICHARDO ROGNIONO / ESPULSO DI VAL TAVEGIA, / Musico dell'Eccellentissimo Duca di Terranova Governator Generale / nella Stato di Milano per Sua Masetà Cattolica. / Parte Seconda. / CON PRIVILEGIO. / [Printer's mark] / IN VENETIA, / Appresso Giacomo Vincenti. M. D. XCII.

Preface to Part Two on fol. C1ᵛ headed: "AI VIRTUOSI LETTORI L'AUTTORE."

Part One contains various figuration patterns (scales, ascending and descending thirds in several rhythmic patterns, and so forth) for practice. Part Two contains cadence formulas and other stereotyped figures along with elaborate diminutions on them. Several complete individual voice parts (listed below) with diminutions are included at the end of Part Two. HorsS, HorsWT and KuV, p. 136, include examples from this volume. A microfilm of the copy that was in D:Bgk is now in the Deutsches Musikgeschichtliches Archiv in Cassel (D: Km).

	fol.	
1	H2	*Domine quando veneris*
2	H2ᵛ	*Ancor che col partire* (SCMA VI, 45: Rore)
	H3	The same "Per sonar con ogni sorte di Stromento"
	H4	The same "Facile per la Viola bastarda"
	H4ᵛ	The same "Per la Viola bastarda"
3	I1ᵛ	*Un gai Bergier Per Diminuire sopra una parte* (RieH II, 462: Crecquillon)
	I2ᵛ	The same "Facile per la Viola bastarda"
	I3	The same "Per la Viola bastarda in altro modo"

1592_{11}

VEROVIO, SIMONE

DILETTO / SPIRITUALE / CANZONETTE / A tre et a quattro voci / composte da diver/si ecc.ᵐⁱ Musici / Con L'intavolatura del Cimbalo / Et Liuto / ROMA / 1592

24 fols. Mensural notation, keyboard score, and Italian lute tablature. The title is placed within an ornamental border; at the top is "Te Deum laudamus," beneath the title "Martin van Buyten incidit." Dedication on fol. 2 headed "Al Ill.ᵐᵒ et molto R.ᵒ Sig.ʳᵉ et mio Padrone oss.ᵐᵒ il Sig.ʳᵉ Antonio Boccapadule," and signed "Di Roma alli x di Novembre M. D. Lxxxxii. D. V. S. Ill.ʳᵉ et molto R.ᵈᵃ Ser.ʳᵉ humiliss. Simone Verovio," reprinted in SartMS, p. 54, after 1586_8. On fol. 23ᵛ: table of contents. The compositions identified by the superior letter *a* (ᵃ) are reprinted in AV II, 184–194. The following canons appear at the bottoms of the right-hand pages:

	fol.	
1	title page	*Laudate Dominum*
2	3	*Ad Dominum cum tribularer a4*
3	7	*Auxilium meum a4*
4	8	*In te Domine speravi a5*
5	10	*De profundis clamavi a4*
6	13	*Illumina oculos meos a3*
7	14	*In Domino letabitur a4*

In each case only one part is written out. For other editions see 1586_8. The vocal setting of each piece appears on the left page of each opening, keyboard and lute intabulations on the right page. Nos. 1–15 are *a3*, nos. 16–22 *a4*.

Copy in: I:Bc.

	fol.	
1	2v	*Jesu decus angelicum*[1] Felice Anerio
2	3v	*Spiega mondo maligno*[2] Luca Marentio
3	4v	*Qual paura* Luca Marentio
4	5v	*O Jesu mi dulcissime*[a3] Felix Anerius
5	6v	*Jesu summa benignitas*[a4] Rugieri Giovanelli
6	7v	*JESU sole serenior*[a] Rugieri Giovanelli
7	8v	*Tu mentis delectatio*[a] Rugeri Giovanelli
8	9v	*Tunc amplexus* Felice Anerio
9	10v	*Rex virtutum* Felice Anerio
10	11v	*Giesu sommo conforto*[a5] Simone Verovio
11	12v	*Jesu Rex admirabilis*[6] Joan Petri Aloysii Prenestini [Palestrina]
12	13v	*Tua Jesu dilectio*[7] Joannis Petri Aloysii Praenestini
13	14v	*Se questa valle* Rinaldo del Mel
14	15v	*Deh lasciam dunque* Rinaldo del Mel
15	16v	*Scalda signor* Jacomo Peetrino
16	17v	*Jesu spes penitentibus* Joan Maria Nanini
17	18v	*Quando cor nostrum visitas* Jo. Maria Nanini
18	19v	*O gloriosa donna* Fran.co Soriano
19	20v	*Uscio del Ciel tu sei* Francesco Soriano
20	21v	*Jesu flos matris*[8] Joan Aloysii Praenestini
21	22v	*O beatum incendium* Felice Anerio
22	23v	*Jesus in pace imperat*[9] Jo. Mariae Nanini

1 Mod. ed. in KinO, p. 280.
2 Facs. of fol. 3 in KinsP, p. 153, after 1586₈.
3 Mod. ed. in KinO, p. 281.
4 Facs. of fols. 6v and 7 in WolfH II, 256.
5 Mod. ed. in TebAP, p. 124.
6 Mod. ed. in PalW XXX, 3. Facs. of fols. 12v and 13 in PalW XXX, after p. xix. Tablature repr. in SchlechtG, no. 53.
7 Mod. ed. in PalW XXX, 4.
8 Mod. ed. in PalW XXX, 5.
9 Facs. of fol. 24 in KinsP, p. 153, after 1586₈.

1592₁₂

WAISSEL, MATTHÄUS

Lautenbuch / Darinn / VON DER TA/ bulatur und Application der Lauten / gründlicher und voller Unterricht: Sampt ausserlesenen Deudt/schen und Polnischen Tentzen, Passamezen, Gailliarden, Deudtschen Vi/lanellen, Neapolitanen, und Phantasien: / Auff der Lauten zu schlagen gantz fleissig zugerichtet, und allen Lieb/habern dieser Kunst zu nutz und gefallen in den Druck gegeben, / Durch / MATTHAEUM WAISSELIUM / Bartensteinensem Borussum. / [Cut of a lutenist] / Gedruckt zu Franckfurt an der Oder, durch Andream / Eichorn, Anno: M. D. XCII. / Werden verkaufft bey Paul Brackfelt.

28 fols. German lute tablature. On fol. A1v: table of contents. Dedication on fol. A2 headed "Den Ehrnvesten, Namhafften, Ehrbarn, unnd wolweisen Herrn: Bürgermeistern, unnd Rhaten, Auch Herrn Richtern, unnd Scheppen, der löblicher Fürstlicher dreyer Stedte Königsberg in Preussen: Altenstad, Kneiphoff, und Lebenich. Meinen grosgünstigen Herrn," and signed "Gegeben zu Franckfurt an der Oder am Tage Margarethe. Anno: 1592. E. E. und W. dienstwilliger Mattheus Waissel von Bartenstein, weyland Pfarrer zu Lanckheim." On fol. A3: poem in Latin headed "In Chelyn Matthaei Waisselii," and signed "Sal. Wey. Sil." On fol. A3v: preface "An den Leser," printed in KosackL, p. 68. Beginning on fol. A4: instructions for playing the lute, headed "Von der Tabulatur und Application der Lauten gründlicher und voller Unterricht." A thematic index of the volume is printed in KosackL, p. 108. The volume is described in GrimmM, pp. 104–107, which includes facsimiles of the title page and of fol F4v. All of the compositions are for solo lute.

Copy in: D:W.[1]

	fol.	
1	D1	*1. Tantz*[2]
	D1	*Sprung*[2]

No.	Fol.	Contents
2	D1	*2. Tantz*
	D1	*Sprung*
3	D1v	*3. Tantz*
	D1v	*Sprung*
4	D1v	*4. Tantz*
	D1v	*Sprung*
† 5	D2	*1. Tantz* [3]
6	D2	*2. Tantz*
7	D2	*3. Tantz*
8	D2	*4. Tantz*
9	D2v	*5. Tantz*
10	D2v	*6. Tantz*
11	D2v	*7. Tantz*
12	D2v	*8. Tantz*
13	D3	*9. Tantz*
14	D3	*10. Tantz*
15	D3	*11. Tantz*
16	D3	*12. Tantz*
17	D3v	*1. Passemezo anticho* [5]
	D4	*El suo Saltarello*
	D4	*Le Represe*
18	D4v	*2. Passemezo anticho*
	E1	*El suo Saltarello*
	E1	*Le Represe*
19	E1v	*3. Passemezo Commune* [6]
	E1v	*Le Represe*
	E2	*El suo Saltarello*
	E2	*Le Represe*
20	E2v	*4. Passemezo Commune* = 1582_1, no. 17a
	E2v	*Le Represe*
	E3	*El suo Saltarello* = 1582_1, no. 17b
	E3	*Le Represe*
21	E3v	*1. Gailliarda. La cara cosa* [7]
	E4	*1. Gailliarda. La cara cosa* (another version)
22	E4v	*2. Gailliarda. La Rocha el fuso* (1571_5, no. 43)
23	F1	*3. Gailliarda. La Traditora* (1571_5, no. 36)
24	F1v	*4. Gailliarda. Chi passa*
	F2	*4. Gailliarda. Chi passa* (another version)
25	F2v	*5. Gailliarda*
26	F2v	*6. Gailliarda*
27	F3	*7. Gailliarda*
28	F3	*8. Gailliarda*
29	F3v	*9. Gailliarda*
30	F3v	*10. Gailliarda*
31	F4	*11. Gailliarda*
32	F4	*12. Gailliarda*
33	F4v	*1. Ohn dich muss ich mich aller Freuden massen* [8] (PubAPTM XIX no. 1: Regnart)
34	F4v	*2. Wen ich gedenck der Stund* (PubAPTM XIX, no. 3: Regnart)
35	F4v	*3. Nu bin Ich einmahl frey* (PubAPTM XIX, no. 3: Regnart)
36	G1	*4. Venus du und dein Kind* (PubAPTM XIX, no. 8: Regnart)
37	G1	*5. Von nöthen ist* [9] (PubAPTM XIX, no. 9: Regnart)
38	G1	*6. Wer wird denn trösten mich* (PubAPTM XIX, no. 16: Regnart)
39	G1	*7. Ich bin zu Lange gewesen*
40	G1	*8. Wenn Ich der Zeit*
41	G1v	*1. Canzonette de amore* [10] (Vogel: Vecchi 21 [1591], no. 1: Vecchi)
42	G1v	*2. Mentre io campai contento* (Vogel: Vecchi 21 [1591], no. 2: Vecchi)
43	G1v	*3. Occhi ridenti io moro* (Vogel: Vecchi 21 [1591], no. 3: Vecchi)
44	G2	*4. Son questi i crispi crini* (Vogel: Vecchi 21 [1591], no. 4: Vecchi)
45	G2	*5. Madonna io v'ho da dir una novella* (Vogel: Vecchi 21 [1591], no. 5: Vecchi)
46	G2	*6. Chi mira gli occhi tuoi* (Vogel: Vecchi 21 [1591], no. 6: Vecchi)
47	G2v	*7. Neapolitana*
48	G2v	*8. Neapolitana*
49	G3	*1. Phantasia* [11]
50	G3v	*2. Phantasia*
51	G3v	*3. Phantasia* [12]
52	G4	*4. Phantasia* [13]

[1] Copies were in D:Bds, and D:SCHLO.

[2] Heading on fol. D1: "Folgen erstlich Deudtsche Tentze." Mod. ed. of no. 1 in EnI, app., p. 1, and TapS, p. 51.

[3] Heading on fol. D2: "Folgen Polnische Tentze."

[4] Mod. ed. in OpieD, no. 3.

[5] Heading on fol. D3v: "Folgen Passemezen."

[6] Mod. ed. in EnI, app., p. 2.

[7] Heading on fol. E3v: "Folgen Gailliarden."

[8] Heading on fol. F4v: "Folgen Deudtsche Vilanellen."

[9] Mod. ed. in RaL, p. 336.

[10] Heading on fol. G1v: "Folgen Neapolitanen."

[11] Heading on fol. G3: "Folgen Phantasien." Mod. ed. of no. 49 in WaissP, no. 1.

[12] Mod. ed. in EnI, app., p. 14.

[13] Mod. ed. in EnI, app., p. 13.

[1592]$_{13}$

WAISSEL, MATTHÄUS

TABULATURA / Allerley künstlicher Preambulen, aus/erlesener Deudtscher und Polnischer Tentze, Passemezen, Gailliar/den, Padoanen, Pavanen, und Branlen: / Auff der Lauten zu schlagen gantz fleissig zugerichtet, und al/len Liebhabern dieser Kunst zu nutz, und gefallen, in den / Druck gegeben / Durch / MATTHAEUM WAISSELIUM / Bartensteinsem, Borussum. / [Cut of a lutenist] / Gedruckt zu Franckfurt an der Oder, durch Andream / Eichorn. Anno MDXCII.

48 fols. (?) German lute tablature. On fol. A1^{v}: table of contents. Dedication on fol. A2 headed "Den gestrengen, Ehrenuesten, Achtbaren, Ehrbaren hoch und wolweisen Herrn: Herrn Burggraven, Bürgermeistern und Herrn des Rhats: Auch Herrn Richtern und Schöppen der löblichen Königlichen Stadt Danzig. Meinen grossgünstigen Herrn," and signed "Gegeben zu Franckfurt an der Oder am Tage Laurentii Anno MDXCII. E. G. Ehrenu. und Hochw: williger Diener Mattaeus Waissel von Bartenstein weiland Pfarrer zu Lanckheim." On fol. A3: poem in Latin headed "Chelyn Matthaei Waisselli Epigramma," signed "Mich. Abelus Franck." On fol. A3^{v}: preface "An den Leser," printed in KosackL, pp. 69–70. A thematic index of this volume is printed in KosackL, pp. 111–119, which includes a brief description of the prefatory matter. Contents = 1591$_{13}$. Copies, now lost, were in D:Bds, D:LÜh, and D:SCHLO. All of the compositions were for solo lute.

1592$_{14}$

WAISSEL, MATTHÄUS

TABULATURA / Guter gemeiner Deudtscher Tentze, / Nicht allein auff einer Lauten in sonderheit, Sondern auch, auff / zweyen Lauten, durch Quarten, zusamen, / zuschlagen. / Für die Schüler dieser Kunst mit fleiss zugerichtet / und in den Druck gegeben. / Durch / MATTHAEUM WAISSELIUM / Bartensteinensem, Borussum, / Zu Ehren und wolgefallen. / Den Edlen und Ehrnvesten, Fabian von Lehndorff, und Bastian / von Lehndorff, Gebrüdern, Erbsass zu Labab, und Steinort, etc: / Und auch / Den Edlen und Ehrvesten Melchiorn Kannachern, und Hectorn / Kannachern, Gebrüdern, zu Paislaken, und Schwansfeld, etc. Erbsass. Besondern / Liebhabern der Music, Und meinen grosgünstigen Junckern. / [Cut of a lutenist] / Gedruckt zu Franckfurt an der Oder, durch Andream / Eichorn. Anno: M. D. XCII.

4 fols. German lute tablature. A thematic index of the volume is printed in KosackL, pp. 120–121. The volume is described in GrimmM, p. 106. All of the compositions are for two lutes.

Copy in: D:W.[1]

	fol.	
1	A1^{v}	*1. Tantz*
	A1^{v}	*Sprung*
2	A1^{v}	*2. Tantz*
	A2	*Sprung*
3	A2	*3. Tantz*
	A2	*Sprung*
4	A2^{v}	*4. Tantz*
	A2^{v}	*Sprung*
5	A2^{v}	*5. Tantz*
	A2^{v}	*Sprung*
6	A3	*6. Tantz*
	A3	*Sprung*
7	A3^{v}	*7. Tantz*
	A3^{v}	*Sprung*
8	A4	*8. Tantz*
	A4	*Sprung*

[1] A copy was in D:SCHLO.

[1592]$_{15}$

BELLÈRE, JEAN, PUBLISHER

Le Jardinet du Cistre vulgaire, contenant fantasies excellentes, et chansons mélodieuses avec des passomezes convenablement changées en plusieurs tons: Paduana, Galliardas, Amandes, Bransles, Voltes et Courantes: et autres choses plaisantes: réduits en tabulature du subdit Cistre nouvellement imprimees. En Anvers, Jean Bellère, 1592.

This volume of music for cittern, now lost, is listed in BrunetML, Supplément, col. 691; DraudiusBC, p. 1622; DraudiusBE, p. 212; and StellMB, p. 24. See also [1575]₇ above.

[1593]₁

BARLEY, WILLIAM

A new booke of Citterne Lessons with a plaine and easie instruction for to learne the Tableture, to conduct and dispose thy hand, sette forth to the Tunes of many Psalmes as they be sung in Churches, also Pavins, Galliards and divers other sweet and easy Lessons. Pri. for William Barley 1593.

This volume, now lost, is listed in DartC, p. 51; DartHL, p. 15; MaunC, p. 18; and SteeleE, p. 101. DeakinO, p. 50, lists the above title but without date. For 1593 DeakinO, p. 50, and also DeakinMB, p. 8, cite the following title: "A most perfecte and true Instruction whereby a man maye learne by his owne industrie to play on the Cytterne without the help of any teacher."

1593₂

CONFORTO, GIOVANNI LUCA

Breve et facile maniera d'essercitarsi ad ogni scolaro. non / solamente a far passaggi sopra tutte le note che si desidera / per cantare, et far la dispositione leggiadra, et in diversi / modi nel loro valore con le cadenze, ma ancora per potere / da se senza maestri scrivere ogni opera et aria passeggiata / che vorranno, et come si notano. et q.^{sto} ancora serve per quei che / sonano di Viola, o d'altri instrom^{ti} da fiato per sciogliere la mano / et la lingua et per diventar possess.^{ri} dell sogg.^{ti} et far altre in/ventioni da se fatte da Gio. Luca Conforto.[1]

20 fols. Mensural notation. The title is placed within an ornamental border. On fol. 1^{v} (= p. 2): "In Roma con licentia de Superiori et Privileggio. 1593 [or 1603?]," printed beneath a cut of Apollo playing the *lira da braccio* to animals. Pages 3–32 contain a systematic table of ornaments. Conforto first gives examples for filling in intervals with *passaggi* (beginning with ascending and descending seconds, then thirds, fourths, fifths, unisons, octaves, and so on). Next (on p. 25) he presents a series of conventional ornaments (*groppi* and *trilli*), and finally he gives examples for decorating several cadential formulas.[2] On pp. 33–40 (= fols. *1–*4) is an explanation of the preceding examples, headed "Dichiaratione sopra li passaggi di Gio. Luca Conforti." The volume is reprinted in facsimile in ConfB, where the date is given as "1593 (?1603)."

Copies in: GB:Lbm, GB:Lbmh, I:Bc.

[1] Facs. of title page in MGG II, col. 1627.
[2] Some of the musical examples are repr. in KuV, p. 115.

1593₃

DIRUTA, GIROLAMO

IL / TRANSILVANO / DIALOGO / SOPRA IL VERO MODO DI SONAR ORGANI, / ET ISTROMENTI DA PENNA, / DEL R. P. GIROLAMO DIRUTA / PERUGINO, / Dell'ordine de' Frati Minori Conu. di San Francesco / ORGANISTA DEL DUOMO / DI CHIOGGIA. / Nel quale facilmente, & presto s'impara di conoscere sopra la Tastatura il luogo di / ciascuna parte, & come nel Diminuire si deveno portar le mani, & il modo d'in/tendere la Intavolatura; provando la verità, & necessità delle sue Regole, con le / Toccate di diversi eccellenti Organisti, poste nel fine del Libro. / Opera nuovamente ritrovata, utilissima, & necessaria a Professori d'Organo. / CON PRIVILEGIO. / [Printer's mark] / In Venetia, Appresso Giacomo Vincenti. M. D. XCIII.[1]

40 fols. Keyboard score. The title is placed within an ornamental border. Dedication on fol. *2 headed "AL SERENISSIMO PRENCIPE DI TRANSILVANIA. IL SIGNOR SIGISMONDO BATTORI." and signed "Di Venetia li. 10. Aprile 1593. D. V. Altezza Serenissima Devotissimo servo & Oratore. Fra Girolamo Diruta."[1] On fol. *2^{v}: preface headed "L'AUTTORE DELL'OPERA AL PRUDENTE LET-

TORE." On fol. *4: foreword headed "A LETTORI. CLAUDIO MERULO da Correggio." All of this prefatory material is printed in SartMS, pp. 77–81. Some of it is reprinted in KrebsD, which includes a German translation of a part of the dialogue. The dialogue begins on fol. *5 (= fol. 1). On fol. 36ᵛ: table of contents. This is the earliest Italian method for keyboard instruments. Contents = 1597₃. There were later editions in 1612 and 1625. For further information see DannMO, pp. 3–9; HaraD; KrebsD; and ReFS, no. 49.[2] The compositions listed below are all for solo keyboard.

† Copies in: H:Ba (imperfect), I:Rla, US:Wc.

	fol.	
1	12ᵛ	*Toccata di grado del primo Tuono*[3] Girolamo Diruta
2	13ᵛ	*Toccata di salto buono del secondo Tuono*[4] Girolamo Diruta
3	15	*Toccata di salto cattivo del sesto Tuono* Girolamo Diruta
4	16ᵛ	*Toccata del terzo Tuono*[5] Claudio Merulo
5	19	*Toccata del sesto Tuono* Andrea Gabrielli
6	22	*Toccata del secondo Tuono*[6] Giovanni Gabrielli
7	24	*Toccata del Quarto Tuono*[7] Luzzasco Luzzaschi
8	25	*Toccata dell'ottavo Tuono* Antonio Romanini
9	26ᵛ	*Toccata dell'ottavo Tuono* Paolo Quagliati
10	29	*Toccata del primo Tuono*[8] Vincenzo Bell'haver
11	31	*Toccata del secondo Tuono* Gioseffo Guami
12	32ᵛ	*Toccata del decimo Tuono*[9] Andrea Gabrielli
13	34	*Toccata dell'undecimo, e duodecimo Tuono*[10] Girolamo Diruta

[1] Facs. of title page and dedication in HaraD, pp. 74 and 78. Facs. of title page only in *Library of Congress. Quarterly Journal of Current Acquisitions* VII (1950) opp. p. 19.

[2] Several musical examples are repr. in FoschA, no. 6.

[3] Mod. ed. in KrebsD, p. 383.

[4] Mod. ed. in KrebsD, p. 384.

[5] Mod. ed. in DallaA, no. 9; DallaL I, no. 4; and GuilC, p. 20.

[6] Mod. ed. in Gabri(G)CO I, no. 2; Gabri(G)W, p. 34; TorA III, 137 (after the 1625 ed.); and ValentinTo, no. 6.

[7] Mod. ed. in FoschA, no. 6, and FuserC, no. 24.

[8] Mod. ed. in DallaA, no. 8.

[9] Mod. ed. in DallaA, no. 6; DallaLO IV, no. 6; MOM, vol. 66; TorA III, 77 (after the 1625 ed.); and ValentinTo, no. 4.

[10] Mod. ed. in KrebsD, p. 386.

1593₄

GABRIELI, ANDREA AND GIOVANNI

INTONATIONI D'ORGANO / DI ANDREA GABRIELI ET DI GIO. SUO NEPOTE / ORGANISTI DELLA SERENISS. SIG. DI VENETIA IN S. MARCO / Composte sopra tutti li Dodeci Toni della Musica / Novamente Stampate & poste in luce / LIBRO PRIMO / [Printer's mark] / In Venetia Appresso Angelo Gardano / MDXXXXIII.[1]

44 fols. Keyboard score. On fol. 43ᵛ: table of contents. There is a modern edition of the compositions by Andrea in Gabri(A) I. There is a modern edition of the compositions by Giovanni in Gabri(G)W and Gabri(G)CO I, and a modern edition of the intonations by Giovanni in TorA III, 131. The complete keyboard music of Andrea Gabrieli was published in six volumes: I (1593₄), II (1595₃), III (1596₇), IV (now lost), V (1605; see SartMS, p. 133), and VI ([1571]₂ and 1605; see SartMS, p. 133). All of the compositions are for solo keyboard.

Copies in: CH:Bu, F:Pc, F:Pthibault, GB:Ob, I:Bc.

	fol.	
1	1ᵛ	*Intonationi di Gio: Gabrieli, Del Primo Tono*[2]
2	2	*Del Primo Tono. Trasportado alla Quarta alta*[3]
3	2ᵛ	*Del Secondo Tono*[4]
4	3	*Del Secondo Tono. Trasportado alla Quinta alta*
5	3ᵛ	*Del Terzo et Quarto Tono*[5]
6	4	*Del Terzo et Quarto Tono. Trasportado alla Quarta alta*[6]
7	4ᵛ	*Del Quinto Tono*
8	5	*Del Quinto Tono. Trasportado alla Quarta alta*

9	5ᵛ	*Del Sesto Tono*
10	6	*Del Sesto Tono. Trasportado alla Quarta alta*
11	6ᵛ	*Del Settimo Tono*[7]
12	7	*Del Settimo Tono. Trasportado alla Quinta bassa*
13	7ᵛ	*Del Ottavo Tono*
14	8	*Del Ottavo Tono. Trasportado alla Quarta alta*
15	8ᵛ	*Del Nono Tono*[8]
16	9	*Del Nono Tono. Trasportado alla Quinta bassa*
17	9ᵛ	*Del Decimo Tono*
18	10	*Del Decimo Tono. Trasportado alla Quarta alta*
19	10ᵛ	*Del Undecimo Tono*[8]
20	11	*Del Undecimo Tono. Trasportado alla Quarta bassa*
21	11ᵛ	*Duodecimo Tono*
22	12	*Duodecimo Tono. Trasportado alla Quinta bassa*
23	12ᵛ	*Intonationi di Andrea Gabrieli. Del Primo Tono*[9]
24	13	*Del Secondo Tono*[10]
25	13ᵛ	*Del Terzo Tono*[11]
26	14ᵛ	*Del Quarto Tono*[11]
27	15ᵛ	*Del Quinto Tono*
28	17	*Del Sesto Tono*
29	18	*Del Settimo Tono*[12]
30	20	*Del Ottavo Tono*
31	21	*Toccata di Andrea Gabrieli. Del Primo Tono*
32	23	*Toccata di Andrea Gabrieli. Del Sesto Tono*[13]
33	30	*Toccata di Andrea Gabrieli. Del Ottavo Tono*
34	36	*Toccata di Andrea Gabrieli. Del Nono Tono*

[1] Facs. of title page in MGG VI, col. 1367.
[2] Mod. ed. in BiggsT, p. 28, and FuserC, no. 6.
[3] Facs. of fol. 2 in BedbK, pl. IX.
[4] Mod. ed. in AdlerH, p. 350. Facs. of fol. 2ᵛ in MGG VI, col. 1368.
[5] Mod. ed. in DallaLO I, no. 5.
[6] Mod. ed. in WasG, no. 27b.
[7] Mod. ed. in FuserC, no. 7.
[8] Mod. ed. in ApelM I, 24, and BiggsT, p. 28.
[9] Mod. ed. in CarlH, p. 4.
[10] Mod. ed. in EinSH, no. 21.
[11] Mod. ed. in DallaA, nos. 3–4.
[12] Mod. ed. in ApelMK, p. 54; HAM, no. 135; and WasG, no. 27a.
[13] Mod. ed. in WasG, no. 28.

1593_5

MASCHERA, FIORENZO

LIBRO PRIMO DE CANZONI / DA SONARE, A QUATTRO VOCI, / DI FLORENTIO MASCHERA / Organista nel Duomo di Brescia. / Novamente con ogni diligenza ristampate. / [Printer's mark] / In Venetia Appresso Angelo Gardano. / M. D. LXXXXIII.

Four part books in mensural notation, each of 12 fols. On fol. 12ᵛ (= p. 22): table of contents. Contents = 1584_{10}. All of the compositions are for instrumental ensemble *a 4*.

Copy in: B:Br.

1593_6

RAVAL, SEBASTIANO

IL PRIMO LIBRO / DI CANZONETTE / A QUATTRO VOCI, / COMPOSTE PER IL SIG. SEBASTIANO RAVAL / Gentil'huomo Spagnuolo dell'Ordine di ubidientia di / San Gio. Battista Gierosolimitano. / [Printer's mark] / IN VENETIA, Appresso Giacomo Vincenti. 1593.

Four part books in mensural notation, each of 13 fols. The title is placed within an ornamental border. Dedication on fol. 1ᵛ of each part book headed "ALL'ILLUSTRISSIMO ET ECELL.ᴹᴼ SIGNORE ET PATRONE MIO OSSERVANDISS. IL SIGNOR MARC'ANTONIO COLONNA DUCA Di Talliacozzo, Prencipe di Paliano, Gran Conte Stabile, e Grande per la Maestà Catholica di Spagna," and signed "di Roma a di 24. Marzo. 1593. Di V. Ecclenza Illustriss. & Eccellentiss. Minor creato F. Sebastiano Raval," reprinted in GaspaC III, 252, and SartMS, p. 76. On fol. 13ᵛ (= p. 24) of each part book: table of contents. SartMS, p. 77, gives a complete list of the contents. The volume contains 20 canzonets with Italian text, and three pieces for instrumental ensemble *a 4*.

Copy in: I:Bc (S lacks title page).

p.
1 20 *Ricercar a 4. sopra una stessa fuga del nono tuono*
2 22 *Ricercar a 4. del decimo tuono*
3 23 *Ricercar a 4. del primo tuono*

1593_7

TERZI, GIOVANNI ANTONIO

DI GIO. ANTONIO TERZI / DA BERGAMO, / INTAVOLATURA DI LIUTTO, / ACCOMODATA CON DIVERSI PASSAGGI / per suonar in Concerti a duoi Liutti, & solo. / LIBRO PRIMO. / IL QUAL CONTIENE, MOTETTI, CONTRAPONTI, / Canzoni Italiane, & Francese, Madrigali, Fantasie, & Balli di diverse sorti, / Italiani, Francesi, & Alemani. / CON PRIVILEGGIO. / [Printer's mark] / IN VENETIA, / Appresso Ricciardo Amadino, / M D XCIII.

68 fols. Italian lute tablature. The title is placed within an ornamental border. Dedication on fol. 1ᵛ headed "AL MOLTO ILLUSTRE MIO SIGNORE, ET PADRONE OSSERVANDISSIMO IL SIG. CAVALIER BARTOLOMEO FINO," and signed "Di Venetia. il dì 15 di Luglio. 1593. Di V. S. Molto Illustre Divotissimo Servitore Gio: Antonio Terzi." The music begins on fol. 2 (= p. 1). On p. 134: table of contents. 1599_{11} is a second volume in the same series. The compositions identified by the superior letter *a* ([a]) are reprinted in ChilLS, pp. 98–135. MoeDM contains a thematic index of the dances (p. 470) and concordances for them (p. 282). Nos. 10–16 are arranged to be played either by two lutes "in concerto," or by solo lute. Nos. 17–27 are arranged to be played by solo lute, or as part of an instrumental ensemble (see note 4). All of the other compositions are for solo lute.

Copies in: D:W, I:Bc, I:Fn, US:NYp.

MUSIC FOR SOLO LUTE

p.
1 1 *Diligam te Domine*[1] Andrea Gabrieli *a4* (Gabr(A)C [1576], no. 1)
2 3 *Ego rogabo* Andrea Gabrieli *a4* (Gabr(A)C [1576], no. 10)
3 4 *Virgo prudentissima* Giulio Renaldi *a4*
4 7 *Tu es Pastor ovium* Palestina *a4* (PalW VI, 21)
5 9 *Angelus ad pastores*[2] Palestina *a4*
6 11 *Surrexit* Marc'Antonio Ingegnero *a5* (RISM 1583_2, no. 14)
7 13 *Qui me confessus* Claudio [Merulo] da Correggio *a5*
8 14 *Veni in hortum meum* Orlando Lasso *a5* (LassoW V, 120)
9 17 *Ad dominum cum tribularer* Gio. Cavaccio *a5*

MUSIC FOR TWO LUTES, OR FOR SOLO LUTE

10 19 *Vestiva i colli* Palestina *a5* (PalO IX, 117)
20 *Contraponto sopra Vestiva i colli per sonar a duoi liutti in quarta o in concerto*
24 2a pars *Cose le chiome mie*
25 *Contraponto sopra il predetto per suonar come di sopra*
11 28 *S'ogni mio ben*[a] Striggio *a6* (Vogel: Striggio 3 [1566], no. 20)
29 *Contraponto sopra S'ogni mio ben, per suonar come di sopra, ma a l'unisono*[a]
31 *Un'altro Contraponto sopra l'istesso a l'unisono*[a]
12 34 *Anchor ch'io possa dire* Striggio *a6* (Vogel: Striggio 3 [1566], no. 3)
35 *Contraponto sopra Anchor ch'io, &c. a l'unisono per suonar a doi liutti, & in concerto*
13 38 *Susanne un jour. Canzon Francese a la quarta* (LassoW XIV, 29: Lasso)
39 *Contraponto sopra Susanne un jour di Orlando a 5: per suonare a doi liutti in quarta, & in Concerto*
14 43 *Petit Jaquet, Canzon francese*[3] Claudio [Merulo] da Correggio *a4* (compare 1592_7, no. 9, and I:Bc, MS Q 26, no. 27: Courtois)
44 *Contraponto sopra Petit Jaquet, Canzon francese di Clau. da Coreggio per suonar come di sopra*

15 48 *Canzone a doi liutti unisoni* Claudio [Merulo] da Correggio *a 4*

50 *Secondo liutto in risposta*

16 52 *Canzone a duoi liutti unisoni* Claudio [Merulo] da Correggio *a 4*

55 *Secondo Liutto*

MUSIC FOR SOLO LUTE, OR FOR LUTE "IN CONCERTO"[4]

17 57 *Canzone Prima* Mascara (= Fiorenzo Maschera) (1584_{10}, no. 1: "Canzon La Capriola")

18 59 *Canzone seconda* Maschera (1584_{10}, no. 2: "Canzon [La Martinenga]")

19 61 *Canzone terza* Maschera (1584_{10}, no. 4)

20 63 *Canzone quarta* Maschera (1584_{10}, no. 5: "Canzon La Maggia")

21 65 *Canzone quinta*[5] Maschera (1584_{10}, no. 6)

22 67 *Canzone Sesta* Maschera (1584_{10}, no. 8)

23 69 *Canzone Settima* Maschera (1584_{10}, no. 10: "Canzon La Rosa")

24 73 *Canzone ottava*[a] Maschera (1584_{10}, no. 11: "Canzon [L'Averolda]")

25 74 *Canzone nona* Maschera (1584_{10}, no. 13: "Canzon [La Girella]")

26 76 *Canzone decima* Maschera (1584_{10}, no. 15)

27 79 *Canzone undecima & ultima* Maschera (1584_{10}, no. 17)

MUSIC FOR SOLO LUTE

28 81 *Quando fra bianche perle* Gio. Maria Nanino *a 5* (RISM 1574_4, p. 20)

83 2a pars *Sentomi aprirsi*

29 84 *D'un si bel fuoco* Giaches Wert *a 5* = 1584_6, no. 29

86 2a pars *Scorgo tant'alto*

30 87 *Caro dolce ben mio* Andrea Gabrieli *a 5* (RISM 1576_5, p. 28)

31 88 *Quando i vostri begli occhi* Marenzio *a 5* (MarenW I, 10)

32 90 *Verra ma il dì* Costanzo Porta *a 5* (RISM 1576_5, p. 16)

91 2a pars *Ma a che dolermi più*

33 92 *Fera gentil* *a 5* (Vogel: Rore 31 [1574], p. 15: Cipriano da Rore)

92 2a pars *Perche si stretto è il nodo*

34 93 *Ahi chi mi rompe il sonno* Filip. de Monte *a 5* (MonteO XXV, 51)

94 2a pars *Di ch'ella mossa*

35 95 *Fantasia prima*[6] Terzi

36 96 *Fantasia seconda* Terzi

37 97 *Fantasia terza* Terzi

38 99 *Fantasia quarta* Terzi

39 100 *Fantasia quinta* Terzi

40 101 *Fantasia sesta* Terzi

41 102 *Pass'e mezzo per b molle in trei modi*[a]

104 *Gagliarda del prescritto pass'e mezzo*[a][7]

42 105 *Gagliarda detta herdsona*

43 106 *Gagliarda nova de l'Autore*

44 106 *Pass'e mezzo per ♮ quadro in trei modi*

108 *La sua gagliarda*

45 110 *Gagliarda nova de l'Autore*

46 111 *Gagliarda*

47 111 *Pass'e mezzo in trei parti*

113 *Saltarello del pass'e mezzo*

48 114 *Gagliarda*

49 115 *Ballo Tedesco, & Francese*[a]

117 *Il Saltarello del prescritto ballo*[a]

50 117 *Pass'e mezzo*[a][8]

119 *Saltarello*[a]

51 120 *Gagliarda nova*[a]

52 121 *Nova gagliarda del padre de l'Autore*[a][9]

53 121 *Pass'e mezzo per b molle*

123 *Gagliarda del prescritto*

54 124 *Gagliarda nova de l'Autore*

55 124 *Ballo Tedesco novo de l'Autore*[a][10]

125 *Gagliarda del ditto ballo Tedesco*[a]

56 125 *Pass'e mezzo per ♮ duro*

127 *Gagliarda del pass'e mezo*

57 128 *Pass'e mezzo per b molle in altro tuono*

129 *Gagliarda*[a]

58 130 *Gagliarda*[a]

59 131 *Gagliarda*[a]

60 132 *Courante francese*

61 133 *Courante francese*

[1] Facs. of p. 1 in MGG IV, col. 1191.
[2] Beginning pr. in ReMR, p. 521.
[3] Mod. ed. in GaspCM, p. 8.
[4] Heading on p. 17: "Segue undeci canzoni del Mascara per suonar in concerto, & solo." Since a second lute part is not provided, the phrase "in concerto" presumably means that the lute intabulation may be played with the ensemble versions (see 1584_{10}).
[5] Mod. ed. in McKeeM, p. 108.
[6] Heading on p. 95: "Segue sei fantasie de l'Autore."
[7] Mod. ed. in FischV, no. 23.
[8] Mod. ed. in EC, pt. I, vol. II, p. 665.
[9] Mod. ed. in KlaemM II, no. 12.
[10] Mod. ed. in NeemAM II, no. 18.

1593_8

GARDANO, ANGELO, PUBLISHER

FANTASIE RECERCARI / ET CONTRAPUNTI A TRE VOCI, / Di Adriano & de altri Autori, appropriati per Cantare & Sonare / d'ogni sorte di Stromenti, Con due Regina celi, l'uno / di Adriano & l'altro di Cipriano, Sopra / uno medesimo Canto Fermo. / Novamente con ogni diligenza Ristampate. / [Printer's mark] / In Venetia Appresso Angelo Gardano. / M. D. LXXXXIII.

Three part books in mensural notation, each of 16 fols. (?). On the last verso of each part book: table of contents. Contents = 1551_6. Nos. 1 and 2 are fully texted; the other compositions are for instrumental ensemble *a3*.

Copy in: GB:Lbm (SB).

1593

DOUBTFUL WORKS

1. Vogel II, 284, suggests that Orazio Vecchi, *Canzonette A Quattro voci* (Nuremberg, Gerlach, 1593), contains one fantasia for instrumental ensemble *a4*. In fact the collection includes no instrumental music.

2. DeakinO, p. 50, dates William Barley, *A new Booke of Tabliture*, 1593. The collection is listed in this bibliography as $1596_{4,\ 5,\ \text{and}\ 6}$.

3. On November 19, 1593, John Danter was licensed to print *A moste perfect and true Instruction whereby a man maye learne by his owne industrie to playe on the Cytterne without the helpe of any teacher*. See ArberT II, 640.

1594_1

BARIOLLA, OTTAVIO

CAPRICCI, / OVERO / CANZONI / A' QUATTRO, / D'OTTAVIO BARIOLLA / Organista alla Gloriosa Madonna presso / Santo Celso di Milano. / LIBRO TERZO. / [Printer's mark] / IN MILANO, / Appresso gl'heredi di Francesco, & Simon Tini, fratelli. / M. D. XCIIII.

Four part books in mensural notation, each of 16 fols. (?). The title is placed within an ornamental border. Dedication on fol. *1ᵛ headed "AL SIGNOR ALESSANDRO VISTARINI," and signed "Di Milano, li 6. di Marzo. 1594. Ottavio Barioli," reprinted in SartMS, p. 83. Fol. *2 = p. 1. On p. 30: table of contents, followed by the colophon: "In Milano, Nella Stamparia di Pacifico Pontio. M. D. LXXXXIIII." All of the compositions are for instrumental ensemble *a4*.

Copy in: I:Bc (SA).

	p.	
1	1	*Canzone Prima*
2	2	*Canzone Seconda*
3	4	*Canzone Terza*
4	5	*Canzone Quarta*
5	7	*Canzone Quinta*
6	8	*Canzone Sesta*
7	10	*Canzone Settima*
8	11	*Canzone Ottava*
9	13	*Canzone Nona*
10	15	*Canzone Decima*
11	16	*Canzone Undecima*
12	18	*Canzone Duodecima*
13	19	*Canzone Decimaterza*
14	21	*Canzone Decimaquarta*
15	22	*Canzone Decimaquinta*
16	24	*Canzone Decimasesta*
17	25	*Canzone Decimasettima*
18	26	*Famela Pietr'Antonio. Canzone 18*
19	28	*Il Gobo Nan. Canzone 19*
20	29	*La Todesca. Canzone 20*

1594₂

BOTTRIGARI, ERCOLE

IL DESIDERIO / OVERO, / De' Concerti di varii Strumenti Musicali, / DIALOGO, / DI ALEMANNO BENELLI; / Nel quale anco si ragiona della participatione di essi / Stromenti, & di molte altre cose pertinenti / alla Musica. / [Printer's mark] / In Venetia appresso Ricciardo Amadino, / M D XCIIII.

32 fols. The title is placed with an ornamental border. On p. *2: a list of the authors cited, headed "Nomi de' Musici cosi Theorici, come Pratici, & di alcuni Poeti, & Filosofi allegati nel Dialogo." On pp. *3–*12: table of contents. The treatise begins on p. *13 (= p. 1). On p. 52: a list of errata headed "Errori piu importanti scorsi nello stampare." This treatise, in the form of a dialogue, "is mainly concerned with the practical problems of ensemble performance, including the tuning of instruments in order that they may be played together" (quoted from ReFS, no. 50). No complete compositions are included among the musical examples. For a later edition see 1599_4. There was a third edition in 1601. The second edition is reprinted in facsimile in BottrigD, and translated into English in BottrigDE. BrunetML, item 10156, mentions a 1590 edition, which is not otherwise known. For further information see ReFS, no. 50.

Copies in: B:Br, CH:Lcortot, F:Pc, GB:Lbmh, I:Bc, US:Cn, US:Wc.[1]

[1] A copy was in the Wolffheim library (see WolffC I, no. 528).

1594₃

BOVICELLI, GIOVANNI BATTISTA

REGOLE, / PASSAGGI / DI MUSICA, /MADRIGALI, E MOTETTI / PASSEGGIATI: / [D]I GIO. BATTISTA BOVICELLI / D'ASSISI, / Musico nel Duomo di Milano. / ALL'ILLUSTRISS. ET ECCELLENTISS. SIG. / IL SIG. GIACOMO BUONCOMPAGNI, / Duca di Sora, &c. / CON PRIVILEGIO. / [Printer's mark] / IN VENETIA, / APPRESSO GIACOMO VINCENTI. / M. D. XCIIII. / A instantia delli Heredi di Francesco, e Simon Tini, Librari in Milano.

44 fols. Mensural notation. Dedication on fol. 2–2ᵛ (= pp. 3–4) headed "ALL'ILLUSTRISS.ᴹᴼ ET ECCELL.ᴹᴼ PRENCIPE IL SIGNOR GIACOMO BUONCOMPAGNO, DUCA DI SORA, Marchese di Vignola, Sig. d'Arpino, & Arce, e Generale de gli huomini d'Arme nello Stato di Milano, & patron mio Colendiss.," and signed on p. 4 "Di Milano, a 12. d'Agosto, 1594. Di V. E. Illustriss. Devotiss. & obligatiss. Servitore Gio: Battista Bovicelli." On pp. 5–6: preface headed "AI LETTORI L'AUTTORE." On p. 88: table of contents. Although Bovicelli's rules for adding *passaggi* to written music are intended primarily for singers, the volume is included in this bibliography because it is so closely related to similar volumes intended for both singers and instrumentalists (for instance, 1592_{10} and 1593_2). The volume is organized in the following way:

pp. 7–9	"Avertimenti per li Passaggi, quanto alle parole" [general remarks on texting decorated passages]
10–16	"Avertimenti intorno alle note" [general remarks on how and when to add *passaggi*, and what kinds to add]
17–36	"Diversi modi di diminuire" [Systematic table of ornaments: Bovicelli first gives examples for filling in intervals with *passaggi* (ascending seconds, thirds, fourths, fifths, and sixths, and descending seconds, thirds, and so on), and then examples for ornamenting scalewise ascents and descents, long notes, and various cadences] [1]
37–87	The superius parts of various compositions (listed below) are given in plain and decorated versions, one printed above the other. This section is introduced by a note (on p. 37) headed "Al Virtuoso Lettore L'Autore."

The volume is reprinted in facsimile in BoviR.

Copies in: F:Pc (imperfect), I:Bc.

	p.	
1	38	*Io son ferito*[2] Palestina *a5* (PalW XXVIII, 179; another version of no. 2 below)
2	42	*Ave verum corpus*[3] Pallestina (another version of no. 1 above)
3	46	*Ancor che co'l partire*[4] Ciprian de Rore (SCMA VI, 45)
4	50	*Angelus ad Pastores ait* Ciprian de Rore
5	53	*Vadam & circuibo*[5] Tomaso Lodovico de Vittoria *a6* (VicO I, 97)
	59	2a pars *Dilectus tuus*
6	64	*In te Domine speravi* Claudio [Merulo] da Correggio *a6*
7	68	*Assumpsit Jesus* Claudio [Merulo] da Correggio *a6*
8	73	[*Falsobordone*] *Secondo Tono*[6] Giulio Cesare Gabucci *a4*
9	74	*Magnificat del Secondo Tono* Gabucci
10	78	*Falsi bordone primo Tono* Ruggiero Giovanelli *a4*
11	79	*Et exultavit* Giovanelli
12	83	[*Falsobordone*] *Sesto Tono* G[iovanni] B[attista] B[ovicelli] *a4*
13	84	*Salmo Dixit Dominus domino* Bovicelli [text begins: "Sede a dextris meis"]

[1] Some of the musical examples are repr. in KuV, p. 118.

[2] Mod. ed. in KuV, p. 122, and PalW XXXIII, 63. Facs. of p. 38 in MGG II, col. 174.

[3] Mod. ed. in PalW XXVIII, iv, and PalW XXXIII, 63.

[4] Mod. ed. in GoldV, p. 121. Facs. of p. 46 in MGG VI, col. 1103.

[5] Mod. ed. in KuV, p. 126.

[6] Mod. ed. in GoldV, p. 119.

1594₄

CARRARA, MICHELE

In questa carta s'insegna il vero et si/curo modo per potere presto scompartire ogni musica / et ridurla facilmente in qual si voglia sorte dintavolatura di / liuto commodissima per sonare.

This set of instructions for playing the lute, printed on one large folio, is a second edition of 1585₅ (see there for details). The title, reproduced above, is printed on the belly of the lute, above the strings; below the strings is the legend "Autore M. Michele paduanis Carrara, perito sonatore di liuto, et musico eccellente." A composition for solo lute, in Italian lute tablature, headed "toccata o preludo sopra il liuto cosa rara" is added above the intabulations of "Laudate eum." At the bottom of the page: "Superiorum permissu Joan Antoni de Paulis formis. Romae .1.5.9.4." The figure of the lute has been newly engraved, and the contents have been slightly rearranged on the page. The dedication from 1585₅ is missing here as are the statements "Ector Ruberti formis," and "Cum Privilegio e Cum licentia de Superiori," printed on the belly of the lute in 1585₅. Except for the changes noted, and minor revisions of the text, the contents of the two editions are the same.

Copy in: I:Fc.[1]

[1] EitQ II, 344, says that a copy was in the Wagener library.

1594₅

DENSS, ADRIAN

FLORILEGIUM / OMNIS FERE GENERIS / CANTIONUM SUAVISSIMARUM / AD TESTUDINIS TABULATURAM AC/COMMODATARUM, LONGE JUCUN/DISSIMUM. / IN QUO PRAETER FANTASIAS LEPIDISSIMAS, / continentur diversorum Authorum cantiones selectissimae, utpote: / Motetae, Neapolitanae, Madrigales trium, quatuor, quinque, sex / vocum. Item Passemezi, Galiardae, Alemandi, Courantes / Voltae, Branles, & eius generis Choreae variae: Om/nia ad Testudinis tabulaturam fideliter / redacta, per / Adranum Denss. / Indicem cantionum & chorearum post praefationem videre licebit. / [Printer's mark] / COLONIAE AGRIPPINAE. / Excudebat Gerardus Grevenbruch. Anno redemptionis, / M. D. XCIV.

4 + 96 = 100 fols. French lute tablature and mensural notation. On fol. *2: the pre-

face headed "AD PHILOMUSEN," followed by two Latin quatrains, the first headed "In Zoilum Tetrastichon M. G. M. G.," and the second, "Aliud in Zoilum I. L. R." On fol. *2^v: two poems in Latin, the first headed "Panegyris ad Ornatissimi et Musices Peritissimi Adriani Denss Florilegium Suavissimum. Scripta a M. Gulielmo Maio Gottingensi Saxone. Musices Amatore," and the second, "Ad Lectorem Exhortatio Eiusdem." Dedication on fol. *3 headed "REVERENDO, ILLUSTRI, AC GENEROSO DOMINO D. ARNOLDO EX COMITIBUS DE MANDERSCHEIDT ET BLANCKENHEIM, BARONI IN JUNCKERAID ET DAUN &c. METROPOLITANARUM ET CAthedralium Ecclesiarum Treuiren. Praeposito. Colonien. & Argentinensis Scholastico, nec non D. Andreae Ecclesiae Colonien. Praeposito. Domino suo clementiss.," and signed "Datae Coloniae Agrippinae. 4. Nonar. Septemb. Anno 1594: aera novata. Reverendae & Illustri Generositati vestrae perpetua observante voluntate deditissimus. Adrianus Denssius." On fol. *3^v: table of contents. Fol. *5 = fol. 1. Attributions to composers are taken from the table of contents. Two or more voices of the vocal model in mensural notation are included on the page facing the lute arrangement for nos. 1–85. These voices are indicated in the following list by S, A, T, and B. Nos. 86–148 are for solo lute.

Copies in: A:Wn, D:KNu, D:LEm, D:Mbs, D:TR, D:W, PL:WRu.[1]

fol.

1 *4^v *Quam gloriosum* (SB) Lodovvicus à Victoria *à4* (VicO I, 1)

2 2^v *Domine non sum dignus* (SB) Victoria *à4* (VicO I, 39)

3^v 2a pars *Miserere mei*

3 4^v *Laudate Dominum* (SB) Bernardin Mosto *à4*

4 5^v *Gustate & videte*[2] (SB) Orlandus Lassus *à5* (LassoW V, 73)

8^v 2a pars *Divites eguerunt*

5 10^v *Ogni vita*[3] (STB) Lodovvicus Torti *à3* (Vogel: Torti [1584], no. 7)

6 10^v *Dal primo giorno* (STB) Torti *à3* (Vogel: Torti [1584], no. 11)

7 11^v *Vaghe bellezze* (STB) Torti *à3* (Vogel: Torti [1584], no. 9)

8 11^v *Delle vostre sciocchesse* (STB) Gaspar Costa *à3* (Vogel: Costa 4 [1584], no. 2)

9 12^v *Assai promette* (STB) Costa *à3* (Vogel: Costa 4 [1584], no. 6)

10 12^v *La venenosa vista* (STB) Costa *à3* (Vogel: Costa 4 [1584], no. 7)

11 13^v *Se del mar si seccasser* (STB) Costa *à3* (Vogel: Costa 4 [1584], no. 21)

12 13^v *Crudel lascia sto core* (STB) Costa *à3* (Vogel: Costa 4 [1584], no. 20)

13 14^v *O chiome rilucenti* (STB) Costa *à3* (Vogel: Costa 4 [1584], no. 19)

14 14^v *Amor è fatto* (STB) Costa *à3* (Vogel: Costa 4 [1584], no. 18)

15 15^v *Udite novi amanti* (STB) Costa *à3* (Vogel: Costa 4 [1584], no. 12)

16 15^v *Fuggirò fuggirò* (STB) Paulo Bellasio *à3*

17 16^v *Fuggit'amore* (STB) Giov: Dominico danola *à3* (Vogel: Nola 4 [1569], no. 15)

18 16^v *Non puo sentir* (STB) Gio. Giac: Gastoldi *à3* (Vogel: Gastoldi 30 [1592], no. 9)

19 17^v *Lieto cantai* (STB) Caesar Borgo *à3* (Vogel: Borgo 1 [1584], no. 2)

20 17^v *La gratia e la beltade* (STB) Borgo *à3* (Vogel: Borgo 1 [1584], no. 3)

21 18^v *Ahi filli* (STB) Gio: Giac. Gastoldi *à3* (Vogel: Gastoldi 30 [1592], no. 2)

22 18^v *S'in fede del mio amore* (STB) Gastoldi *à3* (Vogel: Gastoldi 30 [1592], no. 7)

23 19^v *Ahi che mi tiene* (STB) Gastoldi *à3* (Vogel: Gastoldi 30 [1592], no. 16)

24 19^v *Mentre scherzava* (STB) Gastoldi *à3* (Vogel: Gastoldi 30 [1592], no. 10)

25 20^v *Non si sa dimmi* (SB) Joannin Favereo *à3* (Vogel: Favereo [1593], no. 1)

26 20v *Madonna di cucagna* (SB) Favereo *à 3* (Vogel: Favereo [1593], no. 6)

27 21v *Gut Singer und* (SB) Leonardus Lechnerus *à 3* (LechN, no. 1)

28 21v *Adonis zart* (STB) Lechner *à 3* (LechN, no. 9)

29 22v *Cosa non vada*[4] (SB) Orazio Vecchi *à 4* (Vogel: Vecchi 21 [1591], no. 8)

30 22v *Occhi ridenti* (SB) Vecchi *à 4* (Vogel: Vecchi 21 [1591], no. 3)

31 23v *Mentre io campai* (SB) Vecchi *à 4* (Vogel: Vecchi 21 [1591], no. 2)

32 23v *Mentre io vissi. Risposta* (SB) *à 4*

33 24v *O tu che vai* (SB) Vecchi *à 4* (Vogel: Vecchi 21 [1591], no. 18)

34 24v *Il cor che mi rubasti* (SB) Vecchi *à 4* (Vogel: Vecchi 21 [1591], no. 21)

35 25v *Lucilla io vo morire* (SB) Vecchi *à 4* (Vogel: Vecchi 24 [1582], no. 19)

36 25v *Cor mio se per dolore* (SB) Vecchi *à 4* (Vogel: Vecchi 34 [1590], no. 11)

37 26v *Dormiva amor*[5] (SB) Ferabosco *à 4* (Vogel: M. Ferrabosco [1585], no. 3)

38 26v *O monti o fiumi*[5] (SB) Ferabosco *à 4* (Vogel: M. Ferrabosco [1585], no. 4)

39 27v *Che giovarebbe haver* (SB) Ferabosco *à 4* (Vogel: M. Ferrabosco [1585], no. 5)

40 27v *Danzar vidd'io* (SB) Ferabosco *à 4* (Vogel: M. Ferrabosco [1585], no. 6)

41 28v *Donna ben ch'io* (SB) Ferabosco *à 4* (Vogel: M. Ferrabosco [1585], no. 7)

42 28v *Io stanco & lasso* (SB) Ferabosco *à 4* (Vogel: M. Ferrabosco [1585], no. 8)

43 29v *E un sol in cielo* (SB) Ferabosco *à 4* (Vogel: M. Ferrabosco [1585], no. 9)

44 29v *Che mi giova servir* (STB) Ferabosco *à 4* (Vogel: M. Ferrabosco [1585], no. 11)

45 30v *Meraviglia d'amore* (SB) Ferabosco *à 4* (Vogel: M. Ferrabosco [1585], no. 14)

46 30v *Mi trá d'hoggi* (SB) Gastoldi *à 3* (Vogel: Gastoldi 30 [1592], no. 5)

47 31v *Desir che tanto salli* (SB) Gaspar Costa *à 4* (Vogel: Costa 2 [1580], no. 1)

48 31v *Godi pur del bel sen* (SB) Costa *à 4* (Vogel: Costa 2 [1580], no. 14)

49 32v *Io vorrei pur hormai* (SB) Costa *à 4* (Vogel: Costa 2 [1580], no. 3)

50 32v *Lottava sfera* (SB) Costa *à 4* (Vogel: Costa 2 [1580], no. 2)

51 33v *Giovani vaghi* (SB) Costa *à 4* (Vogel: Costa 2 [1580], no. 8)

52 33v *Come faró* (SB) Costa *à 4* (Vogel: Costa 2 [1580], no. 13)

53 34v *Al dipartir* (STB) Costa *à 4* (Vogel: Costa 2 [1580], no. 17)

54 34v *Amor s'io posso* (SB) Costa *à 4* (Vogel: Costa 2 [1580], no. 11)

55 35v *Se doppo mille manifeste prove* (STB) Costa *à 4* (Vogel: Costa 2 [1580], no. 5)

56 36v *Di pianti e di sospiri* (STB) Costa *à 4* (Vogel: Costa 2 [1580], no. 6)

57 37v *Mentre lontan* (STB) Costa *à 4* (Vogel: Costa 2 [1580], no. 16)

58 38v *Non si puo piu* (STB) Costa *à 4* (Vogel: Costa 2 [1580], no. 12)

59 39v *Per pianto la mia carne* (STB) Costa *à 4* (LassoW VIII, 13: Lasso)

60 40v *La virginella* (SB) Baldasar Donato *à 4* (Vogel: Donato 11 [1568], no. 25)

61 41v *Gl'occhi* (SB) Gaspar Costa *à 4* (Vogel: Costa 2 [1580], no. 10)

62 41v *Venite maghi* (SB) Costa *à 4* (Vogel: Costa 2 [1580], no. 15)

63 42v *Disse á l'amata mia* (SB) Luca Marenzo *à 4* (Vogel: Marenzio 74 [1587], no. 2)

64 43ᵛ *Veggo dolce mia* (STB) Marenzio *à 4* (Vogel: Marenzio 74 [1587], no. 3)

65 44ᵛ *Ridon di maggio* (SB) Haslerus *à 4* (Vogel: Hassler 2 [1590], no. 1)

66 44ᵛ *Chi mi dimandarà* (SB) Hassler *à 4* (Vogel: Hassler 2 [1590], no. 2)

67 45ᵛ *Mir hab ich gentzlich* (SB) Leonardus Lechnerus *à 4* (LechW IX, no. 12)

68 45ᵛ *Wo jemandt lust* (SB) Lechner *à 4* (LechW IX, no. 2)

69 46ᵛ *O dolce vita mia*[6] (STB) Giulio Renaldi *à 5* (Vogel: Renaldi 2 [1576], no. 15)

70 47ᵛ *Veux tu ton mal* (STB) Orlandus [Lasso] *à 5* (LassoW XIV, 71)

71 48ᵛ *Le voules vous. Responce* (STB) (LassoW XIV, 74: Lasso)

72 49ᵛ *Que me servent*[7] (SB) Philip. de Monte *à 5* (MonteO XXV, 59)

73 50ᵛ *Est il possible* (STB) Orlandus [Lasso] *à 5* (LassoW XIV, 112)

74 51ᵛ *Dell'auro crin* (STB) Lassus *à 5* (LassoW VIII, 112)

52ᵛ 2a pars *Con le stelle*

75 53ᵛ *Hor pensat'al mio mal* (STB) Ivo de vento *à 5* (Vogel: Vento 1 [1575], no. 6)

76 54ᵛ *Verament'in amore*[8] (STB) Philip. de monte *à 5* (MonteO XXV, 66)

77 54ᵛ *Elle s'en va* (STB) Orlandus [Lasso] *à 5* (LassoW XIV, 105)

78 56ᵛ *Madonna se volete* (STB) Hieron. Vespa *à 5* (Vogel: Vespa 2 [1576], no. 7)

79 57ᵛ *Madonna poi ch'uccider* (STB) Luca Marenz. *à 5* (Vogel: Marenzio 39 [1582], no. 1)

80 58ᵛ *Amor deh dimmi* (SB) Gio: Maria Nanino *à 5* (Vogel: Nanino 5 [1587], no. 8)

81 58ᵛ *Ohn dich muss ich mich* (SB) Lechnerus *à 5* (PubAPTM XIX, no. 1)

82 59ᵛ *Chiamo la morte* (SB) Theodor Riccius (Vogel: Riccio 2 [1577], no. 3)

83 59ᵛ *Mamma mia cara* (SB) Riccio *à 5* (Vogel: Riccio 2 [1577], no. 6)

84 60ᵛ *Se tu m'ami*[9] (STB) Andrea Gabrielis *à 6* (Vogel: A. Gabrieli 4 [1580], no. 6)

85 61ᵛ *Non ti sdegnar* (STB) A. Gabrieli *à 6* (Vogel: A. Gabrieli 4 [1580], no. 17)

86 62ᵛ *Fantasia Prima*[10]

87 63 *Fantasia 2*

88 64 *Fantasia 3*

89 65 *Fantasia 4*

90 65ᵛ *Fantasia 5*

91 67 *Fantasia 6*

92 67ᵛ *Fantasia Gregorii Howet*

93 68ᵛ *Fantasia alia eiusdem*

94 69ᵛ *Fantasia 10* [sic]

95 70 *Fantasia 9* [sic]

96 70ᵛ *Fantasia 11*

97 71ᵛ *Gaillarde*

98 72 *Gaillarde*

99 72ᵛ *Gaillarde*

100 73 *Gaillarde*

101 73ᵛ *Gaillarde*

102 73ᵛ *Galiarde*

103 74 *Galiarda*

104 74ᵛ *Galiarda nova*

105 74ᵛ *Galiarda nova*

106 75 *Galiarde*

107 75 *Passemezo in C sol fa ut, per b mol*

76 *Galliarde*

108 76ᵛ *Passemeso in G. sol re ut. b mol*

77 *Galiarda*

109 77ᵛ *Gagliarda di Ferabosco*

110 78 *Passemeso in F. b mol*

78ᵛ *Galiarda*

111 79 *Passemeso in D la sol re, b mol*

80 *Galiarda*

112 80ᵛ *Passemeso in G sol re ut, b dur*

81 *Galiarda*

113 81ᵛ *Passemezo in C sol fa ut. b durum*

82 *Galiarda*

114 83 *Passemezo in F fa ut, B duro*

84 *Gaillarde*

115 84ᵛ *Passemezo in D la sol re, b dur*

85 *Gaillarde*

116 85ᵛ *Allemande*

117 85ᵛ *Allemande*

118 86 *Allemande*[11]

119	86v	*Allemande*
	86v	*Ripresa*
120	87	*Allemande dalliance*
121	87	*Allemande Brunette*
122	87v	*Allemande Ich dancke Gott*
123	87v	*Allemande*
124	88	*Allemande de Fleur*
125	88	*Allemande*
126	88v	*Allemande*
127	88v	*Allemande*
128	89	*Allemande*
	89	*Variatio praecedentis*
129	89v	*Allemande*
	89v	*Variatio praecedentis*
130	90	*Allemande*
	90	*Reprinse*
131	90v	*Allemande d'amour*
	90v	*Variatio praecedentis*
132	91	*Allemande Imperial*
133	91	*Allemande*
134	91v	*Courante de Victor Montbuisson*
135	92	*Courante eiusdem*
136	92	*Courante*
137	92v	*Courante de Victor de Montbuisson*
138	93	*Volte*
139	93	*Volte*
140	93v	*Vray Dieu disoit une fillette* Orlandus [Lasso] (LassoW XII, 72)
141	94	*Branle*
142	94v	*Branle double*
143	94v	*Branle de Poitou*
144	94v	*Courante*
145	95	*Ronde*
146	95v	*Branle*
147	95v	*Allemande*
148	96	*Pauren Tantz* [12]
	96	*Reprise*
	96	*Variatio*

[1] A copy was in D:Hs.

[2] Facs. of fols. 5v and 6 in MGG VII, col. 1337.

† [3] Heading on fol. 10v: "Neapolitanae. Trium Vocum."

[4] Heading on fol. 22v: "Neapolitanae et Madrigales Quatuor Vocum."

[5] Facs. of fol. 27 in EF II, 45, and MGG IV, col. 46.

[6] Heading on fol. 46v: "Madrigales Quinque Vocum."

[7] Mod. ed. in MonteO XXV, 12.

[8] Mod. ed. in MonteO XXV, 15.

[9] Heading on fol. 60v: "Sex Vocus."

[10] Heading on fol. 62v: "Fantasiae et Choreae." Mod. ed. of no. 86 in NeemAM II, no. 15.

[11] Mod. ed. in NeemAM II, no. 16.

[12] Facs. of fol. 96 in MGG III, col. 196.

[1594]$_6$

GABRIELI, ANDREA, AND ANNIBALE PADOVANO

DIALOGHI MUSICALI / DE DIVERSI ECCELLEN/TISSIMI AUTORI, / A Sette, Otto, Nove, Dieci, Undeci & Dodici voci, / Novamente posti in luce. / CON DUE BATTAGLIE A OTTO VOCI, / Per sonar de Istrumenti da Fiato, di Annibale Podoana / & di Andrea Gabrieli, già Organisti della Serenissima Signoria di Venetia / in San Marco. / CON PRIVILEGIO. / [Printer's mark] / In Venetia Appresso Angelo Gardano M. DLXXXXIIII

Twelve part books in mensural notation. Contents = 1590_2. A copy of the altus part book is listed in SartMS, p. 84, as having been in the Antiquariatbuchhandlung Albert Cohn in Berlin (see his catalogue for 1878, p. 9). The volume contained compositions with Italian text, and two pieces for instrumental ensemble *a8*.

1594_7

GASTOLDI, GIOVANNI GIACOMO

BALLETTI / A TRE VOCI / Con la intavolatura del Liuto, per cantare, / sonare, & ballare. / DI GIO. GIACOMO GASTOLDI DA CARAVAGGIO / Maestro di Cappella nella Chiesa Ducale di S. Barbara / di Mantova. / Novamente composti, & dati in luce. / [Printer's mark] / IN VENETIA, Appresso Ricciardo Amadino. / M D XCIIII.

Three part books in mensural notation and Italian lute tablature (S, 17 fols.; TB, each of 10 fols.). The title is placed within an ornamental border. Dedication on fol. 2 (= p. 1) of each part book headed "ALL'ILLUSTRISS. SIGNORE mio Signore, & Patrone colendissimo, IL SIGNOR ALESSANDRO ANGOSCIOLA, Cameriero del Serenissimo Sig. Duca di Mantova," and signed "Di Venetia il dì 29 di Genaro 1594. Di V. S. Illustrissima Servitore affetionatissimo Gio. Giacomo Gastoldi," partly reprinted in Vogel: Gastoldi 35 (1594). The compositions identified by the superior letter *a* ([a]) are reprinted in ZfSM XXXIII without text (the lute intabulation is included only for no. 4). Contents = 1598_6. For later editions see Vogel I, 279–281. Lute intabulations of the *balletti* appear in the canto part book only; the intabulation and vocal superius of each piece are printed on facing pages. Pagination in the following inventory is taken from the tenor part book. The inventory lists the first words of text for each piece followed by the title (in parentheses).

Copies in: D:As, D:Hs.

	p.	
1	2	*Sonatemi un balletto* (*Il Ballerino*)[a]
2	3	*La mia amorosa* (*La Cortigiana*)[a]
3	4	*Poi ch'el mio foco* (*Lo Spensierato*)[a]
4	5	*Non morirò* (*Lo Sdegnato*)[a]
5	6	*Vive vive Bacco ogn'hor* (*Il Todesco*)[a]
6	7	*O vezzosetta* (*Il Prigioniero*)
7	8	*Vita mia per che* (*Il Luchesino*)
8	9	*Se mi fai saltar* (*L'Humorista*)
9	10	*Per voler d'Amore* (*Il Felice*)
10	11	*Dimmi ch'è del mio core* (*Il Curioso*)
11	12	*Che pensi tu* (*Il Risentito*)
12	13	*Non mi dar* (*Il Tormentato*)
13	14	*Fin c'havrò vita* (*Il Costante*)
14	15	*Vo lodar* (*Il Fortunato*)
15	16	*O che diletto* (*L'Invaghito*)[a]
16	17	*E vivo a mio despeto* (*El Passionao*)[a]

1594₈

LUPACCHINO, BERNARDINO, AND JOAN MARIA TASSO

DI BERNARDINO LUPACHINO / ET DI JOAN MARIA TASSO, / IL PRIMO LIBRO A DUE VOCI / Aggiontovi alcuni Canti de diversi Auttori, / Novamente Ristampato. / [Printer's mark] / In Venetia Appresso Angelo Gardano. / M. D. LXXXXIIII.

Two part books in mensural notation, each of 20 fols. Contents = 1559_6. All of the compositions are *a 2* and without text or title.

Copy in: I:Bc (S).[1]

[1] A copy was in D:Bds.

[1594]₉

METALLO, GRAMMATICO

Canzoni alla napolitana a 4 & a 5, con due canzoni alla francese per sonare. Libro quarto. Venezia, 1594.

This volume, now lost, is listed in DraudiusBE, p. 270. It contained compositions with Italian text, and two pieces for instrumental ensemble *a 4* or *a 5*. Thirteen compositions[1] from this volume are intabulated for the organ (using new German keyboard tablature) in CH:Bu, MS F. IX. 43, between fols. 129 and 178. The two *canzoni alla francese per sonare* may have had text, for on fol. 174 of the manuscript is "Metallo Canzon di Francese per sonar / Ch'in freta." According to FétB VI, 109, the title page stated that Metallo was maestro di cappella of the cathedral at Bassano.

[1] And not 31 as stated in EitQ, s.v. "Metallo."

1594₁₀

PAIX, JAKOB

SELECTAE, AR/TIFICIOSAE ET ELEGAN/TES FUGAE DUARUM, TRI/UM, QUATUOR, ET PLURIUM VOCUM, / partim ex veteribus & recentibus Musicis summa Diligen/tia & acurato iudicio collectae, partim Compositae / à JACOBO PAIX, Organico / Palatino Lauingano. / Tertia, locupletior & correctior aeditio: / BOETIUS. / Musica obtinet principatum: nihil enim sine illa manet. / [Printer's mark] / LAUINGI / Excusum per Leonhardum Reinmichaelium. / cIↄ cI VIC.

20 fols. Mensural notation. The title is placed within an ornamental border. On fol. 1ᵛ: same cut of Jakob Paix as in 1590_6; beneath the cut a canon headed "Psal. 142. Trio in homophonia," and with the text beginning "Domine ad te confugi." Dedication on fol. 2 headed "NOBILITATE ET ERUDITIONE ORNATISS. VIRO D. Marco Thennio, Patricio August. Domino suo observando. Jac. Paix. S. P. D.," and

dated "Lauingae idib. Febr. Anno 94." On fol. 2v: a paragraph by Zarlino on canons, headed "Dele Fughe, o consequenze, over Reditte, Che dire le vogliano." On fol. 19v: a table headed "Tabula Signorum Resolutoria." On fol. 20: a note on proportions headed "De Proportionibus Musicis." For the first edition see [1587]₇. Contents = 1590₆, except that nos. 3–5 (fols. 3v–4) of the first edition are replaced here by a composition *a 4* ("Si vis laudari") by J[acobo] P[aix] O[rganico]. The title page states that this is a third edition. All of the compositions are canons for two, three, four, and more voices; some have complete text, and some do not.

Copies in: D:Mbs, D:Rp.[1]

[1] A copy was in PL:WRu.

[1594]₁₁

PICCININI, ALESSANDRO

Trattato sopra la Tabulatura. Bologna 1594.

This treatise on tablature, now lost if it ever existed, is included in the list of Italian tablatures in WolfH II, 69. It is not mentioned in KinsAP. It may be the volume, once in the library of King John IV of Portugal, listed in VasJ, p. 108, as: "Intavolatura de Laude, & Chitarrone de Alessandro Picini Bolognese. lib. 1. & advirtimentos para com facilidade tanger os ditos instrumentos."

[1594]₁₂

STIVORI, FRANCESCO

Il Secondo Libro de Ricercari a 4 voci di Francesco Stivori. Venezia 1594. Amadino.

This volume, now lost, was in USSR:K (SAB). EitQ IX, 291, says that it contained 20 ricercares *a 4*. For other volumes by Stivori see 1589₇, note 1.

1595₁

AICHINGER, GREGOR

LIBER SECUNDUS / SACRARUM CANTIONUM / (Quas vulgo Motettas vocant) tum Festis / precipuis, tum cuiuis tempori accom/modatae 6. 5. & 4 Vocum./ His quoque accedunt Missa, & Magnificat, nec non / Dialogi aliquot Octo, & Decem Vocum, / AUCTORE / Gregorio Aichinger, Illustris ac generosi Domini / Jacobi Fuggeri Senioris &c. Organista. / [Printer's mark] / Venetiis, Apud Angelum Gardanum. / M. D. LXXXXV.

Eight part books in mensural notation (S, 25 fols.; ATB, each of 26 fols.; 5, 22 fols.; 6, 11 fols.; 7 and 8, each of 8 fols.). The title is placed within an ornamental border. On fol. 1v: the Fugger coat of arms. Dedication on fol. 2 headed "PERILLUS.RI ET GENEROSO D: DOMINO JACOBO FUGGERO SENIORI, Baroni Kirchberge & Veissenhorni, Babenhausique Domino, Patrono suo, Gregorius Aichinger Ratisponensis DD.," and signed "Vale Augustae Vindelicorum Primum Calendis Januarii, Anno M D XCV." Fol. 2v = p. 2. On p. 48: table of contents. The volume contains 42 compositions with Latin texts (40 motets, one Mass, and one Magnificat), and three pieces for instrumental ensemble *a 4*.

Copies in: A:Wn (imperfect), D:Kl, D:Rp (imperfect).

	p.		
1	36	*Ricercar Primi Toni*	*a 4*
2	38	*Ricercar per sonare & cantare*	*a 4*
3	40	*Ricercar per sonare & cantare*	*a 4*

1595₂

BANCHIERI, ADRIANO

CONCERTI / ECCLESIASTICI / A OTTO VOCI / DI D. ADRIANO BANCHIERI DA BOLOGNA / Monaco Olivetano, Discepolo del Sig. Gioseffo Guami, / Aggiontovi nel Primo Choro la Spartitura per sonare / nell'Organo commodissima, / Nuovamente Composti, & dati in luce. / BASSO DEL [Printer's mark] SECON.

CHORO / IN VENETIA, Appresso Giacomo Vincenti. M. D. XCV.

Nine part books, eight in mensural notation, each of 12 fols., the ninth in keyboard partitura, of 20 fols. The title is placed within an ornamental border. Dedication on fol. 2 of each part book headed "ILLUST.MO AC REVER.MO D. D. PHILIPPO SEGAE S. R. E. CARD. AMPLISS. F.," and signed "Bononiae, ex Coenobio S. Michaelis in Nemore. Idib. Julii 1595." On fol. 12v: table of contents. The organ part book has a separate title page, placed within an ornamental border:

> SPARTITURA / PER SONARE / NEL ORGANO / Accommodata al Primo Choro nei Concerti di D. ADRIANO / BANCHIERI da Bologna Monaco Olevitano, Discepolo / del Signor Gioseppe Guami / ALL'ILL.mo ET R.mo SIG. CARD. DI PIACENZA / [Printer's mark] / IN VENETIA Appresso Giacomo Vincenti. 1595.

On fol. 20v of the organ part book: a note headed "A GLI SIG. ORGANISTI," reading: "Volendo la Spartitura di tutti due Chori, sarà facil cosa accommodarla prestissimo, pigliando la parte acuta & grave del Secondo Choro, & dove in questa dice à 8. lasciarlo, & aggiungendo quella à questa, vi saranno tutti due: ma l'Autore non l'ha fatta, atteso che l'intentione sua è per concertarla à Chori separati. In tanto vivete felici." This note is followed by the table of contents. The organ part includes the bass and superius voices of the first chorus in score. The collection contains 15 compositions for double chorus *a8*,[1] and 3 compositions for instrumental ensemble *a4* and *a8*. No 2 is for the second chorus alone; no. 3 is for the first chorus alone.

Copies in: D:Kl (partitura wanting), I:Bc (S1, B2, and partitura), I:FEc.

	p.	
1	14	*Canzon Francese detta la Carissima à8*
2	15[2]	*Canzon Francese del Secondo Tuono, detta la Galluppa à4* = 1596_3, no. 3
3	15[3]	*Canzon Francese dell'Ottavo Tuono, detta la Sirifina à4*

[1] These compositions are: p. 1: *Ecce sacerdos magnus*; 2: *Factum est silentium*; 3: *Ego flos campi*; 4: *Salve regina*; 5: *Angelus ad pastores ait*; 6: *Omnes gentes plaudite manibus*; 7: *Confitemini Domino in Ecco*; 8: *Verbum caro factum est*; 9: *Paratum cor meum*; 10: *Magnificat Secundi Toni*; 12: *Magnificat Octavi Toni*; 13: *Laudate Dominum*; 16: *Magnificat* [*Sexti Toni*] *à versetti*; 17: *Missa, Paratum cor meum*; 22: *Adoramus te.*

[2] No. 2 is on p. 15 of the second chorus part books.

[3] No. 3 is on p. 15 of the first chorus part books.

1595_3

GABRIELI, ANDREA

> RICERCARI DI ANDREA GABRIELI / ORGANISTA IN S. MARCO DI VENETIA / Composti & Tabulati per ogni sorte di Stromenti da Tasti, / Novamente stampati & dati in luce. / LIBRO SECONDO. / [Printer's mark] / In Venetia Appresso Angelo Gardano. / M. D. LXXXXV.

44 fols. Keyboard score. Fol. A2 – fol. 1. The compositions by Andrea are reprinted in Gabri(A)RO I and II. The compositions by Giovanni are reprinted in Gabri(G)W and Gabri(G)CO I. For other volumes in this series see 1593_4. All of the compositions are for solo keyboard.

Copies in: CH:Bu, I:Bc.[1]

	fol.	
1	A1v	*Ricercar del Primo Tuono*[2]
2	4	[*Ricercar del*] *Primo Tuono Alla Quarta alta*[3]
3	7	[*Ricercar del*] *Secondo Tuono Alla Quarta alta*
4	9v	[*Ricercar del*] *Terzo Tuono*[4]
5	13	[*Ricercar del*] *Quarti Toni*
6	16v	[*Ricercar del*] *Quinti Toni*
7	19v	[*Ricercar del*] *Sesto Tono*
8	24	[*Ricercar del*] *Settimo Tono*
9	28	[*Ricercar del*] *Ottavo Tono*[5] Gio: Gabrieli
10	30v	[*Ricercar del*] *Nono Tono*
11	33v	[*Ricercar del*] *Decimo Tono*[6] Gio: Gabrieli
12	38v	[*Ricercar del*] *Undecimo Tono*
13	40v	[*Ricercar del*] *Duodecimo Tono*

[1] SeiffG, p. 35, erroneously dates the Basel copy 1575 and the Bologna copy 1585.

[2] Mod. ed. in TorA III, 61.

[3] Mod. ed. in GaussO I, no. 1, and WasG, no. 20.

[4] Mod. ed. in TagA I, no. 20.

[5] Mod. ed. in BarthaZ, no. 68; FuserC, no. 25; GottA, no. 76; KörnO V, no. 18; and TagA II, no. 17.

[6] Mod. ed. in DallaA, no. 13; RieM, no. 52; TagA II, no. 19; and WasG, no. 21.

1595₄

GUMPELZHAIMER, ADAM

COMPENDIUM / MUSICAE LATINO/ GERMANICUM. / Studio & opera Adami Gum/pelzhaimeri, Trospergii / Bavari, editum. / NUNC ALTERA HAC EDITI/one alicubi mutatum & auctum. / AUGUSTAE /Excusum typis Valentini Schoenigii. / Anno M. D. XCV.

82 fols. Mensural notation. The title is placed within an ornamental border depicting musicians playing various instruments. Dedication on fol. *2, headed

> ORNATISSIMUS ADOLESCENTIBUS, NEC NON INDOLIS AC SPEI OPTImae pueris Conrado Hoermanno, Philippo Hellero, Joanni Scharschmidio Franco, Tobiae & Matthaeo Christoph: Ehemiis, Philippo Hoechstettero, Johan: Berlohero, Christophoro Fronmillero, Matthaeo Millero, Hieremiae Laubio, Johanni Gassero, Davidi Wagnero, Adamo Reisnero, Laurentio Neogeorgo, Andreae Schellero, Christophoro Nachtrubio, Sebastiano Heidenrico Misnico, Georgio Hindermario, Davidi & Hieremiae Ehingeris, Johan: Baptistae Heinzelio, Adolpho Leschenprandio, Johan: Jacobo Rumlero, Wolgango Hoeschlio, Christophoro Christelio, Salomoni Jenischio, Andreae Zeilnero, Lucae Schallero, philomusis, Adamus Gumpelzhaimerus S. P. D.

and dated "Postridiè Kal: April. 1595. Augustae." On fol. *2ᵛ: dedication to the first edition (1591₆),[1] headed

> SPLENDORE GENERIS ORNATIS, PIETATIS, VIRTUTIS ET DOCTRINAE STUDIOSIS ADOLESCENTIBUS JOAN: GEORGIO Hoermanno, Hieronymo Herwarto, Paulo Ramo, Johan: Huldarico Linckio, Friderico & Johan: Friderico Saliceis Grisonibus, Matthaeo Menharto; Nec non optimae spei pueris Georgio Sigismundo Fabricio, Matthaeo Sturzelio, Hieremiae Puraunero, Philippo Henischio, Danieli Oppenridero Reinhartshofensi, Matthaeo Henningo, Joachimo Prinnero, Joan: Leuchsnero Franco, Hieronymo & Tobiae Zaehiis, Marcello Theodorico Neoburgensi, Christophoro Hafnero, Antonio & Magno Jacobo Seitziis, Henrico Schot Tyrolensi, Friderico Davidi & Marco Antonio Schalleris, discipulis percharis S. P. Adamus Gumpelzhaimerus T[rospergii]

and dated "Mense Novemb: 1590. Augustae Vindelicorum." This second dedication is followed (on fol. *3) by a two-line Latin epigraph headed "Ad Zoilum" On fol. *3ᵛ: preface headed "Dem Leser glück und heil," and signed "Geschriben in Augspurg, den 2. tag Aprilis, im Jar Jesu Christi unsers Seligmachers, 1595. Adam Gumpelzhaimer von Trosperg." On fol. *4 (= fol. 1): table of contents. Two folios are numbered 13, an error not corrected in the following inventory. On fols. 75–76: an index of all of the musical examples. This is a revised, second edition of 1591₆, which is a revision and expansion of Heinrich Faber's *Compendiolum musicae pro incipientibus* (Brunswick, 1548); for further information on the relation between Faber's work and Gumpelzhaimer's revision, and for a list of later editions of the Gumpelzhaimer work, see MGG III, cols. 1648–1688, and MGG V, cols. 1112–1119. The text is printed in Latin on the left side of each page, and in German on the right side.

This elementary introduction to the rudiments of music is divided into ten chapters: "Musica (der Singkunst)," "Clavibus (den Schlüsseln)," "Vocibus (den Stimmen)," "Cantu (dem Gesang)," "Mutatione (der verenderung der Stimm)," "Figura & Signis (der gestalt der Noten und zaichen)," "Ligatura (der zusamenbindung der Noten)," "Pausis & Punctis (den Pausen unnd Puncten)," "Proportionibus (der Proportion)," and "Tonis seu Modis (dem Ton)." Each chapter is illustrated with musical examples, mostly canons, some without text. Chapter 10 (not included in 1591₆) is illustrated with 12 untexted examples *a 4*, each demonstrating the "properties" of a mode. A list of the modes and their characteristics follows:

fol.

13v Dorian. Hilaris
14 Hypodorian. Moestus
14v Phrygian. Austerus
15 Hypophrygian. Blandus
15v Lydian. Asper
16 Hypolydian. Lenis
16v Mixolydian. Indignans
17 Hypomixolydian. Placabilis
17v Aeolian. Suavis
18 Hypoaeolian. Tristis
18v Ionian. Jucundus
19 Hypoionian. Flebilis

The 12 pieces are reprinted after the 1611 edition in GumpelzKF. The 1611 examples differ in some details from the 1595 examples.

Following chapter 10 there are a great many musical examples. On fols. 19v–41v: canons *a2* to *a8*, with Latin or German text, or without text.[2] Four of the textless canons are called "fantasiae" in the index; the other textless canons are called "exemplum," "fuga," "Sex voces musicales," or "mutatio vocum." Some but not all of the canons are identical with those in 1591_6. On fols. 42–61v: pieces *a2* with German or Latin text, and the six ricercares without text listed below (not present in 1591_6). The duos are preceded by a separate title page (fol. 42) headed "Sequuntur Bicinia Sacra, in usum juventutis Scholasticae collecta."[3] On fols. 62v–74v: pieces *a3*, *a4*, and *a5*, with Latin or German text.

Copies in: D:Lr (imperfect), D:Mbs, F:Pm.[4]

	fol.		
1	56v	[*Ricercare 1.*][5]	Pomponio Nenna = 1590_{12}, no. 45
2	57v	[*Ricercare 2.*]	Gio. Pietro Gallo
3	58v	[*Ricercare 3.*][6]	Giovanni de Antiquis
4	59v	[*Ricercare 4.*]	Stefano Felis
5	60v	[*Ricercare 5.*]	Cola Vincenzo Fanelli = 1591_7, no. 80
6	61v	[*Ricercare 6.*]	D'Incerto = 1591_7, no. 79

[1] See 1591_6 for several names included in the dedication in the first edition but omitted here.
[2] Some of them are repr. in DTB X/2.
[3] Facs. of the title page of this second section in MGG I, col. 1841.
[4] According to FétB IV, 162, a copy was in Strasbourg.
[5] The six ricercares are headed "Ricercari, sive Fantasiae 6, elegantes diversorum Autorum."
[6] Mod. ed. in DoflS, no. 3, and MI IV, 12.

[1595]₅

METALLO, GRAMMATICO

Ricercari a canto e tenore. In Venetia. Apresso Giacomo Vincenti, 1595.

This volume of ricercares *a2*, now lost, is mentioned in FétB VI, 109. A first edition of this work may have appeared in 1591 or before, for the trade catalogue of the firm of Vincenti for that year lists "Metalo L 10 [= the price]" under "Musica a due voci" (see VincenI, fol. 2, and ThibaultD). For later editions of these Metallo ricercares *a2* see SartMS 1605e, 1609i, 1614i, 1617g, 1626l, and so forth.

1595₆

MORLEY, THOMAS

OF / THOMAS MORLEY / THE FIRST BOOKE OF / CANZONETS / TO / TWO VOYCES. / [Printer's mark] / IN LONDON / BY THOMAS ESTE. / CIↃ. IↃ. XC. V.[1]

Two part books in mensural notation, each of 14 fols. Dedication on fol. 2 headed "TO THE MOST VERTUOUS AND GENTLE LADIE THE LADIE PERIAM," and signed "From London the 17. of November. 1595. Your Ladieships Ever to commaund, Thomas Morley," reprinted in EMS I, vii, and MorlCB, p. 4. On fol. 2v: table of contents. A second edition appeared in 1619. John Playford, *A Catalogue of all the Musick Bookes that have been printed in England*, 1653, mentions an Italian edition of which no copies survive (see *The Musical Times* for July 1, 1926, p. 637, for a facsimile of the catalogue). MorlCB is a modern edition of the entire volume (with a facsimile of the title page and of fol. B1). MorlCU is a facsimile edition of the entire volume. EMS I is a modern edition of the canzonets only. MorlF and MorlFV are modern editions of the fantasies only. The compositions identified by the superior letter *a* ([a]) are reprinted in DoflS. The volume contains 21 canzonets *a2* and nine fantasies *a2*.

Copies in: EIR:Dm, GB:Lbm, GB: Lcm, US:SM (T), US:Ws (S).

	fol.	
1	5	*Fantasie: Il doloroso?*
2	6	*Fantasie: La Girandolo?*[a]
3	8	*Fantasie: La Rondinella?*
4	10	*Fantasie: Il Grillo?*
5	11	*Fantasie: Il Lamento?*[a]
6	12	*Fantasie: La Caccia?*[a]
7	13	*Fantasie: La Sampogna?*[a 2]
8	14	*Fantasie: La Serena?*
9	14ᵛ	*Fantasie: La Torello?*[a] [recte: *La Tortorella?*]

[1] Facs. of the title page in KinsP, p. 101; MGG IX, col. 593 (along with one page of vocal music from this volume); and SubHM I, 440.
[2] Mod. ed. in MI IV, 10.

[1595]₇

NEWSIDLER, MELCHIOR

Mel. Neysidler: Il primo libro intabulatura di liuto di Melchior Neysidler Alemanno ove sono Madrigali, Canzon Framesi [*sic*], Passemetzi, Saltarelli, &c. Venetiis 1595. fol.

This volume of music for solo lute, now lost, is listed in DraudiusBE, p. 268. FétB VI, 307, lists the same title for 1576 (see [1576]₂) as a later edition, in Italian tablature, of 1574₅.

1595₈

SPONGA, FRANCESCO

RICERCARI / ET ARIE FRANCESI / à Quattro Voci / DI FRANCESCO SPONGA / Discepolo di Andrea Gabrieli / Nuovamente composte, e date in luce. / IN VENETIA, / Appresso Giacomo Vincenti. / MDXCV.

Four part books in mensural notation, each of 12 fols. The title is placed within an ornamental border. Dedication on fol. *1ᵛ headed "ALL'ILLUSTRE ET ECCELLENTISSIMO SIG. MIO COLENDISSIMO IL SIG. LODOVICO USPER," and signed "Di Venetia il dì 21. Decembre. M. D. XCIV. Di V. S. Illustre, & Eccellentissima Devotissimo Servitore Francesco Sponga," reprinted in SartMS, p. 86. Fol. 2 = p. 1. On p. 22: table of contents. All of the compositions are for instrumental ensemble *a4*.

Copies in: CH:Bu, GB:Lbm (B).

	p.	
1	1	*Ricercar Primo*
2	2	*Ricercar Secondo*
3	3	*Ricercar Terzo*
4	5	*Ricercar Quarto*
5	7	*Ricercar Quinto*
6	8	*Ricercar Sesto*
7	9	*Ricercar Settimo*
8	10	*Ricercar Ottavo*
9	11	*Ricercar Nono*
10	12	*Ricercar Decimo*
11	13	*Ricercar Undecimo*
12	14	*Ricercar Duodecimo*
13	15	*Ricercar Decimoterzo*
14	16	*Ricercar Quartodecimo*
15	17	*Aria Francese Prima*
16	18	*Aria Francese Seconda*
17	19	*Aria Francese Terza*
18	21	*Aria Francese Quarta*

1595₉

VECCHI, ORAZIO

SELVA / DI VARIA RICREA/TIONE / DI HORATIO VECCHI. / Nella quale si contengono Varii Soggetti, / A 3. à 4. à 5. à 6. à 7. à 8. à 9. & à 10 voci, / cioè Madrigali, Capricci, Balli, Arie, Justiniane, Canzo/nette, Fantasie, Serenate, Dialoghi, un Lotto amo/roso; con una Battaglia à Diece nel fine, / & accomodatovi la Intavolatura di / Liuto alle Arie, ai Balli, et / alle Canzonette. / Novamente Ristampata & Corretta. / CON PRIVILEGIO / [Printer's mark] / In Venetia Appresso Angelo Gardano. / M. D. LXXXXV.

Ten part books in mensural notation and Italian lute tablature. On fol. 1^v: same dedication as in 1590_8, but dated August 5, 1595. On fol. 30^v: table of contents. Contents = 1590_8. The volume contains compositions with Italian and French text, and 13 pieces using instruments. Eleven of the 13 are printed as part songs (with texts), and with lute accompaniment. Two of the 13 are for instrumental ensemble *a 5* and *a 4* (one of the two includes a lute part as well).

Copies in: D:As (8 wanting), D:MÜs (T7), F:Pc (S wanting), F:Pn (S), GB:Lbm (8), I:Bc (5), I:Fr (8), I:Vnm.[1]

[1] A copy of AB was in D:Bds.

1595_{10}

VEROVIO, SIMONE

LODI DELLA MUSICA / A .3. VOCI. Composte da diversi Ecc^{tl} / Musici con $L'intavolat^a$ / del Cimbalo e Liuto / Libro Primo. / Raccolto intagliato et / stampato da Simone / Verovio In / Roma / 1595 / Con licentia de Superiori.

20 fols. Mensural notation, keyboard score, and Italian lute tablature. The title is placed within an ornamental border. On fol. 19: imprimatur given by Pompeo Ugonio. The vocal setting of each piece is printed

LODI DELLA MVSICA
A.3.VOCI.
Composte da diuersi Ecc.ti
Musici con L'intauolat.a
del Cimbalo et Liuto
Libro Primo.
Raccolto intagliato et
stampato da Simone
Verouio In
Roma
.1595.
Con licentia de Superiori

Title page of 1595_{10}

across the top of each opening; the keyboard intabulation appears on the lower left-hand page, and the lute intabulation on the lower right-hand page.

Copies in: D:Mbs, GB:Lbm, I:Bc, I:Pca.

	fol.	
1	1v	*Ai dolci e vaghi accenti* Gio: Maria Nanino
2	2v	*E se tal'hor affetti* Gio: Maria Nanino
3	3v	*Cosi un leggiadro canto* Gio: Maria Nanino
4	4v	*Onde spieghin sue lodi* Gio: Maria Nanino
5	5v	*Spesso il Canto* Gio. de Macque
6	6v	*E sopra gl'arbuscelli* Gio. de Macque
7	7v	*E i travagliati amanti* Gio. de Macque
8	8v	*Se dunque il dolce Canto* Gio. de Macque
9	9v	*All'hor che di bei fiori* Ruggiero Giovanelli
10	10v	*E da verdi boschetti* Ruggiero Giovanelli
11	11v	*Al suon di Cornamusa* Felice Anerio
12	12v	*Quand'il fido Pastore* Rinaldo del Mel
13	13v	*Al tremolar de l'onde* Felice Anerio
14	14v	*L'amoroso Delfino lascia i profondi* [vocal setting only]
15	15v	*E le celesti sfere* Rinaldo del Mel
16	16v	*Mentr'il canoro Cigno* Gio. Bernardino Nanino
17	17v	*Ecco del Canto* Bernardino Nanino
18	18v	*E voi muse gradite* Bern.no Nanino.

1595

DOUBTFUL WORKS

1. FétB III, 51, erroneously dates John Dowland, *The First Booke of Songs or Ayres*, 1595. The volume is listed in this bibliography as 1597_4.

1596_1

ARBEAU, THOINOT

ORCHESOGRAPHIE, / METODE, ET TEORIE / EN FORME DE DISCOURS ET TABLATURE / POUR APPRENDRE A DANCER, BATTRE LE / Tambour en toute sorte & diversité de batte/ries, Jouër du fifre & arigot, tirer des armes / & escrimer, avec autres honnestes / exercices fort convenables / à la Jeunesse. / AFFIN / D'estre bien venue en toute Joyeuse compagnie & y monstrer sa dexterité / & agilité de corps, / Par Thoinot Arbeau demeurant a Lengres. / Tempus plangendi, & tempus saltandi. / Eccle. 3. / [Printer's mark with the motto "TELLE EST LA GLOIRE DES HOMMES"] / A LENGRES, / Par Jehan des Preyz Imprimeur & Libraire, tenant sa bouti/que en la ruë des merciers dicte les Pilliers. / M. D. XCVI. / Avec Privilege du Roy.[1]

104 fols. Mensural notation. The same dedication as in 1589_1, on fol. 1v, headed "A maistre Guillaume Tabourot," reprinted in WeckC, p. 27. This volume is described in WeckC, pp. 26–30. Contents = 1589_1 and 1597_1. This treatise on dancing, in the form of a dialogue, gives detailed choreography and music for a large number of sixteenth-century dances. All of the complete musical examples are notated as single voices, except for one composition *a 4*.

Copies in: A:Wn, F:Pc.

[1] Facs. of title page in MagB, p. 46. Facs. of fol. 30 in SubHM I, 452.

1596_2

ASOLA, GIOVANNI MATTEO

CANTO FERMO / SOPRA MESSE, / HINNI, / ET ALTRE COSE ECCLESIASTICHE / Appartenenti à' Sonatori d'Organo, per giusta/mente rispondere al Choro, / Accommodato dal R. D. GIO. MATTEO / ASOLA VERONESE, / Nuovamente Ristampato, & Corretto. / [Printer's mark] / IN VENETIA, / Appresso Giacomo Vincenti, M. D. XCVI.

32 fols. Mensural notation. On fol. 1v (= p. 2): cut of the Virgin and Child surrounded by angels, including one playing recorder and another lute. On pp. 60–64: table of contents. The volume contains plain chants for the entire church year, to be used as cantus firmi by church organists. The volume includes four Mass ordinaries (without Credos), three separate Credos, hymns for the whole liturgical year, one Magnificat in each mode, four antiphons, and the Te Deum. According to the title page this is not the first edition. EitQ I, 221, lists later editions in 1607, 1615, and 1635. FétB I, 156, lists later editions in 1602 and 1615.

Copy in: I:Bc.

1596_3

BANCHIERI, ADRIANO

CANZONI ALLA FRANCESE / A QUATTRO VOCI / PER SONARE / Dentrovi, un Echo, & in fine una Battaglia a Otto, & dui Concerti / fatti sopra Lieto godea. / DI ADRIANO BANCHIERI BOLOGNESE / Organista in S. Michele in Bosco. / LIBRO SECONDO. / Novamente composte, & date in luce. / [Printer's mark] / In Venetia appresso Ricciardo Amadino. / M D XCVI.

Four part books in mensural notation, each of 10 fols. The title is placed within an ornamental border. Dedication on fol. 1v of each part book headed "AL MOLTO REVERENDO P. VICARIO GENERALE DIGNISSIMO DI MONTE OLIVETO. IL P. D. CIPRIANO ROVATI Mio Padron Colendissimo," and signed "Di Bologna il dì 8 dì Aprile. 1596. Di V. P. M. R. Servitore Affettionatissimo. Adriano Banchieri," reprinted in SartMS, p. 88. Fol. 2 = p. 1. On p. 18 of each part book: table of contents. According to MGG I, col. 1208, there was a second edition of this collection in 1603. Nos. 12 and 13 are completely texted in each voice. All of the other compositions are for instrumental ensemble *a 4*.

Copy in: I:Bc.

	p.	
1	1	*Canzon Prima. La Rovattina*
2	2	*Canzon seconda. L'Ardina*
3	3	*Canzon Terza. La Galluppa* [*Revista*] = 1595_2, no. 2
4	4	*Canzon Quarta. La Rustica* Sopra "Vitam eternam"
5	5	*Canzon Quinta. La Pomponazza*
6	6	*Canzon Sesta. L'Alcenagina* Sopra "Vestiva i Colli" (compare PalO IX, 117: Palestrina)
7	6	*Canzon Settima. La Guamina* Gioseffo Guami (1599_7, no. 68)
8	8	*Canzon Ottava. La Banchierina*
9	9	*Canzon Nona. La Camerina* Sopra "Veni dilecte mi" (compare PalO XI, 197: Palestrina)
10	10	*Canzon Decima. La Feliciana*
11	11	*Canzon Undecima. La Organistina Bella*[1] In Echo
12	12	*La Battaglia*[2] *a 8* [*Concerto primo*]
13	14	*Magnificat a 8* [*Concerto secondo*] Sopra "lieto Godea" (compare IMAMI I, 35: Giovanni Gabrieli)
	16	2a pars *Suscepit Israel* [*Concerto terzo*]

[1] Dynamics (*piano* and *forte*) are included in no. 11.

[2] The text begins: "Udite ecco le trombe."

1596_4 †

BARLEY, WILLIAM

A new Booke of Tabliture, Containing / sundrie easie and familiar Instructions, shewing howe to attaine to the knowledge, to / guide and dispose thy hand to play on sundry Instruments, as the Lute, Orpharion, / and Bandora: Together with divers new Lessons to each of these Instruments. / Whereunto is added an introduction to Prickesong, and certaine familliar rules of Descant, with other / necessarie Tables plainely shewing the true use of the Scale or Gamut, and also how to set any Lesson / higher or lower at your pleasure. / Collected together out of the best Authors professing the practise of these Instruments. / [Cut of a lute lying on an open music book] / Printed at London for William Barley and are to be sold at his shop in Gratious street, 1596.

25 fols. French lute tablature. The title is placed within an ornamental border. Dedication on fol. A2 headed "To the Right honorable & vertuous Ladie Bridgett Countesse of Sussex, W. B. wisheth health of bodie, content of minde, with increase of all Honourable perfection, and eternall happinesse in the worlde to come." On fol. A3: a poem headed "Certaine Verses upon the Alphebet of her Ladyships Name." On fol. A3^v: preface headed "To the Reader." On fol. A4: a poem beginning "Thoughts make men sigh, sighes make men sick at hart." On fol. A4^v: a poem beginning "Your face, Your tongue, Your wit," followed by another poem beginning "Flow forth abundant teares, bedew this dolefull face." Beginning on fol. B1: "An Instruction to the Lute" (a partial translation of Le Roy's lute instructions; see $[1557]_1$). Cuts of a lute appear on fol. B1 and on fol. B2. Items a and b in the index below are given as examples in the course of the instructions. For other volumes in this series, see 1596_5 and 1596_6.[1] The dedication, the preface, and the four poems are reprinted in BolleG, pp. 112–119. For further information on all three volumes, see CaseyP. All of the compositions are for solo lute.

Copies in: GB:Lbm, GB:Lcm, US:SM.[2]

	fol.	
a	C1	*The x. Commandements*
b	C3^v	[Textless example]
1	D1^v	*A Pavan for the Lute* F[rancis] C[utting]
2	D3	*A Pavan for the Lute* F[rancis] C[utting]
3	E1	*Lacrime* [*Pavane*] J[ohn] D[owland]
4	E3	*A Paven for the Lute* [*Pipers Pavan*] J[ohn] D[owland]
5	F1^v	*An Almaine for the Lute* F[rancis] C[utting]
6	F3^v	*Fortune* J[ohn] D[owland]
7	F4	*A Galliard for the Lute* Fr[ancis] C[utting]

[1] The three volumes, 1596_4, 1596_5, and 1596_6, are usually listed as one (see, for example, RISM 1596_{20}), but since they each have a separate title page, preface, and introductory matter, and each is signed beginning with fol. A1, they are here listed separately. DeakinMB, p. 9, dates these three collections 1599; DeakinO, p. 50, dates them 1593.

[2] A copy was in the library of W. H. Cummings (see CummC, no. 1182).

1596_5 †

BARLEY, WILLIAM

A new Booke of Tabliture for the Orpha/rion: Contayning sundrie sorts of lessons, collected together out of divers good Authors, for / the furtherance and delight of such as are desirous to practise on this Instrument. / Never before Published. / [Cut of an orpharion with the frets lettered *b* to *q*] / Imprinted at London for William Barley; and are to be sold at his shop in Gratious / street neare Leaden-Hall.

16 fols. Letter tablature for the seven-course orpharion.[1] On fol. A4: preface headed "To the Reader." For other volumes in this series see 1596_4 and 1596_6. All of the compositions are for solo orpharion.

Copies in: GB:Lbm, GB:Lcm.

	fol.	
1	B1	*The Countesse of Sussex Galliard* P[hilip] R[osseter]
2	B2	*Another galliard of the Countesse of Sussex* P.P. (= Philip Rosseter?)
3	B3	*Another galliard of the Countesse of Sussex* P[hilip] R[osseter]
4	B3^v	*Solus cum Sola made by J[ohn] D[owland]*
5	B4^v	*A Galliard made by J[ohn] D[owland]*
6	C1	*A Galliard made by F[rancis] C[utting]*
7	C1^v	*A Galliard made by Ed[ward] J[ohnson]*
8	C2	*An Almaine* Frances Cuting
9	C2^v	*Go from my Windowe made by J[ohn] D[owland]*
10	C4^v	*Bockingtons Pound* Fr[ancis] C[utting]
11	D1	*Mistris Winters Jump made by J[ohn] D[owland]*
12	D1^v	*Cuttings Comfort* [Francis Cutting]
13	D2	*Walsinggam made by Francis Cutting*

14 D3[v] *Master Birds Pavan set by Francis Cutting*

[1] The seven-course orpharion is tuned C′ G C F a d g′.

† 1596_6

BARLEY, WILLIAM

A new Booke of Tabliture for the Bando/ ra: Contayning sundrie sorts of lessons, collected together out of divers good Authors for / the furtherance and delight of such as are desirous to practise on this Instrument. / Never before Published. / [Cut of a bandora with the frets lettered *b* to *q*] / Imprinted at London for William Barley; and are to be sold at his shop in Gratious / street neere Leaden-Hall.

16 fols. Letter tablature for the seven-course bandora,[1] with mensural notation for the voice part in nos. 5–8. On fol. A3: preface headed "Gentle Reader." On fol. D4: texts for nos. 5 and 6 and a third poem beginning "Short is my rest whose toyle is overlong." The three poems are reprinted in BolleG, pp. 119–121. For other volumes in this series, see 1596_4 and 1596_5. Nos. 1–4 and 9 are for solo bandora; nos. 5–8 are for voice and bandora.

Copies in: GB:Lbm, GB:Lcm.

	fol.	
1	A4	*The Quadron Pavan*
	B2	*The Quadron Galliard*
2	B3	*A Perludium* A[ntony] H[olbourne]
3	B3[v]	*The new Hunt sundry waies made by Frances Cutting*
4	C1[v]	[Textless piece.] A[ntony] H[olbourne]
5	C2[v]	*Those eies which set my fancie on a fire* [voice and bandora]
6	C3[v]	*How can the tree but waste and wither away*[2] [voice and bandora]
7	C4[v]	*One joy of joyes I only felt* [voice and bandora]
8	D1[v]	*But this & then no more it is my last of all*[3] [voice and bandora]
9	D2[v]	*Treschoses*

[1] In his preface Barley describes the bandora as an instrument with six courses tuned B♭ C F b♭ d g′. His tablature, however, calls for a seventh course tuned to F′.

[2] The poet, named at the end of the text, is Thomas Lord Vaux. For concordances see RubsS, p. 274.

[3] The voice part appears to have no relation to the bandora part in no. 8. Possibly Barley printed the voice part of one song with the accompaniment to another.

1596_7

GABRIELI, ANDREA

IL TERZO LIBRO DE RICERCARI / DI ANDREA GABRIELI, ORGANISTA IN S. MARCO DI VENETIA. / Insieme uno Motetto, Dui Madrigaletti, & uno Capricio sopra il Pass'è mezo Antico, / In cinque modi variati, & Tabulati per ogni sorte di Stromenti da Tasti. / Novamente stampati, & dati in luce. / [Printer's mark] / In Venetia Appresso Angelo Gardano. / M. D. LXXXXVI.

44 fols. Keyboard score. Fol. A2 = fol. 1. On fol. 42[v]: table of contents. The compositions identified by the superior letter *a* ([a]) are reprinted in Gabri(A)RO II, nos. 1–6, 9, and 10. For other volumes in the same series see 1593_4. All of the compositions are for solo keyboard.

Copies in: CH:Bu, I:Bc.

	fol.	
1	A1[v]	*Ricercar del Primo Tono*[a]
2	3	*[Ricercar del] Secondo Tono*[a]
3	7	*[Ricercar del] Quinto Tono*[a]
4	9[v]	*[Ricercar del] Quinto Tono*[a1]
5	11[v]	*[Ricercar del] Nono Tono*[a]
6	14[v]	*[Ricercar del] Nono Tono*[a]
7	21[v]	*Fantasia Allegra Del Duodecimo Tono*[2]
8	25[v]	*Cantate Domino*[a] *a 5* Motetto d'Andrea Gabrieli (IMAMI I, no. 1)
9	30	*Canzon Ariosa*[3]
10	33	*Anchor che co'l partire*[a4] Madrigale *a 4* di Cipriano de Rore (SCMA VI, 45)
11	34[v]	*Io mi son giovinetta*[5] Madrigale *a 4* di Giachet (EinIM III, no. 30: D. Ferabosco)
	35[v]	2a pars [*Io vo per verdi prati*]
12	38[v]	*Pass'e mezo Antico*[6]

[1] Mod. ed. in FuserC, no. 8.
[2] Mod. ed. in Gabri(A)CR, no. 1; RitZ, no. 1; TagA I, no. 21; TorA III, 67; and WasG, no. 22. Facs. of fol. 23v in MGG III, col. 1768.
[3] Mod. ed. in DallaLO I, no. 3; FuserC, no. 10; Gabri(A)I, no. 13; TagA I, no. 19; and WasG, no. 23.
[4] Mod. ed. in TagA I, no. 18.
[5] Mod. ed. in Gabri(A)I, no. 14.
[6] Mod. ed. in CorteA, no. 60; Gabri(A)I, no. 15; KleinO, p. 90; MOM, vol. 66; TagA, 89; and TorA III, 71.

1596_8

MASCHERA, FIORENZO

LIBRO PRIMO / DE CANZONI / DA SONARE, / A QUATTRO VOCI, / DI FLORENTIO MASCHERA / Organista nel Duomo di Brescia. / Di nuovo con diligenza ristampate. / [Printer's mark] / IN MILANO, / Appresso gli heredi di Francesco, & Simon Tini. / M. D. XCVI.

Four part books in mensural notation, each of 12 fols. (?). On fol. 1v: preface headed "A'gl'amatori delle virtù," and signed "Di Milano li 12. di Giugno, 1596. Li heredi di Francesco, & Simon Tini," reprinted in SartMS, p. 90. Contents = 1584_{10}. All of the compositions are for instrumental ensemble *a 4*.

Copy in: I:A (B).

1596_9

MAZZI, LUIGI

RICERCARI A QUATTRO / ET CANZONI A QUATTRO, / A CINQUE, ET A OTTO VOCI / Da Cantare, & Sonare con ogni sorte / d'Istrumenti / DI LUIGI MAZZI / Organista delli Reverendi Padri di San / Benedetto di Ferrara, / [Printer's mark] / IN VENETIA, / Appresso Giacomo Vincenti. M. D. XCVI.

Four part books in mensural notation (SAT, each of 12 fols.; B, 14 fols.). The title is placed within an ornamental border. Dedication on fol. 1v (= p. 2) of each part book headed "AL MOLTO MAGNIFICO SIG. MIO OSSERVANDISSIMO IL SIG. ANTONIO GORRETTI," and signed "Di Venetia il Primo di Gennaro 1596. Di V. S. Affettionatissimo per servirla Luigi Mazzi," reprinted in SartMS, p. 87. On p. 28 of the bass part book: table of contents. All of the compositions are for instrumental ensemble *a 4*.

Copies in: I:Fn, I:MOe (SB).

	p.	
1	3	*Ricercar Primo*
2	5	*Ricercar Secondo*
3	7	*Ricercar Terzo*
4	8	*Ricercar Quarto*
5	10	*Ricercar Quinto*
6	12	*Ricercar Sesto*
7	14	*Ricercar Settimo*
8	15	*Ricercar Ottavo*
9	17	*Canzon prima a 4*
10	17	*Canzon Seconda a 4*
11	18	*Canzon Prima a 8*
12	20	*Canzon Seconda a 8*
13	21	*Canzon prima a 5*
14	22	*Canzon Seconda a 5*
15	23	*Canzon terza a 5*
16	24	*Canzon quarta a 5*

$[1596]_{10}$

NEWSIDLER, MELCHIOR

Melchioris Neusidleri Teutsch Lautenbuch, darinnen künstliche Muteten, liebliche Italiänische, Frantzösische teutsche Stücke, fröliche teutsche Däntz, Passomezo, Saltarelle, und drey Fantaseyen, Strassburg, 1596. in fol.

This volume of music for solo lute, now lost, is listed in DraudiusBLG, p. 552. It is a later edition of 1574_5. See also $[1576]_2$ and $[1595]_7$.

1596_{11}

RAVAL, SEBASTIAN

El Primo Libro / di Ricercari / a quatro voci cantabili / Per Liuti Cimbali, et Viole d'arco, quattro o sei opere con parole spirituali, / in Canoni ad Echo, ad otto, et a dodeci voci, che cantano in quattro parte /

conjunti et divisi chori. E Ricercar in contreponti osservati sciolti, / et in quattro fughe d'accordio di Studi particulari, / et utilissimi per studiosi. / Composte per FRA SEBASTIAN RAVAL, dell'Ordine di San Gio. Battista, / Maestro della Cappelle Reale di San Pietro di Palermo. / All'Illustrissimo et Eccellentissimo Signor / Il Conte Don Giovanni Vintimillia Marchese de Hieraci, / Principe di Castel Buono, Presidente et Capitan / Generale per Sua Maesta nel Regno di Sicilia. / [Coat of arms] / In Palermo, per Gio. Antonio de Franceschi M. D. XCVI.

Four part books in mensural notation, each of 12 fols. On fol. 1^v: dedication, reprinted in AngAM, p. 106. On fol. 12^v: table of contents. All of the compositions are for instrumental ensemble *a4*, except nos. 19–22, which are canons *a8* and *a12*.

Copy in: E:V.

	fol.	
1	2	[*Ricercar*] *Del Primo Tono trasportato*
2	2^v	[*Ricercar*] *Del Secondo Tono trasportato*
3	3	[*Ricercar*] *Del Undecimo Tono naturale*
4	3^v	[*Ricercar*] *Del Ottavo Tono trasportato*
5	4	[*Ricercar*] *Del Undecimo Tono trasportato*
6	4^v	[*Ricercar*] *Del Duodecimo Tono trasportato*
7	5	[*Ricercar*] *Del Nono Tono trasportato*
8	5^v	[*Ricercar*] *Del Primo Tono naturale*
9	6	[*Ricercar*] *Del Primo Tono naturale*
10	6^v	[*Ricercar*] *Del Secondo Tono naturale*
11	7	[*Ricercar*] *Del Terzo Tono naturale*
12	7^v	[*Ricercar*] *Del Quarto Tono naturale*
13	8	[*Ricercar*] *Del Quinto Tono naturale*
14	8^v	[*Ricercar*] *Del Sesto Tono naturale*
15	9	[*Ricercar*] *Del Settimo Tono naturale*
16	9^v	[*Ricercar*] *Del Ottavo Tono naturale*
17	10	[*Ricercar*] *Del Duodecimo Tono naturale*
18	10^v	*Viderunt te aque Deus, per Organum*
19	11	*Congregate sunt gentes* (Canon *a8*)
20	11^v	*Haec dies* (Canon *a12*)
21	12	*Da pacem Domine* (Canon *a8*)
22	12^v	*Misit Dominus* (Canon *a12*)

†

1596

DOUBTFUL WORKS

1. DeakinMB, p. 8, lists a 1596 edition of William Bathe, *A Briefe Introduction to the skill of Song*. A license to print the work was applied for on September 29, 1596; see ArbertT III, 71. The volume is listed in this bibliography as $158?_2$.

1597_1

ARBEAU, THOINOT

ORCHESOGRAPHIE, / METODE, ET TEORIE / EN FORME DE DISCOURS ET TABLATURE / POUR APPRENDRE A DANCER, BATTRE LE / Tambour en toute sorte & diversité de batte/ries, Jouër du fifre & arigot, tirer des armes / & escrimer, avec autres honnestes / exercices fort convenables / à la Jeunesse. / AFFIN / D'estre bien venue en toute Joyeuse compagnie & y monstrer sa dexterité / & agilité de corps, / Par Thoinot Arbeau demeurant a Lengres. / Tempus plangendi, & tempus saltandi. / Eccle. 3. / [Printer's mark with the motto "TELLE EST LA GLOIRE DES HOMMES"] / A LENGRES, / Par Jehan des Preyz Imprimeur & Libraire, tenant sa bouti/que en la ruë des merciers dicte les Pilliers. / M. D. XCVII. / Avec Privilege du Roy

104 fols. Mensural notation. The same dedication as in 1589_1 on fol. 1^v headed "A maistre Guillaume Tabourot." Contents = 1589_1 and 1596_1. This treatise on dancing, in the form of a dialogue, gives detailed

choreography and music for a large number of sixteenth-century dances. All of the complete musical examples are notated as single voices, except for one composition *a 4*.

Copy in: GB:Lrc.

1597_2

CAVACCIO, GIOVANNI

MUSICA DI GIOVANNI CA/VACCIO DA BERGAMO, / Ove si contengono due fantasie, che dan principio e fine / all'opera, Canzoni alla Franzese, Pavana co'l / Saltarello, Madrigali, & un Proverbio / non so se antico, o moderno. / A QUATTRO VOCI. / [Printer's mark] / IN VENETIA M D XCVII.

Four part books in mensural notation, each of 14 fols. The title is placed within an ornamental border. Dedication on fol. A1^v of each part book headed "AL ILLUSTRE SIGNORE ET MIO PATRON OSSERVANDISSIMO. IL SIGNOR CAMILLO NICOLINI," and signed "Da Bergamo alli 28 Novembre. 1596. Di V. S. Illustre. Servitore di cuore. Giovanni Cavaccio." Fol. 2 = p. 1. Nos. 6, 10, 14, and 19 are supplied with text in all voices. All of the other compositions are for instrumental ensemble *a 4*.[1]

† Copy in: I:Bc.

	p.	
1	1	*La Bertani*
2	2	*La Nicolina*
3	3	*La Verità*
4	4	*La Lafranchina*
5	5	*La Brigientia*
6	6	*Dal tempo che canta il Cucco. Il proverbio*
7	7	*La Solcia*
8	8	*La Foresta*
9	9	*La Fina*
10	10	*Mentre mia stella*
11	11	*La Bignani*
12	12	*La Nova*
13	12	*La Morari*
14	14	*Argo son le miserie*
15	15	*La Villa chiara*
16	16	*L'Agosta*
17	17	*La Marina*
18	18	*La Pasti*
19	18	*Ero cosi dicea*
20	20	*La Benaglia*
21	20	*La Massaina*
22	22	*La Moiola*
23	23	*L'Aresia*
24	24	*Pavana*
	25	*Saltarello*
25	26	*La Gastolda*

[1] FétB II, 223, lists "Musica a 5 da sonare. Venezia. 1585" as a volume by Cavaccio; he probably refers to Vogel: Cavaccio 3 (1585), which contains no instrumental music.

1597_3

DIRUTA, GIROLAMO

IL / TRANSILVANO / DIALOGO / SOPRA IL VERO MODO DI SONAR / Organi, & istromenti da penna. / DEL R. P. GIROLAMO DIRUTA / PERUGINO, / Dell'Ordine de' Frati Minori Conu. di S. Francesco. / ORGANISTA DEL DUOMO / DI CHIOGGIA. / Nel quale facilmente, & presto s'impara di conoscere sopra la Tasta/tura il luogo di ciascuna parte, & come nel Diminuire si deveno / portar le mani, & il modo d'intendere la Intavolatura; provando / la verità, & necessità delle sue Regole, con le Toccate di diversi / eccellenti Organisti, poste nel fine del Libro. / Opera nuovamente ritrovata, utilissima, & necessaria / a Professori d'Organo. / AL SERENISSIMO PRENCIPE / di Transilvania. / CON PRIVILEGIO. / [Printer's mark] / In Venetia, Appresso Giacomo Vincenti. M. D. XCVII.[1]

32 fols. Keyboard score. The title is placed within an ornamental border. On pp. 3–4: the same dedication, preface and foreword as in 1593_3. The dialogue begins on p. 5. On p. 64: table of contents. Contents = 1593_3. The complete compositions in this instruction book for keyboard instruments are all for solo keyboard.

Copies in: D:Bds;Tü,[2] D:Tu, GB: †
Lbm, I:Bc.

[1] Facs. of title page in MGG III, col. 558. Facs. of two pages in KinsP, p. 126.

[2] This copy was in the Wolffheim library (see WolffC I, no. 597). A copy was in the Landau-Finaly library in Florence (see RoedigC I, 512).

1597₄

DOWLAND, JOHN

THE / FIRST BOOKE / of Songs or Ayres / of fowre partes with Ta/bleture for the Lute: / so made that all the partes / together, or either of them seve/rally may be song to the Lute, / Orpherian or Viol de gambo. / Composed by John Dowland Lute/ nist and Batcheler of musicke in / both the Universities. / Also an invention by the sayd / Author for two to playe up/on one Lute. / Nec prosunt domino, quae prosunt omnibus, artes. / Printed by Peter Short, dwelling on / Bredstreet hill at the sign of the Starre, 1597[1]

24 fols. French lute tablature and mensural notation. The title is placed within an ornamental border showing various figures from the ancient world, from mythology, and representing disciplines of learning. On fol. *1ᵛ: a coat of arms. Dedication on fol. *2 headed "TO THE RIGHT HONORABLE SIR GEORGE CAREY, OF THE MOST HONORABLE ORDER OF THE GARTER KNIGHT, Baron of Hunsdon, Captaine of her Majesties Gentlemen Pensioners, Governor of the Isle of Wight, Lietenant of the Countie of Southt. Lord Chamberlaine of her Majesties most Royall house, and of her Highnes most honourable privie Counsell," and signed "Your Lordships most humble servant, John Dowland." On fol. *2ᵛ: preface headed "To the courteous Reader," and including a laudatory letter in Italian, signed "Di Roma a' 13. di Luglio. 1595. D. V. S. Affettionatissimo servitore, Luca Marenzio," both reprinted in WarA, p. 29. On fol. A1 (= fol. *3): a poem in Latin headed "Tho. Campiani Epigramma de instituto Authoris," followed by the table of contents. The entire collection except for no. 22 is reprinted in a modern edition in MB VI, which includes a facsimile of fols. B1–B1ᵛ. All of the songs are reprinted in a modern edition for solo voice and lute in EL, ser. 1, vols. I–II, which includes a facsimile of the title page and reprints all of the prefatory material. See there for information concerning later editions (in 1600, 1606, and 1613). Versions *a4* are all reprinted in DowlS. The compositions identified by the superior letter *a* (ᵃ) are reprinted in DowlL, nos. 3, 6–7, 11, and 17 (arranged for voice and guitar). All of the compositions in the volume except for no. 22 are printed in alternate versions for lute and one or more voices, and for voices *a4*.

Copies in: EIR:Duc, GB:Lbm, US:Bp, US:SM.

	fol.	
1	A1ᵛ	*Unquiet thoughts*[2]
2	A2ᵛ	*Who ever thinks or hopes of love for love*[a3]
3	B1ᵛ	*My thoughts are wingde with hopes*[4]
4	B2ᵛ	*If my complaints could passions moove*[5]
5	C1ᵛ	*Can shee excuse my wrongs*
6	C2ᵛ	*Now, O now I needs must part*[6]
7	D1ᵛ	*Deare, if you change, ile never chuse againe*
8	D2ᵛ	*Burst forth my teares*
9	E1ᵛ	*Go christall teares*
10	E2ᵛ	*Thinkst thou then by thy fayning*
11	F1ᵛ	*Come away, come sweet love*[7]
12	F2ᵛ	*Rest awhile you cruell cares*
13	G1ᵛ	*Sleep wayward thoughts*[a]
14	G2ᵛ	*Al ye whom love or fortune*
15	H1ᵛ	*Wilt thou unkind thus reave me*[a8]
16	H2ᵛ	*Would my conceit*
17	I1ᵛ	*Come againe: sweet love doth now envite*[a9]
18	I2ᵛ	*His golden locks*
19	K1ᵛ	*Awake sweet love*[a10]
20	K2ᵛ	*Come heavy sleepe*[11]
21	L1ᵛ	*Away with these selfe loving lads*
22	L2ᵛ	*My Lord Chamberlaine his galliard*[12] ("for two to play upon one lute")

[1] Facs. of title page in KommaM, p. 117; MGG III, col. 720; and WarA, frontispiece. FétB III, 51, incorrectly dates this volume 1595.

[2] Facs. of fol. A2 in MGG III, col. 721.

[3] Facs. of fols. A2ᵛ and B1 in PN, p. 90.

[4] Mod. ed. for voice and lute in EinSH, no. 23, and ParrishT, no. 34.

[5] Mod. ed. for voice and lute in LowT, p. 55.

[6] Mod. ed. of the version *a4* in ScherG, no. 146.

[7] Mod. ed. in DowlSS, no. 6 (arr. for voice and guitar).

[8] Mod. ed. in DowlTS, no. 3 (arr. for voice and guitar).

[9] Mod. ed. for voice and lute in BarthaZ, no. 64; BruAL I, 36; and LowT, p. 57. Mod. ed. arr. for voice and guitar in DowlTS, no. 1.

[10] Mod. ed. in DowlTS, no. 2 (arr. for voice and guitar). Facs. of fols. K1ᵛ and K2 in HarmM, pl. 19.

[11] Mod. ed. for voice and lute in BruAL I, 35; MagniSM I, 308; and MU I, app., p. 28. Facs. of fols. K2ᵛ and L1 in KinsP, p. 101, and PinchIH, p. 64.

[12] Mod. ed. in BruAL I, 37.

1597₅

GABRIELI, GIOVANNI

SACRAE / SYMPHONIAE, / JOANNIS GABRIELII. / SERENISS. REIP. VENETIAR. ORGANISTAE / IN ECCLESIA DIVI MARCI. / Senis, 7, 8, 10, 12, 14, 15, & 16, Tam / vocibus, Quam Instrumentis. / Editio Nova. / CUM PRIVILEGIO. / [Printer's mark] / VENETIIS, Apud Angelum Gardanum. / M. D. XCVII.

Twelve part books in mensural notation (SATB56, each of 34 fols.; 7, 31 fols.; 8, 29 fols.; 9 and 10, each of 14 fols.; 11 and 12, each of 12 fols.). Dedication on fol. A1ᵛ headed "Illustriss: ac Generosis: Dominis Georgio, Antonio, Philippo, et Alberto Fratribus Fucharis, Liber. Bar. In Chirchberg, & Weissenhorn, &c. Joannes Gabrielus. S. P. D." On fol. A2: poem in Latin headed "Ad Eosdem"; the poem and the dedication are reprinted in SartMS, p. 96. The music begins on fol. A2ᵛ (= p. 2). On p. 65: table of contents. On p. 66: printer's mark. All of the instrumental compositions are reprinted in IMAMI II, which includes (after p. viii) facsimiles of the title page (canto), the dedication, the table of contents, and p. 62. For further information see FlowerG. A complete list of the contents is given in SartMS, p. 95. The volume contains compositions with Latin text, omitted from this inventory, and compositions for instrumental ensemble *a8*, *a10*, *a12*, and *a15*.

† Copies in: A:Wn, D:As (S wanting), D:Rp (AB wanting), GB:Lbm (5), I:BRd (11 and 12 wanting), I:PCd (12), US:Cn (T).[1]

	p.	
1	30	*Canzon Primi Toni*[2] *a8*
2	31	*Canzon Septimi Toni*[3] *a8*
3	32	*Canzon Septimi Toni*[4] *a8*
4	33	*Canzon Noni Toni*[5] *a8* = 1597₁₂, no. 1
5	34	*Canzon Duodecimi Toni* *a8* = 1597₁₂, no. 2
6	35	*Sonata Pian & Forte*[6] *a8* *Alla Quarta Bassa*
7	44	*Canzon Primi Toni*[7] *a10*
8	45	*Canzon Duodecimi Toni* *a10*
9	46	*Canzon Duodecimi Toni* *a10*
10	47	*Canzon Duodecimi Toni*[8] *a10*
11	48	*Canzon in Echo Duodecimi Toni*[9] *a10*
12	49	*Canzon sudetta accomodata per concertar con l'Organo*[10] *a10*
13	57	*Canzon Septimi & Octavi Toni* *a12*
14	58	*Canzon Noni Toni* *a12*
15	59	*Sonata Octavi Toni*[11] *a12*
16	62	*Canzon Quarti Toni*[12] *a15*

[1] A copy was in D:Bds (9–12 wanting).

[2] Mod. ed. in MUB, vols. 91 and 415 (arr. for brass and organ), and WasI, no. 3.

[3] Mod. ed. in Gabri(G)CS.

[4] Mod. ed. in MUB, vol. 28.

[5] Mod. ed. in MUB, vols. 53 and 408 (arr. for brass and organ); the beginning is pr. in WintG III, 119.

[6] Scored for cornetto, violin and six trombones. Mod. ed. in CorteA, no. 62; Gabri(G)S; Gabri(G) SP; HAM, no. 173; MUB, vols. 45 and 406 (arr. for brass and organ); RoyM, p. 33; ScherG, no. 148; WasI, no. 4; and WasV. Facs. of p. 35 in KinsP, p. 106.

[7] The beginning is pr. in CorteA, no. 61.

[8] Cornetto is specified for the superius part.

[9] Scored for eight cornetti and two trombones. Mod. ed. in MUB, vol. 34, and SchneidA, p. 95.

[10] Scored for eight cornetti and two trombones. In the S and 7 part books no. 11 is headed "Questo Soprano serve alla Canzone in Echo a numero 49, che e l'istessa, & si sona con l'Organo." In the other part books no. 12 is headed "Pigliate li Soprani della Canzon in Echo antecedente à numero 48, che è questa istessa, & si soni com'è scritta qui, Variata di Concerto, con l'Organo insieme, che cosi va Concertata." Mod. ed. in MUB, vol. 401.

[11] Mod. ed. in MUB, vol. 10.

[12] Scored for two cornetti, violin and twelve trombones. Mod. ed. in MUB, vol. 19.

1597₆

HOLBORNE, ANTONY

THE / CITTHARN / SCHOOLE, / BY / ANTONY HOLBORNE / Gentleman, and servant to her most / excellent Maiestie. / Hereunto are added sixe short AERS / Neapolitan like to three voyces, with/out the Instrument: done by his bro/ther WILLIAM HOLBORNE. / [Printer's mark] / AT LONDON. / Printed by Peter Short, dwelling on / Breadstreet hill at the signe of / the Starre 1597.

68 fols. Letter tablature for cittern in Italian tuning; added instrumental parts and voice parts are in mensural notation. Dedication on fol. A2 headed "TO THE RIGHT HONORABLE, NOBLE, AND MOST WORTHY LORD, THOMAS LORD BURGH, BARON GAINSBURGHE, LORD GOVERNOUR FOR HER MAIESTY OF HER TOWNE OF BREILL, AND THE FORTS OF CLAYBURGH AND MEWENNOORT IN THE COUNTIE OF HOLLAND IN THE LOWE CONTRYES, KNIGHT OF THE MOST HONORABLE ORDER OF THE GARTIER, LORD DEPUTY AND GOVERNOR GENERALL FOR HER MAIESTY OF HER REALME OF IRELAND," and signed on fol. A2^v "Your L. ever most faithfullie devoted Antony Holborne. Ni merear moriar." On fol. A3: preface headed "To the proficient Scholler or lover of the Cittharn." Colophon on fol. R4: "1597. [Printer's mark with motto "SUBLIME DEDIT OS HOMINI"] AT LONDON. Printed by Peter Short, dwelling on Breadstreet hill at the signe of the Starre." Nos. 34–55 and 58 have a part for a bass instrument (in mensural notation) added to the cittern part. Nos. 56 and 57 have three instrumental parts as well as the cittern version. Nos. 59–64 are for voices *a 3*. All of the other compositions are for solo cittern.

Copies in: GB:Cu, GB:Lcm.[1]

MUSIC FOR SOLO CITTERN

	fol.	
1	B1	*Praeludium*
2	B1	*Praeludium*
3	B1^v	*Praeludium*
4	B1^v	*Praeludium*
5	B2	*Praeludium*
6	B2	*Praeludium*
7	B2^v	*Pavane passamezo*
8	B2^v	*Galliarde*
9	B3	*Pavane Quadro*
10	B3^v	*Pavane la vecchio*[2]
11	B4^v	*The oulde Almaine*
12	C1	*The voyce*
13	C1^v	*In pescod time*
14	C2^v	*The Spanish pavane*[3]
15	C3	*Qui passi*
16	C3^v	*As I went to Walsingham*
17	C4	*Mounsiers Almayne*
18	C4^v	*The Miller*
19	D1	*What you will*
20	D1^v	*The maydens of the Countrey*
21	D1^v	*A Jyg*
22	D2	*Bonny sweet Robin*
23	D2	*A French toy*
24	D2^v	*Go from my window*
25	D3	*Sicke sicke and very sicke*
26	D3^v	*Pavane Quadro*
27	D4^v	*Pavane passamezo*
28	E2^v	*Pavane passamezo*
29	E4^v	*Galliard pessamezo* [sic]
30	F1^v	*Pavane Quadro*
31	F3	*Pavane la vecchio*[4]
32	F4^v	*Pavane Quadro*
33	G2^v	*A Hornepype*

MUSIC FOR CITTERN AND ONE BASS INSTRUMENT

34	G4^v	*Pavane*
35	H1^v	*Maister Earles pavane*
36	H2^v	*Pavane*
37	H3^v	*Pavane*
38	H4^v	*Pavane*
39	I1^v	*Almayne*
40	I2^v	*Galliarde*
41	I3^v	*Maister Birds Galliard*
42	I4^v	*Galliarde*
43	K1^v	*Galliard*
44	K2^v	*Galliard*
45	K3^v	*Galliard*
46	K4^v	*Galliarde*
47	L1^v	*Almaine*
48	L2^v	*Galliard*
49	L3^v	*Galliarde*
50	L4^v	*Almaine*
51	M1^v	*Almayne*
52	M2^v	*Galliard*
53	M3^v	*Almaine*
54	M4^v	*Galliard*
55	N1^v	*The Lullaby* (1599_6, no. 4)
56	N2^v	*Fantasia. Trium vocum*[5] (for cittern and/or three other instruments)
57	O2^v	*Fantasia. Trium vocum*[5] (for cittern and/or three other instruments)
58	P2^v	*The farewell* (for cittern and one bass instrument)

CANZONETS *a 3* BY WILLIAM HOLBORNE[6]

59	Q1^v	*Change then for lo she changeth*
60	Q2^v	*Since Bonny-boots*

61 Q3v *Heere rest my thoughts*
62 Q4v *Sweet I grant*
63 R1v *Gush foorth my teares*
64 R2v *Sit still & sturre not*

[1] The London copy was in the library of Edward F. Rimbault; the Cambridge copy was in the library of Dr. John Bull.

[2] Quasi-facs. and mod. ed. in WolfH II, 134.

[3] On this dance see PoulN.

[4] Facs. of fol. F3 in SteeleE, pl. 37.

[5] Mod. ed. of the three lines in mensural notation in HolF.

[6] Heading on fol. Q1: "Hereafter do follow Sixe short Aers or Canzonets to three voyces, being the first fruites of Composition, doone by his brother William Holborne."

1597[7]

LÜTKEMAN, PAUL

Der Erste Theil. / Newer Lateinischer und deut/scher Gesenge auff die vornembsten Feste und etliche / Sontage im Jahr nebenst nachfolgenden schönen Fantasien, / Paduanen und Galliarden lustig zusingen unnd gar lieblich auff / allerley art Instrumenten zu gebrauchen, mit 5. 6. und / mehr Stimmen Componiret, und in / Druck verordnet / Durch / PAULUM LUTKEMAN COLBERGENSEM: / Instrumentalem Musicum in der Fürstlichen und Löbli/chen See Stadt Alten Stettin. / DISCANTUS. / Daselbst Gedruckt, durch Andree Kellnern Erben. Anno 1597.[1]

Six part books in mensural notation (S, 37 fols.; A, 34 fols.; TB, each of 33 fols.; 5, 35 fols.; 6 wanting from unique set of part books). The title is placed within an ornamental border. On fol. A1v: a coat of arms. Dedication on fol. A2 headed "Den Ehrenvesten, Achtbarn, Hochgelarten, Erbarn und Wolweisen Herrn Burgemeistern unnd Rathmannen der Stadt, Straelsund, Gryphswald, Anclam, Pasewalch, Wolgast, und Demmin, Meinen Grossgünstigen Herrn und beforderern," and signed on fol. A3 "Datum Alten Stettin den 12 Martii Anno 97. E. E. A. W. und G. Dienstwilliger: Paul Lütkeman Musicus." On fol. A3v of the discant part book: table of contents of the first part of the volume. On fol. G1 of the discant part book: table of contents for the second part of the volume. All of the compositions are by Lütkeman (in the volume they are headed "P. L."). Nos. 1–28 are for voices; nos. 29–51 are for instrumental ensemble *a5*; and nos. 52–60 are for instrumental ensemble *a6*.

Copy in: D:W (6 wanting).

MUSIC FOR VOICES

fol.

1 A4 *Nu kom der Heiden Heilandt à5*
2 A4v *Hodie Christus natus est à6*
3 B1 *Der Engel sprach zu den Hirten à5*
4 B1v *Beatus autor seculi à5*
5 B2 *Angelus ad pastores ait à5*
6 B2v *Nunc dimittis à6*
7 B3 *Christe der du bist tag à5*
8 B3v *Quare tristis es à5*
9 B4 *Da Jesus an dem Creutze stundt à6*
10 B4v *O Lamb Gottes à5*
11 C1 *Jesu nostra Redemptio à5*
C1v 2a pars *Inferni claustra penetrans à4*
C1v 3a pars *Ipsa te cogat*
C2 4a pars *Tu esto nostrum gaudium à4*
12 C2 *Christ lag in todes banden à5*
13 C3 *Congratulamini mihi omnes à5*
C3v 2a pars *Recedentibus discipulis*
14 C4 *Laudate dominum in sanctis eius à5*
C4v 2a pars *Laudate eum in tympano & choro*
15 D1 *Laudate dominum omnes gentes à8*
16 D2 *Misericordias domini à5*
17 D3 *In partu dolor est à5*
18 D3v *Cantate Domino à5*
19 D4 *Exultate iusti in domino à5*
D4v 2a pars *Cantate ei*
20 E1 *Ascendit Deus in jubilo à5*
21 E2 *Exaudi Deus à6*
E2v 2a pars *Cor meum*
22 E3 *Nu bitten wir den heiligen Geist à5*
23 E3v *Dum complerentur à5*
24 E4 *Venit magna à5*
25 E4v *Sancta trinitas à7*
26 F1v *Duo Seraphin à6*
27 F2v *Wenn wir in höchsten nöten sein à5*
F3 2a pars *Wir heben unser Augn*
F3v 3a pars *Drumb kommen wir*

	F4	4a pars *Auff das von Hertzen können wir*
28	F4ᵛ	*Es ist nicht liebers à 5*

MUSIC *a 5* FOR INSTRUMENTS

29	G1ᵛ	*Fantasia* [2]
30	G2	*Fantasia*
31	G2ᵛ	*Fantasia*
32	G3	*Fantasia, Isspruch ich muss dich:* (compare DTO XIV/28, p. 15: Isaac)
33	G3ᵛ	*Fantasia*
34	G3ᵛ	*Fantasia. Ich ruff zu dir:* [3] (compare LassoW XVIII, 4: Lasso)
35	G4ᵛ	*Fantasia*
36	H1	*Fantasia*
37	H1ᵛ	*Fantasia. Er setz* [4]
38	H2	*Paduan*
39	H2ᵛ	*Galliard*
40	H2ᵛ	*Galliard*
41	H3	*Paduan*
42	H3	*Galliard*
43	H3ᵛ	*Fantasia*
44	H4	*Galliard*
45	H4ᵛ	*Paduan*
46	I1	*Paduan. Ohn dich muss:* (compare PubAPTM XIX, no. 1: Regnart)
47	I1	*Galliard*
48	I1ᵛ	*Paduan*
49	I1ᵛ	*Galliard*
50	I2	*Galliard*
51	I2	*Galliard Offt wünsch ich ihr* (compare 1584_8, no. 17: Langius)

MUSIC *a 6* FOR INSTRUMENTS

52	I2ᵛ	*Fantasia*
53	I3	*Galliard*
54	I3ᵛ	*Paduan*
55	I3ᵛ	*Galliard*
56	I4	*Paduan*
57	I4ᵛ	*Galliard*
58	I4ᵛ	*Galliard*
59	K1	*Fantasia*
60	K1ᵛ	*Galliard*

[1] LütkeF includes a facs. of the title page, the dedication, and the table of contents for the instrumental music.
[2] Mod. ed. in LütkeF, no. 3.
[3] Mod. ed. in LütkeF, no. 1.
[4] Mod. ed. in LütkeF, no. 2.

1597_8

MANCINUS, THOMAS

DUUM VOCUM / CANTIUNCULARUM / THOMAE MANCINI MEGAPOLI/tani, Chori Musici in aula Wolferby/tana magistri, liber. / VOX SUPERIOR. / HELMAESTADII / Excudebat Jacobus Lucius, Anno / M. D. XCVII.

Two part books in mensural notation, each of 28 fols. The title is placed within an ornamental border. Dedication on fol. A1ᵛ headed "REVERENDISSIMO, ET ILLUSTRISSIMO PRINCIPI, AC DOMINO, DN. HENRICO JULIO EPISCOPO HALBERstadensi, Duci Brunsvicensi, & Lunaeburgensi, Domino suo clementissimo S. PL.," and signed on fol. A2 "Rᵐᵒ, Eᵗ Illᵐᵒ C. T. Obsequentissimus, Thomas Mancinus." On fol. G4ᵛ: table of contents. All of the compositions are *a 2*; nos. 1–10 are fully texted; nos. 10–26 are without text or title. Nos. 24–26 are notated as mensuration canons.

Copy in: D:Kl.

MUSIC FOR TWO VOICES

	fol.	
1	A2ᵛ	*Nasce la pena mia*
2	A3ᵛ	*Ein glück ohn Neide*
3	A4ᵛ	*Il cor che mi rubasti*
4	B1ᵛ	*Avecque vous mon amour finera*
5	B2ᵛ	*Anchor che col partire*
6	B3ᵛ	*La dipartita è amara*
7	B4ᵛ	*Liquide perle*
8	C1ᵛ	*Vorria morire*
9	C2ᵛ	*Voce mero flammis*
10	C3ᵛ	*O sole o stelle o luna*

MUSIC FOR TWO INSTRUMENTS

11	C4ᵛ	XI.
12	D1ᵛ	XII.
13	D2ᵛ	XIII.
14	D3ᵛ	XIIII.
15	D4ᵛ	XV.
16	E1ᵛ	XVI.
17	E2ᵛ	XVII.
18	E3ᵛ	XVIII.
19	E4ᵛ	XIX.
20	F1ᵛ	XX.
21	F2ᵛ	XXI. = nos. 25 and 26 below
22	F3ᵛ	XXII.
23	F4ᵛ	XXIII. = no. 24 below

24 G1^{v} XXIIII. Per Diapason infra = no. 23 above
25 G2^{v} XXV. = no. 21 above
26 G3^{v} XXVI. Per Diapason infra = no. 21 above.

1597₉

MARINO, ALESSANDRO

DI ALESSANDRO MARINO, / IL PRIMO LIBRO / DE MADRIGALI SPIRITUALI / A SEI VOCI, / Con una Canzone a dodeci nel fine. / Novamente composti, & dati in luce. / [Printer's mark] / In Venetia appresso Ricciardo Amadino, / M D XCVII.

Six (?) part books in mensural notation, each of 14 fols. (?). The title is placed within an ornamental border. Dedication on fol. 1^{v} headed "AL MOLTO ILL.^{RE} ET REVEREND.^{MO} mio Signore, & Patron Colendissimo, IL REVEREND.^{MO} PADRE DON ASCANIO MARTINENGO Generale della Congregatione de Canonici Regulari Lateranensi & Abbate dignissimo di S. Giovanne in Verdara de Padoa," and signed "Di Venetia il dì primo d'Aprile 1597," reprinted in SartMS, p. 90. On fol. 14^{v}: table of contents. SartMS, p. 90, and Vogel: Marino 2 (1597) both give a complete list of the contents. The volume contains 12 compositions with Italian text, and one piece for instrumental ensemble *a12*.

Copy in: I:Bc (T).

1 fol. 12^{v} *La bella Roncinetta. Canzone a12*

1597₁₀

MORLEY, THOMAS

CANZONETS / OR / LITTLE SHORT AERS / TO FIVE AND SIXE / VOICES. / BY / THOMAS MORLEY / Gentleman of her Highnesse Chappell. / LONDON. / Printed by Peter Short / dwelling on Bredstreet hil / at the signe of the Star. / M. D. XCVII

Five part books in mensural notation and French lute tablature (AB5, each of 14 fols.; T, 16 fols.; S, 22 fols.). The title is placed within an ornamental border. Dedication on fol. 2 headed "TO THE RIGHT HONORABLE SIR GEORGE CAREY; KNIGHT MARSHALL OF HER MAJESTIES HOUSEHOLD, GOVERNOR OF THE ILE OF WIGHT, CAPTAINE OF THE HONORABLE BAND OF HER HIGHNES GENTELMEN PENSIONERS, BARON OF HUNDSDON, AND LORD CHAMBERLAINE OF HER MAJESTIES HOUSE." On fol. 23^{v}: table of contents. Arrangements of the canzonets *a5* for solo voice and lute are included in the cantus part book. The lute parts are intabulations of the lower four voices of each canzonet. The vocal compositions without the lute accompaniments are reprinted in EMS III, which includes the dedication. Foliation is taken from the cantus part book. The pieces *a6* are not included in the following inventory.

Copies in: GB:En (A), GB:Lbm, GB:Ob, US:SM.[1]

	fol.	
1	2^{v}	*Flie love that are so sprightly*
2	3^{v}	*False Love did me inveagle*
3	4^{v}	*Adiew adiew adiew you kind and cruel*
4	5^{v}	*Loves follke in greene araying*
5	6^{v}	*Love tooke his bowe and arrow*
6	7^{v}	*Lo where with floury head*
7	8^{v}	*O griefe even on the Bud*
8	9^{v}	*Soveraigne of my delight*
9	10^{v}	*Our bony bootes could toote it*
10	11^{v}	*Ayme the fatall arrow*[2]
11	12^{v}	*My nymphe the deere*
12	13^{v}	*Cruell wilt thou persever*
13	14^{v}	*Said I that Amarillis*
14	15^{v}	*Damon and Phillis squared*
15	16^{v}	*Lady you thinke you spite me*
16	17^{v}	*You blacke bright starres*
17	18^{v}	*I follow loe the footing*

[1] A copy was in the library of W. H. Cummings (see CummC, no. 1124).

[2] Facs. of the superius (fol. 11^{v}) and of the lute intabulation (fol. 12) in SteeleE, figs. 38 and 39.

1597₁₁

OROLOGIO, ALEXANDER

INTRADAE / ALEXANDRI / OROLOGII, / Quinque & sex vocibus, / quarum in omni genere instru/mentorum musicorum usus esse potest. / LIBER PRIMUS. / [Printer's mark] / CANTUS. / HELMAESTADII / In Officina typographica Jacobi Lucii. / M. D. XCVII.[1]

Six part books in mensural notation (SATB5, each of 8 fols.; 6, 6 fols.). The title is placed within an ornamental border. Dedication on fol. 1ᵛ headed "SERENISSIMO POTENTISSIMOQUE PRINCIPI AC DOMINO, DN. CHRISTIANO IV. Daniae, Norvegiae, Gothorum & Vandalorum regi, Duci Slesvici, Holsatiae, Stormariae & Ditmarsiae, Comiti in Oldenburgk & Delmenhorst, Domino suo clementissimo," and signed "Datae Helmaestadii in ac. IUL 24. Augusti An. 97. Regi M.ᵗⁱˢ T. addictissimus cliens Alexander Orologius," reprinted in SartMS, p. 91. For further information see NefI, which includes a modern edition of no. 3. All of the compositions are for instrumental ensemble *a5* and *a6*.

Copies in: D:Kl, DK:Kk.[2]

	fol.		
1	2	*1* [*Intrada*]	*à5*
2	2	*2* [*Intrada*]	*à5*
3	2ᵛ	*3* [*Intrada*]	*à5*
4	2ᵛ	*4* [*Intrada*]	*à5*
5	3	*5* [*Intrada*]	*à5*
6	3	*6* [*Intrada*]	*à5*
7	3ᵛ	*7* [*Intrada*]	*à5*
8	3ᵛ	*8* [*Intrada*]	*à5*
9	4	*9* [*Intrada*]	*à6*
10	4	*10* [*Intrada*]	*à6*
11	4ᵛ	*11* [*Intrada*]	*à6*
12	4ᵛ	*12* [*Intrada*]	*à6*
13	5	*13* [*Intrada*]	*à6*
14	5	*14* [*Intrada*]	*à6*
15	5ᵛ	*15* [*Intrada*]	*à6*
16	5ᵛ	*16* [*Intrada*]	*à6*
17	6	*17* [*Intrada*]	*à6*
18	6	*18* [*Intrada*]	*à6*
19	6ᵛ	*19* [*Intrada*]	*à6*
20	6ᵛ	*20* [*Intrada*]	*à6*
21	7	*21* [*Intrada*]	*à6*
22	7	*22* [*Intrada*]	*à6*
23	7ᵛ	*23* [*Intrada*]	*à6*
24	7ᵛ	*24* [*Intrada*]	*à6*
25	8	*25* [*Intrada*]	*à6*
26	8	*26* [*Intrada*]	*à6*
27	8ᵛ	*27* [*Intrada*][3]	*à6*
28	8ᵛ	*28* [*Intrada*][3]	*à6*

[1] Facs. of title page in KinsP, p. 160, and MGG X, col. 409.

[2] An incomplete set of part books was in PL:L.

[3] Nos. 27 and 28 are headed "Instrumentis eiusdem generis."

1597₁₂

KAUFMANN, PAUL, PUBLISHER

FIORI / DEL GIARDINO / DI DIVERSI ECCEL/LENTISSIMI AUTORI / à / Quattro, cinque, sei, sette, otto, & nove [*sic*] voci. / Raccolta con molta diligentia & / novamente date in luce. / [Fleuret] / NORIMBERGO / Appresso Paulo Kaufmann. / M. D. XCVII.

Six part books in mensural notation (SA5, each of 40 fols.; T, 38 fols.; B, 32 fols.; 6, 18 fols.). On fol. a1ᵛ: preface headed "Omnibus Musices amatoribus Typographus S. D.," reprinted in SartMS, p. 93. On fol. k3ᵛ: table of contents. SartMS, p. 93, and Vogel 1597₂ both give a complete list of the contents. The volume contains compositions with Italian text,[1] and two pieces for instrumental ensemble *a8*.

Copies in: B:Br, D:Bhm (B), D:F (S56), D:Hs, D:Kl (SATB5), D:Mbs, US:BU (T).[2]

	fol.		
1	I4ᵛ	*Canzon. Noni Toni a8*	Giov. Gabriel. = 1597₅, no. 4
2	K1	*Canzon. Duodecimi Toni a8*	Gio. Gabrieli = 1597₅, no. 5

[1] "Chiar'Angioletta" (fol. I1ᵛ) by Giovanni Gabrieli is marked "Aria per sonar." This is the same as 1590₂, p. 48.

[2] Copies were in D:DS and PL:GD.

[1597]13

HASKINS, WILLIAM, PUBLISHER

A playne and perfect Instruction for learnynge to play on ye virginalles by hand or by booke both by notes and by letters or Tabliture never heretofore sett out by any, etc.

This volume of instructions for playing the virginals, now lost if it ever were printed, is listed in ArberT III, 81, dated March 7, 1597. It is also listed in DartHL, p. 16; DeakinMB, p. 9; and SteeleE, p. 100. DeakinO, p. 54, states that it was licensed on May 7, 1597, to be printed by William Haskins.

1597 14

VECCHI, ORAZIO

CANZONETTE / A TRE VOCI / DI HORATIO VECCHI, / Et di Gemignano Capi Lupi / Da Modona. / Novamente poste in luce. / CON PRIVILEGIO. / [Printer's mark] / In Venetia Appresso Angelo Gardano. / M. D. LXXXXVII.

Three part books in mensural notation and Italian lute tablature, each of 18 fols. The title is placed within an ornamental border. Dedication on fol. A1v of each part book headed "AL MOLTO ILLUSTRE SIG: ET PATRON MIO OSSERVANDISS. IL SIGNOR PAOLO CALORI," and signed "Di Venetia il dì 20. Marzo 1597. Di V. S. Molto Illustre Affettionatiss. Servitore Horatio Vecchi." Fol. A2 = p. 1. On the last page of the cantus secondo and basso part books: table of contents. Lute intabulations of the *canzonette* appear in the canto part book only.

Copies in: D:As (SB), GB:Lbm (ST), I:Bc, I:Fr (S).[1]

	p.	
1	1	*Deh cant' Aminta* Horatio Vecchi
2	2	*Per l'ottavo miracolo* Horatio Vecchi ("Alla M. Ill. S. Laura Calori Cortese")
3	3	*Hora ch'ogn'animal* Horatio Vecchi
4	4	*L'amara dipartita* Gemignano Capi Lupi
5	5	*Nisa dolce ben mio* Capi Lupi
6	6	*Mentre l'Aquila* Capi Lupi
7	7	*Gia l'ond'e'l vento* Horatio Vecchi
8	8	*Al tremend'e potente* Horatio Vecchi
9	9	*La fiamma che m'incende* Capi Lupi
10	10	*Temerario Fetonte* Capi Lupi
11	11	*Io dissi e dico* Horatio Vecchi
12	12	*Mentre belle signore* Horatio Vecchi
13	13	*A l'acqua a l'aria* Capi Lupi
14	14	*Piu che mai vaga e bella* Capi Lupi
15	15	*S'udia un Pastor* Horatio Vecchi
16	16	*O Felice Nocchiero* Horatio Vecchi
17	17	*Hor ch'è lungi il mio bene* Horatio Vecchi
18	18	*Non date fede o amanti* Horatio Vecchi
19	19	*Non piu saette al core* Capi Lupi
20	20	*Piangete occhi miei* Capi Lupi
21	21	*Chi brama di veder* Capi Lupi
22	22	*Il marmo fino* Horatio Vecchi
23	23	*Odo da tutti dire* Horatio Vecchi
24	24	*Amar Donna che strugge* Capi Lupi
25	25	*Non ho piu vit'Amore* Capi Lupi
26	26	*L'ultima volta ch'io Ti viddi* Horatio Vecchi
27	27	*Chi scuopr'hoggi fra noi* Horatio Vecchi
28	28	*Lusinghiero desio* Horatio Vecchi
29	29	*O dolcezz'amarissime d'amore* Capi Lupi
30	30	*Ti chiamo e non rispondi* Capi Lupi
31	31	*Care amorose* Capi Lupi
32	32	*Amanti Corrette tutti quanti* Capi Lupi
33	33	*Udite udite amanti* Horatio Vecchi
34	34	*Questo è troppo signora* Horatio Vecchi

[1] Copies were in D:Bds (S) and the library of Georg Becker (SB). Paul Kaufmann of Nuremberg published the same collection in the same year but without the lute intabulations (see Vogel: Vecchi 40 [1597]).

1597

DOUBTFUL WORKS

1. MLE, 1904, pp. 17 and 109, dates Claudio Merulo, *Toccate d'Intavolatura d'organo . . . Libro Primo*, 1597. The volume is listed in this bibliography as 1598_9.

1598_1

BASSANO, GIOVANNI

RICERCATE / PASSAGGI / ET CADENTIE / Per potersi essercitar nel diminuir terminatamente, con / ogni sorte d'Istrumento: & anco diversi pas/saggi per la semplice voce. / DI GIOVANNI BASSANO / Musico dell'Illustriss. Signoria di Venetia, / Novamente Ristampate. / [Printer's mark] / IN VENETIA, / Appresso Giacomo Vincenti. 1598.

12 fols. Mensural notation. The title is placed within an ornamental border. On fol. 2: same preface as in 1585_4. Contents = 1585_4. The volume contains highly decorated monophonic ricercares, a series of formulas for ornamenting a given melodic line, and the superius of a madrigal supplied with *passaggi*.

Copy in: I:Fn (imperfect).[1]

[1] A copy was in D:Bgk.

1598_2

CAVENDISH, MICHAEL

14. Ayres in Tabletorie to the Lute expressed with two / voyces and the base Violl or the voice & Lute only. / 6. more to 4. voyces and in Tabletorie. / And / 8. MADRIGALLES to 5. voyces. / By / MICHAELL CAVENDISH / Gentleman. / [Printer's mark] / AT LONDON / Printed by Peter Short, on bredstreethill / at the signe of the Starre: 1598.[1]

24 fols. French lute tablature and mensural notation. Dedication on fol. A2 headed "TO THE HONOURABLE protection of the Ladie Arbella [Stuart]," and signed "Yours humbly to be commaunded: MICHAELL CAVENDISH. From Cavendish this 24 of July." On fol. M1v: additional texts for some of the songs. On fol. M2: table of contents. The eight madrigals *a 5* added after the lute songs and omitted from this inventory are reprinted in EMS XXXVI. The songs with lute are all reprinted in EL, ser. 2, vol. VII, which includes the dedication. The compositions identified by the superior letter *a* ([a]) are reprinted in WarEA, vols. III–IV. As the title page explains, nos. 1–14 include along with the lute part cantus and bass parts in mensural notation, fully texted; nos. 15–20 include alternate versions for lute and for voices *a 4*.

Copy in: GB:Lbm (imperfect).

MUSIC FOR LUTE AND/OR SOPRANO AND BASS VOICES

	fol.	
1	A2v	*Stay, Glicia, stay*
2	B1	*Why should my muse*
3	B1v	*Mourne, Marcus, mourne*[a]
4	B2	*Have I vow'd and must not breake it*
5	B2v	*Finetta, faire and feat*
6	C1	*Love is not blind*
7	C1v	*Love the delight*[a]
8	C2	*The hart to rue*
9	C2v	*Silvia is faire*[a]
10	D1	*Curst be the time*[a]
11	D1v	*Faire are those eies* (practically identical to no. 17 below)
12	D2	*Wandring in this place*
13	D2v	*Everie bush new springing*
14	E1	*Down in a valley*[a]

MUSIC FOR LUTE AND/OR VOICES *a 4*

15	E1v	*Wanton, come hither*
16	E2v	*Say shepherds say*
17	F1v	*Faire are those eies* (practically identical to no. 11 above)
18	F2v	*Farewel, farewell, dispaire*
19	G1v	*Slie theefe*
20	G2v	*What thing more cruell*

[1] The top part of the title page is missing from the unique copy.

1598₃

FONGHETTI, PAOLO

CAPRICII, / ET / MADRIGALI / DI PAOLO FONGHETTI / Veronese, / Nuovamente composti, & dati in luce. / A DUE VOCI. / [Printer's mark] / IN VERONA, / Appresso Francesco dalle Donne, & Scipione / Vargnano suo Genero. M D IIC.

Two part books in mensural notation, each of 16 fols. The title is placed within an ornamental border. On fol. 1ᵛ of each part book: a cut illustrating the motto "VERITAS FILIA TEMPORIS." Dedication on fol. 2 of each part book headed "A GLI ILLUSTRI SIGNORI CONTI, IL CONTE GASPARO, ET MARC'ANTONIO VERITA Miei Signori, & Patroni osservandiss.," and signed "Di Verona il di 12. Marzo 1598. Di V. S. Illustri Affetionatiss. Servitore. Paolo Fonghetti." Fol. 2ᵛ = p. 1. On p. 29 of each part book: table of contents. The collection contains nine completely texted duos (nos. 1–9) and 16 textless duos (nos. 10–25).[1]

Copy in: I:Bc.

MUSIC FOR TWO VOICES

	p.	
1	1	*Se da quel vago viso*
2	2	*Deh dove senza me*
3	3	*A caso un giorno*
	4	2a pars *Vaga d'udir*
	5	3a pars *Con quel poco di spirto*
	6	4a pars *Mentre ch'ella*
4	7	*Fingo di non amare*
5	8	*Vidi da dui bei lumi*
6	9	*Un vostro sì*
7	10	*Voi bramate ben mio*
8	11	*Deh torna à me mio Sol*
9	12	*Io me ne vò la notte*

MUSIC FOR TWO INSTRUMENTS

10	13	*Il Conforme*
11	14	*Lo Spaventoso*
12	15	*Il Penseroso*
13	16	*Il Cortese*
14	17	*Lo Aereo*
15	18	*Lo Estravagante*
16	19	*Polia*
17	20	*Polifilo*
18	21	*Lo Amoroso*
19	22	*Il Philarmonico*
20	23	*Fetonte*
21	24	*Lo Aspettato*
22	25	*Lo Espedito*
23	26	*Il Corriero*
24	27	*La Biscia*
25	28	*Il Fantastico*

[1] This volume is apparently the one referred to in FétB III, 288, with the title *Madrigali a due voci co'l liuto ossia ghitarone. Verona, app. Franc. delle Donne et Scipione Vergne suo genero, 1598, in-4°.*

1598₄

GALLUS, JOSEPH

Totius Libri primi / SACRI OPERIS / MUSICI ALTERNIS / MODULIS CONCINENDI / PARTITIO, / Seu quam praestantiss. Musica PARTITURAM vocant. / AUTORE M. R. D. JOSEPHO GALLO / Mediolanensi, Religionis Somaschae: / Studio tamen & labore R. D. Aurelii Ribrochi Nobilis Dertho/nensis in gratiam Organistarum in lucem edita. / [Printer's mark] / MEDIOLANI, / Apud haeredes Francisci, & Simonis Tini. / M. D. XCVIII.

104 fols. Keyboard partitura and organ bass.[1] The title is placed within an ornamental border. Dedication on p. 2 headed "PIETATE, ET ERUDITIONE INSIGNI VIRO ADMODUM REV.ᵈᵒ DOMINO, D. BALTHASARI DE CORNEIS NUNCUPATO, PROTHONOTARIOQUE APOSTOLICO plurimum observando. AURELIUS RIBROCHUS foelicitatem," and signed "Dat. Mediolani Calendis Januariis M. D. XCIIX." On p. 3: preface headed "Aurelius Ribrochus candidissimus cum Organorum, tum caeterorum instrumentorum musicorum pulsatoribus, aliisque Musicis prestantissimis, S. P. I." On p. 208: table of contents. The volume contains compositions in score and organ basses.

Copies in: D:Mbs, GB:T.

COMPOSITIONS IN SCORE (FOR TWO CHORUSES: ONE OF INSTRUMENTS AND ONE OF VOICES)

	p.	
1	4	*Hodie nobis de coelo* Concentus duplex vocum & Instrumentorum, continens cantionem, quam vocant la Magia (compare 1584_{10}, no. 5)
	21	2a pars *Dies sanctificatus*
2	40	*Gaudent in coelis* Concentus duplex vocum, & Instrumentorum, continens cantionem nuncupatam la Cortesa (compare 1592_7, no. 4)
3	57	*Veni electa mea* Concentus duplex vocum, & Instrumentorum, continens cantionem la Ben venuta nuncupatam (compare 1592_7, no. 5)
4	76	*Ecce Angelus de coelo*
5	96	*Magnificat*

ORGAN BASSES FOR POLYCHORAL COMPOSITIONS

6	132	*Missa sine nomine, novenis vocibus, Partitiones, Bassus utriusque Chori*
7	154	*Hodie nobis indignis*
	157	2a pars *Puer qui natus est*
8	158	*Ornaverunt faciem templi*
9	162	*Veni in hortum meum*
10	164	*Petre amas me*
11	168	*Quis es tu?*
12	170	*Quam pulchra es & quam decora*
13	174	*Nigra sum sed formosa*

INSTRUMENTAL PIECES IN SCORE

14	176	*La Mantegazza* Cantio alternis modulis pulsanda
15	193	*La Grassa* Cantio quaternis instrumentorum sonis modulanda
16	200	*La Biuma* Cantio quaternis instrumentorum sonis modulanda

[1] This is apparently the one remaining part from a set of part books. EitQ IV, 138, lists a copy of the cantus part, now lost, in the library of Professor Fr. Zelle in Berlin. For further information see KinO, pp. 198ff.

1598_5

GASTOLDI, GIOVANNI GIACOMO

DI GIO. GIACOMO / GASTOLDI / MAESTRO DI CAPELLA / nella Chiesa Ducale di S. Barbara / in Mantova, / E d'altri Eccellentiss. Musici di Milano, / IL PRIMO LIBRO / DELLA MUSICA / A DUE VOCI. / [Printer's mark] / IN MILANO, / Appresso l'herede di Simon Tini, & Gio. Francesco Besozzo. / M. D. XCVIII.

Two part books in mensural notation, each of 20 fols. The title is placed within an ornamental border. Dedication on fol. A1v headed "AL SIG. FRANCESCO BAGLIONE nostro osservandissimo," and signed "Dalle nostre Stampe il dì 6. Maggio 1598. D. V. S. L'herede dil quon. Simon Tini, e Gio. Francesco Besozzo," reprinted in SartMS, p. 99. Fol. A2 = p. 1. The compositions identified by superior letters are reprinted as follows: ([a]) in DolS, nos. 4–8; ([b]) in HM XXIII; ([c]) in HM XXIV. All of the compositions are for instrumental ensemble *a 2*.

Copy in: D:As.

	p.	
1	1	[Gastoldi][a]
2	2	[Gastoldi]
3	3	[Gastoldi]
4	4	[Gastoldi][c]
5	5	[Gastoldi][ac]
6	6	[Gastoldi][c]
7	7	[Gastoldi][c]
8	8	[Gastoldi][1]
9	9	[Gastoldi][ac]
10	10	[Gastoldi]
11	11	[Gastoldi][a]
12	12	[Gastoldi]
13	13	[Gastoldi][b]
14	14	[Gastoldi][b]
15	15	[Gastoldi][ab2]
16	16	[Gastoldi]
17	17	*A voci pari*[b] [Gastoldi]
18	18	*A voci pari* [Gastoldi]
19	19	*A voci pari*[b] [Gastoldi]
20	20	*A voci pari*[b] [Gastoldi]
21	20	Orfeo Vecchi
22	22	Orfeo Vecchi
23	24	d'Incerto
24	25	d'Incerto

25 26 Serafin Canton
26 27 Serafin Canton
27 28 *Canon in diapason* Richardo Rogniono
28 29 *Canon al unison* Richardo Rogniono
29 30 Gio. Domenico Rognoni
30 31 *Canon al Semiditono acuto per contrari movimenti* Gio. Dominico Rognoni
31 32 Giovan Paulo Cima
32 34 Giovan Paulo Cima[c]
33 35 d'Incerto
34 36 d'Incerto
35 37 Hieronimo Baglioni
36 38 Hieronimo Baglione

[1] Mod. ed. in EinVG, p. 365.
[2] Mod. ed. in MU III, app., p. 83.

1598_6

GASTOLDI, GIOVANNI GIACOMO

BALLETTI / A TRE VOCI / Con la intavolatura del Liuto, per cantare, / sonare, & ballare. / DI GIO. GIACOMO GASTOLDI DA CARAVAGGIO / Maestro di Cappella nella Chiesa Ducale di S. Barbara / di Mantova. / Novamente ristampati. / [Printer's mark] / In Venetia appresso Ricciardo Amadino / 1598.

Three part books in mensural notation and Italian lute tablature (S, 17 fols. (?); T, 10 fols. (?); B, 10 fols.). The title is placed within an ornamental border. Dedication on fol. 2 of each part book (?) headed "ALL'ILLUSTRISS. SIGNORE mio Signore, & Padrone colendissimo, IL SIGNOR ALESSANDRO AGOSCIOLA, Cameriero del Serenissimo Sig. Duca di Mantova," and signed "Di Venetia il dì 20 di Ottobre. 1598. Di V. S. Illustrissima. Servitore affettionatissimo, Gio. Giacomo Gastoldi." The dedication is the same as the one in 1594_7 except for the date. On the verso of the last folio of each part book (?): table of contents. Contents = 1594_7. The volume contains compositions with Italian text with their intabulations for solo lute. The intabulations probably appeared in the canto part book only (as in 1594_7).

Copy in: D:Bhm (B).

$[1598]_7$

HAUSSMANN, VALENTIN

Neue artige und liebliche Täntze, zum theil mit Texten, dass man kan mit Menschlicher Stimme zu Instrumenten singen, zum theil ohne Text gesetzt, und denen, welche sich etwas neues gelieben lassen, zu gefallen publiciert Durch Valentinum Haussmann Gerbipol: Saxonem. Gedruckt zu Nürnberg, durch Paulum Kauffmann. 1598.

Four part books in mensural notation, each of 20 fols. (?). Contents = 1599_5. An incomplete set of part books was in D:Bds, according to EitQ V, 53, and MeyeM, p. 213. All of the compositions were *a4*; nos. 1–21 were fully texted, and nos. 22–46 were without text.

1598_8

LASSO, ORLANDO DI

NOVAE ALIQUOT ET AN/TE HAC NON ITA USITATAE AD / DUAS VOCES CANTIONES SUAVISSIMAE, / omnibus Musicis summè utiles: nec non Tyronibus / quàm eius artis peritioribus summopere / inservientes. / AUTHORE / ORLANDO DI LASSO, / Illustrissimi Bavariae Ducis Alberti / Musici Chori Magistro. / Summa diligentia compositae, correctae, & nunc / primùm in lucem editae. / LONDINI. / Excudebat Thomas Este. / 1598.

Two part books in mensural notation, each of 10 fols. On fol. 10^v: table of contents. Contents = 1577_2. The volume contains 24 compositions *a2*; nos. 1–12 have Latin text; nos. 13–24 are without text and title.

Copies in: GB:Lbm (imperfect), US:SM.

1598_9

MERULO, CLAUDIO

TOCCATE / D'INTAVOLATURA / D'ORGANO DI CLAUDIO / MERULO DA CORREGGIO / organista del Sereniss.°

/ Sig. Duca di Parma / et Piacenza Ec. / Nuovamente da lui date in luce, et / con ogni diligenza corrette. / LIBRO PRIMO. / [Printer's mark] / In Roma appresso Simone Verovio / MD. XCVIII. / Con licenza de Superiori.[1]

43 fols. Keyboard score. Dedication on fol. A1ᵛ headed "All'Ill.ᵐᵒ et R.ᵐᵒ et Patron mio Col.ᵐᵒ il Sig. Card. Farnesio," and signed "Di Roma questo di 20 d'agosto. 1598. Di V. S.ʳⁱᵃ Ill.ᵐᵃ et Ecc.ᵐᵃ Devotissimo et Humiliss.ᵐᵒ Servitore Simone Verovio," reprinted in BigiM, p. 50; CasSV, p. 197; CatM, p. 49; and SartMS, p. 99. Fol. A2 = fol. 1. On fol. 43: table of contents. The entire collection is reprinted in MeruT I, which includes a facsimile of fol. 1. A second volume of toccatas by Merulo was printed in 1604 (see SartMS, p. 124). All of the compositions are for solo keyboard.

† Copies in: B:Br,[2] D:Bds, D:Mbs, F:Pc,[3] GB:Lbm, I:Bc, I:Fn, I:Vnm, US:CA.[4]

	fol.	
1	1	*Primo Tuono. Toccata Prima*[5]
2	4	*Primo Tuono. Toccata Seconda*
3	11	*Secondo Tuono. Toccata Terza*
4	16	*Secondo Tuono. Toccata 4.ª*[6]
5	19	*Secondo tuono. Toccata Quinta*
6	23	*Terzo Tuono. Toccata Sesta*[7]
7	27	*Terzo Tuono. Toccata Settima*[8]
8	33	*Quarto tuono. Toccata Ottava*
9	39	*Quarto Tuono. Toccata Nona*[9]

[1] Facs. of title page in GaspCM, p. 16.
[2] This copy was in the library of François J. Fétis.
[3] This copy was in the library of Gaetano Gaspari.
[4] A copy was in the library of A. H. Littleton (see MLE, 1904, pp. 17 and 109, where the date is given as 1597).
[5] Mod. ed. in ValentinTo, no. 5. Facs. of fol. 1 in MGG VIII, col. 139, and WolfH II, 257.
[6] Mod. ed. in TagA II, no. 3.
[7] Mod. ed. in KrausCO II, no. 1.
[8] Mod. ed. in BarthaZ, no. 66; FétT, p. 157; KleinO, p. 105; TagA II, no. 1; and WeitzG, no. 1.
[9] Mod. ed. in BedbI I, no. 1, and SchlechtG, no. 56.

1598_{10}

REYMANN, MATTHAEUS

NOCTES / MUSICAE, / STUDIO / ET / industriâ / MATTHAEI REYMANI / TORONENSIS BORUSSI / CONCINNATAE. / [Cut of a lutenist with one foot on a lion, and the motto "NON VI SED CHELY"] / Editio est VOEGELIANA. / ANNO CHRISTI / CIↃ. IↃ. XCVIII. / Cum privilegio S. Caes. Maiest. & Septemuir. Saxon.[1]

100 fols. French lute tablature. Dedication in Latin verse on fols. 2–3ᵛ headed "GENEROSIS STRENUIS, EX VERE NOBILI, ANTIQUA ET SPLENDIDA PROSAPIA, EQUITIBUS AURATIS; Tum doctrina, tum rerum experientia eximiis viris, Fratribus, DOMINIS JOHANNI, ADAMO, CAROLO ET NICOLAO CZEYKYS IN CAZOW ET OLBRAMOWITZ, DOMINIS." On fol. 4: preface headed "Lectoris," and signed "Datae Kal. Sext. Anno Christi M. D. XCVIII.," explaining the notation of the seventh and eighth courses on the lute, and summarizing the contents of the volume. On fol. 4ᵛ: two poems in Latin, the first headed "Genii et ingenii elegantioris Dn. Matthaeo Reymano," and signed "M. Joannes Suevius Annament.," and the other headed "Ad Eundem Elegëidion," and signed "Paullus Frobergius F." At the end: three pages of errata (missing from the Brussels copy). The volume was printed by Voegelin in Heidelberg. The contents were reprinted in 1600 as part of a larger work by Johann Ruden (see RISM 1600_{5a} and BohnMD, p. 345). All of the compositions are for solo lute.

Copies in: B:Br (imperfect), D:W, PL:WRu.[2]

	fol.	
1	A1	*Praeludii primi ad notam G sol re ut, melos molle*
2	A1ᵛ	*2. Praeludium harmoniae eiusdem*
3	A2	*3. Praeludium harmoniae eiusdem*[3]
4	A2ᵛ	*1. Praeludii primi ad notam G sol re ut, melos durum*
5	A3	*2. Praeludium harmoniae eiusdem*
6	A3ᵛ	*3. Praeludium harmoniae eiusdem*
7	A4	*1. Praeludii primi ad notam F fa ut, melos molle, tono ficto*
8	A4ᵛ	*2. Praeludium harmoniae eiusdem*
9	A5	*3. Praeludium harmoniae eiusdem*
10	A5ᵛ	*1. Praeludii primi ad notam F fa ut, melos durum*
11	B1	*2. Praeludium harmoniae eiusdem*
12	B1ᵛ	*3. Praeludium harmoniae eiusdem*

13 B2 *Praeludium unum ad notam D la sol re, ficti toni, melos durum*
14 B2v *Praeludii primi ad notam C sol fa ut, melos molle, tono ficto*
15 B3 *2. Praeludium harmoniae eiusdem*
16 B3v *Praeludii primi ad notam C sol fa ut, melos durum*
17 B4 *3. Praeludium harmoniae eiusdem*
18 B4v *1. Praeludii primi ad notam E la mi, melos durum*
19 B5 *2. Praeludium harmoniae eiusdem*
20 B5v *Praeludium unum ad notam E la mi, tono ficto, melos molle*
21 B6 *Praeludium unum ad notam B fa b mi, tono ficto, melos molle*
22 B6v *Fantasia super Nu kom der heiden Heylandt*[4] (compare BäumK, p. 244, and ZahnM I, no. 1174)
23 C2 *Fantasia super Von Himmel hoch da komm ich her*[5] (compare ZahnM I, no. 346)
24 C3v *Fantasia super Erhalt uns Herr bey deinem Wort* (compare ZahnM I, no. 350)
25 C4v *Fantasia super Es spricht der unweizen mundt wol* (compare ZahnM III, no. 4436)
26 D1 *Fantasia super Erbarm dich mein O HERRE Gott* (compare BäumK, p. 257, and ZahnM III, no. 5851)
27 D3v *Fantasia super Ich ruffe zu dir Herr Jesu Christ*[6] (compare ZahnM IV, no. 7400)
28 D5v *Fantasia super Nu frewt euch lieben Christen gemein* (compare ZahnM III, no. 4427)
29 E1v *Fantasia super Durch Adams fall ist ganz verderbt* (compare ZahnM IV, no. 7549)
30 E3v *Fantasia super Wenn mein stündlein verhanden ist* (compare ZahnM III, no. 4482)
31 E6 *Fantasia*
32 F2 *Fantasia*
33 F4 *Fantasia*
34 F5 *Fantasia*
35 F6v *Fantasia*[7]
36 G1v *Fantasia*[7]
37 G3 *Fantasia*
38 G4v *Passemezae 1 ad notam G sol re ut, Melos molle*
39 H1v *Passemezae 2 ad notam G sol re ut, Melos durum*
40 H5v *Passemezae 3 ad notam F fa ut, melos molle, tono ficto*
41 I3 *Passemezae 4 ad notam F fa ut, melos durum*
42 I6v *Passemezae 5 ad notam D la sol re, Melos molle*
43 K4v *Passemezae 6 ad notam D la sol re, melos durum, ficto tono*
44 L1v *Passemeze 7 ad notam C sol fa ut, melos molle, tono ficto*
45 L4v *Passemeze 8 ad notam C sol fa ut, melos durum*
46 M1v *Passemeze 9 ad notam E la mi, melos molle, tono ficto*
47 M4v *Passemeze 10 ad notam E la mi, melos durum, tono ficto*
48 N1 *Passemeze 11 ad notam B fa b mi, melos molle, tono ficto*
49 N4 *Passemeze 12 ad notam B fa b mi, melos durum, tono ficto*
50 N6v *Pavana 1*
51 O1v *Pavana 2*
52 O2v *Pavana 3*
53 O3v *Pavana 4*
54 O4v *Pavana 5*
55 O5 *Galliarda 1*
56 O5v *Galliarda 2*
57 O6 *Galliarda 3*
58 O6v *Galliarda 4*
59 P1 *Galliarda 5*
60 P1v *Galliarda 6*
61 P2v *Galliarda 7*
62 P3v *Galliarda 8*
63 P4v *Galliarda 9*
64 P5 *Galliarda 10*
65 P5v *Chorea 1*
66 P6 *Chorea 2*
67 P6v *Chorea 3*[8]
68 Q1v *Chorea 4*
69 [*Chorea 5*]
70 [*Chorea 6*]
71 [*Chorea 7*]
72 [*Chorea 8*]
73 [*Chorea 9*]

[1] The inventory was made from a microfilm of the incomplete Brussels copy, which lacks a title page and all fols. after fol. Q1v. The title page and information concerning the last 5 fols. are taken from BohnMD, p. 331.
[2] A copy was in D:Hs.
[3] Mod. ed. in WustM, p. 221.
[4] Beginning pr. in WustM, p. 234.
[5] Beginning and end pr. in WustM, p. 232.
[6] Beginning pr. in WustM, p. 235.
[7] Beginning of no. 35 pr. in WustM, p. 231; mod. ed. of no. 36 in NeemAM II, no. 22.
[8] Mod. ed. in WustM, p. 242.

1598₁₁

VINCENTI, GIACOMO, PUBLISHER

INTAVOLATURA D'ORGANO / FACILISSIMA, / Accommodata in versetti Sopra gli Otto Tuoni / ECCLESIASTICI, / Con la quale si può giustamente risponder à Messe, à Salmi, & à tutto / quello che è necessario al Choro. / Novamente data in luce. / [Printer's mark] / IN VENETIA, Appresso Giacomo Vincenti. M. D. XCVIII.

17 fols. Keyboard score. Music is printed only on the recto of each fol.; the versos are blank. Fol. A2 = fol. 1. The entire collection is reprinted in KastnV. For further information see KastnI, which includes facsimiles of the title page and fol. 1. All of the compositions are for solo keyboard.

Copy in: I:Bc.

	fol.	
1	1	[*Verso*] *primo del primo tuono*
2	2	[*Verso*] *secondo del primo tuono*
3	3	[*Verso*] *primo del secondo tuono*
4	4	[*Verso*] *secondo del secondo tuono*
5	5	[*Verso*] *primo del terzo tuono*
6	6	[*Verso*] *secondo del terzo tuono*
7	7	[*Verso*] *primo del quarto tuono*
8	8	[*Verso*] *secondo del quarto tuono*
9	9	[*Verso*] *primo del quinto tuono*
10	10	[*Verso*] *secondo del quinto tuono*
11	11	[*Verso*] *primo del sesto tuono*
12	12	[*Verso*] *secondo del sesto tuono*
13	13	[*Verso*] *primo del settimo tuono*
14	14	[*Verso*] *secondo del settimo tuono*
15	15	[*Verso*] *primo dell'ottavo tuono*
16	16	[*Verso*] *secondo dell'ottavo tuono*

1599₁

ALLISON, RICHARD

THE / PSALMES OF / David in Meter, / The plaine Song beeing the com/mon tunne to be sung and plaide upon / the Lute, Orpharyon, Citterne or Base / Violl, severally or altogether, the sing/ing part to be either Tenor or Treble / to the Instrument, according to / the nature of the voyce, or / for foure voyces: / With tenne short Tunnes in the end, to / which for the most part all the Psalmes / may be usually sung, for the use of / such as are of mean skill, and / whose leysure least serveth / to practice: / By / Richard Allison Gent. Practitioner in / the Art of Musicke: and are to be solde / at his house in the Dukes place / neere Alde-gate. / LONDON / Printed by William Barley, the / Assigne of Thomas Morley. / 1599. / Cum Privilegio Regiae / Majestatis.

75 fols. French lute tablature, cittern tablature (for the four-course cittern using Italian tuning), and mensural notation. The title is placed within an ornamental border. On fol. A1ᵛ: a coat of arms. Dedication on fol. A2 headed "To the right Honorable and most ver[t]uous Lady, the Lady Anne Countesse of Warwicke," and signed on fol. A2ᵛ "Your Honors humbly devoted in all duety Richard Allison." On fol. A3: three poems in English headed "John Dowland Batcheler of Musicke in commendation of Richard Allison, and this most excellent work," "William Leighton Esq. in praise of the Author," and "John Welton in prayse of the Author." On fol. A3ᵛ: an excerpt from the royal printing privilege headed "The extract and effect of the Queenes Maiesties Patent to Thomas Morley, for the Printing of Musicke." On fol. A4: a table listing the compositions which can be used for more than one psalm, headed "A Table containing what notes are to be sung to these particular Psalmes following." On fol. T3: a coat of arms. The volume contains psalm settings arranged with various alternative methods of performance in mind. On the left page of each opening is the cantus part of the vocal setting, a lute intabulation, and (printed upside down) a cittern intabulation. On the right page of each opening are the three lower parts of the vocal setting.

Copies in: GB:En, GB:Lbm, US:Cn, US:SM (imperfect).[1]

	fol.	
1	A4ᵛ	*Come holy Ghost eternall God* (Veni Creator)
2	B1ᵛ	*O Lord of whom I do depend* (The humble sute of a Sinner)
3	B2ᵛ	*O come & let us now rejoice*[2] (Venite exultemus)
4	B3ᵛ	*We praise thee God* (Te Deum)

5 B4^{v} *O all yee workes of God* (The Song of the three Children)

6 C1^{v} *My soule doth magnifie the Lord* (Magnificat)

7 C2^{v} *O Lord, because my harts desire* (Nunc dimittis)

8 C3^{v} *What man so ever he be* (Quicunque vult)

9 C4^{v} *O Lord turne not away thy face* (The Lamentation)

10 D1^{v} *Our Father which in heaven art* (The Lords prayer)

11 D3^{v} *Harke Israell & what I say* (The x. Commandements)

12 D4^{v} *Where righteousnes doth say* (The complaint of a Sinner)

13 E1^{v} *The man is blest that hath not bent* (Psalme. 1.)

14 E2^{v} *O Lord how are my foes increast* (Psalme. 3.)

15 E3^{v} *Lord in thy wrath reprove me not* (Psalme. 6.)

16 E4^{v} *There is no God as foolish men* (Psalme. 14.)

17 F1^{v} *O God my strength & fortitude* (Psalme. 18.)

18 F2^{v} *O Lord how joyful is the King* (Psalme. 21.)

19 F3^{v} *O God my God, wherefore dost thou* (Psalme. 22.)

20 F4^{v} *I lift my hart to thee* (Psalme. 25.)

21 G1^{v} *All laud & praise with hart and voice* (Psalme. 30.)

22 G2^{v} *The man is blest that carefull is* (Psalme. 41.)

23 G3^{v} *Our eares have heard our fathers tell* (Psalme. 44.)

24 G4^{v} *The Lord is our defence* (Psalme. 46.)

25 H1^{v} *The mighty God th'eternal hath thus spoke* (Psalme. 50.)

26 H2^{v} *O Lord consider my distresse* (Psalme. 51.)

27 H3^{v} *Why dost thou tyrant boast abroad* (Psalme. 52.)

28 H4^{v} *Send ayd & save mee from my foes* (Psalme. 59.)

29 I1^{v} *Regarde O Lord for I complaine* (Psalme. 61.)

30 I2^{v} *Let God arise & then his foes* (Psalme. 68.)

31 I3^{v} *Save me O God and that with speed* (Psalme. 69.)

32 I4^{v} *Lord give thy judgments to the King* (Psalme. 72.)

33 K1^{v} *Bee light & glad in God rejoice* (Psalme. 81.)

34 K2^{v} *Attend my people to my Law* (Psalme. 78.)

35 K3^{v} *My soule give laud unto the Lord* (Psalme. 103.)

36 K4^{v} *My Soule praise the Lord* (Psalme. 104.)

37 L2^{v} *With hart I doe accord* (Psalme. 111.)

38 L4^{v} *Ye children which do serve the Lord* (Psalme. 113.)

39 M2^{v} *Blessed are they that perfect are* (Psalme. 119.)

40 M4^{v} *I lift mine eyes to Sion hill* (Psalme. 121.)

41 N1^{v} *I did in hart rejoyce*[3] (Psalme. 122.)

42 N3^{v} *Now Israell may say I that truely* (Psalme. 124.)

43 N4^{v} *Such as in God the Lord doe trust* (Psalme. 125.)

44 O1^{v} *When that the Lord againe his Sion* (Psalme. 126.)

45 O3^{v} *Lord to thee I make my mone* (Psalme. 130.)

46 O4^{v} *Remember Davids troubles Lord* (Psalme. 132.)

47 P1^{v} *O Praise the Lord* (Psalme. 135.)

48 P2^{v} *Praise ye the Lord for hee is good* (Psalme. 136.)

49 P4^{v} *When as wee sat in Babilon* (Psalme. 137.)

50 Q1^{v} *O Lord upon thee doe I call* (Psalme. 137.)

51 Q2^{v} *Thee will I laud my God and King* (Psalme. 145.)

52 Q3^{v} *Praise ye the Lord for it is good* (Psalme. 147.)

53 Q4^{v} *Give laude unto the Lord* (Psalme. 148.)

54 R1^{v} *Attend my people and give eare* (Audi Israel)

55 R2^{v} *Our father which in heaven art* (The Lords prayer)

56 R3^{v} *All my beliefe and confidence* (The Creede)

57 R4^{v} *Give peace in these our daies O Lord* (Da pacem)

58 S1^{v} *O Lord in thee is all my trust* (The Lamentation)

59 S2ᵛ *Preserve us lord by thy deare word* (A prayer)
60 S2ᵛ *O God that art my righteousnesse* (Psalme. 4.)
61 S3ᵛ *Helpe Lord for good & godly men* (Psalme. 12.)
62 S3ᵛ *O Lord give eare* (Psalme. 17.)
63 S4ᵛ *The God of Gods the Lord* (Psalme. 50.)
64 S4ᵛ *How pleasant is thy dwelling place* (Psalme. 84.)
65 T1ᵛ *Lord God of health the hope and stay* (Psalme. 88.)
66 T1ᵛ *It is a thing both good and meete* (Psalme. 92.)
67 T2ᵛ *I love the Lord because my voice* (Psalme. 116.)
68 T2ᵛ *Those that doe put their confidence* (Psalme. 125.)

[1] A copy of this volume came to America on the *Mayflower* (see ChaseA, p. 12). A copy was in the library of J. F. R. Stainer (see MLE, 1904, p. 58).
[2] Facs. of fols. B2ᵛ and B3 in SmithL, p. 32.
[3] Facs. of fol. N2 in SteeleE, fig. 41.

1599₂

BELLANDA, LODOVICO

CANZONETTE / SPIRITUALI / A DUE VOCI / Con altre à Tre, & à Quattro / da Sonare, / Novamente da Lodovico Bel/ landà date in luce. / In Verona per Francesco dalle / Donne, et Scipione Vargna/no suo Genero. 1599. / Con licenza de' Superiori.

Two part books in mensural notation, each of 12 fols. The title is placed within an ornamental border. Dedication on fol. *1ᵛ of each part book headed "ALLE NOBILISSIME, ET VIRTUOSISSIME MIE SIGNORE, Et Patrone osservandissime LE SIGNORE CECILIA, ET CATERINA RICCIARDELLE," and signed "Di Verona li 22. Maggio 1599. Humilissimo Servitore Lodovico Bellandà." Fol. *2 = p. 1. On p. 22 of each part book: table of contents. Since this volume is not indexed in Vogel the following inventory lists all of the compositions. Nos. 1–9 are fully texted duos; nos. 10–13 are for instrumental ensemble *a 3* and *a 4*.

Copy in: I:VEcap.

MUSIC FOR VOICES *a 2*

	p.	
1	1	*O Musa tù*
	2	2a pars *Tu spira al petto mio*
2	3	*O più bella del Sole*
3	4	*Fu ben la prima donna*
4	5	*Nel bel seno chiudesti*
5	6	*Scorgi'l mio debil legno*
6	7	*Morte m'hà teso il laccio*
7	8	*Tu che l'interno effetto*
8	9	*Vergine pura d'ogni parte* Don Paolo Fonghetti
	10	2a pars *Sola tu fosti eletta*
9	11	*O più rara del Sole*

MUSIC FOR INSTRUMENTAL ENSEMBLE

10	12	[*Canzone*] *Da Sonare a 3* R. P. Ambrogio Bresciano
11	14	[*Canzone*] *Da Sonare a 3* R. P. Ambrogio Bresciano
12	16	[*Canzone*] *Da Sonare a 4*
13	18	[*Canzone*] *Da Sonare a 4*

[1599]₃

BORGO, CESARE

Canzoni alla francese à 4. Lib. 2. Venetia 1599.

This volume of music for instrumental ensemble *a 4*, now lost, is listed in FétB II, 28; PiciA, p. 137; and SartMS, p. 105.

1599₄

BOTTRIGARI, ERCOLE

IL / DESIDERIO, / OVERO / De' Concerti di varii Strumenti Musicali. / DIALOGO / DEL M. ILL. SIG. CAVALIERE / Hercole Bottrigaro: / Nel quale anco si ragiona della Participatione di essi / Strumenti, & di molte altre cose pertinenti / alla Musica. / [Printer's mark] / IN BOLOGNA. / Appresso Gioambattista Bellagamba. M D IC. / Con licenza de' Superiori.[1]

35 fols. Dedication on p. *3 headed "ALL'ILLUSTRISSIMO, ET REVER.ᴹᴼ MONSIG. PATRON MIO COL.ᴹᴼ IL SIGNOR Cardinale Aldobrandino," and

signed "Di Bologna il dì 26. di Ottobre. 1599. Di V. S. Illustriss. & Reverendiss. Humilissimo servitore Gratia Lodi Garisendi," reprinted in SartMS, p. 103. On p. *5: preface headed "A' Benigni, e Cortesi Lettori." On pp. *8–*13: table of contents. On p. *14: a list of authorities cited, headed "Nomi de' Musici così Teorici, come Prattici, & di alcuni Poeti, & Filosofi, allegati nel Dialogo." The treatise begins on p. *15 = p. 1.[2] On p. 52: a list of errata headed "Errori piu importanti scorsi nello stampare." On pp. 53–54: a list of errata headed "Errori scorsi nello Stampare, & corretti." Except for the prefatory material and a few minor changes in the text, the contents = 1594₂. This second edition is reprinted in facsimile in BottrigD. BottrigDE is an English translation.

Copies in: B:Br, GB:Lbmh, I:Bc.

[1] Facs. of title page in KinsP, p. 109.
[2] Facs. of p. 1 in MGG II, cols. 155–156.

1599₅

HAUSSMANN, VALENTIN

Neue artige und liebliche Täntze, / zum theil mit Texten, dass man kan mit Menschlicher / Stimme zu Instrumenten singen, zum theil ohne Text gesetzt, / und denen, welche sich etwas neues gelieben lassen, / zu gefallen publiciert / Durch / Valentinum Haussmann / Gerbipol: Saxonem. / CANTUS. / Gedruckt zu Nürnberg, durch / Paulum Kauffmann. / M. D. XCIX.

Four part books in mensural notation, each of 20 fols. (?). Dedication on fol. A2 headed "Dem Ehrwirdigen, Edlen, Gestrengen und Ehrnvesten Herrn Joachimo Johann-Georg von der Schulenburg, dess Hohen Stiffts Halberstatt Thomherrn u. Meinem grossgünstigen Herrn und Patronen," and signed on fol. A2ᵛ "Datum Gerbstedt, den. 5. Maii, Anno 1598. E. E. und G. Dienstwilliger Valentinus Haussmann Gerbipol," reprinted in DDT XVI, viii. On fol. A3: table of contents for the dances with German text. For the first edition of this collection see [1598]₇. Later editions are listed in MeyeM, p. 213. The compositions identified by superior letters are reprinted as follows: (a) in DDT XVI, 115–122; (b) in NM, vol. 80. Nos. 1–21 are dances with German text; nos. 22–46 are without text; all of the compositions are *a 4*.

Copies in: D:Bds (B), D:Hs (ST).

DANCES WITH GERMAN TEXT

	fol.	
1	A3ᵛ	*Jungfrau wolt ir nicht mit mir ein Täntzlein*[1]
	A3ᵛ	Nach Tantz *So tantzen wir*
2	A4	*Ach hett ich die, so je begert mein hertze*
	A4	Nach Tantz *Was Gott beschert*
3	A4ᵛ	*Venus hat mir gar vest gebildet ein*
	A4ᵛ	Nach Tantz *Drumb ist mein hertz*
4	B1	*Ach Gott wie schwere pein*
	B1	Nach Tantz *Wolan Göttin schon*
5	B1ᵛ	*Holdseligs Bild mich nicht betrübe*
	B1ᵛ	Nach Tantz *Vil lügn die falschen Kläffer dichten*
6	B2	*Feins Lieb dein günstig ohren wend zu*
	B2	Nach Tantz *Solchs wil ich nun von dir*
7	B2ᵛ	*Ein hitzigs Feur mein hertz thut brinnen*
	B2ᵛ	Nach Tantz *Darumb wünsch ich in zucht und ehren*
8	B3	*Ein Fräulein zart, hab ich mir ausserkorn*
	B3	Nach Tantz *Bleib nicht lang auss*
9	B3ᵛ	*Megdlein was zeichst du dich*
	B3ᵛ	Nach Tantz *Was nicht bleiben wil*
10	B4	*Megdlein jung mein Sonnenschein*
	B4	Nach Tantz *Mägdlein jung du edles Blut*
11	B4ᵛ	*Das mein betrübtes Hertz*
	B4ᵛ	Nach Tantz *Schau an mein gemüt*
12	C1	*Feins Lieb in ehren, thu ich mich kehren*
13	C1ᵛ	*Jungkfrau ich wolt euch wol gern*
14	C2	*Auff mein Gsang unnd mach dich ring*
15	C2ᵛ	*Kein Mensch auff Erden*
16	C3	*Ein Jungfrau mir gefellt*
17	C3ᵛ	*LIEB hat mein hertz, auss freud*

18 C4 *Jungfrau wenn wolt ir euch eins besinnen*
19 C4ᵛ *Dass ich mein leben, dir gantz ergeben*
20 D1 *Soll ich dir mein Lieb nicht versagen*
21 D1ᵛ *Weil mich deine Pfeil so schmerzlich plagen*

DANCES WITHOUT TEXT

22 D2 *XXII.* [*Tantz*][ab 2]
D2 *Nach Tantz*[ab]
23 D2ᵛ *XXIII.* [*Tantz*][ab]
D2ᵛ *Nach Tantz*[ab]
24 D2ᵛ *XXIIII.* [*Tantz*][a]
D3 *Nach Tantz*[a]
25 D3 *XXV.* [*Tantz*][a 3]
D3 *Nach Tantz*[a]
26 D3ᵛ *XXVI.* [*Tantz*][4]
D3ᵛ *Nach Tantz*
27 D3ᵛ *XXVII.* [*Tantz*][a]
D4 *Nach Tantz*[a]
28 D4 *XXVIII.* [*Tantz*][b]
D4 *Nach Tantz*[b]
29 D4ᵛ *XXIX.* [*Tantz*]
D4ᵛ *Nach Tantz*
30 D4ᵛ *XXX.* [*Tantz*][a]
E1 *Nach Tantz*[a]
31 E1 *XXXI.* [*Tantz*]
E1 *Nach Tantz*
32 E1ᵛ *XXXII.* [*Tantz*]
33 E1ᵛ *XXXIII.* [*Tantz*][5]
34 E2 *XXXIIII.* [*Tantz*]
35 E2 *XXXV.* [*Tantz*][b]
36 E2 *XXXVI.* [*Tantz*][ab]
37 E2ᵛ *XXXVII.* [*Tantz*][a]
38 E2ᵛ *XXXVIII.* [*Tantz*][a]
39 E2ᵛ *XXXIX.* [*Tantz*]
40 E3 *XL.* [*Tantz*]
41 E3 *XLI.* [*Tantz*]
42 E3 *XLII.* [*Tantz*]
43 E3ᵛ *XLIII.* [*Tantz*][b]
44 E3ᵛ *XLIIII.* [*Tantz*]
45 E3ᵛ *XLV.* [*Tantz*][a]
46 E4 *XLVI.* [*Tantz*]

[1] Heading on fol. A3ᵛ: "Folgen Täntze nach Teutscher und Polnischer art mit Texten."
[2] Heading on fol. D2: "Folgen Täntze nach Teutscher und Polnischer Art ohne Text." Mod. ed. of no. 22a in MFH IX, 9.
[3] Mod. ed. in FortI I, 12.
[4] Mod. ed. in ZfSM LVI, no. 5.
[5] Mod. ed. in ZfSM LVI, no. 3.

1599₆

HOLBORNE, ANTONY

PAVANS, / GALLIARDS, ALMAINS, AND / other short AEirs both grave, and light, / in five parts, for Viols, Violins, / or other Musicall Winde / Instruments. / Made by Antony Holborne Gentleman and / Servant to her most excellent / Maiestie. / [Printer's mark with the motto "DEUS IN AETERNUM"] / Imprinted at London in little Saint Hellens by William Barley, the / Assigne of Thomas Morley, and are to be sold at his / shop in Gratious-streete. / 1599. / Cum privilegio ad Imprimendum solum.

Five part books in mensural notation, each of 18 fols. Dedication on fol. A2 of each part book headed "TO THE RIGHT WORSHIPFULL AND VERTUOUS GENTLEMAN SIR RICHARD CHAMPERNOWNE KNIGHT," and signed "Yours in all love and due reverence, Antony Holborne." On fol. E2ᵛ of each part book: table of contents. HolPG is a modern edition of the entire collection. There is a modern edition of two compositions in MUB, vol. 6. The compositions identified by superior letters are reprinted as follows: (ᵃ) in ARC, vol. 17; (ᵇ) in ARC, vol. 50; (ᶜ) in ARC, vol. 51; (ᵈ) in ARC, vol. 52; (ᵉ) in HolSE; (ᶠ) in MUB, vol. 93. All of the compositions are for instrumental ensemble *a 5*.

Copies in: GB:Lbm (imperfect), GB:Och, US:Cn, US:SM (SB).

fol.
1 A3 *Bona Speranza*
2 A3 *The teares of the Muses*
3 A3ᵛ *Pavan*
4 A3ᵛ *Lullabie* (1597₆, no. 55)
5 A4 *The Cradle*[1]
6 A4 *The New-yeeres gift*[f 1]
7 A4ᵛ *Pavan*[2]
8 A4ᵛ *The Marie-golde*[f 2]
9 B1 *Pavan*
10 B1 *Galliard*[2]
11 B1ᵛ *Pavan*[c]
12 B1ᵛ *Galliard*[d]
13 B2 *Pavan*
14 B2 *Galliard*
15 B2ᵛ *Pavan*[3]
16 B2ᵛ *Galliard*[3]

17 B3 *Paradizo*[b]
18 B3 *The Sighes*[b]
19 B3v *Sedet Sola*[b]
20 B3v *Galliard*[b] (1592_6, no. 71)
21 B4 *Infernum*
22 B4 *Galliard*[d]
23 B4v *Spero*
24 B4v *Galliard*
25 C1 *Patiencia*[f 4]
26 C1 *Hermoza*[4]
27 C1v *The image of Melancholly*
28 C1v *Ecce quam bonum*
29 C2 *Mens innovata*
30 C2 *Galliard*
31 C2v *The funerals*
32 C2v *Galliard*
33 C3 *Heres paternus*
34 C3 *Muy linda*[d]
35 C3v *Decrevi*
36 C3v *My selfe*
37 C4 *Pavan*
38 C4 *Galliard*
39 C4v *Pavan*[a]
40 C4v *Galliard*[a]
41 D1 *Pavan*
42 D1 *Galliard*[a]
43 D1v *Amoretta*
44 D1v *Nec invideo*
45 D2 *Pavan*
46 D2 *Galliard*[e]
47 D2v *Pavan*
48 D2v *Galliard*
49 D3 *Pavana Ploravit*[c]
50 D3 *Sic semper soleo*[c]
51 D3v *Galliard Posthuma*
52 D3v *Galliard*
53 D4 *Last will and testament*[df]
54 D4 *Galiard*
55 D4v *The night watch*[a]
56 D4v *Almayne*
57 E1 *Almaine*[c]
58 E1 *The fruit of love*[e 5]
59 E1 *The Choise*[bef]
60 E1v *The Honie-suckle*[a]
61 E1v *Wanton*[b]
62 E1v *The widowes myte*[d]
63 E2 *The Fairie-round*[ce]
64 E2 *As it fell on a holie Eve*[e]
65 E2 *Heigh ho holiday*[a 5]

[1] Mod. ed. in HolQ.
[2] Mod. ed. in HolTQ.
[3] Mod. ed. in ARS, vol. 31.
[4] Mod. ed. in ARC, vol. 26 (no. 25 as "Pavan," and no. 26 as "Galliard").
[5] Mod. ed. in HolP.

1599_7

MOLINARO, SIMONE

INTAVOLATURA / DI LIUTO / DI SIMONE MOLINARO / GENOVESE / LIBRO PRIMO / Nel quale si contengono Saltarelli, Pass'e mezi, / Gagliarde, e Fantasie. / Novamente composto, & dato in luce. / [Printer's mark] / IN VENETIA M D XCIX. / Appresso Ricciardo Amadino.[1]

74 fols. Italian lute tablature. The title is placed within an ornamental border. Dedication on fol. *1v headed "AL MOLTO MAGNIFICO SIG. CHRISTOFFARO PAPA Patrone mio sempre Osservandissimo," and signed "Di Genova il primo di Settembre. 1599. Di V. S. Affettionatissimo Servitore Simone Molinaro," reprinted in GiazMG, p. 304. Fol. *2 = p. 1. On p. 146: table of contents. All of the compositions except those by Gostena are reprinted in a modern edition in MolinL, which includes facsimiles of the title page, the dedication, and p. 77. The Gostena compositions, except for those missing from the Florence copy, are reprinted in a modern edition in GostL. The compositions identified by the superior letter *a* ([a]) are reprinted in ChilLS, pp. 136–175. Two saltarelli arranged for keyboard and recorder are printed in MolinS. MoeDM contains a thematic index of the dances (p. 483) and concordances for them (p. 285). For further information see RoncM. All of the compositions are for solo lute.

Copies in: GB:Cu, GB:Lbm, I:Fn (imperfect).

	p.	
1	1	*Saltarello*
2	2	*Saltarello*
3	3	*Saltarello*[a]
4	4	*Saltarello*
5	5	*Saltarello*[a]
6	6	*Saltarello*
7	7	*Saltarello*[a]
8	8	*Ballo detto il Conte Orlando*[a 3]
	8	*Saltarello del predetto ballo*[a]
9	9	*Pass'e mezo*
	13	*Gagliarda*
10	14	*Pass'e mezo*
	20	*Gagliarda*

11 21 *Pass'e mezo*
29 *Gagliarda*
12 31 *Pass'e mezo*[a]
36 *Gagliarda*
13 37 *Pass'e mezo*
39 *Gagliarda*
14 40 *Pass'e mezo*
42 *Gagliarda*
15 43 *Pass'e mezo*
45 *Gagliarda*
16 46 *Pass'e mezo*[a]
49 *Gagliarda*[a]
17 50 *Pass'e mezo*[a]
53 *Gagliarda*
18 55 *Pass'e mezo*[a 4]
58 *Gagliarda*[a]
19 59 *Pass'e mezo*[a]
61 *Gagliarda*[a]
20 62 *Fantasia prima*
21 63 *Fantasia seconda*
22 65 *Fantasia terza*
23 66 *Fantasia quarta*
24 68 *Fantasia quinta*
25 69 *Fantasia sesta*
26 71 *Fantasia settima*
27 73 *Fantasia ottava*
28 75 *Fantasia nona*[a 5]
29 77 *Fantasia decima*
30 78 *Fantasia undecima*
31 80 *Fantasia XII*
32 82 *Fantasia XIII*
33 83 *Fantasia XIIII*
34 85 *Fantasia XV*
35 86 *Fantasia prima*[6] Gostena
36 88 *Fantasia seconda* Gostena
37 89 *Fantasia terza* Gostena
38 90 *Fantasia quarta* Gostena
39 92 *Fantasia quinta* Gostena
40 93 *Fantasia sesta* Gostena
41 95 *Fantasia settima* Gostena
42 97 *Fantasia ottava* Gostena
43 100 *Fantasia nona* Gostena
44 102 *Fantasia decima* Gostena
45 103 *Fantasia undecima* Gostena
46 105 *Fantasia XII* Gostena
47 108 *Fantasia XIII* Gostena
48 109 *Fantasia XIIII* Gostena
49 110 *Fantasia XV* Gostena
50 112 *Fantasia XVI* Gostena
51 113 *Fantasia XVII* Gostena
52 115 *Fantasia XVIII* Gostena
53 117 *Fantasia XIX* Gostena
54 118 *Fantasia XX* Gostena
55 120 *Fantasia XXI* Gostena
56 121 *Fantasia XXII* Gostena
57 123 *Fantasia XXIII* Gostena
58 124 *Fantasia XXIIII* Gostena
59 125 *Fantasia XXV*[a 7] Gostena
60 127 *Mais que sert la richesse a l'homme* Canzone Francese a quattro di Gulielmo Costelii Intavolata dal Gostena (MMRF III, no. 2: Costeley)
61 128 *Pis ne me peult venir* Thomas Crecquillon *a 4* intabulated by Gostena (RISM 1572₂, fol. 25)
62 130 *Susane un jour*[8] Orlando Lasso *a 5* intabulated by Gostena (LassoW XIV, 29)
63 133 *Fantasia di Giulio Severino sopra Susane un jour*[8]
64 135 *Ung gaii bergier* Thomas Crecquillon *a 4* intabulated by Molinaro (RieH II, 462)
65 137 *Rossingnolet* [*qui chante*] Clemens non papa *a 4* intabulated by Molinaro (ClemensO X, 41)
66 139 *Frais & gaillard* Clemens non papa *a 4* intabulated by Molinaro (ClemensO X, 17)
67 142 *Canzone a quattro di Gioseppe Guami* intabulated by Molinaro
68 144 *Canzone a quattro di Gioseppe Guami* intabulated by Molinaro (1596₃, no. 7: "La Guamina")

[1] Facs. of title page and p. 1 in GiazMG, pls. xxxi and xxxiii.
[2] On this copy see DartM.
[3] Mod. ed. in EC, pt. I, vol. II, p. 666.
[4] Mod. ed. in no. 18a in BruS II, no. 63.
[5] Mod. ed. in BossiC, no. 3.
[6] Heading on p. 86: "Seguono vinticinque fantasie di Gio: Battista dalla Gostena zio e maestro del Molinaro."
[7] Mod. ed. in EC, pt. I, vol. II, p. 667.
[8] For a discussion of the chanson and the fantasia based on it, see WardP, pp. 209–212.

1599₈

MORLEY, THOMAS

THE / FIRST BOOKE OF CON/sort Lessons, made by divers exqui/site Authors, for six instruments to / play together, the Treble Lute, the / Pandora, the Cittern, the Base-/Violl, the Flute & the Treble-Violl. / Newly set forth at the coast & / charges of a

Gentle-man, for his pri/vate pleasure, and for divers o/thers his frendes which de/light in Musicke. / Printed at London in Little Saint / Helens by William Barley, the / Assigne of Thomas Morley, / and are to be solde at his shop / in Gratious-streete. / CUM PRIVILEGIO AD / Imprimendum solum. 1599.[1]

Six part books, in mensural notation (bass viol, flute, treble viol) and French tablature for lute, pandora (tuned C D g c e a′), and cittern (tuned b g d e). The flute and bass viol part books each have eight folios, and the cittern and pandora part books 12 folios. The title is placed within an ornamental border. Dedication on fol. A2 of each part book headed "TO THE RIGHT HONORABLE, SIR STEPHEN SOME KNIGHT, LORD MAYOR OF THE CITTY OF LONDON AND TO THE RIGHT WORSHIPFUL THE Aldermen of the same, Thomas Morley Gent. of her Majesties Chappell, wisheth long health and felicitie." On the verso of the last folio of each part book: table of contents. The foliation in the following inventory is after the flute part book. BecFB is a modern edition of the entire collection, reconstructed with the aid of part books from the second edition of 1611 and of manuscript copies of some of the compositions; BecFB includes facsimiles of the title page and dedication. Concordances for the pieces and reasons for the attributions are given in detail in the critical notes in BecFB. For further information see DartCL. All of the compositions are for instrumental ensemble *a6*: treble and bass viols, flute, lute, pandora and cittern.

Copies in: GB:Lbm (bass viol), GB:Ob (cittern), GB:Och (pandora and flute).

	fol.	
1	A3	*The Quadro pavin*[3] [Richard Allison]
	A3	*The Galliard to the Quadro Pavin*
2	A3ᵛ	*De la Tromba Pavin* [Richard Allison?]
3	A3ᵛ	*Captaine Pipers Pavin* [John Dowland?]
	A4	*Captayne Pipers Galliard* [John Dowland?] (compare 1597₄, no. 4: "If my complaints could passions moove")
4	A4	*Galliard, Can shee Excuse* [John Dowland?] (compare 1597₄, no. 5)
5	A4	*Lacrime Pavin* [John Dowland?] (compare EL, ser. 1, vol. V, no. 2: "Flow my tears")
6	A4ᵛ	*Phillips pavin* [Peter Phillips?]
	A4ᵛ	*Galliard to Phillips Pavin*
7	B1	*The frogge galliard* [John Dowland or Thomas Morley?] (compare 1597₄, no. 6: "Now, O now I needs must part")
8	B1	*Alisons knell*[2] [Richard Allison]
9	B1ᵛ	*Goe from my Window*[2] [Richard Allison]
10	B2	*In Nomine Pavin* [Nicholas Strogers]
11	B2	*My Lord of Oxenfords Maske* [William Byrd?]
12	B2ᵛ	*Mounsiers, Almaine*[3] [William Byrd?]
13	B2ᵛ	*Michels galliard*
14	B2ᵛ	*La Volto* [Thomas Morley?]
15	B2ᵛ	*Balowe* [Thomas Morley?]
16	B2ᵛ	*O Mistresse mine* [Thomas Morley?]
17	B3	*Sola Soleta* [Thomas Morley?] (compare Vogel: Conversi 2 [1572], p. 9, and RISM 1590₂₉: "When al alone my bony love was playing")
18	B3	*Joyne hands* [Thomas Morley] (compare EMS I, no. 1 *a3*: "See, mine own sweet jewel")
19	B3ᵛ	*La Coranta* [Thomas Morley?] (compare 1589₁, no. 3: "Belle qui tiens ma vie")
20	B3ᵛ	*The Lord Sowches Maske* [Thomas Morley?]

[1] Facs. of title page in MGG IX, pl. 37.

[2] Mod. ed. in MorlTL.

[3] For information about manuscript sources of the missing lute parts, see SpencerT.

1599₉

PELLEGRINI, VINCENZO

CANZONI: / DE INTAVOLATURA D'ORGANO / FATTE ALLA FRANCESE / DI VINCENZO PELLEGRINI CANONICO DI PESARO / Novamente da lui date in luce, & con ogni diligenza corrette. / LIBRO PRIMO. / ALL'ILLUSTRISSIMA SIGNORA LIVIA DELLA ROVERE. / [Printer's mark] / IN VENETIA, Appresso Giacomo Vincenti. M. D. LXXXXIX.

61 fols. Keyboard score. Dedication on fol. A2 headed "ALL'ILLUSTRISS.MA SIGNORA LIVIA DELLA ROVERE, VINCENZO PELLEGRINI DA PESARO DEVOTISSIMO SERVO," and signed on fol. A2v "Di Venetia il dì 27. Marzo. 1599," reprinted in GaspaC IV, 59, and SartMS, p. 104. Fol. A3 = p. 1. On p. 98: table of contents. All of the compositions are for solo keyboard.

Copy in: I:Bc.

	p.	
1	1	*Canzone detta La Berenice*
2	9	*Canzon detta la Gentile*
3	14	*Canzon detta la Cassiodora*
4	22	*Canzon detta la Serpentina* [1]
5	28	*Canzon detta la L'Archangiola*
6	37	*Canzon detta la Nota*
7	43	*Canzon detta la Serafina*
8	48	*Canzon detta la Mariana*
9	56	*Canzon detta la Diana*
10	63	*Canzon detta la Capricciosa* [2]
11	72	*Canzone detta la Gratiosa*
12	81	*Canzone detta la Pellegrina*
13	89	*Canzone detta la Barbarina*

[1] Mod. ed. in DallaLO I, no. 7, and TorA III, 49.

[2] Mod. ed. in FuserC, no. 28, and TorA III, 51.

1599$_{10}$

STIVORI, FRANCESCO

RICERCARI / CAPRICCI ET / CANZONI / A QUATTRO VOCI. / DI FRANCESCO STIVORI / Organista della Magnifica Communita / di Montagnana. / LIBRO TERZO. / Novamente composti, & dati in luce. / [Printer's mark] / In Venetia, Appresso Ricciardo Amadino. / M D XCIX.

Four part books in mensural notation, each of 12 fols. (?). The title is placed within an ornamental border. Dedication on fol. 1v headed "AL MOLTO MAGNIFICO MIO SIGNOR OSSERVANDISSIMO IL SIGNOR GIOVANNI GABRIELI Organista della Sereniss. Signoria di Venetia," and signed "Di Venetia il dì 20. Febraio. 1599. Di V. S. Molto Magnifica Servitore obligatiss. Francesco Stivorio," reprinted in SartMS, p. 102. Fol. 2 = p. 1. For other volumes by Stivori see 1589$_{7}$, note 1. All of the compositions are for instrumental ensemble *a 4*.

Copy in: A:Wn (SA).

	p.	
1	1	*Ricercar Primo*
2	2	*Ricercar Secondo*
3	4	*Ricercar Terzo*
4	5	*Ricercar Quarto*
5	6	*Capriccio*
6	7	*Ricercar quinto*
7	8	*Ricercar Sesto*
8	9	*Ricercar Settimo*
9	10	*Ricercar ottavo*
10	11	*Ricercar Nono*
11	12	*Ricercar Decimo*
12	13	*Ricercar Undecimo*
13	14	*Ricercar Duodecimo*
14	15	*Canzone prima*
15	16	*Capriccio*
16	17	*Canzone seconda*
17	18	*Canzone terza*
18	19	*Capriccio*
19	20	*Canzone quinta*
20	21	*Canzone sesta detta la saporita*
21	22	*Capriccio*

1599$_{11}$

TERZI, GIOVANNI ANTONIO

IL SECONDO / LIBRO / DE INTAVOLATURA / DI LIUTO / DI GIO. ANTONIO TERZI / DA BERGAMO. / Nella quale si contengono Fantasie, Motetti, Canzoni, Madri/gali Pass'e mezi, & Balli di varie, & diverse sorti. / Novamente da lui data in luce. / [Printer's mark] / IN VENETIA, / Appresso Giacomo Vincenti 1599.

64 fols. Italian lute tablature. The title is placed within an ornamental border. Dedication on fol. *1v headed "AL MOLTO ILLUSTRE ET ECCELL.MO SIGNOR MIO OSSERVANDISSIMO IL SIGNOR SILLANO LICINO," and signed "Di

Venetia il di 10. Novembre 1598. Di V. Sig. molto Illustre, & Eccellentissimo Devotissimo Servitore Gio. Antonio Terzi," reprinted in GaspaC IV, 175. The music begins on fol. 2 (= p. 1). On p. 124: table of contents. On p. 125: a note headed "Ai Virtuosi Lettori" concerning printing errors. MoeDM contains a thematic index of the dances (p. 475) and concordances for them (p. 283). The compositions followed by an asterisk are completely texted (that is, they are for lute and voice, but the voice part is not otherwise differentiated). Nos. 30, 38, and 87 are for two lutes; no. 93 is for four lutes; and no. 55 is a lute part for a large ensemble. The other compositions are for solo lute.

Copies in: D:W, I:Bc.

	p.	
1	1	*Preludio de l'Autore*[1]
2	2	*Fantasia de l'Autore*
3	4	*Gagliarda Prima*
4	4	*Gagliarda detta Tamburin*
5	6	*Leggiadre Ninfe* Marenzio *a6* (Vogel: Marenzio 16 [1591], p. 3)
6	7	*Candide perle* [Antonio] Bicci (Vogel: Marenzio 16 [1591], p. 4)
7	8	*Quando mirai sa bella faccia**[2] Horatio Vecchi (Vogel: Vecchi 21 [1591], p. 19)
8	9	*Di pianti e di sospir** Juliano Paratico (Vogel: Paratico [1588], p. 2)
9	9	*Ahi chi mi tien'il core** Gio. Giacomo Gastoldi (Vogel: Gastoldi 30 [1592], no. 16)
10	9	*Come faro cor mio** Antonio Mortaro (Vogel: Mortaro 4 [1594], p. 21)
11	10	*Fantasia in modo di Canzon Francesa*[3] [Francesco] Guami (1588_8, no. 4)
12	12	*Un'altra Fantasia del detto* (1588_8, no. 3)
13	14	*Jouisans canzon Francesa* Adriano [Willaert] (RISM 1545_{14}, fol. 2: "Jouissance vous donneray")
14	16	*Gagliarda terza dell'autore*
15	17	*Gagliarda Quarta*
16	18	*Nasce la pena mia con Passaggi* Striggio (MonteO XVI, app.)
17	21	*Balletto Francese*
18	22	*Balletto Alemano*[4]
19	22	*Volta Francese*
20	23	*Volta seconda Francese*
21	23	*Volta terza Francese*[5]
22	23	*Volta quarta Francese*
23	24	*Ballo Alemano*
24	25	*Ballo secondo Alemano*
25	25	*Balo 3. Alemano*
26	26	*Ballo 4. Alemano*
27	26	*Toccata de l'Auttore*
28	26	*In te Domine speravi* Claudio [Merulo] da Correggio *a6*
29	28	*Padouana*
30	30	*Liquide perle* Marenzio *a5* (two lutes) (MarenW I, 1)
	31	*Contrapunto sopra Liquide perle per sonare insieme*
31	33	*Bariera balletto con tutte le sue repliche*
32	38	*Toccata Seconda dell'Autore*
33	39	*Fantasia Seconda dell'Autore*
34	41	*Pass'e mezo per ♮ duro*
	42	*Gagliarda del Pass'e mezo*
35	43	*Gagliarda Seconda* [recte: "Quinta"]
36	44	*Gagliarda Sesta*
37	45	*Gagliarda Settima*
38	46	*Alermifault. Canzon Francese* Adriano [Willaert] *a5* (two lutes) (AttainCK II, no. 1: "Aller my fault sur la verdure," Janequin)
	49	*Secondo Liutto*
39	52	*Non hebbe tante foglie**
40	52	*Non ved'hoggi'l mio sole** [Ruggiero] Giovanelli (Vogel: Giovanelli 27 [1591], p. 4)
41	53	*Mi parto ahi sorte** Giovanelli (Vogel: Giovanelli 27 [1591], p. 29)
42	53	*Se di dolor** Giulio Renaldi *a5* (Vogel: Renaldi 2 [1576], p. 11)
43	55	*In Deo speravit cor meum* Claudio [Merulo] da Correggio *a6*
44	56	*Hodie completi sunt* Andrea Gabrieli *a4*
45	58	*Padoana Seconda*
46	60	*Padoana Terza*
47	61	*Fantasia in modo di Canzon Francese dell'Autore*
48	62	*Fantasia in modo di Canzon Francese*[6] Gio. Gabrielli [sic]
49	64	*Un'altra* [*fantasia*] Paolo Tusti

50	67	*Branle Francese duble*
51	67	*Branle Secondo*
52	68	*Branle Terzo*
53	68	*Branle Simple Francese*
54	69	*Gagliarda dell'Autore Ottava*
55	70	*Chi farà fede accommodato à modo di Viola bastarda per suonar in Concerto con Liutto grande* Striggio *a5* (RISM 1583_{15}, fol. 20^{v})
56	74	*Mandatum novum do vobis** Pietro Vinci *a5* (MacC, no. 47, fol. 20)
57	75	*Domine Deus* Annibale Padoano *a6*
	76	2a pars *Exaudi*
58	77	*La velenosa vista** Oratio Scaletta *a3*
59	78	*Qual piu crudel martire** Scaletta [*a3*]
60	78	*Canzon la Vilachiara, over fantasia* Mascara (1584_{10}, no. 18)
61	80	*Gagliarda Decima* [sic]
62	81	*Erano i capei d'oro* Gio. Maria Nanino *a5* (Vogel: Nanino 2 [1582], p. 4)
	82	2a pars *Non era l'andar suo*
63	83	*Amorosa Fenice* Gio. Maria Cavaccio *a5*
64	84	*Ballo Alemano quinto dell'Autore*
65	84	*Ballo Alemano Sesto*
66	85	*Donna la bella mano* Arcangelo da Bergamo *a5* (RISM 1582_{4}, p. 19)
67	86	*O bella Ninfa mia* Gianetto Palestina *a5* (PalW XXVIII, 152)
68	86	*Se dal soave, & amoroso sguardo*[7] Gio. Andrea Dragone *a5* (RISM 1582_{4}, p. 12)
69	87	*Pass'e mezo Paganina*
	88	*Gagliarda del ditto*
70	89	*Fantasia seconda in modo di Canzon Francese dell'autore*
71	91	*Fantasia come di sopra* Vicenzo Bellaver
72	92	*Ballo Alemano Settimo*
73	92	*Ballo Alemano Ottavo*
74	93	*Fantasia Terza dell'Autore*
75	95	*Preambulo de l'Auttore* [*sopra le Corente Francese*]
76	95	*Cuorrente Francese*
77	96	*Corrente Secondo*
78	96	*Cuorrente Terzo*
79	97	*Corrente Quarto*
80	97	*Cara la vita mia* Giaches Wert *a5* (Vogel: Wert 3 [1564], p. 13)
	97	2a pars [*Poi che con gl'occhi*]
81	99	*Gagliarda de l'autore nona* [sic]
82	100	*Gofred. Canzon Francese* Incerto *a5*
83	102	*Beatus homo qui invenit sapientiam* Cipriano [da Rore] *a5* (RoreO I, no. 8)
84	104	*Gagliarda undecima*
85	105	*Gagliarda 12* S. Agostina Vertoa da Bergamo
86	106	*Ballo Polaco*
87	106	*Non mi toglia il ben mio* Marco Antonio Ingegnero *a4* (two lutes) (Vogel: Rore 33 [1569], p. 5: Rore)
	107	*Contrapunto dell'Auttore sopra Non mi toglia*
88	110	*Pass'e mezo ultimo*
	112	*Gagliarda del Pass'e mezo*
89	114	*Un giorno passeggiando** Angelo Barbato (RISM 1587_{7})
90	115	*L'amata Ninfa** Gio. Maria Nanino (Vogel: Nanino 7 [1593], p. 15)
91	115	*Torneo Amoroso balletto Italiano*
92	117	*Balletto Alemano ultimo*
93	117	*Canzone a Otto Voci de l'Auttore per suonar a 4. Liutti overo fantasia*

[1] Mod. ed. in NeemAM II, no. 17.

[2] Note on p. 8: "Le parole per cantare sono sotto al Basso." Some of the other completely texted pieces in this volume have similar notes.

[3] Facs. of p. 10 in MGG III, col. 1765.

[4] Mod. ed. in MoeDM, p. 347.

[5] Mod. ed. in NeemAM II, no. 19.

[6] Mod. ed. in Gabri(G)CO III, no. 13.

[7] Facs. of p. 86 in MGG III, col. 741.

[1599]12

PIMENTEL, PEDRO

Livro de cifra de varias obras para se tangerem no Orgao. 1599.

This volume of music for solo organ, now lost, is listed in BarbB III, 610, and FétB VII, 59. Pimentel was a Portuguese organist who died in 1599 (see EitQ VII, 450).

1599

DOUBTFUL WORKS

1. DeakinMB, p. 9, dates William Barley, *A new Booke of Tabliture*, 1599. The collection is listed in this bibliography as $1596_{4,\,5,}$ and $_6$.

[159?]$_1$

JOAO DE ARRATIA, BERNARDO CLAVIJO, AND DIEGO DEL CASTILLO

Tentos para Orgao de Joao de Arratia, Bernardo Clavijo, & Diogo [= Diego] del Castillo.

VasJ, no. 455, lists this volume of music for solo keyboard, now lost, as being in the library of King John IV of Portugal. For information on Clavijo and Castillo, see MGG II, cols. 901, 1473–1475. Organ music by Castillo is mentioned in Francisco Correa de Arauxo, *Libro de tientos y discursos de musica practica* (Alcalá, 1626) (see MME VI, 40).

159?$_2$

BYRD, WILLIAM

Psalmes, Sonets, & songs of sadness and / pietie, made into Musicke of five parts: whereof, some / of them going abroade among divers, in untrue coppies, are / heere truely corrected, and th'other being Songs very rare / and newly composed, are heere published, for the recreation / of all such as delight in Musicke: By William Byrd one / of the Gent: of the Queenes Maiesties / Royall Chappell. / [Cut of the coat of arms of Sir Christopher Hatton] / Printed at London by Thomas Este, / dwelling in Aldergate streete, over / against the signe of the George.

Five part books in mensural notation, each of 24 fols. The prefatory matter is the same as that in 1588_2 save that the list of errata is omitted and the corrections made in the text. Contents = 1588_2. The volume contains 35 fully texted compositions *a 5*, 26 of which were originally composed for solo voice with four instruments (probably viols).[1]

Copies in: GB:Cu (ATB5, plus a second B and S), GB:Eu (S), GB:Lbm, GB:Lcm, GB:Lk, GB:Och, US:SM.

[1] I am grateful to Mrs. Geoffrey Wilson of Cambridge, England, for checking my description of this volume against the Cambridge copies.

[159?]$_3$

MARENZIO, LUCA

Villanelle a 3, para tanger no Laude.

VasJ, no. 849, lists this volume of music for solo lute, now lost, as being in the library of King John IV of Portugal.

[159?]$_4$

PERAZA, FRANCISCO DE

Tentos de Tecla, tresladados de hum livro, que Francisco de Peraça tangedor, & Racioneiro da Sè de Toledo trouxe a Villa Vicosa de varios Autores.

VasJ, no. 435, lists this volume of music for solo keyboard, now lost, as being in the library of King John IV of Portugal. Organ music by Peraza is mentioned in Francisco Correa de Arauxo, *Libro de tientos y discursos de musica practica* (Alcalá, 1626) (see MME VI, 40).

Appendix

EDITIONS WITH BASSO CONTINUO PARTS NOT LISTED ELSEWHERE IN THE BIBLIOGRAPHY

1575 Placido Falconi. *Introitus et Alleluia per omnes festivitates totius anni cum quinque vocibus Placidi Falconii Asulani. Venetiis Apud Filios Antonii Gardani. 1575* (see EitQ III, 385; GaspaC II, 68; and KinO, p. 194).

1591 Giovanni Pietro Flaccomio. *Vespere, Missa Sacraeque cantiones. 1591* (see TreB, p. 500).

1594 Giovanni Croce. *Mottetti a Otto Voci di Giovanni Croce Chiozzotto Vice Maestro di Capella della Serenissima Signoria di Venetia, in San Marco. Commodi per le Voci, e per Cantar con ogni Stromento, Novamente Ristampati, & Corretti. Con Privilegio. In Venetia, Appresso Giacomo Vincenti. 1599.* (The organ score is from a 1594 ed.; see EitQ III, 107; FétB II, 393; GaspaC II, 411; and KinO, p. 196.)

1595 Guglielmo Arnone. *Magnificat a 4 e 8 voci con b. c. Milano, 1595* (see DonaSM, p. 122).

1596 Giovanni Croce. *Messe a Otto Voci di Giovanni Croce Chiozzotto Vice Maestro di Capella della Serenissima Signoria di Venetia in San Marco, Nuovamente composte, e date in luce. Con Privilegio. In Venetia, Appresso Giacomo Vincenti, 1596* (see GaspaC II, 64, and KinO, p. 197).

1596 Orfeo Vecchi. *Psalmi integri in totius anni solemnitatibus, Magnificat 2, Antiphonae 4 ad B. V. post completorium et modulationes 8, quae vulgo Falsibordoni nuncupantur. 5 vocibus. Mediolani, apud haeredes Francisci, & Simonis Tini. 1596* (see DonaSM, p. 90, and EitQ X, 44).

1598 Giovanni Bassano. *Motetti per Concerti ecclesiastici A 5. 6. 7. 8. & 12. Voci, di Giovanni Bassano Musico della Serenissima Signoria di Venetia, Et Maestro di Musica del Seminario di San Marco. Novamente Composti, & dati in luce. In Venetia, Appresso Giacomo Vincenti, 1598.* (see EitQ I, 368; GaspaC II, 378, which says, "La parte dell'organo ha la data del 1559 (!)"; and KinO, p. 200).

1598 Antonio Mortaro. *Partitio Sacrarum Cantionum Tribus vocibus Antonii Mortarii Brixiensis In Ecclesia Divi Francisci Mediolani Organistae. Per illustri Domino D. Amadeo Puteo Ponderani, ac Rheani Comiti. Mediolani, Apud haeredem. Simonis Tini, & Jo. Franciscum Bisutium. 1598* (see DonaSM, p. 91; EitQ VII, 72; GaspaC II, 467; and KinO, p. 200).

1598 Lucretio Quintiani. *Partitura de Bassi delle Messe et Motetti a otto voci di D. Lucretio Quintiani, Maestro di Capella di S. Ambrosio maggiore di Milano. Libro primo. In Milano appresso l'herede di Simon Tini, & Francesco Besozzi. 1598* (see DonaSM, p. 91; EitQ VIII, 105; and KinO, p. 198).

1598 Augustinus Soderinus. *Sacrarum Cantionum 8 & 9 voc. lib. I. cum 3 aliis canticis voc. et instrum. alternatim. Mediolani, Apud Augustinum Tradatum, 1598* (see DonaSM, p. 109; EitQ IX, 196; and KinO, p. 200).

1598 Orfeo Vecchi. *Basso Principale da sonare delli Salmi interi a Cinque voci di Orfeo Vecchi. In Milano, Appresso l'herede di Simon Tini, & Gio: Francesco Besozzo. 1598* (see DonaSM, p. 91; EitQ X, 44; GaspaC II, 323; and KinO, p. 200).

1598 Orfeo Vecchi. *Orphei Vecchi Mediolanensis in Ecclesia Divae Mariae Scalen.*

Reg. Duc. Musicae, & Chori Magistri Motectorum Quinque vocibus Liber secundus. Mediolani, Apud haeredem Simonis Tini, & Jo. Franciscum Bisutium. 1598 (see DonaSM, p. 91; EitQ X, 44; and GaspaC II, 508).

1598 Orfeo Vecchi. *Orphei Vecchi Mediolanensis in Ecclesia Divae Mariae Scal. Reg. Duc. Musicae, & Chori Magistri, Missarum Quinque Vocibus Liber secundus. Quibus Missa pro defunctis, aliquotque sacrae Cantiones accessere. Mediolani, Apud haeredem Simonis Tini, & Jo. Franciscum Besutium. 1598* (see DonaSM, p. 92; EitQ X, 44; GaspaC II, 149; and KinO, p. 200).

1599 Guglielmo Arnone. *Partitura del Secondo Libro delli Motetti à cinque & otto voci, Di Guglielmo Arnone Milanese Organista nella Chiesa Metropolitana di Milano. Al M.to Ill.ro Sig. Lucio Castelnovate Signor & Padrone colendissimo. In Milano, appresso l'herede di Simon Tini, & Gio. Francesco Besozzi, 1599* (see DonaSM, p. 92; EitQ I, 208; GaspaC II, 340; and KinO, p. 201).

1599 Giovanni Bassano. *Concerti Ecclesiastici A Cinque, Sei, Sette, Otto, & Dodeci Voci. Di Giovanni Bassano Musico della Sereniss. Signoria di Venetia, & Maestro di Musica del Seminario di San Marco. Libro Secondo. Novamente composti, & dati in luce. In Venetia, appresso Giacomo Vincenti. 1599* (see EitQ I, 368; GaspaC II, 378; and KinO, p. 201).

1599 Serafino Cantone. *Sacrae cantiones . . . octo vocibus . . ., Mediolani, apud Augustinum Tradatum, 1599* (see DonaSM, p. 109; EitQ II, 312; KinO, p. 201; and PiciA, p. 490).

1599 Antonio Mortaro. *Messa, salmi, motetti et Magnificat a tre chori. Di Antonio Mortaro da Brescia, alla Santa Casa di Loreto. In Milano, appresso l'herede di Simon Tini, & Francesco Besozzi, 1599* (see DonaSM, p. 93; EitQ VII, 72; GaspaC II, 113; and KinO, p. 201).

1599 Lucretio Quintiani. *Musica D. Lucretii Quintiani Cremonensis Monacis Cistercensis Quatuor vocum in introitus Missarum super cantu plano, quae in solemnitatibus Sanctorum omnium toto anno celebrantur juxta morem S. R. E. nunc primum in lucem edita. Mediolani apud haer. Simonis Tini, et Franciscum Besutium, M. D. XCVIIII* (see DonaSM, p. 93, and EitQ VIII, 105).

1599 *Motetti e Salmi a otto voci, Composti da Otto Eccellentiss. Autori, con la parte de i Bassi, per poter sonarli nell'Organo dedicati al molto Rever. Sig. Cesare Schieti Dignissimo Canonico di Urbino. Venezia, Giacomo Vincenti, 1599* (see EitQ X, 94; KinO, p. 201; and SchneidA, p. 70).

LIST OF WORKS CITED

The following list does not contain a complete bibliography, but comprises manuscripts, books, articles, and periodicals referred to in the text. The sigla are taken from Gustave Reese, *Music in the Renaissance*, 1954 (ReMR); similar sigla have been devised for those works not in Reese.

Manuscripts

Austria

A:Wn — Vienna, Österreichische Nationalbibliothek: Cod. 18827.

Belgium

B:Bc — Brussels, Bibliothèque du Conservatoire royal de musique: MS 26660; MS 26661.

B:Br — Brussels, Bibliothèque royale de Belgique, MS 9085 ("Brussels Basse Dance Manuscript").

Switzerland

CH:Bu — Basel, Universitätsbibliothek: MS F. IX. 43; MSS F. X. 1–4.

CH:SGs — St. Gall, Stiftsbibliothek: Cod. 463 ("Tschudi Liederbuch").

Germany

D:Bds — Berlin, Deutsche Staatsbibliothek: Mus. MS 40115.

D:LO — Löbau: MS s.n.

D:Mbs — Munich, Bayerische Staatsbibliothek: Mus. MS 1511b; Mus. MS 1516.

D:Rp — Regensburg, Proskesche Musikbibliothek: MS A. R. 855; MSS B. 211–215.

Denmark

DK:Kk — Copenhagen, Det kongelige Bibliotek: MS Ny. Kgl. S.2°.1848.

Spain

E:E — Biblioteca de San Lorenzo del Escorial: MS Plut. 53.

E:SE — Segovia, Catedral: MS s.n.

E:TZ — Tarazona, Catedral: MS 2.

France

F:CA — Cambrai, Bibliothèque municipale: MS 124.

F:Pn — Paris, Bibliothèque nationale: MS fonds fr. 1596; MS fonds fr. 22103; MS fonds fr. 22537; MS nouv. acq. fr. 4599; Rés. Vm[7] 676.

Great Britain

GB:Cmc — Cambridge, Magdalene College: MS Pepys 1760.

GB:Lbm — London, British Museum: Add. MS 31922; Add. MS 35087.

GB:Lcm — London, Royal College of Music: MS 2088.

GB:Ob — Oxford, Bodleian Library: Canonici Misc. MS 213.

Italy

I:Bc — Bologna, Biblioteca comunale annessa al Conservatorio musicale G. B. Martini: MS Q 17; MS Q 19; MS Q 26.

I:BGid — Bergamo, Istituto musicale "Donizetti": MS 1209.

I:Fc — Florence, Biblioteca del Conservatorio di Musica: MS Basevi 2439; MS Basevi 2440.

I:Fn — Florence, Biblioteca nazionale centrale: MS Magl. XIX, 59; MS Magl. XIX, 107; MS Magl. XIX, 117; MSS Magl. XIX, 164–167.

I:Fr — Florence, Biblioteca Riccardiana: MS 2356.

I:Rvat — Rome, Biblioteca Apostolica Vaticana: Cappella Sistina MS 13.

I:Vas — Venice, Archivio di Stato: Registre Notatorio XXIII, 1499–1506.

I:Vnm — Venice, Biblioteca nazionale Marciana: MSS It. Cl. IV, 1795–1798.

I:VEcap — Verona, Biblioteca capitolare: Cod. MCXXVIII.

Netherlands

NL:DHk — The Hague, Koninklijke Bibliotheek: MS 74.H.7.

Portugal

P:C — Coimbra, Biblioteca Geral da Universidade: MS M.M. 9.

Poland

PL:B — Brieg, Gymnasialbibliothek: MS s.n.

PL:L — Legnica (formerly Liegnitz), Biblioteca Rudolfina der Rittersakademie, MS s.n.

United States

US:Nf — Northampton, Mass., Smith College, Forbes Library: Alfred Einstein Collection.

US:Wc — Washington, D.C., Library of Congress: Laborde Manuscript.

Books, Articles, and Periodicals

AbbS — Abbiati, Franco, *Stòria della musica*, 1939.

AdlerH — Adler, Guido, *Handbuch der Musikgeschichte*, 1924; 2nd ed., 2 vols., 1929. Written by Adler with collaboration of outstanding specialists. References are to the second edition.

AdrT — Adriansen, Emanuel, *Zwei festliche Tanzstücke*, ed. A. Wölki, 1941.

AgricolaIG — Agricola, Martin, *Instrumentische Gesänge um 1545*, Heinz Funck, 1933.

AmbG — Ambros, August W., *Geschichte der Musik*, 5 vols., 1862–1878, 1882; 3rd ed., 1887–1911. The first edition was completed by Hugo Leichtentritt. Volume V consists of Otto Kade's supplement of musical examples. References are to the third edition.

AmeH — Ameln, Konrad, Christhard Mahrenholz, W. Thomas, and others, eds., *Handbuch der deutschen evangelischen Kirchenmusik*, 3 vols., 1933–1940.

AndrewsP — Andrews, H. K., "Printed Sources of William Byrd's 'Psalmes, Sonets and Songs'," *Music and Letters*, XLIV (1963), 5.

AngAM — Anglés, Higinio, "El Archivo musical de la catedral de Valladolid," *Anuario musical*, III (1948), 59.

AngCM — Anglés, Higinio, and José Subirá, *Catálogo musical de la Biblioteca nacional de Madrid*, 3 vols., 1946–1951.

AngME — Anglés, Higinio, *La Música española . . . Catálogo de la Exposición histórica . . .*, 1941.

AngMF — Anglés, Higinio, "Dades desconegudes sobre Miguel de Fuenllana, vihuelista," *Revista musical catalana*, XXXIII (1936), 140.

AngO — Anglés, Higinio, "Orgelmusik der Schola Hispanica," in *Peter Wagner–Festschrift* (1926), p. 11.

AngPL — Anglés, Higinio, "El 'Pange Lingua' de Johannes Urreda, maestro de capilla del Rey Fernando el Católico," *Anuario musical*, VII (1952), 193.

AntoniK — Antoni, Fritz and Wilhelm, eds., *Klingend Spiel. Allerlei Tanz- und Bläserstücklein, auch von Streichern auszuführen, zu vier Stimmen*, 1926.

ApelL — Apel, Willi, "Neapolitan Links between Cabezón and Frescobaldi," *The Musical Quarterly*, XXIV (1938), 419.

ApelM — Apel, Willi, *Musik aus früher Zeit*, 2 vols., 1934.

ApelMK — Apel, Willi, *Masters of the Keyboard*, 1947.

ApelN Apel, Willi, *The Notation of Polyphonic Music, 900–1600*, 1942; 4th ed., 1953. References are to the fourth edition.

ApelOR Apel, Willi, "The Early Development of the Organ Ricercar," *Musica disciplina*, III (1949), 139.

ApelQ Apel, Willi, "Attaingnant: Quatorze Gaillardes," *Musikforschung*, XIV (1961), 361.

ApelR Apel, Willi, "A Remark about the Basse Danse," *Journal of Renaissance and Baroque Music*, I (1946), 139.

ApelSM Apel, Willi, "Early Spanish Music for Lute and Keyboard Instruments," *The Musical Quarterly*, XX (1934), 289.

ApelTA Apel, Willi, "Tänze und Arien für Klavier aus dem Jahre 1588," *Archiv für Musikwissenschaft*, XVII (1960), 51.

ArbOB *Thoinot Arbeau: Orchesography (1588)*, trans. C. W. Beaumont, 1925.

ArbOE *Thoinot Arbeau: Orchésographie, et Traicté en Forme de Dialogue (1588)*, English trans. by M. S. Evans, 1948.

ArbOF *Thoinot Arbeau: Orchésographie (1588)*, ed. L. Fonta, 1888.

ArberT Arber, Edward, ed., *A Transcript of the Registers of the Company of Stationers of London; 1554–1640 A.D.*, 5 vols,, 1875–1877, 1894.

ARC Archive of Recorder Consorts, London, Schott, 1951—.

ARC 16 *Six Sixteenth-Century Quartets*, ed. Walter Bergmann, 1954.

ARC 17 *Antony Holborne: Suite for Five Recorders*, ed. John Parkinson, 1952.

ARC 26 *Antony Holborne: Pavan & Galliard*, ed. Edgar Hunt, 1953.

ARC 50 *Antony Holborne: A First Set of Quintets*, ed. Royston Barrington, 1955.

ARC 51 *Antony Holborne: A Second Set of Quintets*, ed. Royston Barrington, 1956.

ARC 52 *Antony Holborne: A Third Set of Quintets*, ed. Royston Barrington, 1956.

ARC 73 *Florentio Maschera: Canzon Seconda "La Martinenga,"* ed. Margaret and Francis Grubb, 1958.

ARC 74 *Florentio Maschera: Canzon Quarta*, ed. Margaret and Francis Grubb, 1958.

ARS American Recorder Society Editions, ed. Erich Katz, 1950—.

ARS 13 *Andrea Gabrieli: Ricercare del 12° Tono*, ed. Bernard Krainis, 1954.

ARS 31 *Antony Holborne and Robert Parsons: 3 Dance Movements*, ed. Elna Sherman, 1958.

AttainC *Pierre Attaingnant: Chansons und Tänze. Pariser Tabulaturdrucke aus dem Jahr 1530 von Pierre Attaingnant*, facsimile ed. with commentary by Eduard Bernoulli, 5 vols., 1914.

AttainCK *Pierre Attaingnant: Transcriptions of Chansons for Keyboard*, ed. Albert Seay, 1961.

AttainS *Pierre Attaingnant: Suite de Branles pour piano*, ed. Emile Bosquet, 1922.

AudaL Auda, Antoine, *La Musique et les musiciens de l'ancien pays de Liége*, 1930.

AulerS Auler, Wolfgang, ed., *Spielbuch für Kleinorgel oder ander Tasteninstrumente*, 2 vols., 1942.

AV *Anthologia vocalis*, 6 vols., ed. F. Hamma, O. Ravanello, and others, 1921–1928.

AzpiaA Azpiazu, José de, ed., *Alte spanische Meister (Milan, Mudarra, Narváez)*, 1955.

AzpiaG Azpiazu, José de, *Gitarrenschule*, 4 vols., 1954–1958.

AzzaiV *Azzaiolo, Filippo: Villotte del fiore*, ed. Francesco Vatielli, 1921.

BachV Bacher, Joseph, *Die Viola da gamba*, 1932.

BalF Bal y Gay, Jesús, "Fuenllana and the Transcriptions of Spanish Lute Music," *Acta musicologica*, XI (1939), 16.

BalR Bal y Gay, Jesús, ed., *Romances y villancicos españoles del siglo XVI*, 1939. Modern arrangements with piano accompaniment.

BanchC Banchieri, Adriano, *Conclusioni nel suono dell'organo, 1608*, facsimile ed., 1934.

BarbB Barbosa Machado, Diogo, *Bibliotheca Lusitana*, 4 vols., Lisbon, 1741–1759.

BarbiC Barbieri, Francisco A., ed., *Cancionero musical de los siglos XV y XVI*, 1890.

BarkT Barker, E. Phillips, "Master Thoinot's Fancy," *Music & Letters*, XI (1930), 383.

BarthaZ Bartha, Dénes von, ed., *A Zenetörténet Antológiaja*, 1948.

BasseC Basse, Nicolas, *Collectio in unum corpus*, Frankfurt, 1952.

BaumD — Baumann, Otto A., *Das deutsche Lied und seine Bearbeitungen in den frühen Orgeltabulaturen*, 1934.

BäumK — Bäumker, Wilhelm, ed., *Das katholische deutsche Kirchenlied in seinen Singweisen von den frühesten Zeit bis gegen Ende des 17. Jahrhunderts*, 3 vols., 1883–1891.

BeauB — *Baltasar de Beaujoyeulx: Balet Comique de la Royne (1582)*, facsimile ed. with commentary by Giacomo Alessandro Caula, 1962.

BecFB — Beck, Sydney, ed., *The First Book of Consort Lessons for Treble and Bass Viols, Flute, Lute, Cittern and Pandora Collected by Thomas Morley, 1559–1661*, 1959.

BecherC — Becherini, Bianca, *Catalogo dei manoscritti musicali della Biblioteca nazionale di Firenze*, 1959.

BeckH — Becker, Carl Ferdinand, *Die Hausmusik in Deutschland in dem 16., 17., und 18. Jahrhunderte*, 1840.

BeckT — Becker, Carl Ferdinand, *Die Tonwerke des XVI. und XVII. Jahrhunderts*, 1855.

BedbI — Bedbrook, Gerald S., ed., *Early Italian Keyboard Music*, 2 vols., 1954–1956.

BedbK — Bedbrook, Gerald S., *Keyboard Music from the Middle Ages to the Beginnings of the Baroque*. 1949.

BehD — Behrend, Siegfried, ed., *Altdeutsche Lautenmusik für Gitarre*, 1959.

BehF — Behrend, Siegfried, ed., *Altfranzösische Lautenmusik für Gitarre*, 1959.

BehI — Behrend, Siegfried, ed., *Altitalienische Lautenmusik für Gitarre*, 1959.

BehS — Behrend, Siegfried, ed., *Altspanische Lautenmusik für Gitarre*, 1959.

BerH — Bernoulli, Eduard, *Aus Liederbüchern der Humanistenzeit*, 1910.

BergT — Bergmans, Paul, *La Typographie musicale en Belgique au XVIe siècle*, 1930.

BermuD — Bermudo, Fray Juan, *Declaración de instrumentos musicales (1555)*, facsimile ed. by Macario Santiago Kastner, 1957.

BermuM — Bermudo, Fray Juan, *Mira Nero de Tarpeya: Romance viejo*, ed. José de Azpiazu, N.d.

BermuOO — Bermudo, Fray Juan, *Oeuvres d'orgue (1555) publiées d'après la Declaración de instrumentos musicales*, ed. Pierre Froidebise, 1960.

BesM — Besseler, Heinrich, *Die Musik des Mittelalters und der Renaissance*, 1931–1935.

BFS — Notenbeilagen zum "Blockflötenspiegel," Hanover, Adolph Nagel, 1931–1932.

BiggsT — Biggs, E. Power, ed., *Treasury of Early Organ Music*, 1947.

BigiM — Bigi, Quirino, *Di Claudio Merulo da Correggio*, 1861.

BinchoisC — Binchois, Gilles, *Die Chansons von Gilles Binchois (1400–1460)*, ed. Wolfgang Rehm, 1957.

BlochL — Bloch, Suzanne, "Lute Music, Its Notation and Technical Problems in Relation to the Guitar," *The Guitar Review*, IX (1949), 15.

BlumeS — Blume, Friedrich, *Studien zur Vorgeschichte der Orchestersuite im 15. und 16. Jahrhundert*, 1925.

BodeH — Bode, "Anfrage in Betreff des Ursprunges der Melodie: Herzlich lieb hab ich dich, O Herr," *Monatshefte für Musikgeschichte*, V (1873), 123.

BoettB — Boetticher, Wolfgang, *Bibliographie des sources de la musique pour luth (extrait de Studien zur solistischen Lautenpraxis, 1943)*, 1957.

BoettL — Boetticher, Wolfgang, *Orlando de Lasso und seine Zeit, 1532–1594*, 1958.

BöhA — Böhme, Franz M., *Altdeutsches Liederbuch*, 1877.

BöhT — Böhme, Franz M., *Geschichte des Tanzes in Deutschland*, 2 vols., 1886.

BohnMD — Bohn, Emil, *Bibliographie der Musik-Druckwerke bis 1700 welche in der Stadtbibliothek, der Bibliothek des Academischen Instituts für Kirchenmusik und der Königlichen und Universitäts-Bibliothek zu Breslau aufbewahrt werden*, 1883.

BolleG — Bolle, W., "Die gedruckten englischen Liederbücher bis 1600," *Palestra* XXIX (1903), 112.

BonnA — Bonnet, Joseph, ed., *An Anthology of Early French Organ Music*, 1942.

BonnO — Bonnet, Joseph, ed., *Historical Organ Recitals*, 6 vols., 1917–1945.

BorD — Van den Borren, Charles, *Guillaume Dufay: Son importance dans l'évolution de la musique au XVe siècle*, 1926.

BossR — Bossinensis, Francesco, *20 Recercari da sonar nel lauto (1511) dall'unicum di Brera*, ed. Benvenuto Disertori, 1954.

BossiC — Bossi, Renzo, ed., *Cinque Pezzi antichi*, 1953.

BottrigD — Bottrigari, Ercole, *Il Desiderio, 1594*, ed. Käthi Meyer, 1924.

BottrigDE — Bottrigari, Ercole, *Il Desiderio, or Concerning the Playing together of Various Musical Instruments*, trans. Carol MacClintock, 1962.

BoviR — Bovicelli, Giovanni Battista, *Regole Passaggi di musica, 1594*, facsimile ed. by Nanie Bridgman, 1957.

BoydE — Boyd, Morrison C., *Elizabethan Music and Musical Criticism*, 1940.

BoylM — Boyleau, Simon, *Simonis Boyleau Genere Galli, Juvenis in arte musica eximii motetta Quatuor vocum*, Venice, Girolamo Scotto, 1544.

BranR — Branzoli, Giuseppe, *Ricerche sullo studio del liuto*, 1889.

BrauH — Braun, Walter, "Ein Hallesches Exemplar von Arnold Schlicks 'Spiegel der Orgelmacher und Organisten,'" *Musikforschung*, VII (1954), 66.

BraunS — Braungart, Siegfried, *Die Verbreitung des reformatorischen Liedes in Nürnberg in der Zeit von 1525 bis 1570*, 1939.

BrayF — Brayssing, Gregoire, *Three Fantasies from Adrian le Roy's Quart Livre de Tabulature de Guiterre (1553)*, ed. Deric Kennard, 1956.

BrenN — Brenet, Michel, "Notes sur l'histoire du luth en France," *Rivista musicale italiana*, V (1898), 637, and VI (1899), 1.

BridgmE — Bridgman, Nanie, "Christian Egenolff, imprimeur de musique (A propos du recueil Rés. Vm⁷ 504 de la Bibl. nat. de Paris)," *Annales musicologiques*, III (1955), 77.

BroC — Brown, Charles Canfield, "Chanson Transcriptions in the Attaingnant Keyboard Books," unpub. thesis, Columbia University, n.d.

BrownM — Brown, Howard Mayer, *Music in the French Secular Theater, 1400–1550*, 1963.

BrownTC — Brown, Howard Mayer, ed., *Theatrical Chansons of the Fifteenth and Early Sixteenth Centuries*, 1963.

BruA — Bruger, Hans, ed., *Pierre Attaingnant (1529), zwei- und dreistimmige Solostücke für die Laute*, 1927.

BruAL — Bruger, Hans, ed., *Alte Lautenkunst aus drei Jahrhunderten*, 2 vols., 1923.

BruD — Bruger, Hans, ed., *Deutsche Meister des ein- und zweistimmigen Lautensatzes*, 1926.

BruS — Bruger, Hans, *Schule des Lautenspiels*, 1926; reprinted, 1961.

BrunetML — Brunet, J. C., *Manuel du libraire et de l'amateur de livres*, 1860–1865.

BS — Blätter der Sackpfeife, 60 vols., Hanover, Adolph Nagel, n.d.

BU — *Biographie universelle ancienne et moderne*, 85 vols., 1811–1862.

BuH — Burney, Charles, *General History of Music*, 4 vols., 1776–1789; mod. ed. with notes by Frank Mercer, 2 vols., 1935. References are to the 1957 Dover reprint of the Mercer edition.

BuggR — Buggert, Robert, "Alberto da Ripa, Lutenist and Composer," unpub. diss., University of Michigan, 1956.

BukMB — Bukofzer, Manfred, *Music in the Baroque Era*, 1947.

BukMR — Bukofzer, Manfred, *Studies in Medieval and Renaissance Music*, 1950.

BurnsAV — Burns, Joseph A., "Antonio Valente, Neapolitan Keyboard Primitive," *Journal of the American Musicological Society*, XII (1959), 133.

BuusR — Buus, Jacques, *Ricercari III° e IV° dell'Intabolatura d'Organo (Venezia, 1549)*, ed. Macario Santiago Kastner, 1957.

ByrdW — *The Collected Works of William Byrd*, ed. Edmund H. Fellowes, 20 vols., 1937–1950.

CabezonC — Cabezón, Antonio de, *Claviermusik. Obras de Musica para Tecla, Arpa y Vihuela*, ed. Macario Santiago Kastner, 1951.

CabezonF — Cabezón, Antonio de, *4 Tientos für Orgel, mit oder ohne Pedal*, ed. Max Drischner, 1953.

CabezonP — Cabezón, Antonio de, *Pavana italiana*, ed. José de Azpiazu, n.d.

CabezonT — Cabezón, Antonio de, *Tientos und Fugen aus den Obras de Musica para Tecla, Arpa y Vihuela*, ed. Macario Santiago Kastner, 1958.

CafS — Caffi, Francesco, *Stòria della musica sacra nella già Cappella Ducale di S. Marco in Venezia dal 1318 al 1797*, 2 vols., 1854–1855; reprinted, 1931.

CaravI — Caravaglios, Nino, "Una nuova 'Intavolatura di Cimbalo' di Antonio Valente Cieco," *Rivista musicale italiana*, XXIII (1916), 491.

CarlH — Carl, William C., ed., *Historical Organ Collection*, 1919.

CarpAC — Carpenter, Hoyle, "The Works of Antonio de Cabezón," unpub. diss., University of Chicago, 1957.

CarrB — Carruth, John Robert, "The Organ Works of Sperindio Bertoldo," unpub. thesis, Cornell University, 1948.

CarraI — *Intavolatura di Liuto di Michele Carrara MDL XXXV*, facsimile ed. by Benvenuto Disertori, n.d.

CasSV — Casimiri, Raffaele, "Simone Verovio da Hertogenbosch," *Note d'archivio*, X (1933), 189.

CaseyP — Casey, William S., "Printed English Lute Instruction Books, 1568–1610," unpub. diss., University of Michigan, 1960.

CatM — Catelani, Angelo, *Memorie della vita e delle opere di Claudio Merulo*, 1859, revised by G. Benvenuti, 1931.

CatulP — *The Poems of Gaius Valerius Catullus*, ed. and trans. F. W. Cornish, Loeb Classical Library, 1935.

CauO — Cauchie, Maurice, "L'Odhecaton, recueil de musique instrumentale," *Revue de musicologie*, VI (1925), 148.

CauT — Cauchie, Maurice, "A propos des trois recueils instrumentaux de la série de l'Odhecaton," *Revue de musicologie*, IX (1928), 64.

CavazzO — Cavazzoni, Girolamo, *Orgelwerke*, ed. Oscar Mischiati, 2 vols., 1958.

CavazzR — Cavazzoni, Girolamo, *Ricercare*, ed. Pieter Fischer, n.d.

CDMI — I Classici della musica italiana (Raccolta nazionale), ed. Gabriele d'Annunzio, 36 vols. (152 quaderni), 1918–1921. Quaderni 23–27: Girolamo Cavazzoni, *Composizioni*, ed. G. Benvenuti, 1919.

CEK — Corpus of Early Keyboard Music, ed. Willi Apel, 1963—.

  CEK II — *Marco Facoli: Collected Works*, ed. Willi Apel, 1963.

CellerO — Celler, Ludovic, *Les Origines de l'opéra et Le Ballet de la Reine (1581)*, 1868.

CesF — Cesari, Gaetano, Raffaello Monterosso, and Benvenuto Disertori, eds., *Le Frottole nell'edizione principe di Ottaviano Petrucci*, 1954.

CesM — Cesari, Gaetano, "Musica e musicisti alla corte sforzesca," in F. Malaguzzi Valeri, *La Corte di Lodovico il Moro*, IV (1923), 183. Printed previously, with fewer musical examples and the like, in *Rivista musicale italiana*, XXIX (1922), 1. References are to Valeri's volume.

ChaillFM — Chaillon, Paule, "Les Fonds musicaux de quelques bibliothèques de province," *Fontes artis musicae*, II (1955), 154.

ChaseA — Chase, Gilbert, *America's Music, from the Pilgrims to the Present*, 1955.

ChaseG — Chase, Gilbert, "Guitar and Vihuela: A Clarification," abstract, *Bulletin of the American Musicological Society*, no. 6 (1940), 13.

ChilB — Chilesotti, Oscar, ed., Biblioteca di rarità musicali, 9 vols., 1884–1915.

  ChilB I — *"Nobiltà di Dame" del ... Caroso ... "Le gratie d'amore" ... di ... Negri ...*, [1884?].

  ChilB V — *Arie, Canzonette e Balli ... di Horatio Vecchi ...*, [1892].

  ChilB VIII — *Musica del Passato (da intavolature antiche)*, [1914].

ChilC — Chilesotti, Oscar, "Una Canzone celebre nel Cinquecento: 'Io mi son giovinetta' del Ferabosco," *Rivista musicale italiana*, I (1894), 446.

ChilCI — Chilesotti, Oscar, "Chansons françaises du XVIe siècle en Italie (transcrites pour le luth)," *Revue d'histoire et de critique musicales*, II (1902), 63, 202.

ChilCM — Chilesotti, Oscar, *Claudio Merulo nelle intavolature di liuto*, 1904.

ChilCS — Chilesotti, Oscar, ed., *Canzonette del secolo XVI a voce sola con accompagnamento di pianoforte ricostrutte sull' intavolatura di liuto*, n.d.

ChilF — Chilesotti, Oscar, "Francesco da Milano," *Sammelbände der Internationalen Musikgesellschaft*, IV (1903), 382.

ChilHN — Chilesotti, Oscar, "Di Hans Newsidler," *Rivista musicale italiana*, I (1894), 48.

ChilJ — Chilesotti, Oscar, "Jacomo Gorzanis, liutista del Cinquecento," *Rivista musicale italiana*, XXI (1914), 86.

ChilL — Chilesotti, Oscar, ed., *Da un codice Lauten-Buch del Cinquecento*, 1890.

ChilLI — Chilesotti, Oscar, "Note circa alcuni liutisti italiani della prima metà del Cinquecento," *Rivista musicale italiana*, IX (1902), 36, 233.

ChilLS Chilesotti, Oscar, ed., *Lautenspieler des 16. Jahrhunderts*, 1891.

ChilLV Chilesotti, Oscar, "Il primo Libro di liuto di Vincenzo Galilei," *Rivista musicale italiana*, XV (1908), 753.

ChilP Chilesotti, Oscar, "Il Pater noster di Adriano Willaert," *Sammelbände der Internationalen Musikgesellschaft*, III (1902), 468.

ChilPF Chilesotti, Oscar, "Perino Fiorentino, liutista del secolo XVI," *Rivista fiorentina*, I (1908), 23.

ChilR Chilesotti, Oscar, "'La Rocca e'l fuso,'" *Rivista musicale italiana*, XIX (1912), 363.

ChilS Chilesotti, Oscar, *Saggio sulla melodia popolare del Cinquecento*, 1889.

ChrysS Chrysander, Friedrich, "A Sketch of the History of Music Printing," *Musical Times*, XVIII (1877), 265, 324, 375, 470, 524, 584.

ClemensCS V Clemens non Papa, Jacobus, *Liber Quintus Cantionum Sacrarum*, Louvain, Pierre Phalèse, 1559.

ClemensCS VI Clemens non Papa, Jacobus, *Liber Sextus Cantionum Sacrarum*, Louvain, Pierre Phalèse, 1559.

ClemensO *Jacobus Clemens non Papa: Opera omnia*, ed. Karel P. Bernet Kempers, 1951—.

ClosBD Closson, Ernest, ed., *Le Ms. dit des Basses Danses de la Bibliothèque de Bourgogne*, 1912. Facsimile edition with commentary.

CM Collegium Musicum, ed. Milos Velimirović, Yale University, New Haven, 1960—.

CM II *Thirty Chansons for Three and Four Voices from Attaingnant's Collections*, ed. Albert Seay, 1960.

CMI I Classici musicali italiani, 1924—.

CMI I *M. A. Cavazzoni, J. Fogliano, J. Segni ed Anonimi: Composizioni per organo*, ed. G. Benvenuti, 1941.

ColinM II Colin, Pierre, *Petri Colin, Apud Insignem Haeduorum Ecclesiam Pueris symphoniacis praefecti, Modulorum (quos vulgo Moteta vocant) in quatuor, & quinque voces partitorum Liber Secundus*, Paris, Nicolas Du Chemin, 1561.

CollaerAH Collaer, Paul, and Albert van der Linden, *Atlas historique de la musique*, 1960.

CombDF Combarieu, Jules, "Danses françaises et musique instrumentale du XVIe siècle," *Revue d'histoire et de critique musicales*, I (1901), 138.

ConfB *Giovanni Luca Conforto: Breve et facile maniera d'essercitarsi a far passaggi, 1593 (1603?)*, facsimile ed. with German trans. by Johannes Wolf, 1922.

CoopI Cooper, Gerald M., "Italian Instrumental Music of the 16th Century," *Proceedings of the Musical Association*, LVI (1929), 55.

CortP Cortés, Narciso A., "Diego Pisador, algunos datos biográficos," *Boletín de la Biblioteca Menéndez y Pelayo*, III (1921), 331.

CorteA Corte, Andrea della, *Scelta di musiche per lo studio della stòria*, 5th ed., 1949.

CortotC Cortot, Alfred and Frederick Goldbeck, *Bibliothèque Alfred Cortot. Première partie: Théorie de la musique. Traités et autres ouvrages théoriques des XVe, XVIe, XVIIe et XVIIIe siècles*, n.d.

CouN Coussemaker, Charles Edmond H. de, *Notice sur les collections musicales de la Bibliothèque de Cambrai*, 1843.

CremaI Crema, Joan Maria da, *Intavolatura di Liuto Libro Primo*, ed. Giuseppe Gullino, 1955.

CremaR Crema, Giovanni Maria da, *Recercar Undecimo y Recercar Tredecimo*, ed. José de Azpiazu, 1960.

CrockerC Crocker, Eunice C., "An Introductory Study of the Italian Canzona for Instrumental Ensembles," unpub. diss., Radcliffe College, 1943.

CromM Crombie, A. C., *Medieval and Early Modern Science*, 2 vols., 1959.

CummC *Catalogue of the Famous Musical Library . . . the Property of the Late W. H. Cummings, Mus. Doc.*, 1917. A Sotheby auction catalogue.

CurtisD Curtis, Alan, ed., *Dutch Keyboard Music of the 16th and 17th Centuries*, 1961.

CW Das Chorwerk, ed. Friedrich Blume, 1929—. For titles of individual volumes see Gustave Reese, *Music in the Renaissance* (1954), p. 897.

CzerG Czerwinski, Albert, *Geschichte der Tanzkunst*, 1862.

CzerT Czerwinski, Albert, *Die Tänze des 16. Jahrhunderts und die alte französische Tanzschule vor Einführung der Menuett*, 1878.

DallaA — Dalla Libera, Sandro, ed., *Antología organistica italiana*, 1957

DallaL — Dalla Libera, Sandro, ed., *Il Libro dei versi*, 1955.

DallaLO — Dalla Libera, Sandro, ed., *Liber organi*, 7 vols., 1955–1961.

DannMO — Dannreuther, Edward, *Musical Ornamentation*, n.d.

DartC — Dart, Thurston, "The Cittern and Its English Music," *The Galpin Society Journal. An Occasional Publication*, I (1948), 46.

DartCL — Dart, Thurston, "Morley's Consort Lessons of 1599," *Proceedings of the Royal Musical Association*, LXXIV (1947), 1.

DartHL — Dart, Thurston, "A Hand-List of English Instrumental Music Printed before 1681," *The Galpin Society Journal. An Occasional Publication*, VIII (1955), 13.

DartM — Dart, Thurston, "Simone Molinaro's Lute-Book of 1599," *Music & Letters*, XXVIII (1947), 258.

DavB — Davidsson, Åke, *Bibliographie der musiktheoretischen Drucke des 16. Jahrhunderts*, 1962.

DavC — Davidsson, Åke, and Rafael Mitjana, *Catalogue critique et descriptif des imprimés de musique des XVIe et XVIIe siècles, conservés à la Bibliothèque de l'Université royale d'Upsala*, 3 vols., 1911–1951.

DazaE — Daza, Esteban, *Enfermo estaba Antioco. Romance*, ed. José de Azpiazu, 1958.

DDT — Denkmäler deutscher Tonkunst, ed. R. von Liliencron, H. Kretzschmar, H. Albert, and A. Schering, ser. 1, 65 vols., 1892–1931. For the titles of individual volumes, see Gustave Reese, *Music in the Renaissance* (1954), p. 898. See also Denkmäler deutscher Tonkunst, ser. 2 (DTB).

DeakinMB — Deakin, Andrew, *Musical Bibliography*, 1892.

DeakinO — Deakin, Andrew, *Outline of Musical Bibliography*, 1899.

DeffU — Deffner, Oskar, *Über die Entwicklung der Fantasie für Tasteninstrumente*, 1927.

DegenB — Degen, Dietz, *Zur Geschichte der Blockflöte in den germanischen Ländern*, n.d.

DehnC — Dehn, Siegfried W., "Compositionen des XVI. Jahrhunderts zu weltlichen Texten," *Caecilia, eine Zeitschrift für die musikalische Welt*, XXV (1846), 29.

DehnS — Dehn, Siegfried W., ed., *Sammlung älterer Musik aus dem 16. und 17. Jahrhundert*, 1837.

DevP — Devoto, Daniel, "Poésie et musique dans l'oeuvre des vihuelistes," *Annales musicologiques*, IV (1956), 85.

DieL — Dieckmann, Jenny, *Die in deutscher Lautentabulatur überlieferten Tänze des 16. Jahrhunderts*, 1931.

Die Laute — *Die Laute. Monatsschrift der Musikantengilde zur Pflege des deutschen Liedes und guter Hausmusik*, ed. Fritz Jöde, 5 vols., 1917–1922. Succeeded by *Die Musikantengilde* (MU) in 1922.

DisK — Dischner, Oskar, ed., *Kammermusik des Mittelalters. Chansons der 1. u. 2. niederländischen Schule für drei bis vier Streichinstrumente herausgegeben*, 1927.

DiseC — Disertori, Benvenuto, "L'Unica Composizione sicuramente strumentale nei codici tridentini," *Collectanea historiae musicae*, II (1957), 135.

DiseCT — Disertori, Benvenuto, "Contradiction tonale dans la transcription d'un 'Strambotto' célèbre," in *Le Luth et sa musique*, ed. Jean Jacquot (1958), p. 37.

DiseF — Disertori, Benvenuto, *Le Frottole per Canto e Liuto Intabulate da Franciscus Bossinensis*, 1964.

DiseM — Disertori, Benvenuto, "Le Canzoni strumentali da sonar a quattro di Claudio Merulo," *Rivista musicale italiana*, XLVII (1943), 305.

DoA — Dodge, Janet, "Les Airs de cour d'Adrien Le Roy," *Revue musicale de la Société internationale de Musique*, III (1907), 1132.

DoL — Dodge, Janet, "Lute Music of the XVIth and XVIIth centuries," *Proceedings of the Musical Association*, XXXIV (1908), 123.

DoflS — Doflein, Erich, ed., *Spielmusik für Violine: Alte Musik*, vol. II, 1932.

DolDE — Dolmetsch, Mabel, *Dances of England and France from 1450 to 1600*, 1949.

DolDS — Dolmetsch, Mabel, *Dances of Spain and Italy from 1400 to 1600*, 1954.

DonaSM — Donà, Mariangela, *La Stampa musicale a Milano fino all'anno 1700*, 1961.

DoniL Doni, Antonio Francesco, *La Libraria del Doni, fiorentino*, Venice, G. Giolito de' Ferrari, 1558.

DorezM Dorez, Léon, "Francesco da Milano et la musique du Pape Paul III," *Rivista musicale italiana*, XI (1930), 104. Also in Dorez's *La Cour du Pape Paul III*, I (1932), 221.

DorfS Dorfmüller, Kurt, "Studien zur Lautenmusik in der ersten Hälfte des 16. Jahrhunderts," unpub. diss., Ludwig-Maximilian Universität, Munich, 1952.

DowlL Dowland, John, *18 Lieder bearbeitet für Singstimme und Gitarre*, ed. Siegfried Behrend, 1960.

DowlLM Dowland, John, *The Lute Music of John Dowland*, transcr. and ed. for piano by Peter Warlock, 1927.

DowlS Dowland, John, *The First Set of Songs, in Four Parts*, ed. William Chappell, Musical Antiquarian Society, 1844.

DowlSS Dowland, John, *Six Songs*, ed. Desmond Dupré, 1954.

DowlTS Dowland, John, *Three Songs for Voice and Guitar*, ed. Karl Scheit, 1955.

DraudiusBC Draudius, Georg, *Bibliotecha classica, sive Catalogus officinalis, in quo philosophici artiumque adeo humanicorum, poetici etiam et musici libri omnes . . . continentur*, Frankfurt, 1611. References are to the edition of 1625.

DraudiusBE Draudius, Georg, *Bibliotheca exotica, sive Catalogus officinalis librorum peregrinus linguis usualibus scriptorum*, Frankfurt, 1610. References are to the edition of 1625.

DraudiusBLG Draudius, Georg, *Bibliotheca librorum germanicorum classica, das ist: Verzeichniss aller und jeder Bücher, so fast bey dencklichen Jaren, bis auffs Jahr nach Christi Geburt 1625 in teutscher Spraach von allerhand Materien hin und wider in Truck aussgangen*, Frankfurt, 1611. References are to the edition of 1625.

DraudiusV Draudius, Georg, *Verzeichnisse deutscher musikalischer Bücher, 1611 und 1625*, ed. Konrad Ameln, 1957.

DressSC Dressler, Gallus, *Opus sacrarum cantionum, quatuor, quinque et plurium vocum*, Nuremberg, Catherine Gerlach, 1577.

DrozT Droz, Eugénie, Geneviève Thibault, and Yvonne Rokseth, eds., *Trois chansonniers francais du XVe siècle*, 1927.

DTB Denkmäler deutscher Tonkunst, ser. 2: Denkmäler der Tonkunst in Bayern, ed. Adolf Sandberger, 36 vols., 1900–1931. For titles of individual volumes, see Gustave Reese, *Music in the Renaissance* (1954), p. 900.

DTO Denkmäler der Tonkunst in Österreich, ed. Guido Adler, 1894—. For titles of individual volumes, see Gustave Reese, *Music in the Renaissance* (1954), p. 900.

Du Verdier Du Verdier, Antoine, sieur de Vauprivas, and François La Croix du Maine, *Les Bibliothèques françoises*, 6 vols., Paris, 1772–1773.

DuyL Van Duyse, Florimond, ed., *Het oude Nederlandsche Lied*, 3 vols., 1903–1907.

EC *Encyclopédie de la musique et Dictionnaire du Conservatoire*, ed. A. Lavignac and L. de la Laurencie, 1913–1931. Vols. I–V: *Partie I: Histoire de la musique*; vols. VI–XI: *Partie II: Technique, pédagogie et esthétique.*

EcorC *Catalogue des livres rares et précieux composant la collection de feu M. Jules Écorcheville*, 1920.

EcorL Écorcheville, Jules, "Le Luth et sa musique," *Sammelbände der Internationalen Musikgesellschaft*, VIII (1907–08), 131.

EDMR Das Erbe deutscher Musik, Reichsdenkmale, 1935—. For titles of individual volumes, see Gustave Reese, *Music in the Renaissance* (1954), p. 901.

EF *Encyclopédie de la musique*, 3 vols., Paris, Fasquelle, 1958.

EggeT Eggebrecht, Hans H., "Terminus 'Ricercar,'" *Archiv für Musikwissenschaft*, IX (1952), 137.

EhmL Ehmann, Wilhelm, ed., *Alte Liedsätze für Orgel oder Klavier*, 1939.

EI *Enciclopedia italiana di scienze, lettere ed arti*, 36 vols., 1929–1939.

EinAR "Die Aria di Ruggiero," *Sammelbände der Internationalen Musikgesellschaft*, XIII (1912), 444.

EinIM Einstein, Alfred, *The Italian Madrigal*, 3 vols., 1949.

EinN — Einstein, Alfred, "Narrative Rhythm in the Madrigal," *The Musical Quarterly*, XXIX (1943), 475.

EinSH — Einstein, Alfred, *A Short History of Music*, 1938.

EinVG — Einstein, Alfred, "Vincenzo Galilei and the Instructive Duo," *Music & Letters*, XVIII (1937), 360.

EinZ — Einstein, Alfred, *Zur deutschen Literatur für Viola da Gamba im 16. und 17. Jahrhundert*, 1905.

EisenV — Eisenberg, Jacob, "Virdung's Keyboard Illustrations," *The Galpin Society Journal. An Occasional Publication*, XV (1962), 82.

EitGA — Eitner, Robert, "Giulio Abondante's Lautenbücher," *Monatshefte für Musikgeschichte*, VIII (1876), 119.

EitK — Eitner, Robert, and Otto Kade, "Katalog der Musik-Sammlung der Kgl. öffentlichen Bibliothek zu Dresden (im japanischen Palais)," *Monatshefte für Musikgeschichte*, XXI, Supplement (1890).

EitQ — Eitner, Robert, *Biographisch-bibliographisches Quellenlexikon der Musiker und Musikgelehrten der christlichen Zeitrechnung bis zur Mitte des 19. Jahrhunderts*, 10 vols., 1899–1904. Additions and corrections published from 1912 to 1914 in a quarterly, *Miscellanea Musicae Bio-bibliographica*, ed. H. Springer, M. Schneider, and W. Wolffheim. A new edition, including the *Miscellanea*, with other additions and corrections was published in 1947.

EitS — Eitner, Robert, *Bibliographie der Musik-Sammelwerke des XVI. und XVII. Jahrhunderts, 1877*.

EitSW — Eitner, Robert, "Schulwerke von 1535 etc.," *Monatshefte für Musikgeschichte*, XX (1888), 17.

EitT — Eitner, Robert, "Tänze des 15. bis 17. Jahrhunderts," *Monatsheft für Musikgeschichte*, VII, Supplement (1875).

EL — The English School of Lutenist Song Writers, ed. Edmund H. Fellowes, ser. 1 and 2, 16 vols., 1920–1932. For titles of individual volumes see Gustave Reese, *Music in the Renaissance* (1954), p. 903.

ElúsA — Elústiza, Juan B. de, and G. C. Hernandez, eds., *Antología musical, siglo de oro de la música litúrgica de España. polifonia vocal siglos XV y XVI*, 1933.

EMS — English Madrigal School, ed. Edmund H. Fellowes, 36 vols., 1914–1924. For titles of individual volumes see Gustave Reese, *Music in the Renaissance* (1954), p. 904.

EnI — Engel, Egon, *Die Instrumentalformen in der Lautenmusik des 16. Jahrhunderts*, 1915.

EngL — Engel, Hans, ed., *Das mehrstimmige Lied des 16. Jahrhunderts in Italien, Frankreich und England*, n.d.

EnglertBS — Englert, Anton, "Bernhard Schmid und Johann Fischart," *Zeitschrift für deutsche Philologie*, XXXVIII (1906), 245.

EP — *Encyclopédie de la Pléiade: Histoire de la musique, Vol. I: Des origines à Jean-Sébastien Bach*, ed. Roland Manuel, 1960.

ExF — Expert, Henry, ed., *La Fleur de musiciens de Pierre de Ronsard*, 1923.

FaisstH — Faisst, Immanuel, "Über die Entstehung der Melodien 'Herzlich lieb hab ich dich, O Herr, etc.' und 'Innsbruck, ich muss dich lassen, etc.,'" *Monatshefte für Musikgeschichte*, VI (1874), 26, 33, 49.

FedM — Federmann, Maria, *Musik und Musikpflege zur Zeit Herzog Albrechts: zur Geschichte der Königsberger Hofkapelle in den Jahren 1525–1578*, 1932.

FelWB — Fellowes, Edmund H., *William Byrd*, 1936; 2nd ed., 1948.

FellJ — Fellerer, Karl G., "Josquins Missa Faisant regrets in der Vihuela-Transkription von Mudarra und Narváez," *Gesammelte Aufsätze zur Kulturgeschichte Spaniens*, XVI (1960), 179.

FerandB — Ferand, Ernst T., "Die Motetti, Madrigali, et Canzoni Francese . . . Diminuiti . . . des Giovanni Bassano (1591)," in *Festschrift Helmuth Osthoff zum 65. Geburtstage* (1961), p. 75.

FerandIM — Ferand, Ernst T., ed., *Die Improvisation in Beispielen aus neun Jahrhunderten abendländischer Musik*, 1956.

FerandM — Ferand, Ernst T., *Die Improvisation in der Musik*, 1938.

FétB — Fétis, François J. *Biographie universelle des musiciens*, 2nd ed., 8 vols., 1860–1865. Two-volume supplement by A. Pougin, 1878–1880.

FétC — *Catalogue de la bibliothèque de F. J. Fétis acquise par l'état belge*, 1877.

FétT — Fétis, François J., *Traité complet de la théorie et de la pratique de l'harmonie*, 4th ed., 1849.

FinschC — Finscher, Ludwig, "Loyset Compère and His Works," *Musica disciplina*, XII (1958), 105.

FischV — Fischer, Kurt von, ed., *Die Variation*, 1955.

FlechaE — *Mateo Flecha: Las Ensaladas (Praga, 1581)*, ed. Higinio Anglés, 1954.

FlowerG — Flower, John A., "Giovanni Gabrieli's Sacrae Symphoniae (1597)," unpub. diss., University of Michigan, 1956.

ForkA — Forkel, J. Nicolaus, *Allgemeine Geschichte der Musik*, 2 vols., 1788–1801.

FortI — Fortner, Wolfgang, ed., *Instrumentalspielbuch. Alte Originalsätze feierlichen Charakters, Festmusiken und deutsche Tänze (16.–18. Jahrhundert)*, 2 vols., 1939.

FoschA — Foschini, Gaetano F., ed., *Antología classica italiana*, 1931.

FoxA — Fox, Charles Warren, "Accidentals in Vihuela Tablatures," abstract, *Bulletin of the American Musicological Society*, no. 4 (1938), 22.

FoxED — Fox, Charles Warren, "An Early Duet for Recorder and Lute," *The Guitar Review*, IX (1949), 24.

FoxP — Fox, Charles Warren, "A Pleasant and Very Useful Book (1529)," abstract, *Bulletin of the American Musicological Society*, no. 2 (1937), 22.

FranF — Francesco da Milano, *3 Fantasien für Gitarre*, ed. Siegfried Behrend, 1960.

FrerA — Frerichs, Elly, "Die Accidentien in den Orgeltabulaturen," *Zeitschrift für Musikwissenschaft*, VII (1924–25), 99.

FroideA — Froidebise, Pierre, ed., *Anthologie de l'orgue des primitifs à la Renaissance*, 2 vols., 1957.

FrotO — Frotscher, Gotthold, *Geschichte des Orgelspiels und der Orgelkomposition*, vol. I, 1935.

FrotOI — Frotscher, Gotthold, ed., *L'Organo italiano. 7 Pezzi*, n.d.

FuenD — Fuenllana, Miguel de, *De antequera sale el moro. Romance viejo*, ed. Emilio Pujol, n.d.

FuenF — Fuenllana, Miguel de, *Fantasia*, ed. Graciano Tarragó, 1957.

FunA — Funck, Heinz, *Martin Agricola, ein frühprotestantische Schulmusiker*, 1933.

FuserC — Fuser, Ireneo, ed., *Classici italiani dell'organo*, 1955.

Gabr(A)C — *Andreae Gabrielis Sereniss. Rep. Venetiarum in Templo S. Marci Organistae Ecclesiasticarum Cantionum Quatuor Vocum . . . Liber primus*, Venice, Angelo Gardane, 1576.

Gabr(A)CF — Gabrieli, Andrea, *Canzoni alla francese*, ed. Pierre Pidoux, 1952.

Gabr(A)CR — Gabrieli, Andrea, *Canzonen und ricercari ariosi*, ed. Pierre Pidoux, 1952.

Gabr(A)I — Gabrieli, Andrea, *Intonationen*, ed. Pierre Pidoux, n.d.

Gabr(A)R — Gabrieli, Andrea, *Three Four Part Ricercari*, ed. Hans T. David, 1940.

Gabr(A)RDT — Gabrieli, Andrea, *Ricercar del duodecimo tuono*, ed. A. Lumsden, 1957.

Gabr(A)RO — Gabrieli, Andrea, *Ricercari für Orgel*, ed. Pierre Pidoux, 2 vols., 1941–1952.

Gabr(A)RST — Gabrieli, Andrea, *Ricercar del sesto tuono*, ed. A. Lumsden, 1957.

Gabr(G)C — Gabrieli, Giovanni, *Canzoni per sonar a quattro*, Antiqua, eine Sammlung alter Musik, ed. Alfred Einstein, 1933.

Gabr(G)CO — Gabrieli, Giovanni, *Composizioni per organo*, ed. Sandro dalla Libera, 3 vols., 1957–1958.

Gabr(G)CS — Gabrieli, Giovanni, *II. Canzone für acht Instrumentalstimmen in zwei Chören (1597)*, ed. Paul Winter, 1960.

Gabr(G)S — Gabrieli, Giovanni, *Sonata pian e forte*, ed. Fritz Stein, 1932.

Gabr(G)SP — Gabrieli, Giovanni, *Sonata pian'e forte*, ed. Reginald Johnson, 1961.

Gabr(G)W — Gabrieli, Giovanni, *Werke für Tasteninstrumente*, ed. Gerald S. Bedbrook, 1957.

GalR — Galilei, Vincenzo. *Zwölf Ricercari zu vier Stimmen*, ed. Franz J. Giesbert, 1959.

GallLP — Gallico, Claudio, *Un libro di poesie per musica dell'epoca d'Isabella d'Este*, 1961.

GanB — Gandolfi, Riccardo, "Biblioteca," in *Annuario del R. Istituto musicale di Firenze e atti dell'Accademia* (1899).

GanaF *Silvestro Ganassi: Opera intitulata Fontegara . . . 1535*, facsimile ed., 1934.

GanaOF *Silvestro Ganassi: Opera intitulata Fontegara*, ed. Hildemarie Peter, 1956; 2nd ed. with English trans. by Dorothy Swainson, 1959. The second edition is referred to in this book as GanaOFE.

GanaR *Silvestro Ganassi: Regola Rubertina, 1542–1543*, facsimile ed. with preface by Max Schneider, 1924.

GardI *Indice delli libri di musica che si trovano nelle stampe di Angelo Gardano*, 1591.

GaspCM Gasperini, Guido, Nestore Pelicelli, Pompeo Molmenti, and others, *Claudio Merulo da Correggio, 1533–1604*, 1904.

GaspaC Gaspari, Gaetano, *Catalogo della biblioteca del Liceo musicale di Bologna*, 5 vols., 1890–1943; reprinted 1961.

GastN Gastritz, Mathias, *Novae harmonicae cantiones*, Nuremberg, 1569.

GaussO Gauss, Otto, ed., *Orgelkompositionen aus alter und neuer Zeit*, 4 vols., 1909–1913.

GE *La Grande Encyclopédie, inventaire raisonné des sciences, des lettres et des arts*, 31 vols., 1886–1902.

GeorgK Georgii, Walter, ed., *400 Jahre europäischer Klaviermusik*, 1950.

GerbH Gerber, Rudolf, "Spanische Hymnensätze um 1500," *Archiv für Musikwissenschaft*, X (1953), 165.

GerbS Gerber, Rudolf, ed., *Spanisches Hymnar um 1500* (Das Chorwerk, vol. 60), 1957.

GéroB Gérold, Théodore, ed., *Le Manuscrit de Bayeux*, 1921.

GhiA Ghisi, Federico, "Un Aspect inédit des Intermèdes de 1589 à la cour médicéenne," in *Les Fêtes de la Renaissance*, ed. Jean Jacquot (1956), p. 145.

GhiFM Ghisi, Federico, ed., *Feste musicali della Firenze medicea (1480–1589)*, 1939.

GiazMG Giazotto, Remo, *La Musica a Genova nella vita pubblica e privata dal XIII al XVIII secolo*, n.d.

GiesA Giesbert, Franz J., ed., *Pierre Attaingnant: Pariser Tanzbuch aus dem Jahre 1530*, 1950.

GiesIF Giesbert, Franz J., ed., *Instrumental-Fantasien des 16. Jahrhunderts für vierstimmigen Blockflöten-, Violen- oder Fidelchor*, 1954.

GiesK Giesbert, Franz J., ed., *Klassiker des Lautenspiels, Vol. I: Fantasien und Tänze aus der Blütezeit der Lautenmusik*, 1925.

GiesS Giesbert, Franz J., ed., *Ein altes Spielbuch, Liber Fridolini Sichery*, 1936.

GlarDE Miller, Clement A., "The Dodecachordon of Heinrich Glarean," unpub. diss., University of Michigan, 1951.

GodB Godman, Stanley, "Bach's Copies of Ammerbach's 'Orgel oder Instrument Tabulatur' (1571)," *Music & Letters*, XXXVIII (1957), 21.

GoldV Goldschmidt, Hugo, "Verzierungen, Veränderungen und Passagien im 16. und 17. Jahrhundert," *Monatshefte für Musikgeschichte*, XXIII (1891), 111.

GolosT Golos, G. S., "Tre intavolature manoscritte di musica vocale rintracciate in Polonia," *L'Organo*, III (1962) 123.

GomCF Gombosi, Otto, "The Cultural and Folkloristic Background of the Folia," *Papers Read by Members of the American Musicological Society*, 1940 (1946), 88.

GomF Gombosi, Otto, "Zur Frühgeschichte der Folia," *Acta musicologica*, VIII (1936), 119.

GomH Gombosi, Otto, "Der Hoftanz," *Acta musicologica*, VII (1935), 50.

GomI Gombosi, Otto, "Italia, patria del basso ostinato," *La rassegna musicale*, VII (1934), 14.

GomM Gombosi, Otto, "Die Musikalien der Pfarrkirche zu St. Ägidien in Bártfa," in *Festschrift für Johannes Wolf* (1929), 38.

GomO Gombosi, Otto, *Jacob Obrecht, eine stilkritische Studie*, 1925.

GomRF Gombosi, Otto, "A la recherche de la forme dans la musique de la Renaissance: Francesco da Milano," in *La Musique instrumentale de la Renaissance*, ed. Jean Jacquot (1955), p. 165.

GomVB Gombosi, Otto, *Bakfark Bálint élete és müvei* (*Der Lautenist Valentin Bakfark, Leben und Werke*), Musicologia Hungarica, vol. II (Hungarian and German text), 1935.

GomVC Gombosi, Otto, ed., *Compositione di Meser Vincenzo Capirola. Lute-Book (circa 1517)*, 1955.

GombertMT I Gombert, Nicolas, *Del primo Libro de i motteti a quattro voci*, Venice, Girolamo Scotto, 1539.

GombertMT II Gombert, Nicolas, *Nicolai Gomberti, Musici Imperatorii, Motectorum, nuperrime maxima diligentia in lucem aeditorum Liber secundus. Quatuor vocum*, Venice, Girolamo Scotto, 1541.

GombertMT II a 5 Gombert, Nicolas, *Nicolai Gomberti, Musici Solertissimi, Motectorum Quinque vocum, Maximo studio in lucem editorum Liber secundus. Quinque vocum*, Venice, Girolamo Scotto, 1541.

GombertO *Nicolas Gombert: Opera omnia*, ed. Joseph Schmidt-Görg, 1951—.

GoovH Goovaerts, Alphonse, *Histoire et bibliographie de la typographie musicale dans les Pays-Bas*, 1884; reprinted, 1963.

GostL *Giovanni Battista della Gostena: Intavolatura di Liuto*, ed. Giuseppe Gullino, 1949.

GottA Gottschalg, A. W., ed., *Historisches Album für Gesang, Pianoforte, Harmonium, Pedalflügel oder Orgel*, 1884.

GottronMM Gottron, Adam, *Mainzer Musikgeschichte von 1500 bis 1800*, 1959.

GrandT Grand-Carteret, John, "Les Titres illustrés et l'image au service de la musique," *Rivista musicale italiana*, V (1898), 1.

GravA Gravisi, Anteo, "Andrea Antico da Montona," in *Atti e memorie della Società istriana di archeologia e stòria patria*, I (1885), 141.

GressE Gress, Richard, *Die Entwicklung der Klaviervariation von Andrea Gabrieli bis zu Johann Sebastian Bach*, 1929.

GreuB Greulich, Martin, *Beiträge zur Geschichte des Streichinstrumentenspiels im 16. Jahrhundert*, 1934.

GrimmM Grimm, Heinrich, *Meister der Renaissancemusik an der Viadrana*, 1942.

GuerrM Guerrero, Francisco, *Francisci Guerrero Hispalensis sacrae cantiones, vulgo moteta nuncupata quinque vocum*, Seville, Martin a Montesdoca, 1555.

GuerrO Guerrero, Francisco, *Opera omnia*, ed. Miguel Gavaldá and Vicente García, Monumentos de la música española, vols. XVI, XIX, 1955—.

GuilC Guilmant, Alexander, ed., *Concert historique d'orgue*, 1896.

GumpelzKF Gumpelzhaimer, Adam, *Zwölf kleine Fantasien*, ed. Franz J. Giesbert, n.d.

GünthB Günthert, Ernst, ed., Beiträge zur Klaviermusik (Sudetendeutsche Monatshefte. Im Auftrag des Musikwissenschaftlichen Institutes der deutschen Universität, Prague), 1936–1937.

GurB Gurlitt, Willibald, "Burgundische Chanson und deutsche Liedkunst," in *Bericht über den Musikwissenschaftlichen Kongress in Basel* (1925), p. 153.

HaasA Haas, Robert, *Aufführungspraxis der Musik*, 1930.

HahneIL Hahne-Overmann, Elisabeth, "Ikonographie der Lautengriffe," *Zeitschrift für Musikwissenschaft*, XII (1929–30), 527.

HalbK Halbig, Hermann, ed., *Klaviertänze des 16. Jahrhunderts*, 1928.

HalfT Halfpenny, Eric, "Tantivy: an Exposition of the 'Ancient Hunting Notes,'" *Proceedings of the Musical Association*, LXXX (1953–1954), 43.

HAM Davison, Archibald T., and Willi Apel, eds., *Historical Anthology of Music*, vol. I, 1946; rev. ed., 1949. References are to the first edition.

HamC Hambraeus, Bengt, *Codex Carminum Gallicorum. Une étude sur le volume Musique vocale du manuscrit 87 de la Bibliothèque de l'Université d'Upsala*, 1961.

HambF Hamburger, Povl, "Die Fantasien in Emanuel Adriansens Pratum Musicum (1600)," *Zeitschrift für Musikwissenschaft*, XII (1929–30), 148.

HammerI Hammerstein, Reinhard, "Instrumenta Hieronymi," *Archiv für Musikwissenschaft*, XVI (1959), 117.

HarZ Harich-Schneider, Eta, and Ricard Boadella, "Zum Klavichordspiel bei Tomàs de Santa Maria," *Archiv für Musikforschung*, II (1937), 243.

HaraD Haraszti, Émile, "Les Rapports italo-transylvains de Il Transilvano de Girolamo Diruta," in *Mélanges de musicologie offerts à M. Lionel de la Laurencie* (1933), p. 73.

HaraL Haraszti, Émile, "Un Grand Luthiste du XVIe siècle: Valentin Bakfark," *Revue de musicologie*, X (1929), 159.

HarmM Harman, Alec, Anthony Milner, and Wilfrid Mellers, *Man and His Music: The Story of Musical Experience in the West*, 1962.

HawkH Hawkins, Sir John, *A General History of the Science and Practice of Music*, 5 vols., 1776; new ed., 3 vols., 1853, 1875; mod. ed., 2 vols., 1963. References are to the first edition.

HawkeO Hawke, H. William, ed., *Elkan-Vogel Organ Series*, 5 vols., n.d.

HeartzBD Heartz, Daniel, "The Basse Dance," *Annales musicologiques*, VI (1958–1963), 287.

HeartzC Heartz, Daniel, "La Chronologie des recueils imprimés par Pierre Attaingnant," *Revue de musicologie*, XLIV (1959), 176.

HeartzE Heartz, Daniel, "An Elizabethan Tutor for the Guitar," *The Galpin Society Journal. An Occasional Publication*, XVI (1963), 3.

HeartzP Heartz, Daniel, "Parisian Music Publishing under Henry II: A Propos of Four Recently Discovered Guitar Books," *The Musical Quarterly*, XLVI (1960), 448.

HeartzS Heartz, Daniel, "Les Styles instrumentaux dans la musique de la Renaissance," in *La Musique instrumentale de la Renaissance*, ed. Jean Jacquot (1955), p. 61.

HeartzSF Heartz, Daniel, "Sources and Forms of the French Instrumental Dance in the Sixteenth Century," unpub. diss., Harvard University, 1957.

HeartzSM Heartz, Daniel, "A Spanish 'Masque of Cupid,'" *The Musical Quarterly*, XLIX (1963), 59.

HenzeG Henze, Bruno, *Das Gitarrespiel*, 14 vols., 1950.

HeronF Heron-Allen, Edward, *De fidiculis bibliographie*, 2 vols., 1890–1894.

HerpN Herpol, Homer, *Novum et insigne opus musicum*, Nuremberg, 1565.

HewO Hewitt, Helen, ed., *Harmonice Musices Odhecaton A*, 1942.

HeyerV *Versteigerung von Musikbüchern, praktischer Musik und Musiker-Autographen des 16. bis 18. Jahrhunderts aus dem Nachlass des Herrn Kommerzienrates Wilhelm Heyer in Köln*, 4 vols., 1927.

HillM Hill, Richard S., "Music from the Collection of Baron Horace de Landau," in *LCQA*, VII (1950), 14.

HirK Hirsch, Paul, and Käthi Meyer, *Katalog der Musikbibliothek Paul Hirsch, Frankfurt am Main*, 4 vols., 1928.

HirthK Hirth, Georg, *Kulturgeschichtliches Bilderbuch aus drei Jahrhunderten*, 3 vols., 1881–1890.

HM Hortus Musicus. Small volumes of music published by Bärenreiter Verlag, Kassel and Basel, 1941—.

HolF Holborne, Antony, *Two Fantasias (1597)*, ed. Thurston Dart, 1948.

HolP Holborne, Antony, *Two Pieces: "The Fruit of Love" and "Heigh Ho Holiday,"* ed. Harvey Sartorius, 1940.

HolPG Holborne, Antony, *Pavans, Galliards, Almaines and Other Short Airs in Five Parts for Viols, Violins or Wind Instruments*, ed. Sydney Beck, 1940.

HolQ Holborne, Antony, *Two Quintets*, ed. Edgar Hunt, 1959.

HolSE Holborne, Antony, *Suite for an Ensemble of Brass or Other Instruments*, ed. Thurston Dart, 1959.

HolTQ Holborne, Antony, *Three Quintets*, ed. Edgar Hunt, 1961.

HolzTVC Holzmann, Klaus, "Hieronymus Formschneyders Sammeldruck Trium Vocum Carmina. Nürnberg 1538," unpub. diss., Albert-Ludwigs-Universität, Freiburg in Breisgau, 1956.

HorsE Horsley, Imogene, "Improvised Embellishment in the Performance of Renaissance Polyphonic Music," *Journal of the American Musicological Society*, IV (1951), 3.

HorsS Horsley, Imogene, "The Solo Ricercar in Diminution Manuals: New Light on Early Wind and String Techniques," *Acta musicologica*, XXXIII (1961), 29.

HorsV Horsley, Imogene, "The Sixteenth-Century Variation and Baroque Counterpoint," *Musica disciplina*, XIV (1960), 161.

HorsWT Horsley, Imogene, "Wind Techniques in the Sixteenth and Early Seventeenth Centuries," *Brass Quarterly*, IV (1960), 49.

HuntR Hunt, Edgar, *The Recorder*, 1957.

HuntingC Huntington, Archer, *Catalogue of the Library of Ferdinand Columbus. Reproduced in Facsimile from the Unique Manuscript in the Columbine Library of Seville*, 1905.

HuskC Husk, W. H., *Catalogue of the Library of The Sacred Harmonic Society*, 1872.

HutchV Hutchinson, Loving, "The Vihuela Music of Diego Pisador," unpub. thesis, Eastman School of Music, Rochester, N.Y., 1937.

IISM Istituto italiano per la stòria della musica, Rome.

IISM I *Villanelle alla napolitana a tre voci di musicisti Baresi del secolo XVI raccolte da Giovanni de Antiquis per le stampe del Gardano del 1574*, ed. S. A. Luciani, 1941.

IMAMI Istituzioni e monumenti dell'arte musicale italiana, 6 vols., 1931–1939.

IMAMI I *Andrea e Giovanni Gabrieli e la musica strumentale in San Marco, I*, ed. G. Benvenuti, 1931.

IMAMI II *Andrea e Giovanni Gabrieli e la musica strumentale in San Marco, II*, ed. G. Benvenuti with preface by G. Cesari, 1932.

IMAMI IV *La Camerata fiorentina: Vincenzo Galilei*, ed. F. Fano, 1934.

ImelS Imelmann, Rudolf, "Zur Kenntnis der vor-Shakespeare'schen Lyrik," *Jahrbuch der deutschen Shakespeare-Gesellschaft*, XXXIX (1903), 168.

JachetMT I Jachet of Mantua, *Celeberrimi Maximeque delectabilis musici Jachet, chori Sancti Petri urbes Mantuae magistri: Motecta Quatuor vocum . . . Liber primus*, Venice, Girolamo Scotto, 1539.

JackBD Jackman, James L., ed., *Fifteenth Century Basse Dances* (The Wellesley Edition, no. 6), 1964.

JacobsTN Jacobs, Charles, *Tempo Notation in Renaissance Spain*, 1964.

JanT Janequin, Clément, *Trente chansons à trois et quatre voix*, ed. Maurice Cauchie, 1928.

JepK Jeppesen, Knud, ed., *Der Kopenhagener Chansonnier*, 1927.

JepO Jeppesen, Knud, *Die italienische Orgelmusik am Anfang des Cinquecento*, 1943; rev. ed., 2 vols., 1960. References are to the first edition.

Josq *Josquin des Prés: Werken*, ed. Albert Smijers, 1921—.

JosqMS *Missen*, 1931—.

JosqMT *Motetten*, 1926—.

JosqWW *Wereldlijke Werken*, 1925—.

KallLO Kaller, Ernst, ed., *Liber organi*, 7 vols., 1931–1935.

KastnI Kastner, Macario Santiago, "Una Intavolatura d'organo italiana del 1568," *Collectanea historiae musicae*, II (1956), 237.

KastnMM Kastner, Macario Santiago, "Los Manuscritos musicales n° 48 y 242 de la Biblioteca general de la Universidad de Coimbra," *Anuario musical*, V (1950), 78.

KastnP Kastner, Macario Santiago, "Parallels and discrepancies between English and Spanish Keyboard Music of the Sixteenth and Seventeenth Century," *Anuario musical*, VII (1952), 77.

KastnR Kastner, Macario Santiago, "Relations entre la musique instrumentale française et espagnole au XVIe siècle," *Anuario musical*, X (1955), 84.

KastnSI Kastner, Macario Santiago, ed., *Silva ibérica de música para tecla de los siglos XVI, XVII y XVIII*, 1954.

KastnV Kastner, Macario Santiago, ed., *Altitalienische Versetten in allen Kirchentonarten für Orgel oder andere Tasteninstrumente*, 1957.

KatzF Katz, Erich, ed., *Fantasias & Ricercares of the 16th and 17th Centuries*, 1954.

KemE Kempers, Karel P. Bernet, "Die Messe 'En Espoir' des Jacobus Clemens non Papa," in *Festschrift für Joseph Schmidt-Görg* (1957), p. 10.

KenN Kendall, Raymond, "Notes on Arnold Schlick," *Acta musicologica*, XI (1939), 136.

KiesS Kiesewetter, Raphael, *Schicksale und Beschaffenheit des weltlichen Gesanges*, 1841.

KiesT Kiesewetter, Raphael, *Die Verdienste der Niederländer um die Tonkunst*, 1829.

KinDT Kinkeldey, Otto, "Dance Tunes of the Fifteenth Century," in *Instrumental Music*, ed. David Hughes (1959), p. 3.

KinO Kinkeldey, Otto, *Orgel und Klavier in der Musik des 16. Jahrhunderts*, 1910.

KinsAP Kinsky, Georg, "Allessandro Piccinini und sein Arciliuto," *Acta musicologica*, X (1938), 103.

KinsP — Kinsky, Georg, *A History of Music in Pictures*, 1930.

KlaemM — Klaembt, Fritz, ed., *Musik für Liebhaber des Gitarrenspiels*, 1960.

KleinO — Klein, John, ed., *The First Four Centuries of Music for the Organ*, 2 vols., 1948.

KnappC — Knapp, J. Merrill, "The Canzone Francese and Its Vocal Models," unpub. thesis, Columbia University, 1941.

KoczD — Koczirz, Adolph, "Die Gitarrekompositionen in Miguel de Fuenllana's Orphénica lyra (1554)," *Archiv. für Musikwissenschaft*, IV (1922), 241.

KoczJ — Koczirz, Adolph, "Der Lautenist Hans Judenkünig," *Sammelbände der Internationalen Musikgesellschaft*, VI (1905), 237.

KoczM — Koczirz, Adolph, "Die Fantasien des Melchior de Barberis für die siebensaitige Gitarre," *Zeitschrift für Musikwissenschaft*, IV (1921), 11.

KölZ — Köler, David, *Zehen Psalmen Davids*, Leipzig, 1554.

KörL — Körte, Oswald, *Laute und Lautenmusik bis zur Mitte des 16. Jahrhunderts*, 1901.

KörnO — Körner, G. W., and A. G. Ritter, eds., *Der Orgel Freund. Vor- und Nachspiele, figurirte Choräle, Trio's, Fughetten, Fugen, Fantasien u.s.w. in allen Formen*, n.d.

KommaM — Komma, Karl Michael, *Musikgeschichte in Bildern*, 1961.

KosI — Kosleck, J., ed., *Instrumentalsätze älterer Zeit*, n.d.

KosackL — Kosack, Hans-Peter, *Geschichte der Laute und Lautenmusik in Preussen*, 1935.

KrI — Kroyer, Theodor von, *Die Anfänge der Chromatik im italienischen Madrigal des XVI. Jahrhunderts*, 1902.

KrausCO — Kraus, Eberhard, ed., *Cantantibus organis*, 3 vols., 1958–1959.

KrebsD — Krebs, Carl, "Girolamo Diruta's Transilvano," *Vierteljahrsschrift für Musikwissenschaft*, VIII (1892), 307.

KriegerME — Krieger, Ferdinand, *Musica ecclesiastica catholica*, 1872.

KuV — Kuhn, Max, *Die Verzierungs-Kunst in der Gesangs-Musik des 16.–17. Jahrhunderts (1535–1650)*, 1902.

LangL — Langius, Gregorius, *Newer deudscher Lieder, mit dreyen Stimmen*, Breslau, Johannes Scharffenberg, 1584.

LassoCDV — Lasso, Orlando di, *Cantiones duarum vocum. Magnum opus I–XXIV*, ed. by Paul Boepple, Dessoff Choir Series, 2 vols., 1941–1942.

LassoF — Lasso, Orlando di, *Fantasien aus Magnum opus musicum*, ed. Gerd Ochs, n.d.

LassoW — Lasso, Orlando di, *Sämtliche Werke*, ed. F. X. Haberl and A. Sandberger, 1894—.

LauC — Laurencie, Lionel de la, A. Mairy, and G. Thibault, eds., *Chansons au luth et airs de cour français du XVIe siècle*, 1934.

LauLL — Laurencie, Lionel de la, *Les Luthistes*, 1928.

LB — Lose Blätter der Musikantengilde. Small volumes of music published by G. Kallmeyer Verlag, Wolfenbüttel, [ca. 1930—].

LCQA — *Library of Congress. Quarterly Journal of Current Acquisitions*, 1943—.

LCReport — *Library of Congress. Annual Report*, 1866—.

LechM — Lechner, Leonhard, *Motectae sacrae, quatuor, quinque, et sex vocum*, Nuremberg, Catharine Gerlach and the heirs of Johannes Montanus, 1576.

LechN — Lechner, Leonhard, *Der erst und ander Theil der teutschen Villanellen . . . mit 3 Stimmen*, Nuremberg, Catharine Gerlach, 1590.

LechW — Lechner, Leonhard, *Werke*, ed. Konrad Ameln, 1954—.

LefL — Lefkoff, Gerald, ed., *Five Sixteenth Century Venetian Lute Books*, 1960.

LeiH — Leichtentritt, Hugo, ed., *Deutsche Hausmusik aus vier Jahrhunderten*, 1907.

LeMaiG — Le Maistre, Matthaeus, *Geistliche und weltliche teutsche Geseng*, Wittemberg, 1566.

LenK — Lenaerts, René B., ed., *Die Kunst der Niederländer*, 1962.

LenN — Lenaerts, René B., *Het Nederlands polifonies Lied in de 16de Eeuw*, 1933.

LenneC — Lenneberg, Hans, "The Critic Criticized: Sebastian Virdung and His Controversy with Arnold Schlick," *Journal of the American Musicological Society*, X (1957), 1.

Le RoyF — Le Roy, Adrian, *Fantaisies et danses extraites de A briefe and essaye Instruction (1568)*, ed. Pierre Jansen and Daniel Heartz, 1962.

Le RoyFM — Le Roy, Adrian, *Premier Livre de Tabulature de luth (1551)*, ed. André Souris and Richard de Morcourt, 1960.

Le RoyP — Le Roy, Adrian, *Psaumes* (*Tiers livre 1552—Instruction 1574*), ed. Richard de Morcourt, 1963.

LesAC — Lesure, François, Nanie Bridgman, Isabelle Cazeaux, M. Levin, Kenneth Levy, and D. P. Walker, eds., *Anthologie de la chanson parisienne au XVIe siècle*, 1952.

LesD — Lesure, François, "Danses et chansons à danser au début du XVIe siècle," in *Recueil de travaux offerts à M. Clovis Brunel* (1955), p. 176.

LesDC — Lesure, François, and Geneviève Thibault, "Bibliographie des éditions musicales publiées par Nicolas du Chemin (1549–1576)," *Annales musicologiques*, I (1953), 269.

LesE — Lesure François, "L'*Épitome musical* de Philibert Jambe de Fer (1550)," *Annales musicologiques*, VI (1958–1963), 340.

LesGF — Lesure, François, "La Guitare en France au XVIe siècle," *Musica disciplina*, IV (1950), 187.

LesLRB — Lesure, François, and Geneviève Thibault, *Bibliographie des éditions d'Adrian Le Roy et Robert Ballard (1551–1598)*, 1955.

LesP — Lesure, François, and Richard de Morcourt, "G. P. Paladino et son 'Premier Livre' de luth (1560)," *Revue de musicologie*, XLII (1958), 170.

LevyS — Levy, Kenneth, "'Susanne un jour': The History of a 16th Century Chanson," *Annales musicologiques*, I (1953), 375.

LiliH — Liliencron, Rochus von, "Die Horazischen Metren in deutschen Kompositionen des 16. Jahrhunderts," *Vierteljahrsschrift für Musikwissenschaft*, III (1887), 26.

LitaDP — Litaize, Gaston, and Jean Bonfils, eds., *Da Pacem Domine, Versets de Schlich, Sweelinck, Raison*, n.d.

LiuM — Liuzzi, Fernando, *I Musicisti in Francia* (*L'Opera del Genio Italiano all'Estero*), 1946.

LittC — Littleton, Alfred H., *A Catalogue of One Hundred Works Illustrating the History of Music Printing*, 1911.

LLiuQ — LLiurat, Q., "Quelques erreurs sur Cabezon 1510–1566," *Revue musicale de la Société internationale de Musique*, VI (1910), 604.

LM — *Larousse de la musique*, 2 vols., 1957.

LockVR — Lockwood, Lewis, "Vincenzo Ruffo and Musical Reform after the Council of Trent," *The Musical Quarterly*, XLIII (1957), 357.

LowE — Lowinsky, Edward, "Early Scores in Manuscript," *Journal of the American Musicological Society*, XIII (1960), 126.

LowG — Lowinsky, Edward, "The Goddess Fortuna in Music," *The Musical Quarterly*, XXIX (1943), 45.

LowT — Lowinsky, Edward, *Tonality and Atonality in Sixteenth-Century Music*, 1961.

LSM — *Le Luth et sa musique*, ed. Jean Jacquot, 1958.

LU — *Liber usualis*. References are to the 1947 Belgian edition.

LütkeF — Lütkeman, Paul, *Fantasien über Kirchenmelodien der pommerschen Reformationszeit*, ed. Erdmann Werner Böhme, 1931.

LumE — Lumsden, David, "English Lute Music, 1540–1620, An Introduction," *Proceedings of the Royal Musical Association*, LXXXIII (1956–57), 1.

LumS — Lumsden, David, "The Sources of English Lute Music (1540–1620)," *The Galpin Society Journal. An Occasional Publication*, VI (1953), 14.

MacC — MacClintock, Carol, "A Court Musician's Songbook: Modena MS C311," *Journal of the American Musicological Society*, IX (1956), 177.

MagB — Magriel, Paul, *A Bibliography of Dancing*, 1936.

Maggs28 — *Maggs Brothers Catalogue. Music, Early Books, Manuscripts, Portraits and Autographs*, catalogue no. 512, London, 1928.

Maggs58 — *Maggs Brothers Catalogue. Florence and Tuscany, Music*, catalogue no. 849, London, 1958.

MagniSM — Magni Dufflocq, Enrico, *Stòria della musica*, vol. I, 1933.

MainB — Mainerio, Giorgio, *Il primo Libro de balli*, ed. Manfred Schuler, 1963.

MalAR — Malecek, Anton R., "Anton Rotta, eine biographische Skizze," in *Festschrift Adolph Koczirz zum 60. Geburtstag* (1930), 20.

MalR — Malecek, Anton R., "Der Paduaner Lautenmeister Antonio Rotta (ca 1495–1548)," unpub. diss., University of Vienna, 1930.

Mald — Maldeghem, Robert van, ed., *Trésor musical*, 1865–1893.
  MaldP — *Musique profane*, 29 vols., 1865–1893.
  MaldR — *Musique religieuse*, 29 vols., 1865–1893.
MarenW — Marenzio, Luca, *Sämtliche Werke*, ed. Alfred Einstein, Publikationen älterer Musik . . . der Deutschen Musikgesellschaft, vol. I, Jahrgang IV[1], 1929; vol. II, Jahrgang VI, 1931.
MaryO — Mary, André, "'L'Orchésographie' de Thoinot Arbeau," *Les Trésors des bibliothèques de France*, V (1935), 85.
MaunC — Maunsell, Andrew, *The Seconde Part of the Catalogue of English Printed Books*, 1595.
MB — Musica Britannica. A National Collection of Music, 1951—.
  MB I — *The Mulliner Book*, ed. Denis Stevens, 1951; 2nd ed., 1954.
  MB VI — *John Dowland: Ayres for Four Voices*, ed. Edmund H. Fellowes, Thurston Dart, and Nigel Fortune, 1953.
  MB XVIII — *Music at the Court of Henry VIII*, ed. John Stevens, 1962.
McKeeM — McKee, William E., "The Music of Florentio Maschera (1540–1584)," unpub. diss., North Texas State College, 1958.
MeM — Meyer, Käthi, "Michel de Toulouze," *The Music Review*, VII (1946), 178.
MeiC — Meiland, Jacob, *Cantiones sacrae*, Nuremberg, 1569.
MeiN — Meiland, Jacob, *Newe ausserlesene teutsche Liedlein*, Nuremberg, 1569.
MendP — Mendel, Arthur, "Pitch in the 16th and Early 17th Centuries," *The Musical Quarterly*, XXIV (1948), 28, 199, 336, 575.
MerT — Merian, Wilhelm, *Der Tanz in den deutschen Tabulaturbüchern*, 1927.
MeruC — Merulo, Claudio, *Canzonen, 1592*, ed. Pierre Pidoux, 1941.
MeruCan — Merulo, Claudio, *Sei Canzoni da Sonar a 4*, ed. Benvenuto Disertori, 1950.
MeruO — Merulo, Claudio, *Livre IV des Oeuvres d'Orgue . . . Venise, 1568*, ed. J. B. Labat, [1865?].
MeruT — Merulo, Claudio, *Toccate per organo*, ed. Sandro Dalla Libera, 3 vols., 1959.
MeyeM — Meyer, Ernst H., *Die mehrstimmige Spielmusik des 17. Jahrhunderts in Nord- und Mitteleuropa*, 1934.
MeyerC — *Collection Musicale André Meyer*, ed. François Lesure, 1960.
MFH — Musikalische Formen in historischen Reihen, ed. Heinrich Martens, 20 vols., 1930–1937.
MfMG — *Monatshefte für Musikgeschichte*, 1869–1905.
MGG — Die Musik in Geschichte und Gegenwart, ed. Friedrich Blume, 1949—.
MI — Musica instrumentalis, ed. Helmut Mönkmeyer, 6 vols., 1960.
MilanC — Milán, Luis, *Con pavor recordó el moro. Romance*, ed. José de Azpiazu, 1958.
MilanF — Milán, Luis, *Fantasia 4 & Fantasia 14*, ed. Pieter van der Staak, 1958.
MilanFa — Milán, Luis, *Fantasia*, ed. Graciano Tarragó, 1962.
MilanL — Milán, Luis, *Levayme amor d'agnesta terra*, ed. José de Azpiazu, n.d.
MilanM — Milán, Luis, *Musikalische Werke*, ed. Leo Schrade, Publikationen älterer Musik . . . der Deutschen Musikgesellschaft, vol. II[1], 1927.
MilanSP — Milán, Luis, *6 Pavanes and a Fantasia*, ed. Alexander Bellow, 1961.
MilanT — Milán, Luis, *Toda mi vida os amé*, ed. Fernandez Lavie, 1955.
MilanT (Puj) — Milán, Luis, *Toda mi vida os amé. Villancico*, ed. Emilio Pujol, n.d.
MIR — *La Musique instrumentale de la Renaissance*, ed. Jean Jacquot, 1955.
MischR — Mischiati, Oscar, "Tornano alla luce i ricercari della 'Musica Nova' del 1540," *L'Organo*, II (1961), 73.
MitU — Mitjana, Rafael, Jesús Bal y Gay, and Isabel Pope, eds., *Cancionero de Upsala*, 1944.
MLE, 1904 — *An Illustrated Catalogue of the Music Loan Exhibition held . . . by the Worshipful Company of Musicians at Fishmonger's Hall, June and July, 1904*, 1909.
MLI — *Music Libraries and Instruments*, ed. Unity Sherrington and Guy Oldham, 1961 ("Hinrichsen's Eleventh Music Book").
MME — Monumentos de la música española, ed. Higinio Anglés, 1941—. For titles of individual volumes see Gustave Reese, *Music in the Renaissance* (1954), p. 923.
MMFTR — Les Monuments de la musique française au temps de la Renaissance, 10 vols., ed. Henry Expert, 1924–1930. For titles of individual volumes see Gustave Reese, *Music in the Renaissance*, p. 923.

MMRF — Les Maîtres musiciens de la Renaissance française, 23 vols. plus supplementary vols., ed. Henry Expert, 1894–1908. For titles of individual volumes see Gustave Reese, *Music in the Renaissance* (ReMR), p. 923.

ModF — *Jacques Moderne: Fröhliche Musik* (*Musique de joye*), ed. Franz J. Giesbert, 1934.

MoeDM — Moe, Lawrence H., "Dance Music in Printed Italian Lute Tablatures from 1507 to 1611," 2 vols., unpub. diss., Harvard University, 1956.

MohrA — Mohr, Ernst, *Die Allemande*, 2 vols., 1932.

MohrH — Mohr, Peter, *Die Handschrift B.211–215 der Proske-Bibliothek zu Regensburg*, Schriften des Landesinstituts für Musikforschung Kiel, vol. VII, 1955.

MolinL — Molinaro, Simone, *Intavolatura di Liuto, Lib. primo.*, ed. Giuseppe Gullino, 1940.

MolinS — Molinaro, Simone, *2 Saltarelli*, ed. Reginald Smith-Brindle, 1957.

MollM — Moll Roqueta, Jaime, "Músicos en la corte del Cardenal J. Tavera (1523–1545): Luis Venegas de Henestrosa," *Anuario musical*, VI (1951), 155.

MolmS — Molmenti, Pompeo, *La Stòria di Venezia nella vita privata dalle origini alla caduta della repubblica*, 5th ed., 2 vols., 1911.

MolzHN — Molzberger, Ernst, ed., *Lautenstücke von Hans Newsidler*, 1939.

MOM — Masterpieces of Organ Music. Selected Compositions of the Old Masters, ed. Norman Hennefield, 1944—.

MonkS — Mönkemeyer, Helmut, ed., *Hans Gerle. Spielstücke*, 2 vols., 1964.

MonteO — Monte, Philippe de, *Opera*, ed. Charles van den Borren and J. van Nuffel, 1927—.

MorL — Morphy, Guillermo, ed., *Les Luthistes espagnols du XVI*[e] *siècle*, 2 vols., 1902.

MoralesMS II — Morales, Cristóbal de, *Missarum Liber II*, Lyons, Jacques Moderne, 1551.

MoralesO — Morales, Cristóbal de, *Opera omnia*, ed. Higinio Anglés, 1952—.

MorcouA — Morcourt, abbé Richard de, "Adrian le Roy et les psaumes pour luth," *Annales musicologiques*, III (1955), 179.

MorcouB — Morcourt, abbé Richard de, "Le Livre de tablature de luth de Domenico Bianchini (1546)," in *La Musique instrumentale de la Renaissance*, ed. Jean Jacquot (1955), p. 177.

MorlCB — Morley, Thomas, *Two Part Canzonets for Voices and Instruments*, ed. D. H. Boalch, 1950.

MorlCU — Morley, Thomas, *Canzonets for Two Voices*, facsimile ed. by John E. Uhler, 1954.

MorlF — Morley, Thomas, *Nine Fantasies for Two Viols*, ed. Edmund H. Fellowes, 1928.

MorlFV — Morley, Thomas, *Neun Fantasien für zwei Viola da Gamba*, ed. Nathalie Dolmetsch, 1956.

MorlTL — Morley, Thomas, *Two Consort Lessons Collected by Thomas Morley*, ed. Thurston Dart, 1957.

MorlayeC — Morlaye, Guillaume, *Psaumes de Pierre Certon réduits pour chant et luth*, ed. François Lesure and Richard de Morcourt, 1957.

MornableP — Mornable, Antoine, *Livre second contenant XVII. pseaulmes de David traduictz de Latin en Francois par Clement Marot et naguères mis en musique en quatre parties separees par maistre Anthoine de Mornable*, Paris, Pierre Attaingnant, 1546.

MorrA — Morrow, Michael, "Ayre on the F♯ String," *The Lute Society Journal*, II (1960), 9.

MosGR — Moser, Hans J., ed., *Gassenhawerlin und Reutterliedlin* (*1535*), facsimile ed. (with missing discant supplied by the editor), 1927.

MosL — Moser, Hans J. and Eduard Bernoulli, eds., *Das Liederbuch des Arnt von Aich*, 1930.

MosPH — Moser, Hans J., *Paul Hofhaimer*, 1929.

MU — *Die Musikantengilde*, 7 vols., 1922–1929. This journal succeeded *Die Laute*.

MUB — Music for Brass. Small volumes of music published by the Robert King Music Co., North Easton, Mass., ca. 1950—.

- MUB 6 — *Antony Holborne: Two Pieces*
- MUB 10 — *Giovanni Gabrieli: Sonata Octavi Toni.*
- MUB 19 — *Giovanni Gabrieli: Canzon quarti toni.*

MUB 22 *Tielman Susato: Three Dances.*
MUB 28 *Giovanni Gabrieli: Canzon Septimi Toni.*
MUB 34 *Giovanni Gabrieli: Canzon Duodecimi Toni.*
MUB 45 *Giovanni Gabrieli: Sonata pian'e forte.*
MUB 53 *Giovanni Gabrieli: Canzon Noni Toni.*
MUB 91 *Giovanni Gabrieli: Canzon Primi Toni.*
MUB 93 *Antony Holborne: Five Pieces.*
MUB 401 *Giovanni Gabrieli: Canzon Duodecimi Toni.*
MUB 406 *Giovanni Gabrieli: Sonata pian'e forte.*
MUB 408 *Giovanni Gabrieli: Canzon Noni Toni.*
MUB 415 *Giovanni Gabrieli: Canzon Primi Toni.*

MudF Mudarra, Alonso de, *Fantasia X*, ed. Graciano Tarragó, 1957.

MudG Mudarra, Alonso de, *Gallarda*, ed. Graciano Tarragó, 1957.

MudI Mudarra, Alonso, *Isabel, perdiste la tu faxa*, ed. José de Azpiazu, 1958.

MudR Mudarra, Alonso de, *Romanesca*, ed. Andrés Segovia, n.d.

MudT Mudarra, Alonso de, *Triste estaba el Rey David*, ed. José de Azpiazu, 1958.

MülleG Müller-Blatau, Joseph, *Grundzüge einer Geschichte der Fuge*, 1931.

MurphF Murphy, Richard M., "Fantasia and Ricercare in the Sixteenth Century," unpub. diss., Yale University, 1954.

MusetS Muset, Joseph, ed., *Early Spanish Organ Music*, 1948.

NagM Nagler, Georg, *Die Monogrammisten*, 5 vols., 1879–1919.

NaglerT Nagler, A. M., *Theatre Festivals of the Medici, 1539–1637*, 1964.

NarC Narváez, Luis de, *Con que la lavare*, ed. José de Azpiazu, 1958.

NarG Narváez, Luis de, *Siete Variaciones (Diferencias) sobre "Guardame las Vacas,"* ed. Graciano Tarragó, 1957.

NarT Narváez, Luis de, *Tema y Variaciones sobre un Aire popular*, Clásicos españoles de la música, publicados por la Asociación patriótica española, vol. I, ed. Ernesto Barreda, 1938.

NarV Narváez, Luis de, *Ventidos Variaciones sobre "Conde Claros,"* ed. Graciano Tarragó, 1962.

NeemAM Neemann, Hans, ed., *Alte Meister der Laute*, 4 vols., n.d.

NeemL Neemann, Hans, ed., *Alte deutsche Lautenlieder*, n.d.

NefI Nef, Karl, "Die Intraden von Alexander Orologio," in *Gedenkboek aangeboden aan Dr. D. F. Scheurleer* (1925), p. 219.

NefV Nef, Karl, "Seb. Virdungs Musica getutscht," in *Bericht über den musikwissenschaftlichen Kongress in Basel* (1925), p. 7.

NettlE Nettl, Paul, "Die Tänze Jean d'Estrées," *Musikforschung*, VIII (1955), 437.

NeuP Neusidler, Hans, *Präambulum und Tanz*, ed. Karl Scheit, n.d.

NewmM Newman, Joel, "Francesco Canova da Milano, A Lutenist of the Sixteenth Century," unpub. thesis, New York University, 1942.

NiemOL Niemöller, Klaus, "Othmar Luscinius, Musiker und Humanist," *Archiv für Musikwissenschaft*, XV (1958), 41.

NijM Nijhoff, W., "Een merkwaardig Muziekboek te Antwerpen nij Vorsterman uitgegeven, 1529," *Het Boek*, XXII (1934), 267.

NixB Nixon, H. M., "The Book of XX Songs," *British Museum Quarterly*, XVI (1951), 33.

NM Nagels Musikarchiv. Small volumes of music published by Adolph Nagel Verlag, Hanover, 1927—.

NoskeL Noske, Frits, "Remarques sur les luthistes des Pays-Bas (1580–1620)," in *La Musique instrumentale de la Renaissance*, ed. Jean Jacquot (1955), p. 179.

NoskeS Noske, Frits, ed., *Das ausserdeutsche Sololied*, 1958.

NowakH Nowak, Leopold, "Paul Hofhaymers 'Nach willen dein' in den Lautentabulaturen des 16. Jahrhunderts. Ein Vergleich," in *Festschrift Adolph Koczirz zum 60. Geburtstag* (1930), p. 25.

Obr Obrecht, Jakob, *Werken*, ed. Johannes Wolf, 1912–1921.
ObrMS *Missen*, 24 vols.
ObrMT *Motetten*, 4 vols.
ObrWW *Wereldlijke Werken*, 2 vols.

OHM *Oxford History of Music*, ed. Sir Henry Hadow, 7 vols. 1901–1934.

OL — Orgue et liturgie, ed. Norbert Dufourcq, Félix Raugel, and Jean de Valois, ca. 1945—.

OL 2 — *L'Orgue en Europe aux XVIe et XVIIe siècles*, ed. Norbert Dufourcq, n.d.

OL 5 — *Ricercari de Luzzaschi à Antoine Reboulot*, ed. Norbert Dufourcq, n.d.

OL 8 — *Hymnes et antiennes*, ed. Norbert Dufourcq, n.d.

OL 12 — *Notre Dame*, ed. Jean de Valois, 1951.

OL 14 — *A la vierge*, ed. Norbert Dufourcq, 1952.

OL 30 — *Antonio de Cabezón, I*, ed. Norbert Dufourcq, Félix Raugel, and Jean de Valois, 1956.

OL 34 — *Antonio de Cabezón, II*, ed. Norbert Dufourcq, Félix Raugel, and Jean de Valois, 1957.

OLI — L'Organiste liturgique, ed. Gaston Litaize and Jean Bonfils, ca. 1945—.

OLI 14 — *Ascension Pentecôte*, 1956.

OLI 21 — *Salve Regina*, n.d.

OpieD — Opienski, Henryk, ed., *Dawne Tánce Polskie z XVI i XVII wieku* (*Altpolnische Tänze aus dem XVI. und XVII. Jahrhundert*), 1911.

OppelF — Oppel, Reinhard, "Einige Feststellungen zu den französischen Tänzen des 16. Jahrhunderts," *Zeitschrift der Internationalen Musikgesellschaft*, XII (1911), 213.

OrtizR — Ortiz, Diego, *Recercada* (no. 2). *Verzierungen über den Supran der Chanson "Doulce memoire,"* ed. Christian Döbereiner, 1936.

OrtizT — Ortiz, Diego, *Tratado de glosas sobre clausulas y otros generos de puntos en la música de violones* (*1553*), ed. Max Schneider, 1913; 2nd, revised ed., 1936; 3rd, revised ed., 1961.

OsG — Osthoff, Helmuth, *Der Lautenist Santino Garsi da Parma*, 1926.

OsM — Osthoff, Helmuth, "Magnificat bei Josquin," *Archiv für Musikwissenschaft*, XVI (1959), 230.

OsN — Osthoff, Helmuth, *Die Niederländer und das deutsche Lied* (*1400–1640*), 1938.

PadovanoR — Padovano, Annibale, *13 Ricercari for Organ, 1556*, ed. N. Pierront and J. P. Hennebains, 1934.

PaixZ — Paix, Jakob, *Zway neue teutsche Liedlein mit 4 Stimmen*, n.d. [ca. 1580].

PalO — Palestrina, Pierluigi da, *Le Opere complete*, ed. Raffaele Casimiri, 1939—.

PalW — Palestrina, Pierluigi da, *Werke: Erste kritisch durchgesehene Gesammtausgabe*, ed. F. Espagne, F. X. Haberl, and others, 33 vols., 1862–1907.

PanS — Panum, Hortense, *The Stringed Instruments of the Middle Ages*, English ed., rev. and ed. Jeffrey Pulver, n.d.

ParaC — Parabosco, Gerolamo, *Composizioni a due, tre, quattro, cinque e sei voci*, ed. Francesco Bussi, 1961.

ParisC — Paris, Gaston, and Auguste Gevaert, eds., *Chansons du XVe siècle*, 1875; reprinted 1935.

ParrishM — Parrish, Carl, and John F. Ohl, *Masterpieces of Music before 1750*, 1951.

ParrishT — Parrish, Carl, *A Treasury of Early Music*, 1958.

PastorE — Pastor, Perez, "Escrituras de concierto para imprimir libros," *Revista de archivos, bibliotecas y museos*, I (1897), 363.

PedAO — Pedrell, Felipe, ed., *Antología de organistas clásicos españoles*, 2 vols., 1908.

PedB — Pedrell, Felipe, ed., *Juan Bermudo: Versillos de salmos e interludios de himnos*, n.d.

PedC — Pedrell, Felipe, *Catàlech de la Biblioteca musical de la Disputació de Barcelona*, 2 vols., 1908–1909.

PedCP — Pedrell, Felipe, ed., *Cancionero musical popular español*, 4 vols., 1919–1920.

PedH — Pedrell, Felipe, ed., *Hispaniae schola musica sacra*, 8 vols., 1894–1898.

PedOL — Pedrell, Felipe, ed., *El Organista litúrgico español*, 1905.

PeetA — Peeters, Flor, ed., *Anthologia pro organo*, 2 vols., 1949.

PeetM — Peeters, Flor, ed., *Oudnederlandsche Meesters voor het Orgel*, 1945.

PeterM — Peter de Vallier, Otto, "Die Musik in Johann Fischarts Dichtungen," *Archiv für Musikwissenschaft*, XVIII (1961), 205.

PetrO — Petrucci, Ottaviano, *Odhecaton* (*Venice, 1501*), facsimile ed., 1932.

PhalAT — Phalèse, Pierre, "*Antwerpener Tanzbuch*" *Galliarden, Balli, Allemanden zu vier Stimmen* (*1583*), ed. Helmut Mönkemeyer, 2 vols., 1962.

PhalCh VI — Phalèse, Pierre, publ., *Sixiesme livre des chansons a quatre parties nouvellement composez et mises en musique par maistre Jehan de Latre*, Louvain, 1555.

PhalLT — Phalèse, Pierre, "*Löwener Tanzbuch.*" *Fantasien, Pavanen, Gaillarden zu vier Stimmen (1571)*, ed. Helmut Mönkemeyer, 2 vols., 1962.

PiciA — Picinelli, Filippo, *Ateneo dei letterati milanesi*, 1670.

PidP — Pidoux, Pierre, "Les Psaumes d'Antoine de Mornable, Guillaume Morlaye et Pierre Certon," *Annales musicologiques*, V (1957), 179.

PierO — Piersig, Johannes, ed., *Europäische Orgelmusik. Ausgewählte Orgelmusik des 16.–18. Jahrhunderts*, 1958.

PinchIH — Pincherle, Marc, *An Illustrated History of Music*, trans. Rollo Myers, 1959.

PirC — Pirro, André, *Les Clavecinistes*, 1925.

PirF — Pirro, André, "Les 'Frottole' et la musique instrumentale," *Revue de musicologie*, III (1922), 3.

PirH — Pirro, André, *Histoire de la musique de la fin du XIVe siècle à la fin du XVIe*, 1940.

PisG — Pisador, Diego, *Guarte guarte el Rey don Sancho. Romance viejo*, ed. José de Azpiazu, 1958.

PisM — Pisador, Diego, *La Mañana de San Juan. Romance viejo*, ed. José de Azpiazu, 1958.

PisMA — Pisador, Diego, *Madonna mia fa* (*Villanesca*), ed. Pieter van der Staak, 1959

PisQ — Pisador, Diego, *Quien tu viese tal poder* (*Villancico*), ed. Pieter van der Staak, 1958.

PisS — Pisador, Diego, *Si la noche hace oscura* (*Villancico*), ed. Pieter van der Staak, 1958.

PlamEC — Plamenac, Dragan, "'Excerpta Colombina': Items of Musical Interest in Fernando Colon's 'Regestrum,'" in *Miscelánea en homenaje a Monseñor Higinio Anglés*, II (1961), 663.

PlamF — Plamenac, Dragan, ed., *Facsimile Reproduction of the Manuscripts Sevilla 5-I-43 and Paris N.A.Fr. 4379* (Part I), 1962.

PlamML — Plamenac, Dragan, "Music Libraries in Eastern Europe: A Visit in the Summer of 1961," *Music Library Association Notes*, XIX (1962), 217.

PlamSC — Plamenac, Dragan, "The 'Second' Chansonnier of the Biblioteca Riccardiana (Codex 2356)," *Annales musicologiques*, II (1954), 105.

PN — *The Printed Note. 500 Years of Music Printing and Engraving*, The Toledo Museum of Art, Toledo, Ohio, 1957.

PoulN — Poulton, Diana, "Notes on the Spanish Pavan," *The Lute Society Journal*, III (1961), 5.

PraM — Pratt, Waldo S., *The Music of the French Psalter of 1562*, 1939.

ProdM — Prod'homme, Jacques-Gabriel, "Guillaume Morlaye, éditeur d'Albert de Ripe, luthiste et bourgeois de Paris," *Revue de musicologie*, VI (1925), 157.

PruB — Prunières, Henry, *Le Ballet de cour en France*, 1914.

PubAPTM — Publikation älterer praktischer und theoretischer Musikwerke, ed. Robert Eitner, 29 vols., 1873–1905. For titles of individual volumes see Gustave Reese, *Music in the Renaissance* (1954), p. 930.

PujA — Pujol, Emilio, "Joan Carlos Amat en la historia de la guitarra." *Anuario musical*, V (1950), 125.

PujBG — Pujol, Emilio, ed., *Bibliothèque de musique ancienne et moderne pour guitare*, n.d.

PujHC — Pujol, Emilio, ed., *Hispanae citharae ars viva*, 1955.

QueI — Querol-Garalda, Miguel, "Importance historique et nationale de romance," in *Musique et poésie au XVIe siècle* (Paris, 1954), p. 306.

QuittH — Quittard, Henri, "'L'Hortus Musraum' de 1552–53 et les arrangements de pièces polyphoniques pour voix seule et luth," *Sammelbände der Internationalen Musikgesellschaft*, VIII (1907), 254.

RaL — Radecke, Ernst, "Das deutsche weltliche Lied in der Lautenmusik des 16. Jahrhunderts," *Vierteljahrsschrift für Musikwissenschaft*, VII (1891), 285.

RadiA — Radino, Giovanni Maria, *Il primo Libro di Balli d'Arpicordo, 1592*, ed. Rosamond E. Harding, 1949.

RadiL — Radino, Giovanni Maria, *Intavolatura di Balli per sonar di Liuto*, ed. Giuseppe Gullino, 1949.

RanR — Ranke, Friedrich, and Josef M. Müller-Blattau, "Das Rostocker Liederbuch," *Schriften der Königsberger Gelehrten Gesellschaft*, IV (1927), 193.

RauM — Raugel, Félix, ed., *Les Maîtres français de l'orgue aux XVIIe et XVIIIe siècles*, n.d.

RauQ — Raugel, Félix, ed., *Quarante-six pièces pour orgue ou Harmonium d'anciens auteurs français et étrangers*, n.d.

ReFS — Reese, Gustave, *Fourscore Classics of Music Literature*, 1957.

ReMR — Reese, Gustave, *Music in the Renaissance*, 1954; rev. ed., 1959. References are to the first edition.

ReO — Reese, Gustave, "The First Printed Collection of Part-Music: The Odhecaton," *The Musical Quarterly*, XX (1934), 39.

ReR — Reese, Gustave, "The Repertoire of Book II of Ortiz's *Tratado*," in *The Commonwealth of Music*, G. Reese and R. Brandel, eds., 1965, p. 201.

ReaneyMS — Reaney, Gilbert, "The Manuscript Oxford, Bodleian Library, Canonici Misc. 213," *Musica disciplina*, IX (1955), 73.

ReedC — Reed, Edward B., *Christmas Carols Printed in the 16th Century*, 1932.

RegnC I — Regnart, Jakob, *Il primo Libro delle canzone italiane à cinque voci*, Vienna, 1574.

RegnC II — Regnart, Jakob, *Il secundo Libro delle canzone italiane a cinque voci*, Nuremberg, 1581.

RegnS — Regnart, Jakob, *Sacrae aliquot cantiones quas Moteta 5 et 6 voci*, Munich, 1575.

RehA — Rehberg, Willy, ed., *Alte Hausmusik für Klavier (1550–1780)*, 2 vols., 1934.

ReissmA — Reissmann, August, *Allgemeine Geschichte der Musik*, 3 vols., 1863–1864.

ReyD — Reysschoot, Dorsan van, ed., "Danses du XVIe siècle d'après le recueil 'Chorearum Molliorum Collectanea' (1583) conservé à la Bibliothèque I. et R. de Berlin," *La Revue musicale*, supplements to vols. VI (1906), VII (1907), and VIII (1908).

ReynaB — Reyna, Ferdinando, *Des origines du ballet*, 1955.

RibF — Ribeiro, Sampayo, "Sobre o fecho do 'Auto da Cananeia,'" *Brotéria*, XXVIII (1938).

RiccS I — Riccio, Theodore, *Sacrae cantiones, quas vulgo motecta vocant, quinque, sex, et octo vocum*, Nuremberg, 1576.

RieH — Riemann, Hugo, *Handbuch der Musikgeschichte*, 4 vols., 1901–1913; 2nd ed., 1920–1923. References are to the first edition.

RieM — Riemann, Hugo, *Musikgeschichte in Beispielen*, 1912.

RieMF — Riemann, Hugo, "Das Lautenwerk des Miguel de Fuenllana (1554)," *Monatshefte für Musikgeschichte*, XXVII (1895), 81.

RieT — Riemann, Hugo, "Tänze des 16. Jahrhunderts à double emploi," *Die Musik*, XXI (1906–07), 140, plus musical supplements.

RiessO — Riess, Carl, ed., *Old Spanish Organ Music*, 1960.

RISM — *Répertoire international des sources musicales publiés par la Société internationale de musicologie et l'Association internationale des bibliothèques musicales. Recueils imprimés, XVIe–XVIIe siècles, Vol. I: Liste Chronologique*, ed. François Lesure, 1960.

RitZ — Ritter, August G., *Zur Geschichte des Orgelspiels*, 1884.

RodioR — Rodio, Rocco, *Cinque Ricercate, Una Fantasia*, ed. Macario Santiago Kastner, 1958.

RoedigC — Roediger, Karl E., *Catalogue des livres, manuscrits et imprimés composant la bibliothèque de M. Horace de Landau*, 2 vols., 1885–1890.

RoksM — Rokseth, Yvonne, "Un Motet de Moulu et ses diverses transcriptions pour orgue," in *Bericht über den musikwissenschaftlichen Kongress in Basel* (1925), p. 7.

RoksMO — Rokseth, Yvonne, *La Musique d'orgue du XVe siècle et au début du XVIe*, 1930.

RoksO — Rokseth, Yvonne, ed , *Deux livres d'orgue édités par Pierre Attaingnant (1531)*, 1925.

RoksT — Rokseth, Yvonne, ed., *Treize motets et un prélude pour orgue, édités par Pierre Attaingnant (1531)*, 1930.

RoncM — Roncaglia, Gino, "Simone Molinaro," *Rivista musicale italiana*, XLV (1941), 184.

RoreMT — Rore, Cipriano de, *Cypriani Rore musici excellentissimi Motetta . . . Quinque vocum*, Venice, Antonio Gardane, 1545.

RoreO — Rore, Cipriano de, *Opera omnia*, ed. Bernhard Meier, 1959—.

RossiM — Rossi, Giacomo, *Il Minuetto*, 1896.

RothB — Roth, F. W. E., "Zur Bibliographie der Musikdrucke des 15.–17. Jahrhunderts in der Darmstädter Hofbibliothek," *Monatshefte für Musikgeschichte*, XX, Supplement (1888).

RothGH — Roth, F. W. E., "Zur Geschichte der Hofmusik zu Heidelberg im 16. Jahrhundert," *Neues Archiv für die Geschichte der Stadt Heidelberg*, VI (1905), 103.

RoyM — Roy, Otto, ed., *Musik des Mittelalters und der Renaissance*, 2nd ed., 1960.

Rubio — Rubio, Samuel, ed., *Polifonía española*, 1955.

RubsS — Rubsamen, Walter, "Scottish and English Music of the Renaissance in a Newly-Discovered Manuscript," in *Festschrift Heinrich Besseler zum sechzigsten Geburtstag* (1961), p. 259.

SaA — Santa Maria, Fray Tomás de, *Oeuvres transcrites de l'Arte de tañer fantasia* (*Valladolid 1565*), ed. Pierre Froidebise, 1961.

SaV — Santa Maria, Fray Tomás de, *Wie mit aller Vollkommenheit und Meisterschaft das Klavichord zu spielen sei*, 1937. This volume is a German translation by Richard Boadella and Eta Harich-Schneider of the theorist's *Libro llamado Arte de tañer fantasia* (1565).

SachsPM — Sachs, Curt, *The Evolution of Piano Music, 1350–1700*, 1944.

SachsRD — Sachs, Curt, "Der Rhythmus der basse danse," *Acta musicologica*, III (1931), 107.

SachsW — Sachs, Curt, *World History of the Dance*, 1937. This volume is an English translation of *Eine Weltgeschichte des Tanzes*, 1933.

SainzF — Sainz de la Maza, Regino, ed., *Cuatro fantasias del siglo XVI*, 1954.

SaliM — Salinas, Francisco, *De Musica libri septem* (*1577*), facsimile ed. by Macario Santiago Kastner, 1958.

SalmL — Salmen, Walter, *Das Lochamer Liederbuch*, 1951.

SalvaC — Salvá y Mallen, Pedro, *Catálogo de la Biblioteca de Salvá*, 2 vols., 1872.

SartC — Sartori, Claudio, "Precisazioni bibliografiche sulle opere di Girolamo Cavazzoni," *Rivista musicale italiana*, XLIV (1940), 359.

SartD — Sartori, Claudio, *Dizionario degli editori musicali italiani*, 1958.

SartFB — Sartori, Claudio, "A Little Known Petrucci Publication: The Second Book of Lute Tablatures by Francesco Bossinensis," *The Musical Quarterly*, XXXIV (1948), 234.

SartMS — Sartori, Claudio, *Bibliografia della musica strumentale italiana stampate in Italia fino al 1700*, 1952.

SartN — Sartori, Claudio, "Nuove conclusive aggiunte alla 'Bibliografia' del Petrucci," *Collectanea historiae musicae*, I (1953), 175.

SartP — Sartori, Claudio, *Bibliografia delle opere musicali stampate da Ottaviano Petrucci*, 1948.

SartUD — Sartori, Claudio, "Una Dinastia di editori musicali," *La bibliofilia*, LVIII (1956), 178.

ScanL — Scandello, Antonio, *Nawe und lustige weltliche deudsche Liedlein*, Dresden, 1570.

ScanN — Scandello, Antonio, *Newe teutsche Liedlein mit vier und fünf Stimmen*, Nuremberg, 1568.

SchaalM — Schaal, Richard, "Die Musikbibliothek von Raimund Fugger d.J.," *Acta musicologica*, XXIX (1957), 126.

ScherG — Schering, Arnold, ed., *Geschichte der Musik in Beispielen*, 1931.

ScheurC — Scheurleer, Daniel F., *Catalogus der Muziekbibliotheek van D. F. Scheurleer*, 1893.

ScheurCM — *Muziekhistorisch Museum van Dr. D. F. Scheurleer. Catalogus van de Muziekwerken en de Boeken over Muziek*, 1923.

SchlechtB — Schlecht, Raymond, "Ein Beitrag zur Musikgeschichte aus dem Anfange des 16. Jahrhunderts nach dem 'Spiegel der Orgelmacher und Organisten von Arnold Schlick,' 1511," *Monatshefte für Musikgeschichte*, II (1870), 165, 181, 197.

SchlechtG — Schlecht, Raymund, *Geschichte der Kirchenmusik*, 1879.

SchlechtK — Schlecht, Raymund, "Ein Beitrag zur ältesten Klavier-Literatur," *Monatshefte für Musikgeschichte*, II (1870), 122.

SchlickS (Eitner) — Schlick, Arnold, *Spiegel der Orgelmacher und Organisten*, ed. Robert Eitner and W. Bethge, published in *Monatshefte für Musikgeschichte*, I (1869), 77.

SchlickS (Flade) — Schlick, Arnold, *Spiegel der Orgelmacher und Organisten*, ed. Ernst Flade, 1932; second printing, 1951.

SchlickS (Miller) — Schlick, Arnold, *Spiegel der Orgelmacher und Organisten*, English trans. by Frank S. Miller, published in *Organ Institute Quarterly*, VII (1959), 13.

SchlickS (Smets) — Schlick, Arnold, *Spiegel der Orgelmacher und Organisten*, ed. Paul Smets, 1959.

SchlickT (Eitner) — Schlick, Arnold, *Tabulaturen etlicher Lobgesang und Lidlein* (*Mainz, 1512*), ed. Robert Eitner, published in *Monatshefte für Musikgeschichte*, I (1869), 115.

SchlickT (Harms) — Schlick, Arnold, *Tabulaturen etlicher Lobgesang und Lidlein* (*Mainz, 1512*), ed. Gottfried Harms, 1924.

SchmidOP — Schmid, Anton, *Ottaviano dei Petrucci da Fossombrone*, 1845.

SchmidT — Schmid, Ernst Fritz, ed., *Tänze des 16. Jahrhunderts für vier Instrumenten*, 1926.

SchmidtgG — Schmidt-Görg, Joseph, *Nicolas Gombert, Kapellmeister Kaiser Karls V: Leben und Werk*, 1938.

SchneidA — Schneider, Max, *Die Anfänge des Basso Continuo und seiner Bezifferung*, 1918.

SchneiderV — Schneider, Marius, "Un Villancico de Alonso de Mudarra procedente de la música popular granadina," *Anuario musical*, X (1955), 79.

SchraG — Schrade, Leo, "Eine Gagliarde von Ciprian de Rore," *Archiv für Musikwissenschaft*, VIII (1926), 385.

SchraI — Schrade, Leo, *Die handschriftliche Überlieferung der ältesten Instrumentalmusik*, 1931.

SchraLM — Schrade, Leo, "Luys Milan the Vihuelista," *The Guitar Review*, IX (1949), 19.

SchraTI — Schrade, Leo, "Tänze aus einer anonymen italienischen Tabulatur, 1551," *Zeitschrift für Musikwissenschaft*, X (1928), 449.

SCMA — Smith College Music Archives, ed. Ross L. Finney, 1935—. For titles of individual volumes see Gustave Reese, *Music in the Renaissance* (1954), p. 937.

SeayFC — Seay, Albert, ed., *French Chansons. Early Chansons with English and French Texts*, 1957.

SeiffG — Seiffert, Max, *Geschichte der Klaviermusik*, vol. I, 1899 (based on Karl Weitzmann's *Geschichte des Klavierspiels und der Klavierliteratur*, 1863; 2nd ed., 1879).

SeligG — Selig, Karl-Ludwig, "A German Collection of Spanish Books," *Bibliothèque d'humanisme et Renaissance*, XIX (1957), 51.

SenflW — Senfl, Ludwig, *Sämtliche Werke*, ed. E. Löhrer and O. Ursprung, 1937—.

SermM — Sermisy, Claudin de, *Nova et prima motettorum editio 6.5.4. et 3 voc.*, Paris, Pierre Attaingnant and Hubert Jullet, 1542.

SharpD — Sharp, Cecil, and A. P. Oppé, *The Dance: An Historical Survey of Dancing in Europe*, 1924.

SlimCA — Slim, H. Colin, "Keyboard Music at Castell'Arquato by an Early Madrigalist," *Journal of the American Musicological Society*, XV (1962), 35.

SlimK — Slim, H. Colin, "The Keyboard Ricercar and Fantasia in Italy, ca. 1500–1550, with Reference to Parallel Forms in European Lute Music of the Same Period," unpub. diss., Harvard University, 1961.

SlimMN — Slim, H. Colin, ed., *Musica Nova* (Monuments of Renaissance Music, vol. 1), 1964.

SmijO — Smijers, Albert, ed., *Van Ockeghem tot Sweelinck*, 7 vols., 1939–1956.

SmijT — Smijers, Albert, and A. Tillman Merritt, eds., *Treize livres de motets parus chez Pierre Attaingnant en 1534 et 1535*, 1934—.

SmithFC — Smith, Margaret Dean, "A Fifteenth Century Dancing Book," *Journal of the English Folk Dance and Song Society*, III (1937), 100.

SmithL — Smith, Carleton Sprague, "Religious Music and the Lute," *The Guitar Review*, IX (1949), 31.

SolA — Solerti, Angelo, *Gli albori del Melodramma*, 3 vols., 1905.

SolMus — Solerti, Angelo, *Musica, ballo e drammatica alla corte Medicea dal Seicento al 1637*, 1905.

SommL — Sommer, Hermann, *Die Laute*, 1920.

SonnD — Sonneck, O. G., "A Description of Alessandro Striggio and Francesco Corteccia's Intermedi 'Psyche and Amor' 1565," *The Musical Antiquary*, III (1911–1912), 40.

SpencerT — Spencer, Robert, "Two Missing Lute Parts for Morley's Consort Lessons," *The Lute Society Journal*, IV (1962), 31.

SpiessA — Spiessens, Godelieve, "Emmanuel Adrianssen et son Pratum musicum," *Acta musicologica*, XXXVI (1964), 142.

StaakF — Staak, Pieter van der, ed., *Four Royal Dances*, 1957.

StaakS — Staak, Pieter van der, ed., *7 Easy 16th Century Pieces*, 1959.

StarkeHGL — Starke, Reinhold, "Hieronymus Gregorius Langius Havelbergensis," *Monatshefte für Musikgeschichte*, XXXI (1899), 116.

SteeleE — Steele, Robert, *The Earliest English Music Printing*, 1903.

SteinitA — Steinitzer, Max, *Musikgeschichtlicher Atlas*, 1908.

StellMB — Stellfeld, Jean-Auguste, "Het muziekhistorisch Belang der Catalogi en Inventarissen van het Plantinsch Archief," *Vlaamsch Jaarboek voor Muziekgeschiedenis*, XXIII (1940), 5.

StevnsnJB — Stevenson, Robert, *Juan Bermudo*, 1960.

StevnsnS — Stevenson, Robert, *Spanish Music in the Age of Columbus*, 1960.

StolI — Stoltzer, Thomas, *Ich klag den Tag und Entlaubet ist der Walde*, ed. Wilhelm Twittenhoff, n.d.

StraM — Straeten, Edmond van der, *La Musique aux Pays-Bas avant le XIXe siècle*, 8 vols., 1867–1888.

StraubeM — Straube, Karl, ed. *Alte Meister des Orgelspiels. Neue Folge*, 2 vols., 1929.

SubHM — Subirá, José. *Historia de la música*, 2nd ed., 2 vols., 1951.

SubHME — Subirá, José, *Historia de la música española e hispano americana*, 1953.

SubM — Subirá, José, *La Música en la Casa de Alba*, 1927.

SumnO — Sumner, William L., *The Organ, Its Evolution, Principles of Construction and Use*, 3rd ed., 1962.

SusaD — Susato, Tielman, *Danserye zeer lustich . . . om spelen op alle musicale instrumenten (1551)*, ed. Franz J. Giesbert, 2 vols., 1936.

SutherR — Sutherland, Gordon, "The Ricercari of Jacques Buus," *The Musical Quarterly*, XXXI (1945), 448.

SutherS — Sutherland, Gordon, "Studies in the Development of the Keyboard and Ensemble Ricercare from Willaert to Frescobaldi," unpub. diss., Harvard University, 1942.

SzmolyanAL — Szmolyan, Walter, "Das Archiv für alte Lautenmusik in Maria Enzersdorf bei Wien," *Österreichische Musikzeitschrift*, XVI (1961), 538.

TagA — Tagliapietra, Gino, ed., *Antologia di musica antica e moderna per pianoforte*, 14 vols., 1931–1932.

TapL — Tappert, Wilhelm, "Die Lautenbücher des Hans Gerle," *Monatshefte für Musikgeschichte*, XVIII (1886), 101.

TapS — Tappert, Wilhelm, ed., *Sang und Klang aus alter Zeit*, 1906.

TautA — Taut, Kurt, *Die Anfänge der Jagdmusik*, n.d.

TBI — *Trésors des bibliothèques d'Italie, IVe–XVIe siècles. Bibliothèque nationale, Paris*, 1950.

TebAP — Tebaldini, Giovanni, *L'Archivio musicale della Cappella Antoniana in Padova*, 1895.

ThibaultC — Thibault, Geneviève, "Les Collections privées de livres et d'instruments de musique d'autrefois et d'aujourd'hui," *Fontes artis musicae*, VI (1959), 55.

ThibaultD — Thibault, Geneviève, "Deux catalogues de libraires musicaux: Vincenti et Gardane (Venise, 1591)," *Revue de musicologie*, X (1929), 177, and XI (1930), 7.

TischA — Tischer, G., and K. Burchard, "Aus einer alten Bibliothek," *Sammelbände der Internationalen Musikgesellschaft*, II (1900–01), 158.

TomasA — Tomasin, Don Pietro, and G. Piber, *Andrea Antico, chierico di Montona nell'Istria, primo calcografo musicale*, 1880.

TorA Torchi, Luigi, ed., *L'Arte musicale in Italia*, 7 vols., 1897–1908.

TorM Torchi, Luigi, "La Musica istrumentale in Italia nei secoli XVI, XVII e XVIII," *Rivista musicale italiana*, V (1898), 64, 281, 455; VI (1899), 255, 693; VII (1900), 233; VIII (1901), 1.

TornC Torner, Eduard M., ed., *Colección de vihuelistas españoles del siglo XVI*, 1923.

TornCM Torner, Eduard M., ed., *Cancionero musical*, 1928.

TorriC Torri, Luigi. "Nel terzo centenario della morte di Giovanni Croce detto il Chiozzotto," *Rivista musicale italiana*, XVI (1909), 550.

TouA Toulouze, Michel, *L'Art et instruction de bien dancer* (*1496*), facsimile ed. with commentary by Victor Scholderer, 1936.

TreB Trend, John B., "Musikschätze auf spanischen Bibliotheken," *Zeitschrift für Musikwissenschaft*, VIII (1926), 499.

TreBM Trend, John B., "Catalogue of the Music in the Biblioteca Medinaceli, Madrid," *Revue hispanique*, LXXI (1927), 485.

TreL Trend, John B., *Luis Milan and the Vihuelistas*, 1925.

TreM Trend, John B., *The Music of Spanish History to 1600*, 1926.

TrichT Trichet, Pierre, *Le Traité des instruments de musique*, ed. François Lesure, published in *Annales musicologiques*, IV (1956), 175.

TwittT Twittenhoff, Wilhelm, ed., *Tanzsätze des 16. Jahrhunderts*, 3 vols., n.d.

UtenF Utendal, Alexander, *Fröhliche newe teutsche unnd frantzösische Lieder . . . mit vier, fünff und mehr Stimmen*, Nuremberg, 1574.

ValVS Valente, Antonio, *Versi spirituali per organo*, ed. Ireneo Fuser, 1958.

ValdeA Valderrábano, Enriquez de, *Ay de mi! Romance viejo*, ed. José de Azpiazu, 1958.

ValdeY Valderrábano, Enriquez de, *Ya cavalga calamos*, ed. José de Azpiazu, 1958.

ValentinTo Valentin, Erich, ed., *The Toccata*, 1958.

ValleA Valle de Paz, Giacomo del, *Annibale Padovano*, 1933.

VasE Vasconcellos, Josquim de, *El Rey D. João o 4*^{to}, 1900.

VasJ Vasconcellos, Josquim de, *Primeira parte do index da Livraria de musica do Rey Dom João IV*, 1873.

VasquezVC Vásquez, Juan, *Villancicos i canciones de Juan Vasquez a tres y a quatro*, Ossuna, 1551.

VentoM Vento, Ivo de, *Liber Mottetorum quatuor vocum, nunc primum in lucem editus*, Munich, 1571.

VentoN Vento, Ivo de, *Newe teutsche Liedlein, mit fünff Stimmen*, Munich, 1569.

VerA Verchaly, André, ed., *Airs de cour pour voix et luth* (*1603–1643*), 1961.

VernO Vernarecci, Augusto, *Ottaviano de' Petrucci da Fossombrone*, 2nd ed., 1882.

VicO Victoria, Tomás Luis de, *Opera omnia*, ed. Felipe Pedrell, 8 vols., 1902–1913.

VicenO Vicentino, Nicola, *Opera omnia*, Henry Kaufman, ed., 1963.

VillalbaCE Villalba Muñoz, P. Luis, ed., *Diez canciones española*, 1914.

VinS Vindel, Francisco, *Solaces bibliográficos*, 1942.

VincenI Vincenti, Giacomo, *Indice di tutte l'opera di musica che si truova alla stampa della pigna*, Venice, 1591.

VirdungM (Schrade) Virdung, Sebastian, *Musica getutscht* (*1511*), facsimile ed. by Leo Schrade, 1931.

VNM Vereeniging voor Nederlandsche Muziekgeschiedenis. Uitgaven. 1869—. For titles of individual volumes see Gustave Reese, *Music in the Renaissance* (1954), p. 943.

Vogel Vogel, Emil, *Bibliothek der gedruckten weltlichen Vocalmusik Italiens aus den Jahren 1500–1700*, 2 vols., 1892; reprinted, 1962.

Vogel Einstein *Bibliography of Italian Secular Vocal Music Printed between the years 1500–1700, by Emil Vogel*, revised and enlarged by Alfred Einstein, in *Music Library Association Notes* II (1945), 185, 275; III (1945), 51, (1946), 154, 256, 363; IV (1946), 41, (1947), 201, 301; V (1947), 65, (1948), 277, 385, 537. Einstein's revisions are also printed at the end of the 1962 reprinting of Vogel.

WagMP Wagner, Peter, "Das Madrigal und Palestrina," *Vierteljahrsschrift für Musikwissenschaft*, VIII (1892), 423.

WaissP Waisselius, Matthaeus, *Phantasia und deutscher Tanz*, ed. Karl Scheit, n.d.

WaissT Waisselius, Matthaeus, *Meisterwerke alter Lautenkunst: Matthäus Waissel, Tänze, Fantasien, Präambeln*, ed. Walther Pudelko, 1925.

WalS — Wallner, Bertha A., "Sebastian Virdung von Amberg," *Kirchenmusikalisches Jahrbuch*, XXIV (1911), 85.

WaldC — Waldbauer, Ivan F., "The Cittern in the Sixteenth Century and Its Music in France and the Low Countries," unpub. diss., Harvard University, 1964.

WalkerI — Walker, D. P., ed., *Musique des Intermèdes de "La Pellegrina,"* 1963.

WalkerM — Walker, D. P., "La Musique des intermèdes florentins de 1589 et l'humanisme," in *Les Fêtes de la Renaissance*, ed. Jean Jacquot (1956), p. 133.

WalthW — Walther, Johann, *Wittembergisch deudsch geistlich Gesangbüchlein*, Wittemberg, 1551.

WarA — Warlock, Peter, *The English Ayre*, 1926.

WarEA — Warlock, Peter, and Philip Wilson, eds., *English Ayres, Elizabethan and Jacobean*, 6 vols., 1927–1931.

WardDVM — Ward, John, ed., *The Dublin Virginal Manuscript*, 1954.

WardH — Ward, John, "Le Problème des hauteurs dans la musique pour luth et vihuela au XVIe siècle," in *Le Luth et sa musique*, ed. Jean Jacquot (1958), p. 171.

WardL — Ward, John, "The Lute in 16th-Century Spain," *The Guitar Review*, IX (1949), 27.

WardLM — Ward, John, "The Lute Music of MS Royal Appendix 58," *Journal of the American Musicological Society*, XIII (1960), 117.

WardM — Ward, John, "Music for A Handefull of Pleasant Delites," *Journal of the American Musicological Society*, X (1957), 151.

WardP — Ward, John, "Parody Technique in 16th-Century Instrumental Music," in *The Commonwealth of Music*, G. Reese and R. Brandel, eds., 1965, 208.

WardU — Ward, John, "The Use of Borrowed Material in 16th-Century Instrumental Music," *Journal of the American Musicological Society*, V (1952), 88.

WardV — Ward, John, "The Vihuela da mano and Its Music (1536–1576)," unpub. diss., New York University, 1953.

WardVH — Ward, John, "The Editorial Methods of Venegas de Henestrosa," *Musica disciplina*, VI (1951), 105.

WasG — Wasielewski, Joseph von, *Geschichte der Instrumentalmusik im XVI. Jahrhundert*, 1878.

WasI — Wasielewski, Joseph von, ed., *Instrumentalsätze vom Ende des XVI. bis Ende des XVII. Jahrhunderts*, 1874.

WasV — Wasielewski, Joseph von, *Die Violine im 17. Jahrhundert*, 1874.

WeckB — *Balet comique de la royne (Paris, 1582)*, ed. with piano reduction by Jean-Baptiste Weckerlin, 1882.

WeckC — Weckerlin, Jean-Baptiste, *Bibliothèque du Conservatoire national de musique et de déclamation: Catalogue bibliographique*, 1885.

WeitzG — Weitzmann, Karl, *Geschichte des Klavierspiels und der Klavierliteratur*, 1863; 2nd ed., 1879. See also SeiffG.

WertM — Wert, Giaches de, *Musices, vel (ut dicunt) Motectorum Quinque vocum Liber primus*, Nuremberg, 1569.

WhythA — *The Autobiography of Thomas Whythorne*, ed. James Osborn, 1961.

WhythFD — Whythorne, Thomas, *Fifteen Duos in Canon (1590) for divers Recorders*, ed. Walter Bergmann, 1955.

WieM — Wienandt, Elwyn A., "Musical Style in the Lute Compositions of Francesco da Milano (1498–1543)," unpub. diss., University of Iowa, 1951.

WieP — Wienandt, Elwyn A., "Perino Fiorentino and His Lute Pieces," *Journal of the American Musicological Society*, VIII (1955), 2.

WillO — Willaert, Adrian, *Opera omnia*, ed. Hermann Zenck and Walter Gerstenberg, 1950—.

WillR — Willaert, Adrian, *Ricercari a 3 voci*, ed. Hermann Zenck, 1933.

WintG — Winterfeld, Carl von, *Johannes Gabrieli und sein Zeitalter*, 3 vols., 1834.

WinterR — Winternitz, Emanuel, "Alcune rappresentazioni di antichi strumenti italiani a tastiera," *Collectanea historiae musicae*, II (1956), 466.

WohlT — Wohlgemuth, Gerhard, ed., *Tänze des 16. Jahrhunderts*, n.d.

WolfEA — Wolf, Johannes, "Ein alter Lautendruck" *Zeitschrift der Internationalen Musikgesellschaft*, I (1899), 29.

WolfH Wolf, Johannes, *Handbuch der Notationskunde*, 2 vols., 1913, 1919.

WolfHM Wolf, Johannes, *Historia de la música*, Spanish translation and additions by Higinio Anglés and José Subirá, 4th ed., 1957.

WolfME Wolf, Johannes, ed., *Music of Earlier Times (13th Century to Bach)*, 1946 (American reprint of *Sing- und Spielmusik aus älterer Zeit*, 1930).

WolfMS Wolf, Johannes, ed., *Musikalische Schrifttafeln*, 1923.

WolffC *Versteigerung der Musikbibliothek des Herrn Dr. Werner Wolffheim*, 4 vols., 1928–1929.

WotC Wotquenne-Plattel, Alfred, *Chansons italiennes de la fin du XVI*me *siècle*, n.d.

WotHM Wotquenne-Plattel, Alfred, "Étude sur l'Hortus Musarum de Pierre Phalèse," *Revue des bibliothèques et archives de Belgique*, I (1903), 65.

WustA Wustmann, Gustav, "Elias Ammerbach," *Sammelbände der Internationalen Musikgesellschaft*, XI (1909), 137.

WustM Wustmann, Rudolf, *Musikgeschichte Leipzigs*, vol. I, 1909.

YaF Yates, Frances A., *The French Academies of the Sixteenth Century*, 1947.

YoungBS Young, Clyde W., "The Keyboard Tablatures of Bernhard Schmid, Father and Son," unpub. diss., University of Illinois, 1957.

YoungKM Young William, "Keyboard Music to 1600," *Musica Disciplina*, XVI (1962), 115, and XVII (1963), 163.

ZahnM Zahn, Johannes, *Die Melodien der deutschen evangelischen Kirchenlieder*, 6 vols., 1889–1893.

ZanG Zanoskar, Hubert, ed., *Gitarrespiel alter Meister*, 2 vols., 1955.

ZfSM Zeitschrift für Spielmusik. Small volumes of music published by Hermann Moeck Verlag in Celle, ed. Helmut Mönkemeyer, Felix Oberborbeck, Gerd Ochs, and Wilhelm Twittenhof, ca. 1930—.

ZontaS Zonta, Giuseppe, *Storia della letteratura italiana*, 3 vols., 1928–1932.

ZurM Zur Westen, Walter von, *Musiktitel aus vier Jahrhunderten*, 1921.

ZuthH Zuth, Josef, *Handbuch der Laute und Gitarre*, 1926.

INDEX I: LIST OF LIBRARIES AND THEIR HOLDINGS

The sigla are taken from RISM; similar sigla have been devised for those libraries not in RISM. "L" (in parentheses) following an entry means that the volume is now lost. "D.W." following an entry refers to the "Doubtful Works" listed at the end of the year in question. For references to volumes that were in private libraries see Index IV (Index of Names) under: C. P. E. Bach, J. S. Bach, C. F. Becker, Georg Becker, John Bull, Charles Burney, Albert Cohn, W. H. Cummings, Jules Écorcheville, François J. Fétis, Fugger library, Gaetano Gaspari, Wilhelm Heyer, Ben Jonson, Horace Landau-Finaly, Alfred Littleton, J. E. Matthew, Henry Prunières, Edward F. Rimbault, Daniel F. Scheurleer, J. F. R. Stainer, T. W. Taphouse, Wilhelm Tappert, Wagener library, Werner Wolffheim, Alfred Wotquenne-Plattel, and Friedrich Zelle.

AUSTRIA

A: Gu Graz, Universitätsbibliothek, 1589_5

A: Iu Innsbruck, Universitätsbibliothek, 1511_3, 1554_3

A: Wgm Vienna, Gesellschaft der Musikfreunde, 1511_3, 1523_2, 1529_1, 1553_2, 1572_1, 1573_2, 1575_1, 1583_4

A: Wn Vienna, Österreichische Nationalbibliothek, 1504_1, 1508_2, 1509_1, 1511_3, $151?_1$, 1521_1, 1523_2, 1529_1, 1530_2, 1532_1, 1536_3, 1536_4, 1536_8, 1536_9, $[1538]_3$ (L), 1539_1, 1540_1, 1543_3, 1546_1, 1546_6, 1546_7, 1546_9, 1546_{10}, 1546_{11}, 1546_{13}, 1546_{15}, 1546_{17}, 1546_{19}, 1546_{20}, 1547_2, 1547_3, 1547_5, 1547_8, 1547_9, 1547_{10}, 1548_1, 1548_4, 1549_1, 1549_2, $154?_4$, 1550_4, 1552_1, 1554_1, 1554_2, 1554_3, 1555_1, 1560_3, 1561_3, 1562_1, 1562_3, 1562_4, 1563_2, 1563_3, 1563_5, 1563_6, 1563_7, 1563_{11}, 1564_4, 1565_2, 1568_1, 1568_6, 1568_7, 1569_1, 1569_6, $156?_3$, 1572_1, 1573_2, 1574_5, 1574_6, 1581_1, 1582_3, 1584_3, 1586_5, 1587_1, 1587_3, 1588_4, 1589_5, 1591_9, 1592_2, 1592_3, 1594_5, 1595_1, 1596_1, 1597_5, 1599_{10}

A: Wu Vienna, Universitätsbibliothek, 1581_1

BELGIUM

B: Bc Brussels, Bibliothèque du Conservatoire royal de musique, 1542_2, 1543_2, 1552_{11}, 1553_{10}, 1583_4, 1591_6

B: Br Brussels, Bibliothèque royale de Belgique, 1508_2, 1523_2, 1529_1, 1536_4, 1536_7, 1546_{15}, 1552_4, 1553_8, 1553_9, 1554_4, 1554_7, 1554_8, 1555_4, 1558_3, 1558_4, 1558_6, 1562_4, 1564_1, 1567 D.W., 1568_5, 1571_3, 1573_1, 1573_3, 1577_6, 1578_3, 1584_5, 1586_5, 1586_8, 1589_8, 1590_2, 1590_8, 1592_3, 1592_8, 1593_5, 1594_2, 1597_{12}, 1598_9, 1598_{10}, 1599_4

SWITZERLAND

CH: Bu Basel, Universitätsbibliothek, 1511_3, 1562_4, 1577_6, 1583_6, 1588_8, 1589_3, 1591_3, 1591_4, 1592_7, 1593_4, 1595_3, 1595_8, 1596_7

CH: BEsu Bern, Stadt- und Universitätsbibliothek, 1536_6

CH: E Einsiedeln, Stiftsbibliothek, 1529_1, 1591_6

CH: Lcortot Lausanne, Bibliothèque Alfred Cortot, 1533_2, 1536_4, 1542_1, 1546_6, 1546_7, 1546_{10}, 1546_{13}, 1546_{15}, 1548_1, 1549_2, 1555_1, 1565_5, 1581_1, 1582_3, 1583_4, 1584_5, 1589_1, 1594_2

CH: SGv St. Gall, Stadtbibliothek (Vadiana), 1551_1, 1552_5, 1552_6, 1553_4

CH: Zz Zürich, Zentralbibliothek (and Bibliothek der Allgemeinen Musikgesellschaft), 1560_3, 1572_1, 1573_2, 1575_3

CH: ZO Zofingen, Stadtbibliothek, 1536_6

CZECHOSLOVAKIA

CS: B Brno, Hudební oddělení Zemského Musea, 1523_2

CS: Os Olomouc (formerly Olmütz), Studienbibliothek, 1536_4 (L)

CS: Pdobi Prague, Bibl. Josef Dobrovský, 1517_1

GERMANY

D: As Augsburg, Staats- und Stadtbibliothek, 1529_1, 1545_1, 1555_2, 1555_3, 1584_7, 1587_3, 1589_5, 1590_{12}, 1592_3, 1594_7, 1595_9, 1597_5, 1597_{14}, 1598_5

D: Bds Berlin, Deutsche Staatsbibliothek, 1507_1 (L), 1507_2 (L), 1537_1 (L), 1538_1 (L), 1546_2 (L), $[1547]_{11}$ (L), $[1547]_{12}$ (L), 1550_4 (L), 1551_8 (L), 1552_1 (L), $[1552]_{10}$ (L), 1554_3 (L), 1556_5 (L), 1558_5 (L), 1559_5 (L), 1562_4, $[1562]_{12}$ (L), 1565_1 (L), 1565_4 (L), 1565_5 (L), 1566_1 (L), 1566_2 (L), 1566_3 (L), 1567_2 (L), 1568_2 (L), 1571_6 (L), 1572_1 (L), 1573_1 (L), 1573_2 (L), 1575_1 (L), 1577_5 (L), 1577_6 (L), 1578_3, 1579_3 (L), 1583_4 (L), 1583_6 (L), 1584_6 (L), 1585_3 (L), 1586_5 (L), 1586_8, 1588_5 (L), 1589_3 (L), 1589_5 (L), 1589_8, 1590_8 (L), 1592_6 (L), 1592_{12} (L), $[1592]_{13}$ (L), 1594_8 (L), 1595_9 (L), 1597_5 (L), 1597_{14} (L), $[1598]_7$ (L), 1598_9, 1599_5

D: Bds-Tü Stiftung Preussischer Kulturbesitz, Tübinger Depot der ehemaligen Preussischen

DENMARK

SPAIN

E:Mn Madrid, Biblioteca nacional, 1536_4, 1536_5, 1538_1 (2 copies), 1546_{14}, 1547_5 (2 copies), 1549_3 (2 copies), 1550_1, 1552_7 (2 copies), 1553_6, 1554_3 (4 copies), 1555_1, 1557_2 (2 copies), $[1564]_3$, 1576_1, 1578_3
E:S Seville, Biblioteca Colombina, 1502_1 (L), 1503_1, 1504_1 (L), 1507_1 (L), 1507_2 (L), 1508_2 (L), 1509_1, 1511_1 (L), 1511_3 (L), 1517_1 (L), 1529_2, 1530_5
E:Tp Toledo, Biblioteca provincial, 1538_1
E:V Valladolid, Archivo de la Catedral, 1555_1, 1565_5, 1596_{11}
E:VAc Valencia, Catedral, 1547_5

IRELAND

EIR:Dm Dublin, Marsh's Library, 1595_6
EIR:Duc Dublin, University College, 1597_4

FRANCE

F:Ameyer Paris, Collection Musicale André Meyer, 1551_7, 1582_3
F:AS Arras, Bibliothèque municipale, 1592_6 (L)
F:B Besançon, Bibliothèque municipale, 1545_3, 1582_3
F:CA Cambrai, Bibliothèque municipale, 1552_{11} (L)
F:CV Charleville, Bibliothèque municipale, 1536_4, 1566_1
F:DU Dunkirk, Bibliothèque municipale, 1552_{11} (L), 1553_{10} (L)
F:G Grenoble, Bibliothèque municipale, 1577_6
F:MD Montbéliard, Bibliothèque municipale, 1584_6, 1589_6
F:Nd Nantes, Bibliothèque du Musée Dobrée, 1582_3
F:O Orléans, Bibliothèque municipale, 1578_6
F:Pa Paris, Bibliothèque de l'Arsenal, 1582_3
F:Pc Paris, Bibliothèque du Conservatoire, 1504_1, 1504_2, 1509_1, 1511_3, 1532_1, 1536_4, 1536_5, 1537_1, 1543_2, 1544_2, 1546_9, 1552_8, 1554_3, 1556_7, 1561_3, 1579_4, 1581_1, 1582_3, 1584_5, 1589_1, 1589_8, 1590_8, 1590_{12}, 1593_4, 1594_2, 1594_3, 1595_9, 1596_1, 1598_9
F:Pm Paris, Bibliothèque Mazarine, 1551_3, 1552_3, 1553_3, 1554_4, 1556_8, 1577_6 (L), 1582_3, 1592_6, 1595_4
F:Pn Paris, Bibliothèque nationale, 1507_1, 1507_2, 1512_1, 1536_5, 1536_9, 1542_3, 1547_6, 1550_5, 1550_6, 1552_7, 1554_2, 1554_3, 1554_9, 1555_1, 1555_5, 1557_3, 1557_4, 1562_1, 1574_2, 1574_3, 1581_1, 1582_3 (7 copies), 1583_4, 1584_5, 1585_6, 1589_1, 1592_6, 1595_9
F:Po Paris, Bibliothèque de l'Opéra, 1582_3
F:Pthibault Paris, Bibliothèque G. Thibault, 1546_7, 1546_{10}, 1546_{15}, 1547_2, 1548_3, 1549_2, 1552_4, 1552_8, 1554_2, 1554_6, 1554_7, 1554_8, 1555_4, 1556_3, 1556_5, 1558_3, 1559_7, 1561_2, 1562_3, 1563_8, 1564_4, 1569_2, 1581_1, 1582_3, 1584_5, 1593_4
F:Psg Paris, Bibliothèque Sainte-Geneviève, 1558_1, 1559_1, 1559_2, 1559_3
F:RO Roanne, Bibliothèque municipale, 1502_3
F:Ssc Strasbourg, Séminaire catholique, 1578_5, 1580_2
F:Ssp Strasbourg, Séminaire protestant, 1536_6, 1536_7
F:T Troyes, Bibliothèque municipale, 1573_5, 1573_8, 1574_7
F:VE Vesoul, Bibliothèque municipale, 1553_1 (L), 1553_8 (L), $[1586]_3$ (L)

GREAT BRITAIN

GB:Ctc Cambridge, Trinity College, 1588_2, 1589_2
GB:Cu Cambridge, University Library, 1571_1, 1588_2, 1589_2, 1597_6, 1599_7, $159?_2$
GB:En Edinburgh, National Library of Scotland, 1597_{10}, 1599_1
GB:Eu Edinburgh, University Library, 1511_3, $159?_2$
GB:Ge Glasgow, Euing Musical Library, 1565_5, 1584_5, 1588_2, 1589_2
GB:Gu Glasgow, University Library, 1545_1, 1581_1
GB:Lam London, Royal Academy of Music, 1589_2
GB:Lbm London, British Museum, 1511_3, 1523_1, 1529_1, 1532_1, 1532_2, 1533_1, 1536_4, 1536_5, 1538_1, 1540_2, 1543_3, 1545_1, 1546_2, 1546_5, 1546_6, 1546_7, 1546_{10}, 1546_{13}, 1546_{16}, 1547_3, 1547_5, 1548_4, 1549_4, 1549_5, 1549_7, 1549_8, 1551_3, 1552_3, 1552_7, 1553_2, 1553_3, 1554_3, 1554_4, 1555_1, 1556_8, 1558_1, 1558_5, 1559_1, 1559_2, 1559_3, 1562_1, 1564_2, 1565_5, 1566_2, 1566_3, 1568_3, 1569_2, 1571_1, 1571_4, 1572_1, 1574_2, 1574_7, 1575_1, 1578_3, 1578_8, 1579_3, 1581_1, 1582_3, 1584_5, 1585_1, 1585_3, 1585_6, 1586_8, 1587_3, 1588_2, 1588_6, 1589_1, 1589_2, 1589_3, 1589_5, 1589_8, $158?_2$ (2 copies), 1590_7, 1590_{11}, 1591_6, 1591_7, 1591_{11}, 1592_1, 1592_3, 1592_6, 1593_2, 1593_8, 1595_6, 1595_8, 1595_9, 1595_{10}, 1596_4, 1596_5, 1596_6, 1597_3, 1597_4, 1597_5, 1597_{10}, 1597_{11}, 1598_2, 1598_6, 1598_9, 1599_1, 1599_6, 1599_7, 1599_8, $159?_2$
GB:Lbmh London, British Museum, Paul Hirsch Collection, 1511_2, 1511_8, 1532_2, 1533_1, 1546_{18}, 1546_{20}, 1547_7, 1547_9, 1559_5, 1562_3, 1568_2, 1573_8, 1577_6, 1582_3, 1583_4, 1584_3, 1593_2, 1594_2, 1599_4
GB:Lcm London, Royal College of Music, 1556_9, 1558_1, 1562_3, 1573_4, 1580_3, 1589_2, 1595_6, 1596_4, 1596_5, 1596_6, 1597_6, $159?_2$
GB:Lk London, King's Music Library, 1589_2, 1589_3, 1590_7, $159?_2$
GB:Lrc London, Royal College of Physicians, $148?_1$, 1597_1
GB:Lsc London, Sion College, $158?_2$ (L)
GB:Lu London, University Library, 1588_2, 1589_2
GB:LI Lincoln, Cathedral Library, 1588_2
GB:Mp Manchester, Public Library, 1588_2
GB:Ob Oxford, Bodleian Library, 1563_{12}, 1568_7, 1571_6, 1574_2, 1588_2, 1589_2, 1590_{11}, 1591_5, 1593_4, 1597_{10}, 1599_8
GB:Och Oxford, Christ Church, 1589_2, 1599_6, 1599_8, $159?_2$
GB:T Tenbury, St. Michael's College, 1589_2, 1598_4
GB:Y York, Minster Library, 1588_2

HUNGARY

H:Ba Budapest, Magyar Tudományos Akadémia Könyvtára, 1593_3
H:Bn Budapest, Országos Széchényi Könyvtár, 1573_3
H:BA Bártfa, St. Aegidius Church, 1573_3 (L)

ITALY

I:A Assisi, Biblioteca comunale, 1574_3, 1577_5, 1596_8
I:Bc Bologna, Biblioteca comunale annessa al Conservatorio musicale G. B. Martini, 1501_1, 1502_1, 1535_1, 1536_4, 1540_3, 1542_2, 1543_1 (2 copies), 1543_2, 1546_{16}, 1547_1, 1549_7, $154?_2$, $154?_3$, 1551_5,

U.S.S.R.

INDEX II: VOLUMES DESCRIBED, ARRANGED BY TYPES OF NOTATION

French tablatures use letters to represent frets (a = open string, and b = first fret); Italian tablatures use numbers to represent frets (O = open string, and ɪ = first fret). Further details about the notation of instrumental music may be found in ApelN, part I, and WolfH II.

INDEX III: VOLUMES DESCRIBED, ARRANGED BY PERFORMING MEDIUM

When sixteenth-century editors and publishers prepared their volumes for the press they took into account the great freedom of choice left to performers in deciding on the instrumentation of a specific composition. Many volumes of instrumental music are arranged in such a way that various combinations of instruments can play from the same printed music. This characteristic flexibility complicates the task of preparing this index, which clearly cannot indicate every possible instrumentation. John Dowland's first book of ayres (1597_{4}), for example, includes one lute part and four voice parts. The volume is listed in this index under "Lute solo," "Lute and solo voice," "Lute and several voices," and "Vocal music." Although these entries by no means exhaust the possibilities for the performance of these Dowland ayres, this example will help the reader to understand the scope and limitations of this index. "D.W." following an entry refers to the "Doubtful Works" listed at the end of the year in question. Treatises and instructions for adding ornamentation are included in this index even though these entries do not refer to performing medium.

INDEX IV: NAMES

INDEX V: FIRST LINES AND TITLES

Titles are entered under the first main word, omitting any initial article; first lines are entered under the initial article (for example, both *La Alfonsina* and *A tirannie not lasting long* are entered under A). In view of the casual attitude of the sources toward consistent spelling it seemed needlessly pedantic to record every variant. Variant spellings are entered only when they affect the alphabetic order, or cause ambiguity (for example "A bien gran tort" is ignored as a variant of "A bien grant tort," but "Amour ne scauriez vous aprendre" is cross-referenced to "Amour me scauriez vous aprendre"). Names of dances have been standardized; for example, all dances called Padoana, Padouana, Paduana, Pavana, Pavenne, Pavin, and so on are entered under Pavane.

Each entry includes, after the title or the first line, the last name of the composer (not the intabulator) if he is known, and the second and later parts of longer compositions. Second and later parts are entered separately and cross-referenced. One entry has been made for each composition (that is, if two composers made settings of the same text, there will be two separate entries in this index). For various titles of abstract compositions, see the entry "Abstract Compositions." For combinations of dances, see the entry "Suite."

Since second and later editions of volumes are not inventoried, references to individual compositions in this index are to first editions only.